P9-ASH-869

ENCYCLOPEDIA OF EVANGELICALISM

ALSO BY RANDALL BALMER

Growing Pains: Learning to Love My Father's Faith

Religion in Twentieth Century America

Blessed Assurance: A History of Evangelicalism in America

Grant Us Courage: Travels Along the Mainline of American Protestantism

The Presbyterians (cowritten with John R. Fitzmier)

Mine Eyes Have Seen the Glory: A Journey into the Evangelical Subculture in America

A Perfect Babel of Confusion: Dutch Religion and English Culture in the Middle Colonies

ENCYCLOPEDIA OF EVANGELICALISM

Randall Balmer

Westminster John Knox Press
LOUISVILLE • LONDON

Book design by Sharon Adams
Cover design by Jennifer K. Cox
Cover illustration: Billy Graham With Arms Raised. © Bettmann/CORBIS

First edition
Published by Westminster John Knox Press
Louisville, Kentucky

This book is printed on acid-free paper that meets the American National Standards Institute Z39.48 standard. ♾

PRINTED IN THE UNITED STATES OF AMERICA

02 03 04 05 06 07 08 09 10 11 — 10 9 8 7 6 5 4 3 2 1

Library of Congress Cataloging-in-Publication Data

Balmer, Randall Herbert.

Encyclopedia of evangelicalism / Randall Balmer.
p. cm.
Includes bibliographical references.
ISBN 0-664-22409-1 (alk. paper)
1. Evangelicalism—Encyclopedias. 2. Evangelicalism—United States—Encyclopedias. I. Title.

BR1640 .B35 2001
270.8'2'03—dc21

200102690

for Catharine
and for all *the saints*

PREFACE

For some years now, in addition to other scholarly projects, I have been engaged in this quixotic venture of writing an encyclopedia of evangelicalism, one that would provide a sense of both the history and the extraordinary breadth of this popular movement. The task, though maddening at times, has also provided moments of insight and fascination as one topic led to another and still another, like tributaries leading off the beaten path into the brambles.

While I have made every effort to be fair and accurate, I make no pretense of being definitive—that is, because it emanates from one man's pen, this work inevitably bears some biases and interpretations, some of which are apparent simply in what has been chosen for inclusion. For the purposes of this project I have defined *evangelicalism* rather broadly, even though I know that many of the people and organizations treated here prefer a more restrictive interpretation. My latitudinarian approach has yielded, I believe, a far more complex and textured portrait of evangelicalism in all of its diversity.

I recognize that this encyclopedia—with its entries on individuals, organizations, denominations, theological terms, events, and movements—will be used primarily as a reference work. While I have no objection to that, I think this volume also offers a glimpse into evangelical mores and folkways; entries like "Fellowship," "Just," "Testimony," "Sword Drill," and "Gnomic Hebrew Moniker" (to name just a few) provide a sense of evangelicalism as a "lived" tradition, which is appropriate for a movement that, in the United States at least, is the culture's dominant folk religion.

The purview for this book, however, extends beyond the United States. I have sought to include relevant entries from Canada, Latin America, Great Britain, and elsewhere, although I readily acknowledge that the volume is weighted heavily toward North America. Evangelicalism itself, I believe, is a quintessentially North American phenomenon, deriving as it did from the confluence of

Pietism, Presbyterianism, and the vestiges of Puritanism. Evangelicalism picked up peculiar characteristics from each strain—warmhearted spirituality from the Pietists (for instance), doctrinal precisionism from the Presbyterians, and individualistic introspection from the Puritans—even as the North American context itself has profoundly shaped the various manifestations of evangelicalism: fundamentalism, neo-evangelicalism, the holiness movement, pentecostalism, the charismatic movement, and various forms of African-American and Hispanic evangelicalism.

Although I bear ultimate responsibility for this work, several people made my task easier. Holly Folk drafted most of the entries on evangelical colleges and Bible institutes as well as several of the pieces on Christian contemporary music groups. Tommy L. Faris drafted entries on various evangelical denominations, David DiSabatino did the same for the events and personalities surrounding the Jesus movement, and Philemon Sevastiades supplied text for many of the entries on theology. Michael L. Peterson provided information on the Society of Christian Philosophers and several related entries. Jesse T. Todd and J. Shawn Landres each supplied the first draft of an article. I am grateful for their contributions.

Donald Dayton looked over my initial list of entries and offered useful suggestions, and a gift from Lee and Deb Wilson financed some of the student assistance I received. Carey Newman helped me to rescue this manuscript from the clutches of another publisher, and his colleagues at Westminster John Knox Press expertly shepherded it to publication.

A final note. The References section at the end of many of the articles is suggestive rather than exhaustive. I make no pretense of having included a reference to everything a person has published or to all of the relevant literature on a topic.

R. B.
Palm Sunday 2001
Ridgewood, New Jersey

Aberhart, William (1878–1943) Born in southwestern Ontario, William Aberhart graduated from Queen's University in Kingston, Ontario. Although he had been shaped theologically by Presbyterianism, he entered the dispensationalist orbit of *C. I. SCOFIELD around the turn of the century; Aberhart began to teach about the *RAPTURE and the premillennial return of Christ. He migrated west to Calgary, Alberta, in 1905, where he taught at Crescent Heights High School and preached at Westbourne Baptist Church.

Aberhart, known to many as "Bible Bill," attracted large audiences to his "Prophetic Bible Conferences," dispensationalist Bible studies that emphasized biblical *INERRANCY, the imminent return of Jesus, and the imperative of *CONVERSION before it was too late. The conferences became so popular that they moved from Westbourne Baptist to the Grand Theatre, where he illustrated his teachings with a dispensational chart that measured six feet by twenty-one feet. In October 1924 his organization, Calgary Prophetic Bible Conference, began publishing *Prophetic Voice,* a monthly magazine that propagated dispensationalist and fundamentalist doctrines. Aberhart bitterly opposed the formation of the United Church of Canada in 1925, which he saw as the incarnation of liberal or "modernist" theology. He formed the Calgary Prophetic Bible Institute in the fall of that year with the hope that graduates would fill rural pulpits and thereby resist the incursion of *MODERNISM; the new building for the school was dedicated in October 1927. Like Scofield, his mentor, Aberhart also started a correspondence course, called Radio Sunday School, in 1926, and in 1929 he began broadcasting his Prophetic Bible Conference over the radio.

Aberhart's success bred a kind of insularity, and his doctrines began to veer away from evangelical orthodoxy in the 1920s and into what Aberhart himself characterized as "extreme *FUNDAMENTALISM." He taught that the Authorized Version, or King James Version, of the *BIBLE was inerrant, and that it had been translated from original manuscripts that had been hidden in the Swiss Alps, free from the accretions of Roman Catholicism. He held to the "Jesus only" doctrine of believer's *BAPTISM, the notion that the candidate for *BAPTISM is baptized in the name of Jesus alone, not the Father or the Holy Spirit. Aberhart also arrogated to himself the title of "Apostle"; the Westbourne congregation was subsumed under the umbrella of the Calgary Prophetic Bible Institute Church and withdrew from its parent denomination, the Baptist Union of Western Canada.

In the throes of the Great Depression, Aberhart discovered the economic theories of C. H. Douglas, which blamed distant government and financial powers for economic hardship and advocated the idea of "Social Credit," a kind of pump-priming scheme similar to Franklin Roosevelt's New Deal, to promote recovery. Aberhart took these ideas into the political arena, and in the 1935 elections, when the governing party, the United Farmers of Alberta, was plagued with scandal, Aberhart and his Social Credit Party prevailed, making Aberhart the province's premier. The party won again five years later, but Aberhart died in office in 1943; the Social Credit Party, under the leadership of E. C. Manning, one of Aberhart's Bible Institute students, dominated Alberta's provincial politics until 1971.

References: William Aberhart, *God's Great Prophecies* (1922); idem, *An Introduction to the Study of Revelation* (1924); idem, *The Douglas System of Economics* (1933); John G. Stackhouse Jr., s.v. "William Aberhart," in Charles H.

Lippy, ed., *Twentieth-Century Shapers of American Popular Religion* (1989).

Abilene Christian University (Abilene, Texas) Abilene Christian University was founded in 1906 when A. B. Barret, a graduate of Nashville Bible School, persuaded members of the local Church of Christ to sponsor a Bible school in Abilene, Texas. First known as Childers Classical Institute, the school was renamed Abilene Christian College six years later. By 1919, Abilene had become the first college in the Churches of Christ denomination to offer bachelor's degrees.

The college has been on its current campus since 1929. Like many church colleges, Abilene faced financial difficulties in its first few decades; during the Great Depression, for instance, faculty voluntarily returned half their salaries to the school to help balance its budget. In recent years, however, the school has prospered and now offers a wide range of graduate and undergraduate degrees, including graduate programs in divinity, biblical studies, journalism, business, public administration, and gerontology, among others. Abilene's library holds several special collections: the Robbins Railroad Collection, Omar Burleson Archives, Herald of Truth Radio and Television Archives, and the Sewell Bible Library, which contains research materials on the Restoration. In conjunction with this latter collection, Abilene's Center for Restoration Studies sponsors exhibits, lectures, and tours on church and Restoration history.

References: *Abilene Christian University Graduate Catalog 1995–97* (1995); William C. Ringenberg, *The Christian College: A History of Protestant Higher Education in America* (1984).

Abolitionism From the sixteenth to the nineteenth century, approximately fifteen million Africans were forcibly removed to the Americas to work as slaves. The first organization to emerge in the abolitionist movement was the Abolition Society, founded in England in 1787 under the leadership of Thomas Clarkson and *WILLIAM WILBERFORCE. The society succeeded in persuading Parliament in 1807 to abolish the slave trade with its colonies. When slavery itself persisted, the Anti-Slavery Society was founded in Britain in 1823 under the leadership of Thomas Fowell Buxton, a member of Parliament. In 1833, nearly four decades after France had outlawed slavery in its colonies, Parliament passed a law abolishing slavery in all British colonies.

The debate over the abolition of slavery and the slave trade bitterly divided America's evangelicals. Following the lead of such eighteenth-century opponents of slavery as John Woolman, a Quaker, several denominations in the early national period took stands against slaveholding. The most notorious statement came from the Methodists, who in the articles of their founding in 1784 tried to deny membership to slaveholders. The Methodists never enforced that provision, however, so it was left to individuals to work for the abolition of slavery.

Although the slave trade was abolished in 1807, slavery itself continued in the South, in part because of the robust demand for cotton. Northern evangelicals, however, became especially exercised about the perpetuation of what they regarded as a barbaric practice, although the solutions they proposed ranged widely from outright abolition to gradual emancipation to the colonization of blacks to Liberia in Africa. The pressure intensified in 1831 when William Lloyd Garrison began publishing the *Liberator,* and the formation of the American Anti-Slavery Society two years later abetted new avenues of resistance, especially the Underground Railroad.

As the chasm between North and South widened over the issue of slavery, Protestant denominations divided in anticipation of the Civil War. The *SOUTHERN BAPTIST CONVENTION was organized in 1845 after a split with Northerners over abolition; the Methodist Episcopal Church, South was formed the same year. Southern Presbyterians seceded from the larger Presbyterian denomination in 1861. Methodists reunited in 1939, and the Presbyterians in 1983. The Southern Baptists have never reunited with those in the North.

Reference: C. C. Goen, *Broken Churches, Broken Nation: Denominational Schisms and the Coming of the American Civil War* (1985).

Abortion A controversial issue among Christians for centuries, abortion emerged in the 1970s as a major point of political and religious division. While the Roman Catholic hierarchy has been steadfast in its opposition to abortion, Protestants have generally (though not universally) followed suit. Paul Ramsey, a Methodist and an ethicist at Princeton University, consistently articulated a theological case against abortion, but some liberal Protestants equivocated, employing the language of privacy, individual conscience, and women's rights.

In the United States, the Supreme Court's 1973 *Roe* v. *Wade* decision, which opened the way for legalized abortion, sharpened the issue. Initially, the response on the part of evangelicals was muted—the famously conservative *SOUTHERN BAPTIST CONVENTION, in fact, endorsed *Roe* v. *Wade* in 1973 and for several years thereafter as a landmark decision affirming the separation of church and state—but as the *RELIGIOUS RIGHT began to gather force later in the 1970s, abortion became a matter of religious debate. *PAUL WEYRICH, one of the architects of the *RELIGIOUS RIGHT, for example, insists that only in the late 1970s, after evangelical conservatives had cooperated on other political issues, was opposition to abortion added to the agenda. Sensing a political opportunity, *RONALD REAGAN, the Republican candidate for president in 1980 who, as governor of California, had signed a law legalizing abortion, loudly proclaimed his opposition to abortion. That position helped him win the votes of politically conservative evangelicals in 1980 and again in 1984.

The antiabortion movement (which generally prefers the moniker "pro-life") was most visible in the 1980s, and the activism took many forms, from blockades of abortion clinics to moves in Congress to outlaw abortion by constitutional amendment (something that Reagan had promised to push for in both of his campaigns). More liberal elements of the evangelical community generally concurred, although **SOJOURNERS* magazine, for example, linked opposition to abortion to a wider "pro-life" agenda, including opposition to capital punishment and help for the poor. Among many politically conservative evangelicals, opposition to abortion became a kind of litmus test for faith itself, and *RELIGIOUS RIGHT activists were so adamant that they succeeded in demanding that Republican politicians accede to their view in order to win their votes.

The election of Bill Clinton to the presidency in 1992 effectively ended—or at least tabled—hopes for an outright legal ban on abortion, either through legislation or through the appointment of antiabortion jurists to the Supreme Court. Sensing that the issue was losing some of its potency, leaders of the *RELIGIOUS

Right, while not abandoning their stand on abortion, shifted their rhetoric in the 1990s to other issues, such as opposition to homosexuality.

References: Dallas A. Blanchard, *The Anti-Abortion Movement and the Rise of the Religious Right: From Polite to Fiery Protest* (1994); Cynthia Gorney, *Articles of Faith: A Frontline History of the Abortion Wars* (1998).

Acadia University (Wolfville, Nova Scotia) Acadia College was formed in 1838 in the aftermath of the *Revival in the Maritimes, sometimes called the *Canada Fire, led by *Henry Alline. Founded and supported by the Baptists of Nova Scotia, Acadia was not established solely for the training of ministers; instead, backers of the school believed that education should not be for the elites alone, but for the common people as well. Acadia University, which includes Acadia Divinity College, represents one of the many contributions of the dissenting tradition to higher education in Canada.

Reference: Barry M. Moody, "Breadth of Vision, Breadth of Mind: The Baptists of Acadia College," in G. A. Rawlyk, ed., *Canadian Baptists and Christian Higher Education* (1988).

Accrediting Association of Bible Colleges The Accrediting Association of Bible Colleges (AABC), formerly known as the American Association of Bible Colleges, was established several decades ago as an alternative to (secular) regional accrediting agencies, whose standards were often incompatible with the priorities of many Bible institutes. The Accrediting Association of Bible Colleges now has nearly one hundred member institutions, including Baptist Bible College, *Moody Bible Institute, *Multnomah Bible College, and *Philadelphia College of Bible. As a federally recognized accrediting agency, the AABC makes it possible for its member schools to participate in certain federal programs (by providing an assurance that certain standards are upheld) without additional reviews from the government. In addition to its accrediting services, the association also offers support services for its member schools, including the production and distribution of relevant publications, holding annual and regional meetings, and sponsoring professional development for faculty and administrators.

Reference: Virginia Lieson Brereton, *Training God's Army: The American Bible School, 1880–1940* (1990).

Addams, Jane (1860–1935) Jane Addams's mother died when she was three, so she was reared in Cedarville, Illinois, by her father, who was a successful miller, a Quaker, an eight-term Illinois state senator, and a friend of Abraham Lincoln. At seventeen Addams entered the Rockford Female Seminary (now Rockford College) and later studied medicine at the Women's Medical College of Pennsylvania, although poor health forced her to curtail her medical studies. On the advice of doctors she took two trips to Europe; after the first she returned to Cedarville and joined the Presbyterian Church. In the course of her second trip, which lasted from 1887 to 1889, Addams visited Toynbee Hall, an institution designed to meet the needs of London's poor. When she returned to the United States she moved to Chicago and, with her college friend Ellen Gates Starr, founded Hull House in a shabby old mansion on Halstead Street in the city's Nineteenth Ward, an area of tenements and sweatshops.

Within months Addams and Starr had transformed the building into a center of cultural activity and social outreach: a theater, a day nursery, a boys' club, and a home for working girls. The success of the enterprise attracted support from private philanthropists, and it gave Addams public exposure as an advocate for the urban poor. She worked for legislation to improve the lot of urban laborers, and she became increasingly interested in issues surrounding women; she addressed prostitution and feminine psychology in her writings.

Addams's *Twenty Years at Hull-House,* published in 1910, earned her an international reputation. During World War I she helped to form the Women's Peace Party and lobbied extensively in Europe for an end to hostilities. In 1920, Addams helped to organize the American Civil Liberties Union and was elected the first president of the Women's International League for Peace and Freedom. Her efforts on behalf of the poor, for peace, and for women were recognized in 1931 when, with Nicholas Murray Butler, she was named recipient of the Nobel Peace Prize.

By the time of her death in 1935, Hull House had expanded to cover an entire city block, with buildings centered around a courtyard. In 1961, plans were made to tear down Hull House to make room for the Chicago campus of the University of Illinois. Despite worldwide protests against such plans, the properties were sold in 1963, although the original building was preserved as a memorial to Addams. Hull House settlement work was relocated to other venues in Chicago.

References: Jane Addams, *Democracy and Social Ethics* (1902); idem, *Newer Ideals of Peace* (1907); idem, *The Spirit of Youth and the City Streets* (1909); idem, *Twenty Years at Hull-House* (1910); idem, *A New Conscience and an Ancient Evil* (1911); idem, *The Long Road of Women's Memory* (1916); idem, *The Second Twenty Years at Hull-House* (1930).

Adopting Act of 1729 The Adopting Act of 1729, drafted primarily by *JONATHAN DICKINSON, forged a compromise between the New England and Scots-Irish factions of American Presbyterianism over the issue of subscription to the *WESTMINSTER STANDARDS. The *SUBSCRIPTION CONTROVERSY, which reflected similar disputes back in Great Britain, pitted people who demanded strict adherence to Westminister against the "Puritan" faction, which wanted to allow for expressions of piety. The Adopting Act stitched the two sides together, at least until the *GREAT AWAKENING exposed the fissure yet again and divided Presbyterians into Old Lights and *NEW LIGHTS.

Reference: Randall Balmer and John R. Fitzmier, *The Presbyterians* (1993).

Adoption Five references in the New Testament, all found in the writings of Paul, refer to the concept of adoption as it pertains to the new relationship between God and humanity through Jesus Christ. The Old Testament does not stipulate specific laws regarding adoption; in a number of cases, however, adoptions took place. In Genesis, Jacob takes two of Joseph's sons as his own (Gen. 48:5). Also in Genesis, a type of adoption is suggested by the taking of a child between an adult's knees, thereby demonstrating a family relationship henceforth (Gen. 48:12; 50:23). In Ruth, Naomi verbally adopts Ruth's son (Ruth 4:16–17). Two clear examples of God's adoption and the filial relationship deriving from it are the prophet Nathan's conveying God's will about David's successor: "I will be a father to him, and he shall be a son to me" (2 Sam. 7:14). Again in Psalm 2:7, God states about his anointed king: "You are my son; today I have begotten you."

These examples, along with Roman law that was applicable during Paul's lifetime, serve as the model for the concept of adoption in the New Testament. By adoption Christians are made "sons of God." This familial relationship is very important in understanding how evangelicals understand their relationship to God and Jesus Christ. While Paul no doubt understood and modeled the concept of adoption upon his extensive knowledge of Old Testament scripture and Roman law, he develops a new spin on adoption in the New Testament. That spin, which has become central to evangelical understanding of the believer's relationship with Jesus Christ, focuses upon a personal adoption by God through Jesus Christ. Thus, believers redeemed by Christ are all made "children of God." As a child of God, the believer is no longer a slave literally, nor a slave to the material order of the universe. Believers are by adoption what Christ is by birthright, and as such, they become co-inheritors along with Christ (Rom. 8:17) of God's Kingdom and all that it implies. However, the process of adoption is not quite complete in the evangelical understanding until the final deliverance when the body will be freed completely from the material world and admitted into the world to come (Rom. 8:23). This understanding is one reason why evangelicals are focused upon the time of waiting with anticipation as well as focused on the eschaton, or the end of time, when the struggle to maintain a relationship with Christ by carrying out his commandments will be ended.

Adoration This term describes a strong sense of worship, in evangelical practice directed appropriately only to God and Jesus Christ. Occasionally, especially in pentecostal circles, this worship is directed to the Holy Spirit as well, but often in a context together with the first two persons of the Holy Trinity.

Adoration can also have a negative connotation, such as the idol worship that is repeatedly depicted throughout the *BIBLE as humans turning away from the true God. Evangelicals understand the proper use of adoration as "giving glory to God," usually expressed in prayer or song or even in personal comportment. Thus, for adoration to be true worship and not fall into idolatry, all glory must be directed to God or to the Trinity.

Advent Christian Church The Advent Christian Church is a denomination that traces its roots to the millennial prophecies of *WILLIAM MILLER, who predicted that Jesus would return to earth on October 22, 1844. After the *GREAT DISAPPOINTMENT of the *MILLERITE movement in 1844 the Adventists scattered in various directions. Many people went back to the churches from which they had come. Other Millerites attempted to find the error that *WILLIAM MILLER must have made so that they could prepare more adequately for Jesus' *SECOND COMING. One of the latter groups decided that Miller had been off in his calculations by ten years. Accordingly, they looked to 1854 for Jesus' return. After this final disappointment some of this group pulled together to form the Advent Christian Church.

One of the foundational beliefs of the Advent Christians is that of "Life Only in Jesus Christ." According to this belief, immortality of the soul is conditional, applying only to those who qualify for it through faith in Christ. Furthermore, the Advent Christians believe that the soul remains in an unconscious state until the return of Christ and that the souls of the wicked become extinct rather than pass into eternal torment. Advent Christians also continue to maintain the *MILLERITE belief in the imminent return of Jesus Christ, though without Miller's date-setting. The *POLITY of the churches is congregational, and the denomination has no formal creedal statements. The Advent Christian Church merged with the Life and Advent Union in 1964.

Headquarters for the Advent Christian General Conference of America are in Charlotte, North Carolina. The denomination maintains two colleges, Aurora University in Aurora, Illinois, and Berkshire Christian College in Haverhill, Massachusetts. Approximately twenty thousand members are spread among 350 churches in the United States and Canada. The denomination joined the *NATIONAL ASSOCIATION OF EVANGELICALS in 1987.

References: Frank S. Mead and Samuel S. Hill, *Handbook of Denominations in the United States*, 10th ed. (1996); J. Gordon Melton, *The Encyclopedia of American Religions*, 3d ed. (1993).

Adventism While more liturgical traditions observe Advent, the season leading to Christmas and commemorating the advent of Jesus, evangelicals are more likely to be concerned about adventism, which denotes the *SECOND COMING of Jesus. Adventists, then, are people who look for the *SECOND COMING; most adventists, moreover, are premillennialists, who believe that Jesus will return at any moment, before the *MILLENNIUM predicted in the book of Revelation. In a less generic sense of the word, adventism also refers to the *SEVENTH-DAY ADVENTISTS, an evangelical denomination.

Africa Inland Mission Founded in 1895 by *PETER CAMERON SCOTT, who died the following year, the Africa Inland Mission is an interdenominational missionary agency. From its early years the organization has emphasized to the mission field the importance of social issues. With offices in Bristol, England, the African Inland Mission operates as a faith mission, meaning that it does not engage in the solicitation of funds.

African Methodist Episcopal Church. *See* **Methodism.**

African Methodist Episcopal Zion Church. *See* **Methodism.**

Alaska Bible College (Glenallen, Alaska) Alaska Bible College began as a project of Central Alaska Missions, Inc., a missionary organization established by Vincent J. Joy. As early as 1957, Joy's organization formed a Christian Education Committee, which allocated eighty acres of leased land for a new *BIBLE INSTITUTE. Alaska Bible College opened nine years later with twelve students and three teachers; the first commencement exercises took place in 1970. In 1971, Central Alaska Missions merged with SEND International, another evangelistic association. The *ACCREDITING ASSOCIATION OF BIBLE COLLEGES has accredited the college since 1982. Alaska Bible College also has legal status with the state of Alaska, but no regional accreditation. Beginning in 1976, Alaska Bible College has developed extension programs in Anchorage, Fairbanks, and Juneau.

Although Alaska Bible College's curriculum now includes courses in math, psychology, and Western civilization, the overall structure is still that of a traditional Bible school. Every four-year student completes a major in *BIBLE, choosing a second major from one of the following areas: pastoral, missions, Christian education, Christian camping, or integrated studies in ministry. The college also offers an associate of arts degree for students seeking basic training in ministry, as well as a certificate in *BIBLE and a non-degree program in Christian Service ministries. All students are expected to do Christian fieldwork. They are also expected to complete work assignments in the dining hall, which helps keep down operating costs. Toward this end, college employees are also expected to make financial contributions. Faculty and staff are responsible for raising their own salaries.

Alaska Bible College's standards of conduct are fairly vague; students are asked to refrain from alcohol, drugs, tobacco, and "any other conduct that might adversely reflect on Christ." The absence of language regarding *DANCING or entertainment, however, should not be taken as a sign of *LIBERALISM. "Recognizable Christian living" and "commitment to Biblical truth compatible with the Doctrinal Standard of the College" are two requirements for graduation. Furthermore, Alaska is unusually specific about its doctrinal positions, which suggest a very conservative theology. In the school's "Doctrinal Standard," Alaska states unequivocally that it is not a "Charismatic college." In fact, students from charismatic traditions are required to sign a pledge promising not to propagate spiritual miracles, double election, or *SPEAKING IN TONGUES, which is considered especially outside the pale of "normative Christianity." Students who disagree with these positions are encouraged to "seek their education at an institution of like mind."

Reference: *Alaska Bible College 1996–1998 Catalog* (1996).

Aldrich, Joseph C(offin) (1940–) An evangelical preacher and educator, Joseph C. Aldrich graduated from Multnomah School of the Bible, Southern Oregon State College, and *DALLAS THEOLOGICAL SEMINARY, where he earned both the master's and the Th.D. degrees. After serving several pastorates, he succeeded his father, Willard Aldrich, as president of Multnomah School of the Bible, in Portland, Oregon, in 1978. Under the direction of the younger Aldrich, Multnomah moved away from some of the more strident *FUNDAMENTALISM that characterized its past and toward a more inclusive, cooperative evangelicalism. Aldrich was active in other evangelistic organizations, including the *BILLY GRAHAM School of Evangelism. Aldrich served as chair of the *BILLY GRAHAM crusade in Portland held in September 1992. Poor health forced him to step down from the presidency at Multnomah, and Dan Lockwood succeeded him in 1997.

Alexander, Archibald (1772–1851) Archibald Alexander, arguably the progenitor of the *PRINCETON THEOLOGY, spent many of his early years as an itinerant minister in eastern Virginia. He was educated under the tutelage of William Graham, rector of Liberty Hall, and was ordained in the Presbyterian Church in 1794. In 1807, at the age of thirty-five, Alexander was elected moderator of the General Assembly, and during his address the following year he spoke of the need for a theological seminary. Following a term as president of Hampden-Sydney College and immediately preceding his appointment as professor of didactic and polemic theology at Princeton, he was pastor of the Pine Street Presbyterian Church in Philadelphia.

References: Archibald Alexander, *A Brief Outline of the Evidences of the Christian Religion* (1825); idem, *Evidences of the Authenticity, Inspiration, and Canonical Authority of the Holy Scriptures* (1826); idem, *The Log College* (1851); Mark A. Noll, ed., *The Princeton Theology, 1812–1921* (1983).

Alexander, Joseph Addison (1809–1860) The son of *ARCHIBALD ALEXANDER, the founder of Princeton Theological Seminary, Joseph Addison Alexander was a precocious child who learned to read the Old Testament in original Hebrew by the age of ten. An accomplished linguist, he graduated with highest honors from the College of New Jersey in 1826, where he later served as adjunct professor of languages and literature from 1830 until 1833. After study in Europe, Alexander became instructor (1834), associate professor (1838), and then professor of oriental and biblical literature (1840–1851) at Princeton Seminary. In 1851, he was named to the Chair of Biblical and Ecclesiastical History and then finished his career as professor of hellenistic and New Testament literature from 1859 until his death. Alexander's many commentaries brought him renown in both the United States and Great Britain. He contributed frequently to the *Biblical Repertory* and served as one of its editors for many years.

Allen, A(sa) A(lonzo) (1911–1970) Born into poverty in Sulphur Rock, Arkansas, A. A. Allen became an itinerant *EVANGELIST, an evangelical radio personality, and a publisher. Allen, who later characterized himself as "an ex-jailbird drifting aimlessly through life," was converted from drunkenness and dissipation in a "*TONGUES speaking" Methodist church in 1934. Shortly thereafter he became a licensed minister in the *ASSEMBLIES OF GOD. After a stint as pastor of a small church in Colorado, Allen forged a career—though not much of a living—as an itinerant revivalist for the *ASSEMBLIES OF GOD. In 1947 he accepted a more stable post as pastor of an Assembly of God in Corpus Christi, Texas.

Though initially suspicious of the "healing *REVIVALS" taking place throughout the South, Allen drove to Dallas in 1949 to hear *ORAL ROBERTS and returned convinced that this activity was a work of God. When his congregation refused to support a radio program, however, Allen once again became an itinerant, this time with an emphasis on healing. Ever the showman, he purchased a large tent in 1951, set up headquarters in Dallas, and started a radio program, the *Allen Revival Hour,* in 1953. His message was both sensational and populist, articulating the concerns and frustrations of the destitute and the handicapped; his campaigns took him to Cuba and Mexico, and his radio broadcast was carried on stations throughout Latin America as well as in the United States.

After an arrest for drunk driving in fall 1955, while he was conducting a crusade in Knoxville, Tennessee, Allen skipped bail rather than standing trial. The incident brought to the fore the persistent rumors of his drinking, even though Allen tried to portray himself as victim of an elaborate kidnapping scheme. Rather than face expulsion from the *VOICE OF HEALING, a loose organization of Assemblies' healing evangelists, Allen, like *JIMMY SWAGGART several decades later, surrendered his ministerial credentials and became independent. He also became increasingly paranoid, attacking his critics as atheists, communists, and unsympathetic to *REVIVALS. Stung by the criticism of other pentecostals, Allen even tried to set up a kind of denomination, Miracle Revival Fellowship, for clergy and laity. His publication, *Miracle Magazine,* which had a circulation of two hundred thousand in 1956, also provided a means of communication outside of denominational conduits.

In 1958, Allen established Miracle Valley, a permanent headquarters and training center, near Bisbee, Arizona. There he developed some of the ideas linking physical and financial well-being that became part of the pentecostal "faith movement" a decade later. In 1967, he divorced his wife of more than thirty years, and three years later he died alone in a San Francisco motel room.

References: A. A. Allen, *My Cross* (1957); David Edwin Harrell Jr., *All Things are Possible: The Healing and Charismatic Revivals in Modern America* (1975).

Allen, Richard (1760–1831) Born into slavery, Richard Allen grew up on a plantation near Dover, Delaware, and was converted in 1777. He began preaching in local Methodist churches and on the plantation, where his owner became one of Allen's early converts. Allen was allowed to purchase his freedom, whereupon he became a protégé of *FRANCIS ASBURY, preaching on Methodist circuits in the mid-Atlantic region and supporting himself with odd jobs.

In 1786, Allen joined St. George's Methodist Church in his native Philadelphia, a predominantly white congregation. The prayer and Bible study sessions Allen offered attracted other blacks to the church, but their presence kindled resentment among white congregants and led to a segregated seating arrangement for worship services, with blacks consigned to the gallery. Offended, Allen and Absalom Jones led a contingent of African Americans out of St. George's to form the Free African Society.

Allen then set on a determined course for distinctive black religious identity. He organized his followers in 1784 as the Bethel African Methodist Episcopal Church, with *FRANCIS ASBURY's blessing. St. George's, however, resisted Allen's efforts at independence; a court ruling finally allowed for the formation of the African Methodist Episcopal Church in April 1816.

References: Richard Allen, *The Life, Experience, and Gospel Labors of the Rt. Rev. Richard Allen* (1793); Carol V. R. George, *Segregated Sabbaths: Richard Allen and the Emergence of Independent Black Churches, 1760–1840* (1973).

Alliance Defense Fund An organization associated with the *RELIGIOUS RIGHT, the Alliance Defense Fund is a legal defense fund that was created in 1994 to counteract the influence of the American Civil Liberties Union on matters of religious freedom. *DON WILDMON of the *AMERICAN FAMILY ASSOCIATION, *BILL BRIGHT of *CAMPUS CRUSADE FOR CHRIST, *D. JAMES KENNEDY of Coral Ridge Ministries, *JAMES DOBSON of *FOCUS ON THE FAMILY, and *LARRY BURKETT of *CHRISTIAN FINANCIAL CONCEPTS are its founders.

Alliance Theological Seminary (Nyack, New York). *See* **Nyack College and Alliance Theological Seminary.**

Alline, Henry (1748–1784) Sometimes called "the Whitefield of Nova Scotia," after the famous revivalist *GEORGE WHITEFIELD, Henry Alline was born in Newport, Rhode Island, and moved with his parents to Falmouth, Nova Scotia, at the age of twelve. In 1775, after many years of spiritual seeking, Alline had a dramatic and emotional *CONVERSION experience, one with arguably mystical overtones. He began preaching throughout the Maritime Provinces and found especially receptive audiences in rural Nova Scotia.

While Alline, a Baptist, urged on his audiences the importance of evangelical regeneration, his preaching also had the effect of reinforcing sentiments of political neutrality among Nova Scotians during the American Revolution. Alline's fervent piety lent itself to the writing of music (a volume called *Hymns and Spiritual Songs* was published posthumously), and his revival successes in the Maritimes emboldened him to make forays into New England. He died of tuberculosis in 1784, shortly after undertaking a preaching tour to New Hampshire.

References: G. A. Rawlyk, *Ravished by the Spirit: Religious Revivals, Baptists, and Henry Alline* (1984); idem, *The Canada Fire: Radical Evangelicalism in British North America, 1775–1812* (1994).

Alma White College. *See* **White, Alma.**

Almira College. *See* **Greenville College.**

Alpha An evangelical renewal movement, Alpha began in 1977 at a Church of England parish, Holy Trinity Brampton. Nicky Gumbel and other leaders in the congregation sought to devise a program that would provide spiritual nurture for their parishioners. The Alpha course produced remarkable results in Brampton, an evangelical, charismatic congregation. Beginning in 1993, designers of the Alpha materials made them available to other churches throughout Great Britain, then to the Continent, to North America, and eventually around the world. Approximately half a million people attended Alpha courses in 1997, led by people who have taken a two-day intensive training course.

The ten-week Alpha curriculum places a strong emphasis on *EVANGELISM and on the charismatic gifts. Aside from its obvious connotations, the name Alpha also represents an acronym: *A*=anyone interested in learning more about Christianity; *L*=learning and laughter; *P*=pasta (eating together is emphasized as a community-building activity); *H*=helping one another; *A*=ask anything.

Reference: Timothy C. Morgan, "The Alpha-Brits Are Coming," *Christianity Today*, February 9, 1998.

Alston, William P(ayne) (1921–) Born in Shreveport, Louisiana, William P. Alston grew up in ***METHODISM**, although he later changed his denominational affiliation to Episcopal. He earned the bachelor's degree from Centenary College in 1942 and the Ph.D. from the University of Chicago in 1951. A philosopher of religion, he taught at the University of Illinois at Champaign-Urbana, Rutgers University, and the University of Michigan before becoming a professor of philosophy at Syracuse University. Alston has held various research fellowships and has served as president of various philosophical societies, including the ***SOCIETY OF CHRISTIAN PHILOSOPHERS**, from 1978 until 1981.

Alston has played a significant role in the renewal among professional philosophers of academic interest in Christian belief. In the 1970s, he moved from a nominal religious life to a more genuine Christian faith (as he recounted in a 1994 essay entitled "A Philosopher's Way Back to the Faith"). As a consequence of this "*CONVERSION" in 1978, Alston helped conceive and was elected the first president of the ***SOCIETY OF CHRISTIAN PHILOSOPHERS**; his reputation as a first-class philosopher of language was one of several factors that gave early credibility and momentum to the Society. In 1982, he became editor of ***FAITH AND PHILOSOPHY**, a journal published by the Society, and served in that capacity until 1990.

Alston's philosophical interests include the rationality of religious belief, issues between realism and antirealism, and the philosophy of religious language. Much of his speaking and publishing has been on the epistemology of religious experience (how we know), and he is widely known for defending a position that identifies parallels between sense perception and religious experience, arguing that the ways in which we form beliefs about God bear important similarities to the ways in which we form beliefs about external sensory objects. This position refutes critics who dismiss religious belief as falling outside our normal epistemological processes.

References: William P. Alston, *Philosophy of Language* (1964); idem, *Epistemic Justification* (1989); idem, *Divine Nature and Human Language* (1993); idem, *The Reliability of Sense Perception* (1993).

Altar Call For most evangelicals the term "altar call" is a misnomer in that their churches have no physical altar. Most evangelicals subscribe to a "memorialist" interpretation of the *LORD'S SUPPER, which insists that the bread and wine of *HOLY COMMUNION merely represent the body and blood of Christ; they are not changed, as in the Roman Catholic doctrine of transubstantiation, into the actual body and blood of Christ. For that reason, an altar call, which is generally an invitation by the preacher to step toward the pulpit for *CONVERSION, *BAPTISM, or church membership, is really an invitation to a spiritual rather than a physical location.

Throughout American history various *EVANGELISTS have had signature altar calls. *BILLY SUNDAY, for instance, would invite—more often, taunt—his auditors to "hit the *SAWDUST TRAIL" and shake the preacher's hand as an indication of their intention to give their lives to Jesus (the term came from the practice of sprinkling sawdust on the aisles during tent meetings). *BILLY GRAHAM had his choir sing verse after verse of "Just As I Am," sometimes pausing between verses while he issued yet another plea for people to come forward and "make a decision for Christ." Not all evangelical services culminate in an altar call. Some preachers use it only on occasion, when they sense a special moving of the Holy Spirit. Among other groups, however, notably the Southern Baptists, altar calls at the conclusion of services are so customary that they might qualify as a ritual.

Amazing Grace Mission. *See* **Farmers for Christ International.**

American Association of Bible Colleges. *See* **Accrediting Association of Bible Colleges.**

American Association of Christian Schools Founded in 1972, the American Association of Christian Schools claims more than one thousand affiliated schools in the United States, reaching a student population of approximately 150,000. With strong associations with such *RELIGIOUS RIGHT organizations as the *FAMILY RESEARCH COUNCIL, its stated purpose is "to aid in promoting, establishing, advancing, and developing Christian schools and Christian education in America." Its headquarters are in Independence, Missouri, with an additional office in Washington, D.C.

American Baptist Churches in the USA The history of Baptists in America dates back to the founding of the First Baptist Church in Providence, Rhode Island, in 1638. Baptist ideals and churches continued to spread through much of the colonies, and the first association of Baptist churches, the Philadelphia Baptist Association, was formed in 1707. The two principles of the autonomy of congregations and of voluntary association have guided much of the life, work, and growth of the Baptist churches in America.

The number of Baptists began to grow significantly after the American Revolution, due in large measure to the *SECOND GREAT AWAKENING. By the early nineteenth century, considerable disagreement had arisen among the Baptists concerning the role and propriety of establishing mission work in the United States and other countries. Baptists had originally come out of the *SEPARATIST Puritan/Reformed tradition, with its grounding in *CALVINISM, including the doctrine of election. Most felt that, according to the Reformed teaching of that day, it was inappropriate to send out missionaries. The Calvinist doctrines of predestination and election meant that it was not in the power or purview of Christians to extend the *GOSPEL to new places other than by the migration of believers. The quarrel came to a head in 1814. *ADONIRAM JUDSON, along with his wife, *ANN, and *LUTHER RICE, had been sent to India by the Congregational churches of Massachusetts to establish a mission in South Asia. On the ocean voyage, however, Judson and his party became convinced of Baptist doctrines and announced upon arrival in India that they were Baptists, whereupon they sent word of their change of heart and mind back to the United States. Rice returned to try to raise support for this mission work among the Baptists; Judson moved the site of his work to Burma. Without ever meaning to do it, American Baptists had taken their first step into missionary endeavor.

Rice's efforts led to the founding of the General Missionary Convention of the Baptist Denomination in the United States of America for Foreign Missions, later known as the American Baptist Foreign Mission Society. This group met every three years and was known popularly as the *TRIENNIAL CONVENTION. In 1824, the American Baptist Home Mission Society was established, and the American Baptist Tract and Publication Society was formed in 1832. These three societies formed the nucleus of what would become the American Baptist Churches in the USA (ABCUSA) and the *SOUTHERN BAPTIST CONVENTION. When the societies refused to appoint unmarried women as missionaries, American Baptist women formed their own foreign and home mission societies in the 1870s.

By the 1840s, the issue of slavery had begun to undermine the unity of the societies. When both the foreign and home mission societies refused to appoint slaveholders as missionaries, the Baptist churches in the South withdrew to form their own societies. These churches established a much more centralized form of government and became the *SOUTHERN BAPTIST CONVENTION. The three original societies continued their work until 1907, when the various appeals for funds had become confusing and unsatisfactory. The Northern Baptist Convention was formed to coordinate the efforts of the three societies, which became cooperating organizations of the convention. The convention reorganized in 1950 and changed the name to the American Baptist Convention. Another reorganization in 1972 led to the final name change to the current American Baptist Churches in the USA.

The doctrinal base of the ABCUSA is strictly noncreedal. At various times there have been statements of faith, most notably the *NEW HAMPSHIRE CONFESSION, but

American Baptists have resisted the adoption of creeds. Instead, the ABCUSA emphasizes the concepts of soul freedom and the priesthood of believers. American Baptists believe that every believer has the ability to read and to interpret Scripture according to the leading of the Holy Spirit within him or her. No believer needs any intermediary either to understand Scripture or to pray. This belief has led to the proliferation of theological positions on many issues. In recent years, American Baptists have emphasized the diversity within the denomination while, at the same time, maintaining the presence of a unified core of belief in the person and work of Jesus Christ.

Most American Baptists are evangelical in belief and practice, affirming the divine inspiration, though not always the *INERRANCY, of Scripture. The ABCUSA is strongly Trinitarian. The churches observe the ordinances of *BAPTISM by immersion for adult believers and, usually monthly, the *LORD'S SUPPER. Baptists in America have often been at the forefront on the issues of the separation of church and state. From *JOHN LELAND and *ISAAC BACKUS in the colonial period and the early Republic to the current work of the interdenominational Baptist Joint Committee on Public Affairs, Baptists have striven for the freedom of all believers and churches without influence or interference from governmental authority.

The diversity among American Baptists has taken its toll. Controversies in the 1920s and 1940s led to the formation of the *GENERAL ASSOCIATION OF REGULAR BAPTIST CHURCHES in 1932 and of the *CONSERVATIVE BAPTIST ASSOCIATION in 1947. In both of these controversies the groups that left the denomination were on the more conservative theological side of various doctrinal issues, notably the inspiration and *INERRANCY of the *BIBLE. Even so, the conservative evangelical presence has remained strong in the ABCUSA, especially in recent years in the form of the American Baptist Evangelicals, an evangelical caucus within the larger American Baptist body.

American Baptists have long been proponents of ecumenism and interfaith cooperation. The ABCUSA was among the founding denominations of the Federal Council of Churches (now the National Council of Churches in Christ) and has also maintained membership in the *BAPTIST WORLD ALLIANCE and the World Council of Churches. While not a formal member of the *NATIONAL ASSOCIATION OF EVANGELICALS (NAE), the ABCUSA does have relationships with member denominations of that group and has had observer status in NAE meetings.

Since the founding of the mission societies, American Baptists have been aggressive and unwavering in their support for foreign and home mission endeavors. Overseas, the ABCUSA works closely with indigenous leadership among the churches, often taking a supportive role in the work of the national churches. In the United States, American Baptists, most obviously Walter Rauschenbusch, pastor and later a seminary professor, were among the leaders in developing the *SOCIAL GOSPEL movement. The American Baptist churches also worked closely with Baptists among immigrants to the United States.

ABCUSA *POLITY is staunchly congregational. The mission societies, now called the Board of International Mission, the Board of National Mission, and the Board of Educational Mission, continue their work with the support of affiliated churches. The churches send delegates to a biennial convention. Between biennial meetings the general board oversees the work of the mission boards, and the office of the general secretary has general oversight of denominational efforts. While the majority of the denomination is generally evangelical, the leadership of the ABCUSA has tended to be more liberal in theology. Today, while the validity of any blanket statement concerning the ABCUSA is questionable, the denomination is usually considered among the mainline Protestant churches.

Headquarters for the ABCUSA are in Valley Forge, Pennsylvania, and the denomination claims more than fifty-eight hundred American Baptist churches and in excess of 1.5 million members. The denomination supports several colleges and five seminaries across the country.

References: Frank S. Mead and Samuel S. Hill, *Handbook of Denominations in the United States*, 10th ed. (1996); J. Gordon Melton, *Encyclopedia of American Religions*, 3d ed. (1993).

American Baptist Foreign Mission Society. *See* **Southern Baptist Convention** *and* **Triennial Convention.**

American Bible Society The American Bible Society (ABS) is a nonprofit, "interconfessional" or interdenominational organization, whose purpose is to "Provide the Holy Scriptures to every man, woman, and child in a language and form each can readily understand, and at a price each can easily afford." With national headquarters in New York City, the American Bible Society translates Scripture and prints *BIBLES, New Testaments, individual books of the *BIBLE, and short tracts and, with the help of a network of volunteers—the "Scripture Sharers"—distributes them at or below cost across the United States and overseas. Through this work, the American Bible Society sees itself as fulfilling the Great Commission of Matthew 28:19, the injunction in which all Christians are commanded to "Go therefore and make disciples of all nations."

The impulse to distribute the vernacular *BIBLE can be traced to Martin Luther's insistence on the priesthood of believers. Luther himself translated the New Testament into German, thereby laying the linguistic foundation for the German language and triggering a rise in literacy, as the common folk sought to read and interpret the Scriptures for themselves.

In the United States, evangelicals have been eager to place copies of the *BIBLE into the hands of the people. By the early nineteenth century more than one hundred societies had been established for this purpose, but the formation of the American Bible Society in New York City in 1816, modeled loosely on the British and Foreign Bible Society, represented by far the largest *BIBLE distribution effort. The Society seized on the emerging print technologies to produce *BIBLES at a furious pace—in the 1820s, the American Bible Society had more Treadwell presses than did the publishing company Harper & Brothers—and it made use of local auxiliaries both to distribute the Bibles and to collect money.

The Bible society movement relied on the efforts of the *COLPORTEURS, the individual *BIBLE and tract distributors who worked in the United States in the nineteenth century. Leadership of the organization, on the other hand, was illustrious. Elias Boudinot, president of the United States Continental Congress, was the first president of the society, and John Jay, the first chief justice of the Supreme Court, succeeded Boudinot. Other early officials included John Quincy Adams, sixth president of the United States, and Francis Scott Key, composer of "The Star-Spangled Banner." In its ability to work across denominational lines, the American Bible Society became the model for many other religious organizations, such as the *AMERICAN TRACT SOCIETY, the *AMERICAN SUNDAY SCHOOL UNION, and the American Temperance Union.

As the American market became saturated with *BIBLES, the Society eventually turned its efforts toward other languages, working closely with missionaries from various denominations. From its headquarters on Columbus Circle in New York City, the Society has printed *BIBLES in more than a thousand languages and distributes approximately three million *BIBLES annually. Since its establishment, the American Bible Society has distributed more than 6.9 billion copies of *BIBLES and other materials.

In the United States, languages of translation include Navajo, Gullah (a Creole language spoken off the coast of South Carolina), and Yup'ik for the Inuits in Alaska. In 1946, the American Bible Society helped found the United Bible Societies, which has grown to become an international fellowship of more than one hundred national societies. Through the United Bible Societies, the American Bible Society supports translation teams working in more than five hundred languages. Currently, the American Bible Society and the United Bible Societies distribute materials in more than three hundred languages each year.

The American Bible Society is responsible for publishing the *Today's English Version New Testament,* better known as the *Good News for Modern Man Bible.* When this translation was released in 1966, it was one of the first contemporary-language *BIBLES, and it enjoyed great success for that reason. In more recent years, the society also has published the *Contemporary English Version Bible,* the "Bible for Today's Family." It was completed in 1995.

American Board of Commissioners for Foreign Missions Founded in 1810, the American Board of Commissioners for Foreign Missions was the first missions agency in American history. The impetus for the Board came from students who had been present at the famous *HAYSTACK PRAYER MEETING in 1806. A cohort of students concerned about foreign missions were studying at *ANDOVER SEMINARY and successfully petitioned the Congregationalists of Massachusetts to organize a missions agency. The first five missionaries, including two from the Haystack Meeting, sailed for India in 1812. *ADONIRAM JUDSON and *LUTHER RICE, however, changed their views on *BAPTISM during the voyage; they eventually left the American Board to form the American Baptist Foreign Mission Society, reflecting their newfound Baptist convictions.

The American Board of Commissioners for Foreign Missions was never exclusively Congregational; missionaries from other Reformed denominations also served under its aegis. Mission work extended around the world and was especially strong in Hawai'i, India, China, Japan, Sri Lanka, and southern Africa. At the height of its influence, the American Board claimed over seven hundred missionaries in 1920. The organization became the United Church Board for World Ministries in 1961, under the auspices of the United Church of Christ.

American Board of Missions to the Jews. *See* **Chosen People Ministries.**

American Center for Law and Justice Founded by *PAT ROBERTSON in July 1990, the American Center for Law and

Justice is "dedicated to the promotion of pro-liberty, pro-life, and pro-family issues." Robertson sought specifically to counteract what he saw as "anti-Christian bigotry" in American society, especially as embodied in the American Civil Liberties Union. "All over this country a frightening trend continues," Robertson wrote in 1992. "The civil and religious liberties of American citizens—especially *Christian* citizens—are being trampled."

The American Center for Law and Justice has its headquarters in Virginia Beach, Virginia, and a number of satellite offices throughout North America (including Ottawa, Ontario, where the organization is known as the Canadian Center for Law and Justice). In 1992, Robertson hired *JAY SEKULOW as chief counsel for the organization; Sekulow, one of the rising stars of the *RELIGIOUS RIGHT, has argued a number of important cases and has emerged as a spokesman for conservative interests. Not infrequently, the American Center for Law and Justice has sought to blur the line of separation between church and state. In the winter 1992 issue of *Law & Justice*, the Center's glossy magazine, Keith Fournier, executive director of the organization, urged that the wall of separation, which he compared to the Berlin Wall, be torn down altogether: "'TEAR DOWN THIS WALL!' Let our children pray again and our preachers preach again."

Reference: *The Religious Right: The Assault on Tolerance & Pluralism in America* (1994).

American Christian Commission
After the Civil War a group of evangelicals, inspired by *JAMES YEATMAN from St. Louis, organized the American Christian Commission in Cleveland in September 1865. The organization of clergy and laity, many of whom had been involved in the *UNITED STATES CHRISTIAN COMMISSION during the war, sought to address the religious and social needs of the cities, the first such organization to do so.

American Colonization Society
Founded in December 1816, the American Colonization Society (originally known as the American Society for the Colonization of Free Persons of Colour) sought to "repatriate" blacks to Africa. The organization raised money to purchase the freedom of slaves, with the condition that they resettle in Africa. The American Colonization Society drew its support from a broad, sometimes contradictory coalition: politicians who wanted to align themselves with the antislavery forces without giving up Southern support, evangelicals who thought that returning Christianized blacks to Africa might provide an opening for the Christianization of the entire continent, those who sought to demonstrate to skeptical Southerners that blacks could govern themselves, and those who despaired of ever attaining social harmony after the emancipation of slaves.

African Americans themselves viewed the proposal with some ambivalence. Some indeed saw it as an opportunity to escape the oppression of the white man in North America; second- and third-generation slaves found it unsettling to contemplate "returning" to a place they had never been. Among the most vigorous opponents was *RICHARD ALLEN, a freedman and founder of the African Methodist Episcopal Church. Allen feared that the initiatives of the American Colonization Society might lead to the forced deportation of all blacks to Africa.

A delegation from the society, led by *SAMUEL J. MILLS, located and secured territory in West Africa for a colony that would become known in 1922 as Liberia. By 1830, over fourteen thousand blacks accepted the offer of settlement in Africa as a condition of their emancipation. Another wave of migrants headed to Africa in the years immediately following the Civil War and after the end of Reconstruction.

American Council of Christian Churches A militantly fundamentalist and separatist organization, the American Council of Christian Churches was formed in New York City on September 17, 1941, with *CARL MCINTIRE as its first president. McIntire and others feared the encroachment of theological *LIBERALISM or "*MODERNISM," especially as embodied in the Federal Council of Churches (later, the National Council of Churches). The new organization challenged the cozy relationship between the United States government and the Federal Council of Churches on matters of religion. Specifically, the American Council of Christian Churches argued that both the quota of chaplains in the armed forces and the Federal Communications Commission's allocation of free radio time through the Federal Council was unfair to fundamentalist interests. The American Council of Christian Churches won concessions on both of those issues.

McIntire's leadership of the organization lasted until 1968, when his uncompromising *SEPARATISM, even from other fundamentalists who did not share precisely his views, led to internal divisions. He unsuccessfully sought to reverse his ouster two years later. The American Council of Christian Churches remains committed to biblical *INERRANCY and to a strict separation from denominations it regards as apostate. The organization, which is a member of the International Council of Christian Churches, publishes a magazine, *Christian Beacon,* and maintains offices in Valley Forge, Pennsylvania.

American Family Association Founded in 1977 by *DONALD WILDMON, a Methodist minister in Tupelo, Mississippi, the American Family Association describes itself as a "Christian organization promoting the biblical ethic of decency in American society with primary emphasis on TV and other media." The organization grew out of Wildmon's National Federation for Decency and Christian Leaders for Responsible Television (CLeaR-TV); it took the name American Family Association in 1987, as it sought to broaden its agenda. Wildmon has crusaded against what he views as anti-Christian biases in the media; his most visible efforts include the protest against Martin Scorsese's film *The Last Temptation of Christ* and his excoriation of Andres Serrano's photograph "Piss Christ." He has orchestrated boycotts of companies that advertise on programs that he deems objectionable; those targets have included General Motors, S. C. Johnson Wax, Kellogg, Ford Motor Company, Eastman Kodak, and Pepsico, among others. In the political arena, Wildmon himself expressed support for Pat Buchanan in the 1990s.

American Indian Evangelical Church The American Indian Evangelical Church was organized in 1945 among American Indians living in the Minneapolis/St. Paul area, a group that numbered about eight thousand at that time. Originally formed as the American Indian Mission, the church adopted the current name in 1956. The first president was Iver C. Grover, a Chippewa.

The church's doctrine is typical of *EVANGELICALISM. The doctrinal statement begins with the Apostles' Creed. Further, it affirms the Trinity and the divinity of Jesus, both foundational beliefs among evangelicals. The church practices *BAPTISM by immersion and observes the *LORD'S SUPPER. *POLITY in the American Indian Evangelical Church is congregational, with the pastor held to be the spiritual overseer of the congregation. The church does not report its membership or the number of its individual congregations.

Reference: J. Gordon Melton, *The Encyclopedia of American Religions*, 3d ed. (1993).

American National Baptist Convention. *See* **National Baptist Convention of the U.S.A., Inc.**

American Protective Association The American Protective Association, a nativist, anti-Catholic organization, was formed in Clinton, Iowa, in 1887 by Henry F. Bowers and a group of businessmen. The Association tapped into the fears of many Protestants in the Midwest that the Roman Catholic Church intended to undermine American democratic institutions. Members of the American Protective Association, which grew to somewhere between .5 to 2.5 million members in the 1890s, pledged never to vote for a Roman Catholic or to hire one when another worker was available. The organization supported the Republican Party and held its own conventions, the last one in 1898. The American Protective Association disbanded entirely in 1911.

American Sunday School Union Founded in 1824, the American Sunday School Union was primarily a lay society dedicated to the propagation of evangelical Christianity and the teaching of democratic values. The union published books and a *SUNDAY SCHOOL curriculum, organized and trained *SUNDAY SCHOOL leaders, and sought to develop *SUNDAY SCHOOLS "wherever there is a population." In the antebellum period the American Sunday School Union organized national conventions and, as part of its missionary function, founded thousands of *SUNDAY SCHOOLS, especially in the frontier area of the Mississippi Valley.

After the Civil War, however, individual denominations increasingly assumed the task of organizing and administering *SUNDAY SCHOOLS. The American Sunday School Union was relegated to a supporting role and to organizing *SUNDAY SCHOOLS in rural areas. In 1970, in recognition of its task of helping ethnic and multicultural groups, the organization changed its name to the American Missionary Society.

American Tract Society A nondenominational publisher with distinct Protestant sympathies, the American Tract Society played a major role in the propagation of evangelical literature early in the nineteenth century. Formed by a merger of the Massachusetts and New York tract societies in 1825, the American Tract Society emerged as a pioneer in publishing technology, printing and distributing more than five million tracts annually by the late 1820s.

Over the course of the nineteenth century, the American Tract Society sought new means for disseminating its literature, which usually took the form of brief homilies on common vices, such as drinking, coupled with a plea for *SALVATION. With the emergence of the railroads, the Society helped to organize a network of traveling agents, known as *COLPORTEURS, who peddled tracts, *BIBLES, and literature to other travelers.

Amsterdam 2000 Organized by the *BILLY GRAHAM EVANGELISTIC ASSOCIATION, Amsterdam 2000 was a gathering in

July and August 2000 of more than ten thousand Christian leaders from 209 countries and territories. Over the course of nine days the group heard from a number of evangelical luminaries, including *JOHN R. W. STOTT and *ANNE GRAHAM LOTZ. The gathering also issued *The Amsterdam Declaration: A Charter for Evangelism in the 21st Century,* which outlined the importance of evangelical theology, the probity of *EVANGELISTS, and *EVANGELISM itself.

Reference: Gustav Niebuhr, "Religion Conference Sets Goals for Evangelists," *New York Times,* August 19, 2000.

Amy's Friends In 1998, Amy Dupree, a topless dancer in Dallas, formed an organization called Amy's Friends to help women in the sex-entertainment business leave their work. Dupree herself had decided to quit dancing after hearing a sermon about the body being a temple of the Holy Spirit. With the assistance of the Preston Road Church of Christ, the organization functions as a kind of halfway house, offering support groups and assistance in finding childcare and alternative employment.

Reference: Jim Jones, "Exotic Dancers Find Escape Route," *Christianity Today,* May 24, 1999.

Anabaptism Literally *to baptize again,* the term "Anabaptism" refers to the so-called left wing of the Protestant Reformation of the sixteenth century, which began in Zurich among followers of Ulrich Zwingli, a Swiss Protestant reformer. Martin Luther's injunction that everyone should read the *BIBLE for himself or herself sent many Protestants scurrying to the New Testament. There, some found no reference to the Roman Catholic (or Lutheran) practice of infant *BAPTISM. In fact, the New Testament seemed to suggest that only adults—believing adults—should be baptized. Luther objected to this interpretation, but he was unable to control those people who insisted on rebaptizing adult believers (they were rebaptized because most of the followers had already been baptized as infants, before their *CONVERSION into the Anabaptist movement).

Because they challenged both Luther and the Roman Catholic Church, and because of an abortive attempt on the part of some Dutch Anabaptists to establish a theocracy in Münster, the Anabaptists became a persecuted minority, highly decentralized and dispersed throughout Europe, Asia, and, eventually, North America, where many found refuge. They divided into different groups or bands, including the Amish (followers of Jakob Ammann), the Mennonites (followers of Menno Simons), and the Hutterites (followers of Jakob Hutter). Taking as their warrant the Sermon on the Mount (Matthew 5–7), Anabaptists continue to emphasize pacifism, missions, the separation of church and state, *BAPTISM (and church membership) for adult believers only, and a recovery of the purity of the New Testament church.

References: George Hunston Williams, *The Radical Reformation* (1962); William R. Estep, *The Anabaptist Story* (1963).

Anderson, John B(ayard) (1922–) Born in Rockford, Illinois, and reared in the *EVANGELICAL FREE CHURCH, John B. Anderson earned the bachelor's degree from the University of Illinois in 1942 and the J.D. in 1946. He earned a second law degree, from Harvard, in 1949 and was a member of the U.S. Foreign Service from 1952 until 1955. Campaigning as a conservative Republican, Anderson won election to the U.S. House of Representatives in 1960 and was reelected nine times. He rose within the Republican Party to become chair of the House Republican Conference, thereby making him the third-ranking Republican in the House.

Over the course of his career Anderson became increasingly liberal, first on the matter of civil rights and then on women's issues. "My heart is on the left and my pocketbook is on the right," he once remarked. Anderson's decision to support the articles of impeachment against Richard Nixon in 1974 was one of the precipitating factors in Nixon's decision to resign. In his legislative career Anderson earned a reputation for his oratorical skills, and in 1980, having decided not to seek reelection to Congress, he chose instead to pursue the Republican nomination for president. Despite acknowledging his intellectual gifts—Michael Gartner, then the editor of the *Des Moines Register*, for example, praised Anderson as having a "seventeen-jewel mind"—the press and the pundits regarded his candidacy lightly. Anderson, however, did surprisingly well in the early primaries, in part because he offered a liberal alternative to a field dominated by *RONALD REAGAN and George Bush; he also possessed a quick, rapier wit, as when he remarked in the New Hampshire debate that the only way Reagan could accomplish his stated goal of balancing the federal budget and increasing military spending at the same time was "with smoke and mirrors."

As the conservative juggernaut developed and Anderson realized that he could not win his party's nomination, he decided to mount a third-party candidacy, choosing Patrick Lucey, formerly the governor of Wisconsin, as his running mate. As the campaign developed, some hard-right conservatives within Anderson's denomination, the *EVANGELICAL FREE CHURCH, sought to embarrass him with a censure for his pro-choice stand on *ABORTION. In a general election that featured three candidates for president who all claimed to be evangelicals—Anderson, Reagan, and *JIMMY CARTER, the incumbent—Anderson, the independent candidate, finished a distant, yet respectable, third, with 6.5 percent of the popular vote.

References: John B. Anderson, *Between Two Worlds: A Congressman's Choice* (1970); idem, *Vision and Betrayal in America* (1976).

Anderson University and Anderson School of Theology (Anderson, Indiana) Affiliated with the *CHURCH OF GOD (ANDERSON, INDIANA), Anderson University grew out of the educational department of a publishing house for religious tracts, music, and a paper called *The Gospel Trumpet*. Founded in 1917, the school's first name was the Anderson Bible Training School. It was later renamed Anderson College and Theological Seminary, and then Anderson College. The college adopted the name Anderson University in 1992, the year it opened its business school. The university is well-known for its program in music. Christian pop singer *SANDI PATTY and songwriter *BILL GAITHER both graduated from Anderson College.

Anderson School of Theology is the seminary for the *CHURCH OF GOD (ANDERSON, INDIANA). Established in 1950, it achieved regional accreditation fifteen years later.

Reference: William C. Ringenberg, The *Christian College: A History of Protestant Higher Education in America* (1984).

Andover Controversy. *See* **Andover Theological Seminary.**

Andover-Newton Theological School. *See* **Andover Theological Seminary.**

Andover Theological Seminary (Boston, Massachusetts) Andover Theological Seminary, the first theological seminary in the United States, was formed in 1808 on the campus of Andover Academy in Massachusetts. The catalyst was the appointment of Henry Ware, a Unitarian, to the Hollis Chair of Divinity at Harvard, a move that signaled the departure of Harvard from the Reformed orthodoxy of its Puritan founders. Andover was meant to carry on the Reformed tradition, at least as it was interpreted by such *NEW DIVINITY theologians as Jedediah Morse, *TIMOTHY DWIGHT, and *LEONARD WOODS, who became head of the faculty.

Between 1886 and 1893, the school experienced what became known as the Andover Controversy. Although the seminary had required its faculty to subscribe to the Andover Creed, a blend of Calvinist and Edwardsean theology, many faculty, led by E. C. Smyth, became restive in the post–Civil War era and pressed for more liberal interpretations of theological principles, including the notion that people who die without hearing the *GOSPEL will have the opportunity to accept or reject Christ before the final judgment. Conservatives succeeded in ousting Smyth, but the Massachusetts Supreme Court voided his dismissal in 1892.

By the turn of the twentieth century, Andover was reeling from internal dissension and threatened by diminished enrollments. The school moved to Cambridge, Massachusetts, in 1908 and became affiliated, ironically, with Harvard Divinity School. The schools contemplated a merger in 1922, but Andover's board of visitors invoked a long-dormant requirement that Andover's faculty subscribe to an orthodox creed. The faculty resigned in protest. The seminary ceased operations until 1931, when it merged with a Baptist school, Newton Theological Institute, to form Andover-Newton Theological School.

Reference: Leonard Woods, *History of Andover Theological Seminary* (1885).

Andre Kole Ministry Andre Kole Ministry is an outreach program of *CAMPUS CRUSADE FOR CHRIST INTERNATIONAL. Andre Kole is a "Christian illusionist" who has performed for more than thirty years and appeared in almost eighty countries. He uses his act as a tool for *EVANGELISM by performing standard magic tricks like making people and objects appear and disappear and sawing assistants in half. Kole then challenges audience to "contrast the illusion of empty philosophies with the reality of Jesus Christ." The ministry has a home office in Tempe, Arizona.

Reference: Information provided by Campus Crusade for Christ International.

Andrews, Emerson (1806–1884) Born into an evangelical household in Mansfield, Massachusetts, Emerson Andrews moved with his family to Westmoreland, New Hampshire, at the age of eighteen. A year later he fell ill with a virus; although he survived, his father and six siblings died. He became a schoolteacher in several schools in Vermont and New Hampshire, attended school himself, and finally wandered into a *REVIVAL meeting conducted by *ASAHEL NETTLETON. After several weeks of consideration, Andrews decided to "stand up for God, and for religion, and for righteousness" and "trust my Savior with all my heart and soul."

Feeling called to the ministry, Andrews was baptized in the Mohawk River and enrolled in Union College, Schenectady, New York. His application to the Baptist Board of Foreign Missions was denied because he was not married (and, in fact, he remained single all of his life). He was licensed to preach, however, and assumed the pulpit of a small Baptist church in Waterford, New York, and then moved to another Baptist congregation in West Troy, New York, and to another in Lausingbury, New York. His ability to unite fractious congregations earned him the praise of Baptist officials, and he was ordained an *EVANGELIST in the Regular Baptist Church in 1836. During his pastorate in Troy, New York, amid the *REVIVAL fires in the "burned-over district," Andrews enjoyed considerable success. He turned down an offer to become chaplain to the United States Congress and soon left the Troy church to devote himself to *EVANGELISM. In 1845, after years of *ITINERANCY, Andrews briefly became pastor of a Baptist church in Reading, Pennsylvania, and then relocated to Philadelphia and finally to Saratoga Springs, New York.

Andrews participated in the meetings of the *EVANGELICAL ALLIANCE and of the World Temperance Conference, both of which were held in London in 1846. Andrews continued his travels as an *EVANGELIST after his return to the United States. He preached throughout the South and in California, but he often gravitated to out-of-the-way places. "In choosing my preaching point," Andrews wrote, "I have always tried to select the poor, weak, or neglected churches or villages, and give them the whole *GOSPEL."

References: Emerson Andrews, comp., *Revival Songs* (1870); idem, *Revival Sermons* (1871); idem, *Travels in Bible Lands* (1872); idem, *Living Life* (1872).

AnGeL Ministries. *See* **Lotz, Anne Graham.**

Angelica, Mother (née Rita Antoinette Rizzo) (1923–) Mother Angelica, a Roman Catholic nun who is popular with many charismatics, especially Catholic charismatics, was born Rita Antoinette Rizzo in Canton, Ohio. She grew up in poverty, endured ostracism because of her parents' divorce, and began working full-time at the age of eleven. After being healed from severe abdominal pains, she entered a Franciscan convent in 1944. "Sister Angelica" injured her leg while working in the Santa Clara monastery and promised God that she would open a monastery in the South if her leg were healed; she founded Our Lady of the Angels Monastery outside Birmingham, Alabama, in 1961.

The fledgling monastery sold everything from books to peanuts and fishing lures to keep afloat, and the books by "Mother Angelica" gradually gave her a national reputation. She ventured into television in 1978, taping a series of talks that were aired on *PAT ROBERTSON's *700 Club* and *JIM BAKKER's PTL network. The unlikely specter of a diminutive, pre-Vatican II nun dressed in full habit talking extemporaneously on a variety of religious topics caught on. *Mother Angelica Live,* produced out of her Birmingham facility and distributed by Eternal Word Television Network, opens with her trademark greeting, "Let's get on with it!" It features some interviews with guests, but the host clearly is the star, projecting an amiable, homespun image but with the tut-tutting air of a baseball umpire who brooks no nonsense.

Reference: "Mother Angelica: Nun Better," *Christianity Today*, October 2, 1995.

Angelus Temple (Los Angeles, California). *See* **McPherson, Aimee Semple (née Aimee Elizabeth Kennedy).**

Angley, Ernest W. (1921–) The son of a Baptist deacon and textile worker from Gastonia, North Carolina, Ernest W. Angley was baptized in the Spirit while still in his teens. He studied at the Church of God Bible Training School (now *LEE COLLEGE) in Cleveland, Tennessee. After being divinely healed of ulcers, Angley embarked on a healing ministry at the age of twenty-three, established the Healing Stripes Evangelistic Association, and eventually settled at Grace Cathedral, an independent church in Akron, Ohio, although he took his healing crusades around the world. A flamboyant and controversial figure who preached in a white suit and whose services often lasted for five hours, Angley was arrested in Munich, Germany, in 1984 for practicing medicine without a license. His television program, *The Ernest Angley Television Hour,* gave him wider exposure during the 1980s, but it also exposed Angley as one of the more risible of the televangelists.

References: Ernest W. Angley, *Faith in God Heals the Sick* (1983); idem, *Cell 15* (1984); Patsy Simms, *Can Somebody Shout Amen!* (1988).

Anglo-Israel Association. *See* **British Israelism.**

Anglo-Saxon Federation of America. *See* **Rand, Howard R.**

Ankerberg, John (1941–) Born in Chicago, the son of Floyd Ankerberg, an early leader of *YOUTH FOR CHRIST, John Ankerberg graduated from the University of Illinois, Chicago, and from *TRINITY EVANGELICAL DIVINITY SCHOOL. A precocious *EVANGELIST, Ankerberg had organized a Youth for Christ Bible club in his high school, and he became involved in various parachurch organizations, including *INTERVARSITY CHRISTIAN FELLOWSHIP. After graduating from Trinity Divinity School in 1973, he became a founding member of *WILLOW CREEK COMMUNITY CHURCH until he left to begin his own organization, the John Ankerberg Theological Research Institute, in 1976.

Ankerberg, an ordained Baptist minister, ventured into television in 1982 with a discussion-show format centered around theological issues. The program, which took the name *The John Ankerberg Show* in 1983, evolved into a kind of showdown between the proponents of various belief systems—Mormonism, Baha'i, Roman Catholicism, Jehovah's Witnesses—and evangelical Christianity, as represented by Ankerberg. The program, which has appeared on the *CHRISTIAN BROADCASTING NETWORK, the *TRINITY BROADCASTING NETWORK, and the Family Channel, also addresses social and moral issues as well as apocalyptic themes. During the televangelist scandals of the 1980s, Ankerberg brought allegations of *JIM BAKKER's homosexuality to the attention of the *ASSEMBLIES OF GOD.

Reference: John Ankerberg, *One World: Bible Prophecy and the New World Order* (1990).

Anointing Anointing is the practice of pouring or spreading oil on the body or certain parts of the body. This practice, which can have cosmetic and religious significance, is quite common in the Near and Middle East. Many Eastern and Western faiths still use anointing in religious rituals. Oil was also used medicinally. Evangelicals use the term to mean God's unique selection of an individual. It often was understood to convey a sense of elevation or glorification when its cosmetic effects were set in a religious context. Anointing was and is seen as conferring a spiritual power that sanctifies and makes one holy (Exod. 30:22–32). The Old Testament speaks of this effect when it talks about anointing kings, prophets, and priests. Saul, David, and Solomon received the right to rule over Israel through anointing. The priests of the temple were also anointed with oil, making them able to act with *AUTHORITY in the religious sphere. The *BIBLE sometimes uses the term to mean unique selection by God to carry out a specific task or mission. Eventually, the concept of an "anointed one" (*mashiah* in Hebrew, *christos* in Greek) became the refrain of the Hebrew prophets as a means of deliverance from exile and restoration of the Jewish national identity and strength. In coming to identify this restoration with God's will and eventually with the kingdom of God, understood as being unique to Israel's relationship with God because of the covenant, the political restoration came to have eschatological interpretations as well. These eschatological or *END-TIMES interpretations had repercussions beyond Israel's relationship with God and transformative implications for "all the nations," the whole of humanity. The name Jesus Christ thus means "Jesus the anointed one" or "Jesus the Messiah."

In the Christian period, anointing became sacramental in nature, an action taken to heal the sick using the application of oil to convey a spiritual power or grace. The anointing of people baptized in water became the symbol for many Christians of being "sealed" in the Holy Spirit, thus symbolizing reception by the baptized person. Many Christians in a variety of settings used anointing with oil. In Europe, monarchs and some bishops were anointed to signify the spiritual significance of their leadership and being chosen by God for their people. A few evangelicals, pentecostals, and holiness people in particular still use oil literally in this fashion, while all evangelicals refer to anointing as a signifier of "chosenness," and to Christ as God's anointed. This phrase, "God's anointed," can also be used to describe people who are children of God by *ADOPTION.

Anti-Saloon League of America Formed in December 1895 by a coalition of *TEMPERANCE organizations, the Anti-Saloon League of America was founded for the ostensible purpose of closing saloons, but it aimed at more broadly eradicating the consumption of alcohol. Dominated by evangelical Protestant reformers, the organization attracted little support from Jewish and Catholic leaders. Under the guidance of the first general superintendent, *HOWARD HYDE RUSSELL, a Congregationalist minister, the League advocated grassroots action. It encouraged its members first to work for the passage of local option laws, then state legislation, and finally congressional regulation of alcohol shipments across state lines. Passage of the Eighteenth Amendment in 1919 represented the high-water mark for *TEMPERANCE activists, but its repeal in 1933 dealt a crippling blow to the Anti-Saloon League, as well as other *TEMPERANCE organizations. The League collapsed its operations into the National Council on Alcohol Problems in 1964.

Anxious Bench Also knows as the mourner's bench, the anxious bench became a fixture of American revivalism in the antebellum period. Although it often had a physical location—the area just in front of the preacher or the first few rows of seats or benches—the purpose was spiritual. It was a place where people who were affected by the preaching could congregate and contemplate their eternal fate.

*CHARLES GRANDISON FINNEY popularized the anxious bench as one of his

"*NEW MEASURES" to encourage *CONVERSIONS. As such, the anxious bench is grounded firmly in Arminian (as opposed to Calvinist) theology because it posits the centrality of human volition in the *SALVATION process. An individual need not depend on the Calvinist notion of election or predestination; instead, prospective converts controlled their own destinies, and the anxious bench provided a convenient—and conducive—venue for deciding their eternal fates.

In the twentieth century, the most visible expression of the anxious bench took place at *BILLY GRAHAM's evangelistic crusades. Graham, like Finney and *BILLY SUNDAY and numerous other evangelists, invited auditors to walk forward, pray the "*SINNER'S PRAYER," and "accept Jesus into their hearts." For Graham, the twentieth-century equivalent to the anxious bench was the patch of artificial turf directly in front of his lectern in the sports stadium. His invitation to "make a decision for Christ" underscores the affinity between Arminian theology and American revivalism.

Apocalypticism Apocalypticism refers generally to a set of beliefs concerning the end of time. Many evangelicals, because of their penchant for biblical *LITERALISM, believe that the prophetic utterances in the *BIBLE, particularly those found in the books of Daniel and Revelation, indicate that human history will soon screech to a halt and the world will end in some kind of apocalyptic judgment. Apocalypticism takes many forms, in large measure because biblical prophecies are subject to many interpretations, but apocalypticism is especially popular among premillennialists, who believe that Jesus will return to earth before the *MILLENNIUM predicted in the book of Revelation (20:1–10).

Apostasy The term "apostasy" means an intentional denial of Jesus Christ, denying belief in him; someone who denies Christ is an apostate. Evangelicals also use the term to describe one who was once part of the community of believers and now has left that community. In some cases, evangelicals might use the term to describe a member of their specific community or denomination who has gone to another church that they feel is not fully Christian. In Christian history, an emperor, Julian the Apostate (332–363), earned this appellation due to his pagan beliefs. Though reared a Christian, he renounced belief in Jesus and reinstituted pagan practices in temples and attempted a reorganization of the pagan religious community along the lines of the Christian one.

Apostolic Assembly The Apostolic Assembly evolved from gatherings of Mexican and Mexican-American believers in Los Angeles after the *AZUSA STREET REVIVAL. Three of the early leaders, Luis Lopez, Juan Navarro, and Marcial de la Cruz, organized churches in California, especially on both sides of the California-Mexico border; many of the congregants came from the Mexican Methodist Church, drawn to the *PENTECOSTALISM of the Apostolic Assembly. The denomination is especially popular among farm workers in the Coachella, Ventura, Imperial, and San Joaquin Valleys.

Reference: Daniel Ramírez, "Pentecostal Praxis: A History of the Experience of Latino Immigrants in the Apostolic Assembly Churches of the United States" (unpublished paper).

Apostolic Faith Mission. *See* **Azusa Street Mission.**

Apostolic Faith Movement. *See* **Parham, Charles Fox.**

Argue, Don (1939–) Don Argue, born in Winnipeg, Manitoba, graduated from *CENTRAL BIBLE INSTITUTE in Springfield, Missouri, and earned graduate degrees at the University of Santa Clara and the University of the Pacific. He was director of *EVANGELISM for *TEEN CHALLENGE in New York City and served as pastor of churches in San Jose and Morgan Hill, California. Following a stint as campus pastor and dean of students at *EVANGEL COLLEGE, Argue was named president of North Central College in Minneapolis, Minnesota, in 1979. Under his leadership, the school became the fastest-growing Bible college during the 1980s. On December 13, 1994, Argue was unanimously elected president of the *NATIONAL ASSOCIATION OF EVANGELICALS (NAE), a post he assumed on April 1, 1995. Argue's mandate was to move the organization of approximately forty-three thousand evangelical congregations away from its close association with the *RELIGIOUS RIGHT and to forge closer ties with other Protestants, including mainline Protestant denominations.

During his three years at the NAE, Argue tried to revitalize the organization, which he characterized as "too old, too white, and too male." In 1996, at his behest, the NAE issued an "Evangelical Manifesto," which decried *EVANGELICALISM's growing fragmentation. He worked toward racial reconciliation among evangelicals and served as cochair of the State Department's Subcommittee on Religious Freedom and Religious Persecution Abroad. Argue left the *NATIONAL ASSOCIATION OF EVANGELICALS to become president of *NORTHWEST COLLEGE in Kirkland, Washington, in 1998.

Arizona Association of Christian Schools. *See* **Association of Christian Schools International.**

Arkansas Holiness College. *See* **Southern Nazarene University.**

Arlington College. *See* **Azusa Pacific University.**

Arminianism Arminianism is the doctrine that *SALVATION is available to anyone who exercises faith; it contrasts with the Calvinistic understanding that God alone determines who is and who is not among the elect. In 1610, the disciples of Jacobus Arminius, a Dutch theologian, produced a manifesto called the *Remonstrance,* which they viewed as a corrective to the Calvinist doctrine of election. The *Remonstrance* held that one's election to *SALVATION was based on God's foreknowledge of faith on the part of the believer; that Christ died for all humanity (although only believers benefited); that grace was resistible; and that the believer's perseverance in the faith was dependent upon his or her actions. The Reformed Synod of Dordt, a gathering of Dutch Reformed leaders, firmly repudiated Arminian doctrines in 1618, thereby contributing the mnemonic TULIP to the vocabulary of Reformed theology: total depravity; unconditional election; limited *ATONEMENT (limited to the elect); irresistible *GRACE; perseverance of the saints.

Despite the conclusions of Dordt, Arminianism became enormously popular among American evangelicals, especially after the American Revolution when Americans, who had only recently taken their political destiny into their own hands, responded to a message that assured them that they controlled their religious destinies as well. Whereas *JONATHAN EDWARDS, a Calvinist, had insisted that the Great Awakening was "a surprising work of God," *CHARLES GRANDISON FINNEY, apologist for the *SECOND GREAT AWAKENING, insisted that *REVIVAL—and *SALVATION itself—was "the work of man." "Revival of religion is not a miracle," Finney declared in his *Lectures on Revival.* "There is nothing on religion beyond the ordinary powers of nature. It consists entirely in the right exercise of the powers of nature." Finney's emphasis on human volition in the *SALVATION process stood in opposition to the Calvinist notion of predestination and election, but his Arminian theology was exquisitely suited to the American context and to the temper of the times.

The almost wholesale adoption of Arminian theology on the part of antebellum evangelicals was a source of consternation to people who sought to uphold the Calvinist tradition, especially the theologians at Princeton Theological Seminary. The *PRINCETONIANS emphasized the importance of an educated clergy, for example, as a way of dampening the enthusiasm of the *REVIVALS, which were hotbeds of Arminianism. They failed, however, and the Arminian emphasis on individual volition and self-determination came to dominate American *EVANGELICALISM. *BILLY GRAHAM, for instance, uses the language of Arminianism in his crusades when he implores his auditors to "make a decision for Christ," language that Edwards would find utterly foreign to his understanding of salvation.

Armstrong, Annie (Walker) (1850–1938) Born into an affluent family in Baltimore, Annie Armstrong joined a local Baptist church at age nineteen and quickly devoted her life to the promotion of missions. At Richmond, Virginia, in 1888, she led the efforts to organize the Women's Missionary Union within the *SOUTHERN BAPTIST CONVENTION. Armstrong was elected corresponding secretary, an unsalaried post that she retained until 1906.

Armstrong proved to be a strong and influential leader within the *SOUTHERN BAPTIST CONVENTION, despite the highly conservative nature of the denomination and its dim views of women in leadership roles. She instituted the famous Lottie Moon Christmas Offering, in honor of the venerable Southern Baptist missionary, and Armstrong herself was later honored by the creation of the Annie Armstrong Offering for Home Missions.

Reference: Alma Hunt, *History of the Women's Missionary Union* (1976).

Armstrong, Ben(jamin) (1923–) Born in Newark, New Jersey, Ben Armstrong graduated from New York University and from Union Theological Seminary. He was ordained by the United Presbyterian Church in 1949 and served several churches in New York and New Jersey before signing on with *TRANS WORLD RADIO, a shortwave ministry, in 1958. In 1967, the *NATIONAL RELIGIOUS BROADCASTERS tapped him to head the organization, where he remained until 1989.

Armstrong presided over a period of unprecedented growth in evangelical broadcasting. He eagerly promoted the emerging electronic media and placed the "awesome technology of broadcasting" into a theological grid. We are living, he said, in the "last days" before the *SECOND COMING of Christ. God has placed this technology at the disposal of evangelicals to provide "a revolutionary new form of the worshiping, witnessing church that existed twenty centuries ago."

References: Ben Armstrong, *The Electric Church* (1979); Quentin J. Schultze, *Televangelism and*

American Culture: The Business of Popular Religion (1991).

Armstrong, William L(ester) (1937–) William L. Armstrong, an evangelical, was born in Fremont, Nebraska, and educated at Tulane University and the University of Minnesota. After a brief career with a radio station and as a banker, he entered Colorado politics as a Republican. Armstrong rose steadily from one term as a state representative to the state senate, where he became majority leader. In 1972, he was elected to Congress and was twice reelected. He won election to the United States Senate in 1978, was reelected six years later, and retired from elective politics at the conclusion of his second Senate term.

Arterburn, Steve. *See* **Women of Faith.**

Aryan Nations. *See* **Butler, Richard Girnt.**

Asbury, Francis (1745–1816) Born near Birmingham, England, Francis Asbury became involved with the evangelical Methodist connection within the Church of England at an early age. He began preaching while still in his teens and in 1766 became one of the traveling preachers associated with *JOHN WESLEY. Five years later, Asbury responded to Wesley's appeal for missionaries to America; he arrived in Philadelphia in October 1771.

Asbury was the only Methodist missionary to remain in America through the Revolutionary War. Wesley's opposition to the cause of patriotism had made *METHODISM suspect to many Americans, but Asbury stayed in contact with various Methodist societies throughout the war, and when the conflict ended he emerged as the leader of the movement. Asbury was one of the central figures at the 1784 Christmas Conference in Baltimore, which formed the Methodist Episcopal Church in America. He and Thomas Coke, Wesley's representative to the conference, were designated general superintendents of the new denomination.

Asbury advocated the use of *CAMP MEETINGS and encouraged the formation of *SUNDAY SCHOOLS and the development of higher education among Methodists. He promoted the denomination's "Book Concern," which evolved into a Methodist publishing house called Cokesbury.

For forty-five years, Asbury was an itinerant *EVANGELIST throughout America, especially in the South and the Southwest, traveling some three hundred thousand miles and delivering sixteen thousand sermons. The settled nature of the American clergy distressed Asbury, and he sought to lead by example, establishing the Methodist system of circuits and *CIRCUIT RIDERS. Asbury himself had no home, finding shelter wherever he could; at one point he instructed a correspondent in England to address mail simply to Francis Asbury "in America."

Reference: Elmer T. Clark, ed., *The Journal and Letters of Francis Asbury* (1958).

Asbury College (Wilmore, Kentucky) Asbury College opened in 1890 under the name Kentucky Holiness School. The school, founded by *EVANGELIST John Wesley Hughes as fulfillment of a pledge he had made ten years earlier while a student at Vanderbilt, was renamed in honor of Bishop *FRANCIS ASBURY, one of the leading figures in early American *METHODISM. The first president was *EVANGELIST *HENRY CLAY MORRISON.

Asbury College is now interdenominational, but it remains aware of its Methodist and holiness roots. Asbury's literature proclaims, "Every facet of college life is shaped by the Wesleyan-Arminian understanding of *SIN, *GRACE, and the possibility of full *SALVATION." Periodically, however, Asbury's conservative theological perspective has more closely resembled *FUNDAMENTALISM than *METHODISM. Especially in the 1920s and 1930s, encroaching "*MODERNISM" was a cause of concern to its leaders.

Even compared to other Christian colleges, the percentage of Asbury's graduates who attend seminary has historically been disproportionately high, a fact that may account in part for its students' reputation for religious enthusiasm. In 1970, Asbury College was the starting point for a widely publicized *REVIVAL, called the *ASBURY REVIVAL, which caused classes to be canceled for a full week when a service went on for 185 hours without interruption. Students who participated traveled to other church colleges spreading the news, and similar *REVIVALS occurred at several other evangelical schools, including *HOUGHTON COLLEGE, *WHEATON COLLEGE, and *ORAL ROBERTS UNIVERSITY.

Reference: William C. Ringenberg, *The Christian College: a History of Protestant Higher Education in America* (1984).

Asbury Revival On Tuesday morning, February 3, 1970, the students of *ASBURY COLLEGE in Wilmore, Kentucky, filed into Hughes Auditorium for required chapel. The scheduled preacher was Custer Reynolds, the college's academic dean and a Methodist layman. Rather than offering a sermon, however, Reynolds spoke briefly about his own spiritual life and invited students to do the same. One by one, students came forward to give their testimonies. Many prayed, wept, or sang quietly, and what would become known as the Asbury Revival was underway.

By Thursday, news of the *REVIVAL had spread to newspapers and television; strangers came to campus to join the gatherings, which lasted long into the night. Other schools invited Asbury faculty and students to visit their campuses, and the *REVIVAL followed them, from California to New York and even to South America. By summer, the Asbury Revival had touched well over one hundred Bible schools, colleges, seminaries, and congregations.

Asbury Theological Seminary (Wilmore, Kentucky) Although Asbury Theological Seminary is interdenominational, it graduates more United Methodist pastors than any other divinity school, a testimony to the appeal of its conservative doctrinal positions. The school began in 1923, when faculty from *ASBURY COLLEGE met with President *HENRY CLAY MORRISON to discuss founding a graduate theological school. Asbury Seminary opened that fall. The seminary was part of the college until 1931, when it was incorporated as a separate institution, and while Asbury Seminary moved onto its own campus in 1939, these changes did not represent a complete break with the college. In addition to serving as president of the college, Morrison headed the seminary until his death in 1942.

Now known as Asbury Theological Seminary, the school offers master's degrees in religious studies, divinity, world mission, and *EVANGELISM, as well as doctorates in missiology and ministry. It runs a cooperative program with the University of Kentucky for a joint degree in social work and religion. The library holds a research collection on biblical studies in addition to extensive holdings on international missions, *METHODISM, the Wesleyans, and the *HOLINESS MOVEMENT.

Reference: William C. Ringenberg, *The Christian College: A History of Protestant Higher Education in America* (1984).

Ashcroft, John (1942–) Born to a pentecostal preacher and his wife, John Ashcroft grew up in Springfield, Missouri, near the world headquarters of his denomination, the *ASSEMBLIES OF GOD. He was converted at age twelve. He earned his baccalaureate degree from Yale University in 1964 and his J.D. from the University of Chicago Law School three years later. After practicing law for several years he ran unsuccessfully for Congress and then held several appointive offices in Missouri. He was the state's attorney general from 1976 until he was elected governor in 1984. Ten years later, he was elected U.S. senator.

Ashcroft, a conservative and a Republican, considered running for president in 2000 but decided instead to run for reelection. His Democratic opponent, Mel Carnahan, the governor of Missouri, was killed in a plane crash three weeks prior to the election, although the state election laws would not allow the Democratic Party to place another name on the ballot. The new governor, who had succeeded Carnahan, pledged to appoint Carnahan's wife, Jean, to the seat should Carnahan defeat Ashcroft.

Ashcroft lost by approximately forty-nine thousand votes. His political career was rescued, however, when President George W. Bush appointed Ashcroft U.S. attorney general. Ashcroft's record came under intense scrutiny during the confirmation process, with opponents picking up on his praise of Confederate soldiers as "patriots," his successful opposition to the confirmation of an African American judge, and his efforts to block school desegregation as indications of racism. Ashcroft, an ardent opponent of *ABORTION, gay rights, and the United Nations, strongly disputed charges that he was racist, and, after a strong lobbying effort by the *CHRISTIAN COALITION and other *RELIGIOUS RIGHT groups, he was eventually confirmed by the Senate.

References: Laurie Goodstein, "Ashcroft's Life and Judgments Are Steeped in Faith," *New York Times*, January 14, 2001.

Assemblies of God The Assemblies of God was formed in April 1914 during a meeting at Hot Springs, Arkansas. The meeting of pentecostal leaders from around the country was called to determine doctrinal standards; to develop a policy of cooperation; to clarify missionary, ministerial, and educational interests; and to establish the requirements for the religious government of the churches.

The theology of the Assemblies of God was formulated only through great struggle in the churches. The "Jesus Only" issue (the idea of *BAPTISM in the name of Jesus alone, rather than invoking the entire Trinity) proved especially difficult, but the Assemblies settled on a Trinitarian stance. The Assemblies' theology can be characterized as fundamentalist, with a belief in the infallibility and inspiration of the *BIBLE. They also believe in the fall and redemption of humanity, *BAPTISM in the Holy Spirit, divine healing, eternal punishment for the wicked, and eternal reward for believers. The Assemblies of God recognizes the ordinances of *BAPTISM and the *LORD'S SUPPER. There is a special emphasis on the *BAPTISM OF THE HOLY SPIRIT being evidenced in *GLOSSOLALIA, or *SPEAKING IN TONGUES. The

Assemblies believe that all the gifts of the Spirit should be present in the churches.

The *POLITY of the Assemblies of God is essentially congregational, but the General Council, which consists of all ordained ministers, has centralized control of missionary, educational, ministerial, publishing, and doctrinal issues. There are more than 2.57 million members in twelve thousand churches in the United States, with over 16 million members worldwide. The organizational headquarters of the Assemblies of God are in Springfield, Missouri. The denomination endorses seventeen institutions of higher education, including Bible schools, colleges, and a seminary.

References: Frank S. Mead and Samuel S. Hill, *Handbook of Denominations in the United States*, 10th ed. (1996); J. Gordon Melton, *The Encyclopedia of American Religions*, 3d ed. (1993).

Assemblies of God Theological Seminary (Springfield, Missouri) Assemblies of God Theological Seminary is the denominational seminary for the *ASSEMBLIES OF GOD. The seminary is currently located in the denomination's international headquarters in Springfield, Missouri, but in 1996, a groundbreaking ceremony was held to build a separate facility on five acres of land adjacent to *EVANGEL COLLEGE in Springfield. Although the General Council of the *ASSEMBLIES OF GOD approved establishing a seminary in 1961, the General Presbytery, the denomination's ruling body, took ten years to accept a recommendation from other committees that plans for the school be implemented. In 1972, a preliminary constitution and bylaws were drawn up, and formal incorporation followed later that year. The school was first known as Assemblies of God Graduate School and renamed Assemblies of God Theological Seminary in 1984.

In keeping with the pentecostal ties of its parent denomination, the library at Assemblies of God Theological Seminary has extensive holdings on the pentecostal movement. Moreover, the hiring policy requires that all full-time faculty members be "full gospel believers," despite the fact that the school serves individuals from many "church and parachurch persuasions." The seminary offers a master of divinity program with several concentrations: pastoral ministries, global missions, pentecostal studies, historical studies, and biblical languages. It also grants the master of arts in theological studies, Christian ministry, missiology, and counseling, and plans to introduce a doctoral program in ministry. Assemblies of God Theological Seminary has fraternal and exchange agreements with many other schools, including seminaries and Bible colleges in the Philippines, Singapore, Belgium, Kenya, India, and Togo, West Africa, among other places.

Like many pentecostal schools, Assemblies of God Theological Seminary does not have a written stance on the acceptability of *DANCING, though alcohol and tobacco are not allowed—on- or off-campus—for enrolled students. Attendance at daily chapel services is encouraged but not required.

Reference: Assemblies of God Theological Seminary 1996–98 Catalog (1996).

Assent Protestant Christians have affirmed assent of faith by a variety of means, including reason, *AUTHORITY, freedom, *GRACE, and experiential certainty. Protestant Christian theologians have focused on different means or placed differing emphasis on a variety of means in an effort to better understand assent.

Another way of understanding this process has been to see the interaction of intellect and experience in understanding Scripture and traditions that have over time accrued meaning for Christians. Reason would help the mind understand the meaning of texts, traditions, and explanations, and experience of the Spirit in the context of living out a Christian life would ground intellectual understanding in a living experience of the Divine. For evangelical Christians, especially pentecostals and charismatics, faith is often affective—not merely an intellectual assent, but a faith grounded as well in some experience of God, such as *SPEAKING IN TONGUES or divine healing.

Associated Canadian Theological Schools A consortium of Canadian evangelical seminaries, the Associated Canadian Theological Schools dates to discussions held in 1985 among representatives from four denominations: the Fellowship of Evangelical Baptist Churches of Canada, the *ASSOCIATED GOSPEL CHURCHES of Canada, the *EVANGELICAL FREE CHURCH of Canada, and the *BAPTIST GENERAL CONFERENCE of Canada. As a consequence of these discussions, the *BAPTIST GENERAL CONFERENCE established Canadian Baptist Seminary, and the Evangelical Free Church along with *TRINITY WESTERN UNIVERSITY established *TRINITY WESTERN SEMINARY. These two, together with *NORTHWEST BAPTIST SEMINARY, form the Associated Canadian Theological Schools, which is located adjacent to Trinity Western Seminary.

Although the three seminaries maintain their separate identities, their point of unity is "sharing a vision for proclaiming the *GOSPEL and building the church." The purpose of the organization is "to facilitate through a cooperative arrangement effective and efficient achievement of each seminary's mission and fulfillment of their common vision: to strengthen present pastoral and other ministries and aggressively to plant new churches in Canada and around the world by equipping dynamic leaders who have a love and burden for people based on a strong commitment to Jesus Christ and the *WORD OF GOD."

Associated Gospel Churches The moving force behind the Associated Gospel Churches, a Canadian denomination of evangelicals, was *PETER W. PHILPOTT, although its roots lay in the *REVIVAL and missionary movement of the late nineteenth century. In 1921, several of the congregations either founded by or inspired by Philpott, who later became pastor of *MOODY MEMORIAL CHURCH in Chicago, gathered to form the Associated Gospel Churches, a loose denomination with an aggregate membership of about ten thousand in more than one hundred congregations.

Associated Mennonite Biblical Seminary (Elkhart, Indiana) Associated Mennonite Biblical Seminary is an inter-Mennonite institution founded and supported by the Mennonite Church and General Conference Mennonite Church; the seminary evolved from the merger of the schools run by the two denominations. In 1933, the Mennonite Church's *GOSHEN COLLEGE in Indiana began to offer a bachelor's degree in theology, and by 1946, the college's Bible school had become known as Goshen Biblical Seminary. The year before, Mennonite Biblical Seminary was established in Chicago by the General Conference Mennonite Church, a group largely descended from Russian immigrants, rather than Swiss or Germans. Joint summer sessions began in

1954, and a joint program was launched four years later under the name Associated Mennonite Biblical Seminaries, when Mennonite Biblical Seminary moved to Elkhart, Indiana. The two schools did not merge at that time, however, but continued to cooperate for thirty-five more years. Goshen Biblical Seminary joined Mennonite Biblical Seminary in Elkhart in 1969, and in 1993, the schools were finally incorporated as one seminary.

The seminary exists primarily to train pastors, missionaries, teachers, *EVANGELISTS, and church workers. Two thirds of the students at Associated Mennonite Biblical Seminary are enrolled in the master of divinity degree program. The school also offers a master of theological studies, and an M.A. in theological studies and in peace studies. Nondegree students can earn a certificate in theological studies. Associated Mennonite Biblical Seminary enrolls many non-Mennonite students, especially Methodists. The seminary has cross-registration with Goshen College.

In keeping with its Mennonite heritage, the library at Associated Mennonite Biblical Seminary holds a Peace Resource Center, with newsletters from international agencies that make up the peace movement. The school also runs an Institute of Mennonite Studies, which sponsors research and publishes occasional collections of papers on *ANABAPTISM and Mennonite history.

References: C. J. Dyck, "The AMBS Story" [pamphlet] (1996); *Associated Mennonite Biblical Seminary 1996–1998 Catalog* (1996).

Association for Church Renewal The Association for Church Renewal was formed in 1996 as a coalition of evangelical, reform-minded groups within seven mainline Protestant denominations: Christian Church (Disciples of Christ), *AMERICAN BAPTIST CHURCHES U.S.A., Evangelical Lutheran Church in America, United Methodist Church, Episcopal Church, Presbyterian Church (U.S.A.), and United Church of Christ. The organization, chaired by James Heidinger Jr. of the Methodist group *GOOD NEWS, seeks collectively to push mainline Protestantism toward more conservative stands on such issues as homosexuality, *ABORTION, religious freedom, and feminism.

Association for Native Evangelism. *See* **Osborn, T(ommy) L(ee).**

Association of Christian Schools International The Association of Christian Schools International (ACSI) is the largest evangelical Christian school organization in the world, with member schools in all fifty states, all ten Canadian provinces, and in eighty-two other nations. The organization was founded in 1978, the result of a merger of three associations: the National Christian School Education Association (NCSEA), an outgrowth of the National Association of Christian Schools; the Ohio Association of Christian Schools (OACS); and the Western Association of Christian Schools (WACS), which had been formed in 1975 from the merger of the Arizona Association of Christian Schools and the California Association of Christian Schools. The following year, the Northwest Fellowship of Christian Schools joined WACS. In the years immediately following the initial merger of NCSEA, OACS, and WACS in 1978, several other Christian school associations merged with the newly formed Association of Christian Schools International: the Southeast Association of Christian Schools, the Association of Teachers of Christian Schools, the Great Plains Association of Christian Schools, and the Texas Association of Christian Schools.

From its headquarters in Colorado

Springs, Colorado, ACSI produces and distributes textbooks and curricular materials for Christian schools throughout North America and the world. The organization has regional offices both inside and outside the United States: Lancaster, Pennsylvania; Snellville, Georgia; North Canton, Ohio; Dallas, Texas; Mesa, Arizona; Vancouver, Washington; Sacramento, California; La Habra, California; Minesing, Ontario; Three Hills, Alberta; Washington, D.C.; Budapest, Hungary; Guatemala City, Guatemala; and Kiev, Ukraine.

The organization claims that the student enrollment in ACSI member schools and colleges has increased from 185,687 to 796,867 since 1978. In that same period of time its school membership has grown from 1,051 schools to 3,770.

Association of Evangelical Lutheran Churches. *See* **Lutheran Church—Missouri Synod.**

Association of Teachers of Christian Schools. *See* **Association of Christian Schools International.**

Association of Vineyard Churches Formed in 1985, the Association of Vineyard Churches is the denominational rubric for the network of *VINEYARD CHRISTIAN FELLOWSHIPS around the world. The Vineyard at Anaheim, California, founded by *JOHN WIMBER, is generally considered the flagship congregation for the movement, which emphasizes a kind of neopentecostal "signs and wonders" theology.

Assurance Many Christians throughout history have claimed or rejected the idea of assurance, the theological notion of knowing one's place in the afterlife. John Calvin taught that the elect, living a good life, could view the fruits of that good life as an objective demonstration of their assurance of God's *SALVATION. This teaching gave the doctrine of assurance a basis in predestination, which also absolved individuals of responsibility for their own *SALVATION. During eighteenth-century revivals, people like *JOHN WESLEY, the founder of *METHODISM, were opposed to Calvin's idea of predestination. Instead, Wesley sought to explain assurance through scriptural interpretation of Romans 8:17: "When we cry, 'Abba! Father!' it is that very Spirit bearing witness with our spirit that we are children of God, and if children, then heirs, heirs of God and joint heirs with Christ." For Wesley, various spiritual marks attested to the veracity of the assurance of *SALVATION promised by the Holy Spirit in the characteristics of one's life. These marks included awareness of the change from death to life, and the "fruits of the Spirit" (love, joy, peace). Wesley perceived a danger in using feelings as a barometer for assurance; he thought that the criteria of love, joy, and peace, especially as demonstrated toward others, could be used as specific measures. While contemporary Methodist doctrine does not dwell much on assurance, evangelicals often speak of their assurance of *SALVATION.

Athletes in Action Athletes in Action is the sports ministry of *CAMPUS CRUSADE FOR CHRIST INTERNATIONAL. Athletes in Action works directly with coaches and athletes at all levels. The organization uses the platform of sports as a tool for the *EVANGELISM of the general public as well. Its mission is rooted in the belief that a "society looking up to athletes as heroes must find heroes looking up to God."

Since its founding in the 1960s, Athletes in Action has grown to a full-time staff of more than three hundred people, working across the country and in the Athletes in Action headquarters in Cincinnati. Athletes in Action sponsors training and competitive athletic programs, such as youth internships, running clubs, and the Summer International Track & Field Projects. It is better known, however, for its outreach to college and professional athletes. Athletes in Action has ministries serving professional sports teams in twenty major American cities, from New York to San Francisco, and its staff also works on nearly fifty college and university campuses. The connections made through these programs help make possible another endeavor: the Legends of the Hardwood Breakfasts—high-priced meals with celebrities. Speakers at these events have included coaches and commentators from Big Ten universities and political figures like Stephen Goldsmith, the mayor of Indianapolis, Indiana.

Athletes in Action sells athletic clothing and evangelistic materials featuring testimonies by *BORN-AGAIN sports figures, like three-time Super Bowl participant Joe Gibbs and All-Pro wide receiver Irving Fryar. In addition to videos, pamphlets, and study guides, however, Athletes in Action carries "NFL Player Testimony Cards." The organization also offers "Super Bowl Kits" for evangelistic use at parties during halftime.

Athletes in Action is a prime example of "*MUSCULAR CHRISTIANITY," a form of *EVANGELISM that appeals primarily to men. Unlike organizations like the *PROMISE KEEPERS, however, Athletes in Action does not actively discriminate against women but simply seeks men out in an area of life where they predominate. A similar organization is the *FELLOWSHIP OF CHRISTIAN ATHLETES, which also appeals primarily to men.

Reference: Information provided by Athletes in Action and Campus Crusade for Christ.

Atlantic Baptist University (Moncton, New Brunswick) In 1949, the United Baptist Convention of the Atlantic Provinces established the United Baptist Bible Training School to provide a Bible-college education and also to keep evangelical students from leaving Atlantic Canada, particularly the Maritime Provinces. Originally the school was a *BIBLE INSTITUTE and a high school, but by 1968, it had fully developed into a Bible college and liberal arts junior college.

In 1970, the name was changed to Atlantic Baptist College, and accreditation as a four-year college followed in 1983. In 1996, the college opened a new campus in Moncton and changed its name to Atlantic Baptist University. The school has a requirement that all students complete a minor in religious studies.

Reference: Atlantic Baptist University Academic Calendar 1996–1997 (1996).

Atonement This term describes a doctrine of reconciliation pertaining to Jesus Christ's suffering, death, and resurrection. The doctrine has evolved through various understandings of the term and concept. It appears in the King James Version of the *BIBLE in both the Old and New Testaments. The English word comes from the phrase "at one," a condition in which two or more people have reconciled a difference. The term "atonement" came to reflect the actual action of repayment or restitution through which good relations were once again achieved. The word occurs but once in the New Testament in Paul's letter to the Romans (Rom. 5:11), a translation of a Greek word *katallage* which means "downing the otherness." In 2 Corinthians it is translated as "reconciliation." In the Old Testament "atonement" is used to define acts through which guilt can be expiated. The best example of this is the high priest's annual atonement for the *SINS of the people on a specific day, Yom Kippur or the Day of Atonement (Lev. 23:26ff.). As a Christian doctrine, central to evangelical understanding of the purpose of God's actions through Jesus Christ, the doctrine of atonement must be understood through the interpretation of the New Testament of Jesus' unique place in history. Thus, Paul states that "Christ died for our sins" (1 Cor. 15:3).

Atter, (Gordon) Francis (1905–) Born into a Methodist household, Francis Atter's parents became pentecostals when he was a young child; they went as missionaries to China in 1908 and then returned to Canada for a preaching career that spanned three decades. Atter himself began preaching at age seventeen, became pastor of a congregation two years later, and continued on to a distinguished career as a pastor, an educator, and a leader of *PENTECOSTALISM in Canada. He served as district official for the *PENTECOSTAL ASSEMBLIES OF CANADA as well as on that body's executive committee.

Reference: Francis Atter, *The Third Force* (1962).

Au Sable Institute. *See* **DeWitt, Calvin B.**

Auburn Affirmation The Auburn Affirmation, a statement drafted in 1923 and signed by liberal or "modernist" members of the Presbyterian Church U.S.A., urged toleration of doctrinal differences within the denomination. Officially entitled *An Affirmation Designed to Safeguard the Unity and Liberty of the Presbyterian Church in the United States of America,* the Auburn Affirmation ostensibly reaffirmed the action of the 1910 General Assembly, which essentially adopted the tenets of **THE FUNDAMENTALS,* but the Auburn Affirmation also allowed that some within the denomination might have other, equally valid formulae for explaining these truths. The proposal was turned away at the 1925 General Assembly, but in 1926 the General Assembly adopted a commission report that embodied the principle of doctrinal toleration articulated in the Auburn Affirmation. Conservatives interpreted this as a movement away from orthodoxy, and the fundamentalist schism within the northern Presbyterian Church began shortly thereafter.

References: Lefferts A. Loetscher, *The Broadening Church* (1954); Bradley J. Longfield, *The Presbyterian Controversy: Fundamentalists, Modernists, and Moderates* (1991); Randall Balmer and John R. Fitzmier, *The Presbyterians* (1993).

Auburn Convention The Auburn Convention was a gathering of New School Presbyterians in 1837 in response to the excision of four New School synods by the Old School majority at the 1837 General Assembly. The Old School charged the New School with heresy for compromising the *WESTMINSTER STANDARDS by articulating a modified *CALVINISM, one that compromised the Calvinist doctrine of election. The 1837 Assembly claimed that the four synods in question—Western Reserve, Utica, Genessee, and Geneva—were illegal because they came into the denomination under the aegis of the 1801 Plan of Union with Congregationalists, whom the Old School blamed for the supposed theological innovations.

The Auburn Convention was an attempt, first of all, by the New School to protest its theological orthodoxy and, second, to regroup. The 1838 General Assembly, however, refused to reverse the previous year's decision, and after a tumultuous session, both sides adjourned to different venues, and each side claimed the name Presbyterian Church in the United States of America. The two sides eventually reconciled in 1870.

Reference: George M. Marsden, *The Evangelical Mind and the New School Presbyterian Experience* (1970).

Audio Adrenaline Audio Adrenaline, one of the hippest evangelical musical groups of the late 1990s, formed in the late 1980s when rhythm guitarist and songwriter Bob Herdman approached three students at Kentucky Christian College—guitarist Barry Blair, lead vocalist Mark Stuart, and bassist Will McGinniss—who were playing together in a group called A180. Herdman asked for their help in recording a song he had written, a heavy-metal/rap piece called "My God." Soon after, A180 asked Herdman to join, and the foursome became known as Audio Adrenaline.

The recording of "My God" was not only responsible for Audio Adrenaline's formation as a band; in 1989, it earned them a record contract with ForeFront Communications. The group's debut album on ForeFront, *Audio Adrenaline,* was released in 1992. The following year the band recorded *Don't Censor Me,* which sold 250,000 copies. The album was also released in long-form video under the name *Big House,* which won a Dove Award for Best Long Form Video and nominations from Billboard Music Awards and America's Christian Music Awards. Another recording, *Live Bootleg,* followed in 1995. Then, in 1996, Audio Adrenaline released its most successful album to date; *Bloom* resulted in three Top Ten hits, two of which made it to number-one on the Christian music charts. For the ensuing tour, drummer Ben Cissell joined the original four band members.

Audio Adrenaline continues to tour periodically with ***DC TALK**, but they have branched out to open for the ***NEWSBOYS** on their *Going Public* tour. Like these better-known bands, however, Audio Adrenaline has already proven itself capable of breaking down the barriers between mainstream and Christian music. Audio Adrenaline was the first Christian rock group to perform in either the Hard Rock Cafe or the House of Blues in Los Angeles.

Reference: Information provided by ForeFront Communications Group, Inc.

Authority Evangelicals diverge widely on defining the concept and nature of authority. All would affirm that the authority of the church centers upon Jesus Christ. They would also understand that the means of verifying Jesus' sovereignty over the church is the ***BIBLE**, and so the ***BIBLE** is equivalent to the authority of Jesus Christ for many evangelicals because the ***BIBLE** contains God's revelation to humanity. The ***POLITY** of the church and its exercise of authority vary among evangelicals. For some denominations there is a collegial quality based upon interpretations of Christian community as patterned after the early Christian communities portrayed in the ***BIBLE**. In this way, the ***BIBLE** is also the blueprint for structure while also the literal and figurative "***WORD OF GOD**."

Avila, Yiye (1926–) Widely known as the Spanish-speaking ***BILLY GRAHAM**, Yiye Avila is a former bodybuilder from Puerto Rico who won the title of Mr. North America in 1954. His health began to deteriorate, however, because of rheumatoid arthritis. He saw ***ORAL ROBERTS** on television, dedicated his life to God, and claimed divine healing. Avila became a pentecostal preacher and faith healer shortly thereafter. His radio and television programs are heard throughout Latin America, and his preaching throughout the Americas has led a large number of Hispanics to convert to evangelical Christianity.

Reference: Blaine Harden, "Hispanic Evangelicals Flock to Hear a Force in Their Faith," *New York Times*, September 5, 2000.

Awana Clubs International The term Awana derives from the acrostic, "Approved Workmen Are Not Ashamed," taken from 2 Timothy 2:15. Founded in the 1940s by Lance "Doc" Latham, pastor of the North Side Gospel Center in Chicago, the organization began as a way of reaching girls and boys from the community who did not attend church on Sundays. Latham, who relied on the assistance of Art Robinson, a member of the congregation, emphasized the mastery and the ***MEMORIZATION** of the ***BIBLE**, and the organization developed Scout-style uniforms, handbooks, and award systems to encourage participation. The Awana Youth Organization was formed in 1950, after word of the program's success prompted inquiries from other evangelical churches. Since the 1950s, the organization, now based in Streamwood, Illinois, has developed a network of subgroups:

Cubbies (boys and girls ages three and four)
Sparks (boys and girls in kindergarten, first grade, and second grade)
Pals (boys in third and fourth grade)
Chums (girls in third and fourth grade)
Pioneers (boys in fifth and sixth grade)
Guards (girls in fifth and sixth grade)
CrossTrainers (urban youth)
Friends (mentally challenged)
Jr. Varsity (youth in seventh and eighth grade)
Varsity (teenagers in grades nine through twelve)

Awana, which changed its name to Awana Clubs International in 1986, emphasizes the importance of working through local churches. Congregations that wish to use the Awana program and curricular materials secure an annual charter from the organization (ninety-five dollars in 1998), "an agreement between Awana Clubs International, a nondenominational organization, and a church whereby the Awana ministry may be operated in that church." The organization betrays its fundamentalist leanings by stipulating that no charter will be granted to a congregation that is affiliated with either the ***CHARISMATIC MOVEMENT** or with the National Council of Churches or World Council of Churches.

Ayer, William Ward (1892–1985) Born in New Brunswick, Canada, William Ward Ayer was converted in Boston in 1916 at a ***BILLY SUNDAY *REVIVAL** meeting. Ayer graduated from ***MOODY BIBLE INSTITUTE** in 1919 and went on to serve as pastor of churches in Illinois, Indiana, and Ontario, before becoming pastor of Calvary Baptist Church in New York City in 1936. In the course of his thirteen-year tenure, Calvary Baptist grew from four hundred to sixteen hundred members. Ayer's radio broadcast, called *Marching Truth,* reached an estimated quarter-million listeners.

Ayer was a fervent fundamentalist whose rhetoric sometimes veered into anti-Communism and anti-Catholicism. Although he was no stranger to theological argumentation, he warned fundamentalists against being too contentious, once characterizing them as "such unloving and acrimonious folk." Ayer wrote ten books, including *God's Answer to Man's Doubts* (1943), served as trustee for *BOB JONES UNIVERSITY and for *EASTERN BAPTIST THEOLOGICAL SEMINARY, was chosen as the first president of the *NATIONAL RELIGIOUS BROADCASTERS, and was a popular speaker at Bible conferences.

References: William Ward Ayer, *Questions Jesus Answered* (1941); idem, *God's Answer to Man's Doubts* (1943).

Azusa Pacific University (Azusa, California) Originally known as the Training School for Christian Workers, Azusa Pacific University was started in 1899 by California Quakers inspired by the *HOLINESS MOVEMENT. In 1965, having changed its name to Azusa College, the school merged with Los Angeles Pacific College to become Azusa Pacific College. This merger made Azusa Pacific the official church college of the *FREE METHODIST CHURCH in the southwestern United States. Three years later, the school absorbed another institution—Arlington College of Long Beach, California, a *CHURCH OF GOD (ANDERSON, INDIANA) school founded in 1954 by the Church of God in southern California.

Since 1981, Azusa Pacific has introduced numerous graduate programs and changed its name to Azusa Pacific University. Today, the school maintains affiliations with no fewer than five denominations—the Brethren in Christ, Church of God, *FREE METHODIST CHURCH, the Missionary Church, and the *SALVATION ARMY. More than forty denominations are represented in the student body.

Azusa Pacific is divided into six separate schools: the College of Liberal Arts and Sciences, the Schools of Education and Behavioral Studies, Music, Nursing, and Business and Management, and the C. P. Haggard School of Theology. All the schools award graduate degrees; even the College of Liberal Arts and Sciences has programs in teaching English as a second language and computer science. The only doctorate conferred, however, is the Ed.D. in the School of Education. The library holds special collections on the Missionary in the American West, American Catholic Church History, Lincolniana, French and German classics, and Western Americana.

References: *Azusa Pacific University 1995–1996 Graduate Catalog* (1995); Virginia Lieson Brereton, *Training God's Army: The American Bible School, 1880–1940* (1990); William C. Ringenberg, *The Christian College: A History of Protestant Higher Education in America* (1984).

Azusa Street Mission The address 312 Azusa Street in Los Angeles, formally known as the Apostolic Faith Mission and popularly known as the Azusa Street Mission, is one of the formative venues for the pentecostal movement. The building, which measured only forty-by-sixty feet, had once been home to an African Methodist Episcopal congregation, but more recently had been a stable and a warehouse before it was appropriated by a fledgling group of pentecostals in April 1906. The group required larger quarters because *WILLIAM J. SEYMOUR, an African American preacher who taught the necessity of *SPEAKING IN TONGUES, was attracting large crowds to Bonnie Brae Street, where he preached from the front porch of Richard Asberry's home. The Azusa Street Mission soon became a hive of activity, with meetings as frequent as three times a day and visitors from around the world. Eventually, however, the revival fervor waned, although meetings continued at the Azusa Street Mission until 1931, when the city of Los Angeles condemned and razed the building.

Azusa Street Revival The Azusa Street Revival began in 1906 when *WILLIAM J. SEYMOUR, an African American holiness preacher who had moved west from Houston early that year, began holding cottage meetings with a small band of followers. Seymour, formerly a waiter, had been an apprentice briefly under *CHARLES FOX PARHAM, the progenitor of the pentecostal *REVIVAL in 1901. Under Seymour's leadership, a gathering in a home at 214 North Bonnie Brae Street was convulsed with *GLOSSOLALIA on April 9, 1906. As word spread, the curious and the faithful came, and within a week Seymour and his followers sought larger quarters.

They settled on a dilapidated building in an industrial section of downtown Los Angeles, and for the next three years 312 Azusa Street, with its enthusiastic, interracial throngs and *SPEAKING IN TONGUES, became a place both of spiritual renewal and pilgrimage. At the height of the *REVIVAL, which grew in intensity after the San Francisco earthquake, meetings were held three times daily. "The night is made hideous," the *Los Angeles Times* wrote, "by the howlings of the worshippers."

Seymour incorporated the ministry as the Pentecostal Apostolic Faith Movement by the end of 1906. Many participants in the Azusa Street Revival reported miraculous healings, and countless participants served as emissaries, taking the Azusa pentecostal message around the world, fortified by the conviction that Jesus would return at any time.

By 1909, a gradual enervation of *REVIVAL enthusiasm had set in. Some of Seymour's early followers turned against him, motivated either by jealousy or by doctrinal differences or some combination of the two. Despite Seymour's waning influence, however, the Azusa Street Revival left an indelible mark on American *EVANGELICALISM—especially *PENTECOSTALISM—in the twentieth century.

Reference: A. C. Valdez Sr., *Fire on Azusa Street* (1980).

■ ■ ■

Babcock Tragedy On February 13, 1805, Amasa Babcock, of eastern New Brunswick, acted on the prophecies of his daughter, Sarah Babcock. Sarah, at the encouragement of a *NEW LIGHT Baptist minister, Jacob Peck, had declared that the end of the world, as predicted in the *BIBLE, was imminent and that Jesus had commanded her to convert the local inhabitants, Acadian Roman Catholics, to evangelical Christianity. Amasa, Sarah's father, gathered his sister Mercy, his brother Jonathan, Amasa's wife, and nine children in the family's kitchen and sprinkled a handful of flour on the floor, proclaiming "This is the bread of Heaven." He removed his shoes and ran out into the deep snow, yelling, "The world is coming to an end, and the stars are falling." Returning to the kitchen, Amasa Babcock commanded his brother and sister to sit on a bench while he sharpened a long "clasp knife." After a long silence, Amasa instructed his sister and his brother to disrobe and fall on their knees to prepare for eternity. Amasa screamed "The Cross of Christ!" and fatally stabbed his sister.

Jonathan, apparently the next in line, fled the house naked and summoned neighbors. Amasa, obviously deranged, cried "Gideon's men arise!" He was captured, convicted of murder, and hanged on June 28, 1805. The "Babcock Tragedy" drew public attention to the excesses of the *NEW LIGHT *REVIVAL, the "*CANADA FIRE," in the Maritimes as well as to the millennial underpinnings of the *REVIVAL.

References: G. A. Rawlyk, *Ravished by the Spirit: Religious Revivals, Baptists, and Henry Alline* (1984); idem, *The Canada Fire: Radical Evangelicalism in British North America, 1775–1812* (1994).

Back to the Bible *Back to the Bible,* a radio broadcast, went on the air from Lincoln, Nebraska, on May 1, 1939. *THEODORE H. EPP, a young preacher from Oklahoma, had come to Nebraska with sixty-five dollars and a vision of starting a radio broadcast that would propagate evangelical ideas and encourage missions. Epp steadily added other radio stations to his network and began broadcasting by means of shortwave radio to other countries. In 1954, the organization opened an international office in Canada, followed over the ensuing five years by offices in England, Sri Lanka, France, the Philippines, Australia, South Africa, India, Ecuador, and Jamaica. By the early 1970s, offices had opened in Italy, Costa Rica, Ecuador, Mexico, Venezuela, and Colombia.

In 1980, Warren Wiersbe, formerly the pastor of *MOODY CHURCH in Chicago, became assistant Bible teacher, as Epp edged toward retirement; Wiersbe eventually took over as general director in 1984. Back to the Bible added a new radio ministry for women, called *Gateway to Joy,* with *ELISABETH ELLIOT in 1988. *WOODROW KROLL joined Back to the Bible in 1990 as the new general director and Bible teacher, replacing Wiersbe, who retired. The organization moved into new headquarters in February 1995 and has expanded its operations into China and Eastern Europe. At the turn of the twenty-first century, Back to the Bible moved aggressively into new media technologies, including the Internet.

References: Harold J. Berry, *I Love to Tell the Story: Back to the Bible's Adventure of Faith* (1989); Randall Balmer, "Wireless Gospel," *Christianity Today,* February 19, 2001.

Backsliding Depending on what theology informs an evangelical's understanding of the faith, the issue of backsliding can be crucial. Whereas Calvinist soteriology insists that God's *GRACE is irresistible and that those who are truly among the elect will persevere, a soteriology informed by *ARMINIANISM would worry about backsliding, someone making a profession of faith and then falling back into unregenerate behavior. Among devout evangelicals, someone identified as a backslider would be the subject of intense concern, prayer, and (doubtless) curiosity.

Backus, Isaac (1724–1806) Considered one of the pioneers of the notion of church-state separation, Isaac Backus was born in Norwich, Connecticut, and converted in 1741, during the *GREAT AWAKENING. He founded the New Light church in Titicut, Massachusetts, and in 1751, he became convinced that adult *BAPTISM was preferable to infant *BAPTISM. That position placed Backus and his congregation outside the mainstream of the Congregationalist establishment. In 1756, he assumed the pastorate of the Baptist church in Middleborough, Massachusetts, and was one of the organizers of the Warren Baptist Association in 1767.

Backus is best remembered for his agitations against the Congregationalist establishment in favor of religious liberty. Representing the Warren Baptist Association, for instance, Backus in 1774 presented the Massachusetts delegation to the Continental Congress with a petition in favor of religious liberty. He served a prison term for refusing to pay church taxes, arguing that religious affiliation should be voluntary and that churches should rely on the contributions of their adherents.

Reference: William G. McLoughlin, ed., *The Diary of Isaac Backus*, 3 vols. (1980).

Bakke, Ray(mond) J(ohn) (1938–) Reared in rural Washington state, Ray Bakke attended *MOODY BIBLE INSTITUTE in Chicago, where he became interested in urban ministry. He became pastor of an inner-city church in Seattle and then moved to another congregation in Chicago, where he has spent the bulk of his career as pastor, professor, writer, and consultant on urban ministry. He is senior associate of International Urban Associates, an organization that seeks to facilitate and coordinate evangelical activities in cities throughout the world.

"People should study the city not because it's so different from the rest of America," Bakke said in a 1997 interview, "but because it's pointing the way the rest of the country is going." Bakke contends that evangelicals, many of whom fled to the suburbs in the middle decades of the twentieth century, have failed to grasp the importance of urban ministry. "All those people who believed that 'greater is he that is in you than he who is in the world' were running away from the city," he said, "people who loved foreign missions, just when foreigners were arriving here in big numbers."

References: Ray Bakke, *A Theology as Big as the City* (1997); Richard A. Kauffman, "Apostle to the City," *Christianity Today*, March 3, 1997.

Bakker, James Charles "Jay" (1976–) The son of *JIM and *TAMMY FAYE BAKKER, Jay Bakker, known then as "Jamie Charles," appeared frequently on his parents' television programs. Afflicted with dyslexia, Bakker struggled in school. When his father was sentenced to prison in 1989, Jay turned to drink and eventually to drugs. "I thought about killing myself," he recalled later, "but feared that hell would consist of a series of acid flashbacks that never went away."

After enrolling in a twelve-step program, Bakker eventually embraced his parents' faith. His arms are thickly tatooed, and he is a pastor for a youth ministry in Atlanta called Revolution.

References: Jay Bakker, *Son of a Preacher Man: My Search for Grace in the Shadows* (2001); Ken Garfield, "PTL's Prodigal Son Lays Down His Burden," *Charlotte Observer*, February 12, 2001.

Bakker, James Orsen "Jim" (1940–) Without doubt the most notorious televangelist in the scandal-plagued 1980s, Jim Bakker was born into a family of modest means in Muskegon Heights, Michigan, and reared in the *ASSEMBLIES OF GOD. Afflicted with shyness throughout his school years, Bakker experienced a religious *CONVERSION in 1958 after a crisis in which he ran over a young boy in his church's parking lot. After graduating from high school the following year, he matriculated at North Central Bible College in Minneapolis, an Assemblies of God school. There Bakker met Tammy Faye La Valley; the couple's decision to marry in 1961 brought about their expulsion from the college because marriage while still a student violated school policy.

Jim and *TAMMY FAYE BAKKER became itinerant *EVANGELISTS, specializing in children's work, and Jim Bakker soon acquired ministerial credentials in the *ASSEMBLIES OF GOD. In 1965, *PAT ROBERTSON hired the Bakkers and their puppet show for his fledgling *CHRISTIAN BROADCASTING NETWORK (CBN). *The Jim and Tammy Show* became popular with viewers, and Jim Bakker's tearful pleas for money produced a flood of contributions. Robertson quickly seized on Bakker's potential and installed him as host of a new program, *The 700 Club,* modeled on the *Tonight Show, starring Johnny Carson*. *The 700 Club* premiered November 28, 1966, and Bakker remained with CBN until 1973, when he became cofounder of *TRINITY BROADCASTING NETWORK in Santa Ana, California.

The Bakkers began their own operation the following year in Charlotte, North Carolina. *The PTL Club*—variously known as "Praise the Lord," "People That Love," and, by cynics, "Pass the Loot"—featured both of the Bakkers and became the foundation for the PTL Network. The network soon moved into state-of-the-art production facilities at Heritage USA, the Bakkers' Christian theme park, which included a hotel, campground, shopping mall, restaurants, condominiums, and a water amusement park.

Bakker had been a tireless proponent of the so-called *PROSPERITY GOSPEL, the "health-and-wealth" doctrine that God was eager to bestow worldly goods to anyone who contributed generously to God's work (read "PTL"). "We preach prosperity," Bakker said. "We preach abundant life. Christ wished above all things that we prosper." In his eagerness to raise capital for Heritage USA, which was located near Fort Mill, South Carolina, Bakker offered lifetime timeshares to people who contributed large sums of money. That tactic would prove to be his legal undoing when it came to light that he had vastly oversold the timeshares and had no way of fulfilling his obligations.

Bakker's spiritual and moral undoing came in the person of Jessica Hahn, a church secretary from Long Island. On March 19, 1987, Bakker abruptly resigned the chairmanship of PTL. He spoke of a "hostile force" that was threatening him with blackmail in order to take over his religious empire. It later emerged that the "force" was fellow televangelist *JIMMY SWAGGART, who excoriated Bakker as a "pretty boy preacher" and a "cancer" on the body of Christ. At issue was a 1980 tryst between Bakker and Hahn, which Bakker had attempted to conceal with hush money delivered by one of his surrogates, Richard Dortch. Bakker tried to save PTL by turning it over to another televangelist, *JERRY FALWELL. Still another televangelist, *JOHN ANKERBERG, stepped forward with charges that Bakker was bisexual.

The drama played out in the media—including *Good Morning America, Nightline,* and *Time* and *Newsweek* cover stories. The Bakkers' lifestyle of conspicuous consumption—gold-plated bathroom fixtures, Rolls Royces, air-conditioned doghouses—soon came to light, along with a salary and bonus package that exceeded a million dollars annually, all while Heritage and PTL sank deeper and deeper into debt. PTL petitioned for bankruptcy, the Internal Revenue Service launched an investigation, and the *ASSEMBLIES OF GOD defrocked Bakker for sexual misconduct.

Bakker stood trial in 1989 for financial improprieties surrounding PTL and Heritage USA. He was convicted and initially sentenced to forty-five years in prison, a sentence later reduced to eight years, of which he served five. While in prison Bakker renounced his *PROSPERITY THEOLOGY. "I began to look up all the Scriptures used in prosperity teaching, such as 'Give and it shall be given unto you,'" he recalled in a 1998 interview. "When I put that Scripture back into its context, I found

Christ was teaching on forgiveness, not on money. He was teaching us that by the same measure that we forgive, we will be forgiven." He added, "I believe the harlot of the book of Revelation is materialism."

While in prison, Bakker also learned that Tammy Faye wanted a divorce; she remarried in October 1993. Upon his release in 1994, Jim Bakker initially settled quietly near Charlotte, North Carolina, and became active in *SAMARITAN'S PURSE, the organization headed by *FRANKLIN GRAHAM, who had visited Bakker regularly in prison. Bakker, who remarried in the fall of 1998, later relocated, in his words, to "the ghetto of Los Angeles," where he assisted in various street ministries.

References: Jim Bakker, *Eight Keys to Success* (1980); idem, *I Was Wrong* (1997); idem, *Prosperity and the Coming Apocalypse* (1999); Charles E. Shepard, *Forgiven: The Rise and Fall of Jim Bakker and the PTL Ministry* (1989); "The Reeducation of Jim Bakker," *Christianity Today,* December 7, 1998.

Bakker, Tammy Faye. *See* **Messner, Tammy Faye (née LaValley) (Bakker).**

Balmer, Clarence R(ussel) (1929–1997) Born in Columbus, Nebraska, on the eve of the Great Depression, Clarence R. Balmer listened to *CHARLES FULLER's *Old Fashioned Revival Hour* as a teenager while working the family farm. At age nineteen, he attended a Sunday evening service at the new *EVANGELICAL FREE CHURCH in Columbus and there gave his heart to Christ. Within six months he had enrolled at Trinity Seminary and Bible College (now *TRINITY INTERNATIONAL UNIVERSITY) in Chicago to prepare for the ministry. After marriage to Nancy R. Froberg in 1953, he briefly attended Wheaton Graduate School and then completed studies for the bachelor's degree in education at the University of Nebraska.

After serving as an interim pastor in Phillips, Nebraska, Balmer's first church was a large rural congregation in East Chain, Minnesota, where he was ordained into the ministry of the *EVANGELICAL FREE CHURCH in 1960. A gifted preacher and a dedicated pastor, his quiet and humble demeanor endeared him to the congregations he served in Minnesota, Michigan, Iowa, and Illinois. He served the denomination in various capacities, including Mission U.S.A. from 1969 to 1974 and the denomination's board of directors for nearly two decades. In June 1982, he was elected to a two-year term as moderator of the denomination.

Balmer, while en route with his sons to a church meeting on the other side of the state of Michigan, discovered a large, wooded tract of five hundred acres. In 1967, he negotiated the purchase of the property on behalf of the Free Churches in the state for use as a camp; Spring Hill Camps, located in Evart, Michigan, now attracts more than ten thousand campers annually. In addition, he directed several building programs during his ministry, including one in Bay City, Michigan, and another in Freeport, Illinois. While in Des Moines, Iowa, he guided the Highland Park Evangelical Free Church to a new building in the northwest section of town, where it took the name Westchester Evangelical Free Church and enjoyed substantial growth under his leadership. He also played a pivotal role in the formation of *MARK IV PICTURES and appeared in several of the company's films, including *A Thief in the Night*. Balmer spent the final six years of his ministry as district superintendent of the central district of California, with offices in Turlock. He and his wife, Nancy, retired to Ankeny, Iowa, in 1996.

Bangs, Nathan (1778–1862) Born in Stratford, Connecticut, into an Episcopalian household, Nathan Bangs migrated to Upper Canada in his early twenties and there fell under the influence of Methodist preaching, which, he recounted, "came like a dagger to my heart." Bangs was converted in August 1800: "With an ecstasy of holy joy did I lay hold upon the cross of the Lord Jesus as my Saviour." After his experience of *SANCTIFICATION in February 1801, Bangs heeded the call to preach and helped to spread the Methodist *REVIVAL, the "*CANADA FIRE," throughout what is now eastern Ontario. Bangs was ordained by the New York Conference in 1804, whereupon he returned to Upper Canada, this time to the western part of the colony. In the summer of 1806, Bangs moved to Québec City and later to Montréal, but his message of Methodist enthusiasm met with indifference, even resistance, in the colony so shaped by French Roman Catholicism.

Returning to New York in 1808, Bangs spent the remainder of his career in the United States. He founded the Methodist Missionary Society and served as its first secretary from 1836 to 1841. He sought to raise the educational standards of Methodist ministers and, toward that end, served briefly, from 1841 to 1842, as president of Wesleyan University. A staunch opponent of *CALVINISM, Bangs published *The Errors of Hopkinsianism Detected and Refuted* in 1815 and wrote a four-volume *History of the Methodist Episcopal Church*, which appeared from 1838 to 1840.

Reference: G. A. Rawlyk, *The Canada Fire: Radical Evangelicalism in British North America, 1775–1812* (1994).

Bannockburn Seven The moniker Bannockburn Seven was applied to seven students at *TRINITY EVANGELICAL DIVINITY SCHOOL, located in the affluent Bannockburn section of Deerfield, Illinois. Led by *JIM WALLIS, this group led protests and demonstrations in the early 1970s on an evangelical campus more accustomed to white, Republican, middle-class sensibilities. Wallis and his confrères distributed leaflets opposing racism, discrimination against women, militarism, and American policies in Southeast Asia. This cohort, with additions and defections, eventually formed a Christian community in the Rogers Park neighborhood of Chicago and published the *Post-American* tabloid, later renamed **SOJOURNERS* magazine.

Baptism Among evangelicals, the ancient rite of baptism has been the focus of considerable debate and controversy. While the Roman Catholic Church believes that the sacrament of baptism, usually done in infancy, removes the taint of original *SIN, most evangelicals offer different interpretations. Some, following Martin Luther and John Calvin, see infant baptism as the rite of initiation into the community of faith. A larger number of evangelicals, however, follow the Baptist tradition, which insists upon adult (or believer's) baptism. In this theology, inherited from Conrad Grebel and *ROGER WILLIAMS, among many others, baptism—by immersion, not sprinkling—follows *CONVERSION; it is a public testimony on the part of the believer to his or her *SALVATION and therefore cannot be done in infancy.

While those evangelicals who believe in infant baptism defend it as the New Testament counterpart to circumcision, Baptists point out that no clear instance of a child being baptized appears in the New Testament. Even the baptism of Jesus, as recorded in the Gospels, took place when Jesus was an adult, not an infant.

Baptism of the Holy Spirit Though rooted in the New Testament, the notion of baptism of the Holy Spirit emerged out of the *HOLINESS MOVEMENT in the nineteenth century, and it was often used synonymously with *SANCTIFICATION or the "*SECOND BLESSING" of the Holy Spirit. With the advent of *PENTECOSTALISM, however, *GLOSSOLALIA (*SPEAKING IN TONGUES) was taken as evidence of the baptism of the Holy Spirit, and it came to be seen by many pentecostals as the only true evidence of Spirit *BAPTISM.

*SPEAKING IN TONGUES became the issue dividing the *HOLINESS MOVEMENT from pentecostalism. *A. B. SIMPSON, a holiness leader and founder of the *CHRISTIAN AND MISSIONARY ALLIANCE, insisted, for example, that the baptism of the Holy Spirit could occur in a believer without *GLOSSOLALIA.

Baptist Bible College and Graduate School of Theology (Springfield, Missouri) Baptist Bible College was organized by the *BAPTIST BIBLE FELLOWSHIP, an independent Baptist group that split from *J. FRANK NORRIS's World Baptist Fellowship. Among the principal leaders in the schism were G. Beauchamp Vick, minister of the Temple Baptist Church in Detroit, and W. E. Dowell, pastor of the High Street Baptist Church in Springfield, Missouri. Clearly a fundamentalist institution from its founding, Baptist Bible's most famous alumnus is *JERRY FALWELL, who modeled both his ministry at *THOMAS ROAD BAPTIST CHURCH and the curriculum at *LIBERTY UNIVERSITY after the *BAPTIST BIBLE FELLOWSHIP and its college.

The school began when the Fellowship's ministers met in a hotel in Fort Worth, Texas, in May 1950 to discuss plans to establish a "Christian school that would be free from all forms of ecclesiastical despotism," perhaps alluding to the fact that they had broken ties with Norris when he dismissed Vick from the presidency of his seminary without the approval of its trustees. That summer the Fellowship bought a tract of land that had once been a city park in Springfield, Missouri. Classes opened the same fall in Dowell's High Street Baptist Church, but by mid-autumn the school had bought and refurbished four army-type barracks and was able to move onto its own campus. Vick was named the first president and served until his death in 1975. Dowell became the vice president and succeeded Vick in the presidency. Dowell stepped down in 1983 but continued to serve as chancellor.

Baptist Bible College earned accreditation from the *AMERICAN ASSOCIATION OF BIBLE COLLEGES in 1978, but it does not have regional accreditation. Correspondence courses are available for students who cannot attend the school. The college runs an FM radio station with the call letters KWFC, for "Keep Witnessing For Christ."

Baptist Bible College has always tried to keep its tuition very low. Between 1978 and 1979, tuition was only eight dollars per credit hour, and the school still has the lowest tuition of colleges in the *ACCREDITING ASSOCIATION OF BIBLE COLLEGES. While these measures ensure that education is financially accessible to all students, the application process reflects unusually strict criteria for admission. Not only must applicants demonstrate evidence of *CONVERSION as a condition of admission, married applicants must account for their own marital history as well as that of their spouse, and the application process requires a physical examination, including a test for HIV status. Prospective students must also provide full details of their mental health history.

Baptist Bible Graduate School of Theology was established in 1985, and classes started the following year. The graduate school offers the master of divinity as well as the master of arts in biblical studies, biblical counseling, missions, and intercultural studies. In 1996, the graduate school had no full-time women faculty, and only one of the adjunct faculty was a woman. These hiring rates are not the only indicator of the school's belief in distinct roles for women and men. The missions program has separate course requirements for the sexes. The men's track includes courses in theology and anthropology. Women must choose a vocational minor in education, business, or music; their program, therefore, substitutes vocational courses like word processing, "keyboarding," or teaching of reading for the advanced courses in theology. Only married women with children are allowed to pursue a missions degree without a minor, and they must sign a waiver indicating their awareness that their degree does not give them a marketable skill.

Baptist Bible College and Graduate School of Theology is still affiliated with *BAPTIST BIBLE FELLOWSHIP INTERNATIONAL. The biology and religion departments both teach "creation science." Lifestyle standards include a ban on attending public movie theaters, and music listened to in college dormitories is also subject to censure.

References: *Baptist Bible College Undergraduate Studies Catalog 1995–1999* (1995); *Baptist Bible Graduate School of Theology Graduate Studies Academic Catalog 1996–1997* (1996); Virginia Lieson Brereton, *Training God's Army: The American Bible School, 1880–1940* (1990); Ed Dobson, Ed Hindson, and Jerry Falwell, *The Fundamentalist Phenomenon*, 2d ed. (1986).

Baptist Bible Fellowship Baptist Bible Fellowship was organized by a group of ministers who split from *J. FRANK NORRIS's World Baptist Fellowship. Among the principal leaders in the schism were G. B. Vick, minister of the Temple Baptist Church in Detroit, and W. E. Dowell, pastor of the High Street Baptist Church in Springfield, Missouri. *BAPTIST BIBLE COLLEGE was founded as one of the main endeavors of the Fellowship, and it remains the group's flagship institution.

References: Martin E. Marty, ed., *Fundamentalism and Evangelicalism* (1993); C. Allyn Russell, *Voices of American Fundamentalism: Seven Biographical Studies* (1976).

Baptist Bible Institute. *See* **Cedarville College.**

Baptist Bible Union Formed in 1923, the Baptist Bible Union, an alliance of Baptist fundamentalists, drew its support from three geographically diverse sources: from Southern fundamentalists, led by *J. FRANK NORRIS; from fundamentalists, led by *WILLIAM BELL RILEY, in the Northern Baptist Convention; and from Canadian fundamentalists, led by *T. T. SHIELDS of Toronto. Shields, elected president of the organization, declared that the Baptist Bible Union's purpose was "declaring and waging relentless and uncompromising war on *MODERNISM."

The war was carried out on two fronts: missions and education. The Union brought a resolution before the Northern Baptist Convention in 1925 that would put an end to the denomination's "inclusive policy," which they regarded as theological *LIBERALISM. When the motion failed, the Baptist Bible Union sought to create its own mission society, but the idea foundered. Two years later, the Union purchased *DES MOINES UNIVERSITY with the idea of transforming it into a citadel of *FUNDAMENTALISM. Many of the students and faculty, however, did not share that vision, and the school closed in 1929 after a student riot. Riley eventually dissociated himself from the Union, Norris became distracted when forced to defend himself against a murder charge, and Shields eventually retreated to Toronto. The final meeting of the Baptist Bible Union took place in 1932, but a new organization of Baptist fundamentalists was formed to carry on a similar agenda: the *GENERAL ASSOCIATION OF REGULAR BAPTIST CHURCHES.

Baptist General Conference The Baptist General Conference traces its roots to Rock Island, Illinois, where in 1852 a Swedish preacher baptized three converts and organized a Swedish Baptist church. The church spread and, in 1879, organized a national conference called the Swedish Baptist General Conference of America. Initially the group received support from the American Baptist Home Missionary Society and the American Baptist Publication Society, but the Conference became completely independent in 1944. The group changed its name the following year by dropping "Swedish." With the language and national identification removed, the Conference grew rapidly.

The theology of the Baptist General Conference is decidedly evangelical, with a clear affirmation of the *INERRANCY and inspiration of the *BIBLE, and of the Trinity. The Conference's *POLITY is congregational, supporting the usual Baptist tenets of soul liberty, separation of church and state, autonomy of local churches, and voluntary cooperation of churches (the associational principle).

Headquarters for the Baptist General Conference are in Arlington Heights, Illinois. Conference churches are clustered in the North Central and Pacific Northwest areas of the United States, but they can be found throughout much of the country. There are currently more than 875 local churches in 13 regional districts in the United States, the Caribbean, and the Bahamas. The Conference supports *BETHEL COLLEGE and Bethel Seminary in St. Paul, Minnesota.

References: Frank S. Mead and Samuel S. Hill, *Handbook of Denominations in the United States*, 10th ed. (1996); J. Gordon Melton, *The Encyclopedia of American Religions*, 3d ed. (1993).

Baptist General Conference of Canada The entity that became known as the Baptist General Conference of Canada organized its first church in 1894, the result of *EVANGELISM and church planting among newly arrived Swedish immigrants. For ninety years, the Canadian churches were affiliated with the Baptist General Conference in the United States, with a number of its pastors being trained at Bethel Seminary in St. Paul, Minnesota. Feeling a need for Canadian identification and wanting to embark on a campaign for *EVANGELISM and church growth, the Canadian churches in 1981 moved to organize the Baptist General Conference of Canada. By the mid-1990s, the denomination had eighty congregations in British Columbia, Alberta, Saskatchewan, Manitoba, Western Ontario, and Québec. The Baptist General Conference of Canada also supports missionaries in several other countries. The denomination's seminary is Canadian Baptist Seminary, a member of the *ASSOCIATED CANADIAN THEOLOGICAL SCHOOLS.

Baptist Missionary Training School (Chicago, Illinois) The Baptist Missionary Training School was founded in Chicago in 1881. It was the first missionary training institute of its kind, predating

*A. B. SIMPSON's Missionary Training Institute, *MOODY BIBLE INSTITUTE, and *A. J. GORDON's Boston Missionary Training School. The Baptist Missionary Training School's enrollment was all female, for at the time seminaries were closed to women. In its endeavor to train women church workers and missionaries, Baptist Missionary Training School was soon followed by the three other aforementioned schools, which are generally regarded as the earliest *BIBLE INSTITUTES.

Reference: Virginia Lieson Brereton, *Training God's Army: The American Bible School, 1880–1940* (1990).

Baptist National Education Convention. *See* **National Baptist Convention of the U.S.A., Inc.**

Baptist Union Theological Seminary. *See* **Bethel College and Bethel Theological Seminary.**

Baptist World Alliance Organized at a meeting in Exeter Hall in London in 1905, the Baptist World Alliance is an international consortium of Baptist organizations. Members of the Alliance, which has its headquarters in McLean, Virginia, support missions and evangelization, relief efforts, and the two fundamental tenets of Baptist belief: congregational autonomy (the self-governance of individual churches) and religious freedom (no state interference).

Barnhouse, Donald Grey (1895–1960) Though born to devout Methodist parents in Watsonville, California, Donald Grey Barnhouse became one of the best-known Presbyterian preachers in the first half of the twentieth century. After attending the *BIBLE INSTITUTE OF LOS ANGELES (BIOLA), where he learned dispensational premillennialism at the feet of *REUBEN A. TORREY, Barnhouse went briefly to the University of Chicago and then to Princeton Theological Seminary. He left seminary in 1917 to join the army signal corps and remained in Europe after the war to serve as a missionary in Brussels and in France.

Barnhouse settled in Philadelphia upon his return to the United States in 1925. He did some graduate work at the University of Pennsylvania, earned a Th.M. at Eastern Baptist Theological Seminary, and served as pastor of Grace Presbyterian Church. In 1927, he accepted the pulpit at Tenth Presbyterian Church, where he stayed for the remainder of his life. Barnhouse's skill as a preacher, writer, and lecturer catapulted him and his church into the front ranks of Presbyterianism. He became a leading voice for the conservative or fundamentalist wing of the denomination, often unleashing criticism against both liberal Protestantism and Roman Catholicism. He started a network radio program in 1928 and a monthly magazine, *Revelation*, in 1931, which was renamed *Eternity* in 1950.

As part of the so-called neo-evangelical movement, Barnhouse became somewhat more irenic toward the end of his life. His "New Year's Resolution" of 1953 expressed a willingness to work more in harmony with other Christians. Although opposed to the Federal Council of Churches, he indicated a willingness to work with the National and World Councils, and, in a break with many fundamentalists, he supported the publication of the Revised Standard Version of the *BIBLE.

References: Donald Grey Barnhouse, *His Own Received Him Not* (1933); idem, *Life by the Son* (1939); idem, *Guaranteed Deposits* (1949);

C. Allyn Russell, "Donald Grey Barnhouse: Fundamentalist Who Changed," *Journal of Presbyterian History,* LIX (1981).

Barrington College. *See* **Gordon College.**

Bartlesville Wesleyan College (Bartlesville, Oklahoma) Affiliated with the *WESLEYAN CHURCH, Bartlesville Wesleyan College evolved in a series of mergers of smaller schools dating back to the beginning of the twentieth century, starting with Colorado Springs Bible College, founded in Colorado in 1910. Over the next fifty years that school merged with several others, including Pilgrim Bible College of Pasadena, California (founded in 1917) and Holiness Evangelistic Institute of El Monte, California (established in 1932), which was later renamed Western Pilgrim College. Colorado Springs Bible College moved to Bartlesville, Oklahoma, in 1959 and changed its name to Central Pilgrim College. Nine years later the school became known as Bartlesville Wesleyan College, after the Wesleyan Methodist and Pilgrim Holiness churches merged.

At that point, the school offered a four-year ministerial program and a two-year degree in liberal arts. When Miltonvale Wesleyan College, a junior college established by the *WESLEYAN METHODIST CHURCH in 1909, merged with Bartlesville Wesleyan, the combined schools decided to introduce a baccalaureate program in liberal arts. Bartlesville received four-year accreditation two years later.

Basham, Don(ald) (Wilson) (1926–1989) One of the leaders of the controversial *SHEPHERDING MOVEMENT, which set up strict accountability structures for new converts to *EVANGELICALISM, Don Basham studied at Phillips University in Enid, Oklahoma, where he and his wife experienced the *BAPTISM OF THE HOLY SPIRIT, including *SPEAKING IN TONGUES. After graduation and seminary, he was ordained by the Christian Church (Disciples of Christ) and served churches in Washington, D.C., Toronto, and Sharon, Pennsylvania. Basham became more and more devoted to the *CHARISMATIC MOVEMENT. In 1967, he resigned his church and moved to Fort Lauderdale, Florida, to become editor of *New Wine* magazine.

While in Fort Lauderdale, Basham joined with *BOB MUMFORD, *CHARLES SIMPSON, *DEREK PRINCE, and *ERN BAXTER to developed the "shepherding" system of spiritual accountability. Their organization, *CHRISTIAN GROWTH MINISTRIES, collapsed in the mid-1980s amid charges of abuse and excessive meddling into the personal lives of followers. After *New Wine* ceased publication in 1987, Basham relocated to Ohio and briefly published *Don Basham's Insights.*

References: Don Basham, *Face Up with a Miracle* (1967); idem, *A Handbook on Tongues, Interpretation, and Prophecy* (1971); idem, *True and False Prophets* (1973).

Basic Communities This term most often refers to a movement within Christianity in which small groups of people form a community that reflects, in turn, their common view of a Christian life. Very often the community is set up as a response to the secular forces of consumer society, materialism, or political disaffection with the status quo as perceived by the community.

The phenomenon of "basic communities" usually has its roots in socioeconomic dislocations that result from highly stratified classes in complex societies, such as the United States, or in societies with large classes of poor dominated by a smaller but powerful class of wealthy power brokers. The pressures facing disaffected groups in both these types of societies has led to the establishment of alternative communities, based on a common vision of Christian community derived from the New Testament. Even in the organized structures of denominational churches, some believe that too much hierarchy and direction are wielded from above. The communities coalesce around ideals of love, *POLITY, and social service as derived from New Testament sources, and they administer these Christian ideals within a self-contained and defined *AUTHORITY within the community. Every member brings personal gifts to the community. The members live their faith and understand the Christian community primarily through their relations with each other within the community.

This phenomenon expresses itself in widely differing fashions. Some of the groups live communally, while others have contact only at their meetings, with many variations in between. The most common traits are fewer formal structures, a collective leadership, an emphasis upon common liturgical celebrations, and generally compatible interpretations of the *BIBLE. Basic communities are not necessarily exclusively composed of individuals who define themselves as "evangelical"; they often include people from a variety of traditions or denominations. They often reflect, however, an evangelical sensibility with regard to preaching, social action, and organization.

Bauer, Gary L(ee) (1948–) Born into a blue-collar family in Newport, Kentucky, Gary L. Bauer found his way to the local Baptist church and soon became involved in a Republican crusade to reform the town's taverns. After graduating with a law degree from Georgetown University in 1973, he worked in the Reagan administration first as a low-level functionary and later as a domestic policy advisor, where he pushed the *RELIGIOUS RIGHT's "family values" agenda. After making the acquaintance of *JAMES DOBSON, head of *FOCUS ON THE FAMILY, Bauer took over Dobson's *FAMILY RESEARCH COUNCIL, a public-policy group loosely associated with Dobson's empire. The council's growing partisanship on behalf of Republican causes—in 1991, for example, Bauer chaired a group called the Citizens Committee to Confirm Clarence Thomas—forced *FOCUS ON THE FAMILY to divorce itself officially from the Family Research Council, although Bauer and the organization maintained strong ties to Dobson and *FOCUS ON THE FAMILY. With its headquarters in Washington, D.C., the *FAMILY RESEARCH COUNCIL had seventy-five employees in 1996 and an annual budget of $10 million. Bauer has proven remarkably effective in organizing grassroots political activity on behalf of politically conservative evangelicals, and in 1999 he announced his candidacy for the 2000 Republican presidential nomination, but dropped out early in the primaries.

References: Gary L. Bauer, *Our Journey Home: What Parents Are Doing to Preserve Family Values* (1992); Jason DeParle, "A Fundamental Problem," *New York Times Magazine*, July 14, 1996.

Bauman, Louis S(ylvester) (1875–1950) Born into a Brethren household in Nora Springs, Iowa, Louis S. Bauman began preaching at the age of seventeen, was ordained in 1894, and became one of the leading evangelists in the *BRETHREN CHURCH (ASHLAND, OHIO). In 1900, he assumed the pulpit at First Brethren Church in Philadelphia; the same year he became a charter member of the Foreign Missionary Society, which he later served as board member and board secretary.

In addition to his advocacy for missions, Bauman imbibed premillennialist ideas, which he articulated for the remainder of his life—in books, preaching, and evangelistic campaigns. After a successful campaign in Long Beach, California, in 1911, Bauman founded a Brethren congregation there that became the largest church in the denomination. Bauman, disturbed about the drift toward *LIBERALISM at the denomination's schools, Ashland College and Ashland Theological Seminary, joined in the founding of *GRACE THEOLOGICAL SEMINARY and, two years later, the National Fellowship of Brethren Churches (now the Fellowship of Grace Brethren Churches).

References: Louis S. Bauman, *The Faith Once for All Delivered to the Saints* (1909); idem, *Light from Bible Prophecy* (1940).

Baxter, (William) (John) Ern(est) (1914–) Ern Baxter was born in Saskatoon, Saskatchewan, and reared in the Presbyterian Church in Canada. His parents became pentecostals, and Baxter, after initial resistance, followed suit in 1932 with his *BAPTISM OF THE HOLY SPIRIT, including *SPEAKING IN TONGUES. After serving in the *PENTECOSTAL ASSEMBLIES OF CANADA, he became pastor of Evangelistic Temple in Vancouver, British Columbia. In 1948, he accepted *WILLIAM MARRION BRANHAM's invitation to join Branham's ministry. After five years of touring with the healing *EVANGELIST, Baxter returned to Evangelistic Temple in 1953.

In the 1960s, Baxter was drawn into the fledgling *CHARISMATIC MOVEMENT. He forged a friendship with *DENNIS J. BENNETT, rector of St. Luke's Episcopal Church in Seattle, and started his own monthly magazine, *New Covenant Times.* In 1974, at a conference in Montreat, North Carolina, Baxter met *BOB MUMFORD of *CHRISTIAN GROWTH MINISTRIES in Fort Lauderdale, Florida, font of the controversial *SHEPHERDING MOVEMENT, which demanded strict accountability on the part of new converts to Christianity. Baxter moved to Fort Lauderdale and joined the organization as one of the principals. In 1984, he relocated to El Cajon, California, after the group decided to decentralize.

References: Ern Baxter, *Thy Kingdom Come* (1977); idem, *The Chief Shepherd of His Sheep* (1987).

Baylor University (Waco, Texas) Baylor University was originally established in 1845 by an act of the Texas Republic. Forty years later, the unification of the Texas Baptists' general conventions led to the merger of Baylor with the church college in Waco.

Baylor was the alma mater of archfundamentalist *J. FRANK NORRIS, the "Texas Tornado" whose attacks changed the university's policies on more than one occasion. As an undergraduate, Norris successfully led a student uprising against Baylor's president, O. H. Cooper, a former Yale professor. When, as a joke, some students smuggled a dog into a chapel service, Cooper angrily threw the howling animal out the window. Enraged at the president's loss of control, Norris brought the matter to the attention of both the Society for the Prevention of Cruelty to Animals and Baylor's board of trustees. This event brought about Cooper's resignation.

Norris graduated in 1903, but twenty years later he would use his newspaper, *The Baptist Standard*, to accuse the school of making accommodations to "*MODERNISM" (theological *LIBERALISM) and evolution, which he equated with heresy. Beginning around 1921, Norris launched a series of attacks on Baylor faculty. Norris especially criticized Samuel Dow, a sociology professor who had written a book discussing the apparent development of contemporary humans from less civilized and less socialized beings. Dow was driven from his position at Baylor as a result of Norris's attacks. Norris also called for the resignation of two biology professors, Lula Pace and Ora Clare Bradbury, who stated they believed Genesis but thought the language may have been allegorical. Baylor's president, Samuel P. Brooks, defended the teachers, but Bradbury resigned nonetheless. Pace stayed at the school until her death in 1925, and Norris continued to call for her resignation until then. Norris also used his paper to effect the transfer of Baylor's theological seminary to Fort Worth, where it became known as Southwestern Baptist Theological Seminary.

Somehow, the school survived these run-ins with its most famous student. Today, Baylor enjoys a reputation as one of the *SOUTHERN BAPTIST CONVENTION's strongest universities. Its medical school is especially well-known, operating seven satellite hospitals across Texas. Nonetheless, Baylor bears the marks of its fundamentalist past. The school is still quite conservative, and its decision finally to allow social *DANCING attracted national media attention in 1996.

References: Thomas C. Hunt and James C. Carper, eds., *Religious Higher Education in the United States: A Source Book* (1996); Martin E. Marty, ed., *Fundamentalism and Evangelicalism* (1993); C. Allyn Russell, *Voices of American Fundamentalism: Seven Biographical Studies* (1976).

Beall, James (Lee) (1925–) The son of *MYRTLE D. BEALL, founder of the Bethesda Missionary Temple in Detroit, James Beall succeeded his mother as pastor of the congregation in the late 1970s. He was a leader in the *CHARISMATIC RENEWAL MOVEMENT, and his radio broadcast, *America to Your Knees*, was broadcast nationwide.

Beall, Myrtle D. (née Monville) (1896–1979) Born into a devout Roman Catholic household in Hubbell, Michigan, Myrtle Beall fell under the influence of *METHODISM and eventually felt called to begin an independent evangelistic outreach in the early 1930s. She started a *SUNDAY SCHOOL in Detroit, which evolved into a congregation known as Bethesda Missionary Temple. Beall, who maintained a grueling schedule that included three daily radio broadcasts, obtained *ASSEMBLIES OF GOD credentials in 1937, and ten years later the congregation began construction of an "armory," with seating for three thousand. In 1948, with the outbreak of the *LATTER RAIN REVIVAL in Saskatchewan, Beall traveled twenty-five hundred miles by automobile to witness the event. Upon her return to Detroit, Bethesda became a center of the *LATTER RAIN MOVEMENT, drawing visitors from across North America. When the *ASSEMBLIES OF GOD began to oppose the *REVIVAL, Beall and the Bethesda Missionary Temple left the denomination in 1949.

Beecher, Catharine (Esther) (1800–1878) The daughter of *LYMAN and Roxana (Foote) BEECHER, Catharine Beecher was born in East Hampton, New York, and, try though she did, she could never appropriate the kind of evangelical *CONVERSION that her father expected of her. She became a moral reformer nevertheless, especially in the field of women's education. Beecher founded the Hartford

Female Seminary, which trained women for work as ministers' wives and as missionary teachers who would bring a kind of Christian literacy to the frontier. Beecher, more than anyone else, was responsible for the nineteenth-century cult of domesticity, which insisted that women belonged in the home and that they assume responsibility as the moral guardians of their families. Paradoxically, she traveled throughout the country encouraging women to do just that, and she wrote a number of devotional and advice books.

Reference: Kathryn Kish Sklar, *Catharine Beecher: A Study in American Domesticity* (1973).

Beecher, Lyman (1775–1863) Born in New Haven, Connecticut, Lyman Beecher matriculated at Yale College in 1793, where he came under the influence of ***TIMOTHY DWIGHT**, who became president in 1795 and initiated an aggressive campaign to root out infidelity and Enlightenment influences among the students. Beecher was one of Dwight's first converts, and the two men became colleagues and friends. After his graduation in 1797, Beecher studied with Dwight for another year, whereupon he accepted the pulpit of the East Hampton Presbyterian Church on Long Island. Beecher came to public attention when he launched a campaign against dueling after Alexander Hamilton had been killed in a duel with ***AARON BURR** in Weehawken, New Jersey.

Beecher moved from East Hampton to the Congregational Church at Litchfield, Connecticut, in 1810, where he became an ardent defender of establishment status for the Congregational Church, warning that disestablishment would sound the death knell for religion. Shortly after Connecticut disestablished Congregationalism in 1818, however, Beecher recanted his earlier sentiments. The voluntary principle, he concluded, had been the best thing to happen to organized religion because it forced the churches to compete openly in the free market of religion. During his Litchfield years, Beecher added another cause to his crusade against vice: ***TEMPERANCE**.

In 1826, Beecher moved to the Hanover Street Congregational Church in Boston, where he hoped to combat Unitarianism at its source. Beecher also became sympathetic to the "***NEW MEASURES**" of revivalism, much to the consternation of old-line Calvinists, who accused him of betrayal.

Concerned about the "invasion" of foreigners (Roman Catholic immigrants), especially in the West, Beecher accepted the presidency of Lane Theological Seminary in Cincinnati in 1932, where he also served as pastor of the Second Presbyterian Church. In his fundraising and recruiting trips on behalf of the seminary, Beecher became more and more vociferous about the threat of Roman Catholicism. In 1834, after Beecher had spoken in Boston, an angry mob burned the Ursuline convent in Charlestown, Massachusetts; many contemporaries believed that Beecher's incendiary rhetoric had galvanized the mob.

Beecher's tenure at Lane was checkered. He tried unsuccessfully to mediate between the pro- and antislavery factions during the ***LANE REBELLION**. Beecher himself was brought up on charges of heresy in 1835, on the grounds that he did not subscribe strictly enough to the Westminster Confession of Faith, the doctrinal standard for Presbyterians. Although he was exonerated, Old Side Presbyterians continued to regard him as suspect for his sympathies with revivalism.

References: Lyman Beecher, *The Autobiography of Lyman Beecher*, 2 vols. (1961); Stuart C. Henry,

Unvanquished Puritan: A Portrait of Lyman Beecher (1973); Marie Caskey, *Chariot of Fire: Religion and the Beecher Family* (1978).

Beeson Divinity School. *See* **Samford University.**

Behold, Inc. *See* **Stapleton, Ruth Carter.**

Belhaven College (Jackson, Mississippi) Belhaven College for Young Ladies was chartered in 1894 by Lewis Fitzhugh. The school first operated in the former home of Col. Jones S. Hamilton, whose house was named Belhaven in honor of his ancestral home in Scotland, and the school adopted the name as well. It was twice destroyed by fire—once in 1895 and again in 1911. After the second fire, the school merged with McComb Female Institute and reopened on a new campus as Belhaven Collegiate and Industrial Institute; four years later it changed its name to Belhaven College. In 1939, the college incorporated another school, Mississippi Synodical College, which had been established in 1883, and for that reason Belhaven considers 1883 its official founding date. The college became coeducational in 1954.

The Synod of Mississippi of the Presbyterian Church in the United States owned and operated the college until 1972, at which time an independent board of trustees assumed control of the school. Belhaven College maintains an affiliation with three Presbyterian denominations—the Presbyterian Church of the United States, the *PRESBYTERIAN CHURCH IN AMERICA, and the *EVANGELICAL PRESBYTERIAN CHURCH—but it is most closely tied to the Synod of the Living Waters of the Presbyterian Church (USA).

Belhaven College has unusually extensive programs in both fine and performing arts. It is one of nine liberal arts colleges accredited by the National Association of Schools of Arts and Design, and in conjunction with the Ballet Magnificat School of Dance, Belhaven offers a minor in ballet. The college sponsors social dances on campus.

Reference: Belhaven College 1996–97 Catalog (1996).

Bell, B. Clayton (1932–2000) Born in China to missionary parents *L. NELSON BELL and his wife, B. Clayton Bell graduated from *WHEATON COLLEGE in 1954 and from Columbia Theological Seminary in 1958. He was ordained in the Presbyterian Church (USA) and served as pastor of congregations in Alabama and Georgia. In 1973, he became pastor of the Highland Park Presbyterian Church in Dallas, Texas, one of the largest in the denomination, retiring early in 2000.

Bell, Eudorus N. (1866–1923) The first general chairman of the General Council of the *ASSEMBLIES OF GOD, Eudorus N. Bell was born in Lake Butler, Florida, and pursued a career as a Baptist minister. He graduated from Stetson University and Southern Baptist Theological Seminary and studied for three years at the University of Chicago, earning the B.A. in 1903. He spent seventeen years as a Southern Baptist pastor, primarily in Texas.

His career took a different turn after his Spirit *BAPTISM on July 18, 1908. Bell had taken a leave of absence from his church in Fort Worth, Texas, in order to investigate the pentecostal outpouring at *WILLIAM DURHAM's North Avenue Mission in Chicago. He left his Baptist church the following year and assumed leadership of a pentecostal congregation in Malvern, Arkansas. He published a monthly paper, *The Apostolic Faith* (later known as *Word and Witness*), the publication that in December 1913 issued the first "call" for pentecostals to gather in Hot Springs, Arkansas, for the purpose of forming a denomination. When the *ASSEMBLIES OF GOD was founded the following year, Bell gave *Word and Witness* to the new denomination and became the group's first general chairman. He edited the *Pentecostal Evangel* (also known as *Weekly Evangel* and *Christian Evangel*) from 1917 to 1919, served as secretary of the *ASSEMBLIES OF GOD until 1920, and then served again as general chairman until his death in 1923.

Reference: Edith L. Blumhofer, *Restoring the Faith: The Assemblies of God, Pentecostalism, and American Culture* (1993).

Bell, L(emuel) Nelson (1894–1973) A medical missionary and influential evangelical leader, L. Nelson Bell was born in Longsdale, Virginia, and experienced an evangelical *CONVERSION at the age of eleven. After graduating from Washington and Lee College and the Medical College of Virginia, he spent twenty-five years as a medical missionary to China, under the auspices of the Southern Presbyterian Church. After the Japanese occupation of China, Bell returned to the United States in 1941 and practiced medicine in Asheville, North Carolina.

An unwavering voice for conservativism within the Presbyterian Church in the U.S., Bell founded the *Southern Presbyterian Journal* in 1942 (later renamed *The Presbyterian Journal*). In 1950, he led the successful opposition to the proposed merger with the Presbyterian body of the North, the Presbyterian Church in the U.S.A., which he regarded as too liberal. In 1972, he was elected moderator of the Southern Presbyterian body. Bell's wider contribution to *EVANGELICALISM in the twentieth century was the establishment of **CHRISTIANITY TODAY*, which he founded together with his son-in-law, *BILLY GRAHAM. Bell wrote a column, "A Layman and his Faith," for the new magazine, managed production, and served on its board of directors.

Bellamy, Joseph (1719–1790) One of the main proponents of the *NEW DIVINITY, Joseph Bellamy was born in Cheshire, Connecticut, and graduated from Yale College in 1735. After his religious *CONVERSION, Bellamy studied for the ministry under *JONATHAN EDWARDS in Northampton, Massachusetts, and was ordained in Bethlehem, Connecticut, in 1740. He became an itinerant preacher during the *GREAT AWAKENING and returned to Bethlehem in 1742. Bellamy's theological writings attempted to perpetuate the experiential *CALVINISM of Edwards's thought.

References: Joseph Bellamy, *True Religion Delineated* (1750); idem, *The Wisdom of God in the Permission of Sin* (1758); Mark Valeri, *Law and Providence in Joseph Bellamy's New England: The Origins of the New Divinity in Revolutionary America* (1994).

Beman, Nathan S(idney) S(mith) (1785–1871) Nathan S. S. Beman, a Presbyterian clergyman and educator, was born in New Lebanon, New York, to Samuel and Silence (Douglass) Beman. Although he matriculated at Williams College in 1803, Beman withdrew after the second term and, following a year's teaching at Fairhaven, Vermont, continued his studies at Middlebury College. Upon graduation in 1807, he became preceptor at Lincoln Academy, Newcastle, Maine, where he studied theology with Kiah Bailey. He returned to Middlebury as tutor in 1809.

His trajectory as an educator already established, Beman began the second part of his *CALLING, the ministry, the following year when he was ordained as pastor of the First Presbyterian Church, Portland, Maine, on March 14, 1810. Poor health forced his resignation two years later, whereupon Beman relocated to Mount Zion, Georgia, and formed both an academy and a Presbyterian church. With the exception of a single year, 1818–1819, when Beman was president of Franklin College in Athens, Georgia, he remained at Mount Zion until he assumed the pastorate of the First Presbyterian Church in Troy, New York, on June 14, 1823.

Amid the *REVIVAL fires of the "burned-over district," the region of upstate New York repeatedly singed by *REVIVAL, Beman would enjoy his greatest success as an *EVANGELIST, a leader of New School Presbyterianism, and a polemicist. His advocacy of *REVIVAL also drew criticism, however, as suggested by the anonymous publication of a pamphlet in 1827, entitled *A Brief Account of the Divisions in the First Presbyterian Church in the City of Troy*. Over the course of his forty-year tenure at First Presbyterian Church, Beman, an eloquent and powerful preacher, established himself as a leader in ecclesiastical, educational, and community affairs. He became a trustee of Middlebury College in 1824 and declined an election to the presidency of that institution in 1846. He also became associated with Rensselaer Polytechnic Institute. In 1842, he was elected vice president and in 1845 president, a post he held concurrently with his pastorate until 1865.

Many of his sermons and discourses were published, some separately and some collected into volumes. *Four Sermons on the Doctrine of the Atonement* appeared in 1825 and was reprinted in England; *The Old Minister* was published in 1839. Beman could be pugnacious and his rhetoric biting. He directed much of his fire toward the Roman Catholic Church and the Protestant Episcopal Church, belittling their claims of apostolic succession, the doctrine that the spiritual *AUTHORITY of the bishopric can be traced in a direct line to the apostles. He supported various social reform movements, and as the Civil War approached Beman stood resolutely and vociferously in the camp of those calling for the abolition of slavery.

Beman's advocacy of *REVIVAL thrust him into the cauldron of Presbyterian politics in the 1820s and 1830s. Old School Presbyterians, led by *CHARLES HODGE and the theologians at Princeton Seminary, looked askance at the Arminian theology of *CHARLES GRANDISON FINNEY, the Presbyterian revivalist whose "*NEW MEASURES" Beman and other revival-minded Presbyterians had adopted. Beman's *REVIVALS in 1826 drew the ire of these Old School conservatives, and he was reprimanded by a convention the same year. Beman's stature, nevertheless, was such that he was elected moderator of the General Assembly five years later, in 1831.

Although Beman tried to act as peacemaker between the Old School conservatives and the New School revivalists—he brokered a meeting, the *NEW LEBANON CONVENTION, between the two sides at New Lebanon, New York, in 1827—his sympathies clearly lay with the New School, in part because of his friendship with Finney. When the Old School wrested control of the denomination in 1837 and exscinded the synods with New School sympathies, the revivalists chose Beman as leader of their New School movement. He contributed further to their cause by compiling the *Church Psalmist*, a collection of hymns that the

New School Presbyterians adopted. Beman's own contributions to nineteenth-century hymnody bear the unmistakable stamp of postmillennial optimism, the conviction that evangelicals must be active in bringing about the kingdom of God through social reform.

References: Nathan S. S. Beman, *Episcopacy Exclusive; A Review of Dr. Coit's Sermon and Pamphlet* (1856); idem, *Letters to Rev. John Hughes* (1857); George M. Marsden, *The Evangelical Mind and the New School Presbyterian Experience* (1970).

Ben Lippen School. *See* **Columbia International University.**

Benediction. *See* **Blessing.**

Bennett, Belle Harris (1852–1922) Born into a socially prominent family near Richmond, Kentucky, Belle Harris Bennett had a religious *CONVERSION in her early twenties, whereupon she joined the local Methodist church. She became interested in foreign missions and soon was appointed by the Woman's Foreign Mission Board to raise funds for a school to train women for foreign missions. As a result of her travels throughout the South, she was able to establish Scarritt Bible and Training School in Nashville, Tennessee. Bennett continued her activities on behalf of missions, first as president of the Woman's Home Missionary Society, from 1896 until 1910, then as head of the Woman's Missionary Council, which grew out of the merger of the foreign and home missions bodies. Bennett advocated the rights of blacks and women and, in 1902, persuaded the Methodist Episcopal Church, South to establish an order of deaconess for foreign missions, thereby allowing women to serve as foreign missionaries.

Bennett, Dennis J(oseph) (1917–1991) Born in London and reared in California, Dennis J. Bennett studied at San Jose State College and at Chicago Theological Seminary. Initially he became a Congregationalist minister, but in 1951 he chose to become a priest in the Episcopal Church because of its liturgy and its adherence to the historic creeds. In 1959, while rector of the affluent St. Mark's Episcopal Church in Van Nuys, California, Bennett received the *BAPTISM OF THE HOLY SPIRIT. Soon thereafter, on a Sunday morning, Bennett informed his stunned parishioners of his Spirit *BAPTISM and that he had spoken in *TONGUES. At the first of the three morning services, he recalled later, he detected a kind of reserved acceptance. During the second service, his assistant ripped off his vestments and stormed out of the church, and during the third service, Bennett tendered his resignation. Bennett's announcement, together with the spread of the spiritual gifts to other members of the congregation, is generally considered the genesis of the *CHARISMATIC RENEWAL MOVEMENT within the Episcopal Church.

"We're Episcopalians," one relieved parishioner told *Time* magazine after Bennett's resignation, "not a bunch of wild-eyed hillbillies." Bennett accepted an invitation from William Fisher Lewis, bishop of the Episcopal diocese of Olympia, Washington, to "bring his fire" to St. Luke's Episcopal Church, a blue-collar mission in Ballard, Washington, that was about to be closed for the third time. The *CHARISMATIC RENEWAL spread there as well, revitalizing the church and making it a showcase of charismatic influence within mainline Protestantism. Bennett wrote a number of books, including *Nine O'Clock in the Morning;* preached and lectured widely; and was one of the founders of the Episcopal Charismatic Fellowship (now *EPISCOPAL RENEWAL MINISTRIES).

References: Dennis J. Bennett, *Nine O'Clock in the Morning* (1970); idem, *The Trinity of Man* (1979); Edith L. Blumhofer, *Restoring the Faith: The Assemblies of God, Pentecostalism, and American Culture* (1993).

Bennett, John G., Jr. (1937–) Born in Olney, Pennsylvania, John G. Bennett Jr. struggled to overcome an impoverished childhood. He taught school, studied medicine for a time, and eventually went into finance. Despite a past checkered with financial irregularities, Bennett established the Foundation for New Era Philanthropy in 1989. He promised investors that he would double their money in six months, and he made special appeals to not-for-profit evangelical organizations, colleges, and seminaries. By the time the *NEW ERA SCANDAL, Bennett's pyramid scheme, came to light in 1995, investors had lost $135 million. Bennett was sentenced to twelve years in prison on September 22, 1997, after conviction on eighty-two counts of fraud and related charges, despite his claim that "religious fervor," not avarice, motivated his actions.

Reference: Tony Carnes, "New Era's Bennett to Prison," *Christianity Today*, October 27, 1997.

Benson, David V. (1929–) An alumnus of *WHEATON COLLEGE, Harvard University, the University of California at Los Angeles, and *FULLER THEOLOGICAL SEMINARY, David V. Benson, an expert in Slavic languages, used Hollywood Presbyterian Church to launch his Russian-language radio *EVANGELISM in the mid-1950s. In 1958, he organized *RUSSIA FOR CHRIST MINISTRIES, which distributed *BIBLES and a radio broadcast, *Christ's Warrior*, behind the Iron Curtain. Benson traveled extensively, making contact with Russian-speaking evangelicals. Following the collapse of the Soviet Union, he faced opposition from leaders of the Russian Orthodox Church, who resented his evangelistic efforts.

References: David V. Benson, *Christianity, Communism, and Survival!* (1967); idem, *Miracle in Moscow* (1973).

Berachah Church (Houston, Texas). *See* **Thieme, R(obert) B(unger), Jr.**

Berg, "Moses" David (1919–1992) Through his mother, Virginia Brandt Berg, David Berg was introduced to the hippie scene of the 1960s. She had initiated an evangelistic outreach in Huntington Beach, California, distributing free peanut butter sandwiches and preaching on the beach. After his mother died, David Berg took over her ministry, eventually parlaying his charisma into control of a former *TEEN CHALLENGE coffeehouse, the beginnings of his "*END-TIMES ministry."

Originally referring to his followers as "Teens for Christ," Berg preached a radical "100 percent commitment to Christ," suggesting that his group was the "true remnant of faith" in these last days. As with many similar evangelistic efforts during that time, Teens for Christ saw significant growth by recruiting transient hippies. Berg began to teach that he carried a "special anointing from God" and that he was "God's end-time prophet," even affixing the name "Moses" to his own.

As the ministry grew, others began to take notice of the group's intensity and its fanatical doomsday proclamations. A newspaper reporter, noting their militant style, dubbed them the "Children of God." Berg liked the name, and it began to surface in their internal literature, a series of "divinely inspired" directives penned by Berg, called "Mo Letters." More publicity ensued as the Children of God became known as "the radical element of the Jesus people movement." Although early media reports were favorable, citing their zealousness, their barnstorming techniques to disrupt other church services, and their public "sackcloth and ashes" demonstrations, the tide began to turn as disaffected former members began to surface. Media stories turned negative. Charges of kidnapping prompted a number of anxious parents to form an alliance group intent on rescuing their children from Berg's clutches. Cult deprogrammer Ted Patrick also turned his gaze on the reclusive Berg and his followers. With legal problems hanging over his head, Berg and the Children of God fled North America to establish colonies first in England and then in other European countries.

Though the main portion of their activities were overseas, the North American media were jarred in 1973 by reports that Moses David Berg had disseminated teachings that promoted the doctrine of "Flirty Fishing," proselytization through sexual relations. Berg called his band of female fishers "hookers for Jesus" who proclaimed a "message of universal love." Since Berg's words held equal status with the *BIBLE, the doctrine of Flirty Fishing was spread throughout the various Children of God communities, although they were not always carried out. Berg continued to spread his "message of love" throughout the world into the 1990s, establishing communities in forty different countries. Rarely seen in public since 1971, Berg died in 1992.

References: Deborah Berg Davis, *The Children of God: The Inside Story* (1984); David E. Van Zandt, *Living in the Children of God* (1991).

Berkeley Blitz The Berkeley Blitz was an evangelistic initiative conducted by *CAMPUS CRUSADE FOR CHRIST at the University of California, Berkeley in 1967. The idea motivating the Berkeley Blitz was that if *CAMPUS CRUSADE could penetrate Berkeley, the seat of radical student unrest, then other campuses would follow. The organization mobilized under the slogan "Solution: Spiritual Revolution" and conducted a week of rallies on campus, which culminated in *BILLY GRAHAM's address to a large audience at Berkeley's Greek Theater. In the highly charged atmosphere at Berkeley at the time, however, the Berkeley Blitz had little effect. "Dollar for dollar," one *CAMPUS CRUSADE veteran later admitted, "I think it was one of the weakest things we ever did." A later initiative at the University of California, Los Angeles also yielded disappointing results.

Reference: William Martin, *With God on Our Side: The Rise of the Religious Right in America* (1997).

Berkshire Christian College. *See* **Boston Bible School.**

Bertermann, Eugene (1914–1983) Born in Bittern Lake, Alberta, Eugene Bertermann studied at *CONCORDIA COLLEGE and at Washington University in St. Louis. In 1940, he was ordained in the *LUTHERAN CHURCH—MISSOURI SYNOD. Bertermann had received a scholarship from the Lutheran Laymen's League, which he served as business manager for nearly a quarter of a century. From 1957 until 1975, he was president of *NATIONAL RELIGIOUS BROADCASTERS.

Bertermann was also involved in other missions and evangelistic efforts. He served as executive director of his denomination's television department for eight years and helped to organize Lutheran Bible Translators in 1964. He worked for the *FAR EAST BROADCASTING COMPANY and was one of the planners for *KEY '73, an interdenominational evangelistic effort.

Bethany Nazarene College. *See* **Southern Nazarene University.**

Bethany-Peniel College. *See* **Southern Nazarene University.**

Bethel Bible College (Topeka, Kansas) Also known as "The Parham School of Tongues," founded by evangelist *CHARLES FOX PARHAM, Bethel Bible College opened in 1900 near Topeka, Kansas. Forty students enrolled. In many ways Parham's school imitated the more established *BIBLE INSTITUTES; students were charged to study the *BIBLE in the morning and spend each afternoon in some form of practical Christian service, but some evidence suggests that academics at Bethel were remarkably weak, to the point of nonexistence.

On January 1, 1901, one of Parham's students, *AGNES OZMAN, began to speak in *TONGUES, validating the idea that authentic *BAPTISM OF THE HOLY SPIRIT would bring on the "gift of the Spirit." This event marked the beginning of the modern pentecostal movement. One of Parham's students, *WILLIAM J. SEYMOUR, preached the experience at the *AZUSA STREET MISSION in Los Angeles, thereby precipitating the *AZUSA STREET REVIVAL. Parham's Bible College, however, had dispersed by the end of the summer of 1901.

Reference: Virginia Lieson Brereton, *Training God's Army: The American Bible School, 1880–1940* (1990).

Bethel Bible Training School. *See* **Gordon College.**

Bethel College (Mishawaka, Indiana) Bethel College was founded in 1947 by the Missionary Church, a denomination with pietist origins. The College's library contains the Missionary Church Archives and Historical Collections. Graduate programs are available in business and ministry.

Neither occult practices nor social *DANCING are permitted on campus or at school-sponsored events. Bethel College does, however, condone "ethnic games and the use of choreography in drama, musical productions, athletic events, and other formal academics."

Reference: Bethel College 1996–1997 Catalog (1996).

Bethel College (North Newton, Kansas) Bethel College was established in 1887 at Newton, Kansas, by Mennonite immigrants from Central and Eastern Europe. The college maintains its affiliation with the General Conference Mennonite Church, and today approximately half the student body comes from a Mennonite or pietist background.

Bethel's founding represented a new openness to education for Mennonites. Previously, higher education had been seen as "dangerous to faith," but the college opened with the promise of instruction in Latin, Greek, and other humanistic subjects, in addition to study of the *BIBLE. Since its beginnings, Bethel has been coeducational.

Bethel is first among Kansas colleges and universities in the percentage of graduates who go on to earn doctoral degrees. Since 1920, about five percent of its graduates have earned doctorates, a statistic that demonstrates Bethel's continuing commitment to the liberal arts tradition.

Bethel College and Bethel Theological Seminary (St. Paul, Minnesota) Bethel

Theological Seminary was founded by John Elexis Edgren in 1871 to respond to the need for trained ministers in the Baptist Churches of Swedish immigrants. From 1874 to 1888, the seminary was located in St. Paul, Minnesota, and Stromsberg, Nebraska. At other points in its first fifty years, however, it periodically existed as the Swedish department of the University of Chicago, and the university's predecessor, the Baptist Union Theological Seminary.

In 1914, the Baptist General Conference assumed full support of the seminary, and it moved back to St. Paul, Minnesota, where it joined with Bethel Academy (founded 1905) under the name Bethel Academy and Seminary of the Swedish Baptist General Conference. In 1977, a branch of the seminary opened in San Diego, with the assistance of San Diego's College Avenue Baptist Church.

Bethel College began as Bethel Academy, a junior college and secondary school, first established in 1905. A junior college curriculum was introduced in 1931, and the college started its baccalaureate program sixteen years later. In 1961, the trustees bought the current campus. Bethel is affiliated with the *BAPTIST GENERAL CONFERENCE, and it was one of the founding members of the *CHRISTIAN COLLEGE CONSORTIUM.

Reference: William C. Ringenberg, *The Christian College: A History of Protestant Higher Education in America* (1984).

Bethel Mission (St. John's, Newfoundland). *See* **Garrigus, Alice Belle.**

Bethune, Mary McLeod (1875–1955) Born to former slaves in Mayesville, South Carolina, Mary McLeod Bethune graduated from the Bible Institute for Home and Foreign Missions (later known as *MOODY BIBLE INSTITUTE) in 1895. Although she aspired to be a missionary to Africa, she was rejected twice and so turned her attention to the education of African Americans. She taught in Georgia and Florida and in 1904 opened her own school, the Daytona Normal and Industrial School for Girls, in Daytona Beach, Florida, which eventually became Bethune-Cookman College, a fully accredited liberal arts institution.

Early on in the school's history, Bethune developed a relationship with the National Association for Colored Women, which raised funds to help support the school. In 1927, Bethune became president of the organization which, under her leadership, advocated school desegregation, prison reform, antilynching legislation, and women's training programs. Bethune also founded the National Council of Negro Women in 1935, a coalition of women's organizations. From 1935 to 1943, Bethune served as director of the Division of Negro Affairs and as a member of Franklin Delano Roosevelt's "Black Cabinet." "If I have a legacy to leave my people, it is my philosophy of living and serving," she wrote in her last will and testament. "As I face tomorrow, I am content, for I think I have spent my life well. I pray now that my philosophy may be helpful to those who share my vision of a world of peace, progress, brotherhood, and love."

References: Mary McLeod Bethune, "My Last Will and Testament," *Ebony*, August 1955; Rackham Hold, *Mary McLeod Bethune: A Biography* (1964); Judith Weisenfeld, s.v. "Bethune, Mary McLeod," in Jack Salzman, et al., eds., *Encyclopedia of African-American Culture and History* (1996).

Beulah Heights College. *See* **Southern Nazarene University.**

Beyond the Blue Beyond the Blue, a *CONTEMPORARY CHRISTIAN MUSIC trio, was formed in 1994, when Steve Smith, once a performer for Sea World, joined forces with producer and songwriter Marty Funderburk. The duo quickly recruited Richard Kelly, who had begun singing with the Interdenominational Mass Choir of Atlanta at age fourteen. The name of the group refers to heaven, the ultimate goal of all their work. When they formed, Beyond the Blue was signed to Word Records without even a demo tape—testimony to all three members' longstanding involvement in the music industry. The son of a pastor, Smith also previously sang at Disney World and Epcot Center and recorded jingles for commercial advertising. A "Showcase Winner" on *The Price Is Right* game show, Kelly's résumé included traveling with Earth, Wind & Fire as a backup singer on their "Touch the World" tour and performing with Robin Brown and the Triumphant Delegation. He was invited to be a guest vocalist at the 1988 Democratic National Convention. In addition to his experience in music production and songwriting, Funderburk toured for six years as a singer with Life Action Ministries and once sang at the White House for George Bush's private Christmas party.

Reference: Information provided by Word Records.

Bible For evangelicals of all stripes, the Bible provides their epistemological foundation. As God's revelation to humanity, the Bible—both the Hebrew Scriptures (Old Testament) and the New Testament—provide the basis for faith, theology, and practice. Any doctrine or behavior deemed "unbiblical" is open to suspicion.

Because evangelicals, beginning with Martin Luther, rejected the primacy of the Roman Catholic Church, thereby setting aside Rome's twin bases of *AUTHORITY, Scripture and tradition, evangelicals rely on the authority of the Bible alone (**SOLA SCRIPTURA*). For this reason, evangelicals view the Bible with particular reverence; they often refer to it as the "*WORD OF GOD" (*word* usually is capitalized), and they have devised various doctrines, including the doctrine of biblical *INERRANCY, to defend its integrity and reliability. Some evangelicals have even invested the Bible with a kind of iconic significance. They insist that a copy of the Bible should never touch the floor or that it should never be placed beneath another book.

Bible Belt The term *Bible Belt* was coined by H. L. Mencken of the *Baltimore Sun* and was meant as an unflattering reference to the large concentration of fundamentalists in America, especially in the South. The term has endured—and often without the pejorative overtones that Mencken intended—as a way of denoting regions with a high density of evangelicals. From time to time, moreover, various pundits have tried to locate the various "buckles" of the Bible Belt. Although such speculation is, of course, an inexact science, some of the candidates for such a designation would include Wheaton/Carol Stream, Illinois; Dallas/Fort Worth, Texas; Grand Rapids, Michigan; Lynchburg and Virginia Beach, Virginia; Toronto and Hamilton, Ontario; Colorado Springs, Colorado; and Orange County, California.

Bible Institute for Home and Foreign Missions of the Chicago Evangelization Society. *See* **Moody Bible Institute.**

Bible Institute of Los Angeles. *See* **Biola University.**

Bible Institute of Pennsylvania. *See* **Philadelphia College of Bible.**

Bible Institutes and Bible Colleges Beginning in the late nineteenth century, many Bible institutes were founded by various denominations, Bible fellowships, and independent individuals. The three earliest such schools were *A. B. SIMPSON's Missionary Training Institute (now known as *NYACK COLLEGE), founded in New York in 1882; *MOODY BIBLE INSTITUTE, which began in Chicago in 1886; and A. J. Gordon's Boston Missionary Training School, established in Boston in 1889.

In general, Bible institutes were established to train laypeople and church workers rather than to prepare ordained clergy. They were often started as single classes in Bible study at local churches, with the study not culminating in a degree at all but rather leading to a certificate of completion. From the beginning, the schools had a high representation of female students; some schools, like that of *EMMA DRYER in Chicago, were all-women. The primary focus at the institutes was Bible study, with courses in English and related subjects offered as needed to supplement that main endeavor. "Practical skills" in areas such as church music or missionary work were also stressed. At the same time, founders of Bible institutes were often highly suspicious of secular learning—study of the liberal arts was sometimes seen as "dangerous to faith." Such hostility was related, no doubt, in part to the controversies regarding biblical criticism and Darwinism that raged in the late nineteenth century, but it also found its source in the social and financial circumstances of the supporters of many of the schools. In their early years, Bible institutes tended to be extremely marginal; the schools often only knew from month to month whether or not they could stay open.

Such financial hardship continues to plague the smaller Bible institutes to this day; indeed, most of the roughly six hundred institutes run by local churches in the United States operate under these circumstances. Over time, however, some of the more successful institutes have adopted the trappings of secular education, including at least a smattering of liberal arts. Some of the institutes developed full degree programs that culminated not only in a certificate, but often also in an associate's or bachelor's degree in *BIBLE. Although the terms are sometimes used interchangeably, the main separator between Bible institutes and Bible colleges tends to be their size, with the larger and more stable schools choosing the latter name and also adopting a liberal arts curriculum.

Today, some Bible colleges have adapted, so they more closely resemble Christian colleges or even secular schools. Liberal arts courses are offered side by side with courses in theology and *BIBLE, and although students at Bible colleges tend to continue to major in biblical studies, they often complete a second major in a field such as psychology, church music, or education. Bible colleges remain distinctive from Christian liberal arts colleges, however, in the continued emphasis of the former on Bible study.

The longer-established Bible colleges and institutes participate in their own national association, the *ACCREDITING ASSOCIATION OF BIBLE COLLEGES (AABC). While some of these schools also pursue regional accreditation, most rely on the AABC's accrediting standards alone. As "training grounds for Christian workers," Bible colleges have generally maintained rigorous standards of conduct. It is testimony to the normalcy of such restrictions that they are codified in written form far less often than at *CHRISTIAN COLLEGES, where the faith commitments of individual students might vary considerably.

Reference: Virginia Lieson Brereton, *Training God's Army: The American Bible School, 1880–1940* (1990).

Bible Presbyterian Church Formed in 1938 under the leadership of *CARL MCINTIRE, the Bible Presbyterian Church was, in part, a reaction against the tendencies toward *MODERNISM that many saw in the Presbyterian Church in the USA (PCUSA). McIntire, along with *J. GRESHAM MACHEN and other dissatisfied Presbyterians, had departed from the PCUSA in 1936 to form the Presbyterian Church of America. Soon afterward, however, that church divided over three issues: the use of alcoholic beverages, premillennial theology, and support of the Independent Board of Presbyterian Foreign Missions. When there clearly could be no unity on these points, McIntire led a group to form the Bible Presbyterian Church. The remaining faction was not allowed to use the name Presbyterian Church of America and became instead the *ORTHODOX PRESBYTERIAN CHURCH.

With McIntire as their leader, the Bible Presbyterians diligently opposed *MODERNISM, communism, and pacifism. The church especially targeted the National Council of the Churches of Christ and the World Council of Churches as centers of apostasy in the twentieth century. McIntire founded both the *AMERICAN COUNCIL OF CHRISTIAN CHURCHES and the International Council of Christian Churches in the 1940s to provide a place where—in his view—true Christian churches could separate themselves from the apostate councils.

In the 1950s, considerable opposition to McIntire's leadership arose. This opposition formed the larger faction in the Bible Presbyterian Church and left to form the *REFORMED PRESBYTERIAN CHURCH, *EVANGELICAL SYNOD, which now is a part of the *PRESBYTERIAN CHURCH IN AMERICA. McIntire's faithful followers declared themselves a new and independent synod of the Bible Presbyterian Church.

The doctrine of the Bible Presbyterians is fundamentalist, subscribing to the Westminster Confession of Faith and the Larger and Smaller Westminster Catechisms, the historic touchstones of Presbyterian orthodoxy. The church is premillennial; opposes all forms of the *SOCIAL GOSPEL and liberation theology, which it regards as Marxist; and requires belief in the *INERRANCY and infallibility of Scripture and in the virgin birth and deity of Jesus Christ, his blood *ATONEMENT, bodily resurrection, and literal *SECOND COMING. The church takes strong stands against the use of alcohol as a beverage, new evangelicalism, the Revised Standard Version of the *BIBLE, evolution, civil disobedience, and the United Nations.

*POLITY in the church is presbyterian, but with significant emphasis given to congregational authority. Congregations own their property, call their own pastors, and may withdraw at any time for any reason they deem sufficient. Meetings of presbyteries and synods are for edification and fellowship rather than administration. The church claims a membership of about ten thousand in the United States and Canada.

References: Frank S. Mead and Samuel S. Hill, *Handbook of Denominations in the United States*, 10th ed. (1997); J. Gordon Melton, *The Encyclopedia of American Religions*, 3d ed. (1993).

Bible Revival Evangelistic Association. *See* **Nunn, David (Oliver).**

Bible Standard, Inc. *See* **Open Bible Standard Churches.**

Bible Training School. *See* **Lee College.**

Bibletown Conference/Retreat Center (Boca Raton, Florida) Founded in 1950 by *IRA LEE ESHELMAN and located in Boca Raton, Florida, Bibletown Conference/Retreat Center represents an attempt to perpetuate the late nineteenth-century Bible Conference movement among present-day evangelicals. "I felt the gold coast of Florida was entitled to something better than a diet of night clubs and race tracks, or cheap and valueless entertainment," Eshelman recalled forty years later. "A center had to be built in this vacationland, appealing to those people coming to Florida with a love for those values contributing to America's greatness!" Like the prophetic conferences and the *CAMP MEETINGS of earlier generations, Bibletown attracts evangelicals who want to combine vacation in modest, affordable accommodations in Florida with an opportunity to hear gospel music and evangelical preaching.

Reference: Ira Lee Eshelman, *A Gold Coast Miracle: "Great Things He Hath Done"* (n.d.).

Biederwolf, William (Edward) (1867–1939) A native of Monticello, Indiana, William Biederwolf was converted to evangelical Christianity as a teenager. He studied at Wabash College, Princeton University, and Princeton Theological Seminary as well as several European universities. He returned to Indiana in 1897 as pastor of a Presbyterian church at Logansport before signing on as an assistant to *J. WILBUR CHAPMAN in 1900.

Six years later, Biederwolf struck out on his own, becoming an itinerant revivalist. Like *BILLY SUNDAY, his contemporary, Biederwolf combined an emphasis on *EVANGELISM with advocacy of civic and social reform, especially prohibition. In 1922, he was named director of the *WINONA LAKE BIBLE CONFERENCE, making it into a gathering place both for the devout and for many evangelical luminaries. The following year, he added the title director of the Winona Lake Bible School of Theology. Biederwolf later became an ardent premillennialist, and he also served as pastor of the Royal Poinciana Chapel in Palm Beach, Florida, known as the "richest congregation in the world."

Reference: William Biederwolf, *The Millennium Bible* (1924).

Bilezikian, Gilbert (1930–) According to *BILL HYBELS, founder and senior pastor of *WILLOW CREEK COMMUNITY CHURCH, "There would be no Willow Creek without Gilbert Bilezikian." Hybels had met Bilezikian when the two were at *TRINITY COLLEGE in Deerfield, Illinois—Bilezikian as teacher and Hybels as student. When Hybels decided to form a new church in 1975, he asked Bilezikian to join the enterprise as a kind of pastor-teacher and theologian-in-residence.

The child of Armenian refugees, Bilezikian grew up in occupied France. He was converted to evangelical Christianity at a *SALVATION ARMY meeting. He migrated to Boston, where he studied at *GORDON-CONWELL THEOLOGICAL SEMINARY and then earned the Ph.D. from Boston University. He returned to France for military service and several years of teaching. He taught at *WHEATON COLLEGE, served as president of a university in Lebanon, and then came to Trinity, where he met Hybels.

Bilezikian, a member of the Bible department at Trinity, emphasized the importance of Christian community, based on the Acts of the Apostles. "Without community," he wrote, "there is no Christianity." Those convictions have led him to insist on gender equality. "I am not a feminist," he told an interviewer in 2000, but "authentic community necessarily implies full participation of women and men on the basis of spiritual gifts, not on the basis of sex." Despite some early opposition from other staff members at the fledgling church—including Hybels himself—Willow Creek adopted a policy of gender equality, and it now requires potential members to affirm that they "joyfully submit to the leadership of women in various leadership positions at Willow Creek."

References: Gilberet Bilezikian, *Beyond Sex Roles* (1985); Lauren F. Winner, "The Man Behind the Megachurch," *Christianity Today,* November 17, 2000.

Billy Graham Center. *See* **Billy Graham Evangelistic Association.**

Billy Graham Evangelistic Association During the course of *BILLY GRAHAM's 1950 crusade (revival campaign) in Portland, Oregon, a group of advisors prevailed upon him to establish a not-for-profit corporation that would manage the financial affairs related to the evangelistic career of the promising young evangelist. George Wilson, the business manager at Northwestern Schools in Minneapolis, a fundamentalist Bible institute that Graham served as president (though largely in a titular role), had taken the lead in proposing the corporation. The Billy Graham Evangelistic Association (BGEA), with Graham as president and Wilson as secretary-treasurer, was incorporated in Minnesota, with its headquarters in Minneapolis.

The association handles all the business affairs related to Graham's worldwide operations, including the salaries and the scheduling of Graham and associate *EVANGELISTS, the *Hour of Decision* radio broadcasts, *Decision* magazine, World Wide Pictures (begun in 1951, but since disbanded), and Graham's writings—his books and his syndicated newspaper column, "My Answer." The organization also runs various other support services, including schools on *EVANGELISM and training for crusade volunteers. The association also is responsible for overseeing the Billy Graham Center, including a museum and a library, housed at Graham's alma mater, *WHEATON COLLEGE, Wheaton, Illinois.

Through the years the Billy Graham Evangelistic Association has acquired a well-earned reputation for corporate efficiency. Its careful attention to detail, however, and its financial accountability are at least partially responsible for the fact that no serious charge of malfeasance has been laid at Graham's feet throughout a career that spanned more than half a century. In 1995, the association had a staff of 525 employees, a mailing list of 2.7 million active donors, and $88 million in annual revenues.

Reference: William Martin, *A Prophet with Honor: The Billy Graham Story* (1991).

Billy James Hargis Evangelistic Association. *See* **Hargis, Billy James.**

Biola University (La Mirada, California) Biola University began as the Bible Institute of Los Angeles, a school that developed out of weekly classes in Bible study and Christian *EVANGELISM known as the Fishermen's Club for men and

Lyceum Club for women. The Bible Institute's founding was the result of the vision of two men: T. C. Horton, who had founded the Fisherman's Club, and *LYMAN STEWART, a cofounder of the Union Oil Company, who also would underwrite the cost of producing and distributing **THE FUNDAMENTALS*, the series of pamphlets, published between 1910 and 1915, that would give fundamentalism its name. Stewart and Horton created an organization in 1908 to establish an interdenominational school. Shortly afterward, classes began in two rooms above a pool hall in downtown Los Angeles. The Bible Institute hired *REUBEN A. TORREY as the first dean by 1912, and the following year Stewart laid the cornerstone of the first building for the Institute's own campus. By 1915, the school was able to move to its new site in Los Angeles.

In the 1920s, the Bible Institute of Los Angeles was famous as a major proponent of *DISPENSATIONALISM and *FUNDAMENTALISM. Several faculty worked on **THE FUNDAMENTALS*, and the Institute also published *The King's Business,* a popular fundamentalist magazine. When radio station KJS began broadcasting in 1922, the school became one of the first Bible schools to launch a radio station. Originally established as a training school for Christian workers, the Bible Institute attracted mostly older students in its early years; until the 1930s, the average age was twenty-five. The Institute always emphasized missionary work; the Institute sponsored two missions in Australia and founded a sister Bible school in China. The school also had several domestic missionary programs, including departments specifically designed to proselytize factory workers, Mexican immigrants, sailors, and Jews.

During the Great Depression, the Institute experienced several periods of financial crisis. Starting in 1932, *LOUIS T. TALBOT, a radio evangelist and pastor of Church of the Open Door, assumed the presidency, and more than once the school was rescued from imminent bankruptcy by Talbot's appeals to his congregation and radio audiences. The Bible Institute weathered the 1930s but was forced to cut back on its missionary activities; despite economic recovery in subsequent decades it did not restore the original emphasis on missions but chose instead to strengthen its academic programs. During Talbot's twenty years as president, the school introduced degree programs in theology, Christian education, and sacred music. It also changed to a four-year curriculum, and the age of the average student dropped to twenty years. In 1949, the Institute changed its name to Biola College (Biola is an acronym for Bible Institute of Los Angeles). Biola's change in emphasis from foreign missions to Christian academics was sealed in the 1950s when the school severed its ties with the *BIBLE INSTITUTE in China.

With the establishment of Talbot Theological Seminary, Biola's first graduate school, the college rapidly outgrew its original facilities. Biola College moved onto its present, seventy-five-acre campus in La Mirada in 1959.

In the past twenty years, Biola has developed several divisions, in addition to the School of Arts and Sciences. In 1977, Biola College acquired the graduate programs of Rosemead Graduate School of Professional Psychology and merged them four years later with the college's own undergraduate psychology department to form the Rosemead School of Psychology. Biola College became known as Biola University in 1981. Talbot Theological Seminary took the name Talbot School of Theology in 1983, in order to reflect the merger of Biola's graduate and undergraduate departments of religion. Ten years later, the School of Business was created, and the School of Continuing Studies was added in 1994.

Today, the university offers master's degrees in divinity and theological studies and the master of arts in education, Christian education, ministry, and practical theology. The university has doctoral programs in ministry, psychology, and education. The library's special holdings include collections in Bible history and translation, the history of *FUNDAMENTALISM and evangelical Christianity, and international Christian missions.

References: *Biola University Undergraduate Catalog 1996–97* (1996); Virginia Lieson Brereton, *Training God's Army: The American Bible School, 1880–1940* (1990); Martin E. Marty, ed., *Fundamentalism and Evangelicalism* (1993); William C. Ringenberg, *The Christian College: A History of Protestant Higher Education in America* (1984).

Black, William (1760–1834) A Methodist itinerant preacher during the *CANADA FIRE, the evangelical *REVIVAL in Nova Scotia around the turn of the nineteenth century, William Black initially embraced the *REVIVAL but came in time to reject it as a species of "fanaticism." Black had moved with his family from Yorkshire to Nova Scotia in 1775. Four years later, at the age of seventeen, Black had an emotional evangelical *CONVERSION. "I was determined never to rest," he recalled, "until I found rest in Christ."

Black and *HENRY ALLINE were spiritual allies during the age of the American Revolution; both preached the importance of spiritual rebirth and godly living, and both were determined opponents of *CALVINISM. Denominational loyalties, however, prompted a split. Black, known as the "father of *METHODISM" in the Maritimes, would accuse Alline, a Congregationalist, of poaching from the Methodists.

References: G. A. Rawlyk, *The Canada Fire: Radical Evangelicalism in British North America, 1775–1812* (1994).

Blackstone, William E(ugene) (1841–1935) A zealous dispensationalist, William E. Blackstone in 1878 published the immensely popular book *Jesus Is Coming,* an explanation of how historical and current events pointed to the imminent return of Jesus. His dispensationalist convictions led to initiatives aimed at the *CONVERSION of Jews to Christianity and to the restoration of Jews to Palestine, both of them, according to dispensationalists, necessary preconditions to the unfolding of events in the book of Revelation. In 1887, Blackstone was one of the founders of the Chicago Hebrew Mission (later the American Messianic Fellowship), which he served as superintendent from its founding until 1891. Blackstone sent a "Memorial" to President Benjamin Harrison in 1891 urging that persecuted Russian Jews be allowed to settle in Palestine. In 1916, a similar representation to President Woodrow Wilson may have been influential in the United States government's support for the Balfour Declaration, which endorsed a homeland for Jews in Palestine.

References: William E. Blackstone, *Jesus Is Coming* (1878); Paul Boyer, *When Time Shall Be No More: Prophecy Belief in Modern American Culture* (1992).

Blackstone Memorial (1891) In 1891, *WILLIAM E. BLACKSTONE, an ardent dispensationalist, sent a "Memorial" to President Benjamin Harrison, with over four hundred signatories, urging the resettlement of persecuted Russian Jews in Palestine. Such a scheme would not only have eased the crowding at Ellis Island, it would also have been a step toward the restoration of Jews to Palestine, thereby realizing dispensationalist expectations about the fulfillment of biblical prophecies.

Reference: Paul Boyer, *When Time Shall Be No More: Prophecy Belief in Modern American Culture* (1992).

Blair, Samuel (1712–1751) Samuel Blair, born in Ulster, Ireland, emigrated to the Middle Colonies at a young age. He studied theology at *WILLIAM TENNENT's *LOG COLLEGE in Neshaminy, Pennsylvania, and was licensed by the Presbytery of Philadelphia in 1733. He served as pastor of two churches in New Jersey and accepted a call to the Faggs Manor Presbyterian Church near New Londonderry, Pennsylvania, in 1739. A *REVIVAL broke out there in March 1740, and Blair soon emerged as a forceful preacher and one of the leaders of the revivalist New Side Presbyterians during the *GREAT AWAKENING.

Blanchard, Charles A(lbert) (1848–1925) Charles A. Blanchard, who was born in Galesburg, Illinois, when his father, *JONATHAN, was president of Knox College, followed in his father's footsteps as a preacher, a president, and a polemicist. The younger Blanchard graduated from *WHEATON COLLEGE with a bachelor's degree in 1870, while his father was president of that school. After a brief stint as principal of the preparatory school at Wheaton, Charles became professor of English language and literature at Wheaton, then vice president of the college, and finally succeeded his father as president in 1882, a post he held until his death in 1925.

Ordained in 1878, Charles Blanchard served as pastor of several Presbyterian churches, the College Church in Wheaton, and the Illinois Street Church in Chicago, better known as *MOODY CHURCH. Toward the end of his life, Blanchard emerged as a conservative voice in the fundamentalist-modernist controversies, serving as first vice president of the National Fundamentalist Association. He published several books, including one on *ESCHATOLOGY and another attacking secret societies.

Blanchard, Jonathan (1811–1892) Born in Rockingham, Vermont, Jonathan Blanchard studied at Middlebury College, *ANDOVER SEMINARY, and Lane Theological Seminary. In 1834, he became a dedicated abolitionist and an articulate and passionate foe of slavery, at one time taking on Stephen A. Douglas. Blanchard also railed against secret societies, especially the Masonic order. After his graduation from Lane, Blanchard was ordained in 1838 as pastor of the Sixth Presbyterian Church in Cincinnati, known derisively as the "nigger church" because of its *ABOLITIONISM. The church grew significantly during Blanchard's tenure, and in 1843 he was elected to the American vice presidency of the World's Anti-Slavery Convention in London.

Blanchard's greatest achievements were in the area of educational administration. As president of Knox College (Galesburg, Illinois) from 1845 to 1857, he proved to be remarkably gifted in the recruitment both of students and of contributions, even as he continued to be outspoken on social issues. In 1860, Blanchard accepted the invitation of Congregationalists to be the first president of *WHEATON COLLEGE, in Wheaton, Illinois, a position he held until yielding to his son, *CHARLES A. BLANCHARD, in 1882. During his tenure at Knox, the elder Blanchard had founded a religious periodical, *The Christian Era*; at Wheaton he founded and edited the *Christian Cynosure*, a publication sharply critical of secret societies.

Reference: Donald W. Dayton, *Discovering An Evangelical Heritage* (1988).

Blessed Trinity Society Formed in 1960 to support the *CHARISMATIC MOVEMENT in mainline churches, the Blessed Trinity Society was organized by *JEAN STONE WILLANS, who had been active at St. Mark's Episcopal Church in Van Nuys, California, when *DENNIS J. BENNETT, the rector, received his Spirit *BAPTISM. Bennett's ouster demonstrated the importance of a support network for charismatics who wished to remain in mainline denominations. From 1961 until 1966, the Blessed Trinity Society published a quarterly magazine, *Trinity*, which contained news about the movement and also assisted in the placement of charismatic ministers.

Blessing In the simplest and most ancient understanding of this term, something that describes a goodness in one's life is a blessing. The opposite condition or event would be a curse. People who trust in God and follow God's commandments are blessed, and this state of goodness can be requested through prayer for others as well as for oneself. In the Hebrew *BIBLE, the priests were instructed to ask for and to give the priestly blessing to the people. By the time of the New Testament, the act of "blessing" God was associated with giving thanks and praise to the one who grants all blessings. Christians were also encouraged to bless their enemies as a way of transforming their evil intentions and negating their danger. The idea of a blessing in a larger context, such as the blessing of Abraham, generally is interpreted as extending to all Gentiles, and the priest-king Melchizedek becomes the prototype of the consecrated agent who is able to impart the blessing of God upon the people and the material world. Some distinction also exists between spiritual blessings and general blessings. The former refer to charisms, or gifts of the Spirit, and sometimes to a speculation about the nature of heavenly life. In evangelical gatherings, the pastor will often offer a blessing to the congregation in the form of a benediction, and evangelicals themselves often acknowledge the blessings of God in their lives, a reference to their sense that God looks after their well-being, even in adversity.

Blessitt, Arthur (1942–) Ordained at age nineteen, Arthur Blessitt did not finish degrees begun at both Mississippi College or Golden Gate Baptist Seminary, claiming that the needs of the mission field were more pressing. After serving as pastor in a number of different Baptist churches (in Mississippi, Montana, and Nevada), Blessitt claimed that he was "ordered by God to Los Angeles" at the height of the emerging counterculture. Beginning in Hollywood, California, the *EVANGELIST opened the His Place nightclub as a twenty-four-hour spiritual way station in 1968. Later that same year, he gained international attention when a preaching stint at a local strip club was picked up by the media. His Place became the site of regularly scheduled "toilet services," where newly converted junkies disposed of their drugs to symbolize the flushing away of the old life.

Blessitt also organized Jesus marches and the picketing of pornographic bookstores, and he called for week-long periods of fasting to return the nation to its Christian roots. In 1969, when neighboring club owners began to pressure police to get Blessitt out of the area, the coffeehouse came under threat of having its lease terminated. In response, Blessitt chained himself to a twelve-foot cross, proclaiming that he would fast until he was allowed to reopen the coffeehouse.

In 1970, Blessitt announced that he would "blitz the nation for Jesus Christ," that God had told him to carry the twelve-foot cross (by now fitted with a small wheel) through the country on a seven-month, thirty-five-hundred-mile journey from Los Angeles to Washington, D.C. For a brief period Blessitt set up a similar coffeehouse outreach in the heart of New York's Times Square. Always in search of publicity, Blessitt ran for the Democratic presidential nomination in 1976; he won a few votes in the New Hampshire and Florida primaries before bowing out of the race. He traveled extensively during the 1970s, carrying the cross through numerous countries in Europe and Asia, and he has continued traveling with the cross into the 1990s. "By 1987, I had carried a larger cross to many countries," he explained, "and I felt Jesus speak clearly to me during a visit to Germany. He said, 'I want you to give your life to carrying the cross to every nation before the year 2000.'"

Reference: Arthur Blessitt and Walter Wagner, *Turned On to Jesus* (1971).

Blood of Christ In both the Old and New Testaments, blood is associated with sacrifice and death, although at times it is a symbol of life. The evangelical understanding of the blood of Christ is associated with the passion and death of Jesus. Through Jesus' death, the *SINS of the world have been cleansed. Thus, evangelical Christians identify with the blood of Christ, believing that they have been "washed in the blood of Christ," a theme that recurs in evangelical hymnody. This sacrifice of God's son, also known as the *ATONEMENT, was the central event in the cleansing of *SINS, and the phrase generally extends to the entire salvific action of Christ's life, death, and resurrection.

Bluffton College and Bluffton Theological Seminary (Bluffton, Ohio) Founded in 1899 under the name Central Mennonite College, Bluffton College was established to keep Mennonite youth "within the fold" by training leaders and combating "*MODERNISM." The college provided general academic and vocational education to youth from the Middle District of the General Conference of the Mennonite Church. Bluffton also indoctrinated them in European Mennonite culture and the *BIBLE. Nevertheless, the college has been both coeducational and interracial from its beginnings.

Like many church-related colleges, Bluffton began as an academy and then developed into a junior college. The school reorganized in 1914, at which time it adopted its present name. The first bachelor's degrees were granted in 1915. Bluffton Theological Seminary was added in 1921, but for the first ten years the seminary was considered an independent institution—Witmarsum Theological Seminary. In 1931, it was incorporated as part of the college. Bluffton College and Theological Seminary have excellent archives on Mennonites in the Mennonite Historical Library.

Reference: William C. Ringenberg, *The Christian College: A History of Protestant Higher Education in America* (1984).

Boardman, George Dana (1801–1831) A Baptist missionary to Burma, George Dana Boardman was born in Livermore, Maine, and graduated from Maine Literary and Theological Institute (now Colby College), where he also taught briefly. Responding to a call to missionary service, he enrolled at *ANDOVER THEOLOGICAL

SEMINARY and was ordained by the Waterville (Maine) Baptist Church on February 16, 1825. He and his wife, Sarah Hall, sailed to India that same year under the auspices of the Baptist Missionary Board. After two years in Calcutta, they moved to Moulmein, Burma, to establish a mission station; the next year, they founded another station at Tavoy, where Boardman enjoyed considerable success in his evangelistic work among the Karen people. Following Boardman's untimely death in 1831, his widow remained on the mission field and married *ADONIRAM JUDSON, founder of the Burmese missions, three years later.

Boardman, W(illiam) E(dwin) (1810–1886) W. E. Boardman was born in Smithfield, New York, and had an experience of *SANCTIFICATION while working in Potosi, Wisconsin, a small mining town. He studied at Lane Theological Seminary for three years, beginning in 1843, and started a church in Greenfield, Indiana. Boardman became a missionary with the *AMERICAN SUNDAY SCHOOL UNION, spending time in New Haven, Connecticut, and Detroit, before settling in Gloucester City, New Jersey. His wife, Mary, wrote the first draft of *The Higher Christian Life,* which W. E. Boardman revised and published under his name in 1858. The book sold briskly in North America and in Britain, and its popularization of *KESWICK "higher life" piety became enormously influential among evangelicals.

Boardman went to California briefly, but his abolitionist sentiments led him back to New England, where he became secretary of the *UNITED STATES CHRISTIAN COMMISSION, a mission to soldiers during the Civil War, and came into contact with the divine healing principles articulated by *CHARLES CULLIS. After the war, the Boardmans traveled in Europe and Britain, where W. E. Boardman organized the International Conference on Divine Healing and True Holiness in 1884.

References: W. E. Boardman, *The Higher Christian Life* (1858); idem, *He that Overcometh; or, a Conquering Gospel* (1869); idem, *The Lord that Healeth Thee* (1880); Donald W. Dayton, *Theological Roots of Pentecostalism* (1987); David Bundy, "Keswick and the Experience of Evangelical Piety," in Edith L. Blumhofer and Randall Balmer, eds., *Modern Christian Revivals* (1993).

Bob Jones University (Greenville, South Carolina) *BOB JONES SR., a well-known *EVANGELIST and the son of an Alabama sharecropper, founded the university that bears his name in St. Andrews Bay, Florida, in 1926. The college relocated to Cleveland, Tennessee, in 1933, following the stock market crash of 1929, which forced the school to liquidate its assets. Fourteen years later, in 1947, it moved to its current campus in Greenville, South Carolina.

A fundamentalist, biblical worldview infuses every aspect of daily life at Bob Jones University, including strict codes governing personal appearance and comportment. Over the water fountains hang signs quoting Isaiah 12:3 (KJV): "Therefore with joy shall ye drink water out of the wells of salvation." In fact, the school has the reputation for being one of the most fundamentalist colleges in America; the school code of conduct forbids students from wearing beards or listening to music recorded after 1960. Bob Jones University has chosen to foreswear regional accreditation since the beginning, out of a desire to remain autonomous with regard to governance, curriculum, and student life. In spite of—or perhaps because of—its reputation, Bob Jones University has grown to approximately five thousand students a year, and U.S. Senator Strom Thurmond has served on the board of trustees.

Throughout most of its history, the college was run by the Jones family. The senior *BOB JONES was succeeded by his son, and later by his grandson, who collectively gave the school a reputation for having an authoritarian government. In the 1950s, when faculty complained about low salaries, *BOB JONES senior and junior changed the by-laws to prohibit all criticism of the college by employees, establishing such criticism as grounds for dismissal. Some faculty resigned in protest, and the senior Jones responded by preaching a sermon on Judas. One departing administrator noted that Jones made it clear that "Judas was a much finer fellow, for he did have the grace to hang himself."

The school's "Champions for Christ" karate team is known in Greenville, but its art museum enjoys a much wider reputation. Bob Jones University holds one of the most extensive collections of religious art in the world. Although students at Bob Jones University must adhere to limitations on the movies that are deemed acceptable, the school nonetheless has one of the best film departments in the country, housing its own production company, Unusual Films. Since its founding in 1950, Unusual Films has completed several feature-length productions, including *Wine of Morning,* which was selected to represent the United States at the International Congress of Schools of Cinema at the Cannes Film Festival.

One of the distinctive characteristics of Bob Jones University is the parietal rules. Men must wear ties and women skirts. Attendance at chapel is mandatory, and all dates are chaperoned. In the spring of 2000, during the course of the Republican presidential primaries, Bob Jones University became a political issue, with the media focusing on the visit of George W. Bush and his failure to denounce the school's well-publicized ban on interracial dating and its strident anti-Catholic rhetoric. In a March 3 appearance on *Larry King Live,* *BOB JONES 3D announced that the university would rescind the ban on interracial dating.

References: *The Glory and the Power,* PBS documentary (1992); William C. Ringenberg, *The Christian College: A History of Protestant Higher Education in America* (1984); Gustav Niebuhr, "On the Campus in the Center of the Storm, Life Goes On," *New York Times,* March 5, 2000.

Bob Jones University* v. *the United States *Bob Jones University* v. *the United States* is alternately seen as an effort by conservatives to protect freedom of religion and oppose government interference with property, or as the Reagan administration's attempt to use the tax code to promote segregation. In 1970, the Internal Revenue Service (IRS) instituted a policy denying tax-exempt status to segregated private schools. *BOB JONES UNIVERSITY in Greenville, South Carolina, lost its tax-exempt status a year later under the new IRS regulations. *BOB JONES UNIVERSITY originally refused African Americans admission entirely. Married blacks were not admitted until 1971, and it took four additional years before unmarried African Americans could attend. Even after changing its admission policies, the university retained a strict prohibition on interracial dating, citing biblical injunctions against the mixing of the races.

*BOB JONES UNIVERSITY first sued for restoration of its tax-exempt status in 1971 and initiated a second suit four years later to recover unemployment taxes. The IRS countersued for recovery of $490,000 owed in back taxes. When *RONALD

REAGAN took office in 1981, his Department of Justice, led by William Bradford Reynolds, assistant attorney general for civil rights, joined the university in a suit against the IRS, seeking to overturn the policy. This act precipitated considerable public outcry, for Justice was seen as trying to force the IRS to grant the tax exemption.

In January 1982, the Reagan administration proposed nullifying the IRS regulations by statute, rather than solving the issue through the courts. The measure was strongly supported by Senators Jesse Helms and Strom Thurmond, the latter of whom was a trustee of the university. In conjunction with the administration's new tactic, the Department of Justice attempted to withdraw its suit from the Supreme Court but was unsuccessful. The case was finally decided in May 1983 when the Supreme Court reaffirmed the position of the IRS, with Associate Justice William Rehnquist writing the sole dissenting opinion. The Court's decision established a precedent that the IRS could deny tax-exempt status to an organization whose goals were not in "harmony with the public interest" and "at odds with the common community conscience." This decision has been cited in other suits of discrimination at religious colleges, such as *Gay Rights Coalition* v. *Georgetown University*, in which the federal appeals court ruled that despite the college's religious opposition to homosexuality, it had to provide facilities and services to gay students.

References: Thomas C. Hunt and James C. Carper, eds., *Religious Higher Education in the United States: A Source Book* (1996); Jack Greenberg, *Crusaders in the Courts* (1994); William C. Ringenberg, *The Christian College: A History of Protestant Higher Education in America* (1984); Tinsley E. Yarbrough, *The Reagan Administration and Human Rights* (1985).

Boddy, Alexander (Alfred) (1854–1930) One of the leaders of *PENTECOSTALISM within the Church of England, Alexander Boddy was the son of an Anglican rector and was influenced by the *KESWICK MOVEMENT. While serving as vicar at All Saints Church, Sunderland, Boddy and his wife, Mary, conducted revival services, which included divine healing, beginning in the 1890s. Boddy participated in the *WELSH REVIVAL and the pentecostal outpouring in Oslo; he and his wife both experienced *BAPTISM in the Spirit in September 1907. Boddy traveled widely throughout North America promoting the cause of *PENTECOSTALISM. The acknowledged leader of the pentecostal movement in Britain, Boddy also hosted the Annual Whitunside Pentecostal Conventions at Sunderland from 1908 to 1914.

References: Alexander Boddy, *The Laying On of Hands, a Bible Ordinance* (1895); Edith L. Blumhofer, "Alexander Boddy and the Rise of Pentecostalism in Britain," *Pneuma*, VIII (1996).

Body Life. *See* **Stedman, Ray C.**

Boice, James Montgomery (1938–2000) Born in Pittsburgh, James Montgomery Boice earned degrees from Harvard University, Princeton Theological Seminary, and the University of Basel. He was licensed by the Presbytery of Pittsburgh in 1963, and after working on the staff of **CHRISTIANITY TODAY* he became pastor of the prestigious Tenth Presbyterian Church in Philadelphia in 1968. Boice, a noted biblical expositor and a prolific writer, has contributed to numerous religious periodicals. He was a founder of the Alliance for Confessing Evangelicals and speaker on its radio program, *The Bible Study Hour*.

References: James Montgomery Boice, *Witness and Revelation in the Gospel of John* (1970); idem,

The Sermon on the Mount (1972); idem, *Commentary on the Gospel of John,* 5 vols. (1975–1979); idem, *The Sovereign God* (1978); idem, *Christ's Call to Discipleship* (1986); idem, *The King Has Come* (1992).

Boltz, Ray Christian musician Ray Boltz was born and reared in Muncie, Indiana. A graduate of Ball State University in Indiana with a degree in business and marketing, Boltz began his music ministry in the mid-1980s by performing in evangelistic and Sunday night services, prisons, and youth meetings. His first album, *Watch the Lamb,* was released in 1986. Since then, Boltz has recorded eight more albums, including *Moments for the Heart* (1995), which remained on the Billboard charts for three years. Boltz's album *No Greater Sacrifice* (1996) recounts his experiences as a volunteer with Mission of Mercy, a Christian relief organization in India. Boltz has won two Dove Awards from the *GOSPEL MUSIC ASSOCIATION, and his *The Concert of a Lifetime* (1995) video has "gone gold." When not on tour, he lives with his wife and four children in his hometown of Muncie.

Reference: Information provided by Word Records.

Bonnke, Reinhard (1940–) Born in Königsberg, Germany, Reinhard Bonnke, a pastor's son, attended the Bible College of Wales and was ordained by the German Pentecostal Church in 1964. Three years later he began work as a missionary, and in 1974 he founded Christ for All Nations, an evangelistic organization centered around Bonnke's *REVIVAL campaigns and his mass-mailing strategy for the distribution of evangelistic booklets. Bonnke's weekly television program, *Reinhard Bonnke Ministries,* began airing over the *TRINITY BROADCASTING NETWORK in 1995.

Bonnke, whose evangelistic rallies feature divine healing, invested most of his energies in Africa at the turn of the twenty-first century, earning him the sobriquet "the *BILLY GRAHAM of Africa." His *REVIVAL campaign in Lagos, Nigeria, late in 2000, for example, drew nearly 6 million people, including 1.6 million in a single night.

Reference: Corrie Cutrer, "'Come and receive your miracle,'" *Christianity Today,* February 5, 2001.

Boone, Charles Eugene "Pat" (1934–) One of the more risible characters in twentieth-century pop culture, Pat Boone was born in Jacksonville, Florida, but grew up in Nashville, Tennessee. He recorded his first hit record, "Two Hearts," in 1955, three years before he graduated from Columbia University. Boone starred in the motion picture *Bernadine,* and he was improbably cast as the streetwise preacher in the screen adaptation of *DAVID WILKERSON's *The Cross and the Switchblade.* In part because of his contact with Wilkerson during production of the movie, Boone received the *BAPTISM OF THE HOLY SPIRIT early in 1969, which he recounted in his autobiography the following year, *A New Song.* Boone and his family became active in *JACK HAYFORD's Church on the Way in Van Nuys, California.

Many evangelical parents responded positively to Boone's clean-cut, milk-and-cookies image, especially during the years of the counterculture. Boone remained determinedly out of step with that culture; his trademark throughout the seventies, for example, was white shoes. Late in 1996, however, long after heavy metal music had passed its heyday, Boone released an album of heavy metal music and labored hard immediately thereafter to persuade critics that the effort was indeed a serious one.

References: Pat Boone, *'Twixt Twelve and Twenty* (1958); idem, *A New Song* (1970); idem, *A Miracle a Day Keeps the Devil Away* (1974).

Booth, Catherine (née Mumford) (1829–1890) Born in Derbyshire, England, Catherine Mumford moved with her family to London in 1844, where she became a lay worker in a Wesleyan society. She married *WILLIAM BOOTH in 1855; a decade later, the couple established the Christian Mission, an evangelistic outreach, in London's East End. When the mission changed its name to the *SALVATION ARMY in 1878 and adopted the accouterments and nomenclature of the military, Catherine Booth became known as the "Army Mother." Booth pressed for women's rights, and her sympathy with Quaker theology led her and her husband to deemphasize sacramentalism within the *SALVATION ARMY as divisive and confusing to new converts.

References: Frederick de Lautour Booth-Tucker, *The Life of Catherine Booth*, 2 vols. (1892); Roy Hattersly, *Blood and Fire: William and Catherine Booth and Their Salvation Army* (1999).

Booth, Evangeline Cory (1865–1950) The seventh child of eight children born to *WILLIAM and *CATHERINE BOOTH, founders of the *SALVATION ARMY, Evangeline Cory Booth directed *SALVATION ARMY operations in Canada from 1896 to 1904 and in the United States from 1904 until 1934. A gifted administrator, "Commander" Booth became the fourth "General" of the *SALVATION ARMY in 1934, a post she held until retirement in 1939.

Reference: Edward H. McKinley, *Marching to Glory: The History of the Salvation Army in the United States, 1880–1980* (1980).

Booth, William (1829–1912) Born in Nottingham, England, William Booth worked as a pawnbroker's apprentice in Nottingham and later in London. He was converted at the age of fifteen and became a Methodist minister in 1852; three years later, he married *CATHERINE MUMFORD, who would become his partner in evangelistic and social amelioration enterprises. Booth became an independent *EVANGELIST in 1861, and in 1865, the Booths opened the Christian Mission in London's East End.

Booth changed the organization's name to the *SALVATION ARMY in 1878 and adopted military trappings and a military organization, with "General" Booth in command. Booth taught the holiness doctrine of *SANCTIFICATION, and he recognized early on the importance of social relief in order to reach the indigent of the cities. "Obedience is only another word for the active side of religion, and a very important side it is," Booth wrote, "and unless it is well understood, and, better still, well practiced, all other sides of religion will disappear." Under Booth's energetic leadership, the *SALVATION ARMY spread rapidly throughout Great Britain and to Europe, Australia, and North America.

References: William Booth, *In Darkest England and the Way Out* (1890); George Scott Railton, *The Authoritative Life of General William Booth, Founder of the Salvation Army* (1912); Roy Hattersly, *Blood and Fire: William and Catherine Booth and Their Salvation Army* (1999).

Born Again Taken from the third chapter of St. John, where Jesus tells Nicodemus that in order to enter the kingdom of heaven he must be "born again," the term has come to be synonymous with evangelical *CONVERSION. An evangelical will often talk about her *CONVERSION—which is often a dramatic turning away from *SIN—as a born-again experience or describe himself as a "born-again Christian." The latter designation is generally meant to distinguish the evangelical believer from a "liberal" or "nominal" Christian who claims the designation falsely, many evangelicals believe, because the nominal Christian cannot point to a datable experience of *GRACE when she or he was born again.

Boston Bible School (Boston, Massachusetts) Boston Bible School was founded in 1897 by several prominent Advent Christians, who saw a need for denominational schools to educate ministers and skilled laypeople. Classes began the following year with twelve students. When Boston Bible School opened, its founders faced the objections of other Advent Christians, who believed that the call from God was the only necessary qualification to preach and were therefore suspicious of "minister factories." Ironically, most of the school's students were men in training for the ministry. In this respect, Boston Bible School can be seen as an exception to the general tendency of *BIBLE INSTITUTES to enroll mostly women and laypeople. Women were allowed, however, to take pastoral courses along with men, in preparation for ordination.

Like many *BIBLE INSTITUTES, Boston Bible School encouraged students to apply regardless of ability to pay or previous academic preparation. Perhaps as a result, the school's financial stability was very marginal in the early years; sometimes the ability to pay faculty and employees was only certain on a week-to-week basis. Furthermore, through the 1930s the school rarely enrolled more than twenty students.

In 1958, Boston Bible School, now renamed New England School of Theology, moved from Boston to Lenox, in western Massachusetts. In later years, it was known as Berkshire Christian College. The school closed in the 1980s.

Reference: Virginia Lieson Brereton, *Training God's Army: The American Bible School, 1880–1940* (1990).

Boston Missionary Training Institute. *See* **Gordon College.**

Bosworth, F(red) F(rancis) (1876–1958) Influenced by *JOHN ALEXANDER DOWIE's church in Chicago, F. F. Bosworth also joined Dowie's utopian city of healing in *ZION CITY, Illinois. After his *BAPTISM OF THE HOLY SPIRIT, however, Bosworth left Zion and by 1910 formed a church in Denver, Colorado. In 1912, Bosworth sponsored an extraordinarily successful six-month-long *REVIVAL crusade led by *MARIA B. WOODWORTH-ETTER, which provided her a great deal of notoriety in pentecostal circles. Bosworth became a successful itinerant *EVANGELIST himself; he also became one of the pioneers in radio *EVANGELISM and founded the National Radio Revival Missionary Crusaders, based in Chicago.

An early leader of the *ASSEMBLIES OF GOD, Bosworth nevertheless led a small splinter group affirming that *SPEAKING IN TONGUES was merely one of the evidences of *BAPTISM OF THE HOLY SPIRIT. He joined with the *CHRISTIAN AND MISSIONARY ALLIANCE and later signed on with *WILLIAM MARRION BRANHAM's evangelistic team as a kind of senior mentor to young *EVANGELISTS. He devoted the last years of his life to mission work in Africa.

Bowers, Sam (Holloway) (Jr.) (1924–) Born in New Orleans, Louisiana, Sam Bowers became Imperial Wizard of the

White Knights of the *KU KLUX KLAN in Mississippi, the man responsible for inciting violence against blacks and against civil rights workers in the 1960s. A member of the Hillcrest Baptist Church in Laurel, Mississippi, Bowers had two religious experiences that shaped him profoundly. The first occurred in the navy, just after V-J Day in August 1945, when he climbed to the ship's deck and thanked God for sparing his life and dedicated himself to "seek to understand the purpose of your mercy, and to live accordingly." After an honorable discharge from the military, Bowers studied engineering at Tulane and the University of Southern California but returned to Laurel, Mississippi, and opened a vending-machine business called the Sambo Amusement Company. Bowers began immersing himself in Nazi and racist literature.

His second epiphany occurred on a two-lane highway in southern Mississippi. Bowers had been depressed by his sense of failure and was contemplating suicide. He had an experience of "unmerited *GRACE," however, which convinced him that God had appointed him to a special task. Study of the King James Version of the *BIBLE further convinced Bowers that his mission lay in preserving the purity of his race.

As Imperial Wizard, Bowers combined racist, anti-Semitic, and anticommunist ideologies with a skewed interpretation of Scripture that led him to rail against "the prophets of Baal," who were destroying the Southern way of life. The tactic for resisting this incursion from the North was not so much public demonstration as harassment. "The purpose of harassment," Bowers recalled later, "is to stir up and fret the enemy, then step back and wait for him to make a mistake, meanwhile preparing calmly and soberly to exploit any mistake that he does to the maximum advantage to ourselves." Harassment took many forms, from the burning of crosses on courthouse lawns to stink bombs, from sugar and molasses in fuel tanks to "the proper use of the Telephone," presumably as a tool of intimidation. Under Bowers's leadership the Mississippi Klan, formally organized on February 15, 1964, engaged in a campaign of harassment, terror, intimidations, and beatings. Bowers was especially exercised by the prospect of civil rights activists from the North coming to desegregate the South. In preparation, Bowers addressed his followers. "We must always remember that while law enforcement officers have a job to do, we, as Christians, have a responsibility and have taken an oath to preserve Christian civilization," he admonished. "May Almighty God grant that their job and our oath never come into conflict; but should they ever, it must be clearly understood that we can never yield our principles to anyone, regardless of our position."

Bowers, according to government authorities, masterminded the killings of three civil rights activists—James Chaney, Andrew Goodman, and Michael Schwerner—in Neshoba County on June 21, 1964; their bodies were later found buried in an earthen dam on the property of a Klansman. Bowers boasted that a "jury would not dare convict a white man for killing a nigger in Mississippi." Indeed, Bowers stood trial several times for the Neshoba murders and four times for the killing of another man, Vernon Dahmer; he escaped conviction each time. On October 20, 1967, however, he was convicted on federal charges for conspiracy to violate the civil rights of Chaney, Goodman, and Schwerner. Bowers spent six years in prison and in 1976 returned to Laurel and to his work as a "Mississippi native pinball operator and preacher of Jesus the Galilean."

Reference: Charles Marsh, *God's Long Summer: Stories of Faith and Civil Rights* (1997).

Bowery Mission Modeled on *JEREMIAH MCAULEY'S *WATER STREET MISSION, the Bowery Mission was founded in 1879. As the New York City neighborhood degenerated amid the steady urbanization of the late nineteenth century, the mission's task of social reclamation became more and more crucial. The magazine **CHRISTIAN HERALD* took over the operations of the mission in 1895, and it remains an important evangelical beacon more than a century later.

Reference: Norris Magnuson, *Salvation in the Slums: Evangelical Social Work, 1865–1920* (1977).

Bowman, Robert H. (1915–) While a student at *SOUTHERN CALIFORNIA BIBLE COLLEGE, Robert H. Bowman sang baritone in the famous Haven of Rest quartet, which performed for ever-larger radio audiences in southern California. In the 1940s, Bowman joined with *JOHN BROGER and William J. Roberts to form the *FAR EAST BROADCASTING COMPANY, a mission agency that would carry evangelistic programming over the radio airwaves. Christian Radio City Manila, their flagship station, opened in 1947, and the addition of more than thirty transmitters expanded the range considerably. After several years managing *FAR EAST BROADCASTING COMPANY, Bowman accepted a position with the Pentagon in 1954.

Reference: Eleanor Bowman, *Eyes Beyond the Horizon* (1991).

Boyd, Myron (1909–1978) Following his graduation from *SEATTLE PACIFIC COLLEGE in 1932, Myron Boyd was ordained and served several churches in Washington state before assuming the pulpit of First Free Methodist Church in Seattle in 1939. There he became the preacher for a regional radio program, *Gospel Clinic,* and then became host of *Light and Life Hour,* broadcast from Winona Lake, Indiana. A charter member of the *NATIONAL RELIGIOUS BROADCASTERS, Boyd resigned his church in 1947 to devote his full energies to radio. In 1976, he left *Light and Life Hour* to become a bishop in the *FREE METHODIST CHURCH.

Brainerd, David (1718–1747) A Presbyterian missionary to the Delawares, David Brainerd was born in Haddam, Connecticut, and became converted in 1739, during the *GREAT AWAKENING. He entered Yale College to prepare for the ministry but was expelled in 1742 after he chastised school authorities for their lack of piety, remarking that one tutor had "no more grace" than a chair. Undeterred, Brainerd secured a commission from the Society in Scotland for Propagating Christian Knowledge to become a missionary among the Mohican Indians along the Hudson River.

Brainerd remained there less than a year. He was ordained by the presbytery of New York in 1744 and then relocated to Pennsylvania to work among the Delawares. Chronically impatient and afflicted with bouts of depression and physical illness, he moved on to central New Jersey the following year, where he enjoyed modest success. Brainerd continued his *ITINERANCY but died of tuberculosis in 1747 at the home of his fiancée, Jerusha Edwards, the daughter of *JONATHAN EDWARDS.

Although Brainerd's accomplishments as a missionary were less than overwhelming—he seldom stayed in one place long enough to learn the language or to understand native customs—he nevertheless cast a long shadow over evangelical missions in America. The posthumous publication of Brainerd's journal by *JONATHAN EDWARDS, his prospective father-in-law, inspired countless missionaries, especially in the nineteenth century.

References: Jonathan Edwards, "The Life of David Brainerd," in Norman Pettit, ed., *The Works of Jonathan Edwards*, vol. 7 (1984).

Brainerd, John (1720–1781) John Brainerd, born in Haddam, Connecticut, was commissioned as a missionary to the Indians in 1748 by the Society in Scotland for Propagating Christian Knowledge. He took over the work that his older brother, *DAVID BRAINERD, had begun in central New Jersey and stayed with it for nearly three decades. John Brainerd taught his charges the virtues of farming and the dangers of alcohol. In 1758, he followed the Delawares to their reservation at Brotherton, where they languished. Eventually Brainerd expanded his missionary work to whites, organizing seven congregations in the vicinity of the Brotherton mission.

Branham, William Marrion (1909–1965) A mystic from an early age, William Marrion Branham was born in a log cabin in eastern Kentucky, but his family soon relocated to Jeffersonville, Indiana. He headed to Phoenix at age nineteen, where he worked on a ranch and became a professional boxer, but he returned to Indiana following the death of his brother. Branham aspired "to seek and find God"; within months, he resolved to become a preacher. Ordained as an independent Baptist, he began preaching and enjoyed such extraordinary success in Jeffersonville that he established a church there, known as Branham Tabernacle.

Branham considered and then for a time rejected the controversial "Jesus only" pentecostal doctrine that *BAPTISM was in the name of Jesus alone, not the entire Trinity. His stories about growing up in poverty resonated with many listeners during the Great Depression. He told of losing his wife and child to the flooded Ohio River in 1937, an event he would later ascribe to his rejection of the "Jesus only" doctrine.

Because his congregation was so poor, Branham had to support himself with other work, including that of a game warden for the state of Indiana. While working that job on May 7, 1946, Branham had a vision about his future as a healing *EVANGELIST. In the vision a large figure approached and said: "Fear not. I am sent from the presence of Almighty God to tell you that your peculiar life and your misunderstood ways have been to indicate that God has sent you to take a gift of divine healing to the people of the world. IF YOU WILL BE SINCERE, AND CAN GET THE PEOPLE TO BELIEVE YOU, NOTHING SHALL STAND BEFORE YOUR PRAYER, NOT EVEN CANCER." Branham began his healing ministry almost immediately, healing a woman in St. Louis and then continuing on to Jonesboro, Arkansas, and Shreveport, Louisiana. Reports of miraculous healings followed him everywhere (including attestations that he had revived the dead), and he enjoyed the support of such pentecostal *EVANGELISTS as *F. F. BOSWORTH and *ORAL ROBERTS. The postwar healing *REVIVAL was in full swing.

As the crowds grew larger, Branham expanded the orbit of his travels across the country. Exhaustion prompted him to announce his retirement in May 1948, but he was back on the road five months later. In that time other healing evangelists had emerged, most of them working under the doctrinal umbrella of the *Voice of Healing* magazine, edited by *GORDON LINDSAY. In January 1950, Branham held a campaign in Houston, where a lens flare on a photographer's camera produced an image of Branham with what was interpreted by his followers as a supernatural aura. He took the healing *REVIVAL to Scandinavia later that same year and returned to Europe in 1955.

A man of intense piety and deep humility, Branham inspired other young preachers in the healing *REVIVAL. Although he remained in demand, the size of his crowds waned in the 1950s, and in 1956 the Internal Revenue Service charged him with tax evasion for what may have been an inadvertent mistake. So revered was he by some pentecostals that after his death in 1965 many followers believed that he would rise from the dead.

References: Gordon Lindsay, *William Branham: A Man Sent from God* (1950); David Edwin Harrell Jr., *All Things Are Possible: The Healing and Charismatic Revivals in Modern America* (1975); C. Douglas Weaver, *The Healer-Prophet, William Marrion Branham: A Study of the Prophetic in American Pentecostalism* (1987).

Bredesen, Harald (1918–) An ordained Lutheran and one of the leaders of the *CHARISMATIC MOVEMENT, Harald Bredesen received his Spirit *BAPTISM at a pentecostal summer camp in 1946, whereupon he tendered his resignation to Lutheran church authorities. When the resignation was refused, Bredesen took this as a sign that he should remain within the mainline fold and advocate pentecostal renewal. He became pastor of the Mount Vernon Dutch Reformed Church in 1957, where he initiated charismatic prayer meetings. Among those affected were *PAT BOONE and *PAT ROBERTSON, who served as Bredesen's student assistant from 1958 to 1959. Bredesen cooperated with *JEAN STONE in the formation of the *BLESSED TRINITY SOCIETY in 1960 and was at least partially responsible for coining the term "*CHARISMATIC RENEWAL" in 1963 to describe the movement of pentecostal impulses within mainline churches. Bredesen left the Mount Vernon church in 1970 and served as pastor of Trinity Christian Center in Victoria, British Columbia, from 1971 until his retirement in 1980.

Breese, David W. "Dave" (1926–) An alumnus of *JUDSON COLLEGE (Elgin, Illinois) and Northern Baptist Theological Seminary, Dave Breese worked as an *EVANGELIST for *YOUTH FOR CHRIST in the 1950s and founded his own organization, *CHRISTIAN DESTINY MINISTRIES, in 1963. A popular conference speaker, Breese expanded into the media beginning in 1978 with *Dave Breese Reports*, a thirty-minute radio broadcast that eventually became a television program. In 1987, Breese added another program, *The King Is Coming*, which provided a showcase for his premillennialist teachings.

References: Dave Breese, *The Five Horsemen* (1975); idem, *The Exciting Plan of God for Your Life* (1978); J. Gordon Melton, Phillip Charles Lucas, and Jon R. Stone, *Prime-Time Religion: An Encyclopedia of Religious Broadcasting* (1997).

Bresee, Phineas (Franklin) (1838–1916) Born in Franklin County, in the "burned-over district" of western New York, Phineas Bresee was converted at a Methodist meeting in 1856 and moved to Iowa as a Methodist itinerant preacher. He served a succession of circuits and congregations, beginning with his appointment to Holland, Iowa, in 1858. During *REVIVAL meetings in 1866, Bresee had an experience of *SANCTIFICATION that would shape his spirituality for the remainder of his life. Financial embarrassment prompted Bresee to leave Iowa for California (he held a financial interest and had sold stock in a mine that was flooded in 1883). In Los Angeles, Bresee became pastor of the First Methodist Church and once again, in the Methodist tradition, served a succession of congregations in addition to a brief stint as presiding elder of the Los Angeles district.

Bresee found that his advocacy of holiness and *SANCTIFICATION placed him in conflict with the Methodist hierarchy. In 1894, he asked for assignment to the Peniel Mission, an interdenominational holiness center in Los Angeles. When the conference refused, Bresee withdrew from the Methodist discipline and moved to Peniel Mission. The arrangement turned out not to be a good one, and in October 1895, Bresee, together with J. P. Widney, formed the *CHURCH OF THE NAZARENE a few blocks from the Mission. The church grew rapidly, built a tabernacle the next year, formed a satellite congregation in Berkeley in 1897, and launched a periodical, *The Nazarene* (later changed to *The Nazarene Messenger*). The fledgling denomination merged with the Association of Pentecostal Churches in 1907 and then with the Holiness Church of Christ a year later to form the Pentecostal *CHURCH OF THE NAZARENE denomination, which would drop the term "Pentecostal" in 1919. Bresee served as general superintendent of the new denomination until his death in 1916.

References: Phineas Franklin Bresee, *The Certainties of Faith* (1958); Carl Bangs, *Phineas F. Bresee: His Life in Methodism, the Holiness Movement, and the Church of the Nazarene* (1996); Timothy L. Smith, *Called Unto Holiness* (1962).

Bresee College. *See* **Southern Nazarene University.**

Brethren in Christ Church The Brethren in Christ is one of the bodies to come out of the informally organized River Brethren. The Brethren in Christ formed in 1863, in part to gain legal recognition for its members who refused to participate in the Civil War. The name was adopted then, but the Church did not incorporate until 1903.

The Brethren in Christ Church believes in the inspiration of the *BIBLE; the Trinity; the deity and virgin birth of Jesus Christ; Christ's death as *ATONEMENT for human *SIN; his resurrection from the dead; the imminent return of Christ; and the resurrection of the dead, with punishment for the unbeliever and reward for the believer. The Church practices a triune *BAPTISM by immersion, teaches *TEMPERANCE and modesty of apparel and life, and opposes war. The Brethren in Christ has a congregational *POLITY, but six regional conferences and a General Conference carry out Church programs. The Church supports two colleges: *MESSIAH COLLEGE in Grantham, Pennsylvania, and Niagara Christian College in Fort Erie, Ontario. The Brethren in Christ Church claims more than nineteen thousand members in the United States and Canada.

References: Frank S. Mead and Samuel S. Hill, *Handbook of Denominations in the United States,* 10th ed. (1996); J. Gordon Melton, *The Encyclopedia of American Religions,* 3d ed. (1993).

Brethren Church (Ashland, Ohio) The Brethren Church (Ashland, Ohio) was formed in 1882 from a split in the Church of the Brethren. The crisis centered on the issues of a lack of educational opportunities, an unlearned clergy, and plain dress. The dissenting party, under the leadership of Henry R. Holsinger, finally left the Church of the Brethren to form what was called the Progressive Dunkers, a reference to the *BAPTISM performed by the church.

The Progressive body is much like the Church of the Brethren in most aspects of its theology. The Brethren Church does not have a statement of faith, claiming that the New Testament is its creed. The Church practices a threefold *BAPTISM by immersion, and communion services include footwashing.

The Church has a congregational *POLITY, and an annual conference conducts the business of the body. Headquarters are in Ashland, Ohio, which is also the home of the Church's theological seminary and university. There are approximately fifteen thousand members in 125 churches. The Brethren Church is a member of the *NATIONAL ASSOCIATION OF EVANGELICALS.

References: Frank S. Mead and Samuel S. Hill, *Handbook of Denominations in the United States,* 10th ed. (1996); J. Gordon Melton, *The Encyclopedia of American Religions,* 3d ed. (1993).

Bride When Bride, a Kentucky-based, Christian heavy-metal band, rose to fame in the early 1990s, it precipitated a change in Christian contemporary music, which to that point had welcomed few metal bands into the fold. Bride was formed in 1983 by two brothers, Dale and Troy Thompson, and was originally known as Matrix. The band changed its name in 1986 to distinguish itself from a secular group of the same name.

Bride's first album was released in 1986 on Pure Metal, a subsidiary of Refuge Records. Not until 1990, however, did the band have a hit single, with "Everybody Knows My Name." Since then the group has racked up more than a dozen number-one songs on the Christian contemporary charts, with singles like "Rattlesnakes," "The Worm," "Beast," and "Psychedelic Super Jesus." By 1997, Bride had released a total of nine recordings, first on Pure Metal, then on Star Song, which acquired the smaller label in 1990, and most recently on an independent label called Rugged Records. Their latest album is *The Jesus Experience.* Over time, however, the band's musical style has changed somewhat, from heavy-metal, "thrash" music, to more mainstream rock. This transition may account for their increasing commercial appeal as well as new accolades from evangelical critics. In the 1990s, Bride won four Dove Awards from the *GOSPEL MUSIC ASSOCIATION, including the commendation for Metal Album of the Year in 1995, for *Scarecrow Messiah.*

Reference: Information provided by Bride's official Web site.

Bright, William Rohl "Bill" (1921–) Born into a Methodist household in Coweta, Oklahoma, Bill Bright moved to southern California after graduating from Oklahoma's Northeastern State College. He founded Bright's California Confections, a specialty foods company, which became a commercial and financial success. His association with Hollywood Presbyterian Church, however, and especially with the church's Christian education director, *HENRIETTA MEARS, altered the direction of his life. In 1945, Bright had a *CONVERSION experience that led him to remove the alcohol content from the brandied items in his product line. He matriculated at Princeton Theological Seminary in 1946 but transferred to *FULLER SEMINARY in Pasadena the following year in order to be closer to his business interests. He left Fuller in 1951 without graduating and soon thereafter sold his business and rented a house near the campus of the

University of California, Los Angeles, in order to devote his energies to student *EVANGELISM. That same year he founded *CAMPUS CRUSADE FOR CHRIST, with an independent board of directors. Bright was unabashedly autocratic in control of the organization. He warned staff members that "this is not a democratic organization" and instructed them that any criticism of him or his surrogates would be construed as "evidence of disloyalty to Christ" and "shall be accepted as an act of resignation."

Bright's evangelistic efforts, nevertheless, soon bore fruit. Campus Crusade expanded to other colleges and universities in the West and eventually became an international organization. Bright's focus has always been on *EVANGELISM, and toward that end he has developed a number of evangelistic tools, including the popular "Four Spiritual Laws" booklet used by legions of evangelicals throughout the world. In the early 1970s, Bright and Campus Crusade organized a mass *EVANGELISM campaign, called *KEY '73, which featured yellow bumper stickers with "I Found It!" emblazoned in black letters. These bumper stickers, which were intended to provoke conversation and, hence, an opportunity for *EVANGELISM ("What did you find?"), became commonplace among evangelicals. Bright has traveled widely, led evangelistic efforts in the former Soviet Union, and in 1996 was awarded the prestigious Templeton Prize.

References: Bill Bright, *Have You Heard of the Four Spiritual Laws?* (1965); idem, *Come Help Change the World* (1979); Richard Quebedeaux, *I Found It! The Story of Bill Bright and Campus Crusade* (1977); William Martin, *With God on Our Side: The Rise of the Religious Right in America* (1997).

British Israelism The key ideological component behind the *CHRISTIAN IDENTITY movement, British Israelism is the belief that the British are the "ten lost tribes" of ancient Israel. These views were first articulated by Richard Brothers and then developed by *JOHN WILSON, who drew a distinction between the two tribes of Israel (those who claim to be Jews) and the ten lost tribes of Judah (Britons and northern Europeans, many of whom are unaware of their true identity as Jews). As a consequence of Wilson's *EVANGELISM, British-Israel associations emerged in England in the 1870s, and by 1886 the Anglo-Israel Association counted twenty-seven affiliates.

Although the movement peaked in England in the 1920s (about five thousand adherents), the ideology of British Israelism, which is heavily laced with millenarian thought, caught on among white supremacists in the United States, who used it as a warrant for their racism and anti-Semitism. It was advanced by Henry Ford and by *WESLEY SWIFT, who founded the Church of Jesus Christ Christian in 1946. Other groups associated with Smith and with British-Israelitism include the Posse Commitatus, the violent arm of the movement, begun by William Potter Gale, and the Church of Jesus Christ Christian-Aryan Nations, founded in Idaho by *WILLIAM GIRNT BUTLER in 1979.

References: Michael Barkun, *Religion and the Racist Right: The Origins of the Christian Identity Movement* (1994); David Ostendorf, "Countering Hatred," *Christian Century*, September 8–15, 1999.

Broaddus, Andrew (1770–1848) Born into an Anglican household in Caroline County, Virginia, Andrew Broaddus became a Baptist in 1789 and was ordained to the ministry two years later. A skilled preacher, Broaddus emerged as a leader of Virginia Baptists. He published several books, but his most enduring contribution was to evangelical hymnody, both as a writer and as a compiler. He published three volumes of hymns: *Collection of Sacred Ballads* (1790); *The Dover Selection of Spiritual Songs* (1828); and *The Virginia Selection of Songs, Hymns, and Spiritual Songs* (1836).

Broadus John A(lbert) (1827–1895) Born in Culpepper County, Virginia, John A. Broadus remained in Charlottesville as pastor of the Baptist church and as tutor and chaplain at the University of Virginia, where he had graduated in 1850. In 1857, he became one of the founders of Southern Baptist Theological Seminary; he designed a curriculum for a "theological university," which emphasized a range of electives. When the new seminary convened at Greenville, South Carolina, in 1859, Broadus was one of the charter faculty members. The onset of the Civil War forced the fledgling seminary to suspend its operations, something that Broadus viewed as regrettable, but necessary. "I am not a secessionist—the word angers me now," he wrote, "but I am a Virginian."

After service as a chaplain in the Confederate army, Broadus returned to the classroom to resume teaching and writing. When the seminary moved to Louisville, Kentucky, in 1877, Broadus followed and eventually succeeded James Boyce as president in 1889, thereby becoming the school's second president. His preaching skills were legendary and prompted invitations from the North as well as the South, including appearances at *DWIGHT L. MOODY's Northfield Conferences, the *CHAUTAUQUA INSTITUTION, and the Yale Lectureship on Preaching. His introductory textbook on homiletics, *On the Preparation and Delivery of Sermons*, remains in print and is still used in seminary classrooms.

References: John A. Broadus, *On the Preparation and Delivery of Sermons* (1870); idem, *Harmony of the Gospels* (1893); William Henry Brackney, *The Baptists* (1988).

Broger, John C(hristian) (1913–) Born in Nashville, Tennessee, John C. Broger studied at the Georgia Institute of Technology, *SOUTHERN CALIFORNIA BIBLE COLLEGE, and Texas A&M University. He was one of the founders of the *FAR EAST BROADCASTING COMPANY in 1945, and in 1954 he went to work for the Defense Department as a consultant in troop indoctrination. Two years later, Broger became deputy director of Armed Forces Information and Education (later, Armed Forces Information Service). In 1961, he was promoted to director of the agency, a post he held until 1984.

Broger used his position to advance evangelical and nationalistic sentiments in the military. A dedicated foe of communism, he coined the term "militant liberty" to describe the aggressive vigilance needed to vanquish communist ideology, and he incorporated these ideas into troop information programs. Broger, an energetic Cold Warrior, also became a popular speaker on the evangelical lecture circuit, where his anticommunist rhetoric played well among politically conservative evangelicals.

Reference: Ann C. Loveland, *American Evangelicals and the U.S. Military, 1942–1993* (1996).

Brookes, James Hall (1830–1897) James Hall Brookes, one of the founders of the *NIAGARA BIBLE CONFERENCE, attended Miami University (Ohio) and Princeton Theological Seminary before being ordained as a Presbyterian minister in 1854. He served a church in Dayton,

Ohio, and in 1858 accepted a call to the Second Presbyterian Church in St. Louis. Six years later, he assumed the pulpit at the Sixteenth & Walnut Street Church, where he remained until his retirement.

A prolific author, Brookes was one of the first evangelicals in America to adopt *JOHN NELSON DARBY's dispensationalist ideas. He became an ardent champion of dispensational *PREMILLENNIALISM, promoting this interpretive scheme through his preaching, his lectures at Bible conferences (including Niagara), and a journal entitled *The Truth,* which he edited from 1875 until his death. Brookes roundly assailed the incursion of *LIBERALISM into American Protestantism, he railed against feminism, and he numbered among his disciples *CYRUS INGERSON SCOFIELD, author of the **SCOFIELD REFERENCE BIBLE*.

Brothers, Richard (1757–1824) One of the earliest proponents of *BRITISH ISRAELISM, the belief that the Britons are the "ten lost tribes" of Israel, Richard Brothers was a retired naval officer who began having apocalyptic visions in 1791. One of his visions instructed him to lead the Jews back to Palestine, although he also became convinced that the Jews were intermingled with the European population and that most were unaware of their true identity. Brothers came to believe that he was himself a scion of the House of David, and he took on royal pretensions. He was declared insane and was institutionalized from 1795 to 1806.

Reference: Michael Barkun, *Religion and the Racist Right: The Origins of the Christian Identity Movement* (1994).

Broughton, Leonard G. (1865–1936) Born into poverty in rural North Carolina, Leonard G. Broughton nevertheless graduated from Wake Forest College and earned a medical degree from the Kentucky School of Medicine. He had been converted at age fourteen and had aspired to become a minister, however; after a bout of typhoid fever, Broughton gave up his medical practice for the ministry. After serving Baptist churches in Winston, North Carolina, and Roanoke, Virginia, Broughton went to Third Baptist Church in Atlanta in 1897. The following year, after a disagreement over relocation, he led a faction of about two hundred members to form Tabernacle Baptist Church. Membership grew rapidly (over three thousand members within a decade) as Broughton implemented his ideas for an "institutional church," with a home for "helpless women," an annual Bible conference, and an infirmary that evolved first into a nursing school and eventually into Georgia Baptist Hospital.

Broughton's visits to *DWIGHT L. MOODY's Northfield Bible Conferences in the 1890s had put him in touch with dispensationalist and *KESWICK ideas. He brought them south and used his own Bible conferences to disseminate fundamentalist doctrines. Broughton's conferences became so popular that hundreds, even thousands, were often turned away; audiences reached ten thousand. Broughton, unlike many other dispensationalists, however, insisted on the importance of social amelioration and retained that emphasis throughout his ministry. His success in Atlanta brought invitations to go elsewhere. Broughton refused them all until an invitation arrived from Christ Church in London. He left Atlanta for England in 1912 but returned to the United States and served as pastor of several Baptist churches in the South, including a return to Tabernacle Baptist Church from 1929 to 1931.

Reference: William R. Glass, "The Ministry of Leonard G. Broughton at Tabernacle Baptist Church, 1898–1912: A Source of Southern Fundamentalism," *American Baptist Quarterly,* IV (March 1985).

Brown, Antoinette (Louisa) (1825–1921) The first ordained woman minister in America, Antoinette Brown was converted at the age of nine, following her parents' *CONVERSION during *CHARLES FINNEY's revival in Rochester, New York. She graduated from Oberlin College in 1850 and then became a lecturer on *TEMPERANCE, women's rights, and *ABOLITIONISM. Discerning a call to the ministry, Brown was ordained at the Congregational church in South Butler, New York, on September 15, 1853. She resigned her post a year later, however, amid some theological doubts. She eventually became a Unitarian.

Reference: Nancy A. Hardesty, *Women Called to Witness* (1984).

Brown, Harold O(gden) J(oseph) (1933–) An evangelical theologian, ethicist, and conservative activist, Harold O. J. Brown was born in Tampa, educated at Harvard University, and ordained to the Congregationalist ministry in 1958. Throughout his career, Brown has been affiliated with a number of evangelical agencies, organizations, and educational institutions on both sides of the Atlantic, including Park Street Church in Boston, **CHRISTIANITY TODAY,* the International Fellowship of Evangelical Students, and *TRINITY EVANGELICAL DIVINITY SCHOOL. His scholarly writing, Brown says, derives from "a deep desire to state the case for the historic Christian faith in such a way that it will make sense even to those who do not accept it and will be stronger and fuller for those who do."

In 1975, Brown founded the Christian Action Council, an antiabortion lobbying group with offices in Washington, D.C. His political conservativism has attracted the attention of such conservative stalwarts as William F. Buckley Jr.

References: Harold O. J. Brown, *The Protest of a Troubled Protestant* (1969); idem, *The Reconstruction of the Republic* (1977); idem, *Death before Birth* (1977); idem, *Heresies: The Image of Christ in the Mirror of Heresy and Orthodoxy* (1983).

Brown, Huntley (1963–) Born in Brownstone, Jamaica, Huntley Brown learned to play the piano from his brothers and from his father, who played piano and the accordion. After a brief stint on the nightclub circuit in Jamaica, Brown enrolled at *JUDSON COLLEGE in Elgin, Illinois, where he became a star attraction of the college's music program and also performed regularly for *WILLOW CREEK COMMUNITY CHURCH. He is the resident pianist for WCFC-Television, the religious station in Chicago, and also travels and performs for the *BILLY GRAHAM EVANGELISTIC ASSOCIATION.

Brown, James H. (1912–1987) A pentecostal leader within the Presbyterian Church, James H. Brown was born in Pittsburgh and educated at *GROVE CITY COLLEGE and Princeton Theological Seminary. Early in the 1950s, while pastor of the Upper Octorara Presbyterian Church in Parkesburg, Pennsylvania, Brown came under the influence of a pentecostal Bible study. He was baptized in the Spirit toward the end of the 1950s, whereupon his church became famous for its charismatic Saturday evening prayer and praise services. Brown, because he remained within the Presbyterian Church, became one of the leaders of the *CHARISMATIC RENEWAL MOVEMENT within Presbyterianism.

Brown, John (1800–1859) A fervent and violent abolitionist, John Brown was reared in a Calvinist home in Connecticut. He assisted runaway slaves in the Underground Railroad during the 1820s and 1830s, but he became increasingly impatient for the eradication of slavery. Brown joined antislavery forces in Kansas in 1855, led the Pottawatomie Massacre in 1856, and the following year began plotting a slave uprising in the South that would finally bring an end to the "peculiar institution."

As Brown's plans began to unfold, he clearly had taken on a messianic mantle. During a planning meeting held in Canada in 1858, for instance, Brown outlined a provisional government for the South that would take effect after the uprising; Brown designated himself commander-in-chief of the new government. On October 16, 1859, Brown led a raid on the federal armory at Harper's Ferry, (West) Virginia, that was to trigger the insurrection. Slaves in the area failed to rally, however. Brown was captured the following day and was hanged on December 2, a symbol of Northern conspiracy to Southern slaveholders and a martyr to Northern abolitionists.

Reference: Stephen B. Oates, *To Purge This Land with Blood: A Biography of John Brown* (1970).

Brown, John Wayne "Punkin" (1964–1998) A serpent-handler from rural Newport, Tennessee, Punkin Brown preached a literal interpretation of Mark 16:18, in the King James Version of the *BIBLE: "They shall take up serpents; and if they drink any deadly thing, it shall not hurt them; they shall lay hands on the sick, and they shall recover." Brown had been bitten twenty-two times before a yellow timber rattler delivered a fatal bite in October 1998. Brown's wife, Melinda, had also died from a rattlesnake bite three years earlier.

Reference: Dennis Covington, *Salvation on Sand Mountain: Snake Handling and Redemption in Southern Appalachia* (1995).

Brown, R(obert) R. (1885–1964) R. R. Brown, born in Dagus Mines, Pennsylvania, studied for the ministry at the Missionary Training Institute (now *NYACK COLLEGE). After serving as pastor of *CHRISTIAN AND MISSIONARY ALLIANCE churches in Chicago and in Beaver Falls, Pennsylvania, Brown accepted the pastorate of the Omaha Gospel Tabernacle in Omaha, Nebraska, in 1923. That same year a new radio station in town, WOW, asked Brown to preach on its first Sunday of operation. Initially skeptical of this new medium, Brown warmed to the possibilities when he learned that a listener had been converted after hearing his first radio sermon. "Hallelujah!" Brown exclaimed. "Unction can be transmitted!"

Radio Chapel Service became a weekly fixture until 1977, and Brown, known as the "*BILLY SUNDAY of the air," served as host until his death in 1964. He treated his audience, which numbered nearly half a million, as a kind of extended congregation, a "church of the airwaves." He sent listeners official membership cards in the World Radio Congregation and solicited money for various evangelistic and humanitarian causes.

Brownsville Revival Begun on Father's Day, 1995, the Brownsville Revival, also known as the Pensacola Outpouring, combines the ecstatic worship characteristic of the *AZUSA STREET REVIVAL with highly moralistic teachings on matters of personal behavior. The movement, located at the Brownsville Assembly of God in Pensacola, Florida, preaches against the evils of alcohol, drugs, tobacco, pornography, and homosexuality. Some of those affected by the *REVIVAL claim to have been exorcized of demons. Similar in style and influence to the *TORONTO BLESSING, the Brownsville Revival attracted more than a million visitors within the first two years. The faithful and the curious have, at times, waited in line from four o'clock in the morning for evening services, held four nights a week. Services last until the early morning hours, and at any given time hundreds of worshipers might be moaning and writhing on the floor in a state of spiritual possession.

John Kilpatrick, the congregation's pastor, professed surprise at the Brownsville Revival. "During *REVIVAL, the Holy Spirit draws a lot of people in here who never had anybody love them," Kilpatrick told **CHRISTIANITY TODAY* in 1997, trying to explain the more dramatic manifestations of the *REVIVAL. "When they feel love for the first time, they don't know how to act."

The Brownsville Revival can also lay claim to prophecy. *PAUL YONGGI CHO, pastor of one of the world's largest churches, located in Seoul, South Korea, claimed that in the course of praying for *REVIVAL in America God prompted him to look at a map of the United States. His finger went to Pensacola, which is known as the "gay Riviera" because of its general toleration of homosexuals. "I sensed the Lord say, 'I am going to send *REVIVAL to the seaside city of Pensacola, and it will spread like a fire until all of America has been consumed by it,'" Cho wrote in the foreword to Kilpatrick's book, *Feast of Fire*. The *REVIVAL began in 1995 during a sermon by Steve Hill, a former-drug-user-turned-evangelist whom the Brownsville congregation had supported. Approximately half the congregation (nearly a thousand people) responded to Hill's altar call. Many of them, Kilpatrick included, fell to the floor under the influence of the Holy Spirit.

Kilpatrick and Hill formed a partnership; Kilpatrick preached on Sunday mornings, while Hill conducted the evening gatherings, Wednesday through Saturday nights. With the influx of visitors the Brownsville Assembly of God undertook a large building program, conducted conferences for pastors, and opened the Brownsville Revival School of Ministry in 1997. An investigative report by the *Pensacola News-Journal* that same year, however, revealed that some "converts" had been coached and that Hill, one of the pastors, had significantly exaggerated his preconversion life in order to increase the "impact" of his autobiography, *Stone Cold Heart*. The newspaper also raised the possibility of financial irregularities in regard to an orphanage in Argentina that was putatively supported by proceeds from the *REVIVAL. Church officials denied any wrongdoing.

References: John Kilpatrick, *Feast of Fire* (1995); Steve Rabey, "Pensacola Outpouring Keeps Gushing," *Christianity Today*, March 3, 1997; idem, "Brownsville Revival Rolls Onward," ibid., February 9, 1998; Leo Sandon, "Pentecost in Pensacola," *Christian Century*, August 27–September 3, 1997; Bob Jones IV, with Edward E. Plowman, "The Pensacola Revival: Shaken or Stirred?" *World*, December 20, 1997.

Brownsville Revival School of Ministry. *See* **Brownsvile Revival.**

Bruce, F(rederick) F(yvie) (1910–1991) One of the premier evangelical biblical scholars of the twentieth century, F. F. Bruce earned the M.A. from Cambridge University and another master's degree from the University of Aberdeen. He was Rylands Professor of Biblical Criticism and Exegesis at the University of Manchester in England. He wrote numerous biblical commentaries and other books and served as editor of the New International Commentary for the New Testament.

References: F. F. Bruce, *The History of the Bible in English: From the Earliest Versions to Today* (1978); idem, *The Hard Sayings of Jesus* (1983); idem, *The Canon of Scripture* (1998); Mark A. Noll, *Between Faith and Criticism: Evangelicals, Scholarship, and the Bible in America* (1986).

Bryan, William Jennings (1860–1925) William Jennings Bryan, the "Great Commoner," cut a wide swath through American culture as attorney, orator, editor, congressman, three-time Democratic nominee for president, and secretary of state. The inveterate populist was also a devout Presbyterian layman.

After graduating from college and law school, Bryan settled in Lincoln, Nebraska, in 1887. Three years later, he won election to Congress and soon emerged as leader of the free-silver Democrats. His electrifying "Cross of Gold" speech at the 1896 Democratic National Convention, in which he railed against monopolistic business interests, won him the Democratic nomination for president at the age of thirty-six. Although Bryan also captured the nomination of the Populists and campaigned in twenty-six states, the "Boy Orator of the Prairie" lost the election to William McKinley. Four years later, a rematch yielded the same result.

After capturing the Democratic nomination again in 1908, losing this time to William Howard Taft, Bryan threw his support to Woodrow Wilson in 1912. The new president rewarded the Great Commoner with appointment as secretary of state, but as war approached in Europe Bryan dissented from Wilson's move toward engagement and resigned from the cabinet in June 1915.

The eclipse of Bryan's political career allowed him to devote his energies to such progressive causes as prohibition, peace, and women's suffrage. He is probably best remembered, somewhat unfairly, for his final public act in Dayton, Tennessee, assisting in the prosecution of John T. Scopes for teaching evolution in the public schools, thereby violating the state's newly minted *BUTLER ACT. Bryan had long been suspicious of Darwinism, not so much because it challenged the Genesis account of creation but because, as a true progressive, he feared the effects of social Darwinism. Clarence Darrow, Bryan's adversary in the courtroom, transformed the trial into a showdown between biblical *LITERALISM and scientific progress. In the trial's most dramatic moment, duly recorded by H. L. Mencken and a phalanx of journalists, Bryan took the stand himself, whereupon Darrow succeeded in making Bryan—and, by extension, all fundamentalists—look foolish. Exhausted and humiliated, Bryan died in his sleep five days after the trial.

References: William Jennings Bryan, *The First Battle: A Story of the Campaign of 1896* (1896); idem, *The Prince of Peace* (1909); idem, *The Memoirs of William Jennings Bryan* (1925); Robert W. Cherny, *A Righteous Cause: The Life of William Jennings Bryan*; Lawrence W. Levine, *Defender of the Faith: William Jennings Bryan, The Last Decade, 1915–1925* (1965); Garry Wills, *Under God: Religion and American Politics* (1990); Edward J. Larson, *Summer for the Gods: The Scopes Trial and America's Continuing Debate over Science and Religion* (1997).

Bryan College (Dayton, Tennessee) Chartered in 1930 under Tennessee law as a "general welfare corporation" with the purpose of providing "for the higher education of men and women under auspices distinctly Christian and spiritual," Bryan College was named for *WILLIAM JENNINGS BRYAN, who prosecuted the Scopes "Monkey Trial" in Dayton, Tennessee. During the *SCOPES TRIAL, Bryan had remarked that he wished for the establishment of a religious preparatory school in or near Dayton. Following the orator's death in Dayton on July 26, 1925, the Bryan Memorial University Association was created to establish a college in his honor. It launched a national campaign to raise $5 million—half for endowment and half for buildings—but the onset of the Great Depression precipitated the collapse of the organization, and construction of the new campus was halted. Nevertheless, classes did begin in September 1930 in what previously had been Rhea County High School. The college was known as Bryan University until 1958, when it adopted its present name.

Bryan College is connected to the *SCOPES TRIAL in the present as well as the past. Every summer, students and faculty perform a reenactment of the trial in conjunction with the Dayton Chamber of Commerce, as part of a summer-long festival celebrating that famous contest between the forces of *FUNDAMENTALISM and *MODERNISM.

References: William C. Ringenberg, *The Christian College: A History of Protestant Higher Education in America* (1984); *Mine Eyes Have Seen the Glory*, three-part PBS documentary (1992).

Bryant, Anita (1940–) Anita Bryant made her singing debut at the age of two in a rural Baptist church in Oklahoma. She began singing on a weekly radio program at eight years old, the same year she was baptized. She had her own weekly television show at age twelve, and the next year she cut her first record. At sixteen, she became a favorite on Arthur Godfrey's CBS television show and soon thereafter signed a contract with Carlton Records. Bryant also entered beauty contests, winning Miss Tulsa, Miss Oklahoma, and placing second runner-up in the 1959 Miss America Pageant. In addition to her performances at conventions and state fairs, Bryant also tapped into the lucrative advertising market, doing commercials for Coca-Cola, Holiday Inn, and Kraft. In 1968 she became the "sunshine girl" for the Florida Citrus Commission, touting the virtues of orange juice.

Aside from her unwittingly hilarious cameo in Michael Moore's 1989 documentary *Roger & Me*, Bryant's brush with notoriety occurred in 1977 after the Metropolitan Dade County Commission passed an ordinance that would have required that qualified homosexuals be hired as teachers in parochial and private schools. Bryant responded with a campaign to repeal the measure, crusading under the banner of her newly formed organization, the Save Our Children Federation (later renamed Protect America's Children). Bryant argued that homosexuality was a sin and that if gays and lesbians were allowed to flaunt their "deviate lifestyles," then the American family and the American way of life would disappear. "Homosexuals cannot reproduce—so they must recruit," she warned. "And to freshen their ranks, they must recruit the youth of America." In large measure because of Bryant's efforts, the voters overturned the ordinance in June 1977.

Despite Bryant's jubilation, her campaign raised the ire of many liberals and gay-rights advocates. In 1978, she estimated that her activism had cost her half a million dollars in bookings. Bryant was relieved of her one-hundred-thousand-dollar-a-year contract with the Florida Citrus Commission, although the contract was later reinstated.

References: Anita Bryant, *The Anita Bryant Story* (1977); "Playboy Interview: Anita Bryant," *Playboy*, May 1978.

Buechner, (Carl) Frederick (1926–) Although Frederick Buechner would not rush to claim the label *evangelical*, his writings have become popular among many evangelicals, who admire their literary quality and the author's overwhelming sense of *GRACE. Born in New York City, Buechner graduated from Princeton University in 1948 and published his first novel, *A Long Day's Dying*, to critical acclaim just two years later. One reviewer heralded "a new American novelist of the greatest promise and the greatest talent." While pursuing his vocation as a writer, Buechner started attending the Madison Avenue Presbyterian Church near his apartment in New York. On the occasion of Queen Elizabeth's coronation, the minister was preaching about the coronation of Jesus in the believer's heart, which, he said, should take place amid confession and tears. "And then with his head bobbing up and down so that his glasses glittered," Buechner recounted in *The Alphabet of Grace*, "he said in his odd, sandy voice, the voice of an old nurse, that the coronation of Jesus took place among confession and tears and then, as God was and is my witness, great laughter, he said. Jesus is crowned among confession and tears and great laughter, and at that phrase great laughter, for reasons that I have never satisfactorily understood, the great wall of China crumbled and Atlantis rose up out of the sea, and on Madison Avenue, at 73rd Street, tears leapt from my eyes as though I had been struck across the face." Buechner was twenty-seven years old at the time.

He entered Union Theological Seminary to study for the ministry and graduated in 1958, whereupon he was ordained a minister in the United Presbyterian Church. Buechner's *CONVERSION and ordination, he believes, cost him credibility in literary circles. "I am too religious for the secular reader," he said, "and too secular for the religious reader." He wrote a quartet of novels about Leo Bebb, an evangelist-exhibitionist, and an invitation to give the Noble Lectures at Harvard Divinity School led to *The Alphabet of Grace* and a series of other nonfiction and autobiographical books on faith and belief.

References: Frederick Buechner, *A Long Day's Dying* (1950); idem, *The Return of Ansel Gibbs* (1958); idem, *The Alphabet of Grace* (1970); idem, *Lion Country* (1971); idem, *Open Heart* (1972); idem, *Love Feast* (1974); idem, *Wishful Thinking: A Theological ABC* (1974); idem, *Treasure Hunt* (1977); idem, *Telling the Truth: The Gospel as Tragedy, Comedy, and Fairy Tale* (1977); idem, *Godric* (1980); idem, *The Sacred Journey* (1982); idem, *Telling Secrets* (1991); Marie-Helene Davies, *Laughter in a Genevan Gown: The Works of Frederick Buechner, 1970–1980* (1983); Philip Yancey, "The Reverend of Oz," *Books & Culture*, March/April 1997.

Buffalo Male and Female Institute. *See* **Milligan College.**

Buies Creek Academy. *See* **Campbell University.**

Burkett, Larry (1939–) Larry Burkett was born in Winter Park, Florida, into a family that was, in his words, "somewhere between poor and very poor." After graduating from high school, Burkett joined the air force; he received a medical discharge, attended Orlando Junior College, and worked for a succession of technology companies. Through the influence of his wife, Judy, Burkett was converted to evangelical Christianity in the fall of 1971. He began to study the *BIBLE, paying particular attention to passages that he believed shed light on financial matters, such as tithing and borrowing.

Following a conversation with *BILL BRIGHT, Burkett joined the staff of Bright's organization, *CAMPUS CRUSADE FOR CHRIST, early in 1973. After an uneven start, Burkett developed materials and lectures on Christian financial responsibility out of the organization's Atlanta offices. In 1974, he contacted several publishers about the possibility of producing a book on personal finances but, hearing no interest, he wrote and published five thousand copies of *Your Finances in Changing Times.* The book did well enough for Burkett to resign from *CAMPUS CRUSADE and start his own organization, Christian Financial Concepts, in May 1976. Burkett's reputation as a financial advisor grew steadily within *EVANGELICALISM, in part because of exposure on Christian radio. By the late 1990s, *Your Finances in Changing Times,* republished by Moody Press, had sold approximately 1.3 million copies. By 1998, Christian Financial Concepts had a staff of 135 people and an annual operating budget of over $8.5 million.

Politically, Burkett has aligned himself with the *RELIGIOUS RIGHT. He was one of the founders of the *ALLIANCE DEFENSE FUND in 1994, and he has worked on behalf of Republican candidates. Some of his works, notably *The Coming Economic Earthquake* and *Whatever Happened to the American Dream?*, venture into the realm of public policy, combining apocalyptic themes with the ideas of Ludwig von Mises, an Austrian libertarian economist. Burkett spins out his conspiracy theories even more boldly in popular novels: *The Illuminati* and *The Thor Conspiracy*. In 2000, Burkett merged his Christian Financial Concepts with Crown Ministries, which was headed by Howard Dayton, to form Crown Financial Ministries.

References: Larry Burkett, *Your Finances in Changing Times* (1975); idem, *Hope When It Hurts* (1998); Larry Eskridge, "When Burkett Speaks, Evangelicals Listen," *Christianity Today,* June 12, 2000.

Burr, Aaron (1715–1757) Born in Fairfield, Connecticut, Aaron Burr graduated from Yale College in 1735 and remained in New Haven, Connecticut, for graduate study under the auspices of the Berkeley Foundation. In the course of that year, Burr experienced a spiritual awakening that prompted a shift in his theology. "Before this," he said later, "I was strongly attached to the Arminian scheme, but then was made to see those things in a different light, and seemingly felt the truth of the Calvinian doctrines." Burr decided to enter the ministry, serving churches in Greenfield, Massachusetts, and Hanover, New Jersey, before assuming the pulpit of the First Presbyterian Church in Newark, New Jersey, in December 1736.

Burr was sympathetic toward—though not uncritical of—the *GREAT AWAKENING. As a settled minister himself, he took issue with *GILBERT TENNENT's famous Nottingham, Pennsylvania, sermon, "The Danger of an Unconverted Ministry," fearing ecclesiastical chaos if converts heeded Tennent's call to separate "from their minister under a notion of his being unconverted."

Following the death of *JONATHAN DICKINSON, the College of New Jersey's first president, in 1747, the college students moved from Elizabeth to Newark, where they sat under the tutelage of Burr, an expert in classical languages. Burr was appointed president of the college the following year, holding both positions—pastor in Newark and president of the college—until 1755, when he devoted his full energies to the college. He supervised the move to Princeton in 1756, but his efforts on behalf of the school took a toll on his health. He fell ill in August 1757 and died a month later.

Burwash, Nathanael (1839–1918) Born into a devout Methodist household in Lower Canada, Nathanael Burwash moved with his family to a farm in Upper Canada when he was five. He attended Victoria College in nearby Cobourg, graduating with the B.A. in 1859. After six years in the ministry, Burwash then pursued a lifelong career in education and theology, studying briefly at Yale and earning two degrees from Garrett Biblical Institute in Evanston, Illinois. He became dean of Victoria College in 1863 and set about to upgrade theological training for Methodist ministers. Although his theology was conservative, Burwash nevertheless maintained an open mind on the matter of contemporary biblical scholarship, opening the way for higher criticism, a discipline that sometimes cast doubt on the authenticity of the *BIBLE, to be taught in the theological institutions of the Methodist Church in Canada.

Burwash became president and chancellor of Victoria University in 1887 and in 1906 was elected to the prestigious Royal Society of Canada. In addition to being the foremost theologian of *METHODISM in Canada, Burwash worked tirelessly for the expansion and the availability of education opportunities. When negotiations on church union opened in 1902 among Presbyterians, Congregationalists, and Methodists, Burwash served as president of the subcommittee on doctrine.

References: Nathanael Burwash, *A Handbook of the Epistle of St. Paul to the Romans* (1887); idem, *Inductive Studies in Theology* (1896); idem, *Manual of Christian Theology on the Inductive Method* (1900); Marguerite Van Die, *An Evangelical Mind: Nathanael Burwash and the Methodist Tradition in Canada, 1839–1918* (1989).

Bushyhead, Jesse (1804–1844) Born into the Cherokee Nation, Jesse Bushyhead, although educated by the Presbyterians, became a Baptist and the first ordained Cherokee minister. He founded an indigenous Cherokee church at Amohee, Tennessee, and was appointed as a justice to the Cherokee Supreme Court, later serving as chief justice. He lobbied unsuccessfully against the Cherokee removal and accompanied his people on the Trail of Tears to Indian Territory (Oklahoma) during the winter of 1838–39. Just before his death in Westville, Oklahoma, northern Baptists published erroneous information that Bushyhead had been a slaveowner, and this controversy contributed to the split between northern and southern Baptists in 1844.

References: William G. McLoughlin, *Cherokees and Missionaries, 1789–1839* (1984); Diane Glancy, *Pushing the Bear: A Novel of the Trail of Tears* (1996).

Businessman's Revival. *See* **Prayer Meeting Revival.**

Buswell, J(ames) Oliver, Jr. (1895–1977) A native of Mellon, Wisconsin, J. Oliver Buswell Jr. graduated from the University of Minnesota, the University of Chicago, and New York University, where he eventually earned his Ph.D. in 1949. Buswell had been ordained by the Presbyterian Church, U.S.A. in 1918, but his antimodernist scruples led him to affiliate with a fundamentalist mission board, which prompted his ouster from the Presbyterian ministry in 1936.

Buswell served as president of *WHEATON COLLEGE (Illinois) from 1926 until 1940, during which time the school grew rapidly and gained some measure of academic respectability, all the while remaining true to its fundamentalist constituency. Upon leaving Wheaton, Buswell spent the remainder of his career associated with institutions that were even more conservative and separatist than Wheaton. He taught at *FAITH THEOLOGICAL SEMINARY, the National Bible Institute (which became Shelton College), *COVENANT COLLEGE, and Covenant Theological Seminary.

Reference: Joel A. Carpenter, *Revive Us Again: The Reawakening of American Fundamentalism* (1997).

Butcher, Samuel J. (1939–) Born into a poor family in Jackson, Michigan, Samuel J. Butcher demonstrated artistic ability early in life, often painting scenes from the *BIBLE. He was converted to evangelical Christianity in a country church, and he resolved to use his talent only "for the Lord." Butcher became the staff artist for Child Evangelism Fellowship, an evangelical organization based in Warrenton, Missouri, and in 1974 he created his first "Precious Moments" drawing. This became the basis for an extensive line of commercial products—paintings, drawings, figurines—all featuring his sentimental, stylized rendition of children. In 1989, Butcher opened his Precious Moments Chapel in Carthage, Missouri, which has become one of the most popular tourist attractions in the Ozarks. "It is my prayer," Butcher said, "that through my work in the Chapel, I might share my faith with others and that the Spirit of God might touch the visitors' hearts and bring them to the saving knowledge of Jesus Christ, our Lord."

Butler, Brett (Morgan) (1957–) One of the premier outfielders in Major League Baseball during the 1980s and 1990s, Brett Butler, born in Los Angeles, was selected in the twenty-third round by the Atlanta Braves in June 1979. Traded to the Cleveland Indians in 1983, he signed with the San Francisco Giants as a free agent in 1987 and with the Los Angeles Dodgers three years later. Butler went to the New York Mets as a free agent in 1995 but was traded later that year to the Dodgers, where he finished his career. In May 1996, Butler entered a hospital in Atlanta for a tonsillectomy but was diagnosed with a cancerous tumor in one of his tonsils. The tumor and lymph nodes were removed, followed by six weeks of radiation therapy. Butler rejoined the team August 26 and played for the remainder of the season as well as the 1997 season, after which he retired.

Throughout his career and especially during his medical ordeal, Butler spoke openly about his evangelical faith. He had been converted at a *FELLOWSHIP OF CHRISTIAN ATHLETES gathering in 1973, and he was active in baseball chapels and in speaking to evangelical groups.

Reference: Brett Butler, with Jerry Jenkins, *Field of Hope: An Inspiring Autobiography of a Lifetime of Overcoming Odds* (1997).

Butler, Richard Girnt (1917–) One of the leaders of the *CHRISTIAN IDENTITY movement, Richard Girnt Butler was a disciple of *WESLEY SWIFT and tried, briefly, to take over Swift's Lancaster, California, congregation following Swift's death in 1970. In 1973, Butler moved to Coeur d'Alene, Idaho, where in 1979 he founded the Church of Jesus Christ Christian-Aryan Nations, which became one of the centers of *CHRISTIAN IDENTITY. In addition, Butler organized a political group for the propagation of his white supremacist views, the Aryan Nations; the annual Aryan Nations World Congresses take place in the heavily armed compound north of Hayden Lake, Idaho, where Butler houses the church. As early as 1980, Butler advocated the formation of a separate white "homeland" free of Jews, African Americans, and the intervention of the federal government. On September 7, 2000, Butler was found liable for $6.3 million to compensate for the actions of his security guards who, two years earlier, shot at, terrorized, and beat a mother and her son whose car had backfired in front of the group's compound.

References: Michael Barkun, *Religion and the Racist Right: The Origins of the Christian Identity Movement* (1994); David Ostendorf, "Countering Hatred," *Christian Century*, September 8–15, 1999.

Butler Act Introduced into the Tennessee general assembly by John Washington Butler, the Butler Act of 1925 forbade the teaching of "any theory that denies the story of the Divine Creation of man as taught in the *BIBLE" by any public school teacher in the state. The willingness of John T. Scopes of Dayton, Tennessee, to stand trial for violating the Butler Act set up one of the most colorful and dramatic trials in American history, pitting Clarence Darrow for the defense against *WILLIAM JENNINGS BRYAN, who assisted the prosecution.

On July 21, 1925, Scopes was convicted of violating the Butler Act and fined one hundred dollars. The conviction was later overturned by the Supreme Court of Tennessee on a technicality, although the court simultaneously upheld the constitutionality of the Butler Act. The statute remained on the books until its repeal in 1967.

Reference: Edward J. Larson, *Summer for the Gods: The Scopes Trial and America's Continuing Debate over Science and Religion* (1997).

■ ■ ■

Caban, Fred (1951–) Born and reared in Azusa, California, Fred Caban came of age during the counterculture movement of the 1960s. Immersing himself in the rock 'n' roll lifestyle, the young teenager garnered a reputation as an up-and-coming guitar player. By 1968, Caban was on a spiritual quest for truth when he and his bandmates happened to stop by a Christian coffeehouse in Huntington Beach, California. The Lightclub Outreach, formerly a *TEEN CHALLENGE drop-in center, had just been taken over by *DAVID BERG and family, who would later become known as the Children of God. Caban was offered a small booklet of the Gospel of John, which he claimed "for the first time answered some of the questions that had been going through my mind." Later that same night, Caban prayed to "whoever was out there" to reveal himself. Caban recalled that he experienced a theophany "where Jesus came to me and touched me on the shoulder and I actually saw him and he basically called me to follow him." Caban returned to the coffeehouse, where he shared his experience with the leaders and was baptized that same night.

Returning to his hometown of Azusa, Caban decided to synthesize his newfound faith with his musical talents. He formed a band called Agape, the Greek word for God's love. Where previously their goal had been to gain the attention of local recording companies, Agape functioned as one of the first musical evangelistic *JESUS PEOPLE bands. Within six months, a group of fifty young converts had joined the trio as a loose amalgamation of spiritually searching teenagers who gathered for Bible studies and strategy sessions to promote the band's concerts. Over the course of their career, the band released two albums, *Gospel Hard Rock* (1971) and *Victims of Tradition* (1972). The albums stand as two of the earliest efforts of this avant garde gospel music in the rock 'n' roll vernacular of the street culture. The band toured as rock 'n' roll missionaries for over six years. In his insistence that the message of the *GOSPEL could be communicated through a driving, hard rock beat, Fred Caban was the Jimi Hendrix of the *JESUS MOVEMENT.

Cadle, E. Howard (1884–1942) E. Howard Cadle, born in Fredericksburg, Indiana, was converted to evangelical Christianity in 1914 out of a life of drunkenness and gambling, a story that he would recount throughout his ministry. He established a base of operations in Indianapolis, Indiana, where he built a nondenominational, ten-thousand-seat auditorium, known as Cadle Tabernacle, in 1921. Despite early success, Cadle lost control of the building two years later in a dispute with the Tabernacle's board. He then engaged in a number of activities, including land speculation, politics, and itinerant *EVANGELISM, until 1931, when he was able to purchase the Tabernacle from the bank that had repossessed it. He rededicated the Tabernacle with an elaborate ceremony on October 10, 1931.

One of the pioneers of radio *EVANGELISM, Cadle began broadcasting over a local Indianapolis station and expanded to a daily broadcast, *The Nation's Family Prayer Period,* over Cincinnati's WLW in 1932. For fifteen minutes daily and half an hour on Sunday, Cadle's voice could be heard across the country until 1939, when the station's five-hundred-thousand-watt "superpower" license was revoked, thereby diminishing somewhat the extent of his audience.

By that time, however, Cadle had established a unique ministry to Appalachia. A program called *MOUNTAIN CHURCH WORK, begun in 1937, placed radio receivers, which he had purchased for twenty-five dollars each, in small Appalachian communities that were too small or too poor to hire a full-time pastor. The faithful in rural parts of Indiana, Ohio, Kentucky, Tennessee, Virginia, and West Virginia would gather in their churches on Sunday morning and listen to the radio transmission from Cadle Tabernacle by way of WLW, complete with the Tabernacle's fourteen-hundred-voice choir and Cadle's preaching. E. Howard Cadle, who promoted himself as a "modern *CIRCUIT RIDER," became well known throughout Appalachia as the vicarious pastor of more than six hundred churches.

Cadle was an innovator and an entrepreneur in other ways; *Time* magazine called him "a smart businessman" in 1939, the same year, paradoxically, that WLW's signal was reduced to fifty thousand watts, thus limiting the range of Cadle's broadcasts, although the Mutual Network eventually picked them up. At one time Cadle owned a sawmill, a farm and retreat center outside of Indianapolis, and an apple orchard. He purchased an airplane and conducted "one-night *REVIVALS." Following his death in 1942, his widow and various pastors sought to keep the ministry alive, but the Tabernacle was razed in 1968, and only a vestige of the original operation, now known as Cadle Chapel, remains.

References: E. Howard Cadle, *How I Came Back* (1932); Ted Slutz, "Selling Christ: E. Howard Cadle's Big Business for God" (unpublished paper).

Cadle Tabernacle (Indianapolis, Indiana). *See* **Cadle, E. Howard.**

Calgary Prophetic Bible Conference. *See* **Aberhart, William.**

Calgary Prophetic Bible Institute. *See* **Aberhart, William.**

California Association of Christian Schools. *See* **Association of Christian Schools International.**

California Baptist College (Riverside, California) California Baptist College was started in 1950 by the Los Angeles Baptist Association. During the early years, classes were held in the First Southern Baptist Church in El Monte, and in 1955 the college moved to Riverside, California. California Baptist has graduate programs in counseling psychology and education. The college prohibits the use of alcohol and tobacco on campus, and occult practices are outlawed in the standards of student conduct.

References: California Baptist College Catalog, 1995–1996 (1995).

Call to Renewal Formed in May 1995, Call to Renewal is a coalition of religious leaders who took umbrage at the assumption on the part of *PAT ROBERTSON, *RALPH REED, and the *CHRISTIAN COALITION that they articulated the political views of all Christians, even evangelical Christians. The group released a statement, "The Call to Renewal: Let Other Voices Be Heard," a week after the *CHRISTIAN COALITION had issued its "Contract with the American Family." "The almost total identification of the *RELIGIOUS RIGHT with the new Republican majority in Washington is a dangerous liaison with political power," the statement read. "Christian faith must not become another casualty of the culture wars." The "Call to Renewal" statement was drafted by *JIM WALLIS, editor of **SOJOURNERS* magazine, and by *TONY CAMPOLO, a professor at *EASTERN COLLEGE, both of whom describe themselves as "progressive evangelicals," but a wide spectrum of religious leaders was represented among the eighty signatories.

On December 7, 1995, leaders of Call to Renewal were arrested in the United States Capitol for protesting cutbacks in welfare, and at the organization's conference the following year Campolo castigated the *RELIGIOUS RIGHT, specifically the *CHRISTIAN COALITION, for not being sufficiently "pro-life." Campolo said that "if you're going to be pro-life, you ought not only have a discussion about *ABORTION, you also have to have a discussion about tobacco, an industry that kills 450,000 Americans and a million worldwide" every year. "You're not pro-life," he continued, "if you're not talking about guns." Wallis called on both the pro-choice and the antiabortion forces "to collaborate together to radically reduce the rate of *ABORTION in this country by working on teenage pregnancy, by working on adoption reform, by changing the moral climate in which we treat women and children."

Reference: Richard A. Kauffman, "Does Call to Renewal Skirt Partisan Politics?" *Christianity Today*, October 28, 1996.

Calling The idea of having "a calling" occurs quite frequently in both Testaments. The calling is God's attempt to fulfill God's will in the person who is being called. God can call individuals such as Moses or John the Baptist, or God can also call a whole people, such as Israel. In the New Testament, and in the evangelical understanding of calling, the call is a summons to participate in building the kingdom of God and in the *SALVATION made possible through the person of Christ. Individuals are called into *FELLOWSHIP with Christ, as well as to share the attributes of Christ, such as the peace of Christ, freedom, and love. Certain individuals are called to specific tasks, such as apostleship, teaching, *SPEAKING IN TONGUES, or healing.

Evangelical understandings of being called are often seen in eschatological terms, because the end of this world is imminent. This frames the idea of being called as the individual's participation in a unique election, which will at the last judgment set him or her apart from fallen humanity. Evangelicals also talk about call in the sense of vocation, particularly a call to the ministry, to the mission field, or to some form of Christian service.

Calvary Chapel (Santa Ana, California) The original Calvary Chapel was a small congregation in Costa Mesa, California, that was on the verge of disbanding when *CHUCK SMITH, a former Foursquare minister, became pastor in 1965. Shortly after his arrival, Smith initiated an outreach to the hippies then swarming the beaches of southern California. Soon these *JESUS PEOPLE came in droves, attracted by Smith's teaching from the *BIBLE and the kind of "soft *PENTECOSTALISM" that he espoused. Smith's brand of *PENTECOSTALISM expressed itself in dreamy worship music, for example, and in an allowance for—but not an insistence upon—*SPEAKING IN TONGUES.

Calvary Chapel soon outgrew its physical plant and relocated to its present site, on the corner of Fairview and Sunflower, in Santa Ana. The movement spread as those affiliated with the church moved elsewhere and began new congregations. By 1999, more than seven hundred congregations were affiliated with the Calvary Chapel in the United States (Smith resists calling it a denomination) and another five hundred or so worldwide.

References: Randall Balmer, *Mine Eyes Have Seen the Glory: A Journey into the Evangelical Subculture in America,* 3d ed. (2000); Donald E. Miller, *Reinventing American Protestantism: Christianity in the New Millennium* (1997).

Calvin College and Calvin Theological Seminary (Grand Rapids, Michigan) Calvin College and Calvin Theological Seminary are affiliated with the *CHRISTIAN REFORMED CHURCH in North America. They have a common history and share a campus, but each has its own faculty and academic life. The college and seminary began in 1876 as a single theological school for Dutch members of the *CHRISTIAN REFORMED CHURCH. Founded by Egbert Boer, the school initially had only seven students. By 1894, students who did not plan to enter the ministry were admitted to the first four years of the program, and the school developed into a theological seminary and a general preparatory academy. Six years later, the curriculum was broadened, and the academy changed its name to John Calvin Junior College. In 1920, when baccalaureate programs were introduced, the college became known as Calvin College, and the secondary school was discontinued.

Calvin Theological Seminary now offers the master of divinity degree, several master's of arts, the master of theological studies, as well as doctoral degrees. The seminary moved onto its current campus in Grand Rapids in 1960, and by 1974 the college had joined it there. The Hekman Library houses several special collections. Among them are the Colonial Origins Collection, which contains archives and records of the *CHRISTIAN REFORMED CHURCH, and the H. H. Meeter Calvinism Research Collection—the world's largest collection of material about *CALVINISM and its founder, John Calvin. Unlike many other Christian colleges, Calvin, though Reformed and generally conservative in theology, does not impose a lot of behavioral strictures on its students; smoking, drinking, and *DANCING, for instance, are not specifically proscribed in statements regarding student conduct.

References: *Calvin College Catalog 1995/96* (1995); William C. Ringenberg, *The Christian College: A History of Protestant Higher Education in America* (1984).

Calvinism A system of theology dating to John Calvin, Calvinism refers to several formative doctrines that lie at the bedrock of evangelical theology in the Reformed tradition, which, in turn, is virtually synonymous with Calvinism. This system is sometimes abbreviated as the "Five Points of Calvinism":

Unconditional Election (God chooses some for salvation according to God's inscrutable will)
Limited *ATONEMENT (Christ died to redeem only the elect)
Total Depravity of all humanity (all have inherited Adam's *SIN and are therefore unworthy of *SALVATION)
Irresistible Grace (God saves those God elects)
Preservation (perseverance) of the saints (once saved, always saved)

These doctrines are sometimes referred to by the acronym TULIP: *T*otal depravity; *U*nconditional election; *L*imited atonement; *I*rresistible *GRACE; *P*erseverance of the saints.

These doctrines were hashed out at the Synod of Dordt by the Reformed Churches of the Netherlands in response to the Remonstrant Party, which placed more emphasis on human volition in the *SALVATION process. The Remonstrants were led by Jakob Hermanszoon (Jacobus Arminius), Simon Episcopius, Johann Oudenbarneveldt, and Hugh De Groote (Hugo Grotius—the jurist). Anti-Remonstrant Reformed stalwarts included Francis Gomarus, Pieter Platevoet (Petrus Plancius), and others.

These heads were also adopted, with varying degrees of rigor, by those who identified with the Reformed tradition elsewhere, including Scotland, the Reformed cantons of Switzerland, the Puritans in England, and the Reformed strain of *EVANGELICALISM in America.

References: John T. McNeill, *The History and Character of Calvinism* (1954); John H. Leith, *An Introduction to the Reformed Tradition: A Way of Being in the Christian Community*, rev. ed. (1977).

Cambridge Declaration Adopted April 20, 1996, during a meeting of the Alliance of Confessing Evangelicals held in Cambridge, Massachusetts, the Cambridge Declaration is an extended statement by conservative evangelicals who wish to reclaim the central tenets of Reformation theology. The preamble, for instance, reads: "Evangelical churches today are increasingly dominated by the spirit of this age rather than by the Spirit of Christ. As evangelicals, we call ourselves to repent of this *SIN and to recover the historic Christian faith."

Lamenting that "the light of the Reformation has been significantly dimmed," the signatories, which included ***R. C. SPROUL**, ***DAVID F. WELLS**, ***MICHAEL HORTON**, and ***J. A. O. PREUS**, among others, reiterated what they believed were the distinctives of the Protestant Reformation on matters of biblical *AUTHORITY, Christocentric theology (Jesus stands at the center of the redemptive scheme), justification by *GRACE through faith (we can do nothing to earn *SALVATION), and "God-centered worship." They berated evangelicals for succumbing to the blandishments of contemporary culture: "Therapeutic technique, marketing strategies, and the beat of the entertainment world often have far more to say about what the church wants, how it functions, and what it offers, than does the Word of God." The Cambridge Declaration concludes with "A Call to Repentance & Reformation," which includes a repudiation of the notion "that evangelicals and Roman Catholics are one in Christ Jesus even where the biblical doctrine of justification is not believed." This statement, aimed at evangelicals who seek theological agreement with Catholics, reiterates the differences between Protestant and Catholic theology.

Cambridge Inter-Collegiate Christian Union. *See* **InterVarsity Christian Fellowship.**

Camp Meeting The camp meeting in North America evolved from the Scottish practice of "sacramental seasons," protracted gatherings of the faithful that featured preaching, socializing, and sacramental observances, especially the *LORD'S SUPPER. Evangelicals quickly adapted this tradition to the American scene, and camp meetings became a staple of antebellum religious life, especially in the South. Typically, the announcement of a camp meeting would draw settlers from the surrounding area for singing, preaching, and spectacular *CONVERSIONS attended by all manner of religious "exercises"—the jerks, barking, falling, and the like. Toward the middle of the nineteenth century, camp meetings had become a bit tamer, and the 1845 publication of B. W. Gorham's *Camp Meeting Manual* signaled a kind of routinization; Gorham offered precise directions for the planning and the execution of camp meetings. After the Civil War, camp meetings were again used, this time in an attempt to infuse—or to reinfuse—piety and holiness principles into denominations, especially *METHODISM, that had become rather lax and had departed from the fervor of the previous generations. Camp meetings are still plentiful in North America. Some have evolved into large, extended family gatherings, where piety is little in evidence, while others maintain their adherence to holiness principles, which emphasize godly living and a separation from the blandishments of the world.

References: Leigh Eric Schmidt, *Holy Fairs: Scottish Communions and American Revivals in the Early Modern Period* (1989); John R. Boles, *The Great Revival, 1787–1805: The Origins of the Southern Evangelical Mind* (1972); Dickson D. Bruce Jr., *And They All Sang Hallelujah: Plain Folk Camp-Meeting Religion, 1800–1845* (1974); Randall Balmer, "From Frontier Phenomenon to Victorian Institution: The Methodist Camp Meeting in Ocean Grove, New Jersey," *Methodist History*, XXV (April 1987); Charles H. Lippy, "The Camp Meeting in Transition: The Character and Legacy of the Late Nineteenth Century," *Methodist History*, XXXIV (October 1995).

Campbell, Alexander (1788–1866) Born in Ireland and educated briefly at the University of Glasgow, Alexander Campbell and his family migrated to western Pennsylvania in 1809, where he joined his father, who had preceded him by two years. Convinced that the existing denominations had departed from the teachings of the New Testament, both father and son left Presbyterianism and formed the Christian Association of Washington, which would become the genesis of the Disciples of Christ and the Churches of Christ, also known as the *RESTORATION MOVEMENT. Alexander Campbell also organized a congregation at Brush Run, Pennsylvania, and was ordained by that congregation on May 4, 1811. From 1813 until about 1830, the reform movement was associated with the Redstone Baptist

Association, and Campbell itinerated through West Virginia, Kentucky, Tennessee, Ohio, and Indiana with the message of a primitive, New Testament Christianity that avoided the distortions and the creedalism of existing denominations. His followers became known officially as Disciples of Christ, although many outsiders referred to them as Campbellites.

The movement grew rapidly, in part because of Campbell's effectiveness as a preacher and a debater, but also because of his use of periodicals—the *Christian Baptist* (1822–1830) and the *Millennial Harbinger* (1830–1866). In 1840, Campbell founded Bethany College in Bethany, Virginia (now West Virginia); he served as its president from 1840 until 1860.

References: Alexander Campbell, *Psalms, Hymns and Spiritual Songs* (1834); idem, *The Christian System* (1835); idem, *Christian Baptism* (1854); Richard T. Hughes and C. Leonard Allen, *Illusions of Innocence: Protestant Primitivism in America, 1630–1875* (1988).

Campbell, Ivey G(lenshaw) (1874–1918) A seamstress reared in a Presbyterian household in East Liverpool, Ohio, Ivey G. Campbell had an experience of *SANCTIFICATION, which placed her at odds with the pastor of her Presbyterian church. Campbell joined with other holiness people to open the Broadway Mission in East Liverpool. In 1906, after word arrived from Los Angeles about the pentecostal *REVIVAL on Azusa Street, Campbell traveled west and received the *BAPTISM OF THE HOLY SPIRIT at the *AZUSA STREET MISSION. Upon her return to Ohio she conducted services at Claude A. McKinney's Union Gospel Mission in Akron and launched *REVIVAL campaigns as far afield as Cleveland and Pittsburgh. Campbell (along with McKinney and Levi R. Lupton) was one of the organizers of the pentecostal *CAMP MEETING in Alliance, Ohio, which helped to spread *PENTECOSTALISM to the Northeast.

Campbell, Thomas (1763–1854) The cofounder, with his son *ALEXANDER, of the *RESTORATION MOVEMENT, Thomas Campbell graduated from the University of Glasgow in 1786 and became a minister in the Seceder Presbyterian Church of Scotland. He served as pastor of a Seceder congregation in Ahorey, Ireland, from 1798 until his migration to North America in April 1807. Campbell ran afoul of his fellow Presbyterians in western Pennsylvania, where he had settled, over doctrinal matters and organized the Christian Association of Washington, which advertised the *BIBLE as its only creed: "Where the Scriptures speak, we speak; where the Scriptures are silent, we are silent."

In September 1809, Campbell issued his manifesto for the new *RESTORATION MOVEMENT, his *Declaration and Address,* in which he deplored the divisions within Christendom as a "horrid evil" and declared that "the church of Christ upon earth is essentially, intentionally, and constitutionally one." When his son Alexander joined him in Washington County that same year, the two founded the Brush Run Church, which became the nucleus of the movement that evolved into the Christian Church and the Disciples of Christ.

References: Alexander Campbell, *Memoirs of Elder Thomas Campbell,* 2 vols. (1861); Richard T. Hughes and C. Leonard Allen, *Illusions of Innocence: Protestant Primitivism in America, 1630–1875* (1988).

Campbell University (Buies Creek, North Carolina) Campbell University began in 1887 as a coeducational school, Buies Creek Academy. It was founded by

North Carolina preacher James Archibald Campbell. The North Carolina Baptist State Convention acquired Buies Creek Academy in 1925, and the following year the school attained junior college status and became known as Campbell Junior College. In 1961, the college began offering bachelor's degrees and changed its name to Campbell College. The college established graduate programs in law, education, and business in the late 1970s and took the name Campbell University in 1979 to reflect these additions. The Baptist State Convention of North Carolina owns Campbell, but it claims to be nonsectarian. The school has Division I status for athletics.

Campbellites. *See* **Campbell, Alexander** *and* **Christian Churches.**

Campbellsville University (Campbellsville, Kentucky) Campbellsville University is affiliated with the Kentucky Baptist Convention of Southern Baptists. Like many other church colleges founded at the beginning of the twentieth century, Campbellsville was originally a secondary school, Russell Creek Academy. Members of Russell Creek Baptist Association of Salem Baptist Church began raising funds for the academy in 1900, but classes did not begin for seven more years. The academy was renamed Campbellsville College in 1924, when it became a junior college. Baccalaureate programs were added in 1957. Campbellsville College took the name Campbellsville University in 1992, with the introduction of master's degree programs.

Campolo, Anthony "Tony" (1935–) One of the most colorful and articulate proponents of a politically progressive *EVANGELICALISM, Philadelphia-born Tony Campolo was ordained to the gospel ministry in 1957. He studied at *EASTERN COLLEGE and *EASTERN BAPTIST THEOLOGICAL SEMINARY and earned the Ph.D. from Temple University in 1968. Campolo, a sociologist based at *EASTERN COLLEGE, has founded a number of organizations that address social problems from a theologically conservative perspective. In 1969, for example, he founded the Evangelical Association for the Promotion of Education, which seeks to encourage education and economic development in America's cities and in Third World countries. He has been active in social reform efforts in Haiti and in the Dominican Republic, where he founded the Technological University of the South, in Azua, Dominican Republic.

Campolo won the Democratic nomination for Pennsylvania's fifth congressional district in 1976, but he was defeated in the general election. Throughout his career he has consistently articulated a progressive political agenda—with particular emphasis on care for the poor—from within a theologically conservative ambit. Such a posture has placed him at odds with *PAT ROBERTSON, *JERRY FALWELL, *RALPH REED, and other leaders of the *RELIGIOUS RIGHT. Campolo has acknowledged that he represents a minority view within *EVANGELICALISM, but he insists that it is a larger minority than most Americans realize; the difference, he says, is that the *RELIGIOUS RIGHT enjoys greater access to the media and therefore appears to represent a larger percentage of evangelicals.

Campolo, an extraordinarily gifted and entertaining orator, lectures and preaches extensively throughout North America. He forged a close friendship with Bill Clinton and served as the president's spiritual advisor during the Monica Lewinsky scandal and the impeachment crisis of 1998. Campolo, together with

*JIM WALLIS, founded *CALL TO RENEWAL, an organization of progressive evangelicals, in 1995.

References: Anthony Campolo, *A Reasonable Faith: Responding to Secularism* (1983); idem, *It's Friday, But Sunday's Coming* (1984); idem, *Wake Up America!* (1991); idem, *Sociology Through the Eyes of Faith* (1992); idem. *Revolution and Renewal* (2000); idem, *Is Jesus a Republican or a Democrat?* (1995); "Dissident Evangelical: An Interview with Tony Campolo," *Christian Century,* February 22, 1995; Joseph B. Modica, ed., *The Gospel with Extra Salt* (2000).

Campus Crusade for Christ, International Campus Crusade for Christ, International is the largest evangelistic organization in the world. With headquarters in Orlando, Florida, the nondenominational organization has more than thirteen thousand full-time staff and one hundred thousand volunteers in 167 countries. Its operating budget in 1995 was more than $250 million.

Campus Crusade was founded by a businessman and former *FULLER THEOLOGICAL SEMINARY student *WILLIAM R. ("BILL") BRIGHT and his wife, Vonette. After several years of successful *EVANGELISM at the University of California at Los Angeles, the couple pledged to become "slaves of Jesus," liquidating their business interests in 1951 to finance a fledgling ministry to college students. Their original goal was to "saturate" campuses across the United States, and their strategy was simple: preach the *GOSPEL, gain converts, and train them to convert other people to evangelical Christianity. Bright's team quickly became known for their efforts to recruit charismatic student leaders, with the notion that these individuals would be most successful in gaining converts. Campus Crusade was the organization responsible for the "evangelistic blitz" at Berkeley in 1967, when six hundred volunteers arrived at the California flagship school. About this time, the organization began to expand its domestic and international outreach to other segments of the population. Five years later its Christian convention brought out a crowd of more than eighty thousand at the Dallas Cotton Bowl, and more than one hundred thousand more attendees arrived later for a Christian rock concert. This event, Explo '72, made Campus Crusade a pioneer force in *CONTEMPORARY CHRISTIAN MUSIC. In the 1970s, Campus Crusade sponsored "I Found It!" bumper-sticker campaigns here and abroad.

Campus Crusade has staff on 650 university campuses in the United States, and 400 more in other countries. The organization still sends thousands of young *EVANGELISTS to Florida's beaches during spring break to preach to college students, but its programs have expanded far beyond this group and now number more than forty subministries divided into three sections: national, international, and professional.

The professional arm of Campus Crusade has its own departments to publish and distribute books and other evangelistic materials. Arrowhead Productions International coordinates video, radio, and multimedia productions for outreach by Campus Crusade's other ministries as well as external religious organizations. *Worldwide Challenge* magazine has a circulation of almost one hundred thousand, and many more people are reached by *World Changers Radio,* a fifteen-minute daily broadcast. In San Bernardino, California, Campus Crusade runs a religious training school, the International School of Theology, as well as the Arrowhead Springs Conference Center, a facility for meetings and retreats for Christian groups and organizations.

Some of the national programs, such as *ATHLETES IN ACTION and the Josh

McDowell Ministry, are well-known in their own right. There are also missions to homeless people, single adults, soldiers, Latinos, and African Americans. The organization uses a variety of methods to reach people, such as music, magic, Bible study, and the Internet. Relying on the same impulses as the *PROMISE KEEPERS and other forms of "*MUSCULAR CHRISTIANITY," Campus Crusade helps build "godly men" through its M.A.N. (Man's Authentic Nature) program, which is balanced by an outreach effort for women. The organization also has specialized ministries to the members of many professions, including diplomats, lawyers, doctors, university professors, and Hollywood actors. Campus Crusade's Executive Ministries witnesses to business professionals through an "evangelistic dinner party strategy."

The international division of Campus Crusade serves mainly youth and students. Two of the organization's largest domestic endeavors also have significant international components. In 1979, with the help of a generous donation from Texas oil billionaire Nelson Bunker Hunt, the organization filmed *Jesus,* a feature-length account of Christ's life based on the Gospel of Luke. Since that time the film has been shown to more than 800 million people worldwide and has become the most widely translated film in history, with versions produced in more than 370 languages to date. Its international distribution is buttressed by a domestic program to make video copies available to every American household. Also, in 1987, Campus Crusade launched New Life 2000, a campaign to evangelize every person on earth by the year 2000. Through this endeavor, the organization aspired to fulfill Christ's Great Commission of witnessing to all people. Specific objectives of the campaign included converting one billion people and planting a million new churches around the world.

Despite—or perhaps because of—its tremendous success, Campus Crusade sometimes comes in for criticism. Former volunteers have noted the lack of support for new converts to help them live a Christian life. The organization's emphasis on *EVANGELISM, criticized as shallow, simplistic, or even impersonal, has led detractors to deride it as the "McDonald's" of religious organizations. One area in which Campus Crusade is rarely censured, however, is its meticulous financial accountability (its annual budget is approximately $250 million). All employees must raise the money to pay for their own salaries, including *BILL and Vonette *BRIGHT. This policy is only one example of an overall commitment to use financial contributions on program expenses, rather than overhead, and it has enabled Campus Crusade to have some of the best efficiency ratings of any nonprofit organization. In 1993 *Money* magazine rated it the "most efficient" religious organization in the United States. In 2000, Bright announced that he would step aside as head of Campus Crusade the following year in favor of Stephen Douglass, the organization's executive vice president.

Reference: Information provided by Campus Crusade for Christ, International.

Campus Life. *See* **Youth for Christ, International.**

Canada Fire The name "Canada Fire," taken from a contemporary account by Methodist itinerant *NATHAN BANGS, refers to the evangelical *REVIVAL of religion in Upper Canada and the Maritimes that took place in the period roughly from the American Revolution to the War of 1812. According to *G. A. RAWLYK, the preeminent historian of Canadian *EVANGELICALISM, this *REVIVAL was led by such preachers as Bangs, *HARRIS HARDING, *DAVID GEORGE, *FREEBORN GARRETTSON, and especially *HENRY ALLINE. The *EVANGELICALISM of the Canada Fire, Rawlyk argues, was more radical and more egalitarian than the *GREAT AWAKENING in the American colonies. The earliest harbinger of the *SECOND GREAT AWAKENING, according to Bangs and *LORENZO DOW, was the revival preaching of *HEZEKIAH CALVIN WOOSTER in Upper Canada.

Reference: G. A. Rawlyk, *The Canada Fire: Radical Evangelicalism in British North America, 1775–1812* (1994).

Canadian Baptist Seminary (Langley, British Columbia). *See* **Baptist General Conference of Canada** *and* **Associated Canadian Theological Schools.**

Canadian Center for Law and Justice. *See* **American Center for Law and Justice.**

Canadian Protestant League The Canadian Protestant League, a nativist organization, was formed in the fall of 1941 by Protestant clergymen in Toronto, who were exercised about what they saw as the outsized influence of Roman Catholicism on Canadian life. The group chose fundamentalist firebrand *T. T. SHIELDS, pastor of the Jarvis Street Baptist Church, as their president. The League, according to its constitution, had three purposes: to defend "the traditional, civil, and religious liberties of British subjects"; to affirm and to propagate "the great doctrines and principles of the Protestant Reformation"; and to resist the imperial ambitions of Rome and its "political methods of propagating its tenets, and of extending and exercising this illegitimate authority."

The organization's membership grew to eighteen hundred by the end of the year, and Shields's tour of the West tripled that number. The League distributed anti-Catholic literature, staged mass rallies, and supported political candidates sympathetic to nativism. Shields published his own anti-Catholic polemic in 1943: *Canadians Losing at Home the Freedom for Which They Are Fighting Abroad.* That same year, Parliament considered a resolution to gag Shields, but the prime minister, W. L. M. King, opposed the move because he did not want to make a martyr out of Shields, a man whom King held in "utter contempt." The Canadian Protestant League continued its protests throughout the 1940s, but the fervor faded by the end of the decade.

References: T. T. Shields, *Canadians Losing at Home the Freedom for Which They Are Fighting Abroad* (1943); John G. Stackhouse Jr., s.v. "Thomas Todhunter Shields," in Charles H. Lippy, ed., *Twentieth-Century Shapers of American Popular Religion* (1989).

Candler, Warren Akin (1857–1941) Born in Villa Rica, Georgia, Warren Akin Candler attended Emory College and joined the North Georgia Conference of the Methodist Episcopal Church, South in 1875. He became president of Emory in 1888, a post he held until his election as bishop a decade later. Throughout his life, Candler, a conservative, steadfastly opposed reunification with the northern Methodists. He pushed for the relocation of Emory to Atlanta in 1914, where it became Emory University. Candler served as chancellor of the school until 1921, and Emory's Candler School of Theology was named in his honor.

Cane Ridge The most famous and most spectacular *REVIVAL in American history took place at Cane Ridge, Kentucky, in August 1801. Organized by *BARTON W. STONE and other frontier revivalists, the Cane Ridge *CAMP MEETING attracted anywhere from ten thousand to twenty-five thousand participants, many of whom were overcome by the Holy Spirit. Under the preaching of various Baptist, Methodist, and Presbyterian *EVANGELISTS, who set aside their sectarian differences, many people experienced religious *CONVERSION (although critics insisted that more souls were conceived than converted). Cane Ridge is also notable for the religious enthusiasm that attended the gathering. According to contemporaries, those who came under the influence of the Holy Spirit were overtaken by various involuntary "exercises." These included *DANCING, the "jerks," falling, barking, singing, and running. Although it was never matched, Cane Ridge set the standard for *CAMP MEETING religion throughout the antebellum period.

References: John R. Boles, *The Great Revival, 1787–1805: The Origins of the Southern Evangelical Mind* (1972); Paul K. Conkin, *Cane Ridge: America's Pentecost* (1990).

Cannon, James, Jr. (1864–1944) James Cannon Jr., a *TEMPERANCE advocate and Methodist bishop, was born in Salisbury, Maryland, on the Delmarva Peninsula. Initially intent on pursuing a career in law, he graduated from Randolph-Macon College, but a shift in career ambitions led him to pursue the ministry with degrees from Princeton Theological Seminary and from Princeton University. After serving several churches in Virginia, Cannon became principal of Blackstone Female Institute in Virginia in 1894, a post he held for almost a quarter century. His strong convictions about the ruinous traffic in alcoholic beverages received a wide hearing through his editorship of denominational and *TEMPERANCE newspapers, the *Methodist Recorder* and the *Baltimore-Richmond Christian Advocate.*

Cannon was active in the *ANTI-SALOON LEAGUE and in the push for a Prohibition amendment to the U.S. Constitution. In 1918, Cannon was elected bishop in the Methodist Episcopal Church, South; he supervised mission activities in Latin America, Turkey, and Africa; chaired the Commission on Temperance and Social Service; and advocated ecumenism, or unity among Protestant Christians. Cannon's political activism culminated in his refusal to support Al Smith, the Democratic (and "wet" Roman Catholic) candidate for president in 1928; Cannon's relentless campaigning for Herbert Hoover earned him the gratitude of the Republican president but also the enmity of Cannon's fellow Southerners. His enemies, with scant evidence, accused him of being a "bucketshop gambler," a stock speculator, because of the financial schemes he used to support the Blackstone Institute and the Southern Assembly, a conference center he had developed for the denomination at Lake Junaluska, North Carolina. When Cannon, who had been widowed, married his private secretary in 1930, the enemies had further cause to gloat. The denomination's Board of Temperance and Social Service, which Cannon headed, was eliminated in 1934, although Cannon continued his activities on behalf of *TEMPERANCE until his death a decade later.

References: James Cannon Jr., *Bishop Cannon's Own Story: Life As I Have Seen It*, ed. Richard L. Watson (1955); Virginius Dabney, *Dry Messiah: The Life of Bishop James Cannon Jr.* (1949); Daniel Swinson, s.v. "James Cannon Jr.," in Charles H. Lippy, ed., *Twentieth-Century Shapers of American Popular Religion* (1989).

Capstone Cathedral (Phoenix, Arizona). *See* **Frisby, Neal (Vincent).**

Card, Michael (1957–) Born in Madison, Tennessee, Michael Card, a singer and songwriter, graduated from Western Kentucky University in 1979 and earned a master's degree in biblical studies there the following year. *First Light,* his debut album, appeared in 1981. He has earned five Dove Awards from the *GOSPEL MUSIC ASSOCIATION, and he has written several books, including children's books.

Reference: Wendy Murray Zoba, "Incarnating Mystery," *Christianity Today,* July 10, 2000.

Carey, Lott (c. 1780–1829) Born into slavery in tidewater Virginia, Lott Carey became a hired laborer in Richmond, Virginia, where he attended night school and participated in religious meetings at the First Baptist Church. He was converted and then baptized in 1807, whereupon he began to preach to various gatherings of African Americans around the city. Carey purchased his own freedom and that of his two children in 1813, and he began to take an interest in missionary work. He was instrumental in the formation of the Richmond African Missionary Society in 1815. In 1821, the *AMERICAN COLONIZATION SOCIETY chose Carey to begin a mission in western Africa. In 1822, he and his company settled in the new colony of Cape Montserado, later known as Liberia. Despite the ubiquitous threats of starvation, disease, and local hostility, Carey founded several schools and the Providence Baptist Church; he taught in the schools and helped in the administration of medical care in the colony. He was chosen vice governor in 1828 and later became the acting governor of Liberia. Although his life was cut short by the explosion of a powder magazine, Carey managed to regularize some of the colony's affairs and to finalize the purchase of lands from regional chieftains.

References: Leroy Fitts, *Lott Carey: First Black Missionary to Africa* (1978); William Henry Brackney, *The Baptists* (1988).

Carey, William (1761–1834) Born in Northamptonshire, England, William Carey was a cobbler's apprentice and a self-educated man. His readings of the *BIBLE and theological writings led him to embrace Baptist teachings; he began preaching in local meetinghouses, was baptized, and became pastor of a small congregation in Moulton. Carey's concern for missions and *EVANGELISM led to the publication of *An Enquiry into the Obligations of Christians to use means for the conversion of the Heathens.* This work, which appeared in 1792, was a clarion call for missionary work, which Carey pressed with his formula: "pray, plan, pay."

With the assistance of *ANDREW FULLER, Carey pushed for the formation of the Baptist Missionary Society, founded in Kettering, England, in 1792. The next year, Carey left for India as the Society's first missionary. Over the course of a career that lasted three decades, Carey founded Baptist churches, a college, and an indigo plantation, the proceeds of which he used to publish and distribute copies of the *BIBLE. An accomplished linguist, Carey translated the Scriptures into Bengali, Marathi, Panjabi, Sanskrit, Kanarese, and Telugu; he produced grammars and dictionaries for several other languages, and some regard him as the father of modern Bengali. Carey also made his voice heard in social and political matters. He urged the conservation of forests, founded the Agricultural Society of India, and called for an end to infanticide and *sati,* the Indian practice of a widow throwing herself onto her husband's funeral pyre.

References: William Carey, *An Enquiry into the Obligations of Christians to use means for the conversion of the Heathens* (1792); Eustace Carey, *Memoir of William Carey, D.D.* (1837); John Clark Marshman, *The Life and Times of Carey, Marshman, and Ward,* 2 vols. (1859); Mary Drewery, *William Carey, A Biography* (1978); William Henry Brackney, *The Baptists* (1988).

Carey College. *See* **Oklahoma Baptist University.**

Carman (né Licciardello, Carman Dominic) (1956–) Born Carman Dominic Licciardello, Carman, a singer and pentecostal *EVANGELIST, has been a fixture in *CONTEMPORARY CHRISTIAN MUSIC since the 1970s. His mother played in all-girl bands, and Carman himself once sang in bars on the New Jersey shore and performed on the nightclub circuit in Las Vegas. His life changed, however, in 1976, when he attended a gospel concert by *ANDRAÉ CROUCH and the Disciples in southern California. He was *BORN AGAIN. Carman soon became an *EVANGELIST in his own right, selling recordings of his Christian music out of the trunk of his car.

Since then, Carman has released more than a dozen albums and numerous videos, several of which have been certified gold or platinum, with total sales of more than seven million copies. He has won four Dove awards from the *GOSPEL MUSIC ASSOCIATION. Carman's 1990 release, *Revival in the Land,* earned him two awards from *Billboard,* for Album of the Year and Contemporary Christian Artist of the Year. Two years later, *Addicted to Jesus* won in the same two categories. In 1993, *The Standard* went to number one on *Billboard*'s Christian charts. And in 1994, Carman broke the record for the largest Christian music concert when more than seventy thousand people attended his October 22 show at Dallas's Texas Stadium. Carman's 1995 album, *R.I.O.T., the Righteous Invasion of Truth,* made its debut at number-one on *Billboard*'s Christian Contemporary Music chart.

Unlike musical acts such as *AMY GRANT or *MICHAEL W. SMITH, Carman's music has not gained popularity in non-Christian circles, and he has never shown interest in becoming a "crossover artist." Carman contents himself with a great following among young evangelical teenagers. Ironically, his music draws on a variety of secular sources, including "acid house" and Latin-American rap; Carman has made several recordings in Spanish. He is known for his ability to create a pastiche of sounds, incorporating clips from the 1960s and doing impressions of Elvis, the Bee Gees, and Michael Jackson. Such stylings are only one reason Carman has the reputation for being "flashy." His current stage show includes four large video screens and six stage dancers. One of his best-known songs, "No Monsters," is performed in concerts with the dancers dressed as monsters and angels. This kind of dark imagery and literal depictions of good and evil have caused *Z MUSIC Television, the twenty-four-hour Christian music channel, to refuse to air some of Carman's videos.

Carman also receives criticism in evangelical circles for having an overly strict moral certainty, and he is often cited, positively and negatively, for the extreme success of his tie-in marketing. The singer has published two books, *Raising the Standard* and *The R.I.O.T. Manual,* to accompany two of his albums, and *R.I.O.T.* also has inspired a two-part video. Carman and the staff from his charity, Carman Ministries, Inc., claim that such tie-ins are needed because in general he does not charge admission to shows but only asks for a "love offering." The proceeds from the associated merchandise have, however, been plentiful enough to help Carman Ministries work in partnership with Feed the Children, a domestic hunger-relief agency, and to establish R.I.O.T. centers in Houston, Detroit, and Los Angeles. These centers offer social services and referrals. Carman Ministries, Inc. aspires to set up similar facilities in thirty-six other inner-city areas across the United States.

Reference: Information provided by Sparrow media relations.

Carmichael, Ralph (1927–) Although his musical compositions and arrangements seem tame by the Christian rock standards of the 1980s and 1990s, Ralph Carmichael was one of the pioneers in the remaking of "church music" from the old standards of eighteenth- and nineteenth-century hymnody to the "*PRAISE MUSIC" so popular in evangelical circles at the end of the twentieth century. Born in Quincy, Illinois, to an *ASSEMBLIES OF GOD pastor and his wife, Carmichael learned the violin, piano, and trumpet and became enamored of the big band music of the era. He studied for the ministry at *SOUTHERN CALIFORNIA BIBLE COLLEGE but dropped out because of his relentless pursuit of music. Carmichael spent five years as the minister of music at a Los Angeles Baptist church, where he wrote "The Savior Is Waiting." He scored nature films produced by the Moody Institute of Science in Santa Monica, California, and scored and wrote songs for *BILLY GRAHAM films (World Wide Pictures) such as *Joni, The Cross and the Switchblade*, and *The Restless Ones*.

Carmichael wrote and arranged music for *The Dinah Shore Show* and for such performers as Nat "King" Cole, Bing Crosby, Ella Fitzgerald, Rosemary Clooney, *PAT BOONE, and others. When rock 'n' roll began to take hold in the 1960s, Carmichael set about updating church music to fit the changing times—and his teenage daughter's taste. He wrote several songs that became the staple of evangelical youth gatherings: "He's Everything to Me," "A Quiet Place," and "We Are More Than Conquerors," among others. Carmichael founded Light Records and sponsored such Christian contemporary artists as *ANDRAÉ CROUCH, Dino, and Bryan Duncan. In the 1990s, Carmichael was the musical director for the Young Messiah tour, the highest-grossing Christian musical tour in history.

"I don't think groups like *JARS OF CLAY and 4HIM feel the stigma I did growing up," Carmichael recalled. "I think they are enjoying the freedom that exists now to go out and communicate the gospel without anybody saying, 'That's worldly.' It's wonderful that we have fought for and won the right to have this freedom of expression."

Reference: Ralph Carmichael, *He's Everything to Me* (1986).

Carnell, E(dward) J(ohn) (1919–1967) One of the brightest stars in *EVANGELICALISM's intellectual firmament, E. J. Carnell was born into a Baptist parsonage in Antigo, Wisconsin. He earned the B.A. from *WHEATON COLLEGE in 1941, where his thought was profoundly shaped by *GORDON H. CLARK, a philosopher who sought to provide rational defenses for Christianity. Carnell continued on to *WESTMINSTER THEOLOGICAL SEMINARY, where he studied apologetics with *CORNELIUS VAN TIL, and then to Harvard University, where he wrote a dissertation on Reinhold Niebuhr. Carnell also completed a second doctorate (in 1949, one year after his Harvard doctorate), this one at Boston University, with a dissertation entitled "The Problem of Verification in Søren Kierkegaard."

Concurrent with his graduate studies, Carnell taught at *GORDON COLLEGE and Divinity School, and by the time he accepted an appointment at the newly formed *FULLER THEOLOGICAL SEMINARY in 1948, he had already earned a reputation as an evangelical *wunderkind*. His award-winning *Introduction to Christian Apologetics,* published in 1948, was acclaimed by evangelicals and nonevangelicals alike. Over the course of his nineteen years at Fuller, Carnell served the school in several capacities—as professor of ethics and philosophy of religion and as president from 1954 to 1959. Throughout the last years of his life, he was haunted by emotional and psychological problems, and he began to imbibe doubts about some of the "cultish" dimensions of *EVANGELICALISM.

References: E. J. Carnell, *An Introduction to Christian Apologetics* (1948); idem, *Christian Commitment* (1957); idem, *The Kingdom of Love and the Pride of Life* (1960); George M. Marsden, *Reforming Fundamentalism: Fuller Seminary and the New Evangelicalism* (1987); Rudolph Nelson, *The Making and Unmaking of an Evangelical Mind: The Case of Edward Carnell* (1988).

Carothers, Warren Fay (1872–1953) A self-taught attorney, Warren Fay Carothers was admitted to the Texas bar in 1894. He started preaching in 1896 and received his license as a "local preacher" from the Methodists three years later. In 1905, while pastor of Texas Holiness Church in Beeville, Texas, Carothers came upon the teachings of *CHARLES FOX PARHAM; he affiliated with the pentecostal movement and became Parham's field director in the Apostolic Faith movement, with responsibility for training evangelists and pastors.

Carothers and Parham severed their relationship in 1912, apparently over the organizational form of the Apostolic Faith, and Carothers joined the *ASSEMBLIES OF GOD two years later. As an executive with that newly formed denomination, Carothers argued against allowing women to preach, and he worked tirelessly for greater cooperation among the various pentecostal bodies. His efforts at ecumenism, however, met with little effect, and in 1923 he withdrew from the Assemblies to form an independent church in Houston. He also continued his practice of law in Houston and was appointed a federal judge in 1933.

References: Warren Fay Carothers, *The Baptism with the Holy Ghost* (1906); idem, *Church Government* (1909).

Carradine, Beverly (1848–1919) Born in Yazoo County, Mississippi, Beverly Carradine was converted to Christianity in 1874 and shortly thereafter joined the Mississippi Conference of the Methodist Episcopal Church, South. Stationed at Vicksburg, he was ordained a deacon in 1876 and then served a succession of churches in Mississippi before transferring to Louisiana in 1882. While there, he vigorously opposed proposals for a state lottery, and in 1889, while stationed at Carondelet, Louisiana, he experienced the *BAPTISM OF THE HOLY SPIRIT, which, according to holiness teachings, conferred *SANCTIFICATION.

Carradine, a fiery preacher, moved on to St. Louis, and in 1890 he published *Sanctification,* a volume setting forth holiness doctrines, and the first of several books. In the face of hostility from Methodist bishops who opposed the *HOLINESS MOVEMENT within the denomination, Carradine initially urged the holiness people to remain in the Methodist Episcopal Church, South. By 1893, however, faced with determined opposition from the Methodist hierarchy, he himself left the denomination to become an itinerant *EVANGELIST.

Carroll, B(enajah) H(arvey) (1843–1914) A native of Mississippi and a graduate of *BAYLOR, B. H. Carroll served briefly in the Texas Rangers and for the Confederate cause in the Texas Infantry before heeding a call to the ministry. His first church, in Burleson County, Texas, opened a school to teach literacy to war veterans, and his second pulpit, First Baptist Church in Waco, provided Carroll the opportunity to teach at Baylor, where he quickly became a classroom favorite. Carroll's success in the Bible department at Baylor led to the formation of a seminary, initially known as Baylor Theological Seminary, of which he became the first president; he shepherded the school, whose name changed to Southwestern Baptist Seminary, to its present Fort Worth location in 1908. Many Southern Baptists regarded him as a statesman, especially for his efforts within the Convention on behalf of education, missions, and *SUNDAY SCHOOLS.

References: B. H. Carroll, *The Genesis of American Anti-Missionism* (1903); idem, *Baptists and Their Doctrines* (1913); Jeff D. Ray, *B. H. Carroll* (1927); J. M. Carroll, *Dr. B. H. Carroll, the Colossus of Baptist History* (1946); William Henry Brackney, *The Baptists* (1988).

Carson, D(onald) A(rthur) (1946–) An evangelical theologian and New Testament scholar, D. A. Carson was born in Montréal and educated at McGill University, Central Baptist Seminary, and Cambridge University. Carson, an ordained Baptist minister, taught at Northwest Baptist Theological College, where he also served as academic dean, and at *TRINITY EVANGELICAL DIVINITY SCHOOL, joining the faculty in 1978. He is widely respected in evangelical circles as a theologian and a scholar.

References: D. A. Carson, *The Sermon on the Mount: An Exposition of Matthew 5–7* (1978); idem, *The King James Version Debate: A Plea for Realism* (1979); idem, *Exegetical Fallacies* (1984); idem, *How Long, O Lord?: Reflections on Suffering and Evil* (1990); idem, *A Call to Spiritual Reformation: Priorities from Paul and His Prayers* (1992); idem, *The Cross and Christian Ministry* (1993).

Carter, James Earl "Jimmy" (1924–) The man who would become the thirty-ninth president of the United States was born in Plains, Georgia, and reared in the Baptist faith by a devout mother. Jimmy Carter attended the U.S. Naval Academy and served in the navy from 1945 to 1953, where he became a protégé of Admiral Hyman Rickover. Following the death of his father, Carter resigned his commission to return to Plains and take over the family's peanut business. In 1962, he won a seat in the Georgia State Senate in a bitterly contested election, recounted in his book *Turning Point,* that pitted Carter against a local political machine. His first bid to become governor of Georgia, which ended in defeat in 1966, prompted a religious *CONVERSION, which Carter recounted as being "*BORN AGAIN."

Carter's second try for the governorship, in 1970, was successful, and he almost immediately plotted a course that would lead to the Democratic presidential nomination six years later. Carter's ascendance from a relatively unknown one-term governor of a Southern state through the Iowa precinct caucuses to the nomination and to the presidency remains one of the more legendary feats of modern-day politics. Throughout his campaign he made no secret that he was a *BORN-AGAIN Christian and a *SUNDAY SCHOOL teacher in his local Southern Baptist church. To a nation still reeling from the ignominy of Vietnam and the sting of Watergate, Carter's obvious probity and his pledge that he would "never knowingly lie to the American people" resonated.

Once in office, Carter faced a series of crises that would test his mettle and eventually erode his popularity—the Arab oil embargo, runaway inflation, the Mariel boat lift, the Iran hostage crisis. Many evangelicals, who had helped elect him to office in 1976, turned against him by the 1980 election, claiming that Carter was too liberal; *JERRY FALWELL, for instance, founded *MORAL MAJORITY in 1979 as little more than a tool to defeat Carter. The 1980 presidential election featured three candidates, all of whom claimed to be evangelical Christians: Carter; *JOHN B. ANDERSON, who had been reared in the *EVANGELICAL FREE CHURCH OF AMERICA; and *RONALD REAGAN, a divorced former movie actor from California. Politically conservative evangelicals threw their support behind Reagan, thereby helping to turn Carter out of office.

It has been said and often repeated that Jimmy Carter was the only man for whom the presidency was a stepping stone. Indeed, while other ex-presidents have been content to dictate memoirs and to collect large fees for lectures or sitting on corporate boards, Carter has vigorously engaged in humanitarian activities, often under the auspices of his presidential library, the Carter Center in Atlanta. He has served as a kind of freelance peacemaker around the world, and he and his wife, Rosalynn, have been active in such causes as *HABITAT FOR HUMANITY.

On October 19, 2000, Carter announced his "very painful decision" to leave the *SOUTHERN BAPTIST CONVENTION because, in his judgment, the denomination's "increasingly rigid creed" represented a betrayal of Baptist principles. "I have been a Baptist for sixty-five years and I have always believed that our denomination's view on creeds was not to have one," he told the *Christian Century.* "I believe in the 'sainthood' of each individual Christian believer to be inspired by the influence of the spirit of Christ in their hearts. Each believer can interpret biblical phrases in accordance with their own conscience." The developments in the *SOUTHERN BAPTIST CONVENTION aimed at changing that tradition, he concluded, "violate the basic tenets of my Christian faith."

References: Jimmy Carter, *Turning Point: A Candidate, a State, and a Nation Come of Age* (1992); idem, *Living Faith* (1996); Dan Arial and Cheryl Heckler-Feltz, *The Carpenter's Apprentice: The Spiritual Biography of Jimmy Carter* (1996); "Carter Cuts SBC Ties," *Christian Century,* November 8, 2000.

Cartwright, Peter (1785–1872) An itinerant Methodist preacher on the American frontier, Peter Cartwright was born in Amherst County, Virginia, and moved with his family to Logan County, Kentucky, in 1790. He was converted in a *CAMP MEETING in 1801, whereupon he joined the Methodist Episcopal Church. Cartwright was licensed in 1802 and began itinerating shortly thereafter, referring to himself as "God's Plowman." After his ordination as a deacon in 1806 and an elder in 1808, he alternated between being a *CIRCUIT RIDER, traveling from settlement to settlement, and a presiding elder until 1826, when he settled finally in the Illinois Circuit.

Cartwright was a masterly preacher whose witty, extemporary style was well received on the frontier, especially in *CAMP MEETINGS, and his *Autobiography* provides colorful and anecdotal insights into antebellum *METHODISM. During nearly half a century in Illinois, Cartwright was active both in ecclesiastical and political affairs. He was elected twice to the Illinois legislature, but he was defeated in his only bid for Congress by a young, up-and-coming politician named Abraham Lincoln.

Reference: Peter Cartwright, *Autobiography of Peter Cartwright* (1956).

Case, William (1780–1855) William Case, one of the leaders of the *HAY BAY CAMP MEETING of 1805, was born in Massachusetts and converted to evangelical *METHODISM in 1803. After being admitted as an itinerant preacher, he was assigned to the Bay of Quinte circuit in Upper Canada. A spellbinding preacher, Case was also a missionary among the Mississauga Indians.

Reference: G. A. Rawlyk, *The Canada Fire: Radical Evangelicalism in British North America, 1775–1812* (1994).

Cash, Johnny (1932–) Born into grinding poverty in Cleveland County, Arkansas, Johnny Cash early in life turned to music as an escape—country, gospel, spirituals, Southern blues, and old railroad songs for which he would eventually become famous. After graduating from high school in 1950, he traveled north and found work in an automobile factory. After a stint in the air force, he married Vivian Liberto; the marriage ended in divorce in 1967. In 1955, while working as an appliance salesman, he formed a group called Johnny Cash and the Tennessee Two and signed with Sun Records in Memphis, the label that had discovered Elvis Presley. "All these years I've been called 'the man in black' because I always wore it," he recalled in 1995. "Started in church in 1955, when I did my first public appearance with the Tennessee Two. We wanted to have a uniform look for church. Nobody had a suit or a white shirt, but all of us had a black shirt, so that's what we wore."

Cash's smoky, brooding voice catapulted him to fame and notoriety in the 1960s and early 1970s. He collected several gold albums and numerous awards, hosted his own network television program, *The Johnny Cash Show,* for three years, and by 1971 was the best-selling country singer ever. But his hard drinking and use of amphetamines finally took their toll. He reached bottom in 1967, and a religious epiphany of sorts finally rescued him. "I felt something—that love, the warm presence of God that I knew as a boy," he recalled. "I understood that I wasn't going to die, there were still things I had to do." With the help and support of his second wife, country singer June Carter, whom he married in 1968, Cash fought his way back to sobriety, although not without some reversals along the way. His testimony about a hard life and dissolute past reclaimed by Jesus, however, plays well with evangelicals. "There is a spiritual side to me that goes real deep," he told *Rolling Stone* in 2000, "but I confess I'm the biggest sinner of them all." One index of Cash's popularity within the evangelical subculture is the frequency of his appearances at *BILLY GRAHAM crusades.

References: Johnny Cash, with Patrick Carr, *Cash: The Autobiography* (1998); Don Cusic, *The Sound of Light: A History of Gospel Music* (1990); Curtis W. Ellison, *Country Music Culture: From Hard Times to Heaven* (1995); Anthony DeCurtis, "Johnny Cash Won't Back Down," *Rolling Stone,* October 26, 2000.

Cashwell, G(aston) B(arnabas) (1860–1916) Born in rural North Carolina, G. B. Cashwell joined the Methodist Episcopal Church, South, but left the Methodists in 1903 to join the Holiness Church of North Carolina, newly formed under the leadership of *A. B. CRUMPLER. Hearing news about the *AZUSA STREET REVIVAL in Los Angeles, Cashwell traveled west in 1906 and there began *SPEAKING IN TONGUES, which he regarded as initial evidence of *BAPTISM OF THE HOLY SPIRIT. Returning to North Carolina, Cashwell's teaching spread through his congregation. After a successful *REVIVAL on December 31, 1906, he rented a three-story tobacco warehouse to accommodate the crowds. The *REVIVAL, which many regarded as the eastern counterpart to the *AZUSA STREET REVIVAL, lasted through January 1907. Cashwell invited fellow Holiness Church ministers to attend his *REVIVAL meetings in Dunn, where most of them also began *SPEAKING IN TONGUES. Cashwell began traveling throughout the South with his pentecostal message, and he counted among his converts *J. H. KING and *A. J. TOMLINSON, leaders, respectively, of the *FIRE-BAPTIZED HOLINESS CHURCH and the *CHURCH OF GOD (CLEVELAND, TENNESSEE). Cashwell, sometimes known as "the pentecostal apostle to the South," also started a periodical, the *Bridegroom's Messenger*, to publicize his efforts.

Cashwell's teachings, however, eventually led to a break with Crumpler, who came to reject the notion that *SPEAKING IN TONGUES was the only initial evidence of spiritual *BAPTISM. Crumpler left the Holiness Church of North Carolina in 1908, and Cashwell left the following year, evidently disappointed that he had not been chosen to lead the denomination.

Reference: Vinson Synan, *The Old-Time Power* (1973).

Catechesis The most common understanding of "catechesis" is the pedagogical or teaching mode of the church as it imparts understanding of faith and doctrine to believers. The purpose of a catechism is to lead the learner to a communion with Christ. Evangelical Christians have not used the formal catechetical models as much as Roman Catholic, Eastern Orthodox, and more traditional Protestant communions. However, since many evangelicals have attempted to reinstate the practice of adult catechism prior to *BAPTISM or full acceptance into the community of believers, they have, either consciously or not, begun the practice of catechetical instruction. While catechisms deal with matters of belief and the experience of Christ, the catechism most often reflects the specific doctrines and tenets of the faith that created it. It is an important method by which a community assures the adherence of its believers to a common belief system. Ideally, catechism as a process of learning and growing in the faith does not stop but continues throughout the life of the believer. While evangelicals emphasize Scripture as the primary source of catechesis, other Christian confessions historically have used additional sources as well; evangelicals in the Reformed tradition, for example, often look to the *WESTMINSTER STANDARDS for catechetical instruction. Evangelical Christians also insist that the personal experience of Jesus Christ is the most important key to any catechetical instruction. For evangelicals, the *experience* of Jesus is more important than knowledge of Jesus.

Cathedral of Hope (Dallas, Texas). *See* **Universal Fellowship of Metropolitan Community Churches.**

Cathedral of Tomorrow (Akron, Ohio). *See* **Humbard, (Alpha) Rex (Emmanuel).**

Catholic Charismatic Renewal The Catholic Charismatic Renewal, a pentecostal movement within the Roman Catholic Church, traces its modern roots to two influences: the *CHARISMATIC MOVEMENT, which emerged in the 1960s, and the Second Vatican Council, which blunted some of the sharper edges of Catholic traditionalism, advocated ecumenism (a drive toward Christian unity), and called attention to the work of the Holy Spirit. The immediate catalysts were two young theology instructors at Duquesne University in Pittsburgh, a Roman Catholic school operated by the Congregation of the Holy Spirit. The lay teachers, Patrick Bourgeois and Ralph Keifer, had been intrigued by *PENTECOSTALISM after reading *The Cross and the Switchblade,* by *DAVID WILKERSON, and *They Speak with Other Tongues,* by John Sherrill. They attended a charismatic gathering run by Presbyterians and soon received the *BAPTISM OF THE HOLY SPIRIT. In mid-February 1967, they conducted a spiritual retreat, which became known as the *DUQUESNE WEEKEND, in the course of which approximately thirty students received Spirit *BAPTISM.

The movement soon spread to the University of Notre Dame and to Michigan State University. During the weekend of April 7–9, 1967, about a hundred students and faculty from these three universities gathered on the Notre Dame campus for spiritual renewal. News of the meeting spread through the Catholic media and through students taking word of this "Catholic *PENTECOSTALISM" home for their summer vacation. Another meeting in South Bend, Indiana, at the end of the summer helped to solidify the movement; the transfer of two early converts, *RALPH MARTIN and Stephen Clark, to the campus of the University of Michigan eventually gave the Catholic Charismatic Renewal a second locus of activity: Ann Arbor, Michigan.

The Catholic Charismatic Renewal has held annual conferences at Notre Dame since 1967, and its influence has spread first to Canada and then to Latin America and around the world. Although it received the sanction of the National Conference of Catholic Bishops, many in the Roman Catholic hierarchy still look askance at the charismatic influences under their care. They distrust the enthusiasm of the Catholic Charismatic Renewal, even as they acknowledge that Catholic charismatics, through their prayer groups and through their innovations in worship, have injected spiritual fervor into moribund parishes.

References: Edward D. O'Connor, *The Pentecostal Movement in the Catholic Church* (1971); Kilian McDonnell, *Charismatic Renewal in the Churches* (1976).

Cattell, Everett L(ewis) (1905–1981) Born in Kensington, Ohio, Everett L. Cattell, a Quaker who was influenced by the *HOLINESS MOVEMENT, graduated from Marion College (now *INDIANA WESLEYAN UNIVERSITY) in 1927 and earned the M.A. in philosophy from Ohio State University three years later. He served as a pastor with the Friends (Quakers), an adjunct professor at Cleveland Bible Institute (now *MALONE COLLEGE), a missionary to India from 1936 until 1957, and president of *MALONE COLLEGE from 1960 to 1972. Throughout his career he was an apologist for missions—"the love of Christ gives us no choice"—although he warned against ethnic or religious superiority in the missions enterprise.

References: Everett L. Cattell, *Spirit of Holiness* (1963); idem, *Christian Mission: A Matter of Life* (1981); David L. Johns, "Everett L. Cattell and a

Theology of Christian Missions," *Quaker Religious Thought*, XXV (July 1992).

Cedar, Paul A(rnold) (1938–) Born in Minneapolis, Minnesota, Paul A. Cedar graduated from Northern State College, Aberdeen, South Dakota, and Northern Baptist Seminary. He was ordained in 1966 and served as pastor for churches of several denominations, including the *EVANGELICAL FREE CHURCH OF AMERICA, a denomination he would later lead as president from 1990 to 1996. He has taught as an adjunct or visiting professor in several seminaries and has served on the advisory boards of numerous evangelical organizations, including the John M. Perkins Foundation, Barnabas International, the Revival Prayer Fellowship, and the Billy Graham Institute of Evangelism.

Cedarville College (Cedarville, Ohio) Cedarville College was affiliated with the *REFORMED PRESBYTERIAN CHURCH when first established in 1887, but it is now a Baptist institution. Financial hardship nearly closed the school after World War II, and the trustees realized Cedarville's survival would depend on its ability to find another supporting denomination. At the same time, the trustees of Baptist Bible Institute of Cleveland were seeking a new campus; Cedarville College and Baptist Bible Institute were merged in 1953 by mutual agreement of both sets of trustees. James T. Jeremiah, the pastor who had first suggested the merger, was the first president after the transfer.

Every student pursuing a bachelor's degree is required to complete a minor in *BIBLE. Social *DANCING and membership in secret societies (including fraternities) are proscribed in the statement regarding student lifestyle.

Reference: Cedarville College Catalog 1995–96 (1995).

Center for Reclaiming America. *See* **Kennedy, D(ennis) James.**

Central Bible Institute (Springfield, Missouri) Central Bible Institute was one of the first pentecostal *BIBLE INSTITUTES. The school was founded in 1922 by the *ASSEMBLIES OF GOD, which also has its headquarters in Springfield, Missouri. The looseness of Central's academic program during its first few decades is testimony to the lenient academic standards many *BIBLE INSTITUTES were willing to tolerate. Central did not require a high-school diploma for admission until 1948, and it was not until the 1940s that the college even offered degrees. Afterward, however, the school began to seek accreditation, and standards were tightened.

From 1949 to 1957, the school was known as Central Bible Institute and Seminary, for while the denomination authorized a separate seminary in Springfield as early as 1961, it did not open until 1973. That seminary, first known as Assemblies of God Graduate School, is now Assemblies of God Seminary.

Reference: Virginia Lieson Brereton, *Training God's Army: The American Bible School, 1880–1940* (1990).

Central College. *See* **Huntington College.**

Central Female Institute. *See* **Mississippi College.**

Central Mennonite College. *See* **Bluffton College and Bluffton Theological Seminary.**

Central Pilgrim College. *See* **Bartlesville Wesleyan College.**

Central Wesleyan College (Central, South Carolina) Central Wesleyan College, established in 1906, is affiliated with the *WESLEYAN CHURCH. In 1994, Central Wesleyan had a minority student enrollment of approximately 20 percent, an enrollment rate significantly higher than the average for Christian colleges. The school maintains a cooperative agreement with nearby Clemson University. Central Wesleyan runs an adult-education program, Leadership Education for Adult Professionals (LEAP), at several extension sites throughout the state.

References: *Peterson's Choose a Christian College: A Guide to Academically Challenging Colleges Committed to Christ-Centered Campus Life*, 4th ed. (1992).

Cerullo, Morris (1931–) Raised in an Orthodox Jewish orphanage in New Jersey, Morris Cerullo was given a New Testament by Helen Kerr, a pentecostal woman who worked at the home. Kerr was fired for her actions, but when Cerullo ran away from the orphanage at age fourteen he sought her out. She arranged for Cerullo to stay with her brother in Paterson, New Jersey, and Cerullo began attending an *ASSEMBLIES OF GOD church. He received a Spirit *BAPTISM, became convinced of a call to preach, and studied at Northeastern Bible College in Essex Fells, New Jersey. After his ordination as an *ASSEMBLIES OF GOD preacher in 1952, Cerullo, who often billed himself as a "converted Jew," became a healing *EVANGELIST, beginning in 1956, linking up with the *VOICE OF HEALING organization.

Cerullo began building his own organization, called World Evangelism, in San Diego in the early 1960s. He started a monthly magazine, *Deeper Life*, in 1963 and moved into television in 1975 with *Helpline*. In addition to his healing *REVIVALS in North America, Cerullo has conducted campaigns elsewhere throughout the world, especially in South America. He has also tried to encourage evangelistic efforts by natives through his National Evangelist Crusades program. After a failed attempt to take over the remains of *JIM BAKKER's PTL empire in 1990, Cerullo managed to salvage the PTL Network, renaming it the Inspirational Network.

References: Morris Cerullo, *My Story* (1965); idem, *The Backside of Satan* (1973); idem, *A Guide to Total Health and Prosperity* (1977); David Edwin Harrell Jr., *All Things Are Possible: The Healing and Charismatic Revivals in Modern America* (1975).

Chafer, Lewis Sperry (1871–1952) The founder of *DALLAS THEOLOGICAL SEMINARY, Lewis Sperry Chafer was born in Rock Creek, Ohio, to a Congregational pastor and his wife. He studied at Oberlin College and in the early 1890s signed on with the *YMCA as an advance man and baritone soloist. Shortly after his marriage in 1896, Chafer became an assistant pastor in the Congregational Church in Painesville, Ohio, and in 1899 took a similar position at the First Congregational Church in Buffalo, New York, where he remained until 1901. He moved to Northfield, Massachusetts, traveled as an itinerant *EVANGELIST, and assisted in the music program at the Northfield summer conferences.

At Northfield, Chafer met *C. I. SCOFIELD, a teacher at the Northfield Training School. Chafer became enamored of Scofield's dispensationalist teachings, relocated to New York in 1915, and became an extension teacher for Scofield's correspondence school. Chafer eventually became pastor of Scofield's former church in Dallas, Texas, where he founded the

Evangelical Theological College in 1924, later renamed *DALLAS THEOLOGICAL SEMINARY. Chafer served as president and professor of systematic theology until his death.

References: Lewis Sperry Chafer, *Satan: His Motive and Methods* (1909); idem, *The Kingdom in History and Prophecy* (1915); idem, *Major Bible Themes* (1926); idem, *Systematic Theology* (1948).

Chalcedon Foundation Founded in 1964 by *ROUSAS JOHN RUSHDOONY, the Chalcedon Foundation is one of the leading think tanks for the *RELIGIOUS RIGHT. In addition to distributing Rushdoony's Reconstructionist materials, Chalcedon (named for the fifth-century church council) operates a Reconstructionist school and church, sponsors seminars, and publishes a monthly magazine, *Chalcedon Report*.

Chapel Car Ministries While riding a train through northern Minnesota in 1890, Wayland Hoyt, pastor of the First Baptist Church of Minneapolis, remarked to his brother about the absence of churches in the small towns along their journey. "Why couldn't a car be built so that it would contain a combination church and parsonage?" he asked. "The car could be sidetracked in these small towns and the people be invited in to hear the *GOSPEL."

Hoyt took his idea to Boston W. Smith, the *SUNDAY SCHOOL missionary for the American Baptist Publication Society in Minnesota. Smith was already using a railroad car for *SUNDAY SCHOOL; the coach would be parked on a siding on Saturday night and then used for *SUNDAY SCHOOL the next morning. Hoyt's idea intrigued Smith, who would eventually serve as superintendent of Chapel Car Ministries, under the auspices of the American Baptist Publication Society, from 1891 to 1907. Hoyt's brother, Colgate, organized a "chapel car syndicate," consisting of Charles L. Colby, John D. Rockefeller, John R. Trevor, James B. Colgate, and E. J. Barney, to underwrite the first car. Built at cost by the Barney and Smith Car Company of Dayton, Ohio, the first car, *Evangel*, was commissioned in 1891. The Northern Pacific Railroad agreed to transport the car wherever the missionaries wanted it. *Evangel* remained in service for thirty-four years, traveling throughout Minnesota, South Dakota, Montana, California, Louisiana, Arkansas, Kansas, Indian Territory (Oklahoma), Nebraska, Colorado, and Wyoming, before it was retired in Rawlins.

A second car, *Emmanuel*, was added in 1893, followed by *Glad Tidings*, *Goodwill*, *Messenger of Peace*, and *Herald of Hope*. The final car, *Grace*, was built in 1914–15. It traveled throughout the West, and from 1943 until 1946 it provided a venue of worship for workers at a World War II steel mill in Orem, Utah. The car, which was retired in 1946, is now on display at the American Baptist Assembly in Green Lake, Wisconsin.

References: R. Dean Goodwin, "On the Rails with the Gospel" (brochure); Wilma Rugh Taylor and Norman Thomas Taylor, *This Train Is Bound for Glory: The Story of America's Chapel Cars* (1999).

Chapel Hill Harvester Church (Atlanta, Georgia). *See* **Paulk, Earl (Pearly), (Jr.).**

Chapman, J(ohn) Wilbur (1859–1918) Born in Richmond, Indiana, J. Wilbur Chapman studied at Oberlin College, Lake Forest College, and Lane Seminary, where he graduated in 1882. After serving as pastor in Reformed and Presbyterian churches, he turned his efforts toward urban *EVANGELISM. As a protégé of *DWIGHT LYMAN MOODY, Chapman both employed and expanded upon Moody's *REVIVAL strategies, including what Chapman called the "simultaneous campaign," in which he coordinated his efforts with those of the local clergy. Chapman's techniques also recalled *CHARLES GRANDISON FINNEY's "*NEW MEASURES": daily preaching, noonday prayer meetings, songfests, extensive publicity, and newspaper coverage.

Chapman remained active in Presbyterian denominational affairs; he served as secretary of the Presbyterian Committee on Evangelism from 1902 to 1918 and was elected moderator of the General Assembly in 1917. Chapman also wrote several books and a number of pamphlets, tracts, hymns, and gospel songs. He compiled several hymnbooks and served as the first director of the *WINONA LAKE BIBLE CONFERENCE in Indiana.

Chapman, Steven Curtis (1962–) An acclaimed Christian songwriter and musician, Steven Curtis Chapman was born in Paducah, Kentucky. As the son of a record-store owner, Chapman grew up more exposed to music than many of his peers; his father also directed the local choir.

Chapman's debut album, *First Hand,* was released in 1987. Since then, he has recorded eight additional albums, including *The Great Adventure* in 1992. His 1996 release, *Sign of Life,* became a "Hot Shot Debut" when it entered the *Billboard* 200 at number twenty, making it the top-selling new release for the week of September 14. That same week "Lord of the Dance," the recording's first single, climbed to the top of the Christian music charts. When it did, it joined the ranks of the twenty-one other songs by Chapman to hit number one.

Over the past decade, Steven Curtis Chapman has toured in the United States, South Africa, South America, Europe, and Asia. Chapman has had three certified gold albums and earned three Grammy Awards and several additional Grammy nominations. His twenty-eight Dove Awards from the *GOSPEL MUSIC ASSOCIATION include being named Songwriter of the Year for seven consecutive years. Glen Campbell, *SANDI PATTY, and Charlie Daniels are only some of the artists who have recorded their own versions of Chapman's songs.

In 1996, Chapman was inducted into the Opryland Starwalk by the Nashville Chapter of the National Academy of Recording Arts and Sciences. He lives in Nashville, Tennessee, with his wife and three children, where he also continues to record on the Sparrow Records label.

References: Information provided by Sparrow Records; Chris Lutes, "Great Expectations," *Campus Life,* September/October 1997.

Charism *Charism* refers most specifically to the gifts of the Spirit that Paul talks about in his writings. These gifts include *SPEAKING IN TONGUES, prophecy, and healing. Love within the community of believers is also a gift of the Holy Spirit, according to Paul: The community is given the gift of love in Christ as the binding principle that allows for unity-in-diversity. The diversity of the community plays out in the variety of gifts that are given to individuals by the grace of God.

The charismatic renewal, brought about by the pentecostal movement, was a revivification of the experience of spiritual gifts within the early Christian community of believers. In 1901, in Topeka, Kansas, a woman who was prayed over received the gift of the Holy Spirit and spoke in *TONGUES. This experience began a movement that led to the splintering of the *HOLINESS MOVEMENT and to the rapid expansion of *PENTECOSTALISM. In the 1960s, the charismatic renewal was felt in the mainstream faiths and eventually influenced the experiential and liturgical life of many traditional churches. The belief that the gifts of the Holy Spirit were attainable by individuals through direct experience of the Spirit's presence has continued to cause division within some churches and even within evangelical Christianity. While all pentecostals are evangelical, not all evangelicals would define themselves as pentecostal, and some would reject the phenomena associated with being "Spirit-filled."

Charismatic The word *charism* is Greek for *GRACE. The evangelical use of the word is understood to include the direct action of God's *GRACE separate from any institutional hierarchy of the earthly church. *Charism* is the operation of the Holy Spirit upon the church as it manifests itself in various observable events. Evangelicals define these events as the fruits or gifts of the Spirit. In the Pauline references to these gifts of the Spirit, in whose writings the church finds its understanding of *charism,* the love of God as manifested by the Holy Spirit is responsible for the gifts given to the believer.

The renewal of these gifts, in unity with a life lived in harmony with the gospels' message, is a state sought by many evangelicals, especially pentecostals and charismatics, who pray for "baptism in the Holy Spirit." People who receive the *charisms,* or gifts, will exhibit them in their worship and in their lives. These include the gift of prophecy, the gift of preaching, healing, and *SPEAKING IN TONGUES (*GLOSSOLALIA).

Charismatic Movement Whereas classical *PENTECOSTALISM traces its origins to *AGNES OZMAN's *SPEAKING IN TONGUES on the first day of the twentieth century, the charismatic movement brought pentecostal fervor—including divine healing and *SPEAKING IN TONGUES—into mainline denominations beginning in the 1960s. The groundwork for such an incursion, however, was laid in the previous decade through the efforts of such pentecostal ecumenists as *DAVID DU PLESSIS, *ORAL ROBERTS, and *DEMOS SHAKARIAN, a California layman and founder of the *FULL GOSPEL BUSINESSMAN'S FELLOWSHIP INTERNATIONAL, a pentecostal organization.

The charismatic movement, also known as the charismatic renewal or neopentecostalism, erupted in 1960 among mainline Protestants with the news that *DENNIS J. BENNETT, rector of St. Mark's Episcopal Church, Van Nuys, California, had received the *BAPTISM OF THE HOLY SPIRIT and had spoken in *TONGUES. About a hundred parishioners followed suit, much to the dismay of other parishioners, members of the vestry, and the Episcopal bishop of Los Angeles. Although Bennett left Van Nuys for Seattle, he remained with the Episcopal Church, taking over a struggling parish, St. Luke's, and transforming it into an outpost of the charismatic movement. Bennett's decision to remain an Episcopalian illustrates the distinction between pentecostals and charismatics, even though both believe in the *BAPTISM OF THE HOLY SPIRIT. Whereas "pentecostal" refers to someone affiliated with one of the pentecostal denominations, such as the *ASSEMBLIES OF GOD or the *CHURCH OF GOD IN CHRIST, a "charismatic" remains identified with a tradition that, on the whole, looks askance at pentecostal enthusiasm.

The movement spread to other mainline Protestant denominations in the 1960s: the American Lutheran Church, the Lutheran Church in America (united in 1988 under the name Evangelical Lutheran Church in America), the United Presbyterian Church (U.S.A.), the American Baptist Church, and the United Methodist Church. Charismatic influences also took root in such unlikely settings as the Mennonites, the Churches of Christ, and the United Church of Christ. The *LUTHERAN CHURCH—MISSOURI SYNOD, however, vigorously resisted charismatic incursions, as did the *SOUTHERN BAPTIST CONVENTION, although *PAT ROBERTSON retained his ordination as a Southern Baptist until his campaign for the presidency in 1988.

Charismatic impulses made their way into the Roman Catholic Church beginning in February 1967, when a group of students from Duquesne University in Pittsburgh attended a spiritual retreat and received the *BAPTISM OF THE HOLY SPIRIT. The *DUQUESNE WEEKEND, as it came to be known, led to other gatherings of Roman Catholics looking for spiritual renewal, notably in South Bend, Indiana, and Ann Arbor, Michigan. Both venues became major centers of the *CATHOLIC CHARISMATIC RENEWAL.

The charismatic movement also finds expression in independent congregations and in a number of larger churches that have begun to form their own network of affiliated congregations, similar to denominations. Notable examples include *CALVARY CHAPEL in Santa Ana, California; Cathedral of Praise in South Bend, Indiana; Victory Christian Center in Tulsa, Oklahoma; Rock Church in Virginia Beach, Virginia; and *VINEYARD CHRISTIAN FELLOWSHIP in Anaheim, California.

Reference: Richard Quebedeaux, *The New Charismatics II* (1983).

Charismatic Renewal. *See* **Charismatic Movement.**

Charismatics Charismatics are those who claim the *charism*, or gifts of the Holy Spirit, and who are associated in some way with the *CHARISMATIC MOVEMENT. Traditionally, the distinction between charismatics and pentecostals has been that pentecostals are members of denominations that are entirely pentecostal (*ASSEMBLIES OF GOD, CHURCH OF GOD IN CHRIST), while charismatics are part of denominations that generally look askance at the spiritual gifts (Episcopal Church, Roman Catholicism, the Southern Baptists). Although that technical distinction remains, the two terms are often used synonymously.

Chastity The evangelical understanding of the term "chastity" means to refrain from sexual intercourse. This state is most often invoked in conjunction with the maintenance of virginity until marriage. However, the early church used the term to mean refraining from sexual intercourse, and it was not at all synonymous with the virginal state. Married people could and might, from time to time, remain chaste and refrain from intercourse for the purpose of religious discipline. Paul refers to this but cautions against the abuse of this practice. The term also referred to widows who remained chaste and virtuous, although not virgins, of course. Evangelicals, in response to the sexual revolution of the twentieth century, have emphasized the importance of chastity by means of teachings and sermons and through such organizations as *TRUE LOVE WAITS.

Chautauqua Institution The Chautauqua Institution, originally known as the Chautauqua Lake Sunday School Assembly, was formed in 1874 by Lewis Miller, an industrialist from Akron, Ohio, and *JOHN HEYL VINCENT, a Methodist bishop, in order to provide training for *SUNDAY SCHOOL teachers. The first gathering took place on August 4, 1874, at a camp-meeting site called Fair Point, on the shores of Lake Chautauqua in western New York, although the founders were anxious to distinguish the goings-on at Chautauqua from the excesses of *CAMP MEETINGS. Vincent, in particular, was "repelled" by *REVIVAL enthusiasm and feared that "the crowd called together on a *CAMP MEETING would not represent the sober, sane, thoughtful element in church life."

Chautauqua quickly evolved into a forum for adult education and cultural enrichment, not only at the grounds in Chautauqua but also through extension programs. In 1878, Chautauqua introduced the Chautauqua Literary and Scientific Circle, a four-year program of guided reading that is the oldest continuous book club in America. As many as one hundred thousand people enrolled in the course at one time; in 1885, for example, the state of Iowa had more than one hundred circles. In 1879, Chautauqua added two new programs, the Chautauqua Teachers Retreat (later called the School of Pedagogy) and the Chautauqua School of Languages. The School of Theology opened two years later. "The schoolhouse should be God's house," Miller declared in 1885. Chautauqua continued to offer a variety of courses, including a class in library science, which was taught by Melvil Dewey; he developed his famous Dewey Decimal System of library classification while at Chautauqua.

In addition to the programs at Chautauqua, an informal network of Chautauqua Assemblies (sometimes known as "little Chautauquas") provided educational programs in localities throughout the Midwest. They also attracted itinerant lecturers and performing artists. With the advent of mass media, the Chautauqua Institution became a summer retreat center and a center for the arts.

Reference: Joseph E. Gould, *The Chautauqua Movement: An Episode in the Continuing American Revolution* (1961).

Chicago Declaration of Social Concern The Chicago Declaration of Social Concern grew out of a workshop of evangelicals in November 1973 organized by *RONALD J. SIDER. The Declaration, which had fifty-three signatories, called upon evangelicals to take seriously the matter of social involvement from an evangelical perspective. It confessed to evangelical complicity in such social ills as racial and economic injustice, militarism, materialism, and sexism. The sentiment regarding sexism, introduced by *NANCY A. HARDESTY, one of only three female delegates, acknowledged that evangelicals "have encouraged men to prideful domination and women to irresponsible passivity." The text, originally drafted by *PAUL HENRY, a political science professor at Calvin College who would later be elected to Congress, was reworked by Stephen Mott, *WILLIAM PANNELL, and *JIM WALLIS. Subsequent meetings of socially concerned evangelicals, also held in Chicago, produced two organizations, the *EVANGELICAL WOMEN'S CAUCUS and *EVANGELICALS FOR SOCIAL ACTION.

Reference: Ronald J. Sider, ed., *The Chicago Declaration* (1974).

Childers Classical Institute. *See* **Abilene Christian University.**

Children of God. *See* **Berg, "Moses" David.**

Children's Bible Hour Begun in November 1942 in Grand Rapids, Michigan, the *Children's Bible Hour* is the longest-running children's program on religious radio. Originally an hour-long live broadcast, *CBH,* as it is known to thousands, was devised by David Otis Fuller, who responded to the plaint of a young girl that there was a lot of religious programming for adults but not much for children. In the 1950s, the show was taped for transmission, and in 1965 a fifteen-minute daily program called *Storytime* was added. The *Children's Bible Hour* airs over six hundred stations across North America and in a hundred foreign countries.

Chili Seminary. *See* **Roberts Wesleyan College.**

China Inland Mission. *See* **Taylor, J(ames) Hudson.**

Chiniquy, Charles (1809–1899) Born in Lower Canada, Charles Chiniquy was ordained a Roman Catholic priest in Québec City in 1933 and earned a reputation as the "apostle of *TEMPERANCE" for his success in securing pledges of abstinence. A bitter opponent of Protestant missions in Québec, Chiniquy attacked French missionaries and, at one point, engaged in a famous debate with *LOUIS ROUSSY, an associate of *HENRIETTE FELLER.

In 1851, Chiniquy was reassigned to St. Anne, Illinois, to serve French-Canadian immigrants, but his refusal to submit to the bishop of Chicago led to his excommunication in 1858. He and many members of his parish became Presbyterians in 1860, and Chiniquy became both an evangelical and a virulently anti-Catholic crusader. A prolific author and a popular, bilingual speaker, Chiniquy railed against Catholic schools and rituals and fueled fears of Catholic conspiracies in his travels in Canada, the United States, Europe, and Australia. Sometimes known as the Luther of Canada, Chiniquy advocated religious liberty against what he regarded as the perils of Catholic censorship.

Reference: K. Richard Lougheed, "The Controversial Conversion of Charles Chiniquy" (Ph.D. thesis: Université de Montréal, 1994).

Cho, Paul Yonggi (1936–) Born in Kyung Nam, Korea, Paul Yonggi Cho is pastor of the largest pentecostal church in the world, the Yoido Full Gospel Central Church in Seoul, Korea. He graduated from the Full Gospel Bible Institute in 1958 and was ordained by the Korean *ASSEMBLIES OF GOD in 1960. Central Church started in 1958, meeting in a makeshift structure pieced together from the remnants of army tents. After joining the *ASSEMBLIES OF GOD in 1962 and employing a system of home cell groups, the congregation grew rapidly, expanding its physical plant and adding more and more services to accommodate the crowds; by the mid-1990s, the church boasted a membership in excess of eight hundred thousand. Cho has emerged as a world leader of *PENTECOSTALISM, in part because of the church's television ministry, which reaches South Korea, Japan, and the United States, especially in cities with large Asian populations.

References: Paul Yonggi Cho, *The Great Power of Faith* (1965); idem, *Beyond the Adversity* (1969); idem, *The Key to Church Growth* (1976); Harvey Cox, *Fire from Heaven: The Rise of Pentecostal Spirituality and the Reshaping of Religion in the Twenty-first Century* (1995).

Chosen People Ministries Shortly after Leopold Cohn arrived in New York City from Hungary in 1892, he forsook his Jewish heritage and converted to Christianity. He founded the Williamsburg Mission in 1894 and started a newsletter, *Chosen People,* in an attempt to apprise Christians of evangelistic initiatives among the Jews. In 1924, Cohn gave the Williamsburg Mission a new name, the American Board of Missions to the Jews; the administration of the organization devolved in 1937 to Joseph H. Cohn, a graduate of *MOODY BIBLE INSTITUTE, after the death of his father, the mission's founder.

The San Francisco arm of the American Board of Missions to the Jews, headed by *MOISHE ROSEN, broke off from the national organization in 1973 to form *JEWS FOR JESUS. The original mission changed its name yet again in 1986, to Chosen People Ministries. The organization, now based in Charlotte, North Carolina, produces a daily radio program, *Through Jewish Eyes,* occasional television specials, and various evangelistic materials.

Reference: Joseph H. Cohn, *I Have Fought a Good Fight: The Story of Jewish Mission Pioneering in America* (1953).

Christ Evangelical Bible Institute (Phoenix, Arizona) "A place where all people can study the word of God," Christ Evangelical Bible Institute (CEBI) is a *BIBLE INSTITUTE for gay and lesbian Christians. Located in Phoenix, CEBI primarily prepares its students for ministry within the gay and lesbian community. The nondenominational school was founded in 1991.

As a Bible-based institution, CEBI does not enthusiastically endorse a "gay lifestyle." For example, the announcement for a course called "Christianity and Homosexuality" describes the class in the following manner: "One cannot effectively minister within the gay and lesbian community until he/she has reconciled his/her sexuality with the *BIBLE and the Christian faith. This course enables the student to consider what the *BIBLE really says about this subject." At the same time, the school's position of inclusivity has set it apart from most evangelicals. For this reason, it is unlikely that CEBI will gain official recognition from the *ACCREDITING ASSOCIATION OF BIBLE COLLEGES in the near future.

Yet while it exists on the margins of the evangelical subculture, CEBI has managed to assemble degree programs leading to either a bachelor's degree in ministry or a Christian worker's certificate. Christ Evangelical Bible Institute also offers correspondence courses. Like many fledgling Bible colleges, tuition is kept very low. In the mid-1990s, the cost was only $12.50 per credit hour.

Reference: Information provided by Christ Evangelical Bible Institute.

Christ for All Nations. *See* **Bonnke, Reinhard.**

Christ for the Nations Institute. *See* **Lindsay, Gordon.**

Christian Action Network A *RELIGIOUS RIGHT organization based in Forest, Virginia, the Christian Action Network was begun by Martin Mawyer, a longtime associate of *JERRY FALWELL, after Falwell disbanded *MORAL MAJORITY in 1989. Mawyer's agenda reads like boilerplate for the *RELIGIOUS RIGHT. He has vowed to resist "radical feminists and militant homosexual groups" and "atheist and amoral secular forces." Mawyer promised to thwart what he claimed was a plot to "put homosexual textbooks into every school by the year 1999," and he has directed considerable energies toward seeking the abolition of the National Endowment for the Arts, at one point issuing a "Declaration of War" to his mailing list.

Overtly political initiatives like this triggered an investigation by the Federal Election Commission (FEC), but the FEC has been notoriously lax in limiting the political activities of groups such as the Christian Action Network. The organization publishes a newsletter, "Family Alert."

Christian Advocates Serving Evangelism. *See* **Sekulow, Jay.**

Christian and Missionary Alliance The Christian and Missionary Alliance (CMA) was founded in 1887 as two separate societies, the Christian Alliance for home mission and the International Missionary Alliance for foreign mission. Both groups grew out of the work of ***A. B. Simpson**, a Presbyterian minister who left that church to pursue an independent ministry with an emphasis on missionary endeavors. The two societies merged in 1897 to form the Christian and Missionary Alliance.

The theology of the Christian and Missionary Alliance is strongly evangelical, holding to a belief in the ***inerrancy** and inspiration of the ***Bible**, the atoning work of Christ, and the premillennial return of Christ. Simpson's core doctrine, called the Fourfold Gospel, looks to Jesus Christ as Savior, Sanctifier, Sealer, and Coming King. The Christian and Missionary Alliance has a Statement of Faith, adopted in 1965 and affirmed several times since then. ***Polity** in the CMA is centered on the annual General Council, which is a conference of delegates from the churches. The council elects the board of managers and oversees the Alliance's affairs. Headquarters are in Nyack, New York. Membership stands at approximately 250,000 in nearly 1,800 churches. The Christian and Missionary Alliance supports over 1,200 missionaries in 53 nations.

References: Frank S. Mead and Samuel S. Hill, *Handbook of Denominations in the United States*, 10th ed. (1996); J. Gordon Melton, *The Encyclopedia of American Religions*, 3d ed. (1993).

Christian Booksellers Association The Christian Booksellers Association (CBA) is the largest trade association for the owners of evangelical retail businesses. Since 1949, the CBA has been committed to its mission of "the development and retail distribution of Christ-honoring product."

The Christian Booksellers Association is best-known for the two trade shows it holds each year: the International Convention and the CBA Expo. More than three thousand prospective vendors attend each of these events, which have become the focus points for marketing Christian products. The conventions showcase not only books but also gift items and inspirational music. The music industry, especially, has gained a considerable boost in the past few years by holding its own events in conjunction with the Expo meetings in Nashville, Tennessee.

The Christian Booksellers Association publishes a four-color monthly trade journal called *CBA Marketplace*. Formerly known as *Bookstore Journal*, it is the standard trade publication for the industry. The association also puts out a supplier's directory, as well as a catalog of materials to help retailers—from laminated labor law posters to customer service manuals and guides to successful direct-mail strategies. This catalog stands out from secular trade catalogs, however, in that it also offers products specifically designed for evangelical businesses, such as marketing kits aimed at churches and videos reviewing the various study *BIBLES available.

Like many trade associations, the Christian Booksellers Association offers a variety of support services to its members. One of these is the CBA Retail Development School, which runs two-day training sessions in connection with the Expo conventions. Furthermore, Christian bookstore owners can buy workers' compensation and property insurance as well as health, dental, life, and disability insurance for their employees. They also can participate in group credit-card services, reduced shipping agreements, and even an automated phone system.

References: Randall Balmer, *Mine Eyes Have Seen the Glory: A Journey into the Evangelical Subculture in America,* 3d ed. (2000); Deborah Evans Price, "Christian Biz Hails Smith's Chart Bow," *Billboard,* September 9, 1995.

Christian Broadcasting Network (CBN) In 1959, *MARION G. "PAT" ROBERTSON, recently graduated from New York Theological Seminary, purchased a defunct UHF television station in Portsmouth, Virginia, for thirty-seven thousand dollars and dubbed it the Christian Broadcasting Network (CBN). Two years later, he started broadcasting three hours of religious television per night in a talk-entertainment format modeled on the *Tonight Show.* In 1965, Robertson hired a husband-and-wife team of *ASSEMBLIES OF GOD evangelists, *JIM and* TAMMY FAYE BAKKER, to augment the programming. Robertson and the Bakkers found that their pentecostal theology coupled with an unabashed emotionalism held considerable appeal for evangelical viewers, and CBN used telethons, often punctuated with tears, in order to raise money and to expand its operations. Early on, Robertson had appealed for seven hundred viewers to pledge ten dollars a month; in 1966, he named his show the *700 Club.*

Financial success prompted expansion in equipment and in the acquisition of new stations, one as far away as Bogotá, Colombia. In 1977, Robertson, having moved his operations to Virginia Beach, began to invest heavily in satellite technology and became, with CNN's Ted Turner, one of the pioneers in that field. The move allowed for the rapid expansion of CBN into the cable television market. By 1987, CBN took in $135 million and had established affiliations with nearly two hundred stations; by the following year it reached nearly nine million homes. The network changed its programming in 1981 to "family-oriented" material and retained the *700 Club* as its sole religious program, bracketed by reruns of such staples as *Gunsmoke* and *The Andy Griffith Show.* In 1987, CBN began charging cable companies for its broadcasts and soon thereafter became a separate corporation, International Family Entertainment, which owns the Family Channel and broadcasts the *700 Club.* Robertson and members of his family made millions of dollars when the corporation went public, and they took personal profits of approximately $227 million when Rupert Murdoch purchased the company in 1997. The following year, CBN agreed to pay a "significant" penalty to the Internal Revenue Service and accepted a two-year, retroactive loss of tax-exempt status for having materially aided Robertson's run for the Republican presidential nomination in 1987 and 1988, thereby violating federal laws.

Christian Broadcasting Network University. *See* **Regent University.**

Christian Catholic Church The Christian Catholic Church uses the term "catholic" to represent the universal character of the church, namely, "catholic" in the sense that all true Christians are welcome. The Church was founded in 1896 by *JOHN ALEXANDER DOWIE, a flamboyant and controversial pentecostal leader. In 1901, he founded *ZION CITY, Illinois, which was named headquarters for the church. For many years, Zion remained a theocratic communal society, a community based—at least ostensibly—on biblical principles. Dowie was critical of the inequities of capitalism and the excesses of labor leaders. He condemned the use of alcohol and tobacco, opposed the use of medicines, and disliked the medical profession, secret societies, and the press.

Theologically, the Christian Catholic Church is orthodox evangelical. The *BIBLE is the rule of faith and practice. The Church also believes in the necessity of repentance from *SIN and a trust in Jesus Christ for *SALVATION, *BAPTISM by triune (three times) immersion, the *SECOND COMING of Christ, and tithing as the method of Christian stewardship. The Church has five places of worship and reports twenty-five hundred members.

References: Frank S. Mead and Samuel S. Hill, *Handbook of Denominations in the United States*, 10th ed. (1996); J. Gordon Melton, *The Encyclopedia of American Religions*, 3d ed. (1993).

Christian Church (Disciples of Christ). *See* **Christian Churches.**

Christian Church of North America This small (13,500 members) body's first General Council was held in 1927 at Niagara Falls, New York. Known originally as the Italian Christian Church, it incorporated in 1948 at Pittsburgh. Though pentecostal, it shies away from what it calls the excesses of some pentecostal churches. The Church observes two ordinances, the *LORD'S SUPPER and *BAPTISM. It is conservative and orthodox in theology. *POLITY in the Christian Church of North America is congregational, but district and national agencies are called presbyteries and are led by overseers. The body maintains relations with the Italian Pentecostal Church of Canada and the Evangelical Christian Churches (*ASSEMBLIES OF GOD in Italy).

References: Frank S. Mead and Samuel S. Hill, *Handbook of Denominations in the United States*, 10th ed. (1996); J. Gordon Melton, *The Encyclopedia of American Religions*, 3d ed. (1993).

Christian Churches The roots of the various modern groups of the Christian churches lie primarily in the work of three Presbyterian ministers: *THOMAS and *ALEXANDER CAMPBELL (father and son), and *BARTON W. STONE. *THOMAS CAMPBELL had come to the United States in 1807 and joined the Philadelphia Synod of the Presbyterian Church. Within only a few months he was removed from that role because of heresy. He then founded the Christian Association of Washington, Pennsylvania. In 1810, he was joined in the work by his son, Alexander. *ALEXANDER CAMPBELL formed the Brush Run Church. In 1813, the Campbells led their flocks into fellowship with the Redstone Baptist Association, and they remained a part of the association until 1830. The Campbells referred to their followers as "Disciples of Christ."

Stone had been a part of the celebrated *CAMP MEETING at *CANE RIDGE, Kentucky, and was pastor of the Presbyterian church there. After the *REVIVAL and because of his work in it, Stone was censured by the Synod of Kentucky. He and four other ministers withdrew from the synod and formed a new presbytery, the Springfield Presbytery. In 1809, they dissolved the presbytery to join what they saw as the wider, larger body of Christ. The group then took the name "Christian Church."

The religious ideas of both the Campbells and Stone are today grouped under the heading of the *RESTORATION MOVEMENT. The purpose of the movement was to restore the church to the ideal of New Testament Christianity. The leaders believed in the essential unity of the body of Christ; they could not accept the sectarianism that they saw all around them. These divisions in the church came from church polity, not from the *BIBLE. The Campbellites and the Stoneites took the *BIBLE as their only creed. They refused to establish any sort of hierarchy or *POLITY beyond the local congregation. Church structures of any and all types usurped the autonomy, the responsibilities, and the rights of the congregations. The leaders advocated *BAPTISM by immersion for adult believers and observed the *LORD'S SUPPER weekly. The Campbells and Stone believed that the local congregations, or societies, acting independently, could restore the whole of Christianity to its roots. In 1832, the "Disciples of Christ" and the "Christians" began joining, and the two names were used more or less interchangeably.

The local congregations gathered regularly in regional meetings for fellowship. These meetings occurred quarterly and annually. The congregations began to establish independent colleges and publishing houses. The first national convention took place in 1849. Its purpose was to further the work of the congregations and to represent them. The convention adopted the name "American Christian Missionary Society" and took on the tasks of church extension, foreign missions, and *EVANGELISM. This beginning step toward formal organization was not universally approved among the Christian churches. Nevertheless, the Missionary Society continued its work and developed other agencies as well until the turn of the twentieth century.

By the early 1900s, the number of agencies had grown to the point where some sort of centralized organization became desirable to some Disciples. In addition, over the years many Disciples congregations had begun using organs and other musical instruments in their worship, although instrumental music had been attacked as early as 1851 because it was seen as a departure from New Testament principles of simplicity. The "noninstrumental" Disciples published a separate yearbook in 1906, which is the date that is generally accepted as the time of their withdrawal from the Disciples. They called themselves the Churches of Christ. The Churches of Christ believe that they are to speak where the *BIBLE speaks and to be silent where the *BIBLE is silent. They accept no creed other than the New Testament. There is no formal organization. The churches do not recognize themselves as a denomination.

A second schism among the Disciples began in the 1920s. Some of the Christian churches reacted against the continuing centralization within the denomination. In 1927, these conservatives formed the North American Christian Convention. The Disciples churches reorganized in 1968 as the Christian Church (Disciples of Christ). When this occurred, four thousand congregations asked to have their names removed from the Disciples directory of churches. What began as a meeting of a particular group within the Disciples fellowship had evolved into a separate group that never has officially organized.

*RESTORATIONISM, which began with the hope of reuniting all believers in Jesus Christ into one church, ironically developed into three major, separate groups of churches: the Churches of Christ (noninstrumental), the Independent Christian Churches and Churches of Christ, and the Christian Church (Disciples of Christ). Only the Disciples have any formal structure. Furthermore, the Churches of Christ have themselves experienced dissension that has led to the birth of several other smaller independent Christian churches. All three groups continue to observe the *LORD'S SUPPER weekly and to practice adult believers' *BAPTISM. In general, the Churches of Christ hold to a more conservative and evangelical theology, differing from the Independent Christian Churches and Churches of Christ primarily on the issue of instrumental music in worship. The Christian Church (Disciples of Christ) has a more liberal theology, but in many ways is not far from its siblings in the *RESTORATION MOVEMENT.

Although exact numbers are difficult to determine due to the independent nature of the churches, the Churches of Christ report having more than 1.6 million members in 13,020 congregations; the Independent Christian Churches and Churches of Christ report nearly 1.1 million members in 5,700 congregations; and the Christian Church (Disciples of Christ) reports 930,000 members in 4,000 congregations. The main strength of these Christian churches is in the South and in the Midwest.

References: Frank S. Mead and Samuel S. Hill, *Handbook of Denominations in the United States*, 10th ed. (1996); J. Gordon Melton, *The Encyclopedia of American Religions*, 3d ed. (1993); *1997 Yearbook of American and Canadian Churches;* Richard T. Hughes and C. Leonard Allen, *Illusions of Innocence: Protestant Primitivism in America, 1630–1875* (1988).

Christian Coalition The Christian Coalition, an organization designed to foster the political activism of religious and political conservatives, grew out of *PAT ROBERTSON's failed attempt at the Republican nomination for president in 1988. At the inaugural festivities for George Bush in January 1989, Robertson met a young political operative, *RALPH REED, and asked Reed for his ideas on how to keep Robertson's political organization intact. Reed responded with a lengthy memorandum, which became the blueprint for the Christian Coalition.

Reed, who had headed the National College Republicans and who had worked for such conservative politicians as Jesse Helms and Newt Gingrich, soon demonstrated his genius for grassroots political organization. He eschewed the high-profile activism (like Robertson's campaign) that had been characteristic of other religiously and politically conservative efforts in favor of organization at the grass roots. The strategy proved quite successful. In November 1990, Christian Coalition-backed candidates were overwhelmingly successful in San Diego County, California; the "San Diego Model," also known as the "stealth campaign" because *RELIGIOUS RIGHT candidates refused to fill out candidate questionnaires or to make public appearances or statements, became the regnant strategy for the Christian Coalition. "It's like guerilla warfare," Reed explained. "If you reveal your location, all it does is allow your opponent to improve his artillery bearings."

The Christian Coalition, which was founded in 1989, the same year that *JERRY FALWELL terminated *MORAL MAJORITY, has proven remarkably effective in the political arena. The organization encourages voter registration of politically conservative evangelicals and distributes "voter guides," which provide highly partisan caricatures of candidates running for local, state, and national offices. The Christian Coalition also provides help for specific candidates, such as with Jesse Helms's imperiled reelection bid in 1990, and coordinates lobbying efforts on behalf of "pro-family" issues. Robertson clearly sees the organization as a tool for political power. "We want to see a working majority of the Republican Party in the hands of pro-family Christians by 1996 or sooner," he told the Coalition's first annual Road to Victory rally in 1991. "Of course, we want to see the White House in pro-family Christian hands, at least by the year 2000 or sooner, if the Lord permits."

In the 1990s, the Christian Coalition had proven itself so effective at grassroots politics that any Republican angling for the presidency had to court Robertson and his organization. That association, however, did not always pay off at the polls; many voters resented the influence of Robertson and the *RELIGIOUS RIGHT. In June 1997, Reed stepped down as executive director to form his own political consulting firm. He was succeeded by two men, *RANDY TATE, formerly a Republican member of Congress from Washington state, and *DONALD P. HODEL, who had served as a Cabinet member in the Reagan administration. Within a year of Reed's departure, the Christian Coalition announced retrenchments, including staff layoffs and a severing of ties to subsidiaries that had sought to reach African Americans and Roman Catholics.

Reference: William Martin, *With God on Our Side: The Rise of the Religious Right in America* (1996).

Christian College Coalition. *See* **Council of Christian Colleges and Universities.**

Christian College Consortium. *See* **Council of Christian Colleges and Universities.**

Christian Colleges and Universities Christian colleges date their founding to the *BIBLE INSTITUTES established in the late nineteenth century; although there are some exceptions, such as *ORAL ROBERTS UNIVERSITY and LeTourneau University, most Christian colleges began as *BIBLE INSTITUTES or secondary schools and gradually developed undergraduate programs in the liberal arts. A second wave of school founding took place after World War II, continuing into the 1960s.

Christian colleges differ from secular institutions by virtue of their attention to both Christian education and the liberal arts. Virtually all Christian colleges have required courses in Scripture and theology, but at the same time, an equal amount of attention is directed toward the sciences, humanities, and professional education—which makes them distinct from traditional Bible colleges. At some schools, however, these subjects might be taught from a religious perspective, so that it would not be unusual to learn the principles of Christian stewardship in a business class, or to study creation science in a biology classroom.

Many Christian colleges are affiliated with evangelical Christian denominations, though a substantial number are nondenominational. Most schools strive after regional accreditation, which is, in fact, a requirement for participation in the colleges' main professional association, the *COUNCIL FOR CHRISTIAN COLLEGES AND UNIVERSITIES.

In keeping with evangelical Americans' strict behavioral standards, the personal conduct of students and teachers is highly regulated. Christian colleges usually maintain "community guidelines," or "lifestyle agreements," in which students, faculty, and staff pledge not to drink, use tobacco, gamble, use or abuse drugs, or engage in proscribed sexual activity. However, the implementation of these codes varies—some schools require year-long obedience, both on and off campus. Others state that these issues reflect personal choices and insist upon compliance only on campus and during the school year. One gauge of the strictness of a college's lifestyle agreement is whether the proscription against smoking tobacco extends beyond campus. Another is whether or not the school permits social *DANCING, or *DANCING of any sort. Some schools attempt to cut a middle way through this injunction—not sponsoring social dances, for instance, or only sponsoring square *DANCING or aerobics classes.

References: *Peterson's Choose a Christian College: A Guide to Academically Challenging Colleges Committed to Christ-Centered Campus Life,* 4th ed. (1992); Thomas C. Hunt and James C. Carper, eds., *Religious Higher Education in the United States: A Source Book* (1996); William C. Ringenberg, *The Christian College: A History of Protestant Higher Education in America* (1984).

Christian Defense League. *See* **Swift, Wesley.**

Christian Destiny Ministries Christian Destiny Ministries, an evangelical media organization, was founded in 1963 by *DAVE BREESE, a popular conference speaker and former *YOUTH FOR CHRIST evangelist. The organization, now based in Hillsboro, Kansas, produces several radio and television broadcasts, including *Dave Breese Reports* and *The King Is Coming.*

Christian Echoes National Ministry. *See* **Hargis, Billy James.**

Christian Endeavor Christian Endeavor, the first evangelical interdenominational youth ministry, was begun in Portland, Maine, in 1881 by *FRANCIS E. CLARK, a Congregationalist minister. By the end of the decade, the movement claimed over half a million members who pledged to read the *BIBLE and pray daily, to adopt a Christian lifestyle, and to attend all the services of their local churches. Christian Endeavor sought to prepare young people for leadership in the church. Although the curriculum, coordinated under the aegis of the United Christian Endeavor Society, was generically evangelical, it allowed for particularities in creed theology according to individual denominations.

As those denominations began to develop their own youth programs, Christian Endeavor saw its influence diminish somewhat. Increasingly, the organization trained its sights on Third World countries.

References: Francis E. Clark, *Christian Endeavor in All Lands* (1906); idem, *The Christian Endeavor Manual* (1925).

Christian Financial Concepts. *See* **Burkett, Larry.**

Christian Flag The Christian flag, which is displayed in many evangelical and fundamentalist churches as a complement to the United States flag, was conceived in 1897 by Charles Carlton Overton, a Presbyterian Sunday school superintendent from New York. It features a red cross on a dark blue canton against a white field. Some time later a pledge was devised, one that students in Christian schools and vacation Bible schools often recite: "I pledge allegiance to the Christian flag, and to the Savior for whose kingdom it stands; one Savior, crucified, risen, and coming again, with life and liberty to all who believe."

Christian Growth Ministries Begun in Fort Lauderdale, Florida, in 1970 by four charismatics—*DEREK PRINCE, *CHARLES SIMPSON, *BOB MUMFORD, and *DON BASHAM—Christian Growth Ministries sought to impose some discipline on the charismatic renewal movement. Also known as the *SHEPHERDING MOVEMENT or the discipleship movement, the organization recruited dozens of churches, who then adopted a pyramid-style scheme of *AUTHORITY, with laity at the bottom, who reported to a church elder or "shepherd," who in turn was responsible to the pastor. The line of *AUTHORITY continued beyond the congregation to regional shepherds and finally to the central authority in Fort Lauderdale.

Allegations of abuse and cultlike behavior quickly emerged. Leaders of Christian Growth Ministries acknowledged some excesses in the mid-1970s, but the *SHEPHERDING MOVEMENT spread to the *CROSSROADS MOVEMENT within the Churches of Christ and to several Roman Catholic charismatic groups. Prince has since dissociated himself with Christian Growth Ministries, and the group moved its headquarters to Simpson's church, Gulf Coast Covenant Church, in Mobile, Alabama.

Christian Herald Christian Herald, an evangelical social service organization, traces its history to 1878 when Joseph Spurgeon, cousin of the redoubtable *CHARLES H. SPURGEON, arrived in New York City to establish an American version of the British weekly newspaper, *Christian Herald and Signs of Our Times.* With contributions from such evangelical titans as *T. DEWITT TALMAGE and *CHARLES SPURGEON, the newspaper increased its circulation and was purchased in 1890 by Louis Klopsch, who guided the continued growth of the publication and added social relief to the organization's agenda. In 1894, after having published reports of destitution among the poor of New York City, many of them newly arrived immigrants, the *Christian Herald* set up a winter food fund. With the surplus from the food fund Klopsch arranged for summertime outings for poor children to an estate owned by a friend in Nyack, New York. Christian Herald eventually purchased the property and operated it as Mont Lawn Camp.

In 1895, Christian Herald purchased the Bowery Mission, which had been established as an evangelical outpost in 1879 but had fallen into financial difficulties. The organization then expanded its evangelistic and relief efforts overseas, to such places as India, China, Japan, Hong Kong, Italy, Scandinavia, Cuba, and Palestine. At one time or another Christian Herald operated eleven orphanages throughout China, Korea, and Hong Kong, all the while continuing its relief efforts in the United States.

In 1948, *Christian Herald* announced the formation of a program called Family Bookshelf, "a club you can trust," which offered readers reliably Christian literature and provided the organization with revenue. Because of the encroachment of the New York City suburbs into the Hudson Valley, the organization moved Mont Lawn Camp to the Pocono Mountains of eastern Pennsylvania in 1961. Citing a decline in circulation and a financial pinch, Christian Herald relocated its offices in 1973 from Manhattan to the suburbs: Chappaqua, New York. In 1992, after more than three thousand issues, *Christian Herald* ceased publication, and the organization, which continued under the same name, devoted its energies to *EVANGELISM and social relief, including after-school programs for at-risk children, substance-abuse programs, and the operation of shelters for the homeless in New York City. Under the direction of Edward H. Morgan Jr., Christian Herald moved its offices back to New York City from Chappaqua in 1998.

Christian Identity Christian Identity refers to a wide variety of white-supremacist groups in North America. These right-wing groups are preoccupied with fears of racial mixing and Jewish conspiracy, and they claim that their beliefs are derived directly from the *BIBLE. The ideology of the Identity movement is heavily millenarian and draws upon the various expressions of *BRITISH ISRAELISM, the conviction that northern Europeans are the "ten lost tribes" of ancient Israel.

References: Michael Barkum, *Religion and the Racist Right: The Origins of the Christian Identity Movement* (1994).

Christian Jugglers Association According to its statement of purpose, the Christian Jugglers Association is a "non-denominational, non-profit association meant to encourage Christian jugglers, through interaction and participation with others of the same interest and the same faith." Membership is limited to jugglers who subscribe to a conservative doctrinal statement that affirms Trinitarianism, the infallibility of the *BIBLE, and the centrality of personal *CONVERSION.

Christian Methodist Episcopal Church. *See* **Methodism.**

Christian Mission. *See* **Salvation Army.**

Christian Reconstructionism. *See* **Reconstructionism.**

Christian Reformed Church in North America The Christian Reformed Church in North America was begun when nineteenth-century settlers from the Netherlands gathered in Michigan to form a church. This group, called the Classis Holland, received aid from the *REFORMED CHURCH IN AMERICA and, in 1850, became a member class of that body. By 1857, however, differences between the parent body and the newer members became too much to overcome, with the immigrants adhering to a more conservative, evangelical understanding of the faith. The Classis Holland split off from the Reformed Church to form the Dutch Reformed Church. Initially, growth was slow, limited primarily to immigrants from Holland. A series of name changes led to the adoption of the name Christian Reformed Church in 1904.

The doctrine and theology of the Christian Reformed Church are strict and conservative. The Church subscribes to three historic, ecumenical creeds: the Apostles' Creed, the Nicene Creed, and the Athanasian Creed. The Church also subscribes to three Reformed confessions: the Belgic Confession, the Heidelberg Catechism, and the Canons of the Synod of Dordt. A final, subordinate statement of faith is a contemporary testimony called "Our World Belongs to God," which the synod adopted in 1986.

The organization of the Christian Reformed Church is typically Reformed. The general synod meets annually to decide issues of church order and practice. Delegates to the synod come from smaller, regional groups, called classes. The classis meets more frequently to deal with matters of a smaller scope. The delegates to the classis are appointed by the councils of the local churches. The decisions of the synod and classis are binding on the local churches.

The denomination owns and operates *CALVIN COLLEGE AND CALVIN SEMINARY in Grand Rapids, Michigan, and is affiliated with several other colleges. The denomination operates its own publishing house. Christian Reformed World Missions sends missionaries to more than thirty countries around the world, and Christian Reformed Home Missions supports missionaries across North America. In 1995, after a bitter and divisive debate, the Christian Reformed Church allowed the ordination of women, prompting many conservatives to leave the denomination, whose numbers dipped below the three-hundred-thousand level of the early 1990s. The Christian Reformed Church in North America, with nearly one thousand churches in the United States and Canada, is based in Grand Rapids, Michigan.

References: Frank S. Mead and Samuel S. Hill, *Handbook of Denominations in the United States,* 10th ed. (1996); J. Gordon Melton, *The Encyclopedia of American Religions,* 3d ed. (1993).

Christian Research Institute Founded in 1960, the Christian Research Institute seeks to combat religious cults, new religious movements, and what it sees as the encroachment of secularism. Based in San Juan Capistrano, California, the organization publishes and distributes information on groups and movements deemed inimical to evangelical Christianity, and it produces a radio commentary, *CRI Perspective,* by Henrik "Hank" Hanegraaff, the organization's director.

Christian Sportsmen's Fellowship Begun in 1994 with the motto, "Our Target to Catch Men for Christ," the Christian Sportsmen's Fellowship is an Atlanta-based evangelistic organization for Christian hunters. The group publishes a magazine, *The Christian Sportsman,* and has nearly three hundred local chapters, which stage wild-game dinners as fundraising and outreach events.

Reference: Emily Yellin, "An Evangelical Group for Hunters," *New York Times,* March 26, 2000.

Christian Union Formed in Columbus, Ohio, in 1864, the Christian Union began as an attempt to draw all Christians into a unity in Christ. The body has no creedal statements, but holds fast to seven principles: (1) the oneness of the church of Christ; (2) Christ as the only head of the church; (3) the *BIBLE as the only rule of faith and practice; (4) good fruits as the one condition of fellowship; (5) Christian union without controversy; (6) self-government by local churches and a cooperative spirit among churches; and (7) avoidance of all partisan political preaching. The Union ordains both men and women and observes the ordinances of *BAPTISM—preferably by immersion—and the *LORD'S SUPPER.

*POLITY in the Christian Union is congregational. State councils and a triennial General Council oversee concerns of the entire body. State councils exist in Oklahoma, Missouri, Iowa, Arkansas, Indiana, and Ohio. The Union has foreign missionaries in several countries. A college, Christian Union School of the Bible, is located in Greenfield, Ohio, and the Christian Union offers an extension course of study through the staff of the college. The Christian Union has six thousand members in 114 churches, the majority of them in Ohio.

References: Frank S. Mead and Samuel S. Hill, *Handbook of Denominations in the United States,* 10th ed. (1996); J. Gordon Melton, *The Encyclopedia of American Religions,* 3d ed. (1993).

Christian World Couriers. *See* **Rader, Paul (Daniel).**

Christianity Today Founded in 1956 at the behest of *BILLY GRAHAM and his father-in-law, *L. NELSON BELL, *Christianity Today* was intended to provide evangelical ministers and laity with a theologically conservative and intellectually rigorous forum for the discussion of theological, ecclesiastical, and social issues. *CARL F. H. HENRY served as editor-in-chief until 1968; he was succeeded by *HAROLD LINDSELL and, in 1978, by *KENNETH S. KANTZER. The magazine, which derived much of its funding from *J. HOWARD PEW in the early years, was also meant to counteract the influence of the *Christian Century*, a similar magazine that identified with mainline Protestantism.

Christianity Today eventually overtook *Christian Century* in circulation, and it remains the most widely quoted religious periodical in the secular press. In 1977, the magazine moved its offices from Washington, D.C., to a new business park in Carol Stream, Illinois, adjacent to Wheaton. Though broadly *NEO-EVANGELICAL in orientation, the magazine has generally hewed to a conservative stance, both theologically and politically.

Reference: John G. Merritt, s.v. "Christianity Today," in Charles H. Lippy, ed., *Religious Periodicals of the United States: Academic and Scholarly Journals* (1986).

Christians for Biblical Equality Christians for Biblical Equality, an organization of evangelical feminists, was founded by Catherine Kroeger and other feminists after the more liberal contingent of the *EVANGELICAL WOMEN'S CAUCUS succeeded in taking over that organization at its 1986 meeting in Fresno, California. Resolutions supporting gay rights at the Fresno conference convinced the more conservative feminists that they could no longer be comfortable in the *EVANGELICAL WOMEN'S CAUCUS. Christians for Biblical Equality has hewed to a more conservative line in theology and on social issues, especially the matter of lesbianism. Its statement of faith includes the following declaration: "We believe in the family, celibate singleness, and faithful heterosexual marriage as the patterns God designed for us."

References: Nancy A. Hardesty, "Evangelical Women," in Rosemary Skinner Keller and Rosemary Radford Ruether, eds., *In Our Own Voices: Four Centuries of American Women's Religious Writing* (1995); Julie Ingersoll, "From Women's Lib to Feminism: A Brief History of the Evangelical Women's Caucus" (unpublished paper).

Christmas Conference. *See* **Methodism.**

Church Growth Movement In 1959, Donald A. McGavran, a missionary to India, founded the Institute of Church Growth, at Eugene, Oregon, an organization dedicated to enlarging evangelical congregations by means of a systematic analysis of large, successful churches, using the tools of the social sciences. McGavran's research led him to the conclusion that the largest and most successful churches are relatively homogeneous congregations, "a section of society in which all the members have some characteristics in common." The key to church growth, then, lay in targeting discrete communities of homogeneous individuals.

McGavran's pragmatic theories have been embraced by many evangelical leaders, who have parlayed them into large and growing congregations, especially in white, middle-class suburbs. In 1965, the Institute of Church Growth became part of the School of World Mission at *FULLER THEOLOGICAL SEMINARY.

Reference: Donald A. McGavran, *How Churches Grow* (1959).

Church of God (Anderson, Indiana) Founded in 1880 by *DANIEL WARNER, the Church of God (Anderson, Indiana) has its roots in the Church of God, General Council. Warner had been affected by the *HOLINESS MOVEMENT and was expelled from the Church of God. He wanted a church organized simply under the *AUTHORITY of God.

The denomination is not associated historically with the pentecostal churches of God but more closely with the churches of the *RESTORATION MOVEMENT. The denomination teaches that all believers are members of the church of God, emphasizing the concept of unity among believers. As a result, the Church of God (Anderson, Indiana) does not keep membership records as such. The Church does not claim that it is the only true church; instead, it offers fellowship to all who are "*BORN AGAIN" believers in Jesus Christ.

The Church of God (Anderson, Indiana) holds traditional evangelical beliefs such as the inspiration and *AUTHORITY of Scripture, and *SALVATION through the *ATONEMENT of Christ and repentance by the believer. In addition, the Church subscribes to the holiness belief in the *SECOND BLESSING of *SANCTIFICATION. The denomination observes the ordinances of *BAPTISM by immersion, the *LORD'S SUPPER, and foot washing. Baptism is regarded as a testimony of *CONVERSION, not for church membership, which the Church of God (Anderson, Indiana) avoids.

Church government is congregational. Ministers meet in voluntary state and regional conventions. The general assembly meets annually in connection with the international convention held at Anderson, Indiana. Although no official membership records are kept, the Church of God (Anderson, Indiana) reported in 1995 that there are 224,061 members in 2,307 churches in the United States. The Church operates *ANDERSON UNIVERSITY AND SCHOOL OF THEOLOGY, *WARNER PACIFIC COLLEGE, and a Bible college.

References: Frank S. Mead and Samuel S. Hill, *Handbook of Denominations in the United States*, 10th ed. (1996); J. Gordon Melton, *The Encyclopedia of American Religions*, 3d ed. (1993); *1997 Yearbook of American and Canadian Churches.*

Church of God (Cleveland, Tennessee) In 1886, at the Barney Creek Meeting House in Monroe County, Tennessee, a group known initially as the Christian Union was formed under the leadership of R. G. Spurling. The newly formed body wanted to preach holiness and the reform and *REVIVAL of the churches. The group experienced little growth for several years until the arrival of *A. J. TOMLINSON, an agent of the *AMERICAN BIBLE SOCIETY, who joined the Church and led the way into a period of rapid growth. Tomlinson introduced the practice of *SPEAKING IN TONGUES, and as the Christian Union grew it suffered persecution for its noisy and raucous worship. In 1907, the Christian Union adopted what it believed was the more biblical name, Church of God.

Tomlinson was elected general overseer of the church in 1909 and in 1914 was elected overseer-for-life. In the 1920s, however, a controversy arose over Tomlinson's authority, especially in regard to church finances. Tomlinson was removed from office and the overseer's authority was reduced. Tomlinson left to form the Church of God of Prophecy.

Church of God (Cleveland, Tennessee) theology is a blending of orthodox Protestant theology and specifically pentecostal themes, including justification by faith, *SANCTIFICATION, the *BAPTISM OF THE HOLY SPIRIT, *TONGUES speaking, and a decided emphasis on the premillennial *SECOND COMING of Jesus Christ. There is no formal creed; rather, the Church places its emphasis on the divine, verbal inspiration of the *BIBLE. The Church also stresses holiness tenets and condemns the use of alcohol and tobacco, the practice of gambling, and many other "negative forces." The Church accepts as ordinances *BAPTISM, the *LORD'S SUPPER, and foot washing.

The government of the Church of God (Cleveland, Tennessee) is centralized. Primary authority for the leadership of the Church resides in the biennial general assembly. Between general assembly meetings, the affairs of the Church of God (Cleveland, Tennessee) are conducted by a supreme council. A general overseer chairs the general assembly. In 1995, the Church of God (Cleveland, Tennessee) reported having 6,060 churches and 753,230 members. The Church operates *LEE COLLEGE in Cleveland, Tennessee, the Church of God School of Theology, and three Bible schools. The denomination also supports an extensive missions program.

References: Frank S. Mead and Samuel S. Hill, *Handbook of Denominations in the United States,* 10th ed. (1996); J. Gordon Melton, *The Encyclopedia of American Religions,* 3d ed. (1993); *1997 Yearbook of American and Canadian Churches.*

Church of God (Seventh Day). *See* **Worldwide Church of God.**

Church of God and Gospel Spreading Association. *See* **Michaux, Lightfoot Solomon.**

Church of God in Christ The Church of God in Christ (COGIC) was legally chartered in 1897 under the leadership of two expelled Baptist ministers. *C. P. JONES and *CHARLES H. MASON had both been dismissed from their respective Baptist churches for preaching the holiness doctrine of *SANCTIFICATION. They met and became friends in 1895. The charter and incorporation took place in Memphis, Tennessee, which became the denomination's home city.

In the early twentieth century, word spread across the country of the *AZUSA STREET REVIVAL in Los Angeles. Mason and two others went to Los Angeles to witness for themselves what was happening. Mason, an African American, himself experienced the *BAPTISM OF THE HOLY SPIRIT and began *SPEAKING IN TONGUES. He started preaching the doctrine as a further step after *SANCTIFICATION. The rest of COGIC was divided over the doctrine. Jones did not accept the belief. The dispute led to a split in which, in 1909, the courts decided that Mason and his group had rights to the COGIC name. Jones and his followers withdrew to form the Church of Christ (Holiness) U.S.A.

In many places COGIC was a racially integrated organization, although integration was more difficult in the South. COGIC ordained many ministers, both black and white, from independent congregations that did not have a denominational authority to do this. Mason even had a white secretary in 1918, William B. Holt, who was later appointed superintendent of Spanish missions in California. In 1914, a number of white pentecostal ministers, many of whom had COGIC ordinations, formed the General Council of the *ASSEMBLIES OF GOD.

The *POLITY of the COGIC has changed through the years. Initially, Mason was named the "General Overseer and Chief Apostle." His authority in matters of Church doctrine and organization was absolute, and he led the Church until his death at the age of ninety-five in 1961. After Mason's death the Church entered a period of study and reorganization, which led to a new constitution in 1972. The general assembly of COGIC is now the legislative and doctrinal authority in the church. Between meetings of the assembly, a twelve-man general board administers the work of the Church. The general assembly elects these twelve bishops from among the board of bishops, which is composed of all the bishops of the Church. One of the twelve bishops on the general board is elected as the presiding bishop.

Especially noteworthy in COGIC is the role of women. Women are not allowed to be ordained, but they may serve as missionaries and may be licensed at the jurisdictional level. Women often start new congregations, whose leadership is then turned over to a male elder to serve as pastor. Since 1911, COGIC has had a women's department, which has been a leader in the development of the missionary program of the Church. The first head of the women's department of COGIC was *LIZZIE WOODS ROBERSON, who gave Mason the funds to open the first COGIC bank account. Today, the department underwrites one third of the budget of the Church.

The doctrine of the Church of God in Christ is typical of the pentecostal *HOLINESS MOVEMENT. The Church believes in the Trinity, holiness, healing, and the premillennial return of Christ. Holiness is considered a prerequisite of *SALVATION. The Church observes the ordinances of *BAPTISM by immersion, the *LORD'S SUPPER, and foot washing.

In 2000, COGIC reported 5.49 million members in 15,300 congregations. The denomination has more than 6.5 million members worldwide. The Church of God in Christ is the largest pentecostal denomination in the world.

References: Frank S. Mead and Samuel S. Hill, *Handbook of Denominations in the United States,* 10th ed. (1996); J. Gordon Melton, *The Encyclopedia of American Religions,* 3d ed. (1993); Joe Maxwell, "Building the Church (of God in Christ)," *Christianity Today,* April 8, 1996; *1997 Yearbook of American and Canadian Churches.*

Church of God, Mountain Assembly The Church of God, Mountain Assembly grew out of a holiness *REVIVAL in 1895 in the South Union Association of the United Baptist Church. In 1903, the United Baptist Church revoked the licenses of all ministers who were preaching the holiness belief in the second work of *GRACE, which imparts *SANCTIFICATION to those who receive it. Three of these ministers met at Jellico, Tennessee, in 1906 and organized the Church of God. The words "Mountain Assembly" were added in 1911 after the group learned that other church bodies were using the name Church of God. In 1906–07, in the wake of the *AZUSA STREET REVIVAL, the group heard of the *BAPTISM OF THE HOLY SPIRIT and of *SPEAKING IN TONGUES as its evidence. The Church adopted this practice, viewing it as a fuller expression of their ideas.

Church of God, Mountain Assembly doctrine is similar to that of the *CHURCH OF GOD (CLEVELAND, TENNESSEE). The Mountain Assembly is very conservative in its faith and uses only the King James Version of the *BIBLE in its worship. The Church of God, Mountain Assembly meets annually. It has offices of general overseer, assistant overseer, and state overseer, but they work within an essentially congregational *POLITY. Headquarters for the assembly remain in Jellico, Tennessee. The latest available figures for church membership are more than twenty years old. In 1977, the Church reported approximately three thousand members in over one hundred churches.

Reference: J. Gordon Melton, *The Encyclopedia of American Religions*, 3d ed. (1993).

Church of Jesus Christ Christian. *See* **Butler, Richard Girnt.**

Church of the Nazarene An outgrowth of the *HOLINESS MOVEMENT of the nineteenth century, the Church of the Nazarene emerged from the merger of three independent holiness groups—the Church of the Nazarene, the Association of Pentecostal Churches in America, and the Holiness Church of Christ—at Pilot Point, Texas, in 1908. For some years, holiness leaders, notably *PHINEAS F. BRESEE, a former Methodist *CIRCUIT RIDER in Iowa, had been agitating to form a national organization. In 1895, after he had relocated to Los Angeles, Bresee had organized the first group to use the name Church of the Nazarene, and he became one of the primary forces behind the merger in 1908. The group originally took the name Pentecostal Church of the Nazarene, but they formally dropped "Pentecostal" in 1919 because the term had become associated with *SPEAKING IN TONGUES, something that the Nazarenes do not endorse.

The Church of the Nazarene derives much of its theology from the articles of faith espoused by British theologian *JOHN WESLEY. Their primary teaching is the doctrine of Christian perfection, or entire *SANCTIFICATION, which holds that the true believer is visited with a second work of *GRACE, subsequent to *CONVERSION. This entire *SANCTIFICATION, according to the Church of the Nazarene, renders the believer "free from original *SIN, or depravity, and brought into a state of entire devotement to God, and the holy obedience of love made perfect." Nazarenes also believe in biblical *INERRANCY, the second advent of Christ, and divine healing. Because of their emphasis on moral perfection, members of the church are expected to hew to strict standards of probity and morality.

Headquarters for the Church of the Nazarene are located in Kansas City, Missouri. The denomination operates a publishing house, a seminary, hospitals, clinics, and a number of liberal arts colleges in the United States, Canada, and Europe.

References: Timothy L. Smith, *Called unto Holiness: The Story of the Nazarenes: The Formative Years* (1962); Rebecca Laird, *Ordained Women in the Church of the Nazarene: The First Generation* (1993).

Church of the United Brethren in Christ The United Brethren grew out of German *PIETISM, a movement that emphasized the importance of spiritual ardor over against mere orthodoxy, which was seen as too intellectualized. The denomination was organized in 1800, and the membership concentrated in Maryland, Virginia, and eastern Pennsylvania. The United Brethren adopted a constitution in 1841, but controversy over the next forty years led to a schism in 1889. The heart of the controversy was the permissibility of church members also being members of secret societies, which were viewed by many as inimical to a healthy Christian life. Proposed changes in the constitution in 1889 allowed membership in secret societies, changed the makeup of lay representation at the general conference, and altered the confession of faith. The split gave rise to two churches, the larger United Brethren in Christ and the Church of the United Brethren in Christ. The former, after two mergers, eventually became a part of the United Methodist Church. The latter has remained independent, holding to the original constitution.

The United Brethren are Trinitarian, believing in the deity, humanity, and atoning work of Christ. The denomination still prohibits membership in secret societies as well as the use of alcoholic beverages. The United Brethren observe the *LORD'S SUPPER and *BAPTISM as ordinances. The church holds local, annual, and general conferences. The general conference is a quadrennial event composed of ministers, district superintendents (presiding elders), general church officials, bishops, and lay delegates. Both women and men are eligible for ordination to ministry. Headquarters are in Huntington, Indiana. The United Brethren in Christ maintain *HUNTINGTON COLLEGE and Graduate School of Christian Ministries, both in the hometown of the headquarters. The United Brethren reports 36,322 members in 390 churches worldwide. About 24,000 of the members and two thirds of the churches are in the United States.

References: Frank S. Mead and Samuel S. Hill, *Handbook of Denominations in the United States,* 10th ed. (1996); J. Gordon Melton, *The Encyclopedia of American Religions,* 3d ed. (1993).

Church of What's Happening Now. *See* **Jenkins, Leroy.**

Church on the Way. *See* **Hayford, Jack (Williams), (Jr.).**

Churches of Christ in Christian Union The Churches of Christ in Christian Union were formed in 1909 when the group withdrew from the *CHRISTIAN UNION due to a dispute over holiness practices. It was organized "to allow a complete freedom in the preaching of full *SALVATION as stated doctrinally by *JOHN WESLEY."

The doctrine of the Churches of Christ in Christian Union is typical of other holiness churches. It stresses divine healing and the *SECOND COMING of Jesus. There is a strong emphasis on *EVANGELISM, with *CAMP MEETINGS, *REVIVAL, and soul-winning crusades being common in the churches. *POLITY is congregational. A general council meets biennially in Circleville, Ohio, home of the headquarters of the Churches of Christ in Christian Union, and the home of the group's college, Circleville Bible College. The churches number 240, with 10,350 members.

References: Frank S. Mead and Samuel S. Hill, *Handbook of Denominations in the United States,* 10th ed. (1996); J. Gordon Melton, *The Encyclopedia of American Religions,* 3d ed. (1993).

Circuit Riders Early in the nineteenth century, the Methodists assigned young preachers to circuits, collections of settlements on the frontier. The preacher assigned to a specific territory would travel, usually on horseback, from one settlement to the next in a regular circuit, organizing congregations, conducting services, and providing the various rites of *BAPTISM, marriage, and funerals. In this way Methodism spread to the frontiers of the new nation, especially to the Cumberland Valley.

Citizens for Excellence in Education One of the organizations that falls under the rubric of the *RELIGIOUS RIGHT,

Citizens for Excellence in Education was founded in 1983 by Robert L. Simonds, a math instructor at Orange Coast College, as the activist arm of another organization, the National Association of Christian Educators. The purpose of the organization, Simonds says, is to implement "our Lord's plans to bring public education back under the control of the Christian community" and to overcome "the atheist dominated ideology of *SECULAR HUMANISM." Citizens for Excellence in Education opposes the teaching of evolution in public schools and advocates censorship of books the organization regards as "occult" or "demonic."

The organization's approach is, in Simonds's words, to "take complete control of all local school boards" by electing politically conservative evangelicals. In November 1992, for example, the group was largely responsible for the election of a majority of conservative evangelicals to the school board in Vista, California. Citizens for Excellence in Education, which claims to have chapters in all fifty states, distributes political action kits and handbooks with titles like *How to Elect Christians to Public Office.* In the late 1990s, however, as part of a larger retrenchment on the part of *RELIGIOUS RIGHT groups, Simonds inaugurated a program called "Rescue 2010," an initiative to encourage all fundamentalist parents to remove their children from public schools by the year 2010. Contributions to the organization, based in Costa Mesa, California, slumped dramatically.

Reference: *"In the Beginning": The Creationist Controversy,* two-part PBS documentary (1994).

Clap, Thomas (Stephen) (1703–1767) Born in Scituate, Massachusetts, Thomas Clap graduated from Harvard College and became pastor of the First Church in Windham, Connecticut. He became rector of Yale College in 1739 and then assumed the office of president in 1745 after a new charter provided for a change in title for the head of the school. Clap strengthened Yale's offerings in mathematics and science, and the student body increased during his tenure. He initially endorsed *GEORGE WHITEFIELD's preaching but later turned against some of the *REVIVAL excesses and supported a 1742 law against *ITINERANCY.

Clap further aroused the ire of evangelicals when he expelled *DAVID BRAINERD for his famous remark that a Yale instructor had no more grace than a chair. Clap switched from the Old Lights to the *NEW LIGHTS in the 1750s, however, principally because he sought to defend Calvinist orthodoxy against the Arminian tendencies of the Old Lights, who opposed the *GREAT AWAKENING. In 1753, he began preaching on campus and soon established the Church of Christ at Yale as an alternative to the Old Light First Church. Throughout his career Clap was no stranger to controversy. His policies gave rise to student riots, which forced him from office in 1766.

Clark, Francis E(dward) (1851–1921) Born in Québec and orphaned at the age of eight, Francis E. Clark graduated from Dartmouth College and from *ANDOVER THEOLOGICAL SEMINARY, whereupon he became pastor of the Williston Congregational Church in Portland, Maine. Clark was searching for a way to integrate young people into the life of his church and in 1881 organized the "Williston Young People's Society of *CHRISTIAN ENDEAVOR." The idea proved so successful that he helped to organize other *CHRISTIAN ENDEAVOR chapters; within six years the interdenominational *CHRISTIAN ENDEAVOR movement claimed over half a million members in seven thousand local societies.

Clark moved to Boston in 1883 as pastor of Phillips Congregational Church. He resigned four years later, however, to devote his full energies to the *CHRISTIAN ENDEAVOR movement, which he consolidated under the aegis of the United Christian Endeavor Society. He expanded his horizons by founding the World's Christian Endeavor Union in 1895. Clark was a tireless apologist for youth ministry; he wrote more than thirty books on the subject and edited a periodical, *Christian Endeavor World.*

References: Francis E. Clark, *Christian Endeavor in All Lands* (1906); idem, *The Christian Endeavor Manual* (1925).

Clark, Glenn (1882–1956) Born in Des Moines, Iowa, Glenn Clark graduated from Grinnell College in 1905. After several teaching and coaching jobs he joined the faculty at Macalester College in 1912, where he earned some recognition with the publication of *The Manual of Short Story Art* in 1921, which became a popular textbook for writing. The death of his father, however, triggered a spiritual crisis, which Clark wrote about in "The Soul's Sincere Desire," an article published in the *Atlantic Monthly*. The overwhelming popularity of the article, a meditation on prayer, prompted Clark to expand it into a book by the same title.

Clark's Bible class at the local Plymouth Congregational Church soon became a kind of laboratory of prayer and spirituality. He drew on his background as a coach to talk about training "spiritual athletes." In 1930, Clark conducted his first spiritual training camp, called Camp Farthest Out, which drew Christians, Jews, even those who were religiously indifferent. These spiritual regimens evolved into an organization that included a loose network of camps, called Camps Farthest Out, and a publisher, Macalester Park Publishing Company, which released the majority of Clark's corpus, more than fifty titles, all told. Clark and his sister, Helen Clark, started a magazine, *Clear Horizons,* in 1940, and Glenn Clark retired from Macalester in 1944 to devote his energies to these various organizations. Clark has become almost a cult figure to some, although there is no evidence that he encouraged such devotion. His camps and his meditations on spirituality have appealed to evangelicals, even fundamentalists, and to those with more liberal theological sympathies.

References: Glenn Clark, *The Soul's Sincere Desire* (1926); idem, *What Would Jesus Do?* (1950).

Clark, Gordon (Haddon) (1902–1985) Gordon Clark, an influential evangelical philosopher, was born in Philadelphia and earned both his baccalaureate and his doctorate from the University of Pennsylvania. He joined the faculty of *WHEATON COLLEGE (Illinois) in 1936, where he helped to shape a number of young evangelical minds, including *EDWARD J. CARNELL and *CARL F. H. HENRY, who later called Clark "one of the profoundest evangelical Protestant philosophers of our time." Clark's intellectual rigor and his unrelenting *CALVINISM, however, did not always sit well at Wheaton, which tended toward *FUNDAMENTALISM in temperament and *ARMINIANISM in theology. Clark was dismissed from the faculty in 1943 and later caught on at Butler University in Indianapolis, where he stayed for the remainder of his career.

Though exiled from evangelical higher education, Clark continued to write for evangelicals from his secular venue. He published a number of books, including *A Christian Philosophy of Education* (1946) and *A Christian View of Men and Things* (1951). He served as a contributing editor of **CHRISTIANITY TODAY* in its early years.

Clarke, Sarah Dunn (1835–1918) Sarah Dunn, born in Cayuga County, New York, spent her early career as a teacher in New York and Iowa before moving to Chicago, where she began a mission *SUNDAY SCHOOL among the poor in 1869. After marrying George Rogers Clarke, the two of them opened an urban mission, called Clarke's Mission, in 1877 (when the mission moved to another location three years later, it became known as the *PACIFIC GARDEN MISSION). More than anyone else, "Mother" Clarke was responsible for the conversion of *BILLY SUNDAY, then a ballplayer for the Chicago White Stockings but later a renowned *EVANGELIST. She was involved in all aspects of the operation until injured in an accident in 1912.

Reference: Carl F. H. Henry, *The Pacific Garden Mission* (1942).

Clarke, William Newton (1841–1911) William Newton Clarke was born into a Baptist parsonage in North Brookfield, Massachusetts. He graduated from Hamilton College in 1861 and served pastorates in Keene, New Hampshire; Newton, Massachusetts; and Montréal. He became an accomplished biblical expositor and in 1881 completed a commentary on the Gospel of Mark, which led to his appointment as professor of New Testament at Toronto Baptist Seminary in 1883. Clarke returned to the pastorate in 1887, this time in Hamilton, New York, but he joined the faculty of what would eventually become Colgate Divinity School in 1890 and quickly emerged as the school's most distinguished professor.

Clarke's theology, as set forth in his monumental *Outline of Christian Theology* in 1909, was unabashedly christological (emphasizing the centrality of Jesus). Christian theology, he insisted, "must have God for its center, the spirit of Jesus for its organizing principle and congenial truth from within and without the *BIBLE."

References: William Newton Clarke, *The Use of the Scriptures in Theology* (1905); idem, *An Outline of Christian Theology* (1909); idem, *Sixty Years with the Bible* (1909); William Henry Brackney, *The Baptists* (1988).

Cleaver, (Leroy) Eldridge (1935–1998) One of the leaders of the Black Panthers who converted to evangelical Christianity, Eldridge Cleaver was born in Wabbaseka, Arkansas, and was educated at a junior college and in Soledad Prison, where he served time for drug dealing and rape from 1954 to 1957 and again from 1958 until 1966. Cleaver wrote his radical treatise on black nationalism, *Soul on Ice,* while in prison, and its literary quality prompted a campaign to win his release. Cleaver, convinced that "there was no hope of effective freedom within the capitalistic system," became minister of information for the Black Panther Party in 1967 and ran for president on the Peace and Freedom Party ticket in 1968.

Cleaver's parole was revoked after a gun battle between police and Black Panthers in Oakland, California, left one Panther dead, another wounded, and a police officer wounded. Rather than face charges, Cleaver left the country late in 1968 and spent the ensuing seven years in exile, primarily in Cuba, Algeria, and France. His visits to various Communist regimes disabused him of some of his idealism; he eventually derided Cuba's economy as "voodoo socialism." Coincident with this political disenchantment Cleaver had a mystical vision, where he saw his own face on the moon, then the faces of his erstwhile heroes—Fidel Castro, Karl Marx, Friedrich Engels—and finally "in dazzling, shimmering light, the image of Jesus Christ appeared." Cleaver fell to his knees and experienced an evangelical *CONVERSION.

He returned to the United States and surrendered to federal authorities. A plea bargain sentenced him to twelve hundred hours of community service, terms so lenient in large measure because of his religious *CONVERSION. "Eldridge changed from one of the most vicious dudes against the system into a person who is reaching out," an ex-Panther remarked. "He's become a nice human being."

Evangelicals were somewhat wary of Cleaver, although he was embraced by some evangelical leaders, including *BILL BRIGHT of *CAMPUS CRUSADE FOR CHRIST. Their suspicions increased somewhat in 1978 when Cleaver opened a boutique in Hollywood that featured his own design for men's trousers, featuring a codpiece. The boutique was short-lived, and Cleaver founded an evangelical organization, Eldridge Cleaver Crusades, the following year. In 1984, he ran unsuccessfully for Congress as an independent conservative.

References: Eldridge Cleaver, *Soul on Ice* (1968); idem, *Soul on Fire* (1978).

Cleveland Bible College. *See* **Malone College.**

Coalition for Christian Colleges and Universities. *See* **Council for Christian Colleges and Universities.**

Coalition on Revival Founded in 1984 by Jay Grimstead, the Coalition on Revival has strong ties with the *RECONSTRUCTIONIST movement. Grimstead advocates the formation of county militias and the abolition of the Internal Revenue Service, public education, and the Federal Reserve Bank. He opposes abortion and gay rights, once declaring that "homosexuality makes God vomit."

The Coalition on Revival has sought to build bridges between Reconstructionist thought and political conservatives, and all members of the coalition's steering committee must sign the Coalition on Revival Manifesto, which includes a pledge to "work to Christianize America and the world." Grimstead added an activist arm in 1990 to the Coalition on Revival: the National Coordinating Council. He wants Christian leaders to "systematically attempt to rebuild our civilization" by means of a "spiritual army." Grimstead has targeted California as the Coalition on Revival's first beachhead: "I can tell you—it is the goal of a number of us to try to Christianize the state of California."

Reference: "The Religious Right: The Assault on Tolerance & Pluralism in America" (1994).

Coe, Jack (1918–1957) Born in Oklahoma City, Oklahoma, and later abandoned by his parents, Jack Coe was raised in an orphanage, which he left at age seventeen. While serving in the army during World War II, he "received a miraculous healing" and began conducting healing *REVIVALS while still in the armed forces. Ordained an *ASSEMBLIES OF GOD minister in 1944, Coe became one of the leaders of the healing *REVIVAL of 1947–1952.

Coe was blunt and plain-spoken, and his preaching drew African Americans as well as whites to his *REVIVALS, a characteristic of many pentecostal *REVIVALS early in the twentieth century. He had a knack for self-promotion and diversification. He published his own magazine, *Herald of Healing,* beginning in 1950, opened a children's home near Dallas, Texas, and in 1954 started a television series that quickly foundered. Coe apparently was obsessed with the size of his *REVIVAL tent, which he boasted was the world's largest. One time he surreptitiously measured *ORAL ROBERTS's tent and ordered one slightly larger, so that he could retain bragging rights.

Coe's dogged independence created friction with *ASSEMBLIES OF GOD officials, and after a long feud Coe was expelled from the denomination, whereupon he opened his own church, the Dallas Revival Center, in 1954. Two years later, while preaching in Miami, Coe was arrested for practicing medicine without a license and was released on a five-thousand-dollar bond. The two-day trial attracted national publicity, but the judge dismissed the case, ruling that he could not "condemn the defendant or anyone who in good faith advocates and practices Divine Healing."

In December 1956, in what one historian has described as "perhaps the greatest shock in the history of the healing revival," Coe became critically ill while preaching in Hot Springs, Arkansas. The man who had always been so outspoken against medical treatment was overweight and overworked; he consented to being treated in a hospital, where he was diagnosed with polio. After his death early the next year, Coe's wife, Juanita, continued his work for a time, but without the force of Coe's relentless ego and personality, the ministry faded.

Reference: David Edwin Harrell Jr., *All Things Are Possible: The Healing and Charismatic Revivals in Modern America* (1975).

Coker, Daniel (né Wright, Isaac) (1780–1846) Born into slavery in Maryland, Daniel Coker ran away to New York as a youth and was ordained a deacon in the Methodist Episcopal Church by *FRANCIS ASBURY. He returned to Maryland, purchased his freedom, and eventually assumed leadership of the African Bethel Church in Baltimore. A literate man, Coker organized a school for black children and worked closely with *RICHARD ALLEN of Philadelphia in the formation of the African Methodist Episcopal Church in 1816. Though elected as the first bishop of the new denomination, Coker refused the office. He left on a missions venture to Africa in 1820, where he organized several churches in Sierra Leone and Liberia.

Coley, Daryl (1955–) Gospel singer Daryl Coley was born in the San Francisco Bay area. His mother reared him and his two siblings alone in Oakland, California, where he sang with the Oakland Children's Chorus. As a young adult, Coley played keyboards for the Hawkins Family until 1977, when he collaborated with a variety of other artists. Coley's career as a singer in his own right began in 1985, when his debut album, *Just Daryl,* was nominated for a Grammy for Best Gospel Performance, Male. Since then, he has released five additional recordings, including *He's Right on Time,* which earned him a second Grammy nomination in 1990. Coley was nominated for a Grammy for the third time in 1993 for *When the Music Stops,* which reached number one on *Billboard*'s Gospel Albums chart. That year he won a Dove Award from the *GOSPEL MUSIC ASSOCIATION in the Contemporary Black Gospel Recorded Song of the Year category, for "Real," along with two other Dove Award nominations. *In My Dreams,* released in

1994, enjoyed a long run in the top ten on *Billboard*'s Gospel chart, and Coley also participated in the Grammy Award–winning *Handel's Messiah: A Soulful Celebration.* In addition, the singer has won two Stellar Awards and seven awards from the Gospel Music Workshop of America.

Coley has been invited to sing at the White House, the Kennedy Center, the Grammy Awards telecast, and the NAACP Image Awards. Like many Christian arrists, he credits God with his commercial success. Coley also cites his faith in God as the force that has helped him wage successful battles against both his own homosexuality and adult-onset diabetes. When not performing, he serves as pastor of the Love Fellowship Tabernacle, the church he founded in Los Angeles. Coley records on Sparrow Records.

Reference: Information provided by Sparrow media relations.

College of the Ozarks (Point Lookout, Missouri) Presbyterian missionary James Forsythe wrote to the Missouri Synod of the Presbyterian Church in 1905 asking for help to found a coeducational boarding school in the Ozarks. A year later, the School of the Ozarks was incorporated with the express purpose of providing education to impoverished but academically promising students from Missouri, Arkansas, Kansas, and Oklahoma. The school enrolled 180 students by the end of the first term.

Forsythe's academy remained a high school for fifty years, long after many other Christian academies developed post-secondary programs. In 1956, however, a junior college was added, and it earned regional accreditation within five years. The board of trustees voted in 1964 to introduce a four-year curriculum. The last high school class graduated in 1967. Full baccalaureate accreditation was granted four years later.

The School of the Ozarks changed its name in 1990 to College of the Ozarks to reflect its full transition to college-level status, yet its commitment to poor students remains as strong as it was in the beginning. The college has a policy that 90 percent of freshman admissions are reserved for students whose families would not otherwise be able to afford higher education. College of the Ozarks maintains what it calls a "covenant relationship" with the Presbyterian Church (U.S.A.).

Reference: College of the Ozarks 1995–97 College Catalog (1995).

Collins, Gary (Ross) (1934–) A prolific author of popular psychology books for evangelicals, Gary Collins was born in Hamilton, Ontario, and earned degrees from McMaster University, the University of Toronto, and Purdue University. Until late in the twentieth century, many evangelicals remained highly suspicious of psychological counseling, but Collins sought to overcome those prejudices. He has taught at a number of evangelical institutions, including *BETHEL COLLEGE, *TRINITY EVANGELICAL DIVINITY SCHOOL, and *LIBERTY UNIVERSITY.

References: Gary Collins, *Search for Reality* (1969); idem, *Overcoming Anxiety* (1971); idem, *Coping with Christmas* (1975); idem, *How to Be a People Helper* (1976); idem, *Psychology and Theology* (1981); idem, *Can You Trust Psychology?* (1988); idem, *The Biblical Basis of Christian Counseling* (1993).

Colorado Baptist University. *See* **Colorado Christian University.**

Colorado Christian University (Lakewood, Colorado) Colorado Christian

University, an interdenominational school, evolved in the 1980s with the merger of three schools. The first, Rockmount College, had been founded in 1914 and achieved regional accreditation in 1981. Rockmount joined with Western Bible College in 1985 to become Colorado Christian College. That college was consolidated four years later with Colorado Baptist University and became known as Colorado Christian University.

Colorado Christian University has graduate programs in counseling, curriculum and instruction, and management, and it operates an extensive adult-education program. Classes are offered on satellite campuses in Colorado Springs, Grand Junction, and Aurora. The university operates three FM radio stations in Colorado: KWBI, KJOL, and KDRH, which together reach listeners across the state, as well as parts of Wyoming and Utah.

Colorado Christian's biology department offers a full course in evolutionary theory, which is somewhat unusual for a Christian liberal arts college. Yet the structure of the course testifies to the religious emphasis of the school. In spite of the inclusion of such subtopics as "phylogenetic pathways," Biology 301—Evolutionary Theory also includes a component called "analysis of the biblical texts relating to creation."

Reference: *Colorado Christian University Undergraduate Studies Academic Catalog 1996–1997* (1996).

Colorado Springs Bible College. *See* **Bartlesville Wesleyan College.**

Colored Fire-Baptized Church of God. *See* **Fire-Baptized Holiness Church of God of the Americas.**

Colored Methodist Episcopal Church. *See* **Methodism.**

Colporteur A colporteur carried the *GOSPEL, usually in the form of *BIBLES and tracts, to the frontier, often riding the railroads. Both the concept and the term were borrowed from France, where itinerant peddlers carried (*porter*) a pack over their shoulders or around their necks (*col*). The *AMERICAN TRACT SOCIETY seized on this idea in 1841 as a way to distribute tracts and *BIBLES to sparsely settled areas in the South and the West. The "colporteur enterprise" expanded from its two original agents to more than five hundred ten years later, and as the commercial economy emerged, colporteurs began to employ the techniques of salesmanship. Other societies and churches also made use of lay itinerants, but the settling of the frontier—and with it the formation of churches—increasingly rendered the colporteurs unnecessary. By the turn of the twentieth century, the *AMERICAN TRACT SOCIETY had only about fifty colporteurs.

Colson, Charles W. "Chuck" (1931–) Charles "Chuck" Colson was one of Richard Nixon's most ruthless operatives in a scandal-plagued administration. He graduated from Brown University, served in the marines, and became "special assistant to the president." Colson once declared that he would do anything to ensure Nixon's reelection in 1972, even if it meant running over his grandmother. His *CONVERSION to evangelical Christianity in the midst of his legal troubles attracted a great deal of skepticism from people who suspected that Colson, like other indicted White House aides who professed *CONVERSIONS, was angling for favorable treatment by the courts.

Colson served time, however, in a minimum security facility, and his evangelical profession held up. Colson's account of his *CONVERSION, *Born Again,* published in February 1976, became a best-seller, and his time in prison led him to form Prison Fellowship, an evangelical ministry to convicts and their families. Colson was honored for his efforts with the Templeton Prize in 1993.

References: Charles Colson, *Born Again* (1976); idem, *Life Sentence* (1979); idem, *How Now Shall We Live?* (1999); Wendy Murray Zoba, "The Legacy of Prisoner 23266," *Christianity Today,* July 9, 2001.

Columbia Bible College. *See* **Columbia International University.**

Columbia Biblical Seminary and Graduate School of Missions. *See* **Columbia International University.**

Columbia International University (Columbia, South Carolina) Columbia International University is the combined name of three affiliated institutions: Columbia Bible College, Columbia Biblical Seminary & Graduate School of Missions, and the Ben Lippen School, which serves children in grades kindergarten–12. None of the schools are denominationally affiliated, and all maintain strict standards for personal behavior; social *DANCING, for instance, is not allowed. The University operates a one-hundred-thousand-watt radio station, WMHK-FM, which broadcasts religious programming and music across central South Carolina twenty-four hours a day.

Columbia Bible College was established in 1923 as Columbia Bible School, a two-year *BIBLE INSTITUTE. The school acquired its first campus four years later and moved to its current site in 1963. Although Columbia Bible College has a liberal arts curriculum, it remains grounded in the study of the *BIBLE. The college offers certificates and associate degrees in *BIBLE, which four-year students complete as part of their general education requirements. All students in bachelor's degree programs earn a major in *BIBLE; they then choose a "professional minor," or a second major. The department of biblical languages is noteworthy because it offers classes in Aramaic, in addition to Greek and Hebrew. The college offers two graduate degrees in education.

Columbia Biblical Seminary & Graduate School of Missions was organized in 1936 as the graduate division of the Bible College. First known simply as the Seminary/Graduate school, it took the name Graduate School of Missions in 1947. In 1973, the graduate school changed its name to Columbia Graduate School of Bible & Missions; fourteen years later, the school took its current name.

The seminary grants the master of arts degree, the master of divinity, as well as doctorates in ministry and theology. Emphasis has always been upon the training of foreign missionaries; though that focus has expanded somewhat to reflect a commitment to work in North America also, the seminary still seeks to impart a cross-cultural perspective to its students. The Seminary offers several concentrations in international or intercultural studies. It also runs an extension center, the Freie Hochschule Fur Mission, in Korntal, Germany.

References: *Columbia Bible College 1996–1998 Academic Catalog* (1996); *Columbia Biblical Seminary & Graduate School of Missions 1996–1997 Academic Catalog* (1996); William C. Ringenberg, *The Christian College: A History of Protestant Higher Education in America* (1984).

Common Sense Realism. *See* **Scottish Common Sense Realism.**

Concerned Women for America Concerned Women for America, one of the most influential components of the *RELIGIOUS RIGHT, was founded in 1979 by *BEVERLY LAHAYE, who resented the assumption on the part of the media that feminists like Betty Friedan spoke for all American women. LaHaye, whose husband, *TIM LAHAYE, had long been active in *RELIGIOUS RIGHT causes, proceeded to form a grassroots organization that grew to more than a half-million women by the 1990s. Concerned Women for America, which is based in Washington, D.C., bills itself as "pro-family" and vigorously opposes *ABORTION, feminism, *SECULAR HUMANISM, and homosexual rights. "Yes, religion and politics do mix," Beverly LaHaye declared in an interview in 1987. "America is a nation based on biblical principles, Christian values. Christian values dominate our government. Politicians who do not use the *BIBLE to guide their public and private lives do not belong in government." In 1997, Concerned Women for America claimed a membership of six hundred thousand.

References: Lori Forman, "The Political Activity of the Religious Right in the 1990s: A Critical Analysis," pamphlet distributed by the American Jewish Committee; Randall Balmer, *Mine Eyes Have Seen the Glory: A Journey into the Evangelical Subculture in America,* 3d ed. (2000).

Concordia Theological Seminary (Fort Wayne, Indiana) Concordia Theological Seminary in Indiana began in 1844, when Lutheran pastor Friedrich C. D. Wyneken was charged with training two missionaries at his parsonage in Fort Wayne. He joined forces two years later with a Bavarian minister, Wilhelm Loehe, who had been training Lutheran students for five years in America, to organize an actual seminary. In 1847, Lutherans in the Midwest organized the German Evangelical Lutheran Synod of Missouri, Ohio, and other States (Missouri Synod), and the new seminary was quickly handed over to the new church body. The Synod resolved in 1860 to merge the seminary in Fort Wayne with its school in St. Louis. The two schools functioned jointly in St. Louis until 1875, when Concordia Theological Seminary was moved to Springfield, Illinois. The seminary remained in Springfield for one hundred years, but it returned to Fort Wayne in 1975 to occupy the campus of Concordia Senior College, which had been absorbed into *CONCORDIA COLLEGE of Ann Arbor, Michigan.

Concordia Theological Seminary is accredited by the Association of Theological Schools in the United States and Canada and offers the master of divinity, master of sacred theology, and master of arts degrees, as well as doctorates in ministry and missiology. Concordia also offers distance learning through its Theological Education by Extension program.

Concordia Theological Seminary is still affiliated with the *LUTHERAN CHURCH—MISSOURI SYNOD and grants preference in admission decisions to members and children of members of that Synod and to members and children of members of other Lutheran church bodies. In keeping with the doctrinal position of the Missouri Synod, the seminary does not admit women into the master of divinity program or to any program that expects entering students to have completed a divinity degree. Women are "encouraged to pursue the master's of arts degree," the only course of study for which they are eligible. Furthermore, the wives of male candidates for the master of divinity degree must also belong to the Lutheran Church. As recently as 1996, Concordia

Theological Seminary had no women full-time faculty members.

The library places special emphasis on the areas of theology and the Lutheran church. Recognizing that many students in seminary make great financial sacrifices to pursue their education, Concordia sponsors a low-cost food cooperative, as well as a clothing cooperative, where students and their families can get free clothing and household items.

Reference: *Concordia Theological Seminary 1996–1997 Academic Catalog* (1996).

Concordia University System The Concordia University System is a consortium of ten colleges and universities across the United States that are affiliated with the *LUTHERAN CHURCH—MISSOURI SYNOD. Although the participating schools were founded as independent institutions, beginning in 1992 they adopted a system known as "simultaneous enrollment." Students at each of the campuses are cross-registered at the other nine institutions and can take a semester or a full year of courses at any other member college. The Concordia University System includes: Concordia College (Ann Arbor, Michigan); Concordia University at Austin (Texas); Concordia College (Bronxville, New York); Concordia University (Irvine, California); Concordia University Wisconsin (Mequon, Wisconsin); Concordia University (Portland, Oregon); Concordia University (River Forest, Illinois); Concordia University (St. Paul, Minnesota); Concordia College (Selma, Alabama); and Concordia University (Seward, Nebraska).

Reference: Roland Lovstad, "The Concordia University System," *Lutheran Witness*, January 2001.

Congregational Holiness Church The Congregational Holiness Church was formed in 1921 out of a controversy over divine healing in the *PENTECOSTAL HOLINESS CHURCH. The leaders of the faction that permitted the use of medicines also objected to the concentration of authority in only a few hands. This stance led to a democratization of church government, which developed into a congregational form of *POLITY.

The Church is Trinitarian in belief (God in three persons) and pentecostal in practice. It emphasizes the *BAPTISM OF THE HOLY SPIRIT, *SPEAKING IN TONGUES, and the inspiration and infallibility of the *BIBLE. The *BIBLE is the sole rule of conduct. The Church condemns the use of tobacco, slang language, membership in secret societies, and other forms of *WORLDLINESS. Ordinances of the Church are *BAPTISM by immersion, the *LORD'S SUPPER, and foot washing. The denomination claims 8,347 members in 174 churches, mostly concentrated in the Southeastern United States and Texas.

References: Frank S. Mead and Samuel S. Hill, *Handbook of Denominations in the United States*, 10th ed. (1996); J. Gordon Melton, *The Encyclopedia of American Religions*, 3d ed. (1993).

Conservative Baptist Association Formally organized on May 17, 1947, in Atlantic City, New Jersey, the Conservative Baptist Association grew out of an earlier organization, the Fundamentalist Fellowship, which had begun in opposition to the liberal or modernist tendencies within the Northern (now American) Baptist Convention. The Fundamentalist Fellowship had demanded that missionaries being sent out subscribe to a fundamentalist doctrine. The Northern Baptist Convention refused to follow the demand. The fundamentalists then established a foreign mission society of their own, the Conservative Baptist Foreign Missionary

Society. The Conservative Baptist Association churches split from the convention in 1947 and formed a separate, loose fellowship of churches.

Conservative Baptist Association doctrine holds to the infallibility of the Scriptures; to Christ's virgin birth, sinlessness, atoning death, resurrection, and ascension; to the Holy Spirit coming from God to convince the world of *SIN, righteousness, and judgment; to the sinfulness of all people and the possibility of regeneration (*SALVATION), *SANCTIFICATION, and comfort through Christ and the Holy Spirit. The group adheres fiercely to the autonomy of local congregations and to the ordinances of *BAPTISM and the *LORD'S SUPPER.

The association supports five schools, including seminaries in Denver, Colorado, and Portland, Oregon. Membership in the Conservative Baptist Association totals two hundred thousand in 1,127 local churches.

References: Frank S. Mead and Samuel S. Hill, *Handbook of Denominations in the United States*, 10th ed. (1996); J. Gordon Melton, *The Encyclopedia of American Religions*, 3d ed. (1993).

Conservative Congregational Christian Conference The roots of the Conservative Congregational Christian Conference date back to 1935, when H. B. Sandine began publishing a mimeographed newsletter. He was concerned over the departure of Congregational Christian churches from their historical and theological beliefs and practices. His concern, shared by many in the churches, led to the formation of the Conservative Congregational Christian Fellowship in Minneapolis, Minnesota, in 1945. During the previous year, news came out of a plan of union between the Congregational Christian Churches and the Evangelical and Reformed Churches. The process of the merger led to the Fellowship becoming a Conference in 1948. Although the merger eventually took place in 1959, giving rise to the United Church of Christ, the Conservative Congregational Christian Conference continued as an independent body.

The conference is staunchly conservative and Trinitarian in theology, holding fast to its fundamentals of the infallibility of the Scriptures, the virgin birth of Christ, the substitutionary *ATONEMENT, Christ's bodily resurrection, and Christ's miracles. The conference also professes the historical Puritan beliefs of the sovereignty of God, the sinfulness of humanity, redemption through Christ, the indwelling of the Holy Spirit, and the sacraments. Membership in the conference is limited to those who profess regeneration.

The conference has its headquarters in St. Paul, Minnesota. By the mid-1990s its membership stood at just under two hundred congregations with a total of 31,178 members.

References: Frank S. Mead and Samuel S. Hill, *Handbook of Denominations in the United States*, 10th ed. (1996); J. Gordon Melton, *The Encyclopedia of American Religions*, 3d ed. (1993).

Consistent Calvinism. *See* **New Divinity.**

Contemporary Christian Music Contemporary Christian music (CCM) is one of the fastest-growing areas of the music business today. Concert and annual album sales of sixty million units gave rise to a $750 million-a-year industry by 1996. Christian contemporary music, also known as devotional or inspirational music, or "white gospel," now amounts to as much as 10 to 13 percent of total sales in American popular music. Since the 1980s, it has outsold both jazz and classical, and by the mid-1990s more than five hundred radio stations in the United States were playing CCM.

The genre started in the 1950s with evangelical singer *LARRY NORMAN, an idiosyncratic songwriter who became the first evangelical performer who dared to combine rock music with Christian lyrics. Norman—who often asked rhetorically, "Why should the devil have all the good music?"—drifted into obscurity, but he paved the way for a number of other Christian musicians who expanded the style during the *JESUS MOVEMENT of the 1960s. After a short slump in the early 1970s, interest revived, thanks to the efforts of gospel partiarchs like *ANDRAÉ CROUCH and Al Green. In the 1980s, however, CCM emerged as a full commercial force, thanks to a Vanderbilt University student named *AMY GRANT, who made history as the first inspirational singer to have a gold record.

Grant's ability to "cross over" into the mainstream market and her subsequent rise to international fame inspired other evangelical performers to seek their fortune among larger audiences. Individuals like *STEVEN CURTIS CHAPMAN and *MICHAEL W. SMITH gave the style its trademark sweet, "pop" sound. At the same time, other musicians sought to incorporate Christian lyrics into a variety of styles. The rock group *PETRA, which had first performed in the 1970s, was joined by bands like *STRYPER and *WHITEHEART, so that by the 1990s Christian performers represented virtually all kinds of music: folk, rap, reggae, grunge, and heavy-metal.

The geographic hub for Christian music is Nashville, Tennessee, because so many gospel recording companies started out as the music division of evangelical publishing houses located there. Today, however, most of the major labels have been taken over by larger recording companies: Gaylord Entertainment owns Word Records; EMI bought Star Song, ForeFront, and Sparrow Records to create the EMI Christian Music Group; and half of Reunion Records—originally founded by *AMY GRANT's brother-in-law—is now controlled by the German music conglomerate BMG.

These acquisitions were shrewd marketing decisions for the parent companies; Reunion alone generates more than $70 million in annual sales. Following suit, other mainstream labels, like Sony and Arista, have begun to organize their own Christian music divisions, but it is not only the recording companies that invested in the growing CCM market. There now is a twenty-four-hour Christian alternative to MTV: *Z MUSIC. Every summer, concert promoters assemble music festivals like Inner Seeds in Atlanta and Cornerstone in the suburbs of Chicago, which attract audiences as large as fifteen thousand people.

The industry is expected to keep growing; in 1995, *Billboard* began to include sales receipts from Christian bookstores, where most inspirational music is sold, into its compilations for top-selling albums. *Billboard*'s new reporting also confirmed the industry's belief that more and more inspirational artists were reaching audiences that were not only evangelical. Not only have Christian artists increasingly made it high into the *Billboard* 200, they also have witnessed similar success on *Billboard*'s specialty charts, such as reggae, rhythm and blues, urban contemporary, and modern rock—thereby challenging the logic of considering CCM a homogeneous genre.

CCM often finds itself pulled in two directions, with dual accountability to Christianity and to the recording companies' bottom lines, for the tastes of secular and religious audiences often conflict. On the one hand, the possibility of entering the mainstream market has tempted many artists to reduce the religious nature of their music. At the same time, however, musicians have long been challenged to maintain a ministry in their music in an effort to mollify the Christian conservatives who can be suspicious of the genre's "worldly" connections. As a result, artists must demonstrate both a strong faith commitment and an ability to uphold evangelicals' lifestyle expectations: Star Song asks all signatories for a written statement of their mission, defining the focus and goals of their music ministry, and other companies have "morality clauses" in their contracts. Performers like *MICHAEL ENGLISH and *SANDI PATTY have found that failure to uphold these standards can cripple a performer's career. In recent years, a third facet has been added to the problem. The Christian music industry now has the monetary power to make the same kinds of artistic demands on performers that until recently only mainstream labels could levy. Artists who venture into new musical territory can find their efforts limited by Christian producers, who attempt to shape the music's content and style. Members of popular groups like *THE NEWSBOYS, *JARS OF CLAY, and *DC TALK have expressed frustration over this situation, but taking into account the fact that CCM emerged with a commercial infrastructure from mainstream music, the development was almost inevitable.

References: Nicholas Dawidoff, "No Sex. No Drugs. But Rock 'n' Roll (Kind of)," *The New York Times,* February 5, 1995; Christopher John Farley, "Reborn to Be Wild: Christian Pop Music Used to Be Soporific," *Time,* January 22, 1996; Jim Long, "We Have Created a Monster," *Christianity Today,* May 20, 1996; Ted Olsen, "Too Holy for the World, or Too Worldly for the Church? Christian Alternative Bands Look for a Home," *Christianity Today,* October 7, 1996; Earl Paige, "NARM Attendees Get Positive Word on Gospel's Potential," *Billboard,* April 3, 1993; Deborah Evans Price, "Michael English Declares his 'Freedom,'" *Billboard,* July 16, 1994; idem, "Christian Biz Hails Smith's Chart Bow," *Billboard,* September 9, 1995; idem, "Gotee Grows into Christian Boutique," *Billboard,* December 7, 1996; idem, "Christian-music Publishers Find their Way in Bigger General-market Companies," *Billboard,* April 19, 1997; idem, "A Field in Flux," *Billboard,* April 26, 1997; Adam Paul Weisman, "Gospel Music Rolls Out of the Church, Onto the Charts," *U.S. News and World Report,* August 25, 1986; Daisann McLane, "Onward, Christian Rockers," *Us,* May 1998; Jay R. Howard and John M. Streck, *Apostles of Rock: The Splintered World of Contemporary Christian Music* (1999).

Conversion Conversion, from the Latin *conversio,* (meaning "turning toward") is the centerpiece of evangelical faith and piety, a definite and decisive transformation from sinfulness to *SALVATION. Evangelical understandings of conversion derive from the third chapter of St. John in the New Testament, where Jesus tells Nicodemus that in order to enter the kingdom of Heaven he must be *BORN AGAIN. Most evangelicals believe that conversion is instantaneous, a datable experience of grace that signals the movement from death to life, from *SIN to *SALVATION, from darkness to light.

Conwell, Russell H(erman) (1843–1925) Born near Worthington, Massachusetts, Russell H. Conwell studied at Yale College, served in the Union Army during the Civil War—at which time he experienced a religious *CONVERSION—and graduated from Albany Law School in 1865. After a career as a lawyer and a journalist, which took him to Minneapolis, Minnesota, and to Boston, Conwell resuscitated a dying congregation in Lexington, Massachusetts, and was ordained in 1879. In 1882, he took on another struggling congregation, Grace Baptist Church, which became known as Baptist Temple, in Philadelphia, which by 1893 had become "the largest Protestant church in America," with a gymnasium, reading rooms, two hospitals, and a thriving *SUNDAY SCHOOL. Conwell, a pioneer in the institutional church movement, taught evening classes to workers who wanted an education but could not afford it; this enterprise evolved into Temple University. His program of theological instruction became Conwell School of Theology, which merged with Gordon Divinity School in 1969 to become *GORDON-CONWELL THEOLOGICAL SCHOOL.

Conwell, a gifted preacher, was one of the precursors of the *PROSPERITY THEOLOGY movement, which was based on the notion that God will make believers wealthy. His most famous sermon, "Acres of Diamonds," delivered over six thousand times, insisted that it was the believer's responsibility to become affluent in order to advance the cause of Christ. "I have come to tell you what in God's sight I believe to be the truth," he preached. "I say that you ought to get rich, and it is your duty to get rich." In contrast to the latter-day prosperity revivalists, however, Conwell made it clear that the purpose of wealth was not self-aggrandizement but the advancement of the *GOSPEL. "Money is power," he said. "Money printed your *BIBLE, money builds your churches, money sends your missionaries, and money pays your preachers."

References: Russell H. Conwell, *Gleams of Grace: Eight Sermons* (1888); idem, *The Life of Charles Haddon Spurgeon: The World's Greatest Preacher* (1892); idem, *How to Live the Christ Life* (1912); idem, *What You Can Do With Your Will Power* (1917); idem, *Borrowed Axes, and Other Sermons* (1923); idem, *Fields of Glory* (1925); Daniel W. Bjork, *The Victorian Flight: Russell H. Conwell and the Crisis of American Individualism* (1979); John R. Wimmer, s.v. "Russell H. Conwell," in Charles H. Lippy, ed., *Twentieth-Century Shapers of American Popular Religion* (1989).

Cook, David C. (1850–1927) David C. Cook, author and publisher of *SUNDAY SCHOOL materials and a leader in the *SUNDAY SCHOOL movement, was born in New York City. Beginning in his teens, he undertook a lifelong task of organizing and teaching mission *SUNDAY SCHOOLS. In order to provide inexpensive curricular materials, Cook and his wife, Marguerite, published *Our Sunday School Quarterly*. In 1875, they founded the David C. Cook Publishing Co., which eventually settled in Elgin, Illinois. The organization, which changed its name to Cook Communications, moved to Colorado Springs, Colorado, in May 1995. It remains an influential evangelical publishing house.

Reference: David C. Cook, *Memoirs: David C. Cook, the Friend of the Sunday School* (1928).

Cook, Robert (1912–1991) Born in Cleveland and educated at *MOODY BIBLE INSTITUTE, *WHEATON COLLEGE, and *EASTERN BAPTIST THEOLOGICAL SEMINARY, Robert Cook was ordained a Northern Baptist in 1935 and served churches in Philadelphia and Chicago. Cook succeeded *TORREY JOHNSON as president of *YOUTH FOR CHRIST in 1948, where he remained for nine years. After several years as vice president of Scripture Press, Cook became president of *THE KING'S COLLEGE, an evangelical school in Briarcliff Manor, New York. He hosted the college's radio program, *The King's Hour*, from 1962 until his death in 1991.

Cooper Memorial College. *See* **Sterling College.**

Cooperative Baptist Fellowship. *See* **Southern Baptist Convention.**

Copeland, Kenneth (1937–) Kenneth Copeland and his wife, Gloria, were converted to evangelical Christianity in 1962, and they moved from Fort Worth, Texas, to Tulsa, Oklahoma, in 1967 to study at *ORAL ROBERTS UNIVERSITY. Though he began working in Roberts's crusades, Copeland drifted more and more to the teachings of another pentecostal healer in Tulsa, *KENNETH E. HAGIN. Copeland, having attended many of Hagin's seminars, decided to drop out of *ORAL ROBERTS UNIVERSITY, return to Fort Worth, and begin his own evangelistic association, Kenneth Copeland Ministries, Inc.

Copeland quickly enjoyed success, in part because of his preaching but also because of his musical talents. In 1973, he started a magazine, *Believer's Voice of Victory*; he went on the radio in 1976, and he moved to television in 1979, where he became one of the best-known televangelists of the 1980s. Along with his mentor, Hagin, and other pentecostal preachers, Copeland preaches the "name it, claim it" theology, which promises believers not only improved health but considerable affluence if they pray with the requisite faith.

Cornerstone College and Grand Rapids Baptist Seminary (Grand Rapids, Michigan) Established in 1941, Cornerstone College in its early years operated as an evening *BIBLE INSTITUTE in the Wealthy Street Baptist Church in Grand Rapids, Michigan. The program had developed by 1944 into a day institute that offered two- and three-year programs and which grew to become two independent schools: *GRAND RAPIDS BAPTIST SEMINARY and Grand Rapids Baptist Bible Institute. Within fifteen years, the *BIBLE INSTITUTE incorporated the graduate school's pre-seminary liberal arts program and changed its name to Grand Rapids Baptist Bible College. The college acquired in 1993 the Grand Rapids School of Bible and Music, which had previously been affiliated with the Independent Fundamentalist Churches of America but was struggling financially. Cornerstone College became the official name of the merged schools a year later.

Cornerstone has a program in missionary aviation which combines FAA-approved training in flying with courses in Bible studies, and the well-established music department offers eight different bachelor's degrees. The college's internship program is also distinctive; every student is required to do an internship relevant to his or her major.

Still very much Baptist in orientation, Cornerstone describes itself as a "theologically conservative institution of Christian higher education." Social *DANCING and attendance at rock concerts are forbidden in its "Lifestyle Agreement."

Reference: *Cornerstone College 1995–1996 Catalog (1995).*

Council for Christian Colleges and Universities The Council for Christian Colleges and Universities (CCCU) is a professional association of evangelical colleges and universities. It was founded in the 1970s as the Coalition for Christian Colleges and Universities by the presidents of colleges that were members of the Christian College Consortium, to act as a "Council for Christian Colleges" that could expand the objectives of the consortium. An informal mailing drew a favorable response from thirty-eight colleges and universities, and in September 1976 the founding meeting of college presidents was held in Washington, D.C. The new organization was established with three objectives: monitoring legislation, public opinion, and judicial activity affecting Christian colleges; developing unified positions to present to the government and public; and creating "an offensive position on potential erosions of religious and educational freedom in the Christian college movement." The Christian College Coalition shared facilities in Washington, D.C., with the Christian College Consortium until 1982, when the consortium moved its headquarters to St. Paul, Minnesota. Also that year, the Christian College Coalition was formally incorporated as an entity independent from the work of its sister organization. By 1995, membership in the Coalition had reached ninety member institutions, and the organization had dramatically expanded its purpose and membership. That same year, the organization was renamed the Coalition for Christian Colleges and Universities, and in 1999 it changed its name yet again to the Council for Christian Colleges and Universities (in part to avoid being confused with the *CHRISTIAN COALITION).

Unlike *BIBLE INSTITUTES, the member colleges in the CCCU all have the liberal arts as their primary focus. To participate in the council, a college must have full, nonprobationary accreditation from the appropriate regional agency and an active hiring policy that requires each full-time faculty member to be a professing Christian. Other criteria include financial integrity consistent with the standards of the *EVANGELICAL COUNCIL FOR FINANCIAL ACCOUNTABILITY and commitment to the cause of Christian higher education through active participation in the council's programs and objectives. Although colleges rarely adopt such priorities merely to participate in the CCCU, such criteria often set the colleges outside the mainstream of American higher education. Many schools have been denied membership in Phi Beta Kappa on the grounds that their stance on religion inhibits academic and intellectual freedom; the CCCU, therefore, like the Christian College Consortium, was established to act as a counter to secular educational organizations.

The Council for Christian Colleges and Universities serves its member colleges through professional development, student programs, leadership initiatives, public advocacy and lobbying, and cooperation on joint endeavors among member schools. The council performs research on demographics, enrollment, and other issues relating to higher education, such as racial and ethnic diversity, an area where many of the schools fall embarrassingly short. The council offers national and regional workshops for faculty and administrators, including an ongoing series of faculty development conferences launched in 1983 with a generous grant from the National Endowment for the Humanities; provides opportunities for sabbaticals; and publishes materials relating to Christian higher education, like the Peterson's guide, *Choose a Christian College.*

The CCCU runs student programs in Washington, D.C., on public policy, a film-studies center in Los Angeles, as well as study-abroad programs in Costa Rica, Egypt, and Russia. The Summer Institute of Journalism is designed to help equip journalism students for future work in the profession. Students from member colleges can also attend classes at Oxford University Summer School, the *AU SABLE INSTITUTE FOR ENVIRONMENTAL STUDIES, and Jerusalem University College, or work at the Center for Urban Studies and the Center for Family Studies, through cooperative agreements with these institutions. To date, nearly three thousand students have participated in these programs.

Institutions that are outside of North America, that are not primarily four-year, undergraduate liberal arts colleges, or that do not meet the council's academic or hiring criteria may still participate in the CCCU as nonvoting affiliates. Currently, nearly twenty other schools are associated with the CCCU, including universities and seminaries in Korea, Canada, and Bolivia, as well as American schools like *FULLER THEOLOGICAL SEMINARY, *WILLIAM TYNDALE COLLEGE, and *PHILADELPHIA COLLEGE OF BIBLE.

Over the past two decades, the CCCU has become the leading organizing force for evangelical higher education. This accomplishment would not have been possible without support from a variety of sources. In the 1970s, the organization was headed by John Dellenback, the former four-term congressman from Oregon who directed the U.S. Peace Corps during the Ford administration. More recently, the council has had former Senator *MARK O. HATFIELD (R.-Oregon) as a member of its board of directors. Hatfield, now a professor at *GEORGE FOX UNIVERSITY, joined the board in early 1997.

Since 1989, the CCCU has received more than five hundred thousand dollars from the Lilly Endowment to assess and improve the fund-raising effectiveness of its member colleges. The council was able to launch a series of conferences and interdisciplinary projects in 1995 on population, consumption, and sustainability issues. This two-year initiative, the CCCU Global Stewardship Project, was funded with a two-hundred-thousand-dollar grant from the Pew Charitable Trusts as part of the Pew Global Stewardship Initiative.

References: Karen A. Longman, "Celebrating Twenty Years of Service: Coalition for Christian Colleges & Universities: Assessing the Mission of Church-Related Higher Education 1976–1996"; idem, "Celebrating Twenty Years of Service—Coalition for Christian Colleges & Universities: Historical Highlights, 1976–1996"; George M. Marsden, *The Soul of the American University: From Protestant Establishment to Established Nonbelief* (1994).

Council for National Policy Organized in 1981 by *TIM LAHAYE, one of the principal figures in the *RELIGIOUS RIGHT, the Council for National Policy provides a forum for leaders of the *RELIGIOUS RIGHT and for funders of politically conservative causes. The council is open by invitation only, and some of the participants have included *PAT ROBERTSON, *ROUSAS JOHN RUSHDOONY, *BEVERLY LAHAYE, *PAUL WEYRICH, *JERRY FALWELL, *PHYLLIS SCHLAFLY, *D. JAMES KENNEDY, *JAMES DOBSON, *GARY L. BAUER, Richard DeVos, and members of the Coors family.

Country Music Combining gospel, bluegrass, and folk music, country music evolved out of the country barn-dance tradition, where the poor people of Appalachia would gather to forget their troubles and celebrate their traditions. The theology that informs country music is unmistakably evangelical and overwhelmingly Arminian, emphasizing the possibility of redemption out of ruin, salvation out of *SIN.

References: Curtis W. Ellison, *Country Music Culture: From Hard Times to Heaven* (1995); Lee Smith, *The Devil's Dream* (1992); Lesley Sussman, *Yes, Lord, I'm Comin' Home!: Country Music Stars Share Their Stories of Knowing God* (1997).

Covenant College (Lookout Mountain, Tennessee) Covenant College is the liberal arts college of the *PRESBYTERIAN CHURCH IN AMERICA, but it was originally affiliated with the *REFORMED PRESBYTERIAN CHURCH, EVANGELICAL SYNOD. When the Evangelical Synod joined the *PRESBYTERIAN CHURCH IN AMERICA in 1982, the college became part of that denomination. Its board of trustees is elected by the *PRESBYTERIAN CHURCH IN AMERICA.

Covenant College was organized in 1955 by the Bible Presbyterian Synod of Reformed Presbyterians. First operating as a Christian liberal arts school in Pasadena, California, classes were held in the Pasadena City Church. The college moved to Creve Coeur, a suburb of St. Louis, in 1956. There, with the help of faculty from *FAITH THEOLOGICAL SEMINARY in Philadelphia, the school grew into a four-year college and three-year seminary. By 1963, both Covenant College and Seminary had outgrown their facilities, and the college had been adopted by the *REFORMED PRESBYTERIAN CHURCH, EVANGELICAL SYNOD. Covenant College therefore made another long-distance move, to Lookout Mountain, Tennessee, in 1964. The Tennessee campus once was a resort, the Lookout Mountain Hotel, also known as the "Castle in the Clouds."

Covenant prohibits the on-campus use of alcohol or tobacco and social *DANCING at all times. The college's "Conduct Statement," however, includes a section addressing "Situations where discretion may be exercised," in which these restrictions are partially waived for older or married students, commuters, and students acting under the authority of their parents or a church, as well as for all students during periods when school is not in session. In addition to its baccalaureate studies, Covenant offers a master's program in education.

References: *Covenant College Academic Bulletin* (1995); *Peterson's Choose A Christian College: A Guide to Academically Challenging Colleges Committed to Christ-Centered Campus Life,* 4th ed. (1992).

Cowboys for Christ Based in Fort Worth, Texas, Cowboys for Christ is an evangelistic organization founded in 1971 by Ted Pressley, a former rodeo cowboy and a graduate of Southwestern Baptist Theological Seminary. The group, which has fifty chapters, holds worship services at rodeos, livestock events, and horse races and conducts weddings and baptisms.

Crandall, Joseph (1771–1858) Although he served in the New Brunswick Assembly from 1818 to 1824, Joseph Crandall's most important work was as a leader of the New Light Baptists in New Brunswick. Born in Tiverton, Rhode Island, Crandall migrated with his parents to Nova Scotia just prior to the American Revolution. After his *CONVERSION in 1795, Crandall became convinced that believer's *BAPTISM was a central tenet of evangelical Christianity. He began preaching throughout Nova Scotia and eastern New Brunswick and was ordained as a Baptist minister in 1799. Crandall soon thereafter embarked on a missionary tour of New Brunswick, prompting *CONVERSIONS and a demand for *BAPTISM by immersion. In one infamous case, Crandall baptized fourteen believers in the icy waters of Saint John River at Kingsclear, New Brunswick.

Reference: G. A. Rawlyk, *The Canada Fire: Radical Evangelicalism in British North America, 1775–1812* (1994).

Crawford, Florence (Louise) (1872–1936) Reared in an atheist home, Florence Crawford had a religious *CONVERSION shortly before she attended the *AZUSA

STREET REVIVAL in 1906. The mother of two, Crawford was baptized in the Spirit and was healed of the spinal meningitis that had been with her since a childhood injury. She recounted that at Azusa Street "a sound like a rushing, mighty wind filled the room, and I was baptized with the Holy Ghost and fire." Crawford's involvement with the *AZUSA STREET MISSION led to a break with her husband, but she persevered and became an itinerant preacher for the Apostolic Faith Church in Canada, Washington, and her native Oregon, where she founded the Apostolic Faith Church in Portland. Crawford disapproved of *WILLIAM J. SEYMOUR's interracial marriage in 1908, and her transfer of the *Apostolic Faith* paper and its mailing list to her base in Portland further alienated her from Seymour.

Crawford, Lois (1892–1986) One of the pioneers of religious broadcasting, Lois Crawford was ordained a Congregationalist in 1923, and she was the first American woman granted a first-class radio telephone license. The station, KFGQ, was created in 1927 in Boone, Iowa, as an evangelistic tool for her father's Bible college. The modest ten-watt transmitter carried the signal of the first religious radio station west of the Mississippi. Lois Crawford, who became the first woman inducted into the *NATIONAL RELIGIOUS BROADCASTERS hall of fame, eventually succeeded her father as pastor of Boone Biblical Church and as president of Boone Biblical Ministries, which included a retirement home, a youth camp, a day school, and a bookstore.

Crawford, Percy (B.) (1902–1960) Born in Minnedosa, Manitoba, Percy Crawford had a *BORN-AGAIN experience at the Church of the Open Door in Los Angeles. He attended the *BIBLE INSTITUTE OF LOS ANGELES (Biola), *WHEATON COLLEGE, *WESTMINSTER THEOLOGICAL SEMINARY, and the University of Pennsylvania. In the 1930s, Crawford organized Saturday-night youth gatherings, which provided the model for the early *YOUTH FOR CHRIST rallies.

Crawford, based in Philadelphia, was also one of fundamentalism's pioneers in the use of media. In 1931, he inaugurated a radio program, *Young People's Church of the Air,* which aired on the Mutual and American broadcasting networks. On October 9, 1949, Crawford aired the first coast-to-coast television broadcast of an evangelistic program in the United States, thus heralding the advent of *TELEVANGELISM. The television program, *Youth on the March,* ran nationwide on Sunday evenings. Crawford, a compelling preacher, also founded the Pinebrook Bible Conference, in Stroudsburg, Pennsylvania, and *THE KING'S COLLEGE, in Briarcliff Manor, New York.

Creationism Also known as scientific creationism or creation science, creationism rests upon the conviction that the Genesis account of creation should be interpreted literally. Since the publication of Charles Darwin's *The Origin of Species* in 1859, creationists have sought to refute Darwin's theories. A showdown between these two camps took place in July 1925 in a steamy courtroom in Dayton, Tennessee. The scorn and ridicule that Clarence Darrow and H. L. Mencken heaped upon fundamentalists at the *SCOPES TRIAL generally discredited creationists in the eyes of the general public, although creationists largely succeeded in keeping Darwinism out of public school curricula until the 1960s.

With the rise of the *RELIGIOUS RIGHT in the 1980s, creationists again sought to thwart the teaching of evolution in the public schools. Some creationist societies tried to bolster their arguments for Genesis with "scientific" evidence, thereby appropriating the moniker "scientific creation." The election of fundamentalist majorities to the school board in several communities set up a showdown between creationists and people who believed that creationism was in fact a religious ideology.

References: Garry Wills, *Under God: Religion and American Politics* (1990); Phillip E. Johnson, *Darwin on Trial* (1991); Duane T. Gish, *Creation Scientists Answer Their Critics* (1993); *"In the Beginning": The Creationist Controversy,* two-part PBS documentary (1994).

Criswell, W(allie) A(mos) (1909–) Born into poverty in Eldorado, Oklahoma, W. A. Criswell was converted to evangelical Christianity at the age of ten; two years later he pledged to enter the ministry. While a student at *BAYLOR UNIVERSITY, Criswell became known as a gifted preacher with a strong voice that, according to legend, could be heard five miles away. He went on to study theology under such Southern Baptist stalwarts as John R. Sampey and *A. T. ROBINSON at Southern Baptist Theological Seminary, where he earned a master's degree and a doctorate.

Criswell assumed his first pastorate in Chickasha, Oklahoma, and became known as the "holy roller preacher with a Ph.D." He continued to hone his preaching at the First Baptist Church in Muskogee, Oklahoma, and then took the pulpit at First Baptist Church in Dallas, Texas, in 1944, where he became known as an expository preacher and a leader of the fundamentalist wing within the *SOUTHERN BAPTIST CONVENTION. Due in part to his preaching and in part because of his emphasis on *EVANGELISM, the church grew to more than twenty-five thousand members by the 1990s, and the congregation became a kind of "full service" church, with gymnasiums, bowling, roller skating, as well as a day school, Criswell Bible College (now known as *CRISWELL COLLEGE), and a Graduate School for the Bible.

Criswell was a fervent opponent of Catholicism throughout most of his career; he vigorously opposed the election of John F. Kennedy to the presidency, for example. He was known for his racist views until the late 1960s; he told the South Carolina legislature in 1956 that integration was "a thing of idiocy and foolishness." By 1968, he had repented of those views and was elected president of the *SOUTHERN BAPTIST CONVENTION, although he remained an arch-conservative politically. As leader of the fundamentalists, Criswell has elevated the doctrine of biblical *INERRANCY to a kind of litmus test for doctrinal orthodoxy, and he has played a major role in the fundamentalist takeover of the *SOUTHERN BAPTIST CONVENTION.

References: W. A. Criswell, *Why I Teach That the Bible Is Literally True* (1969); idem, *What To Do Until Jesus Comes Back* (1975); idem, *The Criswell Study Bible* (1979); idem, *Great Doctrines of the Bible,* 5 vols. (1982–85); Billy Keith, *W. A. Criswell: The Authorized Biography* (1973); Mark G. Toulouse, s.v. "W. A. Criswell," in Charles H. Lippy, ed., *Twentieth-Century Shapers of American Popular Religion* (1989).

Criswell College (Dallas, Texas) Criswell College was started in 1969 by *W. A. CRISWELL, pastor of the First Baptist Church in Dallas, Texas. The school's original purpose was to educate *SUNDAY SCHOOL teachers and Southern Baptist pastors who lacked college degrees. First operating as a night school, Criswell Bible Institute, as it was originally known, began classes in January 1971.

Two years later a day program was introduced. By 1974, the school offered a three-year program in biblical studies; the bachelor of arts in biblical studies curriculum was set in place the following year. A graduate program, known as the Criswell Graduate School of the Bible, was introduced in 1977. The college achieved regional accreditation in 1985 and thereafter became known as Criswell College. It is now part of a larger umbrella organization known as the Criswell Center, which includes not only the college, but also a bookstore and a Christian radio network—KCBI, which runs three one-hundred-thousand-watt stations and reaches north and west Texas as well as southern Oklahoma. For its first twenty years, Criswell held classes in the First Baptist Church of Dallas, but the college acquired the Gaston Avenue Baptist Church in 1989. The school moved onto its own campus there in 1991.

Criswell remains firmly committed to a Bible college curriculum, which reflects the starchy *FUNDAMENTALISM of its founder and namesake. All undergraduate degrees are in biblical studies, with an optional emphasis in counseling, urban ministry, *EVANGELISM and missions, or pastoral ministry. In addition, Criswell requires all incoming students to take a Bible content examination. The school has several master of arts programs and also offers degrees in divinity and missiology. Criswell College is not a member affiliate of the *COUNCIL FOR CHRISTIAN COLLEGES AND UNIVERSITIES.

Criswell is the home of the T. A. Patterson World Mission Research Center, a multimedia resource center that promotes international *EVANGELISM. Using information gathered from Global Mapping International and the World Evangelization Database of the Southern Baptist Foreign Mission Board, the Center maintains a computer system with social and religious information on seventeen thousand people groups around the world. The database, the school claims, is an effective tool for academic researchers and aspiring missionaries alike.

Reference: *The Criswell College 1995–1996 Catalog* (1995).

Crosby, Fanny J(ane) (1820–1915) One of the most prolific hymn writers of the nineteenth century, Fanny J. Crosby was left blind by a physician's mistreatment at the age of six weeks. She turned to religion early in childhood, and by the age of ten could recite the first four books of both the Hebrew *BIBLE and the New Testament from memory. She entered the New York School for the Blind in 1835 and taught there from 1848 to 1858, when she married Alexander Van Alstyne.

Crosby published *The Blind Girl and Other Poems* in 1844, but she is best remembered as lyricist for seemingly countless gospel songs and hymns, including "Blessed Assurance," "Jesus, Keep Me Near the Cross," "To God Be the Glory," and "Tell Me the Story of Jesus." A variety of songwriters put Crosby's words to music, and evangelical hymnals are full of her writings.

Reference: Fanny J. Crosby, *The Blind Girl and Other Poems* (1844).

Crossroads Movement. *See* **International Churches of Christ.**

Croswell, Andrew (1708–1785) Andrew Croswell graduated from Harvard College in 1728 and was ordained at Groton, Connecticut, in 1736. A vocal proponent of the *GREAT AWAKENING, Croswell published a defense of *GEORGE WHITEFIELD, the "grand itinerant," and of *JAMES DAVENPORT, one of the more radical and controversial of the *NEW LIGHT evangelical preachers. Croswell himself became an itinerant preacher in Massachusetts and Connecticut in 1742, attacking the pretensions and the lack of piety in Old Light ministers. He became pastor in 1746 of the Eleventh Church in Boston, a Separate Congregationalist church. Membership in the church dwindled, however, so that only seven members remained at the time of Croswell's death in 1785.

Reference: Leigh Eric Schmidt, "'A Second and More Glorious Reformation': The New Light Extremism of Andrew Croswell," *William and Mary Quarterly*, 3d Ser., XLIII (1986).

Crouch, Andraé (1940–) An enormously influential writer, producer, and interpreter of contemporary gospel music, Andraé Crouch was born in Los Angeles and was converted at the age of nine. Crouch, a gifted musician and performer, signed his first recording contract in 1971. He has performed throughout the world and has won several Grammy and Dove Awards. His score for the Hollywood production of *The Color Purple* received an Oscar nomination.

Crouch, Paul (Franklin) (1934–) Founder and president of the *TRINITY BROADCASTING NETWORK (TBN), Paul Crouch attended *CENTRAL BIBLE INSTITUTE in Springfield, Missouri. In 1961, after working in radio and television, he and his wife, Jan, moved to California in order to oversee media production for the *ASSEMBLIES OF GOD. Crouch established his first station, which would become the flagship station for the *TRINITY BROADCASTING NETWORK, in Santa Ana in 1973. TBN now broadcasts via satellite around the world.

Crumpler, A(bner) B(lackman) (1863–1952) Born in Clinton, North Carolina, A. B. Crumpler became a minister in the Methodist Episcopal Church, South, in the 1880s. In 1890, while listening to the preaching of Beverly Carradine at a district conference in Missouri, Crumpler experienced entire *SANCTIFICATION, which he claimed had rendered him without *SIN. He redirected his career toward *ITINERANCY, spreading holiness teachings throughout North Carolina. He became active in the *NATIONAL CAMP MEETING ASSOCIATION FOR THE PROMOTION OF HOLINESS, and in 1897 he had gathered enough support to organize a state association affiliated with the National Holiness Association.

The Methodist hierarchy, however, looked askance at Crumpler's enthusiasms and in 1899 charged him with "immorality" for conducting a *REVIVAL in Elizabeth City, North Carolina, over the objections of the minister who headed the circuit. Though acquitted, Crumpler left the denomination—the "come-outer" movement, which insisted on separation from those judged less than orthodox, was just then gathering force—and formed the *PENTECOSTAL HOLINESS CHURCH in Goldsboro. In 1900, Crumpler organized about a dozen congregations into the Holiness Church of North Carolina, a small denomination with a *POLITY modeled on the Methodists. He also started a periodical, *Holiness Advocate*, which he published until 1908.

The group was torn asunder after one of the affiliated ministers, *G. B. CASHWELL, began *SPEAKING IN TONGUES in the course of the Azusa Street pentecostal *REVIVAL in Los Angeles and then returned to North Carolina. Cashwell argued that *GLOSSOLALIA was evidence for the *BAPTISM OF THE HOLY SPIRIT, and at a meeting of ministers in Dunn, North Carolina, in 1907, nearly all of the Holiness Church ministers received the blessing of the Holy Spirit and began *SPEAKING IN TONGUES. Crumpler, however, did not. Although he initially reserved judgment on the matter, by the following year he openly opposed *SPEAKING IN TONGUES as the only evidence of Spirit *BAPTISM. At a 1908 meeting of church leaders, Crumpler's position was defeated, although he still managed to be elected president. He left the denomination the next day, however, and returned to the Methodist Episcopal Church, South. He continued preaching for a time but turned more and more of his attentions to the practice of law back in his home town of Clinton. Although he supported Prohibition, he gradually surrendered his passion for holiness teachings.

Cruz, Nicky (1938–) The most famous of *DAVID WILKERSON's converts, Nicky Cruz was born in Puerto Rico and migrated to New York City at the age of fifteen. He soon became a leader of the Mau Mau street gang but responded to the evangelical entreaties of an audacious young pastor, Wilkerson. Cruz's conversion, which led to the breakup of some of New York's gangs, became the focal point of Wilkerson's book, *The Cross and the Switchblade,* which was made into a motion picture. Cruz attended Latin American Bible Institute in La Puente, California, and became an *EVANGELIST in his own right.

References: Nicky Cruz, *Run, Baby, Run* (1968); David Wilkerson, *The Cross and the Switchblade* (1963).

Crystal Cathedral (Garden Grove, California). *See* **Schuller, Robert H(arold).**

Culbertson, William (1905–1971) William Culbertson graduated from the Theological Seminary of the *REFORMED EPISCOPAL CHURCH in 1927 and entered the ministry of that denomination. He served as rector of congregations in Collingdale, Pennsylvania; Ventnor, New Jersey; and Philadelphia, and in 1937 he was elected bishop of the *REFORMED EPISCOPAL CHURCH's New York and Philadelphia synod. He became dean of education at *MOODY BIBLE INSTITUTE in 1942 and then president of the school from 1948 until his retirement in 1970. A gifted preacher and conference speaker, Culbertson's *DISPENSATIONALISM and his advocacy of strict separation from liberals comported well with Moody's *FUNDAMENTALISM.

Reference: Warren W. Wiersbe, *William Culbertson: A Man of God* (1974).

Cullis, Charles (1833–1892) A devout Episcopalian in the Wesleyan and holiness tradition, Charles Cullis studied at the University of Vermont and practiced homeopathic medicine in Boston. On August 19, 1862, he had the experience of entire *SANCTIFICATION after he had "prayed God to sanctify me wholly by the Spirit, and destroy all selfishness and unbelief in my heart." Shortly thereafter, Cullis set up a highly successful home for "indigent and incurable consumptives" and became famous for his "Faith Cures through Prayer." He expanded his enterprises to rescue missions, a deaconess school, a church, homes for spinal and cancer cases, a foreign missions program, and a school for blacks in Virginia. His Willard Tract Repository became a major source of holiness literature in the 1870s and 1880s. He announced the formation of Faith Training College in 1876, and in 1879 he started publishing a periodical, *Times of Refreshing,* "to present Jesus as a full and perfect savior." Cullis's ideas about divine healing influenced such holiness figures as

*W. E. BOARDMAN, *CARRIE JUDD MONTGOMERY, and *A. B. SIMPSON.

References: Charles Cullis, *Faith Cures* (1879); W. E. Boardman, *Faith Work under Dr. Cullis in Boston* (1874); Donald W. Dayton, *Theological Roots of Pentecostalism* (1987).

Culpepper, R(ichard) W(eston) (1921–) Converted during World War II while stationed in Cuba, R. W. Culpepper received a Spirit *BAPTISM in wartime England while praying with other pentecostal soldiers holed up in a hollowed-out haystack. Soon thereafter he claimed that the voice of God told him, "I want you to preach the gospel." Upon his return from military service, Culpepper briefly became an itinerant *EVANGELIST, eventually settling in as pastor of churches in the Los Angeles area. In 1958, he was one of the founders, together with *DAVID NUNN, *W. V. GRANT, and *MORRIS CERULLO, of the World Convention of Deliverance Evangelists. Directing his efforts more and more toward foreign missions, Culpepper supported missionaries and native *EVANGELISTS throughout the 1960s, and in 1970 he moved his operations to Milwaukee, where he became copastor, with *A. C. VALDEZ, of the Milwaukee Evangelistic Temple.

Reference: David Edwin Harrell Jr., *All Things Are Possible: The Healing and Charismatic Revivals in Modern America* (1975).

Cumberland Presbyterian Church The Cumberland Presbyterian Church emerged from the *SECOND GREAT AWAKENING, a series of *REVIVALS over a period of many years that shook the American frontier. The churches and denominations at that time found themselves in the dilemma of having too many people and not enough pastors to lead them. As a result, some churches began the practice of ordaining uneducated men to fill these roles. Some of these men were ordained in the Cumberland Presbytery of the Kentucky Synod of the Presbyterian Church. In 1805, the synod decided that the ordinations needed closer examination. This examination was refused by the presbytery, which led the synod to dissolve the presbytery in 1806. The presbytery appealed to the General Assembly of the Presbyterian Church. The appeal remained unresolved until 1810 when three ministers, Finis Ewing, Samuel King, and Samuel McAdow, constituted a new presbytery, which they named, once again, the Cumberland Presbytery. The new presbytery was formed in Dickson County, Tennessee. Two more groups from the Kentucky Synod joined in the Cumberland Presbytery in 1813 to create the Cumberland Synod. The church had grown so significantly by 1829 that it was able to reorganize itself as the General Assembly of the Cumberland Presbyterian Church.

After the Civil War, efforts began to effect reconciliation between the Cumberland Presbyterians and the Presbyterian Church in the U.S.A. These efforts led to a reunion of the two groups in 1906, but the reunion was far from complete. The terms of reunion were not acceptable to a large portion of the Cumberland Presbyterians; the vote on merger had only carried by a margin of sixty presbyteries to fifty-one. The dissatisfied Presbyterians refused to participate in the union and reorganized themselves to continue as the Cumberland Presbyterian Church.

The first Cumberland Presbyterians had objected to portions of the Westminster Confession, especially the doctrine of strict predestination. They believed in a more Arminian approach that allowed a greater emphasis on individual free will. This emphasis continues to the present day. Not surprisingly, the Cumberland Presbyterians also allowed more flexibility in their standards for ordination. The church affirms the Trinity, the divinity of Jesus Christ, and cooperation with all who accept Jesus as Christ and Lord. The Cumberland Presbyterians practice infant *BAPTISM, which is seen as the seal of the covenant. The *BAPTISM must be affirmed by individuals in a personal profession of faith in Jesus Christ before full membership is conferred on them. The church observes the *LORD'S SUPPER, which is open to all who acknowledge Jesus as the Christ and have faith to understand the significance of the sacrament.

The church continues to have its main strength in the southern and border states, with a few congregations scattered in the midwestern states, Arizona, New Mexico, and California. Headquarters of the Cumberland Presbyterian Church are in Memphis, Tennessee, where the church also maintains a theological seminary. The church claims a membership in the United States of 87,896 in 783 churches.

References: Frank S. Mead and Samuel S. Hill, *Handbook of Denominations in the United States,* 10th ed.; J. Gordon Melton, *The Encyclopedia of American Religions,* 3d ed. (1993); *1997 Yearbook of American and Canadian Churches.*

Cunningham, Loren (1935–) While attending *CENTRAL BIBLE INSTITUTE in Springfield, Missouri, Loren Cunningham, who had been reared in the *ASSEMBLIES OF GOD, came up with an idea for a missions organization that would capitalize on the energy of youth. The organization, *YOUTH WITH A MISSION, began out of his parents' home in California in December 1960. By summer of the following year, the organization had been incorporated with Cunningham as director. He sought to affiliate formally with the *ASSEMBLIES OF GOD, but the astounding success of an eight-week mission effort in the Bahamas in 1964 persuaded him to make the organization interdenominational, with an emphasis on both physical and spiritual well-being.

Under Cunningham's leadership, *YOUTH WITH A MISSION has become a major force for *EVANGELISM around the world. Cunningham heads the operation from his offices in Kailua-Kona, Hawai'i, where the organization's school, Pacific and Asia Christian University, is located.

Reference: Loren Cunningham, *Is That Really You, God?* (1984).

■ ■ ■

Dabney, R(obert) L(ewis) (1820–1898) Reared on a plantation in Louisa County, Virginia, R. L. Dabney had a religious *CONVERSION during a *REVIVAL at Hampden-Sydney College and decided to study for the ministry at Union Theological Seminary in Richmond. After serving as a Presbyterian pastor in Virginia's Shenandoah Valley, he joined the faculty at Union in 1853, where he would remain—except for service during the Civil War on the side of the Confederacy—until 1883.

Dabney was passionately devoted to the South. In 1860, for instance, he was offered both a professorate at Princeton Theological Seminary and the pulpit of Fifth Avenue Presbyterian Church, New York City; he considered neither offer seriously because they would have taken him north. Dabney, a Calvinist, believed that abolitionist sentiments emanating from the North brought on the war and that the South would eventually have given up on slavery if left to its own devices. When secession seemed inevitable, he threw his support wholeheartedly behind the Confederacy. He supported the formation of the Presbyterian Church in the Confederate States of America and opposed any merger between northern and southern Presbyterians. He was so distraught about the outcome of the war and Reconstruction that he tried to organize a migration of southerners to Australia or Brazil. During the 1880s, Dabney led a campaign, ultimately successful, to oust ***JAMES WOODROW**, an erstwhile friend, from his professorate at Columbia Theological Seminary because Woodrow refused unequivocally to oppose Darwinism.

References: Thomas C. Johnson, *Life and Letters of Robert Lewis Dabney* (1903); David Henry Overy, *Robert Lewis Dabney: Apostle of the South* (1967).

Dakota Collegiate Institute. *See* **University of Sioux Falls.**

Dallas Baptist University (Dallas, Texas) Dallas Baptist University began as Decatur Baptist College, which was the first junior college in Texas. In 1897, the Baptist General Convention of Texas bought land from Northwest Texas Baptist College, and Decatur Baptist opened in Decatur, Texas, the following year. The school moved to Dallas in 1965 at the invitation of the Dallas Baptist Association of Southern Baptists, onto a two-hundred-acre campus donated by several Texas businessmen, including John Stemmons and Roland Pelt. When the college moved to Dallas, it began the transition from junior college to four-year institution. Renamed Dallas Baptist College, the first bachelor's degrees were awarded in 1970. The college became Dallas Baptist University in 1985, when it added a master's degree program in business. Since then, the university has added additional graduate programs in management, education, counseling, and biblical studies.

References: *Peterson's Choose a Christian College: A Guide to Academically Challenging Colleges Committed to Christ-Centered Campus Life,* 4th ed. (1992).

Dallas Theological Seminary (Dallas, Texas) ***LEWIS SPERRY CHAFER** founded Dallas Theological Seminary in 1924 as Evangelical Theological College, a three-year graduate school. Two years later, it bought its current campus. The school became known as Dallas Theological Seminary and Graduate School of Theology in 1936. It earned regional accreditation in 1969 and at that time shortened the name to Dallas Theological Seminary.

A protégé of ***C. I. SCOFIELD**, who succeeded him as pastor of the First Congregational Church in Dallas in 1923, Chafer became a noted fundamentalist leader in his own right. The seminary has always been nondenominational and continues, in large measure, to define fundamentalist, especially dispensationalist, theology, much as it did in the 1920s. From 1994 until 2000, Dallas Theological Seminary was headed by big-name fundamentalist writer and evangelist ***CHUCK SWINDOLL**, and ***TOM LANDRY**, retired football head coach for the Dallas Cowboys, served on the school's board of incorporate members.

More than seventy-five years later, the school that Chafer began remains in the vanguard of the most conservative factions of evangelical theology, including no small amount of ambivalence regarding the education and public role of women. For a long time, women were not allowed to serve on the faculty, and in the 1996–97 year, out of fifty-five resident faculty positions, all but three were held by men. Women were also barred from earning master's degrees in theology—the ministry track at Dallas—until 1986. The application for admission to Dallas Theological Seminary is also indicative of the school's fundamentalist orthodoxy. In addition to signing the standard statement of conduct, students must provide information on their history of seeking personal counseling. Married students must submit a statement from their spouses, testifying to their *CONVERSION; divorced or separated applicants have to provide accounts of their separations.

Almost every student at the seminary is required to take courses on all sixty-six books of the *BIBLE, and many are required to complete at least two years of Greek and Hebrew. In addition to the master's in theology, the seminary grants the master of arts degree, as well as doctorates in ministry and biblical and theological studies. Since 1987, Dallas has developed extension sites in Houston and San Antonio, Texas, as well as Chattanooga, Tennessee; Philadelphia; and Tampa.

References: *Dallas Theological Seminary 1996–97 Academic Catalog* (1996); Randall Balmer, *Mine Eyes Have Seen the Glory: A Journey Into the Evangelical Subculture in America,* 3d ed. (2000).

Dancing Although pentecostal communities, which often look to frenetic dancing as a sign of possession by the Holy Spirit, allow—and even encourage—a form of dancing in their worship, many other conservative evangelicals regard all forms of dancing as "worldly." Evangelicals justify this belief with reference to certain New Testament verses (1 Cor. 6:19, 20; 8:8–13; Rom. 14:15–21) which do not mention dance directly at all but rather address the evils of indulging the flesh with physical pleasures. In fact, the proscription against social dancing reflects the evangelical subculture as much as it does a theological perspective. The issue came to the fore in the 1920s, when conservative Christians sought to distance themselves from the flapper era. In the following decades the refusal to engage in social dancing became a litmus test of sorts for the evangelical lifestyle, a proscription that is changing slowly in some circles but is holding fast in others. Today, at most Bible colleges and at many member schools of the *COUNCIL FOR CHRISTIAN COLLEGES AND UNIVERSITIES dancing is not allowed. Some schools, however, make specific allowances for aerobics classes.

Danvers Statement In November 1988, a group called the Council on Biblical Manhood and Womanhood, an organization of fundamentalists and evangelicals, issued the Danvers Statement in an attempt to staunch the spread of biblical feminism in evangelical circles. The group was alarmed by "the increasing promotion given to feminist egalitarianism with accompanying distortions or neglect of the glad harmony portrayed in Scripture between the loving, humble leadership of redeemed husbands and the intelligent, willing support of that leadership by redeemed wives." The Danvers Statement affirmed that "distinctions in masculine and feminine roles are ordained by God as part of the created order, and should find an echo in every human heart."

Reference: Nancy A. Hardesty, "Evangelical Women," in Rosemary Skinner Keller and Rosemary Radford Ruether, eds., *In Our Own Voices: Four Centuries of American Women's Religious Writing* (1995).

Darby, John Nelson (1800–1882) Perhaps no individual has had more effect on

American *FUNDAMENTALISM than John Nelson Darby. Born in London to wealthy Irish parents, Darby graduated from Trinity College, Dublin, and practiced law for a time before entering the ministry of the Church of England in 1825. Although he enjoyed considerable success as a parish priest in County Wicklow, Ireland, Darby disliked the formalism and lack of spiritual ardor that he found in Anglicanism. In 1827, he joined a small group of people in Dublin who met for simple, nonliturgical worship and study of the *BIBLE. Darby left the Church of England in 1831 for the *PLYMOUTH BRETHREN, among whom he became their most influential theologian.

Darby's ideas were shaped by an interpretation of the Scriptures called *DISPENSATIONALISM, which posited that all of human history—as well as the *BIBLE itself—could be divided into different ages or dispensations and that God dealt with humanity in different ways during different dispensations. The present age, Darby insisted, called for the separation of the true believers from nonbelievers in anticipation of the imminent return of Jesus.

Darby propagated these ideas through his many travels, including seven visits to North America between 1859 and 1874. Darby's interpretive scheme eventually caught the attention of such American evangelical figures as *DWIGHT L. MOODY, *A. J. GORDON, and *JAMES H. BROOKES. The general pessimism implicit in *DISPENSATIONALISM fit the temper of America's evangelicals late in the nineteenth century as they surveyed what they saw as the degeneration of American society everywhere around them. Darby's ideas assured evangelicals that this was part of a divine plan, that the world would indeed grow worse and worse just prior to the *RAPTURE, at which time a *TRIBULATION would punish the enemies of righteousness and the millennial kingdom would begin.

*DISPENSATIONALISM, also known as Darbyism, was popularized through the Bible conference movement and especially through the *NIAGARA BIBLE CONFERENCE. The publication of the **SCOFIELD REFERENCE BIBLE* by Oxford University Press in 1909 became an even more effective means for propagating dispensational interpretations to American evangelicals.

Reference: Ernest R. Sandeen, *The Roots of Fundamentalism: British and American Millenarianism, 1800–1930* (1970).

Darbyism. *See* **Dispensationalism.**

Daughters of Sarah Founded in 1978 and published out of Evanston, Illinois, the quarterly magazine *Daughters of Sarah* was begun by Lucille Sider Dayton and other evangelical women who were looking for a forum for their feminist views. Each issue carries the poem, "The Land of Promise," which opens: "We are Christians / We are also feminists. / Some say we cannot be both, / but for us / Christianity and feminism / are inseparable."

The magazine includes theological discussions as well as advocacy for women, often taking positions at odds with many more conservative evangelicals. One editorial, for example, noted that the women's movement was "too often not on the cutting edges for women of Black, Hispanic, or Asian origins, for women of working classes, for women in poverty, for immigrant women. Like Sarah we have often been so concerned about meeting our own needs, legitimate though they are, that we have simply overlooked the Hagars in our midst."

Davenport, James (1716–1757) One of the most spirited revivalists during the *GREAT AWAKENING, James Davenport graduated from Yale College in 1732 and was ordained in 1738 in Southold, on Long Island. The preaching of *GEORGE WHITEFIELD profoundly affected Davenport and prompted him to leave his church and become an itinerant preacher. His extemporaneous preaching, erratic behavior, and refusal to cooperate with settled ministers provided enemies of the *REVIVAL with fodder for their arguments against religious extremism. At the Yale commencement ceremonies in September 1741, for instance, Davenport organized student protests against *THOMAS CLAP, rector of the college, and James Noyes, minister of the Congregationalist church in New Haven. During his tour of Connecticut the following year, Davenport was arrested, tried for disturbing the peace, and deported to Long Island. A subsequent preaching tour of Massachusetts met with a similar fate.

Early in 1743, Davenport was party to the formation of The Shepherd's Tent, putatively a seminary in New London, Connecticut, for the training of revivalist preachers. On March 6, 1743, Davenport and those associated with the school held a book-burning. The fuel for the fire included some of the works of New England divines. The incident galvanized opposition to the Awakening and eventually prompted Davenport to issue a series of *Confessions and Recantations*. From 1747 until his death a decade later, Davenport attained a measure of respectability as pastor of *NEW LIGHT churches in New Jersey. He was elected moderator of the New Side Synod in 1754.

Reference: Harry S. Stout and Peter Onuf, "James Davenport and the Great Awakening in New London," *Journal of American History*, LXX (1983).

David Livingstone Missionary Foundation. *See* **Hargis, Billy James.**

Davies, Samuel (1723–1761) A firebrand preacher whom Patrick Henry acknowledged as the greatest orator he had ever heard, Samuel Davies almost singlehandedly organized Presbyterian churches in the Piedmont region of Virginia. In so doing, he introduced evangelical and revivalist sensibilities into a region putatively dominated by the Church of England. A strong advocate of religious toleration, Davies organized the Hanover Presbytery, thereby providing Presbyterianism with its first foothold in the South.

From 1753 to 1755, Davies and *GILBERT TENNENT visited Britain to raise money for the College of New Jersey. Following the death of *JONATHAN EDWARDS in 1758, Davies consented to succeed Edwards as president of the Presbyterian school; he remained there for only two years, until his own untimely death in 1761 at the age of thirty-eight.

References: Samuel Davies, *The Duty of Christians to Propagate their Religion Among the Heathens* (1758); George W. Pilcher, *Samuel Davies: Apostle of Dissent in Colonial Virginia* (1971).

Day, Stockwell (1951–) Born in Barrie, Ontario, Stockwell Day grew up in Montréal, where he learned to speak French. He attended high school in Ottawa and has lived and worked in the Maritimes, the Northwest Territories, and British Columbia, where he attended the University of Victoria. A pentecostal, he reared his family in Alberta, where he became active in politics. He was elected to the Alberta Legislature in 1986 and went on to serve a number of senior roles, including minister of labour, minister of social services, and, beginning in 1997, provincial treasurer. In 2000, Day was chosen to lead the Canadian Alliance, a conservative coalition. He lost his bid to unseat Jean Chrétien as prime minister of Canada in national elections the following year.

DC Talk The trio known as DC Talk (or dc Talk) was arguably one of the most innovative—and successful—Christian rock bands of the 1990s. This group of "religious rappers turned alternative rockers," as *Time* magazine called them, was formed by Toby McKeehan and Michael Tait, who met at *JERRY FALWELL's *LIBERTY UNIVERSITY in Virginia. They were later joined by classmate Kevin Smith. Their name was a reference to their proximity to Washington, but the record producers at ForeFront who signed them made it a play on words, pointing to their "Decent Christian" lyrics.

DC Talk first toured with *MICHAEL W. SMITH, and the band's mix of rock, soul, and hip-hop styles was well-received. By the mid-1990s, DC Talk had earned two gold records, a Grammy Award, and *Billboard*'s Album of the Year Award; the group was twice named *Billboard*'s Contemporary Christian Artist of the Year. Their third release, *Free at Last,* sold more than a million copies, and the accompanying tour resulted in a film that bore the same name as the album.

DC Talk's fourth recording, *Jesus Freak,* came out in late 1995, and in 1997 *Jesus Freak* won the Grammy Award for Best Rock Gospel Album. In spite of their success, DC Talk remains a trio of committed Christians; the band often appears on worldwide crusades with *BILLY GRAHAM. Writing about their performance at the Mercury Lounge, Jon Pareles of the *New York Times* cautioned his readers that DC Talk were "musical chameleons" who only sought to "proselytize for Christianity." The group countered by describing themselves to that same paper as "Two Honks and a Negro serving the Lord."

Band member Toby McKeehan started his own record company, *GOTEE RECORDS, with the help of two business partners. Gotee has established itself as a successful independent label, most notably with the reggae band Christafari.

References: Information provided by ForeFront Communications Group, Inc.; Christopher John Farley, "Reborn to Be Wild: Christian Pop Music Used to Be Soporific," *Time,* January 22, 1996; Paul O'Donnell, "Rock of Ages," *New Republic,* November 18, 1996; Deborah Evans Price, "It's Not Just for Sundays Anymore," *Billboard,* April 29, 1995.

Deets Bible College. *See* **Point Loma Nazarene College.**

Defenders of the Christian Faith *GERALD BURTON WINROD convened a meeting in 1925 in Salina, Kansas, in order to counteract the pernicious influences of *MODERNISM. Defenders of the Christian Faith, which initially counted about one hundred fundamentalist leaders, emerged from that gathering. The organization selected "Faith of Our Fathers" as its official hymn and adopted a statement of objectives derived from the New Testament book of Jude: "Contend for the faith as it was once delivered unto the saints." Winrod served as executive secretary of the organization throughout his lifetime and used it and the organization's magazine, *The Defender,* as a platform for his political ambitions, his conspiracy theories, and his increasingly anti-Semitic views.

Defenseless Mennonite Church. *See* **Evangelical Mennonite Church.**

DeHaan, M(artin) R(alph) (1891–1965) Martin Ralph DeHaan was known to his many thousands of readers and listeners as M. R. DeHaan. He was born in Zeeland, Michigan, and was reared in the *REFORMED CHURCH OF AMERICA. After attending Hope College for a year he decided to study medicine at the University of Illinois, Chicago, and eventually set up a rural family practice in western Michigan. A medical emergency in 1921 triggered a religious *CONVERSION and prompted him to reexamine his life. He sold his practice, enrolled at Western Theological Seminary, and became enamored of dispensational *PREMILLENNIALISM and an opponent of infant *BAPTISM.

After a contentious nine-year pastorate in Grand Rapids, Michigan, DeHaan suffered a heart attack in 1938, whereupon he resigned his pulpit and restricted his activities to conducting evening Bible classes. At the urging of his mentor, William McCarrell, DeHaan took his Bible classes to a small radio station in Detroit. By 1941, the audiences for *Radio Bible Class* had grown, and the Mutual Broadcasting System carried the program. A second heart attack struck in 1946 while DeHaan was on the air; he managed, however, to complete the broadcast, but his son, *RICHARD DEHAAN, eventually assumed more and more responsibilities for the program and the organization.

The author of twenty-five books, M. R. DeHaan was a master storyteller with a gift for anecdotes and pithy summations. His organization, Radio Bible Class, of Grand Rapids, Michigan, still publishes a daily devotional booklet, "Our Daily Bread," which finds its way into the homes of Christians throughout the English-speaking world.

References: M. R. DeHaan, *508 Answers to Bible Questions* (1952); idem, *Dear Doctor: I Have a Problem* (1961); James R. Adair, *M. R. DeHaan: The Man and His Ministry* (1969).

DeHaan, Richard (1923–) The son of *M. R. DEHAAN, founder of Radio Bible Class, Richard DeHaan studied at *WHEATON COLLEGE, *CALVIN COLLEGE, and Northern Baptist Theological Seminary. After his father's second heart attack in 1946, Richard DeHaan began to assume more and more responsibility within the organization, including the daily radio broadcasts, and he assumed full leadership upon his father's death in 1965. Three years later DeHaan, with the help of Paul Van Gorder, began a television program, *Day of Discovery,* which became one of the ten highest rated religious broadcasts in the country.

Des Moines University (Des Moines, Iowa) In 1927, the *BAPTIST BIBLE UNION, the ultrafundamentalist organization headed by *J. FRANK NORRIS, *WILLIAM BELL RILEY, and *T. T. SHIELDS, purchased Des Moines University, an institution best known for its school of pharmacology, with the idea of turning it into a citadel of fundamentalism. Shields, who was pastor of the Jarvis Street Baptist Church in Toronto, was designated chairman of the board and acting president of the school. Many of the faculty members left immediately, and others followed when presented with the school's new statement of faith, which they were required to sign if they wanted to remain at Des Moines University. The statement included highly specific language affirming special divine creation not only of human life but of animal and vegetable life as well.

Shields disbanded fraternities and sororities, challenged the orthodoxy of faculty members (including the president Shields himself had appointed), and insisted that students sing "God Save the King" at assemblies. Students rioted, and Des Moines University closed its doors in 1929.

References: George S. May, "Des Moines University and Dr. T. T. Shields," *Iowa Journal of History*, LIV (July 1956); John G. Stackhouse Jr., s.v. "Thomas Todhunter Shields," in Charles H. Lippy, ed., *Twentieth-Century Shapers of American Popular Religion* (1989).

Desert Stream Ministries Now based in Anaheim, Desert Stream Ministries was begun in 1980 as an evangelical outreach program to gays and lesbians in West Hollywood, California. This theologically conservative organization, associated with *VINEYARD CHRISTIAN FELLOWSHIP, holds that "sexual brokenness applies to those beset by sexual appetites and/or activities conceived outside of the heterosexual covenant." Desert Stream, which takes its name from Isaiah 43:18–19, describes itself as a "prophetic ministry" that calls homosexuals out of their "sinfulness" and calls on the evangelical church to be more receptive and understanding of people with AIDS and those the organization describes as "sexually broken."

Detroit Bible Institute. *See* **William Tyndale College.**

DeWitt, Calvin B. An evangelical, an environmentalist, and a wetlands ecologist, Calvin B. DeWitt was born into a Christian Reformed household in Grand Rapids, Michigan. He graduated from *CALVIN COLLEGE and did his doctoral work at the University of Michigan. DeWitt is a professor of environmental studies at the University of Wisconsin and teaches in the school's interdisciplinary Institute for Environmental Studies. In addition, he directs the Au Sable Institute, an evangelical study center he founded in Michigan, and he was one of the cofounders of the *EVANGELICAL ENVIRONMENTAL NETWORK in 1993. In addition to his academic work, however, DeWitt has sought to put his environmental ideas into practice. After his election as a town supervisor in Dunn, Wisconsin, just south of Madison, DeWitt succeeded in curbing development and in ensuring the perpetuation of parks and farmland.

References: Calvin B. DeWitt, *Earth-Wise: A Biblical Response to Environmental Issues* (1994); Tim Stafford, "God's Green Acres," *Christianity Today*, June 15, 1998.

Dickinson, Jonathan (1688–1747) After graduating from Yale College in 1706, Jonathan Dickinson, a New Light Presbyterian, began a long ministerial career in Elizabethtown (now Elizabeth), New Jersey. Against those in the Presbyterian Church who argued for strict subscription to the *WESTMINSTER STANDARDS, Dickinson allowed that "experimental" piety should be considered in assessing the qualifications of a ministerial candidate. Although he tried to be a conciliating force between the revivalist New Side faction and the antirevivalist Old Side, Dickinson himself was a thoroughgoing revivalist and was compared by some contemporaries with *JONATHAN EDWARDS.

Dickinson's most significant act may have been his role in the formation of the College of New Jersey. Dickinson and other *NEW LIGHTS recognized the need for an academy to train revivalist ministers, especially after *WILLIAM TENNENT SR. closed his *LOG COLLEGE. Dickinson secured a charter for the new college on October 22, 1746, was elected its first president, and opened classes in his home in May 1747.

References: Jonathan Dickinson, *A Display of God's Special Grace* (1742); Randall Balmer and John R. Fitzmier, *The Presbyterians* (1993).

Dilfer, Trent (Farris) (1972–) Trent Dilfer, a quarterback and an evangelical Christian, was selected in the first round of the National Football League draft in 1994 by the Tampa Bay Buccaneers. After enjoying some success there, he became a backup to Shaun King and was traded to the Baltimore Ravens prior to the 2000 season. Midway through the season Dilfer replaced Tony Banks as the Ravens' quarterback and guided the team to victory in Super Bowl XXXV.

"I nowhere feel that because I'm striving to be faithful that this flip side will be great reward in football," he told a reporter. "But I believe that I am more motivated professionally than I've ever been because God has given me a certain amount of ability, leadership, and other areas that I am called to develop through his strength."

Reference: Jeff M. Sellers, "The Glory of the Ordinary," *Christianity Today,* January 8, 2001.

Disciples of Christ. *See* **Christian Churches.**

Discipleship Movement. *See* **Shepherding Movement.**

Dispensationalism Dispensationalism, also known as dispensational *PREMILLENNIALISM, was a scheme of biblical interpretation that became popular among evangelicals in the late nineteenth and early twentieth centuries. *JOHN NELSON DARBY, an early leader of the *PLYMOUTH BRETHREN in Great Britain, postulated that all of human history could be divided into different ages or dispensations and that God had dealt differently with humanity in each of these dispensations. Dispensationalists further insisted that we are now poised at the end of the final dispensation and that Jesus would return at any moment.

The scheme was especially attractive to evangelicals in America because it allowed them to understand why the postmillennial kingdom so confidently predicted earlier in the nineteenth century had failed to materialize. Rather than looking for the improvement of society, dispensational *PREMILLENNIALISM insisted that the world was growing worse and worse, more and more sinful, and that the imminent return of Jesus offered the only escape from the scourge of the cities, already overrun, in the opinion of evangelicals, by non-Protestant immigrants.

Dispensationalism also offered evangelicals a rubric for understanding Israel and the Jews. Yes, the promises made to Israel in the Hebrew *BIBLE (which evangelicals refer to as the Old Testament) were valid, but the Jews' rejection of Jesus as messiah prompted a postponement of the messianic kingdom and the creation out of the Gentiles a new heir to the promises of ancient Israel, the church.

Darby's ideas caught on with evangelicals in North America and were popularized by means of prophetic conferences, *BIBLE INSTITUTES, and especially the **SCOFIELD REFERENCE BIBLE,* compiled by *CYRUS INGERSON SCOFIELD and published by Oxford University Press in 1909. Scofield insisted upon seven dispensations (although other dispensationalists have come up with other figures), and his scheme became especially popular among *FUNDAMENTALISTS. *DALLAS THEOLOGICAL SEMINARY remains the intellectual center of dispensationalism, which was perpetuated in the twentieth century by such Dallas theologians as *LEWIS SPERRY CHAFER, *JOHN F. WALVOORD, *CHARLES C. RYRIE, and *J. DWIGHT PENTECOST.

References: Ernest R. Sandeen, *The Roots of Fundamentalism: British and American Millenarian-*

ism, 1800–1930 (1970); Timothy P. Weber, *Living in the Shadow of the Second Coming: American Premillennialism, 1875–1982,* enl. ed. (1983); Randall Balmer, *Mine Eyes Have Seen the Glory: A Journey into the Evangelical Subculture in America,* 3d ed. (2000).

Dixon, A(mzi) C(larence) (1854–1925) Born in Shelby, North Carolina, A. C. Dixon graduated from Wake Forest College in 1875 and studied theology in Greenville, South Carolina, under Baptist theologian *JOHN A. BROADUS. Ordained as a Baptist minister, Dixon served several churches in North Carolina and turned down an offer to become president of Wake Forest in favor of another pastorate at Immanuel Baptist Church in Baltimore. He became a popular speaker at Bible conferences in the United States and England, and in 1890 he assumed the pastorate of the Hanson Place Baptist Church in Brooklyn, New York.

Dixon began to attract national attention as an implacable opponent of theological *LIBERALISM during his eleven-year tenure in Brooklyn. During the World's Parliament of Religions, held in Chicago in 1893, for example, Dixon joined *DWIGHT L. MOODY for a month in preaching against that ecumenical and interreligious gathering. Dixon left Brooklyn in 1901 for Ruggles Street Baptist Church in Boston and then moved to *MOODY CHURCH in Chicago, where he served from 1906 until 1911. He continued his itinerant preaching while at *MOODY CHURCH, and during a conference in Los Angeles he met *LYMAN STEWART, a Presbyterian layman and head of Union Oil Company of California. Stewart and his brother, Milton, shared Dixon's suspicions of liberal or "modernist" theology, and as a consequence of their meeting the Stewart brothers gave Dixon the money to compile and distribute the famous booklets called **THE FUNDAMENTALS; OR, TESTIMONY TO THE TRUTH,* a defense of orthodox Protestantism and an attack on *LIBERALISM. Dixon was the first executive secretary and editor of *THE FUNDAMENTALS; he oversaw the production of the first five volumes (out of a total of twelve).

Dixon became pastor in 1911 of the Metropolitan Tabernacle in England, the church that *CHARLES H. SURGEON had made famous in the nineteenth century. Dixon returned to the United States in 1919, and he remained active as a Bible conference speaker, as a dogged proponent of *FUNDAMENTALISM, and as pastor of the University Baptist Church in Baltimore.

Dobson, James C. (1936–) Born in Shreveport, Louisiana, the son, grandson, and great-grandson of holiness ministers, James C. Dobson graduated from Pasadena College in 1958 and studied child development at the University of Southern California, where he earned the doctorate in 1967. A licensed psychologist and the author of more than a dozen books on child-rearing, Dobson taught pediatrics at the University of Southern California School of Medicine and served on the attending staff of Children's Hospital in Los Angeles until 1980. His 1970 book, *Dare to Discipline,* took issue with the permissiveness advocated by Benjamin Spock, whose books on child-rearing had tutored the previous generation of parents.

The success of Dobson's books, his evangelical orientation, and his political conservatism led him to form an organization called *FOCUS ON THE FAMILY in 1977. That group, with its many outlets into the media—publishing, motion pictures, radio programs—propelled Dobson to national prominence in the 1980s as one of the most recognizable figures of the

*Religious Right. He employed the "culture wars" dualism so favored by *Religious Right activists. "Nothing short of a great Civil War of Values rages today throughout North America," he wrote in 1994. "Two sides with vastly differing and incomparable worldviews are locked in a bitter conflict that permeates every level of society." In February 1998, addressing a group of Republican leaders in Phoenix, Dobson castigated the Republican Party for its "betrayal" of politically conservative evangelical voters by relying on that constituency for its votes but failing to deliver on its agenda. Belying the putatively nonpartisan posture of his organization, Dobson criticized Republicans for not caring "about the moral law of the universe" and threatened to lead a defection, adding, "if I go, I will do everything I can to take as many people with me as possible." Defending his jeremiad in a subsequent interview, Dobson declared: "I really do feel that the prophetic role is part of what God gave me to do."

References: James C. Dobson, *Dare to Discipline* (1970); Rolf Zetterman, *Dr. Dobson: Turning Hearts toward Home* (1989); Gil Alexander-Moegerle, *James Dobson's War on America* (1997); Michael J. Gerson, "A Righteous Indignation," *U.S. News & World Report,* May 4, 1998; Wendy Murray Zoba, "Daring to Discipline America," *Christianity Today,* March 1, 1999.

Doddridge, Philip (1702–1751) Philip Doddridge, born in London, was orphaned by 1715 and was trained for the ministry by Samuel Clark and John Jennings. Doddridge took over Jennings's charge in 1723 and also started a small school, which he relocated to Northampton, England, in 1729. He was ordained as pastor of Castle Hill church in Northampton on March 19, 1730, and remained there for the rest of his life. Doddridge enjoyed a productive career as a hymnwriter, preacher, writer, and apologist for the Christian faith; his works were widely circulated both in England and in New England, and several were translated into French, German, and Dutch.

References: Philip Doddridge, *The Family Expositor,* 5 vols. (1738–1756); idem, *The Rise and Progress of Religion in the Soul* (1745); idem, *Course of Lectures* (1763); Geoffrey F. Nuttall, *Richard Baxter and Philip Doddridge* (1951).

Dominion Theology. *See* **Reconstructionism.**

Dordt College (Sioux Center, Iowa) Beginning in 1937, proposals to found a church college circulated among *Christian Reformed Churches in the Midwest, but the project was delayed by the outbreak of World War II. Dordt College was organized in 1953 as the Midwest Christian Junior College, adopting its current name three years later. Dordt College introduced baccalaureate programs in 1961 and awarded its first bachelor's degrees in 1965.

Students are expected to attend church twice every Sunday in addition to chapel twice a week. The college remains affiliated with the *Christian Reformed Church. Consistent with its Low Country heritage, Dordt offers a major in Dutch, and the library maintains a Dutch Archives Collection.

Reference: *Dordt College Catalog* (1995).

Dow, Lorenzo (1777–1834) Lorenzo "Crazy" Dow was born in Coventry, Connecticut, and claimed at age fourteen to have had a dream in which he was called to preach the *gospel. The Methodist Episcopal Church, after some misgivings about both his health and his erratic character, finally ordained him in 1798. He served a circuit in the Maritimes but abruptly left his charge in 1799 to sail for Ireland, where his preaching met with scant success. He returned to the United States in 1801 as an implacable foe of Roman Catholicism. The Methodists accepted him back on trial, and Dow resumed his peregrinations first in Georgia, then in New York, and then throughout the South.

Dow, a forceful and fiery preacher, was a fervent advocate of *CAMP MEETINGS and a bitter opponent of *CALVINISM. He again crossed the Atlantic in 1806 for a preaching tour of Ireland and England. There, his endorsement of *CAMP MEETINGS led to the Mow Cop *CAMP MEETING in June 1807, and the condemnation of the meeting by the Methodist Conference at Liverpool led in turn to the formation of the *PRIMITIVE METHODIST CHURCH.

Dow's unkempt appearance and his frenetic behavior proved attractive and entertaining to audiences in North America. He clashed frequently, however, with the Methodist hierarchy, and Bishop *FRANCIS ASBURY eventually excluded Dow from Methodist gatherings. Dow continued to itinerate and to preach. He returned to England from 1818 to 1820 and planned a utopian city in Wisconsin, which would include refuge for blacks, but that plan was never realized.

References: Lorenzo Dow, *The Chain of Lorenzo* (1804); idem, *The Life, Travel, Labors, and Writings of Lorenzo Dow* (1856); Charles Coleman Sellers, *Lorenzo Dow: The Bearer of the Word* (1928).

Dowie, John Alexander (1847–1907)
Born to a poor family in Edinburgh, Scotland, John Alexander Dowie served as a Congregationalist minister in Australia from 1872 to 1877, during which time a serious plague threatened his congregation. Dowie, having earlier been cured of chronic dyspepsia, prayed for healing and, according to accounts, no more congregants died. In 1882, he founded the International Divine Healing Association, and he organized the Free Christian Church in Melborne in 1883, where healing became a major focus of his ministry.

Dowie emigrated to the United States in 1888 and, after stops in San Francisco and Salt Lake City, eventually settled in Chicago. In 1893, he built a crude tabernacle near the entrance to the World's Fair, where he preached his message of divine healing and his opposition to all medicine. He launched a weekly periodical, *Leaves of Healing,* in 1894, and two years later he incorporated his ministry as the *CHRISTIAN CATHOLIC CHURCH. Dowie's congregation grew to several thousand members, and on New Year's Day, 1900, he unveiled his plans for a utopian colony, *ZION CITY, on more than six thousand acres forty miles north of Chicago. Thousands followed him to *ZION CITY, where he attempted to establish a theocratic society free of liquor, tobacco, pork, and drugstores. Over the enormous platform of the assembly hall, Dowie mounted the crutches, braces, and elevated shoes of those he had healed; on either side, built from old cigar boxes, Dowie erected the letters S and P, which stood for "stinkpot," Dowie's epithet for smokers. Over the course of his career he was arrested more than one hundred times for operating a medical facility without a license.

Dowie, who apparently had been greatly influenced by his visit with the Mormons in Salt Lake City, in 1901 declared himself the fulfillment of Old Testament prophecies and called himself Elijah. Many of his followers, however, remained suspicious. The utopian experiment soon fell into financial disarray, Dowie suffered a stroke in September

1905, and members of the society stripped him of his power the following year.

References: John Alexander Dowie, *The Sermons of John Alexander Dowie* (1979); David Edwin Harrell Jr., *All Things Are Possible: The Healing and Charismatic Revivals in Modern America* (1975).

Dravecky, Dave. *See* **Outreach of Hope.**

Driscoll, Phil (1947–) Christian contemporary recording artist Phil Driscoll began his career in the late 1960s as a secular rock musician. While a first-year student at *BAYLOR UNIVERSITY he had formed a jazz band, and by his second year he was recording his first album, *A Touch of Trumpet,* with the Stockholm Symphony Orchestra. During his senior year he won more than a dozen rounds of the CBS talent search series *The All American College Bowl;* he prevailed over Karen and Richard Carpenter in the final competition.

As a trumpet player and singer, Driscoll has performed with Leon Russell and toured with Joe Cocker; he appeared on *The Ed Sullivan Show, Merv Griffin,* and *The Steve Allen Show.* He also composed music with Stephen Stills and Blood Sweat & Tears. Throughout this time, Driscoll fought a battle with substance abuse. His life was turned around, however, in late 1977, when he was *BORN AGAIN on Christmas Day. In 1982, Driscoll began recording Christian music. Since then, he captured a Grammy Award with Debby Boone for their duet, "Keep the Fire Burning," and also won *GOSPEL MUSIC ASSOCIATION Dove Awards in 1983, 1985, and 1987. He released his eighteenth album, *A Different Man,* in 1996. Recorded in a musical style described as "pop *EVANGELISM," the album included a song written by *MICHAEL W. SMITH and a cover of "The Long and Winding Road" by the Beatles.

Reference: Information provided by Word Records.

Dryer, Emma An associate of nineteenth-century evangelist *DWIGHT L. MOODY, Emma Dryer's early Bible-training efforts in Chicago evolved into *MOODY BIBLE INSTITUTE. Dryer was the principal of the Illinois State Normal University until the Chicago Fire of 1871. After the fire, she changed careers to devote herself to "works of mercy" in Chicago, where she was encouraged by Moody to begin a "Bible Work" in the 1870s and early 1880s. Dryer's relief projects had many facets, one of which was to train women as Bible teachers and urban missionaries. Moody decided in 1886 to expand Dryer's work, and with the help of the Chicago Evangelization Society he began a massive fund-raising drive to develop a year-round training program for home and foreign missionaries, a school still known as *MOODY BIBLE INSTITUTE.

Reference: Virginia Lieson Brereton, *Training God's Army: The American Bible School, 1880–1940* (1990).

Dualism Dualism, the tendency to view the world in bipolar categories—right versus wrong, conservative versus liberal, good versus evil—was one of the overriding characteristics of evangelical theology and approaches to culture in the twentieth century. This reluctance to countenance ambiguity has given rise to judgmentalism, where evangelicals feel obliged to declare whether or not someone is "orthodox" or "Christian" or "saved." These dualistic tendencies toward judgment, which have precedents in the Manichean and Donatist heresies of the early church, were given full expression during the fundamentalist-modernist controversy in the 1920s and 1930s (the name assigned to the dispute itself belies a dualistic construction). A later indication of this continuing inclination toward bipolarity was the warm reception that evangelicals gave to James Davison Hunter's 1991 book *Culture Wars: The Struggle to Define America,* which sought to reduce all political, theological, and sociological debates late in the twentieth century into dualistic categories.

Duncan, David James (1952–) Born in Portland, Oregon, David James Duncan developed a passion for fishing at an early age. "I think by the time I was five I decided, on my own," he said in a 1997 interview, "that the three most important things in my life were creeks, trees, and Jesus." Duncan considers himself devout, but he has little patience for organized religion, especially evangelical Christianity. In *The River Why* he calls door-to-door evangelists "witlesses," and in *The Brothers K,* Duncan, through his narrator, describes another character: "Then there's Papa, who once said He's God's Son all right, and He survived the crucifixion just fine, but that two-thousand-year-old funeral service His cockeyed followers call Christianity probably made Him sorry He did."

A strong sense of faith permeates Duncan's writings, although he prefers to call himself a "follower of Jesus" rather than a "Christian." "I have bet my literary and spiritual life on the belief that Jesus is not a liar," he said. His writing exudes the comforting and haunting sense of *GRACE: "I want to write fiction that dances around the central miracle of our lives—which is that, despite everything, we're loved!"

References: David James Duncan, *The River Why* (1983); idem, *The Brothers K* (1993); idem, *River Teeth: Stories and Writings* (1995); Christine Byl, "A Conversation with David James Duncan," *OE: A Journal of the Oregon Extension,* spring 1997; Sam Alvord, "But Is He a Christian?" *Books & Culture,* September/October 1997.

Du Plessis, David J(ohannes) (1905–1987) Known almost universally as "Mr. Pentecost," David du Plessis was a native of South Africa who served as a pastor and, from 1936 to 1947, as general secretary of the Apostolic Faith Mission Church in South Africa. In 1947, du Plessis became the organizing secretary of the World Pentecostal Fellowship; after moving to the United States in 1948, he affiliated with the *ASSEMBLIES OF GOD and helped to found the Pentecostal Fellowship of North America.

A tireless ecumenist, du Plessis unfurled the banner of *PENTECOSTALISM before such ecumenical groups as the World Council of Churches (WCC) and the National Council of Churches. He was invited to attend the proceedings of Vatican II. Dubbed a "WCC gadfly" by **CHRISTIANITY TODAY,* du Plessis often came in for criticism from separatist evangelicals for comporting with "*MODERNISM" and "ecumenical apostasy." The Assemblies revoked his ministerial credentials in 1962. They were restored in 1980, amid a growing acknowledgment that du Plessis's ambassadorial efforts on behalf of *PENTECOSTALISM had helped to bolster the *CHARISMATIC RENEWAL MOVEMENT in mainline denominations. Pope John Paul II awarded du Plessis the Good Merit Medal in 1983 for "service to all Christianity," the first time a non-Catholic had received that honor. Du Plessis spent his final years at *FULLER THEOLOGICAL SEMINARY, which established the David J. Du Plessis Center for Christian Spirituality in 1985.

References: David J. du Plessis, *The Spirit Bade Me Go* (1970); idem, *Simple and Profound* (1986); Edith L. Blumhofer, *Restoring the Faith: The Assemblies of God, Pentecostalism, and American Culture* (1993).

Duquesne Weekend Generally considered the beginning of the *CATHOLIC CHARISMATIC RENEWAL, the Duquesne Weekend took place in mid-February 1967 when two lay instructors from Duquesne University in Pittsburgh led about thirty students on a spiritual retreat. In the course of the weekend, all of the participants experienced the *BAPTISM OF THE HOLY SPIRIT. Following the Duquesne Weekend, a similar gathering was held at the University of Notre Dame on April 7–9, 1967, the first of the annual *CATHOLIC CHARISMATIC RENEWAL conferences.

Durham, William (1873–1912) Though born and reared a Baptist in Kentucky, William Durham encountered holiness teachings while in Minnesota in 1898 and decided to enter the ministry. He served as pastor of the North Avenue Mission, a small mission in Chicago. Lured to Los Angeles by reports of the *AZUSA STREET REVIVAL, Durham experienced *BAPTISM OF THE HOLY SPIRIT on March 2, 1907. He returned to Chicago and founded a monthly magazine, *The Pentecostal Testimony,* to propagate pentecostal teachings. The North Avenue Mission grew quickly and added ten satellite missions.

Durham's pentecostal theology, however, diverged somewhat from that preached at Azusa. Durham developed the "finished work of Calvary" variant on *PENTECOSTALISM, arguing that both *SALVATION and *SANCTIFICATION were available to all because of Christ's work on Calvary. This stance implied criticism of Azusa's emphasis on instantaneous *SANCTIFICATION and posited instead a kind of progressive *SANCTIFICATION, a doctrine later adopted by the *ASSEMBLIES OF GOD.

Reference: Edith L. Blumhofer, *Restoring the Faith: The Assemblies of God, Pentecostalism, and American Culture* (1993).

Durkin, Jim (1925–1996) Born in Chicago, Jim Durkin served in the U.S. Navy and later worked for the U.S. Forest Service. After converting to evangelical Christianity, he felt a calling to ministry and served a number of pastorates in northern California and Oregon. In the summer of 1970, while Durkin was experiencing dissatisfaction with his ministry, he was approached by several *JESUS PEOPLE who were looking for a place to live and begin their own evangelistic ministry to the hippies. Though initially hesitant, Durkin allowed the young group access to one of his apartment complexes, helping them to open a coffeehouse outreach program. As the ministry blossomed, they looked to him for leadership. He acquired an abandoned coast guard station eleven miles outside of Eureka, California. Moving there with his wife, Dacie, Durkin decided to offer the young Christians spiritual oversight. They called their new home the Lighthouse Ranch.

Building a model of what he felt an effective church should be, Durkin began to gather a number of leaders around him in order to prepare them for active Christian service "wherever the Lord would lead them." In spring 1972, the group began sending out missionary teams to different locations, beginning first with a transplant to Palmer, Alaska, and then to Chicago, Brooklyn, Philadelphia, and other parts of the United States. By 1972, the group had grown to nearly three hundred active members. Throughout the 1970s and 1980s, the evangelistic organization associated with Lighthouse Ranch, known as Gospel Outreach, sent out missionary teams to places as diverse as Germany, Nicaragua, Hawai'i, and Mendocino, California. When Rios Montt, a former member of the Gospel Outreach ministry, came to political power in Guatemala, the organization was accused of manipulating the country through him. With one hundred affiliated churches worldwide, the Gospel Outreach network is one of several denominations to emerge from the *JESUS MOVEMENT.

Dwight, Louis (1793–1854) A graduate of Yale College and *ANDOVER SEMINARY, Louis Dwight became an agent for the *AMERICAN BIBLE SOCIETY. He visited many prisons in the course of his travels and became appalled at the conditions there. As secretary of the Boston Prison Discipline Society, Dwight sought to initiate reforms that would make prisons more humane and would be more conducive to rehabilitation. His ideas, which became known as the Auburn System (because they were first implemented at Auburn, New York), included the use of cell blocks and group labor instead of the Pennsylvania System of solitary confinement. Dwight's reforms, an example of the postmillennial optimism about the perfectibility of society arising from the *SECOND GREAT AWAKENING, became a model for prison reform throughout the world and even changed the nomenclature for the penal system from *prison,* a place of ostracism, to *penitentiary,* where a social deviant could do penance and rehabilitate himself for integration back into society.

Dwight, Timothy (1752–1817) A Congregationalist minister generally regarded as one of the leaders of the *SECOND GREAT AWAKENING in Connecticut, Timothy Dwight was both a grandson and a theological heir of *JONATHAN EDWARDS. A graduate of Yale College, Dwight was a chaplain during the Revolutionary War, during which he wrote his epic poem, *Conquest of Canaan.* After the war, he served as pastor of the Congregational Church at Greenfield, Connecticut, where he remained until he accepted the presidency of Yale in 1795.

Appalled by the popularity of French Enlightenment thought among the students at Yale, Dwight instituted a curriculum of orthodox Christianity which, in the judgment of *LYMAN BEECHER, led to a series of small *REVIVALS among the students. Although he is often identified with the *NEW DIVINITY, Dwight's theology tempered some of the more extreme elements of *NEW DIVINITY "consistent Calvinism." A zealous defender of religious establishment, Dwight earned from his political enemies the sobriquet "Pope of Federalism."

References: Joseph A. Conforti, *Samuel Hopkins and the New Divinity Movement: Calvinism, the Congregational Ministry, and Reform between the Awakenings* (1981); John R. Fitzmier, *New England's Moral Legislator: Timothy Dwight, 1752–1817* (1998).

Dylan, Bob (né Zimmerman, Robert Allen) (1941–) Bob Dylan, born Robert Allen Zimmerman in Duluth, Minnesota, and reared in nearby Hibbing, took the name Dylan while a student at the University of Minnesota because of his admiration for the Welsh poet Dylan Thomas. He spent only a semester at the university, however, where he sang at the campus coffeehouse. His music was influenced by Woody Guthrie, and after Dylan left school he went to New Jersey to visit the dying musician; the two became friends. While in New York City trying to make it as a professional musician, Dylan was discovered by John Hammond of Columbia Records, who found something intriguing in Dylan's plaintive, nasalized singing and soft, soulful strumming. His first album, *Bob Dylan,* released in 1961, met with critical acclaim, as did subsequent offerings. His songs—many of which were picked up by other artists, especially by Peter, Paul & Mary—sounded the note of protest and restlessness during the 1960s. Students for a Democratic Society, an organization of militant radicals, for instance, adopted the nickname "Weathermen" from a line in Dylan's "Subterranean Homesick Blues": "You don't need a weatherman to know which way the wind blows."

Dylan was seriously injured in a motorcycle accident in 1966, breaking his neck. He returned to writing and performing, however, and in 1970 he was awarded an honorary doctorate from Princeton University, the first such honor given a popular singer. His music continued to evolve throughout the 1970s, bringing together elements of folk and rock. The release of *Slow Train Coming* in 1979 bespoke a startling transformation in the Jewish-born singer: his conversion to evangelical Christianity. Many fans were miffed and bewildered, but some critics acknowledged that they detected a new power in Dylan's music. "Dylan's exhortations are certainly at odds with the 'do your own thing' mentality of the '60s," one review read. "But in a curious way, the album is true to Dylan's origins—in fact this LP may be more pure Dylan than anything he's put out in a long time. Dylan has traditionally railed against hypocrisy, materialism, and corruption—the religious themes only serve to intensify the message."

Evangelicals were uncertain about how to greet the news that Dylan was now one of their own. Many remained suspicious because of his unkempt appearance and his association with the radicalism of the 1960s. Dylan publicly renounced his conversion to Christianity early in 1982.

■ ■ ■

Eagle Forum Founded in 1972 by *PHYLLIS SCHLAFLY, a Roman Catholic who had been active in Barry Goldwater's 1964 presidential campaign, Eagle Forum was organized expressly for the purpose of defeating the proposed Equal Rights Amendment to the United States Constitution. After claiming success in that mission, Schlafly kept the organization alive by propagating other *RELIGIOUS RIGHT themes, adding opposition to homosexual rights, for example, to her opposition to feminism. Schlafly has formed alliances with other members of the *RELIGIOUS RIGHT, notably with *BEVERLY LAHAYE, head of *CONCERNED WOMEN FOR AMERICA. The two have declared the existence of two women's movements: the "radical women's movement," represented by the National Organization for Women, and the "real women's movement," which Schafly and LaHaye claim to represent.

References: Phyllis Schlafly, *A Choice, Not an Echo* (1964); Lori Forman, "The Political Activity of the Religious Right in the 1990s: A Critical Analysis," pamphlet distributed by the American Jewish Committee.

Earl Paulk College. *See* **Paulk, Earl (Pearly), (Jr.).**

East Gates International East Gates International traces its history to 1989, when a group of house churches in China sought a supply of legal *BIBLES, rather than risking imprisonment for using smuggled *BIBLES. They asked the assistance of Ned Graham, son of *BILLY and

*RUTH GRAHAM, in part because Ned's grandfather, *L. NELSON BELL, had served as medical missionary in China for twenty-five years. Ned Graham agreed, establishing East Gates International in 1992, which enjoyed a good working relationship with the China Christian Council, the Three-Self Patriotic Movement, and various governmental agencies. The organization has offices in Sumner, Washington, and solicits contributions for *BIBLE distribution from evangelicals in North America.

East Texas Baptist University (Marshall, Texas) William Thomas Tardy, president of the First Baptist Church of Marshall, Texas, began a campaign to found a Bible college in 1911. Although the College of Marshall was incorporated a year later, not until 1915 did the first freshmen arrive. Within two years, however, the school had three hundred students enrolled in its secondary school and junior college. The school switched to a four-year liberal arts program in 1944 and was renamed East Texas Baptist College. In 1984, the Baptist General Convention voted to change the name to East Texas Baptist University. The university grants a master's degree in business administration.

References: *East Texas Baptist University Catalog, 1995–1996* (1995); *Peterson's Choose a Christian College: A Guide to Academically Challenging Colleges Committed to Christ-Centered Campus Life*, 4th ed. (1992).

Eastern Baptist Theological Seminary. *See* **Eastern College.**

Eastern College (St. Davids, Pennsylvania) Eastern College was founded in 1932 as a department of Eastern Baptist Theological Seminary. The school originated as a one-year preparatory course for students seeking training in the ministry, but by 1938 it had developed into a six-year program, offering a combination of college and seminary education. The program expanded a decade later to a seven-year program, culminating in the bachelor's of divinity. Eastern Baptist Seminary's board of trustees voted in 1951 to create a separate undergraduate institution, largely in response to public demand that the preparatory division expand its programs. Known as Eastern Baptist College, the new school opened a year later and attained accreditation by 1954. In 1972, Eastern Baptist College changed its legal name to "Eastern College: A Baptist Institution," in an effort to reflect both its continued affiliation with the American Baptist Church and its wider commitment to teaching evangelical students from a variety of backgrounds. Currently, more than twenty denominations are represented in the student body.

Eastern College offers an individualized major program, in which undergraduates design their own courses of study. The school has graduate programs in business administration, economic development, nonprofit management, health administration, education, and counseling, as well as a dual-degree program in business or economic development and divinity, in conjunction with Eastern Baptist Theological Seminary.

Unlike many Christian colleges, Eastern does not consider marital status in its admission policies and, in fact, states this position formally. The college's regulations in other areas of student life also identify it as slightly more liberal than the average evangelical school. The campus is smoke-free, but there is no off-campus smoking policy. Social *DANCING is not proscribed, and the physical education department even offers a minor in dance. Although the standards of conduct prohibit the use or possession of alcohol on campus or in areas immediately adjacent, and also forbid inappropriate behavior such as being intoxicated on campus, the off-campus use of alcohol is not regulated beyond these stipulations.

References: *Eastern College 1994–1996 Undergraduate Catalog* (1994); William C. Ringenberg, *The Christian College: A History of Protestant Higher Education in America* (1984).

Eastern Mennonite University and Eastern Mennonite Seminary (Harrisonburg, Virginia) Eastern Mennonite University opened in 1917 under the name Eastern Mennonite School. The Bible school, supported by Virginia, Pennsylvania, and Maryland Mennonites, was established as a "fortress to defend the conservative faith." More specifically, the school was meant to be an alternative to the Mennonites' *GOSHEN COLLEGE, which was perceived as being too liberal.

Within one year of its founding, the Bible school offered advanced courses in religion, and by 1937 a four-year Bible program had developed. The school, which became known as Eastern Mennonite College, achieved four-year accreditation in 1944. Since that time, the school has introduced graduate programs in education, counseling, and conflict resolution. Eastern Mennonite Seminary was recognized as an independent institution in 1965 and now offers master's degrees in divinity, religion, and church leadership.

Since 1968, the "Global Village Curriculum" has required a study abroad or stateside "cross-cultural" study program of all students, with an emphasis on peacemaking. The school is conscious of its Christian, pietist heritage but also encourages communication with and understanding of other cultures.

In 1994, the school was renamed Eastern Mennonite University to unify the seminary, graduate, and undergraduate programs. Unlike many *BIBLE INSTITUTES, Eastern Mennonite did not eliminate its secondary school as it introduced a liberal arts college program. The college retained ties with Eastern Mennonite High School until 1981, when the school broke off to operate independently.

Reference: Thomas C. Hunt, James C. Carper, eds., *Religious Higher Education in the United States: A Source Book* (1996).

Eastern Nazarene College (Quincy, Massachusetts) Eastern Nazarene College opened in 1900 as the Pentecostal Collegiate Institute in Saratoga Springs, New York; two years later, the school moved to North Scituate, Rhode Island. The institute became affiliated with the *CHURCH OF THE NAZARENE in 1918, and its name was changed to Eastern Nazarene College. The following year, Eastern Nazarene College took over the old campus of the Quincy Mansion School for Girls in Massachusetts.

The college's bachelor's degree programs were first authorized in 1930. By 1964, a master's degree program in religion was introduced, and additional graduate programs in family counseling and education were added in 1981. Eastern Nazarene College has a semester-long study-abroad program in Romania.

Although most Christian colleges have core curriculums, Eastern Nazarene College's Cultural Perspectives Sequence is distinctive. These courses on Western culture are interdisciplinary in approach and are intended to encourage students to explore the "tensions and possibilities that exist for Christian faith and values in a society permeated with individualism, materialism, and despair," such as discussion of the religious "implications of contemporary science."

The college's lifestyle guidelines are similar to those of most *CHRISTIAN COLLEGES. Nevertheless, the college holds out respect for parental rules: "Since the college does not infringe upon the government of the home, non-resident students who live in their homes are permitted the usual privileges of the home as allowed by their parents."

References: *Eastern Nazarene College 1996–1997 Undergraduate Catalog* (1996); William C. Ringenberg, *The Christian College: A History of Protestant Higher Education in America* (1984).

Ebenezer Bible Institute. *See* **Myland, David Wesley.**

Eclectic Reader. *See* ***McGuffey Reader.***

Ecuador Martyrs Ecuador Martyrs is the name given to a group of five evangelical missionaries—Peter Fleming, Ed McCully, Nate Saint, *JIM ELLIOT, and Roger Youderian—who were slain by the Huaoranis (also know as Aucas) of Ecuador in January 1956. These young missionaries had sought to set up a mission in Huaorani territory, among a people legendary for their savagery and hostility to outside encroachment. Although the initial overtures had been encouraging, shortly after the missionaries arrived in the territory the Huaoranis attacked their encampment on a sandbar in a remote river. A search party later discovered the bodies of all five missionaries, who had been speared to death.

The story of the killings—as well as the evidence that the missionaries refused to defend themselves, despite the fact that they had guns—inspired many young evangelicals to missionary service. In particular, the account of Elliot's widow, *ELISABETH ELLIOT, had the effect of elevating *JIM ELLIOT and the other missionaries to near sainthood among evangelicals.

References: Elisabeth Elliot, *Through Gates of Splendor* (1957); Steve Saint, "Did They Have to Die?" *Christianity Today,* September 16, 1996.

Edman, V(ictor) Raymond (1900–1967) A native of Chicago Heights, Illinois, V. Raymond Edman served in France and Germany during World War I before pursuing an education at the University of Illinois, *NYACK MISSIONARY TRAINING INSTITUTE, and Boston University. He became a missionary to the Quechua in Ecuador in 1923 and remained there until a tropical disease forced his return to the United States in 1928. Edman served as pastor of the *CHRISTIAN AND MISSIONARY ALLIANCE Tabernacle in Worcester, Massachusetts, during which time he earned the Ph.D. in Latin American history from Clark University.

Edman began his career as an educator in 1935, when he taught at *NYACK MISSIONARY INSTITUTE. A year later he moved to *WHEATON COLLEGE, where he was professor of political science for four years and then president of the college for twenty-five years, beginning in 1940. Edman, for whom Wheaton's chapel is named, was a forceful and effective evangelical leader. During his watch, *WHEATON COLLEGE earned accreditation and undertook several building programs. Beyond the campus, Edman served in various capacities as a board member of such evangelical organizations as the *BILLY GRAHAM EVANGELISTIC ASSOCIATION.

References: V. Raymond Edman, *Light in the Dark Age* (1949); idem, *Finney Lives On* (1950); idem, *Out of My Life* (1961).

Education Research Association In 1961, Jim Gabler, a sixteen-year-old student in the public schools in Longview, Texas, began to question some of the material in his school textbooks. Norma Gabler, his mother, appeared before the state board of education objecting to books that she found inaccurate, amoral, or both. Her husband, Mel, who took early retirement as a clerk from the Humble Pipe Line Company, soon joined the effort to vet textbooks in Texas. Because Texas is so large and has a centralized textbook purchasing system, the Gablers and their organization, the Education Research Association, have exerted a considerable influence over the content of textbooks nationwide.

The Gablers, with the assistance of a small staff of researchers, run their not-for profit Education Research Association out of their home in Longview; they receive no salary for their efforts. They routinely raise objections to errors of fact in proposed books, but they also take issue with matters of emphasis. They objected, for example, to an American history textbook that devoted seven pages to Marilyn Monroe but none to Martha Washington, Lyndon Johnson, Richard Nixon, or the assassination of John F. Kennedy. They challenge books that appear to condone homosexuality. They challenge science books that treat evolution as demonstrable fact, insisting that it is only a theory and that it should be taught alongside the Genesis account of creation. The Gablers, who are often accused of censorship, also advocate more parental participation both in textbook selection and in the educational process.

Mel and Norma Gabler and their crusade have attracted nationwide attention, in large measure because Texas is the largest textbook purchaser in the nation and because publishers, wanting a part of that market, revise their textbooks in order to pass muster in Texas. They have appeared on many television programs, including *Donahue* and *60 Minutes,* and have been the subject of countless articles in newspapers. Molly Ivins, a nationally syndicated columnist from Texas, once characterized them as "two ignorant, fear-mongering, right-wing fruitloops who have spent the last twenty years doing untold damage to public education in this state." The Gablers' efforts, however, have not gone unappreciated by parents generally, particularly by those sympathetic to the agenda of the *RELIGIOUS RIGHT. "Let 'em ridicule us and have their fun," Norma Gabler once said about the critics. "With all their griping and complaining and outright lies about us, they can't get over the fact that we're effective. They're squealing because they see the majority of Americans are getting fed up with the way textbooks are attacking traditional values."

References: Mel and Norma Gabler, with James C. Hefley, *What Are They Teaching Our Children?* (1985); *"In the Beginning": The Creationist Controversy,* two-part PBS documentary (1994).

Edwards, Jonathan (1703–1758) Born in East Windsor, Connecticut, the son and grandson of Congregationalist ministers, Jonathan Edwards became a Congregationalist minister himself and also one of the greatest minds ever in American history. A precocious child who ruminated about God and the natural world, Edwards graduated from Yale College at the age of seventeen and stayed an additional two years to study theology, whereupon he was licensed to preach and briefly served as pastor of a Presbyterian church in New York City from 1722 until 1723. He returned to Yale the next year as a tutor, and after two years there he accepted a call as assistant pastor to his grandfather, *SOLOMON STODDARD, in Northampton, Massachusetts. He married Sarah Pierrepont in 1727 and in 1729, upon Stoddard's death, became sole pastor of the Northampton congregation.

During the winter of 1734–35, a *REVIVAL of religion swept through Northampton, a phenomenon that Edwards recounted as a visitation of divine grace in *A Faithful Narrative of the Surprising Work of God* (1737). Three hundred people were added to the church. Religion, according to Edwards, became the dominant topic of conversation among townspeople. After the *REVIVAL waned somewhat, the fires were rekindled with the visit of *GEORGE WHITEFIELD in 1740, during his tour of the Atlantic colonies. By this time the *REVIVAL was widespread, a phenomenon known to historians as the *GREAT AWAKENING.

By the mid-1740s, however, some of the excesses associated with the *REVIVAL began to discredit the Awakening itself. Edwards was placed in the awkward position of defending the *REVIVAL from its enemies by rescuing it from his friends, and he engaged in a protracted pamphlet war with Charles Chauncy of Boston. Edwards's attempts to distinguish between true and counterfeit religious expressions appeared in his most famous work: *A Treatise Concerning Religious Affections,* published in 1746. The *REVIVAL, however, eventually took its toll on Edwards's ministry. Edwards's sharp distinction between the converted and the unconverted led him to renege on Stoddardeanism, his grandfather's practice of allowing anyone to partake of Holy Communion, not merely the regenerate. Eventually, the Northampton congregation forced Edwards's ouster in 1750, whereupon he became a missionary to the Indians in Stockbridge, Massachusetts. During this "Stockbridge exile," Edwards produced some of his most important work, including *Freedom of the Will, The Nature of True Virtue,* and *The History of the Work of Redemption.*

Edwards was chosen in 1757 to succeed his late son-in-law, *AARON BURR, as president of the College of New Jersey. Shortly after assuming office, Edwards died of complications from a smallpox inoculation.

References: Perry Miller, *Jonathan Edwards* (1949); Patricia J. Tracy, *Jonathan Edwards, Pastor: Religion and Society in Eighteenth-Century Northampton* (1979); John E. Smith, *Jonathan Edwards: Puritan, Preacher, Philosopher* (1992).

Edwards, Jonathan, Jr. (1745–1801) One of the *NEW DIVINITY theologians who sought to perpetuate the theology of his father, Jonathan Edwards Jr. was born in Northampton, Massachusetts. The younger Edwards graduated from the College of New Jersey (Princeton) in 1765, studied theology, and was licensed to preach in 1766. Following a stint as tutor at Princeton, Edwards became pastor of the White Haven Church in New Haven, Connecticut, where he was ordained in 1769. He remained in New Haven until 1795, moved to Colebrook, Connecticut, and in 1799 became president of Union College in Schenectady, New York.

In addition to his theological writings, Edwards was one of the earliest opponents of slavery and the slave trade. His zeal for missions impelled him to become one of the prime movers behind the Plan of Union of 1801, which provided for the cooperation of New England Congregationalists and mid-Atlantic Presbyterians in bringing Christianity to the frontier.

References: Jonathan Edwards Jr., *The Impolicy of the Slave Trade and Slavery* (1791); R. L. Ferm, *Jonathan Edwards the Younger, 1745–1801* (1976).

Eliason, Vic (1936–) Vic Eliason grew up in a remote area of northern Minnesota, one hundred miles northwest of Duluth. Having attended a Swedish Baptist Church, where his father served as a lay preacher, Eliason early on imbibed fundamentalist dogma. He enrolled in Open Bible College in Des Moines, Iowa, and was ordained in a nondenominational church. In 1959, Eliason and his wife, Freda, moved to Milwaukee, and two years later started a half-hour radio broadcast called *Voice of Christian Youth,* which soon expanded to a full day of broadcasting. In the 1970s, Eliason purchased radio station WBON, renamed it WVCY, and moved his operation into larger quarters. He ventured into television in 1982.

Eliason's *FUNDAMENTALISM has always been militant, and he has tangled publicly with entities as diverse as the Wisconsin legislature, the public school system, and the *Milwaukee Journal.* He has unleashed special fury against the Roman Catholic Archdiocese of Milwaukee, particularly its archbishop, Rembert Weakland, whom Eliason regarded as a "liberal" for his views on homosexuality and sex education.

Elim Fellowship The Elim Fellowship grew out of the work of graduates of the Elim Bible Institute of Lima, New York. The group came together informally as the Elim Ministerial Fellowship in 1932. The fellowship changed its name in 1947 to Elim Missionary Assembly, and in 1972 the Assembly became the Elim Fellowship. The last change was made so that the name would more nearly represent the purpose and direction of the group.

The doctrine of the fellowship is similar to that of the *ASSEMBLIES OF GOD: an emphasis on the Holy Spirit–filled life and *SANCTIFICATION of the believer. Other doctrines include *PREMILLENNIALISM, the inspiration and infallibility of the Bible, the Trinity, *BAPTISM OF THE HOLY SPIRIT, divine healing, and the resurrection of the saved and unsaved for eternal reward or punishment.

Headquarters for the fellowship are located in Lima, New York, on the campus of the former Genessee Wesleyan Seminary, which the fellowship purchased in 1951. The group claims about 180 churches with twenty thousand members.

References: Frank S. Mead and Samuel S. Hill, *Handbook of Denominations in the United States,* 10th ed. (1996); J. Gordon Melton, *The Encyclopedia of American Religions,* 3d ed. (1993).

Elkhart Institute of Science, Industry and the Arts. *See* **Goshen College.**

Elliot, Elisabeth (née Howard) (1926–) Born to missionary parents in Belgium, Elisabeth Howard graduated from *WHEATON COLLEGE in 1948 and proceeded to prepare for missionary service to Latin America. She began her work in the Andes in 1952 and the next year married another Wheaton graduate, *JIM ELLIOT. The couple concentrated their efforts in the jungles of eastern Ecuador. Elisabeth Elliot was widowed in January 1956 when a group of Huaoranis (Aucas) ambushed her husband and four other missionaries. Though left with an infant daughter, the young widow sought to carry on the missions effort as well as to write about her slain husband. *Through Gates of Splendor,* published in 1957, made the heroism, piety, and sacrifice of the *ECUADOR MARTYRS (*JIM ELLIOT and his coworkers) famous among evangelicals. *Shadow of the Almighty: The Life and Testament of Jim Elliot* appeared the following year and arguably became the most influential biography of an evangelical missionary since *JONATHAN EDWARDS's life of his son-in-law *DAVID BRAINERD.

References: Elisabeth Elliot, *Through Gates of Splendor* (1957); idem, *Shadow of the Almighty: The Life and Testament of Jim Elliot* (1958); idem, *No Graven Image* (1966).

Elliot, James "Jim" (1927–1956) As a student at *WHEATON COLLEGE, Jim Elliot decided to become an evangelical missionary to the Huaoranis (Aucas) living in the jungles of Ecuador. The apparently unprovoked slayings of Elliot and his fellow missionaries Ed McCully, Peter Fleming, Nate Saint, and Roger Youderian—known collectively as the *ECUADOR MARTYRS—in January 1956 shocked the evangelical world and inspired a generation of young evangelicals to missionary service. Elliot's widow, *ELISABETH ELLIOT, wrote an inspiring account of her husband's life and went on to considerable success as an evangelical author.

References: Elisabeth Elliot, *Shadow of the Almighty: The Life and Testament of Jim Elliot* (1958); Steve Saint, "Did They Have to Die?" *Christianity Today,* September 16, 1996.

Ellis, Walter (1883–1944) Born in Derbyshire, England, Walter Ellis migrated to Canada in 1903 and became assistant to the Anglican chaplain of the Barr Colony in Saskatchewan. He earned the bachelor's and master's degrees from the University of Toronto and the B.D. from Wycliffe College. While in Toronto, Ellis came under the influence of *W. H. GRIFFITH THOMAS, from whom he picked up evangelical theology and *KESWICK teachings, with their emphasis on personal holiness, daily communication with God, and Christian service.

Ellis headed west to Vancouver, British Columbia, in 1913 and eventually joined the faculty of Bishop Latimer Hall. He became one of the founders of the *VANCOUVER BIBLE TRAINING SCHOOL in 1918, serving as its principal from its inception until his death in 1944. Ellis, an irenic man, wanted the school to remain unsectarian, and he declared that its purpose was "to furnish a thorough and practical use of the English *BIBLE, and to send forth the workers with an extreme love of souls, and a full realization of the presence and power of the Holy Spirit in their life and service." He vigorously supported missionary work, especially the *CHINA INLAND MISSION, and he held weekly lectures at the school for the benefit of *SUNDAY SCHOOL teachers in the area. Ellis took on additional responsibilities in 1925 as minister of Fairview Presbyterian Church, a conservative congregation that refused to merge into the United Church of Canada.

Reference: Robert K. Burkinshaw, "Conservative Evangelicalism in the Twentieth-Century 'West': British Columbia and the United States," in George A. Rawlyk and Mark A. Noll, eds., *Amazing Grace: Evangelicalism in Australia, Britain, Canada, and the United States* (1993).

Embury, Philip (1728–1773) Philip Embury, a carpenter and Methodist preacher, emigrated from Ireland to New York City in 1760. He became a schoolteacher, but his cousin, *BARBARA HECK, persuaded him to resume his preaching and to join her in the formation of a Methodist society in October 1766. The society grew so rapidly that the congregation constructed its own chapel on John Street in lower Manhattan in 1768. The Emburys and the Hecks moved north into the Hudson Valley in the early 1770s, where they organized other societies in Washington and Albany Counties.

Emmons, Nathaniel (1745–1840) Born in East Haddam, Connecticut, Nathaniel Emmons graduated from Yale College in

1767 and was licensed to preach in 1769. After four years as an itinerant preacher, Emmons became pastor of the Congregational church at Wrentham (later, Franklin), Massachusetts. Emmons was a *NEW DIVINITY theologian, and he trained nearly ninety students for the ministry. He departed from the *NEW DIVINITY, however, on the issue of human depravity. Emmons insisted that *SIN was an act of will rather than a condition inherited from Adam. This gloss on New Divinity theology became known as the "Exercise Scheme" because of Emmons's insistence that *SIN lay in the particular "exercises" of the sinner rather than in imputed guilt.

In addition to his activities as a theologian, Emmons participated in several *REVIVALS. He was one of the founders of the Massachusetts Missionary Society and served as its first president for a dozen years. From 1803 to 1808, he served as editor of the *Massachusetts Missionary Magazine.*

References: Edwards Amasa Park, *Memoirs of Nathaniel Emmons* (1861); Bruce Kuklick, *Churchmen and Philosophers: From Jonathan Edwards to John Dewey* (1985).

Encounter Ministries. *See* **Olford, Stephen F.**

End Times The term "end times" tends to surface in discussions about *ESCHATOLOGY. Evangelicals, the majority of whom hold millennial views of one sort or another, talk about the end times as that sequence of events predicted in the *BIBLE which will lead to the end of time as we know it and the establishment of a millennial kingdom.

English, Michael (1962–) Michael English was once known as the "poster child" of *CONTEMPORARY CHRISTIAN MUSIC, but a scandal caused his near-exile from the industry. English had gained popularity in the early 1990s as both a singer and songwriter, with consistent rankings at the top of *Billboard*'s Christian Contemporary chart. His 1992 release, *Hope,* was the number-five album on that chart for 1993; a year after it was issued, the recording still held a place at number twenty-three. He also sang with the gospel group established by Christian music patriarch *BILL GAITHER and had been asked to sing at the Buffalo Bills' family and team services at two Super Bowls. By 1994, English had already won five Dove Awards from the *GOSPEL MUSIC ASSOCIATION. In April of that year, however, Gaither announced that English would no longer sing with the *BILL GAITHER Vocal Band. Later that month, English went on to win six more Dove Awards, two for his work with the *BILL GAITHER Band, and four others—including Best Male Vocalist for the third consecutive time, Best Inspirational Recorded Song for "Holding Out Hope to You," Best Contemporary Album for *Hope,* and Artist of the Year.

Less than two weeks after the Dove ceremonies, however, English announced he would return all the awards to the *GOSPEL MUSIC ASSOCIATION. In a press conference later revealed to have been convened by his recording company, the singer, who was married at the time, admitted to having had an affair with another Christian artist, Marabeth Jordan, who was a member of a group known as First Call. Jordan, moreover, was pregnant with English's child. The confession came at an inopportune moment, for English and Jordan had just finished performing together in a benefit tour for unwed mothers. Though she later miscarried, Jordan was forced to leave First Call. English found his contract with Warner Alliance indefinitely frozen on the grounds that he had violated its morality clause, and the company released a statement announcing it would no longer market or sell the singer's music. Christian bookstores pulled his albums from the shelves.

English was not entirely banished from Christian music. The *GOSPEL MUSIC ASSOCIATION reinstated his awards after releasing a statement to the effect that the group was not a "policing organization." English continued to write and produce inspirational songs for other singers; he won Dove Awards in both 1995 and 1996, the latter time for Southern Gospel Album of the Year for the recording he produced for the Martins. Some people within the Christian music industry have suggested that English probably could reenter the market were he willing to repent publicly for his conduct. The singer, however, chose to pursue a career in mainstream music instead (although by the end of the decade he had launched a comeback attempt). A few months after the scandal, English signed a new contract with Curb Records, the label that carries Merle Haggard and Lyle Lovett. Late in 1994, Curb released a duet English sang with country singer Wynonna—"Healing"—which came from the soundtrack to the movie *Silent Fall.* The following spring, English recorded another single, "Love Moves in Mysterious Ways." In May 1996 came *Freedom,* his first album since leaving Warner Alliance. Despite his artistic successes and his attempts at a comeback late in the 1990s, English has not attained the same position in the mainstream market that he once enjoyed in Christian contemporary circles.

References: Lisa Collins, "Michael English Soars to the Top with Four Dove Awards," *Billboard,* May 14, 1994; Bob Darden, "Christian Singer Michael English Leaves Industry," *Billboard,* May 21, 1994; Nicholas Dawidoff, "No Sex. No Drugs. But Rock 'n' Roll (Kind of)," *New York Times,* February 5, 1995; Deborah Evans Price, "Curb's Michael English Is 'Healing'; Pop Career Sought Following Scandal," *Billboard,* October 15, 1994; "Michael English Declares His 'Freedom.'" *Billboard,* May 25, 1996.

Episcopal Charismatic Fellowship. *See* **Episcopal Renewal Ministries.**

Episcopal Renewal Ministries Founded in 1973 as the Episcopal Charismatic Fellowship, the Episcopal Renewal Ministries represents a cooperative effort among charismatic Episcopalians for parish renewal. The impetus behind the group came from *DENNIS J. BENNETT and Wesley (Ted) Nelson, who organized the first gathering at St. Matthew's Episcopal Cathedral in Dallas, Texas, early in 1973. The group publishes a newsletter called *ACTS 29,* and its motto reads: "Dedicated to the renewal of people and parishes through Apostolic teaching, biblical preaching, historic worship, and charismatic experience."

Epp, Theodore H(erman) (1907–1985) Born in Oraibi, Arizona, to Mennonite Russian immigrants and reared in rural Oklahoma, Theodore H. Epp was converted in 1927. He studied under the tutelage of his father, J. B. Epp, who had founded the Oklahoma Bible Academy in Meno, Oklahoma. Theodore went on for more education at the *BIBLE INSTITUTE OF LOS ANGELES, Hesston College, and Southwestern Baptist Theological Seminary. Epp was pastor of the Zoar Mennonite Church in Goltry, Oklahoma, from 1932 until 1936, when he became an itinerant preacher, based in Meno, where he had spent his high school years. He also began an apprenticeship to radio evangelist T. Myron Webb, of Enid, Oklahoma, offering Bible teaching over the airwaves. While visiting relatives in Nebraska, a young woman commented, "Why don't some of you radio preachers from Oklahoma come to Nebraska? We have no daily gospel broadcast here."

Epp and his family moved to Lincoln, Nebraska, in 1939 to begin his own radio program, *Back to the Bible Broadcast*, which expanded to more than six hundred stations. One of the founders of *NATIONAL RELIGIOUS BROADCASTERS, Epp published more than sixty books and founded two periodicals: *Good News Broadcaster* (renamed *Confident Living* in 1986) and *Young Ambassador* (now *T.Q.: Teen Quest*).

References: Theodore H. Epp, *45 Years of Adventuring Faith: The Back to the Bible Story;* Harold J. Berry, *I Love to Tell the Story: Back to the Bible's Adventure of Faith* (1989).

Epworth League Named for the place of *JOHN WESLEY's birth, the Epworth League, a Methodist youth organization, was organized in 1889 by C. A. Littlefield and Jesse L. Hurlburt to promote spiritual values, missions, and denominational loyalty among young Methodists in the Methodist Episcopal Church. The idea spread rapidly throughout *METHODISM, including the Methodist Episcopal Church, South and the Methodist Church in Canada. By 1894, the official League organs—*Onward* (Epworth League in Canada) and the *Epworth Herald* (two separate editions: Methodist Episcopal Church, South and the Methodist Episcopal Church)—had a combined circulation in excess of 125,000. Most Epworth League gatherings were held on Sunday evenings—apart from the congregation's regular Sunday evening services, a circumstance that created some tension with local pastors. At its General Conference in 1924, the Methodist Episcopal Church voted to disband the Epworth League and place its youth activities under the auspices of the educational programs of the denomination. The Methodist Episcopal Church, South made a similar ruling in 1930.

Erdman, Charles R(osenbury) (1866–1960) The son of premillennialist leader *WILLIAM J. ERDMAN, Charles R. Erdman graduated from Princeton University and Princeton Theological Seminary, where he assumed the chair of practical theology in 1906. Although he remained at Princeton Seminary until his retirement in 1936, Erdman was very active in denominational affairs. He was pastor of the First Presbyterian Church in Princeton from 1924 to 1934, and he won election as moderator of the General Assembly in 1925. Although Erdman described himself as a fundamentalist, he dealt the fundamentalists a blow when, as moderator, he referred their proposals to a committee, thereby breaking their momentum in their efforts to thwart the spread of *MODERNISM within the denomination. After *J. GRESHAM MACHEN led an exodus from Princeton Seminary to form *WESTMINSTER THEOLOGICAL SEMINARY in 1929, Erdman led an effort to reorganize Princeton Seminary along lines that would make it more inclusive.

Reference: Bradley J. Longfield, *The Presbyterian Controversy: Fundamentalists, Modernists, and Moderates* (1991).

Erdman, William J(acob) (1834–1923) A Presbyterian and a premillennialist, William J. Erdman studied at Hamilton College and at Union Theological Seminary and was ordained in 1860. In the course of serving several pastorates, Erdman became associated with *DWIGHT L. MOODY. Erdman often spoke at the *NIAGARA CONFERENCES, and he served as secretary of the conference throughout its existence. His association with Moody culminated in his term as pastor of Moody's Illinois Street Church, from 1875 to 1878. Erdman, the father of *CHARLES R. ERDMAN, also served as a consulting editor for the **SCOFIELD REFERENCE BIBLE*.

Erskine College and Erskine Theological Seminary (Due West, South Carolina) Erskine Theological Seminary was established in 1837, and Erskine College was founded two years later. The seminary became known as the School of Theology of Erskine College in 1925. The college and seminary share one administration; both are affiliated with the Associate Reformed Presbyterian Church. Today, the seminary awards the master of divinity, the master of arts in Christian ministry, and the doctorate of ministry. Although many Christian colleges do not permit the organization of fraternities and sororities, Erskine College has eight "literary societies" that date to the founding of the school.

Eschatology Literally a study of the *END TIMES, the theological discipline of eschatology holds a special interest for evangelicals because of their conviction that the *BIBLE should be interpreted literally. The prophetic passages in the book of Daniel, for example, and especially the book of Revelation are invested with a great deal of significance because evangelicals generally regard these writings as a blueprint for understanding the sequence of events leading to the end of time. Because these passages are rather recondite, however, they are subject to many interpretations, and so evangelicals often disagree among themselves on eschatological matters.

Eshelman, Ira Lee (1917–) The founder of the *BIBLETOWN CONFERENCE CENTER in Boca Raton, Florida, Ira Lee Eshelman was born in Lancaster, Pennsylvania, and converted to evangelical Christianity in his early twenties. After graduating from *MOODY BIBLE INSTITUTE in 1941, he became pastor of an independent Bible church in Highland Park, Michigan, from 1941 until 1946, when he started a radio program, the *Radio Bible Commentator*. In 1950, he purchased a parcel of land in Boca Raton for use as a Bible conference grounds. He founded the Boca Raton Community Church two years later.

Eshelman retired from the day-to-day management of *BIBLETOWN in 1967, whereupon he took on the task of establishing pregame chapel programs for every team in the National Football League. By 1970, with the endorsement of Pete Rozelle, the league commissioner, Eshelman had succeeded in organizing chapels for every team except the Oakland Raiders. The Raiders followed shortly thereafter when Eshelman, through other owners, applied pressure to Al Davis, the team's owner and general manager. The pregame chapel program, which bears the name Sports World Ministries, has since expanded into Major League Baseball, the Canadian Football League, and professional soccer.

Reference: Ira Lee Eshelman, *A Gold Coast Miracle: "Great Things He Hath Done"* (n.d.).

Estabrooks, Elijah (1756–1825) One of the Baptist leaders of the *CANADA FIRE in the Maritimes, Elijah Estabrooks was born in Haverhill, Massachusetts, and migrated with his family first to Nova Scotia and then to New Brunswick.

Estabrooks's *NEW LIGHT conversion in 1778 led to a career in the ministry. He was baptized by *JOSEPH CRANDALL in 1800, and he played a crucial role in the spread of Baptist sentiments along the Saint John River Valley of New Brunswick.

Reference: G. A. Rawlyk, *The Canada Fire: Radical Evangelicalism in British North America, 1775–1812* (1994).

Eternal Security The issue of "eternal security" has been hotly debated among evangelicals for centuries, the subject of countless discussions around the campfire and in dormitory lounges at evangelical colleges: Can a Christian (by evangelical definition, someone who has been *BORN AGAIN) ever lose *SALVATION? The answer depends, more than anything else, on the theology that informs an evangelical's faith. People in the Reformed tradition, following the lead of John Calvin, would insist that God's grace is irresistible and not dependent upon individual merit. People with Arminian sympathies, who emphasize the individual's role in choosing salvation (to use *BILLY GRAHAM's language, to "make a decision for Christ"), would tend to worry more about the certainty of one's eternal destination. That is, if an individual can determine his own fate by choosing to be *SAVED, presumably he could reverse that choice, either consciously or by exhibiting an indifference toward godly living.

Eternal Word Television Network. *See* **Angelica, Mother.**

Eugene Bell Centennial Foundation The Eugene Bell Centennial Foundation is a nonprofit charitable organization established in 1995. The foundation was named in honor of Eugene Bell, a Presbyterian minister who began missionary service to Korea in 1895. The Bell Foundation's mission is to support educational, humanitarian, and religious projects and exchanges in Korea, both North and South. In 1995, the organization's Food for Life Program distributed nearly seventy thousang bags of rice in the flood-stricken areas of North Korea. The Bell Foundation also works with the *BILLY GRAHAM EVANGELISTIC ASSOCIATION, the United Nations World Food Program, and *WORLD VISION on relief and humanitarian projects in Korea.

Evangel University (Springfield, Missouri) Established in 1955 as Evangel College, Evangel University has always been owned and operated by the General Council of the *ASSEMBLIES OF GOD. It was, in fact, the denomination's first liberal arts college, and its founding was a controversial matter because into the 1950s, the *ASSEMBLIES OF GOD was very suspicious of liberal arts education. While previously the *ASSEMBLIES OF GOD relied almost exclusively on *BIBLE INSTITUTES, at Evangel the humanities were offered alongside courses in religion.

Among Evangel's campus standards and regulations is a proscription against occult practices. On the other hand, students, faculty, and staff are asked to "abstain from all practices that tend to be morally degrading," but decisions regarding television, movies, and other entertainment and social life are left up to the individual.

References: Vision: 1994–1996 Catalog of Evangel College of Arts and Sciences (1994); Thomas C. Hunt and James C. Carper, eds., *Religious Higher Education in the United States: A Source Book* (1996).

Evangelical The term *evangelical* applies to anyone who subscribes to the tenets of *EVANGELICALISM. In a generic sense, an evangelical is someone who believes, first, in the centrality of the *CONVERSION or "*BORN AGAIN" experience as the criterion for entering the kingdom of heaven. Second, an evangelical is someone who takes the *BIBLE seriously as God's revelation to humanity; an evangelical is inclined, more often than not, to interpret the *BIBLE literally.

Defined in this broad fashion, *evangelical* refers to a vast number of people; recent estimates put that number as high as 40 to 46 percent of the population in the United States, for example. Within that broader definition, however, are various permutations of evangelicals: fundamentalists, pentecostals, charismatics, and those in the holiness tradition. Although this rule is not universal, people who call themselves "evangelical" generally pronounce the word with a short "e" (the first two syllables rhyme with "leaven"), while people who are not evangelicals use a long "e" (ee-van-gel-i-cal).

References: Randall Balmer, *Mine Eyes Have Seen the Glory: A Journey into the Evangelical Subculture in America,* 3d ed. (2000); George M. Marsden, *Fundamentalism and American Culture: The Shaping of Twentieth-Century Evangelicalism: 1870–1925* (1980); Christian Smith, *American Evangelicalism: Embattled and Thriving* (1998).

Evangelical Alliance Founded in London in 1846, the Evangelical Alliance brought together evangelicals from Asia, Africa, Europe, America, and Great Britain in an effort to consolidate their activities and avoid duplication of efforts. The notion of such an alliance, which would respect denomination differences, was put forward by *SAMUEL S. SCHMUCKER of Gettysburg Theological Seminary in 1838. Although his *Fraternal Appeal to the American Churches* did not generate immediate action, the treatise became a formative document for the organization; Schmucker was a delegate to the London gathering. The founding meeting gave rise to discussions between the United States and British delegations over the morality of slavery, and the delegates eventually agreed that, rather than forming a worldwide alliance, each country should organize its own alliance.

The Evangelical Alliance in the United States would not take shape until 1867, after the Civil War. It brought together diverse evangelical groups united by a common evangelical theology and, very often, by their antipathy toward Roman Catholicism. Evangelicals associated with the movement also worked for social reform, including *TEMPERANCE. The coalition held conventions in major cities throughout the postbellum period and at the Columbian Exposition in Chicago in 1892. By the turn of the twentieth century, however, the growing tide of industrialization and urbanization had sapped much of the energy from the Evangelical Alliance. The cooperation among Protestants embodied by the Evangelical Alliance was copied by the Federal Council of Churches, organized in 1908.

Evangelical Alliance Mission, The (TEAM) Established in 1890, The Evangelical Alliance Mission, also known as TEAM, is a nondenominational evangelical missionary agency. With an emphasis on *EVANGELISM and church planting, TEAM is active in thirty countries. The organization, headquartered in Wheaton, Illinois, also supports such missionary enterprises as Bible translation, radio broadcasting, and medical assistance.

Evangelical and Ecumenical Women's Caucus. *See* **Evangelical Women's Caucus International.**

Evangelical Association. *See* **Methodism.**

Evangelical Association for the Promotion of Education. *See* **Campolo, Anthony "Tony."**

Evangelical Broadcasting Corporation (EBC) Founded in 1967, the Evangelical Broadcasting Corporation (EBC) is an evangelistic radio and television operation in Hilversum, the Netherlands. The EBC receives financing from the Dutch government and has been honored for the excellence of its educational, cultural, and entertainment programming.

Evangelical Church of North America The Evangelical Church of North America was formed in 1968 by members of the Evangelical United Brethren who objected to that group's merger with the Methodist Church, which created the United Methodist Church. The restive congregations were located primarily in the Pacific Northwest, with fifty churches in the Northwestern Conference and eighteen in the Montana Conference. Many of the pastors in these conferences had been trained at the Western Evangelical Seminary, which was strongly holiness-oriented in its doctrine and emphasis. Shortly after its formation, the Evangelical Church was joined by the Holiness Methodist Church, whose main strength was in the upper Midwest. The Holiness Methodist Church became the North Central Conference in the new denomination.

The theology of the Evangelical Church derives from the Methodist tradition as it was developed in the Evangelical United Brethren church, including a special emphasis on entire *SANCTIFICATION. The *POLITY is also typically Methodist, with conference superintendents overseeing district and annual conferences. The office of general superintendent was created in 1976. The denomination claims a membership of 16,398 in 185 churches, primarily in the Pacific Northwest.

References: Frank S. Mead and Samuel S. Hill, *Handbook of Denominations in the United States,* 10th ed. (1996); J. Gordon Melton, *The Encyclopedia of American Religions,* 3d ed. (1993).

Evangelical Congregational Church The Evangelical Congregational Church was formed out of the 1894 schism in the Evangelical Association. The schismatic faction took the name of the United Evangelical Church. It reunited with the parent group in 1922 as the Evangelical Church. Some members of the schismatic churches objected to the proposed merger. The dissenting churches, located mainly in the East Pennsylvania Conference, voted in special session to remain separate, thus creating the Evangelical Congregational Church.

The church's theology is Trinitarian. It accepts the *BIBLE as the "fully inspired, wholly reliable, solely authentic Word of God." It is the "supreme authority in conscience, creed, and conduct." The church rejects the doctrine of predestination, believing that *GRACE is available to all and that all are able to accept it of their own free will. *POLITY in the church is episcopal, but the *AUTHORITY of the bishops is limited. The churches are autonomous, and ministers are appointed to the congregations. Headquarters for the Evangelical Congregational Church are in Myerstown, Pennsylvania, which is also the home of the church's Evangelical School of Theology. In 1985, the church reported having 159 churches with 35,584 members in the United States.

Reference: J. Gordon Melton, *The Encyclopedia of American Religions,* 3d ed. (1993).

Evangelical Council for Financial Accountability The Evangelical Council for Financial Accountability (ECFA) was founded in 1979 to provide a kind of "Good Housekeeping" seal for evangelical not-for-profit organizations. The impetus had come from *MARK O. HATFIELD, United States senator from Oregon and an evangelical, who warned evangelical leaders in 1977 that members of Congress were prepared to pass legislation to regulate the financial affairs of religious broadcasters unless they found a way to police themselves.

More than 850 religious, charitable, and educational organizations that claim the term "evangelical" are members of the organization, which certifies, in turn, that the organizations adhere to a code of financial conduct and accountability. The council gained prominence in the mid-1980s in the wake of the televangelist scandals as evangelicals sought some guarantee that their contributions to charitable groups claiming to be evangelical would not be misused. The Evangelical Council for Financial Accountability demands of its member organizations, among other things, that they have independent boards of directors, that they adhere to specified guidelines for fund-raising, and that books be audited annually.

Unlike similar secular organizations, ECFA membership standards include the ability to demonstrate a commitment to the evangelical Christian faith. This requirement is not surprising, considering that the council sees its mission as biblically based; the ECFA motto comes from 2 Corinthians 8:21: "For we are taking pains to do what is right, not only in the eyes of the Lord but also in the eyes of men."

ECFA membership is voluntary; organizations seek registration with the council because it helps them earn and retain the public's trust that their donations will be used wisely. All member organizations guarantee their financial integrity by submitting to an annual review. Furthermore, between thirty and forty nonprofits are selected at random yearly for a more indepth review, conducted on-site at each organization's headquarters. When complaints are registered, compliance reviews are held to investigate possible failure to comply with ECFA standards. Like the Better Business Bureau or the National Charities Information Bureau, the Evangelical Council for Financial Accountability makes its membership directory available to the public. This information is available by phone or mail and is posted on the Council's Internet Web site. The ECFA has also published a "Giver's Guide" to help donors make informed decisions, whether or not a nonprofit is a registered member.

Evangelical Environmental Network A project originating out of the cooperation between *EVANGELICALS FOR SOCIAL ACTION and *WORLD VISION, the Evangelical Environmental Network "seeks to nurture a biblically grounded, scientifically informed environmental movement within the evangelical community that understands the urgency of the global crisis and realizes that environmental concern and action are essential to Christian belief and discipleship." The organization sponsors conferences, publishes *Creation Care* magazine, provides curricula for evangelical colleges, and urges evangelicals to be informed about matters of public policy that relate to the environment. The Evangelical Environmental Network also seeks to influence legislation. Early in 1996, for example, the organization lobbied members of Congress in defense of the Endangered Species Act, which itself was endangered by the Republican majority in Congress. One member of the organization, *CALVIN B. DEWITT, a professor of environmental studies at the University of Wisconsin, argued that the legislation in question was "the Noah's ark of our day." The Evangelical Environmental Network encourages evangelical congregations to observe "Creation Sunday," on the Sunday that falls closest to Earth Day, April 22.

Evangelical Fellowship in the Anglican Communion Founded in 1961, the Evangelical Fellowship in the Anglican Communion is an international coalition of evangelicals affiliated with the Church of England and the Anglican Communion. The group seeks a more theologically conservative stance on the *AUTHORITY of Scripture and a return to the doctrines as laid out in the *Thirty-nine Articles.*

Evangelical Fellowship of Canada Begun in Toronto in 1964 as a union of evangelical pastors serving both in evangelical and mainline denominations, the Evangelical Fellowship of Canada is affiliated with the *WORLD EVANGELICAL FELLOWSHIP. The organization, which includes more than twenty denominations with a membership somewhere in the range of one million, also publishes a magazine, *Faith Today.*

Evangelical Free Church of America The Evangelical Free Church of America traces its roots to the free-church movement in Scandinavia, where small congregations of pietistically inclined believers refused to participate in the Lutheranism of the state churches. In the United States, a conference of free churches was held in Boone, Iowa, in 1884. In 1950, the Evangelical Free Church Association (Norwegian-Danish) merged with the Evangelical Free Church of America (Swedish) and took the latter name.

The church, popularly known as the Free Church, is congregational in *POLITY and very conservative, even fundamentalist, in theology. The statement of faith insists upon biblical *INERRANCY and the premillennial return of Christ. Although church theology officially allows for some latitude on other issues, most congregations prefer adult *BAPTISM and generally look askance at the pentecostal gifts of the Spirit.

The denomination, which enjoyed considerable growth in the latter part of the twentieth century, has its offices in Minneapolis and supports missionaries in approximately fifteen foreign countries. Its institutions of higher education include *TRINITY WESTERN UNIVERSITY in Langley, British Columbia, and *TRINITY INTERNATIONAL UNIVERSITY, which encompasses *TRINITY COLLEGE and *TRINITY EVANGELICAL DIVINITY SCHOOL, in Deerfield, Illinois.

References: Arnold Theodore Olson, *The Search for Identity* (1980); idem, *The Significance of Silence* (1981); idem, *Stumbling Toward Maturity* (1981).

Evangelical Friends Alliance A coalition of Friends churches with evangelical sympathies, the Evangelical Friends Alliance was formed in 1965 and includes the religious descendants of the Gurneyites, followers of evangelical revivalist *JOSEPH JOHN GURNEY. The Alliance supports *MALONE COLLEGE, a Christian liberal arts school in Canton, Ohio.

Evangelical-Israel Friendship Council. *See* **Evans, Mike.**

Evangelical Lutheran Joint Synod of Wisconsin and Other States. *See* **Wisconsin Evangelical Lutheran Synod.**

Evangelical Lutheran Joint Synod of Wisconsin, Minnesota, and Michigan. *See* **Wisconsin Evangelical Lutheran Synod.**

Evangelical Mennonite Brethren. *See* **Fellowship of Evangelical Bible Churches.**

Evangelical Mennonite Church The Evangelical Mennonite Church was formed about 1865 as the Defenseless Mennonite Church. Its founder, Henry Egli (or Egly), emphasized the necessity of a personal *CONVERSION experience for believers. Egli taught regeneration, separation, nonconformity to the world, and nonresistance. He believed, as did his followers, that the Amish had lost their piety and had declined into merely an organization. The need for *CONVERSION had been overturned for the inherited culture and practices of the Amish tradition.

In most ways the Evangelical Mennonite Church is indistinguishable from other Mennonite and Amish conferences. It draws its beliefs directly from that tradition. The Church maintains a children's home in Flanagan, Illinois, and a camp near Kalamazoo, Michigan. The denomination has always been open to ecumenical endeavors. It joined the *NATIONAL ASSOCIATION OF EVANGELICALS in 1944. The group claims twenty-nine churches and 4,130 members.

References: Frank S. Mead and Samuel S. Hill, *Handbook of Denominations in the United States,* 10th ed. (1996); J. Gordon Melton, *The Encyclopedia of American Religions,* 3d ed. (1993).

Evangelical Presbyterian Church Formed in 1981, the Evangelical Presbyterian Church (EPC) is a conservative Presbyterian denomination. Beginning with twelve churches, the group now counts nearly 180 churches and a membership of over fifty-six thousand.

Evangelical Presbyterian Church *POLITY is presbyterian (governed by elders), with sessions (local groups), presbyteries (regional), and the general assembly (national). Doctrine in the Evangelical Presbyterian Church is Reformed. The church subscribes to the Westminster Confession, including the sections on the Holy Spirit (chapter 34) and missions (chapter 35), which are excluded by other conservative Presbyterian bodies. Being evangelical in spirit and practice, the Evangelical Presbyterian Church places an emphasis on church planting and world mission. The denomination has been a member of the *NATIONAL ASSOCIATION OF EVANGELICALS since 1982. Headquarters are located in Livonia, Michigan.

References: Frank S. Mead and Samuel S. Hill, *Handbook of Denominations in the United States,* 10th ed. (1996); J. Gordon Melton, *The Encyclopedia of American Religions,* 3d ed. (1993).

Evangelical Teacher Training Association. *See* **Evangelical Training Association.**

Evangelical Theological College. *See* **Dallas Theological Seminary.**

Evangelical Theological Society Founded in Cincinnati on December 27–28, 1949, the Evangelical Theological Society (ETS) is an organization of evangelical scholars who hold at least the master of theology degree (a degree beyond the standard master of divinity for ordination) and who hold to conservative doctrines, especially on the matter of biblical *INERRANCY. The organization grew out of talks earlier that year at Gordon Divinity School (now *GORDON-CONWELL

THEOLOGICAL SEMINARY) about the need for regular discussions about theology and biblical scholarship among people who affirmed *INERRANCY. Aside from academic degrees, the ETS demanded as a condition for membership fidelity to the following statement: "The Bible alone and the Bible in its entirety is the word of God written, and therefore inerrant in the autographs."

In 1958, the society began its own journal, *Bulletin of the Evangelical Theological Society*, later renamed *Journal of the Evangelical Theological Society*. Beginning in the 1970s, the society's statement on biblical *INERRANCY has been challenged, particularly by younger members who question the usefulness of such a construct.

References: Mark A. Noll, *Between Faith and Criticism: Evangelicals, Scholarship, and the Bible in America* (1986); Richard Quebedeaux, *The Worldly Evangelicals* (1978).

Evangelical Training Association (Wheaton, Illinois) One of the oldest and largest evangelical associations, the Evangelical Training Association acts as a link between higher education and the church, seeing itself as a bridge between schools that are training people for Christian service and the churches in which these graduates will ultimately serve. Its membership of approximately two hundred participating institutions in the United States, Canada, and abroad includes seminaries and graduate schools, undergraduate colleges, and non–degree-granting schools, which are often affiliated with local churches. Today, the Evangelical Training Association has two purposes: to promote high standards of Christian education for member schools, and to offer programs, materials, and support services to churches training laypeople for lay ministry. The association is an interdenominational endeavor, and over ninety denominations have used its materials to date.

The Evangelical Training Association was founded in Chicago in 1930 by representatives of five Bible colleges: *MOODY BIBLE INSTITUTE, *BIBLE INSTITUTE OF LOS ANGELES, *PHILADELPHIA SCHOOL OF THE BIBLE, Northwestern Bible and Missionary Training School (now known as *NORTHWESTERN COLLEGE in Minnesota), and Toronto Bible Institute (now known as *ONTARIO BIBLE COLLEGE). Established under the name International Bible Institute Council of Christian Education, the organization's first purpose was to organize for the training of *SUNDAY SCHOOL teachers a set curriculum that would equal in academic rigor the training of public school teachers.

A year later, when the project was expanded to address teacher training for evangelical churches, the International Bible Institute Council became known as the Evangelical Teacher Training Association, the name the association has held for most of its history. In 1956, the association moved from Chicago to nearby Wheaton, Illinois. It moved again in 1972 to Glen Ellyn, Illinois, but returned to Wheaton within five years. The name was changed again in 1989, from the Evangelical Teacher Training Association to the Evangelical Training Association. Since 1989, another Evangelical Teacher Training Association has been established, but the two organizations are separate.

The Evangelical Training Association operates adult- and continuing-education programs through many local churches, which lead to Evangelical Training Association certificates in church ministries. Through its degree-granting member schools, the Evangelical Training Association offers teacher certification and student diploma programs, through which graduates who have completed the Evangelical Training Association's courses receive the organization's diplomas, in addition to degrees from their respective schools. This second degree authorizes the graduates to teach Evangelical Training Association courses in their local churches. The association also offers organizational support, information, and curriculum materials for fledgling *BIBLE INSTITUTES, including a "how-to" manual for churches or individuals interesting in opening a Bible school. The association has its own publishing house that prints an extensive list of titles in both English and Spanish, in addition to many other languages; more than 3 million books have been distributed so far. The Evangelical Training Association also publishes a monthly newsletter, *Profile,* and a twice-yearly journal, the *Journal of Adult Training.*

Evangelical Women's Caucus International The Evangelical Women's Caucus International (EWCI), an organization of evangelical feminists, evolved from a phrase in the *CHICAGO DECLARATION of 1973, which had criticized evangelicals for having "encouraged men to prideful domination and women to irresponsible passivity." Those who approved the *CHICAGO DECLARATION authorized the formation of a women's caucus, which became formalized as the Evangelical Women's Caucus in 1974, the same year that *LETHA SCANZONI and *NANCY A. HARDESTY published their landmark manifesto, *All We're Meant to Be: A Biblical Approach to Women's Liberation.* The Evangelical Women's Caucus (which eventually added "International" to its moniker) functioned both as an organization of like-minded feminists and as a feminist outreach to women in conservative churches.

A fissure between the more conservative and the more liberal elements of the group began to become apparent in 1978 with the publication of *Is the Homosexual My Neighbor?* by Scanzoni and *VIRGINIA RAMEY MOLLENKOTT. That declaration in favor of gay rights alarmed many conservative members of the caucus, who feared that even a remote identification with lesbianism would destroy any possibilities that evangelical feminists could wield influence within *EVANGELICALISM. The coalition crumbled at the 1986 meeting of the Evangelical Women's Caucus International in Fresno, California. Having felt muzzled at previous gatherings, the supporters of gay rights announced an informal meeting of "lesbians and friends," where they planned to introduce a resolution before the larger body. The resolution read: "Whereas homosexual people are children of God, and because of the biblical mandate of Jesus Christ that we are all created equal in God's sight, and in recognition of the presence of the lesbian minority in EWCI, EWCI takes a firm stand in favor of civil rights protection for homosexual persons."

Although the resolution passed, thereby signaling a victory for the liberals, conservative members of the caucus, who were the organization's liaison to the evangelical subculture, felt obliged to abandon the group, however reluctantly. Catherine Kroeger and other conservatives formed a new group, *CHRISTIANS FOR BIBLICAL EQUALITY, while the Evangelical Women's Caucus International changed its name to the Evangelical and Ecumenical Women's Caucus.

References: Nancy A. Hardesty, "Evangelical Women," in Rosemary Skinner Keller and Rosemary Radford Ruether, eds., *In Our Own Voices: Four Centuries of American Women's Religious Writing* (1995); Julie Ingersoll, "From Women's Lib to Feminism: A Brief History of the Evangelical Women's Caucus" (unpublished paper).

Evangelicalism Although the term *evangelical* refers generally to the New Testament and, less generally, to Martin Luther's "rediscovery of the *GOSPEL" in the sixteenth century, the evolution of evangelicalism in America, where it became the most influential religious and social movement in American history, has produced some rather specialized characteristics that set it apart from the mainstream of American Protestantism. The visits of *GEORGE WHITEFIELD, an Anglican itinerant preacher, to the American colonies in the 1730s and 1740s triggered a widespread evangelical *REVIVAL known as the *GREAT AWAKENING. Whitefield built upon and knit together disparate *REVIVALS in the colonies—the pietistic awakenings among the Dutch in the Raritan Valley of New Jersey; the revival in *JONATHAN EDWARDS's congregation in Northampton, Massachusetts; and the sacramental seasons among the Scots-Irish Presbyterians in the Middle Colonies. Despite the persistence of some ethnic and theological differences, all manifestations of the *GREAT AWAKENING emphasized the necessity of some kind of *CONVERSION followed by a piety that was warm-hearted and experiential—or, in the argot of the day, "experimental"—over against the coldly rationalistic religion characteristic of the upper classes and the ecclesiastical establishment. Although generalizing about such a broad and internally diverse movement is perilous, evangelicalism in America has largely retained those characteristics: the centrality of conversion, the quest for an affective piety (perhaps best exemplified by *JOHN WESLEY's Aldersgate experience in 1738, when he found his heart "strangely warmed"), and a suspicion of wealth, *WORLDLINESS, and ecclesiastical pretension.

Eighteenth-century evangelicals, known as *NEW LIGHTS, helped to shape American culture in the Revolutionary era and beyond. Evangelicals generally lined up with the Patriots during the Revolution, and such evangelical leaders as Isaac Backus joined Enlightenment deists such as Thomas Jefferson in an unlikely alliance to press for religious disestablishment. The *SECOND GREAT AWAKENING, which lasted roughly from the 1790s to the 1830s, stoked the *REVIVAL fires once again in three different theaters of the new nation: New England, western New York, and the Cumberland Valley. Each theater made its own distinctive contribution to antebellum evangelicalism. The *REVIVAL fervor in New England gave rise to benevolent and reform societies such as the *TEMPERANCE movement, the female seminary movement, prison reform, and *ABOLITIONISM. *LYMAN BEECHER, for example, invested considerable energy into his campaign to outlaw dueling.

Whereas *JONATHAN EDWARDS had insisted that *REVIVALS were a "surprising work of God," *CHARLES GRANDISON FINNEY in western New York believed that his "*NEW MEASURES" would precipitate *REVIVAL. Finney also emphasized the role of human volition in the salvation process. American evangelicalism ever since has eschewed Calvinist notions about predestination in favor of Finney's Arminian doctrines that exalt the individual's ability to "choose God" and thereby take control of his or her spiritual destiny; such notions doubtless had a certain resonance in the new nation among a people who had, only recently, taken control of their political destiny.

The contribution of the *SECOND GREAT AWAKENING in the South is rather more complex. The *REVIVAL certainly functioned as a civilizing force in a frontier society of widely scattered settlements, prodigious alcohol consumption, and notoriously rowdy behavior. *CIRCUIT

RIDERS, a product of the great organizing genius of American *METHODISM, brought religion to the people; Baptists, the other major religion of the South, ordained their own ministers without regard for clerical education. *CAMP MEETINGS, still a fixture of religion in the South, lured thousands for socializing, preaching, *CONVERSION, and, very often, spectacular displays of religious enthusiasm. Evangelicalism has surely left its mark on Southern culture: Witness the persistence of backwoods *CAMP MEETINGS and *BAPTISMS, evangelical *REVIVALS, and public prayers at high school football games.

The social reforming impulse emanating from Protestantism in the North, however, soon clashed with Southern mores. Evangelicalism in the antebellum South came to be identified with the social order, especially after Nat Turner's rebellion in 1831, which obliterated any public qualms that Southerners harbored about the morality of slaveholding. Southern evangelicals saw themselves at odds with Northern abolitionists over the issue of slavery. Each side marshaled its theological defense of its position on slavery, confident of divine sanction. Southern evangelicalism turned inward and became increasingly insular in the face of attacks from the North. The sectional conflict divided denominations before it sundered the Union, thereby creating institutional schisms that, in some instances, still fester.

The Emancipation Proclamation removed the one adhesive, *ABOLITIONISM, that had united Northern evangelicals, so that after the Civil War evangelicalism in the North began to dissipate in a flurry of theological controversies and denominational disputes. The publication of Charles Darwin's *The Origin of Species* in 1859 had gone virtually unnoticed amid the building sectional tensions, but in the waning decades of the nineteenth century, evangelicals began to recognize its implications for literalistic interpretations of the *BIBLE. The discipline of higher criticism emanating from Germany, moreover, cast further doubt on the infallibility of the Scriptures. American Protestants, especially in the North, waged fierce battles over biblical inspiration. Conservatives—notably A. A. Hodge, B. B. Warfield, and the theologians at Princeton Seminary—reasserted the divine inspiration of the *BIBLE, even insisting upon its *INERRANCY in the original autographs, while liberal theologians such as Charles A. Briggs at Union Theological Seminary took a less rigid view.

Social and economic factors, particularly the industrialization and urbanization of American culture in the decades following the Civil War, exaggerated the divide within American Protestantism. Earlier in the century, evangelical optimism about the perfectibility of both the individual and society had unleashed various reform efforts directed toward establishing the biblical *MILLENNIUM in America; by the close of the century, teeming, squalid tenements populated by immigrants, most of them non-Protestant, hardly looked like the precincts of Zion. In the face of such squalor and the frustrated ambitions for a Protestant empire, disappointed evangelicals adjusted their *ESCHATOLOGY. No longer did they believe that their efforts could bring about the *MILLENNIUM; instead, they adopted an interpretive scheme of the Bible called dispensational *PREMILLENNIALISM that insisted Christ would come at any moment to "*RAPTURE" the true Christians from the earth and unleash his judgment against a sinful world. While evangelicals retreated to *DISPENSATIONALISM and despaired of social reform, their liberal counterparts embraced the *SOCIAL GOSPEL, which held that God redeems not individuals only, but sinful social institutions as well.

Evangelicals and liberals clashed again in the 1910s and 1920s. Responding to various assaults on evangelical orthodoxy, two oil tycoons, *LYMAN and Milton STEWART of Union Oil in California, financed the publication of a series of pamphlets called *THE FUNDAMENTALS*, which outlined what the writers regarded as the essentials of orthodoxy: biblical *INERRANCY, the virgin birth, Christ's *ATONEMENT and resurrection, the authenticity of miracles, and a system of biblical interpretation called dispensational *PREMILLENNIALISM. These "five points of fundamentalism" became the focus of doctrinal struggles in the 1920s, with the "fundamentalists" (hence the name) defending the doctrines against the "modernists" or liberals.

With rare exceptions, the fundamentalists lost those struggles for power within Protestant denominations; while some resolved to stay within mainline churches in hopes of checking the drift toward *LIBERALISM, most left to form independent churches or denominations, such as *J. GRESHAM MACHEN's *ORTHODOX PRESBYTERIAN CHURCH. An even larger defeat for the fundamentalists came in Dayton, Tennessee, in 1925 at the infamous *SCOPES "MONKEY TRIAL." Although fundamentalists, represented in the courtroom by *WILLIAM JENNINGS BRYAN, actually won the case against John T. Scopes (his conviction was later overturned on a technicality), fundamentalists lost badly in the court of public opinion. Merciless lampoons by H. L. Mencken and other journalists covering the trial succeeded in portraying fundamentalists as uneducated country bumpkins, a stereotype that, unfairly, persisted through the end of the twentieth century.

After the 1920s, fundamentalists, perceiving that American culture had turned against them, retreated from public life, but they did not disappear. Instead, they set about building a huge and intricate subculture of churches, denominations, *BIBLE INSTITUTES, colleges, seminaries, Bible camps, mission societies, and publishing houses that provided the foundation for their resurgence in the 1970s. Exactly half a century after the humiliation of the *SCOPES TRIAL and coincident with the presidential campaign of *JIMMY CARTER (a Southern Baptist Sunday school teacher), evangelicals, especially Southerners, began to reassert themselves in the public arena. Although they deserted Carter for *RONALD REAGAN in 1980, evangelicals, led by preacher-activists like *JERRY FALWELL and *PAT ROBERTSON (who himself would mount a credible campaign for the Republican presidential nomination in 1988), have made their presence felt in American politics. During the 1980 campaign, in fact, all three of the major candidates for president—Carter, Reagan, and *JOHN B. ANDERSON, who ran as an independent—claimed to be evangelicals.

Despite the surprise registered by pundits and the media over this political activism, evangelicals in recent years have merely reclaimed their historic place in American public discourse. Evangelicals in the nineteenth century, more than any other group, shaped the nation's political and social agenda, just as they had provided important support for the patriot cause in the eighteenth century. The return of evangelicalism to public life has also served gradually to erode popular perceptions of evangelicals as backwards and somehow opposed to technology and innovation. Evangelicals, in fact, have consistently been pioneers in mass communications—the open-air preaching in the eighteenth century, which prefigured the patriot rhetoric during the Revolution; the Methodist circuits on the frontier, which anticipated grassroots political organizations; and the adroit use of broadcast media in the twentieth century, from the radio preachers of the twenties to the televangelists of the seventies, which provided a model for such acknowledged masters of political communication as Franklin Roosevelt and *RONALD REAGAN.

Evangelicalism—from the *REVIVAL tradition of the eighteenth and nineteenth centuries to the militant *FUNDAMENTALISM of the 1920s to *PENTECOSTALISM with its emphasis on *SPEAKING IN TONGUES and other gifts of the Holy Spirit—is deeply imbedded in American life, in part because of its promise of easy *SALVATION, intimacy with God, and a community of fellow believers. H. L. Mencken, no friend of evangelicals, remarked in 1925 that if you threw an egg out of a Pullman window almost anywhere in America, you would hit a fundamentalist. Pullman cars are obsolete now; fundamentalists are still around.

References: Randall Balmer, *Mine Eyes Have Seen the Glory: A Journey into the Evangelical Subculture in America,* 3d ed. (2000); George M. Marsden, *Fundamentalism and American Culture: The Shaping of Twentieth-Century Evangelicalism: 1870–1925* (1980); Timothy L. Smith, *Revivalism and Social Reform in Mid-Nineteenth-Century America* (1957); Jon R. Stone, *On the Boundaries of American Evangelicalism: The Postwar Evangelical Coalition* (1997); Christian Smith, *American Evangelicalism: Embattled and Thriving* (1998); David Harrington Watt, *A Transforming Faith: Explorations of Twentieth-Century American Evangelicalism* (1991).

Evangelicals for Social Action Evangelicals for Social Action, formally organized in 1978, traces its roots to the *CHICAGO DECLARATION OF SOCIAL CONCERN, which was adopted in November 1973 by a group of evangelicals concerned about social apathy and political conservativism on the part of many evangelicals. Led by *RONALD J. SIDER, of *EASTERN BAPTIST THEOLOGICAL SEMINARY, the organization publishes a monthly magazine, *Prism,* and seeks, according to the organization, "to integrate *EVANGELISM and social transformation." The organization promotes Sider's "consistent life ethic," opposing *ABORTION-on-demand but also supporting arms control, nuclear disarmament, education, and protection of the environment.

Evangelism Evangelism, the process of spreading the *GOSPEL, the "good news" of *SALVATION through Jesus Christ, is something that evangelicals take seriously as part of their mandate from the Scriptures. When Jesus appeared to his disciples after the Resurrection, he told them: "Go into all the world and proclaim the good news to the whole creation" (Mark 16:15). Evangelicals have engaged in various forms of *EVANGELISM, from systematic efforts, such as missions and *REVIVAL campaigns, to individual "witnessing" to others.

Evangelist An evangelist proclaims the "good news" of the *GOSPEL to others. While every Christian who engages in *EVANGELISM would be considered an evangelist, the term very often refers to professional preachers, such as *DWIGHT L. MOODY or *BILLY SUNDAY or *BILLY GRAHAM, who have taken on the task of *EVANGELISM as a full-time vocation.

Evans, Anthony "Tony" (1949–) Born in Baltimore, Tony Evans, the cofounder and senior pastor of the Oak Cliff Bible Fellowship in Dallas, Texas, is a popular African American speaker in evangelical circles. He has served as chaplain of the Dallas Mavericks basketball team, and he has frequently addressed *PROMISE KEEPERS rallies with an uncompromising message demanding that men take charge of their households. Evans, a graduate of *DALLAS THEOLOGICAL SEMINARY, is also founder and president of an organization called the Urban Alternative, which seeks "spiritual renewal in urban America through the church and radio outreach."

References: Tony Evans, *Returning to Your First Love* (1995); idem, *What Matters Most* (1997); idem, *What a Way to Live* (1997).

Evans, Dale (née Smith, Frances Octavia) (1912–2001) Born October 13, 1912, in Uvalde, Texas, Francis Octavia Smith moved with her family to Osceola, Arkansas, where she attended high school and showed promise as a singer. She married Thomas Frederick Fox in 1928, at the age of fourteen, but the marriage ended in divorce by the time she was seventeen. She began singing on the radio in Memphis, Tennessee, and then in Dallas, Texas, and Louisville, Kentucky. Evans married a second time while in Dallas, but that marriage ended in 1945. At the suggestion of a radio station manager, and after trying several stage names, Smith took the name Dale Evans because it was easy to pronounce. She moved to CBS Radio in Chicago in 1940 as a vocalist on the weekly program *News and Rhythm* and launched a career in the movies three years later with *Swing Your Partner.* She appeared frequently in radio shows and Western films with *ROY ROGERS; the couple married in 1947. They performed in rodeo shows and concerts and in the early 1950s started their own television series, *The Roy Rogers Show,* which ran from 1951 to 1957 and became one of NBC's top-rated programs. Evans wrote many of the religious songs and romantic ballads for their programs. Her musical compositions include, "Aha, San Antone," "The Bible Tells Me So," "Happy Birthday, Gentle Savior," and "Happy Trails."

Evans appeared frequently with *BILLY GRAHAM in the 1950s, and at times she seemed conflicted about her *CALLING. "I wanted to be an entertainer as long as I could remember," she told the *Houston Chronicle* in 1968. "I knew it was dangerous spiritually because it is based squarely in the ego, and the *BIBLE says pride is an abomination." On the other hand, Evans recognized the religious importance of her work. "I would love to be an *EVANGELIST," she once said, "but I think God has revealed to me that I can serve him best by just remaining at my post."

References: Dale Evans, *Happy Trails: Our Life Story* (1994); James Barron, "Dale Evans, No-Nonsense Queen of the West, Dies at 88," *New York Times,* February 8, 2001.

Evans, Harry L(ouis) (1930–) One of the more thoughtful and intellectually curious leaders in evangelical higher education in the 1960s and 1970s, Harry L. Evans was ordained in the *EVANGELICAL FREE CHURCH OF AMERICA in 1952 after having attended that denomination's Trinity Seminary and Bible College. He served as pastor of churches in New York, Nebraska, and Illinois before becoming president of Trinity. He presided over the school's move from Chicago to Deerfield, Illinois, in Chicago's northern suburbs, where it divided into two institutions, *TRINITY COLLEGE and *TRINITY EVANGELICAL DIVINITY SCHOOL (now, collectively, *TRINITY INTERNATIONAL UNI-

VERSITY). Evans allowed the deans of the institutions, *J. EDWARD HAKES of Trinity College and *KENNETH S. KANTZER of the divinity school, a great deal of latitude in building their respective schools. The results were impressive. Kantzer attracted a number of prominent evangelical scholars to the divinity school, and Hakes recruited an extraordinary cohort of freshly minted Ph.D.s who transformed the college into a place of considerable intellectual vitality in the early 1970s, especially by the standards of *EVANGELICALISM.

In 1974, at Evans's behest, the *EVANGELICAL FREE CHURCH agreed to separate the two schools and to allow *TRINITY COLLEGE to become quasi-independent of the denomination. Evans eventually left the presidency of the divinity school to devote his full energies to the college. Fundamentalists within the denomination, however, eventually forced his ouster. Although the ostensible reason was Evans's second marriage—following the sudden death of his first wife, Evans married a woman who had been divorced—the fundamentalists had long been suspicious of his intellectual curiosity and his "liberal" ideas. In his congenial and jovial way, Evans intermittently pushed against some of the shibboleths of *FUNDAMENTALISM; conservatives were incensed, for instance, when he allowed a square dance on campus in 1977 (which took place under the euphemism "folk games"). After his removal from office, Evans held a variety of jobs and finally settled in southern California, where he became active as a layman in All Saints Episcopal Church in Pasadena.

Evans, Louis (Hadley), (Sr.) (1897–1981) Born in Goshen, Indiana, Louis Evans received degrees from Occidental College and from McCormick Theological Seminary. He was ordained a Presbyterian in 1922 and served churches in North Dakota, California, and Pennsylvania before accepting the pulpit of First Presbyterian Church in Hollywood, California, where he remained from 1941 until 1953. He wrote a number of popular devotional books, was active in denominational affairs, and preached and lectured throughout North America and abroad. Evans was a founder of the *FELLOWSHIP OF CHRISTIAN ATHLETES and served as its president from 1955 to 1958.

References: Louis Evans, *The Kingdom Is Yours* (1952); idem, *This Is America's Hour* (1957); idem, *Youth Seeks a Master* (1964); idem, *Christ on Trial* (1980); idem, *Can You Really Talk to God?* (1982).

Evans, Mike (1947–) Once touted as a successor to *JIM BAKKER on the *PTL Club*, Mike Evans is an *ASSEMBLIES OF GOD minister and a televangelist based in Euless, Texas. He is president of Mike Evans Ministries International and the Evangelical-Israel Friendship Council (which advocates the designation of Jerusalem as capital of Israel), and is one of the founders of the Church on the Move in Euless.

Evans, an ardent premillennialist, has conducted evangelistic campaigns around the world. Late in 1994, he was forced to abort *REVIVAL meetings in Cambodia when an angry mob stormed his luxury hotel and demanded a refund of their travel expenses after Evans had failed to perform healing miracles as advertised. Evans and his organization blamed the contretemps on the Khmer Rouge rebels.

Ewart, Frank J. (1876–1947) A leader in the Oneness Pentecostal movement, Frank J. Ewart was born in Australia and emigrated to Canada in 1903. His pentecostal experience in 1908 led to a break with his Baptist congregation in Portland, Oregon; he moved to Los Angeles, became an associate of *WILLIAM H. DURHAM, and took over Durham's pastorate when Durham died in 1912. Ewart became convinced the following year that water *BAPTISM should be performed in the name of Jesus only, not with the traditional Trinitarian formula of Father, Son, and Holy Ghost. On April 15, 1914, Ewart and Glenn A. Cook rebaptized one another in the name of Jesus only and proceeded to rebaptize other pentecostals. Ewart spread his teachings through a periodical, *Meat in Due Season*, and he presented the Oneness doctrine to the general council of the *ASSEMBLIES OF GOD in 1916; the Assemblies, however, soundly rejected the teaching and reaffirmed the Trinitarian formula. Ewart founded his own church in Belvedere, California, in 1919 and was ordained by the denomination that eventually became known as the United Pentecostal Church.

References: Frank J. Ewart, *The Name and the Book* (1936); idem, *The Phenomenon of Pentecost* (1947).

Exodus International Founded in 1976, Exodus International bills itself as a "Christian referral and resource network." Working from a theologically conservative doctrinal position, the organization "upholds heterosexuality as God's creative intent for humanity, and subsequently views homosexual expression as outside God's will." Exodus International disputes the notion that homosexuality is genetically determined and castigates those who opt for "the homosexual lifestyle" as indulging in sinfulness. The organization, with offices in Seattle, teaches that "freedom from homosexuality is possible through repentance and faith in Jesus Christ." Exodus International, which has accepted financial assistance from the *CHRISTIAN COALITION, includes a number of people on its board of directors who have "overcome homosexuality."

In 2000, the Exodus International board ousted its chairman, John Paulk, after disclosures that Paulk had visited a gay bar in Washington, D.C., and then lied about it. Paulk, married to a woman who described herself as a former lesbian, was also head of the homosexuality and gender division of *FOCUS ON THE FAMILY.

References: "Ex-gay Ministry Ousts Board Chairman," *Christian Century*, October 25, 2000; John Paulk, *Not Afraid to Change: The Remarkable Story of How One Man Overcame Homosexuality* (1998).

■ ■ ■

Fairmount Bible School. *See* **Indiana Wesleyan University.**

Faith and Philosophy *Faith and Philosophy: Journal of the Society of Christian Philosophers* is the official publishing vehicle of the *SOCIETY OF CHRISTIAN PHILOSOPHERS. *Faith and Philosophy* describes itself as advancing the aims of the society by contributing to the continuing effort of the Christian community to articulate its faith in a way that will withstand critical scrutiny, and to explore the implications of that faith for all aspects of human life. The journal publishes articles that address philosophical issues from an evangelical Christian perspective, for discussions of philosophical issues that arise within the Christian faith, and for articles from any perspective that deal critically with the philosophical credentials of the

Christian faith. *Faith and Philosophy* represents a resurgence of interest in such intellectual activity in the later decades of the twentieth century.

Published from its beginning from the campus of *ASBURY COLLEGE in Wilmore, Kentucky, *Faith and Philosophy* has grown to have one of the largest circulations of all scholarly periodicals in the field of philosophy. Since its inception, the journal has been published quarterly under the guidance of its managing editor, *MICHAEL PETERSON. *Faith and Philosophy* encourages "a type of literature that is relatively rare in current English language philosophical journals, a literature at once philosophically disciplined and religiously engaged." The editors of the journal believe the task of critical and reflective self-understanding should be carried out in dialogue with those who do not, as well as with those who do, share their Christian commitment. The influence of *Faith and Philosophy* has been acknowledged by intellectuals who clearly do not share its Christian orientation.

Along with full-length articles, *Faith and Philosophy* features back-and-forth critical discussions, symposia, and reviews of books. Each October issue is devoted to a single topic and contains both commissioned and submitted papers. A sampling of topical issues published to date includes: Christianity and Ethical Theory, Religious Pluralism, the Bible and Philosophy, Christianity and Social Philosophy, the Religious Significance of Contemporary Continental Philosophy, and Christian Philosophy and the Mind-Body Problem. The quantity of scholarly articles appearing in *Faith and Philosophy* is often noted as a significant influence in the profession of philosophy, and the quality of the contents has led some to declare it "the world's most prestigious journal in philosophy of religion."

References: Tony Pasquarello, "Humanism's Thorn: The Case of the Bright Believers," *Free Inquiry,* winter 1992/93; Kristine Christlieb, "Suddenly, Respect: Christianity Makes a Comeback in the Philosophy Department," *Christianity Today,* April 17, 1987.

Faith Center. *See* **Scott, Eugene V. "Gene."**

Faith Journey. *See* **Testimony.**

"Faith Principles" "Faith principles," a theory for evangelical fundraising, was devised by *GEORGE MÜLLER, a Prussian-born evangelical in the nineteenth century. Müller established an orphanage and Bible school in England in 1834–35 in order to test his belief that God would sustain anyone and any cause that simply depended on God. If the believer made needs known to God through prayer, Müller believed, no further action would be necessary; God would supply those needs as long as the believer abided by the "faith principles," which entailed never going into debt and never asking directly for money.

Müller's idea was taken up by a number of nineteenth-century evangelicals, notably the British missionaries Amy Carmichael and *J. HUDSON TAYLOR. Several organizations, such as the *AFRICAN INLAND MISSION and the Latin America Mission, also abided by Müller's "faith principles," and the ideology was popular among many American evangelical groups well into the twentieth century.

Reference: Michael S. Hamilton, "The Financing of American Evangelicalism, 1945–1995," paper presented at "The Financing of American Evangelicalism Consultation," Naperville, Illinois, December 3–5, 1998.

Faith Theological Seminary (Wilmington, Delaware) *CARL MCINTIRE organized Faith Theological Seminary in 1937 after he had broken with the *PRESBYTERIAN CHURCH IN AMERICA to found the *BIBLE PRESBYTERIAN CHURCH. Faith Seminary was doggedly fundamentalist, drawing on independent fundamentalist churches for students and support. One of its most famous alumni was *FRANCIS A. SCHAEFFER.

Reference: Joel A. Carpenter, *Revive Us Again: The Reawakening of American Fundamentalism* (1997).

Faith Training College. *See* **Cullis, Charles.**

Falwell, Jerry (1933–) Born in Lynchburg, Virginia, Jerry Falwell entered Lynchburg College in 1950 to study engineering. In 1952, however, he was converted through the influence of *CHARLES E. FULLER and his popular radio program, *The Old Fashioned Revival Hour.* Falwell transferred to the *BAPTIST BIBLE COLLEGE in Springfield, Missouri, and graduated in 1956, whereupon he was ordained by the *BAPTIST BIBLE FELLOWSHIP. Returning to Lynchburg the same year, Falwell and thirty-five members founded the Thomas Road Baptist Church, which met in a building recently vacated by the Donald Duck Bottling Company. Falwell soon began radio broadcasts of his church services, and in 1968 he moved into television with a program called (reminiscent of Fuller's moniker) *The Old Time Gospel Hour.* Falwell formed Liberty Baptist College (now *LIBERTY UNIVERSITY) as a fundamentalist undergraduate institution in 1971, openly touting it as the Harvard of *EVANGELICALISM.

Although he had earlier disclaimed any political involvement, Falwell over the course of the 1970s became more and more vocal in espousing politically conservative positions on such issues as *ABORTION and civil rights, all the while supporting Bible reading and prayer in the public schools. At times, he called for an end to public schools altogether. "I hope I live to see the day when, as in the early days of our country, we won't have any public schools," he wrote in 1979. "The churches will have taken them over again and Christians will be running them. What a happy day that will be!"

In 1979, Falwell set up a conservative political organization called *MORAL MAJORITY, Inc., which included educational activities and a legislative lobby. "When I started *MORAL MAJORITY, I was leading the evangelical church out from behind their walls," Falwell recounted in 1996. His 1980 book, *Listen America!*, a political screed, warned that there was "no doubt that the sin of America is severe" and that the United States was "literally approaching the brink of national disaster." Falwell's support for *RONALD REAGAN in the 1980 presidential election, together with *MORAL MAJORITY's help in registering millions of politically and religiously conservative voters, helped to elect—and eventually to reelect—Reagan to the presidency. In a radio interview in 2000, Falwell looked back on his political legacy: "*RONALD REAGAN would not have been president unless *BIBLE-believing Christians in 1979 and 1980 by the millions said we had had enough and threw *JIMMY CARTER out and put *RONALD REAGAN in, to put it bluntly."

Falwell remained a fixture on the landscape of American politics throughout the 1980s. He took stands against pornography and homosexuality. While offering unqualified support for the state of Israel and for Ferdinand Marcos, the deposed president of the Philippines, Falwell criticized the work of Desmond Tutu, the Anglican archbishop of South Africa.

In 1987, wanting to devote more of his energies to *LIBERTY UNIVERSITY, Falwell stepped down as president of *MORAL MAJORITY. The next year he briefly took over the scandal-ridden organization of fellow televangelist *JIM BAKKER, whose excesses, both sexual and financial, had recently come to light. Falwell, however, a self-proclaimed fundamentalist rather than a pentecostal, found the PTL organization too unwieldy; he felt that he could not win the confidence of Bakker's pentecostal following. *TAMMY FAYE BAKKER later suggested that Falwell's motive was to acquire PTL's satellite capabilities, to which Falwell responded, "Tammy Faye, she's a loony. I don't think there was a time when her elevator went to the top floor."

Falwell dissolved *MORAL MAJORITY on June 10, 1989, ten years after its founding and the same year that *PAT ROBERTSON organized his *CHRISTIAN COALITION. Bedeviled by financial problems in the 1980s and discredited somewhat by his association with PTL, Falwell attempted a comeback in the mid-1990s. He struck financial deals with Kenneth Keating, who had been convicted in the Reagan-era savings-and-loan scandals, and Falwell also accepted money from Sun Myung Moon's Unification Church, which most evangelicals regard as a cult.

Despite such unsavory associations, Falwell persisted in portraying himself as a prophet. "God has called me to be a voice crying in the wilderness," he told *CHRISTIANITY TODAY in 1996. "God has called me to mobilize, inform, and inspire the evangelical church in America." He attempted to revive his flagging popularity with ritual execrations of liberals, "secular humanists," "violent Muslims," and Bill Clinton, who Falwell referred to as an "ungodly liar." Falwell also peddled two videotapes, *Clinton Chronicles* and *Circle of Power,* which, with no corroborating evidence, accused the president of all manner of crimes.

Early in 1999, Falwell broadened his attack to include Tinky Winky, a character from the popular children's television program *Teletubbies.* Issuing a "parent alert" in his *National Liberty Journal,* Falwell enumerated the reasons that he thought the animated character was homosexual: "He is purple—the gay pride color; and his antenna is shaped like a triangle—the gay pride symbol."

References: Jerry Falwell, *Listen America!* (1980); idem, *The Fundamentalist Phenomenon: The Resurgence of Conservative Christianity* (1981); idem, *Falwell: An Autobiography* (1996); Shelley Baranowski, s.v. "Jerry Falwell," in Charles H. Lippy, ed., *Twentieth-Century Shapers of American Popular Religion* (1989); John W. Kennedy, "Jerry Falwell's Uncertain Legacy," *Christianity Today,* December 9, 1996; Susan Friend Harding, *The Book of Jerry Falwell: Fundamentalist Language and Politics* (2000).

Family Research Council Originally founded in 1981 to formulate and to propagate a "family values" agenda for the *RELIGIOUS RIGHT, the Family Research Council merged with *JAMES DOBSON's *FOCUS ON THE FAMILY and remained a satellite until its reorganization in October 1992, a reorganization calculated to protect *FOCUS ON THE FAMILY's tax-exempt status. The organizations, however, maintained close ties. "We will be legally separate," Dobson declared, "but spiritually one." Under the leadership of *GARY L. BAUER, who had worked as a domestic policy advisor in the Reagan White House, the council grew significantly and became increasingly vocal with its politically conservative agenda. With offices in

Washington, D.C., by 1996 it counted seventy-five employees and an annual budget of $10 million.

When Bauer decided to pursue the 2000 Republican presidential nomination, he stepped down from the leadership of the organization in January 1999. Ken Connor, a Florida trial attorney and an antiabortion activist, was appointed president of the council the following year.

Reference: Lori Forman, "The Political Activity of the Religious Right in the 1990s: A Critical Analysis," pamphlet distributed by the American Jewish Committee.

Far East Broadcasting Company Organized in 1945, the Far Eastern Broadcasting Company was begun by *JOHN BROGER, formerly a communications expert in the navy, and *ROBERT BOWMAN, formerly a baritone in the Haven of Rest quartet. Their idea was to harness the communications power of radio to evangelize Asian peoples. Broger set up a station in Manila, the Philippines, and the first signal went out on June 4, 1948, with the singing of "All Hail the Power of Jesus' Name." Despite modest beginnings, the Far Eastern Broadcasting Company expanded rapidly; ten years later, it was sending signals into the People's Republic of China. The organization, with headquarters in La Mirada, California, now transmits to Asia, Eastern Europe, Latin America, and Australia.

Farmers for Christ International Farmers for Christ International, which bills itself as "a ministry in the world of agriculture," is technically a division of Amazing Grace Ministries, founded in 1983 by *JAMES H. GARDNER, a Baptist minister, as an evangelistic outreach at state and county fairs. (The former entity was established, according to Gardner, because some of the fairs refused to allow Amazing Grace Ministries onto their premises, but the two organizations are functionally indistinguishable.) A fundamentalist mission, Farmers for Christ International sets up a tent or a booth, tended by volunteers, at a fair. "The front half contains tables with tracts and curiosity items to draw people in to look around," the organization's brochure reads. "The back half of the tent or booth has tables and chairs. We sit down with them and show them from the *BIBLE how to be saved, and urge them to pray and receive the Lord right then." The organization then gives the names of converts "to fundamental Baptist churches in their area."

Farmers for Christ International, which is based in Dayton, Tennessee, also produces and distributes Bible lessons, and its statement of faith includes such fundamentalist nostrums as biblical *INERRANCY, *PREMILLENNIALISM, and *SEPARATISM: "We believe the Revised Standard Version of the *BIBLE is a perverted translation of the original languages, and that collaboration or participation with all forms of *MODERNISM, whether in the National Council of Churches or otherwise is wrong, and demands separation on our part."

Reference: Amazing Grace Mission brochure.

Fee, Gordon D(onald) (1934–) Born in Ashland, Oregon, Gordon D. Fee earned the bachelor's and master's degrees from *SEATTLE PACIFIC COLLEGE (now University) and was ordained in the *ASSEMBLIES OF GOD in 1959. After a pastorate in Des Moines, Washington, Fee earned the Ph.D. from the University of Southern California in 1966 and then joined the faculty of *SOUTHERN CALIFORNIA COLLEGE as professor of *BIBLE. In 1969, Fee went to

*WHEATON COLLEGE as associate professor of New Testament and then to *GORDON-CONWELL THEOLOGICAL SEMINARY in 1974. Fee and his wife spent part of each year teaching theology in Third World settings. Fee's scholarship was motivated by "a strong desire to present an evangelical theological position with as much scholarly integrity as I can give it, so that it might have a fair hearing as a valid option in the theological enterprise."

References: Gordon D. Fee, *New Testament Exegesis: A Handbook for Students and Pastors* (1982); idem, *First and Second Timothy: A Good News Commentary* (1984); idem, *Paul's Letter to the Philippians* (1996).

Feller, Henriette (née Odin) (1800–1868) Born in Vaud, Switzerland, during the Napoleonic Wars, Henriette Feller was converted during the Genevan Revival, conducted by Merle d'Aubigné and *ROBERT HALDANE, a Scottish *EVANGELIST. Feller became active in evangelistic work herself, especially after the death of her husband during a typhus epidemic. She emerged as a leader in an independent church in Lausanne, which adopted the practice of believer's *BAPTISM sometime in the late 1820s.

Feller, having divested herself of her considerable wealth, sailed for North America in 1835 as a missionary with the Swiss Independent Missionary Society. She settled initially in Montréal and established a small church with the help of *LOUIS ROUSSY. Shortly thereafter, she established a Baptist school, the Institut Feller, at Grande-Ligne, south of Montréal, as well as Canada's first francophone Protestant church, at Marieville in 1837. Opposition from Roman Catholic *patriotes* the following year, however, forced Feller briefly into exile in the United States, where she continued to raise money for the school and to establish contacts with evangelical leaders in New England. She returned to rebuild the school, renamed Ecole de Grand-Ligne, and eventually to expand the Grande-Ligne Mission, affiliating with the Canadian Baptist Missionary Society in 1845.

References: John M. Cramp, *A Memoir of Madame Feller* (1876); Walter N. Wyeth, *Henrietta Feller and the Grande Ligne Mission* (1898); Randall Balmer and Catharine Randall, "'Her Duty to Canada': Henriette Feller and French Protestantism in Québec," *Church History*, 70 (March 2001).

Fellowship In the argot of *EVANGELICALISM, "fellowship" can be a noun, an adjective, or a verb. As a noun it refers, when used in a broad sense, to the community of faith, but it can also denote a small-group gathering, an organization (such as the *FELLOWSHIP OF CHRISTIAN ATHLETES), or even a federation of congregations. As an adjective, "fellowship" is most often used in "Fellowship Hall," which is generally a place for socializing in, say, the basement of a church. Finally, although grammatically incorrect, "fellowship" takes the form of a verb in evangelical jargon: "Let's fellowship together."

Fellowship of Associates of Medical Evangelism Located in Columbus, Indiana, and established in the early 1970s, the Fellowship of Associates of Medical Evangelism (F.A.M.E.) exists to evangelize and help plant churches by providing medical personnel and supplies, funding hospitals and clinics, and working in partnership with Christian missionaries. Since its inception, the facilities built by the fellowship have included a nutrition center and small hospital in Haiti, and a hospital in Madras, India, for leprosy victims.

The organization maintains an office of only three people in the United States, but it has a staff of ninety missionaries and medical personnel overseas. In 1995, F.A.M.E. treated one million people at seventy hospitals, clinics, and mobile medical units in twenty-nine countries. The fellowship currently has projects in Asia, Africa, Latin America, and the Caribbean, as well as several European countries: Albania, Portugal, Russia, and Ukraine.

The Fellowship of Associates of Medical Evangelism is not the first missionary group to provide medical services as part of its Christian witness, nor is it the largest or most famous organization to do so, but it is representative of other similar relief agencies, both historically and in the present day. F.A.M.E. records the number of *BAPTISMS performed each year (ten thousand in 1995), and also reports the number of indigenous people who burn their traditional religious objects in rejection of idolatry—a tally recorded by missionaries around the world for more than one hundred years.

Reference: Information provided by the Fellowship of Associates of Medical Evangelism.

Fellowship of Christian Athletes The Fellowship of Christian Athletes (FCA) is an interdenominational sports ministry whose mission is "To present to athletes and coaches, and all whom they influence, the challenge and adventure of receiving Jesus Christ as Savior and Lord, serving Him in their relationships and in the fellowship of the church." The organization was founded in 1954 by a basketball coach from Norman, Oklahoma, named Don McClanen. With the help of its famous national spokesman, *TOM LANDRY, former head coach for the Dallas Cowboys, the Fellowship of Christian Athletes grew to a national organization with an annual budget approaching $15 million.

Now operating out of Kansas City, Missouri, the Fellowship of Christian Athletes serves several hundred thousand youths and adults each year through sports camps and school programs known as "FCA Huddles"—student-led fellowships of athletes and coaches. These local groups have adult chapters of volunteers who help out at local events, raise funds, and help run "accountability groups," where students share concerns about their spiritual progress and seek help for living a life in keeping with evangelical standards. The FCA claims to have chapters in 16 percent of American schools.

The organization has for a long time understood the strategic potential of "hero worship" as a tool for *EVANGELISM. The Fellowship of Christian Athletes has solicited the support of athletes like David Robinson of the San Antonio Spurs, Brent Jones of the San Francisco Forty-Niners, and golfer Steve Jones, 1996 U.S. Open Champion, to encourage children and teenagers to give their lives to Christ. Celebrities like these athletes also urge young people to join the FCA's antidrug campaign, One Way 2 Play—Drug Free!, by pledging not to use drugs or alcohol. The organization also gets out its message with an extensive array of sports clothing bearing evangelical messages; the line of "Team Gear" includes hats, T-shirts, shorts, and sweatshirts.

The Fellowship of Christian Athletes is one of the most established and best-known organizations in the tradition of "*MUSCULAR CHRISTIANITY"—the evangelical movement that targets men and boys through a very masculine interpretation of Jesus. The Fellowship, for example, regularly hosts booths at *PROMISE KEEPERS conferences. Unlike the *PROMISE

KEEPERS, however, the Fellowship of Christian Athletes is by no means closed to women and girls, who can attend single-sex or coed sports camps. Female athletes like LPGA professional Betsy King and synchronized swimmer Becky Dyroen-Lancer, who as captain led her team to win the gold medal at the 1996 Olympics, are in fact central figures in the organization's outreach to women. In 1996, the FCA signed a covenant with *ATHLETES IN ACTION to work cooperatively on a national level, including evangelistic outreach at the Summer Olympics in Atlanta.

Reference: Information provided by Fellowship of Christian Athletes.

Fellowship of Christian Magicians The Fellowship of Christian Magicians, based in Plymouth, Minnesota, is an international organization of people dedicated to the "encouragement and promotion of a high standard of presentation of the *GOSPEL of our Lord and Savior Jesus Christ, and to the winning of souls to Christ." Membership is limited to people who subscribe to a conservative evangelical doctrinal statement. The organization, which publishes a magazine, *The Christian Conjurer,* provides instruction in "how to use the visual illustrations and develop talent for *GOSPEL presentation using sleight of hand, optical illusion, ventriloquism, puppets, balloons, clowning, juggling, storytelling, and other visual arts as they develop for this one cause: visually promoting the *WORD OF GOD."

Fellowship of Christians in Universities and Schools. *See* **Moore, Peter C(lement).**

Fellowship of Evangelical Bible Churches The Fellowship of Evangelical Bible Churches, founded in 1889, grew out of the merger of two conservative Mennonite bodies. Originally named the United Mennonite Brethren of North America, the group went through a series of name changes before settling on the current name in 1987.

From its inception, the Fellowship was strongly evangelistic. Leaders insisted on true repentance, *CONVERSION, *BAPTISM on confession of faith, and living lives committed to Jesus Christ. The church supports over 150 missionaries in a variety of mission agencies worldwide and reports forty-four hundred members in its thirty-seven churches. The Fellowship of Evangelical Bible Churches holds to the belief in the *BIBLE as the inerrant, inspired *WORD OF GOD and to dispensational interpretation. The fellowship joined the *NATIONAL ASSOCIATION OF EVANGELICALS in 1948 under the name Evangelical Mennonite Brethren.

References: Frank S. Mead and Samuel S. Hill, *Handbook of Denominations in the United States,* 10th ed. (1996); J. Gordon Melton, *The Encyclopedia of American Religions,* 3d ed. (1993).

Fellowship of Southern Churchmen Begun in 1934 as a nondenominational fellowship of "liberal and progressive young ministers" dedicated to social reform, the Fellowship of Southern Churchmen was organized by James Dombrowski of the Highlander Folk School in Monteagle, Tennessee, and by Howard A. Kester from the Committee on Economic and Racial Justice in Nashville. Reinhold Niebuhr addressed the first Conference of Younger Churchmen of the South (which became the Fellowship of Southern Churchmen). The group, which drew much of its theology from *NEO-ORTHODOXY, adopted resolutions condemning capitalism, war, and racism.

Members of the Fellowship supported union organizing and investigated lynchings. They worked for the improvement of race relations. In 1938, the organization published a statement, signed by fifty prominent Southerners, calling for "full citizenship rights" for African Americans. Membership declined in the 1950s as other religious groups took up the cause of civil rights. The Fellowship of Southern Churchmen was reorganized in 1964 as the Committee of Southern Churchmen, under the leadership of Will D. Campbell.

Reference: Anthony P. Dunbar, *Against the Grain: Southern Radicals and Prophets, 1929–1951* (1981).

Fellowship of Witness Fellowship of Witness, formed in 1965, is an evangelical advocacy group within the Episcopal Church. The organization seeks a return to more conservative doctrines, a stronger view of the authority of Scripture, and an adherence to the ecumenical councils and the Church of England's *Thirty-nine Articles.* Fellowship of Witness, which publishes a quarterly magazine, *Kerygma,* is governed by a board made up of clergy and laity, and is part of the larger Evangelical Fellowship in the Anglican Communion.

Ferguson, Miriam Amanda "Ma" (née Wallace) (1875–1961) Born in Bell County, Texas, Ma Ferguson is considered to be the second woman to serve as governor of a U.S. state. She was elected governor of Texas on November 4, 1924, the same day that Nellie Taylor Ross was elected governor of Wyoming; because Ross was inaugurated sixteen days before Ferguson, however, Ross is considered the first female governor.

Ferguson, a fundamentalist, served as governor of Texas from 1925 until 1927 and again from 1933 to 1935. She claimed her election was vindication of her husband, James E. Ferguson, also governor of Texas, who was impeached and removed from office in 1917. In the fall of 1925, shortly after the conclusion of the *SCOPES TRIAL in nearby Tennessee, Ma Ferguson ordered the Texas textbook commission to delete references to evolutionary theory from high school textbooks, a ban that remained in effect for decades thereafter and which forced textbook publishers to produce specially edited books for Texas.

Reference: Edward J. Larson, *Summer for the Gods: The Scopes Trial and America's Continuing Debate over Science and Religion* (1997).

Finkenbinder, Paul (1921–) Known throughout Latin America for his radio broadcasts, Paul Finkenbinder was born in Santurce, Puerto Rico, to Spanish-speaking missionary parents. He studied at *ZION BIBLE INSTITUTE of Rhode Island and at *CENTRAL BIBLE COLLEGE in Springfield, Missouri. He became a missionary to El Salvador, where he earned the nickname "Hermano Pablo" (Brother Paul), because Salvadorans found his surname too difficult to pronounce. Ordained in the *ASSEMBLIES OF GOD in 1948, Finkenbinder began broadcasting a radio program, which eventually took the name *Un Mesaje a la Conciencia* ("Message to the Conscience") in 1955. He expanded from radio into television and in 1969 moved his headquarters to Costa Mesa, California.

Finley, Samuel (1715–1766) A native of County Armagh, Ireland, Samuel Finley emigrated to the Middle Colonies in 1734. He was licensed to preach in 1740 by the revivalistic Presbytery of New Brunswick; he was ordained two years later. Finley was an itinerant preacher during the *GREAT AWAKENING and in the process established himself as a leader of the New Side Presbyterians. He became a settled minister in 1744 when he accepted the pulpit at the Presbyterian church in Nottingham, Maryland, where he remained for seventeen years, establishing a school for ministerial candidates. In 1761, Finley became president of the College of New Jersey (now Princeton University), a post he retained until his death in 1766.

Finnan, Dennis (1944–) An alumnus of *MOODY BIBLE INSTITUTE, Dennis Finnan began broadcasting a radio program, *The World, the Word & You,* from Benton Harbor, Michigan, on May 11, 1980. The program features a fundamentalist perspective on matters as diverse as angels, prophecy, parenting, and Christianity in cyberspace. The broadcast now originates from St. Charles, Minnesota, where Finnan is pastor of the St. Charles Bible Church.

Finney, Charles Grandison (1792–1875) On October 10, 1821, a religious *CONVERSION occurred that would change the course of one man's life as well as redirect the course of American *EVANGELICALISM. Until that moment, Charles Grandison Finney had prepared to practice law, but he now believed that he had been given "a retainer from the Lord Jesus Christ to plead his cause." The St. Lawrence presbytery licensed him to preach in 1823 and ordained him the following year. He began preaching in upstate New York under the auspices of the Female Missionary Society of the Western District in 1824.

Early in his career, Finney harbored doubts about *CALVINISM, not so much on theological as on pragmatic grounds; Finney was convinced that Calvinistic determinism simply did not lend itself to *REVIVALS. Instead, he preached that by the mere exercise of volition anyone at all could repent of *SIN and thereby claim *SALVATION. For a people who had only recently taken their political destiny into their own hands, Finney assured them that they controlled their religious destiny as well.

Finney experimented with many ideas for promoting *REVIVALS, including protracted meetings, allowing women to pray or exhort in public, and the "*ANXIOUS BENCH" for wavering auditors, who could come forward and contemplate the choice between heaven and hell. These innovations eventually became known as "*NEW MEASURES," and they have been present in American revivalism ever since. Whereas *JONATHAN EDWARDS, the primary apologist for the *GREAT AWAKENING, had argued that *REVIVAL was a gracious visitation, in his words "a surprising work of God," Finney argued that it was "the work of man," that simply following the proper formula (which he provided in his *Lectures on Revivals of Religion*) would bring about *REVIVAL.

Finney's *REVIVALS in Rochester and in upstate New York spread to major eastern cities. They attracted national attention as well as spirited opposition from Old School Calvinists. Finney nevertheless remained adamant in his conviction about the importance of human volition in the salvation process, just as he believed in the perfectibility of both human nature and society.

A bout of cholera in 1832 prompted Finney to retire from active leadership in the western New York phase of the *SECOND GREAT AWAKENING. He served as pastor, successively, of the Second Presbyterian Church and the Broadway Tabernacle in New York City and the First Congregational Church in Oberlin, Ohio.

In 1835, Finney accepted an appointment in the newly formed Oberlin Collegiate Institute (now Oberlin College) as professor of theology, and he served as president of the college from 1851 to 1866.

References: Charles Grandison Finney, *Lectures on Revivals of Religion* (1835); idem, *Sermons on Important Subjects* (1836); idem, *Lectures on Systematic Theology,* 2 vols. (1846–47); Keith J. Hardman, *Charles Grandison Finney, 1792–1875* (1987); Charles E. Hambrick-Stowe, *Charles G. Finney and the Spirit of American Evangelicalism* (1996).

Finster, Howard (1916–2001) An American folk artist and Baptist preacher whose work often features evangelical and apocalyptic themes, Howard Finster was born in Valley Head, Alabama, and attended school for approximately six years. He was *SAVED during a Methodist *REVIVAL meeting at age thirteen. "That night the whole heavens looked new, the stars looked new," he recalled many years later. "It was the sweetest night I ever owned."

Finster served as pastor of Baptist churches and preached in *CAMP MEETINGS for the better part of four decades, and in 1965, after retiring as pastor of the Chelsea Baptist Church in Menlo, Georgia, he began repairing bicycles and lawn mowers in Pennville, Georgia, near Summerville. He began painting in 1976. Finster had a vision from God instructing him to build *Paradise Garden* in the vicinity of his repair shop. *Paradise Garden,* for which Finster has received a grant from the National Endowment for the Arts, is constructed out of "other people's junk"; it features a thirty-foot tower built out of bicycle parts, an assortment of structures and curiosities, and Finster's own church, The World's Folk Art Church, Inc.

Although Finster works in a variety of media, his primary medium is tractor enamel, which he paints onto plywood, masonite, heavy canvas, tin, mirror, gourds, or whatever else might be at hand. A visionary, Finster's art often illustrates his own visions, and the pieces are replete with scriptural citations and warnings about the imminent apocalypse, as predicted in the Bible. His "sermon art," Finster says, was mandated by God because "preaching don't do much good; no one listens—but a picture gets painted on a brain cell." Finster, whose art has received critical acclaim and has been shown in prestigious museums and galleries, also is fond of *ELVIS PRESLEY, whose visage also appears in Finster's work. "Elvis appeared to me while I was working in the garden," Finster told a reporter in 1995. "I was in the flower bed. He was wearing a light shirt and blue pants. I talked to him and asked him to stay a while with me. But he said, 'Howard, I'm on a tight schedule.'"

References: Howard Finster and Tom Patterson, *Howard Finster: Stranger from Another World, Man of Visions Now on This Earth* (1989); J. F. Turner, *Howard Finster: Man of Visions* (1989); Robert Peacock and Annibe Jenkins, *Paradise Garden: A Trip through Howard Finster's Visionary World* (1996); Patricia Leigh Brown, "Losing Paradise, Keeping His Faith," *New York Times,* June 29, 1995.

Fire-Baptized Holiness Church of God of the Americas Organized as the Colored Fire-Baptized Holiness Church of God in 1908, the Fire-Baptized Church of God of the Americas, an African American group, split off from the Fire-Baptized Holiness Church of God, a predominately white pentecostal body. The white group merged with the International Pentecostal Holiness Church in 1911. At some point the word "Colored" was dropped from the Church's name.

Ecclesiastical authority in the Church

resides in the general council that meets quadrennially and in the eleven-member executive council composed of bishops, district elders, and pastors. Headquarters for the denomination are located in Atlanta. The Fire-Baptized Holiness Church of God of the Americas joined the *NATIONAL ASSOCIATION OF EVANGELICALS in 1978.

References: Frank S. Mead and Samuel S. Hill, *Handbook of Denominations in the United States*, 10th ed. (1996); J. Gordon Melton, *The Encyclopedia of American Religions*, 3d ed. (1993).

First Baptist Church (Hammond, Indiana). *See* **Hyles, Jack.**

First German Evangelical Lutheran Synod. *See* **Wisconsin Evangelical Lutheran Synod.**

Fischer, John (Walter) (1947–) John Fischer, born in Pasadena, California, graduated from *WHEATON COLLEGE in 1969 and studied for the ministry under *RAY C. STEDMAN of Peninsula Bible Church in Palo Alto, California. A talented and versatile performer, Fischer spent much of the 1980s as artist-in-residence at *GORDON COLLEGE, Wenham, Massachusetts. His first album, *The Cold Cathedral*, released in 1969, helped to spark a spiritual renewal coincident with the *JESUS MOVEMENT, and subsequent albums remain popular with younger evangelicals. Fischer's concerts feature a mix of humor, speaking, and music, and he writes an award-winning column in *Contemporary Christian Music* magazine. In addition to his nonfiction writings, Fischer branched out into fiction with the publication of *Dark Horse* in 1983 and *Saint Ben* a decade later.

References: John Fischer, *Dark Horse* (1983); idem, *Real Christians Don't Dance* (1988); idem, *True Believers Don't Ask Why* (1989); idem, *Saint Ben* (1993); idem, *The Saints' and Angels' Song* (1994); idem, *On a Hill Too Far Away* (1994); idem, *What on Earth Are We Doing?* (1997); idem, *Ashes on the Wind* (1998).

Flannelgraph Generations of evangelical *SUNDAY SCHOOL students are well familiar with the flannelgraph, a board covered with flannel fabric and usually resting on an easel. *SUNDAY SCHOOL teachers, especially at the elementary level, use the flannelgraph to illustrate stories from the *BIBLE. They move representations of Moses or Noah or the pillar of fire, all of which are also backed with flannel, around the board in an attempt to bring the stories to life for young audiences. Although the flannelgraph is by no means the sole property of evangelicals, the extent of its use by evangelicals provides an indication of the importance they attach to biblical literacy.

Fletcher, John (William) (né de la Fléchère, Jean Guillaume) (1729–1785) John Fletcher, who was *JOHN WESLEY's designated successor, was born in Nyon, Switzerland, and studied classics at Geneva. Fletcher went to England in 1750, where he eventually befriended *CHARLES and *JOHN WESLEY and became well-known in Methodist circles. He experienced a religious awakening in 1754 and was ordained in the Church of England three years later. In 1760, he became vicar of Madelay, and by the end of the decade he agreed to become president of Trevecka College, a seminary founded by his patron, *LADY HUNTINGDON.

Fletcher left the seminary several years later during a controversy with the Calvinistic Methodists, when he cast his lot with Wesley, who asked Fletcher to be his successor. Fletcher initially demurred, but he continued to support Wesley's efforts through his organizing and through his writings, which sought to explain and to systematize Wesleyanism.

References: John Fletcher, *Discours sur la régénération* (1759); idem, *The Works of Rev. John Fletcher*, 9 vols. (1877).

Focus on the Family Focus on the Family was founded in 1977 by *JAMES C. DOBSON, a licensed psychologist and author of several books on child-rearing. His best-known book, *Dare to Discipline*, took issue with Benjamin Spock's permissiveness of an earlier generation and urged parents to discipline their children beginning at an early age. Dobson's ideas were well-received by evangelicals, many of whom lamented what they saw as the decline in morality in American society. Though nominally (and legally) nonpartisan, Focus on the Family seeks to promote "family values" by working against pornography, the "homosexual agenda," and the teaching of evolution in public schools.

In 1991, the organization relocated its national headquarters from Pomona, California, to Colorado Springs, Colorado. Dobson and the organization were active proponents of Colorado's Amendment 2, a 1992 ballot initiative that sought to restrict civil rights for gays. Focus on the Family publishes a number of magazines for specialized audiences, distributes the publications of Dobson and other conservative evangelicals, and produces several syndicated radio shows, including *Adventures in Odyssey, Focus on the Family*, and *Weekend*.

Reference: Gustav Niebuhr, "Advice for Parents, and for Politicians," *New York Times*, May 30, 1995.

Foote, Julia (1823–1900) Born in upstate New York, Julia Foote became a member of the African Methodist Episcopal Church as a teenager and, when she moved with her husband to Boston, joined the African Methodist Episcopal Zion Church. She sought ordination and, when denied, became an itinerant preacher, whereupon she was excommunicated from her church in Boston. She continued preaching, however, and on May 20, 1894, she became the first woman to be ordained a deacon in the African Methodist Episcopal Zion Church.

References: Julia Foote, *A Brand Plucked from the Fire: An Autobiographical Sketch* (1879); William Andrews, ed., *Sisters of the Spirit: Three Black Women's Autobiographies of the Nineteenth Century* (1986); Judith Weisenfeld, s.v. "Foote, Julia," in Jack Salzman, et al., eds., *Encyclopedia of African-American Culture and History* (1996).

Forbes, James A(lexander), Jr. (1935–) James A. Forbes, a gifted preacher and a pentecostal, graduated from Howard University, Union Theological Seminary, and Colgate-Rochester Divinity School. He holds his ordination with the Original United Holy Church International, although his theology is no longer evangelical in the way that most white evangelicals would recognize the term. In 1976, Forbes accepted an invitation to teach at Union Theological Seminary, where he became the Joe R. Engle Professor of Preaching. He left his full-time post at Union in 1991 to become the first African American senior minister at Riverside Church, which is located just across the street from Union in the Morningside Heights section of New York City.

Ford, Leighton (1930–) In 1955, after completing seminary and marrying *BILLY GRAHAM's sister Jeanie, Leighton Ford decided to assist his brother-in-law in evangelistic ministry. He signed on with the *BILLY GRAHAM EVANGELISTIC

ASSOCIATION, intending to stay for a year. He lasted for thirty years, becoming a well-known evangelistic preacher in his own right. He finally left the organization and formed Leighton Ford Ministries in 1986, working to train younger leaders within *EVANGELICALISM. He developed an eighteen-month curriculum called Arrow Leadership Program, which he left in 1998 to devote more of his energies to spiritual direction.

References: Leighton Ford, *Transforming Leadership: Jesus' Way of Creating Vision, Shaping Values, and Empowering Change* (1993); idem, *The Power of Story: Rediscovering the Oldest, Most Natural Way* (1994); Lauren F. Winner, "From Mass Evangelist to Soul Friend," *Christianity Today,* October 2, 2000.

Foreign Mission Baptist Convention of the U.S.A. *See* **National Baptist Convention of the U.S.A., Inc.**

Fort Wayne Female College. *See* **Taylor University.**

Forum for Scriptural Christianity. *See* **Good News.**

"Four Spiritual Laws." *See* **Bright, William Rohl "Bill."**

Fox, Lorne (Franklin) (1911–) An itinerant *EVANGELIST under the auspices of the *ASSEMBLIES OF GOD, Lorne Fox was healed of heart disease through the ministry of *CHARLES S. PRICE. Fox, a Canadian, edited a publication called *Golden Grain* and began his own *REVIVAL campaigns in 1947. His evangelistic efforts took him around the world.

Frank, Douglas (William) (1941–) Douglas Frank grew up in a missionary household and graduated from *WHEATON COLLEGE. He earned the Ph.D. in history from the State University of New York at Buffalo, writing a dissertation on Harvard philosopher William Earnest Hocking. Frank taught at *TRINITY COLLEGE in Deerfield, Illinois, and in 1975 he, along with Sam Alvord and several other colleagues, founded the *OREGON EXTENSION, a college extension program that takes place in a former logging camp in the Cascade Mountains of southern Oregon. Frank's various writings have called into question some of the shibboleths of *EVANGELICALISM, including its rationalism and its identification with American middle-class values.

References: Douglas Frank, *Less than Conquerors: How Evangelicals Entered the Twentieth Century* (1986); Randall Balmer, *Mine Eyes Have Seen the Glory: A Journey into the Evangelical Subculture in America,* 3d ed. (2000).

Franson, Fredrik (1852–1908) Fredrik Franson was born into a pietistic household in Pershyttan, near Nora, Westmoreland, Sweden. His father died when he was five, but his mother was passionately interested in missions, and she helped to instill in him a love for piety and the Scriptures. Franson excelled in school, especially in languages, and in 1869 he emigrated with his family to the United States, settling in Saunders County, Nebraska. Stricken with malaria, Franson read the *BIBLE and experienced an evangelical *CONVERSION in 1872. Upon his recovery, he undertook an extensive study of the *BIBLE, became affiliated with a local Baptist church, and began preaching. He went to Chicago in 1875 to hear *DWIGHT L. MOODY and became a member of Moody's Illinois Street Church, an affiliation that Franson maintained for the remainder of his life.

Franson also began an itinerant ministry in 1875, initially among the Scandinavians in Minnesota, and from there he traveled west to Utah, Colorado, and Nebraska, where he triggered a large *REVIVAL beginning in October 1880. Franson was ordained into the gospel ministry on January 20, 1881, at the Free Church in Phelps Center, Nebraska. He continued his itinerations to the East and then embarked on a missionary trip to Europe and Scandinavia. During the voyage across the Atlantic early in 1881 Franson met *GEORGE MÜLLER, founder of the Faith Orphanage in Bristol, England; Franson picked up some of Müller's teachings on "*FAITH PRINCIPLES," the idea that God's work would receive financial blessings if only the workers relied on faith alone and desisted from making direct financial appeals.

Franson conducted *REVIVAL meetings throughout Scandinavia, healing the sick and recording many *CONVERSIONS. In Roeskilde, Denmark, however, a woman afflicted with rheumatism accused Franson of making her illness worse. He was arrested, spent thirty-eight days in jail, and was banished from the country. Franson continued his evangelistic efforts throughout Europe, returning to the United States in 1890. Shortly thereafter he founded the Scandinavian Alliance Mission in Chicago, which provided training for foreign missionaries. Franson, himself a fervent premillennialist who preached that Jesus would return at any moment, traveled throughout the world in order to encourage missionary work.

Reference: O. C. Grauer, *Fredrik Franson, Founder of the Scandinavian Alliance Mission of North America: An Evangelist and Missionary in World-Wide Service* (n.d.).

Free Congress Research and Education Foundation The Free Congress Research and Education Foundation, headed by *PAUL WEYRICH, evolved from the Committee for the Survival of a Free Congress, founded with money from the archconservative Coors Foundation in July 1974. Weyrich had been a press aide to U.S. Senator Gordon Allot (R.-Colorado), and he was the first president of the Heritage Foundation, from 1971 to 1974. Recognizing the electoral potential of politically conservative evangelicals, Weyrich began building coalitions between political and religious conservatives beginning in the mid-1970s. He and the Free Congress Foundation have been intimately involved in several *RELIGIOUS RIGHT organizations and initiatives, including the Conservative Caucus, *MORAL MAJORITY, the *RELIGIOUS ROUNDTABLE, and National Empowerment Television (NET).

Reference: Lori Forman, "The Political Activity of the Religious Right in the 1990s: A Critical Analysis," pamphlet distributed by the American Jewish Committee.

Free Methodist Church of North America The Free Methodist Church of North America was formed in western New York state in 1860 when several Methodist Episcopal ministers and lay people in the Genesee Conference were expelled from that conference. Under the leadership of *BENJAMIN TITUS ROBERTS, the group founded the Free Methodist Church on the concept of radical freedom. Many in the group were abolitionists and supported freedom for all human beings, and the church objected to the developing practice in the Methodist churches of selling pews, believing instead that the worship of God should be free of discrimination on the basis of economics. The leaders also urged the Methodist church to return to its Wesleyan roots. They stressed the teaching of entire

*SANCTIFICATION by means of *GRACE through faith.

Other than the particular emphasis on holiness, the Free Methodists had little disagreement with the Methodist Episcopal Church. In theology, the Free Methodists stress the virgin birth, the deity of Jesus, and his vicarious *ATONEMENT and resurrection. Membership requires confession and forgiveness of *SIN, and the experience of entire *SANCTIFICATION is sought in all believers. The *BIBLE is the rule for all matters of faith and life. In practice, the Church has rules of conduct spelled out in its membership covenant; it stresses social concern for all people and prohibits membership in secret societies. The denomination supports Christian education in several colleges and at *ASBURY SEMINARY in Wilmore, Kentucky. It also has an active *EVANGELISM and mission program.

Church government is a modified episcopacy. A general conference meets every four to five years to review the *POLITY and programs of the denomination and to elect bishops. Annual conferences meet in thirty-six districts in the United States and Canada. All church property is held in trust for the denomination. In 1995, the Free Methodist Church reported 1,068 churches with 74,707 members. Headquarters are located in Indianapolis, Indiana.

References: Frank S. Mead and Samuel S. Hill, *Handbook of Denominations in the United States*, 10th ed. (1996); J. Gordon Melton, *The Encyclopedia of American Religions*, 3d ed. (1993).

Freed, Paul E. (1918–1996) The son of missionary parents, Paul E. Freed was reared in the Middle East. After serving as a pastor in Greensboro, North Carolina, and as director of a local chapter of *YOUTH FOR CHRIST, he began radio *EVANGELISM out of Morocco. Political opposition in 1959 forced his Voice of Tangiers to relocate to Monaco, where he christened a larger operation, *TRANS WORLD RADIO. The steady addition of transmitters has expanded the reach of his ministry (now headquartered in Cary, North Carolina) to approximately 80 percent of the world's population.

Reference: J. Gordon Melton, Phillip Charles Lucas, and Jon R. Stone, *Prime-Time Religion: An Encyclopedia of Religious Broadcasting* (1997).

Freedmen's Aid Society of the Methodist Church In 1866, the Methodist Episcopal Church withdrew from the national commissions that had been formed to deal with the education of freed slaves during Reconstruction and established the Freedmen's Aid Society as its own denominational organization. In the late nineteenth century, the society established twelve colleges, most of which still exist. One of the schools, New Orleans University, merged with Straight College, a Congregational school, in 1935 to form Dillard University. Another, Central Tennessee College in Nashville, Tennessee, later known as Walden College, closed in 1935. Along with those two institutions, the following colleges also trace their founding back to the Freedmen's Aid Society:

Bennett College (Greensboro, North Carolina)
Claflin University (Orangeburg, South Carolina)
Clark Atlanta University (Atlanta, Georgia)
Huston-Tillotson College (Austin, Texas)
Morristown College (Morristown, Tennessee)
Morgan College (Baltimore, Maryland)
Shaw University (Holly Springs, Mississippi)
Philander Smith College (Little Rock, Arkansas)

George R. Smith College (Sedalia, Missouri)

Wiley University (Marshall, Texas)

In addition, the Freedmen's Aid Society founded twenty academies and one medical school, Meharry Medical School. Established in Nashville in 1876, Meharry remains the largest private institution for African American health professionals in the United States.

Reference: Thomas C. Hunt and James C. Carper, eds., *Religious Higher Education in the United States: A Source Book* (1996).

Frelinghuysen, Theodorus Jacobus (1691–c. 1747) An influential—and divisive—pietist within the Dutch Reformed Church, Theodorus Jacobus Frelinghuysen was educated at the University of Lingen, where he was influenced by the pietistic followers of Gysbertus Voetius. He served two pastorates in the Lowlands before inadvertently accepting a call to the Raritan Valley of New Jersey (Frelinghuysen was initially under the impression that Raritan was in Flanders). He made good on his acceptance, however, and arrived in New York in 1720.

Frelinghuysen almost immediately ran afoul of the orthodox Dutch clergy in the Middle Colonies. He chided them for their vanity (one minister had a mirror in his home) and for their use of formal prayer (The Lord's Prayer) during worship. Once installed in the Raritan churches, Frelinghuysen proceeded, in good pietist fashion, to deny access to *HOLY COMMUNION to anyone he judged to be unconverted or wanting in piety. People excluded tended to be the more affluent members of his congregations, and they eventually responded with a document called the *Klagte* ("Complaint"), a bill of particulars against Frelinghuysen. The *Klagte* upbraided Frelinghuysen for flouting church authority and included allegations, apparently unrefuted, that Frelinghuysen was homosexual, a telling charge against someone who repeatedly urged probity on his congregants. Although he married, in part to quiet the rumors, Frelinghuysen refused to relent on his demands for high standards of morality from his congregants.

Frelinghuysen's *ITINERANCY and his evangelical fervor contributed to the onset of the *GREAT AWAKENING in the Middle Colonies. *GILBERT TENNENT, who often shared his pulpit with Frelinghuysen (and vice versa), acknowledged that Frelinghuysen had taught him about piety and *REVIVAL, and both *JONATHAN EDWARDS and *GEORGE WHITEFIELD praised Frelinghuysen's ministry. Frelinghuysen's suspicions of the traditionalist Classis of Amsterdam, which claimed responsibility for the Dutch Reformed churches in the colonies and which took a dim view of *PIETISM, led him and others to press for an American ecclesiastical body, a Coetus, which was formed in 1747.

References: James Tanis, *Dutch Calvinistic Pietism in the Middle Colonies: A Study in the Life and Theology of Theodorus Jacobus Frelinghuysen* (1968); Randall Balmer, *A Perfect Babel of Confusion: Dutch Religion and English Culture in the Middle Colonies* (1989).

Fresno Pacific College (Fresno, California) Fresno Pacific College was founded in 1944 by the Pacific District Conference of the Mennonite Brethren Church. Although the U.S. Conference of the *MENNONITE BRETHREN CHURCH held control between 1956 and 1979, today the college is again operated by the Pacific District Conference. In its early years, the school was known as Pacific Bible Institute and held classes in the *YMCA in downtown Fresno. In 1956, the name changed to Pacific Bible Institute and Christian College, and a year later, a junior college program was instituted. The school was again renamed in 1960, becoming Pacific College. The first bachelor's degrees were awarded in 1965, and Fresno Pacific College added graduate programs in 1976.

Fresno Pacific College's Graduate Division offers master of arts degrees in several areas of education, as well as in administration and conflict resolution. Its Hiebert Library holds the archives to the *MENNONITE BRETHREN CHURCH. The college's science building, the twenty-four-sided Marpeck Center, was mentioned in *Time* magazine for its unusual shape. *DANCING is not allowed on campus.

Reference: *Fresno Pacific College 1995–96 Catalog* (1995).

Friends Bible Institute and Training School. *See* **Malone College.**

Frisbee, Lonnie (1951–1993) One of the first true hippie converts of the *JESUS MOVEMENT, Lonnie Frisbee was the quintessential Jesus freak of the 1960s' outbreak of countercultural Christianity. Converted while high on LSD in a California desert, Frisbee claimed that he had an experience of theophany where he was commissioned to become an *EVANGELIST. Not long after this experience, he met a group of street Christians who had begun an evangelistic outreach in the Haight-Ashbury district of San Francisco. He moved into their communal home for a short time before moving on to southern California to join a small church in Costa Mesa.

Frisbee and his wife, Connie, joined the fledgling congregation of *CALVARY CHAPEL through a chance meeting with their pastor, *CHUCK SMITH. Although inclined more toward the conservative mind-set of the Orange County constituents, Smith and his wife, Kay, were interested in reaching the youth of the counterculture with the *GOSPEL. They asked their children to bring a "real live hippie" home with them so that they could better understand the generation they wanted to reach. Smith was immediately struck by Frisbee's charisma. "I was not at all prepared for the love that this young man would radiate," Smith recalled. "His love of Jesus and his Spirit-filled personality lit up the room."

Smith invited the Frisbees to lead a drug rehabilitation house called the House of Miracles and offered Lonnie Frisbee charge over the Wednesday night Bible study at the church. Frisbee's Bible study soon became the central night of activity for the church, drawing thousands of young people from the surrounding areas. Frisbee was the charismatic spark that ignited the tremendous burst of spiritual activity at *CALVARY CHAPEL. During the four-year period that he was at *CALVARY CHAPEL, from 1968 to 1971, Frisbee brought thousands of new converts into evangelical Christianity. His influence over a number of current *CALVARY CHAPEL leaders—Mike MacIntosh and *GREG LAURIE, in particular—helped to shape the *CALVARY CHAPEL movement.

By 1971, Frisbee was looking to move on. Marital difficulties and theological conflicts with Smith prompted him to join charismatic teacher *BOB MUMFORD in Fort Lauderdale, Florida, in the beginnings of what became known as the *SHEPHERDING MOVEMENT. After suffering a divorce in 1973, Frisbee remained under a number of authority figures before returning to the *CALVARY CHAPEL staff in 1976. He caught the attention of *JOHN WIMBER, whose Yorba Linda church had just become part of the *CALVARY CHAPEL Fellowship. After a couple of meetings, Wimber invited Frisbee to speak at his church on Mother's Day, 1980. Wimber recalls that occasion as a watershed for the church, the real beginning of the "signs and wonders" that became a trademark of Wimber's ministry. In the six months following that service, Wimber's congregation quintupled in size, from five hundred to twenty-five hundred. Many people believe that Frisbee was the most important precursor of Wimber's "signs and wonders" ministry and the subsequent rise of the *VINEYARD CHRISTIAN FELLOWSHIP churches. Frisbee, therefore, played a pivotal role in the emergence of the two largest denominations associated with the *JESUS MOVEMENT.

Frisbee's story, however, had a tragic ending. He contracted AIDS and died early in 1993. At his funeral service he was eulogized as a Samson figure.

Frisby, Neal (Vincent) (1933–) Born in Strong, Arkansas, much of Neal Frisby's life is shrouded in mystery. "I always had a desire to be a conqueror, a champion," he confessed, without elaboration, in his autobiography. He moved to California, completed the ninth grade, and went to barber college. Following the birth of her second child, Frisby's wife, still in her teens, committed suicide, which Frisby later attributed to demon possession. He attended an *ASSEMBLIES OF GOD church shortly thereafter and was converted, spoke in *TONGUES, and concluded that "the Spirit of God bade me go preach and pray for the sick." Frisby, by his own account, descended into alcoholism instead and neglected his family and his barber shop. He spent time in hospital psychiatric wards and in the state mental asylum, where he witnessed all manner of demon possession. Concluding that his sickness was spiritual and not physical, Frisby finally "had it out with the devil." After a spiritual breakthrough he embarked on a forty-day fast, in the course of which God endowed him with the extraordinary power of "creative miracles."

Frisby also became convinced of his calling as a prophet. He claims *WILLIAM MARRION BRANHAM, among others, as his mentor, but Frisby believes that he is the "Rainbow Angel" of Revelation 10. Frisby, who also claims the powers of healing, organized his followers into a church called the Capstone Cathedral, a pyramid-shaped structure in Phoenix. He is a recluse, but he preaches regularly at the church and issues tapes, booklets, and "prophetic scrolls," which contain his prophecies, to several hundred followers across the country.

References: W. V. Grant, *Creative Miracles* (n.d.); Randall Balmer, *Mine Eyes Have Seen the Glory: A Journey into the Evangelical Subculture in America,* 3d ed. (2000).

Full Gospel Business Men's Fellowship International Founded by *DEMOS SHAKARIAN, a California dairyman, the Full Gospel Business Men's Fellowship International is an organization of laymen associated with the *CHARISMATIC MOVEMENT. Part of its appeal lay in the growing sense on the part of laymen that the clergy in pentecostal denominations had become too powerful and that the laity was not consulted enough in the governance of church affairs. The group became allied with independent revivalists. It received early and crucial support from *ORAL ROBERTS, for example, who in turn benefited from the publicity and the financial support that the members provided.

The organization, which explicitly

excluded clergy from membership, started a periodical, *Voice,* in 1953 and later that same year held its first annual convention, in Los Angeles. The organization grew rapidly, with local chapters formed across the country in the wake of pentecostal *REVIVAL campaigns. By 1972, the Full Gospel Business Men's Fellowship reported a membership of three hundred thousand and an annual budget in excess of $1 million. Its effect was to provide a kind of social legitimation for the *CHARISMATIC MOVEMENT. By meeting in dignified settings (usually in hotel banquet rooms) and thereby demonstrating the support of businessmen, the Full Gospel Business Men's Fellowship helped to move the *CHARISMATIC MOVEMENT from tents and sawdust to suburbs and office suites, thereby showcasing its white-collar constituency.

Reference: David Edwin Harrell Jr., *All Things Are Possible: The Healing and Charismatic Revivals in Modern America* (1975).

Full Gospel Central Church (Seoul, Korea). *See* **Cho, Paul Yonggi.**

Fuller, Andrew (1754–1815) Andrew Fuller, born in Cambridgeshire, England, was converted and baptized at the age of sixteen. Not long thereafter, he took over as pastor of the local Baptist congregation in Soham, and his reading of *JONATHAN EDWARDS turned Fuller against the hyper-*CALVINISM then popular among the Particular Baptists. Fuller believed that strict Calvinistic predestination militated against *EVANGELISM. He argued for human freedom without compromising the notion of divine sovereignty, and he eventually published his views in 1785 as *The Gospel Worthy of All Acceptation*.

In 1782, he left Soham for Kettering, where he remained for the rest of his life. Along with other like-minded Baptists, Fuller organized the Baptist Missionary Society in October 1792 and was selected its first secretary. Fuller championed the cause of missions, often in the face of great resistance, arguing that faith in Christ was the duty of all who hear the *GOSPEL.

References: Andrew Fuller, *The Gospel Worthy of All Acceptation* (1785); idem, *The Calvinistic and Socinian Systems Examined and Compared as to their Moral Tendency* (1793); idem, *The Gospel its Own Witness* (1799); William Ward, *A Sketch of the Character of the Late Rev. Andrew Fuller* (1817).

Fuller, Charles E(dward) (1887–1968) Charles E. Fuller spent his early years in the family orange business near Redlands, California. After graduating from Pomona College in 1910, he returned to the orange groves and soon expanded his interests into real estate, leasing land for oil drilling, and trucking. Under the fundamentalist preaching of *PAUL RADER, pastor of *MOODY CHURCH in Chicago, Fuller experienced a dramatic *CONVERSION in 1916 and began teaching an adult *SUNDAY SCHOOL class at his church, Placentia Presbyterian Church. Increasingly dissatisfied with his secular pursuits, Fuller set them aside and enrolled at the *BIBLE INSTITUTE OF LOS ANGELES (BIOLA), where, under the influence of *REUBEN A. TORREY, he learned dispensational *PREMILLENNIALISM.

Unhappy with the emphasis on social action at Placentia Presbyterian, Fuller resigned from the board of elders and founded Calvary Church as an independent congregation in 1925. He was ordained by a group of Baptist churches associated with the *BAPTIST BIBLE UNION, a fundamentalist organization, and soon became an itinerant preacher. He began broadcasting the church's worship services and a program of Bible studies over local radio stations in 1930. His congregation eventually grew impatient with Fuller's attention to radio *EVANGELISM; he submitted his resignation in 1933 and formed the Gospel Broadcasting Association to support his radio and evangelistic ministry. After experimenting with several formats, Fuller settled on a Sunday evening *REVIVAL service, called *Radio Revival Hour,* complete with a studio audience. By 1937, the program, renamed *The Old Fashioned Revival Hour,* was aired nationwide over the Mutual Broadcasting System, and Fuller's broadcasts were more popular than Amos 'n' Andy, Bob Hope, and Charlie McCarthy. "We are allied with no denomination," Fuller declared in 1937. "We are fundamental, premillennial, and our desire is to bring up no controversial questions, but only to preach and teach the *WORD OF GOD."

Mutual dropped the program in 1944, however, but Fuller was able to knit together a collection of local independent stations until a new network, ABC, picked it up in 1949. The advent of television signaled a long decline for Fuller's program. His attempts to adapt to the new medium ended in failure, and ABC Radio finally forced him off the network in 1963.

Fuller's other contribution to American Protestantism was in the field of education. He provided the money to begin a "Christ-centered, Spirit-directed training school" that would provide education and training for ministers and missionaries. *FULLER THEOLOGICAL SEMINARY opened its doors in Pasadena, California, in 1947 under the direction of *HAROLD JOHN OCKENGA, who also served as pastor of the Park Street Church in Boston. Ockenga and other members of the faculty, however, shared a vision for the seminary that would be somewhat at odds with Fuller's. Ironically, the school sought to shed the legacy of a narrow premillennialist *FUNDAMENTALISM with its mechanical insistence on biblical *INERRANCY, characteristics that applied to Charles Fuller's own theology.

References: Wilbur M. Smith, *A Voice for God: The Life of Charles E. Fuller, Originator of the Old Fashioned Revival Hour* (1949); Daniel P. Fuller, *Give the Winds a Mighty Voice: The Story of Charles E. Fuller* (1972); George M. Marsden, *Reforming Fundamentalism: Fuller Seminary and the New Evangelicalism* (1987); L. David Lewis, s.v. "Charles E. Fuller," in Charles H. Lippy, ed., *Twentieth-Century Shapers of American Popular Religion* (1989).

Fuller, Millard (1934–) The founder of Habitat for Humanity, Millard Fuller was born into poverty but graduated from Auburn University and the University of Alabama Law School. After passing the bar exam, he and his partner, Morris Dees, opened a highly successful law firm in Montgomery, Alabama. Fuller's long working hours, however, caused a crisis in his marriage, and he resolved to give away all of his money. The Fullers relocated to Sumter County, Georgia, where they joined *CLARENCE JORDAN's Koinonia Community. In the late 1960s, Fuller came up with the idea to cooperate with the poor to build houses for them. The homes would be built at cost, the mortgages financed at no interest, and the owner would also invest "sweat equity" into the construction.

He tried the idea in Sumter County and then as a missionary for the United Church of Christ in Zaire. When he and his wife, Linda, returned from Africa, they began Habitat for Humanity in 1976. The organization, in cooperation with community groups, corporations, and religious organizations, has built thousands of homes in the United States and around the world. "Habitat is a small organization with a big idea," Fuller explained in a 1999 interview, "and the idea is that everybody who gets sleepy now will have a place to sleep. There's a profound theological basis for that, because God, clearly revealed in the *BIBLE, is the God of the whole crowd. . . . He wants everybody fed, everybody watered, everybody clothed, everybody housed."

Reference: Michael G. Maudlin, "God's Contractor," *Christianity Today*, June 14, 1999.

Fuller Theological Seminary Founded in Pasadena, California, in 1947 as a "Christ-centered, Spirit-directed training school," Fuller Theological Seminary received its inspiration and early funding from *CHARLES E. FULLER and his radio program, *The Old Fashioned Revival Hour*. Under the absentee guidance of the school's first president, *HAROLD JOHN OCKENGA (who remained as pastor of Park Street Church in Boston), Fuller Seminary sought to soften some of the harder edges of *FUNDAMENTALISM and engage modern scholarship and biblical criticism. With a founding faculty consisting of *CARL F. H. HENRY (theology), Everett Harrison (New Testament), *WILBUR SMITH (apologetics), and *HAROLD LINDSELL (church history and missions), Fuller Seminary attracted some of *EVANGELICALISM's best and brightest students.

The "*NEW EVANGELICALISM" emanating from Fuller Seminary was uneasy with the militancy, the *SEPARATISM, and the anti-intellectualism of fundamentalists. Many fundamentalists, in turn, viewed Fuller with suspicion, especially as members of the faculty seemed sympathetic with *NEOORTHODOXY and tempered their enthusiasm for biblical *INERRANCY. *CHARLES WOODBRIDGE and *HAROLD LINDSELL, among others, became openly critical of the "*LIBERALISM" at Fuller, and after the appointment of *DAVID ALLAN HUBBARD as president in 1963, a number of faculty members moved to more conservative, fundamentalist institutions, such as *TRINITY EVANGELICAL DIVINITY SCHOOL.

Fuller earned accreditation in 1957 from the American Association of Theological Schools. The 1960s witnessed the founding of Fuller's Schools of Psychology and World Mission as well as the introduction of doctoral programs in ministry and theology in the School of Theology. All three divisions of the seminary earned regional accreditation from the Western Association of Schools and Colleges in 1969. Since then, Fuller has developed master of arts programs in Christian leadership and intercultural and cross-cultural studies, a master of science program in marital and family therapy, as well as master's programs in divinity and theology. Fuller also awards doctorates in psychology, therapy, theology, missiology, and ministry. The seminary has extension sites in Seattle; Phoenix and Tucson, Arizona; and throughout California, including the San Francisco Bay area, Bakersfield, Sacramento, Santa Barbara, Costa Mesa, Ventura, and San Diego.

Although the seminary is interdenominational, more than four hundred students belong to the Presbyterian Church (USA). Fuller has a ministry office for Presbyterian students who are seeking denominational ordination. It also hosts a similar office for *REFORMED CHURCH IN AMERICA students. Fuller runs special training and support programs for African American and Latino pastors who have not yet earned undergraduate degrees. The seminary also has a Center for Deaf Ministries that offers support services both to deaf students and deaf and hearing students who plan to minister with deaf people. Fuller's minority and international student ratios reflect the seminary's commitment to diversity: Nineteen percent of the student body are American members of minority groups, and another 25 percent are international students.

Fuller Theological Seminary's library has strong collections in the areas of the Wesleyan *HOLINESS MOVEMENT, women and the church, third-world theological writing, and the social witness of various American churches, including abolitionist churches, African American churches, and peace movements. The library also has a rare book room with volumes dating to the sixteenth century; it houses the recently established *DAVID DU PLESSIS Center for Christian Spirituality.

References: *Fuller Theological Seminary Catalog, 1995–1996* (1995); George M. Marsden, *Reforming Fundamentalism: Fuller Seminary and the New Evangelicalism* (1987).

Fulton Street Prayer Meeting Generally regarded as the catalyst for the *PRAYER MEETING REVIVAL of 1857–1859, the Fulton Street Prayer Meeting began on September 23, 1857, at the Old North Dutch Reformed Church, which had hired businessman *JEREMIAH C. LANPHIER as a lay *EVANGELIST to the neighborhood. Lanphier convened the meetings at noon for the benefit of businessmen in the area. Soon the weekly prayer meetings became daily, as the *REVIVAL took hold and spread to other cities in North America. The Fulton Street Prayer Meeting remained popular for a quarter of a century.

Fundamental Baptist Mission of Trinidad and Tobago Founded in 1921, the Fundamental Baptist Mission of Trinidad and Tobago performs evangelistic work and produces a weekly radio broadcast. Much of its support comes from affiliate offices in South Charleston, West Virginia, and Hamilton, Ontario.

Reference: J. Gordon Melton, Phillip Charles Lucas, and Jon R. Stone, *Prime-Time Religion: An Encyclopedia of Religious Broadcasting* (1997).

Fundamentalism The term *fundamentalism* derives from a series of pamphlets that appeared between 1910 and 1915 called **THE FUNDAMENTALS; OR, TESTIMONY TO THE TRUTH.* *The Fundamentals* contained conservative statements on doctrinal issues that were meant to counteract the perceived drift toward liberal theology or "*MODERNISM" within Protestantism. People who subscribed to these doctrines became known as *fundamentalists,* and *fundamentalism* came to refer to the entire movement.

Fundamentalism has also been described as a militant antimodernism, but that characterization must be qualified. Fundamentalists are not opposed to modernism in the sense of being suspicious of innovation or technology; indeed, fundamentalists (and evangelicals generally) have often been in the forefront in the uses of technology, especially communications technology. Fundamentalists have an aversion to modernity only when it is invested with a moral valence, when it represents a departure from orthodoxy or "traditional values," however they might be defined.

Finally, fundamentalism can be characterized as confrontational, at least as it has developed in the United States; *JERRY FALWELL, for instance, insists that he is a fundamentalist, not an evangelical. This militancy—on matters of doctrine, ecclesiology, dress, personal behavior, or politics—has prompted George M. Marsden, the preeminent historian of fundamentalism, to remark that the difference between an evangelical and a fundamentalist is that a fundamentalist is "an evangelical who is mad about something."

References: George M. Marsden, *Fundamentalism and American Culture: The Shaping of Twentieth-Century Evangelicalism: 1870 to 1925* (1980); Joel A. Carpenter, *Revive Us Again: The Reawakening of American Fundamentalism* (1997); Robert D. Woodberry and Christian S. Smith, "Fundamentalism et al.: Conservative Protestants in America," *Annual Review of Sociology,* XXIV (1998).

Fundamentalist Fellowship. *See* **Conservative Baptist Association.**

Fundamentals, The; or, Testimony to the Truth A series of twelve booklets, *The Fundamentals* represented an attempt on the part of conservative Protestants to counteract the drift toward liberal theology or "*MODERNISM" in the early decades of the twentieth century. Subtitled *Testimony to the Truth,* these booklets contained articles on doctrinal matters by respected evangelicals in North America and Great Britain. The idea for such a series came from *LYMAN STEWART of Union Oil Company of California; he and his brother Milton financed their publication and set up a fund to distribute them to Protestant workers throughout the English-speaking world.

Out of the ninety articles contained in the pamphlets, approximately one third addressed the controverted issue of biblical inspiration. Others articulated conservative positions on such issues as the virgin birth of Jesus, the authenticity of miracles, the resurrection, and the Genesis account of creation. People who subscribed to the doctrines set forth in these pamphlets came to be called "fundamentalists."

References: Ernest R. Sandeen, *The Roots of Fundamentalism: British and American Millenarianism, 1800–1930* (1970); George M. Marsden, *Fundamentalism and American Culture: The Shaping of Twentieth-Century Evangelicalism: 1870 to 1925* (1980).

Furman, Richard (1755–1825) An early Baptist leader and apologist for slavery, Richard Furman was born in Esopus (Kingston), New York, but grew up in South Carolina. Largely self-educated, he learned languages and literature and taught himself medicine. Furman was converted in 1771, and the "boy preacher" began preaching at the age of sixteen, becoming well-known in Baptist circles for his oratorical skills. Furman's loud support for the Patriot cause prompted Lord Cornwallis to hunt him down during the Revolutionary War; Furman fled to Virginia. He was a member of the South Carolina constitutional convention, where he argued for the separation of church and state.

Beginning in 1778, Furman served as a Baptist pastor in various venues, and in 1787, he became pastor of the First Baptist Church in Charleston, South Carolina, the most prominent Baptist pulpit in the South. Furman held this post for the rest of his life and used it as a platform to organize Baptists and coordinate their efforts. He was the first president of the *TRIENNIAL CONVENTION, the first national organization of Baptists. He was also the first president of the South Carolina Baptist Convention. Furman's advocacy on behalf of education—he was known in Baptist circles as the "apostle of education"—led to the founding of Columbian College (now George Washington University) in Washington, D.C. Furman University, organized in 1827 as the first Baptist college in the South, was named in his honor.

Furman was an aristocrat and a slave-owner. In 1822, he published a "biblical" defense of slavery, and his notions about Baptist cooperation together with his own pro-slavery sentiments helped to lay the foundation for the formation of the *SOUTHERN BAPTIST CONVENTION in 1845.

References: Harvey T. Cook, *A Biography of Richard Furman* (1913); J. A. Rogers, *Richard Furman: Life and Legacy* (1985).

Fyfe, Robert Alexander (1816–1878) Robert Alexander Fyfe, born in Laprairie, Lower Canada, prepared for the Baptist ministry at Canada Baptist College and Newton Theological Institute. Beginning in 1843, he served briefly as principal of Canada Baptist College and then began the first of two tours of duty as pastor of what eventually became the Jarvis Street Baptist Church in Toronto. Fyfe worked for cooperation among Baptists in Canada, especially in the realm of education and missions. He was the guiding force behind the formation of both the Canadian Literary Institute in 1860 and the Regular Baptist Foreign Missionary Society of Canada a decade later.

Reference: T. T. Gibson, *Robert Alexander Fyfe* (1988).

■ ■ ■

Gabelein, Arno C(lemens) (1861–1945) Born in Germany, Arno C. Gabelein emigrated to the United States in 1879 after discerning a call to the ministry. Following a stint as an assistant at the German Methodist Episcopal Church in New York City, Gabelein was ordained in 1885 and went on to serve Methodist congregations in Maryland, New York, and New Jersey. Having subscribed enthusiastically to *JOHN NELSON DARBY's notions about dispensational *PREMILLENNIALISM, Gabelein returned to New York in 1894 and became affiliated with the Hope of Israel Mission. He founded a periodical, *Our Hope,* which he used to propagate his interpretations about biblical prophecy and his convictions about Christian missions to the Jews.

With his flawless Yiddish and long beard, Gabelein became a kind of showcase converted Jew for American evangelicals late in the nineteenth century, who were just then revising their eschatological notions to provide an argument for the *CONVERSION of Jews and their restoration to Palestine. Gabelein became a regular speaker at Bible and prophecy conferences. Like other dispensationalists, Gabelein discerned social decay everywhere around him but insisted that these were the "signs of the times," that they heralded the imminent *SECOND COMING of Jesus. He also, like other dispensationalists, urged a separation from "liberal" Protestants. He left the Methodist Church himself in 1899 because of its supposed apostasy.

References: Arno C. Gabelein, *Conflict of the Ages* (1933); Paul Boyer, *When Time Shall Be No More: Prophecy Belief in Modern American Culture* (1992).

Gabler, Mel. *See* **Education Research Association.**

Gabler, Norma. *See* **Education Research Association.**

Gaither, Gloria (née Sickal) (1942–) The "principal lyricist" for the Gaither songs, which she wrote with her husband, Bill, Gloria Gaither graduated from *ANDERSON COLLEGE (now Anderson University). She met and eventually married *BILL GAITHER while both were teaching in Alexandria, Indiana, and the two became a formidable songwriting duo. In 1985, Gloria Gaither received the Dove Award from the *GOSPEL MUSIC ASSOCIATION for "Upon This Rock."

References: Gloria Gaither, *Make Warm Noises* (1971); idem, *Rainbows Live at Easter* (1974); idem, *Because He Lives* (1974); idem, *Decisions: A Christian's Approach to Making Right Choices* (1982); Stephen R. Graham, s.v. "Bill and Gloria Gaither," in Charles H. Lippy, ed., *Twentieth-Century Shapers of American Popular Religion* (1989).

Gaither, William J. "Bill" (1936–) A native of Alexandria, Indiana, Bill Gaither, often called the "patriarch of gospel music," became enamored of gospel quartets as a child and began his own short-lived group after high school. He switched his aspirations to high school teaching and enrolled in *ANDERSON COLLEGE (now Anderson University), where he received the bachelor's degree in English in 1959. Two years later, he graduated with a master's degree in guidance from Ball State University.

While still in school, Gaither published his first song, "I've Been to Calvary," and he continued to pursue his musical interests while he taught high school in his hometown of Alexandria. There he met and married *GLORIA SICKAL, a fellow teacher who became his musical and songwriting partner. Bill Gaither continued his composing and achieved a breakthrough with "He Touched Me" in 1963; the song was nominated for a Grammy Award and was recorded by *ELVIS PRESLEY.

Gaither eventually left his teaching job to devote full energies to writing and performing with the Bill Gaither Trio. His songs, which feature an easy, almost hypnotic melody, invite audience participation, and they have become a staple of contemporary evangelical worship. Gaither has received several awards for his contemporary gospel compositions. In 1981, he formed the New Gaither Vocal Band; his variety television show, *Bill Gaither,* was broadcast by the *TRINITY BROADCASTING NETWORK.

References: Stephen R. Graham, s.v. "Bill and Gloria Gaither," in Charles H. Lippy, ed., *Twentieth-Century Shapers of American Popular Religion* (1989); Jim Bessman, "Gaither Sees Bigger Home for Gospel; Series to Market Music to Wider Audience," *Billboard,* May 3, 1997.

Gardner, James H(arrison) (1931–) Born in St. Paul, Minnesota, James H. Gardner attended Michigan State College, where he experienced an evangelical *CONVERSION. He prepared for the ministry at *GRACE THEOLOGICAL SEMINARY in Winona Lake, Indiana, and was a pastor in Indiana for twenty-five years. During this time, he did evangelistic work part-time at state and county fairs, and he founded Amazing Grace Mission in 1983 as "an independent, Fundamental, soul-Winning Mission." Both Amazing Grace Mission and *FARMERS FOR CHRIST INTERNATIONAL (which are functionally indistinguishable) use state and county fairs as a venue for *EVANGELISM and for incorporating new converts into "fundamental Baptist churches in their area." Gardner (and, by extension, his organizations) holds to such fundamentalist dogmas as *PREMILLENNIALISM, separation from liberals, and the *INERRANCY of the *BIBLE as God "has preserved it for the English-speaking world in the Authorized King James Version."

Reference: Amazing Grace Mission brochure.

Garnet, Henry Highland (1815–1882) Henry Highland Garnet was born into slavery in Kent County, Maryland. He escaped from bondage with his parents and his sister in 1824, and the family found its way to New York City. The family broke up, however, when slave-catchers ransacked their home and destroyed their possessions. Garnet went to school at the abolitionist-sponsored Canaan Academy in New Hampshire and continued his education at the Oneida Institute in Whitestown, New York, graduating in 1840. He then became an abolitionist lecturer under the aegis of the *AMERICAN ANTI-SLAVERY SOCIETY. Garnet's radicalism—he once called upon slaves to rise up in insurrection and slay their white masters—soon attracted opposition, including that of Frederick Douglass, who was then emerging as the nation's most influential abolitionist.

Garnet was ordained a Presbyterian in 1842 and served churches in Troy, New York, New York City, and Washington, D.C. He recruited African Americans for the Union Army during the Civil War, and on February 12, 1865, he preached a sermon before the United States House of Representatives commemorating the passage of the Thirteenth Amendment to the Constitution. Though once an opponent of colonization, Garnet took an avid interest in African affairs toward the end of his life. He accepted an appointment as minister to Liberia in 1881, but he died shortly after his arrival the following year.

References: W. M. Brewer, "Henry Highland Garnet," *Journal of Negro History,* XIII (January 1928); J. Schor, *Henry Highland Garnet: A Voice of Black Radicalism in the Nineteenth Century* (1977).

Garr, A(lfred) G(oodrich), (Sr.) (1874–1944) One of the first to receive the *BAPTISM OF THE HOLY SPIRIT during the *AZUSA STREET REVIVAL, A. G. Garr was born in Danville, Kentucky, and studied at Center College and *ASBURY COLLEGE. While pastor of the Burning Bush Mission in Los Angeles, Garr attended the meetings on Azusa Street, where he received the *BAPTISM OF THE HOLY SPIRIT and began *SPEAKING IN TONGUES on June 16, 1906. Garr's experience led to conflict with his congregation, prompting his resignation and a resolve to carry the Azusa message to India. Upon announcing his intention, the Azusa Street gathering contributed hundreds of dollars; Garr and his family sailed for India with the assumption that the pentecostal gift of *TONGUES would allow them to preach in a foreign language without having studied that language (**XENOLALIA*).

That expectation, however, was never realized. Garr preached to a group of missionaries upon his arrival in Calcutta in 1907, and many received a Spirit *BAPTISM. The Garrs continued on to Bombay, Ceylon (Sri Lanka), and Hong Kong, where two of their daughters died. After a furlough, the Garrs returned briefly to China in 1911 before settling into an itinerant healing ministry in the United States. Garr's evangelistic efforts over the ensuing two decades met with success, but a particularly fruitful *REVIVAL in Charlotte, North Carolina, in 1930 convinced him to settle there. The congregation he founded there became known as Garr Memorial Church.

Reference: Vinson Synan, *The Holiness-Pentecostal Movement in the United States* (1971).

Garrettson, Freeborn (1752–1827) Freeborn Garrettson, the son of a wealthy slaveholder, was born in Hartford County, Maryland, near the mouth of the Susquehanna River. Garrettson fell under the influence of several itinerant Methodist preachers, and after his own New Birth in

1775, he freed his slaves and became a Methodist itinerant preacher himself. He traveled and organized churches in Maryland, Virginia, North Carolina, New York, and Delaware. In Baltimore in 1874, at the founding "Christmas Conference" of the Methodist Episcopal Church in the United States, Garrettson was dispatched to Nova Scotia.

Arriving in Halifax in February 1785, Garrettson took part in the second wave of the Awakening in the Maritimes. A charismatic leader and a gifted preacher whose voice, according to contemporaries, projected "a quarter of a mile," Garrettson soon emerged as leader of the Maritime Methodists. His return south in 1787 left a leadership void; *FRANCIS ASBURY was reluctant to assign his most fervent preachers to the Maritimes, so leadership among the Methodists devolved upon ill-equipped imports from Britain. Garrettson eventually married Catharine Livingston and settled in Rhinebeck, New York, but he was largely responsible, through his itinerations, for the push of *METHODISM westward beyond the Allegheny Mountains.

Reference: G. A. Rawlyk, *The Canada Fire: Radical Evangelicalism in British North America, 1775–1812* (1994).

Garrigus, Alice Belle (1858–1949) Having attended Mount Holyoke Female Seminary, Alice Belle Garrigus taught school, worked in a home for poor women and children, and was an itinerant preacher in New Hampshire. In 1910, she moved to St. John's, Newfoundland, as a missionary, where she organized the Bethesda Mission and preached, in her words, "the full *GOSPEL—Jesus as Savior, Sanctifier, Baptizer, Healer and Coming King." Garrigus effectively brought *PENTECOSTALISM to Newfoundland; her Bethesda Mission eventually became the cornerstone of a denomination, Bethesda Pentecostal Assemblies, later known as the Pentecostal Assemblies of Newfoundland.

Gee, Donald (1891–1966) Converted in 1905 at London's Finsbury Park Congregational Church, Donald Gee became a pentecostal in 1913. His first pastorate, in a suburb of Edinburgh, saw considerable growth in the congregation, and in 1928 he accepted an invitation to be a Bible teacher in Australia and New Zealand, which led to other lectures around the world. Known as the "apostle of balance" for his conciliatory demeanor and his eagerness to avoid doctrinal controversies, Gee argued insistently that the pentecostal *REVIVAL should be regarded as a worldwide phenomenon and not restricted to any one country. Toward the goal of a transnational understanding of *PENTECOSTALISM, Gee helped to organize several international conferences. A gifted musician and writer, Gee wrote more than thirty books and contributed to pentecostal publications; in 1947, he was appointed editor of *Pentecost,* a post he retained until his death.

References: Donald Gee, *Concerning Spiritual Gifts* (1928); idem, *Upon All Flesh* (1935); idem, *After Pentecost* (1945).

Geisler, Norman L(eo) (1932–) Born in Warren, Michigan, Norman L. Geisler was ordained in 1956. He graduated from *WHEATON COLLEGE, Detroit Bible College (now *WILLIAM TYNDALE COLLEGE), and Loyola University. Geisler, a creationist, a philosopher, and a systematic theologian, taught at Detroit Bible College and at *TRINITY COLLEGE before joining the faculty of *TRINITY EVANGELICAL DIVINITY SCHOOL in 1969. Geisler left for

*DALLAS THEOLOGICAL SEMINARY in 1979 and remained there until becoming a dean at *JERRY FALWELL's *LIBERTY UNIVERSITY from 1989 until 1991. He was named dean of Southern Evangelical Seminary in Charlotte, North Carolina, in 1992 and became president in 1997.

Geisler's theology is conservative and dispensational. His relations with colleagues have often turned sour because he accuses fellow evangelicals of heresy for departing from his understanding of orthodoxy on some point of doctrine.

References: Norman L. Geisler, *The Christian Ethic of Love* (1973); idem, *Christian Apologetics* (1976); idem, *The Roots of Evil* (1978); idem, *False Gods of Our Time* (1985); idem, *The Infiltration of the New Age* (1989); idem, *Answering Islam* (1993); Randall Balmer, *Mine Eyes Have Seen the Glory: A Journey into the Evangelical Subculture in America,* 3d ed. (2000).

General Association of General Baptists Starting with the work of *BENONI STINSON in Indiana, a group of dissident Baptists, sometimes called Stinsonites, formed the Liberty Association of General Baptists in 1824. The churches in the association, which held Arminian beliefs emphasizing free will, had felt ostracized by the predominant Calvinist Baptists in the state. From southwestern Indiana the movement spread west into Illinois and south into Kentucky. The General Association of General Baptists was organized in 1870.

Doctrinally, the General Baptists believe that Christ died for all; that failure to achieve *SALVATION lies with the individual; that humankind is depraved; and that regeneration is necessary for *SALVATION, which comes by repentance and faith in Christ. People who persevere are *SAVED; the wicked are punished eternally. The *LORD'S SUPPER and *BAPTISM by immersion are the only ordinances and should be open to all believers. Some General Baptist churches practice foot washing.

*POLITY is similar to other Baptist bodies. Congregations are autonomous and voluntarily gather in associations. Ordinations are approved by local bodies of ministers and deacons. The association supports a liberal arts college with a theological department at Oakland City, Indiana, and the group's headquarters are located in Pine Bluff, Missouri. The General Baptists report 876 churches with 74,156 members.

References: Frank S. Mead and Samuel S. Hill, *Handbook of Denominations in the United States,* 10th ed. (1996); J. Gordon Melton, *The Encyclopedia of American Religions,* 3d ed. (1993).

General Association of Regular Baptist Churches At the 1922 annual meeting of the (then) Northern Baptist Convention, a group of pastors attempted to convince the convention to adopt the moderately Calvinist *NEW HAMPSHIRE CONFESSION as the basis of the convention's doctrine. When the move failed, the pastors and their churches formed the *BAPTIST BIBLE UNION within the denomination. The purpose of the union was to rid the convention of all traces and effects of the modernist movement. The union became the General Association of Regular Baptist Churches (GARBC) in 1932, as churches from eight states withdrew from the Northern Baptist Convention.

The GARBC does not consider itself a denomination, as such. It is an association of like-minded Baptist churches with no overarching denominational structure or hierarchy. Each church in the association is allowed to send up to six voting delegates, called messengers, and as many nonvoting members as it likes, to the annual meeting. All decisions concerning the association are made in that meeting.

Voting members must subscribe to the Articles of Faith before being seated in the meeting.

The kinds of work usually falling under the purview of a denominational organization—mission work, publishing, curriculum development and distribution, and the like—are carried out by autonomous organizations. Six approved agencies oversee all mission endeavors. Associational approval is given annually after a close review of the work and doctrine of the agencies. Likewise, the approved colleges, seminaries, and Bible colleges must undergo an annual review before retaining approved status. Strict adherence to the Articles of Faith is required.

The Articles of Faith are typical of fundamentalist doctrine. The Articles affirm the verbal, plenary inspiration of the Scriptures and their infallibility and *INERRANCY. The Articles are Trinitarian, express a belief in creation as literally described in the book of Genesis, and assert the reality and personality of the devil. The association further stresses the virgin birth and substitutionary *ATONEMENT of Jesus and his premillennial return. There are two ordinances, *BAPTISM by immersion and the *LORD'S SUPPER.

As is usual with Baptist groups, *POLITY is congregational. The local church is the locus of authority. A council of eighteen makes recommendations to the annual meeting, but it has only limited authority to act on its own or on behalf of the churches. At each annual meeting, nine members of the council are elected to a two-year term. A national representative is nominated by the council and elected by the annual meeting.

Other Baptist-distinctive characteristics, such as soul freedom and the separation of church and state, are also emphasized in the churches. Separation for the GARBC, however, also extends to separation from any church body or organization that allows—or even has fellowship with any group that allows—any taint of *LIBERALISM or *MODERNISM in its midst.

The GARBC has its home office in Schaumburg, Illinois. In 1994, the association reported 1,458 churches and a total membership of 136,380.

References: Frank S. Mead and Samuel S. Hill, *Handbook of Denominations in the United States*, 10th ed. (1996); J. Gordon Melton, *The Encyclopedia of American Religions*, 3d ed. (1993); *1997 Yearbook of American and Canadian Churches.*

General Missionary Convention of the Baptist Denomination in the United States of America for Foreign Missions. *See* **Southern Baptist Convention** *and* **Triennial Convention.**

Geneva College (Beaver Falls, Pennsylvania) Geneva College began in 1848, when Reformed Presbyterian minister J. B. Johnston built a small brick building with the help of a couple of students in Northwood, Ohio. Johnston named the structure Geneva Hall. The school soon accepted women as well as men, and Geneva Hall was a station on the Underground Railroad in the 1860s; freed slaves constituted half the enrollment during Reconstruction. In 1873, Geneva Hall was renamed Geneva College, and the school moved from Ohio to Beaver Falls, Pennsylvania, seven years later. Four-year accreditation was granted in 1923.

Historically, Geneva is noteworthy in several respects. The college offered courses in biblical literature and church history—the forerunners of a liberal arts curriculum—from its founding in 1848. For a brief period, Geneva was almost entirely given over to the training of ministers, which was unusual for a *BIBLE INSTITUTE. Most important, however, is that Geneva was one of the first, if not the first, colleges to play competitive college basketball. Springfield, Massachusetts, native C. O. Beamis introduced the sport at the college in 1892, and both women and men played, albeit in separate sports programs. Four years later, the men's team played its first intercollegiate game. Geneva lost to the University of Chicago, 15–12.

Reference: William C. Ringenberg, *The Christian College: A History of Protestant Higher Education in America* (1984).

Geneva Hall. *See* **Geneva College.**

Genevan Revival The Genevan Revival, also known as the *Réveil génévois,* began around 1819 in Geneva, Switzerland, under the preaching of Merle d'Aubigné, *ROBERT HALDANE, and a small band of Moravians. The *REVIVAL emphasized the interiority of faith as opposed to formalistic observances. One of the most famous converts was *HENRIETTE FELLER, who sold her considerable possessions and became the first Protestant missionary to francophone Canada.

George, David (1743–1810) David George was born into slavery in Virginia. He escaped from a brutal slaveholder but took with him at least a rudimentary knowledge of evangelical theology. His *NEW LIGHT *CONVERSION in 1774 prompted a desire to become literate, so that he could read the *BIBLE, and led to a preaching career. George and his family were part of the exodus of black Loyalists from the South to Nova Scotia during the American Revolution. As a Baptist preacher, George, described by a contemporary as "rather tall and slender," was very effective. He baptized blacks and whites alike.

In part because of the racism he faced from outside the evangelical community, George decided in 1792 to lead a group of Maritime blacks to West Africa, under the aegis of the Sierra Leone Company. There, due to the harsh realities of a new environment, some of George's *NEW LIGHT fervor waned.

Reference: G. A. Rawlyk, *The Canada Fire: Radical Evangelicalism in British North America, 1775–1812* (1994).

George Fox University (Newberg, Oregon) Sponsored by the Evangelical Friends (Quakers) Church, George Fox College was established in 1885 as Pacific Friends Academy. It adopted the name Pacific College in 1891 and became known as George Fox College in 1949. In July 1996, George Fox College merged with Western Evangelical Seminary of Tigard, Oregon, and the combined schools adopted the name George Fox University. The school has graduate programs in psychology, education, Christian studies, and business management.

From the beginning, the university has had a political flavor. Pacific Friends Academy's most famous student was Herbert Hoover, who later became the thirty-first president of the United States. More recently, Republican Senator *MARK O. HATFIELD from Oregon was an active board member from 1959 until 1986, when he was named an honorary board member for life. Hatfield taught at the university upon his retirement from the Senate in 1997 as the Herbert Hoover Distinguished Professor.

The library maintains special collections on Quakers, conflict resolution and international peacekeeping, and the

Hoover administration. George Fox University also has a small museum with materials on Quaker history and missions, the history of the college, and early Pacific Northwest Americana.

Reference: *George Fox University Catalog 1996–97* (1996).

German Evangelical Lutheran Synod of Missouri, Ohio, and Other States. *See* **Lutheran Church—Missouri Synod.**

Gibson, Christine A(melia) (1879–1955) The head of Zion Bible Institute in East Providence, Rhode Island, Christine A. Gibson was born in British Guyana. She was orphaned as a small child, was converted at the age of twenty-one, and found her way to a holiness faith home in East Providence in 1905. She became pastor of the church associated with the home and was baptized in the Holy Spirit. In addition to the church, the home, and the *BIBLE INSTITUTE, Gibson also ran a worker training school. She advocated what she called "*FAITH PRINCIPLES" for the operation of these various enterprises; that is, she refused to rely on fees or advance pledges but rather on prayer. She established the *ZION EVANGELISTIC FELLOWSHIP in 1935, a federation of independent churches in the Northeast, to provide prayer and financial support.

Gideons International Inspired by the Protestant impulse to provide the *BIBLE in the vernacular, the Gideons arose from an 1898 meeting between Samuel Hill and John Nicholson in the Central Hotel in Boscobel, Wisconsin. The next year, these men, together with another businessman, W. J. Knights, formed an association of traveling laymen dedicated to *EVANGELISM, chiefly through the distribution of *BIBLES. The original name of the organization was the Christian Commercial Travelers Association of America, but they quickly became known as the Gideons, from the account in Judges 7 of Gideon and the Israelites, armed only with torches and pitchers, prevailing over the Midianites. The organization's logo depicts a torch and a double-handled pitcher.

In 1908, the Gideons began distributing *BIBLES to hospitals, hotel rooms, schools, and prisons, and they have distributed millions of *BIBLES and New Testaments since, averaging about a million worldwide every forty-six days. Today the organization, based in Nashville, Tennessee, and supported by contributions from churches and from individuals, claims about twenty thousand members around the world. They distribute *BIBLES and conduct services in senior citizens' homes, missions, and penal institutions.

Gilbeah Bible Institute. *See* **Myland, David Wesley.**

Giminez, Anne (née Nethery) (1932–) A pentecostal *EVANGELIST and co-founder (with her husband, John) of the Rock Church in Virginia Beach, Virginia, Anne Nethery was born in Houston and converted in 1949 during a *T. L. OSBORN tent *REVIVAL. She became an itinerant revivalist herself at the age of thirty, and in the course of her travels she met and eventually married *JOHN GIMINEZ, a reformed drug addict from the Bronx, New York. In 1968, a year after their wedding, Anne and John Giminez appeared on *PAT ROBERTSON's *700 Club,* where they would become popular guests in the ensuing years. They founded Rock Church just a few blocks from CBN headquarters, and their popularity with the CBN audience led them to begin their own television program, *Rock Alive,* in 1978, which in turn augmented attendance at the church. Anne Giminez's fiery preaching provided the centerpiece of the program, although her visibility often drew fire from fundamentalists who did not approve of women preachers.

Giminez, John (1931–) Born in New York City, John Giminez became a school dropout, a drug addict, and a convicted felon before his *CONVERSION to evangelical Christianity at the age of thirty-one. In 1967, he married Anne Nethery, an itinerant pentecostal preacher, and a year later the couple established Rock Church in Virginia Beach, Virginia. The church grew rapidly, in part because of its television program, *Rock Alive.* The church also operates its own *BIBLE INSTITUTE, Rock Christian Academy, and a children's home in India. Giminez is founder of the National Association for the Advancement of Hispanics.

Global Outreach. *See* **Prince, (Peter) Derek.**

Glossolalia Popularly known as "speaking in tongues," glossolalia refers to an ecstatic speech usually in a language unknown to the speaker and often to the auditors. People who speak in tongues, usually associated with the pentecostal and the *CHARISMATIC MOVEMENTS, claim to do so under the influence of the Holy Spirit, and they regard the "gift" of glossolalia as a latter-day manifestation of a New Testament phenomenon, particularly the passage in Acts 2 when the Holy Ghost descended upon the early Christians at Pentecost.

Especially in the early part of the twentieth century, pentecostals regarded glossolalia as evidence for *BAPTISM OF THE HOLY SPIRIT, also known in some circles as the "*SECOND BLESSING" (after the first blessing, *CONVERSION). People who have spoken in tongues describe it as a beautiful experience of both spiritual and emotional release and communion with God.

In the New Testament, Paul talks both about the gift of tongues and another gift of interpreting tongues. In some pentecostal circles, then, glossolalia is regarded as a conduit for a message of general edification from the Holy Spirit to the community of believers. Another variation is **XENOLALIA* or *xenoglossolalia,* where the person under the influence of the Holy Spirit speaks in a recognizable foreign language that she or he had never learned.

Reference: H. Newton Malony and A. Adams Lovekin, *Glossolalia: Behavioral Science Perspectives on Speaking in Tongues* (1985).

Gnomic Hebrew Monikers As some fundamentalists became more and more separatist in the final decades of the twentieth century—insisting on *HOME SCHOOLING or sectarian schools for their children, for instance—many adopted the practice of using obscure Old Testament names for their children. These gnomic Hebrew monikers—Naphtali, Shadrach, and the like—were often intended as a "witness" to others and were, not incidentally, flashed to other fundamentalists as a badge of the parents' piety.

Goetschius, John Henry (1717–1774) Arriving in Philadelphia in 1735, John Henry Goetschius, though only seventeen years old, immediately began preaching in various churches in the Delaware Valley. When he applied for ordination, the Presbytery of Philadelphia turned him down because of his lack of learning. Goetschius undertook a course of study with Peter Henry Dorsius in Bucks

County and was later ordained in the Dutch Reformed Church by Dorsius, *THEODORUS JACOBUS FRELINGHUYSEN, and *GILBERT TENNENT.

Both the Classis of Amsterdam (which claimed jurisdiction over the Dutch Reformed Church in the colonies) and the Dutch Reformed ministers in the Middle Colonies had opposed Goetschius's ordination because of his pietistic leanings and his schismatic tendencies. In 1740, however, amid the enthusiasm of the *GREAT AWAKENING, Goetschius managed to secure an appointment among the Dutch churches on Long Island. Like Frelinghuysen, Goetschius sought to bar from *HOLY COMMUNION congregants whom he found lacking in piety. This act caused bitter contention in the churches and, eventually, an ecclesiastical inquiry into Goetschius's probity and his handling of church matters. He reluctantly submitted to an ordination examination and transferred to the Dutch Reformed church at Hackensack, New Jersey, which he served until his death.

References: Randall Balmer, *A Perfect Babel of Confusion: Dutch Religion and English Culture in the Middle Colonies* (1989); idem, "John Henry Goetschius and *The Unknown God*: Eighteenth-Century Pietism in the Middle Colonies," *Pennsylvania Magazine of History and Biography,* CXIII (October 1989).

Gong, Dong (c. 1850–c. 1900) Born in China, Dong Gong emigrated to the United States with his parents and settled in San Francisco, where he became a laborer. Gong was converted by the Chinese mission established by the First Baptist Church of San Francisco. He was licensed to the ministry about 1869, and in 1874 he accepted an invitation from the First Baptist Church in Portland, Oregon, to set up a mission to the growing Chinese community there. Gong ran a church school that generated a large number of converts to Christianity. He also worked as a preacher and a translator and in 1875 became the first Asian American to be fully ordained by the Baptists in the United States.

Gong employed female teachers in his schools, according them equal status with men. In the course of his work in Portland and later with the Chinese community at Puget Sound, Gong resisted Chinese gangs and the traffic in opium. He went to China in 1878, probably to work as a missionary, but he returned to the United States and died in California.

Reference: William Henry Brackney, *The Baptists* (1988).

Good News Also known as the Forum for Scriptural Christianity, Good News is an evangelical advocacy group within the United Methodist Church. It grew in response to an article by Charles W. Keysor in the July 1966 issue of the *New Christian Advocate,* the official magazine for Methodist clergy. The article, "Methodism's Silent Majority," argued that the denomination seriously underestimated the evangelical sentiments of its clergy and its membership. The response to the article was overwhelming, and Good News was formed in 1967 to press evangelical causes within what is now the United Methodist Church.

The organization, based in Wilmore, Kentucky, publishes a magazine as well as educational materials for congregations sympathetic to its conservative theology. On July 20, 1975, the group's board of directors met at Lake Junaluska, North Carolina, and adopted a statement of faith, "An Affirmation of Scriptural Christianity for United Methodists." The statement, also known as the *JUNALUSKA AFFIRMATION, was rooted firmly in the

Wesleyan tradition and restated theologically conservative doctrines on such matters as biblical *AUTHORITY, human depravity, and the importance of *SANCTIFICATION.

Gordon, A(doniram) J(udson) (1836–1895) Shortly after his *CONVERSION at age fifteen, A. J. Gordon decided to prepare for the ministry. He entered Brown University in 1856 and after graduation entered Newton Theological Seminary and was ordained as a Baptist minister in 1863. Gordon accepted the pulpit at Clarendon Street Baptist Church in Boston on 1869; he stayed there for a quarter century, the remainder of his active ministry, and the size of the congregation grew steadily during his tenure.

Gordon introduced congregational singing to his church, and he produced a hymnal, *Congregational Worship,* published in 1872. Gordon also fell under the influence of *PLYMOUTH BRETHREN writings, particularly dispensational *PREMILLENNIALISM. When *DWIGHT L. MOODY came to Boston in 1877 and conducted *REVIVAL meetings in a tent next to Gordon's church, Gordon found that he had much in common with the revivalist. The two men cooperated with one another in a number of evangelistic ventures, and Gordon became a regular teacher at Moody's summer conferences in Northfield, Massachusetts.

Gordon joined the Prohibition Party in the 1880s and tried to resist the growing influence of Roman Catholics in city government. He supported the women's suffrage movement and advocated a woman's right to preach. Although he believed in divine healing, Gordon attacked Mary Baker Eddy and the fledgling Christian Science movement in a book entitled *The Ministry of Healing* (1873). Gordon also directed much of his energies to missions, both domestic and foreign. He was active in the American Baptist Missionary Union, and in 1889 he founded the Boston Missionary Training School, known today as *GORDON COLLEGE and *GORDON-CONWELL THEOLOGICAL SEMINARY.

Gordon College (Wenham, Massachusetts) Gordon College traces its recent history to two different schools, Gordon College and Barrington College, which merged on Gordon's campus in 1985. The combined school is the only nondenominational *CHRISTIAN COLLEGE in New England.

Originally chartered to train foreign missionaries, Gordon College was one of the first Bible colleges. Gordon was founded in Boston in 1889 as the Boston Missionary Training Institute. *ADONIRAM JUDSON GORDON, pastor of Boston's Clarendon Street Baptist Church, led the drive to establish the school, which first held classes in the vestry.

The school was renamed in Gordon's honor when he died in 1895. Between 1907 and 1914, the school was affiliated with Newton Theological Institution, but the schools broke off ties with each other because of theological differences as well as Gordon Bible College's increasing involvement in the training of Baptist clergy. The school was awarding college degrees by 1917 and was renamed Gordon College of Theology and Missions in 1921. In the following years, Gordon developed into both a liberal arts college and a divinity school, now known as Gordon-Conwell Theological Seminary.

In its early years, Gordon's enrollment was predominantly women, which was not unusual for Bible colleges. However, as the college's programs developed—especially the track for ordained ministry—the administration sought more male than female students. This objective solidified in 1930 when the trustees voted to limit women to only one third of the total enrollment. The college has abandoned this rule since then, and women once again make up slightly more than half of the student body.

Gordon College moved to its present campus in Wenham in 1955, onto the former estate of financier Frederick H. Prince. Fifteen years later, however, Gordon's seminary merged with Conwell School of Theology from Philadelphia and moved to its own site in nearby Hamilton, Massachusetts. Gordon-Conwell Theological Seminary, one of the leading evangelical seminaries in North America, now operates completely independently from the college.

Barrington College was founded in 1900 as the Bethel Bible Training School in Spencer, Massachusetts. Later based in Dudley, Massachusetts, and then Providence, Rhode Island, the school moved to Barrington, Rhode Island, in 1959 and took the name Barrington College.

While the college has a strong identity as a Christian institution, Gordon may in certain ways reflect its Northeastern location. *DANCING, for instance, is not prohibited in the "Life and Conduct Guidelines." Furthermore, 11 percent of Gordon's students in 1996 were of color. Although this percentage is below the national average for population, it represents a high rate of diversity in comparison with other evangelical colleges.

References: *Gordon College Academic Catalog, 1995–1996* (1995); Virginia Lieson Brereton, *Training God's Army: The American Bible School, 1880–1940* (1990); William C. Ringenberg, *The Christian College: A History of Protestant Higher Education in America* (1984).

Gordon-Conwell Theological Seminary. *See* **Gordon College.**

Gorman, Marvin (1933–) A charismatic and flamboyant preacher whose services often feature *SPEAKING IN TONGUES, exorcisms, and divine healing, Marvin Gorman was pastor of a highly successful *ASSEMBLIES OF GOD congregation in New Orleans, Louisiana, when *JIMMY SWAGGART summoned him to his headquarters in Baton Rouge, Louisiana, in June 1986 and confronted him with rumors of Gorman's adulteries. Swaggart passed this information on to the *ASSEMBLIES OF GOD hierarchy; Gorman immediately resigned his church and was defrocked by the denomination a week later. The congregation's schools were closed, and Gorman's radio and television programs were canceled.

Gorman retaliated against Swaggart two years later, releasing to the press photographs of Swaggart leaving a motel room, apparently after an encounter with a prostitute. The disclosures eventually forced Swaggart's public humiliation and ouster from the Assemblies' ministry. Gorman also filed a $90 million defamation suit against Swaggart; he eventually received $185,000.

In the early 1990s, Gorman tried to resurrect his ministry. He opened the Temple of Praise in New Orleans and has resumed local radio and television broadcasts.

Gortner, Hugh "Marjoe" Ross (1944–) One of the more famous—and notorious—of the child *EVANGELISTS, Marjoe Gortner was the son of pentecostal preachers who was ordained at the age of five. Billed as "the world's youngest ordained preacher," Gortner preached memorized sermons, played several musical instruments, and traveled across the nation from 1949 until 1957. By the age of thirteen, however, Gortner had become disillusioned and retired from the

*REVIVAL circuit. After several personal and professional setbacks, he returned briefly to preaching and then tried—in a book and a movie—to make a name by "exposing" other *EVANGELISTS as charlatans.

Reference: David Edwin Harrell Jr., *All Things Are Possible: The Healing and Charismatic Revivals in Modern America* (1975).

Goshen Biblical Seminary. *See* **Associated Mennonite Biblical Seminary.**

Goshen College (Goshen, Indiana) Goshen College began in 1894 as a night school: the Elkhart Institute of Science, Industry, and the Arts. Its founder was physician Henry A. Munhaw, a member of Prairie Street Mennonite Church, who acted under the encouragement of Elkhart's church leader, John Frank.

When the Elkhart Institute moved to Goshen in 1903 it adopted a liberal arts curriculum. At that time, the school—now known as Goshen College—faced considerable opposition from the Lancaster County (Pennsylvania) Mennonite Conference, which feared that the new curriculum was a sign of encroaching *MODERNISM. Goshen's students did not help matters any when they began to wear nontraditional clothing. The crisis over "*MODERNISM" became so pressing that Goshen was closed in 1923 for one year. In spite of these early controversies, however, the college still maintains strong denominational ties to the Mennonite Church, and around two thirds of the student body are Mennonites or from Mennonite-related denominations.

Goshen's general education requirements are unique in that all students are expected to complete a study-service term abroad. Most students choose to travel to the Caribbean or Central America, but the college also operates sites in Asia, Germany, and the Ivory Coast.

Goshen College is the home of the Archives of the Mennonite Church and the Mennonite Historical Library, which maintains one of the largest collections of information on *ANABAPTISM and the Reformation in America. *Mennonite Quarterly Review* is also published out of Goshen. The college has affiliate degree programs with Case Western Reserve University, Washington University, Pennsylvania State University's University Park Campus, and the University of Illinois.

References: *Goshen College Catalog 1995–97* (1995); William C. Ringenberg, *The Christian College: A History of Protestant Higher Education in America* (1984).

Gospel The gospel is the "good news" of salvation, as proclaimed in the New Testament. Evangelicals believe that they have appropriated that gospel by acknowledging Jesus as their savior, and they believe it is incumbent on them to spread the gospel, the "good news," to others.

Gospel Missionary Union At a *YMCA Bible conference near Ottawa, Kansas, in 1889, a young man named Will Mitchell responded to the appeals of the organizers for missionaries to the Sudan. Later that same day, however, Mitchell drowned, making a deep impression on everyone in attendance at the conference. Several from the conference, notably George S. Fisher, secretary of the Kansas *YMCA, became fervent about missions, traveling the state and recruiting missionaries.

Fisher, together with *R. A. TORREY and A. E. Bishop, organized the World's Gospel Union in Topeka in 1892. Within a few years, the organization—later renamed Gospel Missionary Union—sent missionaries to Sierra Leone and later to Colombia, Ecuador, and the French Sudan. Today, the organization, which has its headquarters in Kansas City, Missouri, supports approximately four hundred full-time and more than one hundred short-term missionaries.

Gospel Music Gospel music, especially Southern gospel music, emerged from slave spirituals, rural singing conventions (including shape notes), and songbook publishing dating back to the nineteenth century. One of the characteristics of white gospel music has been multipart harmony, as exemplified in the gospel quartets, with a low bass counterbalanced by a high tenor, whereas black gospel has tended to be more creative and less regimented. Gospel music, with its biblically based message and, very often, its confessional style, has comported well with *EVANGELICALISM's emphasis on personal *CONVERSION.

References: Bill C. Malone, *Southern Music, American Music* (1979); James R. Goff Jr., "The Rise of Southern Gospel Music," *Church History,* LXXVII (December 1998).

Gospel Music Association The Gospel Music Association (GMA) is a nonprofit organization that acts as an umbrella organization to support and promote the development of all forms of gospel and Christian music. The GMA's three thousand members come from all sections of the music industry and include recording producers, radio and television personnel, promoters, agents, and publishers.

Since 1969, the Gospel Music Association has been best known for its sponsorship of the annual Dove Awards. With honors in more than thirty categories, the Dove Awards is the premier ceremony in Christian music. The awards presentations have been held in Nashville's *GRAND OLE OPRY for several years and routinely harness big-name performers like *AMY GRANT to serve as host. Beginning in 1995, the Gospel Music Association teamed up with the Family Channel and Target Stores to promote the awards ceremony. That year, the association developed a twelve-track sample cassette of inspirational music called *It's Not Just for Sundays Anymore.* The sampler was distributed through Target and advertised on the Family Channel. The success of this partnership has led to Target's becoming a key sponsor of the Dove Awards, which are now broadcast annually on the Family Channel.

The Gospel Music Association has also developed a training course for aspiring inspirational performers. Known as the Gospel Music Academy, the program holds seminars on topics such as career development, songwriting, stage presentation, legal issues, and the best way to land a recording contract. In addition, participants have the chance to learn from artists in residence, who in the past have included *MICHAEL W. SMITH and *CINDY MORGAN. The Gospel Music Academy also sponsors "Spotlight" competitions, regional and national talent contests in which unsigned musicians compete for recording contracts as well as a variety of support services from GMA member business, including studio time, Internet Web sites, and a promotional mailing to industry publishers.

As the Christian music industry grew in the 1980s and 1990s, the Gospel Music Association expanded its activities and influence. The GMA's success brought on a new wave of reproach, however, from within and outside the music circles, because of its name. More specifically, critics have contended that the association has inappropriately adopted the use of the word "gospel" in its name. While "gospel" often is understood to refer to African American church music, the musical style is not African American, and artists represented by the GMA are almost all Caucasians. This discrepancy has led to the suggestion that the organization be more circumspect and call its music "white gospel."

Reference: Patricia Bates, "Growing Pains Discussed at CBA," *Billboard,* February 17, 1996.

Gospel Spreading Church. *See* **Michaux, Lightfoot Solomon.**

Gospel Spreading Tabernacle Building Association. *See* **Michaux, Lightfoot Solomon.**

Gotee Records Gotee Records, an independent recording company, was founded by *DC TALK member Toby McKeehan and two friends, who collectively became known as the Gotee Brothers. The business started as a production company in the early 1990s. Its first release was Out of Eden's *Lovin the Day* in 1994, but the company hit its stride the following year when it signed the reggae band Christafari, which combined Christian lyrics with a reggae beat. Now known as Gotee Brothers Entertainment, it has managed, so far, to avoid being acquired by one of the major Christian recording labels, such as Sparrow, Star Song, or Word Records. Along the way, Gotee has earned widespread praise for the diversity and innovativeness of the music it releases.

References: Deborah Evans Price, "From SoundScan to Christian Label Acquisitions, It was a Notable Year," *Billboard,* December 23, 1995; "Gotee Grows into Christian Boutique," *Billboard,* December 7, 1996.

Gothard, William "Bill" (1934–) A graduate of *WHEATON COLLEGE (B.A., 1957, and M.A., 1961), Bill Gothard was ordained by the LaGrange Bible Church in the suburbs of Chicago. In 1964, he developed a six-day seminar for evangelical youth, which came to be known as the Institute in Basic Youth Conflicts. He officially founded the organization in 1973 and in the mid-1970s offered his seminar in cities across North America, filling such auditoriums as the Arie Crown Theater in Chicago. Gothard, who became known for his "chain of command" schemes of *AUTHORITY, offered fairly standard fundamentalist, even legalistic, notions about biblical, parental, and pastoral *AUTHORITY, male headship of the household, and *DISPENSATIONALISM. Gothard changed the name of his organizationin 1990 to Institute in Basic Life Principles, based in Oak Brook, Illinois. In addition to the seminars, Gothard has developed a home school curriculum and operates the Oak Brook College of Law and Government Policy.

Reference: Wilfred Bockelman, *Gothard, the Man and His Ministry: An Evaluation* (1976).

Gourley, Thomas Hampton (1862–1923) Born in Peru, Indiana, Thomas Hampton Gourley spent his childhood in Nebraska and Iowa. Converted to evangelical Christianity about 1894, at which time he also claimed physical healing, Gourley became an itinerant *EVANGELIST in the Kansas-Missouri area. Gourley's *REVIVAL meetings in Lawrence, Kansas, in 1897 attracted the opposition of locals, who complained of late-night noise emanating from Gourley's *REVIVAL tent. Some townspeople and others associated with the University of Kansas sought to drive Gourley out of Lawrence, storming the tent after one of his meetings, leaving it demolished. The local newspaper had described the preacher as a man "of uncouth appearance, dress, and language" who demonstrated "no personal charms except this power to throw his convert into a cataleptic state." Gourley persevered, however, relocating the *REVIVAL to a sporting field.

Gourley continued to preach in the Kansas-Missouri area until he headed west to Los Angeles about 1904 and then to Seattle by 1906, where he brought the pentecostal emphasis on *SPEAKING IN TONGUES that had been the hallmark of the *AZUSA STREET REVIVAL. In Seattle, Gourley conducted another revival; launched a periodical, *The Midnight Cry*; and opened a Bible school at 1617 Seventh Avenue. In March 1911, believing that the *END TIMES were fast approaching, Gourley and a band of 150 followers relocated to Lopez Island, one of the San Juan Islands in Puget Sound. On Lopez Island, Gourley's disciples lived in tentlike structures and operated a communal bakery and dining hall. After being acquitted in 1919 on charges of making seditious remarks during the course of a sermon, Gourley abandoned his colony and resettled in St. Louis in 1921. He was killed in a train derailment in Georgia two years later.

Reference: James R. Goff Jr., "The Limits of Acculturation: Thomas Hampton Gurley and American Pentecostalism," paper given at the Society for Pentecostal Studies in Toronto, March 1996.

Grace The word *grace* is the translation of the Greek word *charis* from the New Testament. It is a loving gift, the gift of love, bestowed by God upon a person or people. Specific examples of God's grace and its manifestations appear in the New Testament. Eventually, the term came to have a broader meaning, especially for evangelicals. Grace is the cause of human election as one of God's chosen people. By grace, otherwise unredeemable individuals are set apart from the inevitable death and damnation of this world. Grace is the way in which people are "*SAVED" from death and brought to eternal life in God through belief in Christ. This gift of grace from God is different from the gift of life, for it is bestowed freely upon those whom God chooses, most often those who have demonstrated their understanding of their sinful state and submitted themselves to God's mercy. Thus, the evangelical understanding of grace is that it is indispensable for being guaranteed eternal life in Christ beyond this world.

Grace College and Grace Theological Seminary (Winona Lake, Indiana) Grace College is the only liberal arts college affiliated with the Fellowship of Grace Brethren Churches, a pietistic denomination organized in 1939. The college was founded in 1948 by Alva J. McLain, the school's first president, and Herman A. Hoyt, who served as dean.

The Morgan Library's special collections include the papers of evangelist *BILLY SUNDAY, who spent a great deal of time in Winona Lake. Single students under the age of twenty-three must live in the dormitories. *DANCING is not allowed on campus.

References: *Grace College 1995–97 Catalog* (1995); Thomas C. Hunt and James C. Carper, eds., *Religious Higher Education in the United States: A Source Book* (1996).

Grace University (Omaha, Nebraska) Grace Bible Institute was founded as a

Mennonite Bible training school in 1943, its founders heavily influenced by dispensational *PREMILLENNIALISM. Over the ensuing decades, certain Mennonite distinctives—*ARMINIANISM, nonresistance, rigorous *SEPARATISM—steadily disappeared, contributing to the impression that Grace was more fundamentalist than it was Mennonite. Graduates in the early years, for example, did not have to be pacifist, but they had to affirm that "the next great event in the fulfillment of prophecy will be the pre-tribulation coming of Christ into the air to receive to Himself His own"; the school hired its first non-Mennonite president, Robert Benton, in 1971. Grace University, which now bills itself as private and nondenominational, encompasses Grace College of Graduate Studies, Grace College of Continuing Education, and Grace College of the Bible.

Reference: William Vance Trollinger Jr., "Grace Bible Institute and the Advance of Fundamentalism among the Mennonites," *Mennonite Life*, 53 (June 1998).

Graham, Anne. *See* **Lotz, Anne Graham.**

Graham, Billy. *See* **Graham, William Franklin, (Jr.) "Billy."**

Graham, Ruth (McCue) Bell (1920–) The daughter of American missionaries to China, *L. NELSON BELL and his wife, Virginia, Ruth McCue Bell grew up in China and returned to the United States to attend *WHEATON COLLEGE. She was courted assiduously by *HAROLD LINDSELL, but another Wheaton student, young *BILLY FRANK GRAHAM, caught her eye and eventually captured her heart. They were married in Montreat, North Carolina, on August 13, 1943, and Ruth Bell Graham settled into the life of homemaker, mother, and wife to a peripatetic husband. Graham, however, has also made a name for herself in evangelical circles through her lectures and her books.

References: Ruth Bell Graham, *It's My Turn* (1982); idem, *Sitting by My Laughing Fire* (1977); Patricia Cornwell, *Ruth, A Portrait: The Story of Ruth Bell Graham* (1997).

Graham, Sylvester (1794–1851) Sylvester Graham overcame a troubled childhood and a nervous breakdown to become, first of all, a Presbyterian minister and then one of the nineteenth century's most passionate and influential advocates of good food, health, and personal hygiene. After the death of his father, Sylvester was reared in a succession of relatives' homes. He studied briefly at Amherst Academy but left after fellow students circulated derogatory reports about him. A nervous breakdown ensued, and Graham eventually married his nurse, Sarah Earle, in 1826.

He was ordained by the Presbyterians two years later, assumed the pastorate at Bound Brook, New Jersey, and soon began studying physiology and nutrition, doubtless because of his own poor health, but also because he sought medical grounds to substantiate his claim that the consumption of alcohol was unhealthy. Graham came to believe that the violation of physical laws was an offense against God and that sexual excesses both before and during marriage rendered the individual susceptible to disease and premature death. Emboldened by these "discoveries," Graham began lecturing on food and what he called "the science of human life."

Graham's message of *TEMPERANCE, sexual moderation, and vegetarianism stirred controversy along the Atlantic seaboard; Ralph Waldo Emerson, for example, derided Graham as the "poet of bran bread and pumpkins." Graham, nevertheless, railed against the millers who, when grinding grain for flour, bolted out much of the bran and thereby lost the grain's vitamins and minerals. In his *Treatise on Bread and Breadmaking,* published in 1837, he attacked commercial bakers, insisting that bread should be made of whole grain, coarsely ground, and that it should be baked at home by the wife and mother of the household. The so-called Graham system included other spartan tenets as well. Graham eschewed all tobacco, caffeine, liquor, and most condiments; he believed in chastity, cold showers, fresh air, and firm mattresses.

Students at Williams College, Wesleyan University, and Oberlin College lived by Graham's brown-bread doctrine. The Graham cracker became a staple in many nineteenth-century households, and from 1837 to 1839 the *Graham Journal of Health and Longevity,* edited by David Campbell, promoted the Graham system.

Graham, William Franklin, (Jr.) "Billy" (1918–) Born November 7, 1918, near Charlotte, North Carolina, William Franklin Graham Jr., better known as Billy Graham, went to one of *MORDECAI HAM's *REVIVAL meetings in 1934 and there experienced a religious *CONVERSION that shaped the direction of his life. By the time he graduated from *WHEATON COLLEGE in 1943, he had developed the preaching style for which he would become famous. In 1946, Graham joined the staff of *YOUTH FOR CHRIST and later became, for a time, president of Northwestern Schools in Minneapolis, all the while continuing his evangelistic campaigns.

Graham's successful Los Angeles crusade in 1949 brought him national attention, in no small measure because newspaper magnate William Randolph Hearst, impressed with the young evangelist's preaching and his anticommunist rhetoric, instructed his papers to "puff Graham." From Los Angeles, Graham took his evangelistic crusades around the country and the world, thereby providing him with international renown.

Graham, by his own account, has enjoyed close relationships with American presidents from Dwight Eisenhower to Bill Clinton. (Even though Graham met with Harry Truman in the Oval Office, the president was little impressed with the young evangelist.) Although he purported to be apolitical, Graham's most notorious political entanglement was with Richard Nixon, whom he befriended when Nixon was Eisenhower's vice president. During the 1960 presidential campaign, Graham met in Montreaux, Switzerland, with *NORMAN VINCENT PEALE and other Protestant leaders to devise a way to derail the campaign of John F. Kennedy, the Democratic nominee, thereby assisting Nixon's electoral chances. Although Graham later mended relations with Kennedy, Nixon remained his favorite, with Graham all but endorsing Nixon's reelection effort in 1972 against George McGovern. As the Nixon presidency unraveled amid charges of criminal misconduct, Graham reviewed transcripts of the hitherto secret Watergate-era tape recordings. Although the tapes provided irrefutable evidence of Nixon's various attempts to subvert the Constitution, Graham professed to be physically sickened by his friend's use of foul language.

Throughout his career, Graham's popular appeal lay in his extraordinary charisma, his forceful preaching, and his simple, homespun message: Repent of your *SINS, accept Christ as savior, and you shall be *SAVED. Behind that simple message, however, stood a sophisticated organization, the *BILLY GRAHAM EVANGELISTIC ASSOCIATION, which provided extensive advance work and a follow-up program for new converts. Even though he pioneered the use of the television for religious purposes, Graham has always shied away from the label "televangelist." During the 1980s, when other television preachers were embroiled in sensational scandals, Graham remained above the fray, and throughout a career that has spanned more than half a century, few people questioned his integrity. In 1996, Graham and his wife, Ruth, received the Congressional Gold Medal, the highest honor that Congress can bestow upon a citizen.

Graham claims to have preached in person to more people than anyone else in history, an assertion that few would challenge. His evangelistic crusades around the world, his television appearances and radio broadcasts, his friendships with presidents and world leaders, and his unofficial role as spokesman for America's evangelicals made him one of the most recognized religious figures of the twentieth century.

References: Billy Graham, *Just As I Am* (1997); William Martin, *A Prophet with Honor: The Billy Graham Story* (1991); Larry Eskridge, "'One Way': Billy Graham, the Jesus Generation, and the Idea of an Evangelical Youth Culture," *Church History*, LXVII (1998); *Crusade: The Life of Billy Graham*, PBS documentary (1993).

Graham, (William) Franklin, (3d) (1952–) Born July 14, 1952, in Montreat, North Carolina, Franklin Graham spent most of his early years trying to elude the shadow of his famous father, *BILLY GRAHAM. A strong-willed child, Franklin engaged in desultory acts of rebellion not at all uncommon for a preacher's kid: smoking, alcohol, firearms, rock music, fast cars, and motorcycles. In 1974, however, during a trip to the Middle East, Franklin became *BORN AGAIN and shortly thereafter became involved with an evangelical relief organization, *SAMARITAN'S PURSE. Early in the 1980s, he started preaching, loosely under the aegis of the *BILLY GRAHAM EVANGELISTIC ASSOCIATION, in evangelistic campaigns in small towns.

By the mid-1990s, as *BILLY GRAHAM's health began to falter, and especially after the elder Graham became too ill to preach at a crusade in Toronto in June 1995, *BILLY GRAHAM and the board of the *BILLY GRAHAM EVANGELISTIC ASSOCIATION began serious discussions about succession. On November 7, 1995, the board unanimously installed Franklin as vice chair of the board, with direct succession as chair and chief executive officer "should his father ever become incapacitated." Franklin Graham increasingly took on a more visible role, offering, for example, the invocation at the inauguration of President George W. Bush on January 20, 2001.

References: David Van Biema, "In the Name of the Father," *Time*, May 13, 1996; John W. Kennedy, "The Son Also Rises," *Christianity Today*, December 11, 1995.

Grand Canyon University (Phoenix, Arizona) Grand Canyon University is owned and operated by Arizona Southern Baptists, and its board of trustees is elected by the state convention. The school was begun by a few students and faculty of a failed Baptist college in New Mexico and was finally established in the mid-1940s, when L. D. White, pastor of Calvary Baptist Church in Casa Grande, began collecting funds for a school. In 1946, the Baptist General Convention of Arizona Southern Baptists voted to organize a college, and alumni and faculty of the New Mexico school joined the endeavor as faculty and trustees. Grand Canyon College opened in 1949 in an old armory building in Prescott, Arizona. It moved to Phoenix two years later.

Originally established as a school for preachers, the Grand Canyon education program developed rapidly. Today the school is divided into six separate colleges: liberal arts and social sciences, business, communications and fine arts, nursing, education, and science and allied health; it offers master's degrees in education and business. Grand Canyon College changed its name to Grand Canyon University in 1989, the fortieth anniversary of its founding.

References: *Grand Canyon University Catalog 1996–1997* (1996); Virginia Lieson Brereton, *Training God's Army: The American Bible School, 1880–1940* (1990).

Grand-Ligne Mission. *See* **Feller, Henriette.**

Grand Ole Opry The Grand Ole Opry, which evolved out of the country barndance tradition, received its name in 1927. Combining various musical traditions, including gospel, bluegrass, and folk music, the Grand Ole Opry quickly emerged as a showcase for country music talent. The broadcast of shows over the clear-channel radio station WSM made the Opry, its music, and its performers household names throughout much of Appalachia. By 1933, the radio station had formed a booking agency for Opry performers, and appearance on the Opry stage provided a kind of imprimatur; if listeners heard and enjoyed an artist on the Opry, they could be assured of a good show when that artist visited their community. The Grand Ole Opry, which has had six homes in its history (including *Ryman Auditorium from 1943 to 1974 and its present venue at Opryland Park), has consistently celebrated both poverty and Protestantism, ruin and redemption.

Reference: Curtis W. Ellison, *Country Music Culture: From Hard Times to Heaven* (1995).

Grand Rapids Baptist Bible Institute. *See* **Cornerstone College** *and* **Grand Rapids Baptist Seminary.**

Grand Rapids Baptist Seminary (Grand Rapids, Michigan) Grand Rapids Baptist Seminary and its undergraduate counterpart, *Cornerstone College, share a campus and operate under one board of trustees, but they maintain separate facilities, administration, and faculty. The two schools grew out of a series of evening Bible classes begun in 1941 at Wealthy Street Baptist Church in Grand Rapids, Michigan. Within four years, the night program had developed into a day *Bible institute and seminary, and it received authorization from the State of Michigan to grant a bachelor's degree in divinity. Both graduate and undergraduate programs continued to develop over the next several decades, with the fledgling seminary adding a master of divinity degree in 1968 and later introducing master's programs in religious education, theology, and theological studies. A doctor of ministry track began in 1991.

Grand Rapids Baptist Seminary is accredited by the North Central Association of Colleges and Schools and the American Theological Association. Affiliated with the Regular Baptist Church, the school is on the conservative end of the evangelical spectrum. As recently as 1996, the seminary had no women faculty, and only one woman served on the board of trustees. Grand Rapids Baptist Seminary runs an Asian extension program, which lets students attend classes four weeks a year in Singapore and study in their home countries the rest of the time. With *CORNERSTONE COLLEGE, the seminary hosts an internationally known Bible conference each winter.

Reference: *Grand Rapids Baptist Seminary 1996–1998 Catalog* (1996).

Grand Rapids School of Bible and Music. *See* **Cornerstone College** *and* **Grand Rapids Baptist Seminary.**

Grant, Amy (1962–) Since the early 1980s, Amy Grant has reigned as the uncontested queen of *CONTEMPORARY CHRISTIAN MUSIC and has enjoyed unprecedented success in both the inspirational and mainstream pop music markets. By the mid-1990s her albums had sold more than 15 million copies in the United States and overseas.

Grant was born in Augusta, Georgia, but grew up in Nashville, Tennessee, where her father was a physician. She began playing piano in third grade and started writing music as a teenager. Grant was only fifteen when she signed her first contract with Word Records, which came about when her church leader played a tape of her music over the phone to a producer. Grant made history in 1981 with the first Christian contemporary album to be certified as a gold record. Two years later, the former student from Vanderbilt University went on to win a Grammy award for *Age to Age*. Also in 1983, she was nominated for six Dove Awards from the *GOSPEL MUSIC ASSOCIATION.

In the secular market, Grant occasionally faced minor difficulties due to her faith commitment; in 1990, she sued Marvel Comics for using her likeness on the cover of a Dr. Strange comic book. Grant and her lawyer argued that the comic featured "vampires, sorcerers, and occult themes" and that its distribution would damage her reputation as a Christian singer. Such difficulties seemed trivial, however, in light of the ten million albums Grant had sold by 1991. When *Heart in Motion* came out that year, Grant's bouncy, pop-music style helped her make history once again. The album, which sold more than four million copies and was certified "multiplatinum," reached number ten on *Billboard*'s Top 200 Chart. The five singles—including the popular "Baby, Baby"—helped the album hold a place in the Top 200 for fifty-two weeks.

With mainstream success, however, came accusations from some evangelical circles that the singer had let her Christianity lapse. For the video companion to the single "Baby, Baby," Grant, who was married to an inspirational songwriter named Gary Chapman, was filmed cavorting with actor Jamie Stone. This launched criticism that she should not have appeared in romantic scenes with someone other than her husband. Grant and Chapman separated early in 1999, and the couple divorced the following year; she then married country singer Vince Gill. Other people within and outside the Christian recording business complained about the use of the word "baby" in Grant's lyrics, criticizing it as being sexually seductive, as well as the perceived reduction in the number of references to Jesus in her songs. No amount of criticism from evangelical circles, however, could remove Grant from her place at the top of the Christian music industry, and in 1992 the singer won the *GOSPEL MUSIC ASSOCIATION's Dove Award for Artist of the Year.

Despite her success in the mainstream market, Grant does not seem eager to abandon Christian music in favor of a wholly secular career. Without any doubt, she opened a door to mainstream audiences, through which other groups, like *JARS OF CLAY and *DC TALK, have managed to pass. Grant now records jointly on Myrrh Records and A&M.

References: "Amy Grant Meets Dr. Strange," *Christianity Today,* June 18, 1990; Dolly Carlisle, "Christian Music's Best-Seller is the Sweet-Sounding Gospel According to Amy Grant," *People Weekly,* April 18, 1983; Lisa Collins, "Amy Grant Lands Dove's Top Honor," *Billboard,* April 25, 1992; Patrick M. Connolly, "Amy Grant: Charting a New Course," *Saturday Evening Post,* November-December 1991; Paul O'Donnell, "Rock of Ages," *New Republic,* November 18, 1996; Deborah Russell, "A&M, Myrrh Build Grant's 'House' on Solid Ground," *Billboard,* July 30, 1994.

Grant, W(alter) V(inson) (1913–1983) Born in rural Arkansas, W. V. Grant became a successful businessman and then an *ASSEMBLIES OF GOD minister and an important figure in the charismatic revival. He established an independent ministry in 1949, billing himself as "the ploughboy preacher from Arkansas," but then was forced by poor health to scale back his *ITINERANCY. He was associated with the *VOICE OF HEALING organization as vice president and in 1962 started a magazine called *Voice of Deliverance.* He organized a small network of churches, built a *REVIVAL center in Dallas, preached on radio programs, and maintained a limited schedule of REVIVAL campaigns.

References: W. V. Grant, *Raising the Dead* (n.d.); David Edwin Harrell Jr., *All Things Are Possible: The Healing and Charismatic Revivals in Modern America* (1975).

Grant, W(alter) V(inson), Jr. (1956–) W. V. Grant Jr. sought to follow his father's footsteps as a faith healer, and he spent the early part of his career marketing his father's writings. In 1996, however, the younger Grant was sentenced to prison for tax evasion, following an 1991 exposé on televangelists by ABC News.

Gray, James M(artin) (1851–1935) Born in New York City and ordained in the *REFORMED EPISCOPAL CHURCH, James M. Gray served several churches and in 1893 became associated with *DWIGHT L. MOODY when Gray began teaching at Moody's Northfield summer conferences. In 1904, he became the first dean of *MOODY BIBLE INSTITUTE in Chicago, where he remained until his death; Gray was designated president of the institution in 1925. Under his leadership the school's music curriculum was expanded; a radio station, WMBI, was begun; and a magazine, *Moody Bible Institute Monthly,* published (now known as *Moody Monthly*).

Gray, an ardent fundamentalist, became one of the major voices during the fundamentalist-modernist controversy of the 1920s. He was one of seven editors of the **SCOFIELD REFERENCE BIBLE,* and he contributed an article, "The Inspiration of the Bible," to **THE FUNDAMENTALS.*

Great Awakening Although contemporaries described a "great and general *REVIVAL of religion," the term "Great Awakening" is most likely a convention used by historians to refer to the religious upheaval in the Atlantic colonies during the 1730s and 1740s. The harbingers of *REVIVAL reached back to the "harvests" in *SOLOMON STODDARD's congregations in 1690s in the Connecticut Valley and to Guiliam Bertholf's peregrination among the Dutch in northern New Jersey. The *REVIVAL at Northampton, Massachusetts, in the winter of 1735–1736, was documented by the town's pastor, *JONATHAN EDWARDS, in *A Faithful Narrative of a Surprising Work of God*.

The *REVIVAL fires were rekindled during a preaching tour of the colonies by *GEORGE WHITEFIELD in 1740, whose effective preaching prompted many colonists to embrace the New Birth. The Awakening tended to level ethnic barriers—the Dutch Reformed pietists in New Jersey cooperated with the Presbyterians in revival efforts—and also showcase the preaching of itinerant *EVANGELISTS, whose activities often threatened the settled clergy. The *REVIVALS also established lines of communication among the colonists, which would become crucial to the success of the Patriot cause leading up to the American Revolution.

The fervor of the Awakening began to wane in the mid-1740s (although it was just beginning in the Chesapeake region). Many colonists in New England became disillusioned with *REVIVAL excesses, as when *JAMES DAVENPORT and his supporters burned the works of Puritan divines on a wharf in New London, Connecticut. The legitimacy of the *REVIVAL was debated in a pamphlet war between Edwards and Charles Chauncy of the Brattle Street Church in Boston. Chauncy, who later became a Unitarian, argued that religious *CONVERSIONS were intellectually based and gradual, while Edwards allowed in his classic statement, *Religious Affections*, for the legitimacy of religious enthusiasm, provided such expressions met certain criteria, as a reflection of "a divine and supernatural light." In the short run, the opponents of *REVIVAL prevailed, and Edwards himself was ousted from his pulpit in Northampton. The Great Awakening, however, had enduring effects on American culture, in religion, in social organization, and in politics.

References: Edwin S. Gaustad, *The Great Awakening in New England* (1957); Harry S. Stout, *The Divine Dramatist: George Whitefield and the Rise of Modern Evangelicalism* (1991).

Great Disappointment *WILLIAM MILLER's calculations had narrowed the *SECOND COMING of Christ to sometime between March 21, 1843, and March 21, 1844. When Jesus failed to materialize, Miller declared that he had neglected to account for a "tarrying time," which would place the *SECOND COMING at October 22, 1844. Miller's adventist followers, known as *MILLERITES, again went into a frenzy of *EVANGELISM and preparation. The passing of the second date is known in adventist history as the Great Disappointment, as thousands of Miller's followers returned to their homes and endured the ridicule of their neighbors.

Much of Miller's following dispersed after the Great Disappointment; other disciples organized into smaller, even more sectarian groups. The largest group to emerge out of the Great Disappointment was the *SEVENTH-DAY ADVENTIST CHURCH, organized by *ELLEN GOULD WHITE in 1863.

Reference: David L. Rowe, *Thunder and Trumpets: Millerites and Dissenting Religion in Upstate New York, 1800–1850* (1985).

Great Plains Association of Christian Schools. *See* **Association of Christian Schools International.**

Great Revival. *See* **Second Great Awakening.**

Greater Europe Mission The idea that evolved into Greater Europe Mission, an evangelical, nondenominational mission agency, came to Robert P. Evans, a Navy chaplain in World War II, while convalescing in a French hospital from injuries suffered in the Normandy invasion. After a stint with *YOUTH FOR CHRIST, Evans sought to provide training for Europeans so that they could carry on the task of evangelization. Evans and his wife moved to Paris in 1949 to begin the European Bible Institute as one of the subsidiaries of Greater Europe Mission. The first of ten schools, located now in Austria, Germany, France, Belgium, Greece, Italy, Portugal, Spain, and Sweden, the institute was staffed by missionaries from North America. The mission also founded seminaries in Germany and Belgium, and Tyndale Seminary in the Netherlands.

Although the original focus was Bible training, with a view toward making European missions self-sustaining, the Greater Europe Mission is still largely a North American operation (headquarters are in Carol Stream, Illinois). The emphasis of mission work has also shifted somewhat from education toward church planting.

Reference: Robert P. Evans, *Let Europe Hear* (1963).

Green, Keith (1953–1982) Regarded as something of a saint in the world of *CONTEMPORARY CHRISTIAN MUSIC, Keith Green was born in Sheepshead Bay (Brooklyn), New York, and reared in Canoga Park, California. He showed musical abilities at an early age, winning a five-year record contract from Decca at age eleven. Although he was touted by the national press as the next teen idol, Green lost out to Donnie Osmond. During his teen years, Green became enmeshed in the counterculture, with its fixation on drugs and the religions of the East. His searching eventually led him to Jesus Christ. On December 16, 1972, Green wrote in his journal, "Jesus, you are hereby welcomed officially into me."

He continued to pursue music, both writing and performing. His debut album as a Christian was *For Him Who Has Ears to Hear,* released in 1977. After a second album with Sparrow Records, Green asked out of his contract so that he could start his own label and distribute recordings for whatever the buyer could afford to pay. Sparrow agreed, and Green made good on his promise with *So You Wanna Go Back to Egypt,* released on his own Pretty Good Records label. His final album, *Songs for the Shepherd,* was released on April 12, 1982, just weeks before Green was killed in a small-plane crash.

Reference: Mark Joseph, *The Rock & Roll Rebellion: Why People of Faith Abandoned Rock Music—and Why They're Coming Back* (1999).

Green, Steve (1956–) Christian singer Steve Green is almost as well-known as an advocate for "family values" as he is for his music. Green grew up in Argentina, where his father was a missionary. He attended *GRAND CANYON COLLEGE in Phoenix, Arizona, but left in 1976 to sing with a Christian group called Truth. While with this band, he met his wife. Green later performed in radio and television commercials, but he returned to school in 1978. Then he and his wife were asked to join the Gaither Vocal Band as backup singers. After a brief stint as lead vocalist for the band *WHITEHEART, Green decided that Christian rock music was not his style, and he began a solo music career in 1983. Two years later, he was named *GOSPEL MUSIC ASSOCIATION Male Vocalist of the Year, and his debut recording, *Steve Green,* was nominated for a Dove Award for Inspirational Album of the Year.

Green has won seven Dove Awards, been nominated for four Grammy Awards, and has had numerous hit songs on the Christian music charts, including "People Need the Lord," "The Mission," "He Holds the Keys," and "God and God Alone." Green has recorded eighteen albums, several of which are in Spanish. He maintains the tradition of his missionary family and has done several mission trips to Latin America, which have helped him become one of the most popular Christian contemporary singers in Spanish-speaking countries.

Green's persona is more traditionally "clean-cut" than many popular Christian singers, and he willingly identifies himself with conservative political and religious movements. Green wrote "Teach Me to Love" for the *PROMISE KEEPERS. He plays video clips of *FOCUS ON THE FAMILY's *JAMES DOBSON in his concerts and encourages people to subscribe to that organization's magazine. The Dobson clips are not the only unusual use of video in Green's concerts; he often shows his wedding pictures and photos of his children on a large screen. Green also makes a point of calling his wife, Marijean, at home in the middle of each concert and inviting children from the audience up on stage to sing with him. He sees all these elements as supporting a broader message of family values. When not touring, Green lives in Franklin, Tennessee, outside Nashville, with his wife, daughter Autumn, and son Josiah.

Reference: Information provided by Sparrow media relations.

Greenville College (Greenville, Illinois) Affiliated with the *FREE METHODIST CHURCH, Greenville College dates its official founding to 1892. The campus, however, has been a site for Christian higher education for more than 140 years. In 1855, New Hampshire native Stephen Morse opened a women's college in Greenville, and named it in honor of his wife, the former Almira Blanchard. Almira College was a Baptist institution; ownership of the college changed hands in 1878, and although the school remained Baptist, it became coeducational at that time. Fourteen years later, Almira College's campus and property were bought by the Central Illinois Conference of the Free Methodist Church, and the school was reincorporated as Greenville College. The first students of the new college were graduated in 1898.

Like many *CHRISTIAN COLLEGES, Greenville faced considerable financial hardship during the Great Depression. The college, however, came up with an innovative means to keep poor students employed: The chemistry laboratory was transformed into a manufacturing plant for medicines, toiletries, and flavorings, which other students sold on commission across the country. In addition to news and music, the college radio station, WGRN-FM, broadcasts both collegiate and religious programming, including Sunday services from several area churches as well as home basketball and football games. Ernest Boyer, former head of the Carnegie Foundation for the Advancement of Teaching, was an alumnus of the college, and the Christian music group *JARS OF CLAY began when band members were students there.

References: Greenville College 1996–1997 Catalog (1996); William C. Ringenberg, *The Christian College: A History of Protestant Higher Education in America* (1984).

Griffith, Andy (1926–) Actor Andy Griffith is an American household name because of his television career that has spanned six decades. Less well-known is his long-standing connection to church music, though he won the 1997 Grammy

Award for the Best Southern, Country or Bluegrass Gospel Album, for his collection of hymns, *I Love to Tell the Story.*

Born in Mount Airy, North Carolina, he contemplated majoring in ministry at the University of North Carolina but trained as a classical singer instead and graduated with a music degree in 1949. His first job after college was teaching high school choral music; in this period, he also served as choir director for the First Baptist Church in Goldsboro, North Carolina.

In the early 1950s, Griffith moved to New York hoping to launch a career in music. When that proved unsuccessful, he began performing comedy routines in nightclubs. Griffith made his television debut in 1955 on *The U.S. Steel Hour.* Two years later, he starred in his first feature film, *A Face in the Crowd,* directed by Elia Kazan. From 1960 to 1968, Griffith starred in *The Andy Griffith Show,* which was one of the top-ranked programs on American television for the length of its run. Griffith later starred in several other series, including *Matlock,* which ran from 1986 to 1995. He also acted in several miniseries, including *Roots: The Next Generations,* as well as *Murder in Texas,* for which he received an Emmy nomination. Griffith was inducted into the Academy of Television Arts and Sciences Hall of Fame in 1992 and given the Lifetime Achievement Award from the National Association of Television Program Executives.

In 1996, producers from Sparrow Records and Tyrell Music Group invited Griffith to make an album of old gospel hymns. *I Love to Tell the Story—25 Favorite Hymns* is actually Griffith's eleventh album; his recording career began in 1953 with his comedy routine, *What It Was Was Football,* and he continued to make comedy albums into the early 1970s. *I Love to Tell the Story* is a collection of familiar songs, such as "Shall We Gather at the River," "Will the Circle Be Unbroken," and "Amazing Grace." Through ads strategically placed on cable and network television, the recording sold more than four hundred thousand copies and brought one of the highest awards in music to a man who had all but abandoned hope of a musical career.

Reference: Information provided by Sparrow media relations.

Grimké, Angelina (Emily) (Weld) (1805–1879) The youngest of fourteen children born to slave-holding parents who were active in South Carolina politics and in the Episcopal church, Angelina Grimké was converted under the auspices of a Presbyterian *REVIVAL. She eventually joined her older sister, Sarah Grimké, as a member of the Quakers. The Grimké sisters moved to Philadelphia in 1821 where they became active in the abolitionist movement and eventually joined the Philadelphia Anti-Slavery Society. The sisters moved to New York in 1836, and Angelina's tract, *An Appeal to Christian Women in the South,* which appeared the same year, became one of the manifestos of the abolitionist movement. Widely read and praised in the North, the publication was publicly burned in her hometown, Charleston, South Carolina.

Angelina addressed the first Anti-Slavery Convention of American Women in 1837. The Grimké sisters traveled throughout New England as agents of the American Anti-Slavery Society, speaking before various audiences, including "mixed" audiences of men and women, something of a scandal at the time. (The Massachusetts General Association of Congregationalist Minsters, for example, condemned the practice of female pulpit oratory.) The Grimké sisters thereby became doubly suspect in the eyes of many; they advocated both *ABOLITIONISM and women's rights.

Angelina married abolitionist *THEODORE DWIGHT WELD in Philadelphia in 1838. They moved, with Sarah, to New Jersey, where the sisters settled somewhat into domestic life and attenuated their public presence. They assisted Weld, however, in the writing of his important book, *Slavery As It Is.*

References: Angelina Grimké, *An Appeal to Christian Women of the South* (1836); idem, *Letters to Catharine Beecher, in Reply to an Essay on Slavery and Abolition* (1838); K. D. Lumpkin, *The Emancipation of Angelina Grimké* (1974).

Grimké, Sarah (Moore) (1792–1873) Born in Charleston, South Carolina, Sarah Grimké's parents were prominent citizens, Episcopalians, and slave-holders. Sarah developed abolitionist convictions, however, after her involvement in Presbyterian and Methodist *REVIVALS. With her younger sister, Angelina, Sarah moved north to Philadelphia in 1821, joined the Quakers, and became active in the abolitionist movement. Her *Epistle to the Clergy of the Southern States,* published in 1836, refuted the biblical arguments in support of slavery. As the Grimké sisters traveled in support of *ABOLITIONISM, their practice of addressing "mixed" audiences of both men and women created a stir. Sarah responded to criticism of the practice in *Letters on the Equality of the Sexes and the Condition of Women,* which offered a biblical defense of women's rights.

Following Angelina's marriage to *THEODORE DWIGHT WELD in 1838, Sarah moved with the couple to New Jersey, where her public role diminished somewhat. In 1863, the Grimké sisters relocated to Massachusetts and continued their campaign for women's rights.

References: Sarah Grimké, *Epistle to the Clergy of the Southern States* (1836); idem, *Letters on the Equality of the Sexes and the Condition of Women* (1838).

Grimshaw, William (1708–1763) Known as "Mad Grimshaw" for his bold and boisterous preaching, William Grimshaw was ordained in the Church of England in 1731 and became the architect of the evangelical *REVIVAL in northern England. Grimshaw himself was dissolute during his early years of ministry, but by the time he settled at Haworth in 1742 he was a fervent evangelical. In Haworth and throughout his large parish, Grimshaw's preaching brought *CONVERSIONS and a rapid increase in the number of communicants. He was closely affiliated with *METHODISM, although he was a high churchman and vigorously opposed any efforts to break with the Church of England.

Reference: Frank Baker, *William Grimshaw, 1708–1763* (1963).

Grimstead, Jay. *See* **Coalition on Revival.**

Grinnell, Josiah Bushnell (1821–1891) It was to Josiah Bushnell Grinnell that Horace Greeley issued his famous dictum, "Go west, young man, go west." Grinnell was born in New Haven, Vermont, and was educated at Castleton Seminary in Vermont and at the Oneida Institute in Whitesboro, New York. In 1844, he served as agent for the *AMERICAN TRACT SOCIETY in Wisconsin and then attended Auburn Theological Seminary, graduating in 1847. He became pastor of the Congregational church in Union Village, New York, and he organized the First Congregational Church in Washington, D.C., in 1851.

Grinnell became profoundly troubled by slavery; he preached what some believe was the first sermon against slavery in Washington, a stand that eventually forced him to leave Washington for a church in New York City. There, having briefly lost his voice and having grown increasingly frustrated by the lack of progress in the crusade against slavery, Grinnell applied to Greeley, his friend, for counsel. Grinnell obeyed the famous advice and headed to Iowa in 1854, where he purchased six thousand acres in Poweshiek County, founded the town that bears his name, started a Congregational church, and laid plans for Grinnell University. In 1859, Iowa College, which had been founded in Davenport in 1846 by the *IOWA BAND, moved to Grinnell and merged with the school to form what is known today as Grinnell College.

Grinnell attended the organizing convention for the Republican Party in Iowa in 1856. That same year he was elected to the state senate on a three-part platform: "No Liquor Shops; Free Schools for Iowa; No Nationalizing of Slavery." Grinnell quickly emerged as the leading abolitionist in the state. He publicly criticized the *Dred Scott* decision and hosted *JOHN BROWN and a band of escaped slaves to his home in 1859; Brown wrote part of his famous Virginia Declaration in Grinnell's parlor. A vigorous supporter of Abraham Lincoln, Grinnell was elected to Congress in 1862, serving from 1863 to 1867, when he lost the Republican nomination for governor. In 1872, his support of Greeley's candidacy for president (in part because of Grinnell's strong reservations about Ulysses Grant's qualifications) effectively ended his political career as a Republican. He turned increasingly to other pursuits, including raising money for the college, the promotion of Iowa beyond the state's borders, the development of railroads, and pushing for higher standards in agriculture, an initiative that led to his election as president of the American Agricultural Association in 1885.

Following Grinnell's death in 1891 the *Iowa State Register* (now the *Des Moines Register*) remarked: "Mr. Grinnell by residence belonged to Grinnell, by faith to the Congregational church, and by politics to the Republican party; but in a wider, truer sense he belonged to no sect and no party, but to the people, to the state, and to the cause of the greatest good for all men."

Reference: Josiah Bushnell Grinnell, *Men and Events of Forty Years* (1891).

Grinnell College. *See* **Grinnell, Josiah Bushnell.**

Griswold, Alexander Viets (1766–1843) Alexander Viets Griswold was denied admission to Yale College because of his parents' Anglican and Loyalist sympathies. He became a farmer instead and educated himself in law and theology. He applied for ordination in the Episcopal Church in 1794 and was ordained a deacon the following year. After serving a number of parishes in Connecticut, Griswold became rector of St. Michael's Church in Bristol, Rhode Island, in 1805, and in 1811 he became bishop of the Eastern Diocese (all of New England except Connecticut). He continued his parish ministry, however, moving from St. Michael's to St. Peter's in Salem, Massachusetts, in 1830. In 1835, he left the parish to devote full energies to his diocese, which grew dramatically under his care. Following the death of William Whyte in 1836, Griswold became the fifth presiding bishop of the Episcopal Church.

Although he was a high churchman early in his career, Griswold gravitated toward evangelical and Methodist expressions during the course of a religious *REVIVAL in his Bristol, Rhode Island, parish in 1812. Prayer meetings and special services were among the "*NEW MEASURES" that Griswold introduced, to great effect. A number of Episcopal clergy came to Bristol to observe these evangelical phenomena and to study with Griswold. He taught the importance of "free" (nonliturgical) prayer meetings and argued that revivalism was in no way inimical to the Episcopal Church.

Griswold steadfastly resisted the movement toward Anglo-Catholicism in the Episcopal Church, especially as the influence of Tractarianism began to be felt in America. His 1843 treatise, *The Reformation: A Brief Exposition of Some of the Errors and Corruptions of the Church of Rome,* attacked Roman Catholic claims to be the true and only church. He insisted that the Episcopal Church remain true to its Protestant theological heritage.

References: Alexander Viets Griswold, *The Reformation: A Brief Exposition of Some of the Errors and Corruptions of the Church of Rome* (1843); W. W. Manross, "Alexander Viets Griswold and the Eastern Diocese," *Historical Magazine of the Protestant Episcopal Church,* IV (1935).

Grounds, Vernon C(arl) (1914–) Born in Jersey City, New Jersey, Vernon C. Grounds studied at Rutgers University, *FAITH THEOLOGICAL SEMINARY, *WHEATON COLLEGE, and Drew University. Throughout a long career in evangelical higher education, Grounds has called on evangelicals to develop and exercise a social conscience. He spent the bulk of his career at Conservative Baptist Seminary in various capacities, including professor, president, and president emeritus.

References: Vernon C. Grounds, *The Reason for Our Hope* (1945); idem, *Evangelicalism and Social Concern* (1968); idem, *Revolution and the Christian Faith* (1971); idem, *Radical Commitment: Getting Serious about Christian Growth* (1984).

Guest, John (1936–) A native of Oxford, England, John Guest was converted to evangelical Christianity at a *BILLY GRAHAM crusade in London. He was ordained a priest in the Episcopal Church, where he strongly supported efforts to return the denomination to its historic Christian roots. From 1970 to 1990, he was rector of St. Stephen's Church, Sewickley, Pennsylvania, at that time one of the most rapidly growing Episcopal parishes in the United States. He was one of the principal founders of *TRINITY EPISCOPAL SCHOOL OF MINISTRY in 1975, and he has traveled widely under the auspices of the John Guest Evangelistic Team.

References: John Guest, *In Search of Certainty* (1983); idem, *This World Is Not My Home* (1988); idem, *Finding Deeper Intimacy with God: Only a Prayer Away* (1992); idem, *Beating Mediocrity: Six Habits of the Highly Effective Christian* (1993).

Gullicksen, Kenn. *See* **Vineyard Christian Fellowship.**

Gurney, Joseph John (1788–1847) Born in Norwich, England, Joseph John Gurney became a recorded Quaker minister in 1818, at the age of twenty-nine. Throughout an impressive career as an *EVANGELIST, banker, and humanitarian, he was able to combine Quaker rigor in matters of plain dress and pacifism with evangelical revivalism and Bible study. During a three-year visit to North America beginning in 1837, Gurney sought to persuade Congress to end slavery, and his efforts to reorient the Society of Friends toward *EVANGELICALISM prompted schisms in the New England and the Ohio Yearly Meetings. His followers became known as *GURNEYITES, and his legacy survives most clearly in the Friends United Meeting and the *EVANGELICAL FRIENDS ALLIANCE.

Gurneyites The Gurneyites were members of the Religious Society of Friends (Quakers) who derived their inspiration from *JOSEPH JOHN GURNEY, an English Quaker who, on a tour of North America from 1837 to 1840, urged Quakers to adopt evangelical styles of Bible study, warm-hearted piety, and revivalism. Gurneyite sentiment sparked divisions in the New England and the Ohio Yearly Meetings, and Gurneyites adopted the pastoral system of ministry rather than the traditional Quaker use of itinerant, unpaid, and untrained ministers.

Gustavson, E. Brandt (1936–2001) President of the *NATIONAL RELIGIOUS BROADCASTERS during the 1990s, E. Brandt Gustavson was born in Rockford, Illinois, and studied at *NORTHWESTERN COLLEGE (St. Paul, Minnesota) and Loyola University (Chicago). He began his career in broadcasting with shortwave radio under the aegis of *TRANS WORLD RADIO and in 1960 began a long association with *MOODY BIBLE INSTITUTE. He also worked for the radio division of the *BILLY GRAHAM EVANGELISTIC ASSOCIATION and again for *TRANS WORLD RADIO before assuming the post with the *NATIONAL RELIGIOUS BROADCASTERS. Gustavson was widely credited with restoring a measure of integrity to evangelical broadcasting after the televangelist scandals of the 1980s.

■ ■ ■

Hagin, Kenneth E(rwin), Sr. (1917–) A sickly child born prematurely in McKinney, Texas, Kenneth E. Hagin was converted while confined to bed at the age of fifteen. He studied the *BIBLE and became convinced of the possibility of divine healing after reading Mark 11:24: "What things soever ye desire, when ye pray, believe that ye shall receive them, and ye shall have them." Hagin, who was frequently given to visions, claimed healing in August 1934 and shortly thereafter began preaching in the local Baptist church in Roland. He soon drifted toward the pentecostals, however, and in August 1937 began *SPEAKING IN TONGUES, which he interpreted as a *BAPTISM OF THE HOLY SPIRIT. Hagin became a minister in the *ASSEMBLIES OF GOD and served small congregations in east Texas from 1937 until 1947, when he gave up his pulpit to become an itinerant *EVANGELIST.

Hagin formed the Kenneth E. Hagin Evangelistic Association in 1962 (later renamed Kenneth Hagin Ministries, Inc.) and eventually severed his ties with the *ASSEMBLIES OF GOD. In 1966, Hagin moved his operations to Tulsa, Oklahoma, where he expanded to a radio ministry (*Faith Seminar of the Air*), launched a magazine (*The Word of Faith*), and started the Rhema Correspondence Bible School. Hagin began the Rhema Bible Training Center in 1974, which is located in Broken Arrow, Oklahoma, adjacent to Hagin's Rhema Bible Church.

Beginning in the late 1970s, Hagin became one of the most vocal proponents of what he calls "faith teaching," also known as the *PROSPERITY GOSPEL or the "name it, claim it" movement. According to this theology—which was also propagated by other pentecostal *EVANGELISTS, including Hagin's disciples *KENNETH COPELAND and *FREDERICK K. C. PRICE—God will bestow all manner of material blessings upon the faithful who only ask God with the requisite faith in their hearts. This notion became very popular among evangelicals in the 1980s, during the Reagan era of self-aggrandizement.

References: Kenneth E. Hagin, *Redeemed from Poverty, Sickness and Death* (1960); idem, *The Woman Question* (1975); idem, *How You Can Be Led by the Spirit of God* (1978); idem, *You Can Have What You Say* (1979); idem, *I Went to Hell* (1982); idem, *Signs of the Times* (1985); Paul G. Chappell, s.v. "Kenneth Hagin, Sr.," in Charles H. Lippy, ed., *Twentieth-Century Shapers of American Popular Religion* (1989).

Hague, Dyson (1857–1935) Dyson Hague, born in Toronto, studied at the University of Toronto and Wycliffe College before his ordination in the Anglican Church of Canada in 1883. He served as rector of several Anglican parishes as well as St. James' Cathedral in Toronto before becoming professor of apologetics, liturgics, and theology at Wycliffe College in 1897. He was a prolific author as well as a prominent evangelical leader within the Church of England. A churchman with strong fundamentalist leanings, Hague contributed to **THE FUNDAMENTALS*, thereby adding the voice of a prominent Anglican to the call for orthodoxy within North American Protestantism.

Reference: Dyson Hague, *The Church of England before the Reformation* (1897).

Haines, Ralph E. Ralph E. Haines was reared an Episcopalian and graduated from the United States Military Academy in 1935. He had been sympathetic to religious matters in his various commands, but a 1971 invitation to speak at a military breakfast sponsored by the *FULL GOSPEL BUSINESS MEN'S FELLOWSHIP INTERNATIONAL in Buffalo, New York, led to Haines's *SPEAKING IN TONGUES. "I experienced a bubbling up and finally an active eruption of the Holy Spirit which had been living within me for many years," the four-star general later recounted. "On that day the entire room was filled with the Holy Spirit and it seemed I was the number-one lightning rod!"

Haines, who referred to himself as a private in God's army, became concerned about the "moral mooring" of people in his charge, and Haines's *BAPTISM OF THE HOLY SPIRIT prompted him to speak publicly—and frequently—about the experience. "I've changed from a shy, private worshipper to a bold soldier of the Lord," he said. His flurry of speaking engagements before civilian groups, however, attracted the attention of Congress and the media, and the Pentagon finally asked Haines to retire in September 1972, six months ahead of schedule. Haines continued his promotion of evangelical and pentecostal views after his retirement—before civilian and military audiences alike.

Reference: Ann C. Loveland, *American Evangelicals and the U.S. Military, 1942–1993* (1996).

Hakes, J(oseph) Edward (1916–) Born to a Baptist minister and his wife, J. Edwards Hakes was reared in New York City and attended *WHEATON COLLEGE, where he majored in history and lettered in basketball. Upon graduation in 1937, he accepted a scholarship and studied for one year at the School of Law at Columbia University. Feeling called to the ministry, Hakes transferred to Eastern Baptist Theological Seminary and graduated in 1941 with the bachelor of divinity degree. In 1967, he received a doctorate from the University of Pittsburgh.

Hakes served as pastor of churches in New York, Ohio, and Michigan before moving into Christian higher education. He accepted the presidency of *GRAND RAPIDS THEOLOGICAL SEMINARY and *GRAND RAPIDS BIBLE COLLEGE in 1954. He taught on the faculty of *WHEATON COLLEGE from 1958 until 1966 and then became chair of the division of Christian education at *TRINITY EVANGELICAL DIVINITY SCHOOL. In 1969, Hakes responded to the challenge of building a faculty of liberal arts at *TRINITY COLLEGE in Deerfield, Illinois. Hakes hired a group of young Ph.D.s and created an atmosphere of intellectual excitement and daring in the early 1970s. During his tenure as dean, Trinity came to be highly regarded in evangelical higher education, and Hakes established himself as a leading theorist and spokesman for the entire *CHRISTIAN COLLEGE movement. In addition to his professional work, Hakes served for a time as publisher of *Christian Scholar's Review* and was active in various human rights efforts and liberal political causes.

Reference: J. Edward Hakes, ed., *An Introduction to Evangelical Christian Education* (1964).

Haldane, Robert (1764–1842) Born in London, Robert Haldane was orphaned at an early age and reared by relatives. He studied at the University of Edinburgh and joined the Royal Navy in 1780. He had an evangelical *CONVERSION in 1795, whereupon he became active in the Society for the Propagation of the Gospel, organized *SUNDAY SCHOOLS, and became a patron of missionary work, especially on the Continent. Haldane became convinced of Baptist views and was (re)baptized by immersion in 1808. He went to Europe himself in October 1816, where he participated in the *GENEVA REVIVAL and spent several years in Montauban, France.

Haldeman, I(saac) M(assey) (1845–1933) Ordained to the Baptist ministry in 1870, I. M. Haldeman served churches in Chadds Ford, Pennsylvania, and Wilmington, Delaware, before accepting a call to Calvary Baptist Church, New York City, in 1884, where he remained for nearly half a century. An unrelenting polemicist and a stirring orator who often preached to standing-room-only crowds, Haldeman railed against "*WORLDLINESS" in its various forms. His dispensationalist theology led him to forsake programs of social amelioration and to muse at length on the *END TIMES. His 1910 volume, *The Signs of the Times,* set forth the tenets of dispensational *PREMILLENNIALISM for a popular audience.

Hall, Franklin (1907–) An itinerant healing *EVANGELIST in the pentecostal tradition, Franklin Hall left the *METHODISM of his childhood because "They didn't take to divine healing." He began his itinerant ministry during the Great Depression and became convinced of the restorative powers of fasting. Hall, who considered himself a teacher more than a preacher, published *Atomic Power with God through Prayer and Fasting* in 1946 and founded a magazine, *Miracle Word,* in 1965. His insistence on fasting as a spiritual discipline placed him at odds with other pentecostals, but he continued to teach that a regimen of fasting and prayer would cure tiredness, sickness, even body odor. In 1956, he formed Deliverance Foundation, a federation of churches that followed his teachings.

References: Franklin Hall, *Atomic Power with God through Prayer and Fasting* (1946); idem, *Formula for Raising the Dead* (1960); David Edwin Harrell Jr., *All Things Are Possible: The Healing and Charismatic Revivals in Modern America* (1975).

Hall, Ralph J. (1891–1973) Known as the "cowboy preacher," Ralph J. Hall, who grew up in west Texas, began his career as a lay missionary to the ranch people of the Mountain West, especially New Mexico.

He was ordained as a Presbyterian in 1916, even though he had never attended college or seminary. Over the course of a career that spanned nearly half a century, Hall established camp conferences for young people, well over one hundred mission *SUNDAY SCHOOLS, and annual "cowboy *CAMP MEETINGS." Typically, Hall would join a gathering of cowboys and ranchers, work with them over the course of several days, and conduct religious services around the campfire at night. After singing gospel songs, Hall would preach and then ask for some kind of religious commitment. "Some of you have told me of your problems, of your great concerns," Hall recalled telling one gathering. "I know my Lord can and will help you if you will accept him as your Savior."

Throughout his journeys—he estimated that he traveled over 2 million miles in the course of his career, by horseback, truck, and automobile—Hall would encounter people hungry for the *GOSPEL and for *GOSPEL preaching. "It seems to me that of all the loneliness and the yearning of the Christian heart," he wrote, "the one that goes deepest and causes the most suffering is to be cut off from the privileges of Christian worship and Christian fellowship."

References: Ralph J. Hall, "Memoirs of a Cowboy Preacher," *Presbyterian Life,* November 15, 1971; idem, *The Main Trail,* ed. Vic Jameson (1971).

Hall, Tony (Patrick) (1942–) Born in Dayton, Ohio, Tony Hall received the A.B. degree from Denison University in 1964 and served in the Peace Corps from 1966 to 1967. He was elected to the Ohio General Assembly in 1968 and to the State Senate four years later. A Democrat and a Presbyterian, Hall ran successfully for Congress in 1978. While attending a *PRAYER BREAKFAST in Dayton in 1980, Hall was impressed with the sincerity and the evangelical commitment of the event's speaker, *CHUCK COLSON; Hall's ensuing year-long spiritual quest ended with his *CONVERSION to evangelical Christianity.

Despite his evangelical convictions, such *RELIGIOUS RIGHT organizations as the *CHRISTIAN COALITION have opposed Hall because of his party affiliation and for his support of such "liberal" issues as gun control, human rights, and alleviating hunger. In April 1993, after the House of Representatives abolished its Select Committee on Hunger, which Hall had headed, he fasted for three weeks; Congress eventually responded by setting up the Hunger Caucus and the Congressional Hunger Center. Despite opposition from the *RELIGIOUS RIGHT, left-leaning evangelicals, on the other hand, find in him an ally. "Tony Hall is the perfect example of what we want," said *RON SIDER, president of *EVANGELICALS FOR SOCIAL ACTION. "He supports the family, opposes *ABORTION and gay marriage, but combines that with a conviction that the poor matter, as to racial justice and environmental concerns." Hall has also earned the respect of his colleagues, both Republican and Democratic. "Tony is the conscience of Congress," *FRANK R. WOLF, a Republican from Virginia, said. "Everyone on both sides listens to him, and he's someone I look to for leadership."

Reference: Frederica Mathewes-Green, "The Hungry Congressman," *Christianity Today,* September 1, 1997.

Halverson, Richard C(hristian) (1916–1995) Born in Pingree, North Dakota, Richard C. Halverson drifted to Hollywood in the 1930s to pursue a career as an entertainer. He soon turned his sights toward theology, however, graduating from *WHEATON COLLEGE in 1939 and from Princeton Theological Seminary. Following his ordination as a Presbyterian minister in 1942, Halverson served as pastor of a number of churches and worked for several evangelical agencies. After a stint as minister of new life at Hollywood Presbyterian Church he was named pastor of Fourth Presbyterian Church, in Washington, D.C., in 1958. The church grew under his leadership and his evangelical preaching. After Republicans gained control of the United States Senate following the 1980 elections, *MARK O. HATFIELD of Oregon persuaded his colleagues to elect Halverson chaplain of the Senate, a post he held until his retirement in 1995.

References: Richard C. Halverson, *Christian Maturity* (1956); idem, *Man to Man: A Devotional Book for Men* (1961); idem, *Walk with God between Sundays* (1965); idem, *How I Changed My Thinking about the Church* (1972); idem, *A Day at a Time: Devotions for Men* (1974); idem, *No Greater Power: Perspectives for Days of Pressure* (1986).

Ham, Mordecai (Fowler), Jr. (1877–1961) Born in Scottsville, Kentucky, the son and grandson of Baptist preachers, Mordecai Ham at the age of twenty-two turned his back on a budding career in business and an offer from a theater company to become an itinerant *EVANGELIST. Circulating primarily in the South, Ham conducted tent *REVIVAL meetings and was known for his confrontational style. Very often he would identify some local figure as the personification of evil and entreat his listeners to mend their own ways and presumably to avoid the fate of the person held up as the personification of evil.

Ham's rhetoric of demonization, however, often verged into racism, anti-Catholicism, and anti-Semitism. In 1924, for instance, Ham wrongly accused Julius Rosenwald, a Jew who was president of Sears-Roebuck, of operating houses of prostitution in Chicago. Though tarnished with the brush of racism, Ham continued his itinerant preaching. His most famous convert by far was a young man who attended Ham's revival meetings in Charlotte, North Carolina, in 1934. At the conclusion of one of the meetings, young *BILLY FRANK GRAHAM accepted Ham's invitation to become "*BORN AGAIN." *BILLY GRAHAM's career would far eclipse Ham's (in part because Graham studiously avoided any tinge of racism). During his last years, Ham confined most of his preaching to the radio.

Hamblen, (Carl) Stuart (1908–) One of *BILLY GRAHAM's earliest and most famous converts, Stuart Hamblen was born in Kellyville, Texas, where his musical influences were black field hands and the cowboy songs of ranchers. He attended McMurry College in Abilene, Texas, with the ambition of becoming a teacher, but he ended up in Hollywood at KFI-Radio as "Cowboy Joe." After a brief stint at KMPC-Radio, Hamblen landed his own show on KMIC in Inglewood, California, and hired a cast of supporting musicians and wrote his own songs. Hamblen moved to KMTR in Hollywood two years later, where he produced two programs daily, *Covered Wagon Jubilee* in the mornings and *Lucky Stars* in the evening. In addition to his work on radio in the 1940s, Hamblen also appeared in several films, usually cast in a villainous role.

Hamblen's hard living came to an end after his visited Graham's *REVIVAL tent at the famous Los Angeles crusade in 1949, the same year that his single *But I'll Be*

Chasin' Women became a hit. "I'd always been a rough man," Hamblen recalled in 1976, "but my big problem was not being able to leave the booze alone. My daddy was a Methodist minister and I guess I was the original juvenile delinquent. I just loved to fight too, and I suppose I got thrown into jail a few times." After his *CONVERSION to evangelical Christianity, Hamblen wrote "It Is No Secret (What God Can Do)," which became a popular evangelistic song. Most of his music thereafter had religious themes, and his sacred albums included *Of God I Sing*, *Grand Old Hymns*, *It Is No Secret*, and *Beyond the Sun*. In 1971, after many years' hiatus, Hamblen went back on radio with *Cowboy Church of the Air*, a weekly program on KLAC in Hollywood. "But the one thing I want to make clear is I'm no preacher," Hamblen said. "And we don't accept donations even though some people, bless 'em, choose to send money. I just say thank you and send it right back."

Reference: Billy Graham, *Just As I Am: The Autobiography of Billy Graham* (1997).

Hampstead Academy. *See* **Mississippi College.**

Happy Church (Denver, Colorado). *See* **Hickey, Marilyn.**

Hardesty, Nancy A(nn) (1941–) Born and reared in Lima, Ohio, Nancy A. Hardesty graduated from *WHEATON COLLEGE, earned a degree in journalism from Northwestern University, and earned the Ph.D. in the history of Christianity from the University of Chicago. While teaching in the English department at *TRINITY COLLEGE (Deerfield, Illinois), Hardesty became more and more outspoken for the cause of evangelical feminism. She was one of only three women in attendance at the November 1973 workshop that gave rise to the *CHICAGO DECLARATION OF SOCIAL CONCERN. Hardesty's contribution to the Declaration was a phrase acknowledging that evangelicals "have encouraged men to prideful domination and women to irresponsible passivity." In 1974, Hardesty and *LETHA DAWSON SCANZONI published *All We're Meant to Be: Biblical Feminism for Today*. The book, which has gone through several editions, prompted heated discussions among evangelicals about the place of women in twentieth-century *EVANGELICALISM.

References: Nancy A. Hardesty and Letha Dawson Scanzoni, *All We're Meant to Be: Biblical Feminism for Today* (1974, 1986, 1992); Hardesty, *Women Called to Witness: Evangelical Feminism in the Nineteenth Century* (1984); idem, *"Your Daughters Shall Prophesy": Revivalism and Feminism in the Age of Finney* (1991).

Harding, Harris (1761–1854) More than any other man, Harris Harding was responsible for translating *HENRY ALLINE's *NEW LIGHT revivalism into Baptist practice in early nineteenth-century Nova Scotia and New Brunswick. Born in Horton, Nova Scotia, Harding moved with his family to Connecticut and was imprisoned by the British during the Revolutionary War. Returning to Nova Scotia, Harding became a schoolteacher and began attending *NEW LIGHT meetings. He was converted late in 1785, when he "seemed all at once to obtain a view of Jesus."

Harding took it on himself to spread the Allinite *GOSPEL. He played a major role in Nova Scotia's Second Awakening, but a sexual liaison with Hetty Huntington, whom he married in 1796, six weeks before their child was born, eroded some of his support among evangelicals. Harding was able to rebound, however. His decision to be baptized in 1799 contributed to yet another *REVIVAL in Yarmouth, prompting a *NEW LIGHT opponent to remark that "several hundreds have already been baptized, and this plunging they deem to be absolutely necessary to the *CONVERSION of their souls." Although Harding broke for a time with the Baptist Association, he more than any other figure is responsible for the Baptist presence in the Yarmouth region of Nova Scotia.

Reference: G. A. Rawlyk, *The Canada Fire: Radical Evangelicalism in British North America, 1775–1812* (1994).

Hargis, Billy James (1925–) Born in Texarkana, Texas, Billy James Hargis studied briefly at Ozark Bible College and was ordained at the Rose Hill Christian Church (Disciples of Christ) in 1943. After serving churches in Arkansas, Missouri, and Oklahoma, he founded Christian Echoes National Ministry, in Tulsa, Oklahoma, as a vehicle for his antiliberal and anticommunist sentiments.

Hargis and his crusade flourished during the McCarthy era. In 1953, he attempted to airlift copies of the *BIBLE into eastern Europe by means of balloons. In 1960, he published *Communist America—Must It Be?*, which gained wide circulation in fundamentalist circles. He denounced sex education as satanic and communistic. These efforts and others earned Hargis the admiration of other anticommunist fundamentalists; he received honorary degrees from Defender Seminary in Puerto Rico and from *BOB JONES UNIVERSITY, in Greenville, South Carolina.

As the civil rights movement gathered force, Hargis spoke out against it, vilifying Martin Luther King Jr. as a "stinking racial agitator." Hargis soon widened his attacks to include John and Robert Kennedy, and, later, Lyndon Johnson. In 1962 he conducted his First National Anti-Communist Leadership School and continued to publish books decrying *LIBERALISM and communism, which he viewed as inseparable. His political activities, however, led to a loss of tax-exempt status for his organization.

Hargis withdrew from the Disciples of Christ in 1966 and organized the Church of the Christian Crusade, based in Tulsa. He also organized a missionary arm called the David Livingstone Missionary Foundation and a college, the American Christian Crusade College, whose mission was to teach "anti-Communist patriotic Americanism." All three organizations came under attack in 1974, however, when students of both sexes at the college accused Hargis of having sexual relations with them. The charges had surfaced when a newly married couple confessed to one another on their honeymoon that each had had prior sexual relations—each of them with Hargis. Other students substantiated similar charges to the satisfaction of school officials, who forced Hargis into retirement.

Hargis managed a year later to regain control of the church and the missionary organization, but he failed in his bid to reclaim the college, which eventually closed in 1977. Hargis founded the Billy James Hargis Evangelistic Association in 1975, and in 1981 he was granted a license to operate a television station. Despite these efforts, however, he was never able to regain the influence or the prominence he enjoyed prior to the disclosures about sexual misconduct. Hargis published a rueful autobiography, *My Great Mistake,* in 1986.

References: Billy James Hargis, *Communist America—Must It Be?* (1960); idem, *Why I Fight for a Christian America* (1974); idem, *Riches and*

Prosperity Through Christ (1978); idem, *The Cross and the Sickle—Super Church* (1982); John Harold Redekop, *The American Far Right: A Case Study of Billy James Hargis and Christian Crusade* (1968); Michael R. McCoy, s.v. "Billy James Hargis," in Charles H. Lippy, ed., *Twentieth-Century Shapers of American Popular Religion* (1989).

Harper, Elijah (1949–) A Cree-Ojibwa and the son of an evangelical pastor, Elijah Harper was born in northeastern Manitoba and studied at the University of Manitoba, where his political activism was kindled by the black civil rights movement. He became active in opposing the so-called White Paper issued in 1969 by the minister of Indian affairs, Jean Chrétien (who later became prime minister of Canada). The White Paper proposed to deny all special status for aboriginals in Canada, the first move in a series that would rouse Canadian Indians out of their passivity. In 1990, Harper, now a member of the Manitoba legislature, successfully blocked consideration of the Meech Lake Accord, which supporters believed would have finally ended the French-English conflict that had been festering in Canada for centuries. Harper and other Indians believed that granting Québec special status as a "distinct society" would further erode the political status of aboriginals, and his success in blocking the accord made him something of a hero and instilled a sense of pride among Canada's Native Americans.

Harper's faith combines Native spirituality and evangelical piety. "He is the most spiritual person I know," one of Harper's associates declared. "I watch miracles happen around the guy." In 1995, he was afflicted with a mysterious ailment that eluded medical diagnosis and treatment, but Harper finally was healed when he looked to Jesus, a *CONVERSION that he sees as the culmination of his Native spirituality. For Harper, that transformation led to a kind of moral vision; he invited Canadian leaders to join him for a "Sacred Assembly." More than two thousand showed up in December 1995 at the *Palais des Congres* in Hull, Québec, for four days of speeches and meetings among Native American leaders, politicians, evangelicals, and mainline Christians. "I want to reiterate what the Creator wants to do," Harper told the assembled crowd. "What he wants to do is heal this land and heal this people." A second Sacred Assembly convened in August 1997, reflecting Harper's desire to reconcile competing factions in Canadian society. "Some people mistake the Sacred Assembly as a Christian event or as an aboriginal event," he said. "It's not either. But it's up to God what he decides to do with it from there."

Reference: David di Sabatini, "Elijah Harper: For Such a Time as This," *Prism*, May/June 1998.

Harper, William Rainey (1856–1906) William Rainey Harper was the first president of the University of Chicago. He was born in New Concord, Ohio, and his father was a Presbyterian storekeeper. Harper showed great intellectual promise at a young age, graduating from the Presbyterians' Muskingum College before he was fourteen. After studying at home for a few years, he entered Yale in 1873 and two years later received the Ph.D. in ancient languages. Harper began teaching at Denison University in Ohio in 1876. Soon after, he had a *CONVERSION experience while attending a Baptist prayer meeting, an event that sealed his commitment to low-church Protestantism. Harper's religion was a combination of Methodist and Baptist sentiments, in which individual responsibility and the involvement of the laity were stressed. He called for the universal primitive authority of the *BIBLE and a rejection of external intellectual and political *AUTHORITY and tradition.

Harper took a job in 1879 teaching Hebrew at Morgan Park Theological Seminary, a Baptist institution outside Chicago. In 1886, however, he went to Yale, where he was appointed as the first chair of English *BIBLE four years later. Harper was an enthusiastic supporter of popular education, and in the 1880s he established a series of seven-week courses on religion as part of the *CHAUTAUQUA movement. While still at Yale, he was named principal of *CHAUTAUQUA's College of Liberal Arts, which placed him in charge of the national *CHAUTAUQUA curriculum. Even after he left the *CHAUTAUQUA movement, he continued to run a series of summer institutes modeled after it, but he was forced to abandon this project after he began to help organize the University of Chicago in 1891.

Harper's principal benefactor at Chicago was John D. Rockefeller, whose generous financial backing helped build the new school quite quickly. Harper was often censured by Rockefeller, however, for his "*LIBERALISM"—his willingness to experiment with the *BIBLE. Harper wanted to affirm traditional theology, but he sought ways to reconcile it with some aspects of biblical criticism and science, for he was confident that scientific inquiry would reveal the irreducible supernatural and divine aspects of Scripture, minus the human elements of its authors. Some of Rockefeller's objections were assuaged by the educator's fervor for the *BIBLE. A highly energetic leader, Harper strove to institute national Bible study, organizing the *RELIGIOUS EDUCATION ASSOCIATION, editing *Biblical World*—a scholarly journal that reached many nonacademic people—and participating in correspondence curricula through the American Institute of Sacred Literature. These endeavors were representative of his antiélitist approach to education, for Harper was well-known for his emphasis on practical teaching.

Reference: George M. Marsden, *The Soul of the American University: From Protestant Establishment to Established Nonbelief* (1994).

Harrington, Bob (1927–) Known as "the chaplain of Bourbon Street," Bob Harrington made a name for himself among evangelicals by preaching to drug users, prostitutes, pimps, gamblers, and alcoholics in New Orleans, Louisiana. His flamboyant dress and demeanor attracted attention, and his accounts of *EVANGELISM in what he called "the devil's boot camp" were popular among viewers of the PTL network in the 1970s. He also had his own television and radio programs in the New Orleans area, but his stock among evangelicals fell when his marriage dissolved.

Harrison, William K., Jr. Known as "the *BIBLE-reading general," William K. Harrison Jr. was probably the most prominent self-described evangelical in the post-World War II military. A graduate of the United States Military Academy, Harrison rose steadily through the ranks of the army to become a general. Throughout his long and influential career, and even after his retirement in 1957, Harrison frequently offered public attestations to his evangelical faith; he became president of the Officer's Christian Union in 1954 and remained in that capacity until 1972. Harrison supported and encouraged religious activities in the military, and he spoke out against pacifism in general and against antiwar protesters during the

Vietnam War. In 1966, writing in the pages of **CHRISTIANITY TODAY,* Harrison defended the bombing of North Vietnam as strategically and morally justified. "The whole problem of the war in Viet Nam is complicated by the sincere but erroneous idea that mankind can in some way bring peace to the world," he declared. "Wars will continue until man's rebellion runs its full course, terminating in the wars of the great *TRIBULATION at the end of this age. Only the *SECOND COMING of the Lord Jesus Christ, as so often foretold in the *BIBLE, will end the rebellion and bring an age of peace and prosperity."

References: William K. Harrison Jr., *My Life as a Christian in the United States Army* (1950); D. Bruce Lockerbie, *A Man Under Orders: Lieutenant General William K. Harrison Jr.* (1979); Ann C. Loveland, *American Evangelicals and the U.S. Military, 1942–1993* (1996).

Hartsville College. *See* **Huntington College.**

Harvard Veritas Forum Harvard Veritas Forum was founded in 1992 by Kelly Monroe in order to create, in her words, "a place where students could ask their deepest questions about the art of life, a place where we could explore the unity and beauty of the truth of Jesus Christ." The organization sponsors lectures and events to foster religious life on campus, reminding students and faculty that Harvard was founded by the Puritans in the seventeenth century to perpetuate the faith.

Hatch, Nathan O. (1946–) A respected historian and one of the highest ranking administrators in American higher education, Nathan O. Hatch graduated from *WHEATON COLLEGE and from Washington University, where he earned the Ph.D. in American history in 1974. He joined the faculty of the University of Notre Dame in 1975, where he rose to the rank of full professor. In addition to his scholarship, much of it centering on *EVANGELICALISM in the eighteenth and nineteenth centuries, Hatch has served as an administrator at Notre Dame, first as associate dean, then, beginning in 1989, as vice president for graduate studies and research. In 1996, he assumed the office of provost, creating the anomaly of an evangelical serving such a high position in a Roman Catholic university.

References: Nathan O. Hatch, *The Sacred Cause of Liberty: Republican Thought and the Millennium in Revolutionary New England* (1977); idem, *The Democratization of American Christianity* (1989).

Hatfield, Mark O(dom) (1922–) One of the more thoughtful and articulate evangelical politicians in American history, Mark O. Hatfield has often taken stands that placed him at odds with more politically conservative evangelicals. His opposition to the war in Vietnam, for instance, as well as his work for nuclear disarmament provoked resistance from many evangelicals and inspired one of Hatfield's books, *Conflict and Conscience.*

Born in Dallas, Oregon, Hatfield graduated from Willamette University in 1943 and received the master's degree in political science from Stanford University. He returned to teach at Willamette and in 1957, after serving in both the Oregon House of Representatives and the State Senate, he became the youngest secretary of state in Oregon history, at age thirty-four. In 1958, he was elected to the first of two terms as governor, and he won election to the U.S. Senate in 1966. He was reelected four times before deciding to retire in 1996; Hatfield, a Republican, has never lost an election.

A devout Baptist, Hatfield was very nearly chosen as Richard Nixon's vice presidential running mate in the 1968 presidential election. Nixon had asked *BILLY GRAHAM, a close friend and advisor, for his suggestions; Graham argued for Hatfield, but Nixon chose Spiro Agnew, governor of Maryland, instead. In subsequent years, after the scandals surrounding the Nixon administration came to light, Hatfield would express relief that he was not tainted by Nixon's perfidiousness.

Throughout his career, Hatfield, an admirer of Abraham Lincoln, took principled stands on a number of issues, from opposition to the war in Vietnam to casting the deciding vote in 1995 against the so-called balanced-budget amendment, which was one of the centerpieces of Newt Gingrich's Contract with America. Hatfield also came to resent what he viewed as the takeover of the Republican Party in the 1980s and 1990s by *PAT ROBERTSON and the *RELIGIOUS RIGHT. "My party," he remarked, has been overrun by "converted Confederates."

References: Mark O. Hatfield, *Not Quite So Simple* (1967); idem, *Conflict and Conscience* (1971); idem, *Between a Rock and a Hard Place* (1976); idem, *Against the Grain: Reflections of a Rebel Republican* (2001).

Hawes, Joel (1789–1867) Born in Medway, Massachusetts, Joel Hawes graduated from Brown in 1813 and went on to study theology at *ANDOVER SEMINARY. He was ordained in 1818 at the First (Center) Congregational Church in Hartford, Connecticut, where he spent his entire career. Hawes, though suspicious of some of its excesses, especially rampant emotionalism, was a proponent of revivalism. "Let your hearts be much set on *REVIVALS of religion," he wrote in 1830. "Never forget that the churches of New England were planted in the spirit of *REVIVALS; that they have hitherto existed and prospered by *REVIVALS, and that if they are to exist and prosper in time to come, it must be by the same cause which has from the first been their glory and defence." Hawes presided over a number of *REVIVALS in his congregation; *CHARLES GRANDISON FINNEY preached there on several occasions.

His prorevivalist views placed Hawes in opposition to one of his Congregational colleagues in Hartford, Horace Bushnell, pastor of North Congregational Church. In *Christian Nurture* and elsewhere, Bushnell had opposed *REVIVALS as a throwback to the old Calvinist notion that a child was depraved and in need of a radical evangelical *CONVERSION. Hawes was among those who brought Bushnell to trial for heresy. Bushnell protested his innocence to Hawes and tried, unsuccessfully, to repair the breach between them and to reestablish an association between their respective congregations.

References: Joel Hawes, *Lectures to Young Men* (1828); idem, *A Tribute to the Memory of the Pilgrims, and a Vindication of the Congregational Churches of New-England* (1830); Edward A. Lawrence, *The Life of Rev. Joel Hawes, D.D.* (1873).

Hay Bay Camp Meeting In the summer of 1805, three Methodist itinerant preachers, *NATHAN BANGS, Henry Ryan, and William Case, planned a *CAMP MEETING *REVIVAL in the Bay of Quinte circuit in Upper Canada. The venue was "the land of Peter Huff on the shore of Hay Bay," in the precise region where the preaching of *HEZEKIAH CALVIN WOOSTER had ignited the *CANADA FIRE a decade earlier. The organizers of the *CAMP MEETING sought to replicate the success of the infamous *CANE RIDGE

*CAMP MEETING in Kentucky four years earlier.

The *CAMP MEETING began on September 27, 1805, and continued for three days. Approximately twenty-five hundred Upper Canadians attended. The results, according to a contemporary accounting, were impressive: "30 Justified, 28 Backsliders reclaimed and 39 Sanctified 97 in all." News of the Hay Bay *REVIVAL "excited great interest far and near." The site was revered as sacred space by Methodists for a long time, and the *CAMP MEETING fostered a sense of religious community among the Methodists of Upper Canada.

Reference: G. A. Rawlyk, *The Canada Fire: Radical Evangelicalism in British North America, 1775–1812* (1994).

Hayford, Jack (Williams), (Jr.) (1934–) Having attended *L.I.F.E. BIBLE COLLEGE in Los Angeles, Jack Hayford became affiliated with that school's parent body, the *INTERNATIONAL CHURCH OF THE FOURSQUARE GOSPEL. He served a church in Indiana and then became an administrator for the denomination and for the school, including a term as president of *L.I.F.E. Hayford accepted the pulpit of a small Foursquare congregation of eighteen members in Van Nuys, California, in 1969. Under his leadership the church grew to more than eight thousand members and changed its name to Church on the Way. Hayford, who has written several hundred songs, including "Majesty," also produces a television program and a daily radio broadcast, both called *Living Way*.

Reference: Jack Hayford, *Church on the Way* (1982).

Haygood, Atticus Greene (1839–1896) A transitional figure in nineteenth-century southern *METHODISM, Atticus Greene Haygood was born in Watkinsville, Georgia, and graduated from Emory College in 1859. Admitted to the Georgia Conference of the Methodist Episcopal Church, South, he served as a chaplain to Confederate troops during the Civil War and as pastor after the war; in 1870, he was elected *SUNDAY SCHOOL secretary for the denomination and editor of *SUNDAY SCHOOL publications. As president of Emory College from 1875 to 1884, Haygood expanded the curriculum and pushed for the education of African Americans, an initiative that aroused opposition in the South. During his time at Emory, Haygood also edited the *Wesleyan Christian Advocate*.

He resigned the presidency in 1884 to become an agent for the Slater Fund, a foundation promoting education for blacks. Toward that end, Haygood helped in the formation of Paine College in Augusta, Georgia, and his book on the subject, *Our Brother in Black: His Freedom and Future*, became an influential treatise on education for African Americans.

Haygood was elected bishop in 1890 and moved to Los Angeles, where he worked to establish churches in the West. Poor health, however, forced him to return to Georgia three years later.

References: Atticus Greene Haygood, *Our Brother in Black: His Freedom and Future* (1881); Harold W. Mann, *Atticus Greene Haygood: Methodist Bishop, Editor, and Educator* (1965).

Hays, Richard B. (1948–) Reared in a Methodist household in Oklahoma City, Oklahoma, Richard B. Hays attended Yale University, where he was influenced by both William Sloane Coffin and *FRANCIS SCHAEFFER. He briefly attended Perkins School of Theology in Dallas, Texas, but then relocated to Massachusetts and participated in a Christian community called Metanoia Fellowship. He enrolled in Yale Divinity School, earned the Ph.D. at Emory University, and returned to Yale as faculty member before moving on to Duke Divinity School as professor of New Testament. Hays's publications seek to engage the church more than the academy: "Nothing I or anyone writes commending the faith will have much of an impact unless there is a community living that faith."

References: Richard B. Hays, *Echoes of Scripture in the Letters of Paul* (1989); idem, *The Moral Vision of the New Testament: A Contemporary Introduction to New Testament Ethics* (1996); Tim Stafford, "Richard Hays: Recovering the Bible for the Church," *Christianity Today*, February 8, 1999.

Haystack Prayer Meeting Students at Williams College, Williamstown, Massachusetts, were engaged in one of their regular prayer meetings in 1806 when a thunderstorm sent them scampering for cover under a haystack. In the course of the meeting, the participants, including such figures as *LUTHER RICE and *SAMUEL J. MILLS JR. felt called to foreign missions. In 1808, they formed the Society of the Brethren and took as their motto, "We can do it if we will." *ADONIRAM JUDSON and others later joined the group at *ANDOVER SEMINARY. Their appeal to the General Association of the Congregational Ministers in Massachusetts in 1810 led to the founding of the *AMERICAN BOARD OF COMMISSIONERS FOR FOREIGN MISSIONS.

Haywood, G(arfield) T(homas) (d. 1931) G. T. Haywood, born in Greencastle, Indiana, and reared in Indianapolis, gravitated to *PENTECOSTALISM around the turn of the twentieth century and became pastor of a large *ASSEMBLIES OF GOD congregation in Indianapolis. Early in 1915, he became enamored of the new "oneness only" doctrine of *BAPTISM as espoused by Glenn Cook. Haywood and his entire congregation were rebaptized in the "Jesus only" rubric rather than the Trinitarian formula of Father, Son, and Holy Spirit. Leaders of the recently formed *ASSEMBLIES OF GOD denomination tried unsuccessfully to dissuade Haywood of his views.

Haywood, who was a gifted songwriter, attracted others within the *ASSEMBLIES OF GOD to his "oneness only" doctrine, especially other African Americans. In 1917, he became secretary of the new Pentecostal Assemblies of the World, a "oneness only" group, and he remained pastor of the Indianapolis congregation until his death in 1931.

References: G. T. Haywood, *Before the Foundation of the World* (1923); Edith L. Blumhofer, *Restoring the Faith: The Assemblies of God, Pentecostalism, and American Culture* (1993).

Healing Stripes Evangelistic Association. *See* **Angley, Ernest W.**

Heard, Mark (1952–1992) Born and reared in Macon, Georgia, this sensitive singer-songwriter came of age during the *JESUS MOVEMENT, although the corpus of his work did not see release until the 1980s. A former *CAMPUS CRUSADE youth worker, Mark Heard was tremendously influenced by a brief visit to *FRANCIS SCHAEFFER's *L'ABRI FELLOWSHIP in Switzerland, where he found answers to some of the conundrums raised by his fundamentalist background.

Heard left his hometown in 1975 and moved to California to join *LARRY NORMAN's Solid Rock Artist troupe, where he recorded *Appalachian Melody* (1979). When that company disbanded, he signed with

Chris Christian's Home Sweet Home label and released a string of low-selling but critically acclaimed albums throughout the 1980s. In the latter part of the decade, Heard began recording and releasing his music on his own Fingerprint label and garnering attention from the wider musical community; Canadian singer Bruce Cockburn, for example, has called him one of the "greatest songwriters of our generation." In 1992, after a performance at the Cornerstone music festival in Illinois, Heard had a massive heart attack and died a few months later. Travailing in obscurity for most of his musical career, Heard's music has been rediscovered by a number of fledgling artists who have been touched by his ability to relate the human condition through the gift of song.

Hebrew Christian Fellowship Founded in 1944, Hebrew Christian Fellowship is an association of evangelical individuals and churches who seek to convert Jews to Christianity. Based in the greater Philadelphia area, the organization distributes *BIBLES and evangelistic literature around the world, conducts seminars, publishes a quarterly magazine, *Shalom,* and airs a radio broadcast both within the United States and into eastern Europe.

Heck, Barbara (née Ruckle) (1734–1804) Born in Rathkeale, Ireland, Barbara Ruckle sailed for New York City with her husband, Paul Heck, and others in 1760. Five years later, Barbara Heck, concerned about the religious indifference of other Irish immigrants, organized a Methodist society with the help of *PHILIP EMBURY. The society had become so large by 1768 that they built a chapel on John Street in lower Manhattan. In the early 1770s, the Hecks and the Emburys relocated to the Hudson Valley, and with the outbreak of the American Revolution the Hecks moved to Canada, first to Montréal and then to Upper Canada, where they started the first Canadian Methodist society, in Augusta.

Henry, Carl F(erdinand) H(oward) (1913–) Born in New York City to German immigrants and reared on Long Island, Carl F. H. Henry became editor of the *Smithtown Star* at nineteen, but after an evangelical *CONVERSION in 1933 he decided to attend *WHEATON COLLEGE, graduating in 1938. While continuing with a master's degree at Wheaton, he simultaneously undertook doctoral studies at Northern Baptist Theological Seminary, earning the Th.D. in 1942, one year after his ordination to the Baptist ministry. Henry published *Remaking the Modern Mind* in 1946, which argued that *EVANGELICALISM should engage the life of the mind as well as the larger culture.

Henry went on to do a Ph.D. in philosophy at Boston University, and in 1948 he joined the faculty of the newly opened *FULLER THEOLOGICAL SEMINARY in Pasadena, California. His book *The Uneasy Conscience of Modern Fundamentalism,* published in 1948, called evangelicals to a "*NEW EVANGELICALISM," a move beyond the *SEPARATISM and anti-intellectualism of the fundamentalists in order to develop a worldview that included the social and political realms.

In 1956, *BILLY GRAHAM and *L. NELSON BELL lured Henry away from Fuller to edit a new magazine, **CHRISTIANITY TODAY,* which was founded as an evangelical response to the more liberal and mainline journal, **CHRISTIAN CENTURY.* The magazine prospered under Henry's leadership and catapulted him to prominence within the evangelical subculture and beyond. He left the editorship in 1968, however, in part apparently because of differences with *J. HOWARD PEW, the politically conservative financier and backer of the magazine. After a year's hiatus at Cambridge University, Henry taught at *EASTERN BAPTIST THEOLOGICAL SEMINARY from 1969 to 1974 and turned his efforts toward the publication of his six-volume systematic theology: *God, Revelation, and Authority* (1976–1983). He became a lecturer-at-large for *WORLD VISION from 1974 until his retirement four years later. Even in retirement, however, Henry continued his writing and lecturing. His son, *PAUL HENRY, was elected to Congress from Michigan in 1984, and the elder Henry became an advisor of sorts for evangelicals, especially politically conservative evangelicals, involved in the public arena.

References: Carl F. H. Henry, *The Uneasy Conscience of Modern Fundamentalism* (1948); idem, *Faith at the Frontiers* (1969); idem, *Evangelicals in Search of Identity* (1976); idem, *God, Revelation, and Authority*, 6 vols. (1976–1983); Richard A. Purdy, s.v. "Carl F. H. Henry," in Walter A. Elwell, ed., *Handbook of Evangelical Theologians* (1993).

Henry, Paul B(rentwood) (1942–1993) Paul B. Henry, son of evangelical theologian *CARL F. H. HENRY, was born in Chicago and earned the baccalaureate degree from *WHEATON COLLEGE in 1963. He served as a Peace Corps volunteer in Liberia and Ethiopia for two years before returning to school. He earned the M.A. and the Ph.D. from Duke University in 1970 and then taught political science at *CALVIN COLLEGE from 1970 to 1978, also serving as a member of the Michigan Board of Education. Henry left Calvin in 1978 to pursue public office. That same year he was elected as a Republican to the Michigan State House of Representatives and, four years later, to the State Senate. During the 1980 presidential campaign he assisted the candidacy of *JOHN B. ANDERSON but left the campaign when Anderson dropped out of the Republican primaries to mount an independent candidacy. Henry was elected to the U.S. House of Representatives in November 1984, where he served until his untimely death in July 1993. In 1997, *CALVIN COLLEGE established the Paul B. Henry Institute for the Study of Christianity and Politics in his honor.

Reference: Paul B. Henry, *Politics for Evangelicals* (1974).

Hensley, George Went (?-1955) According to tradition, George Went Hensley was the first to handle serpents in obedience to a literal interpretation of Mark 16:18, in the King James Version of the *BIBLE: "They shall take up serpents; and if they drink any deadly thing, it shall not hurt them; they shall lay hands on the sick, and they shall recover." Hensley, an illiterate preacher, took up a poisonous viper about 1910 in a holiness gathering near Sale Creek, Tennessee. He preached throughout southern Appalachia and was bitten dozens of times. He died from a snake bite in north Florida in 1955.

Reference: Dennis Covington, *Salvation on Sand Mountain: Snake Handling and Redemption in Southern Appalachia* (1995).

Heritage U.S.A. *See* **Bakker, James Orsen "Jim."**

Hickey, Marilyn (née Seitzer) (1931–) Marilyn Hickey, pastor of Happy Church, an Assembly of God in Denver, Colorado, and head of Marilyn Hickey Ministries, was born in Dalhart, Texas, and earned her baccalaureate degree from the University of Northern Colorado. She was a high school teacher before joining her husband, Wallace, in the ministry, having experienced a call from God to "cover the earth with His Word." Indeed, Hickey has conducted *REVIVAL campaigns across the nation and in such foreign venues as Pakistan. Her skills at teaching the *BIBLE also led her into broadcast media, both radio and television, and to found a two-year *BIBLE INSTITUTE called Marilyn Hickey Training Center.

Hicks, Roy (H.) (1920–) Born in Big Sandy, Tennessee, Roy Hicks graduated from *L.I.F.E. BIBLE COLLEGE in 1943 and became an executive with the *INTERNATIONAL CHURCH OF THE FOURSQUARE GOSPEL. He was associated with such groups as the *FULL GOSPEL BUSINESS MEN'S FELLOWSHIP INTERNATIONAL as well as Christ for the Nations Institute.

Hicks, Tommy (1909–1973) An *EVANGELIST and faith healer, Tommy Hicks saw his greatest success in Latin America, especially in Argentina, in the mid-1950s. He drew exceedingly large crowds in Buenos Aires in 1954; enjoyed the support of Argentina's president, Juan Perón; and claimed to have converted key political figures as well as thousands of Argentinians. His missionary activities were underwritten in part by the *FULL GOSPEL BUSINESS MEN'S FELLOWSHIP INTERNATIONAL.

References: Tommy Hicks, *Capturing the Nations in the Name of the Lord* (1956); idem, *It's Closing Time* (1958); David Edwin Harrell Jr., *All Things Are Possible: The Healing and Charismatic Revivals in Modern America* (1975).

Hill, E(dward) V(ictor) (1934–) Named "one of the most outstanding preachers in the United States" by *Time* magazine, E. V. Hill has served as pastor of the Mount Zion Missionary Baptist Church in Los Angeles since the early 1960s. Hill, an African American and an evangelical, is also a board member for the *BILLY GRAHAM EVANGELISTIC ASSOCIATION and the National Institute on Biblical Inerrancy.

Hillman College. *See* **Mississippi College.**

Hills, Marilla Turner (Marks) (Hutchins) (1807–1901) Born in Vermont, Marilla Turner Hills devoted her life to the advance of missions, higher education, and women among the Freewill Baptists in the United States and Canada. Hills studied at Oberlin College from 1842 until 1845, while her husband, evangelist David Marks, was itinerating from a base in Ohio. Hills became active in support of the Underground Railway and made the acquaintance of such classmates as Lucy Stone, *FRANCES WILLARD, and *ANTOINETTE BROWN. Her husband's death cut short her education, but her second marriage (to another leader of the Freewill Baptists) allowed Hills to participate in the organization of the first women's missionary society among the Freewill Baptists. She undertook extensive correspondence with Baptist missionaries throughout the world and used this intelligence to organize local female missions support organizations.

Reference: Marilla Turner Hills, *Missionary Reminiscences* (1885).

Himes, Joshua V(aughan) (1805–1895) A preacher and social reformer at the Chardon Street Chapel in Boston, Joshua V. Himes was a close friend of William Lloyd Garrison and worked for such causes as *ABOLITIONISM, peace, and *TEMPERANCE. His life changed direction in 1839, however, when he became convinced of *WILLIAM MILLER's calculations about the imminent end of the world.

Himes provided Miller with publicity and marketing savvy, translating this farmer and Baptist preacher from Low Hampton, New York, into a national figure by means of publications, hymnals, and what was then the largest tent in North America. Himes founded *Signs of the Times*, a ***MILLERITE** publication, in 1840 and turned his Chardon Street Chapel into a major center of ***MILLERITE** activity. After Miller's early predictions failed to materialize, Himes tried to rally the faithful, but he, too, ultimately became disillusioned, left the movement, and became an Episcopal priest in the Dakotas.

Reference: Gary Land, ed., *Adventism in America* (1986).

Hindustan Bible Institute Established in 1950, Hindustan Bible Institute operates training schools in Sri Lanka and Madras, India. The independent missions organization plants churches, does medical and social service work, and broadcasts a radio program, *Voice of India*, to India and Sri Lanka. Hindustan Bible Institute also publishes a monthly magazine, which is also called *Voice of India*.

Hine, Edward (1825–1891) One of the early propagandists for ***BRITISH ISRAELISM**, Edward Hine converted to the British-Israel movement in 1840, although he did not give his first public lecture until 1869. Hine's ideological contribution to the movement was to nudge it away from the Anglo-Saxon emphasis that ***JOHN WILSON** had articulated and to limit the claims of "ten lost tribes" status to the British, thereby explicitly excluding the Germans. Hine came to North America in 1884, and in the course of a four-year visit he spread the ***BRITISH ISRAELISM** doctrine throughout New England, the New York metropolitan area, as far west as Chicago, and throughout Ontario.

Reference: Michael Barkun, *Religion and the Racist Right: The Origins of the Christian Identity Movement* (1994).

Hinn, Benedictus "Benny" (1952–) One of the more flamboyant and controversial of the pentecostal televangelists, Benny Hinn was born in Jaffa, Israel; he was reared in a Greek Orthodox household, although he attended a private Roman Catholic school. The family moved to Toronto in 1968, after the Six Day War, and shortly thereafter Hinn was converted to evangelical Christianity. He studied the ***BIBLE**, and a turning point in his life occurred when he attended a service conducted by ***KATHRYN KUHLMAN** in Pittsburgh. There, Hinn was impressed by Kuhlman's rhetoric of intimacy with the Holy Spirit. Upon returning to Toronto, according to his own account, Hinn prayed, "Holy Spirit, ***KATHRYN KUHLMAN** said you are her friend. I don't think I know you. Can I meet you?"

Hinn had been afflicted throughout childhood with a stutter, but when he rose at the Trinity Assembly of God in Oshawa, Ontario, on December 7, 1974, to tell about his spiritual experiences, he spoke fluently. That moment, he claims, marked the beginning of a lifetime of miracles. Indeed, Hinn claims that he was commanded to preach by a voice, which said, "If you do not preach, everyone who falls will be your responsibility."

Hinn founded the Orlando Christian Center in Orlando, Florida, in March 1983. Now known as the World Outreach Center, Inc., the congregation numbers around ten thousand. In addition, Hinn has taken his "Miracle Crusades" around the world. His claims of spectacular healing powers, his natty suits, and his unusual hairstyle, which defies both the laws of gravity and powers of description, have also translated well onto television. His daily half-hour program, *This Is Your Day,* airs across North America and to stations in places as diverse as Latin America, Russia, India, and South Africa.

Hinn's flamboyant tactics, his "health-and-wealth" theology, and his opulent lifestyle—expensive home and automobiles, a Rolex wristwatch—came under attack from the media and from fellow evangelicals in the 1990s. Although Hinn often dismisses such criticisms by saying he wished he had a "Holy Ghost machine gun," he at times has issued a public recantation of his "health-and-wealth" theology, only to return to it again.

Reference: Benny Hinn, *Good Morning, Holy Spirit* (1990).

Hobbs, Herschel H(arold) (1907–1995) Born in Talladega Springs, Alabama, Herschel H. Hobbs began preaching at age nineteen and became one of the most powerful preachers and theologians in the *SOUTHERN BAPTIST CONVENTION. After graduating from Howard College (now *SAMFORD UNIVERSITY), Hobbs earned the master's and doctorate degrees in New Testament interpretation from Southern Baptist Theological Seminary. Following his ordination in 1929, he served a number of churches before assuming the pastorate of the First Baptist Church in Oklahoma City, where he remained until his retirement in 1972.

In addition to a number of books, Hobbs wrote a column, "Baptist Beliefs," which appeared regularly in Baptist newspapers, and his sermons were broadcast weekly over hundreds of radio stations on *The Baptist Hour.* Hobbs exerted an influence in ecclesiastical affairs far beyond that of a successful preacher. From 1961 to 1963, he served two terms as president of the *SOUTHERN BAPTIST CONVENTION, and he was also vice president of the *BAPTIST WORLD ALLIANCE from 1965 to 1970. He is best known, however, for heading a panel charged with revising the Southern Baptists' Faith and Message statement, which was adopted by the Convention in 1963. That theologically conservative manifesto represents the closest thing to a creedal statement ever issued by the Southern Baptists.

Hocking, David L(ee) (1941–) Born in Long Beach, California, David L. Hocking graduated from *BOB JONES UNIVERSITY, *GRACE THEOLOGICAL SEMINARY, and Western Graduate School of Theology. Ordained in 1961 by the National Fellowship of Brethren Churches, Hocking served as the national youth director for the Brethren churches until 1964, when he began Grace Brethren Church in Columbus, Ohio. In 1968, he became pastor of First Brethren Church in Long Beach, California.

Hocking, an accomplished Bible expositor, began his career as a radio *EVANGELIST in 1974, with a program called *Sounds of Grace.* From 1979 to 1989, he was host of *The BIOLA Hour,* a weekly program of Bible study out of *BIOLA UNIVERSITY in La Mirada, California. A dispute with the board of directors led to another radio program, *Solid Rocks Radio,* and in 1995 he began *Hope for Tomorrow,* a daily, half-hour radio program. Hocking, who espouses *PREMILLENNIALISM, preaches and lectures around the country and, since 1992, has been affiliated with the *CALVARY CHAPEL movement.

References: David L. Hocking, *Spiritual Gifts* (1974); idem, *The Nature of God in Plain Language* (1984); idem, *The Coming World Leader: Understanding the Book of Revelation* (1988).

Hodel, Donald P(aul) (1935–) Born in Portland, Oregon, Donald P. Hodel graduated from Harvard University in 1957, where he had been a member of the Harvard Young Republican Club. He returned to Oregon, earned a law degree from the University of Oregon Law School, and eventually became a corporate attorney for Georgia-Pacific, the lumber and paper products company. Hodel became chairman of the Oregon Republican State Central Committee in 1966, and in 1969 he was named deputy administrator of the Bonneville Power Administration, the federal agency that markets electrical power generated by dams in the Pacific Northwest. He was promoted to the top job three years later.

Despite the surplus of inexpensive electricity, Hodel relentlessly advocated the construction of nuclear and coal-fired plants, a plan that put him on a collision course with environmentalists, whom he called the "Prophets of Shortage" and accused of "choking off our individual and collective aspirations for ourselves and our children." The election of *JIMMY CARTER brought calls for Hodel's dismissal as head of the Bonneville Power Administration. He resigned, took a job as president of an industry group, the National Electric Reliability Council, and then moved to Washington in 1981 as undersecretary for the Department of the Interior in the Reagan administration.

As second-in-command to *JAMES G. WATT, secretary of the Interior, Hodel was responsible for carrying out Watt's "pro-growth" initiatives, such as oil exploration in protected areas and the sale of wilderness lands. *RONALD REAGAN named Hodel secretary of the Department of Energy in November 1982, where he continued policies favorable to industry interests. At the beginning of Reagan's second term, Hodel moved back to Interior as secretary. There he generally continued Watt's policies, although his low-key, nonconfrontational style attracted less rancor from environmentalists.

After leaving office, Hodel became increasingly active in the *RELIGIOUS RIGHT. In 1997, after a stint as interim vice president of *FOCUS ON THE FAMILY, Holdel was designated by *PAT ROBERTSON to become president and chief executive officer of the *CHRISTIAN COALITION. Hodel stepped down less than two years later, however, and Robertson again became president of the organization.

Hodge, Archibald Alexander (1823–1886) The son of *CHARLES HODGE who was named for *CHARLES HODGE's mentor, *ARCHIBALD ALEXANDER, the founder of Princeton Theological Seminary, Archibald Alexander Hodge attended both the College of New Jersey and Princeton Seminary. Before succeeding his father as professor of theology from 1878 until his death, A. A. Hodge was a missionary to India and a professor at Western Theological Seminary. In the early 1880s, he coedited the *Presbyterian Review* with Union Theological Seminary's Charles A. Briggs. Hodge's *Outlines of Theology* (1860), a dialectical treatise on the essentials of Christian doctrine, went through two editions during his lifetime.

Reference: Mark A. Noll, ed., *The Princeton Theology, 1812–1921* (1983).

Hodge, Charles (1797–1878) Probably the most famous proponent of the *PRINCETON THEOLOGY, Charles Hodge graduated from the College of New Jersey (Princeton University) in 1815 and from Princeton Theological Seminary in 1819. He was ordained by the New Brunswick Presbytery in 1821, but he found that he was ill-suited for pastoral responsibilities. He accepted an invitation from *ARCHIBALD ALEXANDER to teach at Princeton Seminary, where he was elected professor of Oriental and biblical literature in 1822. From 1826 until 1828, he took a two-year hiatus to study in Europe, where he spent most of his time in Halle, Germany, under the tutelage of F. A. D. Tholuck, with whom he forged a lasting friendship. Hodge was appointed professor of theology at Princeton Seminary in 1840, a post he retained until his death.

Hodge is best known for his three-volume *Systematic Theology* (1872–1873) and for his work as founding editor of the *Biblical Repertory*, later known as the *Biblical Repertory and Theological Review* and later still as the *Biblical Repertory and Princeton Review*. Hodge's discursive comments over nearly four decades in the *Biblical Repertory* show the real range of his considerable intellect. He offered his Reformed perspective on everything from higher criticism to Jacksonian democracy, from science to slavery.

References: Charles Hodge, *The Way of Life* (1841); idem, *Theological Essays* (1846); idem, *Essays and Reviews* (1857); idem, *Systematic Theology*, 3 vols. (1872–1873); idem, *What Is Darwinism?* (1874); Mark A. Noll, ed., *The Princeton Theology, 1812–1921* (1983).

Hofer, David (1917–) A 1936 graduate of the *BIBLE INSTITUTE OF LOS ANGELES (BIOLA), David Hofer was active in a gospel quartet and in *YOUTH FOR CHRIST before settling in his boyhood home of Dinuba, California. There he and his brother, Egon, founded an evangelical radio station, KRDU, in 1946. The success of the station led to David Hofer's appointment to a three-year term as president of the *NATIONAL RELIGIOUS BROADCASTERS, beginning in 1979.

Holiness Evangelistic Institute. *See* **Bartlesville Wesleyan College.**

Holiness Movement One of the strains of American *EVANGELICALISM, the holiness movement emerged from *JOHN WESLEY's emphasis on Christian perfection, the doctrine that the believer could attain "perfect love" in this life, after the *BORN-AGAIN experience. Wesley's notion of perfect love freed the believer from the disposition to sin, although he allowed for failings rooted in "infirmity" and "ignorance." The *Cyclopedia of Methodism*, published in 1881, defined *holiness* as the belief that every believer is capable of "perfection of his nature by which he is infinitely averse to all moral evil."

Fittingly, holiness teachings achieved their best hearing in Methodist circles, but as *METHODISM expanded, became more respectable, and acquired middle-class trappings in the nineteenth century, holiness doctrines faded into the background. Though rooted in the Methodist Episcopal Church, the holiness movement was interdenominational and sought to revitalize the piety in *METHODISM and other denominations. Holiness—also called *SANCTIFICATION or *SECOND BLESSING (after the first, conversion)—was promoted in the antebellum period by *SARAH LANKFORD and *PHOEBE PALMER in their *TUESDAY MEETINGS FOR THE PROMOTION OF HOLINESS, by *TIMOTHY MERRITT in his *Guide to Holiness* magazine, and by *CHARLES FINNEY and *ASA MAHAN at Oberlin College. After the Civil War, holiness thrived in independent *CAMP MEETING associations, such as those at Ocean Grove, New Jersey, and Oak Bluffs, Massachusetts.

By the final decade of the nineteenth century, holiness *EVANGELISTS numbered more than three hundred. The

Methodist hierarchy grew uneasy about the holiness influence, especially the apparent lack of denominational loyalty of holiness people. As they came under increased pressure, some submitted to the Methodist hierarchy, while others joined emerging holiness denominations, such as the *CHURCH OF GOD (ANDERSON, INDIANA), the *CHURCH OF THE NAZARENE, the *PENTECOSTAL HOLINESS CHURCH, or the *FIRE-BAPTIZED HOLINESS CHURCH, among others. These groups generally emphasize the importance of probity and ask their adherents to shun *WORLDLINESS in all its insipid forms. The holiness movement also survives in regular *CAMP MEETINGS throughout North America.

References: Melvin E. Dieter, *The Holiness Revival of the Nineteenth Century* (1980); Charles E. Jones, *Perfectionist Persuasion: The Holiness Movement and American Methodism, 1867–1936* (1974).

Holmes, Marjorie (Rose) (1910–) Born in Storm Lake, Iowa, Marjorie Holmes attended Buena Vista College and Cornell College, where she earned the B.A. in 1931. Holmes spent her career as a freelance writer, columnist, and teacher of writing. She has published extensively for the evangelical market, although her books, especially her novels, have also reached a wider audience. *Two from Galilee,* a novel about Mary and Joseph, released in 1972, made the *New York Times* bestseller list and became one of the years' best-sellers. The book, according to Holmes, was an attempt to take Joseph and Mary "out of the art galleries and take away the gold frames and halos which create a barrier for us." *Two from Galilee,* Holmes continued, "means more to me than anything else I have ever written. If I had never written anything else besides this book, I would still feel like I had accomplished something."

References: Marjorie Holmes, *World by the Tail* (1943); idem, *Cherry Blossom Princess* (1960); idem, *Wanted: Someone to Talk To* (1967); idem, *Two from Galilee* (1972); idem, *Lord, Let Me Love* (1978); idem, *God and Vitamins: How Exercise, Diet, and Faith Can Change Your Life* (1980).

Holy Communion. *See* **Lord's Supper.**

Holy Eucharist. *See* **Lord's Supper.**

Holy Ghost and Us Bible School. *See* **Sandford, Frank W(eston).**

Holy Ghost People. *See* **Serpent Handling.**

Home Schooling Home schooling, the practice of educating students at home, became increasingly common among evangelicals in the last two decades of the twentieth century. Some of the impetus originated among evangelicals in the South in the wake of the 1954 *Brown* v. *Board of Education* decision that mandated school integration. In the 1980s, many evangelicals were uneasy about what they believed was the rampant *SECULAR HUMANISM in the public schools. Some send their children to church-sponsored schools, while others educate them at home, many with the assistance of curricular materials supplied by evangelical agencies.

Hope Chapel (Hermosa Beach, California, and Kaneohe, Hawai'i) In September 1971, Ralph Moore, a graduate of *L.I.F.E. BIBLE COLLEGE, assumed the pastorate of a small Foursquare congregation in Redondo Beach, California. Moore began targeting young, single adults in the area, and the response was overwhelming; soon the congregation had to seek new facilities, which they found in a former bowling alley in nearby Hermosa Beach. In 1983, responding to what he claimed was a direct revelation from God, Moore left California to start another Hope Chapel, this one in Hawai'i.

Like *WILLOW CREEK COMMUNITY CHURCH in Illinois, Hope Chapel places a great deal of emphasis on cell groups or what they call "MiniChurches," each of which is led by a "shepherd." Once the group reaches a certain size, it is split in order to retain intimacy within the group. In this process of cell division, Hope Chapel has continued its growth. Hope Chapel has maintained its ties to the *INTERNATIONAL CHURCH OF THE FOURSQUARE GOSPEL.

Reference: Donald E. Miller, *Reinventing American Protestantism: Christianity in the New Millennium* (1997).

Hopkins, Samuel (1721–1803) A native of Waterbury, Connecticut, Samuel Hopkins graduated from Yale College in 1741 and studied for the ministry under *JONATHAN EDWARDS in Northampton, Massachusetts. In 1743, he became pastor of the Congregational church in Housatonic (now Great Barrington), Massachusetts. After the death of Edwards, his mentor, in 1758, Hopkins assumed the task of perpetuating Edwardsean thought through several theological works. Hopkins's hyper-Calvinist system was known by various names: Hopkinsianism, Consistent Calvinism, and the *NEW DIVINITY. He was best known for the ethic of "disinterested benevolence," which held that a truly virtuous person would be "willing to be damned for the glory of God." This notion informed Hopkins's own antislavery sentiment, and its acceptance by other Congregationalists helped to drive the missionary movement.

Despite his notoriety in theological circles, Hopkins was dismissed from his church in 1769. The following year he assumed the pulpit of First Congregational Church in Newport, Rhode Island, where he remained for the rest of his life.

References: Samuel Hopkins, *Sin, Thro' Divine Interposition an Advantage to the Universe* (1759); idem, *An Inquiry into the Nature of True Holiness* (1773); idem, *A Dialogue Concerning the Slavery of the Africans, Shewing It To Be the Duty and Interest of the American States to Emancipate Their African Slaves* (1776); idem, *The System of Doctrines contained in Divine Revelation Explained and Defended,* 2 vols. (1793); Joseph A. Conforti, *Samuel Hopkins and the New Divinity Movement* (1981).

Hornshuh, Fred (1884–1982) A pioneer with the Apostolic Faith movement, Fred Hornshuh attended *JOHN ALEXANDER DOWIE's Zion College for two years before graduating from Willamette University in 1908. The following year he received a Spirit *BAPTISM in Portland, Oregon, at an Apostolic Faith meeting, and he became a preacher in the movement for several years. Hornshuh and others left the Apostolic Faith movement to form the Bible Standard Mission, which was eventually folded into the Open Bible Evangelistic Association (now the *OPEN BIBLE STANDARD CHURCHES). Hornshuh, who became an influential pentecostal leader in the Pacific Northwest, founded Lighthouse Temple in Eugene, Oregon, in 1919, the same year he started a magazine, *Bible Standard,* later known as the *Overcomer.*

Horton, Michael S. (1964–) While a sophomore at *BIOLA UNIVERSITY, Michael Horton formed Christians United for Reformation, a group dedicated to reminding evangelicals of their heritage in the Protestant Reformation in the sixteenth century. Soon thereafter he began a radio program, *The White Horse Inn,* and a magazine, *Modern Reformation.* Horton continued his education at *WESTMINSTER THEOLOGICAL SEMINARY, which reinforced his strident *CALVINISM and his suspicion of the cultural accretions that, in his judgment, have compromised twentieth-century evangelical Christianity. "*EVANGELICALISM as a movement," he wrote, "is rushing headlong toward theological ambiguity, which is another way of saying apostasy."

Reference: Michael Horton, *We Believe: Recovering the Essentials of the Apostles' Creed* (1999).

Horton, T(homas) C(orwin) (1848–1932) Born in Cincinnati, T. C. Horton experienced success in business in his twenties but decided to enter Christian work. He became a *YMCA secretary in Indianapolis, Indiana, in 1876 and later served in similar capacities in St. Paul, Minnesota, and Dallas, Texas. He was ordained as a Presbyterian in 1884 and became an associate to *A. T. PIERSON at Bethany Presbyterian Church in Philadelphia. Horton moved on to First Congregational Church (later known as Scofield Memorial Church) in Dallas, before heading west to Los Angeles in 1906.

As pastor of Immanuel Presbyterian Church in Los Angeles, Horton developed what he called the Fisherman's Club to train laymen in the *BIBLE and in *EVANGELISM (a women's counterpart, the Lyceum Club, was begun by Horton's wife, Anna). These clubs led, at least indirectly, to the founding of the *BIBLE INSTITUTE OF LOS ANGELES (now *BIOLA UNIVERSITY) in 1908. Horton served as superintendent of the school while carrying on his pastoral ministry at Immanuel and, later, as an associate at Church of the Open Door. Horton, a dispensational premillennialist, wrote several books and edited two popular periodicals: *The King's Business* and *Fishers of Men.*

References: T. C. Horton, *Personal and Practical Christian Work* (1922); idem, *Potency of Prayer* (1928).

Houghton, William H(enry) (1887–1947) William H. Houghton had an evangelical *CONVERSION experience in Lynn, Massachusetts, in 1901 and joined a holiness church the following year. After a brief career as a vaudeville entertainer he renewed his evangelical commitment in 1909 and entered *EASTERN NAZARENE COLLEGE. Houghton left school within a few months in order to join the evangelistic efforts of John Quincy Adams Henry, serving as a singer for Henry's *REVIVAL campaigns. Houghton accepted a call as pastor of a Baptist church in Canton, Pennsylvania, in 1915, and was ordained in the Northern Baptist Convention; three years later, he moved to another pulpit at New Bethlehem, Pennsylvania.

Early in his evangelistic career, Houghton had developed a friendship with *REUBEN A. TORREY of *MOODY BIBLE INSTITUTE, and he became one of the more outspoken fundamentalist leaders and polemicists. Houghton's magazine, *The Baptist Believer,* lasted for only three issues in 1920, but it was notable for its unrelenting attacks on *MODERNISM. Houghton soon thereafter accepted a call to the First Baptist Church in Norristown, Pennsylvania; in 1924, he moved to the Baptist Tabernacle in Atlanta; in 1930, he was selected to succeed *JOHN ROACH STRATON at Calvary Baptist Church in New York City. Houghton completed his ascent up the ladder of fundamentalist leadership when he succeeded *JAMES M. GRAY as president of *MOODY BIBLE

INSTITUTE in 1934. Houghton developed the faculty and expanded the student body at Moody during his tenure, and he remained active on other fronts as well, including editorial leadership of *Moody Monthly* magazine, a radio program, and the organization of evangelical scientists known as the American Scientific Affiliation.

References: William H. Houghton, *Let's Go Back to the Bible* (1939); Wilbur M. Smith, *A Watchman on the Walls: Life Story of Will H. Houghton* (1951).

Houghton College (Houghton, New York) In the nineteenth century, Houghton College's founder, itinerant preacher *WILLARD J. HOUGHTON, singlehandedly established so many *SUNDAY SCHOOLS in upstate New York that he was dubbed the "Sunday School Man." Late in Houghton's life, recognizing he "was getting old and could not run over these hills much longer," he became determined to found a permanent school, with the help of the Wesleyan Methodists' Lockport Conference. Beginning in 1883, therefore, he began to solicit funds for a Christian academy where "we can mold the [characters] of our boys and girls [and] shape the future of our world." He chose the site of the campus for Houghton Wesleyan Methodist Seminary not only because the spot was at the center of all five circuits of the Wesleyan Methodist denomination but also because it was "free from rum influence" and could offer a strong moral environment.

By 1888, the school had added a department for training ministers. Eight years later, the Wesleyan Educational Society took control of the school's management. The first college-level courses were introduced within a year, and over the next twenty years the school had developed to junior college level. Between 1909 and 1923, Houghton offered up to three years of college education, but baccalaureate-seeking students were still forced to transfer to other institutions. In 1923, the regents of the University of the State of New York gave a provisional charter to the school, which was by this time known as Houghton College. The first bachelor's degrees were awarded two years later. A permanent charter was granted in 1927, with full regional accreditation following in 1935.

Since that time, Houghton College has grown to an enrollment of approximately eleven hundred students, and the school has added an extension campus in suburban Buffalo, New York. The college continues to be operated by the *WESLEYAN CHURCH. The library's Wesleyana/Gunsalus Room houses three collections: a collection of church and college publications, a small collection of rare or valuable books, as well as a personal collection donated by Roy S. Nicholson, who was president of the general conference of the *WESLEYAN METHODIST CHURCH from 1947 to 1959.

References: *Houghton College Catalog 1996–97* (1996); Frieda A. Gillette and Katherine W. Lindley, *And You Shall Remember . . . a Pictorial History of Houghton College* (1982).

House Churches An evangelical movement that flourished in the wake of the counterculture in the late 1960s and 1970s, house churches sought to replicate the New Testament simplicity of the early church, freed from institutional and denominational constraints. The form varied from intentional communities, such as Reba Place Fellowship in Evanston, Illinois, and that which gave rise to the *Post-American* (later **SOJOURN-*

ERS) to Sunday morning gatherings in someone's living room.

Reference: Dietrich Bonhoeffer, *Life Together: A Discussion of Christian Fellowship* (1954).

House of Acts. *See* **Wise, Ted.**

Howard, Thomas (1935–) The son of Philip Howard, editor of the *Sunday School Times,* Thomas Howard spent his early adulthood coming to terms with his fundamentalist upbringing. His autobiographical account, *Christ the Tiger,* traced his struggles with the doctrinal shallowness and aesthetic deprivation of *FUNDAMENTALISM; though overwritten, it provided many young evangelicals with a model of an energetic mind engaging contemporary culture. Howard taught in the English department at *GORDON COLLEGE, and in the 1970s he became enamored of sacramentalism and the historical and liturgical traditions of Christianity. That pilgrimage led to a highly publicized *CONVERSION to Roman Catholicism in 1985 and his resignation from Gordon shortly thereafter.

Reference: Thomas Howard, *Christ the Tiger* (1967).

Howard College. *See* **Samford University.**

Howe, Julia Ward (1819–1910) The author of *The Battle Hymn of the Republic,* Julia Ward Howe and her husband, Samuel, had been active in the abolitionist movement. They edited an antislavery periodical, *Commonwealth,* and helped fugitive slaves. Samuel Howe, a surgeon, was the first director of the first school for the blind in America; Julia Ward Howe was the first president of the New England Woman Suffrage Association.

In December 1861, while visiting Union troops encamped outside the District of Columbia, Howe heard the men singing "John Brown's Body," which had become popular in the North. Her traveling companion suggested that Howe, a poet, might come up with better lyrics to the same tune. That night, unable to sleep, Howe composed new words to the familiar music, verses replete with biblical references, apocalyptic themes, and military imagery. The six-verse poem appeared in the *Atlantic Monthly* in February 1862 under the title "The Battle Hymn of the Republic," which an editor had supplied. A chaplain in the Union Army taught the song to the troops, and it spread like wildfire throughout the North, becoming the anthem for northern opposition to slavery.

Reference: Evelyn Bence, *Spiritual Moments with the Great Hymns* (1997).

Hubbard, David Allan (1928–1996) Born in Stockton, California, to missionary parents, David Allan Hubbard was reared in the pentecostal tradition. Hubbard graduated from *WESTMONT COLLEGE in 1949 and went on to earn two degrees from *FULLER THEOLOGICAL SEMINARY. Ordained into the *CONSERVATIVE BAPTIST ASSOCIATION in 1952, Hubbard earned the doctorate in Old Testament and Semitics from St. Andrews University in 1957. He returned to teach at Westmont, established himself as an Old Testament scholar, and over the course of a productive career published thirty-six books.

Hubbard is best known, however, for his thirty-year tenure as president of Fuller, an evangelical seminary in Pasadena, California. He was chosen for the job in 1963, after a contentious three-year search failed to come up with another acceptable candidate. Hubbard, who was known for his irenic spirit, presided over an expansion of the seminary's student body and the addition of a school of psychology and a school of world missions. In addition, Hubbard took over *CHARLES FULLER's radio program, *Old Fashioned Revival Hour,* in 1967. Two years later Hubbard renamed it *The Joyful Sound,* and he remained the weekly program's chief speaker until he stepped down in 1980.

References: David Allan Hubbard, *With Bands of Love* (1968); idem, *The Second Coming: What Will Happen When Jesus Returns?* (1984); George M. Marsden, *Reforming Fundamentalism: Fuller Seminary and the New Evangelicalism* (1987).

Hudgins, (William) Douglas (1905–) Born in Estill Springs, Tennessee, Douglas Hudgins made a "public profession" of faith in Jesus Christ and was baptized in Taylor's Creek. While a pre-med student at Carson-Newman College, he felt called to the ministry and was ordained a Southern Baptist at the age of twenty. He served as pastor of various churches before enrolling at Southern Baptist Theological Seminary in 1931, graduating in 1934. Hudgins, an eloquent preacher and a man of exquisite decorum, was thrust into the civil rights debate during his long tenure as pastor of the redoubtable First Baptist Church in Jackson, Mississippi, which counted prominent white supremacists among its members, notably Ross Barnett, who would serve as Mississippi's segregationist governor during the early 1960s. Hudgins had opposed the 1954 *Brown* v. *Board of Education* decision, and nine years later he and his congregation turned away a group of black students who attempted to worship at First Baptist Church.

As the "Freedom Summer" of 1964 approached, Hudgins sought to remain apolitical, his theology geared toward personal, rather than public, morality; he refused, for example, to condemn the acts of violence perpetrated against blacks and against civil rights workers, even though he had reason to believe that members of his congregation were engaging in such violence. Hudgins's personalized morality, which was rather common among mid-twentieth-century white evangelicals until the rise of the *RELIGIOUS RIGHT, sought refuge from social upheaval by retreating to an emphasis on personal regeneration and probity.

Reference: Charles Marsh, *God's Long Summer: Stories of Faith and Civil Rights* (1997).

Hughes, Harold E(verett) (1922–) Born into rural poverty near Ida Grove, Iowa, Harold E. Hughes studied briefly at the University of Iowa and served in the military during World War II. He became a truck driver and an alcoholic, at one point reaching the verge of suicide, but his evangelical *CONVERSION turned him in another direction: toward becoming a Methodist lay preacher and, eventually, a politician. After being elected to the Iowa State Commerce Commission, Hughes was elected governor of Iowa in 1962 as a Democrat. He was reelected to a second and then a third term and then won election to the U.S. Senate in 1968. A political liberal who was widely credited with rebuilding the Democratic Party in Iowa, Hughes was a bitter opponent of the Vietnam War and the Nixon administration and briefly sought the Democratic nomination for president in 1972. On September 6, 1973, however, fourteen months before the 1974 election, Hughes stunned the political world by announcing that he would not seek reelection to a safe Senate seat and that he was retiring from politics in order to pursue enterprises more directly related to his faith.

Hughes's affiliation with Doug Coe

and Fellowship Foundation brought him face-to-face with *CHARLES COLSON, the Watergate-felon-turned-evangelical-Christian. In September 1973, in a moment fraught with tension—and poignantly recorded in Colson's autobiography, *Born Again*—Hughes embraced Colson as a brother in Christ, despite their vast political differences. Since leaving the Senate, Hughes has been involved in a number of enterprises, including a spiritual retreat center, Cedar Point, on the Chesapeake Bay near Easton, Maryland, and oversight of the Harold Hughes Centers for Alcoholism and Drug Treatment in Iowa.

References: Harold E. Hughes, *The Man from Ida Grove: A Senator's Personal Story* (1979); James C. Larew, "A Party Reborn: Harold Hughes and the Iowa Democrats," *Palimsest*, LIX (September–October 1978).

Hull House. *See* **Addams, Jane.**

Humbard, (Alpha) Rex (Emmanuel) (1919–) Born in Little Rock, Arkansas, to an itinerant *EVANGELIST and his wife, Rex Humbard became an itinerant preacher himself until he and his wife, Maude Aimee, settled in Akron, Ohio, in 1952. There he formed a nondenominational church that would eventually be called the Cathedral of Tomorrow. Influenced by *KATHRYN KUHLMAN, with whom he sometimes conducted *REVIVAL meetings, Humbard was one of the first preachers to make a foray into television. Maude Aimee, a gospel singer who began singing publicly at the age of nine, appeared regularly on the telecasts.

Humbard's background and theology were vaguely pentecostal, and he preached healing through prayer and anointing with oil, although he did not emphasize the *BAPTISM OF THE HOLY SPIRIT and refused the designation "pentecostal." Questions were raised in 1973 about Humbard's handling of funds, but the church and the television ministry survived. He resigned the pastorate of the Cathedral of Tomorrow in 1983 in favor of Wayne Jones, his brother-in-law.

References: Rex Humbard, *Miracles in My Life: Rex Humbard's Own Story* (1971); idem, *Why I Believe Jesus Is Coming Soon* (1972); idem, *Where Are the Dead?* (1977); David Edwin Harrell Jr., *All Things Are Possible: The Healing and Charismatic Revivals in Modern America* (1975).

Humbard, Maude Aimee (née Jones) (1921–). *See* **Humbard, (Alpha) Rex (Emmanuel).**

Hunter, Charles (Edward) (1920–) A healing evangelist in partner with his wife, *FRANCES HUNTER, Charles Hunter was born in Palo Pinto, Texas, did military service in the air force, and became a successful businessman. Having come out of the *CHURCH OF GOD (ANDERSON, INDIANA), Charles and his wife were baptized by the Holy Spirit relatively late in life. The "Happy Hunters" have conducted "healing explosions" across North America and have written more than thirty books.

Hunter, Frances (née Fuller) (1916–) A partner with her husband, *CHARLES HUNTER, in a healing *EVANGELISM team, Frances Hunter became, in her words, an "instant fanatic" after her *CONVERSION at the age of forty-nine. Born in Saratoga, Illinois, and coming out of the *CHURCH OF GOD (ANDERSON, INDIANA), Frances was baptized by the Holy Spirit not long after she claimed a visit from God while she was in the hospital for eye surgery. The "Happy Hunters" preached about divine healing in the course of their itinerations across North America.

Huntington, Selina, Countess of (née Shirley) (1707–1791) A patron to *EVANGELICALISM and *METHODISM in England, Selina Shirley was born into a noble household. She was a pious child, she married the ninth Earl of Huntington in 1728, and she experienced an evangelical *CONVERSION about a decade later. The Countess of Huntington forged close ties with *JOHN and *CHARLES WESLEY, and she appointed *GEORGE WHITEFIELD as her chaplain. She sponsored evangelical preachers and constructed a network of chapels in various venues, including Brighton, in order to spread the evangelical message, especially in places where the Anglican clergy were not sympathetic. A dedicated Calvinist, the countess sought to provide the proper training for evangelical preachers, who would then become part of her "connexion." An adverse ruling by the ecclesiastical courts in 1780 forced her either to come under the discipline of the Church of England or to seek refuge for her chapels as dissenting places of worship under the Toleration Act; the countess reluctantly chose the latter. In 1790, a year before her death, she transferred the chapels in her connexion to an association, thereby ensuring that they would remain in evangelical hands.

References: F. F. Bretherton, *The Countess of Huntington* (1940); C. Edwin Welch, *Spiritual Pilgrim: A Reassessment of the Life of the Countess of Huntington* (1995).

Huntington College (Huntington, Indiana) Huntington College, owned and operated by the *CHURCH OF THE UNITED BRETHREN IN CHRIST, is perhaps most famous for its claim as the college where former vice president *DAN QUAYLE taught law prior to his election to the United States Senate. Huntington was chartered under the name Central College in 1897. At its founding the college took over the operations of another institution, Hartsville College, originally chartered in 1850. By mutual agreement of both boards of trustees, Central College received all of Hartsville's books and records, and agreed to confer degrees on its senior students. Central College was renamed Huntington College in 1917.

Huntington's Graduate School of Christian Ministries offers three master's degrees in Christian ministry as well as a diploma in pastoral leadership. The library has an archives collection of the *CHURCH OF THE UNITED BRETHREN IN CHRIST.

Huntington College does not have a dress code or require a statement of faith as a prerequisite for admission. In fact, the college strives to seek a balance between Christian faith and conventional student life. While Huntington does not sponsor most forms of social *DANCING, choreographed dramatic productions, aerobics classes, and square dances are all permitted.

Reference: *Huntington College 1996–1998 Catalog (1996).*

Hutchcraft, Ron(ald) (Paul) Called to the ministry at the age of ten, Ron Hutchcraft was profoundly influenced by the *ECUADOR MARTYRS and resolved to do missionary work. He became active in *YOUTH FOR CHRIST during his teens and graduated from *MOODY BIBLE INSTITUTE in 1965. Hutchcraft went on to *WHEATON COLLEGE, all the while continuing his involvement with Chicagoland *YOUTH FOR CHRIST. Hutchdraft headed east in 1970 to begin Metropolitan *YOUTH FOR CHRIST in New York City and New Jersey, before beginning his own organization in 1991, Ron Hutchcraft Ministries, which has its headquarters in

Wayne, New Jersey. Hutchcraft has preached around the world and has served as a faculty member in the Billy Graham Schools of Evangelism. His weekly radio program, *Alive! with Ron Hutchcraft,* was named "talk show of the year" by the *NATIONAL RELIGIOUS BROADCASTERS in 1997.

Hybels, Bill (1951–) Born in Kalamazoo, Michigan, Bill Hybels graduated from *TRINITY COLLEGE (Deerfield, Illinois) in 1975. Having worked as a youth minister at South Park Church in Park Ridge, Illinois, Hybels sought to start his own church in the northwest suburbs of Chicago, so he conducted a door-to-door market research survey to determine why suburbanites stayed away from church. On the basis of his findings, he designed a church to overcome their objections. "Before entering the ministry," he recounted, "I spent a number of years in the marketplace. My genuine love for business and my kinship with businessmen has motivated me to develop a style of communication that relates well to the 'real world.'" Hybels also drew inspiration from two mentors: *ROBERT SCHULLER of the Garden Grove Community Church (now known as the Crystal Cathedral), who spoke in 1977 at the new church's initial fund-raising banquet, and *GILBERT BILEZIKIAN, Hybels's Bible teacher at *TRINITY COLLEGE, whom he credits with instilling a vision for a new kind of Christian community, based on a study of the Acts of the Apostles. "I could not imagine going to my grave without at least trying one time to see if what happened in the first century in that biblically functioning community could happen in the twentieth century in the United States," Hybels recalled. "I could not give my life at that point to a lesser dream, not until I had first tried to do the big one."

Hybels's invention—*WILLOW CREEK COMMUNITY CHURCH, located in South Barrington, Illinois, which began October 12, 1975—became one of the fastest-growing megachurches of the 1970s and 1980s. In addition to his administrative and preaching duties, Hybels has written several books. He lectures frequently to evangelical groups, and he has served as chaplain to the Chicago Bears football team.

References: Bill Hybels, *Caution: Christians Under Construction* (1978); idem, *Christians in the Marketplace* (1982); idem, *Seven Wonders of the Spiritual World* (1988).

Hyles, Jack (1926–2001) Jack Hyles, born in Italy, Texas, became pastor of the First Baptist Church of Hammond, Indiana, in 1959. The congregation grew from a few hundred to more than twenty thousand under his ministry, largely due to his aggressive "bus ministry," which sent *SUNDAY SCHOOL buses to nearby and to far-flung neighborhoods to bring children to the church.

Originally a Southern Baptist and then affiliated with the American Baptist Conference, Hyles eventually broke with both denominations because he believed they were insufficiently fundamentalist. He became a leader of the Independent Fundamental Baptist movement. Hyles founded several Baptist schools in Hammond as well as Hyles-Anderson College.

Reference: Elmer Towns, *World's Largest Sunday School* (1974).

■ ■ ■

Ichthys In Greek, the first letters of each word in the phrase "Jesus Christ, Son of God, Savior" spell *ichthys,* or fish. Christians, therefore, have used a fish as a symbol of their allegiance to Jesus (a symbol that works doubly well because many of the disciples, the earliest followers of Jesus, were fishermen). Especially since the *JESUS MOVEMENT of the early 1970s, the fish has become a popular—and mass-produced—totem for Christians, particularly evangelical Christians.

Idaho Holiness School. *See* **Northwest Nazarene College.**

Illinois Band In 1829, seven students from Yale Divinity School organized what came to be known as the Illinois Band for the purpose of home missions in the West. Responding to a plan put forward by John M. Ellis, a missionary in Illinois, they traveled there under the auspices of the American Home Missionary Society to organize churches and to help found Illinois College in Jacksonville.

Illinois Holiness University. *See* **Olivet Nazarene University.**

Illinois Institute. *See* **Wheaton College.**

Illinois Street Independent Church (Chicago, Illinois). *See* **Moody Church** *and* **Moody, Dwight Lyman.**

Independent Christian Churches and Churches of Christ. *See* **Christian Churches.**

Indiana Wesleyan University (Marion, Indiana) Affiliated with the Wesleyan Church, Indiana Wesleyan University dates its founding to 1920, when two different schools merged. The Wesleyan Methodist Church had opened Fairmount Bible School in Fairmount, Indiana, in 1906. In 1920, the school became the religion department of Marion College (chartered 1890), which was first known as Marion Normal College (from 1890–1912) and then as Marion Normal Institute (1912–1918). By 1928, the combined schools had taken the name Indiana Wesleyan University.

Indiana Wesleyan University has numerous graduate programs, including counseling, business, nursing, and education. For undergraduates, the university's student conduct guidelines are similar to those of most other Christian colleges, and they remain in effect during school breaks, including the summer.

Reference: *Indiana Wesleyan University 1995–1997 Catalog* (1995).

Inerrancy Inerrancy, an interpretation of the doctrine of inspiration, holds that the Scriptures are both divinely inspired and entirely without error in the original manuscripts. Although this had been the general interpretation throughout church history, the doctrine was refined somewhat and stated more emphatically in the latter part of the nineteenth century in response to higher criticism, which cast doubt on the reliability of the *BIBLE. The notion of inerrancy, which received its fullest expression in an 1881 article called "Inspiration," written by *ARCHIBALD ALEXANDER HODGE and *BENJAMIN BRECKINRIDGE WARFIELD and published in the *Presbyterian Review*, came to be the most commonly accepted understanding of inspiration among evangelicals in the twentieth century. Indeed, many evangelicals regard biblical inerrancy as one of the touchstones of orthodox theology.

References: Harold Lindsell, *The Battle for the Bible* (1976); Jack Rogers and Donald McKim, *The Authority and Interpretation of the Bible: An Historical Approach* (1979); John D. Woodbridge, *Biblical Authority: A Critique of the Rogers/McKim Proposal* (1982).

Institut Feller. *See* **Feller, Henriette.**

Institute for Creation Research Established in 1970, the Institute for Creation Research produces information and literature promoting the idea of "scientific creation" as a means of countering the teaching of evolution, especially in the public schools. Begun by creation apologist *HENRY MORRIS, the institute also claims to support geological research that will vindicate the notion of seven-day creation as described in Genesis, but most of the scientific community dismisses such research as jerry-rigged and inconsequential. In addition to sponsoring lectures and debates, distributing literature and videocassettes, and producing radio spots, the organization also maintains a creationist museum at its Santee, California, headquarters.

Reference: *"In the Beginning": The Creationist Controversy,* two-part PBS documentary (1994).

Institute for the Study of American Evangelicals The genesis of the Institute for the Study of American Evangelicals was an April 1977 conference at *TRINITY COLLEGE in Deerfield, Illinois, organized by *MARK A. NOLL, with participation by *NATHAN O. HATCH, Grant Wacker, Harry S. Stout, *GEORGE M. MARSDEN, and others. A subsequent conference, "The Bible in America," held at *WHEATON COLLEGE in November 1979, laid the groundwork for a more permanent institute, housed in the *BILLY GRAHAM CENTER at *WHEATON COLLEGE. The Institute for the Study of American Evangelicals sought to promote scholarship on *EVANGELICALISM, especially in North America, primarily through the organization of conferences, drawing scholars from around the world. Most of these conferences have generated books, such as *Jonathan Edwards and the American Experience,* edited by Hatch and Stout; *Evangelicals and the Mass Media,* edited by Quentin J. Schultze; and *Modern Christian Revivals,* edited by Edith L. Blumhofer and Randall Balmer.

The institute is supported by some individual donations but primarily through foundation grants from the Lilly Endowment and the Pew Charitable Trusts. That money has funded initiatives to study such topics as the missionary impulse and also to support scholars whose work relates to *EVANGELICALISM. The institute, through its funding of various projects and through the scholarship of individuals associated with it (Noll, Hatch, Stout, Marsden, Wacker, and *G. A. RAWLYK) has served to legitimate the study of *EVANGELICALISM in North America within the larger academic community. Indeed, by the mid-1990s some historians of American religion came to regard *EVANGELICALISM as the dominant motif in American religious historiography. The institute's newsletter, *The Evangelical Studies Bulletin,* is published quarterly.

Reference: Tim Stafford, "Whatever Happened to Christian History?" *Christianity Today,* April 2, 2001.

Institute in Basic Life Principles. *See* **Gothard, William "Bill."**

Institute in Basic Youth Conflicts. *See* **Gothard, William "Bill."**

Institutional Church Movement A response to the changing urban environment in the late nineteenth and early twentieth centuries, the Institutional Church movement was an attempt to broaden the programs and services of urban congregations in order to address social ills. Institutional churches—such as the Metropolitan Temple (Methodist) in New York City, Bethany Presbyterian Church in Philadelphia, Berkeley Temple (Congregational) in Boston, and Markham Memorial Presbyterian Church in St. Louis—offered clothing, soup kitchens, employment services, recreational facilities, youth clubs, deaconess homes, and even banking services. Although the Institutional Church movement is most often associated with the *SOCIAL GOSPEL, a number of evangelical congregations, especially Bethany Presbyterian in Philadelphia and Tabernacle Baptist Church in Atlanta, were leaders in the movement.

References: Charles Howard Hopkins, *The Rise of the Social Gospel in American Protestantism, 1865–1910* (1967); William R. Glass, "Liberal Means to Conservative Ends: Bethany Presbyterian Church, John Wanamaker, and the Institutional Church Movement," *American Presbyterians,* LXVIII (1990).

International Bible Institute Council of Christian Education. *See* **Evangelical Training Institute.**

International Church of Christ Begun in the Boston suburb of Lexington, Massachusetts, in 1979 by *KIP MCKEAN, the International Church of Christ teaches that it is the "faithful remnant" of the New Testament church. The International Church of Christ insists on baptizing its followers, even people who have already been baptized by other denominations. The group is known for its aggressive proselytizing, especially on college and university campuses; critics contend that the International Church of Christ, with its claims of exclusivity and its demands that followers provide a weekly detailed accounting of their time, has cultish overtones, and professors complain that students who become involved with the group tend to lose interest in anything but the Church, including their studies.

Typically, Church adherents engage in a strategy they call "love bombing" in order to recruit new followers. This act entails showering praise and attention on the target, and it is especially effective among first-year students, particularly among minorities and engineering students. *EVANGELISTS will learn their targets' class schedules and wait for them after class and eventually invite them to a church activity, often without disclosing who is sponsoring the event. According to a high-ranking defector, commenting on International Church of Christ strategies for proselytizing, "They don't say who they really are. They approach people saying they just want to sit and study the *BIBLE."

Once affiliated with the International Church of Christ, which shuns instrumental music in its worship gatherings, followers submit details of their personal lives to their "discipler," including a detailed accounting of how they spend their time and how many hours they read their *BIBLE. They even consult their discipler about what courses they take. Followers are taught that if they leave they would no longer be following Jesus and they will lose their *SALVATION. The church demands that members, in addition to their rebaptisms, submit to church authorities, and people who threaten to leave are subject to a "breaking session," a confrontation with church authorities intended to intimidate the recalcitrant member into conformity.

The International Church of Christ, which since 1990 has had its headquarters in Los Angeles, claimed attendance of 143,000 in 1997, with nearly three hundred congregations. Its aggressive *EVAN-

GELISM led to an annual increase of about 10 percent in the 1980s and 1990s.

Reference: Randy Frame, "The Cost of Discipleship?" *Christianity Today,* September 1, 1997.

International Church of the Foursquare Gospel The International Church of the Foursquare Gospel was founded by *AIMEE SEMPLE MCPHERSON, who had become an itinerant pentecostal *EVANGELIST with her second husband, Harold S. McPherson. Her first husband, *ROBERT SEMPLE, had died in China, where the couple were serving as missionaries. Sister Aimee, as she was known, continued her itinerant ministry after her divorce from Harold McPherson. Although she encountered a great deal of opposition—partly for being a woman preacher, partly for the flamboyant style of the meetings she conducted—she persevered, settling in Los Angeles in 1918. She built the Angelus Temple in 1923 with the help of her supporters and followers. The International Church of the Foursquare Gospel was incorporated in 1927.

The Church affirms the inspiration and *AUTHORITY of Scripture, the Trinity, and other orthodox Protestant evangelical doctrines and tenets. There are two ordinances, *BAPTISM by immersion and the *LORD'S SUPPER. The International Church of the Foursquare Gospel emphasizes the *BAPTISM OF THE HOLY SPIRIT and *SPEAKING IN TONGUES, but it also emphasizes the importance of living a Spirit-filled life and manifesting the gifts and fruit of the Spirit. Tithing is seen as the method ordained of God for supporting the work and ministries of the Church. The Church actively participates in the *NATIONAL ASSOCIATION OF EVANGELICALS, the *AMERICAN BIBLE SOCIETY, Pentecostal/Charismatic Churches of North America, the Pentecostal World Conference, and the Evangelical Fellowship of Missions Agencies.

The International Church of the Foursquare Gospel is governed by a president, a board of directors, the Foursquare Cabinet, an executive council, and the convention body. The Church's nine districts are overseen by district supervisors. Only the convention body can make or amend the bylaws of the church. Since its founding, the International Church of the Foursquare Gospel has had only three presidents. *AIMEE SEMPLE MCPHERSON served until her death in 1944. She was succeeded by her son, *ROLF KENNEDY MCPHERSON, who served until his retirement in 1988. John R. Holland has held the office since 1988.

From the headquarters in Los Angeles, near the Angelus Temple, the Church maintains an extensive home and foreign missions enterprise. The Church claims 18,577 congregations in eighty-one countries, counting a membership of over 1.8 million. In the United States, the International Church of the Foursquare Gospel reports 1,773 congregations and 229,643 members.

References: Frank S. Mead and Samuel S. Hill, *Handbook of Denominations in the United States,* 10th ed. (1996); J. Gordon Melton, *The Encyclopedia of American Religions,* 3d ed. (1993).

International Congress on World Evangelization Known as the Lausanne Congress because of its venue in Lausanne, Switzerland, the International Congress on World Evangelization, held in 1974, was a ten-day gathering of evangelical leaders to consider the issue of missions throughout the world. With the theme of "Let the Earth Hear His Voice" and with an eye on the year 2000, participants attended workshops and plenary sessions addressing theological, tactical, and methodological issues surrounding the task of *EVANGELISM. The congress adopted a statement, drafted by *JOHN R. W. STOTT and called the *LAUSANNE COVENANT, that upheld the traditional evangelical emphasis on the *AUTHORITY of Scripture and reaffirmed the biblical mandate for missions. The congress rejected the notion, then popular among some theological liberals, that the West should place a moratorium on sending missionaries to the Third World.

Reference: Donald A. McGavran, "A New Age in Missions Begins," *Church Growth Bulletin*, XI (1974).

International Pentecostal Holiness Church The International Pentecostal Holiness Church came into being out of the merger of two groups, the *FIRE-BAPTIZED HOLINESS CHURCH and the Pentecostal Holiness Church. The church dates its founding to 1898, when the former body was founded in South Carolina, and the latter founded in North Carolina. Both groups were southern holiness churches, preaching the message of the *SECOND BLESSING of *SANCTIFICATION. As the pentecostal movement began to gain popularity in the early years of the twentieth century, the two churches realized that they had much in common and began to discuss a merger. That merger, under the name Pentecostal Holiness Church, occurred in 1911. The Church added the word International to its title in 1975.

Theologically, the International Pentecostal Holiness Church follows the development of the denomination. Its roots in Methodist holiness are clear in its doctrinal statement, which derives from the Methodist Articles of Religion. This statement includes affirmations of the Trinity; the virgin birth, death, and bodily resurrection of Jesus; the inspiration, *INERRANCY, infallibility, and *AUTHORITY of Scripture; the *SECOND COMING of Christ; and entire *SANCTIFICATION. The statement also attests to belief in divine healing and the *BAPTISM OF THE HOLY SPIRIT. *SPEAKING IN TONGUES is seen as the initial evidence of the *BAPTISM OF THE HOLY SPIRIT, which will be followed by other manifestations and gifts of the Spirit. In keeping with its Methodist roots, the church allows *BAPTISM by methods other than immersion.

One of the hallmarks of the International Pentecostal Holiness Church is the insistence on three blessings. The first blessing, justification, and the *SECOND BLESSING, *SANCTIFICATION, are commonly held among holiness churches. The International Pentecostal Holiness Church believes that the third blessing, the *BAPTISM OF THE HOLY SPIRIT, can only come to a believer after the first two blessings. Most pentecostals believe that the *BAPTISM OF THE HOLY SPIRIT can come at any time.

*POLITY in the International Pentecostal Holiness Church is episcopal. A general executive board is elected by a quadrennial conference for a four-year term. There is a general superintendent, two assistant general superintendents, and other officers elected to compose the nine-member board. Property is held by the Church. Headquarters are in Oklahoma City, Oklahoma, and the Church reports 157,163 members in 1,653 churches.

References: Frank S. Mead and Samuel S. Hill, *Handbook of Denominations in the United States*, 10th ed. (1996); J. Gordon Melton, *The Encyclopedia of American Religions*, 3d ed. (1993).

International Prison Ministry Begun by Ray Hoekstra in 1970, International

Prison Ministry, based in Dallas, Texas, sends *BIBLES and evangelistic literature to prison inmates in the Caribbean, the United States, Mexico, and the Philippines. The organization also publishes a bimonthly magazine, *Prison Evangelism,* and produces a daily radio broadcast.

International School of Theology. *See* **Campus Crusade for Christ International.**

Internet Revival The Internet Revival began January 22, 1995, when two students from Howard Payne University, a Southern Baptist school, attended a service at the Coggin Avenue Baptist Church in Brownwood, Texas. They publicly confessed to spiritual apathy and complacency, and in the ensuing weeks many others, including students, made similar confessions. *REVIVAL meetings were held on the Howard Payne campus on January 26 and again from February 13 to 15, with many students offering public confessions of *SIN.

On March 1, 1995, John Avant, pastor of the Coggin Avenue Baptist Church, preached at Southwestern Baptist Theological Seminary in Fort Worth, Texas, triggering a seven-hour service of prayer and confession at the largest Protestant seminary in the world. The *REVIVAL spread to other Southern Baptist schools, including *CRISWELL COLLEGE and *SAMFORD UNIVERSITY. On the evening of March 19, a *REVIVAL meeting at *WHEATON COLLEGE lasted from 7:30 until 6:00 the next morning, thereby providing an unprecedented link between students at Southern Baptist schools and those at a northern evangelical campus. The *REVIVAL then spread to other Christian colleges, including Trinity, Greenville, Taylor, Gordon, Eastern Nazarene, Northwestern and Bethel (both in Minnesota), and Biola. Confessions of sin included many instances of sexual indiscretions, but some participants also filled garbage bags with alcohol, drugs, pornography, and compact disks with music regarded as "degrading."

Just as intelligence about the *PRAYER MEETING REVIVAL of 1857 spread from city to city across the telegraph wires, news about the *REVIVAL at Howard Payne spread by word of mouth and by e-mail, thereby giving rise to the moniker Internet Revival. In addition, the visits of students to other campuses called to mind, as an article in *Christian Century* pointed out, the *CIRCUIT RIDERS of the nineteenth century.

Reference: Timothy E. Fulop and Stephen P. Shoemaker, "Campus Confessions," *Christian Century,* July 19–26, 1995.

InterVarsity Christian Fellowship InterVarsity Christian Fellowship emerged from the union of several campus chapters of evangelical organizations in Great Britain. The Cambridge Inter-Collegiate Christian Union, for example, was formed in 1877 and spread to other schools. The first annual InterVarsity conference was held in 1919 for the purpose of organizing and coordinating evangelistic and missionary activities at other schools.

The group expanded to Canada in 1928 and to the United States in 1941. InterVarsity continues to organize evangelical groups and to sponsor evangelistic events on campuses. In addition, it sponsors a triennial missionary conference, called *URBANA, at the University of Illinois, Champaign-Urbana.

References: C. Stacy Woods, *The Growth of a Work of God* (1978); Bruce L. Shelley, "The Rise of Evangelical Youth Movements," *Fides et Historia,* XVIII (1986).

Iowa Band A group of eleven young ministers, newly graduated from *ANDOVER THEOLOGICAL SEMINARY, went to the Territory of Iowa in 1843 as missionaries for the American Home Missionary Society. Their strategy was that each would found a church and that together they would establish a college. Each fulfilled his obligation, and Iowa College opened its doors in Davenport in November 1848. In 1859, the college moved west to Grinnell, Iowa, where it merged with the school there to form Grinnell College.

Reference: Ephraim Adams, *The Iowa Band* (1870).

Ironside, H(enry) A(llen) "Harry" (1876–1951) Born in Toronto into a *PLYMOUTH BRETHREN household, H. A. "Harry" Ironside was a self-educated man who read widely and published more than forty books in the course of his lifetime. After a religious *CONVERSION at age fourteen, Ironside became a *SALVATION ARMY officer, served several posts in California, and became known as "the boy preacher from Los Angeles." He joined the *PLYMOUTH BRETHREN in 1896 and began preaching and teaching throughout the country. In 1930, he accepted the pulpit at *MOODY MEMORIAL CHURCH in Chicago, where he remained until 1948. His lively preaching and his deft expositions of the *BIBLE, which were laced with *DISPENSATIONALISM, made him enormously popular with fundamentalists.

References: Harry A. Ironside, *The Lamp of Prophecy: or, Signs of the Times* (1951); Ernest R. Sandeen, *The Roots of Fundamentalism: British and American Millenarianism, 1800–1930* (1970).

Irwin, B(enjamin) H(ardin) (1854–?) Born near Mercer, Missouri, B. H. Irwin moved to Tecumseh, Nebraska, at the age of nine, where, as a young adult, he practiced law. Irwin experienced a rather dramatic *CONVERSION in 1879, whereupon he became affiliated with and later pastored the Mount Zion Baptist Church. Through the influence of members of the Iowa Holiness Association, Irwin learned the doctrine of *SANCTIFICATION and received it in 1891. He resigned from the Baptist church and became affiliated with the *WESLEYAN METHODIST CHURCH, because of its holiness sympathies. Influenced by the writings of *JOHN FLETCHER, one of the early British converts to *METHODISM, Irwin latched onto the notion of still another spiritual *BAPTISM, "the *BAPTISM of burning love," which came to be known as "fire-baptism."

Irwin became an itinerant preacher throughout the Midwest and published an account of his own fire-baptism, which occurred at Enid, Oklahoma, on October 23, 1895. Irwin organized local fire-baptized holiness associations, left the *WESLEYAN METHODIST CHURCH in 1896, and began to preach divine healing in addition to the other holiness teachings. He formed a national organization in 1898, the *FIRE-BAPTIZED HOLINESS ASSOCIATION, at Anderson, North Carolina, an organization that included groups as far west as Kansas and Oklahoma and as far north as Ontario and Manitoba. Irwin was named general overseer for life, but his ecclesiastical career was cut short when the *Pentecostal Herald* reported in 1900 that Irwin had been seen drunk and smoking a cigar on a street in Omaha. Irwin divorced his wife shortly thereafter and married a younger woman. He left the *FIRE-BAPTIZED HOLINESS ASSOCIATION, resurfaced briefly in 1907 in pentecostal missions in San Francisco and Oakland, but then disappeared from sight.

Italian Christian Church. *See* **Christian Church of North America.**

Itinerancy Itinerant preachers have been an important presence in American religious history, especially in American *EVANGELICALISM. Itinerants would travel from place to place and gather congregations of the faithful and the curious in churches, in barns, in open fields, and, later, in stadiums. Although itinerants such as *GUILIAM BERTHOLF and *ANDREW CROSSWELL were active at the turn of the eighteenth century, itinerancy became more and more common during the *GREAT AWAKENING of the 1730s and 1740s. A large contingent of itinerant preachers, led by the "grand itinerant," *GEORGE WHITEFIELD, took their message of evangelical regeneration throughout the Atlantic colonies.

In the eighteenth century and beyond, the settled clergy (those with regular ecclesiastical appointments) have often looked askance at itinerants because of their enthusiasms but also in no small measure because the itinerants attacked the settled clergy for resisting the evangelical *GOSPEL. The most famous such attack was *GILBERT TENNENT's sermon of 1740, "The Danger of an Unconverted Ministry," in which he upbraided the settled clergy for their resistance to *REVIVAL.

Throughout American history, itinerants have adopted various means for propagating the *GOSPEL. In the early nineteenth century, they were the *CIRCUIT RIDERS of the frontier, and later in the century itinerancy took the form of *COLPORTEURS traveling the rail lines. In the twentieth century, itinerant preachers have taken to the road in automobiles and travel trailers or in large stadium "crusades," the trademark of *BILLY GRAHAM and a host of other *EVANGELISTS. In a sense, however, the alacrity with which *EVANGELISTS have exploited the electronic media suggests that evangelicals have solved forever the problem of itinerancy: The use of radio and television allows the itinerant preacher to be everywhere at once.

References: Timothy D. Hall, *Contested Boundaries: Itinerancy and the Reshaping of the Colonial American Religious World* (1994); Harry S. Stout, *The Divine Dramatist: George Whitefield and the Rise of Modern Evangelicalism* (1991).

■ ■ ■

Jack Van Impe Crusades, Inc. *See* **Van Impe, Jack (Leo).**

Jackson, Sheldon (1834–1909) After graduating from Princeton Theological Seminary in 1858, Sheldon Jackson was rejected for foreign missionary service because he was deemed to be too sickly. He turned his attentions to home missions instead, beginning with a post at Spencer Academy, a mission school among the Choctaw Indians. A bout with malaria ended his service there, but Jackson headed to Minnesota and accepted a commission from the Presbyterian Board of Domestic Missions; over the ensuing decade he organized twenty-three churches, recruited pastors, and raised money for their financial support. On April 29, 1869, Jackson—together with Thomas H. Cleland and John C. Elliott—conducted a prayer meeting near Sioux City, Iowa, in the course of which they dedicated themselves to the task of evangelizing the West. Shortly thereafter, Jackson was commissioned to serve as "superintendent of missions for Western Iowa, Nebraska, Dakota, Idaho, Montana, Wyoming, and Utah, or as far as our jurisdiction extends."

Jackson rose to the challenge. Crisscrossing the West, he established churches, many of them in mining camps, initiated mission work among Native Americans, founded the *Rocky Mountain Presbyterian,* and even tried to challenge the Mormon empire by organizing Westminster College in Utah. Even larger challenges lay to the North. In 1877, ten years after the United States purchased Alaska from Russia, Jackson started Presbyterian churches and missions in the new territory. On his trips back east, he raised money from the churches and lobbied Congress for money to establish schools for the native population. Jackson accepted a civil appointment as general agent of education in Alaska in 1885, all the while maintaining his missionary responsibilities.

References: Hermann N. Morse, "Sheldon Jackson (1834–1909): Christ's Fool and Seward's Folly," in *Sons of the Prophets: Leaders in Protestantism from Princeton Seminary,* ed. Hugh T. Kerr (1963); Norman J. Bender, *Winning the West for Christ: Sheldon Jackson and Presbyterianism on the Rocky Mountain Frontier, 1869–1880* (1996).

Jackson Male Academy. *See* **Union University.**

JAF Ministries. *See* **Tada, Joni Eareckson.**

Jaffray School of Missions. *See* **Nyack College and Alliance Theological Seminary.**

Jakes, T(homas) D(exter) (1957–) A native of West Virginia, T. D. Jakes began his preaching career in the coalfields and environs and began to attract a following. In 1991, he moved his congregation, Greater Emanuel Temple of Faith, from Montgomery to Charleston, West Virginia, where he also served as diocesan bishop in the Higher Ground Always Abounding Assemblies. Jakes began directing his message to women during his pastorate there, developing his "Woman, Thou Art Loosed" conferences, which led to a best-selling book by the same title. He relocated to Dallas, Texas, in 1996 and founded a church he called The Potter's House, which quickly grew into a megachurch; by 2000, the church boasted more than twenty-three hundred worshipers a week, including such local stars as Emmitt Smith and Deion Sanders of the Dallas Cowboys.

Jakes, an African American, preaches a message of healing and reconciliation and the importance of self-esteem. He also advocates some variant of *PROSPERITY THEOLOGY. "When I moved to Dallas, I bought the biggest house I could afford," he declared. "I don't live in a mobile home. There's nothing wrong with being blessed and successful." He is host of a weekly television program, *Get Ready with T. D. Jakes,* which airs over the *TRINITY BROADCASTING NETWORK. In July 1999, he conducted a conference for women in Atlanta, which attracted more than eighty-four thousand people.

References: T. D. Jakes, *Woman, Thou Art Loosed* (1993); idem, *Lay Aside the Weight* (1997); idem, *The Lady, Her Lover, and Her Lord* (1998); Jim Jones, "Swift Growth Shapes Potter's House," *Christianity Today,* January 12, 1998; Lauren F. Winner, "T. D. Jakes Feels Your Pain," *Christianity Today,* February 7, 2000.

James Robison Evangelistic Association. *See* **Robison, James.**

Jarratt, Devereux (1733–1801) Born in Virginia and orphaned at an early age, Devereux Jarratt was reared a nominal Anglican. His evangelical *CONVERSION came under the influence of a Presbyterian minister, however, and he decided to seek ordination. Although attracted to the Presbyterians because of his *CONVERSION, Jarratt finally opted for the Church of England because the two men he admired most, *JOHN WESLEY and *GEORGE WHITEFIELD, both were Anglicans. Jarratt traveled to England and was ordained a deacon by the bishop of London in 1762 and then as priest the following year.

Upon returning to Virginia in 1763, Jarratt assumed the rectorship of Bath parish in Dinwiddie County, a post he held until his death thirty-eight years later. In addition to his parish duties, Jarratt itinerated throughout Virginia and North Carolina, preaching and organizing religious societies. His cooperation with other *NEW LIGHTS, Presbyterians as well as Methodists, helped to trigger a *REVIVAL in 1775–1776, but also earned Jarratt the suspicion and even the enmity of some fellow Anglicans. They derided his enthusiastic preaching and his calls for heartfelt religion and strict morality; Jarratt, in turn, criticized the tepid homilies emanating from "velvet-mouthed" Anglican ministers. The organization of the Methodist Episcopal Church in 1784 dashed Jarratt's hopes that evangelical and revivalist impulses might eventually prevail within the Episcopal (Anglican) Church. Jarratt, who remained with the Episcopal Church, occasionally cooperated with Methodist *EVANGELISTS, but he was disappointed at what he regarded as their defection.

Reference: Devereux Jarratt, *The Life of the Reverend Devereux Jarratt* (1806).

Jars of Clay Although many critics characterize *CONTEMPORARY CHRISTIAN MUSIC as bland, Jars of Clay, a Nashville-based "Christian alternative" band, has proven able to hold its own in the mainstream market. The group, whose name comes from a passage in 2 Corinthians 4:7, was formed by three undergraduate students at *GREENVILLE COLLEGE in Greenville, Illinois. Soon after singer Dan Haseltine teamed up with keyboardist Charlie Lowell and bass guitar player Steve Mason, however, the three were joined by a friend of Lowell's, Matt Odmark, who became the group's guitarist. Their rise to fame was meteoric; the demo tape the students sent out to recording companies brought a barrage of phone calls to the pay phone in their dormitory.

Jars of Clay signed with Essential Records and released a self-titled debut album. *Jars of Clay,* which also was distributed on Silvertone Records, sold more than half a million copies and held its place at number one on *Billboard*'s Contemporary Christian chart for twelve weeks, eventually ascending to double-platinum status. More surprisingly, "Flood," the first single, was released to Christian stations, received good play in the college market, and climbed to number twelve on *Billboard*'s Modern Rock chart—which put the band in the company of Christian pop diva *AMY GRANT as one of the few successful "crossover" acts.

In the fall of 1996, Jars of Clay performed on Conan O'Brian's *Late Night* television show. That year the group also received critical praise when they played as an opening band for former Police member Sting. Their music was included in the soundtrack to *The Long Kiss Goodnight,* an action movie starring Geena Davis and Samuel Jackson, and in such other motion pictures as *Prince of Egypt*.

In a manner somewhat unusual for Christian artists, however, the members of Jars of Clay have been relatively quiet about their faith commitments, which some people suggest has helped rocket the band to success. The amount of positive response from critics across the United States supports the view that the band's penetration of the mainstream market is due to the excellence of its music. These four evangelical musicians, who have combined innovative arrangements with intelligent lyrics, have become formidable rivals to secular artists.

References: Paul O'Donnell, "Rock of Ages," *New Republic,* November 18, 1996; Randall Balmer, *Mine Eyes Have Seen the Glory: A Journey into the Evangelical Subculture in America,* 3d ed. (2000).

Jenkins, Leroy (1935–) In May 1960, Leroy Jenkins, a Presbyterian businessman in Atlanta, had his nearly severed arm healed by *A. A. ALLEN. Jenkins claimed that he had been running from God up to that point, but his healing was followed by a call from heaven: "There is somebody up here that loves you." He procured the ten-thousand-seat tent that had been used by the late *JACK COE and launched an independent ministry. Initially it flourished, winning the approval of many pentecostals, but Jenkins also earned a reputation for erratic behavior. He quarreled with his associates, divorced his wife, and was arrested several times on matters related to drugs and alcohol. Authorities in the Bahamas detained him in 1964 as an "undesirable person."

In the 1970s, he settled in Columbus, Ohio, at the Ohio Theater. He called his congregation the Church of What's Happening Now and declared that it was controlled by a four-person board: "the Father, the Son, the Holy Spirit, and me." He expanded into radio and television and published a quarterly magazine, *Revival of America.* In 1977, still dogged by controversy, Jenkins moved his ministry to his hometown of Greenwood, South Carolina, where he started the Spirit of Truth Church. After fire destroyed some highly insured church property, an investigation ensued, leading to Jenkins's conviction of conspiracy to commit arson and conspiracy to injure a local newspaper reporter. He served three years of a twelve-year sentence, earning a work release in 1982. In 1985, when he was officially paroled, Jenkins again tried to resume his healing and broadcast ministry, this time in Anderson, South Carolina, but his audience had dwindled.

References: Leroy Jenkins, *God Gave Me a Miracle Arm* (1963); idem, *How You Can Receive Your Healing* (1966); David Edwin Harrell Jr., *All Things Are Possible: The Healing and Charismatic Revivals in Modern America* (1975).

Jessup, J. Charles (1916–1993) A pentecostal faith healer who ran afoul of federal authorities, J. Charles Jessup was born in Gulfport, Mississippi, to a pentecostal preacher and his wife. Jessup began preaching on street corners at the age of twelve, and he conducted a *REVIVAL in Dyersburg, Tennessee, at fourteen. Jessup prayed for—and received—the gift of healing, and soon he purchased a large tent from the Ringling Brothers, which he used for his itinerant preaching.

Jessup struck a deal in 1942 with a tiny radio station in Ciudad Acuña, Mexico, just across the border from Del Rio, Texas. The signal was five times more powerful than the FCC allowed in the United States, so Jessup's program could be heard from Canada to Latin America. Billing himself as "the most preachable preacher that ever preached preachable preaching," Jessup parlayed the broadcast into a powerful engine for fund-raising, expanding his network to other stations in the United States and Mexico.

Although he claimed to take only seventy-five dollars a week in salary from his Fellowship Revival Association, Jessup lived the high life, with an expensive house, several Cadillacs, and a seaplane. He also indulged his hobby of cockfighting, and he had at least four wives at various times. The Internal Revenue Service investigated him several times, but he was finally caught by the United States Postal Inspection Service, which led to his indictment on eleven counts of mail fraud in 1964. Jessup pleaded no contest to two charges and was sentenced to a year in prison on December 18, 1968. He served the sentence, but he never preached again.

Reference: Peter J. Boyer, "Miracle Man," *New Yorker*, April 12, 1999.

Jesus Christ Light and Power Company. *See* **Lindsey, Hal.**

Jesus Freaks. *See* **Jesus Movement.**

Jesus Loves Me. *See* **Warner, Anna.**

Jesus Movement In the wake of the counterculture movement in the late 1960s, a number of young people, some of them dropouts from student radicalism and others former drug users, became part of a resurgence of Christianity known as the Jesus movement. The origins of the Jesus movement are difficult to place, but it almost certainly began in California, and one of the most important early leaders was *LONNIE FRISBEE, who connected with *CHUCK SMITH and *CALVARY CHAPEL in Orange County, California. Individuals who became associated with the burgeoning movement, which enjoyed a fertile harvest at Huntington Beach and other beaches in southern California, became known as Jesus Freaks or Jesus People. They were characterized by informal worship, a predilection to maintaining their "hippie" appearance—long hair, beards, casual clothes—and a simple understanding of Christianity that was heavily laced with *APOCALYPTICISM. Jesus People greeted one another with a raised index finger—which signified "one way"—as opposed to the two fingers of the peace sign within the counterculture. Another characteristic of the Jesus movement was its music, some of it rock but more often a kind of sweet, meditative music that was marketed successfully by *MARANATHA! MUSIC. In time, most of those associated with the Jesus movement found their way into mainstream evangelicalism.

References: Robert S. Ellwood, *One Way: The Jesus Movement and Its Meaning* (1973); Steven M. Tipton, *Getting Saved from the Sixties: Moral Meaning in Conversion and Cultural Change* (1982).

Jesus People. *See* **Jesus Movement.**

Jesus People Army. *See* **Meissner, Linda.**

Jewett, Paul K(ing) (1919–1991) Paul K. Jewett, an evangelical theologian, was born in Johnson City, New York, and earned degrees from *WHEATON COLLEGE, *WESTMINSTER THEOLOGICAL SEMINARY, and Harvard University. He was ordained a Presbyterian minister in 1956 and taught at *GORDON DIVINITY SCHOOL from 1950 until 1955, when he moved to *FULLER THEOLOGICAL SEMINARY. His early work was on theologian Emil Brunner, but Jewett's later writings provided a biblical and theological foundation for equality between the sexes.

References: Paul K. Jewett, *Emil Brunner* (1961); idem, *Man as Male and Female: A Study in Sexual*

Relationships from a Theological Point of View (1973); idem, *The Ordination of Women: An Essay on the Office of Christian Ministry* (1980).

Jewish Voice Broadcasts Based in Phoenix, Jewish Voice Broadcasts is an evangelistic outreach to Jews. The organization, founded in 1967 by Louis Kaplan, seeks the *CONVERSION of Jews to Christianity. It publishes *Jewish Prophetic Voice Magazine* and broadcasts a fifteen-minute daily radio program as well as a weekly television program.

Jews for Jesus Incorporated in 1974 by *MOISHE ROSEN, a career missionary with the American Board of Missions to the Jews, Jews for Jesus seeks the *CONVERSION of Jews to evangelical Christianity, although the organization bills itself as promoting "fulfilled Judaism." The fulfillment of Judaism, they argue, lies in the recognition on the part of Jews that Jesus is indeed the messiah. Jews for Jesus has met with vigorous opposition from Jewish leaders, who insist that the organization is merely a front for proselytization and that the claims of converts—namely, that they are still practicing Jews—are disingenuous.

Reference: Moishe Rosen, with William Proctor, *Jews for Jesus* (1974).

John Ankerberg Theological Research Institute. *See* **Ankerberg, John.**

John Birch Society Founded by *ROBERT WELCH and eleven other businessmen in 1958, the John Birch Society is named for a Baptist missionary to China who was killed by the communist regime at the end of World War II. The ultraconservative organization, based in Appleton, Wisconsin, professes to uphold traditional moral values and the Judeo-Christian tradition, but it is best known for its persistent warnings about a communist conspiracy, which is manifest in everything from the United Nations to *RONALD REAGAN. The John Birch Society publishes a biweekly newsmagazine, *New American.*

John Brown University (West Siloam Springs, Arkansas) John Brown University was first known as Southwestern Collegiate Institute, founded in 1919 by John E. Brown, one of the first *EVANGELISTS to use radio broadcasting. Brown sought to give students a balance between academic work, Christian commitment, and practical training—encapsulated in the motto, "Head, Heart, and Hand." Bachelor's degree programs were introduced in 1934, and the school was renamed John Brown University. The college added a master's degree program in counseling in 1995. John Brown University has always been nondenominational. The library has special collections on John E. Brown and another radio evangelist, *J. VERNON MCGEE.

References: *John Brown University 1995–1997 Catalog* (1995); William C. Ringenberg, *The Christian College: A History of Protestant Higher Education in America* (1984).

John Guest Evangelistic Team. *See* **Guest, John.**

Johnson, Harold K(eith) (1912–) A native of North Dakota, Harold K. Johnson was baptized as an Episcopalian and reared as a Methodist. The future chief of staff of the army graduated from the United States Military Academy in 1931, and his fervent evangelical faith was formed during World War II and the Korean War. In the late 1950s, he became active in a military organization called

Protestant Men of the Chapel. After his appointment as army chief of staff in 1964, Johnson became a regular on the evangelical *PRAYER BREAKFAST circuit. "God is the soldier's refuge," he declared. "God is the soldier's strength. God must be the soldier's constant companion." In his official capacity, Johnson sought to curb the use of foul language and barracks humor in the army training schools, and he supported moral and religious instruction within the armed forces.

Reference: Ann C. Loveland, *American Evangelicals and the U.S. Military, 1942–1993* (1996).

Johnson, Phillip E. (1940–) Phillip E. Johnson grew up in Aurora, Illinois, and graduated from Harvard University and from the University of Chicago Law School. He clerked for the chief justice of the California Supreme Court and then became clerk for Earl Warren, chief justice of the U.S. Supreme Court. He accepted a faculty position at Boalt Hall, the law school of the University of California, Berkeley. In the midst of a personal crisis, prompted by his wife's decision to leave the marriage, Johnson, a lifelong agnostic, became enamored of the possibility of belief, especially evangelical belief. He was converted and soon thereafter embarked on an intellectual quest that would take him far afield from the law.

While on sabbatical in England in 1987, Johnson began reading the works of several evolutionists, beginning with *The Blind Watchmaker,* by Richard Dawkins. Johnson took issue with the materialist and naturalistic assumptions that guided their work and concluded that evolutionary theory was the naturalists' "creation myth." He published *Darwin on Trial* and took part in numerous debates with scientists, challenging the fossil record as well as the philosophical assumptions that evolutionists bring to their work. When pressed to present his views of creation, however, Johnson defends the notion of "intelligent design" but refuses to be specific, a position that puts him at odds with the so-called "scientific creationists," who embrace the Genesis account of creation literally. Johnson sees himself engaged in a crusade to topple not only Darwinism but also the other two materialist theorists whose work so shaped rational discourse in the twentieth century: Karl Marx and Sigmund Freud.

References: Phillip E. Johnson, *Darwin on Trial* (1993); idem, *Reason in the Balance: The Case Against Naturalism in Science, Law, and Religion* (1995); idem, *Defeating Darwinism by Opening Minds* (1997); Tim Stafford, "The Making of a Revolution," *Christianity Today,* December 8, 1997; *"In the Beginning": The Creationist Controversy,* two-part PBS documentary (1994).

Johnson, Sherrod C. (1899–1961) Born to sharecroppers in Pine Tree Corner, North Carolina, Sherrod C. Johnson used his skills as a musician and a preacher to escape boyhood poverty. After his pentecostal preaching attracted a modest following to his home in Philadelphia, he hooked up with Robert Clarence Johnson, founder of the Church of Our Lord Jesus Christ of the Apostolic Faith. By 1930, however, Sherrod struck out on his own and opened a storefront church with a slightly different name, the Church of the Lord Jesus Christ of the Apostolic Faith. Johnson's message in many ways echoed that of other African American religious leaders of the era, emphasizing the importance of probity, especially as it related to women. Johnson warned against the observance of "pagan" holidays such as Easter and Christmas and taught his followers to abstain from tobacco, alcohol, and "*WORLDLINESS" in various forms, including television and motion pictures.

He demanded that women wear ankle-length dresses and opaque cotton stockings, although, unlike other preachers of the era, he allowed jewelry and cosmetics. During the Great Depression, Johnson began a radio program, *The Whole Truth*, which eventually enlarged his ministry to other states and abroad to places as diverse as Haiti, the Bahamas, Great Britain, Portugal, and the Maldives.

References: Sherrod C. Johnson, *The Christmas Spirit Is a False Spirit* (n.d.); idem, *False Lent and Pagan Festivals* (n.d.); idem, *Let Patience Have Her Perfect Work* (1964).

Johnson, Torrey (1909–) Torrey Johnson, an alumnus of *WHEATON COLLEGE and Northern Baptist Theological Seminary, became pastor of Chicago's Midwest Bible Church in 1933 and used that platform to become a leader of *EVANGELICALISM. His radio program, *Songs in the Night*, aired over WCFL and later over WMBI, the flagship station of *MOODY BIBLE INSTITUTE. Johnson passed the program on to *BILLY GRAHAM in 1943, and the next year Johnson began conducting youth rallies that eventually became *YOUTH FOR CHRIST, INTERNATIONAL. When the organization was formally constituted in 1945, Johnson was elected the first president, and he proceeded to hire Graham as a traveling *EVANGELIST. Johnson ceded leadership of *YOUTH FOR CHRIST to *ROBERT COOK in 1948. In 1953, he resigned the pulpit at Midwest Bible Church to become an itinerant *EVANGELIST, and from 1968 to 1983 Johnson headed *BIBLETOWN CONFERENCE CENTER in Boca Raton, Florida.

Jones, Charles Colcock (1804–1863) Born in Georgia but educated in the North at Philips Academy, *ANDOVER SEMINARY, and Princeton Seminary, Charles Colcock Jones returned to the South as pastor of the First Presbyterian Church in Savannah in 1831. He left that post the following year in order to devote his energies to the religious instruction of slaves. Although he was well versed in both the theological rationale and the activist strategies of *ABOLITIONISM, Jones vigorously lent a theological defense to the "peculiar institution" of slavery, arguing that Christianity would teach discipline to the slaves and eventually make them worthy of civilization and emancipation. He published several works to assist in the religious instruction of the slaves, and he formed the Association for the Religious Instruction of the Negro.

Jones's prominence as "Apostle to the Blacks" led to his appointment as professor of ecclesiastical history at *COLUMBIA THEOLOGICAL SEMINARY. In 1850, as the sectional crisis was building, Jones was elected to the office of corresponding secretary to the Board of Domestic Missions of the Presbyterian Church, where he sought to ease the tensions between North and South within the denomination. Ill health, however, forced his return to the South from Philadelphia in 1853, where he remained until his death a decade later.

References: Charles Colcock Jones, *A Catechism for Colored Persons* (1834); idem, *Suggestions on the Religious Instruction of the Negroes in Southern States* (1847); Donald G. Mathews, "Charles Colcock Jones and the Southern Evangelical Crusade to Form a Biracial Community," *Journal of Southern History*, XL (August 1975).

Jones, Charles Price (1865–1949) Charles Price Jones was reared as a Baptist and graduated from Arkansas Baptist College in 1891, whereupon he assumed the pastorate of a Baptist church in Searcy, Arkansas, and then Selma, Alabama. While in Selma, Jones encountered holiness teachings; he had his own experience of *SANCTIFICATION in 1894 and began preaching holiness doctrines to his new church, Mt. Helm Baptist Church, in Jackson, Mississippi. Jones published a small book, *The Work of the Holy Spirit in the Churches,* to propagate these beliefs, but they were viewed askance by Baptist officials. By 1902, Jones had left the Jackson Missionary Baptist Association, the National Baptist Convention, and his own congregation, the Mt. Helm Baptist Church, to form the Christ Temple Church.

After an affiliation with *C. H. MASON and the *CHURCH OF GOD, Jones founded the Church of Christ (Holiness) U.S.A. in 1909 because of his disapproval of Mason's move into *PENTECOSTALISM. Jones visited Los Angeles in 1915 to hold *REVIVAL meetings and chose to relocate there two years later. He started the Christ Temple Church of Los Angeles in 1917, where he remained for the rest of his life, all the while continuing his responsibilities as president (later, senior bishop) of the denomination. Jones also wrote many songs and hymns (over one thousand, all told), many of which were published in the *Jesus Only Standard Hymnal.*

Reference: Charles Price Jones, *His Fullness* (1913).

Jones, Clarence W. (1900–1986) Clarence W. Jones graduated from *MOODY BIBLE INSTITUTE in 1921, whereupon he became an assistant to *PAUL RADER at the Chicago Gospel Tabernacle. He helped Rader establish his presence on the radio and in 1928 went to South America in search of a site for a missionary radio station. Jones's initial efforts were unavailing, but his collaboration with Reuben Larson eventually secured a license from the government of Ecuador; the station, HCJB in Quito, Ecuador, began broadcasting on Christmas Day, 1931. A major donation from evangelical philanthropist Robert G. LeTourneau in 1940 provided for the construction of a ten-thousand-watt transmitter, making the station one of the largest and most powerful evangelical voices in the world at that time.

Jones, E(li) Stanley (1884–1973) Born in Clarksville, Maryland, E. Stanley Jones was converted to evangelical Christianity at the age of seventeen, under the preaching of Robert J. Bateman. He decided to enter the ministry and enrolled at *ASBURY COLLEGE in Wilmore, Kentucky, where he imbibed holiness teachings and Wesleyan theology. After graduation in 1907, Jones considered several offers but decided to accept the call to go to India under the auspices of the Mission Board of Northern Methodism, rather than his own Methodist Episcopal Church, South.

Jones arrived in Bombay, India, in November 1907 and enjoyed success as pastor of the Lal Bagh Church in Lucknow. After four years he moved to Sitphar, and he gradually assumed more and more responsibility for Methodist missions in India. After a furlough because of physical and mental exhaustion, Jones returned in 1918 eager to continue his work, although he became less and less sectarian in his presentation of Christianity. His theology did not fit easily into standard categories of liberal and conservative, and he described himself as a man with a modernist mind and a fundamentalist soul. Jones itinerated widely throughout India, seeking to engage members of the intelligentsia in "Round Table" discussions of Christianity; among his acquaintances was Mohandas Gandhi, who greatly impressed the missionary.

In 1930, Jones adapted an Indian form for his own use, establishing a Christian ashram, Sat Tal (Seven Lakes), in the foothills of the Himalayas. Jones found both the setting and the communal lifestyle congenial to study, contemplation, and spiritual renewal. Although he was elected bishop at the Methodist General Conference in 1928, Jones resigned, preferring to remain a roving ambassador for ecumenism, peace, racial understanding, and Gandhian nonviolence.

References: E. Stanley Jones, *The Christ of the Indian Road* (1925); idem, *Christ and Human Suffering* (1933); idem, *The Choice Before Us* (1937); idem, *Mahatma Gandhi: An Interpretation* (1948); idem, *Conversion* (1959); idem, *A Song of Ascents* (1968); Violet Paranjoti, *An Evangelist on the Indian Scene: Dr. E. Stanley Jones* (1970); Daniel Swinson, s.v. "E. Stanley Jones," in Charles H. Lippy, ed., *Twentieth-Century Shapers of American Popular Religion* (1989).

Jones, Howard (Owen) (1922–) In 1957, Howard Jones became the first African American to join *BILLY GRAHAM's crusade team. He had been a jazz musician with aspirations of playing with Duke Ellington and Count Basie, but after his graduation from *NYACK COLLEGE he became pastor of the Bethany Alliance Church in Harlem, where he became acquainted with *JACK WYRTZEN, founder of the *WORD OF LIFE organization. Jones moved to Cleveland in 1952 as pastor of Smoot Memorial Alliance Church, and during his tenure the church sent recordings of their worship services to Africa for broadcast throughout much of the continent. The favorable response prompted Jones to undertake a three-month preaching tour of Ghana, Nigeria, and Liberia. His evangelistic successes in Africa, in turn, led to an invitation from Graham to join his organization as an associate *EVANGELIST. In addition to his evangelistic work, Jones served as the first president of the *NATIONAL BLACK EVANGELICAL ASSOCIATION, and he became the first African American named to the *NATIONAL RELIGIOUS BROADCASTERS' hall of fame. Jones remained with the *BILLY GRAHAM EVANGELISTIC ASSOCIATION until his retirement in 1994.

Reference: Edward Gilbreath, "The 'Jackie Robinson' of Evangelism," *Christianity Today*, February 9, 1998.

Jones, Robert R., Jr. "Bob" (1911–1997) Bob Jones Jr. graduated from *BOB JONES COLLEGE in 1930 and earned the master's degree from the University of Pittsburgh two years later. He became acting president of his father's school in 1932 and served as president from 1947 until 1971. An accomplished Shakespearean actor, Jones sought to make *BOB JONES UNIVERSITY into a center for Christian fine arts; the school's Art Gallery of Religious Paintings, for example, holds many important works.

Bob Jones Jr. shared his father's starchy *FUNDAMENTALISM, including his suspicion of *BILLY GRAHAM as a liberal. When Graham came to Greenville in 1966 to conduct one of his crusades, for example, Jones denied him access to the campus and denounced him in the pages of **CHRISTIANITY TODAY* as "doing more harm to the cause of Jesus Christ than any living man." When John Paul II visited South Carolina, Jones remarked that he would "as soon speak to the devil himself" as talk to the pope.

Jones also resisted the enforcement of antidiscrimination statutes at *BOB JONES UNIVERSITY in the late 1970s, specifically the school's policy of forbidding interracial dating. Jones defended the policy as "biblical," based on his interpretation of the Tower of Babel in the book of Genesis. God intended the races to be separate, Jones insisted, because God separated them into different races and languages at the Tower of Babel, lest humanity become enamored of its material accomplishments and thereby neglect its duty to God. Jones's stand prompted the revocation of the university's tax-exempt status, an action upheld by the U.S. Supreme Court in 1983. After learning of the eight-to-one decision against him, Jones preached in the university chapel: "We're in a bad fix when eight evil old men and one vain and foolish woman can speak a verdict on American liberties. Our nation from this day forward is no better than Russia insofar as expecting the blessings of God is concerned."

References: Bob Jones Jr., *Inspirational and Devotional Verse* (1946); idem, *Ancient Truth for Modern Days: Sermons on the Old Testament Subjects That Particularly Apply to Our Times* (1963); idem, *Old Testament Sermons* (1973); idem, *Cornbread and Caviar* (1985); Edward L. Queen II, s.v. "Bob Jones, Sr., Jr., and III," in Charles H. Lippy, ed., *Twentieth-Century Shapers of American Popular Religion* (1989).

Jones, Robert R., Sr. "Bob" (1883–1968) Born in Skipperville, Alabama, Bob Jones Sr. was a sickly boy, the eleventh and final child born to a former Confederate soldier and his wife. His father demanded that he memorize inspirational and patriotic passages and then recite them for the benefit of household visitors. This early exposure to public oratory paid off; at twelve, Jones spoke at a Populist Party rally, and he began speaking at Farmer's Alliance meetings. His real passion, however, was *EVANGELISM. Having been converted in a Methodist church, Jones preached a *REVIVAL at the age of twelve, and by the following year his brush arbor congregation numbered fifty-four. He was licensed to preach by the Alabama Conference of the Methodist Episcopal Church, South at age fifteen, and he became a *CIRCUIT RIDER the following year.

Orphaned at age seventeen, Jones matriculated at Southern University in Greensboro, Alabama, in December 1900 and supported himself by preaching weekends and during summer vacations. After two years of school, Jones became a full-time *EVANGELIST, itinerating throughout Alabama and the South. His marriage to Mary Gaston Stollenwerk provided him with a helpmeet and a collaborator for his *REVIVALS, which now extended beyond the South.

Jones's travels abated somewhat when he decided to start a school, named for himself, in 1926. Originally located at St. Andrews Bay, near Panama City, Florida, the school fell victim to the stock market crash of 1929. He reopened *BOB JONES COLLEGE in Cleveland, Tennessee, in 1933, where it remained until the need for more space prompted another relocation, this time to Greenville, South Carolina, in 1946, when the school assumed the name *BOB JONES UNIVERSITY. The school's creed trumpeted its commitment to "Christian religion and the ethics revealed in the Holy Scriptures; combating all atheistic, agnostic, pagan and so-called scientific adulteration of the *GOSPEL." It remained racially segregated until 1983, when it lost a case before the U.S. Supreme Court.

Jones was a fiery and combative fundamentalist who denounced communism and Roman Catholicism with equal fervor. He was active in the formation of both the *WORLD'S CHRISTIAN FUNDAMENTALS ASSOCIATION and the *AMERICAN COUNCIL OF CHRISTIAN CHURCHES, and he insisted upon separation from anything that smacked of *LIBERALISM or *MODERNISM. This *SEPARATISM led Jones into conflict with one of his former students, *BILLY GRAHAM; Jones never forgave Graham for enlisting the cooperation of New York City's Protestant

Council, which included some liberal clergy, for his Madison Square Garden crusade in 1957.

References: Bob Jones Sr., *The Modern Woman: A Sermon to Women* (1923); idem, *Comments on Here and Hereafter* (1942); idem, *Bob Jones' Revival Sermon* (1948); idem, *Bob Jones' Sermons* (1983); George Dollar, *A History of Fundamentalism in America* (1973); Edward L. Queen II, s.v. "Bob Jones, Sr., Jr., and III," in Charles H. Lippy, ed., *Twentieth-Century Shapers of American Popular Religion* (1989).

Jones, Robert R., 3d, "Bob" (1939–) Scion of the Bob Jones fundamentalist empire, Bob Jones 3d served in various capacities at ***BOB JONES UNIVERSITY**: dean of men, professor of speech, assistant to the president, and vice president. He succeeded his father, ***BOB JONES JR.**, as president of "The World's Most Unusual University" in 1971. In the spring of 2000, after a spate of bad publicity following George W. Bush's appearance on campus during the Republican presidential primaries, Jones finally rescinded the university's long-standing ban on interracial dating.

References: Bob Jones III, *A Sermon a Day Keeps the Devil Away* (1980); idem, *Biblical Answers to Bothersome Questions* (1981); Edward L. Queen II, s.v. "Bob Jones, Sr., Jr., and III," in Charles H. Lippy, ed., *Twentieth-Century Shapers of American Popular Religion* (1989).

Jones, Sam(uel) (Porter) (1847–1906) Born in Chambers County, Alabama, Sam Jones practiced law but soon fell into alcohol addiction. At his father's deathbed, he promised to forswear liquor; the younger Jones converted to evangelical Christianity in 1872 and was licensed to preach by the Methodist Episcopal Church, South. He served several pastorates between 1872 and 1880, whereupon he became agent of the North Georgia Conference Orphans' Home, in Decatur, Georgia.

As he itinerated more and more widely, Jones's extraordinary preaching skills became more widely known and appreciated. He roundly condemned alcohol, profanity, gambling, and violations of sabbatarianism. His folksy humor and liberal use of slang and sentimentality may have enraged critics, but they held enormous popular appeal. Jones's 1883 ***REVIVAL** campaign in Memphis captured a great deal of media attention, and when ***T. DEWITT TALMAGE** invited him to conduct ***REVIVAL** meetings at the Brooklyn Tabernacle in 1885, Jones made his first significant foray into the North, thereby expanding the geographical range of his peregrinations. He remained, however, strongly identified with his native region and known to many as "the Moody of the South." Jones numbered among his converts a riverboat captain named Thomas Greene Ryman, who would construct a Gospel Tabernacle in 1892, later known as the ***RYMAN AUDITORIUM** of ***GRAND OLE OPRY** fame.

Reference: Laura Jones, ed., *The Life and Sayings of Sam P. Jones* (1907).

Jordan, Clarence (1912–1969) Born in Talbotton, Georgia, Clarence Jordan "accepted Christ" at a ***REVIVAL** meeting at the age of ten and completed a degree in agriculture at the University of Georgia in 1933. While training for his ROTC commission, Jordan was reading the Sermon on the Mount and became a pacifist, resigning his commission in the middle of one of the drills. Choosing to become a licensed Baptist minister, Jordan continued his studies at Southern Baptist Theological Seminary, where he earned the Ph.D. in 1939. While in seminary, Jordan's social conscience was sharpened on such issues as racial equality and pacifism. He became director of the Sunshine Center in Louisville, a ministry to inner-city African Americans. In 1942, Jordan and Martin English founded a racially integrated community, called Koinonia Farm, on four hundred acres near Americus, Georgia. The farm taught local farmers improved farming techniques.

Koinonia (the Greek word for fellowship) prospered under Jordan's leadership until his progressive views on pacifism and racial integration collided with those of the local Baptist congregation. Jordan and his followers were expelled from Rehobeth Baptist Church in 1950, and Koinonia suffered from economic boycotts and occasional violence at the hands of the *KU KLUX KLAN in the years that followed. Beginning in the mid-1950s, Jordan turned his attentions to the production of his "Cotton Patch Version" of the New Testament, a paraphrase of the Scriptures into Southern vernacular. The *Cotton Patch Gospel* was published in four volumes from 1968 to 1973. In 1968, a year before his death, Jordan, with the collaboration of *MILLARD FULLER, reorganized Koinonia Farm as Koinonia Partners, whose activities include the provision of capital for low-income housing under a program called *HABITAT FOR HUMANITY.

References: Clarence Jordan, *The Substance of Faith and Other Cotton Patch Sermons* (1972); Joyce Hollyday, "The Legacy of Clarence Jordan," *Sojourners*, December 1979; Ann Coble, "Cotton Patch Justice, Cotton Patch Peace: The Sermon on the Mount in the Teachings and Practices of Clarence Jordan," *Prism*, September/October 1998.

Josh McDowell Ministry. *See* **McDowell, Josh.**

Joyful Journey. *See* **Women of Faith.**

Judd, Walter H(enry) (1898–1994) Born in Rising City, Nebraska, Walter H. Judd graduated from the University of Nebraska with a bachelor's degree in 1920 and with a medical degree in 1923. From 1924 until 1925, he was traveling secretary for the *STUDENT VOLUNTEER MOVEMENT and then became a medical missionary and hospital superintendent in China under the auspices of the *AMERICAN BOARD OF COMMISSIONERS FOR FOREIGN MISSIONS. He returned to the United States in 1938 and set up a private medical practice in Minneapolis, Minnesota. Judd won election to Congress as a Republican in 1942, and he remained in the House of Representatives until his defeat twenty years later. After leaving Congress, he was a contributing editor for *Reader's Digest* and a radio commentator on government and international relations.

References: Walter H. Judd, *Walter H. Judd: Chronicles of a Statesman* (1980); Lee Edwards, *Missionary for Freedom: The Life and Times of Walter Judd* (1990).

Judson, Adoniram (1788–1850) Adoniram Judson, born to a Congregationalist minister and his wife in Malden, Massachusetts, became America's first Baptist foreign missionary. He entered Brown University at the age of sixteen and graduated as valedictorian in 1807. After teaching for a time and an attempt to become a playwright, Judson enrolled at *ANDOVER THEOLOGICAL SEMINARY in 1808, where he embraced evangelical Christianity and dedicated himself to foreign missions. Judson and five Williams College alumni formed the *AMERICAN BOARD OF COMMISSIONERS FOR FOREIGN MISSIONS in 1812.

Within the space of a fortnight in February 1812, Judson was married, was ordained a Congregationalist minister, and set sail for Calcutta, India, as a foreign missionary. During the voyage Judson and his wife, *ANN HASSELTINE, became convinced of the Baptist practice of immersion. Such a "*CONVERSION" necessitated a break with the Congregationalists, who were supporting the mission, and an affiliation with the Baptists. American Baptists, responding to Judson's overtures as related by *LUTHER RICE, formed the *TRIENNIAL CONVENTION in 1814, later renamed the American Baptist Foreign Mission Society, to support the Judsons' missionary work in Asia. When the East India Company denied them residency in India, they continued on to Rangoon, Burma, where they succeeded in learning the language. Adoniram Judson erected a small hut (*zayat*) and claimed his first convert, Maung Nau, in 1819. He completed his translation of the *BIBLE into Burmese in 1834, and his *Dictionary, English and Burmese* was published in 1849.

Although two of his wives died and his missionary work was interrupted by a seventeen-month stint as a political prisoner, Judson was remarkably effective as an *EVANGELIST. After the death of his second wife, Judson returned briefly to the United States, where his travels helped to promote a missions' consciousness among Baptists in America.

References: Francis Wayland, *A Memoir of the Life and Labors of the Rev. Adoniram Judson, D.D.*, 2 vols. (1853); Courtney Anderson, *To the Golden Shore: The Life of Adoniram Judson* (1956).

Judson, Ann (Nancy) Hasseltine (1789–1826) Two weeks after her marriage to *ADONIRAM JUDSON, Ann Hasseltine Judson sailed for India with her husband under the auspices of the *AMERICAN BOARD OF COMMISSIONERS FOR FOREIGN MISSIONS. During the voyage they decided to become Baptists and were baptized by *WILLIAM CAREY upon their arrival in India. The Judsons, having been denied residency in India by the East India Company, continued on to Burma, where they learned the language and established a mission. Ann Hasseltine Judson did evangelistic work, taught children, and cared for adopted orphans; she translated the biblical books of Daniel, Jonah, and Matthew into Burmese and also wrote a Burmese catechism. Shortly after her husband's release from a seventeen-month incarceration as a political prisoner, Ann Judson died. Her history of the American Baptist mission in Burma, which she wrote in 1823, helped establish her reputation as a formidable missionary.

References: Cecil B. Hartley, *The Three Mrs. Judsons, the Celebrated Female Missionaries* (1863); William Henry Brackney, *The Baptists* (1988).

Judson, Emily Chubbock (1817–1854) Born to a poor family in Eaton, New York, Emily Chubbock attended Utica Female Seminary, where she also taught, beginning in 1841. Chubbock began her career as a writer that same year. She published a *SUNDAY SCHOOL book and wrote for the *New York Mirror* under the pseudonym Fanny Forester. On June 2, 1846, she became the third wife of *ADONIRAM JUDSON, the renowned Baptist missionary to Burma. Chubbock's age—she was twenty-nine years younger than her husband—raised some eyebrows, but the Judsons returned to Burma as missionaries a month after their marriage. In 1848, Emily Chubbock Judson published a memoir of Adoniram Judson's second wife, *SARAH HALL BOARDMAN JUDSON, a volume that became one of the most widely read missionary books of the era.

References: Emily Chubbock, *Charles Linn* (1841); idem, *Memoir of Sarah B. Judson* (1848);

Cecil B. Hartley, *The Three Mrs. Judsons, the Celebrated Female Missionaries* (1863); William Henry Brackney, *The Baptists* (1988).

Judson, Sarah Hall Boardman (1803–1845) Born in Alstead, New Hampshire, and reared in Salem, Massachusetts, Sarah Hall became interested in missionary service at an early age. After she composed a poem about the death of James Colman, a missionary to Burma, *GEORGE DANA BOARDMAN, who had been designated as Colman's successor, took an interest in Sarah Hall. The two were married in 1825 and sailed for India as missionaries the same year. Three years after her husband's death in 1831, Sarah Hall Boardman, who had remained on the mission field, became *ADONIRAM JUDSON's second wife. Sarah Judson organized schools, wrote several tracts, and translated *The Pilgrim's Progress* into Burmese. Following her death in 1845, her biography was written and published by *ADONIRAM JUDSON's third wife, *EMILY CHUBBOCK JUDSON.

References: Emily C. Judson, *Memoir of Sarah B. Judson* (1848); Cecil B. Hartley, *The Three Mrs. Judsons, the Celebrated Female Missionaries* (1863); William Henry Brackney, *The Baptists* (1988).

Judson College (Elgin, Illinois) Judson College was formally incorporated in 1963, but prior to its actual founding it operated for nearly forty years as the college division of Northern Baptist Theological Seminary. When the seminary portion of Northern Baptist moved from Chicago to Lombard in the early 1960s, the college broke off to become an independent entity. It was named after *ADONIRAM JUDSON, the nineteenth-century Baptist missionary to Burma. Judson is affiliated with the American Baptist Church.

The Judson library's special collections include the Edmonson Collection of Contemporary Christian Music recordings (one of the largest in the country), and the Donald G. Peterson Collection of Baptist History and Missions.

Reference: *Judson College Catalog 1996/1997* (1996).

Junaluska Affirmation On July 20, 1975, the board of directors of *GOOD NEWS, an evangelical advocacy group within the United Methodist Church, met at Lake Junaluska, North Carolina, and adopted "An Affirmation of Scriptural Christianity for United Methodists," also known as the Junaluska Affirmation. This statement of faith, grounded firmly in the Wesleyan tradition, affirmed such conservative doctrines as human depravity, the *AUTHORITY of the Bible, the necessity of *SANCTIFICATION, and the centrality of Christ in the *SALVATION process. In addition, the Junaluska Affirmation included a statement about the importance of social amelioration, noting that "faith without works is dead" and urging "unstinting devotion to deeds of kindness and mercy and a wholehearted participation in collective efforts to alleviate need and suffering."

Just By far the most common interjection in evangelical prayers is the word "just." "Lord, we just wanna thank you . . ."; "Lord, just be with us now." While there is no grammatical explanation for that interjection, it is certainly a consequence of the Protestant emphasis on spontaneity in prayer, eschewing liturgy and formalism.

■ ■ ■

Kaiser, Kurt Kurt Kaiser, a composer, arranger, and recording artist, studied at the American Conservatory of Music in

Chicago and earned two degrees from Northwestern University. He has appeared in concerts with George Beverly Shea and has recorded sixteen solo albums at the piano; his album *Psalms, Hymns, and Spiritual Songs* received a Dove Award. He joined Word, Inc. as director of artists and repertoire in 1959 and later became vice president and director of music.

Kaiser, Walter C(hristian), Jr. (1933–) An evangelical theologian and academic administrator, Walter C. Kaiser Jr. was born in Folcroft, Pennsylvania, and educated at *WHEATON COLLEGE and Brandeis University. After teaching at *WHEATON COLLEGE, Kaiser, an Old Testament scholar, joined the faculty of *TRINITY EVANGELICAL DIVINITY SCHOOL in 1966. Kaiser succeeded *KENNETH S. KANTZER as academic dean in 1980. Following a dispute with the faculty at Trinity, Kaiser moved to *GORDON-CONWELL THEOLOGICAL SEMINARY in 1993 as a distinguished professor; he became the seminary's president in 1997.

References: Walter C. Kaiser Jr., *The Old Testament in Contemporary Preaching* (1973); idem, *Toward an Old Testament Theology* (1977); idem, *Toward Old Testament Ethics* (1983); idem, *Hard Sayings of the Old Testament* (1988).

Kantzer, Kenneth S(ealer) (1917–) Kenneth S. Kantzer was born in Detroit and reared in a Lutheran household, although he considered himself an atheist in high school and "came to a firm faith in Christ" while a student in college. Kantzer was initially influenced by the writings of *C. S. LEWIS and Karl Barth, but he narrowly escaped what he would later consider the pitfall of *NEOORTHODOXY. "Other circumstances being different, humanly speaking," Kantzer said in a 1996 interview, "I could have become a follower of Karl Barth."

Kantzer studied at Ashland College, Ohio State University, and the ultrafundamentalist *FAITH THEOLOGICAL SEMINARY. He was ordained into the *EVANGELICAL FREE CHURCH OF AMERICA in 1948. Kantzer earned the doctorate from Harvard University and studied theology in Europe. He taught at *WHEATON COLLEGE and then became dean of *TRINITY EVANGELICAL DIVINITY SCHOOL until accepting the editorship of **CHRISTIANITY TODAY* in 1978, which he held until his official retirement in 1982. Throughout his career, Kantzer was a tireless proponent of biblical *INERRANCY, arguing that anyone who claims the term "evangelical" and yet fails to commit to the doctrine of *INERRANCY was an "inconsistent evangelical." On other matters—the ordination of women, for instance—Kantzer would often equivocate. He occasionally advanced somewhat liberal views and then quickly retracted them in the face of conservative opposition.

References: Kenneth S. Kantzer, *Evangelical Roots* (1978); idem, *Perspectives on Evangelical Theology* (1980); "Standing on the Promises," *Christianity Today*, September 16, 1996.

Karon, Jan (1937–) Jan Karon, reared a Methodist, experienced a religious *CONVERSION at the age of forty-two. She was, she explained in a 1997 interview, "driven to the wall by the circumstances and tragedy of life, being driven to the wall so that, at the end of myself, I could then cry out outside my ego, outside my own self-confidence and self-doing." After a career in advertising, Karon decided at age forty-nine to become a novelist. She moved to Blowing Rock, North Carolina, which she used as the mythical setting for her Mitford series of novels, featuring the gentle, kindly Episcopal rector, Timothy Kavanaugh. The Mitford novels portray an idyllic community where Christian values prevail. Reflecting on the popular success of the novels in the 1990s, Karon offered this explanation: "First of all, when people pick up a Mitford book, they discover *themselves,* their value system. Where else can people find their value system represented in today's world—can you find it in *Vogue* magazine, on *Roseanne,* watching Geraldo? No. What do you find on the bestseller list? Murder and mayhem. But when people go to Mitford, they go home. It's familiar, and it is consoling. And that's what I work to give my readers, the sense of consolation and hope."

References: Jan Karon, *At Home in Mitford* (1994); idem, *A Light in the Window* (1995); idem, *These High, Green Hills* (1996); idem, *Out to Canaan* (1997); Betty Smartt Carter, "Postmarked Mitford," *Christianity Today,* September 1, 1997.

Keillor, Garrison (1942–) One of the most perceptive and witty commentators about Midwestern life, Garrison Keillor was born to descendants of Scottish immigrants in Anoka County, Minnesota. Young Gary, as he was known, was reared in a *PLYMOUTH BRETHREN household, a religious group he would later refer to in his stories as the "Sanctified Brethren." Writing about the taciturn characters that populated his childhood, Keillor commented that his people "were Protestant fundamentalists, who lived by the Word and not by the opinion of others, and were wary of strangers, and didn't go in for small talk, period." Some of his characters in Lake Wobegon shared many of the same characteristics. "If strangers came to the door, they were dealt with and sent on their way," he noted. "They were not people of the Word, and their friendship meant nothing to us."

After graduating from the University of Minnesota, Keillor eventually caught on with the *New Yorker,* an affiliation he maintained until Tina Brown took over as editor. In the course of one of his assignments, a story on the *GRAND OLE OPRY's final performance in Nashville's fabled *RYMAN AUDITORIUM, Keillor hatched the idea of a live radio broadcast celebrating life in the small-town Midwest, a notion that evolved into *A Prairie Home Companion,* a two-hour live radio broadcast on Saturday nights.

The structure of *A Prairie Home Companion* resembles a Protestant church service, with an invocation, plenty of singing (including *GOSPEL MUSIC), announcements (faux advertisements), the sermon (Keillor's "News from Lake Wobegon"), and a benediction. Keillor draws upon the Protestant, evangelical values of his childhood, mixing them with deft characterizations and poignant observations. His novel about Lake Wobegon, *Lake Wobegon Days,* made Keillor the best-selling author of the 1980s.

References: Garrison Keillor, *Lake Wobegon Days* (1985); idem, "In Search of Lake Wobegon," *National Geographic,* December 2000; Michael Fedo, *The Man from Lake Wobegon* (1987); "Door Interviews Garrison Keillor," *The Door,* December-January 1985–1986.

Kellogg, John Harvey (1852–1943) A *SEVENTH-DAY ADVENTIST and a follower of *ELLEN GOULD WHITE's ideas about health, John Harvey Kellogg was born in Tyrone Township, Michigan. He earned the M.D. from the Bellevue Hospital Medical College in New York City with the support of White and her husband, James. In 1876, he was named superintendent of the Western Health Reform Institute in Battle Creek, Michigan, which he renamed the Battle Creek Sanatarium. Kellogg advocated "biologic living" and the importance of "natural medicine," such as vegetarianism, in order to maintain good health. In the 1890s, he set up a laboratory and devised a way to turn cooked grains into dry flakes, which became enormously popular as a breakfast cereal. Kellogg organized a medical missionary college in Chicago in 1895 for the training of Adventist physicians, and although Kellogg left the *SEVENTH-DAY ADVENTISTS in 1907, his lasting contribution to the American table was breakfast cereal, which was mass-produced and marketed under the direction of his brother, Willie Keith Kellogg.

Kennedy, D(ennis) James (1930–) Born in Augusta, Georgia, D. James Kennedy was reared in Chicago and moved with his parents to Florida while in high school. A Sunday morning radio sermon delivered by *DONALD GREY BARNHOUSE of Tenth Presbyterian Church in Philadelphia prompted Kennedy's *CONVERSION in 1953. Shortly thereafter, he quit his job with the Arthur Murray dance studio (he had been honored as Arthur Murray's top dance instructor in the nation in 1953) and became pastor of a mission congregation, Bethel Presbyterian Church, in Clearwater, Florida. He completed his baccalaureate degree at the University of Tampa and entered *COLUMBIA THEOLOGICAL SEMINARY. Upon graduation in 1959, Kennedy accepted a call from the Home Missions Committee of the Everglades Presbytery to take over a mission church in the northern part of Fort Lauderdale, an enterprise that already carried the name Coral Ridge Presbyterian Church. After a rocky start, Kennedy decided to do door-to-door evangelism, the type of grassroots effort that he would later codify in *Evangelism Explosion*. By 1967, Coral Ridge Presbyterian Church had become the fastest growing congregation in the *PRESBYTERIAN CHURCH OF AMERICA; it moved into dramatically expanded quarters in December 1973.

Kennedy's handbook on *EVANGELISM, *Evangelism Explosion,* was first published in 1970, with periodic revisions thereafter. It has been translated and used as an *EVANGELISM tool throughout the world. Kennedy's empire in Fort Lauderdale also includes Coral Ridge Ministries, a radio and television operation; Westminster Academy, a school for kindergarten through twelfth grade, founded in 1971; and Knox Theological Seminary, begun in 1989. Kennedy, the author of more than thirty books, has in recent years angled for a national spotlight. The D. James Kennedy Center for Christian Statesmanship, with offices in Washington, D.C., attests to his aspirations of becoming a major player for the *RELIGIOUS RIGHT. In 1996, Kennedy founded the Center for Reclaiming America, which focuses on fighting the "homosexual agenda" and criticizing public education. "If we are committed and involved in taking back the nation for Christian moral values," Kennedy wrote in his 1994 book, *Character & Destiny,* "there is no doubt we can witness the dismantling of not just the Berlin Wall but the even more diabolical 'wall of separation' that has led to increasing secularization, godlessness, immorality, and corruption in our country."

References: D. James Kennedy, *Character & Destiny: A Nation in Search of Its Soul* (1994); idem, *The Gates of Hell Shall Not Prevail: The Attack on Christianity and What You Need to Know to Combat It* (1996); Herbert Lee Williams, *D. James Kennedy, The Man and His Ministry* (1990).

Kentucky Holiness School. *See* **Asbury College.**

Kenyon, E(ssek) W(illiam) (1867–1948) E. W. Kenyon converted to Christianity in his teens and preached his first sermon in a Methodist church at the age of nineteen. He enrolled at Emerson College in Boston in 1892, where he came into contact with the New Thought movement, which would affect his understanding of Christian doctrine. Kenyon left the Methodists for the Baptists and later became an independent itinerant *EVANGELIST. He founded Bethel Bible Institute but left the school in the early 1920s and headed for California, where he made the friendship of *AIMEE SEMPLE MCPHERSON. He served briefly as pastor of a Baptist church in Pasadena but left to form his own independent church in Los Angeles. He headed to Seattle in 1931, where he began the New Covenant Baptist Church and a radio program, *Kenyon's Church of the Air.*

Though little known during his lifetime, Kenyon's ideas regarding healing and faith became influential after his death. He had published a number of books—*Jesus the Healer* was the most popular—that were picked up by several independent pentecostal *EVANGELISTS, especially *KENNETH E. HAGIN and *KENNETH COPELAND. These preachers used Kenyon's interpretations of the *BIBLE to argue for the so-called *PROSPERITY THEOLOGY so popular in the 1980s, the notion that God will provide health and wealth to the faithful.

Reference: Essek William Kenyon, *The Bible in the Light of Our Redemption* (1969).

Kesler, Jay (1935–) Born in Barnes, Wisconsin, Jay Kesler graduated from *TAYLOR UNIVERSITY in 1958. His long association with *YOUTH FOR CHRIST had begun in 1955, and he became president of the organization in 1973. Kesler—a popular conference speaker, the author of books on parent-teen relations, and host of a daily radio program, *Family Forum*—left *YOUTH FOR CHRIST in 1985 to become president of *TAYLOR UNIVERSITY. He retired from the presidency in 2000 and was named the university's chancellor.

References: Jay Kesler, *Let's Succeed with Our Teenagers* (1973); idem, *Parents and Teenagers* (1984); idem, *Raising Responsible Kids* (1991).

Keswick Movement The Keswick movement, which was dedicated to the notion of personal holiness, takes its name from a gathering place in Keswick, England, but its roots extend to such figures as *JOHN WESLEY, *CHARLES GRANDISON FINNEY, *ASA MAHAN, *W. E. BOARDMAN, *HANNAH WHITALL SMITH, and *ROBERT PEARSALL SMITH. Boardman, a young grocer in Illinois, sought the experience of *SANCTIFICATION in 1843, after having read the testimonies of Finney and Mahan. Boardman studied at Lane Theological Seminary and in 1859 published *The Higher Christian Life,* his treatise on the matter, which argued that "victory" over *SIN was within reach of the evangelical believer. *ROBERT PEARSALL SMITH and his wife, *HANNAH WHITALL SMITH, made a similar discovery in the late 1860s and propagated their views on the matter of the "*SECOND BLESSING" through books, magazines, and holiness gatherings.

During *DWIGHT L. MOODY'S *REVIVAL campaign in Britain in 1873, Boardman and the Smiths held a series of breakfasts to advance their ideas among British evangelicals. At Oxford, England, in 1874, a group of evangelicals gathered for a "Union Meeting for the Promotion of Scriptural Holiness," and the following year eight thousand gathered in Brighton for a "Convention for the Promotion of

Scriptural Holiness." The gatherings adjourned to Keswick three weeks later where, beginning in July 1875, they were conducted annually thereafter.

The theology that emerged from Keswick rejected the traditional notion that justification was immediate but that the process of *SANCTIFICATION was long and arduous. Instead, Keswick promised deliverance from *SIN by claiming "victory in Christ." Although neither *SIN nor the temptation to *SIN was eradicated, both were counteracted by "victorious living" through the power of the Holy Spirit. That power, moreover, equipped the believer for service to the church, especially through *EVANGELISM and missions.

Keswick teachings became enormously popular among American evangelicals in the late nineteenth and early twentieth centuries, in part because the triumphalism implicit in the theology provided a marked contrast to evangelicals' growing sense of beleaguerment in the larger society. Moody's Northfield Conferences became the primary conduit for Keswick ideas, but they spread rapidly throughout the United States and Canada. In 1913, *ROBERT C. MCQUILKIN organized a Keswick conference in Oxford, Pennsylvania, which met the following year in Princeton, New Jersey, and eventually moved to a permanent home in Keswick Grove, New Jersey.

References: Donald W. Dayton, *Theological Roots of Pentecostalism* (1987); George M. Marsden, *Fundamentalism and American Culture: The Shaping of Twentieth-Century Evangelicalism, 1870–1925* (1980); Douglas Frank, *Less Than Conquerors: How Evangelicals Entered the Twentieth Century* (1986); David Bundy, "Keswick and the Experience of Evangelical Piety," in *Modern Christian Revivals*, ed. Edith L. Blumhofer and Randall Balmer (1993).

Ketcham, R(obert) T(homas) (1889–1978) Although he lacked a college education or seminary training, R. T. Ketcham served Baptist churches in Pennsylvania, Ohio, Indiana, and Iowa. He is best known, however, as a tireless champion of fundamentalist doctrines among Northern Baptists. He railed against liberal or modernist ideas and frequently charged that the Northern Baptist Convention was usurping the prerogatives of local congregations. A member of the *BAPTIST BIBLE UNION, Ketchum seceded from the Northern Baptists in 1928 and eventually led in the development of the *GENERAL ASSOCIATION OF REGULAR BAPTIST CHURCHES. Though nearly blind throughout his career, Ketchum traveled widely among Baptist congregations, pointing out the *LIBERALISM of the Northern Baptist Convention and recruiting members for the *GENERAL ASSOCIATION OF REGULAR BAPTISTS.

References: R. T. Ketcham, *Facts for Baptists to Face* (1936); J. Murray Murdoch, *Portrait of Obedience: The Biography of Robert T. Ketcham* (1979).

Key '73 An evangelistic initiative inspired by a 1967 editorial in **CHRISTIANITY TODAY*, Key '73 sought to enlist all evangelicals in a cooperative missions effort during the year 1973. Churches and religious organizations were asked to conduct prayer meetings, Bible studies, and lay *EVANGELISM and to do so without emphasizing divisive doctrines. The most visible representation of this initiative was a bumper sticker with I FOUND IT! emblazoned in black letters on a yellow background, distributed by the hundreds of thousands. Although separatist fundamentalists refused to participate in an effort that they saw as dangerously ecumenical, many evangelical congregations and organizations participated in this grassroots campaign.

Kinchlow, (Harvey) Ben (1936–) A native of Uvalde, Texas, Ben Kinchlow served in the air force for thirteen years and then attended Southwest Texas Junior College. An African American, Kinchlow had been enamored of the teachings of Malcolm X, but a *CONVERSION to evangelical Christianity led to a career in *EVANGELISM. Kinchlow began a ministry to runaways, called His Place, and later led a drug and alcohol rehabilitation program called Christian Farms, during which time he also was ordained in the African Methodist Episcopal Church. He directed the Dallas, Texas, counseling center for *PAT ROBERTSON's *CHRISTIAN BROADCASTING NETWORK (CBN) and moved to the CBN headquarters in Virginia Beach, Virginia, in 1975 to serve with Robertson as cohost of the *700 Club* television program.

King, Joseph Hillery (1869–1946) Born in South Carolina, Joseph Hillery King moved with his family to Georgia during his teens and there was converted during a Methodist *CAMP MEETING. Soon thereafter he embraced the doctrine of entire *SANCTIFICATION. Licensed by the Methodists in 1887, King gravitated toward the holiness wing of *METHODISM. After a brief marriage that ended in divorce, King entered the School of Theology at U. S. Grant University in Chattanooga, although he had only a sparse elementary education. While pursuing his studies, King came into contact with a radical holiness group, the *FIRE-BAPTIZED HOLINESS ASSOCIATION, which taught a "third work of grace" after *SANCTIFICATION, that of "fire baptism." Upon graduation in 1897, King severed his ties with *METHODISM and signed on with the "come-outer" *FIRE-BAPTIZED HOLINESS ASSOCIATION.

King worked briefly as an *EVANGELIST in Canada, then moved to Iowa to assist *B. H. IRWIN, founder of the *FIRE-BAPTIZED HOLINESS ASSOCIATION, and to edit the denomination's periodical, *Live Coals of Fire.* King became general superintendent of the group in 1900, succeeding Irwin, who had departed amid charges of "open and gross *SIN." King moved the headquarters to Georgia, changed the name to *FIRE-BAPTIZED HOLINESS CHURCH OF GOD OF THE AMERICAS, and guided the group into the newly emerging pentecostal ambit. King's book *From Passover to Pentecost,* published in 1914, became an important early defense of *PENTECOSTALISM. The *FIRE-BAPTIZED HOLINESS CHURCH merged with the *PENTECOSTAL HOLINESS CHURCH in 1911, took the latter's name, and established headquarters in Franklin Springs, Georgia. King became president of the group in 1917 and was consecrated its first bishop twenty years later.

Reference: Joseph Hillery King, *From Passover to Pentecost* (1914).

King College (Bristol, Tennessee) When Presbyterians split into two factions over slavery, the three church colleges in eastern Tennessee becamed aligned with the Northern contingent. In response, the Holston Presbytery of the Southern church decided to establish its own college. James King, pastor of the Bristol Presbyterian Church and a large landowner, donated ten acres for the new campus. Named after this benefactor, King College opened in 1867.

Over the next century, King College experienced prosperous moments, but those were outnumbered by times of financial hardship. In 1915, the Synod of

Appalachia was established, and King College became one of its primary targets of support. Two years later, the college was able to move onto a new campus, but by 1938 it was again heavily in debt. King was revisited with financial crises in the 1960s and 1970s, which in 1979 resulted in a transfer of ownership of the college to a new board of trustees of independent Presbyterian clergy and laypeople. Since that time the school has enjoyed greater stability.

In addition to study-abroad sites in Europe and the United States, King College has an exchange program with Han Nam University in South Korea. The library's John Doak Tadlock Collection has materials on regional and Presbyterian history. King College admits students from non-Christian backgrounds. The "Community Life Standards" explicitly prohibit occult practices; social *DANCING is permitted, however, and the school sponsors several dances each year, including a spring formal.

Reference: Bulletin of King College—Announcements for 1996–1997 (1996).

King's College, The (Briarcliff Manor, New York) The King's College, a nondenominational institution, was founded by evangelist *PERCY CRAWFORD in 1938 in Belmar, New Jersey. The college's second president was *The King's Hour* radio personality *ROBERT A. COOK. Although later located in Delaware, the college moved to Briarcliff Manor, New York, in 1955. As one of only two evangelical colleges in the New York metropolitan area—*NYACK COLLEGE being the other—The King's College had both advantages and disadvantages, but a strategic location did not, however, prove enough to save the school from bankruptcy and forced closure in 1994.

Cook was succeeded in 1985 by Friedhelm Radandt, who was widely blamed for the school's decline. Radandt was criticized as an authoritarian leader who forced out professors who refused to sign a statement expressing confidence in his integrity. Radandt also dismissed Samuel Barkat, King's vice president for academic affairs, who resigned his faculty position in protest, citing a pattern of "dishonest and unchristian" treatment of the faculty and staff who challenged Radandt's leadership style. Nor was Barkat the only professor to resign; many other faculty members also left with similar sentiments.

Many other faculty, however, took an opposing side in the argument, claiming that Radandt restored conservative, *BIBLE-based values to a school veering dangerously close to *LIBERALISM. Evidence suggests that in the 1980s some faculty wanted to present a pro-choice stance on the *ABORTION issue as a viable position for evangelical Christians, and a few also suggested that homosexuality should be seen as acceptable. Such theological broadening might make King's seem to have been one of the more "progressive" evangelical colleges, but it also reduced both its enrollment and level of support from churches and alumni. These decreases came at an especially bad time, for the college relied heavily on student tuition in the budget. Radandt hired numerous consultants but never proved himself successful as a fund-raiser. Enrollment fell throughout the 1980s, from 860 in 1980 to 230 by 1993, by which time the college was $21 million in debt.

The Middle States Association of Schools and Colleges announced in 1993 it would not renew King's accreditation due to financial insolvency. The association also cited poor facilities as a second reason to question King's continued accreditation. The campus, once a resort hotel, needed significant improvements. Accreditation was set to expire in June 1994. The impending withdrawal of accreditation caused an exodus of students, who transferred to other schools.

With the accreditation issue under appeal, The King's College hoped to head off closure by selling its campus in Briarcliff Manor to an Irish sports and cultural association and moving to an old research center in nearby Sterling Forest. This plan was thwarted when the college was forced to default on the loan for the new property because a group in Briarcliff Manor, concerned about traffic and noise, requested a long-term environmental impact study, thereby delaying the sale of the old campus. At the end of the fall semester in 1994, the New York State Board of Regents stepped in and ordered the school closed for financial problems and an insufficient number of teachers. By that November, enrollment had dropped to 172 students.

The regents did not, however, revoke King's charter. The King's College continued to exist on paper as a corporate entity. Early in 1998, Radandt announced plans to reopen King's College in the Empire State Building in New York City, with the financial backing of *CAMPUS CRUSADE FOR CHRIST.

References: "School Struggles for Survival," *Christianity Today,* August 16, 1993; John W. Kennedy, "Gift Gives Hope to King's College," *Christianity Today,* December 13, 1993; Warren Bird, "King's College Ordered Closed at Semester's End," *Christianity Today,* November 14, 1994; William C. Ringenberg, *The Christian College: A History of Protestant Higher Education in America* (1984); Joel A. Carpenter, *Revive Us Again: The Reawakening of American Fundamentalism* (1997).

King's University College (Edmonton, Alberta) Beginning in 1965, members of various denominations and independent churches in Western Canada began discussing the creation of a regional Christian college. The Christian College Association (Alberta) was incorporated in December 1970, with an eye to fulfilling this vision. It took several more years for the plans to materialize, but in 1979 the Alberta Legislature granted a charter to King's College.

The school used temporary facilities for more than a decade. In 1993, it moved to its first permanent campus—a new, $13 million complex in Edmonton. That year the school was renamed King's University College.

Kinkade, (William) Thomas (1958–) An artist whose romantic, idyllic paintings have been mass produced, Thomas Kinkade claims inspiration from his faith. He sees himself as a latter-day Impressionist, a "painter of light," whose soft-focus landscapes evoke nostalgia and remind the viewer of traditional values such as faith and family.

Kinkade grew up in a single-parent household in Placerville, California, where he was active in the local *CHURCH OF THE NAZARENE. After an adolescent rebellion, he reconnected with his faith through the *CALVARY CHAPEL movement and forged "a personal relationship with God." His artistic orientation, Kinkade told a reporter from the Religion News Service early in 1998, changed more or less concurrently with his *CONVERSION. "I began to see my art as something not to serve myself but to serve others," he said. Kinkade began signing his paintings with a Bible reference and with the "fish" symbol (the first letters of each word in Greek—Jesus Christ, Son of God, Savior—spell *ichthys,* or "fish"). His works have become so popular that his distribution company, Media Arts Group, Inc., is traded publicly and took in approximately $120 million in revenues in 2000. Kinkade markets lithographs, posters, collector's plates, calendars, greeting cards, home furnishings, and computer screen savers.

"God speaks to people through these paintings," Kinkade says, comparing his work to that of a love song. "At some point, the singer fades into the background, and the voice you are hearing is God's whisper. That's how I feel about my paintings." Kinkade also believes that his work has transformative powers. "Art transcends cultural boundaries," he says. "I want to blanket the world with the *GOSPEL through prints. This is a very thoroughgoing form of *EVANGELISM."

References: Thomas Kinkade, with Philippa Reed, *Thomas Kinkade: A Painter of Radiant Light* (1995); idem, *Beyond the Garden Gate* (1997); idem, with Anne Christian Buchanan, *Lightposts for Living: The Art of Choosing a Joyful Life* (1999); Randall Balmer, "The Kinkade Crusade," *Christianity Today,* December 4, 2000.

Kirkconnell, Watson (1895–c. 1968) Born in Lindsay, Ontario, Watson Kirkconnell studied classics at Queen's University, where he received the M.A. in 1916, and also studied at Oxford before accepting an appointment at Wesley College in Winnipeg, Manitoba. After his wife's death in childbirth in 1925, Kirkconnell embarked on an ambitious program of translating elegies from forty different European languages into English. His academic work coupled with his Baptist convictions—personal freedom and the willingness to defend the rights of others—made Kirkconnell one of the earliest champions of multiculturalism in Canada. He was elected to the Royal Society of Canada in 1936, and in 1940 he became head of the English department at McMaster University. In 1943, after talk of closing humanities departments in Canadian universities for the duration of the war in order to augment scientific and technical education, Kirkconnell was appointed chair of the newly formed Humanities Resource Council in Canada (now known as the Canadian Federation for the Humanities). In 1948, he became president of *ACADIA UNIVERSITY in Wolfville, Nova Scotia, where he argued passionately for provincial support of higher education, even those institutions with church affiliations.

Reference: J. R. C. Perkin, "'There Were Giants in the Earth in Those Days': An Assessment of Watson Kirkconnell," in G. A. Rawlyk, ed., *Canadian Baptists and Christian Higher Education* (1988).

Klopsch, Louis. *See* **Christian Herald.**

Knox Theological Seminary (Fort Lauderdale, Florida, and Colorado Springs, Colorado) Founded in 1989, Knox Theological Seminary began as one of the outreach programs of evangelist *D. JAMES KENNEDY's nine-thousand-member Coral Ridge Presbyterian Church in Fort Lauderdale, Florida. Knox Theological Seminary is named after John Knox, the Scottish reformer; the school is affiliated with the *PRESBYTERIAN CHURCH IN AMERICA but is open to students from other compatible Christian denominations.

Kennedy remains on board as chancellor, and the original campus of Knox Theological Seminary is still located on the grounds of Coral Ridge Presbyterian Church. In the mid-1990s, the school announced plans to build new facilities a few miles away in Fort Lauderdale. A second campus was established in Colorado Springs, Colorado, in 1993. At that site all classes are taught in the evenings to accommodate working students. Since its founding, Knox has also set up extension programs from its campuses in Fort Lauderdale and Colorado Springs to extension campuses in Miami; Savannah, Georgia; Toronto; and Seoul, South Korea. Despite this diverse array of locations, enrollment remains small. In the 1995–1996 school year, the campuses and extension centers enrolled a total of 148 students and registered 200 more people as auditors. The Florida and Colorado campuses together graduated nine students.

Knox is applying for accreditation from the Association of Theological Schools in the United States and Canada and has been granted "Associate Member" status. Currently, the seminary offers the master of divinity and master of theology degrees, as well as the master of arts in religion, biblical and theological studies, religion and society, and Christian ministry—pastoral counseling. The school also has nondegree certificate programs as well as a doctoral program in ministry, which students can complete as an out-of-house program by attending classes two weeks per term in Fort Lauderdale, Toronto, or Colorado Springs.

Even by evangelical standards, the school is very conservative. Not only is the master of divinity degree program open only to men, there are no women on the seminary faculty. Knox Theological Seminary declares it is modeled on the "Old Princeton" approach, characterized by a strong commitment to Calvinist theology; indeed, in many respects, this young institution feels like a throwback to the nineteenth or the early twentieth century. A cornerstone of the institution's mission is "commitment to the sovereignty and *INERRANCY of God's word," and the course offerings appear to address the battles fundamentalists fought against liberals nearly a century ago. One example is a course in the "Philosophy of Science," offered through the Religion and Society degree program. The catalog introduces the course as follows: "True science will never contradict biblical truth. This course examines the underlying philosophical and religious presumptions of current humanistic science and contrasts them with the biblical approach to science." In this class, creation and evolution, historic geology, and old earth and day-age theory are all examined.

Reference: *Knox Theological Seminary Catalog 1995–1997* (1995).

Koop, C(harles) Everett (1916–) Shortly after *RONALD REAGAN's election to the presidency in 1980, many antiabortion evangelicals, having contributed to his electoral victory, pressed the president-elect to make a symbolic appointment to underscore his opposition to *ABORTION. Reagan complied, nominating C. Everett Koop, a respected physician, to the post of surgeon general. Born in Brooklyn, New York, Koop studied at Dartmouth College and the University of Pennsylvania and had been surgeon-in-chief at Children's Hospital in Philadelphia since 1948. Together with *FRANCIS SCHAEFFER, an evangelical theologian, Koop had argued passionately against *ABORTION, although he muted his criticism as a public official. "It's one thing to come to Washington and have firmly held positions," he said, "but it's another thing to take an oath of office to uphold the Constitution, and there may be times when, without abandoning your beliefs, you have to make a political compromise to get the best possible solution to a problem that you can."

As surgeon general, Koop redirected his energies to other issues of public health, including smoking and sexually transmitted diseases. Many of the more extreme voices from the *RELIGIOUS RIGHT criticized him for abandoning the single issue they held most dear. The criticism intensified when Koop, alarmed at the rapid spread of AIDS, urged sex education and the use of condoms in a comprehensive report issued October 22, 1986. *PHYLLIS SCHLAFLY was particularly critical and sarcastic; she told supporters that Koop's advocacy of sex education was a license for teachers to instruct impressionable children how to perform both homosexual and heterosexual acts. Koop responded that Schlafly was "beneath contempt" and someone "whose idea of sex education was something like, 'Don't let anyone touch you where you wear your swimsuit.'"

By 1987, Koop also chided the *RELIGIOUS RIGHT for its lack of tolerance and its growing arrogance. In a speech before the *NATIONAL RELIGIOUS BROADCASTERS he said, "Initially, you sought freedom. In the process, you gained power. And with power, a small minority now want control." After leaving Washington, Koop joined the faculty of Dartmouth College and remained a spokesman on public health.

References: C. Everett Koop, with Francis A. Schaeffer, *Whatever Happened to the Human Race?* (1977); William Martin, *With God on Our Side: The Rise of the Religious Right in America* (1996).

Koresh, David (1959–1993) Born Vernon Howell in Houston on August 17, 1959, David Koresh legally changed his name in August 1990 because he came to believe that he had received the "Cyrus message" (*Koresh* is Hebrew for Cyrus) during a visit to Israel in 1985. Reared in a *SEVENTH-DAY ADVENTIST household, Koresh early on evinced an interest in the prophetic writings of the *BIBLE, although his unconventional views had placed him well outside the mainstream of the denomination.

As the seventh and final prophet, the "angel from the east," Koresh believed that he possessed the keys for unlocking the seven seals predicted in the book of Revelation. He also claimed to be the second Christ, and this status provided the warrant for taking multiple wives, even while demanding celibacy of his followers. By the late 1980s, after a series of maneuverings, Koresh and his followers took over the Branch Davidian compound known as Mount Carmel, near Waco, Texas, which Koresh believed would be at the center of events leading to the end of history. For Koresh and his followers, the end came in a fiery conflagration when the Bureau of Alcohol, Tobacco and Firearms, after a fifty-one-day standoff, laid siege to the compound on April 19, 1993.

Reference: James D. Tabor and Eugene V. Gallagher, *Why Waco? Cults and the Battle for Religious Freedom in America* (1995).

Kroll, Woodrow M(ichael) (1944–) The president and senior Bible teacher for *BACK TO THE BIBLE, Woodrow M. Kroll was born in Ellwood City, Pennsylvania. He received a diploma from Practical Bible College in upstate New York, a bachelor's degree from *BARRINGTON COLLEGE in Rhode Island, and divinity degrees from *GORDON-CONWELL THEOLOGICAL SEMINARY and Geneva-St. Albans Theological Seminary. With his brother Jerry, he was a traveling evangelist with the Kroll Evangelistic Team from 1965 to 1968, when he became pastor of a Baptist church in Middleboro, Massachusetts. He taught at *LIBERTY UNIVERSITY and at Practical Bible

College, where he also served as president from 1981 to 1990. Kroll succeeded Warren W. Wiersbe as head of *BACK TO THE BIBLE in 1990. Under his guidance, the organization branched out into others forms of ministry, including television and the Internet.

References: Woodrow M. Kroll, *Back to the Bible: Turning Your Life Around with God's Word* (2000); idem, *7 Secrets to Spiritual Success* (2000).

Ku Klux Klan The Ku Klux Klan has had various incarnations since its founding in the South following the Civil War. It was revived as a Protestant lodge in Stone Mountain, Georgia, in 1915 by a former Methodist minister, *WILLIAM J. SIMMONS, who introduced religious ritual to the initiatory rites as well as the flaming cross. The Klan, drawing upon a long tradition of nativism in America, reified white, native-born Protestants and directed its anger—and violence—against Jews, African Americans, and Roman Catholics, all of whom it regarded as inimical to traditional morality and small-town values.

During the 1920s, the Klan recruited openly in churches (especially among Methodists, Baptists, and Disciples of Christ), emphasizing its support for law and order, morality, school prayer, and prohibition. The Klan, which often invoked the *BIBLE to justify its racist and anti-Semitic ideology, advocated limits on immigration, and Klansmen boycotted Jewish and Roman Catholic merchants. The Ku Klux Klan added communism to its demonology in the 1930s, and the Klan was responsible for the bombing of synagogues and the burning of black churches during the civil rights movement of the 1950s and 1960s.

References: Robert M. Miller, "A Note on the Relationship between the Protestant Churches and the Revived Ku Klux Klan," *Journal of Southern History*, XXII (August 1956); David Mark Chalmers, *Hooded Americanism: The History of the Ku Klux Klan*, 3d ed. (1987); Wyn Craig Wade, *The Fiery Cross: The Ku Klux Klan in America* (1998); Nancy K. MacLean, *Behind the Mask of Chivalry: The Making of the Second Ku Klux Klan* (1995).

Kuhlman, Kathryn (1907–1976) Born near Concordia, Missouri, and converted at the age of thirteen, Kathryn Kuhlman left town with a tenth-grade education to begin preaching at the age of sixteen. She preached in Idaho, Utah, and Colorado, settling in Denver in 1933. She built the Denver Revival Tabernacle, with seating for two thousand, and used the media to expand her reach. In 1938, Kuhlman married an itinerant *EVANGELIST, Burroughs A. Waltrip Sr., the "Louisiana Pulpiteer," who had left his family for Kuhlman. The marriage forced Kuhlman to leave her Denver congregation. The two evangelists traveled together for a time, but they eventually went their separate ways. Kuhlman, though always elliptical about that chapter in her life, marks her rebirth as an *EVANGELIST (and her *BAPTISM in the Spirit) to her decision to divorce Waltrip; her Spirit *BAPTISM took place on a dead-end street in Los Angeles in 1944, when she and the Holy Spirit "made each other promises."

Kuhlman resumed her career in Franklin, Pennsylvania, in 1946, where she again used the radio to augment her growing congregation. When a woman was healed during one of her services on April 27, 1947, Kuhlman turned toward a healing ministry, although she resented being called a faith healer. "I have no healing virtue," she explained. "I have no healing power. I have never healed anyone. I am absolutely dependent upon the power of the Holy Spirit." Kuhlman moved to Pittsburgh in July 1948, which would become her base for the remainder of her life. In addition, she continued her itinerant ministry of "miracle services" and in the 1960s began a weekly television program on CBS. A dramatic and flamboyant presence, Kuhlman enjoyed considerable success in Los Angeles, and she counted *ORAL ROBERTS among her many admirers. "I will die believing she had the gifts of God," Oral Roberts declared in 1992.

References: Kathryn Kuhlman, *I Believe in Miracles* (1962); idem, *God Can Do It Again* (1969); idem, *Nothing Is Impossible with God* (1974); Wayne E. Warner, *Kathryn Kuhlman: The Woman Behind the Miracles* (1993); Deborah Vansau McCauley, s.v. "Kathryn Kuhlman," in Charles H. Lippy, ed., *Twentieth-Century Shapers of American Popular Religion* (1989); Joel A. Carpenter, *Revive Us Again: The Reawakening of American Fundamentalism* (1997).

■ ■ ■

LaBerge, Agnes N. Ozman. *See* **Ozman, Agnes N. (LaBerge).**

L'Abri Fellowship L'Abri Fellowship was founded in 1955 by *FRANCIS SCHAEFFER and Edith Schaeffer. Nestled in the Swiss Alps, L'Abri (French for "shelter") evolved into a complex of chalets for the study of the *BIBLE and other texts, under the tutelage of the Schaeffers. L'Abri was especially attractive to drifters and various religious seekers, and part of the appeal was a dedication to the arts, a characteristic generally lacking in American *EVANGELICALISM.

Reference: Edith Schaeffer, *Dear Family: The L'Abri Family Letters, 1961–1986* (1989).

Ladd, George Eldon (1911–1982) An influential evangelical scholar of the New Testament, George Eldon Ladd was converted in 1929 and graduated from *GORDON COLLEGE of Theology and Missions four years later. He was ordained a Northern Baptist minister and continued his studies at Gordon Divinity School. He pastored churches in Gilford, New Hampshire; Montpelier, Vermont; and Boston, where he also resumed his graduate work, first at Boston University and then at Harvard, earning the Ph.D. in classics in 1949. Ladd joined the faculty of *FULLER THEOLOGICAL SEMINARY the following year, and for the ensuing three decades he sought to move evangelical scholarship away from *DISPENSATIONALISM and from the defensiveness of *FUNDAMENTALISM toward an acceptance of many of the modern critical methods of New Testament scholarship.

References: George Eldon Ladd, *Crucial Questions about the Kingdom of God* (1952); idem, *Jesus and the Kingdom* (1964); idem, *The New Testament and Criticism* (1967); idem, *A Theology of the New Testament* (1974); Mark A. Noll, *Between Faith and Criticism: Evangelicals, Scholarship, and the Bible in America* (1986); George M. Marsden, *Reforming Fundamentalism: Fuller Seminary and the New Evangelicalism* (1987).

LaHaye, Beverly (Jean) (née Ratcliffe) (1926–) One of the more prominent and influential leaders of the *RELIGIOUS RIGHT, Beverly LaHaye was reared in a forthrightly conservative home and attended *BOB JONES UNIVERSITY, a bastion of *FUNDAMENTALISM. While a student at Bob Jones, she met and married another conservative student, *TIM LAHAYE. The couple served Baptist churches in Pickens, South Carolina, and Minneapolis, Minnesota, before settling in El Cajon, California, where *TIM LAHAYE became pastor of Scott Memorial Baptist Church. Beverly LaHaye became quite active with her husband in various enterprises, including a half-hour television program—*The LaHayes on Family Life*—books, and a lecture series called Family Life Seminars.

Beverly LaHaye became politically active after watching an interview with Betty Friedan, author of *The Feminine Mystique* and founder of the National Organization for Women (NOW). LaHaye took umbrage at the assumption that Friedan spoke for all women in America; she began organizing women in the San Diego area to oppose NOW, the proposed Equal Rights Amendment, and feminist initiatives in general. LaHaye's organization, *CONCERNED WOMEN FOR AMERICA, was chartered in 1979, the same year that *JERRY FALWELL organized *MORAL MAJORITY. Like *MORAL MAJORITY and other *RELIGIOUS RIGHT organizations, *CONCERNED WOMEN FOR AMERICA opposed *ABORTION, gay rights, and *SECULAR HUMANISM; it advocated prayer in schools, so-called family values, and government support for religious schools. LaHaye has conceded that she is "consumed" by the issue of homosexuality. "Of all the problems in America today," she said, "the homosexual movement poses the most serious threat to families and children." By the end of the 1980s, the organization had active chapters in all fifty states, and in 1984, at the height of the Reagan influence, *CONCERNED WOMEN FOR AMERICA moved its offices to Washington, D.C.

References: Beverly LaHaye, *The Spirit-Controlled Woman* (1976); idem, *Spirit-Controlled Family Living* (1978); idem, *I Am a Woman by God's Design* (1980); idem, *The Restless Woman* (1984); David Garrison, s.v. "Tim and Beverly LaHaye," in Charles H. Lippy, ed., *Twentieth-Century Shapers of American Popular Religion* (1989).

LaHaye, Tim (1926–) Born in Detroit, Tim LaHaye enrolled at *BOB JONES UNIVERSITY after a tour of duty in the air force. LaHaye found at Bob Jones a theologically and socially conservative environment congenial to his own background, having been reared in a conservative Baptist tradition. He also found the woman, Beverly Jean Ratcliffe, who would become his wife; Tim and *BEVERLY LAHAYE were married July 5, 1947. Tim LaHaye worked as pastor of a small Baptist church in Pickens, South Carolina, and after graduation moved on to a Baptist church in Minneapolis, Minnesota. The LaHayes headed west to El Cajon, California, in 1956, where Tim became pastor of Scott Memorial Baptist Church.

In part because of his father's death when Tim was nine years old, LaHaye took up the crusade of so-called family values, lashing out against feminism, gays, and secular humanists. The LaHayes had their own half-hour television program, *The LaHayes on Family Life*. They also wrote and distributed books and articles on family life, and developed a lecture series, beginning in 1972, called Family Life Seminars, which they took around the nation and to several foreign countries. LaHaye founded various educational institutions in the San Diego area, including the Christian High School of San Diego and Christian Heritage College.

LaHaye published a number of pop psychology books in the 1960s and 1970s, as well as books on *PREMILLENNIALISM, but the appearance of *The Battle for the Mind* in 1980 signaled his entry into the arena of politics. The book, which was lauded by religious and political conservatives, was a full-throated assault on *SECULAR HUMANISM, which LaHaye found lurking behind such organizations as the National Organization for Women, the American Civil Liberties Union, the

National Association for Education, and the United Nations. LaHaye followed up the book with two others, *The Battle for the Family* (1982) and *The Battle for the Public Schools* (1983). He also followed up with his own *RELIGIOUS RIGHT organization, the American Coalition for Traditional Values, begun in 1984, the same year that his wife's organization, *CONCERNED WOMEN FOR AMERICA, relocated to Washington, D.C. Although LaHaye continued to have an influential voice within the *RELIGIOUS RIGHT, his reputation was tarnished somewhat by his association with Sun Myung Moon and other far-right figures during the 1980s. In 1995, he published (with Jerry Jenkins as coauthor) *Left Behind,* the first of a series of commercially successful novels depicting life during the apocalypse.

References: Tim LaHaye, *The Beginning of the End* (1972); idem, *The Bible's Influence on American History* (1976); idem, *The Unhappy Gays* (1978); idem, *The Battle for the Mind* (1980); idem, *The Battle for the Public Schools* (1983); idem, with Jerry Jenkins, *Left Behind* (1995); David Garrison, s.v. "Tim and Beverly LaHaye," in Charles H. Lippy, ed., *Twentieth-Century Shapers of American Popular Religion* (1989).

Lam, Nora (1932–) Nora Lam was born in Beijing, China, but the essential details of her life thereafter are controverted. Lam claims that she was a prisoner of the Red Army and, while pregnant, faced a firing squad. An electrical storm miraculously diverted the bullets and spared her life, whereupon she vowed that her baby would not be born in China. She claims that the child remained in her womb for twelve months and was born only after her expulsion from China and her arrival in Hong Kong. Soon thereafter, she divorced her first husband and married S. K. Sung, an evangelical leader in Hong Kong; the couple then emigrated to the United States, and Lam began her career as an *EVANGELIST in the early 1970s. Eventually she established Nora Lam Chinese Ministries International, which supports evangelical churches in China.

Lam's story attracted considerable notice in evangelical circles, in part because it confirmed the anticommunist prejudices held by many conservative evangelicals. Lam's autobiography, *China Cry,* was published in 1980 and was made into a feature-length motion picture by *PAUL CROUCH of *TRINITY BROADCASTING NETWORK. Upon release of the film, however, the veracity of Lam's story was called into question, especially at the instigation of John Stewart, an attorney and evangelical radio talk-show host in southern California, who launched his own investigation. Lam's story about her years in China could not be verified, and the chronology of events leading to her divorce and remarriage was also murky, leading critics to charge that she had taken up with Sung well before her divorce.

Despite these charges, and charges of financial irregularities and deceptive evangelistic techniques, Lam continued to enjoy success and popularity among evangelicals. Her organization, based in San Jose, California, takes in several million dollars annually, and she has raised funds through infomercials on television.

References: Nora Lam, *China Cry* (1980); idem, *Bullet-Proof Believer* (1988); "Critics Question Nora Lam's Story," *Christianity Today,* January 14, 1991.

Landmark Movement The Landmark movement emerged among Baptists in the South during the nineteenth century as a protest against any sort of centralization of ecclesiastical authority. Taking its name from Proverbs 22:28 (KJV), "Remove not the ancient landmark, which thy fathers have set," Landmark Baptists asserted the primacy of local congregations, and they argued that the present-day Landmark churches traced their authority back to the New Testament and through an unbroken line of faithful Christians: Montanists, Donatists, Cathars, Waldensians, and Anabaptists. Landmarkers were highly suspicious of any cooperative activity with other churches, even Baptist churches, and would not accept letters transferring church membership, a practice common among other Baptists. They insisted on *BAPTISM by immersion and rejected any non-Baptist rite as an "alien immersion."

The term "Landmark" first appeared in 1854 in an essay by James M. Pendleton, one of the leaders of the movement. The doctrines of Landmarkism, however, have an earlier precedent in the work and theology of James R. Graves, one of the most influential southern Baptists in the nineteenth century.

References: James R. Graves, *Old Landmarkism: What Is It?* (1880); Richard T. Hughes and C. Leonard Allen, *Illusions of Innocence: Protestant Primitivism in America, 1630–1875* (1988): Bill J. Leonard, ed., *Christianity in Appalachia: Profiles in Regional Pluralism* (1998).

Landry, Thomas Wade "Tom" (1924–2000) An evangelical Christian and one of the most successful head coaches in the history of the National Football League, Tom Landry was born in Mission, Texas. He was a defensive back with the New York Giants and became head coach of the Dallas Cowboys in 1960, their inaugural season. In Landry's twenty-nine years at the helm, the Cowboys won eighteen division championships and appeared in five Super Bowls, winning two championships. Landry, wearing his trademark fedora on the sidelines, was known for his stoic demeanor as much as for his effective strategies. When Jerry Jones purchased the team in 1988, he unceremoniously fired Landry, despite Landry's stated desire to coach one more season, which would have been his thirtieth. After his dismissal, however, Landry devoted more time to evangelical causes, including the *FELLOWSHIP OF CHRISTIAN ATHLETES.

Reference: Thomas George, "Tom Landry, 75, Dies; Innovative Coach of Cowboys," *New York Times*, February 14, 2000.

Lane Rebellion By the spring of 1834, students at the recently formed Lane Theological Seminary in Cincinnati responded to the entreaties of *THEODORE WELD, one of their fellow students, to work for the immediate abolition of slavery. That position, as well as the activist measures undertaken by the students, placed them in conflict with the board of trustees at Lane, which advocated a gradualist solution to the slavery question. Meeting over the summer, the board sought to retard the activism of the students. They dismissed John Morgan, a professor who had sided with the students, and resolved that "education must be completed before the young are fitted to engage in the collisions of active life."

At least forty students withdrew from the seminary and set up a "free seminary" across town, where they instructed themselves in theology and continued their work among African Americans. Many of the Lane Rebels, along with Morgan, the fired professor, joined *ASA MAHAN and *CHARLES GRANDISON FINNEY at Oberlin College.

Reference: Donald W. Dayton, *Discovering an Evangelical Heritage* (1988).

Lankford, Sarah (née Worrall) (1806–1896) A vigorous proponent of the doctrine of entire *SANCTIFICATION after her own experience of *SANCTIFICATION on May 21, 1835, Sarah Lankford established the famous *TUESDAY MEETING FOR THE PROMOTION OF HOLINESS at her home in New York City the following year. The *TUESDAY MEETINGS, initially gatherings for women only, consisted of Bible reading, prayer, and personal testimonies, all geared toward engendering the experience of entire *SANCTIFICATION in others. Sarah's younger sister, *PHOEBE PALMER, joined in the gatherings, which they opened to men in December 1839.

The Tuesday Meetings continued under the direction of one or the other sister for half a century. Lankford also organized other *TUESDAY MEETINGS throughout New England and the mid-Atlantic states. Lankford's husband, Thomas, died in March 1872, and *PHOEBE PALMER, her sister, died eight months later. In 1876, Sarah Lankford married her sister's surviving husband, took the name Sarah Lankford Palmer, and edited the *Guide to Holiness* for the remaining two decades of her life.

Reference: J. A. Roche, *The Life of Mrs. Sarah A. Lankford Palmer Who for Sixty Years Was the Able Teacher of Entire Holiness* (1898).

Lanphier, Jeremiah C(alvin) (1809–c. 1890) Born in Coxsackie, New York, Jeremiah C. Lanphier became a successful businessman in New York City and was converted to evangelical Christianity in 1842. In July 1857, the Old North Dutch Reformed Church on Fulton Street retained Lanphier's services as a lay *EVANGELIST to reach the unchurched of the neighborhood. Lanphier, a man of considerable piety, organized what became known as the *FULTON STREET PRAYER MEETING in an effort to reach the businessmen in lower Manhattan. On September 23, 1857, he began weekly prayer meetings at noon. As the *REVIVAL caught on, the weekly meetings became daily, and they formed the core of what became known as the *PRAYER MEETING REVIVAL of 1857–1859. Twenty-five years later, the *FULTON STREET PRAYER MEETINGS were still attracting capacity crowds.

Larson, Bob (1944–) The former lead singer in a rock 'n' roll band, Bob Larson experienced an evangelical *CONVERSION, dropped out of the University of Nebraska, and began lecturing on the dangers of rock music. He published several books on the topic, beginning with *Rock and Roll: The Devil's Diversion.* He created his own organization, Bob Larson Ministries, based in Denver, Colorado, and conducted evangelistic campaigns around the world. After the Jonestown disaster of 1978, when the followers of Jim Jones and the People's Temple committed mass suicide in Guyana, Larson added anticult warnings to his repertoire; his *Larson's Book of Cults,* published by Tyndale House, has been very popular with evangelicals. He also began to warn against something he called "satanic ritual abuse."

Larson's daily two-hour radio talk show, *Talk-Back with Bob Larson,* featured healings and exorcisms and attracted a devoted following. Larson and his combative style also began to attract critics, who claimed that many of his charges were unsubstantiated and that some of the "spontaneous" calls to the radio program were in fact arranged in advance. When Larson and his wife were divorced in 1991, court documents revealed that his compensation from Bob Larson Ministries was, in fact, rather lavish, with earnings well in excess of two hundred thousand dollars annually, exclusive of perquisites.

Employees of Larson's organization also alleged that they were told to use the toll-free 800 line only to accept donations and not for counseling. In addition, the organization tried to pass off previously recorded radio programs as live. By 1995, a dropoff in the number of stations carrying his broadcast prompted Larson to cancel *Talk-Back* and substitute it with a one-hour program, *Bob Larson Live.* The new format replaced calls with Larson's perorations and, occasionally, guests.

References: Bob Larson, *The Day the Music Died* (1973); idem, *Raising Children in the Rock Generation* (1979); idem, *Larson's Book of Cults* (1985); idem, *Satanism: The Seduction of America's Youth* (1989); Timothy C. Morgan, "Personnel Woes Persist at Larson Ministries," *Christianity Today,* September 13, 1993.

Larson, Bruce (1925–) Born in Chicago, Bruce Larson graduated from Lake Forest College, Princeton Theological Seminary, and Boston University. He was ordained a Presbyterian minister in 1952 and served a number of churches. A gifted preacher and a prolific author, Larson became senior pastor of University Presbyterian Church in Seattle in 1980, a post he held for ten years. He was a copastor of *ROBERT SCHULLER's Crystal Cathedral from 1990 until 1994, and he was named adjunct professor of church renewal at *FULLER THEOLOGICAL SEMINARY in 1995.

References: Bruce Larson, *Dare to Live Now!* (1965); idem, *Ask Me to Dance* (1972); idem, *Believe and Belong* (1985); idem, *Faith for the Journey* (1986); idem, *What God Wants to Know* (1993).

Latter Rain Movement A mid-twentieth-century outpouring of pentecostal fervor that proponents compared to the *AZUSA STREET REVIVAL, the Latter Rain movement traces its beginnings to a small pentecostal school in North Battleford, Saskatchewan. In the midst of a Bible study at the Sharon Orphanage and Schools on February 12, 1948, one of the students laid his hands on another student and proceeded to offer a long "prophecy," a spiritually inspired recitation concerning the life and future of the second student. Two days later, according to George Hawtin, leader of the school, "all Heaven broke loose upon our souls and Heaven came down to greet us." Many experienced the gift of healing, and word of the *REVIVAL spread quickly throughout North America. The Latter Rain was characterized by a "laying on of hands" to prompt a visitation by the Holy Spirit, as opposed to the previous practice of "tarrying" for the Holy Spirit.

The term "latter rain" was taken from Joel 2:23, which talks about the "former rain" and the "latter rain." Leaders of the Latter Rain movement read this passage through the grid of *PREMILLENNIALISM: A final outpouring of the Holy Spirit would immediately precede the *SECOND COMING of Christ. One theological justification, *The Feast of Tabernacles,* published by George Warnock, argued that the Feast of Passover had been fulfilled with the death of Christ, and the Feast of Pentecost had been fulfilled when the Holy Spirit descended on the early Christians on the Day of Pentecost; the final manifestation, the Feast of Tabernacles, was now evident in the Latter Rain movement of 1948. As the movement developed, led by such pentecostal *EVANGELISTS as *FRANKLIN HALL and *WILLIAM MARRION BRANHAM, it was marked by numerous reports of healing and other spiritual manifestations.

As some of the leaders demonstrated affinities for sectarianism, however, many of the pentecostals rooted in denominations began to denounce the Latter Rain, sometimes referring to it as the "New Order of the Latter Rain." Some pentecostal denominations, such as the *ASSEMBLIES OF GOD and the *PENTECOSTAL HOLINESS CHURCH, expelled pastors who were associated with the Latter Rain *REVIVAL. Despite the opposition, however, the Latter Rain movement persisted in independent churches and contributed to the *CHARISMATIC MOVEMENT of the 1960s and 1970s.

Laurie, Greg (1952–) Born in Long Beach and raised in a number of troubled homes throughout California, Greg Laurie became immersed in the hippie lifestyle, taking drugs and doing the best he could to avoid *JESUS FREAKS who went "hunting for sinners" in the late 1960s. Typical of many of his generation, Laurie began to search out spiritual questions and looking for "meaning and purpose in life." One day in 1970, he happened to stumble across a meeting conducted by hippie *EVANGELIST *LONNIE FRISBEE on the lawn of the Newport-Harbor High School. The story has two recountings, depending on the participant. Laurie claimed that Frisbee quoted a passage where Jesus stated, "you are either for me or against me," whereupon Laurie "froze" at the thought of making such a decision by and through his actions. Frisbee, on the other hand, claimed that Laurie was disrupting his meeting, and when the *EVANGELIST pointed at the young cynic, Laurie dropped to the ground and started immediately to speak in *TONGUES. Whatever the case, from that day forward, Laurie's aspiration to become an *EVANGELIST like Frisbee never wavered.

While hanging out at *CALVARY CHAPEL, Laurie put his cartoon drawing skills to use, penning a tract called "Living Waters" that he dropped off at the door of *CHUCK SMITH, the church's pastor. Impressed by Laurie's talents, Smith immediately had ten thousand copies made and hired Laurie to do other artwork for various projects at the church. Laurie, who has no formal theological training, took over a congregation of three hundred in 1972 that had been started by Frisbee at All Saints Episcopal Church in Riverside, California. That congregation, now known as Harvest Christian Fellowship, grew into one of the flagships of the *CALVARY CHAPEL movement. This church, which numbers twelve thousand, has also been recognized as one of the ten largest Protestant megachurches in the United States.

In 1990, Smith took his protégé and began billing Laurie as the featured speaker for what has become the annual Harvest Crusade meetings. He has been called the "*EVANGELIST of the MTV generation," touted as a successor to *BILLY GRAHAM, and called one of the rising *EVANGELISTS of the twenty-first century.

Lausanne Congress. *See* **International Congress on World Evangelization.**

Lausanne Covenant The Lausanne Covenant, drafted by British churchman *JOHN R. W. STOTT, was adopted in 1974 by the *INTERNATIONAL CONGRESS ON WORLD EVANGELIZATION, held in Lausanne, Switzerland. The Covenant reaffirmed evangelicals' commitment to biblical *AUTHORITY and to world missions. It became a kind of manifesto and served to rally many evangelicals to the cause of missions.

Laws, Curtis Lee (1868–1946) A native of Virginia and a graduate of Crozer Theological Seminary, Curtis Lee Laws served Baptist churches in Baltimore and in Brooklyn, New York, before assuming the editorship of the *Watchman-Examiner*, a weekly Baptist newspaper, in 1913. From that platform (the Baptist periodical with the widest circulation in the North), Laws established himself as one of the preeminent conservative voices in the fundamentalist-modernist controversy. He tirelessly supported congregational autonomy, biblical *AUTHORITY, and the missions imperative. He coined the term "fundamentalist" in the July 1, 1920, issue of his magazine. Laws was also one of the founders of *EASTERN BAPTIST THEOLOGICAL SEMINARY and the Association of Baptists for World Evangelism.

References: William Henry Brackney, *The Baptists* (1988); Joel A. Carpenter, *Revive Us Again: The Reawakening of American Fundamentalism* (1997).

Laymen's Missionary Movement The Laymen's Missionary Movement grew out of the missionary impulse generated by the *STUDENT VOLUNTEER MOVEMENT. The purpose of the organization, which was conceived by John P. Sleman, was to raise the level of contributions to missions by means of educational presentations throughout North America. Such presentations, usually organized around a banquet, took place across Canada in 1908 and in the United States the following year. The dramatic increase in contributions for missions between 1906 and 1924—from $8.98 million to $45.27 million—can be attributed in part to the success of the Laymen's Missionary Movement.

Reference: John R. Mott, *The Decisive Hour of Christian Missions* (1910).

Lea, Larry (1950–) Larry Lea was converted to evangelical Christianity in 1967 while in a psychiatric ward. He graduated from *DALLAS BAPTIST COLLEGE (now University) in 1972, attended Southwestern Baptist Theological Seminary, became a youth minister at Beverly Hills Baptist Church in Dallas, Texas, and then in 1980 started his own church, Church on the Rock, in the Dallas suburb of Rockwall. The congregation grew spectacularly under Lea's healing-charismatic ministry, claiming a membership of more than eight thousand by 1992.

Lea, who has been influenced by *PAUL YONGGI CHO of South Korea, left the pastorate to pursue his television enterprises and to become dean of theological and spiritual affairs at *ORAL ROBERTS UNIVERSITY, dividing his time between the Dallas area and Tulsa, Oklahoma. His organization was badly discredited on November 21, 1991, when ABC Television's *PrimeTime Live* aired an exposé of Lea and two other Dallas-based televangelists. The program accused Lea of raising large sums of money ostensibly for a church in Auschwitz, Poland, although little of that money, apparently, reached Poland. Lea was also accused of pleading personal poverty after a fire in his Tulsa house, conveniently neglecting to mention that he also owned a furnished home on a lavish five-acre estate in Dallas.

The disclosures forced Lea off the air at the end of 1991. He assumed the senior pastorate of the Lighthouse Church in San Diego in February 1994.

References: Larry Lea, *Could You Not Tarry One Hour?* (1987); Kim Lawton, "Broadcasters Face Ethics Questions—Again," *Christianity Today*, January 13, 1992.

Lee, Daniel (1807–1896) Daniel Lee, the nephew of *JASON LEE, was born in Stanstead, Vermont (now Canada), and was ordained a Methodist elder in 1834. That same year, he accompanied his uncle on a missionary venture to Native

Americans in the Oregon Territory. He set up a mission in The Dalles, Oregon, in 1838 but was forced to return to the East in 1843 because of his wife's health. Lee spent the balance of his career as a pastor in New Hampshire.

Reference: Daniel Lee and J. H. Frost, *Ten Years in Oregon* (1873).

Lee, Jarena (1783–c. 1850) Born in Cape May, New Jersey, to free parents, Jarena Lee was converted in 1804 at the Bethel African Methodist Episcopal Church in Philadelphia, under the ministry of *RICHARD ALLEN. She was later sanctified and became convinced of the call to preach. Allen turned down her initial request in 1809; Lee renewed the plea in 1818 after her husband had died. Allen, then bishop of the African Methodist Episcopal Church, authorized Lee to preach as an itinerant.

Lee preached tirelessly for more than three decades, traveling as far north as Canada. She joined the American Anti-Slavery Society in 1840 and relentlessly advocated the rights of women to be full members of the clergy.

References: William L. Andrews, ed., *Sisters of the Spirit: Three Black Women's Autobiographies of the Nineteenth Century*; Judith Weisenfeld, s.v. "Lee, Jarena," in Jack Salzman, et al., eds., *Encyclopedia of African-American Culture and History* (1996).

Lee, Jason (1803–1845) Born in Stanstead, Vermont (now part of Canada), Jason Lee, the youngest of fifteen children, was converted in 1826. He led a Methodist mission to the Flathead Indians in the Oregon Territory in 1834 and settled near present-day Salem, Oregon, where he established a mission and a school that evolved into Willamette University. Lee, though devout, lacked administrative skills and returned to the East from 1838 until 1840, both to escape discontent at the mission and to recruit other missionaries. Lee and fifty others, dubbed the Great Reinforcement, returned to Oregon in 1840. The mission moved to Salem, a city Lee founded in 1840, and he helped to establish the provisional government for Oregon in 1843. He returned east later that year amid charges that he had failed to file adequate reports with his missionary society. Lee was exonerated the next year, but he retired to Stanstead and never returned to the West.

Reference: C. J. Brosnan, *Jason Lee, Prophet of the New Oregon* (1932).

Lee, Luther (1800–1889) Born into the household of a poor Methodist family in Schoharie, New York, Luther Lee became a Methodist circuit preacher in western New York, where his skills as a revivalist earned him ordination as an elder in 1831. After his stint on the frontier, he moved to northern New York, where he earned the nickname "Logical Lee" for his tenacious debates with local Universalist ministers (those who believed in universal salvation). In 1837, the same year as *ELIJAH P. LOVEJOY's martyrdom, Lee became a fervent abolitionist and obtained reassignment as an agent for the New York Anti-Slavery Society. He helped to form the Liberty Party, with an antislavery platform, and campaigned for James G. Birney for president. He founded two short-lived publications, the antislavery *New England Christian Advocate* and *Sword of Truth,* an anti-Universalist publication.

When antislavery Methodists seceded from *METHODISM to form the Wesleyan Methodist Connection in 1843, Lee became one of the leaders of the new denomination. He was elected president of the General Conference in 1844 and became editor of *The True Wesleyan*. Lee returned to the pastorate in 1852, first in Syracuse and then in Fulton, New York. His *Elements of Theology*, written and published during this time, became a kind of systematic theology for Wesleyan *METHODISM. After a brief stint as professor of theology at Leoni College in Michigan, Lee served several churches in Ohio before accepting a similar professorate at Adrian College in 1864. He rejoined the Methodist Episcopal Church after the Civil War and continued preaching throughout southern Michigan until his retirement.

References: Donald W. Dayton, ed., *Five Sermons and a Tract by Luther Lee* (1975); Paul Leslie Kaufman, *Logical Luther Lee and the Methodist War against Slavery* (2000).

Lee, Richard (1946–) Richard Lee graduated from Mercer University and from Luther Rice Seminary. He became pastor of Rehoboth Baptist Church in the Atlanta metropolitan area in 1982; by 1995, the church claimed five thousand members. Lee has been active in the leadership of the *SOUTHERN BAPTIST CONVENTION, and he appears weekly on Rehoboth's radio and television programs, *There's Hope*.

Lee, Robert G(reene) (1886–1978) Born to a sharecropper's family in South Carolina, Robert G. Lee was converted at age twelve and attended Furman University, where he graduated in 1913. After serving a number of churches, Lee accepted the pulpit at Bellevue Baptist Church, in Memphis, Tennessee, in 1927, where he established a reputation as an accomplished preacher and devoted Baptist leader. He published fifty volumes of sermons, and he preached his most famous sermon, "Payday, Someday," more than twelve hundred times. An ardent opponent of feminism, Lee once remarked that a man's home was his fortress, "where a woman buckles on his armor in the morning as he goes forth to the battles of the day and soothes his wounds when he comes home at night." Lee served as president of the *SOUTHERN BAPTIST CONVENTION from 1948 to 1950, the same year that *Christian Century* designated Bellevue Baptist one of twelve "great churches" in the United States. By the time of Lee's retirement in 1960, Bellevue had received nearly twenty-five thousand new members during his tenure.

References: John E. Huss, *Robert G. Lee: The Authorized Biography* (1967); Randall Balmer, *Grant Us Courage: Travels Along the Mainline of American Protestantism* (1996).

Lee College (Cleveland, Tennessee) Lee College was founded in 1918 by the *CHURCH OF GOD (CLEVELAND, TENNESSEE). First known as Bible Training School, the institution was renamed in honor of its second president, F. J. Lee, in 1947.

Most students are from the Church of God, which has its headquarters in Cleveland. Lee College defines its theological perspective as "conservative, evangelical and Pentecostal," but also professes a strong interest in supporting independent research. All board members, faculty, and staff are required to sign a written statement each year pledging they will not advocate "anything contrary to the Church of God Declaration of Faith."

Lee College is well known for its Christian music program. Two music groups—Lee Singers and Ladies of Lee—have toured throughout Europe and Asia. *DANCING is not proscribed in the code of student conduct. The use of tobacco, however, is forbidden both on and off campus, and the code remains in effect during school vacations.

Reference: Lee College Undergraduate Catalog 1996–97 (1996).

Leighton Ford Ministries. *See* **Ford, Leighton.**

Leland, John (1754–1841) Converted in 1772 at the age of eighteen, John Leland soon thereafter became a preacher, first in his native New England and then, after 1776, in Virginia, whence he itinerated to the Carolinas and as far north as Philadelphia. As a Baptist, Leland agitated for religious freedom and the disestablishment of religion (no state church). He befriended Thomas Jefferson and James Madison and enthusiastically greeted Jefferson's 1786 bill "Establishing Religious Freedom in Virginia." Two years later, fearing that the proposed federal Constitution did not adequately provide for religious freedom, Leland, with the backing of Virginia Baptists, announced his candidacy for the Virginia Convention in order to oppose ratification. Upon Madison's assurance that the matter would be corrected to Leland's satisfaction, Leland withdrew and threw his support behind Madison, who was easily elected.

Leland returned to New England in 1792 and settled in Cheshire, Massachusetts, where he remained (nominally, at least) for the next half century. He traveled and preached widely throughout New England, calling for *CONVERSIONS and pushing for disestablishment. After Jefferson's election to the presidency, Leland marked the occasion by presenting his friend with an enormous cheese, weighing over one thousand pounds. Leland was elected to the Massachusetts House of Representatives in 1811, where he continued to push for religious freedom. He urged liberty of conscience in religious matters and assured his fellow legislators that Christianity could stand on its own merits. Massachusetts eventually disestablished religion in 1833, the last state to do so.

Reference: Edwin S. Gaustad, "The Backus-Leland Tradition," *Foundations,* II (April 1959).

Leroy Jenkins Evangelistic Association. *See* **Jenkins, Leroy.**

Lester Sumrall Evangelistic Association. *See* **Sumrall, Lester (Frank).**

LeTourneau University (Longview, Texas) Nondenominational LeTourneau University was founded in 1946 to serve soldiers returning from the war. It began as LeTourneau Technical Institute, a technical school funded by Robert G. LeTourneau, an industrialist who made his fortune designing heavy-duty earth-moving machinery and offshore drilling platforms.

The school adopted a liberal arts curriculum in 1961 and took the name LeTourneau College. That same year, the college admitted women for the first time. With the introduction of an M.B.A. program in 1989, the college became known as LeTourneau University.

LeTourneau University is distinctive among Christian liberal arts colleges in its retention of technical programs. The school offers a fully accredited engineering major and a strong aviation program, with fifteen planes and its own airstrip.

Reference: LeTourneau University Catalog, 1994–1996 (1994).

Levitt, Zola (1938–) Born in Pittsburgh, into an Orthodox Jewish household, Zola Levitt converted to evangelical Christianity in the 1970s and proceeded to fashion a career out of persuading other Jews to do likewise. From his base in Dallas, Texas, Levitt began with radio—a local program called *The Heart of the Matter* and *Zola Levitt Live,* which was syndicated nationally. Levitt expanded into television in 1978 with *Zola Levitt Presents.* Many of the programs are taped in the Middle East (to emphasize Levitt's contention that evangelical Christianity is the fulfillment of Judaism) with Levitt dressed in flowing white robes. That, together with a full beard, makes him look like a prophetic figure to his many fans (most of whom are evangelicals) and a comic figure to his detractors.

Zola Levitt Ministries runs the Institute of Jewish-Christian Studies, which emphasizes Judaism as the antecedent of Christianity. Levitt has also written a number of books, composes music, and runs his own travel agency, which specializes in tours to Israel. Twice divorced, Levitt in 1994 faced charges of sexual harassment from former employees.

Reference: Zola Levitt, *The Cairo Connection* (1977).

Lewis, C(live) S(taples) (1898–1963) Although C. S. Lewis would never have fit into the theological and cultural categories of twentieth-century American *EVANGELICALISM, much less *FUNDAMENTALISM, his writings exerted an enormous influence on American evangelicals, especially those with intellectual aspirations. Lewis, a Cambridge don and literary scholar, not only studied literature but produced an extraordinary range of literature himself, from science fiction and children's fantasy to autobiography and apologetics.

Lewis's *CONVERSION to Christianity in 1931 had been a tortured one, the intellectual struggle of an atheist who finally surrendered while riding in the sidecar of his brother's motorcycle. Evangelical college students of the 1960s and 1970s, eager to put the anti-intellectualism of *FUNDAMENTALISM behind them, identified with Lewis. They found his writings intelligent and urbane; the fact that Lewis was an Anglican and that he did not share American *EVANGELICALISM's scruples about *TEMPERANCE lent a certain spiciness to that identification. Ironically, the Wade Collection for research on Lewis is housed at *WHEATON COLLEGE, an evangelical school whose theological standards and behavioral requirements would have prevented Lewis from matriculating as a student. Lewis's death on November 22, 1963, was overshadowed by the assassination of President John F. Kennedy the same day.

References: C. S. Lewis, *The Problem of Pain* (1940); idem, *The Screwtape Letters* (1942); idem, *Mere Christianity* (1952); idem, *The Chronicles of Narnia* (1950–1956); Walter Hopper, *C. S. Lewis: A Companion and Guide* (1996).

Lewis, Crystal (1969–) *CONTEMPORARY CHRISTIAN MUSIC artist Crystal Lewis was born in Norco, California, into a preacher's family. She sang in church from an early age and began her recording career at the age of fifteen. She has released more than a dozen albums—including *Gold* and *Beauty for Ashes*—and she has performed at Harvest Crusades.

Liberalism For *EVANGELICALISM, the notion of liberalism has been a protean one, and evangelicals have usually defined themselves as conservative; they have sometimes used the term "orthodox," much to the chagrin of people associated with Eastern Orthodoxy. In theological terms, evangelicals in the nineteenth century distanced themselves from two liberal intellectual currents that cast doubt on the veracity of the *BIBLE: Darwinism and the German discipline of higher criticism. Early in the twentieth century, evangelicals felt embattled by what they reviled as *MODERNISM, the drift toward more liberal formulations of theology within mainline Protestantism. Evangelicals even objected to *NEO-ORTHODOXY as liberal because of what they saw as compromises on the doctrine of biblical *AUTHORITY.

In matters of lifestyle, "liberalism" has often connoted any deviation from a strict fundamentalist behavioral code, which included, typically, proscriptions against *DANCING, card-playing, tobacco (except in the South), or any consumption of alcohol. With the rise of the *RELIGIOUS RIGHT in the late 1970s, some evangelicals added another demonic overtone to the term "liberalism," that of political liberalism.

Liberty Association of General Baptists. *See* **General Association of General Baptists** *and* **Stinson, Benoni.**

Liberty University (Lynchburg, Virginia) Liberty University was founded in 1971 by rising fundamentalist superstar *JERRY FALWELL, who remains on board as chancellor. Originally chartered as Lynchburg Baptist College, Liberty first enrolled only 154 students and held classes in the old high school from which Falwell himself had graduated in 1950. Liberty, which bills itself as the largest private university in Virginia, proudly announces it enrolls nearly five thousand "Young Champions for Christ." In search of a permanent campus, the school bought Candler's Mountain in 1972; since then, the campus has been valued at as much as $200 million, although the school's indebtedness is considerable.

Among evangelical colleges, Liberty's rate of growth is rivaled only by televangelist *ORAL ROBERTS's *ORAL ROBERTS UNIVERSITY in Oklahoma, and *REGENT UNIVERSITY, founded in Virginia by CBN mogul *PAT ROBERTSON. These three schools—arguably the "super-universities" of evangelical America—all bear the distinctive marks of their founders. Liberty still sends many students to worship at Falwell's Thomas Road Baptist Church, and its mission reflects the priorities of Falwell's *MORAL MAJORITY. Built into the "statement of purpose" is a declaration of Liberty's commitment to promoting "an understanding of the Western tradition and the diverse elements of American cultural history, especially the importance of the individual in maintaining democratic and free market processes." Considering that Falwell was at the forefront of the battle to institute the study of "*CREATIONISM" in public schools, it is not surprising that all students are required to take a course on the "History of Life," to ensure a sound background in *CREATIONISM. Liberty University is, in fact, the home of the Center for Creation Studies.

Yet in spite of Falwell's self-positioning as a fundamentalist leader, Liberty shows signs of having made more than a few concessions to contemporary society. The school sponsors numerous Christian rock concerts each year. Liberty has Division I status for all athletic teams, and its basketball team is, in fact, an aspiring contender for the national championship. (The football team was led, at one time, by former Cleveland Browns coach Sam Rutigliano.) Although social *DANCING is proscribed by the college, a nightly aerobics class is held in the student union. Furthermore, students from "God's University," as Falwell refers to the institution, witness on mission trips around the world, distributing tracts not only in distant places such as the former Soviet Union, but also on Florida's beaches during spring break.

At times, the inconsistencies in Liberty's priorities seem to be an exaggerated version of a problem facing many *CHRISTIAN COLLEGES: how to integrate a religious-based program with a liberal arts curriculum. For example, in spite of the "History of Life" requirement, Liberty has a well-developed program in the sciences and offers a pre-med biology track. The situation is possibly more pronounced at Liberty, because the school has ambitions of developing several graduate schools. Currently, it offers graduate programs in education and religion, but it has divided its undergraduate programs into five distinct schools: Education, Communications, Religion, Business and Government, and the College of General Studies, with sights on enlarging each of them in the future.

Faculty at Liberty University are hired on a year-to-year basis. "We don't have tenure," Falwell boasted in 1996, "so it's unlikely that the inmates will be running the asylum here in a few years." In addition to having financial entanglements with Charles Keating, who was convicted in the savings and loan scandals in the 1980s, Falwell early in 1998 acknowledged accepting several million dollars from Sun Myung Moon's Unification Church.

References: *Liberty University 1994–96 Catalog* (1994); John W. Kennedy, "Jerry Falwell's Uncertain Legacy," *Christianity Today,* December 9, 1996.

L.I.F.E. Bible College (San Dimas, California) L.I.F.E. Bible College is affiliated with the *INTERNATIONAL CHURCH OF THE FOURSQUARE GOSPEL, the pentecostal/charismatic denomination started by evangelist *AIMEE SEMPLE MCPHERSON in the 1920s. "L.I.F.E." stands for "Lighthouse of International Foursquare Evangelism." McPherson established the college in Los Angeles in 1924. The school used the facilities of Angelus Temple, the denomination's headquarters, for six decades. L.I.F.E. Bible College then moved onto its own campus in San Dimas, California.

L.I.F.E. Bible College, which numbers *CHUCK SMITH of *CALVARY CHAPEL among its alumni, does not grant graduate degrees, but it runs the series of courses necessary to obtain a ministerial license in the *INTERNATIONAL CHURCH OF THE FOURSQUARE GOSPEL. The college also runs a correspondence school, which grants an associate's degree in *BIBLE. L.I.F.E. is accredited through the *ACCREDITING ASSOCIATION OF BIBLE COLLEGES, though it does not have regional academic accreditation. Occult practices and social *DANCING are both forbidden in the Standards of Student Conduct.

Reference: *L.I.F.E. Bible College Catalog '96–'97* (1996).

Life in the Word, Inc. *See* **Meyer, Joyce.**

LIFE Outreach International. *See* **Robison, James.**

Lifechangers, Inc. *See* **Mumford, Bernard C., Jr. "Bob."**

Lighthouse Temple (Eugene, Oregon). *See* **Hornshuh, Fred.**

Ligonier Ministries Established in 1971 in Ligonier, Pennsylvania, by ***R. C. SPROUL**, Ligonier Ministries produces educational materials from a Reformed—

even arch-Calvinist—perspective, which insists on the Calvinist notions of predestination and election and refutes the idea of free will. The organization, which moved its operations to Orlando, Florida, in 1984, also produces a daily radio program, *Renewing Your Mind with R. C. Sproul.*

Lindsay, Freda (Theresa) (née Shimpf) (1916–) Freda Lindsay, a partner in ministry with her husband, *GORDON LINDSAY, was a leader and organizer of the healing *REVIVAL and helped to found his *VOICE OF HEALING and Christ for the Nations organizations. Upon *GORDON LINDSAY's death in 1973, Freda Lindsay was elected president of the Dallas-based Christ for the Nations Institute, which has seen significant growth under her leadership.

Lindsay, Gordon (1906–1973) Founder and director of Christ for the Nations Institute, Gordon Lindsay was born in *ZION CITY, Illinois, to parents who were part of *JOHN ALEXANDER DOWIE's pentecostal community there. After financial problems surfaced in *ZION CITY, they headed west to Pisgah Grande, California, and then to Portland, Oregon. Gordon Lindsay was converted under the preaching of *CHARLES FOX PARHAM. Lindsay linked up with fellow pentecostal John G. Lake, founder of the Divine Healing missions in Portland and in Spokane, Washington. After itinerating in California and throughout the South, Lindsay settled into pastorates at Avenal, California, and San Fernando, California. After serving as pastor of a church in Ashland, Oregon, Lindsay resigned in 1947 to become manager of *WILLIAM BRANHAM's revival campaigns.

In an effort to publicize the *REVIVALS, Lindsay published *The Voice of Healing,* beginning in 1948, as well as the short-lived *World-Wide Revival* and, later, *Christ for the Nations.* His eagerness to draw attention to other revivalists as well as to Branham led to a break with the latter. Lindsay continued to publish the itineraries of various healing revivalists, who in turn agreed to abide by certain standards of theology and behavior that Lindsay articulated. He organized conventions for healing evangelists—1949 in Dallas, Texas, and 1950 in Kansas City, Missouri—providing a forum as well as guidelines for conducting their *REVIVAL campaigns.

Although he was much more successful in bringing order to the healing *REVIVAL, Lindsay founded Winning the Nations Crusade in 1956 as a missions agency. His business, organizational, and diplomatic skills came to the surface again in 1962, however, when he became one of the prime movers behind the Full Gospel Fellowship of Churches and Ministers International, an organization designed to promote understanding and to minimize the duplication of efforts among pentecostals and charismatics.

In 1967, Lindsay's various ministries were regathered under the rubric of Christ for the Nations, Inc., based in Dallas. Following his death in 1973, Lindsay's widow, *FREDA, was elected president of the organization; it enjoyed even greater growth and influence under her leadership.

References: Gordon Lindsay, *Bible Days Are Here Again* (1949); David Edwin Harrell Jr., *All Things Are Possible: The Healing and Charismatic Revivals in Modern America* (1975).

Lindsell, Harold (1913–1998) Harold Lindsell, one of the more insistent apologists for fundamentalist theology, especially biblical *INERRANCY, was born in

New York City. He graduated from *WHEATON COLLEGE in 1939 and went on for graduate degrees from the University of California, Berkeley, and New York University. An ordained Baptist minister, Lindsell taught at *COLUMBIA BIBLE COLLEGE and Northern Baptist Theological Seminary before becoming professor of missions and church history at the newly formed *FULLER THEOLOGICAL SEMINARY in 1947. He left Fuller for *CHRISTIANITY TODAY in 1964, where he remained until 1978, serving successively as associate editor, editor, and publisher.

Lindsell was exceedingly unhappy about the direction of Fuller Seminary, especially after his departure. He detected a slide toward theological *LIBERALISM, especially on the matter of biblical *INERRANCY. He registered loud noises of protest, notably in his 1976 screed *The Battle for the Bible,* in which he attacked those who, he believed, were compromising orthodox theology.

References: Harold Lindsell, *A Christian Philosophy of Missions* (1949); idem, *Park Street Prophet* (1951); idem, *Christianity and the Cults* (1963); idem, *The World, the Flesh and the Devil* (1973); idem, *The Battle for the Bible* (1976); idem, *The Bible in the Balance* (1979); idem, *The Gathering Storm* (1980); George M. Marsden, *Reforming Fundamentalism: Fuller Seminary and the New Evangelicalism* (1987).

Lindsey, Hal (1930–) Born in Houston in 1930, Hal Lindsey's early Christian life faltered between total apathy, which verged on the point of suicide, and fanatical commitment. He studied briefly at the University of Houston, served in the United States Coast Guard, and then experienced a religious *CONVERSION after going through a divorce. Influenced by his contacts with *FUNDAMENTALISM in the 1950s, Lindsey began to develop a fascination with biblical prophecy. He enrolled in *DALLAS THEOLOGICAL SEMINARY, the intellectual center of dispensational *PREMILLENNIALISM, and served as a domestic missionary for *CAMPUS CRUSADE.

Lindsey left *CAMPUS CRUSADE in 1970 to begin the Jesus Christ Light and Power Company, a youth-oriented ministry on the Los Angeles campus of the University of California (UCLA). Having compiled a number of eschatologically based sermons over the years, he published them under the title *The Late Great Planet Earth.* The book became an overnight best-seller, hitting on a raw nerve of excitement concerning the close proximity of the *SECOND COMING of Christ. With one eye on the Bible and one toward the daily news, Lindsey's book unleashed a wave of *END-TIMES frenzy. His interpretation built upon the rebirth of the nation of Israel in 1948 and the Israeli victory during the Six Day War in 1967, both of which he saw as fulfillment of biblical prophecy and as a foreshadowing of the *SECOND COMING of Christ. Lindsey sometimes taunted his critics, declaring that a person who did not agree with his interpretation scheme did not really believe what was written in the *BIBLE.

Any best-selling book begets sequels. In 1972, he published *Satan Is Alive and Well on Planet Earth,* a book based on the theme of worldwide satanic conspiracies, which fit nicely with the congenital pessimism of American fundamentalists. Next was *There's a New World Coming,* a juxtaposition of the book of Revelation with the menace of twentieth-century technology and nuclear capabilities.

Lindsey's critics were quick to note the apparent contradiction of a man investing heavily in real estate, all the while proclaiming the end of the world. Theologians and historians called his books "biased, manipulative, lacking in integrity, and dangerous," while questioning "the expertise of Lindsey's witnesses and his citation of seemingly minor historical events as having deep significance in prophetic history." Undaunted, Lindsey has continued to be one of the leading experts on biblical prophecy, traveling throughout the world as a popular conference speaker. He continues his prophecies with a weekly radio program, *Saturdays with Hal Lindsey.*

References: Hal Lindsey, *The Late Great Planet Earth* (1970); idem, *Satan Is Alive and Well on Planet Earth* (1972); idem, *The World's Final Hour: Evacuation or Extinction?* (1976); idem, *The 1980s: Countdown to Armageddon* (1980); idem, *The Rapture: Truth or Consequences* (1983); Stephen R. Graham, s.v. "Hal Lindsey," in Charles H. Lippy, ed., *Twentieth-Century Shapers of American Popular Religion* (1989).

Lipscomb, David (1831–1917) Educated at Franklin College in Nashville, Tennessee, David Lipscomb emerged after the Civil War as spokesman for the noninstrumental Churches of Christ. As editor of the *Gospel Advocate,* Lipscomb argued against the use of musical instruments in worship services as well as against organized missionary societies, positions that set the noninstrumental Churches of Christ apart from others in the *RESTORATION MOVEMENT, which sought to restore the church to its New Testament simplicity. In 1891, he founded Nashville Bible School (which later took the name David Lipscomb College).

Literalism *Literalism* refers to the practice of interpreting the *BIBLE literally. Among evangelicals, a literalist would insist, for example, that Adam and Eve were historical figures, that Jonah was indeed swallowed by a large fish, and that the entire book of Revelation, with its apocalyptic beasts and dragons and vials of judgment, will appear exactly as written. The tendency toward literalism derives from at least three sources. First is the fact that evangelicals take the *BIBLE seriously as God's special revelation to humanity. Second, Martin Luther argued for the priesthood of believers, that each individual was responsible before God, which made it incumbent upon each believer to read and interpret the *BIBLE for oneself (Luther also urged the translation of the Scriptures into the vernacular). Finally, the philosophy of *SCOTTISH COMMON SENSE REALISM, which evangelical theologians adopted in the nineteenth century, assured evangelicals that the meaning of Scripture lay in its plainest sense and was available to the ordinary reader when using "common sense."

Living Bible, The In 1954, Kenneth N. Taylor began paraphrasing the *BIBLE into modern English during his daily commute into Chicago from the suburbs. Taylor, an evangelical layman, was concerned that his ten children would not read the *BIBLE because of the unfamiliarity of the cadences of Elizabethan English. By 1962, having failed at finding a publisher for the first installment of his paraphrases, *Living Letters,* Taylor and his wife, Margaret, published the volume themselves under the aegis of *TYNDALE HOUSE PUBLISHERS. The *BILLY GRAHAM organization picked up on it and ordered massive quantities as a promotional device, thereby providing invaluable publicity and ensuring broad acceptance by evangelicals. *TYNDALE HOUSE published Taylor's paraphrases incrementally and then released the entire *BIBLE, called *The Living Bible,* which became enormously popular among evangelicals and has sold more than forty million copies in North America alone.

Livingston, John H(enry) (1746–1825) Born in Poughkeepsie, New York, and educated at Yale College, John H. Livingston studied law for several years before electing to go into the ministry of the Dutch Reformed Church. He studied theology at the University of Utrecht and was ordained by the Classis of Amsterdam. He returned to America in 1770 and became the second English-speaking minister to the collegiate Dutch Reformed churches in New York City.

Livingston became an ardent Patriot during the American Revolution as well as a peacemaker within a church that had long been divided between pietist and traditionalist factions. In 1784, Livingston was elected professor of theology by his Dutch Reformed colleagues, and for many years he offered theological instruction while performing his pastoral duties in New York. From 1810 until his death in 1825, he served as president of Queen's College (now Rutgers University) in New Brunswick, New Jersey, where he also continued offering theological instruction. Those efforts eventually were institutionalized under the rubric of a seminary, now known as New Brunswick Theological Seminary.

Livingston, William (1723–1790) Born in Albany, New York, into a prominent Dutch family, William Livingston graduated from Yale College in 1941. His decision to practice law thrust him into the cauldron of New York politics; he became a populist and a leader of the so-called Presbyterian Party, which challenged the prerogatives and the pretensions of the Anglican Party. In the 1750s, Livingston led the opposition to the formation of King's College (now Columbia University) under Anglican auspices because the organizers wanted to use public funds. Although he failed to block King's College, Livingston succeeded in diverting some of the public lottery money earmarked for the college toward the construction of a jail. More important, his spirited advocacy of the separation of church and state, as published in the *Independent Reflector,* earned for Livingston a place in the history of religious disestablishment in America.

Wearied of the political fray, Livingston retired to New Jersey in 1772. His retirement, however, proved elusive, especially with the onset of the American Revolution. Livingston served on the Essex County Committee of Correspondence, as a delegate to the First Continental Congress, and as commander of the New Jersey militia. The New Jersey legislature elected Livingston as the state's first governor, an office he held for fourteen years.

References: Milton M. Klein, ed., *The Independent Reflector* (1963); John M. Mulder, "William Livingston: Propagandist Against Episcopacy," *Journal of Presbyterian History,* LIV (1976).

Livingstone, David (1813–1873) Doubtless the most famous missionary of the nineteenth century, David Livingstone left his native Scotland for Africa in 1741, having first studied theology, science, and medicine. He had been converted more than a decade earlier after reading *Philosophy of a Future State,* by Thomas Dick, which sought to reconcile science and the *BIBLE. Livingstone began his African sojourn in Cape Town and then headed north to Kuruman, exploring the land, making scientific observations, and learning the Tswana language. He worked in a number of mission stations in the 1840s but always sought to continue north. In 1852, after Transvaal Boers had burned his mission at Kolobeng, Livingstone began a three-year walk north to the upper Zambesi, in central Africa, where he made contact with the Kololo, who also spoke Tswana. Accompanied by members of the Kololo tribe, he continued his trek to the Angola coast. In the course of that leg of his journey, Livingstone discovered evidence of European land-hunger and pillage, including the work of Portuguese slavers. He returned to central Africa—and later to Great Britain—with the conviction that the Zambesi was the surest route for introducing Christianity to Africa, for there the message of the *GOSPEL was as yet untainted by the rapaciousness of Europeans.

At Livingstone's behest, the British government sponsored an expedition in conjunction with the Anglican missionary society, the Universities Mission to Central Africa, but this effort to bring "Christianity and Commerce" to the African interior foundered. The expedition, which lasted from 1858 to 1863, mapped a vast region hitherto unknown to Europeans, but the incursion of Swahili and Portuguese slavers had aroused animosities; many missionaries and staff members died, as did Livingstone's wife, Mary. Discouraged, Livingstone returned to Britain in 1863. Eventually he rallied patrons to his cause of saving eastern Africa from the slavers and left for Africa one final time in 1866.

Livingstone's peregrinations mapped still more of the interior and opened remote parts of Africa to the outside world. His long absences, however, made him the object of popular curiosity in Britain; the *New York Herald* dispatched H. Morton Stanley to "find" him in 1871, and the purported greeting at their encounter, "Dr. Livingstone, I presume," became a popular phrase of English-language repartee. Upon Livingstone's death in 1873, his African friends buried his heart in Africa and transported his body to the British at Zanzibar. His funeral in Westminster Abbey was a national event and triggered a cottage industry of literary works celebrating this heroic missionary.

Reference: David Livingstone, *Missionary Travels and Researches in South Africa* (1857).

Lockerbie, D(onald) Bruce (1935–) Born in Capreol, Ontario, D. Bruce Lockerbie earned both the bachelor's and the master's degrees at New York University. He has taught since 1957 at the Stony Brook School in Stony Brook, New York, an evangelical private school on Long Island. Lockerbie, an Episcopalian, has lectured at *CHRISTIAN COLLEGES, and he has written extensively on matters of faith, parenting, education, theology, and fine arts.

References: D. Bruce Lockerbie, *Patriarchs and Prophets* (1969); idem, *The Way They Should Go* (1972); idem, *The Liberating Word: Art and the Mystery of the Gospel* (1974); idem, *A Man under Orders: Lt. General William K. Harrison Jr.* (1978); idem, *In Peril on the Sea* (1984).

Log College Shortly after settling into the Presbyterian pastorate in Neshaminy, Pennsylvania, in 1726, *WILLIAM TENNENT began providing theological instruction to his sons and to other young men who wanted to be schooled in evangelical theology and piety. He erected in 1736 what his opponents derisively referred to as the Log College, a modest eighteen-by-twenty-foot structure that is generally acknowledged as the precursor of the College of New Jersey (now Princeton University). Old Side Presbyterians, those who insisted on strict subscription to the *WESTMINSTER STANDARDS and who opposed the *GREAT AWAKENING, believed that only the colleges of New England or the universities of the Old

World provided an education worthy of a Presbyterian minister, and so they looked askance at the Log College, its students, and Tennent himself. The Old Side–New Side controversy of the 1730s, however, prompted the organization of the New Brunswick presbytery, controlled by *NEW LIGHTS. Because Presbyterian *POLITY allowed individual presbyteries to train, license, and ordain ministers, the evangelicals of the New Brunswick presbytery could ordain Log College graduates without contending with the Old Side traditionalists who ran the Philadelphia presbytery.

The *REVIVAL of the ensuing decade tipped the balance of power decidedly in favor of Tennent and the *NEW LIGHTS. *GEORGE WHITEFIELD built upon the pietistic awakening already under way among the Dutch in the Raritan Valley of New Jersey. Whitefield quickly formed alliances with *THEODORUS JACOBUS FRELINGHUYSEN, with Tennent, and with his Log College graduates, especially Tennent's eldest son, *GILBERT TENNENT.

The elder Tennent's energies began to flag somewhat in the 1740s, and by his death in 1746 the Log College itself had ceased its operations. Later in the same year, however, New Side Presbyterians organized the College of New Jersey to carry on Tennent's vision of a Presbyterian clergy trained in both theology and, in the argot of the day, "experimental" piety.

References: Archibald Alexander, *The Log College* (1851); Randall Balmer and John R. Fitzmier, *The Presbyterians* (1993).

Lord's Supper Also known as Holy Communion or, in more high-church circles, Holy Eucharist, the Lord's Supper refers to a commemoration of the Last Supper Jesus shared with his disciples before his crucifixion. Because evangelicals have generally shied away from sacramentalism (in part because of its association with Roman Catholicism), many hold to a "memorialist" view of the Lord's Supper. In this interpretation, the bread and the wine of Holy Communion merely remind us of the death of Christ; they do not necessarily impart *GRACE to the believer, as in the Roman Catholic doctrine of transubstantiation, where the bread and wine actually become the body and blood of Christ.

The memorialist view has led, in turn, to a diminution of observance among evangelicals. Whereas faithful Catholics or Episcopalians would receive Holy Communion at least once a week, most evangelical churches offer the Lord's Supper once a month at most, perhaps as seldom as once a quarter or a couple of times a year. The *TEMPERANCE movement in nineteenth-century America also wrought changes in evangelical practice. Unfermented wine—grape juice—was substituted for wine, and the common cup was jettisoned for hygienic reasons in favor of small, individual-sized containers.

Reference: Leonard I. Sweet, *Health and Medicine in the Evangelical Tradition: "Not By Might Nor Power"* (1994).

Los Angeles Pacific College. *See* **Azusa Pacific University.**

Los Angeles University Cathedral. *See* **Scott, Eugene V. "Gene."**

Lott Carey Missionary Convention. *See* **National Baptist Convention of the U.S.A., Inc.**

Lotz, Anne Graham (1948–) An *EVANGELIST and Bible teacher, Anne Graham is the second daughter of *BILLY and *RUTH GRAHAM. Reared in the Montreat

Presbyterian Church, Anne Graham was converted at an early age. In 1966, she married Daniel Lotz, a dentist, reared a family, and became interested in teaching the *BIBLE. She founded AnGeL Ministries (a wordplay on her initials) in 1988, which has catapulted her into speaking situations, often as the first woman to address an evangelical audience. "A lot of places I go I'm the first woman," she told the *New York Times* in 2000. "And I would pray that they're not inviting me because I'm a woman, but because of the message I bring." Lotz defends this role against conservatives by insisting that she speaks from "the *AUTHORITY of Scripture, not from a position of *AUTHORITY over men."

Although Lotz is widely heralded as a superb preacher, she sees her role more as that of teacher to people who are already believers. "Daddy and Franklin are obstetricians, bringing the babies into the family of God," Lotz told a reporter in 2000. "I take them, once they're in the family, and help them to grow."

References: Anne Graham Lotz, *The Vision of His Glory: Finding Hope through the Revelation of Jesus Christ* (1996); idem, *God's Story: Finding Meaning for Your Life in Genesis* (1997); idem, *Just Give Me Jesus* (2000); Gustav Niebuhr, "A Daughter of Graham Is to Address Evangelists," *New York Times,* July 31, 2000; Gayle White, "Her Father's Daughter," *Atlanta Journal-Constitution,* August 19, 2000.

Lovejoy, Elijah P(arish) (1802–1837) The son of a Congregational minister, Elijah P. Lovejoy was born in Albion, Maine, and graduated from Waterville (now Colby) College in 1826. He headed west for St. Louis the following year, where he taught school for several years and for a brief time edited a Whig newspaper. Converted under the preaching of David Nelson, an antislavery *EVANGELIST, Lovejoy returned east in 1832 to study at Princeton Theological Seminary. Licensed to preach by the Philadelphia presbytery in April 1833, he headed back to St. Louis and became editor of the *St. Louis Observer,* a Presbyterian weekly. Lovejoy wielded a fierce editorial pen against Roman Catholics, Baptists, Campbellites, and especially against slavery. Such views were not popular in St. Louis, a river port for the lower South. Protests multiplied, and Lovejoy sought refuge twenty-five miles up the river, in Alton, Illinois.

Although he railed against the evils of slavery, Lovejoy did not at first advocate *ABOLITIONISM; he preferred a gradual end to the institution rather than complete and immediate emancipation. His views became more radical, however, at the Presbyterian General Assembly of 1836, where he sensed that his fellow Presbyterians were equivocating on the issue. Lovejoy returned to Alton with renewed fervor to take up the abolitionist cause. His efforts, however, met with resistance and misfortune. His press arrived from St. Louis on a Sunday, but Lovejoy's sabbatarian scruples compelled him to leave it on the wharf. Sometime during the night it was dumped into the river. A second press was destroyed by angry vigilantes, but, with the assistance of the Ohio Anti-Slavery Society, Lovejoy tooled up again. On one occasion, Lovejoy tried to defend a black man who was burned at the stake, and he met with frequent accusations that he was inciting slaves to revolt.

Lovejoy organized a state auxiliary to the American Anti-Slavery Society in Alton, which aroused further opposition. Local mobs destroyed his press a third time. When the replacement arrived on November 7, 1837, Lovejoy's abolitionist defenders took up arms to guard the warehouse where it sat. An armed mob moved against the warehouse, and someone tried to set it on fire. Lovejoy rushed out to prevent the arson and was shot dead, thereby becoming a martyr both for the cause of abolition and for the freedom of the press.

References: Merton Lynn Dillon, *Elijah P. Lovejoy, Abolitionist Editor* (1961); Paul Simon, *Lovejoy: Martyr to Freedom* (1964).

Ludwig, Wiebo (1941–) An environmental activist and a former Christian Reformed pastor, Wiebo Ludwig graduated from *CALVIN THEOLOGICAL SEMINARY and was pastor of several churches in Ontario. He moved his extended family to the remote Peace River region of western Canada in 1985, setting up a back-to-the-land religious commune on the Alberta–British Columbia border. On April 26, 2000, Ludwig was sentenced to twenty-eight months in prison for sabotaging oil wells in the Canadian north. He claimed that pollution from the oil wells, especially the so-called sour-gas flares used to burn off excess fumes from the wells, was responsible for the poisoning of his land and livestock and for three miscarriages and a stillborn child in his family.

Lutheran Church—Missouri Synod The history of the Lutheran Church—Missouri Synod (LCMS) properly begins with its real founder, *MARTIN STEPHAN, who rarely appears in the sanitized versions of the Synod's history. Stephan was a charismatic, pietist preacher in Saxony who managed to gather around him a coterie of young theological students—as well as, apparently, a coterie of young women. After the authorities shut down Stephan's conventicles, he and his followers made plans to emigrate to the United States. Stephan assumed the title and the elaborate trappings of bishop, and while his followers struggled to gain a foothold in the New World, Stephan began construction of his sumptuous bishop's residence in Perry County, Missouri, using the band's common fund, which Stephan controlled. His followers eventually confirmed their suspicions about Stephan's financial malfeasance and his dalliances with an assortment of women. The clergy finally ousted their leader and sent him into exile, literally rowing him across the Missouri River in 1839 and depositing him in Illinois.

For Stephan's followers, the Stephan debacle provided a formative lesson about the dangers of ecclesiastical autocracy. *C. F. W. WALTHER, pastor of the group's flagship church in St. Louis, stepped forward as leader of the movement, which insisted on congregational autonomy rather than episcopal *AUTHORITY. What became the Lutheran Church—Missouri Synod was formed in 1847 when pastors representing fifteen German Lutheran congregations met in Chicago and signed the constitution of the German Evangelical Lutheran Synod of Missouri, Ohio, and Other States. Ten other pastors signed the constitution as well, but their congregations had yet to approve the document. From these humble beginnings with 3,000 members, the German Evangelical Lutheran Synod grew dramatically to over 68,500 by the end of the nineteenth century and doubled again by the Synod's centennial. German remained the language of the churches until after the First World War. The name was officially changed to the Lutheran Church—Missouri Synod in 1947, the centennial of its founding.

The LCMS is the second largest American Lutheran body, behind only the Evangelical Lutheran Church in America (ELCA). The Missouri Synod is much more conservative than the larger ELCA. The LCMS does not permit the teaching or use of higher criticism of the *BIBLE, nor does the Synod ordain women; in many congregations of the Missouri Synod, women are not even allowed to vote on congregational matters. The LCMS subscribes to the belief in the *BIBLE as inspired, infallible, and inerrant. The Synod is Trinitarian. It upholds the traditional Lutheran confessions and the Lutheran trademarks of "*GRACE alone, Scripture alone, faith alone" as distillations of Luther's teaching.

*POLITY in the LCMS is congregational. The Synod's thirty-nine districts meet triennially in a national convention. The convention elects a president and has oversight of the large mission and educational programs. There are LCMS missions and partners in over fifty countries worldwide. The Synod started more than one hundred new North American ministries each year through the 1980s. The Synod has not participated in any major mergers in its history, and there was only one significant controversy.

During the 1960s, this controversy concerned the understanding of the *BIBLE as the *WORD OF GOD. The conservative faction believed the *BIBLE to be the *WORD OF GOD and that it should be interpreted literally. The more liberal side of the conflict believed the *BIBLE *bears* the *WORD OF GOD, and that, as such, it is open to historical criticism. At the end of the controversy, the more conservative group came out on top, which some historians maintained was the only time in the twentieth century that a conservative group has stemmed a liberal tide in its midst (the fundamentalist takeover of the Southern Baptist Convention in 1979 would belie that claim). The liberal group, numbering approximately one hundred thousand members and two hundred congregations, left the Lutheran Church—Missouri Synod to form the Association of Evangelical Lutheran Churches. This group was a part of the 1988 merger with the American Lutheran Church and the Lutheran Church in America, which created the ELCA.

In 2000, the LCMS reported an aggregate membership of 2.58 million members. There are LCMS churches in all fifty states, mostly concentrated in the Midwest. The Missouri Synod operates sixteen colleges and seminaries in North America. Its churches maintain more than fifteen hundred elementary and secondary schools, making the LCMS educational system the largest among Protestant denominations in the United States. The Synod is a member of the International Lutheran Council, but it does not belong to the Lutheran World Federation, the National Council of Churches, or the World Council of Churches. The LCMS international center is located in Kirkwood, Missouri.

References: Mary Todd, *Authority Vested: A Story of Identity and Change in the Lutheran Church—Missouri Synod* (2000); Frank S. Mead and Samuel S. Hill, *Handbook of Denominations in the United States,* 10th ed. (1996); J. Gordon Melton, *The Encyclopedia of American Religions,* 3d ed. (1993); *1997 Yearbook of American and Canadian Churches.*

Lutheran Congregations in Mission for Christ Lutheran Congregations in Mission for Christ (LCMC) was formed in 2000 by member churches of the Evangelical Lutheran Church in America (ELCA) who were upset by their denomination's approval of the Call to Common Mission, which brought the ELCA into a closer relationship with the Episcopal Church. Dissidents claimed that the cooperation with the Episcopalians compromised key elements of Lutheran theology, especially the priesthood of believers. The LCMC grew out of gatherings of disaffected Lutherans who had formed the Word-Alone Network to resist the approval of the Call to Common Mission.

Lutheran Hour, The. *See* **Maier, Walter A(rthur).**

Lynchburg Baptist College. *See* **Liberty University.**

Lyon, Mary (1797–1849) Born in Buckland, Massachusetts, Mary Lyon was baptized in 1822 and joined the Congregational Church. She taught in a number of schools in western Massachusetts and at the Adams Female Seminary in Londonderry, New Hampshire. She moved to the Ipswich Female Seminary in 1828, but she left in 1834 to pursue her dream of establishing a residential seminary for women. She helped to found Wheaton Female Seminary in Norwich, Massachusetts, in 1835 (now Wheaton College), and the following year she founded Mount Holyoke Female Seminary (Mount Holyoke College). For Lyon, the education of women fit into a larger scheme of building a Christian empire in the new nation. As teacher and as principal at Mount Holyoke, Lyon hewed to a rigorous curriculum, which included courses in mathematics, science, history, and theology.

References: Mary Lyon, *A Missionary Offering* (1843); Amanda Porterfield, *Mary Lyon and the Mount Holyoke Missionaries* (1997).

■ ■ ■

Mabie, Henry Clay (1847–1918) A leader of the fundamentalist faction among northern Baptists, Henry Clay Mabie studied at Chicago University and Seminary and served as a pastor in Illinois, Massachusetts, Indiana, and Minnesota. A tireless advocate of missions, Mabie was elected home secretary of the American Baptist Missionary Union (later renamed the American Baptist Foreign Mission Society) in 1890. As the fundamentalist-modernist controversy heated up toward the end of his life, Mabie sided with the fundamentalists and resisted moves toward centralization within the Northern Baptist Convention.

References: Henry Clay Mabie, *The Divine Right of Missions* (1908); idem, *From Romance to Reality* (1917).

Macartney, Clarence E(dward) (Noble) (1879–1957) Born in Norwood, Ohio, Clarence E. Macartney entered the Presbyterian ministry after studying at the University of Wisconsin, Princeton University, and Princeton Theological Seminary, where he worked with *FRANCIS LANDEY PATTON and *B. B. WARFIELD. His first pastorate was at Paterson, New Jersey; he moved to Philadelphia's Arch Street Presbyterian Church in 1915, where he became a major player in the denomination's fundamentalist-modernist controversy. In the face of liberal (or "modernist") opposition to authoritarian views of Scripture, Macartney called upon the *PRINCETON THEOLOGY of Warfield and *CHARLES HODGE, affirming biblical *INERRANCY and the Westminster Confession of Faith.

Macartney's zealous defense of the *WESTMINSTER STANDARDS catapulted him to the center of the fundamentalist-modernist debate. In 1922, Macartney took strong exception to Harry Emerson Fosdick's famous sermon, "Shall the Fundamentalists Win?" His pointed response was entitled "Shall Unbelief Win?" Macartney soon thereafter brought charges against Fosdick—a Baptist serving a prominent Presbyterian pulpit in New York City—arguing that all incumbents of Presbyterian pulpits must be prepared to affirm the Westminster Confession. The case festered for two years but finally was decided in Macartney's favor, whereupon Fosdick resigned the pulpit (and accepted John D. Rockefeller's invitation to become pastor of Riverside Church).

In part because of his role in the Fosdick case, Macartney was elected moderator of the General Assembly in 1924. He allied himself with *J. GRESHAM MACHEN in his clash with Princeton Seminary. Macartney left the board of the seminary and lent his support to Machen's new *WESTMINSTER THEOLOGICAL SEMINARY, but he refused to leave the Presbyterian Church, U.S.A. when Machen organized the *ORTHODOX PRESBYTERIAN CHURCH in the mid-1930s. Although aligned with the fundamentalists on most matters of theology and morality, Macartney never adopted *DISPENSATIONALISM and refused to become a separatist, preferring to remain as a conservative influence within the denomination. In 1927, he assumed the pulpit of First Presbyterian Church, Pittsburgh, where he stayed for more than a quarter century.

References: Clarence E. Macartney, *The Faith Once Delivered* (1952); C. Allyn Russell, *Voices of American Fundamentalism: Seven Biographical Studies* (1976); Bradley J. Longfield, *The Presbyterian Controversy: Fundamentalists, Modernists, and Moderates* (1991).

MacGregor, James (1759–1830) Born in the Scottish Highlands, James MacGregor studied at the University of Edinburgh, was ordained in Glasgow in 1786, and dispatched as the first Presbyterian missionary to Nova Scotia. A staunch abolitionist who was fluent in both English and Gaelic, MacGregor conducted Nova Scotia's first long communion in 1788 at Pictou. His efforts not only gained a foothold for Presbyterianism in the Maritimes—there were five Presbyterian ministers when he arrived in 1786 and twenty-one when he died in 1830—but also ensured that Presbyterianism bore the stamp of evangelical *CALVINISM.

Reference: G. A. Rawlyk, *The Canada Fire: Radical Evangelicalism in British North America, 1775–1812* (1994).

Machen, J(ohn) Gresham (1881–1937) Without doubt the most famous Presbyterian among the first generation of fundamentalists, J. Gresham Machen was born to a socially prominent family in Baltimore and was educated at Johns Hopkins University, Princeton Theological Seminary, and Marburg and Gottingen in Germany. Although he never lined up fully with *FUNDAMENTALISM—Machen referred to *DISPENSATIONALISM, for example, as a "false method of interpreting Scripture"—he was leader of the conservative forces within Presbyterianism. Machen supported the ouster of Charles A. Briggs from the Presbyterian ranks in the 1890s after Briggs, a professor at Union Theological Seminary (New York), cast doubt on biblical *AUTHORITY. Machen accepted a teaching position at Princeton Seminary in 1906; inherited the mantle of his mentor, *B. B. WARFIELD; and established himself as the last bastion of *PRINCETON THEOLOGY at the seminary.

The *PRINCETON THEOLOGY, with its trademark adherence to biblical *INERRANCY and subscription to the *WESTMINSTER STANDARDS, came increasingly under attack in the 1920s. Machen sought to confront the issue in 1923 with the publication of *Christianity and Liberalism*, which argued, in effect, that the two were mutually exclusive. The Presbyterian Church, U.S.A., however, continued to move in a modernist direction. The denomination adopted the *AUBURN AFFIRMATION in 1925, which allowed broad tolerance on doctrinal matters. Machen and other fundamentalists resisted, albeit unsuccessfully; the seminary was reorganized in 1929 to accommodate the *AUBURN AFFIRMATION. Believing that the reorganization had effectively silenced "Old Princeton," Machen withdrew from the faculty and formed Westminster Theological Seminary in Philadelphia, which was merely the first in a succession of schisms. Machen organized the Independent Board for Presbyterian Foreign Missions, which led to his expulsion from the Presbyterian Church, U.S.A., ministry. In 1936, he and other conservatives founded the *PRESBYTERIAN CHURCH OF AMERICA, which took the name *ORTHODOX PRESBYTERIAN CHURCH in 1939. In a final irony to a life that had aspired to win intellectual respectability for orthodox Christianity, Machen caught pneumonia and died while on a trip to Bismarck, North Dakota, to rally support for his new denomination.

References: J. Gresham Machen, *Christianity and Liberalism* (1923); idem, *The Virgin Birth of Christ* (1930); Bradley J. Longfield, *The Presbyterian Controversy: Fundamentalists, Modernists, and Moderates* (1991); D. G. Hart, *Defending the Faith: J. Gresham Machen and the Crisis of Conservative Protestantism in Modern America* (1994); idem, "When Is a Fundamentalist a Modernist?: J. Gresham Machen, Cultural Modernism, and Conservative Protestantism," *Journal of the American Academy of Religion*, LXV (Fall 1997).

MacNutt, Francis (Scott) (1925–) A leader in the *CATHOLIC CHARISMATIC RENEWAL, Francis MacNutt was born in St. Louis, graduated from Harvard and from the Catholic University of America, and was ordained into the Roman Catholic priesthood in 1956. He received the *BAPTISM OF THE HOLY SPIRIT in 1967 and became a fervent advocate of spiritual gifts, including divine healing, among Roman Catholics. He took the message of charismatic renewal to Latin America as well. MacNutt's credibility in Catholic circles was damaged, however, when he left the priesthood and the Dominican order to marry in 1980. He then became head of the Christian Healing Center in Jacksonville, Florida.

References: Francis MacNutt, *Healing* (1974); idem, *Power to Heal* (1977).

Maddoux, Marlin After stints with churches in Austin and Dallas in his native Texas, Marlin Maddoux started in radio by broadcasting from his garage. By 1975, he had established *Point of View*, a live talk show that presents highly conservative perspectives on theology, politics, and social issues. In addition to the program, Maddoux also founded the USA Radio Network in 1985, which provides programming, supported by commercial advertising, to Christian radio stations around the clock.

Mahan, Asa (1799–1889) Asa Mahan graduated from *ANDOVER THEOLOGICAL SEMINARY in 1827 and became pastor of Cincinnati's Sixth Presbyterian Church and a trustee of nearby Lane Theological Seminary. An opponent of slavery, Mahan supported the *LANE REBELLION and subsequently agreed to become president of Oberlin College. Mahan, who served as president of Oberlin from 1835 to 1850, insisted that the school be integrated and include women and African Americans. The "Oberlin perfectionism" emanating from the college—the notion that holiness is a perfection of the will and is available to everyone after *CONVERSION—derived from the ideas of both Mahan and *CHARLES GRANDISON FINNEY, Oberlin's most famous faculty member.

Mahan resigned the presidency in 1850 and became president of Cleveland University and, later, Adrian College. He joined the *WESLEYAN METHODIST CHURCH in 1871 and became identified later in life with the Higher Christian Life movement.

References: Asa Mahan, *The Baptism of the Holy Spirit* (1870); idem, *Autobiography: Intellectual, Moral, and Spiritual* (1882); Donald W. Dayton, "Asa Mahan and the Development of American Holiness Theology," *Wesleyan Theological Journal*, IX (spring 1974).

Maier, Walter A(rthur) (1893–1950) Walter A. Maier, one of the most influential radio preachers of the twentieth century, was born in Boston. In 1922, as executive secretary of the Walther League, a youth organization for the *LUTHERAN CHURCH—MISSOURI SYNOD, Maier addressed the league's convention, and the address was carried over the radio. Maier realized the potential of this new medium, and by December 1924 he had set up a radio station, KFUO, on the campus of Concordia Seminary in St. Louis, where Maier was professor of Old Testament studies.

On October 2, 1930, Maier went national with the broadcast of *The Lutheran Hour* over the CBS radio network. Maier's simple, biblically based sermons and easygoing demeanor won a large audience. The program switched to the Mutual Broadcasting System in 1935, and by the end of the 1940s, Maier was reaching an audience estimated at 20 million.

References: Walter A. Maier, *The Lutheran Hour* (1931); idem, *Christ for Every Crisis* (1935); idem, *The Radio for Christ* (1939); idem, *For Christ and Country* (1942); idem, *The Airwaves Proclaim Christ* (1948); Paul L. Maier, *A Man Spoke, A World Listened: The Story of Walter A. Maier and the Lutheran Hour* (1963); Guy C. Carter, s.v. "Walter A. Maier," in Charles H. Lippy, ed., *Twentieth-Century Shapers of American Popular Religion* (1989).

Mainse, David R. (1936–) Born in Campbell's Bay, Québec, David R. Mainse studied at Eastern Pentecostal Bible College and became a minister in the *PENTECOSTAL ASSEMBLIES OF CANADA. After preaching occasionally over the radio, Mainse made a foray into television in 1962 with a program called *Crossroads*. The audience grew steadily. In the 1980s, Mainse changed the name of the program, which originates in Toronto, to *100 Huntley Street* and moved to an hour-long program similar to *PAT ROBERTSON's *700 Club*.

Reference: David R. Mainse, *100 Huntley Street* (1983).

Makemie, Francis (1658–1708) Often acknowledged as the "father of American Presbyterianism," Francis Makemie was born in County Donegal, Ireland, and educated at the University of Glasgow because Trinity College, Dublin, was closed to dissenters. He was ordained in Ulster as a missionary by the Irish Presbytery of Laggan in 1682; migrated to Maryland the following year; and immediately began a far-ranging career as an itinerant *EVANGELIST in North Carolina, Virginia, and Maryland, including a stint in Barbados from 1696 to 1698. Makemie returned to Virginia in 1699, received a license to preach, and settled in Accomack County, where he operated a mercantile business (his wife's inheritance), which supported his preaching forays.

Makemie wrote a catechism, no longer extant, in defense of Calvinistic doctrines and the *WESTMINSTER STANDARDS. When George Keith, the Quaker (and, later, Anglican missionary) challenged that apology, Makemie issued a vigorous defense, *An Answer to Keith's Libel*, in which he called Keith "a most Arrogant Spirit" and attacked Quakers and "Papists." Makemie's rejoinder, published in Boston in 1694, won recognition and praise from Increase Mather. After organizing various congregations in the Chesapeake region, Makemie turned his efforts to the formation of the Presbytery of Philadelphia in 1706, the first such presbytery in America, which promptly named him moderator and thereby secured his place in history as "the father of American Presbyterianism."

Makemie can also claim a role in the evolution of religious liberty in America. Edward Hyde, Viscount Cornbury, the governor of New York (who was probably a transvestite), imprisoned Makemie and his colleague John Hampden in 1707 for preaching without a civil license, a tactic that Cornbury employed on various occasions as a means of promoting the Church of England in the colony. Hampden was soon released, but Makemie, labeled a "Disturber of Governments" by the New York governor, spent six weeks in jail and was brought to trial. Although he prevailed in court by demonstrating his compliance with the Act of Toleration, Makemie was assessed court costs as well as the costs of the prosecution. After his acquittal, Makemie publicized his ordeal and argued for religious toleration in *A Narrative of a New and Unusual American Imprisonment of Two Presbyterian Ministers and Prosecution of Mr. Francis Makemie.* The case embarrassed Cornbury, contributed to his recall, and helped to shape the arguments for religious liberty in America.

References: Francis Makemie, *An Answer to Keith's Libel* (1694); idem, *A Narrative of a New and Unusual American Imprisonment of Two Presbyterian Ministers and Prosecution of Mr. Francis Makemie* (1707); James H. Smylie, "Francis Makemie: Tradition and Challenge," *Journal of Presbyterian History*, LXI (1983); Randall Balmer and John R. Fitzmier, *The Presbyterians* (1993).

Malone College (Canton, Ohio) Malone College is affiliated with the Evangelical Friends Church—Eastern Region. The college owes its existence to a very dedicated Quaker couple. Walter and Emma Malone rented a house in Cleveland in 1892 and began the Friends Bible Institute and Training School. For fifteen years, the Malones underwrote all of the school's expenses. The school moved to another campus in Cleveland in 1945 and was renamed Cleveland Bible College. It moved to Canton in 1957 and took the name Malone College to honor its founders. At that time the school adopted a liberal arts curriculum; four-year accreditation soon followed. Graduate programs were begun in education and Christian Ministries in 1992.

References: *Malone College Academic Catalog, 1995–1996* (1995); William C. Ringenberg, *The Christian College: A History of Protestant Higher Education in America* (1984).

Manly, Basil (Sr.) (1798–1868) An educator and advocate of theological education, Basil Manly was born in Pittsborough, North Carolina, was ordained in 1822, and became pastor of the First Baptist Church in Charleston, South Carolina, in 1826. He was named president of the University of Alabama in 1837, where he remained for nearly two decades. From his post as university president, Manly supported the work of Howard College (now *SAMFORD UNIVERSITY), *JUDSON COLLEGE, Furman University, and Southern Baptist Theological Seminary. Manly, an advocate of missions and *EVANGELISM, was also a slave-holder; he led in the formation of the *SOUTHERN BAPTIST CONVENTION in 1845 and the Confederate States of America in 1861.

Manning, Edward (1766–1851) Born in Ireland, Edward Manning moved with his Roman Catholic parents to Falmouth, Nova Scotia, when he was still an infant. After being exposed to the preaching of *HENRY ALLINE, *FREEBORN GARRETTSON, *HARRIS HARDING, and John Payzant, Manning was converted in 1789. He joined Payzant's church but soon thereafter followed his own call to preach. He was ordained in 1795 and then elected believer's *BAPTISM two years later. Manning, reviled by some contemporaries as "the Baptist Pope of the Maritime Provinces," played a major role in the *NEW LIGHT movement of the late eighteenth and early nineteenth centuries.

Reference: G. A. Rawlyk, *The Canada Fire: Radical Evangelicalism in British North America, 1775–1812* (1994).

Manning, James (1738–1791) Born in Piscataway, New Jersey, and educated at Hopewell Academy and the College of New Jersey (now Princeton), James Manning was ordained a Baptist minister in 1763. After the Philadelphia Baptist Association asked him to begin a school for the training of ministers, Manning settled in Warren, Rhode Island, where he became pastor of a Baptist congregation, set up the Warren Baptist Association (the first of its kind in New England), and began a Latin school. Manning became the first president of the College of Rhode Island in 1765, and five years later he moved the school to Providence, where it evolved into Brown University. Manning represented Rhode Island in Congress from 1785 to 1786 and became a champion of public education.

Maranatha! Music One of the most direct descendants of the *JESUS MOVEMENT, Maranatha! Music evolved in 1972 from the music program at *CALVARY CHAPEL in Costa Mesa, California. According to *JOHN FISCHER, this new direction in "church music" emerged when the musical ensemble that was to perform at *CALVARY CHAPEL's upcoming service, a group that called itself Love Song, was asked to offer a preview in the crowded pastor's study before the service. Love Song performed its signature piece, "Welcome Back," with its soft, haunting rhythm, and everyone present knew that something big would come of this new style of "Jesus music."

Maranatha! Music, which eventually became independent of *CALVARY CHAPEL, issued recordings and published sheet music for various artists and groups associated with the *JESUS MOVEMENT, but it has kept abreast of changes in Christian contemporary music. Maranatha!, with offices in San Juan Capistrano, California, bills itself as "the most recognized name in Christian Music."

Marilyn Hickey Ministries. *See* **Hickey, Marilyn (née Seitzer).**

Marion College. *See* **Indiana Wesleyan University.**

Mark IV Pictures Mark IV Pictures, a corporation formed by *DONALD W. THOMPSON and Russell S. Doughton Jr., was begun in Des Moines, Iowa, in 1971 for the purpose of producing evangelistic films. Although both men had considerable experience in filmmaking, the financing for the venture was precarious. As Thompson would recount many times later, a breakthrough occurred when Thompson visited with his pastor, *CLARENCE R. BALMER, senior minister at the Westchester Evangelical Free Church. In the course of a long meeting, punctuated by prayer, the men decided that the venture should go forward; Balmer even offered to put some of his own money behind the effort and agreed to cosign a note.

The corporation's first picture, *A Thief in the Night,* depicting some of the apocalyptic prophecies in the *BIBLE, was released in 1972. The film, unabashedly evangelistic, was enormously successful. While other evangelicals had tried to portray such events as the *RAPTURE and the *TRIBULATION, most efforts had been low-budget "church films." Thompson's directing, however, brought a new sophistication to the genre. Over the course of the next decade, Mark IV Pictures released three sequels in the "prophecy series" as well as a number of other evangelistic films, including *Blood on the Mountain, All the King's Horses,* and *Heaven's Heroes.* A disagreement over management of the corporation and distribution forced Thompson out of the partnership with Doughten in 1984. No pictures have been made since, and Mark IV Pictures, still based in Des Moines, now functions as a distributor of films and videocassettes.

Marsden, George M. (1939–) Arguably the premier historian of American *FUNDAMENTALISM, George M. Marsden grew up in the *ORTHODOX PRESBYTERIAN CHURCH. He earned the B.A. from Haverford College, the B.D. from *WESTMINSTER THEOLOGICAL SEMINARY, and the Ph.D. in American studies from Yale University. After teaching at *CALVIN COLLEGE for more than two decades, Marsden joined the faculty of Duke Divinity School in 1986. He left Duke in 1992 to become the Francis A. McAnaney Professor of History at the University of Notre Dame.

Fundamentalism and American Culture, which appeared in 1980, represented a breakthrough in academic scholarship on *FUNDAMENTALISM. Much the way that Perry Miller's *Orthodoxy in Massachusetts* had triggered a half-century of scholarly interest in Puritanism, Marsden's skill as a historian lent a legitimacy to scholarly inquiry about a movement that had itself generally been regarded as anti-intellectual. The impetus was carried on by a cohort of scholars, including, among others, Grant Wacker, *MARK A. NOLL, and *NATHAN O. HATCH. Each, like Marsden, was associated with the *INSTITUTE FOR THE STUDY OF AMERICAN EVANGELICALS. Following the success of *Fundamentalism and American Culture* and its sequel, *Reforming Fundamentalism,* Marsden embarked on a multiyear project funded by the J. Howard Pew Freedom Trust. Five years of research culminated in *The Soul of the American University,* an extended jeremiad which asserted that people of faith were no longer welcome in the academy—despite the fact that Marsden and his confrères in the *INSTITUTE FOR THE STUDY OF AMERICAN EVANGELICALS held lofty positions at some of the best universities in the English-speaking world. In the mid-1990s, Marsden resumed his more conventional scholarship with work on a biography of *JONATHAN EDWARDS.

References: George M. Marsden, *The Evangelical Mind and the New School Presbyterian Experience* (1970); idem, *Fundamentalism and American Culture: The Shaping of Twentieth-Century Evangelicalism, 1870–1925* (1980); idem, *Reforming Fundamentalism: Fuller Seminary and the New Evangelicalism* (1987); idem, *The Soul of the American University: From Protestant Establishment to*

Established Nonbelief (1994); idem, *The Outrageous Idea of Christian Scholarship* (1997).

Marshall, Daniel (1706–1784) Born in Windsor, Connecticut, Daniel Marshall was converted in 1726 and served as deacon in the Congregational Church for twenty years, until he began to entertain doubts about infant ***BAPTISM**. By 1751, Marshall, along with ***SHUBAL STEARNS**, his brother-in-law, were convinced separatists, having separated themselves from Congregationalism, the established religion in New England. Marshall and his family migrated south to Pennsylvania to do mission work among the Mohawks. The approach of the French and Indian War sent them further south to Virginia, where Marshall organized a church affiliated with the Philadelphia Association in 1754. Marshall was baptized and licensed to preach. He migrated south again, this time to North Carolina, where he was associated with Stearns and the Sandy Creek Association, and then still further south to Georgia, where Marshall organized the first Baptist church in Georgia in 1772.

Reference: William Henry Brackney, *The Baptists* (1988).

Marshall, Peter (1902–1949) An eloquent preacher and chaplain of the United States Senate, Peter Marshall was born in Coatbridge, Scotland, and was a mine worker until he emigrated to the United States in 1927. After working briefly in Birmingham, Alabama, Marshall attended ***COLUMBIA THEOLOGICAL SEMINARY** in Decatur, Georgia. He graduated in 1931, was ordained as a Presbyterian, and served churches in Covington and Atlanta, Georgia, before accepting the prestigious pulpit of the New York Avenue Presbyterian Church in Washington, D.C., in 1937. He became a naturalized citizen that same year and was elected Senate chaplain by the Republican majority a decade later. Marshall's brief prayers, laced with soaring phrases and poetic cadences, conveyed both an intimacy with and a reverence toward the Almighty. He died of a heart attack in 1949.

References: Peter Marshall, *Mr. Jones, Meet the Master* (1949); Catherine Marshall, *A Man Called Peter: The Story of Peter Marshall* (1951); Elise Chase, s.v. "Peter and Catherine Marshall," in Charles H. Lippy, ed., *Twentieth-Century Shapers of American Popular Religion* (1989).

Marshall, (Sarah) Catherine (née Wood) (1914–1983) Born in Johnson City, Tennessee, Catherine Wood graduated from Agnes Scott College in 1936 and married ***PETER MARSHALL**, pastor of the Westminster Presbyterian Church, Atlanta, that same year. The Marshalls moved to Washington, D.C., the following year, where Peter became the pastor of the New York Avenue Presbyterian Church and, ten years later, chaplain to the United States Senate. After Peter's sudden death from a heart attack at the age of forty-six, Catherine collected and published his sermons into a volume entitled *Mr. Jones, Meet the Master.* The commercial success of that volume prompted her to write and publish a biography of her late husband, *A Man Called Peter,* which appeared in 1951, remained on the best-seller list for three years, and was made into a movie in 1955. Marshall's other writings include *To Live Again*; *Beyond Ourselves*; and *Christy*, a novel, which became the basis for a short-lived television series in the 1990s. In 1959, Marshall married Leonard E. LeSourd, executive editor of *Guideposts* magazine, and became editor of the magazine herself in 1961.

References: Catherine Marshall, *A Man Called Peter: The Story of Peter Marshall* (1951); idem, *Christy* (1967); idem, *Meeting God at Every Turn* (1980); Elise Chase, s.v. "Peter and Catherine Marshall," in Charles H. Lippy, ed., *Twentieth-Century Shapers of American Popular Religion* (1989).

Marshman, Joshua (1768–1837) A member of the so-called *SERAMPORE TRIO, Joshua Marshman traveled to India with *WILLIAM WARD and others in 1799 and formed the Serampore mission. Marshman, who was not an effective preacher, devoted himself to the administrative affairs of the mission and to the sometimes ticklish negotiations with the East India Company. Together with *WILLIAM CAREY and Ward, Marshman founded a range of educational institutions, including Serampore College in 1818, the goal of which was to train Indians to replace European missionaries in evangelistic work.

Marshman also learned Chinese and published several translations and grammars; he completed his translation of the entire *BIBLE into Chinese in 1822. Marshman called for various social reforms, including the outlawing of *sati,* the Indian custom of a widow throwing herself onto her husband's funeral pyre.

References: Joshua Marshman, *Elements of Chinese Grammar* (1814); John Clark Marshman, *The Life and Times of Carey, Marshman, and Ward,* 2 vols. (1859).

Martin, Ralph (1942–) A 1964 graduate of the University of Notre Dame, Ralph Martin received a Spirit *BAPTISM in the spring of 1967, after hearing news of the *DUQUESNE WEEKEND. In November of that year, Martin and three others began a prayer meeting in Ann Arbor, Michigan, that evolved into the Word of God community, one of the driving forces behind the *CATHOLIC CHARISMATIC RENEWAL MOVEMENT. Martin, a layman, was the first editor of *New Covenant,* has written a number of books on spiritual renewal, and has a weekly television program, *The Choices We Face.*

References: Ralph Martin, *Unless the Lord Build the House* (1971); idem, *A Crisis of Truth* (1982); idem, *The Return of the Lord* (1983).

Martin, T(homas) T(heodore) (1862–1939) Born in Mississippi and graduated from Mississippi College and Southern Baptist Theological Seminary, T. T. Martin began his preaching career as pastor of churches in Kentucky and Colorado. Although he had preached outdoors to miners in Colorado, Martin's evangelistic work began in earnest in 1900, when he became an itinerant preacher, conducting many of his *REVIVAL campaigns in secondhand circus tents. Martin was an ardent fundamentalist and opponent of Darwinism. A friend of *WILLIAM JENNINGS BRYAN, Martin attended the *SCOPES TRIAL at Dayton, Tennessee, in the summer of 1925, and he was never loath to criticize others in the *SOUTHERN BAPTIST CONVENTION for liberal leanings.

Reference: T. T. Martin, *Redemption and the New Birth* (1913).

Mason, Babbie African American singer Babbie Mason is a Christian contemporary recording artist and songwriter. The daughter of a pastor, Mason once directed the choir in her father's church in Jackson, Michigan. She carries this experience into her present style, which is heavily influenced by African American *GOSPEL MUSIC. Mason's albums include *Heritage of Faith* and *Stand in the Gap.*

Reference: Information provided by Word Records.

Mason, Charles H(arrison) (1866–1961) Born into a Missionary Baptist household near Memphis, Tennessee, Charles H. Mason was healed on September 5, 1880, shortly after his family had moved to Arkansas. Discerning a call to preach, Mason was licensed by the Mt. Gale Missionary Baptist Church. He began preaching in 1893 and that same year claimed *SANCTIFICATION, after having had come into contact with holiness teachings. After a three-month stint as a student in Arkansas Baptist College, Mason abandoned the school for itinerant preaching. In 1894, he joined forces with *CHARLES PRICE JONES, another African American holiness preacher, to form a loose network of holiness congregations called the *CHURCH OF GOD IN CHRIST.

Jones and Mason, who was divorced and remarried, believed that the true Christian had three experiences of grace: *CONVERSION, *SANCTIFICATION, and *BAPTISM OF THE HOLY SPIRIT. When Mason visited the *AZUSA STREET REVIVAL in Los Angeles early in 1907, however, he came into contact with tongues-speaking. He claimed the gift of *GLOSSOLALIA in March and returned persuaded that *SPEAKING IN TONGUES provided evidence of Spirit *BAPTISM. That conviction placed him at odds with Jones, and the two parted company in August 1907; Jones formed the Church of Christ (Holiness) U.S.A., while Mason retained the majority of followers in the *CHURCH OF GOD IN CHRIST. Until his death in 1961, Mason remained active as bishop of the largest African American pentecostal denomination in the United States.

Reference: Joe Maxwell, "Building the Church (of God in Christ)," *Christianity Today,* April 8, 1996.

Massee, J(asper) C(ortenus) (1871–1965) J. C. Massee, born in Marshallville, Georgia, and educated at Mercer University and Southern Baptist Theological Seminary, nevertheless was ordained by the Northern Baptist Convention. He served as pastor of churches in Ohio and in the South before accepting the pulpit at Baptist Temple in Brooklyn, New York, in 1920, where he helped in the formation of the *FUNDAMENTALIST FELLOWSHIP. Elected president of the new group, Massee sought to rein in some of the more ardent fundamentalists within the Northern Baptist Convention. That move cost him support from hard-liners, who eventually bolted to form their own group, *BAPTIST BIBLE UNION, in 1923.

Massee moved in 1922 to Tremont Temple in Boston, where the church grew considerably under his leadership. Wearied of denominational infighting between liberals and fundamentalists, Massee resigned as president of the *FUNDAMENTALIST FELLOWSHIP in 1925, and his call for a six-month truce brought a measure of comity to the Northern Baptist Convention. Massee left Tremont Temple in 1929 to pursue a career as an *EVANGELIST and Bible conference speaker, becoming a regular at *WINONA LAKE BIBLE CONFERENCE.

References: J. C. Massee, *The Second Coming* (1919); idem, *Revival Sermons* (1923); C. Allyn Russell, *Voices of American Fundamentalism: Seven Biographical Studies* (1976).

Matthews, Mark (Allison) (1867–1940) Born in Calhoun, Georgia, Mark Matthews was converted at the age of thirteen and ordained at the age of twenty in the Presbyterian Church in the U.S. (Southern Presbyterians). He served churches in Georgia and Tennessee before moving in 1901 to First Presbyterian Church in

Seattle, where he remained until his death in 1940. An ardent premillennialist, Matthews founded the Bible Institute of Seattle in 1917 and engaged in a wide range of religious and civic activities. His church, First Presbyterian Church, which Matthews claimed was the largest Presbyterian congregation in the world, was the first in the country to own and operate a radio station, KTW-Radio. He started a major hospital, which eventually became affiliated with the University of Washington, and pronounced himself on a number of issues: in favor of cremation and socialized medicine, in opposition to women's suffrage and ordination.

Reference: C. Allyn Russell, *Voices of American Fundamentalism: Seven Biographical Studies* (1976).

Matthews, Randy (1951–) As a thirteen-year-old in 1964, Randy Matthews remembers performing what he then called "gospel rock," which he regarded as a natural outgrowth of having been reared in a home that was founded on the synthesis of music and ministry. His father, Monty Matthews, besides being an ordained minister, had been a member of the Foggy River Boys and the Jordanaires Quartet, which had performed as backup singers for *ELVIS PRESLEY. Randy Matthews's three uncles and grandfather had also been ordained ministers.

He moved to Ohio in 1970 and entered a Cincinnati seminary with designs on continuing the family legacy by becoming a minister. In that same year he and a group of friends turned an old colonial mansion into a Christian communal home that they christened The Jesus House, which functioned as "both coffeehouse and twenty-four-hour-a-day ministry outreach to local prostitutes, runaways, and alcoholics."

In line with his vision to write and perform contemporary *GOSPEL MUSIC, Matthews released an album in 1971 entitled *Wish We'd All Been Ready.* With the success and the exposure garnered by this first release, Matthews became a regular performer at most of the Jesus festivals throughout the country, including the Explo '72 festival at the Cotton Bowl in Dallas, Texas. His second release, *All I Am Is What You See,* appeared in 1972 on a subsidiary label, Myrrh Records. With the recording of these two albums, Matthews established himself as a pioneer of Jesus music; he continued to record and perform into the 1990s.

Maxwell, L(eslie) E(arl) (1895–1984) The founder of *PRAIRIE BIBLE INSTITUTE, L. E. Maxwell had been reared in Kansas and studied at Midland Bible Institute in Kansas City. After his graduation in 1922, Maxwell responded to a request from some farmers in Alberta, Canada, to provide Bible instruction. Although he intended to stay for only a short term, Maxwell remained in Three Hills, Alberta, for sixty-two years. He founded *PRAIRIE BIBLE INSTITUTE and built it into a major center for Bible instruction. The school also includes a graduate school (in Calgary, Alberta) and a high school. Maxwell, who taught at *PRAIRIE BIBLE INSTITUTE until 1980 and who edited the school's periodical, *The Prairie Observer,* insisted that the school retain a strong emphasis on missions and *EVANGELISM.

Reference: L. E. Maxwell, *Born Crucified* (1945).

McAlister, R(obert) E(dward) (1880–1953) Born in Cobden, Ontario, R. E. McAlister became associated with the *HOLINESS MOVEMENT and attended the *AZUSA STREET REVIVAL in 1906. He returned to Canada, was involved in a pentecostal *REVIVAL in the Ottawa Valley, and became one of the founders of the *PENTECOSTAL ASSEMBLIES OF CANADA in 1919. At one point, McAlister championed the "Jesus Only" strain of *PENTECOSTALISM, but the *PENTECOSTAL ASSEMBLIES rejected that doctrine in 1920, under pressure from the *ASSEMBLIES OF GOD in the United States. McAlister was the first editor of the denomination's periodical, *The Pentecostal Testimony,* a post he held from 1920 until 1937.

McAteer, Ed(ward) (A.) (1927–) The organizer of the *RELIGIOUS ROUNDTABLE, Ed McAteer was a marketing specialist with the Colgate-Palmolive Company and active layman in the *SOUTHERN BAPTIST CONVENTION. He founded the *RELIGIOUS ROUNDTABLE in 1979 in an effort to rally fundamentalists to politically conservative causes. McAteer's biggest triumph was in persuading *PAT ROBERTSON, *JAMES ROBISON, *CHARLES STANLEY, *JERRY FALWELL, and *D. JAMES KENNEDY to serve on the organization's board of directors. McAteer himself ran unsuccessfully for the United States Senate in 1984.

McAuley, Jeremiah (1839–1884) Born in County Kerry, Ireland, and abandoned by his parents at age thirteen, Jeremiah McAuley migrated to the United States. He settled in New York and became a streetwise criminal in order to survive. His arrest and conviction on charges of robbery in 1857, however, earned him a fifteen-year sentence at Sing Sing Prison in Ossining, New York. Five years into his incarceration, McAuley had an evangelical *CONVERSION; he was pardoned by the governor two years later and returned to New York City, where he became a desultory *EVANGELIST, lapsing occasionally into petty crime.

McAuley was converted a second time in 1868, and an ensuing friendship with a Wall Street banker, A. S. Hatch, provided the financial backing for a rescue mission, the McAuley *WATER STREET MISSION, which opened in 1872. A decade later, McAuley opened the Cremorne Mission on West Thirty-second Street, which McAuley regarded as the "worst" area he had ever seen. Although he died shortly thereafter, McAuley played a major role in the rescue mission movement. His funeral at the venerable Broadway Tabernacle attracted throngs of people from a range of social classes, and a contemporary noted that more than one hundred rescue missions had been formed at least indirectly because of his influence.

Reference: Norris Magnuson, *Salvation in the Slums: Evangelical Social Work, 1865–1920* (1977).

McAuley Water Street Mission. *See* **Water Street Mission.**

McBirnie, W(illiam) S(tuart) (1922–1994) Born in Toronto, W. S. McBirnie was ordained in the *SOUTHERN BAPTIST CONVENTION at the age of seventeen. He studied at Kletzing College, *BETHEL SEMINARY, Southwestern Baptist Theological Seminary, and California Graduate School of Theology. An ardent premillennialist and a strong supporter of Israel, McBirnie served as pastor of Trinity Baptist Church in San Antonio, Texas, from 1949 to 1959 and in 1961 became pastor of the United Community Church of Glendale, California. Throughout his career he frequently used the radio airwaves to propagate his teachings, and toward the end of his life he was president of the California Graduate School of Theology.

Reference: W. S. McBirnie, *The Antichrist* (1978).

McCartney, William "Bill" (1940–) College football coach and founder of the *PROMISE KEEPERS organization, Bill McCartney was born in 1940 and was converted to evangelical Christianity in 1974 at an *ATHLETES IN ACTION/*CAMPUS CRUSADE FOR CHRIST meeting in Brighton, Michigan. McCartney enjoyed considerable success as the head football coach at the University of Colorado. The Buffaloes won the Associated Press National Championship in 1990, and McCartney won recognition as Kodak Coach of the Year, Bear Bryant Coach of the Year, UPI Coach of the Year, and Walter Camp Foundation Coach of the Year.

On March 20, 1990, McCartney and a friend, Dave Wardell, traveled from Boulder to Pueblo, Colorado, and came up with the idea of organizing evangelical men into a movement that would celebrate the importance of churchgoing, marital fidelity, and parenting. The idea grew in part out of McCartney's own struggles with alcohol, an extramarital affair, and a daughter who became pregnant out of wedlock. Just over three years after the birth of the *PROMISE KEEPERS idea, McCartney filled the University of Colorado's Folsom Stadium with fifty thousand men singing, praying, and listening to exhortations to godliness. At the conclusion of the 1994 football season, McCartney resigned from his coaching position to devote more of his energies to *PROMISE KEEPERS.

Although McCartney insisted that his movement was not political, he maintained close ties with such leaders of the *RELIGIOUS RIGHT as *JAMES DOBSON and *PAT ROBERTSON. In 1992, while still coaching at the University of Colorado, McCartney called a press conference to declare that homosexuality was "an abomination of almighty God" and to announce his support for Amendment 2, a ballot initiative that would negate any laws in Colorado that guaranteed civil rights to gays and lesbians. With McCartney's help, Amendment 2 won approval from Colorado voters, although the United States Supreme Court overturned it in May 1996.

References: Bill McCartney, *From Ashes to Glory*, 2d ed. (1995); idem, *Sold Out: Becoming Man Enough to Make a Difference* (1997); William Martin, *With God on Our Side: The Rise of the Religious Right in America* (1996); Phyllis E. Alsdurf, "McCartney on the Rebound," *Christianity Today*, May 18, 1998; Dane S. Claussen, ed., *The Promise Keepers: Essays on Masculinity and Christianity* (2000).

McClendon, James William (Jr.) (1924–2000) A native of Louisiana, James William McClendon graduated from Southwestern Theological Seminary, was ordained as a Southern Baptist minister, and taught in the theology department at the University of San Francisco. He also taught at Golden Gate Baptist Theological Seminary and at the Church Divinity School of the Pacific. McClendon, who considered himself a Baptist in the tradition of the Anabaptists—Amish, Mennonites, and Brethren—spent the final decade of his life as a distinguished scholar-in-residence at *FULLER THEOLOGICAL SEMINARY. He completed the final volume of his life work, a three-volume *Systematic Theology*, shortly before his death.

Reference: James William McClendon, *Convictions: Defusing Religious Relativism* (1994).

McComb Female Institute. *See* **Belhaven College.**

McDill, Thomas A(llison) (1926–) A native of Chicago, Thomas A. McDill studied at *PHILADELPHIA COLLEGE OF THE BIBLE and earned degrees from

Northern Baptist Theological Seminary, Trinity College, *TRINITY EVANGELICAL DIVINITY SCHOOL, and *BETHEL THEOLOGICAL SEMINARY. After a successful career as pastor of several large congregations within the *EVANGELICAL FREE CHURCH OF AMERICA, McDill became president of the denomination in 1976, a post he held until his retirement in 1990. Throughout his tenure, McDill helped to nudge the denomination away somewhat from its fundamentalist proclivities and into the mainstream of American *EVANGELICALISM. He served, for example, as board member for a number of evangelical agencies, including the *NATIONAL ASSOCIATION OF EVANGELICALS.

McDowell, Josh (1939–) For more than thirty years, Josh McDowell has been a traveling evangelist for *CAMPUS CRUSADE FOR CHRIST, and for several years he has served as head of an international division of that organization, Josh McDowell Ministry. Although he was not reared as an evangelical, McDowell was converted while a student at Kellogg College in Michigan. He soon transferred to *WHEATON COLLEGE in Illinois, where he began to testify at church and evangelistic meetings. McDowell then attended *TALBOT THEOLOGICAL SEMINARY and joined the staff of *CAMPUS CRUSADE FOR CHRIST in 1964.

McDowell started out as a lecturer on the university circuit, but he began to publish books and distribute talks on tape in the 1970s. McDowell eventually added a video series, a radio program, and a religious curriculum as ways to distribute his message, but he remains in high demand as a public speaker, especially at youth gatherings. At these events McDowell often invokes his experience as a parent or, as he prefers to say, "as a dad."

With headquarters in Dallas, Texas, Josh McDowell Ministry now has a staff of sixty people, and in addition to its domestic youth ministry, the organization conducts extensive outreach in the former Soviet Union. Josh McDowell Ministry sends twice-yearly shipments of food, medicine, and gifts to Russia and has distributed more than 14 million books in Russian throughout the former Soviet Union over the last few years.

References: Josh McDowell, *Why Wait?* (1988); idem, *The Myths of Sex Education* (1993); *Mine Eyes Have Seen the Glory*, three-part PBS documentary (1992).

McGee, J(ohn) Vernon (1904–1988) Having decided at an early age to become a minister, J. Vernon McGee graduated from *COLUMBIA THEOLOGICAL SEMINARY and from *DALLAS THEOLOGICAL SEMINARY. After his ordination in the Southern Presbyterian Church he served several Presbyterian congregations in the South and the West before becoming pastor of Church of the Open Door in Los Angeles in 1949, a post he held until his retirement in 1970.

McGee preached on the radio beginning in 1941 with a weekly program called *The Open Bible Hour.* The program changed to daily broadcasts, and the name changed to *Thru the Bible* after McGee moved to Church of the Open Door in 1949. McGee, who was also a popular conference speaker in fundamentalist circles, systematically worked through the entire *BIBLE every five years, with expositions heavily laced with *DISPENSATIONALISM.

McGready, James (1760–1817) Born in western Pennsylvania, James McGready studied for the ministry under two Presbyterian revivalists, John McMillan and Joseph Smith. Licensed by the Redstone

Presbytery in 1788, McGready became an ardent revivalist during a visit to Hampden-Sydney College, which was itself in the throes of *REVIVAL. When McGready began his ministerial career in North Carolina, his *NEW LIGHT tactics met with approval from some and resistance from others. Among his early converts was *BARTON W. STONE, but McGready's assault on various forms of immorality created enemies so fervent that he felt his life was threatened. McGready headed west in 1796, presiding over a three-point charge, serving congregations in Red River, Muddy River, and Gaspar River, all in rural Kentucky.

McGready soon began experimenting with new methods of *EVANGELISM, including the extended *CAMP MEETING. Beginning with the observance of the *LORD'S SUPPER (a carryover from the Scottish practice of "sacramental seasons"), the popular events culminated in the famous *CANE RIDGE *REVIVAL, which became a standard evangelistic event in Southern antebellum religion. McGready's fulsome embrace of revivalism earned him the enmity of Old Side Presbyterians, who were suspicious of his Arminian tendencies. Although he was one of the principals in the formation of the *CUMBERLAND PRESBYTERIAN CHURCH, McGready remained affiliated with the Presbyterian Church and spent his last years planting churches in southern Indiana.

References: John R. Boles, *The Great Revival, 1787–1805: The Origins of the Southern Evangelical Mind* (1972); Randall Balmer and John R. Fitzmier, *The Presbyterians* (1993).

McGuffey, William Holmes (1800–1873) Educated at home by his mother and schooled in Latin by a Presbyterian minister, William Holmes McGuffey demonstrated a prodigious command of languages and literature from an early age, committing long passages of the *BIBLE to memory. After graduating from Washington College in 1826, McGuffey was appointed professor of languages at Miami University, Oxford, Ohio. He was licensed to preach by the Presbyterians in 1829, and although he never held a pastorate, he preached an estimated three thousand sermons over his lifetime—all of them, he boasted, extemporaneous. He accepted the presidency of Cincinnati College in 1836; during his tenure there, McGuffey helped to form the College of Teachers, an organization dedicated to the support of public school education. McGuffey moved on to the presidency of Ohio University in 1839, where he remained until 1843. After two years as a professor at Woodward College, he became professor of moral philosophy at the University of Virginia in 1845, where he remained until his death in 1873.

A tireless advocate of public education, McGuffey left his mark on American public schools in the nineteenth century, in part through his efforts to establish public schools but, more significantly, through his *Eclectic Readers* (often referred to as **MCGUFFEY READERS*). While at Miami University, the Cincinnati publisher Truman & Smith encouraged McGuffey to compile readings for a series of schoolbooks. Drawing from a number of sources, including the *New England Primer,* Noah Webster's *American Spelling Book,* and, of course, the *BIBLE, the *Eclectic Readers* reflected the values of nineteenth-century Protestantism: hard work, industry, loyalty, honesty, *TEMPERANCE, and sabbatarianism. These readers were enormously popular. By 1920, over 122 million copies were sold, and they enjoyed a renaissance in the latter decades of the twentieth century among conservatives and especially among fundamentalists who were either *HOME-SCHOOLING their children or sending them to sectarian schools. Among the new advocates of the **McGUFFEY READERS*, few appeared to be aware of the irony of appropriating the work of such a champion of public education into a sectarian context.

McGuffey Reader Known originally as the *Eclectic Reader*—the name given to each volume of a series of schoolbooks edited by *WILLIAM HOLMES MCGUFFEY in the nineteenth century—the *McGuffey Reader* became commonplace in American public schools in the nineteenth and early twentieth centuries, celebrating Protestant values such as diligence, sobriety, and nationalism. *McGuffey Readers* have again become popular late in the twentieth century among many evangelicals who educate their children at home or who send them to sectarian fundamentalist schools.

McIlvaine, Charles P(ettit) (1799–1873) Charles P. McIlvaine, nineteenth-century leader of the evangelical Episcopalians, was the son of a United States senator. In the course of his studies at the College of New Jersey (Princeton), McIlvaine, under the influence of his mentor, *ARCHIBALD ALEXANDER, experienced an evangelical *CONVERSION. After his graduation in 1816, McIlvaine attended Princeton Theological Seminary from 1817 to 1819. He considered becoming a Presbyterian minister, but Alexander urged him to remain in the Episcopal Church in order to promote evangelical interests there; McIlvaine was ordained a deacon in the Episcopal Church in 1820 and a priest in 1823.

Throughout a long and productive career, McIlvaine became the acknowledged leader of the evangelical party within the Episcopal Church. His first parish was in Georgetown, in Washington, D.C., where he also served twice as chaplain to the United States Senate. As chaplain and professor of ethics at the United States Military Academy (West Point), McIlvaine led a *REVIVAL among the cadets that attracted national attention. He went on to historic St. Ann's Church in Brooklyn in 1827 and taught concurrently as professor of Christian evidences at New York University. McIlvaine was named bishop of Ohio in 1832; he also became president of Kenyon College and founder of Bexley Hall, an Episcopal seminary in Gambier, Ohio.

McIlvaine's renown as an evangelical leader spread across the Atlantic to Great Britain, and he was known on both sides of the Atlantic as a vigorous opponent of Tractarianism, which sought to move the Church of England closer to Roman Catholicism. His book on the matter, *Oxford Divinity*, published in 1841, argued vigorously for the doctrine of justification by *GRACE through faith as the defining tenet of Protestantism. Anglicans (and Episcopalians), he asserted, should remain faithful to their Protestant heritage and not veer toward Rome. While *Oxford Divinity* became a standard text in evangelical seminaries and a tool of defense against Tractarianism, McIlvaine also fought against ritualism in the Episcopal Church. In the 1860s, he tried to keep the increasingly restive evangelical party within the Episcopal Church. Although he succeeded during his lifetime, a schism only seven months after his death led to the formation of the *REFORMED EPISCOPAL CHURCH.

References: Charles P. McIlvaine, *The Evidences of Christianity* (1832); idem, *Oxford Divinity Compared with that of the Romish and Anglican Churches* (1841); idem, *The Truth and the Life* (1855); Diana Hochstedt Butler, *Standing* *against the Whirlwind: The Evangelical Party in the 19th Century Episcopal Church* (1995).

McIntire, Carl (1906–) One of the more colorful and persistent fundamentalists, the P. T. Barnum of American *FUNDAMENTALISM, Carl McIntire was born in Ypsilanti, Michigan, but grew up in Oklahoma. After earning the B.A. from Park College (Missouri), he studied at Princeton Theological Seminary from 1927 until 1929, when he followed *J. GRESHAM MACHEN to *WESTMINSTER THEOLOGICAL SEMINARY as part of the separatist movement. After graduating from Westminster in 1931, McIntire soon formed his own denomination, the *BIBLE PRESBYTERIAN CHURCH, which was even more militantly fundamentalist than Machen's *ORTHODOX PRESBYTERIAN CHURCH. He also organized his own seminary, *FAITH THEOLOGICAL SEMINARY, and two colleges: Shelton College in Cape May, New Jersey, and Highlands College in Pasadena, California. McIntire began publishing a newspaper, *The Christian Beacon,* in 1936 and broadcast the worship services from his congregation in Collingswood, New Jersey, a broadcast that would evolve into *The 20th Century Reformation Hour.*

McIntire founded the *AMERICAN COUNCIL OF CHRISTIAN CHURCHES in 1941 as a counter to the Federal Council of Churches, which he considered too liberal. He also refused to join the *NATIONAL ASSOCIATION OF EVANGELICALS, organized in 1942, considering it insufficiently fundamentalist. In 1948, he organized the International Council of Christian Churches as a worldwide association of like-minded fundamentalists. Throughout his career, McIntire was a tireless crusader against communists, whom he suspected of lurking everywhere from mainline Protestantism to the Public Broadcasting System; he cooperated with the staff of Senator Joseph McCarthy in the late 1940s and early 1950s. Over the years, McIntire expanded his list of enemies to include *BILLY GRAHAM, *ORAL ROBERTS, Martin Luther King Jr., Roman Catholics, antiwar protestors, feminists, the United Nations, the United States Post Office, and the Revised Standard Version of the *BIBLE. In September 1973, McIntire, in defiance of the Federal Communications Commission, operated what he called "*RADIO FREE AMERICA" for a day, a pirate radio station broadcasting from international waters off the coast of Cape May, New Jersey.

Although McIntire continued his diatribes well into his nineties, his audience gradually diminished, and he became more and more a comic figure, beloved even by some he had labeled his enemies. The fortunes of *FAITH THEOLOGICAL SEMINARY declined, and in 1985 the New Jersey Supreme Court upheld the state's Department of Higher Education's decision to withdraw accreditation from Shelton College. By 1999, McIntire had even split off from his own church, the Collingswood *BIBLE PRESBYTERIAN CHURCH, whose elders had asked that he retire after serving as the congregation's senior pastor since 1933. McIntire responded by conducting Sunday services in his home.

References: Carl McIntire, *Twentieth Century Reformation* (1944); idem, *For Such a Time as This* (1946); idem, *The New Bible, Revised Standard Version: Why Christians Should Not Accept It* (1953); idem, *Servants of Apostasy* (1955); idem, *The Death of a Church* (1967); Erling Jorstad, *The Politics of Doomsday: Fundamentalists of the Far Right* (1970); Randall Balmer and John R. Fitzmier, *The Presbyterians* (1993); Shelley Baranowski, s.v. "Carl McIntire," in Charles H. Lippy, ed., *Twentieth-Century Shapers of American Popular Religion* (1989).

McKean, Kip (1954–) Founder and head of the controversial *INTERNATIONAL CHURCH OF CHRIST, Kip McKean grew up in a Methodist home and had a *CONVERSION while a student at the University of Florida. He started a church in 1979 in the Boston suburb of Lexington, Massachusetts; the congregation grew rapidly, began meeting in Boston Garden, and took the name Boston Church of Christ. McKean's movement, known for its aggressive proselytization and for its authoritarianism, became known as the *INTERNATIONAL CHURCH OF CHRIST. "We are not a cult," McKean protested in a 1992 interview. "You don't have to shave your head and give all your money to the church. But you do have to give your heart. In our minds, we're just trying to get back to the *BIBLE."

McKendree, William (1757–1835) William McKendree, the first American-born bishop in the Methodist Episcopal Church, was born in King William County, Virginia, into an Anglican household. He joined a Methodist Society in the mid-1770s, was converted in 1787, and served several circuits. He sided briefly with *JAMES O'KELLY and the *O'KELLY SCHISM over the rights of dissatisfied clergy to appeal their assignments, but he thought better of it and reestablished his ties with the Methodist Episcopal Church. In 1796, McKendree, an effective preacher and administrator, was appointed presiding elder, first in Virginia and later in Kentucky, where he took charge of the Kentucky District of the newly formed Western Conference in 1801. He undertook the task of channeling the *REVIVAL of the frontier into the formation of circuits and churches, and he was rewarded for his efforts with election as bishop in 1808.

McKinney, Claude A(dams) (1873–1940) Born in Oil City, Pennsylvania, Claude A. McKinney was converted in a Methodist setting and became involved with the *SALVATION ARMY in New York City. He attended *A. B. SIMPSON's Bible school and, together with his wife, Elizabeth, served as a missionary to the Belgian Congo. He settled in Akron, Ohio, in 1900 and started the Union Gospel Mission as an outreach to the city's indigent. When *IVEY G. CAMPBELL returned to Ohio from the *AZUSA STREET REVIVAL in Los Angeles, McKinney invited her to conduct services at his mission. McKinney himself was baptized by the Holy Spirit late in 1906. He withdrew from the *CHRISTIAN AND MISSIONARY ALLIANCE two years later and was ordained by the *ASSEMBLIES OF GOD in 1918.

M'Clintock, John (1814–1870) The son of Irish immigrants, John M'Clintock, a Methodist preacher, editor, and educator, was born in Philadelphia and was reared in *METHODISM at St. George's Methodist Episcopal Church. After a stint as clerk in his father's dry goods store, M'Clintock became a bookkeeper for the Methodist Book Concern in New York City at age sixteen. He attended a *REVIVAL at the Allen Street Church, whereupon he determined to enter the ministry. M'Clintock matriculated at the University of Pennsylvania in 1832, and three years later he graduated with honors shortly after he had been admitted on trial in the Philadelphia conference of the Methodist Church.

Poor health forced M'Clintock to relinquish his first charge in Jersey City, New Jersey, in 1836. He became an assistant professor of mathematics at Dickinson College, rising quickly to the rank of full professor, eventually moving to the chair of classical languages in 1840, the same year he was ordained an elder. He resigned his professorship in 1848 to become editor of the *Methodist Quarterly Review,* which he fashioned into a vehicle for the transmission of learning for the Methodist clergy. M'Clintock left the journal in 1856, traveled to the United Kingdom with *MATTHEW SIMPSON as a delegate to the British Wesleyan Conference, and returned to the United States to become pastor of St. Paul's Church in New York City. His tenure at St. Paul's lasted until 1865, but it was interrupted by four years (1860–1864) when he was pastor of the American Chapel in Paris.

The final phase of M'Clintock's career was devoted more explicitly to theological education. An acquaintance with Daniel Drew, who had made a considerable amount of money on Wall Street, led to the formation of Methodism's first theological seminary in America, Drew Theological Seminary, in Madison, New Jersey. Drew wanted M'Clintock to be the first president of the school, and, given his strong commitment to an educated clergy, M'Clintock readily accepted, assuming the office in 1867. Most of the volumes of his magisterial *Cyclopedia of Biblical, Theological, and Ecclesiastical Literature* were published after his death in 1870.

References: John M'Clintock, *Sketches of Eminent Methodist Ministers* (1854); idem, *Cyclopedia of Biblical, Theological, and Ecclesiastical Literature,* 10 vols. (1867–1881); Michael D. Ryan, "John M'Clintock (1814–1870)," in Charles E. Cole, ed., *Something More Than Human: Biographies of Leaders in American Methodist Higher Education* (1986).

McNichol, John (1869–1956) Reared in a Presbyterian home, John McNichol studied at the University of Toronto and Knox College before being ordained as a Presbyterian minister. After pastoral experience in the Ottawa Valley, he began a long-term relationship with Toronto Bible Training School in 1902. Four years later, McNichol became principal of that school (later renamed, successively, Toronto Bible College and *ONTARIO BIBLE COLLEGE); he remained in that capacity for four decades, improving its curriculum and bolstering the caliber of its faculty.

Amid the fundamentalist-modernist controversy, McNichol clearly aligned himself with the conservatives. He contributed an article to **THE FUNDAMENTALS,* although he refused to adopt dispensational *PREMILLENNIALISM. He helped to found the *Christian Evangel* and published his own four-volume work, *Thinking Through the Bible,* in 1944.

Reference: John McNichol, *Thinking Through the Bible,* 4 vols. (1944).

McPherson, Aimee Semple (née Aimee Elizabeth Kennedy) (1890–1944) A woman of indomitable energy and enormous contradictions, Aimee Semple McPherson overcame several personal and professional setbacks to become one of the twentieth century's most intriguing religious personalities. She was born near Ingersoll, Ontario, and reared in both the Methodist and the *SALVATION ARMY traditions. During the winter of 1907–08 a pentecostal *EVANGELIST named *ROBERT JAMES SEMPLE held evangelistic meetings in Ingersoll. Young Aimee Kennedy was one of his converts, and on August 12, 1908, the two were married. They settled briefly in Stratford and in London, Ontario, before moving on to Chicago, where both man and wife were ordained by *WILLIAM H. DURHAM at his North Avenue Mission on January 2, 1909.

The Semples had decided on a career as missionaries. They left for Hong Kong in 1910 with a view toward learning Chinese and then moving on to China. Shortly after their arrival in Hong Kong, however, *ROBERT SEMPLE contracted typhoid fever and died on August 19, 1910, leaving behind a pregnant widow not yet twenty years old. In part because of financial stringency, Aimee remained in Hong Kong until after the birth of her daughter, Roberta Star.

Aimee and Roberta returned to New York City, where they were joined by Aimee's mother, Minnie. They worked with the *SALVATION ARMY mission, and Aimee met and soon married Harold Stewart McPherson. The marriage, however, was an unhappy one. The couple settled briefly in Providence, Rhode Island, but after the birth of the couple's son, Rolf, Aimee moved back with her parents in Ontario, where she soon established herself as an effective preacher with a series of *REVIVAL meetings in Mount Forest, Ontario. McPherson rejoined his wife for a time, serving as an advance man for her *REVIVAL campaigns, but he eventually returned to Rhode Island. The couple divorced in August 1921.

By then "Sister Aimee's" career as a preacher and faith healer had been launched. Her mother took over the advance work and administrative duties. McPherson began publishing a monthly magazine, *Bridal Call,* in 1917; she was ordained as an "*EVANGELIST" by the *ASSEMBLIES OF GOD in 1919, although she resigned that ordination three years later, after her divorce. She dressed in a white nurse's uniform and traveled in her "Gospel Auto," a car with various evangelistic slogans ("JESUS IS COMING—GET READY") emblazoned on the sides.

The "Gospel Auto" attracted a great deal of notice on the drive west to California in 1918. McPherson would pull into a town, wait for a crowd to gather around the car (automobiles themselves were still a curiosity in the late 1910s), preach a sermon, and collect a few contributions. She arrived in Los Angeles in the fall of 1918 and proceeded to establish her base of operations there. She purchased property in Echo Park in 1921, and her magnificent Angelus Temple, with seating for fifty-three hundred, was dedicated January 1, 1923. The temple served as the fulcrum for all of McPherson's operations, including a nascent denomination, which would be incorporated in 1927 as the *INTERNATIONAL CHURCH OF THE FOURSQUARE GOSPEL.

For Sister Aimee, Angelus Temple was a stage and a showplace; she understood that she was competing with the glamour of Hollywood across town. Her "illustrated sermons" very often were delivered against the background of elaborate sets, many of them designed by Thomas Eade, a former vaudeville performer. One Easter Sunday she appeared, dressed entirely in yellow, out of an oversized Easter lily made of plaster of Paris. On another occasion she roared onstage dressed as a cop and straddling a motorcycle. Yet again, she dressed up as George Washington and reviewed the troops at Valley Forge as synthetic snow fell all around her.

In 1922, McPherson became the first woman ever to preach a sermon over the radio, and her station, KFSG ("Kalling Four Square Gospel") was the nation's first station owned and operated by a religious organization. She set up satellite congregations in various venues and broadcast her sermons to those gatherings. McPherson also continued her itinerations, and she established her own school—*L.I.F.E. (LIGHTHOUSE FOR INTERNATIONAL FOURSQUARE EVANGELISM) BIBLE COLLEGE—in 1923.

McPherson's professional success, however, was not matched by personal fulfillment. In May 1926, she "disappeared" while swimming at Venice Beach. She surfaced a month later in Mexico with a story that she had been kidnapped by two drunken desperadoes, Jake and Mexicali Rose. Her return to Los Angeles was greeted by a rousing public welcome, reportedly attended by fifty thousand people. Journalists and others, however, grew suspicious of McPherson's story, especially amid rumors of an affair with Kenneth Ormiston, who had operated KFSG. Faced with legal charges of perpetrating the hoax of her disappearance, McPherson struck back with a "Fight the Devil" fund-raising campaign for her legal expenses and dueled the district attorney to a draw; eventually all charges were dropped.

McPherson's troubles did not abate, however. She became estranged from her mother and from her daughter in the 1930s. She struggled with alcoholism, and on September 13, 1931, she entered into what would become another unhappy marriage, to David L. Hutton. She traveled around the world in 1936 and returned with warnings about totalitarianism, and she became an enthusiastic supporter of the war effort. By 1939, McPherson had regained some of her verve for *EVANGELISM, Angelus Temple, and her denomination.

She appointed her son, *ROLF MCPHERSON, vice president of the *INTERNATIONAL CHURCH OF THE FOURSQUARE GOSPEL in 1944. In September of the same year, she began a *REVIVAL campaign at the Civic Auditorium in Oakland, California. She preached her final sermon on the evening of September 26, returned to her hotel room, and was found dead the next morning of "shock and respiratory failure" following an overdose of medication that may or may not have been suicidal. Sister Aimee was laid to rest on October 9, 1994, at Forest Lawn Cemetery in Glendale, California, following one of the largest funerals ever held in Los Angeles.

References: Aimee Semple McPherson, *This Is That: Personal Experiences, Sermons and Writings* (1919); idem, *The Second Coming of Christ* (1921); idem, *Give Me My Own God* (1936); idem, *The Story of My Life* (1951); Edith L. Blumhofer, *Aimee Semple McPherson: Everybody's Sister* (1993); William G. McLoughlin, "Aimee Semple McPherson: 'Your Sister in the King's Glad Service,'" *Journal of Popular Culture,* I (1967).

McPherson, Rolf (Kennedy) (1913–) The son of pentecostal impresario *AIMEE SEMPLE MCPHERSON, Rolf McPherson was born in Providence, and after his parents' separation accompanied his mother to California in 1918. McPherson graduated from the Southern California Radio Institute in 1933 and studied at his mother's *L.I.F.E. BIBLE INSTITUTE. Following his ordination by the *INTERNATIONAL CHURCH OF THE FOURSQUARE GOSPEL, McPherson edited *Foursquare Magazine.* He became vice president of the denomination early in 1944 and succeeded his mother as president after her death in September of that year. The *INTERNATIONAL CHURCH OF THE FOURSQUARE GOSPEL grew under his leadership, and it joined both the *NATIONAL ASSOCIATION OF EVANGELICALS and the Pentecostal Fellowship of North America. McPherson became president emeritus in 1988.

McQuilkin, Robert Crawford (1886–1952) Born in Philadelphia, Robert Crawford McQuilkin had an evangelical *CONVERSION in 1911 and shortly thereafter became associate editor of *The Sunday School Times,* edited by *CHARLES G. TRUMBULL. McQuilkin remained with the newspaper until his graduation from the

University of Pennsylvania in 1917. He was active in organizing Victorious Life Conferences held first at Oxford, Pennsylvania, and later at Princeton, New Jersey; Stony Brook, Long Island; and Keswick Grove, New Jersey. McQuilkin's passion for evangelical education took several forms. He was the founding president of *COLUMBIA BIBLE SCHOOL, where he remained in office from 1923 to 1952, and president of the *EVANGELICAL TEACHER TRAINING ASSOCIATION from 1931 to 1941. In addition, he founded the Ben Lippen Conference Center in Asheville, North Carolina, in 1928 and the Ben Lippen School in 1940.

References: Robert Crawford McQuilkin, *Victorious Life Studies* (1918); idem, *The Lord Is My Shepherd* (1938).

Mears, Henrietta (Cornelia) (1890–1963) Best known for her long tenure as director of Christian education at First Presbyterian Church, Hollywood, California, Henrietta Mears was influential in the *SUNDAY SCHOOL movement, in the development of Christian education materials, and, perhaps most significantly, in her encouragement of several young men, including *BILLY GRAHAM and *BILL BRIGHT, at early stages of their careers. Born in Fargo, North Dakota, and reared in Minneapolis, Minnesota, Mears attended First Baptist Church, led by *WILLIAM BELL RILEY, and began teaching *SUNDAY SCHOOL at age twelve. After graduating from the University of Minnesota and several stints as a schoolteacher, Mears accepted a position as director of Christian education at Hollywood Presbyterian, where the *SUNDAY SCHOOL grew significantly under her leadership.

After surveying the existing curricular materials for *SUNDAY SCHOOLS and finding them inadequate, Mears began writing her own in 1929. She, together with Cyrus Nelson, founded Gospel Light Press in 1933 (since renamed Gospel Light Publishers) to publish her materials, which soon found wide acceptance among evangelical churches. In addition to her attention to grade school curriculum, Mears also developed a college-level program. In 1937, she negotiated the purchase of Forest Home Camp Grounds, near San Bernardino, California, for use as a spiritual retreat center, and it was here, at a place commemorated by a plaque, that Graham made his famous decision to renounce intellectual pursuits and concentrate simply on preaching the *BIBLE.

Mears inspired many evangelical leaders in postwar America. *WILBUR M. SMITH once remarked that Mears's efforts amounted to "the most significant work among our nation's youth done by a woman in the twentieth century."

Reference: Wendy Murray Zoba, "The Grandmother of Us All," *Christianity Today*, September 16, 1996.

Meissner, Linda (1945–) Reared on an Iowa farm, Linda Meissner, while still a young girl, made a "pact with God" that she would become an *EVANGELIST if God would heal her deathly ill mother. In the early 1960s, Meissner enrolled in an *ASSEMBLIES OF GOD pentecostal college in Springfield, Missouri. After a single semester, she was recruited by *EVANGELIST *DAVID WILKERSON to come work for his *TEEN CHALLENGE outreach among street gangs in New York City. Meissner's role as liaison to female gangs is recounted in a chapter of Wilkerson's best-selling book *The Cross and the Switchblade*.

After leaving the *TEEN CHALLENGE program in the mid-1960s, Meissner still felt a calling to work among youth. After some missionary ventures to the Philippines, Hong Kong, and Mexico City, she stated that a "special visitation of the Holy Spirit" gave her a vision showing "thousands of youth marching for Jesus." The vision also compelled her to begin her evangelistic outreach to youth in Seattle. In 1967, she conducted a number of citywide crusade meetings recruiting young people to help her. Meissner's message was pentecostally charged, centering on the twin emphases of *SPEAKING IN TONGUES (*GLOSSOLALIA) as the initial evidence of the *BAPTISM OF THE HOLY SPIRIT and an eschatological focus on the impending apocalypse and *RAPTURE of the saints. The *JESUS MOVEMENT, with which she was identified, was itself interpreted by members of the movement as the end-time prelude to the *SECOND COMING of Christ.

Meissner had been successful enough by 1969 to open a number of communal homes and a couple of coffeehouses, and to establish a Jesus paper named *Agape,* all under the organizational title of the Jesus People Army (JPA). Meissner took her core evangelistic troupe on a missionary blitz in 1970 that saw the establishment of JPA outposts in Yakima, Everett, and Spokane (all in Washington state); Boise, Idaho; and Vancouver, British Columbia. By 1971, Meissner had become known as the "Joan of Arc of the *JESUS MOVEMENT."

In 1971, Meissner began to worry about the lack of growth and stability of her group in Seattle, compared with other flourishing centers of the *JESUS MOVEMENT. She began to look for a more structured organizational system that would both motivate lax followers and provide financial stability. Hearing of the radical nature of the *CHILDREN OF GOD from a fellow *JESUS PEOPLE leader in Atlanta, Meissner made contact with the group and was invited to their training center in Thurber, Texas, for a week-long visit. Meissner eventually teamed up with the controversial group, despite the protestations of other JPA leaders, local ministers, and her own husband. Leaving behind her husband and his five children, she accompanied the *CHILDREN OF GOD on their North American exodus to Europe in 1972. Meissner took over some of the publishing duties for the group before leaving them in the late 1970s and settling in Denmark.

Melodyland Christian Center. *See* **Wilkerson, Ralph A.**

Mel Trotter Mission A rescue mission in Grand Rapids, Michigan, Mel Trotter Mission was founded by *MEL TROTTER and Harry Monroe. Trotter had been converted under Monroe's preaching at the *PACIFIC GARDEN MISSION in Chicago, and the two men worked together thereafter as itinerant *EVANGELISTS and as promoters of urban missions.

Memorization Evangelicals have long advocated the memorization of Scripture, based on Psalm 119:11 (KJV): "Thy word have I hid in mine heart, that I might not sin against thee." Memorization, evangelicals believe, is an effective tool for *EVANGELISM and personal piety, and at least one organization, *THE NAVIGATORS, is built around the memorization of Scripture. The discipline of memorization has declined, however, with the popularity of translations other than the Authorized or King James Version.

Mendenhall Ministries Mendenhall Ministries, originally founded as *VOICE OF CALVARY MINISTRIES by *JOHN M. PERKINS, is an evangelical organization with headquarters in Mendenhall, Mississippi. Dedicated to the goal of social justice and racial reconciliation, the organization operates a law office, a health clinic, an elementary school, a housing cooperative, a youth center, and other programs for the benefit of the poor, especially African Americans, in the Piney Woods region of central Mississippi.

References: John Perkins, *Let Justice Roll Down* (1976); Randall Balmer, *Mine Eyes Have Seen the Glory: A Journey into the Evangelical Subculture in America,* 3d ed. (2000).

Mennonite Biblical Seminary. *See* **Associated Mennonite Biblical Seminary.**

Mennonite Brethren Churches The founding of the Mennonite Brethren Churches dates to 1860 in the German colonies of southern Russia. A group of the Mennonites there became dissatisfied with the formality of the church meetings, looking instead for a discernible religious experience. The controversy with the church led to the withdrawal of the dissenters to form the Mennonite Brethren Church. Members of the Mennonite Brethren Church carried their convictions with them when they began to immigrate to the United States.

Theologically, the new church was not far from the parent church. The doctrine was the same, but the emphasis on religious experience was different. Accordingly, the church developed a more Baptistic *POLITY in which each local church is autonomous and associates voluntarily with the general conference. The Mennonite Brethren also sought closer attention to prayer and Bible study. The *BIBLE is accepted as infallible and authoritative for life and faith. The churches affirm the Trinity, the virgin birth, sacrificial death, and resurrection of Jesus, and his imminent return. The Mennonite Brethren practice *BAPTISM by immersion and observe the ordinance of the *LORD'S SUPPER. The general conference reports having 20,524 total members. Conference headquarters are in Hillsboro, Kansas.

References: Frank S. Mead and Samuel S. Hill, *Handbook of Denominations in the United States,* 10th ed. (1996); J. Gordon Melton, *The Encyclopedia of American Religions,* 3d ed. (1993); "Contributions to U.S. and Canadian Protestant Churches," *Chronicle of Philanthropy,* vol. IX no. 15.

Mercy The term for mercy, which appears in both the Old Testament and New Testament, refers to two distinct types of action. For evangelicals, the term usually refers to the forgiving activity of God toward humanity. Human beings would otherwise be judged and condemned because of human depravity and the inevitable human tendency toward *SIN. Mercy that God shows toward humanity is theological, that is to say, not grounded in a human ethical or moral structural understanding. However, the mercy that humans show toward each other is of a moral or ethical nature. For evangelicals, the mercy that God shows toward sinful creation requires human beings to show a similar mercy toward other humans who have repented of their *SINS. Only because of the mercy that God has shown are humans able to be *SAVED.

Merritt, Timothy (1775–1845) Born in Connecticut, Timothy Merritt began his career as a Methodist minister in Maine in 1796, where he spent the preponderance of his career. For two brief periods, from 1817 to 1819 and from 1825 to 1827, Merritt was pastor of the First Methodist Episcopal Church in Boston. His real influence on nineteenth-century *METHODISM, however, derived from his writing and editing. In 1831, he was named editor of

Zion's Herald, a post he held for only a year before becoming assistant editor of *METHODISM's *Christian Advocate and Journal*. He was dismissed from the latter assignment in 1836 because of his strong abolitionist sentiments.

Merritt, however, continued as a prolific writer. He was profoundly influenced by *JOHN WESLEY and by *JOHN WILLIAM FLETCHER; his writings on *SANCTIFICATION, holiness, and Christian perfection in the Wesleyan tradition have earned him the sobriquet "father of the American *HOLINESS MOVEMENT." He spoke at churches and at *CAMP MEETINGS and equated Christian perfection with the *BAPTISM OF THE HOLY SPIRIT. Merritt founded and edited the *Guide to Christian Perfection,* which influenced *SARAH LANKFORD and *PHOEBE PALMER (and which was eventually purchased by Walter and *PHOEBE PALMER in 1865). Merritt's *The Christian Manual: A Treatise on Christian Perfection* went through more than thirty printings in the middle decades of the nineteenth century. On related matters, Merritt advocated a democratization of Methodist *POLITY; he supported the development of *SUNDAY SCHOOLS and was active in the abolitionist and *TEMPERANCE movements.

References: Timothy Merritt, *An Essay on the Perseverence of the Saints* (1807); idem, *The Christian's Manual: A Treatise on Christian Perfection, with Directions for Obtaining That State* (1825).

Message In evangelical jargon, "message" is often used to refer to a sermon delivered by a pastor or other religious leader (evangelicals generally eschew the term "homily" because of its high-church connotations). The use would sound something like this: "After a selection from the choir, Brother Larson will bring a message from the *WORD OF GOD," or "That message really spoke to my heart."

Messiah College (Grantham, Pennsylvania) Messiah College opened in 1909 under the name Messiah Bible School and Missionary Training Home. Established by the Brethren in Christ Church in Harrisburg, Pennsylvania, Messiah was originally intended to "educate men and women for home and foreign mission and evangelistic work." The school was renamed Messiah Bible College in 1924 and attained junior college status four years later. The college earned four-year accreditation in 1951 and became known as Messiah College.

Messiah started a satellite campus in Philadelphia in collaboration with Temple University in 1968. Students live in Messiah housing on Temple's campus and take one class a semester with Messiah faculty; the rest of the courses are taught by Temple instructors. Similarly, Messiah College–Africa was initiated in Nairobi, Kenya, in 1983 in conjunction with Daystar University College of Nairobi.

Messiah was owned by the *BRETHREN IN CHRIST CHURCH until 1972, at which time legal control of the college was turned over to its trustees. Messiah maintains a covenant relationship with the Church, but it operates as an independent institution.

Reference: *Messiah College Catalog, 1994–1996* (1994).

Messner, Tammy Faye (née La Valley) (Bakker) (1942–) Born in International Falls, Minnesota, Tammy Faye La Valley met *JIM BAKKER when both were students at North Central Bible College, an *ASSEMBLIES OF GOD school in Minneapolis, Minnesota. Their decision to marry in 1961 forced their ouster from the school because of a policy against married students, and the newlyweds became itinerant *EVANGELISTS, with a specialty in children's ministries. Their break came in 1965 when *PAT ROBERTSON hired them (and their puppets) for his fledgling television operation, the *CHRISTIAN BROADCASTING NETWORK. *The Jim and Tammy Show* became quite popular with viewers, and Robertson took special note of the couple's ability to solicit contributions over the airwaves.

The Bakkers left CBN in 1973 and helped to found the *TRINITY BROADCASTING NETWORK in Santa Ana, California, but returned east the following year to begin what became the PTL Network in Charlotte, North Carolina. Tammy Faye, who became famous for her excessive makeup and her histrionics, became cohost of *The PTL Club*, a talk and variety show that eventually changed its name to *The Jim and Tammy Show.* Fueled by contributions solicited by mail and over the air, the Bakkers' religious empire grew spectacularly during the 1980s, with state-of-the-art production facilities and a Christian theme park, *HERITAGE USA, that ranked third to Disney World and Disneyland in annual number of visitors.

The empire began to crumble, however, early in 1987 when a 1980 tryst between *JIM BAKKER and Jessica Hahn, a church secretary from Long Island, came to light. The media and federal investigators uncovered a multitude of improprieties ranging from the Bakkers' lifestyle of conspicuous consumption to marital troubles to financial irregularities, which eventually landed *JIM BAKKER in prison. In 1993, while her husband was in prison, Tammy Faye announced her intention to seek a divorce. She married Roe Messner, a wealthy developer and old friend, in October 1993.

References: Tammy Faye Bakker, *I Gotta Be Me* (1978); idem, *Run to the Roar* (1980); Tammy Faye Messner, *Tammy: Telling It My Way* (1997); Charles E. Shepard, *Forgiven: The Rise and Fall of Jim Bakker and the PTL Ministry* (1989); *The Eyes of Tammy Faye,* feature-length documentary (1999).

Methodism The story of Methodism in the United States is largely one of division and reunion. This story touches on issues of slavery, race, church politics, the advent of numerous types of theology, and the teachings of *JOHN and *CHARLES WESLEY.

When the Wesleys first visited colonial America, their work was difficult and largely unsuccessful. They had come as missionaries of the Church of England, also known as the Anglican Church, and they returned to England discouraged. On the voyage to America, however, John Wesley had met a group of Moravians and was impressed by their simple piety. On his return to London, John Wesley attended a now-famous religious meeting on Aldersgate Street at which he felt his heart "strangely warmed" by a reading from Martin Luther's "Preface to the Epistle to the Romans." This warming was the start of a *REVIVAL that touched England to its core. The *REVIVAL, ridiculed by the upper and middle classes, was felt most powerfully among the lower classes and working folk.

The Methodist movement was given its shape, and its name, by the method of propagation and organization devised by Wesley. The method included elements such as a circuit system and itinerant ministry, class meetings and class leaders, lay preachers, and annual conferences. Wesley also composed a set of rules that is still used by modern Methodists. It was never Wesley's intention to establish a separate church, and he worked until his death in

1791 to keep his movement within the Church of England.

This effort to maintain a connection with the Anglicans obviously did not hold up in the newly established United States of America. After the Revolutionary War, Wesley recognized that the Methodists in America constituted a separate body. Wesley sent *FRANCIS ASBURY and Thomas Rankin to the colonies in 1771 to be superintendents among the Methodists. Rankin presided over the first conference of Methodists in America at Philadelphia in 1773. After the war, Wesley sent Thomas Coke to join Asbury in superintending the work. Coke was accompanied on the journey by two other preachers who Wesley ordained. In December 1784, the so-called Christmas Conference, at Lovely Land Chapel in Baltimore, organized the Methodist Episcopal Church in America. The conference was composed only of ministers and it adopted the articles of religion as written by Wesley. The conference also declared that Methodists should vow allegiance to the government of the United States. In 1792, the first general conference met and established the quadrennial schedule for general conferences. Annual conferences, obviously, met yearly.

Growth among the Methodists in America was rapid. At the start of the Revolution approximately seven thousand people were followers of the Wesleyan method. By the close of the Revolutionary War, there were fourteen thousand Methodists in thirty-seven circuits. By the middle of the nineteenth century there were over 1.3 million. This same period saw a similar development among African American Methodists with the founding of the African Methodist Episcopal Church in 1787 and the African Methodist Episcopal Zion Church in 1796.

Much of the growth came during the *SECOND GREAT AWAKENING. This series of *REVIVALS spanning the first third of the nineteenth century saw the development of the *CAMP MEETING and mass *REVIVALS. The Methodists, with *CIRCUIT RIDERS traveling the rural areas and the established congregations in the cities, appropriated the *CAMP MEETING and developed its expression with extraordinary results. The Methodist call to personal piety and an experiential faith was well-suited to the *REVIVALS.

The growth, however, did not come easily or without a price. In addition to the African American splits, in 1830 about five thousand clergy and laypeople left the denomination because of a dispute over representation at conferences and the election of presiding elders (district superintendents). The dissenters wanted lay representation and the power to elect their own presiding elders. The schismatics formed the Methodist Protestant Church. It remained a separate and strong denomination until 1939.

The most devastating split to strike the Methodist Episcopal Church came in 1844, over the issue of slavery. Wesley had opposed slavery, but it was not expressly prohibited in church law. The general conference in 1844 suspended Bishop James Andrew of Georgia, who had obtained slaves through marriage and was prohibited by Georgia law from freeing them. Dissidents at the conference met to draw up a plan of separation that would allow annual conferences in slave-holding states to withdraw from the Methodist Episcopal Church to form their own denomination. The controversial plan was adopted by the general conference. A question, which was never resolved, arose about the constitutionality of the separation; nevertheless, in 1845, the Methodist Episcopal Church, South was formed at a meeting in Louisville, Kentucky. The bitter split and accompanying acrimony stayed with both groups well into the twentieth century. In some sections the harsh feelings remained even after the two groups reunited, along with the Methodist Protestant Church, in 1939. The Methodist Episcopal Church, South brought 2.5 million members to the reunited denomination; the Methodist Protestant Church brought around two hundred thousand members; and the Methodist Episcopal Church brought 5 million members to create a church that included 7.7 million Methodists.

The early years of the nineteenth century also saw the development of parallel groups using a discipline modeled after the Methodists' and a theology that was almost identical. Philip Otterbein, a German Reformed pastor, and Martin Boehm, a Mennonite, organized the *CHURCH OF THE UNITED BRETHREN IN CHRIST in 1800. Another church, the Evangelical Association, was founded in 1803 as the result of the preaching of Jacob Albright, a Lutheran farmer who had been converted and nurtured by Methodist instruction. Both churches focused primarily on Germans in Pennsylvania. The Evangelical Association suffered a schism of its own in 1894, which led to the founding of the *UNITED EVANGELICAL CHURCH. The schism was largely repaired by a merger in 1922 that created the Evangelical Church.

The Methodist Episcopal Church, South was in dire condition following the Civil War. Still, even with all of the death and devastation that had ravaged the South, the church was able to recover quickly and to continue its dramatic growth. In 1866, there were at least 225,000 African American members of the Methodist Episcopal Church, South. This number was down considerably from the period before the war. At one point, the slave members of the Methodist Episcopal Church, South in South Carolina actually outnumbered the white members. Significant numbers of freed blacks had left the denomination for the two older African American Methodist groups discussed earlier. At the general conference in 1866, a delegation representing the African American members of the Methodist Episcopal Church, South petitioned to be allowed to establish their own denomination. The request was granted, and the Colored Methodist Episcopal Church was formed in 1870. In 1954, the general conference changed the name of the denomination to the Christian Methodist Episcopal Church, its present name. Today the African Methodist Episcopal Church, the African Methodist Episcopal Zion Church, and the Colored Methodist Episcopal Church number approximately 3.5 million, 1.2 million, and eight hundred thousand members, respectively.

Another significant movement to touch *METHODISM in America was the *HOLINESS MOVEMENT. The period from 1880 to 1914 rocked the Methodists as many people were attracted by the revivalistic movement that focused on the Wesleyan doctrine of perfection. The doctrine states that after a person is *SAVED, he or she should go on to be perfected in love. This perfection will be attended by a "*SECOND BLESSING," which some interpret as the *BAPTISM OF THE HOLY SPIRIT. The growth of this movement led to the formation of two families of churches, the holiness churches and the pentecostal churches. Both families include many separate denominations.

In the 1930s, negotiations had begun between the United Brethren in Christ and the Evangelical Church. Too many similarities existed between the two churches for them to remain separate. Finally, after nearly twenty years of discussion, a merger completed in 1946 formed the Evangelical United Brethren Church. Among the three main white Methodist bodies, negotiations began in 1916. The plan of union put forward in the 1930s was controversial because it divided the denomination into six jurisdictions. Five of these were geographical, but the sixth, called the Central Jurisdiction, was for African American churches wherever they were located geographically. Even with this problematic organization, the general conferences and annual conferences of the three denominations approved the plan overwhelmingly. The Methodist Protestants adopted the plan even though it meant returning to the episcopal form of government that had led to their defection in 1830. In any case, the Methodist Church was formed in 1939. The Central Jurisdiction remained as a part of the structure of the Methodist Church until the merger with the Evangelical United Brethren Church in 1968.

The only significant separation between the constituent bodies of the Methodist Church and the Evangelical United Brethren Church historically had been language. The Methodists used English while the Brethren spoke German. By the mid-twentieth century, even this difference had become negligible. Some concern arose over the role of women in the clergy. The Evangelical Church had never ordained women. The United Brethren had ordained women since 1889. When the two churches merged, the United Brethren accepted the Evangelical practice, and women lost their right to ordination. The Methodist Church had begun ordaining women to full clergy status in 1956. When the merger came in 1968, women were granted full clergy status in the plan of union.

Even in the midst of the merger came dissenting voices. Fifty-one congregations of the Evangelical United Brethren withdrew from the Pacific Northwest Conference to establish the Evangelical Church of North America. In Montana, eighteen of the twenty-three Evangelical United Brethren congregations formed the Evangelical Church of North America in Montana. Other congregations also asked to leave, but they were not given permission.

When the United Methodist Church was created at the general conference in Dallas, Texas, in April 1968, the denomination held about eleven million members. Neither the Evangelical United Brethren nor the Methodists were required to make any significant change in theology or *POLITY, with the exception of the role of women. The *POLITY of the United Methodist Church continued that of the constituent bodies, with sixty-eight annual conferences and a quadrennial general conference. The general conference is now composed half of laity and half of clergy. The general conference is the highest legislative body of the denomination, and its decisions are printed in *Discipline,* which is the church's rulebook. Between the annual conferences and the general conference are five jurisdictional conferences in the United States whose main task is the election of bishops.

Historically the constituent bodies of the United Methodist Church affirmed the traditional beliefs of most of Protestant Christianity. Following the lead of the Wesleys, the Methodists have placed a higher emphasis on personal piety and religious experience. The church holds to two sacraments, *BAPTISM and the *LORD'S SUPPER. The form of the *BAPTISM is optional, but it usually is administered by sprinkling. The frequency of the observance of the *LORD'S SUPPER varies. The twentieth century also saw the Methodists move away from the evangelistic fervor that marked the early republic period, while they have moved forward with an increasingly ambitious social agenda as set forth in the denomination's social creed.

In the mid-1990s, the United Methodist Church had 36,361 churches and over 8.5 million members. It maintains a worldwide presence through its forty-eight foreign annual conferences. It is strongly ecumenical, participating in both the World Council of Churches and the National Council of the Churches of Christ as well as the World Methodist Council.

References: Frank S. Mead and Samuel S. Hill, *Handbook of Denominations in the United States,* 10th ed. (1996); J. Gordon Melton, *Encyclopedia of American Religions,* 3d ed. (1993); *1997 Yearbook of American and Canadian Churches*; Russell F. Richey, *The Methodist Conference in America: A History* (1996); Neil Semple, *The Lord's Dominion: The History of Canadian Methodism* (1996); John Wigger, *Taking Heaven by Storm: Methodism and the Rise of Popular American Religion* (1997).

Methodist Episcopal Church. *See* **Methodism.**

Methodist Episcopal Church, South. *See* **Methodism.**

Methodist Protestant Church. *See* **Methodism.**

Metropolitan Community Churches. *See* **Universal Fellowship of Metropolitan Community Churches.**

Metzger, Bruce M(anning) (1914–) Perhaps the preeminent New Testament textual critic of the twentieth century, Bruce M. Metzger was born in Middletown, Pennsylvania, and educated at Lebanon Valley College, Princeton Theological Seminary, and Princeton University, where he earned the Ph.D. in 1942. He began his long career at Princeton Seminary in 1940 as an instructor, rising through the ranks to full professor in 1954. In addition to his publications, Metzger has headed various New Testament translation and revision committees, notably that of the Revised Standard Version and the New Revised Standard Version.

References: Bruce M. Metzger, *Annotated Bibliography of the Textual Criticism of the New Testament, 1914–1939* (1955); idem, *The New Testament: Its Background, Growth and Content* (1965); idem, *Text Critical Commentary on the Greek New Testament* (1971); Mark A. Noll, *Between Faith and Criticism: Evangelicals, Scholarship, and the Bible in America* (1986).

Meyer, F(rederick) B(rotherton) (1847–1929) F. B. Meyer, born in London and graduated from London University in 1869, was pastor of the Priory Street Baptist Church in York when he befriended ***Dwight L. Moody** and ***Ira Sankey** during their preaching tour of Britain. Moody invited Meyer to Northfield, Massachusetts, in 1891, where Meyer, who espoused ***Keswick** teachings, quickly established himself as a popular favorite on the Bible conference circuit. Meyer made twelve trips to America, all told, where his preaching, biblical exposition, and devotional writings won him a substantial following among American evangelicals. Among those affected by Meyer's preaching was ***J. Wilbur Chapman**, who credited Meyer with changing the direction of his career.

Reference: Ian Randall, "A Christian Cosmopolitan: F. B. Meyer in Britain and America," in George A. Rawlyk and Mark A. Noll, eds., *Amazing Grace: Evangelicalism in Australia, Britain, Canada, and the United States* (1993).

Meyer, Joyce (1942–) The host of *Life in the Word* radio program, which began in

1985, Joyce Meyer claims to have overcome childhood abuse and adversity by reading the *BIBLE and "learning to receive God's *GRACE to bring about changes" in her life. She began her ministry with a home Bible study group in 1976 and was ordained four years later by Life Christian Center in St. Louis. There, she conducted weekly meetings for women, which evolved into a full-time organization, Life in the Word, Inc., and sent Meyer all over the country giving seminars on marriage and women's issues. Her organization, which is based in Fenton, Missouri, a suburb of St. Louis, also publishes a monthly magazine, *Life in the Word.*

Meyer, Kenneth M. (1932–) A pastor and administrator in the *EVANGELICAL FREE CHURCH OF AMERICA, Kenneth M. Meyer grew up on the north side of Chicago, near Wrigley Field. Although he had initially planned to study law, he earned the B.D. from Trinity Seminary and Bible College and was ordained in 1953. He served as pastor of churches in Illinois and Minnesota and as secretary of Christian education for the denomination. Meyer, a gifted fund-raiser, assumed the presidency of *TRINITY EVANGELICAL DIVINITY SCHOOL in 1974 and, a decade later, the presidency of *TRINITY COLLEGE. Just prior to his retirement in 1995, he engineered the merger of those institutions into a larger entity called *TRINITY INTERNATIONAL UNIVERSITY.

Reference: Sharon A. Morris, "Enterprising Servanthood," *Trinity Wellspring,* spring 1996.

Meyer, Lucy (Jane) Rider (1849–1922) Founder of the deaconess movement within American *METHODISM, Lucy Rider Meyer was born in New Haven, Vermont, and converted to *METHODISM at the age of thirteen. She graduated from Oberlin College in 1872 and studied at the Massachusetts Institute of Technology and at the Philadelphia Medical School. At the behest of *JOHN HEYL VINCENT, Meyer wrote *SUNDAY SCHOOL literature, all the while pursuing her interests in science and medicine. She became a professor of chemistry at McKendree College (Lebanon, Illinois) in 1879, received the master's degree from Oberlin the following year, and completed her M.D. at the Women's Medical College of Chicago (Northwestern University) in 1887.

After serving as a delegate to the World Sunday School Association in London in 1880, Meyer returned to the United States to assume the role of field secretary for the Illinois Sunday School Association. She published *Children's Meetings and How to Conduct Them* in 1884 and in 1885 founded the Chicago Training School for City, Home and Foreign Missions (now a part of Garrett-Evangelical Theological Seminary). The Training School gave rise to the first American "deaconess home" for female Training School students who wanted to do medical and social work among the poor of Chicago. The Methodist Episcopal Church formally certified the deaconess movement in 1888, and Meyer remained at the forefront of the deaconess movement for the remainder of her life. She edited *The Deaconess Advocate* and founded numerous philanthropic organizations.

References: Lucy Rider Meyer, *Deaconesses: Biblical, Early Church, European, American* (1889); Isabelle Horton, *High Adventure: Life of Lucy Rider Meyer* (1928).

Michaux, Lightfoot Solomon (1884–1968) Lightfoot Solomon Michaux was born in Buckroe Beach, Virginia, and reared in the Baptist tradition. After making a good living as a seafood merchant, Michaux received his ministerial credentials from the Church of Christ (Holiness) and in 1917 began his own congregation, Everybody's Mission. He broke with the Church of Christ and incorporated his congregation as the Gospel Spreading Tabernacle Building Association in 1921. Michaux, an African American, ran afoul of local authorities in 1922 when he conducted racially integrated baptismal services; he was eventually acquitted.

By 1928, Michaux's preaching, a blend of holiness and positive thinking, had produced several congregations, which he united under the umbrella of the Church of God and Gospel Spreading Association, with headquarters in Washington, D.C. He began a radio ministry, *Radio Church of God,* the following year with a large choir that included Mahalia Jackson among its members. In an era when other African American religious leaders were making their marks on northern cities like Chicago, Philadelphia, and New York, Michaux, who was known to his followers as Elder Michaux, cut a similar figure in Washington. He conducted mass *BAPTISMS annually in the Potomac River, accompanied by parades and gospel singing. His church operated several social welfare programs, provided low-cost housing, and offered an affordable restaurant, Happy News Café. Michaux became an early supporter of Franklin Roosevelt's New Deal, and the preacher's efforts drew many African Americans into the Democratic Party in the 1930s.

Michaux tried to move into television in the late 1940s, but that experiment was short-lived. He reorganized his congregations in 1964, changing the name to the Gospel Spreading Church.

References: Pauline Lark, ed., *Sparks from the Anvil of Elder Michaux* (1950); J. Gordon Melton, Phillip Charles Lucas, and Jon R. Stone, *Prime-Time Religion: An Encyclopedia of Religious Broadcasting* (1997).

MidAmerica Nazarene College (Olathe, Kansas) MidAmerica Nazarene College was established in 1966, and the first students matriculated two years later. Sponsored by the North Central Region of the *CHURCH OF THE NAZARENE, the college is operated by a board of trustees elected from the region's districts in Iowa, Kansas, Minnesota, Missouri, Nebraska, and the Dakotas. In addition to undergraduate liberal arts programs, MidAmerica Nazarene offers master's degrees in education and business. The holiness college has a degree affiliation with European Nazarene Bible College in Germany.

MidAmerica Nazarene's statement of faith is noteworthy for its affirmation of civil liberties. One passage reads, "We believe that people function in a society and that laws are needed for the society to operate efficiently. The form of government and the laws developed in the society are important to the individual and the church. We believe that the American form of democratic government is the finest yet achieved, and fully support its ideals. The importance of the individual, the right of all persons to achieve, and the belief in guaranteed civil liberties are central to American heritage, and are in line with the teachings of the *BIBLE." The inclusion of such a passage is telling, considering that in the 1970s MidAmerica Nazarene was involved in a lawsuit regarding religious civil liberties. In 1972, the Kansas attorney general ruled that the college's students did not qualify for state aid because the school imposed mandatory chapel attendance. The then–

attorney general reversed the ruling in 1979 in a case that was heralded as a victory by Christian-college supporters who sought equal government funding for religious and nonreligious institutions.

Reference: William C. Ringenberg, *The Christian College: A History of Protestant Higher Education in America* (1984).

Midwest Christian Junior College. *See* **Dordt College.**

Midwest Congregational Christian Fellowship When negotiations were underway to form the United Church of Christ, several churches in the Eastern Indiana Association of the Congregational and Christian Churches objected to the liberal direction of the church leadership. In 1958, rather than join in the proposed merger, thirty of these churches withdrew to form the Midwest Congregational Christian Fellowship, with headquarters in Muncie, Indiana.

Doctrine in the fellowship reflects a Puritan heritage, the Christian noncreedal bent, and the evangelical beliefs of the members. The doctrinal statement affirms belief in the Trinity, *SALVATION, the ministry of the Holy Spirit, the resurrection, and the unity of believers. *POLITY in the fellowship is congregational. The fellowship meets quarterly. One quarterly meeting is designated as the annual meeting. The Midwest Congregational Christian Fellowship joined the *NATIONAL ASSOCIATION OF EVANGELICALS in 1964.

Reference: J. Gordon Melton, *The Encyclopedia of American Religions,* 3d ed. (1993).

Mike Evans Ministries International. *See* **Evans, Mike.**

Millenarianism Millenarianism refers generally to beliefs surrounding the *MILLENNIUM, the thousand-year period of righteousness predicted in the book of Revelation. Although evangelicals hold widely divergent views of the millennium, most would fall into the categories of either *PREMILLENNIALISM or *POSTMILLENNIALISM.

Millennium The millennium refers to a thousand-year period expected near the end of the world by many evangelicals, based on their understanding of the biblical prophecies in the book of Revelation, especially Revelation 20:1–7. This millennial age is one in which the righteous will rule either before or after the coming of Jesus Christ at the end of time. For evangelicals, the millennium is one of the events on the apocalyptic calendar leading to the end of the world.

For centuries, millennial ideas have been hotly debated in evangelical circles. Some evangelicals, following the lead of Martin Luther, see the book of Revelation as unfit for inclusion into the biblical canon. They prefer to interpret Revelation itself as a restatement of pre-Christian Jewish apocalyptic thought or as an allegorical source of comfort to the early, persecuted Christians, an assurance that God would eventually avenge their sufferings.

Evangelicals who insist on a literal interpretation of the millennium generally fall into two camps: postmillennialists and premillennialists. Postmillennialists believe that Jesus will return *after* the millennium, this thousand-year period of righteousness. Implicit in postmillennialist belief is the conviction that believers need to work toward the establishment of the millennial kingdom. Much of the impulse for social reform among evangelicals in the nineteenth century, for example, came from postmillennial sentiments.

*PREMILLENNIALISM, on the other

hand, is a theology of despair, at least insofar as it relates to the impetus for reforming society according to the norms of godliness. It holds that Jesus will return *before* the millennium; Jesus may return, therefore, at any moment. Although there are notable exceptions, premillennialists, by and large, have abandoned hopes of widespread social amelioration. They look instead for divine intervention: the *RAPTURE of true believers, the *TRIBULATION, and the millennium.

Miller, Samuel (1769–1850) Samuel Miller, professor of ecclesiastical history and church government at Princeton Theological Seminary, graduated with high honors from the University of Pennsylvania and was ordained by the Presbytery of New York in 1793. A noted preacher, he served as a pastor in New York City before moving to Princeton Seminary in 1813. Miller published *Letters on Unitarianism* (1821) and a *Life of Jonathan Edwards* (1840); he remained at Princeton until poor health forced his retirement in 1849.

Miller, William (1782–1849) Born in Pittsfield, Massachusetts, William Miller was a self-educated man who grew up in Low Hampton, New York. He moved to Poultney, Vermont, after his marriage in 1803. He was a farmer, a sheriff, and a justice of the peace, and he served as an officer in the army during the War of 1812. Miller undertook a systematic study of the *BIBLE after his *CONVERSION in 1816. Two years later he decided that Daniel 8:14 (KJV)—"And he said unto me, Unto two thousand and three hundred days; then shall the sanctuary be cleansed"—held the key for discerning the date for the *SECOND COMING of Christ. Miller's arcane calculations, which posited that a day equaled a year and began numbering from the decree of Artaxerxes to rebuild Jerusalem in 457 B.C.E., led him to conclude that Jesus would return about the year 1843.

Miller began publicizing his calculations in 1831; the following year he published his ideas serially in the *Vermont Telegraph*. Miller hit the lecture circuit, using a huge chart to illustrate his calculations. In 1836, he published *Evidence from Scripture and History of the Second Coming of Christ, About the Year 1843.* Miller and the *MILLERITES, as they were called, received a major boost from *JOSHUA V. HIMES, a Boston minister who proved adept as a publicist. Miller's calculations appeared in a number of periodicals, including *Signs of the Times* and *The Midnight Cry*.

As 1843 approached, the Millerite enthusiasm reached a fever pitch. Horace Greeley thought the threat to public welfare was so great that he published an extra edition of his *New-York Tribune* on March 2, 1843. When Miller was pressed to be specific about the date, he studied Jewish calendars and declared that Christ would return sometime between March 21, 1843, and March 21, 1844. When the Lord failed to materialize, Miller went back to his calculations and announced that he had neglected to account for a "tarrying time" and that the actual date would be October 22, 1844. Once again the Millerites prepared for the *SECOND COMING, and their letdown became known as the *GREAT DISAPPOINTMENT. Miller died in 1849, still convinced that the return of Jesus was imminent.

References: William Miller, *Evidence from Scripture and History of the Second Coming of Christ, About the Year 1843* (1836); David L. Rowe, *Thunder and Trumpets: Millerites and Dissenting Religion in Upstate New York, 1800–1850* (1985).

Millerites The term *Millerites* was given to the followers of *WILLIAM MILLER, adventist prophet and lecturer, in the 1830s and 1840s. Historians estimate the size of Miller's following at anywhere from thirty thousand to one hundred thousand—until the *GREAT DISAPPOINTMENT of 1844, when Jesus did not return, as predicted, on October 22, 1844.

Milligan College (Milligan, Tennessee) Milligan College is affiliated with the Christian Church (Church of Christ), but like many colleges established in the nineteenth century, it was first chartered as an academy by the state legislature. Known as Buffalo Male and Female Institute, the school opened in 1866 under the leadership of Wilson G. Barker. Classes were first held in the Buffalo Church, now Hopwood Memorial Church. In 1875, Kentucky native Josephus Hopwood became the head of the academy. Hopwood introduced a postsecondary curriculum six years later and renamed the college in honor of Robert Milligan of Kentucky University (Transylvania), whom Hopwood regarded as "the embodiment of Christian scholarship and Christian gentility." As the first president of the new college, Hopwood adopted the motto, "Christian Education—the Hope of the World."

During the Second World War many American colleges made their facilities available to the military as training sites, yet Milligan College was the only school completely given over to the navy. The years following World War II were a time of hardship for the college, which found the ties to its civilian alumni difficult to restore even while the navy's pullout mandated a return to nonmilitary programs. The financial picture has been brighter in recent years, for J. Henry Kegley, a 1941 alumnus and frozen-foods entrepreneur, has underwritten a large portion of a $1.3 million project to improve the college's facilities. Kegley has funded a computer laboratory, dormitories, and improvements to existing campus facilities; he has also contributed to the college's endowment.

Milligan College offers numerous bachelor's degrees, including a B.S. in mortuary science, and also has a graduate program in education. The library maintains a special collection on the Restoration.

Reference: *Milligan College 1996–1997 Catalog* (1996).

Mills, Samuel J(ohn), (Jr.) (1783–1818) Converted during an evangelical *REVIVAL in 1801, Samuel J. Mills entered Williams College to prepare for the ministry. An exceptionally pious student, Mills formed a group of fellow evangelicals called Society of the Brethren and was one of the principals in the famous 1806 *HAYSTACK PRAYER MEETING. Mills studied briefly at Yale, where he made the acquaintance of *HENRY OBOOKIAH, a native of Hawai'i, and had a hand in Obookiah's conversion to Christianity.

In 1810, Mills assisted in the formation of the *AMERICAN BOARD OF COMMISSIONERS FOR FOREIGN MISSIONS. He was licensed to preach in 1812, undertook a missionary tour of the South and the Midwest, and was ordained into the Congregational ministry at Newburyport, Massachusetts, in 1815. Although he never served formally as a foreign missionary, Mills was affiliated with several missionary organizations. He served as an agent of the School for Educating Colored Men and helped organize the United Foreign Missionary Society and the *AMERICAN BIBLE SOCIETY. In 1817, Mills accepted an assignment from the *AMERICAN COLONIZATION SOCIETY to purchase land for the "repatriation" of slaves to Africa. Mills secured the land that would eventually become Liberia; he died on the return voyage and was buried at sea.

Miltonvale Wesleyan College. *See* **Bartlesville Wesleyan College.**

Mission Mississippi. *See* **Skinner, Thomas "Tom."**

Missionary Church The Missionary Church was formed in 1969 by the merger of the United Missionary Church and the Missionary Church Association. Both of the former churches came out of a Mennonite, or Anabaptist, heritage but had moved away from their roots toward a more explicitly mission-oriented position.

The Church is conservative and evangelical in theology and congregational in *POLITY. Even though the denomination is congregational, local churches recognize the authority of the general conference, which meets biennially. A president and other officers are elected to four-year terms at a general conference meeting. A general board oversees the various mission endeavors and other agencies of the denomination. The Missionary Church sponsors Bethel College at Mishawalka, Indiana, and its headquarters are in Fort Wayne, Indiana. The church has over three hundred local churches and 29,542 members.

References: Frank S. Mead and Samuel S. Hill, *Handbook of Denominations in the United States,* 10th ed. (1996); J. Gordon Melton, *The Encyclopedia of American Religions,* 3d ed. (1993); "Contributions to U.S. and Canadian Protestant Churches," *Chronicle of Philanthropy,* vol. IX, no. 15.

Missionary Church Association. *See* **Missionary Church.**

Mississippi College (Clinton, Mississippi) Mississippi College is the oldest postsecondary institution in Mississippi. Chartered in 1826 by the state legislature, the school began as Hampstead Academy and was then renamed Mississippi Academy. It took the name Mississippi College in 1830, and a year later the school became the first coeducational college in the United States to grant a college degree to a woman.

The Mississippi Baptist Convention adopted the school in 1850. The Female Department was eliminated at that time. Three years later a separate school for women was established in Clinton. First known as Central Female Institute, the school was later renamed Hillman College. In 1942, Mississippi College bought and absorbed Hillman.

Mississippi College has been nationally recognized by many foundations for the strength of its science programs. At the top of the list, however, is a $1 million award to the biology department from the Howard Hughes Medical Institute to support undergraduate research and support facilities and equipment. Mississippi College's acceptance rate for medical school is 30 percent above the national average.

The college introduced graduate programs in 1950 and has had a full graduate school since 1975, which offers programs in education, arts and sciences, and business. The college also has a law school; total graduate enrollment is more than one thousand students.

Although many *CHRISTIAN COLLEGES prohibit fraternities and sororities of any kind, Mississippi College has four social clubs for women, which run "rush" events. Men can join the collegiate arms of several national service clubs, such as Kiwanis.

References: Mississippi College General 1996–97 Bulletin (1996); Thomas C. Hunt and James C.

Carper, eds., *Religious Higher Education in the United States: A Source Book* (1995).

Mississippi Synodical College. *See* **Belhaven College.**

Modernism. *See* **Liberalism.**

Modesto Manifesto In November 1948, during an evangelistic campaign in Modesto, California, *BILLY GRAHAM asked several of his associates—Cliff Barrows, George Beverly Shea, and Grady Wilson—to recall some of the difficulties that had befallen other *EVANGELISTS and to formulate a strategy to avoid similar setbacks. The group then agreed upon a set of principles, known in the oral tradition as the Modesto Manifesto, although Barrows insists that designation is in no way official.

First, the group agreed that everyone in the Graham organization would consent to strict rules of financial accountability and that everyone would be paid straight salary, not a portion of the offerings. They sought to avoid even the appearance of sexual impropriety, resolving never to have lunch or a counseling session or an automobile ride alone with a woman other than their wives. They resolved to resist inflated publicity, especially regarding attendance at evangelistic rallies, and they determined, finally, not to criticize local clergy. Adherence to the tenets of this Modesto Manifesto has helped to insulate the *BILLY GRAHAM organization from scandal, or even the hint of scandal.

References: William Martin, *A Prophet with Honor: The Billy Graham Story* (1991); *Crusade: The Life of Billy Graham,* PBS documentary (1993).

Moe, Malla (1863–1953) Under the aegis of the Scandinavian Alliance Mission, now known as *THE EVANGELICAL ALLIANCE MISSION (TEAM), Malla Moe spent a remarkable fifty-four years as a missionary in southern Africa, especially Swaziland. Moe, a powerful, domineering woman, assumed responsibilities akin to a bishop on the mission field. She organized churches, conducted evangelistic campaigns, and trained indigenous leaders. Moe spent the last decades of her life as an itinerant *EVANGELIST in Africa, but despite her success and the latitude granted her on the mission field, she was rarely allowed to preach in evangelical churches while on furlough because of evangelical opposition to women's ordination.

Moffett, Samuel A(ustin) (1864–1946) A graduate of Hanover College and McCormick Theological Seminary, Samuel A. Moffett, influenced by *DWIGHT L. MOODY and the *YMCA movement, committed his life to foreign missions in 1886. Three years later, he sailed for Korea under the auspices of the Presbyterian Mission Board and became one of the first Protestant missionaries in inland Korea. In the face of opposition, Moffett began catechism classes and purchased land in Pyongyang, which became the center of Presbyterian theological and medical missions in Korea. In 1907, when four Presbyterian churches formed the Korean Presbyterian Church, Moffett was chosen moderator.

As a consequence of his forty-six years on the mission field, Moffett's legacy to evangelical missions in Korea was strong, indigenous leaders and congregations. His tireless efforts earned him the sobriquet "Looking-up-the-Road Man" from his Korean friends. Moffett participated in the formation of Union Christian College, now known as Soong Jun University, and Presbyterian Theological Seminary. The Japanese forced him out of Korea in 1936, three years before the end of his life.

Mohler, R(ichard) Albert, Jr. (1959–) Born in Lakeland, Florida, R. Albert Mohler Jr. studied at Florida Atlantic University and at *SAMFORD UNIVERSITY, where he earned his baccalaureate degree. He went on to Southern Baptist Theological Seminary, the flagship school of the *SOUTHERN BAPTIST CONVENTION, where he earned the M.Div. and Ph.D. degrees. Mohler was ordained; he served as pastor of several Southern Baptist churches and as editor of *The Christian Index* before becoming the ninth president of Southern Seminary in 1993, at the age of thirty-three.

The presidency of the convention's premier seminary allowed Mohler to press his conservative agenda both at the seminary and within the *SOUTHERN BAPTIST CONVENTION. He stands squarely in the tradition of the conservatives who took over the convention in 1979, and he has expended considerable energy rooting out "moderates" on his faculty and in pushing for ever more conservative doctrinal statements within the *SOUTHERN BAPTIST CONVENTION.

Mollenkott, Virginia Ramey (1932–) One of the leaders in the evangelical feminist movement, Virginia Ramey Mollenkott earned degrees from *BOB JONES UNIVERSITY, Temple University, and New York University. She taught at *CARL MCINTIRE's Shelton College from 1955 until 1963, when she moved to Nyack Missionary College (now *NYACK COLLEGE). In 1967, she joined the faculty of William Paterson College. In addition to her academic work, Mollenkott has articulated a biblical feminism that has often attracted hostility from male evangelicals. Her 1978 book in defense of gay rights, *Is the Homosexual My Neighbor?*, written jointly with *LETHA SCANZONI, helped to precipitate the break within the *EVANGELICAL WOMEN'S CAUCUS over the issue of lesbianism.

References: Virginia Ramey Mollenkott, *In Search of Balance* (1969); idem, *Women, Men, and the Bible* (1977); idem, *The Divine Feminine: Biblical Imagery of God as Female* (1983); idem, with Letha Scanzoni, *Is the Homosexual My Neighbor?* (1978).

Monsma, Stephen V. (1936–) Stephen V. Monsma graduated from *CALVIN COLLEGE, earned the M.A. from Georgetown University, and earned the Ph.D. from Michigan State University. While a professor of political science at Calvin, Monsma was elected to the Michigan House of Representatives on the Democratic ticket, where he served from 1973 until 1979. He was elected to the Michigan Senate in 1978 and served until 1983. After losing a bid for U.S. Congress in 1982 (he lost to another *CALVIN COLLEGE faculty member, *PAUL B. HENRY), Monsma joined the faculty of Pepperdine University as professor of political science.

References: Stephen V. Monsma, *The Unraveling of America* (1974); idem, *Positive Neutrality: Letting Religious Freedom Ring* (1993); idem, *The Challenge of Pluralism: Church and State in Five Democracies* (1997).

Montana Wilderness School of the Bible (Augusta, Montana) Founded in 1981, Montana Wilderness School of the Bible offers a single year of Bible instruction in the Rocky Mountains. The program, which is limited to forty-eight students annually, capitalizes on its wilderness setting, which is twenty-three miles from the nearest town. "Separated from many of life's usual distractions," the catalog reads, "this location provides a unique stage for students to study God's Word (special revelation) while learning firsthand about creation (general revelation) through a heightened awareness of God and His majesty."

The curriculum is unabashedly fundamentalist; the statement of faith includes affirmations of such doctrines as biblical *INERRANCY, the substitutionary *ATONEMENT of Christ (Jesus took on the punishment of sinful humanity), and *PREMILLENNIALISM. Courses are taught by visiting faculty and include such offerings as "Apologetics," "Marriage and Family," "Discipleship," "Scientific Creationism," "Philippians," "Christian Financial Principals" [*sic*], and "Wilderness Backpacking."

Reference: *Montana Wilderness School of the Bible Catalog* (n.d.).

Montgomery, Carrie Judd (1858–1946) Reared in Buffalo, New York, as an Episcopalian, Carrie Judd (she married George S. Montgomery, a mining magnate, in 1890) claimed divine healing as a young woman and published a book, *The Prayer of Peace* (1880), recounting the experience. *A. B. SIMPSON, later the founder of the *CHRISTIAN AND MISSIONARY ALLIANCE, read Judd's book and included her in the growing circle of evangelicals dedicated to healing in the late nineteenth century. Judd began her own monthly magazine, *Triumphs of Faith,* in 1881, and she began speaking about her healing experience. When Simpson organized the *CHRISTIAN AND MISSIONARY ALLIANCE in 1895, Judd became the recording secretary.

Back in Buffalo, Judd turned the room in which she had been healed into a place of prayer, and she established Faith Rest Cottage, a haven of rest and prayer for the sick. In 1893, after a move to Oakland and marriage to Montgomery, Judd opened the Home of Peace, a retreat similar to Faith Rest Cottage. The Montgomerys expanded their affiliations from the *CHRISTIAN AND MISSIONARY ALLIANCE to the *SALVATION ARMY. In 1894, they founded Shalom Training School for missionaries and in 1905 opened an orphanage, later taken over by the *SALVATION ARMY.

The Montgomerys were affected by the *AZUSA STREET REVIVAL, which broke out in 1906. Carrie had spoken in *TONGUES by 1908, and she was ordained by the *CHURCHES OF GOD IN CHRIST in 1914. She later became a charter member of the *ASSEMBLIES OF GOD and was issued credentials as an *EVANGELIST in 1917.

Reference: Donald W. Dayton, *Theological Roots of Pentecostalism* (1987).

Montgomery, John Warwick (1931–) An evangelical scholar and apologist known for his quick mind and acerbic tongue, John Warwick Montgomery was born in Warsaw, New York, and took his baccalaureate degree from Cornell University in 1952; he accumulated numerous advanced degrees in library science, theology, and law. Montgomery joined the faculty of *TRINITY EVANGELICAL DIVINITY SCHOOL as professor of church history in 1964, where he remained for a decade and where he began a European studies program in Strasbourg, France. After leaving Trinity in 1974, Montgomery taught law in various venues, including the Simon Greenleaf School of Law in Anaheim, California, where he served as dean and director of the library, beginning in 1980.

Montgomery, who collects antique Citroen automobiles, has led expeditions in Turkey in search of Noah's Ark. Aside from his legal, theological, and apologetical writings, Montgomery became famous among evangelicals for his debates with Thomas J. J. Altizer on the "God is dead" proposition and with Joseph Fletcher on "situation ethics," debates that, according to most evangelical observers, Montgomery won decisively.

References: John Warwick Montgomery, *The "Is God Dead?" Controversy* (1966); idem, with Thomas J. J. Altizer, *The Altizer-Montgomery Debates: A Chapter in the God Is Dead Controversy* (1967); idem, *Ecumenicity, Evangelicalism, and Rome* (1969); idem, *The Suicide of Christian Theology* (1970); idem, *The Quest for Noah's Ark* (1972); idem, with Joseph Fletcher, *Debate on Situation Ethics* (1972); idem, *The Law above the Law* (1975); idem, *Faith Founded on Fact* (1978).

Montreat-Anderson College. *See* **Montreat College.**

Montreat College (Montreat, North Carolina) Montreat College is affiliated with the Presbyterian Church (U.S.A.). The school was founded in 1916 and was formerly known as Montreat-Anderson College. Today, it offers several two-year and four-year degree programs, including majors in outdoor education and American studies. Montreat expects every student to complete a "cross-cultural learning experience" in either a different region of the United States or in a foreign country. Students have satisfied this requirement with ministry internships and study-abroad programs in places like Chicago, Egypt, Mexico, and Costa Rica.

Moody, Dwight Lyman (1837–1899) One of the most influential preachers in American history, Dwight Lyman Moody was born in Northfield, Massachusetts, and headed east for Boston at the age of seventeen, where he worked in his uncle's shoe store. In Boston, Moody attended Mount Vernon Congregational Church and was converted to evangelical Christianity by his ***SUNDAY SCHOOL** teacher, Edward Kimball.

Moody headed west for Chicago in 1856, where he became a successful shoe salesman. He joined Plymouth Congregational Church, rented four pews, and filled them with acquaintances and business associates. In 1858, "Crazy Moody," as he was sometimes known because of his fervor, started a ***SUNDAY SCHOOL** in the slums, and two years later he quit his business to devote his energies to his religious pursuits. A conscientious objector during the Civil War, Moody did evangelistic and relief work for the ***UNITED STATES CHRISTIAN COMMISSION**, traveling to Shiloh, Murfreesboro, and Chattanooga, and was among the first Union forces to enter Richmond. In 1864, he consolidated his various evangelistic efforts to form the Illinois Street Independent Church (now ***MOODY CHURCH**), and he became president of the Chicago ***YMCA** in 1866.

After the Chicago fire of 1871, which destroyed the ***YMCA**, his church, and his home, Moody built a new building, the Northside Tabernacle, which he used to feed and clothe thousands of people who had lost their homes. Moody then launched out as an itinerant ***EVANGELIST**. He was well-received in Great Britain, and his notoriety across the Atlantic increased his popularity back in North America, where he conducted ***REVIVAL** campaigns in Brooklyn, Philadelphia, New York City, Boston, and Chicago. One of his more notable campaigns was the one he held in conjunction with the Chicago World's Fair in 1892.

Moody's preaching was simple, homespun, and sentimental. He taught the three Rs: ruin by ***SIN**, redemption by Christ, and regeneration by the Holy Spirit. Although he specialized in urban ***EVANGELISM**, Moody's ***ESCHATOLOGY** drifted more and more toward *PREMILLENNIALISM and away from social reclamation. "I look upon this world as a wrecked vessel," he once declared. "God has given me a lifeboat and said, 'Moody, save all you can.'"

Perhaps because he had so little formal education himself, Moody sought to provide grounding in *EVANGELICALISM for people attracted to his preaching. He established Northfield Seminary for girls in 1879 and Mount Hermon School for boys in 1881; Northfield-Mount Hermon, still located in Moody's hometown, is now an elite preparatory school. Moody also conducted summer conferences at Northfield beginning in 1880, and the 1886 gathering gave rise to the *STUDENT VOLUNTEER MOVEMENT. He helped to form a *BIBLE INSTITUTE in Chicago in 1889, a school that became known as *MOODY BIBLE INSTITUTE after his death.

References: J. Wilbur Chapman, *The Life and Work of Dwight L. Moody* (1900); William G. McLoughlin, *Modern Revivalism (*1959); John Pollock, *Moody* (1963); Lyle W. Dorsett, *A Passion for Souls: The Life of D. L. Moody* (1997).

Moody Bible Institute (Chicago, Illinois) Founded in 1889 by the Chicago Evangelization Society, Moody Bible Institute was originally known as the Bible Institute for Home and Foreign Missions of the Chicago Evangelization Society. A reaction to the move toward liberal theology in many seminaries, the institute derived its support from a group of theologically conservative, financially successful businessmen in Chicago. Its credibility in these circles was ensured by the support of *DWIGHT LYMAN MOODY, after whom the school was renamed in 1900.

Moody Bible Institute became a flagship institution of *FUNDAMENTALISM early in the twentieth century, and countless other training schools have patterned their curriculum after Moody's. Although its primary mission was—and remains—the training of pastors and missionaries, the school's influence has reached well beyond the classroom by means of a correspondence school, pastors' conferences, Moody Press publishing house, *Moody Monthly* magazine, a network of radio stations, and a school specializing in the training of missionary pilots.

Moody Church (Chicago, Illinois) Moody Church was organized in 1864 as the Illinois Street Independent Church by *DWIGHT LYMAN MOODY and twelve charter members. The congregation named J. H. Harwood as its first pastor, and Moody, who had enjoyed great success as a *SUNDAY SCHOOL organizer, served as one of its deacons. After the church building was destroyed in the Chicago fire of October 1871, Moody quickly built a new building, Northside Tabernacle, which he used as a relief center for victims of the fire. In the twentieth century, Moody Church, located on North LaSalle Boulevard, was one of the most influential pulpits of American *FUNDAMENTALISM.

Moon, Charlotte "Lottie" Diggs (1840–1912) "Lottie" Moon, reared on a Virginia plantation, graduated from the Abermarle Female Institute in 1861 with a master's degree in classics. After teaching for a time in Georgia, she left for China in 1873 to pursue a career as a teacher and missionary under the auspices of the *SOUTHERN BAPTIST CONVENTION. She briefly considered marriage but broke off her engagement to a fellow missionary because of his sympathy for evolution.

Moon shifted her emphasis to church planting, where she was remarkably successful. In 1889, largely because of Moon's efforts, P'ing-tu became known to Southern Baptists as the "greatest evangelistic center in all China." Moon inaugurated a Christmas Offering for Foreign Missions in 1888 as a fund-raising device within the *SOUTHERN BAPTIST CONVENTION. The offering, still a fixture in Southern Baptist churches, was renamed the Lottie Moon Christmas Offering in 1918, six years after Moon's death from starvation on Christmas Eve, 1912.

Mooneyham, W(alter) Stanley (1926–1991) Born in Houston, Mississippi, W. Stanley Mooneyham served in the navy during World War II, was ordained a Baptist minister in 1947, and graduated from *OKLAHOMA BAPTIST UNIVERSITY in 1950. After serving as pastor of a congregation in Sulphur, Oklahoma, Mooneyham became executive secretary of the National Association of Freewill Baptists from 1953 until 1959, whereupon he worked for the *NATIONAL ASSOCIATION OF EVANGELICALS and the *BILLY GRAHAM EVANGELISTIC ASSOCIATION.

Mooneyham in 1969 took over the presidency of *WORLD VISION INTERNATIONAL, an evangelical relief agency based at the time in Monrovia, California. Under his leadership the organization grew considerably, both in its annual budget and in the reach of its humanitarian work throughout the world. Mooneyham's reputation for integrity made him a logical choice to be one of the cofounders of the *EVANGELICAL COUNCIL FOR FINANCIAL ACCOUNTABILITY in 1979. He left World Vision in 1982 to become pastor of Palm Desert Community Presbyterian Church in Palm Desert, California, where he served for the remainder of his life.

References: W. Stanley Mooneyham, *What Do You Say to a Hungry World?* (1978); idem, *Sea of Heartbreak* (1980); idem, *Dancing on the Straight and Narrow: A Gentle Call to a Radical Faith* (1989); "Stan Mooneyham," *Christianity Today,* July 22, 1991.

Moor's Charity School. *See* **Wheelock, Eleazar.**

Moore, Peter C(lement) (1936–) Peter C. Moore, dean and president of *TRINITY EPISCOPAL SCHOOL OF MINISTRY, grew up in New York City and graduated from Yale University. He earned graduate degrees from Oxford University and the Episcopal Theological School, and a D.Min. from *FULLER THEOLOGICAL SEMINARY. An evangelical, Moore was one of the founders of *TRINITY EPISCOPAL SCHOOL OF MINISTRY in 1975, and he assumed the deanship in 1996 after nearly a decade as rector of Little Trinity Church in Toronto, a flagship parish in the Anglican Church of Canada, and a leader in that denomination's evangelical renewal movement. Before going to Little Trinity he had worked as a parish priest and in the late 1960s founded and directed FOCUS (the Fellowship of Christians in Universities and Schools).

References: Peter C. Moore, *Disarming the Secular Gods: How to Talk So Skeptics Will Listen* (1989); idem, *One Lord, One Faith: Getting Back to the Basics of Your Christianity in an Age of Confusion* (1994); idem, *A Church to Believe In* (1994); idem, ed., *Can a Bishop be Wrong?: Ten Scholars Challenge John Shelby Spong* (1998).

Morgan, Cindy (1968–) Christian contemporary singer and songwriter Cindy Morgan grew up in Snake Hollow, a small town in eastern Tennessee. Her mother was a gospel singer, her father a mechanic who played guitar and wrote songs. After writing her first song at the age of nine, Morgan got her start as a singer in country and gospel shows at Dollywood theme park in nearby Pigeon Forge, Tennessee. She later became a studio singer in Knoxville, where she was noticed by producers from Nashville's Word Records. Word offered her a contract in 1990.

Morgan made her recording debut with *Real Life* in 1990. This album was followed two years later by *A Reason to Live,* and by *Under the Waterfall* in 1995. She also participated in the multiartist projects *My Utmost for His Highest* and *The New Young Messiah.* Morgan was named Best New Artist of the Year by the *GOSPEL MUSIC ASSOCIATION for 1993. She has won three Dove Awards and has been nominated an additional five times.

With songs like "I Know You," "Sweet Days of Grace," "The Days of Innocence," and "Picture Me in Paradise," Morgan attained popularity with a sound evocative of dance-pop music. By the late 1990s, however, this style had given way to acoustic guitars and ballads, as Morgan began recording music she herself had written, as opposed to pieces by other songwriters. Her 1996 recording, *Listen,* best demonstrated this new style.

References: Information provided by Word Records publicity department; Camerin J. Courtney, "The Power of Love," *Today's Christian Woman,* September–October 1997.

Morgan, G. Campbell (1863–1945) Born in Gloucestershire, England, G. Campbell Morgan became a Congregationalist minister, an accomplished preacher, and a biblical expositor, despite his lack of formal theological training. Morgan cooperated with *DWIGHT L. MOODY, in England during Moody's *REVIVAL campaigns, and in North America, where Morgan became a regular attraction at Moody's Northfield Conferences. From 1904 to 1917 and again from 1933 to 1945, Morgan was pastor at Westminster Chapel in London, and he was one of the contributors to **THE FUNDAMENTALS.* Morgan's *FUNDAMENTALISM could at times be biting and contentious, especially when directed against other believers. Pentecostals, for instance, had a hard time forgetting Morgan's remark that *PENTECOSTALISM was "the last vomit of Satan."

Morgan, Marabel (née Hawk) (1937–) Born in Crestline, Ohio, Marabel Hawk married Charles O. Morgan Jr., an attorney, on June 25, 1964. After six years of marriage, Marabel Morgan decided to try to reinvigorate her marriage by submitting unconditionally to her husband. Morgan claimed that this strategy, which she believes is advocated in the *BIBLE, did wonders for her relationship with her husband. "Over a period of about a year,"she testified, "a complete turnaround took place in our marriage." In direct contradiction to emerging feminist sensibilities, Morgan advocated submission as well as a kind of sexual coquettishness, not to mention provocative lingerie, which she claimed made up the "total woman."

Morgan started an organization, Total Woman, Inc., in 1970, which is based in Miami. She published her views in *The Total Woman,* which appeared in 1973. Morgan told her female readers to practice the "Four A's": (1) Accept your husband; disregard his faults and "only think about his virtues"; (2) Admire him, perhaps by calling him at work and saying "I crave your body"; (3) Appreciate your husband; and (4) Adapt to him: "The husband is king and his wife is queen."

With virtually no publicity *The Total Woman* became the bestselling book of 1974. Morgan became an instant celebrity in evangelical circles, capitalizing on evangelical anxieties about the feminist movement.

References: Marabel Morgan, *The Total Woman* (1973); idem, *Total Joy* (1976); idem, *The Total Woman Cookbook* (1980).

Morris, Henry (Madison) (Jr.) (1918–) A native of Dallas, Texas, Henry Morris graduated from Rice University in 1939 with an engineering degree. He worked for the Texas Highway Department and as a civil engineer before returning to Rice as an instructor in engineering in 1942. Four years later, he moved to the University of Minnesota as an instructor and, later, assistant professor. Morris completed a doctorate in hydraulics at Minnesota in 1950 and became professor and head of the department of civil engineering at the University of Southwestern Louisiana. He was professor of hydraulics at Virginia Polytechnic Institute from 1957 until 1970.

A fervent believer in biblical *INERRANCY, Morris developed an avocation in what he called "creation science" in the early 1940s. He published several apologetic books on the subject, beginning with *That You Might Believe* in 1946. Morris became a member of the Creation Research Society in 1963, and he served as president of the organization from 1967 until 1973. His relentless attacks on modern science, especially evolution, made him a favorite with many *FUNDAMENTALISTS. In 1970, Morris and *TIM LAHAYE founded Christian Heritage College in San Diego. Morris served as president of the school for several years until 1980, when he became president of the *INSTITUTE FOR CREATION RESEARCH, another organization that advocates "scientific *CREATIONISM." In addition to his lectures and debates at college campuses, Morris hosts two radio programs—*Back to Genesis*, a daily spot, and *Science, Scripture, and Salvation*, a weekly fifteen-minute program—both of which advocate six-day creation.

References: Henry Morris, *The Bible and Modern Science* (1951); idem, *The Genesis Flood* (1961); idem, *The Twilight of Evolution* (1963); idem, *Evolution and the Modern Christian* (1968); idem, *Scientific Creationism* (1974); idem, *Biblical Creationism* (1993); *"In the Beginning": The Creationist Controversy*, two-part PBS documentary (1994).

Morrison, Henry Clay (1857–1942) Henry Clay Morrison was born in Bedford, Kentucky, and was converted at the age of thirteen. Licensed to preach by the Methodists in 1878, Morrison studied at Vanderbilt University and became a member of the Kentucky Conference of the Methodist Episcopal Church, South. After serving several circuits and stations, all in Kentucky, Morrison was granted permission in 1890 to become a full-time mass *EVANGELIST.

A powerful orator and a fervent proponent of holiness doctrines, Morrison sometimes ran askance of the Methodist hierarchy. He was charged with—and acquitted of—violating church law in 1897 and in 1904, but his stature remained secure enough that he was elected delegate to the General Convention five times. While others of a holiness bent fled the Methodist Episcopal Church, South, Morrison sought to champion holiness doctrines from within the denomination. He founded the *Pentecostal Herald* early in the 1890s and remained its editor for thirty-five years. He became president of *ASBURY COLLEGE in 1910 and in the course of his tenure established *ASBURY THEOLOGICAL SEMINARY in 1923, also serving as its president. Morrison published twenty-five books, all of them directed toward a popular audience.

Reference: Henry Clay Morrison, *Some Chapters of My Life Story* (1941).

Morse, Jedidiah (1761–1826) Jedidiah Morse, born in Woodstock, Connecticut, graduated from Yale College in 1783 and studied theology under the tutelage of Samuel Wales and *JONATHAN EDWARDS JR. Theologically, Morse was a Calvinist, although he sought to avoid the extreme determinism of the *NEW DIVINITY. He was licensed in 1785, taught at Yale, and became pastor of the Congregational church in Charlestown, Massachusetts, in April 1789. Morse sought to combat the rising tide of Unitarianism in the Boston area, and when the Hollis Chair of Divinity became vacant at Harvard, Morse led the charge for the appointment of an orthodox theologian. In 1805, the choice of Henry Ware, a Unitarian, however, effectively signaled the school's turn toward *LIBERALISM. Morse and *LEONARD WOODS then led the move to form *ANDOVER SEMINARY as an orthodox alternative to Harvard.

After the founding of Andover in 1808, Morse turned his attention to other matters. He helped to establish the New England Tract Society in 1814 and the *AMERICAN BIBLE SOCIETY in 1816. He was a member of the *AMERICAN BOARD OF COMMISSIONERS FOR FOREIGN MISSIONS, and his publication of *The American Geography* in 1789 made him the father of geography in America.

References: Jedidiah Morse, *The American Geography* (1789); Henry F. May, *The Enlightenment in America* (1976); J. W. Phillips, *Jedidiah Morse and New England Congregationalism* (1983).

Mother Angelica. *See* **Angelica, Mother.**

Mott, John R(aleigh) (1865–1955) Born in New York and reared in Iowa, John R. Mott was educated at Upper Iowa University and at Cornell University. Mott was one of the one hundred volunteers for foreign missions at *DWIGHT MOODY's Student Conference at Northfield, Massachusetts, in 1886; he soon emerged as chairman of the *STUDENT VOLUNTEER MOVEMENT FOR FOREIGN MISSIONS, an association whose motto was "The world for Christ in this generation." Mott maintained that position for thirty-two years.

At Cornell, Mott's work made the *YMCA chapter the largest in the country, and when he graduated in 1888 Mott became general secretary of the intercollegiate *YMCA, with a mandate to integrate that work with that of the *STUDENT VOLUNTEER MOVEMENT. As an itinerant *EVANGELIST, Mott was extraordinarily effective in recruiting students for missionary service. Both an evangelical and an ecumenist, Mott participated in the founding and early work of such organizations as the World Student Christian Federation, the Foreign Missions Conference of North America, and the World Alliance of *YMCAs. His most important achievement, however, was his involvement in the formation of the World Council of Churches in 1948, an organization he served as president. Because of his relief activities after World War II, Mott was awarded the Nobel Peace Prize in 1946.

References: John R. Mott, *Strategic Points in the World's Conquest* (1897); idem, *The Evangelization of the World in This Generation* (1900); idem, *The Decisive Hour of Christian Missions* (1910); idem, *The Present-Day Summons to the World Mission of Christianity* (1931); idem, *Evangelism for the World Today* (1938); C. Howard Hopkins, *John R. Mott: 1865–1955* (1979); M. Craig Barnes, s.v. "John R. Mott," in Charles H. Lippy, ed., *Twentieth-Century Shapers of American Popular Religion* (1989).

Mount Hermon Hundred Mount Hermon Hundred is the name given to a group of students who pledged themselves to missionary service in the summer of 1886, during the course of a summer conference for *YMCA leaders at Mount Hermon, Massachusetts. This cohort became the basis for the formation of the *STUDENT VOLUNTEER MOVEMENT FOR FOREIGN MISSIONS two years later.

Mount Vernon Nazarene College (Mount Vernon, Ohio) Mount Vernon Nazarene College is the official college of the *CHURCH OF THE NAZARENE's East Central Educational Region, and the board of trustees comprises district representatives from Ohio, Kentucky, and West Virginia. The school was chartered in 1964 by the General Assembly of the *CHURCH OF THE NAZARENE. Its board of trustees was organized two years later, and they soon selected the Lakeholm Farm in Mount Vernon, Ohio, as the site of the campus. Mount Vernon Nazarene College opened in 1968 as a junior college, but it achieved baccalaureate accreditation within six years.

A graduate program in ministry was added in 1991, with the first degrees conferred three years later. Today, Mount Vernon also offers graduate studies in education and has an adult studies program that satisfies the academic component of the requirements for ordination in the *CHURCH OF THE NAZARENE.

In certain respects, Mount Vernon looks like a college of the past, for it has not abandoned the traditional "women-oriented" programs common to many colleges in the earlier part of this century. Although committed to a liberal arts curriculum, the college grants several degrees in home economics and "Family and Consumer Sciences," with optional concentrations in fashion merchandising, interior decorating, or family life management. Social *DANCING is proscribed as contrary to the Nazarene tradition.

Reference: *Mount Vernon Nazarene College 1996–1998 Undergraduate Catalog* (1996).

Mountain Church Work A program begun in 1937 by *E. HOWARD CADLE, pastor of Cadle Tabernacle in Indianapolis, Indiana, Mountain Church Work placed radio receivers in Appalachian churches that were too small or too poor to hire a full-time pastor. The faithful in rural parts of Indiana, Ohio, Kentucky, Tennessee, Virginia, and West Virginia would gather on Sunday mornings and listen to the radio transmission from Cadle Tabernacle by way of Cincinnati radio station WLW. By means of his Mountain Church Work initiative, *E. HOWARD CADLE became well known throughout Appalachia as the vicarious pastor of more than six hundred churches.

Mourner's Bench. *See* **Anxious Bench.**

Mouw, Richard J(ohn) (1940–) A philosopher and educational administrator, Richard J. Mouw earned the baccalaureate degree from *HOUGHTON COLLEGE, a master's degree in philosophy from the University of Alberta, and the Ph.D. in philosophy from the University of Chicago. After teaching for seventeen years at *CALVIN COLLEGE, Mouw joined the faculty of *FULLER THEOLOGICAL SEMINARY as professor of Christian philosophy and ethics in September 1985. Four years later, he was appointed provost and senior vice president of Fuller, and in July 1993 he succeeded *DAVID ALAN HUBBARD as president of the seminary.

References: Richard J. Mouw, *The God Who Commands* (1991); idem, *Uncommon Decency: Christian Civility in an Uncivil World* (1992);

idem, *Consulting the Faithful: What Christian Intellectuals Can Learn from Popular Religion* (1994).

Movie Morality Ministries Based in Richardson, Texas, Movie Morality Ministries was founded in 1986 to "alert families to the decline in the moral content of movies" as well as to "persuade filmmakers to produce more acceptable movies." The organization, founded by John H. Evans, a former petroleum industry executive, publishes *Preview Family Movie and TV Review* twice a month, "offering reviews of current films from a Christian perspective."

Mowat, Oliver (1820–1903) Born in Kingston, Upper Canada, Oliver Mowat practiced law before sitting in the Parliament of the United Province of Canada from 1857 to 1864. In 1872, he became leader of the Ontario Liberal Party and premier of Ontario, a post he retained until 1896, when he was named minister of justice in Wilfrid Laurier's Dominion cabinet. The following year Mowat was appointed lieutenant governor of Ontario. In addition to his political career, Mowat was president of the *EVANGELICAL ALLIANCE of Ontario, a Presbyterian, and an apologist for the Christian faith.

References: Oliver Mowat, *Christianity and Some of Its Evidences* (1890); idem, *Christianity and Its Influence* (1898).

Mühlenberg, Heinrich Melchior (1711–1787) Heinrich Melchior Mühlenberg, the father of Lutheranism in America, was born in Einbeck, Germany, graduated from Göttingen University in 1738, and arrived in Philadelphia four years later only to find that a vagabond preacher had occupied his pulpit. Mühlenberg disposed of the interloper and proceeded to establish some regularized Lutheran organization; the Lutheran Ministerium, the governing body of American Lutheranism, was created in 1748. Although he was active in the spread of *PIETISM during the *GREAT AWAKENING, Mühlenberg remained somewhat suspicious of unbridled revivalism.

Reference: T. G. Tappert and J. W. Doberstein, eds., *The Journals of Henry Melchior Muhlenberg* (1942).

Müller, George (1805–1898) A Prussian, George Müller emigrated to England and in 1834–35 founded an orphanage and the Scriptural Knowledge Institution for Home and Abroad, a combination Bible school and mission society. Müller's primary contribution to *EVANGELICALISM was his "*FAITH PRINCIPLES" ideology, the notion that Christian organizations should rely simply on prayer for their financial needs, never go into debt, and never make direct appeals for money.

Reference: George Müller, *A Narrative of Some of the Lord's Dealings with George Müller* (1850).

Mullins, E(dgar) Y(oung) (1860–1928) Born in Franklin County, Mississippi, E. Y. Mullins graduated from Texas A&M College and from Southern Baptist Theological Seminary. He served as pastor of churches in Kentucky, Maryland, and Massachusetts before accepting the presidency of Southern Baptist Theological Seminary in 1899. Throughout his long tenure, Mullins, who was also professor of theology at the seminary, left his mark on the seminary, on the *SOUTHERN BAPTIST CONVENTION, and on the Baptist movement more broadly. In 1905, he was one of the organizers of the *BAPTIST WORLD ALLIANCE, and he served as president of that body in 1928. Mullins was president of the *SOUTHERN BAPTIST CONVENTION from 1921 to 1924. He was responsible for the seminary's move from downtown Louisville, Kentucky, to its present suburban location, known as "The Beeches." Through the seminary, Mullins, the author of twelve books, advocated an intellectual sophistication among Southern Baptist ministers, but all within the bounds of a conservative theology. When he weighed in on the creationist-evolution debate, for instance, Mullins urged the *SOUTHERN BAPTIST CONVENTION to reject evolutionary theory and to affirm humanity's supernatural origins; at the same time, he cautioned that the *BIBLE was authoritative on "religious opinions" alone. Mullins also persuaded the convention to adopt its first confession of faith, an adaptation of the *NEW HAMPSHIRE CONFESSION OF FAITH.

References: E. Y. Mullins, *Why Is Christianity True?* (1905); idem, *Freedom and Authority in Religion* (1913); idem, *The Christian Religion in Its Doctrinal Expression* (1917); Thomas J. Nettles, s.v. "Edgar Young Mullins," in Walter A. Elwell, ed., *Handbook of Evangelical Theologians* (1993).

Mullins, Rich (1956–1997) Born in Richmond, Indiana, Rich Mullins became an accomplished songwriter and artist in the field of *CONTEMPORARY CHRISTIAN MUSIC. Some of his better-known compositions in evangelical circles included "Hold Me Jesus," "While the Nations Rage," and "Awesome God." His "Sing Your Praise to the Lord" was recorded by *AMY GRANT. Before his sudden death in a traffic accident, Mullins had been working with Compassion International, teaching music to Native American students on a Navajo reservation.

Multnomah Bible College and Biblical Seminary (Portland, Oregon) Multnomah Bible College's longtime president, Willard M. Aldrich, coined the school's motto: "If it's *BIBLE you want, then you want Multnomah." Although the school was founded in the 1930s, Aldrich's evaluation is no less true today. Multnomah remains a Bible college, as opposed to a Christian liberal arts college. All students major in *BIBLE, biblical studies amounting to fifty-two out of approximately 128 credits for four-year students.

Multnomah School of the Bible was started in 1936 by John G. Mitchell, pastor of the Central Bible Church in Portland, Oregon. Mitchell had been a member of the first graduating class of *DALLAS THEOLOGICAL SEMINARY, and Multnomah's theological perspective still resembles that of the fundamentalist Texas school. Classes were first held in a former mortuary, but by the 1950s the school was in need of additional space and facilities. The board of trustees bought the old campus of the Oregon State School for the Blind in 1952.

In addition to the mandatory major in *BIBLE, undergraduate students complete either an additional major or a minor, choosing biblical languages, journalism, elementary education, or women's ministries, among others. The graduate division of the college began offering a graduate certificate in leadership in 1947 and added master's degree programs in biblical studies and sacred ministry in the 1970s. In 1986, the board of trustees established the graduate division as a distinct seminary, Multnomah Graduate School of Ministry, which introduced a master of divinity program the following year. The seminary also offers a master of arts in pastoral or biblical studies.

In 1993, the two schools became known under the common name, Multnomah Bible College and Biblical Seminary. Although some of the stricter behavioral taboos dissipated somewhat under the presidency of *JOSEPH C. ALDRICH, Willard Aldrich's son, Multnomah maintains parietal rules governing the conduct of its students. The consumption of alcohol and tobacco and all forms of *DANCING are proscribed in Multnomah's conduct statement.

References: Randall Balmer, *Mine Eyes Have Seen the Glory: A Journey Into the Evangelical Subculture in America,* 3d ed. (2000); *Multnomah Bible College and Biblical Seminary College Course Listings,* vol. 15, no. 2 (1996).

Mumford, Bernard C., Jr. "Bob" (1930–) Founder and leader of the controversial *SHEPHERDING MOVEMENT, Bob Mumford was born in Steubenville, Ohio. While in the navy he experienced a spiritual renewal that eventually led him to Valley Forge Christian College and later to Reformed Episcopal Seminary, where he earned the master of divinity degree in 1964. After serving as pastor of two churches and as dean and professor at *ELIM BIBLE INSTITUTE, Mumford became involved in pentecostal conferences at Fort Lauderdale, Florida, that led to the formation of the Holy Spirit Teaching Mission. That group, which published *New Wine* magazine, changed its name to *CHURCH GROWTH MINISTRIES, better known as the impetus behind the *SHEPHERDING MOVEMENT.

Mumford left Fort Lauderdale in 1986 for San Rafael, California, where he formed a new organization, Lifechangers, Inc. He became well-known in charismatic circles as an author and lecturer, but he distanced himself from the *SHEPHERDING MOVEMENT in 1984; in 1990, he offered an apology to those who had been hurt by shepherding.

References: Bob Mumford, *The Problem of Doing Your Own Thing* (1973); "An Idea Whose Time Has Gone?" *Christianity Today,* March 19, 1990.

Murch, James DeForest (1886–1973) A vigorous opponent of the National Council of Churches and the World Council of Churches, James DeForest Murch edited *United Evangelical Action,* the newsletter of the *NATIONAL ASSOCIATION OF EVANGELICALS. Murch also had his own radio broadcast, *The Christian's Hour,* and was one of the movers behind the formation of *NATIONAL RELIGIOUS BROADCASTERS; he served briefly as president of the organization from 1956 to 1957.

Reference: James DeForest Murch, *Cooperation without Compromise: A History of the National Association of Evangelicals* (1956).

Muscular Christianity The term "muscular Christianity" originated in a review of Charles Kingsley's novel, *Two Years Ago,* published in Britain in 1857. The reviewer took exception to the book's celebration of heroic Christian activity. The term was pejorative, but it stuck and came to be associated with various activities designed to make Christianity more appealing to men. The background for such efforts is the fact that women have far outnumbered men in church adherence ever since the late seventeenth century. Reformers and revivalists at various moments throughout American history have tried to redress that imbalance, and the appeals to men have taken many forms. The Revival of 1857–58, also known as the Businessmen's Awakening or the *PRAYER MEETING REVIVAL, targeted men engaged in business and commerce. *DWIGHT MOODY and *BILLY SUNDAY fashioned their messages to appeal to men, with Sunday taunting his male auditors to "be a real man" and give their lives to Christ. Around the turn of the twentieth century, a flurry of books—Charles Sheldon's *In His Steps; The Masculine Religion,* by Carl Case; *The Manhood of the Master,* by Harry Emerson Fosdick; and John Pierce's *The Masculine Power of Christ*—all purveyed a Christianity shorn of Victorian sentimentalism so that it might appeal to men.

Muscular Christianity often employs the language of sports and athletics. The Men and Religion Forward Movement of 1911–12, for instance, used rallies and display ads in the sports sections of newspapers to appeal to men, and such groups as *ATHLETES IN ACTION and the *FELLOWSHIP OF CHRISTIAN ATHLETES routinely uphold Christian athletes as paragons of masculine piety. *PROMISE KEEPERS, to cite a more recent example, stands very much in this tradition of muscular Christianity.

References: Gail Bederman, *Manliness and Civilization; A Cultural History of Gender and Race in the United States, 1800–1917* (1995); Tony Ladd and James A. Mathisen, *Muscular Christianity: Evangelical Protestants and the Development of American Sport* (1999).

Muse, Dan T. (1882–1950) Born in Mississippi and reared in Texas, Dan Muse moved onto the Oklahoma Indian Territory as a teenager and had an evangelical *CONVERSION experience in January 1913, which was followed shortly thereafter by *SANCTIFICATION and *SPEAKING IN TONGUES. Answering what he believed was a call to preach, Muse set about organizing congregations throughout Oklahoma for the *PENTECOSTAL HOLINESS CHURCH. Ordained by the Oklahoma Conference in 1918, he quickly demonstrated leadership abilities in the areas of *SUNDAY SCHOOLS and *CAMP MEETINGS and was chosen secretary of the conference in 1925. Thus began a steady rise in the denominational hierarchy, culminating in his election as general superintendent of the church in 1937.

Myers, Paul (1896–1973) A musician during the pioneer era of radio, Paul Myers performed background music for a number of famous programs and was also a radio orchestra leader. After a bout with alcoholism that lasted several years, he heard a ship's bell in the San Diego harbor in February 1934, which he interpreted as the call of God. He found a *GIDEONS *BIBLE in a run-down motel room, began reading, and experienced an evangelical *CONVERSION. He returned to Los Angeles, made amends with his family, and began hosting a radio program, *Haven of Rest,* which had a nautical motif, and which ran from 1934 until Myers's death in 1973. Myers became known to millions of listeners around the world as "First Mate Bob," and he referred to his audience as "shipmates." Myers preached, provided music, with the help of a male quartet, and occasionally hosted "second mates" as guest speakers.

Reference: J. Gordon Melton, Phillip Charles Lucas, and Jon R. Stone, *Prime-Time Religion: An Encyclopedia of Religious Broadcasting* (1997).

Myland, David Wesley (1858–1943) Born in Canada, David Wesley Myland grew up near Cleveland. He professed to have been healed miraculously seven times in his life. His embrace of holiness doctrines and his emphasis on divine healing led him to gravitate away from the Methodist Episcopal Church and toward the more congenial environment of the *CHRISTIAN AND MISSIONARY ALLIANCE in 1890, although he maintained his Methodist credentials throughout his life. Myland held several positions with the new denomination, and he published the *Christian Messenger,* which propagated the fourfold *GOSPEL: *SALVATION, *SANCTIFICATION, healing, and the *SECOND COMING of Christ.

Myland's *BAPTISM OF THE HOLY SPIRIT in 1906 prompted another change in affiliation in 1912, when the *CHRISTIAN AND MISSIONARY ALLIANCE broke with *PENTECOSTALISM over the issue of *GLOSSOLALIA. In 1906, Myland wrote a hymn, "The Latter Rain"—arguably the first hymn of the pentecostal movement—compiled three hymnals, and wrote a definitive theology of *PENTECOSTALISM, *Latter Rain Covenant and Pentecostal Power*, published in 1910. He founded Gilbeah Bible School in Plainfield, Indiana, and also organized the short-lived Association of Christian Assemblies, which disbanded in 1914.

Although Myland never formally affiliated with the *ASSEMBLIES OF GOD, his work—books, articles in the *Christian Evangel* (later the *Pentecostal Evangel*), and hymns—was quite influential in *ASSEMBLIES OF GOD circles. Myland founded Ebenezer Bible Institute in Chicago from 1915 to 1918 and taught at Beulah Heights Bible Institute in Atlanta from 1918 to 1920. He spent the remaining twenty-three years of his life as a pastor to churches in Pennsylvania, Michigan, and Ohio.

References: David Wesley Myland, *Latter Rain Covenant and Pentecostal Power* (1910); idem, *The Revelation of Jesus Christ* (1911).

■ ■ ■

Naismith, James (1861–1939) James Naismith, the inventor of basketball, was born in Almonte, Ontario, and graduated from McGill University before enrolling at the *YOUNG MEN'S CHRISTIAN ASSOCIATION Training School (now Springfield College) in Springfield, Massachusetts. While a student there, Naismith was told by Luther Gulick during the winter of 1891–92 to develop an inexpensive, indoor game to keep young people occupied between the football and baseball seasons. After several failed attempts, Naismith came up with a game that entailed lobbing a round ball into half-bushel–sized peach baskets.

Naismith, a proponent of *MUSCULAR CHRISTIANITY, clearly believed that such a game would be an important tool for character development. "Therefore, while the immediate responsibility of this organization is primarily with intercollegiate contests," he told the annual convention of the National Collegiate Athletic Association in 1914, "yet it should use every means to put basketball, as well as every other sport, on such a basis that it will be a factor in the molding of character, as well as to encourage it as a recreative and competitive sport." In 1898, Naismith accepted the post as director of athletics and of the chapel at the University of Kansas, a position he held until his retirement in 1937.

Reference: Tony Ladd and James A. Mathisen, *Muscular Christianity: Evangelical Protestants and the Development of American Sport* (1999).

Narramore, Clyde M. (1916–) Clyde M. Narramore, who earned a doctorate in psychology from Columbia University, was one of the first Christian psychologists to reach a popular audience. He wrote many books and began his own radio program, which became known as *Psychology for Living*, in the early 1950s. Narramore left his job as psychologist with the Los Angeles County public schools in 1958 and established the Narramore Christian Foundation. In 1970, he founded the Rosemead Graduate School of Psychology, which *BIOLA UNIVERSITY acquired in 1977.

Reference: Clyde M. Narramore, *Why a Psychologist Believes the Bible* (1989).

Nation, Carry (Amelia) (née Moore) (1846–1911) Born in Garrad County, Kentucky, Carry Moore endured an unhappy childhood and a brief first marriage to Charles Gloyd, a physician and an alcoholic who died about a year after their 1867 wedding. Carry moved to Holden, Missouri, with her young daughter and taught school until 1877, when she married David Nation, an attorney, editor, and minister. They relocated to Texas in 1879, where Carry managed a hotel while her husband tried his hand at various jobs.

In 1889, they moved to Medicine Lodge, Kansas, and shortly thereafter Carry A. Nation, a tall and imposing figure, began her crusade against liquor. She joined the Women's Christian Temperance Union in 1892, and by the end of the decade she had developed her trademark protest against the traffic in alcohol: singing hymns, quoting Scripture, smashing liquor bottles, and destroying saloon furnishings with her hatchet. She referred to saloons as "murder mills," "hell holes," and "donkey bedmates of Satan." Though occasionally arrested for disturbing the peace, Nation persisted in her campaign and succeeded in destroying such well-known gathering places as the saloon in Wichita's Hotel Casey and the Senate Saloon in Topeka. In October 1902 and again in November 1904, Nation went to the University of Texas at Austin to campaign against drunken professors who allegedly were corrupting the minds of innocent students.

Nation's protests, which also included demonstrations against tobacco and immodest dress, eventually led her second husband to divorce her in 1901 on grounds of desertion. Nation began lecturing nationally, where she signed autographs and sold her autobiography. Toward the end of her life, she traded on her notoriety as the approach of the Prohibition era diminished the need for violent demonstrations against liquor.

References: Frances Grace Carver, "With Bible in One Hand and Battle-Axe in Another: Carry A. Nation as Religious Performer and Self-Promoter," *Religion and American Culture,* 9 (winter 1999); Fran Grace, *Carry A. Nation: Retelling the Life* (2001).

National Affairs Briefing Arguably the turning point of the 1980 presidential campaign, the National Affairs Briefing was sponsored by the *RELIGIOUS ROUNDTABLE and organized by *JAMES ROBISON and *ED MCATEER. The event, a two-day gathering of politically conservative evangelicals, took place in Dallas, Texas, in August 1980 and opened with the pronouncement of Bailey Smith, president of the *SOUTHERN BAPTIST CONVENTION, that "God Almighty does not hear the prayer of a Jew." Both *JIMMY CARTER and *JOHN B. ANDERSON, sensing a setup, declined to attend the rally, but *RONALD REAGAN saw an opportunity. He had been coached by Robison about what to say at the culmination of the rally when it was finally his turn to speak. After Robison's stemwinder about moral decay in America, the necessity of electing an evangelical Christian to the presidency, and admonitions to "move the hand of God in a mighty crusade of holiness," Reagan strode to the podium and delivered his line: "You can't endorse me, but I endorse you." Reunion Arena erupted in cheers, and Reagan had effectively secured the evangelical vote for the fall election.

Reference: William Martin, *With God on Our Side: The Rise of the Religious Right in America* (1996).

National Association of Christian Educators. *See* **Citizens for Excellence in Education.**

National Association of Christian Schools. *See* **Association of Christian Schools International.**

National Association of Evangelicals An evangelical alternative to the Federal Council of Churches, which evangelicals regarded as too ecumenical and too liberal, the National Association of Evangelicals (NAE) grew out of the *NEW ENGLAND FELLOWSHIP, which *J. ELWIN WRIGHT organized in 1929. The NAE was begun during the National Conference for United Action among Evangelicals, a meeting held at the Hotel Coronado in St. Louis, April 7–9, 1942; the group ratified its constitution at a meeting in Chicago the following year. Its statement of faith opens with a declaration regarding biblical *AUTHORITY: "We believe the Bible to be the inspired, the only infallible, authoritative *WORD OF GOD."

The National Association of Evangelicals hews to a conservative line in both theology and politics, although it took pains in the 1990s to distance itself from the activities and pronouncements of *PAT ROBERTSON, *JAMES DOBSON, and other representatives of the *RELIGIOUS RIGHT. The organization, with headquarters in southern California, also operates several satellite commissions and offices: the Commission on Chaplains; the Office of Public Affairs in Washington, D.C., which attends to legal and political concerns; the Evangelical Foreign Missions Association; the World Relief Commission, the humanitarian arm of the organization; the National Association of Christian Schools; the Commission on Higher Education; and the *NATIONAL RELIGIOUS BROADCASTERS, which severed ties with the NAE in 2001.

More than a half century after its founding, the National Association of Evangelicals has assumed a position of influence in American society. The organization's past president, *DON ARGUE, was named to the twenty-member Presidential Advisory Committee on Religious Freedom Abroad in November 1996. This appointment reflects the group's increasing role as advocate for evangelical Christians in other countries who have been persecuted for their religious beliefs. Argue was also asked by Bill Clinton to lead a prayer in a church service on the morning of Clinton's second inauguration, on January 20, 1997.

Kevin Mannoia, a bishop in the *FREE METHODIST CHURCH OF NORTH AMERICA, succeeded Argue as head of the NAE in July 1999. He moved the organization's offices from Illinois to southern California and changed the bylaws so that denominations could be members of both the NAE and the National Council of Churches.

National Baptist Convention of America, Inc. The National Baptist Convention of America, Inc. was organized in 1915, the result of a dispute in the National Baptist Convention of the U.S.A. (NBCUSA). The dispute was over the ownership of the National Baptist Publishing Board. The publishing board, because it was incorporated earlier than the NBCUSA, felt free to act independently of the convention. The dispute went to trial, where a judge decided that the publishing board did indeed belong to the convention. The publishing board, however, was under the leadership of R. H. Boyd, who was also a leader of the schismatic faction. After the unfavorable decision of the judge, Boyd led his following, and the publishing board, out of the NBCUSA to form the National Baptist Convention, Unincorporated. The group incorporated in 1988.

The National Baptist Convention of

America, Inc. follows the usual doctrines and *POLITY of other Baptist groups. The convention has no national headquarters, but the home offices of the publishing board are located in Nashville, Tennessee. In 1987, the NBCA reported 3.5 million members in twenty-five hundred churches.

References: Frank S. Mead and Samuel S. Hill, *Handbook of Denominations in the United States,* 10th ed. (1996); J. Gordon Melton, *The Encyclopedia of American Religions,* 3d ed. (1993); *1997 Yearbook of American and Canadian Churches.*

National Baptist Convention of the U.S.A., Inc. The National Baptist Convention of the U.S.A., Inc. (NBCUSA), the largest black Baptist body in the world and the fourth largest denomination in the United States, was created in 1895 when three separate bodies, the Foreign Mission Baptist Convention of the U.S.A., the American National Baptist Convention, and the Baptist National Education Convention, merged. A conflict arose within two years of the founding of the NBCUSA. The question had to do with the degree of independence from white Baptists the convention would maintain. A group urging more cooperation between black and white Baptists withdrew to form the Lott Carey Missionary Convention. A more serious controversy occurred in 1915, when a disagreement over the ownership of the National Baptist Publishing Board led to a split in the convention. After the departure of the group that would form the National Baptist Convention, Unincorporated, the NBCUSA itself incorporated to form the National Baptist Convention of the U.S.A., Inc.

The organization developed rapidly under its early leadership. In fact, strong leadership, especially in the office of president, has been one of the hallmarks of the NBCUSA. After the 1915 schism, the denomination acted to unify its organization and administration. By the late twentieth century, however, that restructuring led to allegations of abuses.

Both in doctrine and *POLITY, the NBCUSA is similar to its Baptist siblings, both black and white. Like other African American religious bodies, the NBCUSA has developed its own, more emotionally expressive, style of worship. Headquarters for the NBCUSA are in Nashville, Tennessee, at the Baptist World Center. The Convention reports over 8.5 million members in thirty-three thousand churches in America, Africa, Europe, and the Caribbean.

References: Frank S. Mead and Samuel S. Hill, *Handbook of Denominations in the United States,* 10th ed. (1996); J. Gordon Melton, *The Encyclopedia of American Religions,* 3d ed. (1993); Larry G. Murphy, J. Gordon Melton, and Gary L. Ward, eds., *Encyclopedia of African American Religions* (1993).

National Black Evangelical Association Organized in 1963 as the National Negro Evangelical Association, the National Black Evangelical Association (NBEA) took its present name a decade later. *WILLIAM H. BENTLEY, a prominent evangelical in the African American community, served as the first president of the organization, whose members included *EVANGELIST *TOM SKINNER. Although conservative in theology, the NBEA seeks to encourage evangelicals, both black and white, to be responsive to social needs, especially in the cities. With offices in Portland, Oregon, the organization claims about five hundred members and conducts a variety of programs addressing such issues as theology, youth ministry, pastoral leadership, missions, and *EVANGELISM.

References: "Many Whites Attend Black Conference," *Christianity Today,* October 9, 1970; William H. Bentley, *National Black Evangelical Association: Evolution of a Concept of Ministry* (1979).

National Camp Meeting Association for the Promotion of Holiness. *See* **Ocean Grove Camp Meeting Association.**

National Christian School Education Association. *See* **Association of Christian Schools International.**

National Federation for Decency. *See* **American Family Association.**

National Presbyterian Church. *See* **Presbyterian Church in America.**

National Prayer Breakfast. *See* **Prayer Breakfasts.**

National Religious Broadcasters Organized by the *NATIONAL ASSOCIATION OF EVANGELICALS (NAE) in 1943, the year after that parent body was formed, the National Religious Broadcasters (NRB) seeks to protect the legal, political, and professional interests of evangelical broadcasters. With changes in Federal Communications Commission (FCC) regulations in the 1970s, which provided evangelicals more access to the airwaves, the NRB became more of a political force. Its annual conventions are held in Washington, D.C., and presidents from *JIMMY CARTER to *RONALD REAGAN to George Bush have addressed the convention. Members of the organization are overwhelmingly conservative and have helped advance the political agenda of the *RELIGIOUS RIGHT. Reagan, for instance, delivered his infamous "evil empire" speech before the NRB convention. In 2001, the NRB severed its ties with the NAE.

Navigators, The The Navigators, an organization that promotes evangelical piety as well as knowledge and memorization of the *BIBLE, evolved out of an evangelistic outreach to sailors in San Pedro, California, begun by *DAWSON and *LILA TROTMAN in 1933. *DAWSON TROTMAN had studied briefly at the *BIBLE INSTITUTE OF LOS ANGELES and at Los Angeles Baptist Seminary. His deft combination of evangelical sensibilities with his own energy and charisma led to the expansion of the movement, now called The Navigators, to all branches of the United States military by 1944.

Trotman emphasized "one-on-one discipleship." The organization has enjoyed a close relationship with other evangelical groups, including the *BILLY GRAHAM EVANGELISTIC ASSOCIATION, for which The Navigators has produced follow-up materials used in *BILLY GRAHAM crusades. In 1953, The Navigators moved its headquarters from downtown Los Angeles to Colorado Springs, Colorado. Trotman died from cardiac arrest in 1956 after rescuing a swimmer at the Navigators Conference in Schroon Lake, New York. His longtime assistant, Lorne Sanny, took over the leadership of the organization. By 1986, The Navigators were active in sixty-three countries, with nearly three thousand staff members.

Neo-Evangelicalism Neo-evangelicalism, also known as new *EVANGELICALISM, was a movement among conservative Protestants in the 1940s and 1950s to go beyond the contentious *FUNDAMENTALISM of the 1920s and 1930s and adopt a more irenic posture toward the world in general and other Protestants in particular. *HAROLD JOHN OCKENGA, pastor of Park Street Church in Boston, and president of the newly formed *FULLER THEOLOGICAL SEMINARY, probably coined the term in 1948. He characterized neo-evangelicalism as "progressive *FUNDAMENTALISM with a social message." Ockenga and a cohort of others, including *CARL F. H. HENRY, *EDWARD J. CARNELL, and *VERNON GROUNDS, hoped to counteract the anti-intellectualism associated with *FUNDAMENTALISM, and neo-evangelicalism sought to build an evangelical coalition with the help of such institutions as the *NATIONAL ASSOCIATION OF EVANGELICALS, **CHRISTIANITY TODAY*, the *EVANGELICAL THEOLOGICAL SOCIETY, and *FULLER SEMINARY.

Neo-evangelicals retained a conservative theology, especially on the issue of biblical *INERRANCY, but they cautiously entertained the discipline of biblical criticism. Dispensational theology was called into question, thereby arousing the suspicion and ire of many fundamentalists. *BILLY GRAHAM's cooperation with liberal clergy during his 1957 crusade at Madison Square Garden was interpreted by many fundamentalists as a sellout to "*MODERNISM" all too characteristic of neo-evangelicalism. The new movement prospered, however, because of its willingness to adapt to changing cultural forms, although the insistence on a kind of litmus test over the doctrine of *INERRANCY in the 1970s sapped some of the energy fron neo-evangelicalism at the same time that the televangelists, most of them either *FUNDAMENTALISTS or *PENTECOSTALS, were gathering momentum.

References: Mark A. Noll, *Between Faith and Criticism* (1986); George M. Marsden, *Reforming Fundamentalism: Fuller Seminary and the New Evangelicalism* (1987).

Neoorthodoxy One of the most influential theological movements in twentieth-century Protestantism, neoorthodoxy arose out of the disillusionment with *LIBERALISM after World War I. As the works of Emil Brunner and Karl Barth came to the attention of American theologians in the 1930s, neoorthodoxy, with its emphasis on human depravity and the transcendence (rather than immanence) of God, took hold, especially among mainline Protestants. Many evangelicals were attracted to the neoorthodox emphasis on Scripture as divine revelation, but they were uneasy with Barth's declaration that the *BIBLE *becomes* the Word of God, through the agency of the Holy Spirit, as the individual reads it. Neoorthodoxy, however, also known as the "theology of crisis," shaped theologians on both sides of Protestantism, liberal and evangelical, although it fell into a kind of crossfire: Liberals criticized it for being too pessimistic about human nature, and evangelicals criticized it for being "soft" on biblical *INERRANCY.

Neopentecostalism. See **Charismatic Movement.**

Nettleton, Asahel (1783–1844) Born in Killingworth, Connecticut, Asahel Nettleton was converted in 1800 and attended Yale College, where he became a protégé of *TIMOTHY DWIGHT. After Nettleton's graduation in 1809, he volunteered for missionary service, but poor health prevented him from going abroad. He was ordained in 1811 and became an itinerant preacher in New York and New England, especially Connecticut. Nettleton retained his affinity for the Calvinist theology embodied in the *NEW DIVINITY, which put him at odds with *CHARLES GRANDISON FINNEY's *REVIVAL techniques, known as the "*NEW MEASURES." He also opposed the *NEW HAVEN THEOLOGY of *NATHANIEL WILLIAM TAYLOR and, along with Bennet Tyler, supported the founding of the Theological Institute of Connecticut (later Hartford Seminary).

Reference: Bennet Tyler, *Memoir of the Life and Character of Rev. Asahel Nettleton, D.D.* (1844).

Nevius, John Livingston (1829–1893) After studying at Union College and Princeton Theological Seminary, John Livingston Nevius became a missionary to China under the auspices of the Presbyterian Mission Board. In the course of his several terms there, as well as in Japan, Nevius grew increasingly impatient with the standard missions practice of paying national *EVANGELISTS for their services. He believed that evangelistic work should be self-supporting and operated by indigenous evangelicals. Nevius published his ideas in the 1800s, and in 1890 he accepted an invitation from Korean missionaries to serve as a consultant. The so-called *NEVIUS PLAN, eventually published as *Planting and Development of Missionary Churches,* was remarkably successful in Korea; the Korean Presbyterian Church expanded from one hundred communicants to thirty thousand in 1910 and one hundred thousand by 1933.

Nevius Plan Devised by *JOHN LIVINGSTON NEVIUS, the Nevius Plan provided a blueprint for the expansion of the Korean Presbyterian Church, beginning in the 1890s. Nevius urged an end to the missions practice of paying national *EVANGELISTS and urged that evangelistic work be self-sustaining. The Presbyterians in Korea grew dramatically, from one hundred members to thirty thousand in 1910, to one hundred thousand in 1933, and to eight hundred thousand after World War II. The Nevius Plan has generally received credit for the expansion, although some observers believe that a series of fortuitious circumstances can explain the growth.

New Divinity The New Divinity was a theological system that grew out of the *GREAT AWAKENING and, in particular, out of the thought of *JONATHAN EDWARDS. After Edwards's death in 1758, the task of perpetuating the theology of this formidable intellect fell to a cohort of Congregationalist theologians: *JOSEPH BELLAMY, *SAMUEL HOPKINS, *NATHANIEL EMMONS, and *JONATHAN EDWARDS JR. These theologians, also known as New Divinity men, restated *CALVINISM in its most austere terms. They also justified *REVIVALS and propounded an ethic Bellamy called "disinterested benevolence," which, on a popular level, asked if the believer would be "willing to be damned for the glory of God."

The New Divinity, also known as Consistent *CALVINISM, eventually collapsed beneath its own weight. Although the theology played an important role in the New England phase of the *SECOND GREAT AWAKENING and in the birth of the missions movement, the New Divinity men could not sustain Edwards's thought, the theology became too obtuse for the masses, and *CALVINISM in any form did not comport well with a society inebriated with self-determinism in the early decades of the nineteenth century.

References: Joseph Haroutunian, *Piety Versus Moralism: The Passing of the New England Theology* (1932); Joseph Conforti, *Samuel Hopkins and the New Divinity Movement* (1981); David W. Kling, "The New Divinity and Williams College, 1793–1836," *Religion and American Culture,* 6 (summer 1996).

New England Fellowship The precursor of the *NATIONAL ASSOCIATION OF

EVANGELICALS, the New England Fellowship was organized by *J. ELWIN WRIGHT in 1929 as an association of evangelical churchmen who dissented from the prevailing *LIBERALISM of New England theology. The New England Fellowship attracted such important evangelicals as *HAROLD J. OCKENGA of Boston's Park Street Church, and it became in some respects the launching pad for the neoevangelical movement at mid-century.

New Era Scandal The New Era Scandal unfolded in May 1995 when it became apparent that the Foundation for New Era Philanthropy, headed by *JOHN G. BENNETT JR., had constructed a pyramid scheme that defrauded investors of $135 million. Bennett had solicited money from individuals and from charities—including over 190 evangelical organizations, seminaries, and colleges—with the promise that he would double the investment in six months. Bennett siphoned off about $5 million of the $354 million that passed through New Era, which he had founded in 1989, and another $3 million for his own companies.

On September 22, 1997, Bennett was sentenced to twelve years in prison after conviction on eighty-two counts of fraud and related charges. Some of the money was recovered, but a number of evangelical institutions lost considerable sums.

Reference: Tony Carnes, "New Era's Bennett to Prison," *Christianity Today,* October 27, 1997.

New Evangelicalism. *See* **Neo-Evangelicalism.**

New Hampshire Confession of Faith Drafted in 1833, the New Hampshire Confession of Faith articulated a modified *CALVINISM for the New Hampshire Baptist Convention. A response to the growing impatience with rigid *CALVINISM and the allure of Arminian ideas, the Confession opened with a statement about the *BIBLE that has become classic in Baptist circles: "It has God for its author, *SALVATION for its end, and truth, without any mixture of error, for its matter." The New Hampshire Confession became more and more popular among Baptists over the course of the nineteenth century, although some Baptists resisted formal subscription to the New Hampshire Confession because of their traditional aversion to creedalism.

New Haven Theology New Haven Theology, developed in the antebellum period by *NATHANIEL WILLIAM TAYLOR and other theologians at Yale Divinity School, sought a mediating position between the eighteenth-century *CALVINISM of *JONATHAN EDWARDS and the *ARMINIANISM of *CHARLES GRANDISON FINNEY. Taylor argued that humanity did not inherit Adam's *SIN, that sin lay in particular acts rather than in imputed guilt. In Taylor's words, "there is no such thing as sinning without acting." This New Haven Theology freed antebellum evangelicals from the apparent determinism of *CALVINISM and opened the way for a more aggressive revivalism.

References: Sidney E. Mead, *Nathaniel William Taylor, 1786–1858: A Connecticut Liberal* (1942); Joseph Haroutunian, *Piety Versus Moralism: The Passing of the New England Theology* (1932).

New Lebanon Convention The New Lebanon Convention was a meeting of Calvinist preachers and theologians (Congregationalist and Presbyterian) in New Lebanon, New York, July 18–26, 1827, to discuss *REVIVAL theology and techniques. The participants quickly agreed that *REVIVALS were God's work and that

*REVIVALS would increase at the end of time, but some of the more conservative theologians, such as *LYMAN BEECHER and *ASAHEL NETTLETON, had objected to *CHARLES GRANDISON FINNEY's use of the "*NEW MEASURES" to induce *REVIVALS. Nettleton also sought to place some limits on itinerant revivalists, asking that they secure permission from the settled minister before preaching in a given community. Finally, Nettleton and others objected to the revivalists' use of "audible groaning, violent gestures, and boisterous tones" in the conduct of their religious gatherings.

Although the results of the New Lebanon Convention were ambiguous and the conferees reached no consensus, their failure to censure the "*NEW MEASURES" represented a triumph of sorts for Finney and his aggressive revivalism. The convention also signaled the further ascendance of Finney's Arminian theology over Edwardsean *CALVINISM among antebellum evangelicals.

References: George M. Marsden, *The Evangelical Mind and the New School Presbyterian Experience* (1970); Gary Hiebsch, "A Turning Point in American Revivalism?: The Influence of Charles G. Finney's Memoirs on Historical Accounts of the New Lebanon Convention," *Journal of Presbyterian History*, LXXVI (summer 1998).

New Life Treatment Centers New Life Treatment Centers is a network of evangelical counseling centers. New Life absorbed the Minirth-Meier organization in 1984, making it the largest single provider of psychological counseling for evangelicals. New Life also conducts *WOMEN OF FAITH conferences, which drew more than 450,000 people in twenty-five cities in 1999, and runs Remuda Ranch, a residential treatment center in Arizona for women with eating disorders. Thomas Nelson Publishers purchased a 60 percent interest in New Life Treatment Centers for about $13 million in 2000.

New Lights The term *New Light* was used to designate those sympathetic to the *REVIVALS of the *GREAT AWAKENING in the middle decades of the eighteenth century. New Lights (followers of *THEODORUS JACOBUS FRELINGHUYSEN, *JONATHAN EDWARDS, *GEORGE WHITEFIELD, *GILBERT TENNENT, and others) placed a great deal of emphasis on experiential—or, in the argot of the day, "experimental"—piety, thereby recognizing the importance of what Edwards called the religious affections. New Lights, who insisted on religious *CONVERSION as the beginning of true godliness, also tended to be sympathetic to the itinerant revivalists of the *GREAT AWAKENING, much to the consternation of the settled clergy, who viewed the itinerants as a threat to both the social and religious order. The settled clergy made up the bulk of the Old Lights, people who opposed the *REVIVAL, and several denominations were torn asunder by Old Light–New Light tensions.

Disagreements over revivalism spilled over into the nineteenth century, especially among the Presbyterians, where the parties took slightly different names: New Side *versus* Old Side. The term "New Light" was also applied to the followers of *HENRY ALLINE, a revivalist in Nova Scotia at the end of the eighteenth century.

References: Edwin S. Gaustad, *The Great Awakening in New England* (1957); Harry S. Stout, *The Divine Dramatist: George Whitefield and the Rise of Modern Evangelicalism* (1991); George M. Marsden, *The Evangelical Mind and the New School Presbyterian Experience: A Case Study of Thought and Theology in Nineteenth-Century America* (1970); G. A. Rawlyk, *The Canada Fire: Radical Evangelicalism in British North America, 1775–1812* (1994).

New Measures The "new measures" were *REVIVAL techniques introduced by *CHARLES GRANDISON FINNEY, the principal apologist for the *SECOND GREAT AWAKENING. Unlike *JONATHAN EDWARDS a century earlier, who believed that a *REVIVAL was "a surprising work of God," Finney taught that *REVIVALS could be induced by various means. The "new measures," some of which were already common in Methodist circles, included the use of publicity, protracted *REVIVAL meetings, allowing women to exhort (or testify) in *REVIVAL gatherings, and the mourner's bench or *ANXIOUS BENCH, where a potential convert could come to be persuaded to undergo an evangelical *CONVERSION. The theology underlying the "new measures" was undeniably Arminian in that it emphasized the importance of human volition, both in the planning and execution of *REVIVALS and in the *CONVERSION process itself.

References: Charles E. Hambrick-Stowe, *Charles G. Finney and the Spirit of American Evangelicalism* (1996); Richard Carwardine, *Transatlantic Revivalism: Popular Evangelicalism in Britain and America, 1790–1865* (1978).

New Order of the Latter Rain. *See* **Latter Rain Movement.**

New Side Presbyterianism. *See* **New Lights.**

New Testament Missionary Fellowship. *See* **Phillips, (John) McCandlish, (Jr.).**

New World Order The so-called New World Order is, along with the United Nations and the *TRILATERAL COMMISSION, one of the targets of paranoia from the *RELIGIOUS RIGHT and the *CHRISTIAN IDENTITY movements. According to the demonology of the far right, the New World Order evokes images of, in the words of the *New York Times,* "black helicopters strafing the heartland to establish a world government" and a United Nations takeover of the United States. Such demagogues as *PAT ROBERTSON and Pat Buchanan regularly warned of a New World Order in the 1990s, and George Bush excited the suspicions of the far right during the 1992 presidential campaign by using the term to refer to the emerging global political situation following the collapse of the Soviet Union.

New York Missionary Training College for Home and Foreign Missions. *See* **Nyack College and Alliance Theological Seminary.**

New York Missionary Training Institute. *See* **Nyack College and Alliance Theological Seminary.**

Newsboys The Newsboys are one of the most successful groups in Christian music. The band was formed by Australian natives Peter Furler and John James. They traveled to West Orange, New Jersey, in 1987, with the hope of cutting a record in New York. It sold badly, however, and they returned to Australia. Two years later, the Newsboys tried again, moving to Los Angeles. After several small performances in California and Georgia, the group signed with Star Song Records. Although their first two albums on the Star Song label—*Hell Is for Wimps* and *Boyz Will Be Boyz*—failed to produce more than thirty thousand each in sales, the third recording, *Not Ashamed,* sold four hundred thousand copies and earned a Grammy nomination in 1992 for Best Contemporary Rock Album of the Year. The Newsboys earned a second Grammy nomination in the same category in 1995 for their next album, *Going Public.* The band has also won two Dove Awards from the *GOSPEL MUSIC ASSOCIATION, and they were nominated two other times. In 1996, the Newsboys signed a new contract with Virgin Records. Their first release on Virgin was their most successful recording to date: *Take Me to Your Leader* was a "Hot Shot Debut" at number thirty-five on the *Billboard* 200.

The group tours relentlessly, having averaged two hundred dates a year since 1990. Although they rarely hold *ALTAR CALLS at their concerts, as they did in their early years, the Newsboys are very much in demand as the headline attraction at youth gatherings like the Creation Festival, Jesus Northwest, and the *YOUTH FOR CHRIST SuperConferences. As "Christian Rock Stars," the group has managed to do what few evangelical pop artists have accomplished—achieve a level of commercial success rivaling that of secular performers. The combined sales of their three most recent albums have exceeded 1.2 million copies, and they have been featured on *Good Morning America,* VH-1, *Entertainment Tonight,* and *CNN Headline News.* The Newsboys have survived several changes in band membership, but Furler and James remain; other current members are from the United States and New Zealand.

Reference: Information provided by Star Song Records.

Newton, John (1725–1807) The author of *Amazing Grace,* John Newton, born in London, was the son of a commander in the merchant service. He went to sea at the age of eleven, and in 1743 he was impressed on board the *H.M.S. Harwich.* He soon deserted but was recaptured and demoted to the rank of a common seaman in 1745. Newton, at his own request, was exchanged off Madeira to a slaver, which took him to the coast of Sierra Leone. He suffered brutal persecution as the servant of one slave-trader; another trader treated him more humanely and gave him a share of the business. In 1748, he was rescued by a ship's captain who had been asked by Newton's father to look for him.

Although Newton's mother had died when he was a child, she had imparted to him the rudiments of Christian training prior to her passing. Newton had neglected religion until the voyage back to England, when he was asked to pilot the vessel through a storm. For the remainder of his life he remembered March 21, 1748, as the day of his *CONVERSION, the time of his "great deliverance" from *SIN. Upon his return to England, he was offered command of a slave ship belonging to one of his father's friends; Newton chose, however, to go as first mate. He married in 1750 and went to sea three more times as a captain, during which time he educated himself in literature, mathematics, Latin, and theology. In later years, he never lost his sense of awe that God had *SAVED him out of so depraved a life as that of a slave-ship captain; he could attribute it only to "amazing *GRACE."

Newton retired from a mariner's life in 1754 because of poor health, and from 1755 to 1760 he was surveyor of the tides at Liverpool. The visit of *GEORGE WHITEFIELD during this period rekindled Newton's piety, so much so that he became known as "young Whitefield." He applied to the archbishop of York for holy orders in 1758 but was refused; with the blessing of Lord Dartmouth, however, he was ordained deacon and then priest in 1764 and was assigned to the curacy of Olney, Buckinghamshire. Newton's account of life at sea and his *CONVERSION was published the same year and became an evangelical classic.

Newton's evangelical preaching at Olney and environs soon began to attract crowds (including the poet William Cowper). He published his *Sermons* in 1767 and *Olney Hymns* in 1779, a collection of 280 of his own compositions (including "Amazing Grace, How Sweet the Name of Jesus Sounds!," and "Glorious Things of Thee Are Spoken") and sixty-eight pieces by Cowper.

Newton left Olney for a benefice in London in 1780. The following year he published *Cardiphonia,* which was comprised of selections from his correspondence on religious matters. Here, as in his hymns, Newton again demonstrated his considerable evangelical piety.

References: John Newton, *The Authentic Narrative* (1764); idem, *Sermons, Preached in the Parish Church of Olney* (1767); idem, *Olney Hymns* (1779); idem, *Cardiphonia; or, The Utterance of the Heart* (1781); idem, *Apologia* (1789); idem, *Letters to a Wife,* 2 vols. (1793); *Amazing Grace with Bill Moyers,* PBS documentary (1990); Evelyn Bence, *Spiritual Moments with the Great Hymns* (1997).

Niagara Bible Conference Organized late in the 1860s as the Believers' Meeting for Bible Study, the movement that became known as the Niagara Bible Conference eventually settled at Niagara-on-the-Lake, Ontario, where it met from 1883 until 1900. The annual week-long conferences drew evangelicals for Bible study and preaching heavily laced with dispensationalist and premillennial interpretations. The Niagara Conference became an important tool in the propagation and the popularization of dispensational *PREMILLENNIALISM among American evangelicals.

References: Paul Boyer, *When Time Shall Be No More: Prophecy Belief in Modern American Culture* (1992); Timothy P. Weber, *Living in the Shadow of the Second Coming: American Premillennialism, 1800–1982,* enl. ed. (1983).

Noll, Mark A(llan) (1946–) Evangelical historian and man of letters, Mark A. Noll graduated from *WHEATON COLLEGE with a major in English in 1968. He went on to complete the M.A. in comparative literature at the University of Iowa, the M.A. in church history from *TRINITY EVANGELICAL DIVINITY SCHOOL, and the M.A. and Ph.D. in the history of Christianity from Vanderbilt University. After teaching for three years at *TRINITY COLLEGE (Deerfield, Illinois), Noll joined the faculty of *WHEATON COLLEGE in 1979, becoming McManis Professor of Christian Thought in 1991.

Noll's contributions to *EVANGELICALISM in the late twentieth century were manifold. In addition to his own historical writings, he and *NATHAN O. HATCH founded the *INSTITUTE FOR THE STUDY OF AMERICAN EVANGELICALS in 1982 in order to redress the historiographical neglect of *EVANGELICALISM. Noll, a prolific writer, has published literally hundreds of reviews, essays, poems, and opinion pieces; he was one of the guiding forces behind the founding of *Books & Culture: A Christian Review.* In 1994, he published *The Scandal of the Evangelical Mind,* an extended plaint about the lack of intellectual seriousness among evangelicals, occasioned by the appointment of a dispensationalist as president of *WHEATON COLLEGE.

References: Mark A. Noll, *Between Faith and Criticism: Evangelicals, Scholarship, and the Bible in America* (1986); idem, *Princeton and the Republic, 1768–1822: The Search for a Christian Enlightenment in the Era of Samuel Stanhope Smith* (1989); idem, *A History of Christianity in the United States and Canada* (1992); idem, *The Scandal of the Evangelical Mind* (1994); idem, *Seasons of Grace* (1997).

Nora Lam Chinese Ministries International. *See* **Lam, Nora.**

Norman, Larry (David) (1947–) The "father of Christian rock music" came of age during the height of the hippie counterculture in San Francisco's Haight-Ashbury district. A college dropout after one semester, Larry Norman joined a local band called People, with whom he recorded one album before leaving, citing artistic differences. Norman was signed to a solo recording contract by Mike Curb of Capitol Records in 1969 and released *Upon This Rock,* one of the very first indigenous Jesus rock music albums. Although Norman protested that the album was not recorded as he had envisioned, it gained notoriety as the "Sergeant Pepper of Christianity." His song "I Wish We'd All Been Ready" became the anthem of the *JESUS MOVEMENT with its stark apocalyptic imagery and was used for the title track in the film *A Thief in the Night,* produced and distributed by *MARK IV PICTURES. Norman also was the originator of the "One Way" sign—the index finger pointing towards heaven—that became one of the enduring icons of the *JESUS PEOPLE. The *Time* cover story on "The Jesus Revolution" in 1971 named him the "top solo artist in his field" and established him as the premier contemporary *GOSPEL MUSIC artist of the time.

In the mid-1970s, Norman completed a trio of albums—*Only Visiting This Planet, So Long Ago the Garden,* and *In Another Land*—moving away from the experiential focus of most Jesus music albums and tackling more aggressive sociopolitical issues. He chastised the permissive society and refused to back away from speaking openly about the effects of promiscuity—"gonorrhea on valentine's day (v.d.)"—or with drug problems—"shooting junk until you're half insane"—before imploring the listener to "look in to Jesus, He's got the answer."

Norman established Solid Rock Records in 1975 to record and distribute his own albums and those of other similarly minded artists. Mark Heard, Tom Howard, *RANDY STONEHILL, the tandem of John Pantano and Ron Salsbury, and members of the former *MARANATHA! MUSIC band Daniel Amos all released projects on the short-lived label. Idealism, marital difficulties, and financial naïveté—as well as changing musical tastes—led to the dissolution of the label in the late 1970s.

Suspicious of the Christian record industry's financial mistreatment of their artists, Norman started an underground label named Phydeaux (pronounced Fido), after his dog. He continued to release albums throughout the 1980s and 1990s, although nothing has come close to his impressive Trilogy.

Norris, J(ohn) Frank(lyn) (1877–1952) Born in the slums of Birmingham, Alabama, J. Frank Norris soon moved with his family to Hubbard City, Texas, where they sought better opportunities. His father, however, maintained his reliance on liquor, while his mother turned increasingly to religion, instilling a fanaticism in her young son. In later years, Norris would tell how, after he had recovered from a serious illness, his mother took him to the banks of a nearby river and dedicated him to God's service. Norris's mother, as he recounted the story, heard a voice in response: "You have given the world a preacher." Thereafter, Mary Norris read the *BIBLE to young Frank and assured him that he would become a prophet.

Norris was ordained a Southern Baptist minister in 1899, and despite the family's financial stringency, he graduated from *BAYLOR UNIVERSITY in 1903 and from Southern Baptist Theological Seminary two years later. From 1905 to 1908, he was pastor of McKinney Avenue Baptist Church in Dallas, where the congregation grew tenfold. He then assumed the pulpit of the prestigious First Baptist Church in Fort Worth, a post he held until he died of a heart attack on August 21, 1952.

Norris was not only a forceful and sensationalist preacher, he was a skilled polemicist. His controversial church newspaper, variously titled *The Fence Rail*, *The Searchlight*, and *The Fundamentalist*, had a circulation of more than seventy thousand. He reached even more through his powerful radio station, and the "Texas Tornado" was forever engaged in fighting some evil—liquor, gambling, evolution, Sunday movies, *MODERNISM, or racetrack gambling at the Texas state fair.

Although Norris was one of the founders of Southwestern Baptist Theological Seminary and the head of Baptist Bible Seminary, which was housed in his church, he persisted in portraying himself as a country boy and populist, often deriding "frizzled-headed professors." He would call upon the "fork of the creek boys" to help him destroy *MODERNISM, and he referred to himself as "a country Baptist preacher who lives in a cow town up here and fights the devil for a living."

Norris often looked for fights and even concocted enemies when he could not find real ones, especially among Texas Baptists. He accused other fundamentalists of not being sufficiently conservative, and he leveled charges of *MODERNISM against several professors at Baylor. Finally upset at Norris's machinations, the Texas Baptist convention refused to seat his delegates in 1922 and 1923; in 1924, they ousted his church from the state general association. Undeterred, Norris galvanized other fundamentalists into a separate association, the World Baptist Fellowship. He was one of the three principal figures behind the *BAPTIST BIBLE UNION until its collapse in 1932.

On July 17, 1926, a Fort Worth lumberman, D. Elliot Chipps, angered at Norris's accusations against Henry Clay Meacham, the mayor of Forth Worth, came to Norris's church, unarmed. Apparently fearing for his life, Norris shot and killed Chipps. He stood trial for murder but was acquitted for acting in self-defense. When Norris, characteristically, tried to turn the incident to advantage, claiming that evil forces in Fort Worth had hired Chipps to assassinate him, even many of his supporters became disenchanted, although his own congregation celebrated his return.

In 1932, after conducting a *REVIVAL at Temple Baptist Church in Detroit, Norris agreed to become pastor there, while still maintaining his pulpit in Fort Worth. Many Southerners had been lured to Detroit to work in the automobile factories, and Norris felt at home there. He commuted between the two churches, preaching in each on alternate weeks and printing each week's sermon. He remained as pastor of both—with a combined congregation of twenty-five thousand—until 1948, when he left the Detroit congregation.

References: J. Frank Norris, *Infidelity among Southern Baptists Endorsed by Highest Officials: Exposed by J. Frank Norris* (1946); Patsy Ledbetter, "Defense of the Faith: J. Frank Norris and Texas Fundamentalism, 1920–1929," *Arizona and the West*, 15 (1973); C. Allyn Russell, *Voices of American Fundamentalism: Seven Biographical Studies* (1976); Barry Hankins, *God's Rascal: J. Frank Norris and the Beginnings of Southern Fundamentalism* (1996); Mark G. Toulouse, "A Case Study in Schism: J. Frank Norris and the Southern Baptist Convention," *Foundations*, 21 (January–March 1981).

North American Baptist Conference The North American Baptist Conference

(NABC), formerly the North American Baptist General Conference, was created in the early nineteenth century by German-speaking Americans who had been influenced by Baptists in America. The influx of German immigrants fed the movement. Early work among the Germans focused on the eastern seaboard, especially New Jersey and Pennsylvania. The first conference met in 1851, with 405 representatives from eight churches gathering to form the Eastern Conference. A Western Conference was formed in 1859. The General, now Triennial, Conference first met in 1865.

The conference has twenty associations in the United States and Canada. The local associations oversee the work in their regions. The Triennial Conference is made up of clergy and lay representatives of all the churches. It administers the work of the mission, publication, education, and church planting arms of the denomination. A general council acts for the conference between meetings.

Doctrinally, the NABC follows the typical Baptist doctrines as expressed in the *NEW HAMPSHIRE CONFESSION. The ordinances are *BAPTISM by immersion for believers and the *LORD'S SUPPER. *POLITY is congregational. The home offices of the NABC are in Oakbrook Terrace, Illinois. In 1995, the conference reported having 61,541 members in the U.S. and Canada, 43,928 of them in the United States. There are 388 NABC congregations.

References: Frank S. Mead and Samuel S. Hill, *Handbook of Denominations in the United States,* 10th ed. (1996); J. Gordon Melton, *The Encyclopedia of American Religions,* 3d ed. (1993); "Contributions to U.S. and Canadian Protestant Churches," *Chronicle of Philanthropy,* vol. IX, no. 15.

North American Baptist Seminary (Sioux Falls, South Dakota) North American Baptist Seminary is affiliated with the *NORTH AMERICAN BAPTIST CONFERENCE. The school grew out of the German Department of Rochester Theological Seminary in New York, which had been established in 1858 to train German-speaking immigrants for ministry in the United States and abroad. Over time, the German department gained independent status from its parent seminary, moving to Sioux Falls, South Dakota, in 1949.

Today, North American Baptist Seminary has accreditation from the North Central Association of Colleges and Schools and the Association of Theological Schools in the United States and Canada. The seminary offers two degrees: the master of divinity and master of arts in Christian education. Students can complete a variety of concentrations within these two tracks, including church music, church staff ministries, biblical exposition, and *EVANGELISM. The seminary also offers a combined bachelor of arts–master of divinity program for qualified undergraduates from the University of Sioux Falls or two other local colleges.

North American Baptist Seminary runs a winter-session program in Israel, and a cultural exchange program with sites in Mexico, Cameroon, and Brazil, as well as New York City, Philadelphia, Minneapolis, and Washington, D.C.

The library at the seminary holds a Christian curriculum laboratory with materials for *SUNDAY SCHOOL and Bible school programs. Other special collections include the Harris Memorial Collection on Homiletics (a collection on preaching) as well as archives for the *NORTH AMERICAN BAPTIST CONFERENCE.

Reference: *North American Baptist Seminary 1994–1996 Catalog* (1994).

North American Christian Convention. *See* **Christian Churches.**

North Park College and Theological Seminary (Chicago, Illinois) North Park College and Theological Seminary have grown considerably since their founding by the Evangelical Covenant Church in 1891. From its beginning as the Swedish Covenant School, North Park has grown into a four-year college with a library of more than two hundred thousand books and affiliate degree programs with the University of Illinois, Case Western Reserve University, Washington University, and the University of Minnesota.

North Park College has graduate programs in business, education, and nursing. North Park Theological Seminary, the sister school to the college, offers master's degrees in divinity, theology, and Christian education, the doctorate of ministry in preaching, as well as dual-degree programs with the graduate business program in the college.

North Park has five centers for cultural studies, each of which offers courses, hosts symposia, and produces several publications each year. The centers for African American, Scandinavian, Korean, Middle Eastern, and Latino studies also provide support services to the college's diverse student body. The college serves international students and its local community on the north side of Chicago through an extensive English as a second language program. Students who complete the entire program can transfer directly to the college; the program is available to anyone who hopes to learn English, and matriculation at the college is not required.

The college holds the records for the Evangelical Covenant Church in the Covenant Archives and Historical Library. In addition, the Center for Scandinavian Studies at the college maintains the Swedish-American Archives of Greater Chicago, owned by the Swedish-American Historical Society, and the archives of the Society for the Advancement of Scandinavian Study.

References: *Peterson's Choose a Christian College: A Guide to Academically Challenging Colleges Committed to Christ-Centered Campus Life,* 4th ed. (1992); William C. Ringenberg, *The Christian College: A History of Protestant Higher Education in America* (1984).

Northside Tabernacle (Chicago, Illinois). *See* **Moody, Dwight Lyman.**

Northwest Baptist Seminary (Langley, British Columbia) Owned and operated by the Fellowship of Evangelical Baptist Churches of British Columbia and the Yukon, Northwest Baptist Seminary is the graduate division of Northwest Baptist Theological College; the Evangelical Baptist Churches of Alberta, Saskatchewan, and the Territories also cooperate in the school's governance. Northwest Baptist Seminary emerged in the 1960s from the desire on the part of evangelical Baptists, particularly in western Canada, to establish a school for developing effective church leadership. The seminary, which is part of the *Associated Canadian Theological Schools, offers courses in biblical, theological, historical, and practical studies, all within a Baptist context.

Northwest Bible College. *See* **Northwest College of the Assemblies of God.**

Northwest Christian College (Eugene, Oregon) Northwest Christian College was founded in 1895 by Eugene Sanderson. The college maintains a relationship with the Christian Churches/Churches of Christ and the Christian Church (Disciples of Christ). It also has a cooperative agreement with the University of Oregon at Eugene, which allows Northwest students to take courses at the university and also use its library and recreational facilities.

Northwest is one of a small number of *CHRISTIAN COLLEGES that requires every four-year student to complete a double major—one in *BIBLE and the other in liberal arts. Library special holdings include rare books and *BIBLES and a hymnal collection.

Reference: William C. Ringenberg, *The Christian College: A History of Protestant Higher Education in America* (1984).

Northwest College of the Assemblies of God (Kirkland, Washington) Northwest College of the Assemblies of God has always been affiliated with the Alaska, Montana, Northwest, Southern Idaho, and Wyoming districts of the *ASSEMBLIES OF GOD, representatives from which form the school's board of directors. The institution was founded in 1934 as Northwest Bible Institute. In 1949, a year after changing from a three-year to a four-year curriculum, the school became Northwest Bible College. Seven years later, the curriculum was again expanded, with the introduction of a liberal arts division. The college earned accreditation from the *AMERICAN ASSOCIATION OF BIBLE COLLEGES in 1962. That year the school again changed its name, to Northwest College of the Assemblies of God.

Full regional accreditation was achieved in 1973. Authorized to grant the bachelor of arts degree, Northwest College has a required biblical studies core and offers an advanced biology course that compares contemporary evolutionary theory with the accounts of biblical creation. Students can choose to major in education, behavioral science, business or organizational management, or one of several religious or pastoral concentrations. All students are expected to perform some kind of Christian ministry service.

For the first twenty-five years, Northwest College held classes at Hollywood Temple in Seattle. A new campus ten miles away in Kirkland was acquired in 1958, which has in recent years given the college a unique relationship with the Seattle Seahawks football team. Because the team's training facility is located on the college's campus, students have access to the artificial turf athletic fields.

Northwest College's resources include the Pacific Rim Center for Cross-Cultural Studies, maintained in a covenant relationship with the Division of Foreign Missions of the *ASSEMBLIES OF GOD. The school's Applied Science Center develops agricultural, economic, and nutritional initiatives that aspire to end world hunger, and its Center for Adult Leadership Studies offers adult-education degree programs, including a master's degree program in biblical literature, for which classes meet on campus one week every four months. The master's program is offered in conjunction with Assemblies of God Theological Seminary. Northwest College insists upon a totally drug- and alcohol-free campus.

Reference: *Northwest College Catalog, 1996/97* (1996).

Northwest Fellowship of Christian Schools. *See* **Association of Christian Schools International.**

Northwest Nazarene College (Nampa, Idaho) Eugene Emerson, a holiness layman, sought to create a college in the Northwest that would emulate Nazarene

University in Pasadena, California. His vision was realized with the help of parents of elementary-school children, who perhaps had less grandiose aspirations. The resulting institution, Idaho Holiness School, opened in Nampa, Idaho, in 1913. The school swiftly was transformed from a grammar school to offering a more advanced curriculum, and within two years the first student graduated from the high school. Idaho Holiness changed its name twice in 1916—first to Northwest Holiness College and then to Northwest Nazarene College. By 1920, the grammar school, academy, and *BIBLE INSTITUTE had given way to a baccalaureate curriculum. The college attained junior college accreditation in 1931 and was fully accredited as a four-year school six years later. It now offers graduate programs in education and Christian ministries.

Northwest Nazarene College is the home of the Wesley Center for Applied Theology, which supports academic research on the Wesleyan tradition, assists church leaders, and encourages the application of holiness ideals in both personal and social contexts. In conjunction with Eastern Nazarene College in Massachusetts, Northwest Nazarene offers a study-abroad program in Romania.

Reference: *Northwest Nararene College Undergraduate Catalog 1996–1997* (1996).

Northwestern College (Orange City, Iowa) Seine Bolks, pastor of Orange City, Iowa's, First Reformed Church, established a secondary school in 1882 to prepare students for ministry in the Reformed Church. The school, Northwestern Classical Academy, offered Latin early on, reflecting a commitment to the humanities as well as to religious education. As the academy grew, it also introduced courses in business and education. In 1928, Northwestern Classical Academy added a junior college, and in 1959 the board of trustees decided to eliminate the secondary school and institute a four-year college program. The first baccalaureate degrees were awarded by Northwestern College in 1961, and the last class graduated from the academy. Four years later, the board of trustees voted to adopt a full liberal arts program, representing a new axis for the curriculum. The college earned regional accreditation in 1970.

Northwestern College is affiliated with the *REFORMED CHURCH IN AMERICA, and it remains conscious of the Dutch heritage of its supporting denomination. The library contains a Dutch Heritage Room, which holds both the college's records and also genealogical materials and Dutch artifacts.

Although all students are required to attend three short chapel services each week, Northwestern College has rather permissive behavioral standards in comparison with other *CHRISTIAN COLLEGES. Alcohol is forbidden on campus, in approved off-campus housing, and at campus events, but the school also affirms its commitment to "Christian liberty." All buildings on-campus are smoke-free, but smoking is not specifically forbidden.

References: *Northwestern College 1996–1998 Catalog* (1996); *Peterson's Choose a Christian College: A Guide to Academically Challenging Colleges Committed to Christ-Centered Campus Life,* 4th ed. (1992); William C. Ringenberg, *The Christian College: A History of Protestant Higher Education in America* (1984).

Northwestern College and Northwestern Theological Seminary (St. Paul, Minnesota) Northwestern College began as Northwestern Bible and Missionary Training School in Minneapolis, Minnesota. It was founded in 1902 by fundamentalist pastor *WILLIAM BELL

RILEY, and for the first forty-five years the school shared facilities with Riley's First Baptist Church.

Northwestern Theological Seminary was added in 1935, and the College of Liberal Arts was introduced nine years later. For the last few years of his presidency, Riley devoted himself to developing the liberal arts program, which he envisioned as an alternative to secular, "modernist" education. Riley died in 1947, and the following year the college moved from Minneapolis to St. Paul. There, *EVANGELIST *BILLY GRAHAM assumed the mantle as Riley's successor, although Graham remained a figurehead, spending little time on campus and delegating the management of the school to others. Graham, however, also pushed Northwestern's liberal arts curriculum, which had become unpopular with the Bible school advocates who were suspicious of "secular education." In 1951, Northwestern's Bible school began offering bachelor's degrees, although it remained separate from the liberal arts program. Graham resigned in 1952, and by 1956 the college had split into two entities, with the fundamentalists leaving to create *PILLSBURY BIBLE SCHOOL. The liberal arts college dissolved in 1966 but was able to reopen six years later with the help of a generous gift from the wife of a pizza tycoon. Classes began in 1972 on Northwestern's current campus, a former Roman Catholic seminary. The rebuilt Northwestern was unquestionably a liberal arts college but with a stronger-than-usual emphasis on Bible studies. To this day, every student who enters Northwestern as a first-year student is expected to complete a second major in *BIBLE; transfer students fulfill similar requirements on a proportional basis.

Northwestern is nondenominational but still describes itself as fundamentalist. The "Community Lifestyle Agreement" prohibits social *DANCING and remains in effect even when school is out of session for vacations. Even by the standards of evangelical colleges, Northwestern's Christian outreach programs to the general public are surprisingly vigorous. The college is the annual sponsor of the Lake Johanna Bible Conference, and its network of noncommercial Christian radio stations, which began with KTIS AM/FM in 1949, has six stations, reaching five Midwestern states. In addition, the Skylight Satellite Network radio ministry broadcasts via satellite to 340 more stations across the country. Northwestern's library holds the papers of *WILLIAM BELL RILEY.

References: *Northwestern College Catalog, 1995–1996* (1995); Thomas C. Hunt and James C. Carper, eds., *Religious Higher Education in the United States: A Source Book* (1996).

Nunn, David (Oliver) (1921–) Born and reared in a poor pentecostal household, David Nunn exhibited considerable piety as a child and even claimed a miraculous healing when he stuck a nail in his foot. He served in World War II, however, and became an alcoholic by the age of twenty-two. After his *CONVERSION in November 1946, Nunn claimed to be "delivered from the bondage of drink and all the evil habits of my life" and began preaching for the *ASSEMBLIES OF GOD shortly thereafter. He enjoyed success as a preacher and a healer, but a second call in January 1950 prompted Nunn to become an itinerant: "God spoke to me again and said: 'Get up from here and go into every city, heal the sick therein and preach the kingdom of heaven is at hand.'"

Nunn became affiliated with *GORDON LINDSAY and was a principal *EVANGELIST in the *VOICE OF HEALING organization. When that group began to fade, Nunn formed his own evangelistic association, Bible Revival Evangelistic Association, in 1962, which published *The Healing Messenger,* operated a small radio network, and raised funds for foreign missions.

Reference: David Edwin Harrell Jr., *All Things Are Possible: The Healing and Charismatic Revivals in Modern America* (1975).

Nyack College and Alliance Theological Seminary (Nyack, New York) Nyack College's predecessor, the New York Missionary Training Institute, was one of the first *BIBLE INSTITUTES established. The school began when *ALBERT B. SIMPSON, the Presbyterian pastor who also founded the *CHRISTIAN AND MISSIONARY ALLIANCE, resigned his New York pastorate in 1881 to give himself over fully to the training of "footsoldiers in God's army." A year later, Simpson began holding classes in a theater on Twenty-third Street in Manhattan. The school, also known as New York Missionary Training College for Home and Foreign Missions, relocated several times and eventually acquired space in New York's Gospel Tabernacle.

Simpson believed that lay workers had more spiritual zeal than trained clergy, and the Missionary Training Institute was primarily designed to train laypeople. Within three years of opening, however, the institute introduced courses in "Pastoral Theology," evidence that the training tracks for clergy and laity may not have been totally separate.

Simpson decided in 1897 to move the institute thirty miles north of New York City to Nyack, where the school eventually took the name Nyack Bible Institute. Although the school had indeed outgrown its facilities in New York, Simpson moved the school in order to create a protected environment for his students. In the early years, "worldly amusements" were vigorously monitored, and even "innocent" fiction was forbidden. For five years, between 1907 and 1912, the school ran a Home School and Worker's Training Institute in New York to fill the vacuum created by the move. This program's failure reinforced criticism against Simpson that his new program lacked practical emphasis; efforts to improve academics were seen as a deviation from the original purpose of religious training. Today, however, Nyack College runs two extension sites in New York City. At the Korean Extension School in Flushing, classes are taught in Korean, and English as a second language courses and core curriculum courses are both available. The program is set up to let Korean and Korean American students transfer to the main campus in Nyack. At the New York Center for Christian Studies in Manhattan, students can transfer, too, but they are also able to earn an associate's degree in general education at the extension campus. In 1995, 44 percent of Nyack's enrollment was minority students, perhaps due in part to the success of the extension sites. This percentage is significantly higher than the national average for Christian colleges.

Nyack established its graduate school, the Jaffray School of Missions, in 1960, placing dual emphasis on theology and cultural anthropology in order to train college graduates for missionary work. Jaffray expanded its curriculum in 1974 to include preparation for North American ministries as well as overseas missionary service. At that time, the school changed its name to the Alliance School of Theology and Missions and introduced master's programs in professional ministerial studies. The master's program in divinity was started five years later, and the school became Alliance Theological Seminary, the official seminary of the *CHRISTIAN

AND MISSIONARY ALLIANCE. The seminary also grants master of arts degrees in Old and New Testament and intercultural studies. As of 1996, Alliance Theological Seminary had only one woman full-time faculty member. Nyack College and Alliance Theological Seminary still share facilities, but each has its own faculty.

References: Alliance Theological Seminary Catalog and Applications, 1996–1997 (1996); *Nyack College 1995–96 Catalog* (1995); Thomas C. Hunt and James C. Carper, eds., *Religious Higher Education in the United States: A Source Book* (1996); Virginia Lieson Brereton, *Training God's Army: The American Bible School, 1880–1940* (1990); William C. Ringenberg, *The Christian College: A History of Protestant Higher Education in America* (1984).

■ ■ ■

Oak Brook College of Law and Government Policy. *See* **Gothard, William "Bill."**

Obookiah, Henry (né Opukahaia) (1792–1818) Orphaned at the age of fifteen, Opukahaia (later known as Henry Obookiah) was taken from Honolulu, Hawai'i, to New Haven, Connecticut, by a ship captain. There he met and befriended *SAMUEL J. MILLS, a student at Yale who would become one of the leaders of the foreign missions movement. After following Mills to Andover, Obookiah experienced an evangelical *CONVERSION in 1812, became a member of the Congregational church at Torringford, Connecticut, three years later, and the following year joined the *AMERICAN BOARD OF COMMISSIONERS FOR FOREIGN MISSIONS. He enrolled at the Foreign Mission School in Cornwall, Connecticut, and became an effective *EVANGELIST for the cause of missions. Obookiah died of typhus in 1818, but his autobiography, *Memoirs of Henry Obookiah,* was circulated widely in New England and inspired other missionary efforts, including a highly successful mission to his native Hawai'i.

Occom, Samson (1723–1792) A Mohegan Indian who was converted during the *GREAT AWAKENING, Samson Occom went on to study at Moor's Charity School (now Dartmouth College), run by *ELEAZAR WHEELOCK, to prepare to become an *EVANGELIST among Native Americans. Ordained as a Presbyterian in 1759, he became an itinerant preacher in New England and New York. Occom was a gifted orator; he accompanied Nathaniel Whitaker in 1764 on a two-year, highly successful fund-raising trip to England. After the American Revolution, Occom and several of his followers founded the Brotherton Community of Indians, in Oneida County, New York.

Ocean Grove Camp Meeting Association On June 13, 1867, at the behest of *WILLIAM B. OSBORN, a group of clergy from Pennsylvania and New Jersey met in Philadelphia to discuss how they might use *CAMP MEETINGS for the "promotion of the doctrine and the experience of holiness." The first National Camp Meeting for the Promotion of Holiness was held in Vineland, New Jersey, the following month, July 17–26. Ten thousand people, most of them Methodists, gathered for the event, and more than twenty-five thousand attended the *CAMP MEETING the following year, at Manheim, Pennsylvania.

Organizers of these *CAMP MEETINGS soon came to believe that they should purchase a permanent meeting place. "Let us select a *CAMP-MEETING ground by the seaside," Osborn said, "and then the desired rest and *SALVATION can be secured at the same time." An initial offer for Seven Mile Beach in Cape May, New Jersey, was withdrawn because of concern about mosquitoes. Osborn and *ELWOOD STOKES, who would become the first president of the Ocean Grove Camp Meeting Association, finally decided on a seaside tract in Ocean Grove, New Jersey, and the first *CAMP MEETING was held there in July 1869. Early the following year, a group of thirteen laymen and clergy was chartered by the state of New Jersey as "The Ocean Grove Camp-Meeting Association of the Methodist Episcopal Church." Granted extraordinary powers by the state, the association was able to govern the entire town and to own all of the land within its borders (to this day, homeowners lease the land beneath their dwellings from the association). The association banned the sale of alcohol and tobacco and took sabbatarianism very seriously; it closed its beaches and barred all vehicles from its streets on Sunday (the former prohibition was severely attenuated in 1935, and the latter remained in effect until a court decision until 1980).

After its formation in 1869, the Ocean Grove Camp Meeting Association proceeded to construct a permanent *CAMP MEETING there on the Jersey shore. Whereas the frontier *CAMP MEETINGS earlier in the nineteenth century had been temporary—a gathering place carved out of the wilderness—Ocean Grove offered permanence, but in a way that evoked the frontier gatherings. Semipermanent canvas dwellings still flank the main gathering place. The large wooden tabernacle, completed in 1894, resembles nothing so much as a huge tent. And whereas the frontier gathering places were located in proximity to freshwater for sustenance, the Victorian-era *CAMP MEETING at Ocean Grove was located next to saltwater in order to provide recreation for the weary industrial worker.

References: Kenneth O. Brown, *Holy Ground: A Study of the American Camp Meeting* (1992); Randall Balmer, "From Frontier Phenomenon to Victorian Institution: The Methodist Camp Meeting in Ocean Grove, New Jersey," *Methodist History,* XXV (April 1987); Troy Messenger, *Holy Leisure: Recreation and Religion in God's Square Mile* (1999).

Ockenga, Harold John (1905–1985) Born in Chicago, Harold John Ockenga graduated from *TAYLOR UNIVERSITY in 1927. He began his seminary studies at Princeton Theological Seminary but left to join Princeton expatriate *J. GRESHAM MACHEN at his newly formed *WESTMINSTER THEOLOGICAL SEMINARY in Philadelphia. Upon graduation in 1931, Ockenga served two Presbyterian churches in Pittsburgh before moving on to Park Street Congregational Church in Boston, where he remained for more than three decades. At Park Street, Ockenga began a radio ministry; his scholarly preaching and his publications aimed at a popular audience increased his reputation in evangelical circles throughout New England and eventually across the country. He helped to organize the *NATIONAL ASSOCIATION OF EVANGELICALS in 1941 (a response to the more mainline National Council of Churches), and Ockenga served, from 1942 to 1944, as the new organization's first president.

Following the war, Ockenga sought ways to soften some of the more strident rhetoric and attitudes of the fundamentalists. He coined the term "*NEO-EVANGELICAL" to denote a conservative Protestant theology that was nonseparatist and which sought to engage the larger culture by addressing social issues—something that fundamentalists, with their premillennial *ESCHATOLOGY, were loath to do—and by insisting on intellectual rigor. Ockenga found several ways to promote his vision. He was one of the founders of *FULLER THEOLOGICAL SEMINARY and served two terms as its president, from 1947 to 1954 and again from 1960 to 1963. Both terms, however, were served *in absentia*; Ockenga, despite numerous promises, apparently could not bring himself to leave Boston for Pasadena, California, site of the seminary. Ockenga's other major contribution to *NEO-EVANGELICALISM was his involvement in the founding of **CHRISTIANITY TODAY* in 1956. He served for a quarter of a century as chair of the magazine's board.

Ockenga retired from Park Street Church in 1969 and accepted the presidency of *GORDON COLLEGE and Divinity School. The next year, he became president of the newly merged *GORDON-CONWELL THEOLOGICAL SEMINARY, where he remained until his retirement in 1979.

References: Harold John Ockenga, *These Religious Affections* (1937); idem, *Our Protestant Heritage* (1938); idem, *Our Evangelical Faith* (1946); idem, *The Spirit of the Living God* (1947); George M. Marsden, *Reforming Fundamentalism: Fuller Seminary and the New Evangelicalism* (1987).

Oden, Thomas (Clark) (1931–) A self-described "orthodox evangelical" within the United Methodist Church, Thomas Oden was born into an evangelical household in Altus, Oklahoma. After studying at the University of Oklahoma and at Perkins School of Theology at Southern Methodist University, Oden was ordained a Methodist and then went to Yale for doctoral studies, earning the Ph.D. in 1960. He taught at Phillips University and joined the faculty of Drew University in 1971.

Oden himself divides his intellectual development into two phases: the first, roughly from 1945 to 1965, devoted to modernistic *LIBERALISM, tinged with humanistic psychology; the second, beginning about 1965, characterized by an almost defiant return to evangelical orthodoxy. Social and political developments in the late 1960s contributed to his turnaround. He became distressed at the drug use, sexual attitudes, and violence of the counterculture, especially activities at the 1968 Democratic National Convention in Chicago. Oden began to read the church fathers and embraced what he called "paleo-orthodoxy if for no other reason than to signal clearly that I do not mean once-fashionable *NEOORTHODOXY."

At Drew, Oden's attacks on *LIBERALISM, feminism, and homosexuality made him something of a pariah. Although he managed to continue training a number of students (known, not entirely affectionately, as "Odenites"), Oden himself was increasingly marginalized from the remainder of the faculty beginning in the mid-1990s, in large measure because of the 1995 publication of *Requiem: A Lament in Three Movements. Requiem* was an unstinting attack on the "political correctness" that Oden thought had eviscerated theological education in mainline seminaries. The study of liturgy, he complained, had degenerated into "an experiment in color, balloons, poetry, and freedom," ethics courses had become the study of "political correctness," and classes in pastoral care had evolved into "a support group for the sexually alienated."

References: Thomas Oden, *Agenda for Theology* (1979); idem, *The Living God* (1987); idem, *The Word of Life* (1989); idem, *Life in the Spirit* (1992); idem, *Requiem: A Lament in Three Movements* (1995); Daniel B. Clendenin, s.v. "Thomas Oden," in Walter A. Elwell, ed., *Handbook of Evangelical Theologians* (1993).

Ogilvie, Lloyd John (1930–) An effective author and preacher, Lloyd John

Ogilvie graduated from Lake Forest College and Garrett Theological Seminary. He served as pastor of Presbyterian churches in Illinois and Pennsylvania before accepting the pulpit of First Presbyterian Church, Hollywood, California, one of the twelve "great churches" of 1950, so designated by *Christian Century*. During Ogilvie's tenure, from 1972 to 1995, he developed a television program, *Let God Love You*, and became a prolific lecturer and the author of more than forty books. Because of his stature within the denomination and because of the historic importance of Hollywood Presbyterian Church, Ogilvie emerged as one of the most important evangelical spokesmen within the Presbyterian Church. On January 24, 1995, at the behest of Senator *MARK O. HATFIELD, the U.S. Senate unanimously elected Ogilvie its sixty-first chaplain, a post he assumed on March 13, 1995.

References: Lloyd John Ogilvie, *Let God Love You* (1974); idem, *Life without Limits* (1975); idem, *Loved and Forgiven* (1977); Randall Balmer, *Grant Us Courage: Travels Along the Mainline of American Protestantism* (1996).

Ohio Association of Christian Schools. *See* **Association of Christian Schools International.**

O'Kelly, James (1738–1826) A Methodist *CIRCUIT RIDER and leader of the *O'KELLY SCHISM, James O'Kelly was born in Ireland and immigrated to America during the American Revolution. In 1784, the year of the founding of the Methodist Episcopal Church in the United States, O'Kelly was ordained and appointed a traveling preacher and the presiding elder of the South Virginia district. He became enamored of democratic ideals and sought to translate them into Methodist ecclesiology. O'Kelly argued that a preacher dissatisfied with his appointment should have the right to appeal. Should the conference agree, the bishop would be obliged to reappoint the dissatisfied cleric.

Such views were contrary to the episcopal form of *POLITY (government by bishops) dictated by *JOHN WESLEY and defended by *FRANCIS ASBURY. Asbury and O'Kelly squared off in 1792, during the first General Conference of the Methodist Episcopal Church. When O'Kelly's motion failed, he and his sympathizers bolted from the denomination, a split known as the *O'KELLY SCHISM. O'Kelly, who was also a staunch opponent of slavery, met with a group of his supporters on August 4, 1794, and formed the Republican Methodist Church, which embodied his egalitarianism and his democratic notions on church *POLITY. Seven years later, the denomination changed its name to "Christian Church" and formally adopted a congregational form of *POLITY. "I am for Bible government," O'Kelly declared, "Christian equality, and the Christian name."

References: James O'Kelly, *Essay on Negro Slavery* (1784); F. A. Norwood, "James O'Kelly, Methodist Maverick," *Methodist History*, IV (1966).

O'Kelly Schism The O'Kelly Schism, the first major rift in the Methodist Episcopal Church, was occasioned by the democratic convictions of *JAMES O'KELLY, a *CIRCUIT RIDER in southern Virginia. O'Kelly, an Irish immigrant who had become enamored of republican ideals, introduced a resolution at the first General Conference of the Methodist Church in 1792, providing that "after a bishop appoints the preachers at conference to their several circuits, if anyone thinks himself injured by the appointment, he shall have liberty to appeal to the conference and state his objections." Should the conference agree, the resolution continued, then the bishop would be obligated to appoint the aggrieved cleric to another circuit.

O'Kelly's republican notions about church *POLITY placed him in direct confrontation with Bishop *FRANCIS ASBURY, who believed, with *CHARLES WESLEY, in episcopal *POLITY (government by bishops). The O'Kelly resolution was defeated, whereupon he and a few fellow clergymen, along with perhaps as many as eight thousand church members, left the denomination and formed the Republican Methodist Church. The group was concentrated in North Carolina and in southern Virginia. The O'Kelly Schism officially ended when the remnant of the Republican Methodist Church reunited with the Methodist Episcopal Church in 1934.

References: Charles Franklin Kilgore, *The James O'Kelly Schism in the Methodist Episcopal Church* (1963); Nathan O. Hatch, "The Christian Movement and the Demand for a Theology of the People," *Journal of American History*, LXVII (1980).

Oklahoma Baptist University (Shawnee, Oklahoma) Oklahoma Baptist University represents the third combined attempt by Southern Baptists to found a college in Oklahoma; two previous efforts failed in the early 1900s. In 1906, the State Baptist Convention appointed a commission to found a Baptist university. The school was incorporated in 1910 and opened the following year, first holding classes in the basement of the First Baptist Church and the Convention Hall in Shawnee. That same year another Baptist college opened, Carey College, but it closed within a month. Many of Carey's students and faculty transferred to the new college in Shawnee. The city soon donated sixty acres for a campus, and the college had moved into its new facilities by 1915.

Oklahoma Baptist University is still owned and operated by the Baptist General Convention of Oklahoma. The convention elects the university's board of trustees. Oklahoma Baptist offers a master of science degree in family therapy. The library has a rare book collection of nearly nine hundred volumes, as well as special collections on missions, the Civil War, and World War II.

Oklahoma Baptist's rules regarding student behavior are somewhat more liberal than most other evangelical colleges. *DANCING and rock music are not prohibited; in fact, the guidelines do not include regulations regarding entertainment. While hazing of any kind is expressly prohibited, Oklahoma Baptist is one of the few Christian colleges that allows fraternities.

References: *Oklahoma Baptist University 1996–97 Academic Catalog* (1996); Thomas C. Hunt and James C. Carper, eds., *Religious Higher Education in the United States: A Source Book* (1996).

Oklahoma Holiness College. *See* **Southern Nazarene University.**

Old Lights. *See* **New Lights.**

Old Side Presbyterians. *See* **New Lights.**

Olford, Stephen F. (1918–) The son of missionaries, Stephen F. Olford was born in northern Rhodesia and studied at Oxford University and at St. Luke's College, London. After attending a missionary training institute, he became a chaplain in the British army during World War II. Olford was ordained a Baptist minister in 1953 and became pastor of Duke Street Baptist Church in Richmond, Surrey, England. Six years later, he came to New York City to assume the pastorate of the redoubtable bastion of *FUNDAMENTALISM, Calvary Baptist Church. After a fifteen-year tenure, Olford stepped down in 1973 and founded Encounter Ministries, which includes a radio broadcast, *Encounter.*

Reference: John Phillips, *Only One Life: The Biography of Stephen F. Olford* (1995).

Olivet Nazarene University (Kankakee, Illinois) Olivet Nazarene University began as an elementary school, founded by the Eastern Illinois Holiness Association at Georgetown, Illinois, in 1907. The school moved a year later to Olivet, added a liberal arts college, and was renamed Illinois Holiness University. The *CHURCH OF THE NAZARENE adopted the school in 1912, which became known as Olivet University three years later. The name reverted to Olivet College in 1923. When the campus was destroyed by fire in 1939, the college moved to Kankakee, Illinois, onto the campus of a former Catholic school. At that time, the college adopted the name Olivet Nazarene College. The name changed to Olivet Nazarene University in 1986, which better reflected the diversity of its programs.

Reference: Thomas C. Hunt and James C. Carper, eds., *Religious Higher Education in the United States: A Source Book* (1996).

Olivier, Henri (1799–1864) A spiritual product of the *GENEVA REVIVAL, Henri Olivier was turned down for ordination by the Reformed Church in Lausanne because of his fervent *EVANGELICALISM. He secured ordination in Great Britain, returned to Lausanne, but was expelled in 1824 and moved on to Paris, conducting evangelistic activities there under the patronage of ***ROBERT HALDANE**. As opposition to *EVANGELICALISM thawed in Lausanne later in the 1820s, Olivier returned as pastor of an independent chapel and became associated with the Lausanne Missionary Society.

The Society commissioned Olivier and his wife for service to Upper Canada in 1834. While the Oliviers were spending the winter of 1834–35 in Montréal, English-speaking evangelicals there persuaded them to redirect their evangelistic efforts to the francophone population. Although Henri Olivier's *BAPTISM by immersion in the spring of 1835 alienated some supporters, he persevered in his redefined mission until poor health forced his return to Lausanne in 1836.

Olson, Arnold T(heodore) (1910–) Born in Minneapolis, Minnesota, Arnold T. Olson graduated from Trinity Seminary and Bible College (now *TRINITY INTERNATIONAL UNIVERSITY) and was ordained in 1931. He served as a chaplain during World War II, pastored a number of churches, and chaired a merger committee of several Scandinavian-based Free Churches, which became the *EVANGELICAL FREE CHURCH OF AMERICA in 1950. After serving as moderator and vice president for the new denomination, Olson assumed the presidency, a post he retained until 1976. During his long tenure, Olson presided over the denomination's move from an ethnic enclave to a position closer to the mainstream of American *EVANGELICALISM. The relocation of Trinity Seminary and Bible College from Chicago to suburban Deerfield, Illinois, symbolized that transition; *TRINITY EVANGELICAL DIVINITY SCHOOL, one of the new institutions emerging from the relocation, recognized Olson's contributions by naming its chapel in his honor. In addition to his denominational activities on behalf of the *EVANGELICAL FREE CHURCH, Olson established himself as one of the preeminent evangelical emissaries to Israel.

References: Arnold T. Olson, *This We Believe: The Background and Exposition of the Doctrinal Statement of the Evangelical Free Church of America* (1963); idem, *Believers Only* (1964); *Inside Jerusalem, City of Destiny* (1968); idem, *The Search for Identity* (1980); idem, *The Significance of Silence* (1981); idem, *Stumbling toward Maturity* (1981).

OMF International. *See* **Taylor, J(ames) Hudson.**

Ontario Bible College and Ontario Theological Seminary (North York, Ontario) Ontario Bible College is the oldest Bible college in Canada. Its predecessor, Toronto Bible College, became the third *BIBLE INSTITUTE in North America when it was started in 1894 by Elmore Harris, pastor of the Walmer Road Baptist Church in Toronto. Harris, one of the editors of the **SCOFIELD REFERENCE BIBLE*, also served on *LYMAN and Milton STEWART's committee to oversee the production of **THE FUNDAMENTALS*, the pamphlet series created to defend biblical *INERRANCY and combat "*MODERNISM."

Toronto Bible College merged in 1968 with London, Ontario's, London College of Bible and Missions, which was established in 1935 by J. Wilmot Mahood. At that time the combined schools became known as Ontario Bible College. Eight years later, the college bought its current campus on the outskirts of Toronto and introduced a graduate division under the name Ontario Theological Seminary. Although the college and seminary share a board of governors, library, dormitories, cafeteria, and support staff, they have their own administration, faculty, courses, and buildings. The library has two special collections: the Baldwin Puritan Collection and the Denominational Reference Collection. Ontario Bible College and Ontario Theological Seminary are "transdenominational" and take this concept very seriously. The schools enforce a policy that advocates tolerance across denominational lines and forbids students from imposing denominational beliefs on one another.

Ontario Bible College grants bachelor's degrees in religious studies and religious education. Like most Canadian colleges, the standard undergraduate program at Ontario Bible College is three years instead of four, but students in either division have the option to add a fourth year and earn the bachelor of theology degree. Ontario Theological Seminary grants the master of divinity degree, with concentrations in youth and family ministry, counseling, pastoral care, Chinese studies, educational ministries, and intercultural studies. The seminary also offers a master's of theological studies, in which students concentrate in biblical and theological studies, specialized ministries such as Chinese Church ministries or youth ministry, or Christian foundations, which is a combination of the other two specializations. The M.T.S. is primarily intended as an enrichment program for laity.

In addition to the pastoral and lay programs in Chinese church ministry, the seminary also runs many courses in Korean Christian studies. With a heavy emphasis on intercultural and Asian studies in the curriculum, Ontario is able to maintain impressive ratios of minority student enrollment at both the undergraduate and graduate levels. The seminary has a minority student enrollment of

35 percent, and more than one fifth of the college student body is Chinese or of Chinese descent. On the other hand, while Ontario Bible College and Theological Seminary profess a commitment to the "affirmation" of women students, the college retains only two female full-time faculty members out of a total faculty of sixteen. At the graduate level, Ontario's success at incorporating women is even more ambiguous: Women account for less than 40 percent of the enrollment at the seminary. In spite of the presence of a woman as dean of students, no other women were serving as full-time faculty at the seminary as of 1995. Ontario Bible College is a member of the *ACCREDITING ASSOCIATION OF BIBLE COLLEGES.

Reference: *Ontario Bible College 1995–96 Catalog* (1995).

Open Bible Evangelistic Association. *See* **Open Bible Standard Churches.**

Open Bible Standard Churches The Open Bible Standard Churches came into being through the merger of the Open Bible Evangelistic Association of Des Moines, Iowa, and Bible Standard, Inc., of Oregon. The two former groups had been similar in theology and government and merged in 1935, adopting the name Open Bible Standard Churches, Inc. The headquarters of the churches are in Des Moines, Iowa.

The churches are "fundamental in doctrine, evangelical in spirit, missionary in vision, and pentecostal in testimony." The theology includes an emphasis on the blood *ATONEMENT of Jesus Christ, divine healing, *BAPTISM OF THE HOLY SPIRIT, personal holiness, the premillennial return of Christ, and *BAPTISM by immersion. *POLITY in the churches in congregational. Churches are grouped in districts and regions and are affiliated by charter with the denomination. A general convention meets biennially and includes all licensed and ordained ministers and one lay delegate for each one hundred members. The Open Bible Standard Churches is a member denomination in the *NATIONAL ASSOCIATION OF EVANGELICALS and in the *PENTECOSTAL FELLOWSHIP OF NORTH AMERICA. The denomination claims 360 churches with a total of approximately forty-six thousand members.

References: Frank S. Mead and Samuel S. Hill, *Handbook of Denominations in the United States*, 10th ed. (1996); J. Gordon Melton, *The Encyclopedia of American Religions*, 3d ed. (1993).

Operation Grace World Missions. *See* **Thieme, R(obert) B(unger), Jr.**

Operation Rescue. *See* **Operation Save America.**

Operation Save America Operation Save America, an antiabortion group, was founded in 1984 by Randall Terry as Project Life; it became known as Operation Rescue in 1986 and took its current name in 1999. The group conducts large demonstrations and sit-ins at *ABORTION clinics in an attempt to "rescue" unborn children. Operation Save America, which has clashed with legal authorities, has also published the names of doctors who perform *ABORTIONS and has confronted them in public places. It moved its operations from Binghamton, New York, to Florida, and, in 1994, to Dallas, Texas, under the direction of Philip "Flip" Benham; Terry, because of legal troubles for his previous brushes with the law, had no official role in the organization, although he continued to direct from the sidelines.

The rhetoric of self-righteousness surrounding Operation Save America has occasionally given rise to violence. In 1991, the organization mounted what it called a "Summer of Mercy," a protracted protest in Wichita, Kansas. Better known as the War in Wichita, the confrontation lasted forty-six days, with many of the protesters going to jail in a demonstration of civil disobedience against a court order. After Operation Rescue (as it was then known) circulated "wanted" posters for doctors performing *ABORTIONS, Michael Griffin, who had participated in the organization's protests, murdered David Gunn outside of his clinic in Pensacola, Florida, on March 10, 1993. Terry, who had stated many times that doctors performing *ABORTIONS should be executed, was unrepentant. "I want you to just let a wave of intolerance wash over you," he told a congregation in Indiana later that year. "I want you to let a wave of hatred wash over you. Yes, hate is good." Prior to the 1992 election, Terry asserted that "to vote for Bill Clinton was to *SIN against God."

Reference: William Martin, *With God on Our Side: The Rise of the Religious Right in America* (1996).

Oral Roberts University (Tulsa, Oklahoma) Oral Roberts University was established by *ORAL ROBERTS, the famous pentecostal-holiness-turned-Methodist evangelist. Roberts claims to have received a message from God while having dinner with *PAT ROBERTSON in 1960, commanding him to establish a Bible college. The school was started as an outreach program of the Oral Roberts Evangelistic Association, with strong overlap in the boards of trustees. Around 1961, land was purchased in Tulsa, Oklahoma, for the campus of the new "University of Evangelism," and construction began the following year.

The original image of the school was as a "boot camp" for *EVANGELISM, yet as it began to take shape, Roberts expanded his vision and set out to develop a full-scale university, opening for classes under the name Oral Roberts University in 1965. Many of Roberts's pentecostal associates were horrified to learn that this new university, in a departure from Bible school mentality, allowed female students to wear makeup. Oral Roberts University also presented competition to pentecostals' own Bible colleges, as well as to the *ASSEMBLIES OF GOD's first liberal arts endeavor, *EVANGEL COLLEGE. Furthermore, the Oklahoma-based institution won quick legitimacy from the nonpentecostal world. When the school was formally dedicated in 1967, *BILLY GRAHAM delivered the dedicatory address, proclaiming, "This institution was built by the prayer and the dedication and the money of women and men who love God, who believe the *GOSPEL, and who believe the *BIBLE is the *WORD OF GOD."

Originally, the school had an enrollment of 312 students, but with money from *ORAL ROBERTS's television ministry it was able to add students at a remarkable rate, especially when it secured regional accreditation in 1971. In the 1960s and 1970s, Oral Roberts University was able to build state-of-the-art facilities that earned commendations from the Carnegie and Ford Foundations, despite the ostentation of the two-hundred-foot "Prayer Tower" that has become Roberts's signature piece. By 1975, the campus was valued at $60 million, although wags continue to dismiss it as "Six Flags over Jesus."

In its early years, the university also invested heavily in its interscholastic athletic program, with meteoric results. In 1971, their first year as a member of the

NCAA, Oral Roberts University's basketball team had a 25–1 record and made it to the National Invitational Tournament in Madison Square Garden. By 1974, however, that momentum had collapsed, although the university's "Golden Eagles" sports teams continue to have Division I status.

In the beginning, *ORAL ROBERTS taught a required religion course to every student, and the university retains close ties with the *EVANGELIST, in spite of his "theocratic" style of leadership. Oral Roberts University's "Code of Honor Pledge" requires students to abstain from alcohol and tobacco at all times, whether on or off campus. The dress code is fairly strict and has been repeatedly updated to counter fashions that ring of "immodesty." Roberts has had several battles over students' and faculty's willingness to attend chapel, and beginning in 1975 a mandatory aerobics program was instituted for all students, faculty, and administrators. The physical education requirement is codified in the university's guidelines for student conduct, and the school has even subjected overweight students to disciplinary action for failing to stick to their diets.

Such policies reflect Roberts's own interest in healthy living, but at one time they were the source of one of the more quixotic events in the university's history. In 1977 and 1978, four students were expelled for failing their diets, and several others dropped out from the pressure, being required to lose a pound a week until they met their prescribed weight. By 1978, objection to the policy was tacked onto a lawsuit brought against the university by the American Civil Liberties Union and the Oklahoma Coalition of Citizens with Disabilities. From the point of its founding, Oral Roberts University had excluded students in wheelchairs on the grounds that the campus was not accessible. Facing mounting pressure, the school agreed to make changes to its physical plant and to admit disabled students, but in a tradeoff the plaintiffs dropped the "obesity issue" from the lawsuit, and the weight-loss policy remained intact.

Beginning in the mid-1970s, Oral Roberts University set out to institute graduate programs. First establishing programs in education, business, nursing, and theology, the university aspired to develop schools of medicine, law, and dentistry as well. In 1981, the university's new O. W. Coburn School of Law gained national attention when its forthcoming accreditation by the American Bar Association (ABA) was threatened on the grounds of religious discrimination—in particular, the requirement that students sign a pledge affirming belief in Jesus Christ as Lord and Savior. The issue was hotly debated in ABA meetings, but advocates for the university finally prevailed, and by 1984 all the new graduate programs were in place. The development of graduate programs was not without its cost, however, for the school was almost constantly plagued by financial troubles in the 1980s. The skyrocketing costs of the new programs, especially the cost of building the medical school's new $150 million "City of Faith" hospital, could not be offset by contributions from the Oral Roberts Evangelistic Association, which, faced with a sudden drop in contributions, could not even subsidize undergraduate tuition at the same level after 1980 as it had in years past. When, in 1987 the fund-raising for the medical school was faltering, Roberts began a national appeal to raise $4.5 million, claiming that God would "call him home" should he be unsuccessful.

To date, Oral Roberts University's most famous alumnus is probably Clifton

Taulbert, Pulitzer Prize nominee and best-selling author of *Once Upon a Time When We Were Colored* and *The Last Train North*. Taulbert graduated in the class of 1971.

References: David Edwin Harrell Jr., *Oral Roberts: An American Life* (1985); information supplied by admissions office, Oral Roberts University.

Oregon Extension, The (Ashland, Oregon) Begun in the fall of 1975 by a small group of evangelical scholars, the Oregon Extension offers a fall semester of liberal arts study on the site of an old logging camp in the Cascade Mountains of southern Oregon. The curriculum is interdisciplinary and draws on the expertise of five faculty members, who include *DOUGLAS FRANK and Thomas "Sam" Alvord. The program also seeks to capitalize on its location by punctuating periods of intensive study with wilderness outings.

Originally an extension program of *TRINITY COLLEGE, an evangelical school in Deerfield, Illinois, the college severed ties with the program when a new president, *KENNETH M. MEYER, took the college in a more conservative direction in order to placate fundamentalists within Trinity's parent denomination, the *EVANGELICAL FREE CHURCH OF AMERICA. Since 1986, then, the Oregon Extension has been affiliated with *HOUGHTON COLLEGE, a Wesleyan school in western New York.

Reference: Randall Balmer, *Mine Eyes Have Seen the Glory: A Journey into the Evangelical Subculture in America,* 3d ed. (2000).

Original Sin The term "original sin" and its meaning derive from the story of the expulsion of Adam and Eve from Eden as well as from a passage in the Psalms that refers to human birth as being "born in sin." The concept assumes that due to the fall or expulsion, because of Adam and Eve's rebellion against God's commandment to them, they and all their progeny are born in a state of *SIN. This status accounts for why humans grow old, and why they suffer pain and eventually die. Original sin also accounts for humans' propensity to *SIN and act against God's moral code.

For evangelicals, original sin is wiped clean only by Jesus Christ and the sacrifice of his life on behalf of the sins of humanity. Human beings, reduced to a state of sinfulness and driven by physical and evil forces, cannot by themselves overcome this state of *SIN. Only through the intervention of divine *GRACE, and only because of Jesus Christ, can they break free from the taint of original sin.

Orr, James (1844–1913) An opponent of *MODERNISM, Scottish theologian James Orr studied at the University of Glasgow and became a professor at the United Presbyterian Theological College (1891–1901) and the United Free Church College, Glasgow (1901–1913). An expert in German theology, Orr staunchly defended such doctrines as the virgin birth, the resurrection, and biblical *AUTHORITY. He lectured at prominent institutions in North America, and his contribution of several articles to **THE FUNDAMENTALS* lent intellectual credibility to people engaged in the battle against *MODERNISM.

References: James Orr, *The Christian View of God and the World* (1893); idem, *The Bible under Trial* (1907); idem, *The Resurrection of Christ* (1908).

Ortega, Fernando (1957–) An eighth-generation New Mexican, Fernando Ortega began studying classical piano at age eight and later imbibed the musical influences of James Taylor, the Beatles, Jethro Tull, and Janis Joplin. He spent four years on the staff of *CAMPUS CRUSADE FOR CHRIST and a short stint with the *EVANGELICAL FREE CHURCH in Fullerton, California, led at that time by *CHUCK SWINDOLL. His career as a composer, arranger, and recording artist took some time to evolve, but he has won several Dove Awards, bringing an intelligence and a theological sophistication to the *CONTEMPORARY CHRISTIAN MUSIC scene. One critic lauded "a beautiful, haunting voice that is at once passionate and clear." Ortega quotes the church fathers, Martin Lloyd-Jones, and *A. W. TOZER and describes his music as pop infused with classical training. "It's kind of a hybrid of church music and pop music," he explains. "You can hear the influence of the hymns in what I write." His albums include *Night of Your Return, This Bright Hour,* and *The Breaking of the Dawn.*

References: Melissa Riddle, "Fernando Ortega: Bright Boy," *CCM Magazine,* October 1997; Wendy Murray Zoba, "The Hard Songs of Fernando Ortega," *Christianity Today,* January 11, 1999.

Orthodox Presbyterian Church Founded on June 11, 1936, the Orthodox Presbyterian Church was originally called the Presbyterian Church of America until a court ruling in 1939 forced the change of name. The formation of the new denomination was one of several fundamentalist secessions from the Presbyterian Church (USA), which had begun when *J. GRESHAM MACHEN left Princeton Theological Seminary in 1929 to form *WESTMINSTER THEOLOGICAL SEMINARY. Machen had hoped to rally fundamentalist forces within the larger Presbyterian denomination, but when he became convinced that *MODERNISM would prevail, he started a separate denomination. The Orthodox Presbyterian Church prides itself in its fidelity to historic Christianity and Reformed orthodoxy, especially as formulated in the Westminster Confession of Faith.

Reference: D. G. Hart and John Muether, *Fighting the Good Fight: A Brief History of the Orthodox Presbyterian Church* (1995).

Osborn, Daisy (née Washburn) (1924–) Following her marriage to *T. L. OSBORN in 1941, Daisy Osborn became part of a highly successful team of pentecostal *EVANGELISTS. The Osborns, who maintain their headquarters in Tulsa, Oklahoma, have conducted healing *REVIVALS throughout the world. Daisy Osborn edits their *Faith Digest* magazine and serves as president of the Osborn Foundation, which distributes tapes and literature.

Osborn, T(ommy) L(ee) (1923–) A native of rural Oklahoma, T. L. Osborn was converted at age twelve and discerned a call to preach two years later. He married Daisy Washburn in 1941, and they became partners in an evangelistic team, starting in Oklahoma and spending the next several years in California and in Portland, Oregon, before moving to India as missionaries in 1945. Poor health forced their return the next year, whereupon they settled briefly in McMinnville, Oregon, and returned to Portland in 1947.

While attending one of *WILLIAM MARRION BRANHAM's healing crusades, T. L. Osborn became convinced that he could have a similar ministry as a healing *EVANGELIST. He began in Jamaica in the spring of 1948 and continued in Michigan, Pennsylvania, Tennessee, and Texas. The Osborns expanded their evangelistic efforts to the Caribbean, Latin America, and eventually throughout the world. In 1953, they formed the Association for Native Evangelism, which encourages evangelistic work by trained nationals. They opened their headquarters in a new building in Tulsa, Oklahoma, in 1963 and in 1969 established the Osborn Foundation, which distributes films, audiotapes, and literature.

During the tempestuous 1960s and early 1970s, T. L. Osborn made a special effort to appeal to disaffected youth. "I'm slanting every message in language that makes sense to young people," he explained. "We'd better talk on their level, while we still have the chance." Osborn sprouted a beard, allowed his hair to grow longer, and wore "funky" clothes. As the 1970s unfolded, Osborn promoted the so-called *PROSPERITY GOSPEL, urging supporters to contribute more to his ministry in what he called a "pact of plenty," which would return tangible, material benefits to the contributors.

Reference: David Edwin Harrell Jr., *All Things Are Possible: The Healing and Charismatic Revivals in Modern America* (1975).

Osborn, William B(romwell) (1832–1902) One of the founders of the *OCEAN GROVE CAMP MEETING ASSOCIATION, William B. Osborn was the son of an itinerant Methodist minister and his wife. He was converted after a visit to a *CAMP MEETING. In July 1867, Osborn was one of the organizers of the first national *CAMP MEETING, held in Vineland, New Jersey.

Osborn, buoyed by the success of the Vineland gathering, took it upon himself to locate a parcel of land for a permanent *CAMP MEETING site. After surveying the Jersey shore from Sandy Hook to Cape May, Osborn decided on Ocean Grove, in part because of the absence of mosquitoes. He became superintendent of grounds for the new enterprise and was largely responsible for the physical layout of the *CAMP MEETING grounds. After leaving Ocean Grove in 1872, Osborn became a missionary in Jacksonville, Florida, and a traveling *EVANGELIST in India, Australia, Great Britain, and the Middle East.

Osborn Foundation. *See* **Osborn, T(ommy) L(ee).**

Osteen, John (Hillery) (1921–) Born in Paris, Texas, John Osteen studied at *JOHN BROWN UNIVERSITY and Northern Baptist Theological Seminary and was ordained a Southern Baptist in 1942. After serving churches in California and Texas, and while pastor of the Hibbard Memorial Baptist Church in Houston, Osteen was baptized by the Holy Spirit in 1958. His daughter, who had been afflicted with cerebral palsy since birth, was miraculously healed, whereupon Osteen began a healing ministry. He left the Hibbard Memorial Church and began Lakewood Baptist Church in Houston (later renamed Lakewood Church), a charismatic congregation that grew to more than twenty thousand members. Osteen has written several dozen books, publishes *Manna* magazine, and maintains a television ministry.

Outreach of Hope Based in Colorado Springs, Colorado, Outreach of Hope was founded by Dave Dravecky, a Major League pitcher and an evangelical, whose career was cut short by cancer in his throwing arm, which eventually had to be amputated. The mission of the organization is to "offer hope and encouragement through Jesus Christ to those suffering from cancer or amputation." Outreach of Hope contacts individuals afflicted with cancer or amputees and their families through personal visits, phone calls, and correspondence. As of spring 1996, the group had fifty-two hundred individuals or families on a computer database, people who have either contacted the organization or been referred to it or are interested in the work of the group. Outreach of Hope also offers prayer support for patients and their families through weekly staff prayer and the Prayer Warrior Ministry, which connects those with ongoing prayer needs with an individual "prayer warrior," who commits to pray regularly for them.

References: Dave Dravecky, with Tim Stafford, *Comeback* (1990); idem and Jan Dravecky, *When You Can't Come Back: A Story of Courage & Grace* (1994).

Overhead Projector The overhead projector became a fixture in evangelical—especially pentecostal and charismatic—worship in the final quarter of the twentieth century. The catalyst was the widespread use of so-called *PRAISE MUSIC: simple, lilting melodies with an almost mesmerizing quality. Because these songs were new, most had not been published in hymnals (hymnals themselves came to be regarded as stodgy and passé), so the lyrics were projected onto a screen or a wall. The other fortuitous advantage of overhead projectors was that the congregation, freed now from fumbling with the hymnal, could raise its arms in the pentecostal gesture of openness to the Holy Spirit.

Overseas Missionary Fellowship. *See* **Taylor, J(ames) Hudson.**

Owens, Virginia Stem (1941–) Born in Houston, Virginia Stem Owens claims that "I've never wanted to do anything but write—except for reading." She studied at North Texas State University, the University of Kansas, and Iliff School of Theology. Though once involved in radical politics and the women's movement, Owens, who has also written under the pseudonym Eugenia Adams, claims to have no causes other than her fascination with "the cosmic drama of Christ."

References: Virginia Stem Owens, *The Total Image* (1980); idem, *And the Trees Clap Their Hands* (1983); idem, *Wind River Winter* (1985).

Ozman, Agnes N. (LaBerge) (1870–1937) Born in Albany, Wisconsin, into a Methodist household, Agnes N. Ozman moved with her family to Nebraska as a young child and as a young adult attended several *BIBLE INSTITUTES before settling on *CHARLES FOX PARHAM'S *BETHEL BIBLE COLLEGE in Topeka, Kansas. There, on the first day of the new century, January 1, 1901, Parham laid hands on Ozman and prayed that she would receive the *BAPTISM OF THE HOLY SPIRIT. Ozman responded by *SPEAKING IN TONGUES. "I longed for the Holy Spirit to come in more than for my necessary food," Ozman recalled later, "and at night a desire was felt more than for sleep, and I know it was the Lord."

Parham and others used Ozman's experience as proof that *GLOSSOLALIA attested to Spirit *BAPTISM. As word spread, Ozman's experience became exemplary, thereby beginning what would become known as the pentecostal movement in American Protestantism.

Ozman went on to work as a missionary in Omaha, Nebraska. She married Philemon LaBerge, a pentecostal *EVANGELIST, in 1911, and the two of them worked with struggling congregations across the country. She affiliated in 1917 with the *ASSEMBLIES OF GOD, which issued her credentials as an *EVANGELIST.

Reference: Edith L. Blumhofer, *Restoring the Faith: The Assemblies of God, Pentecostalism, and American Culture* (1993).

■ ■ ■

Pacific and Asia Christian University. *See* **Youth with a Mission.**

Pacific Bible College **(Los Angeles, California).** *See* **Point Loma Nazarene College.**

Pacific Bible College **(Spokane, Washington, and Portland, Oregon).** *See* **Warner Pacific College.**

Pacific Bible Institute. *See* **Fresno Pacific College.**

Pacific Bible Seminary. *See* **Pacific Christian College.**

Pacific Christian College **(Fullerton, California)** Pacific Christian College is affiliated with the Christian Church/Church of Christ, and 70 percent of the student body comes from that background. The college was established in 1928 as Pacific Bible Seminary. At first, classes were held in the Alvarado Church of Christ in Los Angeles, but within two years the seminary moved to Long Beach, where it used the building of the First Christian Church there. The college bought land for a separate campus in 1936, and the first building was completed in 1940.

The school took the name Pacific Christian College in 1962. Full regional accreditation followed seven years later, and by 1973 the college had outgrown its facilities in Long Beach and moved to its current campus in Fullerton. Since then, Pacific Christian College has established a School of Graduate Studies, which offers master's degrees in ministry, counseling, business administration, and international development.

Reference: Pacific Christian College 1996–97 Catalog (1996).

Pacific College. *See* **Fresno Pacific College** *or* **George Fox University.**

Pacific Friends Academy. *See* **George Fox University.**

Pacific Garden Mission Originally called Clarke's Mission after the founders, Sarah Dunn Clarke and George Rogers Clarke, the Pacific Garden Mission opened its doors in Chicago on September 15, 1877, amid saloons, gambling dens, and brothels. The outreach ministry to the down-and-out soon outgrew its one-room facility, and the Clarkes procured the Pacific Beer Garden, a notorious hangout, moved their operations there in 1880, and, at the suggestion of ***Dwight L. Moody**, renamed it the Pacific Garden Mission. The mission offered a variety of social services and conducted gospel meetings, both in the facility and on the streetcorners. Some of the more famous converts included ***Billy Sunday**, then a baseball player with the Chicago White Stockings; Harry Monroe, a counterfeiter from Detroit; and ***Mel Trotter**, a hobo who started a similar urban mission in Grand Rapids, Michigan.

The mission moved again in 1922, this time to a former brothel known as the White House, on State Street. The organization has acquired a number of other buildings in the neighborhood and has added shelters for the homeless and medical and dental services. The Pacific Garden Mission has produced evangelistic films and a radio program, *Unshackled*, which offers stories of wretched lives made new through evangelical ***conversions**. Because of its colorful history and its continued success, it remains one of the flagship operations of the rescue mission movement.

Packer, J(ames) I(nnell) (1926–) Though he never resided in the United States, J. I. Packer has exerted an enormous influence on American *EVANGELICALISM, as a scholar, a teacher, and an author. Born in Gloucestershire, England, Packer earned the bachelor's and the doctorate at Oxford University, where he underwent an evangelical *CONVERSION. After teaching for a time in Britain in 1979, he accepted a professorate in theology at *REGENT COLLEGE in Vancouver, British Columbia.

Packer's theological identity is evangelical and Anglican, but firmly within the Reformed tradition. Throughout his career he has been a resolute defender of biblical *INERRANCY, but he has been critical of the triumphalism that frequently attends *EVANGELICALISM in the United States, and he was one of the signatories of the *CALL TO RENEWAL in May 1995.

References: J. I. Packer, *"Fundamentalism" and the Word of God* (1958); idem, *Knowing God* (1973); Mark A. Noll, "The Last Puritan," *Christianity Today,* September 16, 1996; Alister McGrath, *J. I. Packer: A Biography* (1997).

Palau, Luis (1934–) Born in the province of Buenos Aires, Argentina, Luis Palau was converted at the age of twelve and began preaching at the age of eighteen. He studied at St. Alban's College in Argentina and at *MULTNOMAH SCHOOL OF THE BIBLE in Portland, Oregon. Ordained in 1963, Palau conducted his first evangelistic campaign in Bogotá, Colombia, in December 1966, under the auspices of Overseas Crusades. He formed his own evangelistic organization in 1971; the Luis Palau Evangelistic Association has its international headquarters in Portland. Palau conducts *REVIVAL campaigns throughout the Americas, and he has written numerous books and articles for evangelical publications.

References: Luis Palau, *Calling America and the Nations to Christ* (1994); idem, *The Only Hope for America* (1996).

Palm Beach Atlantic College (West Palm Beach, Florida) In 1964, the John D. MacArthur Foundation offered a two-hundred-acre site in Palm Beach Gardens, Florida, to the Education Commission of the Florida Baptist Convention of Southern Baptists, for the purpose of establishing a church college. Although a steering committee was formed, the project was stalled for several years when *EVANGELIST *BILLY GRAHAM announced his intention to build a university in southern Florida. Graham abandoned his plan in 1968, and the Baptist project was resumed, this time under the auspices of the Palm Lake Baptist Association. That year, the trustees approved the name of the new school as Palm Beach Atlantic College.

From the beginning, Palm Beach Atlantic has been open to students of all religious faiths, not only evangelical Christians. Founded during the height of the countercultural movement, however, Palm Beach Atlantic remains committed to instilling in its students "a love for country, traditional American values, and an understanding of and appreciation for the free enterprise economic system." An economics course on the free-market system is part of the general education requirements for all students.

The school earned four-year accreditation in 1972. Since 1988, the college has introduced master's degree programs in education, business, counseling psychology, and human resource development. All graduate classes are scheduled in the evening to accommodate working adults. The Catherine T. MacArthur School of Continuing Education provides support services for older and nontraditional students. In addition to permitting social *DANCING, the college sponsors "God-vibes Rave"—a "Christian alternative to the underground rave scene."

References: *Palm Beach Atlantic College Undergraduate and Graduate Catalog 1996–97* (1996); Thomas C. Hunt and James C. Carper, eds., *Religious Higher Education in the United States: A Source Book* (1996).

Palmer, Bernard (1914–) Born in Central City, Nebraska, Bernard Palmer achieved notoriety in evangelical circles for his fiction, especially the long series of Danny Orlis books he wrote for *BACK TO THE BIBLE broadcast. Palmer, a member of the *EVANGELICAL FREE CHURCH OF AMERICA, supported himself by working in his family's monument business. He spent only a year in college. "I had failed the English test and was put in the 'dumbbell' class," he recalled many years later. "The teacher, with more courage than wisdom, had us write a short story as an assignment. By the time I had finished setting it on paper, I knew writing was for me. I had never done anything half so intriguing."

Palmer's novels, which number into the hundreds, unfailingly offer a strong evangelistic message along with the admonition for believers to surrender their lives completely to God. Most of the adventures are set on the prairies and in the north woods of Minnesota, places where, since childhood, Palmer has lived and visited on vacations. The one major exception to Palmer's faith-adventure genre was *My Son, My Son*, a story of the life and tragic death of his oldest son, Barry.

References: Bernard Palmer, *Parson John (1942)*; idem, *Danny Orlis and the Angle Inlet Mystery* (1954); idem, *Andy Logan and the Oregon Trail Mystery* (1961); idem, *Danny Orlis and the Ice Fishing Escapade* (1964); idem, *Danny Orlis and Kent Gilbert's Tragedy* (1967); idem, *Felicia Cartwright and the Case of the Bad-Eyed Girl* (1970); idem, *Danny Orlis and DeeDee's Defiance* (1970); idem, *My Son, My Son* (1970).

Palmer, Phoebe (née Worrall) (1807–1874) Reared in a Methodist household, Phoebe Worrall married a Methodist physician, Walter Clarke Palmer, in 1827, and they became active in the Allen Street Methodist Church in New York City. A few months after Phoebe Palmer's sister, *SARAH LANKFORD, had an experience of entire *SANCTIFICATION on May 21, 1835, the Palmers and the Lankfords moved into the same house on Rivington Street, near the Allen Street church. There, the sisters began their famous *TUESDAY MEETINGS FOR THE PROMOTION OF HOLINESS, and Phoebe Palmer had her own *SANCTIFICATION experience on July 26, 1837.

In 1839, Palmer became the first woman to be designated a Methodist class leader in New York. She spoke at *CAMP MEETINGS and, together with her sister, helped to organize other *TUESDAY MEETINGS in New England and the mid-Atlantic states. Her travels took her throughout North America and Great Britain, where she exerted an enormous influence on *WILLIAM and *CATHERINE BOOTH, founders of the *SALVATION ARMY. In addition to her *ITINERANCY, Palmer wrote a number of books on holiness themes. *The Promise of the Father*, published in 1859, offered carefully reasoned arguments for the right of women to preach in churches. The Palmers went into the publishing business with the purchase of the *Guide to Holiness* in 1864, which Phoebe edited for the remainder of her life. They later acquired the *Beauty of Holiness* and *Sabbath Miscellany*, which they merged into the *Guide to Holiness*.

Phoebe Palmer's work and writings were important in both the shaping and the propagation of holiness doctrines in the nineteenth century. She set forth what she called an "altar theology," derived from the Old Testament practice of sacrifice. Palmer urged people who wanted to be sanctified, which she regarded as "full *SALVATION," to lay their desire for holiness on the "altar" and trust God to deliver entire *SANCTIFICATION. She issued "holiness altar invitations" and invited people who had received the experience of entire *SANCTIFICATION to testify to it immediately. Palmer's theology was adopted by such holiness groups as the *SALVATION ARMY, the Free Methodists, the Wesleyan Methodists, and the *CHURCH OF THE NAZARENE.

References: Phoebe Palmer, *The Way of Holiness* (1845); idem, *The Promise of the Father* (1859); Charles E. White, *The Beauty of Holiness: Phoebe Palmer as Theologian, Revivalist, Feminist, and Humanitarian* (1986); Harold Raser, *Phoebe Palmer: Her Life and Thought* (1987).

Palmer, Sarah Lankford. *See* **Lankford, Sarah.**

Palmyra Manifesto Meeting in Palmyra, Missouri, in June 1865, following the Civil War, a group of clergy and laymen from the Methodist Episcopal Church, South sought to chart a direction for southern *METHODISM. The Palmyra Manifesto explicitly rejected the attempts by northern Methodists, led by *MATTHEW SIMPSON, to commandeer church properties in the South and to treat southern Methodists as traitors or penitents. The manifesto asserted the integrity and separateness of the Methodist Episcopal Church, South, and while it welcomed improved relations with "all evangelical churches," it pointedly included the Methodist Episcopal Church, North as merely one among many fraternal denominations.

Palosaari, Jim (1937–) Reared in the Midwest, Jim Palosaari was attracted to the theater as a young man and became involved in a number of avant garde productions. By 1967, he made his way to San Francisco's Haight-Ashbury district for the city's Summer of Love. Two years later, Palosaari and his girlfriend decided to take a trip up the west coast to Canada but were sidetracked by a small pentecostal tent *REVIVAL meeting that changed the course of their lives. After converting and being "filled with the Holy Spirit accompanied by the gift of *TONGUES," they became involved in the emerging *JESUS MOVEMENT and soon affiliated with Linda Meissner's Seattle-based Jesus People Army (JPA). Prior to the disbanding of the various JPA groups, the Palosaaris (now married) were sent out as missionaries to the Midwest. They established a successful *JESUS PEOPLE community in Milwaukee, which had its own underground newspaper, *Street Level,* a discipleship training center, and two rock bands: The Sheep and another that eventually became Resurrection Band.

The Milwaukee *JESUS PEOPLE split into four separate groups in 1972. The Palosaaris took one group to Europe on an itinerant missionary journey, which culminated with their financial rescue by English millionaire Kenneth Frampton. Frampton's anxiety over the fate of his two children, who had been recruited by the *CHILDREN OF GOD, caused him to sponsor the "orthodox *JESUS PEOPLE" in their activities, which included combating controversial groups. Palosaari established the Jesus Family community of believers, similar to the Milwaukee group. The Jesus Family sponsored a coffeehouse, a street paper (*Every Man*), a number of rock concerts, and a multimedia rock opera called *The Lonesome Stone.* Their last event before leaving Europe was the staging of a creative arts festival called Greenbelt, which has become an annual event.

After their European venture came to an end in 1974, members of Palosaari's Jesus Family returned to the United States. They continued to tour their *Lonesome Stone* musical for a brief time before disbanding. Still obsessed with his vision of living out the New Testament ideal in community, Jim Palosaari began to recruit a number of former associates to make another attempt. In 1976, a small group of "committed believers" founded the Highway Missionary Society in Victoria, British Columbia, eventually moving to a large piece of property in Oregon. As with his other efforts, Palosaari centered the ministry around the rock 'n' roll *EVANGELISM of the band Servant. Financial mismanagement created problems by the mid-1980s, and the group disbanded finally in December 1987.

Pannell, William E. (1929–) William E. Pannell graduated from Wayne State University and the University of Southern California. He worked throughout his career to bring a measure of understanding to black-white relations among evangelicals, and his articles appeared in many evangelical periodicals. Pannell was professor of preaching and dean of the chapel at *FULLER THEOLOGICAL SEMINARY.

References: William E. Pannell, *My Friend the Enemy* (1968); idem, *The Coming Race Wars?: A Cry for Reconciliation* (1993).

Paradise Garden. *See* **Finster, Howard.**

Parham, Charles Fox (1873–1929) Founder of the Apostolic Faith movement, Charles Fox Parham was born in Muscatine, Iowa, but grew up in rural Kansas, where he experienced a religious *CONVERSION at age thirteen. Often sick as a child with rheumatic fever and other maladies, Parham claimed divine healing while a student at Southwestern Kansas College. He was licensed to preach by the Methodist Episcopal Church but left the denomination in 1894 to become an independent holiness *EVANGELIST. He preached divine healing, *SANCTIFICATION as a second work of *GRACE, and a "third blessing" of the Holy Spirit.

Parham and his wife, Sarah Thislethwaite, opened Beth-el Healing Home in 1898 in Topeka, Kansas, where residents were taught to rely on God alone for healing. During a summer 1900 visit to Shiloh, *FRANK W. SANDFORD's holiness commune in Maine, Parham became convinced of a "*LATTER RAIN" outpouring of the Holy Spirit just prior to the *END TIMES predicted in the book of Revelation. When he returned to Topeka, Parham founded *BETHEL BIBLE SCHOOL and attracted about forty students. After an extended study of the *BIBLE, Parham and his students became convinced that the initial evidence of *BAPTISM OF THE HOLY SPIRIT was *GLOSSOLALIA. One student, *AGNES N. OZMAN, asked Parham and the other students to pray that she would be baptized by the Holy Spirit. On the first day of the new century, January 1, 1901, Ozman began *SPEAKING IN TONGUES, in what her contemporaries interpreted as Chinese, and she was unable to speak English for the ensuing three days. Parham and some of the other students also spoke in *TONGUES, and Parham carried the news to Kansas City, to Galena, Kansas, and beyond.

As Parham traveled throughout Kansas, Oklahoma, and Texas, he organized converts into a loose federation that became known as the Apostolic Faith Church. He opened a Bible school in Houston in 1905. There, a black holiness preacher, *WILLIAM J. SEYMOUR, appropriated Parham's teachings and took them west with him to Los Angeles, where the *AZUSA STREET REVIVAL broke out in 1906. This event would launch the pentecostal movement into a worldwide phenomenon. Parham, for his part, became disillusioned with Seymour (he accused Seymour of dabbling in spiritualism and hypnotism) and hurled some thinly veiled racial slurs at Seymour, an African American. Parham, however, began to lose favor among pentecostals. Amid charges of sexual misconduct and his espousal of *BRITISH ISRAELISM, Parham retreated to Baxter Spring, Kansas, in 1911, where he continued as an *EVANGELIST and Bible teacher.

References: James R. Goff Jr., *Fields White unto Harvest: Charles F. Parham and the Missionary Origins of Pentecostalism* (1988); Edith L. Blumhofer, *Restoring the Faith: The Assemblies of God, Pentecostalism, and American Culture* (1993).

Park, Edwards Amasa (1808–1900) Edwards Amasa Park was born in Providence, Rhode Island, and graduated from Brown University in 1826. He studied theology under *LEONARD WOODS at *ANDOVER THEOLOGICAL SEMINARY and was ordained in 1831 at Braintree, Massachusetts. Park was also influenced by *NATHANIEL WILLIAM TAYLOR at Yale; Park taught briefly at Amherst College and then moved to Andover in 1835, where he remained until his retirement in 1880. In addition to his teaching and administrative duties, Park was editor of *Bibliotheca Sacra* from 1844 until 1884. Theologically, Park saw himself in the tradition of *JONATHAN EDWARDS (he married Edwards's great-granddaughter, Anna Maria Edwards) and the *NEW DIVINITY theologians, but he also sought, with scant success, to reconcile Edwards with the *NEW HAVEN THEOLOGY of Taylor and Horace Bushnell. Park bitterly opposed the German higher criticism and sought, unsuccessfully, to block its incursion at Andover.

References: Edwards Amasa Park, *The Atonement: Discourses and Treatises* (1859); A. C. Cecil, *The Theological Development of Edwards Amasa Park: Last of the "Consistent Calvinists"* (1974).

Parker, Larstella "Star" (1956–) Star Parker, founder of the Coalition on Urban Affairs, a conservative social policy think tank, was converted to evangelical Christianity in 1981 out of drug abuse, promiscuity, multiple *ABORTIONS, and welfare dependency. An outspoken African American who espouses conservative causes, Parker's entry into media began with a three-hour radio talk show from her home. Her conservative views on topics like welfare, *ABORTION, and the Los Angeles riots in the wake of the Rodney King verdict caught the attention of the secular media and led to talk show appearances, the college lecture circuit, and other opportunities.

"Unfortunately," according to Parker, "the current government welfare system usurps authority from God's people to take care of the poor and destroys the incentive for people to build strong families. The church is the one with the best track record of getting people out of poverty, off drugs, out of lawlessness and sexual promiscuity, into employment, and into lifelong marriage."

References: Star Parker, *Pimps, Whores, and Welfare Brats* (1997); Linda Piepenbrink, "A Star Is Reborn," *Today's Christian Woman*, July/August 1997.

Parkhurst, Charles H(enry) (1842–1933) One of the leaders of the *SOCIAL GOSPEL, Charles H. Parkhurst was born in Framingham, Massachusetts, and graduated from Amherst College. After a pastorate in Lenox, Massachusetts, Parkhurst assumed the pulpit of New York City's Madison Square Presbyterian Church in 1880. In addition to his pastoral duties, he became head of the Society for the Prevention of Crime in 1891, which he used as a platform for civic reform during the progressive era. Parkhurst's most famous sermon was delivered on Valentine's Day, 1892, when he announced a campaign to root out corruption in New York City. He denounced operatives of the Tammany Hall machine as "a lying, perjured, rum-soaked, and libidinous lot" and "the polluted harpies that, under the pretense of governing this city, are feeding day and night on its quivering vitals."

Parkhurst went underground, dressed in disguise, in order to explore—and to expose—the city's underworld of brothels, saloons, and opium dens. He revealed the names of corrupt politicians and dishonest police in his sermons, all the while pushing relentlessly for reform. In part because of his insistence, a commission was formed to investigate the corruption. Parkhurst's efforts led (at least indirectly) to the 1894 election of William L. Strong as mayor on the reform Fusion Party ticket, the appointment of Theodore Roosevelt as head of the police board the next year, and the consolidation of New York City in 1898.

References: Charles H. Parkhurst, *Our Fight with Tammany* (1895); idem, *My Forty Years in New York* (1923).

Parsley, Rod(ney) (1957–) The cofounder and pastor of World Harvest Church in Columbus, Ohio, Rod Parsley was born in eastern Kentucky but grew up in central Ohio. He started a church, Word of Life (originally, Sunrise Chapel) in 1977 and began a television program, *Breakthrough*, in the early 1980s. A dramatic and effective fire-and-brimstone preacher, Parsley attracted larger and larger audiences, both on the radio and in his church, which in 1989 became known as World Harvest Church. Parsley, a faith healer, preaches the so-called *PROSPERITY THEOLOGY—and he lives by it. He has a lavish home and travels by private jet. World Harvest Church also operates a retreat center, a retirement home, World Harvest Christian Academy, and World Harvest Bible College.

Parsons, Henry Martyn (1828–1913) Henry Martyn Parsons, born in Connecticut and graduated from Yale College and Connecticut Theological Institute, served churches in Massachusetts and New York before accepting the pulpit at Knox Presbyterian Church, Toronto, in 1880, where he remained until his death. Parsons was one of the most influential premillennialists at the turn of the century. He helped to organize the *NIAGARA PROPHECY CONFERENCE and served on the board of the Toronto Willard Tract Society. He taught at the Toronto Bible Training School and published many books and articles on *PREMILLENNIALISM.

Partners in Harvest Partners in Harvest, a kind of quasidenomination, was formed early in 1996 as "an open family for autonomous churches." The catalyst was the December 1995 expulsion of the Toronto Airport Christian Fellowship, the progenitor of the *TORONTO BLESSING, from the *ASSOCIATION OF VINEYARD CHURCHES. The Vineyard organization, eager to align more with *EVANGELICALISM proper than with

*PENTECOSTALISM, had taken exception to some of the more charismatic manifestations in Toronto. The Toronto congregation organized Partners in Harvest, which includes both independent congregations and churches formerly affiliated with Vineyard, for those affected by the *TORONTO BLESSING.

Pasadena College. *See* **Point Loma Nazarene College.**

Patterson, Paige (1943–) A contender for sectarianism within the *SOUTHERN BAPTIST CONVENTION, Paige Patterson was a protégé of *W. A. CRISWELL, serving as president of the Criswell Center for Biblical Studies and as managing editor of the *Criswell Study Bible.* He grew up in Texas, started preaching at age fourteen, and received the Th.M. from New Orleans Theological Seminary in 1968. Patterson's theology is unwaveringly conservative and premillennial, and he regards biblical *INERRANCY as a touchstone of the faith. Patterson, in league with Paul Pressler and other conservatives within the *SOUTHERN BAPTIST CONVENTION, was largely responsible for the conservative takeover of the denomination in 1979. "It is not bigotry to insist on doctrinal purity," he wrote in 1968. "It is concern for lost men that should prompt us to guard the great doctrines of the *BIBLE."

In 1992, Patterson became president of Southeastern Baptist Theological Seminary in Wake Forest, North Carolina. Patterson was elected president of the *SOUTHERN BAPTIST CONVENTION in 1998. "Anybody who wants to believe that the *BIBLE is true and is deeply concerned about reaching the world for Christ is going to be increasingly happy in the *SOUTHERN BAPTIST CONVENTION," he announced. "Those with serious questions about the validity and veracity of certain portions of the Word and who do not have a deep commitment to *EVANGELISM and missions will be less comfortable with the *SOUTHERN BAPTIST CONVENTION of the twenty-first century."

References: Paige Patterson, *Living in Hope of Eternal Life* (1968); Charles W. Allen, "Paige Patterson: Contender for Baptist Sectarianism," *Review and Expositor,* LXXIX (winter 1992); John W. Kennedy, "Patterson's Election Seals Conservative Control," *Christianity Today,* July 13, 1998.

Patton, Francis Landey (1843–1932) A Presbyterian clergyman, Francis Landey Patton's lengthy and distinguished career at Princeton began as a student at Princeton Theological Seminary from 1865 to 1869. He was named professor of the relations of philosophy and science to Christian religion at the seminary in 1881, a position he held until assuming the presidency of the College of New Jersey in 1888. In 1884, Landey took over *A. A. HODGE's post as coeditor of the *Presbyterian Review.* Following his tenure at the College of New Jersey, Patton served as president of Princeton Seminary from 1902 until his retirement in 1913.

Patty, Sandi (1956–) Sandi Patty (Sandi Patti) was one of the biggest stars in gospel and inspirational music in the 1980s and early 1990s, but her 1995 disclosure of personal troubles seriously affected her popularity. A graduate of *ANDERSON UNIVERSITY, Patty earned five Grammy Awards for *GOSPEL MUSIC between 1984 and 1991 and earned seven additional Grammy nominations. For 1986, 1987, 1988, and 1989, she was named *Billboard* magazine's "Inspirational Artist of the Year." With three platinum and five gold records, she dominated the *CONTEMPORARY CHRISTIAN MUSIC scene; she performed on six continents, touring with

*BILLY GRAHAM, and appearing on *The Tonight Show* several times. A friendship with George and Barbara Bush ensued, along with invitations to sing at the 1988 and 1992 Republican National Conventions, and the festivities surrounding the 1989 presidential inauguration.

By the mid-1990s Patty had won thirty-four *GOSPEL MUSIC ASSOCIATION Dove Awards, more than any other artist, but rumors of a rocky marriage had an effect on her popularity. In 1992, Patty canceled a leg of her tour and filed for divorce from her husband, to whom she had been married for thirteen years. The following year she came forward with an account of childhood sexual abuse. That same year, with the release of her new album, *Le Voyage*, she changed her last name back to its original spelling; the "Patti" by which she had been known for more than a decade was the result of a misprint on an early album cover. Patty canceled another tour in 1994 and confessed to her Anderson, Indiana, Church of God pastor that she had begun an extramarital affair with Don Peslis, one of her backup singers, three years before, when they were both married to others. Patty also confessed to her church council. Then, eight days after she married Peslis in August 1995, she agreed to an interview with **CHRISTIANITY TODAY* in which she fully disclosed her relationship with the singer and fitness instructor. This admission threatened Patty's place in the Christian music world: Some evangelical book and record stores pulled her recordings from the shelves.

Patty responded by setting up, at her pastor's suggestion, an "accountability group" of acquaintances who have the right to call her to question when they sense her behavior is "straying." By 1996, her career had shown signs of recovery, with prime-time specials on *The Nashville Network* and *The Family Channel,* and a new, heavily promoted Christmas release, "O Holy Night!" Patty also earned two more Grammy nominations in 1996 under the "Best Pop/Contemporary Gospel Album" category for her records *Find It on the Wings* and *My Utmost for His Highest,* which also won her another Dove Award. Patty remains married to Don Peslis, and they have adopted a child, bringing the number of children the couple has from present and past marriages to a total of eight.

References: Sandy Smith, "The Resurrection of Sandi Patti," *Nashville Tennessean,* October 13, 1996; Timothy C. Morgan, "Sandi Patty Stages Comeback," *Christianity Today,* January 12, 1998; information provided by Word Records.

Paulk, Earl (Pearly), Jr. (1927–) Reared in a pentecostal household, Earl Paulk Jr. started preaching in Greenville, South Carolina, at the age of seventeen and later became pastor of the Hemphill Church of God in Atlanta. He studied at Furman University and at Emory University's Candler School of Theology, where he earned the M.Div. in 1952. Together with his brother Don, Paulk founded the Gospel Harvester Church in Atlanta in 1960. When the congregation moved to the suburbs thirteen years later, it took the name Chapel Hill Harvester Church and soon grew into a congregation of more than ten thousand. Paulk has a weekly television program, *Harvester Christian Network,* and his own liberal arts college, Earl Paulk College, which opened in 1986. In December 1992, a former staff member accused Paulk of sexual harassment, prompting others to come forward with similar charges against other pastors. The charges, though vigorously denied, have affected both the membership and the giving at the church.

References: Earl Paulk Jr., *Satan Unmasked* (1984); idem, *Thrust in the Sickle and Reap* (1986); idem, *20/20 Vision: A Clear View of the Kingdom of God* (1988).

Peale, Norman Vincent (1898–1993) Born into a devout Methodist household in Bowersville, Ohio, Norman Vincent Peale graduated from Ohio Wesleyan University in 1920. After a brief flirtation with a career in journalism, where he learned the importance of communicating in simple language, he enrolled in the School of Theology at Boston University in the fall of 1921. After completing his studies three years later, Peale took on a struggling Methodist congregation in Brooklyn, New York. He obtained from the gas company listings of new residents who were moving into a nearby housing development, knocked on their doors, addressed them by name, and invited them to church. After success in Brooklyn, Peale moved on to University Methodist Church in Syracuse, New York, in 1927. He placed advertisements in newspapers asking why it was "suddenly hard to get a seat" in University Church, a tactic similar to one he had used in Brooklyn. The inference was blatantly false in both venues, but in both places it became a self-fulfilling prophecy. While in Syracuse, Peale started a radio ministry; he also met and married Ruth Stafford.

By 1932, Peale was receiving invitations to speak from across the country. He also was offered two pulpits: that of the well-established First Methodist Church in Los Angeles and the Marble Collegiate Church in lower Manhattan, a congregation of the *Reformed Church in America that had declined to around two hundred auditors. With his characteristic pluckiness and appetite for a challenge, Peale chose the latter.

Peale's fortunes at Marble Collegiate, though dismal at first, began to change when he was invited by the Federal Council of Churches to begin a radio broadcast in 1933. *The Art of Living,* a weekly program, remained on the air for four decades. The simple, anecdotal preaching that characterized his pulpit presence played well over the radio airwaves. By the mid-1940s, Peale published *Guideposts,* which contained inspirational meditations.

Peale's theology, like that of his protégé, *Robert Schuller, does not fit neatly into conventional categories, and many evangelicals would protest that his pragmatism and his Dale Carnegie–like theology of positive thinking represent a departure from orthodox *Evangelicalism. Peale's emphasis on prayer and the centrality of Christ as the source of power for the Christian, however, mollified others. Certainly Peale's winsome personality disarmed many critics, some of whom would dismiss him simply as a theological lightweight.

In the realm of politics, Peale was a fervent anticommunist and a thoroughgoing Republican. He opposed Franklin Roosevelt's New Deal and befriended Dwight David Eisenhower and Richard Nixon. During the 1960 presidential campaign, he helped to arrange a meeting with Protestant leaders, including *Billy Graham, for the purpose of derailing the candidacy of John F. Kennedy, a Roman Catholic and the Democratic candidate.

References: Norman Vincent Peale, *The Art of Living* (1937); idem, *You Can Win* (1938); idem, *The Power of Positive Thinking* (1952); idem, *Sin, Sex, and Self-Control* (1965); idem, *Positive Thinking for a Time Like This* (1975); idem, *The True Joy of Positive Living: An Autobiography* (1984); Arthur Gordon, *Norman Vincent Peale: Minister to Millions* (1958); Carol V. R. George, *God's Salesman: Norman Vincent Peale and the Power of Positive Thinking* (1993); Thomas E.

Frank, s.v. "Norman Vincent Peale," in Charles H. Lippy, ed., *Twentieth-Century Shapers of American Popular Religion* (1989).

Pearl River Revival Also known as the "Pearl River Happening," the Pearl River Revival took place in April 2000 at Pearl River Central High School, a public school in Mississippi. It began with a presentation by a student-led group, the local chapter of the *FELLOWSHIP OF CHRISTIAN ATHLETES, on April 12, a nonmandatory event that drew about 90 percent of the school's students. By the end of the presentation, students were weeping, praying, and confessing their sins publicly. News of the *REVIVAL spread by means of Christian radio and the Internet. While detractors worried that the *REVIVAL represented a breach in the wall of separation between church and state, supporters saw it as evidence that God was not excluded from the public schools. Although the fervor died down, students reported some lasting effects in the school. "People now are much more friendly with each other," a sophomore reported. "They're not so critical."

Reference: "Revival Hits Public School," *Christian Century*, June 7–14, 2000.

Peniel College. *See* **Southern Nazarene University.**

Peniel University. *See* **Southern Nazarene University.**

Pennington, Edith Mae (née Patterson) (1902–1974) Edith Mae Patterson, a pentecostal pastor and *EVANGELIST, was born in Pine Bluff, Arkansas, and studied to become a teacher. Her life took an unexpected turn, however, when her aunt submitted Edith Mae's photograph to a newspaper contest for the "Most Beautiful Girl in the U.S." She won the contest, toured the country, developed a nightclub act, pursued a career in Hollywood, and married her business manager, J. B. Pennington.

Edith Mae Pennington's visit to a small pentecostal church in Oklahoma City, Oklahoma, in 1925 again changed the direction of her life. She experienced an evangelical *CONVERSION and, soon thereafter, the *BAPTISM OF THE HOLY SPIRIT. She claimed to be "delivered" from her desire to attend theaters and to wear jewelry. The Penningtons moved to Birmingham, Alabama, where Edith Mae pursued a call to the ministry. She returned to Pine Bluff, Arkansas, became assistant pastor of a newly formed *ASSEMBLIES OF GOD congregation, divorced her husband, and was ordained by the Assemblies in 1930. A gifted orator who railed knowingly against the perils of "*WORLDLINESS," Pennington became an itinerant *EVANGELIST until settling in Shreveport, Louisiana, where she founded Full Gospel Temple, affiliated with the *ASSEMBLIES OF GOD, in 1937. Thirteen years after her ordination, Pennington resigned from the denomination and formed an independent church, The Plant of Renown.

References: Edith Mae Pennington, *From the Floodlights to the Light of the Cross* (n.d.); Edith L. Blumhofer, *Restoring the Faith: The Assemblies of God, Pentecostalism, and American Culture* (1993).

Pensacola Outpouring. *See* **Brownsville Revival.**

Pentecost, George F(rederick) (1842–1920) Born in Albion, Illinois, George F. Pentecost was converted to evangelical Christianity while attending Georgetown College. He left school in

1862 to enlist as a chaplain in the Union Army and soon thereafter became a Baptist minister, serving congregations in Indiana, Kentucky, New York, and Massachusetts. Pentecost earned a reputation as a gifted preacher. He joined with *DWIGHT L. MOODY in evangelistic work in 1878 but accepted the pulpit at Tomkins Avenue Congregational Church in Brooklyn, New York, two years later. Pentecost struck out on his own as an itinerant *EVANGELIST, conducting *REVIVAL campaigns in India and Great Britain, where he served for a time as pastor of London's Marylebone Church. Upon his return to the United States in 1897, Pentecost served as pastor of First Presbyterian Church in Yonkers, New York. He retired for more than a decade but was coaxed out of retirement by a Presbyterian congregation for the final years of his life.

References: George F. Pentecost, *Out of Egypt* (1884); idem, *Grace Abounding in the Forgiveness of Sins* (1897).

Pentecost, J(ohn) Dwight (1915–) A graduate of Hampden-Sydney College and *DALLAS THEOLOGICAL SEMINARY, J. Dwight Pentecost was ordained in the Presbyterian Church. After serving two pastorates in Pennsylvania, Pentecost, who had been steeped in dispensational premillennial theology at Dallas Seminary, joined the faculty of *PHILADELPHIA COLLEGE OF THE BIBLE. He returned to Dallas Seminary for his doctorate in 1953 and chose to concentrate his studies on *ESCHATOLOGY, the doctrine of the *END TIMES.

Pentecost soon established himself as an exponent and a popularizer of dispensational thought. Several of his books were widely read by fundamentalists. Concurrent with his duties at Dallas Seminary, Pentecost served as pastor of Grace Bible Church in Dallas, and he was a popular speaker at Bible and prophecy conferences.

References: J. Dwight Pentecost, *Things to Come* (1958); idem, *The Divine Comforter* (1963); idem, *The Words and Work of Jesus Christ* (1970).

Pentecostal Assemblies of America. *See* **Pentecostal Church of God.**

Pentecostal Assemblies of Canada The Pentecostal Assemblies of Canada, formed in the wake of the *AZUSA STREET REVIVAL, received its charter on May 17, 1919. When the group affiliated with the United States–based *ASSEMBLIES OF GOD the following year, it firmly repudiated the "Jesus Only" doctrine that had been popular among many Canadian pentecostals, whereupon Frank Small of Winnipeg, Manitoba, organized the Apostolic Church of Pentecost in 1921, a Jesus Only group. The Pentecostal Assemblies of Canada and the *ASSEMBLIES OF GOD parted amicably in 1925 because of differences in missions policies.

Canadian pentecostals engaged vigorously in both *EVANGELISM and missions; by 1925, the Canadian Pentecostal Bible College had opened its doors in Winnipeg, Manitoba, and the group began to develop an infrastructure very similar to (and, to some extent, intertwined with) the evangelical subculture in the United States. In addition to educational institutions, the Pentecostal Assemblies has also established shelters for girls, hospitals, and retirement homes. Looking toward the twenty-first century, the denomination undertook an ambitious program of church-planting.

Reference: Thomas William Miller, *Canadian Pentecostals: A History of the Pentecostal Assemblies of Canada* (1994).

Pentecostal Assemblies of Newfoundland. *See* **Garrigus, Alice Belle.**

Pentecostal Church of God Formed in Chicago in 1919 under the name Pentecostal Assemblies of America, this body has had headquarters in Chicago; Ottumwa, Iowa; and, currently, Joplin, Missouri. The church changed its name to the Pentecostal Church of God in America in 1922 and in 1979 dropped "in America."

The theology of the Pentecostal Church of God is evangelical and pentecostal, affirming the evangelical tenets of the *AUTHORITY of Scripture, the Trinity, the deity of Christ, the need for *SALVATION through Christ, and the *SECOND COMING. The church also emphasizes the pentecostal beliefs in the *BAPTISM OF THE HOLY SPIRIT (with the accompanying manifestation of *SPEAKING IN TONGUES) and divine healing. Foot washing is practiced in some congregations. The denomination observes the ordinances of the *LORD'S SUPPER and *BAPTISM by immersion.

Church *POLITY follows a Methodist/holiness/pentecostal model with districts overseen by district superintendents. The church is headed by a general superintendent, with assistance from the general secretary-treasurer and other secretaries and directors. A general convention meets biennially; district conventions usually meet annually. The church claims 119,200 members in 1,224 local churches.

References: Frank S. Mead and Samuel S. Hill, *Handbook of Denominations in the United States,* 10th ed. (1996); J. Gordon Melton, *The Encyclopedia of American Religions,* 3d ed. (1993); *1997 Yearbook of American and Canadian Churches.*

Pentecostal Collegiate Institute. *See* **Eastern Nazarene College.**

Pentecostal Free Will Baptist Church As the name suggests, this body was formed from the merger of several Free Will Baptist associations. The associations, located mainly in North Carolina, had come under the influence of pentecostal teaching in the early years of the twentieth century. The associations had accepted pentecostal doctrine but had remained in the national Free Will Baptist Association. These various bodies formed a general conference in 1943, but many were dissatisfied with the organization. The conference structure was abolished in 1959, to be replaced with a single charter and name for the group: the Pentecostal Free Will Baptist Church.

Church doctrine is a mixture of pentecostal and Baptist beliefs, which include regeneration through faith in the shed blood of Jesus Christ, *SANCTIFICATION as a second (and instantaneous) work of *GRACE, the *BAPTISM OF THE HOLY SPIRIT, divine healing, and the premillennial *SECOND COMING of Christ. *POLITY in the Pentecostal Free Will Baptist Church is congregational. The Church meets in general convention biennially. A general superintendent heads the executive board, which oversees the implementation of church programs. Headquarters are in Dunn, North Carolina. The church has 148 local congregations with 11,757 total members.

References: Frank S. Mead and Samuel S. Hill, *Handbook of Denominations in the United States,* 10th ed. (1996); J. Gordon Melton, *The Encyclopedia of American Religions,* 3d ed. (1993).

Pentecostal Handshake In the early decades of the pentecostal movement, the laity would often make contributions to pastors and missionaries by simply folding currency into their right hands and shaking hands with the pastor or missionary.

This "pentecostal handshake" was a discreet way to demonstrate support and encouragement, without any hint of ostentation. In more recent years, as pentecostals themselves have become more middle class and upwardly mobile, the practice has declined, in part because of the desire for tax-deductible receipts.

Pentecostal Holiness Church. *See* **International Pentecostal Holiness Church.**

Pentecostal Literary and Bible Training School for Christian Workers. *See* **Trevecca Nazarene University.**

Pentecostalism Pentecostalism coalesced as a movement in the early years of the twentieth century. On the first day of the new century, January 1, 1901, a student at *BETHEL BIBLE COLLEGE in Topeka, Kansas, *AGNES N. OZMAN, began *SPEAKING IN TONGUES. This experience, also known as *GLOSSOLALIA, was explicitly linked to the first Pentecost, recorded in Acts 2, when the early Christians were filled with the Holy Spirit. The movement, with its teachings about the *BAPTISM OF THE HOLY SPIRIT, spread to Texas and then to Los Angeles, where it burst into broader consciousness during the *AZUSA STREET REVIVAL.

The roots of pentecostalism, however, reached back into the nineteenth century and the *HOLINESS MOVEMENT, which sought to promote personal holiness (and *JOHN WESLEY's doctrine of Christian perfection) within *METHODISM and other American denominations. By the end of the century, however, holiness advocates were feeling increasingly marginalized, and many left *METHODISM to form their own denominations. The pentecostal movement, with its distinctive emphasis on the second blessing or *BAPTISM OF THE HOLY SPIRIT, as evidenced by *GLOSSOLALIA, spread quickly after the *AZUSA STREET REVIVAL. By the close of the twentieth century, pentecostalism had spread to Latin America; scholars estimate the presence of fifteen to twenty million pentecostals in Brazil, for example, which translates to 10 to 20 percent of the population. In the United States, pentecostalism took various denominational forms, including the *PENTECOSTAL HOLINESS CHURCH, the *CHURCH OF GOD IN CHRIST, the *CHURCH OF GOD (CLEVELAND, TENNESSEE), and the *ASSEMBLIES OF GOD, which was organized in 1914 and is the largest pentecostal denomination in North America.

Pentecostal worship today is characterized by ecstasy and the familiar posture of upraised arms, a gesture of openness to the Holy Spirit. Pentecostals generally believe in the gifts of the Holy Spirit, including divine healing, in addition to *SPEAKING IN TONGUES.

References: Edith L. Blumhofer, *Restoring the Faith: The Assemblies of God, Pentecostalism, and American Culture* (1993); H. Newton Malony and A. Adams Lovekin, *Glossolalia: Behavioral Science Perspectives on Speaking in Tongues* (1985); Harvey Cox, *Fire from Heaven: The Rise of Pentecostal Spirituality and the Reshaping of Religion in the Twenty-first Century* (1995); Richard Schaull and Waldo A. Cesar, *Pentecostalism and the Future of the Christian Churches: Promises, Limitations, Challenges* (2000).

People's Gospel Hour. *See* **Rockwood, Perry F.**

Peretti, Frank E. (1951–) Evangelical novelist and children's book author Frank E. Peretti was born to pentecostal parents in Alberta and moved with his family to Seattle while still an infant. His childhood was marked by a grave and disfiguring illness that left him, even after medical procedures, with a long, black, protruding tongue. His parents took him to *ORAL ROBERTS for divine healing, but the *EVANGELIST was stymied and declared, "I've never seen anything like this before." Peretti recalls in *The Wounded Spirit* the kind of ridicule and abuse he suffered in school.

Some of the darkness of spirit that Peretti endured in those years surfaces in his novels, and his suffering clearly has informed his writing. *The Wounded Spirit* expresses sympathy for other "outcasts," and he credits his survival to his knowledge of "a Savior who taught us to turn the other cheek and forgive."

References: Frank E. Peretti, *The Wounded Spirit: This Is Not Fiction, This Is Real* (2001); idem, *This Present Darkness* (1988); idem, *Prophet* (1992); idem, *The Visitation* (1999).

Perkins, John M. (1930–) Born to black sharecroppers in New Hebron, Mississippi, John M. Perkins left Mississippi for southern California in 1947, shortly after his brother, a decorated military veteran, was killed during an altercation with a deputy marshal. After a stint in the military, Perkins became involved with a series of religious groups, including the Jehovah's Witnesses, Christian Science, and Father Divine Peace Mission, before settling on evangelical Christianity. He "said yes to Jesus Christ" in 1957, and three years later Perkins and his wife, Vera Mae, decided to return to Mississippi with their five children in order to bring both the *GOSPEL and racial reconciliation to the Piney Woods section of Mississippi.

Perkins began *VOICE OF CALVARY MINISTRIES in Mendenhall (the group is known today as *MENDENHALL MINISTRIES), an organization devoted to *EVANGELISM as well as social amelioration. He organized voter registration drives, a housing cooperative, an elementary school, a health center, and a leadership training program. Perkins's activities, however, stirred animosity among whites in the town. In response to the beating of a young African American by the police, Perkins organized a boycott of white businesses in Mendenhall, beginning just before Christmas in 1969. On February 7, 1970, after two vanloads of students associated with *VOICE OF CALVARY were stopped in a nearby county, Perkins went to the Rankin County courthouse and barely survived a night of beatings at the hands of the sheriff and his deputies. Incredibly, criminal charges were brought against Perkins, and Perkins's civil suit ended in compromise settlements.

While convalescing, Perkins resolved "to take a *GOSPEL of love to whites filled with hate." He refined his strategies and moved his base of operations to Jackson, the state capital, where he organized *VOICE OF CALVARY there to address urban needs. In 1981, satisfied that local leadership in Jackson and Mendenhall could continue the work, Perkins moved to a poor section of Pasadena, California, where he has begun similar missions. Another entity, the John M. Perkins Foundation for Reconciliation and Development, has assisted in the organization of other such ministries.

References: John Perkins, *Let Justice Roll Down* (1976); Randall Balmer, *Mine Eyes Have Seen the Glory: A Journey into the Evangelical Subculture in America*, 3d ed. (2000).

Perkins, Spencer (1954–1998) A leader in the emerging racial reconciliation movement among evangelicals and a son of *JOHN M. PERKINS, Spencer Perkins was director of the International Study Center of *VOICE OF CALVARY MINISTRIES. Together with Chris Rice, Perkins edited *Reconcilers* magazine (formerly known as *Urban Family*), an evangelical periodical that advocated reconciliation and community development.

Reference: Spencer Perkins and Chris Rice, *More Than Equals: Racial Healing for the Sake of the Gospel* (1993).

Perry, Troy (Deroy) (1940–) The founder of the *UNIVERSAL FELLOWSHIP OF METROPOLITAN COMMUNITY CHURCHES, Troy Perry was born in Tallahassee, Florida, and became an *EVANGELIST in the *CHURCH OF GOD (CLEVELAND, TENNESSEE) at the age of sixteen. He married Pearl Pinion, the daughter of a Church of God minister, two years later. Perry attended Midwest Bible College and became pastor of a Church of God congregation in Joliet, Illinois. While in Joliet, Perry was caught in a homosexual affair; he shifted his affiliation to the Church of God of Prophecy, which was unaware of Perry's sexual orientation.

Perry attended *MOODY BIBLE INSTITUTE during the 1960–61 academic year and then became pastor of a church in Santa Ana, California, where he made contacts with the homosexual community in southern California. Perry's homosexuality and his conviction that God would not create gay people "just to have something to sit around and hate" led to the dissolution of his marriage and a break of his ties with the Church of God of Prophecy. Perry, who calls himself a "liberal evangelical," held a worship service in his home at Huntington Park, California, in October 1968, which drew only twelve people. A year later, however, his Sunday gatherings filled a Los Angeles theater. The *UNIVERSAL FELLOWSHIP OF METROPOLITAN COMMUNITY CHURCHES, whose trademark is the acceptance of everyone, regardless of sexual orientation, has evolved into the largest religious organization accepting of gays and lesbians.

References: Troy Perry, with Charles L. Lucas, *The Lord Is My Shepherd and He Knows I'm Gay* (1972); idem, with Thomas L. P. Swicegood, *Don't Be Afraid Anymore* (1990); "Gays and the Gospel: An Interview with Troy Perry," *Christian Century*, September 25–October 2, 1996.

Peterson, Eugene H. (1932–) Eugene H. Peterson, the James M. Houston Professor of Spiritual Theology at Regent College in Vancouver, British Columbia, decided early in his career that he would never lead a church composed of more people than he could remember by name. He founded and then ministered to the three hundred members of Christ Our King, in Bel Air, Maryland, for twenty-nine years before joining the faculty of *REGENT COLLEGE. Peterson's writings on prayer and spirituality have been enormously influential among evangelicals.

References: Eugene H. Peterson, *Reversed Thunder: The Revelation of John and the Praying Imagination* (1991); idem, *The Contemplative Pastor: Returning to the Art of Spiritual Direction* (1993); idem, *Leap over a Wall: Earthy Spirituality for Everyday Christians* (1997).

Peterson, Michael L(ynn) (1950–) Born in Linton, Indiana, and educated at *ASBURY COLLEGE, the University of Kentucky, and the State University of New York at Buffalo, Michael L. Peterson has been a leader in *EVANGELICALISM's push into the field of philosophy of religion. He was involved in the significant shift to Christian faith that has taken place among professional philosophers in America since the late 1970s. Peterson was an original member of the *SOCIETY OF CHRISTIAN PHILOSOPHERS, which was founded in 1978. In the early 1980s, he conceived of a scholarly journal as the official publishing arm of the society and served as its managing editor. **THE JOURNAL OF FAITH AND PHILOSOPHY*, published at ***ASBURY COLLEGE**, is widely regarded in the profession as the most prestigious international scholarly journal in the field of philosophy of religion.

Peterson's work has focused on the importance of education in the service of Christianity, the rational integrity of Christian faith, the benefits of philosophy for thinking Christians, and the need for responsible dialogue with people who hold other points of view. Much of his publishing has been aimed at showing that the existence of evil and suffering do not render belief in the Christian God unreasonable, and the reasonableness of believing that the depth of evil we experience may be possible only in a theistic universe. In addition to his work within the academy, Peterson has also sought to bring theological and philosophical issues before the general public through his involvement in a PBS documentary, *Against a Silent Sky*, and his writing in such popular magazines as **CHRISTIANITY TODAY*.

References: Michael L. Peterson, *Evil and the Christian God* (1982); idem, *Philosophy of Education: Issues and Options* (1986).

Petra Petra, one of the oldest Christian rock bands, was formed by lead guitarist Bob Hartman in Fort Wayne, Indiana, in 1972. Their name means "rock" in Greek. Petra struggled commercially throughout the 1970s; at times, their status as one of the original "Jesus Music" bands proved as much a liability as an asset, for their willingness to experiment with rock music was quite controversial. The band was dropped from their original contract with Myrrh Records because of slow sales, and for several years they survived by playing small locations in the Midwest. In the late 1970s, however, Petra was signed by Star Song Records. Soon after, they released their first radio hit, "Why Should the Father Bother." Petra enjoyed additional success in the years that followed, both for new material as well as older songs like "God Gave Rock and Roll to You," "Killing My Old Man," and "Backsliding Blues."

In 1995, Petra released *No Doubt*, their twentieth album, by which time they had also won three Grammy Awards. That year, Bob Hartman announced he would no longer tour with the group. He was replaced by a twenty-one-year-old guitarist, David Lichens, who previously performed with Bon Jovi. Hartman continues to write and produce songs for Petra; he also acts as manager.

Pettingill, William Leroy (1866–1950) One of the founders of ***PHILADELPHIA COLLEGE OF THE BIBLE**, William Leroy Pettingill was ordained by the ***NATIONAL BAPTIST CONVENTION** in 1899 and became pastor of North Church, Wilmington, Delaware. In the course of his thirty-year tenure, Pettingill emerged as a powerful proponent of conservative evangelical theology, as an author, a preacher, and as one of the consulting editors for the **SCOFIELD REFERENCE BIBLE*.

Having worked with ***C. I. SCOFIELD** on the ***BIBLE**, Pettingill and Scofield also collaborated in the founding of ***PHILADELPHIA COLLEGE OF THE BIBLE**, a school dedicated to fundamentalist ideals, in 1914. Scofield served as president and Pettingill as dean, a post he retained until his retirement in 1928. A popular speaker at Bible and prophecy conferences, Pettingill was involved in the formation of the Independent Fundamental Churches of America, and he was a prolific writer. He founded two periodicals,

Serving-and-Waiting (1911) and *Just a Word* (1928), both devoted to fundamentalist and dispensationalist ideas. In 1948, near the end of his life, Pettingill accepted the call to be pastor of First Baptist Church, New York City.

Pew, J(ohn) Howard (1882–1971) A graduate of *GROVE CITY COLLEGE and the Massachusetts Institute of Technology, J. Howard Pew entered his family's business, the Sun Oil Company, as an engineer and quickly worked his way up the ranks until he was appointed president in 1912. During his thirty-five-year tenure, Pew showed himself to be a savvy industrialist, but his real passions lay in conservative theological and religious causes. When he resigned as president in 1947 and became chairman of the board at Sunoco, Pew devoted more of his energies to philanthropy.

His interests ranged from *GROVE CITY COLLEGE (where he served as president of the board of trustees for many years) to *BILLY GRAHAM's fledgling magazine **CHRISTIANITY TODAY* to *CARL MCINTIRE's various fundamentalist enterprises. Following Pew's death in 1971, his philanthropic interests have been perpetrated by the various Pew family foundations, based in Philadelphia and known collectively as the Pew Charitable Trusts.

Phelps, Fred (1929–) A virulent and relentless antihomosexual crusader, Fred Phelps is pastor of the *WESTBORO BAPTIST CHURCH in Topeka, Kansas. He believes that he has been anointed as a latter-day prophet, and he considers himself a latter-day Puritan. "Some are called to preach [God's] message of love," he says, "and I've been called to preach his message of hate. Where are all the old-time preachers who tell people the truth? God hates evildoers and fornicators and fags."

Phelps founded *WESTBORO BAPTIST CHURCH in 1955. He earned a law degree from Washburn University in 1962, whereupon he embarked on a "crusade for righteousness" to strike down Jim Crow laws in Topeka. Phelps's political bearings changed dramatically, however. He began protesting homosexuality and civil rights for gays and lesbians in 1991 when a local park became a gathering place for homosexuals. He soon expanded his protests across North America, picketing in various jurisdictions that were considering civil rights protections for homosexuals. He and his family also picketed the funeral of Matthew Shepard, the young gay man who was brutally beaten and left for dead in 1998.

Reference: Jody Veenker, "Called to Hate?" *Christianity Today*, October 25, 1999.

Philadelphia College of Bible (Langhorne, Pennsylvania) Philadelphia College of Bible was created in 1951, when the Bible Institute of Pennsylvania merged with Philadelphia School of the Bible, in an effort to combine their resources. *C. I. SCOFIELD, famous for his **SCOFIELD REFERENCE BIBLE*, established Philadelphia School of the Bible with *WILLIAM LEROY PETTINGILL in 1914. With Scofield as its first president, Philadelphia School of the Bible initially operated as a night school; a day program was introduced in 1917.

The Bible School of Pennsylvania was founded in 1913 by W. W. Rugh, a former public school teacher who had become an itinerant Bible instructor. The school was originally known as the National Bible Institute of Philadelphia and operated as an extension of the National Bible Institute of New York, from which it gained its independence in 1921. At the time of the merger, the schools took the combined name Philadelphia Bible Institute and offered a three-year diploma in *BIBLE. It was accredited by the *AMERICAN ASSOCIATION OF BIBLE COLLEGES in 1950. In 1958, the institute was authorized by the state of Pennsylvania to offer a bachelor's degree in Bible study and took the name Philadelphia College of Bible. Full regional accreditation followed in 1967.

Philadelphia College of Bible runs an extension campus in Liberty Corner, New Jersey. The college also has a wilderness program in Cable, Wisconsin, where the curriculum is a combination of Bible study and outdoor education.

While all Philadelphia College students major in *BIBLE, they can enhance their biblical studies major with a wide range of additional program options, including not only standard options such as youth ministries or church music, but also programs in "Jewish Evangelism" and "Youth Camping Ministries." For the latter program, students spend up to two years studying and working in the north woods of Wisconsin.

Library special collections include extensive holdings of music, and the Dr. Sang Chan Lee Theological Library. Occult practices and social *DANCING are proscribed in the statement of student standards, but dance choreography is allowed for theater productions. The college, true to its fundamentalist origins, takes its prohibition against gambling extremely seriously as well; the possession of playing cards is not allowed on campus.

Reference: *Philadelphia College of Bible 1995–97 Catalog* (1995).

Phillips, (John) McCandlish, (Jr.) (1928–) After his graduation from high school in 1947, McCandlish Phillips worked for a weekly newspaper in Brookline, Massachusetts. He began attending a Baptist church, but it was a service in a Presbyterian church in Baltimore, five weeks before his discharge from the army in 1952, that eventually determined the course of his life. The preacher closed the service by asking, "Are you willing to go anywhere in the world and do anything Christ asks of you?" Phillips remembered that "every word of that went right through me." Four weeks later, he visited the base chapel and replied yes.

Phillips's call was not the conventional call to full-time pastoral or missionary service. After his discharge, he boarded the train for Boston but felt the urge to get off at Penn Station in New York City. He picked up copies of the *New York Herald Tribune* and the *New York Times* the next morning and, after scanning the classified ads, concluded that the voice of God was telling him that his mission was "to go to the *New York Times* and get a job." Phillips was promoted from copy boy to reporter in 1955, and his reportorial and writing skills soon earned him the praise of his colleagues. One editor, a veteran of several newspapers around the country, told Phillips, "You're the best I've ever seen." Along with his professional successes, however, Phillips tended to matters of faith. Together with Hannah Lowe, a former missionary, Phillips organized a church in Manhattan, the New Testament Missionary Fellowship. The church, located in Morningside Heights, in the vicinity of Columbia University, provides an evangelical community for students as well as local residents.

In December 1973, despite continued professional success and twenty-one years at the newspaper, Phillips resigned from the *Times*. He became an elder and administrator of the New Testament Missionary Fellowship.

References: McCandlish Phillips, *The Bible, the Supernatural, and the Jews* (1970); Ken Auletta, "The Man Who Disappeared," *New Yorker,* January 6, 1997.

Philpott, P(eter) W(iley) (1865–1957) A fundamentalist preacher out of southwestern Ontario, P. W. Philpott was a member of the *SALVATION ARMY from 1884 to 1894, rising to the rank of brigadier, before striking out as an independent *EVANGELIST. In 1896, he founded the Gospel Tabernacle (later renamed Philpott Tabernacle) in downtown Hamilton, Ontario, drawing heavily on migrant Scottish steelworkers. Philpott remained in Hamilton until 1922, when he accepted the pulpit of *MOODY MEMORIAL CHURCH in Chicago. During his seven years in Chicago, the congregation erected a new church building at a cost of over $1 million. He headed west in 1929 as pastor of the Church of the Open Door in Los Angeles and remained there until 1934, whereupon he resumed his career as a traveling teacher and *EVANGELIST.

Reference: David R. Elliott, "Knowing No Borders: Canadian Contributions to American Fundamentalism," in George A. Rawlyk and Mark A. Noll, eds., *Amazing Grace: Evangelicalism in Australia, Britain, Canada, and the United States* (1993).

Pidgeon, George (Campbell) (1872–1971) Born on the south shore of the Gaspé Peninsula of Québec, George Pidgeon attended Morrin College and McGill University and graduated from the Presbyterian Theological College in Montréal. After serving churches in Québec and Ontario, he became professor of practical theology at Westminster Hall in Vancouver, British Columbia, a post he held from 1909 until 1915. He also served as president of the Social Service Council of British Columbia.

Pidgeon's most important appointment was as pastor of the redoubtable Bloor Street Church in Toronto, whose pulpit he occupied from 1915 until his retirement in 1948. There, his formidable preaching skills, his deep piety, and his evangelical theology came to the attention of a wider public. He headed the Board of Moral and Social Reform for the Presbyterian Church in Canada as well as the Board of Home Missions, beginning in 1917. Pidgeon's ecumenical sentiments and his concern about the paucity of churches in western Canada led him to work for church unity. He became moderator of the Presbyterian general assembly in 1925, and when the United Church of Canada—a union of Congregationalists, Methodists, and Presbyterians—was gaveled to order on June 10 of that year, Pidgeon was chosen the first moderator of the new group.

Pidgeon's fondest—and unrealized—hope was that the formation of the United Church of Canada would spark a religious *REVIVAL. In 1930, he was named chair of the interchurch Committee on the Evangelization of Canada, a post he held for a dozen years. In a transition emblematic of the direction of the United Church of Canada, Pidgeon, an evangelical, was succeeded at Bloor Street by E. M. Howse, a theological liberal.

Reference: J. W. Grant, *George Pidgeon: A Biography* (1962).

Pieper, Franz A(ugust) O(tto) (1852–1931) One of the most influential theologians within the *LUTHERAN CHURCH—MISSOURI SYNOD, Franz A. O. Pieper was born in Carwitz, Germany, and immigrated to the United States with his family in 1870. He earned the baccalaureate degree from Northwestern University in Watertown, Wisconsin, and his divinity degree from *CONCORDIA THEOLOGICAL SEMINARY in St. Louis. He was ordained, served two churches in Wisconsin, and returned to Concordia in 1878 as professor and a theological ally of *CARL F. W. WALTHER, leader of the Missouri Synod. Pieper became editor of the seminary's journal, *Lehre and Wehre,* and in 1887 was named president of Concordia, a post he held for the remainder of his life. Beginning in 1899, he served concurrently for twelve years as president of the *LUTHERAN CHURCH—MISSOURI SYNOD.

Pieper was a systematic theologian, a prolific writer, and an able administrator. Under his leadership Concordia grew to become the largest seminary in North America, and the denomination grew as well. He was also an irenic churchman, urging compromise and unity among parties with slightly differing theological views, so long as those doctrines fell within the ambit of Lutheran orthodoxy.

References: Franz A. O. Pieper, *Conversion and Election: A Plea for a United Lutheranism in America* (1913); idem, *Christliche Dogmatik,* 3 vols. (1917–1924).

Piepkorn, Arthur Carl (1907–1973) Arthur Carl Piepkorn, theologian and leader of the *LUTHERAN CHURCH—MISSOURI SYNOD, earned the divinity degree from *CONCORDIA THEOLOGICAL SEMINARY in 1928 and the Ph.D. in archaeology from the University of Chicago in 1932. Early in World War II, he became a military chaplain. He taught at the U.S. Military Chaplain School in Cambridge, Massachusetts, from 1942 until 1950, and became the school's commandant.

Piepkorn returned to Concordia as professor of systematic theology in 1951, and he brought with him strong ecumenical sentiments from his experiences as chaplain and his work with the Federal (later, National) Council of Churches. Piepkorn became especially engaged in the dialogue between Lutherans and Roman Catholics. He was deeply involved in the debates over "orthodoxy" at Concordia Seminary, and his death in 1973 deprived the denomination of sorely needed leadership during a time of crisis.

Reference: Arthur Carl Piepkorn, *Profiles in Belief: The Religious Bodies in the United States and Canada,* 3 vols. (1977–1979).

Pierce, Robert W(illard) "Bob" (1914–1976) A graduate of Pasadena College, Bob Pierce began a missionary career in 1937 that took him to Asia and eventually throughout the world. While visiting Asia in 1947 as a *YOUTH FOR CHRIST *EVANGELIST, Pierce became concerned about people's social and physical needs. In 1950, he founded *WORLD VISION INTERNATIONAL to address those needs, arguing that "we must first treat people's physical needs" before offering the *GOSPEL. Through *WORLD VISION, Pierce raised hundreds of thousands of dollars from evangelicals for world relief. Toward the end of his life, he founded another relief organization, *SAMARITAN'S PURSE, which was taken over by *FRANKLIN GRAHAM when Pierce died of leukemia.

Reference: Franklin Graham and Jeanette Lockerbee, *Bob Pierce: This One Thing I Do* (1983).

Pierson, Arthur T(appan) (1837–1911) Arthur T. Pierson was born in New York City and studied at Hamilton College and at Union Theological Seminary (New York). He was ordained a Presbyterian and served churches in New York, Michigan, Indiana, and Pennsylvania in the 1870s and 1880s. Pierson's notoriety derived from his passion for missions; he wrote over fifty books and for twenty-five years served as editor of the influential *Missionary Review of the World.* Pierson was active in the *STUDENT VOLUNTEER MOVEMENT—he is generally credited with devising the group's slogan: "the evangelization of the world in this generation"—and the Laymen's Missionary Movement. He helped to organize the *AFRICA INLAND MISSION and, after a brief tenure as pastor of *CHARLES H. SPURGEON's Tabernacle in London, assumed the presidency of Gordon's Missionary Training School (now *GORDON COLLEGE) in 1893.

Pierson's *PREMILLENNIALISM lent an urgency to his missions theories. He believed that the *SECOND COMING would occur only after the *GOSPEL had been proclaimed throughout the world. His dispensational and premillennial views made him a welcome guest speaker at such places as *MOODY BIBLE INSTITUTE, *NYACK MISSIONARY TRAINING INSTITUTE, and *KESWICK conferences. Pierson served as one of the editors for the **SCOFIELD REFERENCE BIBLE* and contributed to **THE FUNDAMENTALS.*

References: Arthur T. Pierson, *The Crisis of Missions* (1886); Dana L. Robert, "The Legacy of Arthur Tappan Pierson," *International Bulletin of Missionary Research,* VIII (July 1984).

Pietism One interpretation of *EVANGELICALISM in America is that it emerged from the eighteenth-century fusion of Puritanism, Presbyterianism, and Pietism. While the strand of Puritanism in New England is well known, and the history of Presbyterianism has been amply documented, Pietism remains rather more obscure to most historians, in part because it was borne to North America by people of faith who spoke and worshiped in languages other than English.

The *Oxford English Dictionary* defines "Pietism" as a movement begun by Philipp Jakob Spener at Frankfurt am Main "for the *REVIVAL and advancement of piety in the Lutheran church" and characterized by a "devotion to religious feeling, or to strictness of religious practice." Pietism covers the spectrum from conservative, orthodox, liturgical members of state-church traditions to separatist groups who reviled the "four dumb idols" of the state churches—baptismal font, altar, pulpit, and (in Lutheran lands) confessional—to radical prophetic groups alienated from both social and institutional church life. All pietists, however, emphasized the importance of experiential (or, in the argot of the day, "experimental") religion, a warmhearted piety that was more important than mere intellectual assent to prescribed dogmas. Indeed, Pietism in Europe very often arose as a protest against a cold orthodoxy, which bordered on scholasticism, a highly intellectualized or ratiocinated theology.

In North America, pietists often disrupted ecclesiastical conventions and challenged ecclesiastical hierarchies. The best example of this stance was *THEODORUS JACOBUS FRELINGHUYSEN's all-out assault on the Dutch Reformed clergy in the Middle Colonies, but there are other examples as well, including Peter Henry Dorsius and *HEINRICH MELCHIOR MÜHLENBERG. Pietistic impulses triggered—and were eventually absorbed by—the *GREAT AWAKENING, and the evangelical tradition in America was born.

References: F. Ernest Stoeffler, *The Rise of Evangelical Pietism* (1971); Randall Balmer, *Blessed Assurance: A History of Evangelicalism in America* (1999).

Pilgrim Bible College. *See* **Bartlesville Wesleyan College.**

Pilgrim Holiness Church. *See* **Wesleyan Church.**

Pillar of Fire Ministries. *See* **White, Alma (née Bridewell).**

Pillsbury Baptist Bible College (Owatonna, Minnesota) Pillsbury Baptist Bible College, a "Baptist institution with a separatist frame of reference," represents the culmination of more than one hundred years of effort on the part of conservative Minnesota Baptists to found a postsecondary institution. In 1854, Baptists at Hastings, Minnesota, received a charter from the Minnesota State Legislature to open Minnesota Central University, but the school closed for financial reasons in 1868. The Baptists were undaunted, and nine years later they opened Minnesota Academy, which in 1886 became known as Pillsbury Academy, named in honor of George A. Pillsbury, a member of First Baptist Church in Minneapolis and a onetime mayor of the city. The Baptists dreamed of expanding the school into a university, but it remained a coeducational academy for many years. Then in 1920, it became an all-boys military school.

In 1955, ownership of the school was legally challenged. In a court case that went to the Minnesota Supreme Court, the Baptists were declared the sole owners, and in 1957 the academy officially became Pillsbury Baptist Bible College. In this period, the school benefited from an influx of interest and support from fundamentalists who had previously been affiliated with *NORTHWESTERN COLLEGE and who broke ties with the other Minnesota school in frustration over its transition to a liberal arts curriculum.

As of 1990, Pillsbury Baptist Bible College was a candidate for full regional accreditation. Today, Pillsbury is a "professional college," offering majors in *BIBLE, business, communications, education, history, music, science, and practical theology. The school also operates a two-year course for laypeople and grants the Associate of Applied Science and a Practical Christian Worker's diploma. In spite of its moderate embrace of the liberal arts, however, the school's emphasis remains biblical studies. The forty-nine-hour core curriculum consists mostly of Bible courses, and two years of Christian service is required of all four-year students; two-year students must complete two semesters. The school's biological science survey course compares evolution and the biblical (literal) interpretation of creation.

The regulations on student life are consistent with Pillsbury's position as a very conservative institution. Social *DANCING, secret societies, and movies are all forbidden. In addition, the school's enrollment policies are stricter than many *CHRISTIAN COLLEGES: "Because of Pillsbury's unique purpose as a Bible College whose mission is to offer education for vocational ministry and in light of biblical qualifications for ministry, a divorcee may not be enrolled as a student."

Reference: Pillsbury Baptist Bible College Catalog 1996–1997 (1996).

Pillsbury Bible School. *See* **Northwestern College and Northwestern Theological Seminary and Pillsbury Baptist Bible College.**

Pinnock, Clark H(arold) (1937–) Clark H. Pinnock, born in Toronto, was brought up in a liberal Baptist household, but he was converted to evangelical Christianity in 1949 in part because of the influence of a "Bible-believing grandma and a like-minded *SUNDAY SCHOOL teacher." He became involved with *YOUTH FOR CHRIST rallies and the Canadian Keswick Bible Conference. He graduated from the University of Toronto and did his doctoral studies with *F. F. BRUCE at the University of Manchester. Pinnock was also influenced by *FRANCIS SCHAEFFER and spent a time at Schaeffer's Swiss retreat, *L'ABRI.

Pinnock assumed his first teaching position in 1965, at New Orleans Baptist Theological Seminary. Initially he taught New Testament but moved into systematic theology; he produced several important works early in his career, including *A Defense of Biblical Infallibility* and *Set Forth Your Case.* In 1969, Pinnock accepted a position at *TRINITY EVANGELICAL DIVINITY SCHOOL, where he remained until 1974, when he went to *REGENT COLLEGE in Vancouver, British Columbia. In these years Pinnock became enamored of neopentecostalism, in part because he experienced healing in one of his eyes. He also called into question some of the deterministic elements of Calvinistic theology and drifted toward a more Wesleyan-Arminian perspective, which elevates the notion of self-determination in the individual's relationship with God.

Pinnock returned to Ontario in 1977, to McMaster Divinity College in Hamilton. Over the course of his career, Pinnock had repeatedly addressed the issue of biblical *AUTHORITY, but his tone changed markedly from combative to irenic. He retreated from his earlier insistence on biblical *INERRANCY, although he sought to make clear "in no uncertain terms that I have not changed one whit in the matter of holding to the *BIBLE as the inspired *WORD OF GOD written and as the absolutely trustworthy norm of the church, and whatever changes I may have undergone were in the way of points of clarification as to what it means to believe that." In 1996, reflecting his new appreciation for *PENTECOSTALISM, he wrote: "Revelation is not a closed system of propositional truths but a divine self-disclosure that continues to open up and challenge."

References: Clark H. Pinnock, *Biblical Revelation: The Foundation of Christian Theology* (1971); idem, *The Scripture Principle* (1984); idem, *Three Keys to Spiritual Renewal* (1985); idem, *Tracking the Maze: Finding Our Way through Modern Theology from an Evangelical Perspective* (1990); idem, *Flame of Love: A Theology of the Holy Spirit* (1996); Robert K. Johnston, s.v. "Clark H. Pinnock," in Walter A. Elwell, ed., *Handbook of Evangelical Theologians* (1993).

Pioneer Clubs Pioneer Clubs was created in the mid-twentieth century as a "Bible-based and Christ-centered" alternative to the Boy Scouts and Girl Scouts. In this respect, Pioneer Clubs is best understood as another example of an evangelical alternative to nonevangelical daily life. The clubs serve children from two years old through high school, dividing them by age into seven separate programs: the Skippers, Scooters, Voyagers, Pathfinders, Trailblazers, Challengers, and Explorers.

As in Scouting, Pioneer Club members work on nature projects, do sports, and earn merit badges for skill building, but they also earn merit badges for Bible study and devotional prayer. In the summer, participants can even attend Pioneer Clubs' camping ministry at Camp Cherith, which has twenty locations across the country.

Pioneer Clubs headquarters are in Wheaton, Illinois, home of *WHEATON COLLEGE and assorted other evangelical organizations. Pioneer Clubs have benefited both from this location and an impressive board of reference, which includes the president of the *NATIONAL ASSOCIATION OF EVANGELICALS. The Pioneer Clubs board also has included the presidents of the *EVANGELICAL FREE CHURCH OF AMERICA, the *CHRISTIAN AND MISSIONARY ALLIANCE, and the *BAPTIST GENERAL CONFERENCE, as well as leaders from several other denominations.

Piper, William H(amner) (1868–1911) Born in Lydia, Maryland, and ordained in the Brethren Church in 1893, William H. Piper became part of *JOHN ALEXANDER DOWIE'S *CHRISTIAN CATHOLIC CHURCH and a prominent leader of Dowie's community in *ZION CITY, Illinois. By 1906, however, Piper had become disillusioned with Dowie and with *ZION CITY. He opened the *STONE CHURCH in Chicago on December 9, 1906. Initially averse to *PENTECOSTALISM in the new congregation, Piper relented in June of the following year in the face of declining attendance, whereupon the church began to grow. "Nothing is better calculated to make a minister examine himself than a decrease in his audiences," he said later. "After long days and nights of agony of spirit in earnest prayer, I was finally brought to the decision that what was claimed as the *BAPTISM OF THE HOLY SPIRIT and the *SPEAKING IN TONGUES was really of God." Piper's wife, Lydia Markley Piper, received the Spirit *BAPTISM in July 1907, and her husband followed suit the next February. Piper's influence and the renown of *STONE CHURCH spread throughout *PENTECOSTALISM with the monthly publication of the *Latter Rain Evangel,* beginning in October 1908.

Reference: Edith L. Blumhofer, *Restoring the Faith: The Assemblies of God, Pentecostalism, and American Culture* (1993).

Pippert, Wes(ley) G(erald) (1934–) A graduate of the University of Iowa and *WHEATON COLLEGE, Wes Pippert embarked on his career as a journalist with United Press International in 1955, continuing with brief interruptions until 1988, when he became director of the Washington Program for the University of Missouri School of Journalism. He covered the Watergate scandal and the presidential campaigns of George McGovern in 1972 and of *JIMMY CARTER in 1976 and 1980. Pippert, who holds Local Preacher's credentials in the United Methodist Church, has been a consistent advocate for high ethical standards in journalism.

References: Wes Pippert, *Memo for 1976: Some Political Options* (1974); idem, comp., *The Spiritual Journey of Jimmy Carter* (1978); idem, *An Ethics of News: A Reporter's Search for Truth* (1989); idem, *The Hand of the Mighty: Right and Wrong Uses of Our Power* (1991).

Pittsburgh Experiment. *See* **Shoemaker, Samuel Moor, (Jr.).**

Plantinga, Alvin (Carl) (1932–) Born in Ann Arbor, Michigan, to parents of Dutch descent, Alvin Plantinga studied at *CALVIN COLLEGE and the University of Michigan, and earned the doctorate in philosophy from Yale University in 1958. A member of the *CHRISTIAN REFORMED CHURCH, Plantinga is director of the Center for Philosophy of Religion at the University of Notre Dame. He has numerous published books and articles, and his 1964 edited volume, *Faith and Philosophy,* included pieces by several major philosophers who were Christian in their commitment. This work gave an early signal that professional philosophy would have to take matters of Christian faith seriously in the years ahead.

Richard Swinburne of Oriel College, Oxford University, has called Alvin

Plantinga "the leading philosopher of God" in the contemporary world because he has been a key leader in the revival of academic interest in Christian belief within professional philosophy. Plantinga was involved in the visionary stages and the actual founding of the *SOCIETY OF CHRISTIAN PHILOSOPHERS, and he served as the society's president from 1983 to 1986. Plantinga sees Christian scholarship as a communal task to be undertaken with a certain boldness and one in which Christian faith and conscientious scholarship thrive together. Plantinga has argued that the rationality of Christian and theistic belief is not established by a neutral and universal set of unquestionable criteria and that antitheistic arguments to show that religious belief is either inconsistent or improbable, and thus irrational, fail. Some of his more recent work articulates an alternative understanding of rational belief on the basis of which religious belief, under proper conditions, is indeed rationally warranted.

References: Alvin Plantinga, *God and Other Minds* (1967); idem, *The Nature of Necessity* (1974); idem, *God, Freedom and Evil* (1974); idem, *Does God Have a Nature?* (1980); idem, *Warrant: The Current Debate* (1993).

Plymouth Brethren The Plymouth Brethren, sometimes known as the Christian Brethren or simply the Brethren, trace their history to Dublin, Ireland, in the 1820s. The group, impatient with the formal ritual and clericalism of the established church, sought to replicate the simplicity of New Testament Christianity in their worship and theology. Their worship consisted of gatherings—usually in a member's home—for prayer, teaching from the *BIBLE, and Holy Communion. The first church in England was organized at Plymouth in 1831. The movement, which still has no ordained, salaried clergy, soon spread throughout the British dominions, to Europe (especially France, Switzerland, and Italy), and to the United States.

For American *EVANGELICALISM, the Plymouth Brethren's most significant contribution was the dispensational, premillennial teachings of one of its members: *JOHN NELSON DARBY. Darby's dispensational scheme of biblical interpretation became enormously popular among American evangelicals after the Civil War, even though they were considerably less enamored of Darby's ecclesiastical *SEPARATISM. Today, the Plymouth Brethren have about eleven hundred churches and ninety-eight thousand members in the United States.

Point Loma Nazarene College (San Diego, California) Point Loma Nazarene College began as Pacific Bible College, established in 1902 by the *CHURCH OF THE NAZARENE in Los Angeles. It was renamed Deets Bible College in 1909 in honor of a particularly generous donor. The following year, however, the college moved to Pasadena and was renamed Nazarene University. In 1924, it became Pasadena College, a moniker (and location) it retained for nearly fifty years. The college found itself short of space in 1973 and bought the former campus of California Western University, which had originally been an educational center for the Theosophical Society of America. Pasadena College adopted the name Point Loma College at that time and, later, Point Loma Nazarene College. Point Loma, located on a stunning parcel of land overlooking the Pacific Ocean, has graduate programs in education and religion.

References: *Point Loma Nazarene College 1996–1997 Catalog,* vol. 82 (1996); Thomas C.

Hunt and James C. Carper, eds., *Religious Higher Education in the United States: A Source Book* (1996).

Point of Grace With singles such as "No More Pain," "One More Broken Heart," and "Jesus Will Still Be There," Point of Grace is often called "the Supremes of Christian music." The group of four women in their mid-twenties emerged in the 1990s as Christian music's response to the secular "girl groups" of the previous three decades.

Point of Grace was formed by Heather Floyd, Terry Jones, and Denise Jones (no relation), who sang together as teenagers in a church in Norman, Oklahoma. The three went on to attend Ouichita Baptist University in Arkadelphia, Arkansas, where they sang as a trio with a group known as the Oklahoma Girls. Later joined by college classmate Shelley Phillips, the band took its show on the road, performing in small local spaces across the country. While participating in a religious music workshop at a Colorado ***YMCA** camp, they were discovered by a talent scout from Word Records, which signed the group in 1993. Their name refers to a passage by ***C. S. LEWIS**, who says that human beings live each day on the point of God's ***GRACE**.

With their 1994 debut album, *Point of Grace*, the group broke a record for the number of singles to hit number one. "I'll Be Believing" went straight to the top of *Billboard*'s Christian Contemporary charts, and the album generated five more number-one singles. It also earned them a Dove Award from the ***GOSPEL MUSIC ASSOCIATION** for Favorite New Artist of the Year. The following year, their second recording was also a success: *The Whole Truth* yielded five additional number-one songs. In 1996, Point of Grace was nominated for six Dove Awards and won four, including Group of the Year and Album of the Year for *The Whole Truth*.

Also in 1996, the group released a third recording, *Life, Love and Other Mysteries*. This album was accompanied by a book of the same name, published by Simon & Schuster. Even while being in some ways a "tell-all" about the group, the focus of the book was intended to be "moral living in the '90s," a written stance quite consistent with the member's public support for a Christian lifestyle. Point of Grace acts as a representative for Mercy Ministries of America, a shelter for unwed mothers, and in concert they include messages against drinking and premarital sex, claiming to have made a pact in junior high school to save themselves for marriage. Perhaps because each member has a "morality clause" in her contract with Word Records, the singers also refuse to perform in concert or to be photographed for album covers wearing short skirts.

References: Information provided by Word Records publicity department; Nicholas Dawidoff, "No Sex. No Drugs. But Rock 'n' Roll (Kind of)," *New York Times*, February 5, 1995.

Point of Grace Ministries Point of Grace Ministries, based in Des Moines, Iowa, was begun by Tom Allen after his 1995 ouster from First Federated Church, which he and Don Morris had helped to build into a megachurch. Allen and Morris had come to Iowa from Michigan as a pastoral team in 1970, but a theological dispute over pastoral ***AUTHORITY** led Morris to break with Allen and First Federated in 1990. Morris started his own congregation, Christ Community Church, but on September 15, 1996, the two reunited in the "seeker-friendly" Point of Grace Ministries.

Reference: William Simbro, "'God has brought us back together,'" *Des Moines Register,* September 15, 1996.

Polity Polity is the form of church government used by a particular denomination. Essentially, there are three varieties of polity: episcopal, presbyterian, and congregational (all of them should be understood in the generic sense and therefore rendered in the lower case, not to be identified solely with the Episcopal, Presbyterian, and Congregational denominations). Episcopal polity (as, for example, in the Roman Catholic Church, the Episcopal Church, and various forms of Lutheranism) is church government by bishops, who ultimately decide denominational doctrines and policies and may also control the movement of clergy. The presbyterian polity (the Presbyterian Church and many denominations in the Reformed tradition) is a more representational form of church government, where members of the congregation choose elders, who in turn choose other representatives (sometimes known as presbyters) to the highest body, usually known as the general assembly.

The final form of polity is congregational, where all power rests with the individual congregation—the power to make and approve budgets, to hire and fire clergy, to authorize repairs to the church steeple. The aggregate power of local churches that are congregational in polity—such as in the *SOUTHERN BAPTIST CONVENTION—is, in theory at least, no more than the sum of its parts. While all three forms of polity are represented within evangelical Christianity, congregational polity is by far the most common, which becomes even more apparent when the number of independent, autonomous congregations—those that claim no denominational affiliation—are factored into the equation.

Portland Deliverance One of the pivotal documents in the history of Presbyterianism in the United States, the Portland Deliverance was adopted by the General Assembly of the Presbyterian Church (USA) at its meeting in Portland, Oregon, in 1892. The statement required Presbyterian ministers to affirm the inspiration and *AUTHORITY of the *BIBLE, that "the inspired Word, as it came from God, is without error." Coming at a time when higher criticism had cast doubts on the integrity of the Scriptures and liberal voices were calling for a modification of the denomination's strict adherence to the Westminster Confession, the seventeenth-century standard for Presbyterian orthodoxy, the Portland Deliverance represented a victory for conservatives. Any Presbyterian minister who could not affirm the *BIBLE as "the only infallible rule of faith and practice" was required by the terms of the Deliverance to withdraw from the ministry. Conservatives used the Portland Deliverance as a tool in heresy trials during the 1890s, trials that culminated in the dismissal of Charles A. Briggs in 1893 and Henry Preserved Smith the following year.

References: Lefferts A. Loetscher, *The Broadening Church* (1954); Randall Balmer and John R. Fitzmier, *The Presbyterians* (1993).

Positive Confession Theology. *See* **Prosperity Theology.**

Postmillennialism Postmillennialism, the doctrine that Christ will return *after* the millennium—the thousand years of righteousness predicted in the book of Revelation—was the animating force behind most Protestant social reform efforts in the nineteenth century. The *SECOND GREAT AWAKENING had unleashed a great deal of optimism about not only the perfectibility of individuals through the *SALVATION and *SANCTIFICATION process but also of society itself. Evangelicals in the antebellum era came to believe that they could reform society according to the norms of godliness by dint of their own efforts. They could, in fact, usher in the *MILLENNIUM here on earth, after which Jesus would return.

The effect of postmillennial belief was registered in such movements as *ABOLITIONISM, *TEMPERANCE, prison reform, female seminaries, and *LYMAN BEECHER's campaign against dueling. As the nineteenth century progressed, however, and particularly with urbanization, industrialization, and the influx of non-Protestant immigrants, evangelicals shifted from postmillennialism to *PREMILLENNIALISM, the doctrine that Christ would return at any moment to rescue true believers from a sinful and decaying society.

References: Ernest R. Sandeen, *The Roots of Fundamentalism: British and American Millenarianism, 1800–1930* (1970); Timothy P. Weber, *Living in the Shadow of the Second Coming: American Premillennialism, 1875–1982,* enl. ed. (1983); Paul Boyer, *When Time Shall Be No More: Prophecy Belief in Modern American Culture* (1992).

Potter's House **(Dallas, Texas).** *See* **Jakes, T(homas) D(exter).**

Prairie Bible Institute **(Three Hills, Alberta)** Prairie Bible Institute is the collective name for Prairie Bible College and Prairie Graduate School. Both schools are interdenominational institutions located in Alberta, Canada, and both represent the conservative wing of Canadian *EVANGELICALISM. Prairie Bible Institute began in 1922, when *L. E. MAXWELL, a graduate of Midland Bible Institute, was invited by Alberta farmer Fergus Kirk to teach Bible study in Three Hills, Alberta. The school opened in an abandoned farmhouse with an enrollment of eight students that October.

In the 1950s, when many *BIBLE INSTITUTES began introducing liberal arts curricula, Prairie rejected the tendency, even shunning the process of regional accreditation for fear of encroaching secularization. Prairie Bible College has still not adopted a full liberal arts program, but the school has expanded the courses offered. In addition to biblical studies, the college has specializations such as intercultural studies, sacred music, and missionary aviation. In 1938, Prairie Bible Institute created an interdenominational high school in Three Hills, and an elementary and junior high school have also been added since then.

Prairie Graduate School was founded in 1988. It is located in Calgary, Alberta, seventy miles southwest of the college. The graduate school offers master's degrees of divinity and arts, with concentrations in leadership development, theology, ministry, and intercultural studies.

References: "Shaping Lives to Change the World" (Prairie Bible Institute brochure, n.d.); William C. Ringenberg, *The Christian College: A History of Protestant Higher Education in America* (1984).

Praise Music The term "praise music" is applied to the simple, sweet, melodious music that became very popular in evangelical churches beginning in the 1970s. In part a revolt against the formalism of nineteenth-century hymns, this music, characterized by repetition and a rather narrow musical range, was introduced by the *JESUS MOVEMENT coming out of southern California. Its popularity spread by means of *MARANATHA! MUSIC, which was associated with *CALVARY CHAPEL.

Praise music became common in pentecostal churches, where worshipers would often close their eyes and raise their arms in a gesture of openness to the Holy Spirit. It has also spread—usually by means of *OVERHEAD PROJECTORS—to other evangelical churches.

Prayer Breakfasts The first prayer breakfast took place in Seattle in April 1935 and was organized by Abraham Vereide, a Methodist minister; the gatherings, which included Bible study, were enlarged to include political figures in 1939, and the movement quickly spread to other cities. Prayer breakfasts began in Congress in January 1942, following the bombing of Pearl Harbor the previous month. Henry Wallace, the vice president, and several senators began gathering regularly for morning prayer. The first regular Senate prayer breakfast began shortly thereafter, followed by the House of Representatives, and then other governmental agencies. The National Prayer Breakfast began after Dwight Eisenhower, recently inaugurated as president, asked to join the Senate prayer breakfast in 1953.

The National Prayer Breakfast takes place in Washington, D.C., every January; it is supported by individual contributions, with no government funding. In addition to the National Prayer Breakfast, prayer breakfasts continue in federal, state, and local governments.

Reference: James C. Hefley and Edward E. Plowman, *Washington: Christians in the Corridors of Power* (1975).

Prayer Meeting Revival The Prayer Meeting Revival, which lasted from 1857 until 1859, began with a noontime prayer gathering of six people on September 23, 1857, at the Dutch Reformed Church on Fulton Street in New York City. The meeting had been organized by *JEREMIAH LANPHIER, and it began to grow substantially during the economic panic of October 1857. By early the next year, more than twenty such prayer meetings, led by the laity, were taking place in the city; participants were admonished to stay away from controversial subjects like slavery and *BAPTISM. In Chicago, more than two thousand people gathered daily at the Metropolitan Theater, and the movement spread to other cities in the United States and Canada and even to Great Britain and Ireland.

The Prayer Meeting Revival, also known as the Urban Awakening and the Businessman's Revival, received extensive coverage in the secular press. It crossed denominational lines and contributed substantially to *EVANGELISM, social reform, and the organization of *SUNDAY SCHOOLS. Among those who derived their inspiration from the Prayer Meeting Revival were *DWIGHT L. MOODY, *A. B. SIMPSON, *WILLIAM BOOTH, and *CHARLES SPURGEON.

References: Timothy L. Smith, *Revivalism and Social Reform in Mid-Nineteenth-Century America* (1957); Kathryn Teresa Long, *The Revival of 1857–58: Interpreting an American Religious Awakening* (1997).

Precious Moments. *See* **Butcher, Samuel J.**

Premillennialism Premillennialism is the eschatological doctrine that Jesus will return for the true believers *before* the millennium, the thousand years of righteousness predicted in the book of Revelation. Throughout church history, Christians have debated the precise meaning of the prophetic writings in the *BIBLE—principally the book of Daniel in the Hebrew Scriptures and Revelation at the end of the

New Testament. Although many believed, for example, that Revelation was intended as a source of comfort for the persecuted early Christians, an assurance that God would eventually avenge their sufferings, others have chosen to interpret Revelation as a kind of "prehistory," a prediction of the sequence of events leading to the end of time. These literalists have generally divided between postmillennialists (those who believe that Jesus will return after the millennium) and premillennialists, who hold that the return of Jesus is imminent.

American evangelicals have vacillated to a remarkable degree between premillennialism and *POSTMILLENNIALISM. Although some, notably the *MILLERITES, held premillennial beliefs in the antebellum period, most were postmillennialists: They believed that Christ would return after the *MILLENNIUM, so they took it as their responsibility to bring on the *MILLENNIUM by working to reform society according to the norms of godliness. *POSTMILLENNIALISM, with its general optimism about the perfectibility of individuals and of society, animated most of the social-reform movements of the early nineteenth century—*ABOLITIONISM, *TEMPERANCE, women's suffrage.

Premillennialism began to take hold after the Civil War, however, as evangelicals recognized that the teeming, squalid tenements of the cities, beset by labor unrest, would never resemble the precincts of Zion. Evangelicals also grew increasingly uneasy with the arrival of non-Protestant immigrants, most of whom did not share their scruples about *TEMPERANCE. In response to these social changes, which in turn were prompted by rapid urbanization, industrialization, and unrestrained capitalism, evangelicals shifted their *ESCHATOLOGY from *POSTMILLENNIALISM to premillennialism, which insisted that the world was getting worse and worse and that their only hope was for Christ's return. Specifically, they adopted the variant of premillennialism called *DISPENSATIONALISM, or dispensational premillennialism, which divided all of human history into different ages, or dispensations, and insisted that human history was grinding imminently to a halt, and that Jesus would return at any moment to rescue the true believers from the apocalyptic destruction awaiting the unrighteous. *DISPENSATIONALISM, brought to North America from Great Britain by *JOHN NELSON DARBY, became enormously popular among evangelicals during the decades surrounding the turn of the twentieth century. In contrast to the social optimism implicit in *POSTMILLENNIALISM, premillennialism was a theology of despair because it posited that this world was irredeemable and was careening toward apocalyptic judgment. "I look upon this world as a wrecked vessel," *EVANGELIST *DWIGHT L. MOODY declared toward the end of the nineteenth century. "God has given me a lifeboat and said, 'Moody, save all you can.'"

Evangelicals, especially fundamentalists, held for the most part to premillennialism throughout the twentieth century. They invoked premillennialism as justification for their evangelistic appeals, as demonstrated by *BILLY GRAHAM's crusades or by *A Thief in the Night* by filmmaker *DONALD W. THOMPSON, and for their strong support for the State of Israel, which evangelicals believe will play a central role in the unfolding apocalyptic drama.

On the face of it, the rise of the *RELIGIOUS RIGHT in the late 1970s represents a movement away from premillennialism and back toward *POSTMILLENNIALISM because the leaders of the *RELIGIOUS RIGHT seek, at least according to their own lights, to construct a godly society. While there is some justification for this interpretation—the *RELIGIOUS RIGHT has been greatly influenced, for example, by the postmillennial interpretations of a movement called *RECONSTRUCTIONISM—the majority of evangelicals remain premillennialist in their *ESCHATOLOGY. They may act like postmillennialists, but they profess to be premillennialists.

References: Ernest R. Sandeen, *The Roots of Fundamentalism: British and American Millenarianism, 1800–1930* (1970); Timothy P. Weber, *Living in the Shadow of the Second Coming: American Premillennialism, 1875–1982*, enl. ed. (1983); Paul Boyer, *When Time Shall Be No More: Prophecy Belief in Modern American Culture* (1992); Randall Balmer, *Mine Eyes Have Seen the Glory: A Journey into the Evangelical Subculture in America*, 3d ed. (2000).

Presbyterian Church in America The Presbyterian Church in America was formed out of a split in the Presbyterian Church in the United States (PCUS). Some more conservative members in the PCUS felt that the denomination had moved away from the basic Presbyterian traditions. The conservatives were uncomfortable with PCUS membership in the National Council of Churches in Christ and the World Council of Churches, with the PCUS policy of ordaining women, and with the possible merger with the even more liberal Presbyterian Church in the U.S.A. (PCUSA). In 1972–73, several presbyteries formed with approximately 260 churches and forty-one thousand communicant members that had left the PCUS. In December 1973, these churches organized the National Presbyterian Church. The name was changed the following year to the current name. In 1982, the Reformed Presbyterian Church, Evangelical Synod merged into the Presbyterian Church in America.

Presbyterian Church in America doctrine follows traditional Presbyterian beliefs as outlined in the Westminster Confession of Faith and both the Longer and Shorter Westminster Catechisms. This strict adherence to the conservative Calvinist roots of the Reformed tradition is one of the main points that distinguishes the Presbyterian Church in America from the Presbyterian Church (U.S.A.).

The *POLITY of the Presbyterian Church in America is thoroughly presbyterian. Governance is by the presbyters (or elders) and the graded courts. These are the session for local matters, the presbytery on the regional level, and the general assembly on the national level. Presbyterian Church in America *POLITY also takes seriously the position of the parity of elders, making a distinction between the two classes of teaching elder and ruling elder. The denomination has self-consciously taken a more democratic position (rule from the grass roots up) on presbyterian governance in contrast to a more prelatical approach (rule from the top assemblies down).

With headquarters in Atlanta, the Presbyterian Church in America professes to be one of the most rapidly growing denominations in the United States, reporting 1,299 local congregations with 210,758 communicant members and 57,006 noncommunicant members in 1995. The church supports Covenant College in Lookout Mountain, Georgia, and Covenant Theological Seminary in St. Louis as its educational institutions.

References: Frank S. Mead and Samuel S. Hill, *Handbook of Denominations in the United States*, 10th ed. (1996); J. Gordon Melton, *The Encyclopedia of American Religions*, 3d ed. (1993); "Contributions to U.S. and Canadian Protestant Churches," *Chronicle of Philanthropy*, vol. IX, no. 15.

Presbyterian Lay Committee Formed in 1965 as an independent organization within the United Presbyterian Church in the U.S.A. in order to counter "the increasing emphasis of the Church on social and political action and the lessening emphasis on providing spiritual leadership as a Christian, Bible-believing institution," the Presbyterian Lay Committee seeks to move Presbyterians toward more conservative theological positions. The group sponsors local chapters and publishes a monthly newspaper, *The Presbyterian Layman*.

Presbyterians United for Biblical Concerns Presbyterians United for Biblical Concerns was organized in 1965 to ensure that the proposed Confession of 1967 would not veer too far in the direction of theological *LIBERALISM. The group succeeded to some degree in its original purpose, and it continues to exert a conservative, evangelical influence among Presbyterians.

Presley, Elvis (Aron) (1935–1977) "I believe I will see Elvis Presley in heaven," *BILLY GRAHAM once declared. Whether or not the performer, whose music was a rockabilly fusion of blues, country, and gospel into a new pop idiom, was properly an evangelical is a controverted question among evangelicals themselves. He had no shortage of evangelical critics, who excoriated him for his lifestyle (especially his later dependence on drugs) and for his sexually provocative gyrations. Presley, on the other hand, combined in one persona the two faces of show business illustrated in a pair of cousins from the South: the good-boy *GOSPEL of *JIMMY SWAGGART and the bad-boy rock of Swaggart's cousin Jerry Lee Lewis.

For his part, Presley repeatedly acknowledged his debt to *GOSPEL MUSIC and to the faith that both nurtured him and sustained him in good times and bad. "We were a religious family," he recalled, "going around together to sing at *CAMP MEETINGS and *REVIVALS. . . . It became such a part of my life it was as natural as *DANCING, a way to escape from the problems and my way of release."

References: Peter Guralnick, *Last Train to Memphis: The Rise of Elvis Presley* (1994); Curtis W. Ellison, *Country Music Culture: From Hard Times to Heaven* (1995).

Preus, J(acob) A(all) O(ttesen), Jr. (1920–1994) Born to Norwegian American parents in St. Paul, Minnesota, and baptized into the Norwegian Lutheran Church in America, J. A. O. Preus spent most of his childhood in Highland Park, Illinois, where he came into contact with the *LUTHERAN CHURCH—MISSOURI SYNOD. He graduated with honors from Luther College, Decorah, Iowa, in 1941, whereupon he entered Luther Theological Seminary. Preus, however, became increasingly disenchanted with what he perceived as the theological *LIBERALISM at Luther Seminary; upon graduation in 1945, therefore, he chose ordination in the more conservative Little Norwegian Synod and served several churches in Minnesota. He completed two degrees, including the Ph.D., at the University of Minnesota, alternating his studies with two stints on the faculty of the Synod's Bethany Lutheran College in Mankato, Minnesota.

Preus left Bethany and the Little Norwegian Synod in 1958 for *CONCORDIA THEOLOGICAL SEMINARY (St. Louis) and the *LUTHERAN CHURCH—MISSOURI SYNOD. From his platform as professor of New Testament, Preus acquired more and more power within the denomination. He was named president of Concordia in

1962 and, after intensive politicking, was elected president of the Missouri Synod in 1969 on the third ballot.

Preus emerged as leader of the conservative faction within the denomination when he launched an inquiry into the supposed *LIBERALISM at Concordia. "That godless men take [Scripture] from us is terrifying," Preus declared, "but that theologians and pastors should deprive the church of Scripture by destructive criticism is even more unspeakable." His 1972 *Report of the Synodical President to the Lutheran Church—Missouri Synod* accused Concordia's president, John H. Tietjen, and other members of the faculty of doctrinal irregularities. The denomination upheld Preus, thereby prompting Tietjen and others to form a dissident group, Evangelical Lutherans in Mission. Preus responded in January 1974 by suspending Tietjen and forty-three out of forty-seven members of the Concordia faculty. Most of the students struck in sympathy, and the suspended faculty set up Seminary-in-Exile (known popularly as Seminex, now Christ Seminary). The dissidents, having lost their battle within the Missouri Synod, established the Association of Evangelical Lutheran Churches in 1976, which eventually folded into the Evangelical Lutheran Church in America.

Preus, having beaten back what he regarded as the tides of *LIBERALISM, albeit at considerable cost, stepped down as president of the Missouri Synod in 1981. He returned to the faculty of *CONCORDIA THEOLOGICAL SEMINARY, remaining active in synodical affairs.

References: J. A. O. Preus, *It Is Written* (1971); idem, *Report of the Synodical President to the Lutheran Church—Missouri Synod* (1972); James E. Adams, *Preus of Missouri and the Great Lutheran Civil War* (1977); Mary Todd, *Authority Vested: A Story of Identity and Chance in the Lutheran Church—Missouri Synod* (2000).

Price, Charles S(ydney) (1887–1947) Charles S. Price, trained in the law at Wesley College, Oxford, immigrated to Canada and was later converted at a gathering of Free Methodists in Spokane, Washington. After ordination and ministry among the Methodists, he became disenchanted and gravitated toward Congregationalism, serving as pastor of churches in Valdez, Alaska, and Lodi, California. Some congregants prevailed upon him to attend one of *AIMEE SEMPLE MCPHERSON's *REVIVAL meetings in San Jose. Though initially skeptical, Price changed his mind when "a masterful message came from the lips of the *EVANGELIST and my modernist theology was punctured until it looked like a sieve."

When denominational officials looked askance at Price's preaching about Spirit *BAPTISM at the First Congregational Church, he started Lodi Bethel Temple and soon thereafter began an itinerant healing ministry. He traveled first to Oregon and British Columbia, where a number of miraculous healings attended his preaching. Some of the healings bordered on the spectacular, as in the case of the sister of *DEMOS SHAKARIAN, who would later found the *FULL GOSPEL BUSINESS MEN'S FELLOWSHIP INTERNATIONAL. Shakarian's sister had been badly injured in an automobile accident and had been near death. Price laid hands on her, and she shook for twenty minutes; the next morning, X rays revealed that her shattered pelvis had been completely restored.

In Vancouver, British Columbia, a quarter of a million people attended his meetings over the space of three weeks, and crowds in Edmonton, Calgary, and Winnipeg, Manitoba, frequently resembled mobs. As word of his success spread—in part through the agency of his monthly periodical, *Golden Grain*, started in 1926—Price expanded the range of his peregrination to such places as Toronto; Duluth, Minnesota; and St. Louis; and to England, Scandinavia, and the Middle East. His personal life did not fare so well. His wife divorced him late in the 1920s, and Price was beset by persistent rumors that he was having an affair with his pianist.

Reference: Edith L. Blumhofer, *Restoring the Faith: The Assemblies of God, Pentecostalism, and American Culture* (1993).

Price, Eugenia (1916–1996) Although reared a Methodist, Eugenia Price drifted away from Christianity as a teenager and a young adult. She began writing and soon enjoyed success as a radio script writer for the National Broadcasting Company and for Procter and Gamble. Following a *CONVERSION experience in 1949, Price began to write the scripts for *Unshackled,* the radio program of the *PACIFIC GARDEN MISSION. In the 1950s, she turned to writing books. Her spiritual autobiography, *The Burden Is Light!: The Autobiography of a Transformed Pagan Who Took God at His Word,* appeared in 1955. Ten years later, Price began to publish novels, notably the St. Simons Island trilogy and the Savannah quartet, which demonstrate the incursion of the divine into everyday life.

References: Eugenia Price, *Early Will I Seek Thee: Journal of a Heart that Longed and Found* (1956); idem, *At Home on St. Simons* (1981); idem, *What Really Matters* (1983).

Price, Frederick K. C. (1932–) One of the more brazen proponents of *PROSPERITY THEOLOGY, the notion that God will bless believers with affluence, Frederick K. C. Price was born in Santa Monica, California, and reared as a Jehovah's Witness. He was converted to evangelical Christianity in 1953 and entered the ministry two years later, affiliating with a succession of denominations: Baptist, African Methodist Episcopal, Presbyterian, and *CHRISTIAN AND MISSIONARY ALLIANCE. Price's Spirit *BAPTISM in 1970, however, set him on a denominationally independent course. He founded Crenshaw Christian Center in 1973, which now occupies the former campus of Pepperdine University in Los Angeles. The congregation is multiracial and numbers well above ten thousand. Price, an African American, broadcasts his *PROSPERITY THEOLOGY nationwide with a television program called *Ever Increasing Faith,* begun in 1978. He is unabashed about the pursuit of wealth as a sign of God's blessing and does not shy away from ostentatious displays himself.

References: Frederick K. C. Price, *How Faith Works* (1976); idem, *Faith, Foolishness or Presumption?* (1979); "Increasing Faith: The Price Is Right," *Christianity Today,* October 2, 1995; *Mine Eyes Have Seen the Glory,* three-part PBS documentary (1992).

Pridgeon, Charles Hamilton (1863–1932) A controversial leader of *PENTECOSTALISM, Charles Hamilton Pridgeon was born in Baltimore. He graduated from Lafayette College and Princeton Theological Seminary and undertook further studies in Germany and in Great Britain. Pridgeon was ordained a Presbyterian, but his *BAPTISM OF THE HOLY SPIRIT in 1892 and his embrace of divine healing led to a break with the Presbyterians and a move in the direction of the *CHRISTIAN AND MISSIONARY ALLIANCE. In December 1901, Pridgeon founded the Wylie Avenue Church in Pittsburgh and, shortly thereafter, the Pittsburgh Bible Institute. The spectrum of his ministries soon expanded to include an orphanage, a missions initiative to Africa and India,

*EVANGELISM, a printing operation, and a periodical, *Record of Faith.*

After attending one of *AIMEE SEMPLE MCPHERSON's *REVIVAL campaigns in Dayton, Ohio, Pridgeon returned to Pittsburgh in the winter of 1920 and sparked a *REVIVAL there. He ran afoul of other pentecostal leaders, however, with his views on hell, which constituted a form of universalism. Pridgeon taught that hell was limited in duration, that sinful humanity might be reconciled to the love of God after a period of "restitution." The General Council of the *ASSEMBLIES OF GOD condemned the "Pridgeon Doctrine" or "Pridgeonism" as heresy in 1925.

Reference: Charles Hamilton Pridgeon, *Is Hell Eternal; or, Will God's Plan Fail?*, 3d ed. (1931).

Primitive Methodist Church, USA The Primitive Methodist Church, USA is one of the two Methodist bodies in the United States that does not have its roots in the Methodist Episcopal Church. The Primitive Methodists came out of a *CAMP MEETING in England, led by the American Methodist *EVANGELIST *LORENZO DOW. The Primitive Methodists formed in 1811, when two ministers were expelled from the *WESLEYAN METHODIST CONNECTION. By 1829, Primitive Methodists in the United States were able to secure ministers from England, but by 1840 the American church separated itself from its English parent. Most of the churches were located in the East, with a few in the Midwest.

In its *POLITY, the Primitive Methodist Conference meets annually and is the administrative and legislative body of the church. The conference has direct oversight of all boards, committees, and agencies of the church. The conference is headed by the president, who is elected every four years. There is one full-time salaried officer, the executive director, and equal representation of clergy and laity at all levels of administration. There are six districts; district and local conferences meet quarterly. Headquarters are in Wilkes-Barre, Pennsylvania. The denomination reports eighty-three congregations with 8,487 members.

References: Frank S. Mead and Samuel S. Hill, *Handbook of Denominations in the United States*, 10th ed. (1996); *J. Gordon Melton, The Encyclopedia of American Religions*, 3d ed. (1993).

Primitivism Primitivism, the notion that it is possible to recover the purity of the New Testament church, is a recurrent theme in American *EVANGELICALISM, from the Puritans of the colonial period to the *RESTORATIONIST MOVEMENT and *LANDMARK BAPTISTS in the nineteenth century to *PENTECOSTALISM in the twentieth. All primitivist movements seek to reject the accretions and the corruptions that have leeched onto the church throughout history, and their zeal for New Testament purity at least implies a rebuke to other churches for having departed from what primitivists define as the true *GOSPEL.

Reference: Richard T. Hughes, ed., *The American Quest for the Primitive Church* (1995).

Prince, (Peter) Derek (1915–) Born in Bangalore, India, where his father was stationed by the British army, Derek Prince earned degrees from Cambridge University and also studied at Hebrew University. While serving in the British Royal Army Medical Corps in North Africa during World War II, Prince had an evangelical *CONVERSION and received the *BAPTISM OF THE HOLY SPIRIT several days later. He returned to London after the war and founded a pentecostal church, where he remained until 1956, when he assumed the post of principal of the Nyangori Teacher Training College in Kenya. Prince came to North America in 1962, where he identified with the emerging *CHARISMATIC MOVEMENT and refined his teachings on demon possession, healing, and the *END TIMES.

After serving as pastor of churches in Minneapolis, Minnesota, Seattle, and Chicago, Prince moved to Fort Lauderdale, Florida, in 1968. There, he formed an alliance with *BOB MUMFORD and *DON BASHAM of the *SHEPHERDING MOVEMENT. The three established Good News Church in 1974, and Prince began a radio broadcast, *Today with Derek Prince,* in 1979. Prince broke with Basham and Mumford in 1984 and continues his own activities under the aegis of his Global Outreach organization, based in Fort Lauderdale.

References: Derek Prince, *Discipleship, Shepherding, Commitment* (1976); idem, *The Last Word on the Middle East* (1982); idem, *Chords from David's Harp* (1982); *Derek Prince: The Man and His Ministry* (1984).

Princeton Foreign Missionary Society. *See* **Wilder, Robert Parmelee.**

Princeton Theology Princeton Theology is a name associated with the doctrines espoused by theologians at Princeton Theological Seminary in the nineteenth century, specifically *ARCHIBALD ALEXANDER, *CHARLES HODGE, *ARCHIBALD ALEXANDER HODGE, and *BENJAMIN BRECKINRIDGE WARFIELD, among others. This theology was marked by a strong adherence to Reformed dogma, especially as put forward by the *WESTMINSTER STANDARDS, and by an insistence on human depravity and predestination. As the nineteenth century wore on, Princeton Theology grew increasingly out of favor among American Protestants. The Arminian-inspired revivalism of *CHARLES FINNEY emphasized human agency in the *SALVATION process, something that Hodge and the others regarded as akin to heresy. After mid-century, the German discipline of higher criticism cast doubt upon the reliability of the *BIBLE. The Princeton theologians (also known as the *PRINCETONIANS) responded by emphasizing that the *BIBLE was entirely free from error in the original autographs and that any apparent discrepancies in the text came through the errors of copyists.

The death of Warfield in 1921 marked the passing of the Princeton Theology, especially as Princeton Seminary and the Presbyterian denomination moved away from historic creedal formulations and toward theological *MODERNISM. The departure of *J. GRESHAM MACHEN in 1929 effectively ended the era of Princeton Theology, although many twentieth-century evangelicals at such places as *WESTMINSTER THEOLOGICAL SEMINARY and *TRINITY EVANGELICAL DIVINITY SCHOOL have sought to perpetuate the tradition of Princeton Theology.

Princetonians The Princetonians were a handful of theologians at Princeton Theological Seminary from its founding in 1812 until the 1920s. Although the term can, of course, be applied more broadly, it most often denotes *ARCHIBALD ALEXANDER, *SAMUEL MILLER, *CHARLES HODGE, *ARCHIBALD ALEXANDER HODGE, *FRANCIS LANDEY PATTON, and *BENJAMIN BRECKINRIDGE WARFIELD. These theologians, as well as several lesser lights, propagated and defended a conservative theology that they insisted could be traced back through François Turretin, John Calvin, Augustine, the early church fathers, and to the New Testament itself.

Prison Fellowship. *See* **Colson, Charles W. "Chuck".**

Progressive National Baptist Convention The Progressive National Baptist Convention was formed in 1961 as the result of a dispute in the *NATIONAL BAPTIST CONVENTION IN THE U.S.A. (NBCUSA). The dispute had two parts. The first had to do with the tenure of officers; the second with the civil rights movement. Prior to 1952, the tenure for presidents of the NBCUSA was life. In 1952, however, the convention adopted a four-year term limit. J. H. Jackson was elected president in 1953, but refused to step down when his term expired in 1957. Instead, he ruled that the term-limit provision was a violation of the convention's constitution.

In 1961, the dispute came to a head when Gardner C. Taylor challenged Jackson for the office of president of the convention. The contretemps included physical violence and a court trial. Jackson, however, was reelected as president, and his election was upheld in civil court. Taylor and his supporters refused to accept the defeats. L. V. Booth, pastor of the Zion Baptist Church in Cincinnati, issued a call to form a new Baptist convention, and the Progressive National Baptist Convention was created in November 1961. Booth was elected the first convention president, and Taylor later served in the offices of vice president and president. Until 1990, the convention had a two-year term limit on all offices. In 1990, an amendment to the constitution took effect that allowed any officer to serve a maximum of three consecutive two-year terms. Offices are open to any member of the convention, clergy or lay, male or female.

The second part of the dispute concerned the civil rights movement. The Progressives had been urging the NBCUSA to take a more active role in the movement's leadership. The new convention allowed the leadership that was already in the African American community to come to the fore with the backing of the denomination. Martin Luther King Jr. and Ralph D. Abernathy quickly stepped forward. Through the years the Progressives have continued the struggle for civil rights. Among the leaders in civil rights advocacy who have also been leaders of the Progressives are such men as Jesse Jackson, Benjamin Hooks, William Gray III, and Walter E. Fauntroy.

The Progressive National Baptist Convention is similar to other Baptist denominations in doctrine. With the exception of term limits, the Progressives are also like their parent denomination in *POLITY. The Progressives have been an ecumenical body from the start, maintaining memberships in the World Council of Churches, the National Council of Churches in Christ, the Baptist World Alliance, and the Baptist Joint Committee on Public Affairs, among others. The Progressives' headquarters are in Washington, D.C. In 1995, the convention reported more than 2.5 million members in two thousand churches.

References: Frank S. Mead and Samuel S. Hill, *Handbook of Denominations in the United States*, 10th ed. (1996); J. Gordon Melton, *The Encyclopedia of American Religions*, 3d ed. (1993); Larry G. Murphy, J. Gordon Melton, and Gary L. Ward, eds., *Encyclopedia of African American Religions* (1993); *1997 Yearbook of American and Canadian Churches.*

Project Life. *See* **Operation Save America.**

Promise Keepers On March 20, 1990, *BILL MCCARTNEY, head football coach at the University of Colorado, and his friend

Dave Wardell were traveling to a meeting of the *FELLOWSHIP OF CHRISTIAN ATHLETES in Pueblo, Colorado. In the course of their conversation, they came upon the idea of filling Colorado's Folsom Stadium with men dedicated to the notion of Christian discipleship. This vision spread to a cohort of seventy-two men, who engaged in fasting and prayer in support of the notion.

Over four thousand men showed up for the first gathering, and by July 1993 McCartney's original vision had been fulfilled: Fifty thousand men piled into Folsom Stadium for singing, hugging, and exhortations to be good and faithful husbands, fathers, and churchgoers. By 1996, the organization, Promise Keepers, had an annual budget in excess of $115 million and offices in thirty-two states and provinces throughout North America. More than one million men attended twenty-two rallies at sports stadiums across the country in 1995, and on October 4, 1997, Promise Keepers conducted a mass rally, called Standing in the Gap: A Sacred Assembly of Men, on the Mall in Washington, D.C. The movement quickly faded, however; by February of the following year Promise Keepers announced that it would lay off its entire staff and rely on volunteer labor, although an infusion of contributions and a grant from the Castle Rock Foundation, a politically conservative organization controlled by the Coors brewing empire, kept the organization alive.

References: Gustav Niebuhr, "Men's Group to Lay Off Entire Staff," *New York Times,* February 20, 1998; Randall Balmer, *Blessed Assurance: A History of Evangelicalism in America* (1999); Dane S. Claussen, ed., *The Promise Keepers: Essays on Masculinity and Christianity* (2000).

Prooftexts Because of evangelicals' commitment to **SOLA SCRIPTURA*, the *BIBLE alone, as the source of *AUTHORITY, they have often engaged in providing prooftexts in sermons, writings, and even verbal discourse in order to buttress their arguments. Prooftexts are references to Bible verses, and the practice of "prooftexting" involves inserting these references into the prose. For the preacher, author, or speaker, the use of prooftexts illustrates his or her command of the *BIBLE; in the eyes of some evangelicals, moreover, the more prooftexts the more persuasive the sermon or argument.

Prosperity Gospel. *See* **Prosperity Theology.**

Prosperity Theology Variously known as the prosperity gospel, "name it, claim it," or positive confession theology, prosperity theology posits that God is willing—indeed, eager—to bestow material blessings on the faithful. Although accounts of its origins differ, this doctrine is generally traced to *E. W. KENYON, but it may have its roots in New Thought metaphysical ideas, the notion that anything from health to abundance was available simply through the proper disposition of the mind.

Prosperity theology was taken up by many of the televangelists in the 1970s and 1980s, notably *KENNETH COPELAND, *KENNETH HAGIN, *ROBERT TILTON, and *FREDERICK K. C. PRICE, among others. Not surprisingly, prosperity theology enjoyed its greatest popularity during the 1980s, the Reagan era, with its emphasis on affluence and self-aggrandizement.

Protect Our Children. *See* **Bryant, Anita.**

Providence College and Theological Seminary (Otterburne, Manitoba) Providence College and Theological

Seminary began as the Winnipeg Bible Training School, established in 1925 by H. L. Turner. Five years later, the school was renamed Winnipeg Bible Institute; it became Winnipeg Bible Institute and College of Theology in 1948, upon receipt of a provincial charter to grant theological degrees. In 1963, the college moved completely over to degree-granting programs and became known as Winnipeg Bible College.

In its first forty-five years, the school occupied thirteen different facilities in and around Winnipeg. This transience undoubtedly had an effect on the college's overall stability. Enrollment never exceeded one hundred students. Nonetheless, Winnipeg Bible College did manage to earn Associate membership in the *AMERICAN ASSOCIATION OF BIBLE COLLEGES in 1966. However, by 1970 the college found itself in a period of genuine crisis. In addition to financial and enrollment problems, it was in need of a new campus because the building it occupied was slated for destruction. In response, the college bought an old Catholic high school in Otterburne, Manitoba—thirty miles south of Winnipeg. That fall Winnipeg Bible College opened on its new ninety-three-acre site. It had only seventy students, but within a few years the enrollment had climbed to three hundred, and in 1973 the college earned full accreditation from the *AMERICAN ASSOCIATION OF BIBLE COLLEGES (AABC). The Winnipeg Bible College Graduate Division offered its first full year of courses in 1972. Soon after, the division became known as Winnipeg Theological Seminary. Today, the seminary offers the master of divinity and the doctorate of ministry, in addition to the master of arts in biblical, theological, or global Christian studies, student development, Christian education, and biblical counseling.

In 1992, the college and seminary adopted the name Providence College and Theological Seminary in an effort to reflect both the school's biblical roots and emphasis on liberal arts. Library special resources include collections on missions, contemporary religious movements, and materials for youth drama. The library also has a computer center where students can perform electronic research on ancient Hebrew and Greek texts.

Providence College and Theological Seminary goes to greater lengths than many *CHRISTIAN COLLEGES to regulate students' social life. No social *DANCING is permitted on or off campus. In addition, the school makes clear its expectation that students are to "practise discretion, restraint, and spiritual discernment in inter-personal relationships, the choice of television programs, music, movies, videos, theatre, games and printed matter."

References: *Providence Theological Seminary Catalogue, 1996–1997* (1996); *Providence College Catalogue, 1996–1997* (1996).

■ ■ ■

Quayle, J(ames) Danforth "Dan" (1947–) Born in Indianapolis, Indiana, the scion of a newspaper family, Dan Quayle graduated from DePauw University in 1969 and earned the J.D. from Indiana University in 1974. After briefly practicing law in Huntington, Indiana, he was elected to the U.S. House of Representatives on the Republican ticket in 1976 and reelected two years later. He won election to the Senate in 1980 and reelection in 1986.

Quayle and his wife, Marilyn Tucker Quayle, whom he married in 1972, align themselves with the fundamentalist wing of American *EVANGELICALISM and are especially influenced by the esoteric teachings of *R. B. THIEME. These issues came to light in 1988 when George Bush unexpectedly tapped Quayle to be his vice presidential running mate. Despite Quayle's penchant for malapropisms—he once declared that he did not live in this century—Bush and Quayle won the 1988 election, and Quayle served as vice president of the United States from 1989 until 1993.

Reference: Dan Quayle, *Standing Firm: A Vice Presidential Memoir* (1994).

Quie, Al(bert) (Harold) (1923–) Al Quie was born near Dennison, Minnesota, and served as a navy pilot during World War II. He graduated from St. Olaf College in 1950 and won a special election to the U.S. House of Representatives in 1958 as a Republican. He remained in Congress for two decades, during which time he became friends with other evangelicals such as *HAROLD E. HUGHES and *CHARLES COLSON. Quie was elected governor of Minnesota in 1978 and served until 1983. After leaving the statehouse, Quie worked for Colson's organization, Prison Fellowship, first as area director for North Dakota and Minnesota and, beginning in 1987, as executive vice president. In 2000, he became active in the WordAlone Network, an organization of Lutherans who objected to the Call to Common Mission, a cooperative venture between the Evangelical Lutheran Church in America and the Episocpal Church.

■ ■ ■

Rader, Paul (Daniel) (1879–1938) The son of a Methodist *EVANGELIST, Paul Rader was educated at the University of Denver, the University of Colorado, and the University of Puget Sound prior to becoming a Congregational minister in Boston and in Portland, Oregon. Disillusioned, he left the ministry in Portland in 1908 and found his way to New York, where he became involved with the *CHRISTIAN AND MISSIONARY ALLIANCE and did some street preaching.

After three years at the *CHRISTIAN AND MISSIONARY ALLIANCE Tabernacle in Pittsburgh, Rader became pastor of *MOODY CHURCH in Chicago from 1915 to 1921, during which time he also served as vice president and then president of the *CHRISTIAN AND MISSIONARY ALLIANCE. By the mid-1920s, Rader had left the Alliance and teamed up with *OSWALD J. SMITH in a missionary enterprise called Christian World Couriers.

References: Paul Rader, *The Fight for Light and Other Sermons* (1916); idem, *Round the World* (1922).

Radio Bible Class. *See* **DeHaan, M(artin) R(alph).**

Radio Chapel Service. *See* **Brown, R(obert) R.**

Radio Church of God. *See* **Worldwide Church of God.**

Radio Free America At 12:28 P.M. on Wednesday, September 19, 1973, an AM radio station in Lakewood, New Jersey, noticed interference with its signal at 1170 AM. The source, it turned out, was a World War II–era minesweeper bobbing in international waters in the Atlantic Ocean nine miles off the coast of Cape May. The boat's somewhat less-than-ten-thousand-watt radio signal bounced around several frequencies, prompting complaints from other stations, one in Delaware and others well inland, including KSL in Salt Lake City, Utah. Within two hours, agents of the Federal Communications Commission (FCC) approached the boat in a Coast Guard cutter. By day's end the Lakewood station, WHLW, had threatened to sue; the owner of the rogue signal apologized, ceased his broadcasts about at ten o'clock that night, and instructed his technicians to search for a different frequency. Two days later, Judge Mitchell H. Cohen of the U.S. District Court, at the behest of the FCC, issued a temporary restraining order, which forbade further broadcasting until a full hearing.

Thus began and ended the bizarre saga of Radio Free America—at least the short version of the story. Radio Free America was the brainchild of *CARL MCINTIRE, whose violation of the FCC's Fairness Doctrine had prompted the closure of his radio station, WXUR, in Media, Pennsylvania, which he had used as the flagship station for his *20th Century Reformation Hour* broadcast. McIntire, the implacable fundamentalist and anticommunist crusader, saw himself as a defender of freedom of speech. (He and his confrères, all dressed as the founding fathers, had conducted an elaborate "funeral" for WXUR at Independence Hall in Philadelphia.) Radio Free America—he chose the name as a deliberate rebuke to the government and as a counterpart to Radio Free Europe—succeeded in publicizing his case, and he won the support of many people, including newspaper columnists, members of Congress, and even the redoubtable Sam J. Ervin, Democratic senator from North Carolina. The FCC prevailed in court, however, winning a permanent injunction against McIntire's pirate radio station, and Radio Free America was abandoned.

Railton, George Scott (1849–1913) The first commissioner of the *SALVATION ARMY, George Scott Railton had been associated with *WILLIAM and *CATHERINE BOOTH in Great Britain. Railton brought the *SALVATION ARMY to the United States on March 10, 1880, arriving in New York with seven women "to claim America for God and the Army." Their efforts met with immediate success; Salvationists began publishing *Salvation News* in July, and by the end of the year Railton had traveled to St. Louis in an effort to expand the *SALVATION ARMY to the West. Railton was recalled to London in 1881.

Rand, Howard R. (1889–1991) A second-generation British-Israelitist born in Haverhill, Massachusetts, Howard R. Rand is the man most responsible for the spread of *BRITISH ISRAELISM in the United States and building it into a national organization. He began his organizational work in 1928, and by 1930 he had established his own British-Israel organization, the Anglo-Saxon Federation of America, in Detroit. He traveled throughout the country organizing chapters, and his organization benefited enormously from the zeal—and the financial contributions—of William J. Cameron, an anti-Semitic associate of Henry Ford. Rand's ideas about white supremacy, that whites were God's chosen people, were especially well received during the Great Depression.

Reference: Michael Barkun, *Religion and the Racist Right: The Origins of the Christian Identity Movement* (1994).

Randall, Benjamin (1749–1808) Born in New Castle, New Hampshire, Benjamin Randall was converted upon learning of *GEORGE WHITEFIELD's death in 1770. Randall had heard Whitefield preach but had spurned his evangelical message; with Whitefield's passing, Randall declared, "Whitefield is in heaven, and I am on the road to hell." His *CONVERSION prompted a renewed affiliation with the New Castle Congregational Church, but he soon left because of doubts about the doctrine of infant *BAPTISM. Randall was baptized in 1776 in Madbury, New Hampshire, and became an itinerant preacher who was known for his stentorian voice. He accepted the pulpit of the Congregational church in New Durham and reorganized it as a Baptist church.

Throughout his ministry, Randall had grown increasingly suspicious of Calvinist theology, preferring a doctrine of universal *ATONEMENT, which offered *GRACE to anyone who believes in Jesus Christ. The mainstream Baptists, who still subscribed to the Calvinist notion of predestination, disowned Randall, whereupon he and several friends organized the Freewill Baptist Connexion on June 30, 1780.

References: John Buzzell, *The Life of Elder Benjamin Randall* (1827); William F. Davidson, *The Free Will Baptists in America, 1727–1984* (1985); William Henry Brackney, *The Baptists* (1988).

Rapture A central tenet of premillennial *ESCHATOLOGY, the rapture (sometimes called the rapture of the Church) refers to the taking up of the true believers (generally understood by evangelicals to refer to *BORN-AGAIN Christians) before the *TRIBULATION predicted in the book of Revelation. The doctrine surrounding the rapture derives from 1 Thessalonians 4:15–17, but premillennialists disagree, sometimes heatedly, over when the rapture will occur. While most believe that it will occur before the tribulation, others think it will take place during the tribulation and still others believe the Church will endure the tribulation before being taken up to heaven. With the exception of posttribulationists, most premillennialists draw a distinction between the rapture (when Jesus comes to gather the Church) and the *SECOND COMING (when Jesus returns with his Church to inaugurate the *MILLENNIUM).

Ravi Zacharias Ministries. *See* **Zacharias, Ravi (Kumar).**

Rawlyk, G(eorge) A(lexander) (1935–1995) Reared in a Ukranian-Canadian family, G. A. Rawlyk attended Bethany Baptist Mission in his hometown of Thorold, Ontario, where he learned English and developed a deep and abiding Christian faith. After graduating from McMaster University, he became a Rhodes Scholar in 1957, studied at Oxford University, and completed his graduate studies at the University of Rochester. He taught at Dalhousie University in Halifax, Nova Scotia, beginning in 1963, and went on to teach in the history department at Queen's University in Kingston, Ontario, serving also as chair of the department.

Despite some opposition from within the academy in Canada, Rawlyk, who wrote and edited nearly thirty books, sought to legitimize the study of *EVANGELICALISM in Canada by means of both his own scholarship and his training and encouragement of others. Beginning in 1984, Rawlyk was part of the network of scholars associated with the *INSTITUTE FOR THE STUDY OF AMERICAN EVANGELICALS, encouraging them to include Canada—and, by extension, evangelicals throughout the world—in their scholarly inquiries. An enormously engaging and compassionate man, Rawlyk encouraged countless scholars of *EVANGELICALISM until his untimely death in 1995.

In addition to his strong evangelical convictions, Rawlyk, whose father was a longshoreman and a union organizer, was both a socialist and, in his words, "a staunch Canadian nationalist." He declared in a 1992 interview that "the two sides of my faith are very important. There is a strong pietistic side, but there is also a very strong *SOCIAL GOSPEL side. I am a very committed socialist, largely because of my Christian faith." Rawkyk decried evangelicals' headlong plunge into consumerism. "*EVANGELICALISM as far as I'm concerned isn't destroyed by so-called *MODERNISM, by Biblical criticism, by Darwin," he said. "It's destroyed from within because evangelicals take up consumerism so enthusiastically, and the therapeutic society with such great devotion, and in the process they abandon the essential principles of Christianity—which appear to me to be sacrifice and selflessness rather than selfishness and accumulation." Rawlyk acknowledged that he often found himself, "because of my political and social views, to be anathema to a number of Canadian evangelicals."

References: G. A. Rawlyk, *Ravished by the Spirit: Revivals, Maritime Baptists and Henry Alline* (1984); idem, *Champions of the Truth: Fundamentalism, Modernism and Maritime Baptists* (1990); idem, *"The Canada Fire": Radical Evangelicalism in British North America, 1775–1812* (1994); idem, "Writing about Canadian Religious Revivals," in Edith L. Blumhofer and Randall Balmer, eds., *Modern Christian Revivals* (1993); "Professing History," *LUCAS: An Evangelical History Review*, XIV (1992).

Rayburn, James C., Jr. (1909–1970) The founder of *YOUNG LIFE, James C. Rayburn Jr. studied engineering and mineralogy at Kansas State University and the University of Colorado before enrolling at *DALLAS THEOLOGICAL SEMINARY in 1936. In the course of his fieldwork assignment, Rayburn experimented with several Bible study curricula among his charges in Gainesville, Texas. These, together with his resolve to make meetings fun and to focus on campus leaders, brought considerable success to his evangelistic efforts.

With financial support from *HERBERT J. TAYLOR, a Chicago businessman, Rayburn organized *YOUNG LIFE MINISTRIES in 1941 and founded *Young Life* magazine three years later. The organization eventually moved its operations to a ranch near Colorado Springs, Colorado, called Star Ranch, also provided by Taylor. Rayburn retired in 1964.

Reagan, Ronald (Wilson) (1911–) Born in Tampico, Illinois, to an Irish Catholic father and a Disciples of Christ mother, Ronald Reagan was baptized by the Disciples at age eleven and attended one of the denomination's schools, Eureka College. He became a radio broadcaster and then moved to Hollywood in 1937, where he became a "B" movie actor. Although he originally considered himself to be a New Deal Democrat, he drifted toward conservative politics and emerged as a national figure during Barry Goldwater's run for the presidency in 1964. Reagan was elected to the first of two terms as governor of California two years later.

Though divorced and remarried—something that most evangelicals frowned upon until the 1980s—Reagan formed alliances with conservative evangelicals during the 1970s. By 1980, he had emerged as their champion, even though his own religious commitments remained rather tepid. Reagan's conservative rhetoric as candidate and as president, however, resonated with many evangelicals, and they became his most reliable constituency.

Reconstructionism Reconstructionism, also known as theonomy, dominion theology, or Christian reconstructionism, is a theology and social ethic that advocates restructuring civil society according to the laws contained in the Hebrew Bible (Old Testament). The movement, which dates back to the early 1960s, was begun by *ROUSAS JOHN RUSHDOONY and is perpetuated by Greg Bahnsen and Gary North, Rushdoony's estranged son-in-law.

Reconstructionists believe that the civil government should conform to Mosaic and Levitical laws. Capital punishment, for example, should be imposed for everything from sodomy to the incorrigibility of children. Reconstructionists especially detest the notion of toleration. North, one of the movement's most militant spokesmen, has insisted that "the perfect love of God necessarily involves the perfect hatred of God's enemies," and Rushdoony openly resents that "in the name of toleration, the believer is asked to associate on a common level of total acceptance with the atheist, the pervert, the criminal, and the adherents of other religions." During the 1980s and beyond, Reconstructionist ideas enjoyed considerable influence with leaders of the *RELIGIOUS RIGHT, especially *JERRY FALWELL, *PAT ROBERTSON, and *RANDALL TERRY.

Rededication One of the most common terms in the American evangelical subculture is "rededication," as in, "I've rededicated my life to Christ." After the initial *BORN-AGAIN experience, most evangelicals lapse somewhat in their piety. This "backsliding," as it is often called, can take many forms, from minor trespasses to full-scale rebellion against the norms of the evangelical subculture. Rededication marks the individual's return to the evangelical fold. Similar to *CONVERSION, rededication often occurs in response to preaching, music, or some form of *EVANGELISM, and it is frequently attended by considerable emotion.

Among second-generation evangelicals (people whose parents were converted in some dramatic way), the *CONVERSION and rededication sequence tends to be played out during adolescence. Having been socialized in the church for all or most of their lives, these adolescents still must come up with a credible *CONVERSION narrative for full inclusion in the evangelical community. When their *CONVERSIONS seem to pale next to the stories they have heard from their parents and their parents' generation, these second-generation evangelicals fall away from the faith rather regularly and then make periodic attempts to rededicate their lives to Jesus and thereby reinstate themselves in the evangelical subculture. Because inheriting religious piety (in any tradition) is very difficult, many of these adolescents finally give up the quest and leave the subculture; others leave for a time and then return.

Redeemer College (Ancaster, Ontario) Redeemer College is officially interdenominational, but it derives from a Reformed perspective. The school was actually the second attempt by Reformed Christians to establish a university in Ontario, the first effort in the 1950s having failed. The Ontario Christian College Association was established in 1976 with the purpose of opening such a college; the Ontario Legislature granted a charter to the association in 1980. Two years later, Redeemer College held its first classes in facilities rented from the Board of Education in the city of Hamilton, Ontario. In 1985, the college bought seventy-eight acres of land in Ancaster, Ontario, for its own campus. The following year, Redeemer took occupancy of its new campus, and the same year Redeemer became the first Canadian college to be admitted as a full member of the *CHRISTIAN COLLEGE COALITION. The library holds the Teacher Education Resource Centre, which supports Redeemer's teacher training program. In addition, the library has a six-thousand-volume collection of Dutch language theology, and the Pascal and Custance Collection, which contains three thousand volumes on the relationship between natural science and Christianity.

Reference: *Redeemer College Academic Calendar, 1993–1995* (1993).

Redpath, Alan (1907–) Born in England, Alan Redpath's first career was as an accountant, but he left the secular realm to become a minister. He was pastor of the Duke Street Baptist Church in London before accepting the pulpit at *MOODY MEMORIAL CHURCH in Chicago in 1953. During the course of that pastorate, Redpath sought to expand the church's outreach to Hispanics and African Americans. A popular speaker at Bible conferences, Redpath resigned *MOODY CHURCH in 1962 and returned to Britain as pastor of Charlotte Chapel, in Edinburgh, Scotland.

Reed, Ralph (Eugene), (Jr.) (1961–) Born into a military household in Portsmouth, Virginia, Ralph Reed grew up in Florida, Kentucky, and Georgia; his parents were Methodists and Republicans. Reed attended the University of Georgia from 1979 to 1983, where he became involved in the College Republicans club. "My goal," Reed recalled later of his entry into politics, "was to become the next Lee Atwater—a bare-knuckled, brass-tacks practitioner of hardball politics."

In September 1983, shortly after graduation from college and after moving to Washington as head of College Republicans, Reed experienced a religious *CONVERSION at an *ASSEMBLIES OF GOD church in suburban Washington. Although he did not repent of his conservative politics, he claimed to be sorry for some of his ruthless behavior. "Politics for me had degenerated into a cheap play for power," he recalled of his preconversion days. "I now realize that politics is a noble calling to serve God and my fellow man." In 1984, Reed left Washington for Raleigh, North Carolina, as executive director of a new organization called Students for America. The following year he enrolled in a Ph.D. program at Emory University, where he studied history and eventually received the degree in 1991.

At an inaugural party for George Bush in 1989, Reed met *PAT ROBERTSON, who had failed in his own bid for the Republican presidential nomination the year before. Asked for suggestions about forming a grassroots political organization from Robertson's mailing list, Reed drafted a detailed memorandum, and the two men joined forces to found the *CHRISTIAN COALITION that same year, with Robertson as president and Reed as executive director.

Reed soon displayed his political and organizational savvy, making the *CHRISTIAN COALITION into a formidable force for the *RELIGIOUS RIGHT. "I want to be invisible," Reed once said of his political tactics. "I paint my face and travel by night. You don't know it's over until you're in a body bag. You don't know until election night." Although, according to his own admission, Reed came to the organization as a political operative and not as a "Christian activist," Reed became an effective spokesman for politically conservative evangelicals, often taking softer, more conciliatory positions than Robertson, at least in public. Reed, however, shares Robertson's vision of conservative political dominance. "What Christians have got to do is to take back this country, one precinct at a time, one neighborhood at a time, and one state at a time," Reed said in 1990. "I honestly believe that in my lifetime we will see a country once again governed by Christians . . . and Christian values." Reed stepped down from his post at *CHRISTIAN COALITION in 1997 to form his own political consulting firm.

References: Ralph Reed, *Politically Incorrect* (1994); idem, *Active Faith: How Christians Are Changing the Soul of American Politics* (1996).

Re-enactor's Missions for Jesus Christ Re-enactor's Missions for Jesus Christ was founded in November 1984 by Harold Wyatt and Alan Farley. Both had participated for years in the reenactments of Civil War battles, and they had been looking for someone to conduct church services at the reenactments, both for historical authenticity and for the purposes of *EVANGELISM. Farley and Wyatt began portraying Confederate chaplains, but the group now has chaplains, both Union and Confederate, throughout the United States and in Europe.

According to the organization's materials, its purpose "is to see lost souls saved, lives changed, families put back together, and Christians strengthened all by God's grace and power." The group, which is headed by Farley and has its headquarters in Appomattox, Virginia, reprints and distributes gospel tracts that are contemporaneous to the Civil War. It also publishes a quarterly newspaper, *The Christian Banner,* which contains news about the organization and about reenactments as well as sermons and other evangelistic literature from the Civil War era. The group derives its support from individual congregations, most of which are Baptist, and it conducts Saturday evening tent *REVIVALS and Sunday morning worship services at Civil War reenactments.

Reference: Re-enactor's Missions for Jesus Christ brochure.

Reformed Church in America The Reformed Church in America (RCA) came to the Western Hemisphere as the Dutch Reformed Church well before the Revolutionary War. The first Dutch Reformed church in the colonies was founded by Jonas Michaëlius in 1628 in New Amsterdam (New York City) and is the oldest church in the nation with a continuous, uninterrupted ministry. After decades of infighting between the pietist and the more traditionalist faction—the latter wanted to remain loyal to the Classis of Amsterdam—the American church achieved independence from Holland in 1772. A general synod was organized in 1794, and in 1819 the church was incorporated under the name Reformed Protestant Dutch Church. The present name was adopted in 1867.

The organization of the RCA is presbyterian. Each congregation is governed by an elected consistory, which includes elders, deacons, and pastors. Elders oversee the life of a local church. Several congregations in a geographic region form a classis. Ministers are responsible to a classis, and the classis supervises and advises each congregation in its region. The classis also oversees the ordination, installation, and dismissal of ministers and has oversight of theological students in the region. Regional synods, of which there are eight, supervise regional ministries and provide general superintendence for all the congregations and classes in the region. The general synod, the highest representative body of the denomination, meets annually. It is made up of ministers and elders from each classis and sets the policy and programs for the RCA as a whole.

The doctrinal standards of the RCA are the Belgic Confession, the Heidelberg Catechism, and Canons of the Synod of Dordt. The church has remained theologically conservative. Worship is semiliturgical. Only the liturgies for *BAPTISM and the *LORD'S SUPPER, the two recognized sacraments, are mandatory.

The RCA, as a denomination, is a member of both the National Council of Churches of Christ and the World Council of Churches. The Synod of Mid-America, which is more evangelical in orientation, is a member of the *NATIONAL ASSOCIATION OF EVANGELICALS. As a whole, the RCA reports 306,312 members in 908 churches.

References: Randall Balmer, *A Perfect Babel of Confusion: Dutch Religion and English Culture in the Middle Colonies* (1989); Frank S. Mead and Samuel S. Hill, *Handbook of Denominations in the United States,* 10th ed. (1996); J. Gordon Melton, *The Encyclopedia of American Religions,* 3d ed. (1993); *1997 Yearbook of American and Canadian Churches.*

Reformed Episcopal Church Organized in 1873 by Bishop George David Cummins, the Reformed Episcopal Church was a splinter movement of evangelicals in the Episcopal Church who were upset by the movement away from evangelical principles and toward Anglo-Catholicism on the part of the larger body. Fellow bishops publicly attacked Cummins for participating in an ecumenical communion service in New York City under the aegis of the *EVANGELICAL ALLIANCE. A month after the service, Cummins resigned his office and issued a call for other evangelical Episcopalians to join him.

The new group's *Declaration of Principles* condemned the high church doctrines of moral regeneration through *BAPTISM, transubstantiation, and exclusive adherence to episcopal *POLITY. The Church uses an Episcopal liturgy as it is given in the Book of Common Prayer and holds a sacramental view of the *LORD'S SUPPER and *BAPTISM. The Reformed Episcopal Church is governed by a triennial general council. A presiding bishop is elected from among the serving bishops and acts as executive head of the church. Most authority, however, lies at the diocesan and parish levels. Headquarters for the church are in Philadelphia, and the denomination reports 5,882 members in eighty-three local churches. The Reformed Episcopal Church has been a member denomination in the *NATIONAL ASSOCIATION OF EVANGELICALS since 1990.

References: Alan C. Guelzo, *For the Union of Evangelical Christendom: The Irony of Reformed Episcopalians* (1994); Frank S. Mead and Samuel S. Hill, *Handbook of Denominations in the United States,* 10th ed. (1996); J. Gordon Melton, *The Encyclopedia of American Religions,* 3d ed. (1993).

Reformed Presbyterian Church, Evangelical Synod. *See* **Presbyterian Church in America.**

Reformed Presbyterian Church of North America The roots of the Reformed Presbyterian Church of North America lie in the Covenanter tradition of Scotland. A merger of the Seceders and Covenanters in 1782 created the Associate Reformed Presbyterian Church, now a part of the Presbyterian Church (U.S.A.). Some of the Reformed Presbyterians (Covenanters), however, did not participate in the merger. This group split between *NEW LIGHTS and Old Lights in 1833 over participation in government, specifically, over whether members could vote or hold public office. The *NEW LIGHTS permitted members to vote; the Old Lights did not. The restriction was not removed until 1964. The *NEW LIGHTS formed the Reformed Presbyterian Church, General Synod, which merged with the Evangelical Presbyterian Church in 1965. This group has since also become a part of the Presbyterian Church (U.S.A.).

The doctrine of the Reformed Presbyterian Church of North America is based on the Westminster Confession. The denomination emphasizes the *INERRANCY of Scripture, the sovereignty of God, and the Lordship of Christ over every facet of human life. Worship centers on the reading and exposition of the *BIBLE. Only Psalms are sung in the worship services, and no musical instruments are permitted. Members cannot join secret societies. Although the denomination is thoroughly Presbyterian, there is no general assembly. Most of the group's strength lies in western Pennsylvania and eastern Kansas; there are 68 congregations with 5,174 members.

References: Frank S. Mead and Samuel S. Hill, *Handbook of Denominations in the United States*, 10th ed. (1996); J. Gordon Melton, *The Encyclopedia of American Religions*, 3d ed. (1993).

Regent College (Vancouver, British Columbia) Regent College in Vancouver, British Columbia, was founded in 1968 as an interdenominational school that would focus on the training of the laity. Regent became affiliated in 1973 with the University of British Columbia, which gave the college's students access to the facilities and liberal arts curriculum of the university. Regent's own programs and faith positions remain independent, however, of the larger school.

In addition to continuing education courses for ministers and missionaries, Regent offers master of divinity and master of theology degree programs. The college is accredited by the Association of Theological Schools in the United States and Canada. Although still interdenominational, the school holds a cooperative agreement with the Evangelical Covenant Church for the training of master of divinity students who are candidates for ordination in that denomination.

Regent College also has a large division in Christian studies, in which laypeople can pursue diplomas, certificates, and master's degrees with a variety of concentrations. One such concentration is in Chinese studies, offered through the college's Chinese Studies Program, established in 1985 to minister to the needs of the Chinese in churches in Canada and worldwide. Since 1990, Regent College has also maintained cooperative agreements with *INTERVARSITY CHRISTIAN FELLOWSHIP, *YOUNG LIFE, and *YOUTH FOR CHRIST, under which Regent trains staff workers for these organizations. This degree program culminates in a diploma in Christian studies with a concentration in youth *EVANGELISM.

Reference: *Regent College Catalogue, 1995–1997* (1995).

Regent University (Virginia Beach, Virginia) Regent University was established in 1978 by *MARION G. "PAT" ROBERTSON, founder of both the *CHRISTIAN BROADCASTING NETWORK and, later, the *CHRISTIAN COALITION. Until 1990, the school was known as Christian Broadcasting Network University, and in fact it was built largely from Robertson's media empire. Regent reports its current endowment at $190 million, although that number increased substantially after the sale of the Family Channel to Rupert Murdoch.

Although it opened as a "College of Communication and the Arts" that enrolled seventy-seven students, Regent has always placed a high emphasis on graduate education. In fact, Regent is unusual in that it has no liberal arts college whatsoever but consists of several independent, but affiliated, graduate schools: College of Communication and the Arts; the Robertson School of Government; and the Schools of Law, Divinity, Education, Counseling and Human Services, and Business. These schools each offer master's degrees appropriate to their fields. Regent awards doctorates in education, psychology, ministry and communications, as well as the *juris doctor* degree. In addition, the university's Center for Leadership Studies offers its own Ph.D. program in organizational leadership, with cognates in education, business, or ministry. Currently, Regent's School of Divinity maintains a cooperative agreement with Soonshin University in Seoul, South Korea, whereby the divinity school awards both master's degrees and doctorates of divinity. Regent has plans to institute similar programs in several other countries. Students can enroll in many of these programs on a distance-education option, with little or no on-campus study required. Regent's divinity school operates a field-based master's degree program in practical theology. The School of Business uses taped and at-home study, and most of the other schools offer degree programs by way of the Internet, with new on-line programs added each year.

Robertson comes from the pentecostal tradition, but Regent has managed to attract a diverse body of evangelical students. The name "Regent University" was intended to invoke the school's status as a representative body for Jesus Christ, in both the sacred and secular arenas. Regent also has been called the "Harvard of the *RELIGIOUS RIGHT," a title that reflects not only the school's faith commitment but also the aspirations of its famous founder. Robertson remains on board as chancellor, and Regent continues to share a campus with his other initiatives: the *CHRISTIAN BROADCASTING NETWORK, the *AMERICAN CENTER FOR LAW AND JUSTICE, the American Institute of Missions Strategies, and the Founders Inn and Conference Center.

Reference: Harvey Cox, "The Warring Visions of the Religious Right," *Atlantic Monthly,* November 1995.

Regular Baptist Foreign Missionary Society of Canada. *See* **Fyfe, Robert Alexander.**

Religious Education Association The Religious Education Association was organized by *WILLIAM RAINEY HARPER, the first president of the University of Chicago, who was also a prominent Baptist. Harper saw biblical study as essential to the redemption of American life and organized the Religious Education Association to institute his agenda for making the *BIBLE central. When the association was founded in 1903, John Dewey was one of the speakers at its first convention. Ultimately, the Religious Education Association became a kind of clearinghouse for all of Harper's efforts for educational reform. It promoted many forms of religious education within families, in *SUNDAY SCHOOLS, and up through universities. In an attempt to be universal and free from sectarian infighting, the association claimed to be nondenominational, but both Catholics and the conservatives who would soon earn the name "fundamentalists" were barred from membership, as were African Americans.

Reference: George M. Marsden, *The Soul of the American University: From Protestant Establishment to Established Unbelief* (1994).

Religious Right Sometimes called the Christian Right or the New Christian Right, the Religious Right is a name applied to a loose coalition of personalities and organizations that arose in the late 1970s to articulate a politically conservative agenda. Although evangelicals have long been active in politics, many shied away from political engagement in the political arena in the middle decades of the twentieth century. The immediate catalyst for their return was the presidential campaign of *JIMMY CARTER, a Southern Baptist *SUNDAY SCHOOL teacher who openly declared that he was a "*BORN-AGAIN Christian." While Carter lured many evangelicals out of their apolitical stupor (Southerners especially), many evangelicals turned against him when his administration's Justice Department sought to enforce antidiscrimination laws at *BOB JONES UNIVERSITY, a fundamentalist school in Greenville, South Carolina. This action represented an incursion into the evangelical subculture, which had been so carefully constructed in the decades following the *SCOPES TRIAL.

After evangelical leaders cooperated to resist such a move, they sought to assemble a larger agenda, which in time would include opposition to *ABORTION. Ironically, politically conservative evangelicals turned against Carter in favor of *RONALD REAGAN in 1980, when the Religious Right established itself as an electoral force. *JERRY FALWELL's formation of *MORAL MAJORITY in 1979 was perhaps the most visible eruption of Religious Right impulses, but other organizations that fit beneath that umbrella might include the *RELIGIOUS ROUNDTABLE, *TRADITIONAL VALUES COALITION, *FOCUS ON THE FAMILY, *CONCERNED WOMEN FOR AMERICA, and *CHRISTIAN COALITION, among many others. The highly conservative agenda articulated by Falwell, *PAT ROBERTSON, *RALPH REED, and others, however, represents a departure from the legacy of nineteenth-century *EVANGELICALISM, with its abiding concern for social amelioration and for those less fortunate.

The Religious Right since 1980 has made steady inroads within the Republican Party, often to the chagrin of long-term party members. In 1988, Pat Robertson made a credible showing in the early Republican presidential primaries, and in 1992 Robertson and Pat Buchanan addressed the Republican National Convention in Houston, where they rehearsed themes dear to the hearts of religious conservatives. The success of the Religious Right in the 1980s and 1990s, however, provoked a backlash not only among the electorate (who elected Bill Clinton in 1992 and reelected him four years later) but also among evangelicals whose political sympathies lean to the left on the ideological spectrum. In 1996, Senator *MARK O. HATFIELD, Republican of Oregon, announced his decision not to seek reelection, complaining that "converted Confederates" had taken over his party. That same year *JIM WALLIS, *TONY CAMPOLO, and other politically liberal evangelicals formed an organization called *CALL TO RENEWAL in order to counteract the impression that leaders of the Religious Right spoke for all evangelicals. After Clinton's acquittal on impeachment charges, some leaders of the Religious Right, including *PAUL WEYRICH, Ed Dobson, and Cal Thomas, called on evangelicals virtually to abandon political activity because it had compromised the faith.

References: William Martin, *With God on Our Side: The Rise of the Religious Right in America* (1996); Clyde Wilcox, *Onward Christian Soldiers?: The Religious Right in American Politics* (1996); Dallas A. Blanchard, *The Anti-Abortion Movement and the Rise of the Religious Right: From Polite to Fiery Protest* (1994); Cal Thomas and Ed Dobson, *Blinded By Might: Can the Religious Right Save America?* (1999).

Religious Roundtable Organized in 1979 by *ED MCATEER, one of the architects of the *RELIGIOUS RIGHT, the Religious Roundtable was a caucus of politically conservative evangelicals who sought to promote right-wing political causes and candidates, particularly those who opposed *ABORTION, pornography, and homosexuality. One of the defining moments of the 1980 presidential campaign, which pitted *RONALD REAGAN against the incumbent, *JIMMY CARTER, occurred during the Roundtable's first *NATIONAL AFFAIRS BRIEFING, a rally of fifteen thousand conservatives in Dallas, Texas. After several stemwinding speeches by right-wing preachers, Reagan, who had been seated on the dias, walked the podium and said, "I know this is a nonpartisan gathering, and so I know you can't endorse me, but I . . . want you to know that I endorse you and what you are doing." The crowd rose to its feet and shouted "Amen!," thereby all but ensuring that conservative evangelicals would turn their back on Carter, a fellow evangelical, in favor of Reagan in the November election.

Reparative Therapy Widely advocated and practiced by evangelical groups opposed to homosexuality, the term "reparative therapy" is based on the premise that gays and lesbians have chosen "the homosexual lifestyle" and that homosexuality is not genetically or environmentally determined. Reparative therapy seeks to "treat" gays and lesbians through prayer and intensive counseling, although some evangelical groups have turned to more drastic measures, including hypnosis, deprogramming techniques, behavior modification, and even antipsychotic drugs. One of the more vocal advocates of reparative therapy is *LOU SHELDON of the *TRADITIONAL VALUES COALITION.

Repentance Repentance has various degrees of meaning, most of which center around regret and sadness for sinful actions or thoughts. The term can also suggest a response to Jesus' challenge to prepare for the kingdom of God. In evangelical parlance, repentance becomes an individual's rejection of *SIN and rebellion against the will of God; it focuses on conforming one's will and behavior to the precepts found in the New Testament. This action can be a prelude to the fullness of faith as it is experienced as complete belief in God and Jesus Christ, or it can be the consequence of faith. For most evangelicals, individual repentance is the prelude to acceptance of Jesus Christ as one's personal savior. The larger meaning of repentance becomes a life filled with God's *GRACE given as a gift to the individual who has repented. One grows closer to God through the continuous realization of the gulf between human beings and God and the struggle to live up to a life based upon the high standards of the *BIBLE.

Restoration Movement. *See* **Restorationism.**

Restorationism Restorationism refers specifically to the attempts by *THOMAS and *ALEXANDER CAMPBELL and *BARTON W. STONE early in the nineteenth century to restore Christianity to the primitive simplicity of the New Testament church. Their "no creed but the *BIBLE" motto suggested a deep antipathy toward denominationalism in the early republic. More generically, restorationism connotes a desire to recover the primitive simplicity of the *BIBLE, to leapfrog over centuries of church history in order to restore Christianity to its ideal.

Reference: Richard T. Hughes and C. Leonard Allen, *Illusions of Innocence: Protestant Primitivism in America, 1630–1875* (1988).

Revell, Fleming H(ewitt), (Jr.) (1849–1931) Although Fleming H. Revell left school at the age of ten, he became a successful publisher of evangelical literature at the urging of *DWIGHT L. MOODY, who had married Revell's sister. Moody's tracts and sermons provided the initial material, and his associations with *WHEATON COLLEGE and the *NIAGARA CONFERENCES brought him into the ambit of many dispensationalist authors. Revell's business was destroyed by the Chicago fire of 1871, but he rebuilt, and by 1890 he had become a major publisher. Revell moved his headquarters to New York in 1906, and the company later moved its offices to Englewood Cliffs, New Jersey.

Revival In the parlance of evangelicals, "revival" refers to an upsurge of piety, whether general or localized in a particular region, community, or congregation. It is usually marked by *CONVERSIONS, *REDEDICATIONS, more fervent prayer, and resolutions to enter some form of Christian service.

The theological interpretation surrounding the revival of religion, however, leads to some radically divergent ideas about how revival comes about. In the traditional Calvinist or Reformed understanding of revival, God alone—according to God's own counsels—offers revival as a gift. No one can do anything to bring about revival; it is a gracious visitation from the Almighty. In the Wesleyan or Arminian tradition, which is the dominant motif in American *EVANGELICALISM, revivals can be prompted by the prayers and the work of God's people.

Two of American *EVANGELICALISM's most influential theologians illustrate these divergent perspectives. When he sat down to describe the revival within his congregation at Northampton, Massachusetts, *JONATHAN EDWARDS, a Calvinist, entitled his essay *A Faithful Narrative of a Surprising Work of God.* *CHARLES GRANDISON FINNEY, on the other hand, apologist for the *SECOND GREAT AWAKENING, wrote boldly in his *Lectures on Revivals,* "Revival is the work of man." So prevalent is this latter, Arminian understanding of revival that many churches, especially those within the *SOUTHERN BAPTIST CONVENTION, schedule their annual revivals months in advance. One can only imagine Edwards spinning in his grave in Princeton, New Jersey.

Rhema Bible Training Center. *See* **Hagin, Kenneth E(rwin), Sr.**

Rice, John R(ichard) (1895–1980) Born in west Texas to a pious Southern Baptist family, John R. Rice was converted at age twelve and promptly joined the local Baptist church. He studied briefly at Decatur Baptist College, served in the army, and went on to *BAYLOR UNIVERSITY, graduating in 1920. Rice followed a call to the ministry rather than pursue further studies at the University of Chicago. He enrolled in Southern Baptist Theological Seminary but left before graduating in order to assume pastorates in Plainview, Texas, and later in Shamrock, Texas. Rice left the pastorate in 1926 to become a full-time *EVANGELIST. He hooked up with *J. FRANK NORRIS at First Baptist Church in Fort Worth and started a radio program on Norris's station. His disgust with what he regarded as modernist elements in the *SOUTHERN BAPTIST CONVENTION led Rice to break with the convention in 1927.

Rice founded the Fundamentalist Baptist Church in 1932 in the Oak Cliff section of Dallas. Two years later, he began publishing *The Sword of the Lord,* a periodical of polemics against *LIBERALISM, Catholicism, communism, the civil rights movement, and various other "vices," including *DANCING, alcohol, smoking, and motion pictures. Rice also published more than one hundred books and pamphlets, which were very popular, especially among fundamentalists.

In 1939, Rice resigned his church and moved his operations to Wheaton, Illinois, where he continued publishing *The Sword of the Lord* and resumed full-time *EVANGELISM. Rice's *SEPARATISM continued to manifest itself; he condemned *BILLY GRAHAM, for example, for cooperating with liberal ministers in his evangelistic crusades. Rice moved *The Sword of the Lord* to Murfreesboro, Tennessee, in 1963; he continued as editor and as *EVANGELIST until his death.

References: John R. Rice, *Bobbed Hair, Bossy Wives and Women Preachers* (1941); idem, *When Skeletons Come Out of Closets!* (1943); idem, *Eternal Retribution* (1951); Robert L. Sumner, *A Man Sent from God: A Biography of Dr. John R. Rice* (1959).

Rice, Luther (1783–1836) A graduate of Williams College who was ordained for missionary service by the Congregationalists, Luther Rice sailed for India in 1812 but became convinced on the way over that adult *BAPTISM was the biblical way, not infant *BAPTISM. Upon arrival in Calcutta, he was immersed by an English Baptist missionary and returned the next year to sever his ties with the Congregationalists. Rice then embarked on a career of promoting missions among Baptists. His *ITINERANCY led to the formation of the General Convention of the Baptist Denomination in the United States for Foreign Missions (also known as the *TRIENNIAL CONVENTION), the first national organization of Baptists in America. Rice also founded the *Latter Day Luminary,* the first national Baptist periodical, and Columbian College, a Baptist school in Washington, D.C.

References: Helen Wingo Thompson, *Luther Rice: Believer in Tomorrow* (1983); William Henry Brackney, *The Baptists* (1988); idem, ed., *Dispensations of Providence: The Journal and Selected Letters of Luther Rice, 1803–1830* (1984).

Richard, Cliff (né Webb, Harry Roger) (1940–) Born Harry Roger Webb in Lucknow, India, Cliff Richards (not to be confused with Keith Richard, guitarist with the Rolling Stones) first played guitar and sang with a skiffle band. In 1958, his band adapted to the newly emergent rock 'n' roll and became known as Cliff Richard and the Shadows. Richard became enormously popular in Great Britain, with fifty hit songs in the 1960s, beginning with "Livin' Doll." Very much in contrast to The Who and the Rolling Stones, Richard projected a clean-cut image of moderation, and he also performed as an actor and singer in several films and musicals in London. An evangelical Christian, Richard has appeared frequently in evangelical settings, and he was the lead actor in a *BILLY GRAHAM film about Palestine, *His Land.*

Richey, Raymond T(heodore) (1893–1968) Raymond T. Richey converted to evangelical Christianity after his eyes were healed by a pentecostal *EVAN-

GELIST named Arch P. Collins in Fort Worth, Texas, in 1911. Richey became an assistant pastor in Houston, where he founded the United Prayer and Workers' League. In the course of ministering to the sick at a nearby army camp he contracted tuberculosis, whereupon he went to southern California and was miraculously healed a second time, in September 1919. A year later, he began his career as a healing *EVANGELIST in Hattiesburg, Mississippi, and continued to hold *REVIVAL campaigns through the 1950s. Some of the results were spectacular, as in Tulsa, Oklahoma, in 1923, when *CONVERSIONS totaled more than eleven thousand; people who had been healed formed a parade, with "a truck piled high with discarded crutches."

Riggs, Stephen Return **(1812–1883)** Born in Steubenville, Ohio, and educated at Jefferson College and at Western Seminary in Allegheny, Pennsylvania, Stephen Return Riggs was ordained a Presbyterian in 1836. The following year he and his wife, Mary A. C. Longley, became missionaries to the Sioux under the auspices of the *AMERICAN BOARD OF COMMISSIONERS FOR FOREIGN MISSIONS. Over the course of a career that spanned forty-five years, Riggs, who mastered the various Sioux dialects, established missions in Minnesota and in the Dakota Territory. Having devised a written form of the language, he produced a range of publications, including primers, grammars, a Dakota catechism, and translations of first the New and then the Old Testament.

Reference: Stephen Return Riggs, *Mary and I: Forty Years with the Sioux* (1880).

Riley, William Bell **(1861–1947)** Born on the eve of the Civil War, William Bell Riley grew up in Kentucky and experienced a religious *CONVERSION at age seventeen. Although he had planned to be a lawyer, Riley decided to follow "a divine voice" and pursue the ministry. He attended Valparaiso Normal School and Hanover College (both in Indiana) and graduated from Southern Baptist Theological Seminary in 1888. He served Baptist churches in Illinois, Indiana, and Kentucky before accepting the pulpit of Calvary Baptist Church in Chicago in 1893. He moved on to Minneapolis, Minnesota, four years later as pastor of the First Baptist Church, where he stayed for the remainder of his life.

Shortly after his arrival in Minneapolis, Riley became concerned about the shortage of evangelical pastors in rural areas. He founded the *NORTHWESTERN BIBLE AND MISSIONARY TRAINING SCHOOL to address that need. Riley also tried to stanch the spread of "*MODERNISM" in the Northern Baptist Convention; he railed frequently against Darwinism and published several polemics in the midst of the fundamentalist-modernist controversy, including *The Crisis of the Church* (1914) and *The Menace of Modernism* (1919). Riley also embodied many of the separatist tendencies so common to *FUNDAMENTALISM. He helped to found the *WORLD'S CHRISTIAN FUNDAMENTALS ASSOCIATION in 1919 and later joined with *T. T. SHIELDS and *J. FRANK NORRIS to form the *BAPTIST BIBLE UNION.

By the mid-1930s, Riley turned more of his attention to the religious needs of the cities. In 1935, he founded Northwestern Evangelical Seminary and added still another school, *NORTHWESTERN COLLEGE, in 1944. Following his retirement from the pulpit in 1942, Riley devoted his attention to the schools he had established, and shortly before his death he persuaded a young *EVANGELIST, *BILLY GRAHAM, to take over as president.

References: William Bell Riley, *The Evolution of the Kingdom* (1913); idem, *The Menace of Modernism* (1917); idem, *Inspiration or Evolution* (1926); idem, *The Conflict of Christianity with Counterfeits* (1940); William Vance Trollinger Jr., *God's Empire: William Bell Riley and Midwestern Fundamentalism* (1990); Joel A. Carpenter, *Revive Us Again: The Reawakening of American Fundamentalism* (1997).

Rimmer, Harry (1890–1952) Harry Rimmer, who sought to reconcile science with the *BIBLE, experienced an evangelical *CONVERSION on January 1, 1913. He had dropped out of school in the third grade, but he studied at Hahnemann College of the Pacific, Whittier College, and the *BIBLE INSTITUTE OF LOS ANGELES. Ordained by the Society of Friends, he served as a chaplain in World War I, but he left the Quakers for the Presbyterians in 1919. In 1921, he founded the Research Science Bureau, which was actually a workshop next to his garage in Los Angeles, and "Doctor" Rimmer, as he wanted to be called, became a kind of itinerant lecturer and debater, especially in opposition to Darwinism. A former boxer, his trademark taunt was to offer anyone in his audiences a one-hundred-dollar bill if someone could show him a scientific error in the *BIBLE.

In 1934, Rimmer became pastor of the First Presbyterian Church in Duluth, Minnesota, where he became a prolific author. Later in his career, Rimmer's attention shifted somewhat from apologetic concerns with reconciling science and theology to speculations on apocalyptic themes.

References: Harry Rimmer, *The Harmony of Science and Scripture,* 25 vols. (1925–1934); idem, *Modern Science and the Genesis Record* (1937); idem, *Internal Evidences of Inspiration* (1937); idem, *The Shadow of Coming Events* (1946); Edward B. Davis, "Fundamentalism and Folk Science between the Wars," *Religion & American Culture,* V (summer 1995).

Rivers, Eugene F. (1951–) Born in Boston and reared in north Philadelphia, Eugene F. Rivers was "adopted" by a spiritual father, Benjamin Smith, a holiness minister. Rivers attended Harvard, although he never graduated. As pastor of the Azusa Christian Community, a pentecostal congregation in south Boston that he founded in 1984, Rivers developed a plan, called the Boston Ten Point Coalition, as a blueprint for urban ministry and as a tool to prevent inner-city kids from gravitating to gangs. The success of his scheme led to a cover story in *Newsweek* as well as a role as spokesman for faith-based initiatives during the George W. Bush presidency.

References: C. Stephen Evans and Gail Gunst Heffner, "The Word on the Street," *Books & Culture,* May/June 2000; Gustav Niebuhr, "A Point Man for the Bush Church-State Collaboration," *New York Times,* April 7, 2001.

Rizzo, Rita Antoinette. *See* **Angelica, Mother.**

Roberson, Lizzie Woods (1860–1945) Lizzie Woods Roberson heard the preaching of *CHARLES H. MASON while she was working as matron of women at Demott Arkansas College. In 1911, Mason invited Roberson to start a women's department in his new denomination, the *CHURCH OF GOD IN CHRIST; the department now provides one third of the denomination's annual budget. A gifted teacher and administrator, Roberson also organized the Bible Band and the Home and Foreign Mission for the denomination.

Roberts, B(enjamin) T(itus) (1823–1893) The founder of the *FREE METHODIST CHURCH, B. T. Roberts was expelled from the Methodist Episcopal Church after agitating for reform within the Genessee conference in western New York. In 1860, in Pekin, New York, he and some followers organized the new denomination, insisting upon adherence to the Wesleyan doctrine of entire *SANCTIFICATION, support for *ABOLITIONISM, and opposition to pew rentals, which favored the more affluent (hence the name Free Methodists). Roberts founded Chili Seminary, later renamed *ROBERTS WESLEYAN COLLEGE, in Rochester, New York.

References: B. T. Roberts, *Why Another Sect?* (1879); idem, *Fishers of Men* (1918); Benson Howard Roberts, *Benjamin Titus Roberts: A Biography* (1900).

Roberts, (Granville) Oral (1918–) Oral Roberts was born into poverty in Pontotoc County, Oklahoma, the son of a pentecostal holiness preacher. Roberts was bedridden with tuberculosis in 1935 until a healing *EVANGELIST, George W. Moncey, healed him of his tuberculosis and his stuttering in July of that year. The following year Roberts, after serving an apprenticeship under his father, was ordained by the *PENTECOSTAL HOLINESS CHURCH. He served four congregations between 1941 and 1947 and gained a reputation as one of the up-and-coming preachers within the denomination. Roberts struck out on his own in 1947 with a healing *REVIVAL campaign in Enid, Oklahoma. He began his own monthly magazine, *Healing Waters* (renamed *Abundant Life* in 1956), and early on recognized the utility of the media, specifically radio, to advance his ministry. Having established headquarters in Tulsa, Oklahoma, Roberts stepped up his itinerations, traveling with a huge "tent cathedral"—the biggest ever, he claimed—that provided shelter for more than twelve thousand auditors.

Roberts's message of divine healing helped to revitalize American *PENTECOSTALISM in the postwar era. Following his successful 1951 campaign in Los Angeles, for instance, he endorsed the efforts of *DEMOS SHAKARIAN to organize the *FULL GOSPEL BUSINESS MEN'S FELLOWSHIP INTERNATIONAL. He took his message of healing to the television airwaves in 1955 with a weekly program that soon reached across the nation; by 1980, a Gallup poll indicated that 84 percent of Americans recognized his name. The effect of these efforts was to make *PENTECOSTALISM both more visible and more acceptable to evangelicals. *BILLY GRAHAM, for example, invited Roberts to participate in a 1966 *CONGRESS ON WORLD EVANGELISM. Roberts left the Pentecostal Holiness denomination two years later and was ordained in the United Methodist Church, much to the chagrin of some of his more sectarian admirers.

The Roberts empire expanded considerably in the 1960s with the founding of a coeducational liberal arts college, *ORAL ROBERTS UNIVERSITY, and several graduate schools. In 1981, he opened his City of Faith Medical and Research Center, with the idea of combining faith healing with medical healing. This $250 million project, however, proved cumbersome, especially since it was located in a city, Tulsa, with a surfeit of hospital beds. Roberts was forced to make more and more insistent appeals for money, until in 1987 he warned that God would "call me home" unless his listeners ponied up something like $4.5 million. In a decade already marked by the televangelist scandals of *JIM BAKKER and *JIMMY SWAGGART, Roberts's appeal looked like more of the same, although Roberts was guilty of little more than desperate exuberance.

References: Oral Roberts, *The Drama of the End Time* (1941); idem, *Deliverance from Fear and*

Sickness (1954); idem, *My Story* (1961); idem, *The Baptism with the Holy Spirit* (1964); idem, *The Call* (1972); idem, *Twelve Greatest Miracles of My Ministry* (1972); idem, *Expect a Miracle: My Life and Ministry* (1995); David Edwin Harrell Jr., *Oral Roberts: An American Life* (1985).

Roberts, Richard (1948–) The son of *ORAL and Evelyn ROBERTS and heir apparent to the Roberts's evangelistic empire, Richard Roberts once aspired to be a nightclub singer. He was converted while a student in his father's school, *ORAL ROBERTS UNIVERSITY, and married a singer in his father's ministry at the age of nineteen. That marriage ended in divorce in 1978. Roberts remarried two years later; he and his second wife, Lindsay Salem, have worked together to advance his ministry. He began his own television program, *Richard Roberts Live*, in September 1984, and he has assumed many of the administrative responsibilities for the university and for the Oral Roberts Evangelistic Association.

Reference: Richard Roberts, *He's the God of the Second Chance* (1985).

Roberts Wesleyan College (Rochester, New York) First known as Chili Seminary, Roberts Wesleyan College was founded in 1866 by *BENJAMIN TITUS ROBERTS, the first general superintendent of the *FREE METHODIST CHURCH OF NORTH AMERICA. Roberts claimed he started the college because, "While we cannot prize too highly the benefits of mental culture, we should not lose sight of that moral and religious culture which lies at the foundation of correct principles and good character."

The school's name was changed to A. M. Chesbrough Seminary in 1885, and in 1945 it became known as Roberts Junior College. The college achieved accreditation four years later to grant bachelor's degrees, and the name was changed to Roberts Wesleyan College to reflect the new emphasis on baccalaureate studies. Roberts Wesleyan College introduced its first graduate program in 1991 and now grants master's degrees in education, social work, and organizational management. The standard of student conduct states that, "Some forms of social *DANCING are not permitted on campus or at College-sponsored activities."

Reference: Roberts Wesleyan College 1996–1998 Undergraduate Catalog (1996).

Robertson, Ann Eliza Worcester (1826–1905) A Bible translator and missionary to the Creek Nation, Ann Eliza Worcester was born to Congregationalist parents who were missionaries to the Cherokees. After training in languages, she began working at the newly opened Tullahassee Manual Labor Boarding School in 1850, an enterprise run jointly by the Presbyterians and the Creeks. She married the school's principal, William Schenck Robertson, a Presbyterian minister, and the two collaborated both in mission work and on various translation projects.

The Civil War disrupted their work among the Creeks, but the school reopened in 1868, and over the ensuing dozen years the Robertsons translated portions of the *BIBLE into the Creek language and produced a hymnal. After the death of her husband in 1880, Ann Robertson lived with her daughter Alice in Muskogee, Oklahoma, and completed the translation of the New Testament into Creek in 1887.

Robertson, A(rchibald) T(homas) (1863–1934) A redoubtable New Testament scholar within the *SOUTHERN BAPTIST CONVENTION, A. T. Robertson studied at Wake Forest College and Southern Baptist Theological Seminary, where he graduated in 1888. Over the course of a long and productive career, Robertson published forty-five books, including his massive *Grammar of the Greek New Testament in the Light of Historical Research* (1914). A deeply pious man, Robertson assisted as a counselor in one of *DWIGHT L. MOODY's *REVIVAL campaigns, and he was a strong advocate of the *BAPTIST WORLD ALLIANCE.

References: A. T. Robertson, *A Harmony of the Gospels* (1922); idem, *An Introduction to Textual Criticism* (1925); Everett Gill, *A. T. Robertson: A Biography* (1943).

Robertson, James (1839–1902) James Robertson was born in Scotland and migrated to Canada in 1855. He was educated at the University of Toronto, Princeton Theological Seminary, and Union Theological Seminary (New York) and was ordained by the Presbyterian Church of Canada in 1869. He served churches in Norwich, Ontario, and Winnipeg, Manitoba, before becoming superintendent of Presbyterian missions in western Canada in 1881. Like *SHELDON JACKSON, his contemporary in the United States, Robertson was tireless in his efforts to expand the Presbyterian Church in the Canadian West. Known as "the Presbyterian bishop," he was elected moderator of the denomination in 1895.

Reference: Ian McFadden, *He Belonged to the West: James Robertson* (1958).

Robertson, Marion G(ordon) "Pat" (1930–) Born in Lexington, Virginia, Pat Robertson was the son of A. Willis Robertson, a Democratic congressman and U.S. senator. Pat Robertson enjoyed all the emoluments of a patrician upbringing; he attended a preparatory school in Chattanooga, Tennessee; graduated from Washington and Lee University in 1950; and, after a brief tour of duty with the marines, graduated from Yale Law School in 1955. In 1954, while still in law school, he married Adelia "Dede" Elme, shortly before she gave birth to their first child. Robertson failed the bar exam and decided to forsake law in favor of a career in business.

When Robertson abruptly announced that he was going to be a minister, his mother arranged a meeting with a Dutch *EVANGELIST, Cornelius Vanderbreggen, who was something of a mystic. Robertson had an evangelical *CONVERSION to Christianity and promptly returned home and poured all of his liquor down the drain. He soon left his startled wife, then seven months pregnant with the couple's second child, for a month-long conference sponsored by *INTERVARSITY CHRISTIAN FELLOWSHIP. While there, Robertson received a note from Dede: "Please come back. I need you desperately." Robertson, after prayer and reflection, responded, "I can't leave. God will take care of you." He returned at the conclusion of the conference and devoted himself to prayer and Bible study. At one point, after her husband literally heeded the admonition in Luke 12:23 to sell all and give to the poor, Dede returned to find that Pat had sold all of their furniture and moved them to a friend's house in a Brooklyn slum.

In 1956, Robertson entered the Biblical Seminary of New York (renamed New York Theological Seminary in 1965) and became an associate pastor at the First Reformed Church in Mount Vernon, New York. There, under the influence of the senior minister, Robertson had a pentecostal experience, including *SPEAKING IN TONGUES. After graduation from seminary in 1959, Robertson considered several pastorates and applied to be a missionary in Israel. He mulled the idea of a ministry in the Bedford-Stuyvesant slums, but nothing seemed to capture his interest until he heard that a defunct television station was for sale in Portsmouth, Virginia, for thirty-seven thousand dollars. Robertson visited the station, climbing through a broken window and scaring away a large rat on the glass-strewn floors. He agreed to buy the station on time, grandly dubbed it the *CHRISTIAN BROADCASTING NETWORK, and by 1961, the same year he was ordained a Southern Baptist by the Freemason Street Baptist Church in Norfolk, Virginia, Robertson began broadcasting three hours of religious television per night.

Although the local clergy remained wary of the struggling enterprise, the station—and Robertson's smooth *PENTECOSTALISM—began to catch on with pentecostals and charismatics. In 1965, Robertson hired two young *ASSEMBLIES OF GOD *EVANGELISTS, *JIM and *TAMMY FAYE BAKKER, as additional talent. Fundraising telethons fueled the growth of the station and, eventually, the network. An early telethon solicited seven hundred donors who would pledge ten dollars a month; in 1966, Robertson named his central program, a talk and entertainment format unabashedly based on the *Tonight Show*, the *700 Club*, which became nationally syndicated in 1972.

Aside from his boilerplate *DISPENSATIONALISM and his attraction to various conspiracy theories, Robertson and his theology have always been difficult to categorize. His embrace of pentecostal gifts while putatively a member of the *SOUTHERN BAPTIST CONVENTION, which as a whole frowns upon *SPEAKING IN TONGUES, would classify him as a charismatic. In the mid-1970s, however, Robertson spurned that label in favor of "Spirit-filled evangelical" and by the 1990s insisted upon "evangelical."

On September 17, 1986, Robertson capitalized on his media exposure, which had been enhanced by CBN's use of satellite technology, and announced that he would become a candidate for the Republican presidential nomination if he could obtain three million signatures of support. Less than a year later he declared his candidacy on a far-right political platform. He took a hiatus from CBN, resigned his Southern Baptist ordination in September 1987, and studiously billed himself as a broadcasting executive, bristling when the media referred to him as a televangelist. The media, however, produced a 1985 broadcast of the *700 Club*, when Robertson ordered Hurricane Gloria to change course. "In the name of Jesus," he prayed, "we command you to stop where you are and head northeast, away from land, and away from harm. In the name of Jesus of Nazareth, we command it." In 1995, he took credit for diverting Hurricane Felix from the Virginia coast.

Despite these revelations and with the concerted efforts of politically conservative evangelicals at the grass roots, Robertson won a straw poll in Michigan and finished second to Bob Dole and ahead of George Bush, the eventual nominee, in the Iowa precinct caucuses. In the face of increased scrutiny, however, he faltered in New Hampshire and eventually dropped out of the race.

In January 1989, Robertson met a young political operative, *RALPH REED, at an inaugural party for Bush. Robertson solicited ideas for transforming the grass-roots organizations he had assembled during his campaign into a political lobby for politically conservative evangelicals. Reed's long memorandum in response provided the blueprint for the *CHRISTIAN COALITION, which was formed later that same year. Robertson, as head of the organization (Reed was tapped as executive director), became a major force in American politics and especially within the Republican Party.

With his embrace of such ideologies as Christian *RECONSTRUCTIONISM, Robertson has often been accused of wanting to collapse the First Amendment distinction between church and state. His excoriations of *ABORTION, political liberals, feminists, and homosexuals have earned him the label of intolerant, although such denunciations resonated with many politically conservative evangelicals. Robertson's prime-time address before the Republican National Convention in Houston in 1992 was widely criticized as extremist and as contributing to the defeat of Bush for reelection. On June 8, 1998, Robertson predicted that Orlando, Florida, would be hit with earthquakes, hurricanes, terrorist attacks, "and possibly a meteor" for allowing gay groups to display rainbow flags during "Gay Days" at Walt Disney World. "I don't think I'd be waving those flags in God's face if I were you," he declared on his *700 Club* television program.

In the 1990s, Robertson cashed in on his media empire, which had been built with the tax-deductible contributions of the faithful. In 1997, his sale of International Family Entertainment, which included the Family Channel, to the News Corporation, owned by Rupert Murdoch, raised some eyebrows—and not merely because Robertson had regularly criticized the sleazy programming on Murdoch's Fox Network. Robertson put some of the proceeds from that sale into missions work and millions into Regent University, but he and his son, Tim, reportedly put more than $200 million into their own pockets.

References: Pat Robertson, *Shout It from the Housetops* (1972); idem, with Bob Slosser, *The Secret Kingdom* (1983); idem, *America's Date with Destiny* (1986); idem, *The New Millennium* (1990); idem, *Turning the Tide: The Fall of Liberalism and the Rise of Common Sense* (1993); David Edwin Harrell Jr., *Pat Robertson: A Personal, Religious, and Political Portrait* (1987); Tim Stafford, "Robertson R Us," *Christianity Today*, August 12, 1996.

Robison, James (1943–) A foster child to a Baptist preacher and his wife, James Robison was converted in Pasadena, Texas, at the age of fifteen. Responding to a call to the ministry, he enrolled at East Texas Baptist College and preached frequently while still a student. His demand as a preacher led him to drop out of school, relocate to the Dallas–Fort Worth area, and form the James Robison Evangelistic Association in 1967. With the encouragement of *BILLY GRAHAM, Robison, a Southern Baptist, started preaching on television, using his weekly program, *Restoration with James Robison*, as a platform for his fundamentalist theology and his right-wing political views.

Robison regularly excoriated feminism, evolution, *ABORTION, the National Council of Churches, and *SECULAR HUMANISM on his broadcasts, but he reserved special fire for homosexuals. In February 1979, he unleashed a particularly vicious attack on local gay-rights groups in the Dallas–Fort Worth area, insisting that homosexuality was "perversion of the highest order." The gay community responded with a petition to WFAA-Television for equal time under the provisions of the Federal Communications Commission's Fairness Doctrine, a claim that had been made successfully against Robison by other targets of his criticism, including Christian Scientists and the Mormons. WFAA not only granted the request but canceled Robison's program. It was later reinstated, but several other stations around the country refused to air the program because of Robison's bombast.

Robison turned increasingly political beginning in 1980, when he became vice president of the *RELIGIOUS ROUNDTABLE, a coalition of right-wing evangelicals who promoted conservative candidates, including *RONALD REAGAN. "I'm a preacher," Robison declared, "but I'm no longer just going to be talking about going to heaven." After the 1980 election, he went through a time of personal crisis, which included legal action for a divorce (which was never concluded), but prayer with a friend in 1981, according to Robison, brought about both physical and spiritual healing for his family. Although he refused the label "charismatic," Robison's preaching thereafter bore many of the hallmarks of the *CHARISMATIC MOVEMENT—an emphasis on divine healing, exorcism of demons, the unity of Christian love, and the gifts of the Holy Spirit. Such convictions led to conflict with the *SOUTHERN BAPTIST CONVENTION which, as a whole, frowns upon charismatic expressions; Robison broke with his Southern Baptist church in Euless, Texas.

Other changes followed Robison's turn away from contentiousness. He became more interested in humanitarian causes and in 1992 changed the name of his organization to LIFE Outreach International, which is based in Euless. *Restoration with James Robison,* the television program, became *LIFE Today.*

Reference: James Robison, *Thank God, I'm Free: The James Robison Story* (1988).

Rock Church (Virginia Beach, Virginia). *See* **Giminez, Anne (née Nethery)** *and* **Giminez, John.**

Rockmount College. *See* **Colorado Christian University.**

Rockwood, Perry F. (1917–) A hardline, separatist fundamentalist and fierce anti-Catholic, Perry F. Rockwood was defrocked by the Presbyterian Church in 1947 for his virulent rhetoric. Calling on the help of *T. T. SHIELDS, a fellow Canadian fundamentalist, Rockwood started an independent People's Church in Truro, Nova Scotia. He expanded into radio broadcasting. By 1953, he had extended his reach beyond Canada and to the United States, opening a branch office in Boston; his daily radio broadcast, *People's Gospel Hour,* airs throughout North America. By means of pamphlets, tracts, and the airwaves, Rockwood rails against homosexuality, *MODERNISM, women wearing slacks, charismatics, television, ecumenism, and all versions of the *BIBLE other than the King James Version.

References: Perry F. Rockwood, *Triumph in God: The Life Story of Radio Pastor Perry F. Rockwood* (n.d.); David R. Elliott, "Knowing No Borders: Canadian Contributions to American Fundamentalism," in George A. Rawlyk and Mark A. Noll, eds., *Amazing Grace: Evangelicalism in Australia, Britain, Canada, and the United States* (1993).

Rodeheaver, Homer A(lvan) (1880–1955) Born in Ohio, Homer A. Rodeheaver played in Tennessee's Regimental Band of the Spanish American War before becoming the song leader for *BILLY SUNDAY's evangelistic campaigns. In that capacity, Rodeheaver served the same function that *IRA SANKEY had served for *DWIGHT L. MOODY. Rodeheaver tirelessly sought to popularize gospel singing. He often told stories to introduce various songs, he published both books and music to make them widely available, and he established a

Summer School of Sacred Music at Winona Lake, Indiana.

Rogers, Adrian (1931–) A prominent pastor in the *SOUTHERN BAPTIST CONVENTION and one of the leaders of the conservative takeover of the denomination, Adrian Rogers was born in West Palm Beach, Florida, and ordained in 1951. He graduated from Stetson University in 1954 and from New Orleans Baptist Theological Seminary four years later. His early role models were fellow Southern Baptists *W. A. CRISWELL, *BILLY GRAHAM, and *ROBERT G. LEE, whose pulpit at Bellevue Baptist in Memphis, Tennessee, Rogers would occupy, beginning in 1972.

In the 1980s, Rogers engineered the move of Bellevue Baptist from its downtown location in Memphis to a suburban location in East Cordova, Tennessee. The gigantic new building, completed in 1989 at a cost of $34 million, covers 6.5 acres, with an additional 31 acres of asphalt for parking. The congregation claims twenty-two thousand members, although Rogers conceded in 1989 that "even J. Edgar Hoover couldn't find some of them."

Rogers's theology is unabashedly conservative and fundamentalist; biblical *INERRANCY, for instance, is a central doctrine for him. He was one of the architects of the fundamentalist takeover of the *SOUTHERN BAPTIST CONVENTION, beginning in 1979, and he was elected president of the denomination three times: 1980, 1987, and 1988. His politics are also conservative. Rogers openly supported *RONALD REAGAN over *JIMMY CARTER, a fellow Southern Baptist, in 1980, and he maintained close ties with George Bush.

Reference: Randall Balmer, *Grant Us Courage: Travels Along the Mainline of American Protestantism* (1996).

Rogers, Fred (McFeely) (1928–) Born in Latrobe, Pennsylvania, Fred Rogers graduated from Rollins College and began working for NBC in 1951. He left a couple of years later to develop *Children's Corner* at a new public television station, WQED in Pittsburgh. After a brief foray in Canada as *MisteRogers,* he returned to Pittsburgh and a show that eventually became *Mister Rogers' Neighborhood,* an enormously popular children's television program that began airing nationally on PBS in 1968. Rogers began attending Pittsburgh Theological Seminary part-time in 1954, graduating eight years later. "God, in his great mercy, accepts us exactly as we are," he told a reporter in 2000. "Who could ever stand if God's faithfulness did not endure?"

When he announced his retirement late in 2000, Rogers reflected on legacy. "I invited children to be my neighbor," he told a reporter. "I'd like to think they felt comfortable thinking about and potentially talking about the most important things in life, so that when they're parents—and some are already parents—they're able to know it's OK to talk about feelings." Reflecting further on his success and on the challenge of children's television, Rogers said, "We don't need a lot of loud, fast-paced, violent images to fill the minds of children. I think it's easy to make that kind of thing attractive. I think it's difficult to make goodness attractive."

Reference: Wendy Murray Zoba, "Won't You Be My Neighbor?" *Christianity Today,* March 6, 2000.

Rogers, Roy (né Slye, Leonard) (1911–1998) Roy Rogers, born Leonard Slye in Cincinnati, migrated to California in 1930, where he played guitar and sang in a series of country groups during the 1930s. Together with Bob Nolan and Tim

Spencer he formed the Pioneer Trio in 1933, which later became Sons of the Pioneers. The group's "Tumbling Tumbleweeds" and "Cool Water" soon became classics of country-western music. By 1938, he had taken the stage name Roy Rogers and began a prolific career as a singing, yodeling cowboy in more than one hundred Western films, becoming a master of the romantic ballad. Rogers, dubbed "King of the Cowboys," married *DALE EVANS, who had appeared in a number of his films, in 1947 (his first wife had died the year before). The couple, who demonstrated a simple, evangelical piety, became a team, performing in concerts, rodeo shows, motion pictures, and in their own Western series on television, *The Roy Rogers Show,* which aired on NBC from 1951 to 1957.

Roloff, Lester (1914–1982) Born in Dawson, Texas, and reared on a cotton farm, Lester Roloff attended *BAYLOR UNIVERSITY and Southwestern Baptist Theological Seminary. He served as pastor of several churches and in 1944 began a radio program, *The Family Altar.* The program became successful enough that "Brother Roloff" was able to leave the church ministry and devote his energies to radio and associated enterprises; in 1951, he founded Roloff Evangelistic Enterprises.

Roloff's death in an airplane crash in 1982 did not diminish his presence on the airwaves. Roloff Evangelistic Enterprises still broadcasts reruns of his programs from its headquarters in Corpus Christi, Texas.

Ron Hutchcraft Ministries. *See* **Hutchcraft, Ron(ald) (Paul).**

Root, George F(rederick) (1820–1895) A musician and hymn writer of such songs as "Ring the Bells of Heaven" and "I've Found a Friend," George F. Root was born in Sheffield, Massachusetts, and studied music in Boston. He moved to New York City in 1944 and taught at Union Theological Seminary and the New York State Institution for the Blind, where he met and briefly collaborated with *FANNY J. CROSBY, the famous gospel hymn writer. In 1853, Root opened a school for music teachers, the New York Normal Institute, and began to write music for use in *SUNDAY SCHOOLS. Root moved to Chicago in 1859 as partner in his brother's music publishing firm, Root & Cady, which profited from the popularity of Root's Civil War songs—for example, "Tramp, Tramp, Tramp, the Boys Are Marching" and "The Battle Cry of Freedom." The Chicago fire of 1871, however, doomed the company. Root continued his music teaching and writing—over two hundred published songs, all told—and eventually formed another company, George F. Root & Sons.

Rosedale Bible Institute (Irwin, Ohio) Affiliated with the Conservative Mennonite Conference, Rosedale Bible Institute began as a six-week Bible course in Berlin, Ohio, in 1952. At first, classes were held in the Pleasant View Mennonite Church, with students living in local homes, but in 1966 a junior college was instituted. Rosedale now has a two-year program leading to degrees in pastoral ministries, biblical studies, missions and church planting, music and worship leadership, discipleship in ministry, and *BIBLE and theology, as well as a one-and-one-half-year program in Christian ministries.

Rosedale does not operate on the standard, two-semester basis. Instead, the school runs six five-week terms between September and May, enrolling about one hundred students each term. This structure is only one example of an overall flexibility in Rosedale's program. The school offers short Bible classes to churches around the country through the Congregational Extension Schools program. In addition, Rosedale has an Institute of Pastoral Studies for church leaders and laypeople who cannot attend the regular terms. Students in this program attend classes for one week a term and then complete the rest of their assignments on a correspondence basis.

Rosedale participates in an outdoor education program in Ontario, the Akwachink Leadership School, run by Impact North Ministries. Students on the wilderness program complete a two-week canoe trip and spend the rest of the semester studying Native American issues and ministries. Rosedale sends a faculty member to Kenya each year to teach for two weeks in the Thika area, in conjunction with Regions Beyond Ministry.

In contrast to *GOSHEN COLLEGE, or even *EASTERN MENNONITE UNIVERSITY, Rosedale Bible Institute has kept its original focus as an Anabaptist, Mennonite training school. The catalog states, "There are those today who would try to change the rules, but at RBI, God's Word is still the Authority—*absolutely*" and also lists the primary criteria for admission as "Loyal devotion to Christ and willingness to cooperate with the guidelines of the school," with academics taking a second place. The school requires all students to attend daily chapel. Not only *DANCING, but also rock music, theater attendance, and commercial movies are all prohibited in the student guidelines.

Reference: *Rosedale Bible Institute 1996–97 Catalog* (1996).

Rosen, Martin Meyer "Moishe" (1932–) Moishe Rosen, founder of *JEWS FOR JESUS, was born in Kansas City, Missouri, and reared in a Reform Jewish home. He attended Colorado College, married Ceil Starr, and dropped out of school. A spiritual quest culminated in the couple's *CONVERSION to evangelical Christianity in 1953.

Rosen moved to New York City in 1953 and became affiliated with the *AMERICAN BOARD OF MISSIONS TO THE JEWS, a group that seeks to convert Jews to Christianity. He attended Northeastern Bible College and was ordained a Baptist minister upon his graduation in 1957. That same year he moved to Los Angeles as minister to several Hebrew-Christian groups. He returned to New York a decade later as director of recruitment and training for the *AMERICAN BOARD OF MISSIONS TO THE JEWS. Rosen again relocated to California several years later, this time to San Francisco, in order to work among hippies. There, Rosen founded *JEWS FOR JESUS and its parent organization, Hineni Ministries, in 1974.

His message was that Jews can embrace Christianity without compromising their Jewishness, a claim that most Jews find offensive. Through radio, television, and tracts, however, Rosen emphasized his conviction that Jesus (or *Y'shua*) represents the fulfillment of Judaism. Rosen stepped down as executive director of *JEWS FOR JESUS in May 1996, although he remains involved in the activities of the organization.

Reference: Moishe Rosen, with William Proctor, *Jews for Jesus* (1974).

Ross, (Charles) "Scott" (1939–) Born in Scotland, the son of a working-class minister, Scott Ross became a celebrated disk jockey in the mid-1960s, hobnobbing with rock 'n' roll luminaries such as the Beatles and the Rolling Stones. Ross converted to evangelical Christianity at the height of his popularity within the mainstream rock music industry. Having seen firsthand the devastation of the libertine counterculture (most notably in the deaths of Jimi Hendrix and Brian Jones), he made a decision that he wanted to devote his life to reaching young people with the *GOSPEL through "culturally hip" means.

In 1968, Ross approached *PAT ROBERTSON of the fledgling *CHRISTIAN BROADCAST NETWORK (CBN) with the idea of starting a radio show directed solely toward attracting and meeting the needs of youth. Having had a similar vision, Robertson allowed Ross to host a radio show called *Tell It Like It Is* in January 1969, which was regularly broadcast over five radio stations that CBN had just purchased. Later that same year, Ross opened a Christian community in nearby Freeville, New York, called Love Inn. The community's evangelistic vision included antidrug programs, an underground newspaper, *Free Love,* and the establishment of an early Jesus music label called New Song, which distributed the music of guitar phenom Phil Keaggy.

Ross left the community in 1979 to become more involved in the upper echelons of the authoritarian *SHEPHERDING MOVEMENT. He returned to CBN in the 1980s and continues to work in the family programming department.

Reference: Scott Ross, *Scott Free* (1976).

Roussy, Louis (1812–1880) Louis Roussy, who came from a Huguenot family, was a *COLPORTEUR in his teens and studied for missionary work at the Lausanne Institute. In 1835, he accompanied *HENRIETTE FELLER to Québec, where they worked together as the first Protestant missionaries to francophone Canada, organizing a Baptist congregation in Marieville in 1837. Some years later, Roussy successfully debated *CHARLES CHINIQUY, a Roman Catholic priest who eventually became a Presbyterian, and Roussy's showing provided enormous encouragement to his beleaguered converts.

References: John M. Cramp, *A Memoir of Madame Feller* (1876); Randall Balmer and Catharine Randall, "'Her Duty to Canada': Henriette Feller and French Protestantism in Québec," *Church History,* 70 (March 2001).

Ruibel, Julio Cesar (1953–1995) Born in Sucre, Bolivia, Julio Cesar Ruibel was converted to evangelical Christianity while a student in the United States. He was profoundly influenced by *KATHRYN KUHLMAN and returned to Bolivia in 1972 as an *EVANGELIST. He began with house meetings, but his following grew rapidly; he organized the Neo-Pentecostal Movement in Bolivia at the age of twenty-two. Ruibel moved to Colombia in 1977 and founded the Christian Center and a health clinic in Cali. Ruibel was murdered on December 13, 1995. Apparently, Ruibel's organization had refused to sell some property to the Cali drug cartel, which allegedly killed him in retaliation.

Reference: "Prominent Bolivian Evangelist Murdered," *Christianity Today,* February 5, 1996.

Rushdoony, Rousas John (1916–2001) One of the more influential theorists for the *RELIGIOUS RIGHT, Rousas John Rushdoony was born in New York City to Armenian immigrants. He held a doctorate in educational philosophy, served as a Presbyterian minister and a missionary to Native Americans, and was active in the *JOHN BIRCH SOCIETY. In 1959, Rushdoony launched the movement that came to be known as *RECONSTRUCTIONISM with the publication of an exposition of the apologetics of *CORNELIUS VAN TIL, entitled *By What Standard?* Rushdoony established an organization five years later called Chalcedon Foundation (named for the fifth-century church council) to disseminate his Reconstructionist ideas. The "bible" of *RECONSTRUCTIONISM, a nine-hundred-page volume entitled *The Institutes of Biblical Law,* appeared in 1973.

Rushdoony's *RECONSTRUCTIONISM, which is laced with racism and anti-Semitism, seeks to replace civil law with biblical or Mosaic law. "Christianity is completely and radically anti-democratic," he writes. "It is committed to a spiritual aristocracy." Rushdoony clearly resents the fact that, in a multicultural society, Christians are expected to treat others as their equals—that, in Rushdoony's words, "in the name of toleration, the believer is asked to associate on a common level of total acceptance with the atheist, the pervert, the criminal, and the adherents of other religions." Rushdoony's ideas have been appropriated by such right-wing evangelicals as *PAT ROBERTSON, *JERRY FALWELL, *RANDALL TERRY, *D. JAMES KENNEDY, and *JOHN WHITEHEAD.

References: Rousas John Rushdoony, *By What Standard?* (1959); idem, *The Institutes of Biblical Law* (1973).

Russell, Howard Hyde (1855–1946) Howard Hyde Russell had an evangelical *CONVERSION in 1883, was ordained a Congregational minister two years later, and received the B.D. from Oberlin Seminary in 1888. His brother's alcoholism and his observations about the destructive effects of drinking that he had made while working in Kansas City and Chicago led Russell to form the Ohio Anti-Saloon League in September 1893, which he served as superintendent until 1897. This organization, working through Protestant congregations, sought outright prohibition of the production, sale, and consumption of liquor.

When a national organization, which eventually took the name *ANTI-SALOON LEAGUE OF AMERICA, was formed in Washington, D.C., in December 1895, Russell was chosen as general superintendent, a post he filled until 1903. Using tactics he had honed in Ohio, Russell organized chapters in thirty-six states and made the Anti-Saloon League into the dominant organization within the Prohibition movement. After passage of the Eighteenth Amendment, Russell helped to organize the World League Against Alcoholism.

Russell Creek Academy. *See* **Campbellsville University.**

Russia for Christ Ministries Founded in 1958 by *DAVID V. BENSON, Russia for Christ Ministries distributes Russian-language radio broadcasts to Russia and eastern Europe. The program, called *Christ's Warrior,* offers a mix of stories and Bible readings. In addition, the group has supplied *BIBLES and other evangelistic literature for the use of evangelicals behind the Iron Curtain. Since the collapse of the Soviet Union the organization, now based in Santa Barbara, California, has encountered resistance from the Russian Orthodox Church, which seeks to thwart the evangelistic activities of various American groups.

Rutherford Institute Founded in 1982 to provide legal assistance for right-wing causes, the Rutherford Institute, headed by *JOHN W. WHITEHEAD, has ties to Christian *RECONSTRUCTIONISM, which advocates the rewriting of American legal codes to conform with Mosaic law. The organization, named after Samuel Rutherford, a seventeenth-century Scottish clergyman who rejected the notion of the divine right of kings, engages in litigation—or the threat of litigation—on behalf of people who believe their religious freedoms have been violated. The Rutherford Institute is especially interested in such matters as *HOME SCHOOLING, parental rights, "family values," and school prayer. The organization, which is based in Charlottesville, Virginia, has also been active in trying to stop sex education and condom distribution in public schools; it has opposed school programs that teach tolerance, and it has vowed to prevent the government from forcing a "radical homosexual agenda" on the public. In 1997, Whitehead and the Rutherford Institute became involved in the sexual harassment suit that Paula Corbin Jones brought against Bill Clinton as a way of trying to embarrass the president. Several fund-raising letters for the Rutherford Institute were mailed under Jones's name.

Ryan, Henry (1775–1833) A Methodist missionary in Upper Canada and one of the leaders of the *HAY BAY CAMP MEETING of 1805, Henry Ryan was born in Massachusetts to Irish Catholic parents. He converted to *METHODISM in the 1790s, served several circuits in Vermont and New York, and then volunteered for the Bay of Quinte circuit in Upper Canada, where he would spend the rest of his career. Ryan broke with Canadian *METHODISM in 1828 to form the Canadian Wesleyan Methodist Church.

Reference: G. A. Rawlyk, *The Canada Fire: Radical Evangelicalism in British North America, 1775–1812* (1994).

Ryman Auditorium (Nashville, Tennessee) The storied home of the *GRAND OLE OPRY, Ryman Auditorium in downtown Nashville was actually the fifth venue for the Opry. Named for a Cumberland River steamboat captain, Thomas Greene Ryman, who became an evangelical convert and a foe of alcohol, the auditorium was built in 1892 to accommodate evangelistic church services. In 1896, the famous *EVANGELIST *DWIGHT L. MOODY preached there, and by the early twentieth century the auditorium was used for opera and legitimate theater performances as well as for preaching by the likes of *BILLY SUNDAY.

The Opry moved into Ryman Auditorium in 1943 and remained there until March 1974, when it relocated to Opryland Park. These years were, in many ways, the formative years for the Opry, where *COUNTRY MUSIC and gospel songs wafted from the stage. The favorable acoustics and the intimate setting were conducive to the live performances that were broadcast over radio station WSM. Since the Opry left, Ryman Auditorium, which was listed on the National Register of Historic Places in 1971, has become something of a shrine for the *COUNTRY-MUSIC faithful. More than two hundred thousand fans come annually to visit "the mother church of *COUNTRY MUSIC."

Reference: Curtis W. Ellison, *Country Music Culture: From Hard Times to Heaven* (1995).

■ ■ ■

Sallman, Warner E. (1892–1968) Born in Chicago, Warner E. Sallman was interested in art at an early age, an interest that was encouraged by his parents. He apprenticed at local studios and took night classes at the Art Institute of Chicago. Shortly after his marriage to Ruth Edith Anderson in 1916, Sallman was diagnosed with tuberculosis and told that he had only months to live. Sallman and his wife prayed for recovery, and his health gradually improved.

Sallman enrolled in Bible school with the intention of learning more about the Scriptures so that he could illustrate biblical stories. The dean summoned him to his office one day, affirmed Sallman's aspirations, and added: "Sometime I hope you give us your conception of Christ, and I hope it's a manly one. Most of our pictures today are too effeminate." In January 1924, while he was working on a cover illustration for a denominational magazine, an image of Jesus came to Sallman in a dream. He sketched it quickly and later rendered it into a charcoal drawing. Sallman's *Head of Christ* began to attract wider notice in 1933, when it came to the attention of John T. Stone, president of McCormick Theological Seminary. Copies were distributed by one of the country's largest church-supply houses. Late in 1940, Sallman painted the image in oils; it was copyrighted, and prints were widely distributed throughout the world by Kriebel and Bates. Sallman frequently toured, talking about his famous interpretation of Jesus while doing a charcoal drawing of the image.

References: David Morgan, ed., *Icons of American Protestantism: The Art of Warner Sallman* (1996); Jack R. Lundbom, *Master Painter: Warner E. Sallman* (1999).

Salter, William (1821–1910) Born in Brooklyn, New York, William Salter studied at Union Theological Seminary and at *ANDOVER THEOLOGICAL SEMINARY, where in 1843 he joined forces with ten other young ministers to form the *IOWA BAND, a group of missionaries commissioned by the American Home Missionary Society to preach the *GOSPEL in the Territory of Iowa. Ordained in Denmark, Iowa, on November 5, 1843, Salter preached for two years at Maquoketa before moving to Burlington in April 1846, where he was pastor of the First Congregational Church until his death in 1910. Salter was active in the Underground Railroad and served as a chaplain under the auspices of the Christian Commission during the Civil War. In addition to his pastoral duties, Salter pursued an avocation as a historian.

References: William Salter, *The Progress of Religion in Iowa for Twenty-five Years* (1858); idem, *Our National Sins and Impending Calamities* (1861); idem, The Life of James W. Grimes (1876); idem, *Studies in Matthew* (1880); idem, *Iowa: The First Free State in the Louisiana Purchase* (1905).

Salvation While evangelicals hold differing views on soteriology, the theology of salvation, all agree on its importance: deliverance from *SIN. The salvation of individuals was made possible by the death of Jesus, who took on him the *SINS of humanity. For most evangelicals, citing John 3:16, the work of Christ is appropriated at the moment of *CONVERSION, when the individual turns away from *SIN and accepts Jesus as savior.

Salvation Army In 1865, *WILLIAM and *CATHERINE BOOTH established a mission in the slums of London's East End, an enterprise, originally named Christian Mission, that evolved into the Salvation Army. *WILLIAM BOOTH, who had been ordained in the Methodist New Connexion, had become a freelance *EVANGELIST in 1861, and he intended his Christian Mission to be a supplement to the churches. Other churches, however, did not welcome the Booths' converts, so the mission became a place of worship as well.

The Booths changed the name in 1878 to Salvation Army, and they increasingly adopted the trappings and the nomenclature of militarism. The statement of faith, for instance, was called "Articles of War"; members became known as soldiers; *EVANGELISTS were officers; *WILLIAM BOOTH himself took the title of general. After spreading throughout Great Britain, the Salvation Army arrived in the United States in March 1880, under the direction of *GEORGE SCOTT RAILTON. A year later the Salvation Army landed in France and Australia, and in 1882 the Army reached Canada, led by Jack Addie and Joseph Ludgate. Today the Army's work is carried on by officers speaking 160 languages in 104 countries around the world. In the United States, there are over twelve hundred community corps centers and nearly half a million soldiers in the army.

Although the Booths' original emphasis had been on *EVANGELISM and *SANCTIFICATION (in the Wesleyan tradition), they turned, of necessity, to the task of social amelioration as well. Booth had sought to meet not only the spiritual needs of the crowds in the slums, but the physical needs of the people as well. Today, the Salvation Army runs summer camps and shelters for the homeless, and provides food for the hungry, disaster relief, alcohol and drug rehabilitation, youth camps and programs, senior citizens' camps and programs, hospital and prison visitation, support for unwed mothers, and general assistance for the indigent. Services are provided without cost to any in need, regardless of age, race, sex, religious affiliation, or creed, and funding for this extensive program comes from voluntary donations and subscriptions, federal funds, and annual appeals. In the United States alone, the Salvation Army raises more than $2 billion a year, roughly half from private sources and half from governmental sources.

The structure and *POLITY of the Salvation Army are, by its own admission, unusual. Organized, obviously, on a military model, the international leader holds the rank of general and operates out of the headquarters in London. The United States is under the direction of the national commander, whose offices are in Alexandria, Virginia. For administrative purposes, the nation is divided into four territories: the Central, with headquarters in Des Plaines, Illinois; the East, with headquarters in West Nyack, New York; the South, with headquarters in Atlanta; and the West, with headquarters in Rancho Palos Verdes, California. Each territory is under the leadership of a territorial commander.

The corps center is the basic unit of the army and carries out the religious and social ministries, which are adapted to local needs. Corps centers are led by officers, who act as ministers and administrators. Members of the corps are called soldiers. Officers are trained in one of the four officers' training schools around the country. In the training school, cadets receive formal training as well as field experience in all areas of the army's work. Graduates are appointed to the rank of lieutenant. The appointment is equivalent to ordination in other traditions.

The army is, and always has been, a thoroughly evangelical group. Its wide-ranging social ministries have been so successful that many are unaware that the army is a traditional holiness church, whose mission is "to preach the *GOSPEL of Jesus Christ and to meet human needs in his name without discrimination." The doctrine of the Salvation Army affirms the inspiration and *AUTHORITY of Scripture, the Trinity, the united divine and human natures of Jesus Christ ("truly and properly God and truly and properly man"), human *SIN, the need for repentance and justification, and the privilege of *SANCTIFICATION for all believers.

Other beliefs of the Salvation Army are also distinctive, especially concerning the sacraments, or ordinances, and the role of women. The army looks upon all of life as sacramental, both to the giver and receiver. As a result, the traditional practices of *BAPTISM and communion are not considered as necessary for *SALVATION or growth. With regard to women, the Army very early on opened the ranks of the officers to women, which is to say that women have served, almost from the beginning, in positions of ordained ministry. Women, from General Booth's wife, *CATHERINE BOOTH, on, have been active among the officers, and in 1990 the denomination allowed married women officers to hold ranks equivalent to that of their husbands.

In the late nineteenth century Salvationists operated farm colonies in the American West in an effort to relocate miserable urban dwellers to a more bucolic (and spiritually salubrious) environment. Salvationists maintain their visibility in the cities not only through acts of charity but also by means of brass bands and streetcorner solicitations for funds, much like the bands and the "hallelujah lassies" that attracted attention in the Victorian era.

References: Norman H. Murdoch, *Origins of the Salvation Army* (1996); Edward H. McKinley, *Marching to Glory: The History of the Salvation Army in the United States, 1880–1980* (1980); Clark C. Spence, *The Salvation Army Farm Colonies* (1985); Diane H. Winston, *Red-Hot and Righteous: The Urban Religion of the Salvation Army* (1999).

Samaritan's Purse An evangelical relief organization founded by *BOB PIERCE of *WORLD VISION INTERNATIONAL, to provide food, medicine, and other assistance in areas of crisis, Samaritan's Purse was taken over by *FRANKLIN GRAHAM when Pierce died of leukemia. Under Graham's tenure, from 1978 to 1995, the small organization grew into a $32 million-a-year operation, which provided relief supplies, together with the *GOSPEL, to such places as Haiti, Ethiopia, Bosnia, and the Persian Gulf. The *EVANGELICAL COUNCIL FOR FINANCIAL ACCOUNTABILITY suspended Samaritan's Purse in 1992 because of questions about Graham's compensation and his use of the organization's plane. Graham pulled Samaritan's Purse out of the oversight agency but rejoined two years later.

Samford University (Birmingham, Alabama) First established in 1841, Samford University has become the largest private, accredited, coeducational institution in Alabama, with an enrollment of more than forty-five hundred students. Samford was chartered by Alabama Baptists under the name Howard College. The school opened in 1842 in Marion, Alabama, and moved to Birmingham, Alabama, forty-five years later. By the 1930s, Howard College had attained regional accreditation and added programs in education and pharmacy. It relocated to its current campus in Birmingham in 1957. Four years later, Howard College acquired the Cumberland School of Law, formerly of Lebanon, Tennessee. With the addition of master's degree programs in the 1960s and a large bequest, Howard College was renamed Samford University in 1965. Today, Samford University is divided into eight colleges and schools: Arts and Sciences, Business, Divinity, Education, Law, Music, Nursing, and Pharmacy. The school offers eighty majors and twenty-two degree programs, including graduate degree programs in education, pharmacy, ministry, and law. Samford consistently ranks high in national surveys on education, and was rated "very competitive" by *Barron's Profiles of American Colleges*.

Still affiliated with the Alabama Baptist State Convention of Southern Baptists, Samford University differs from many church-related colleges established in the nineteenth century in that it has not abandoned its Christian roots, although enrollment is open to students of all faiths and denominations. In the 1980s, Samford looked back to its historical roots to found a seminary, Beeson Divinity School, which opened with an entering class of thirty-two students in 1988. Beeson describes itself as an "explicitly evangelical" institution. Beeson and Samford both, however, reject the label "fundamentalist," and it is telling that the first endowed chair at the divinity school was the *BILLY GRAHAM Chair of Evangelism and Church Growth. Special collections in the library include a Religious Education Curriculum Laboratory and the Alabama Baptist Historical Commission's collection of Baptist church minutes and other materials.

Reference: *Beeson Divinity School, Samford University Bulletin 1996–97* (1996).

Sanctification Sanctification is the condition of holiness or consecration, achievable only through God's *GRACE. In the evangelical understanding of holiness, only God is truly holy. However, God's action through the Holy Spirit can sanctify, or "make holy," the human being or human condition. It is God's gift, even as it is an individual goal to be holy. The term may sometimes be associated with cleanliness, in the sense of moral purification. Cleanliness is often understood to mean a state of purity brought about by repentance and acceptance of Jesus Christ. Evangelicals believe that being made holy or sanctified begins with being "washed in the blood of Jesus Christ." It is being saved in spite of *SIN which makes one holy. Among pentecostals and holiness people, sanctification often connotes a particular work of *GRACE, a "*SECOND BLESSING" of the Holy Spirit.

Sandford, Frank W(eston) (1862–1948) An influential and controversial holiness leader, Frank W. Sandford was born in Bowdomham, Maine, and converted on February 29, 1880. After graduating from Bates College in 1886 and beginning his studies for the ministry, Sandford dropped out of Cobb Divinity School and assumed the pulpit at First Baptist Church in Topsham, Maine. During his second pastorate, the Free Baptist Church in Great Falls, New Hampshire, Sandford accepted holiness teachings on *SANCTIFICATION and divine healing; he also imbibed elements of *BRITISH ISRAELISM, which he fused into his millennialist theology, his understanding about the end of time from his reading of the book of Revelation. Sandford entered the orbit of *DWIGHT L. MOODY and his Northfield conferences and also traveled around the world under the auspices of the *STUDENT VOLUNTEER MOVEMENT. Sandford married Helen Kinney, who had been the first *CHRISTIAN AND MISSIONARY ALLIANCE missionary in Japan; the couple eventually settled in Lancaster, Maine.

Sandford conducted evangelistic campaigns, founded the Holy Ghost and Us Bible School, and in 1894 started a periodical, *Tongues of Fire*. Sandford's most ambitious scheme, however, was the construction of a large community, called Shiloh, near Lewiston, Maine. Sandford, who claimed to be Elijah the Restorer (Mal. 4:5), announced that God had instructed him to gather this community of students and followers, who would disperse throughout the world as healing

*EVANGELISTS. With the help of student labor Sandford constructed an imposing Victorian compound: a seven-story tabernacle bedecked with turrets and flags, a healing home, a school, a children's home, and a dormitory with five hundred rooms. By 1904, he had assembled six hundred residents, requiring that they surrender their worldly goods before entering Shiloh.

Sandford's authoritarianism manifested itself in many ways, not least in strict—and abusive—discipline. His missionary concerns and his claims of direct guidance from God led him to acquire two boats, the *Kingdom* and the *Coronet,* to transport members of Shiloh for missionary work. In June 1911, the *Kingdom* was wrecked off the coast of Africa, whereupon Sandford, leading the expedition, ordered the entire contingent to board the *Coronet.* By the time the schooner arrived in Portland on October 21 several passengers had perished from lack of food and water; others were so sick they died within days, bringing the death toll to nine. Amid renewed stories about his abusive practices, Sandford, who had maintained throughout the voyage that he was waiting for divine direction, stood trial for manslaughter and was sentenced to ten years in prison.

Released early from his sentence, Sandford's credibility was so compromised that he retired in near obscurity. At the height of his career, however, he had exerted an enormous influence on such pentecostal leaders as *CHARLES FOX PARHAM, founder of *BETHEL BIBLE COLLEGE in Topeka, Kansas, and *AMBROSE J. TOMLINSON, who would become a leader of the *CHURCH OF GOD (CLEVELAND, TENNESSEE). A remnant of the Shiloh movement, with headquarters in Dublin, New Hampshire, keeps some of Sandford's writings in print.

References: Frank W. Sandford, *The Art of War for the Christian Soldier* (1904); Shirley Nelson, *Fair, Clear, and Terrible: The Story of Shiloh, Maine* (1989).

Sankey, Ira D(avid) (1840–1908) Born in Edinburgh, Pennsylvania, and reared in the Methodist Episcopal Church, Ira D. Sankey served in the Union Army during the Civil War and formed a music club, the "Singing Boys in Blue." After the war, he became active in the ***YMCA** movement. In Indianapolis in 1870, the *EVANGELIST *DWIGHT L. MOODY heard Sankey's dramatic baritone singing at a ***YMCA** convention and enlisted him in Moody's evangelistic work. For the next quarter of a century, Sankey accompanied Moody on his evangelistic tours, where his task was to provide the music and to "warm up" the audiences for Moody's preaching.

Sankey popularized gospel hymns, which were simple melodies with an evangelistic message, often overlaid heavily with emotion. He edited several collections of *REVIVAL songs, the profits of which went to support Moody's schools in Northfield, Massachusetts: *Sacred Songs and Solos* and *Gospel Hymns.*

Reference: Ira D. Sankey, *My Life Story and the Story of the Gospel Hymns and Sacred Songs and Solos* (1906).

Sat Tal. *See* **Jones, E(li) Stanley.**

Satan The Old Testament meaning of "Satan" denotes an adversary, which is the meaning of the word in Hebrew. In other, older Old Testament traditions, Satan is a member of God's heavenly court. From that lofty position Satan was cast down and becomes, by the time of the New Testament, the leader of evil powers and forces in the world. In this role he opposes God and human beings who are beloved of God.

For most evangelicals, Satan is an objective reality, a personal devil who is the author of evil. Satan and his minions, such as demons, use and abuse people by turning them away from God through temptation, guile, and deceit. Evangelicals often define the powers of this world—that is, much of the material world—as inherently evil, a product of Satanic power.

Save the Children Federation. *See* **Bryant, Anita.**

Saved One of the most important questions posed by an evangelical is, "Are you saved?" or "When were you saved?" Although the proper theological answer to the latter question would be something like, "two thousand years ago" (a reference to the crucifixion of Jesus), people who have had a *BORN-AGAIN experience generally reply with the date, the time, and the circumstances of their *CONVERSIONS. For evangelicals, claiming the mantle of *SALVATION—or being "saved"—is, quite literally, a life-or-death matter, because evangelicals believe that the primary criterion for entry into the kingdom of heaven is the *BORN-AGAIN experience.

Sawdust Trail Early in the twentieth century the term "sawdust trail" came to refer to those seeking a *CONVERSION to evangelical Christianity. Lumberjacks in the Pacific Northwest would leave behind trails of sawdust in order to find their way back to camp from working in the woods. *BILLY SUNDAY was probably the first to appropriate the image in revivalism, using it at a 1910 meeting in Bellingham, Washington, to refer to those willing to "find their way home" to Jesus during his *REVIVAL campaign there. The image also worked because very often sawdust was laid down beneath the canvas *REVIVAL tents as a way of soaking up moisture from the ground.

Sunday exploited the metaphor throughout his career. He enjoined his audiences to "hit the sawdust trail" and give their lives to Jesus. "Trail-hitters" would walk up the center aisle, strewn with sawdust, and shake Sunday's hand as a public indication of their *CONVERSIONS. As Sunday's career wound down and as *REVIVAL tents gradually became less important as an evangelistic venue, the term "sawdust trail" fell into desuetude.

Sawyer, Reuben H. (1866–c. 1937) An advocate of *BRITISH ISRAELISM and a leader in the *KU KLUX KLAN, Reuben H. Sawyer was pastor of the East Side Christian Church in Portland, Oregon, which he used as a base to propagate his supremacist views until he resigned the pastorate early in 1921. Sawyer lectured widely throughout the Pacific Northwest and British Columbia. In 1919, he helped in the formation of the British-Israel World Federation, and he addressed the organization's first gathering in 1920 in London. In addition to his work on behalf of *BRITISH ISRAELISM, Sawyer promoted the *KU KLUX KLAN. On December 22, 1921, for example, he addressed six thousand people at Portland's Municipal Auditorium, assuring his auditors that the Klan stood for "a cleansed and purified Americanism where law-abiding citizens will be respected and their rights defended, irrespective of race, religion or color so long as they make an honest effort to be Americans, and Americans only." Sawyer also briefly headed the women's auxiliary of the Oregon Klan, the Ladies of the Invisible Empire (LOTIES), beginning in 1922.

For a time, Sawyer's Klan activities conflicted somewhat with his devotion to

*British Israelism, which at this time still took a rather benevolent view of the Jews. By 1922, however, he was drawing a distinction between authentic and inauthentic Jews, the latter of whom sought the destruction of Christianity.

Reference: Michael Barkun, *Religion and the Racist Right: The Origins of the Christian Identity Movement* (1994).

Scandinavian Alliance Mission. *See* **Franson, Fredrik.**

Scanlan, Michael (1931–) A leader in the *Catholic charismatic renewal, Michael Scanlan was a lawyer when he became a Franciscan in 1957. He was ordained a priest in 1964, whereupon he became dean at the College of Steubenville (Ohio). Shortly after becoming rector of St. Francis Seminary in Loretto, Pennsylvania, he received the *baptism of the Holy Spirit in 1969. He returned to Steubenville in 1974 and made the institution one of the centers of the *charismatic renewal movement. He organized the Steubenville conferences and became a regular speaker at renewal gatherings across North America. Scanlan is a member of the Servants of Christ the King community in Steubenville, which is affiliated with the Sword of the Spirit.

References: Michael Scanlan, *The Power in Penance* (1972); idem, *Inner Healing* (1974); idem, *Let the Fire Fall* (1986).

Scanzoni, Letha Dawson (1935–) Born in Pittsburgh, Letha Dawson Scanzoni attended *Moody Bible Institute from 1954 to 1956 and eventually graduated from Indiana University in 1972. After work with Village Missions in Lookingglass, Oregon, in the late 1950s, Scanzoni began to devote more and more of her energies to writing and lecturing, especially on the issues surrounding evangelical feminism. In 1974, Scanzoni and *Nancy A. Hardesty published *All We're Meant to Be: A Biblical Approach to Women's Liberation*, which argued that feminist sensibilities were very much grounded in the Scriptures; the book sparked a great deal of controversy in evangelical circles and was named the "most influential" book of 1975 by subscribers to *Eternity* magazine. A member of the *Evangelical Women's Caucus, Scanzoni, who was divorced in 1983, also writes and lectures about "biblical interpretation, marriage and family, domestic violence, friendship, sex ethics, and sex education."

References: Letha Dawson Scanzoni, *Youth Looks at Love* (1964); idem, *Sex Is a Parent Affair: Sex Education for the Christian Home* (1973); idem, with Nancy A. Hardesty, *All We're Meant to Be: A Biblical Approach to Women's Liberation* (1974).

Schaeffer, Francis A(ugust) (1912–1984) Born in Philadelphia into a nominally Lutheran family, Francis A. Schaeffer studied engineering at Drexel but then, after a *conversion experience in 1930, completed his bachelor's degree at Hampden-Sidney College. After marrying Edith Rachel Merritt Seville, Schaeffer studied under *Cornelius Van Til at *Westminster Theological Seminary, but he left Westminster when *Carl McIntire and a more fundamentalist faction of premillennialists (who look for the imminent return of Jesus) bolted to form *Faith Theological Seminary and the *Bible Presbyterian Church. Schaeffer completed his seminary training at Faith Seminary, and in 1938 he was ordained by the *Bible Presbyterian Church, the denomination's first ordination. Schaeffer served churches in Pennsylvania and Missouri before moving to Switzerland in

1948 as a missionary under the aegis of both the Independent Board for Presbyterian Foreign Missions and the *AMERICAN COUNCIL OF CHRISTIAN CHURCHES.

Schaeffer and his wife founded *L'ABRI FELLOWSHIP in 1955, a study center in the Swiss Alps that threw its doors open to students and other transients. (An English branch of L'Abri was added in 1958.) In a relaxed, bucolic setting the Schaeffers and, eventually, other Christian apologists offered a critique of modern secularism and an assertion of Christian doctrine. In his lectures and, later, in his books—*The God Who Is There* (1968), *Escape from Reason* (1968), *How Should We Then Live? The Rise and Decline of Western Thought and Culture* (1976), *True Spirituality* (1979), among many others—Schaeffer bemoaned the retreat from moral and intellectual absolutes, which he blamed on the philosopher Georg Friedrich Hegel's notion of synthetical truth and its embrace of relativism. This led, Schaeffer believed, to an abandonment of reason in favor of anything from existentialism to hallucinogenic drugs.

Schaeffer's stern rebuke of social and intellectual indolence in the West and his call for a return to a theologically conservative Christianity resonated with many young people, especially among people who had wearied of the excesses of the counterculture. Schaeffer himself became something of a cult figure among college-age evangelicals in the 1970s. In his later years Schaeffer increasingly turned his attacks on *ABORTION, euthanasia, and suicide, all of which stemmed, he believed, from a renunciation of biblical values. He allied himself with *JERRY FALWELL, *PAT ROBERTSON, and the *RELIGIOUS RIGHT toward the end of his life.

References: Edith Schaeffer, *L'Abri* (1969); Francis A. Schaeffer, *The Complete Works of Francis A. Schaeffer*, 5 vols. (1982); Michael S. Hamilton, "The Dissatisfaction of Francis Schaeffer," *Christianity Today*, March 3, 1997.

Schaeffer, Frank (1952–) The son of *FRANCIS and Edith SCHAEFFER, Frank Schaeffer (also known as Franky Schaeffer) was born in Switzerland and spent the early years of his career involved in many of the same issues that had preoccupied his father, especially opposition to *ABORTION. Frank Schaeffer produced several documentaries, including *Whatever Happened to the Human Race?* which featured his father and *C. EVERETT KOOP. Schaeffer has written several novels, and he moved from the *FUNDAMENTALISM of his father to an affiliation with Eastern Orthodoxy in 1990.

References: Frank Schaeffer, *A Time for Anger: The Myth of Neutrality* (1982); idem, *Portofino: A Novel* (1994); idem, *Dancing Alone: The Quest for Orthodox Faith in the Age of False Religion* (1994); idem, *Letters to Father Aristotle: A Journey through Contemporary American Orthodoxy* (1995); idem, *Saving Grandma* (1997).

Schambach, R(obert) W. (1926–) R. W. Schambach was licensed by the *ASSEMBLIES OF GOD in 1951 and became an associate of *A. A. ALLEN two years later. In 1959, he left Allen, with Allen's blessing, and founded his own itinerant healing ministry, Schambach Miracle Revivals, with headquarters in Elwood City, Pennsylvania. In the 1960s, he started four "Miracle Temples" in the wake of his *REVIVALS—in Newark, New Jersey; Brooklyn, New York; Chicago; and Philadelphia—and these congregations, each led by an assistant, provided the base of his financial support. Like Allen, Schambach appealed especially to the uneducated and to the lower classes. He preferred the old-fashioned tent *REVIVALS and boasted in 1974 that his was the largest tent. "There is something about a tent," he said, "that you can't get in an auditorium."

References: David Edwin Harrell Jr., *All Things Are Possible: The Healing and Charismatic Revivals in Modern America* (1975); Patsy Sims, *Can Somebody Shout Amen!: Inside the Tents and Tabernacles of American Revivalists* (1989).

Schambach Miracle Revivals. *See* **Schambach, R. W.**

Schlafly, Phyllis. *See* **Eagle Forum.**

Schmucker, Samuel Christian (1860–?) Born in Allentown, Pennsylvania, into a Lutheran household, Samuel Christian Schmucker graduated from Muhlenberg College and earned the doctorate in chemistry from the University of Pennsylvania in 1893. Two years later he accepted a post as professor of biological sciences at West Chester State Normal School (now West Chester University), where he remained until his retirement in 1923. Schmucker's real notoriety, however, derived from his longtime association with the Wagner Free Institute of Science in Philadelphia, an organization dedicated to lay education on scientific matters. Schmucker traveled and lectured widely, arguing for free scientific inquiry. "To those of us who have faith in God, and in methods of investigation," he said, "there is no fear but that the outcome will be a higher conception of God and a clearer reverence for investigation." With such views in mind, Schmucker advocated a form of theistic evolution, and he believed as well in a kind of moral evolution for humanity. "Not to believe this," he wrote in 1925, during the age of fundamentalist battles against Darwinism, "is not to see in the working of the world the presence of the Eternal Power whom Jesus taught us to call Father."

References: Samuel Christian Schmucker, *The Study of Nature* (1908); Edward B. Davis, "Fundamentalism and Folk Science between the Wars," *Religion & American Culture,* V (summer 1995).

Schmucker, Samuel S(imon) (1799–1873) A graduate of the University of Pennsylvania and Princeton Theological Seminary, Samuel S. Schmucker served as a pastor in Virginia before becoming the first president of Gettysburg Seminary in 1826. He was instrumental in the formation of the Lutheran General Synod in 1820 and wrote a number of hymns, catechisms, and liturgies for the Lutheran churches. His publication of 1855, *Definite Synodical Platform,* sought to revise the Augsburg Confession, the doctrinal standard of Lutheranism, to make it more palatable to American sensibilities. Schmucker's proposals to eliminate references to the real presence in the *LORD'S SUPPER and to baptismal regeneration (the idea of a new birth through *BAPTISM), however, drew criticism from Lutheran traditionalists.

Though thoroughly Lutheran in theology and identity, Schmucker was a tireless advocate of Christian unity. In *Fraternal Appeal to the American Churches,* published in 1838, he urged a cooperation among Protestants that was eventually embodied in the *EVANGELICAL ALLIANCE, formed in London in 1846.

References: Samuel S. Schmucker, *Fraternal Appeal to the American Churches* (1838); idem, *Definite Synodical Platform* (1855).

School of the Ozarks. *See* **College of the Ozarks.**

Schuller, Robert H(arold) (1926–) Minister in the *REFORMED CHURCH IN AMERICA, televangelist, and purveyor of the gospel of positive thinking, Robert H.

Schuller was born to a farm family in Alton, Iowa, and reared in the *REFORMED CHURCH IN AMERICA. He attended that denomination's school and seminary, Hope College and Western Theological Seminary, both in Holland, Michigan. Upon graduation from seminary in 1950, Schuller was ordained and accepted the pastorate of the Ivanhoe Reformed Church in Riverside, Illinois, whose membership increased tenfold during his four-and-a-half year tenure.

The classis of California (the local jurisdiction of the *REFORMED CHURCH IN AMERICA) summoned Schuller west in 1955 to begin a congregation in Orange County. Schuller, always an innovator, rented the Orange Drive-In movie theater for Sunday worship services and, perched atop the refreshment stand, preached to the automobiles who had responded to his newspaper advertisements: "Come as you are, in the family car." In a culture crazed with the automobile, the idea caught on, and the Garden Grove Community Church quickly grew from one hundred to several thousand. Schuller constructed a church building just down the street from the drive-in, the first of several large building projects he has undertaken on that site, including the massive Crystal Cathedral, designed by Philip Johnson and completed in 1980.

Schuller's theology has been a hybrid between *EVANGELICALISM and a Dale Carnegie–type positive thinking, which Schuller appropriated from his mentor, *NORMAN VINCENT PEALE. Schuller, both in his books and in his sermons, offers simple step-by-step outlines and tidy aphorisms, like, "Turn your hurt into your halo," "Tough times don't last; tough people do," and "Give yourself a spiritual shampoo." Schuller's writings over the years suggest that the language of therapy has overwhelmed the language of theology. One book, *Self-Esteem: The New Reformation,* even argued that the church should abandon theocentric language in favor of the language of pop psychology. Whatever its provenance, however, Schuller's theology has been enormously popular, purveyed through books and his *Hour of Power* television program, which began in 1970.

References: Robert H. Schuller, *You Can Become the Person You Want to Be* (1973); idem, *Be Happy, You Are Loved* (1986); Dennis Voskuil, *Mountains into Goldmines: Robert Schuller and the Gospel of Success* (1983); idem, s.v. "Robert Schuller," in Charles H. Lippy, ed., *Twentieth-Century Shapers of American Popular Religion* (1989).

Scientific Creationism. *See* **Creationism.**

Scofield, Cyrus Ingerson (1843–1921) The man most responsible for the popularization of dispensational *PREMILLENNIALISM, Cyrus Ingerson Scofield was born near Clinton, Michigan, and reared as an Episcopalian. After fighting in the Civil War with a regiment from Tennessee, he settled in St. Louis, married Leontinne Cerre, and studied law. His subsequent move to Atchison, Kansas, allowed him to pursue both a law and a political career, but he returned to St. Louis in 1879, forsaking his career, his two daughters, and his wife, whom he divorced in 1883.

The probable cause of Scofield's difficulties was alcohol abuse, but his evangelical *CONVERSION seemed to set him aright. He helped with *DWIGHT L. MOODY's *REVIVAL campaign in St. Louis and became a protégé of *JAMES HALL BROOKES. Scofield's evangelical zeal took many forms: affiliation with the Plymouth Congregational Church, the Hyde Park Congregational Church, acting superintendent of the *YMCA, and evangelistic work among the railroad men in East St. Louis, Illinois. Mission work took him to Dallas, Texas, in 1882, where a Congregational mission church grew to more than eight hundred members during his thirteen-year tenure.

Sometime during this period Scofield became enamored of the dispensationalist scheme of biblical interpretation that *JOHN NELSON DARBY brought to America. For Scofield, as for countless other evangelicals, Darbyism (as it was sometimes called) explained why America had not developed into the millennial kingdom that evangelicals early in the nineteenth century had so confidently predicted. Instead of the *MILLENNIUM as the next event on the eschatological calendar, Darby, Scofield, and the dispensationalists insisted that Jesus would return for the faithful, the true believers, at any minute and then usher in the *MILLENNIUM after a seven-year period of purgation, known as the tribulation. *DISPENSATIONALISM helped them explain why the society all around them late in the nineteenth century seemed to be in such disarray.

Scofield propagated dispensationalist ideas through several means. He became a fixture on the Bible conference circuit and established a correspondence course, later sold to *MOODY BIBLE INSTITUTE, that enrolled over seven thousand students. He wrote a book, published in 1888, called *Rightly Dividing the Word of Truth.* He became affiliated with Moody's operations in Northfield, Massachusetts, and returned briefly to the Dallas congregation (now known as Scofield Memorial Church), all the while working on a reference *BIBLE that would provide the tools of dispensationalist teaching to the masses.

The publication of the **SCOFIELD REFERENCE BIBLE* by Oxford University Press in 1909 codified dispensationalist ideas and was arguably the most important event in the development of *FUNDAMENTALISM in the twentieth century. Scofield left Dallas for the New York City area, where he ran another correspondence school, New York Night School of the Bible, and helped to found the *PHILADELPHIA SCHOOL OF THE BIBLE in 1914. He revised the **SCOFIELD REFERENCE BIBLE* in 1917, and it remained popular with fundamentalists throughout the twentieth century.

References: Charles Ingerson Scofield, *Rightly Dividing the Word of Truth* (1888); Charles G. Trumbull, *The Life Story of C. I. Scofield* (1920); Larry V. Crutchfield, s.v. "C. I. Scofield," in Charles H. Lippy, ed., *Twentieth-Century Shapers of American Popular Religion* (1989).

Scofield Reference Bible Although Oxford University Press, publisher of the *Scofield Reference Bible,* has long since lost count of the sales figures, the *Scofield Reference Bible* has sold millions since it first appeared in 1909. Written by *CYRUS INGERSON SCOFIELD, the *Scofield Bible* was meant to explain the vagaries of dispensational *PREMILLENNIALISM to the masses. Taken together, the glosses that Scofield provided served as a kind of template for reading the *BIBLE in such a way that the dispensationalist scheme would be apparent. Although other dispensationalists have come up with different interpretations, Scofield held to seven dispensations, beginning with the innocence of the Garden of Eden and concluding with the premillennial *RAPTURE of the faithful. Scofield expanded his edition in 1917, and Oxford issued another revision in 1967.

Scopes Trial The infamous Scopes "Monkey Trial" took place in the Rhea County courthouse in Dayton, Tennessee,

July 10–21, 1925. A science teacher at Dayton High School, John T. Scopes, could not actually recall whether or not he had taught evolution in his classroom, but he had responded nevertheless to an advertisement by the American Civil Liberties Union (ACLU) for someone to test the constitutionality of Tennessee's *BUTLER ACT, which forbade the teaching of evolution in public schools.

Scopes was arrested (by prearrangement) on May 5, 1925, and a grand jury returned an indictment on May 25. The ACLU retained Clarence Darrow for the defense, while *WILLIAM JENNINGS BRYAN, the "Great Commoner" and three-time Democratic nominee for president, assisted the prosecution. As the trial unfolded amid a carnival atmosphere it became clear that Scopes himself was a peripheral figure, that the focus would be a titanic clash between Bryan and Darrow over the legitimacy of scientific inquiry and the literal interpretation of the *BIBLE. The trial turned when Bryan succumbed to Darrow's dramatic ploy to call him, Bryan, as a witness. Darrow fired a series of village-atheist questions at Bryan and succeeded in making him look foolish.

On July 21, after deliberating for nine minutes, the jury found Scopes guilty of violating the *BUTLER ACT. He was fined one hundred dollars, although that judgment was later overturned on a technicality by the Supreme Court of Tennessee. For fundamentalists, however, the damage had been done. The media had blanketed the trial and the goings-on in the courthouse square in Dayton. Radio station WGN in Chicago carried the proceedings live, and the irascible H. L. Mencken of the *Baltimore Sun* led the contingent of journalists. Mencken succeeded in portraying fundamentalists as uneducated backwoods country bumpkins—"gaping primates of the upland valleys"—a caricature that persisted in many quarters through the remainder of the twentieth century.

References: Edward J. Larson, *Summer for the Gods: The Scopes Trial and America's Continuing Debate over Science and Religion* (1997); George M. Marsden, *Fundamentalism and American Culture: The Shaping of Twentieth-Century American Evangelicalism: 1870–1925* (1980); *Mine Eyes Have Seen the Glory,* three-part PBS documentary (1992).

Scott, Eugene V. "Gene" (1929–) Gene Scott, the son of an *ASSEMBLIES OF GOD minister, was born in Buell, Idaho, and was steeped in fundamentalist theology and *CAMP MEETING revivalism. He earned the doctorate from Stanford University and later lapsed into agnosticism. By the early 1960s, however, he was working for *ORAL ROBERTS. He taught briefly at *EVANGEL COLLEGE and in 1969 became pastor of Faith Center in Glendale, California. Scott used the church to launch the nation's first twenty-four hour religious television station, KHOF, which soon provided programming—including Scott's *Festival of Faith*—for national syndication under the rubric of Faith Broadcasting Network.

As host of *Festival of Faith,* Scott sat on a chair, puffing a cigar and wearing different hats and eyeglasses. The show consisted of a sequence of stream-of-consciousness diatribes leveled against a variety of targets: the Internal Revenue Service, the federal government (especially the Federal Communications Commission), labor unions, and other televangelists (especially *JERRY FALWELL, whom he scorned as "Jerry the Fat"). Scott would also harangue his viewers for not sending enough money and would threaten to go off the air unless they ponied up. The FCC took him off the air in May 1983 for various violations. Scott returned to the airwaves in 1990 as voice of the World University Network, which employs medium wave and shortwave stations and reaches around the world.

The Faith Center relocated in 1986 to an old Gothic-style movie theater in downtown Los Angeles, and it is now known as the Los Angeles University Cathedral. Inside, it has a small art museum that holds a Rembrandt and a Monet, along with paintings by Scott. Ironically, Scott does not make himself available to his congregation. Not only does he refuse to meet with them, he ensures his privacy with a security squad of off-duty Los Angeles police officers. In spite of this, however, the congregation has thrived, even though Scott often tells his followers they do not need to go to church to be Christian—as long as they send in their tithes of 10 percent of their incomes. Scott also has no position against profanity, alcohol, *ABORTION, adultery, or homosexuality. While Scott's openmindedness on these issues sets him apart once again from most evangelical pastors, it accurately reflects his life and personality. Scott is famous for cursing figures like *JIMMY SWAGGART on the air, and he was divorced from his first wife, Betty Ann Frazer, after twenty-three years of marriage. Scott has since remarried, and his second wife, Christine Shaw, often appears on his program riding the church's horses.

Reference: Glenn F. Bunting, "The Shock Jock of Televangelism," *Los Angeles Times*, July 7, 1994.

Scott, Orange (1800–1847) Born in Brookfield, Vermont, and converted at a *CAMP MEETING at the age of twenty-one, Orange Scott became a successful revivalist in the Methodist Episcopal Church. His zeal for *ABOLITIONISM, however, which was animated by his belief in the Wesleyan doctrine of entire *SANCTIFICATION (the notion that the believer can be entirely freed from *SIN by the work of the Holy Spirit), eroded his popularity among some Methodists. When Scott pushed abolitionist legislation before the General Conference in 1836 his efforts were rejected. The next year he became a lecturer for the *AMERICAN ANTI-SLAVERY SOCIETY and founded his own periodical, *The Wesleyan Quarterly Review* (later renamed the *American Wesleyan Observer*).

When the General Conference of 1840 again rejected Scott's antislavery overtures, he and Lucius Matlock organized an antislavery convention, held in New York, which led to the formation of the American Wesleyan Anti-Slavery Society. Scott left the Methodist Episcopal Church in 1842 to become the first president of the *WESLEYAN METHODIST CHURCH.

References: Donald W. Dayton, *Discovering an Evangelical Heritage* (1988); Timothy L. Smith, *Revivalism and Social Reform in Mid-Nineteenth Century America* (1957).

Scott, Peter Cameron (1867–1896) Peter Cameron Scott was born in Scotland but emigrated to Philadelphia with his family. During a return visit to Scotland he had something of a spiritual crisis, which prompted him to dedicate his life to missionary service. He sailed for West Africa in 1890 but had to return for reasons of health. While kneeling by the tomb of *DAVID LIVINGSTONE in Westminster Abbey, Scott came up with the idea of establishing a chain of mission stations from east to central Africa, an idea that evolved into the *AFRICA INLAND MISSION, formally organized in 1895. That same year, Scott and the first missionary party sailed for Africa, where Scott died the following year.

Scottish Common Sense Realism An enormously influential school of thought for nineteenth-century evangelicals, Scottish Common Sense Realism was developed in the eighteenth century principally by Thomas Reid, a philosopher at the University of Glasgow, as a response to both the idealism of George Berkeley and the skepticism of David Hume. Scottish Realism (also known as Common Sense Realism) posited that ordinary people could gain a reliable grasp of the world though a responsible use of their senses. In addition to an apprehension of the physical world, the individual also possesses an innate "moral sense" that allows for a grasp of foundational moral principles. In the realm of biblical interpretation, evangelicals used Common Sense Realism to argue that the meaning of the Scriptures was available to the faithful simply by reading the *BIBLE and interpreting it in its plainest sense.

Scottish Realism's first major proponent in America was *JOHN WITHERSPOON, president of the College of New Jersey from 1768 until 1794. The approach spread rapidly among evangelicals in the antebellum period, especially through the agency of the theologians at Princeton Theological Seminary.

References: Sidney E. Ahlstrom, "The Scottish Philosophy and American Theology," *Church History*, XXIV (1955); Mark A. Noll, "Common Sense Traditions and American Evangelical Thought," *American Quarterly*, XXXVII (1985).

Scottish Realism. *See* **Scottish Common Sense Realism.**

Scriptural Knowledge Institution for Home and Abroad. *See* **Müller, George.**

Seattle Pacific University (Seattle, Washington) Seattle Pacific University, which is affiliated with the *FREE METHODIST CHURCH OF NORTH AMERICA, was established in 1891 and has been fully accredited since 1936. Seattle Pacific University was one of the original members of the *CHRISTIAN COLLEGE CONSORTIUM.

The teaching of evolution remains a controversial subject for many *CHRISTIAN COLLEGES. Some schools teach evolution in tandem with creation science; most circumvent the issue by not offering courses in human origins at all. At Seattle Pacific, however, evolution is touched on in a number of biology classes, and the university even offers a full, advanced-level course in evolutionary biology. The university has master's degree programs in education, business, and health sciences.

Rather than demanding attendance at specific chapel sessions, Seattle Pacific lets students design their own program for spiritual life. They are required to earn fifteen Chapel/Forum credits a semester, but they can choose from a number of worship groups, retreats, and community service projects.

References: Seattle Pacific University Undergraduate Catalog 1996–97 (1996); William C. Ringenberg, *The Christian College: A History of Protestant Higher Education in America* (1984).

Second Blessing Second blessing refers to a second movement of the Holy Spirit upon the believer—after the first movement, which is *CONVERSION or new birth. The doctrine derives from *JOHN WESLEY's teaching about Christian perfection or entire *SANCTIFICATION, in which he argued that a second work of *GRACE could render the believer free from the inclination to *SIN. This teaching became common in holiness circles during the nineteenth century. As the pentecostal movement coalesced early in the twentieth century, pentecostals regarded

*GLOSSOLALIA as the evidence for the second blessing.

Second Coming Premillennialists believe that Jesus will return at any moment to *RAPTURE the church (the true believers) and thereby initiate the sequence of events predicted in the book of Revelation. The second coming, or second advent, refers to this return of Jesus to earth (after his first coming, the advent, recorded in the Gospels).

Second Great Awakening The Second Great Awakening was a massive evangelical *REVIVAL that convulsed three theaters of the new nation at the turn of the nineteenth century: New England, the Cumberland Valley, and western New York. Whereas the *GREAT AWAKENING of the eighteenth century had been confined mainly to the Middle Colonies and to New England, the Second Awakening was more diverse and inclusive. The other difference is that, whereas the First Awakening had been overwhelmingly Calvinist in nature—seeing the *REVIVAL, in *JONATHAN EDWARDS's words, as "a surprising work of God"—the Second Awakening was Arminian, with *CHARLES FINNEY, the primary apologist, insisting that *REVIVAL was the work of man and that "*NEW MEASURES" brought on the visitation of *GRACE.

The *REVIVAL on the frontier of the Cumberland Valley, also known as the Great Revival, received its impetus when *JAMES MCGREADY settled in Logan County, Kentucky, and shortly thereafter began conducting *CAMP MEETINGS. The famous *CAMP MEETING in Cane Ridge, Kentucky, in August 1801, attended by as many as twenty-five thousand, greatly abetted the spread of the *REVIVAL, which in turn brought evangelical Christianity to the frontier South.

Whereas the Great Revival had been marked by all manner of spiritual "exercises"—barking, jerking, falling to the ground—the New England theater of the Second Awakening was considerably more contained and cerebral. After *TIMOTHY DWIGHT became president of Yale College in 1795 he instituted a series of courses designed to root out infidelity and a fixation with the Enlightenment among students at the school. Many students were converted, and the *REVIVAL spread, especially through the agency of Dwight's students, notably *LYMAN BEECHER.

The final phase of the Second Awakening took place in western New York, where *REVIVAL fires had blazed so frequently that the region was known as the burned-over district. Especially with the opening of the Erie Canal in 1825, western New York experienced rapid social change, and *REVIVAL preachers, especially Finney, enjoyed considerable success. He employed his "*NEW MEASURES" to promote *REVIVALS in Rochester and elsewhere, and the success of *EVANGELICALISM under Finney's direction also led to a considerable push to reform society according to the norms of godliness.

Taken together, the *REVIVALS that took place in these three theaters profoundly affected American religion, even American history. In the South, the Great Revival stamped the entire region with evangelical sensibilities that persisted into the twenty-first century. The Second Awakening also unleashed a reforming impulse that would transform antebellum America as evangelicals called the nation's attention to such issues as slavery, alcohol, education, and women's rights.

References: John R. Boles, *The Great Revival, 1787–1805: The Origins of the Southern Evangelical Mind* (1972); Whitney R. Cross, *The Burned-*

Over District: The Social and Intellectual History of Enthusiastic Religion in Western New York, 1800–1850 (1950); Paul E. Johnson, *A Shopkeeper's Millennium: Society and Revivals in Rochester, New York, 1815–1837* (1978); Stuart C. Henry, *Unvanquished Puritan: A Portrait of Lyman Beecher* (1973); David W. Kling, *A Field of Divine Wonders: The New Divinity and Village Revivals in Northwestern Connecticut, 1792–1822* (1993); Christine Leigh Heyrman, *Southern Cross: The Beginnings of the Bible Belt* (1997).

Secondary Virginity. *See* **True Love Waits.**

Secular Humanism More than anyone else, *FRANCIS A. SCHAEFFER deserves the credit (or blame) for making "secular humanism" into a household term among conservative evangelicals. Although humanism was a Renaissance ideal that celebrated achievements in literature, arts, and learning as the fullest expression of humanity, which was in turn the apex of God's creation, humanism in the twentieth century took on less religious overtones. The Humanist Manifesto, issued in 1933 and again (with revisions) forty years later, asserted that "the traditional dogmatic or authoritarian religions that place revelation, God, ritual or creed above human needs and experience do a disservice to the human species."

Schaeffer seized upon this exclusion of the divine, arguing that rampant "secular humanism" would lead to moral relativism and ethical bankruptcy. In *How Should We Then Live?* and a spate of other books, Schaeffer portrayed secular humanism as a pernicious and diabolical force undermining the moral and spiritual fabric of America. His acolytes found evidence of secular humanism in everything from situation ethics to the proposed Equal Rights Amendment to the Constitution, from evolution to gay rights. Following Schaeffer's lead, other conservative evangelical leaders issued a call to arms against secular humanism, and widespread popular fear of this menace animated the early efforts of the *RELIGIOUS RIGHT.

References: Francis A. Schaeffer, *How Should We Then Live?* (1976); Tim LaHaye, *Battle for the Mind* (1980); William Martin, *With God on Our Side: The Rise of the Religious Right in America* (1996).

Seeker Churches "Seeker churches" is a generic term for evangelical congregations that employ marketing strategies for luring people to their church services. The undisputed prototype for this approach is *WILLOW CREEK COMMUNITY CHURCH in South Barrington, Illinois, which was begun in 1975 on the basis of a door-to-door market research survey to determine why suburbanites stayed away from church. *BILL HYBELS, the church's founder, proceeded to design a church that would overcome their objections, and the spectacular numerical success at Willow Creek—approximately seventeen thousand people attend Willow Creek's services every weekend—has inspired countless imitators. The list of other seeker churches might include Saddleback Valley Community Church in Orange County, California; Community Church of Joy in Phoenix; Discovery Church in Orlando, Florida; and Second Baptist Church in Houston, among many others.

Reference: Kimon Howland Sargeant, *Re-Forming the Church: Evangelical Seeker Churches, Institutional Innovation, and Cultural Change* (1999).

Seiple, Robert A. (1943–) Robert A. Seiple, a native of Harmony, New Jersey, earned the B.A. degree from Brown University. From 1966 to 1969, he served in the United States Marine Corps, attaining the rank of captain. He flew combat missions in Vietnam and was awarded more than thirty medals, including the Distinguished Flying Cross. Seiple held various posts at Brown, his alma mater, including athletic director, vice president for development, and director of the university's fund-raising campaign. From Brown, Seiple became president of *EASTERN COLLEGE and *EASTERN BAPTIST THEOLOGICAL SEMINARY and in 1987 was named president of *WORLD VISION, the largest privately funded international Christian relief and development agency in the United States.

During Seiple's eleven-year tenure the number of people *WORLD VISION served increased dramatically, as did contributions. He also relocated the agency's headquarters in 1995 to Federal Way, Washington, in an effort to save on overhead costs. Seiple returned to Vietnam in 1988 as *WORLD VISION's president, whereupon he became an advocate for reestablishing diplomatic relations with that country. Seiple received the secretary of state's Distinguished Public Service Award in 1995, and after stepping down as president of *WORLD VISION in 1998 he accepted an appointment from President Bill Clinton to a newly established post of senior adviser for international religious freedom in the Department of State. In announcing the appointment, Clinton declared that Seiple's mandate would be to "make sure that religious liberty concerns get high and close attention in our foreign policy." In September 2000, near the conclusion of Clinton's second term as president, Seiple left that post to join the Institute for Global Engagement, a think tank located at *EASTERN COLLEGE, outside of Philadelphia.

Reference: Robert A. Seiple, *One Life at a Time: Making a World of Difference* (1990).

Sekulow, Jay (1957–) Born into a Jewish household in Brooklyn, New York, and reared on Long Island and in Atlanta, Jay Sekulow converted to evangelical Christianity while a student at Atlanta Baptist College (now Mercer University). He earned a law degree at Mercer and worked as a prosecutor for the Internal Revenue Service before establishing his own law practice in Atlanta. When the firm went bankrupt in the mid-1980s, Sekulow became general counsel for *JEWS FOR JESUS. In that capacity, Sekulow won several cases before the United States Supreme Court, and he expanded his legal advocacy by representing several other *RELIGIOUS RIGHT organizations, including *CONCERNED WOMEN FOR AMERICA and *OPERATION RESCUE. Sekulow also founded an organization called Christian Advocates Serving Evangelism and successfully argued the constitutionality of the Equal Access Act before the Supreme Court in 1990, the law that allows student religious gatherings in public schools.

Sekulow became chief counsel for *PAT ROBERTSON'S *AMERICAN CENTER FOR LAW AND JUSTICE in 1992. In that capacity Sekulow, who refers to the American Civil Liberties Union as the "Anti-Christian Litigation Unit," has argued a number of important cases for the *RELIGIOUS RIGHT, including the defense of antiabortion protesters, the invocation of the First Amendment to protect religious displays and evangelistic efforts on public property, and the defense of students who pray at school functions.

Separates The Separates were strict congregationalists in New England, especially Connecticut, during the middle decades of the eighteenth century. Rather than comport with the established Congregational churches of New England, the Separates formed their own churches, which tended to be more sympathetic to the revivalism of the *GREAT AWAKENING and which imposed exacting demands for church membership. The Separates challenged the New England formula of church and state, which provided public money for the support of Congregational churches and clergy. The Separates, therefore, agitated for disestablishment and for freedom of religious expression.

By the latter half of the eighteenth century, many of the Separate congregations had become Baptist in an effort to maintain their distance from state interference. The Separate conception of church and state, however, eventually was codified in the First Amendment to the United States Constitution and in the subsequent religious disestablishment in Connecticut in 1818 and in Massachusetts in 1833.

References: C. C. Goen, *Revivalism and Separatism in New England, 1740–1800* (1962); William G. McLoughlin, *The New England Dissent, 1630–1833: The Baptists and the Separation of Church and State,* 2 vols. (1971).

Separatism Separatism, the notion of separating from those deemed lacking in piety or orthodoxy, is a recurrent theme in *EVANGELICALISM, especially among fundamentalists in the twentieth century. The biblical warrant fundamentalists usually cite is 2 Corinthians 6:17 (KJV): "Wherefore come out from among them, and be ye separate, saith the Lord, and touch not the unclean *thing;* and I will receive you." During the fundamentalist-modernist controversies in the early decades of the twentieth century, fundamentalists insisted on separating from what they saw as an increasing drift toward *LIBERALISM (or "*MODERNISM") in mainline Protestant denominations. This impulse, which is sometimes called first-degree separatism, took institutional form in such groups as the *BAPTIST BIBLE UNION, which was formed in 1923, and the *GENERAL ASSOCIATION OF REGULAR BAPTISTS, organized in 1932.

With the emergence of *NEO-EVANGELICALISM at mid-century, a movement that sought to tone down some of the militant rhetoric of *FUNDAMENTALISM and to cooperate somewhat with mainline Protestants, second-degree separatism took hold. Second-degree separatists demanded separatism from anyone who would not separate from *LIBERALISM, which they continued to regard as heresy. Thus, *BILLY GRAHAM, who cooperated with the ministerial alliance during his 1957 Madison Square Garden crusade in New York City, became the object of condemnations by the second-degree separatists, many of whom continue to regard him as a flaming liberal. There is some evidence that third-degree separatism emerged among the arch-fundamentalists in the 1970s—a separatism from fundamentalists who refused to practice second-degree separatism.

Serampore Trio At the turn of the nineteenth century, *WILLIAM CAREY, *JOSHUA MARSHMAN, and *WILLIAM WARD established the Serampore mission north of Calcutta, India, under the auspices of the Baptist Missionary Society. Under the direction of these three leaders, known collectively as the Serampore Trio, the mission engaged in an ambitious program of translation, publishing, *EVANGELISM, and education, including the founding of Serampore College.

Reference: John Clark Marshman, *The Life and Times of Carey, Marshman, and Ward,* 2 vols. (1859).

Serpent Handling A variant within the holiness-pentecostal movement, snake handlers (also known as serpent handlers) derive their biblical warrant from a literal interpretation of Mark 16:18 (KJV): "They shall take up serpents; and if they drink any deadly thing, it shall not hurt them; they shall lay hands on the sick, and they shall recover." The earliest recorded incidence of snake handling in a religious context took place in 1910 when *GEORGE WENT HENSLEY picked up a serpent during a *REVIVAL near Cleveland, Tennessee. The practice spread to eastern Kentucky and, eventually, throughout Appalachia, especially among those of Scots-Irish descent. Because of the radical independence of these groups—they have no denominational affiliation—judging their numbers is difficult, but the best estimates suggest that approximately two thousand snake handlers live in Appalachia.

In the course of the snake handler's religious gatherings, as the service reaches a climax amid the sounds of tambourines and guitars and clapping and ecstatic dancing, snake handlers, also known as Holy Ghost people, take poisonous snakes—usually copperheads and rattlesnakes—out of boxes and pass them among members of the congregation. Some place the serpents on their heads or inside their shirts or toss them back and forth to other members of the congregation. The vipers are in no way bound or anesthetized. When someone is bitten, the congregation seeks to "pray them through," and survival is seen as a confirmation of the presence of the Holy Spirit. Variations of snake handling include the drinking of strychnine and the use of fire, sometimes with blowtorches.

The congregations, which typically meet in small buildings or in members' homes, tend to be lesser educated. Many are—or were—coal miners; one of the rites of initiation for a new miner is for fellow miners to throw poisonous snakes at him.

References: Steven M. Kane, "The Holy Ghost People: The Snake-Handlers of Southern Appalachia," *Appalachian Journal,* I (spring 1974); idem, "Holiness Ritual Fire Handling: Ethnographic and Psychophysiological Considerations," *Ethos,* X (1982); Dennis Covington, *Salvation on Sand Mountain: Snake Handling and Redemption in Southern Appalachia* (1995); Deborah Vansau McCauley, *Appalachian Mountain Religion: A History* (1995); Bill J. Leonard, ed., *Christianity in Appalachia: Profiles in Regional Pluralism* (1998); David L. Kimbrough, *Taking Up Serpents: Snake Handlers of Eastern Kentucky* (1995).

Seventh-day Adventist Church The Seventh-day Adventist Church was born in the aftermath of the *MILLERITE *GREAT DISAPPOINTMENT of October 22, 1844. *WILLIAM MILLER, a Baptist preacher, after a long and careful study of the *BIBLE, began to preach his adventist message publicly in 1831. Based on his study, he predicted the imminent return of Jesus Christ. Although initially reluctant to do so, Miller set the probable date as sometime between March 1843 and March 1844. After this first disappointment when Christ did not appear, a movement arose among his followers that reset the date to October 22, 1844. The second disappointment was too much for most of the *MILLERITES. A few, however, remained with the movement, and from this loyal group came both the *ADVENT CHRISTIAN CHURCH and the much larger Seventh-day Adventist Church.

Some of the *MILLERITES had begun keeping the seventh-day Sabbath shortly after the *GREAT DISAPPOINTMENT. One group of these gathered in New Hampshire. It included several leaders in the movement including, most importantly, *ELLEN GOULD WHITE. White, only a teenager at the time of the *GREAT DISAPPOINTMENT, was soon accepted as a prophetess. White confirmed through visions the adoption of the seventh-day Sabbath as well as many other aspects of the Old Testament law. By 1855, the group had relocated to Battle Creek, Michigan. The Church was organized informally under the name Seventh-day Adventist Church at Battle Creek in 1860. Formal organization came in 1863. In 1903, the headquarters were moved to Washington, D.C., and, in 1989, moved again to their present location in Silver Springs, Maryland.

Most Seventh-day Adventist doctrines are the traditional, orthodox Protestant doctrines. The Church believes that the Scriptures are divinely inspired, authoritative, and the infallible revelation of God's will. The Church subscribes to belief in the Trinity, creation *ex nihilo,* and *SALVATION through the atoning death of Jesus Christ. Seventh-day Adventists recognize the ordinances of *BAPTISM by immersion and the *LORD'S SUPPER. The Church also practices foot washing. There is a special emphasis on Old Testament law, especially the Ten Commandments. Believing that the bodies of believers are temples of the Holy Spirit, Seventh-day Adventist members abstain from eating foods declared in Scripture to be unclean, and they foreswear the use of alcohol and tobacco. Church members are urged to follow a healthful diet, exercise regularly, and engage in philanthropy. Seventh-day Adventists, accordingly, sponsor many hospitals and encourage tithing for members.

The Seventh-day Adventists believe that Jesus' *SECOND COMING is imminent but at a time that is, as yet, unknown. According to Church teaching, however, all signs of prophecy indicate that the time will be sooner rather than later. The Seventh-day Adventists have dealt with the *GREAT DISAPPOINTMENT, in part, by saying that in 1844 Jesus Christ began a new phase in his heavenly ministry. His work in the heavenly sanctuary recalls the work done by Hebrew high priests in the ancient earthly sanctuary. The completion of this heavenly ministry will mark the end of the probationary period for humanity and will immediately precede his *SECOND COMING. The Church now teaches that the time of the *SECOND COMING cannot be known and all believers are exhorted to be ready at all times. Seventh-day Adventists give a special place to the spiritual gift of prophecy.

Church *POLITY is a representational democracy. Authority for the Church resides in the membership. There are four levels of organization, from the individual to the worldwide church. Local congregations gather to form local conferences. A number of local conferences form the regional, or union, conference. The highest governmental body is the general conference. At each level delegates and representatives are elected by the membership. The general conference meets every five years. Between quintennial sessions, the executive committee manages administrative tasks. The Church has eleven administrative divisions worldwide.

The Seventh-day Adventist Church has an extensive mission program, emphasizing health and educational ministries as well as spiritual ministries. The Church reports over 8.8 million members around the world. In the United States, there are 838,898 Seventh-day Adventists in 4,636 local churches.

References: Frank S. Mead and Samuel S. Hill, *Handbook of Denominations in the United States,* 10th ed. (1996); J. Gordon Melton, *The Encyclopedia of American Religions,* 3d ed. (1993).

Seymour, William J(oseph) (1870–1922) Born in Centerville, Louisiana, to former slaves, William J. Seymour, who was given to dreams and visions in his youth, was something of a spiritual pilgrim. He was reared a Baptist but became a member of the African Methodist Episcopal church after he migrated north to Indianapolis in 1895. While in Cincinnati from 1900 to 1902, Seymour came into contact with holiness preacher Martin Wells Knapp and joined the Church of God Reformation movement, attracted by their emphasis on entire *SANCTIFICATION and their predictions about an outpouring of the Holy Spirit before the *SECOND COMING of Christ. He was ordained by a small group called the Evening Light Saints movement, and in 1903 he moved to Houston in search of his family.

There he attended Lucy Farrow's holiness church, and when Farrow moved to Topeka, Kansas, to become a governess in *CHARLES FOX PARHAM's household, Seymour took over as pastor of the congregation. Farrow returned to Houston in October 1905 with the claim that she had spoken in *TONGUES, which Parham taught was the "initial evidence" of *BAPTISM OF THE HOLY SPIRIT. When Parham moved his Bible school to Houston two months later, Seymour enrolled and became convinced by Parham's teaching, even though Seymour would not speak in *TONGUES until much later.

Parham and Seymour conducted preaching missions to African Americans in Houston, and Parham was grooming Seymour to be a missionary "to those of his own color" in Texas. In January 1906, however, Seymour accepted an invitation from Neeley Terry, a member of a holiness congregation in Los Angeles, to become a candidate for the church's position as associate pastor. Seymour traveled to Los Angeles by way of Denver, Colorado, where he visited *ALMA WHITE's Pentecostal Union (Pillar of Fire) group. His first sermon in Los Angeles alienated the congregation because of its insistence on *GLOSSOLALIA as evidence of Spirit *BAPTISM; the church barred its doors to Seymour, who was forced to seek shelter in the home of Richard Asberry on North Bonnie Brae Street.

Several weeks of prayer meetings at the house on Bonnie Brae finally led to the gift of *TONGUES for Seymour and others on April 9, 1906. As word of the phenomenon spread, Seymour preached from the front porch to crowds assembled on the street. On April 14, 1906, the crowds reconvened at a forty-by-sixty-foot building, a former warehouse on 312 Azusa Street; four days later, the day of the San Francisco earthquake, the *Los Angeles Times* reported "wild scenes" and "a weird babble of *TONGUES" at the mission on Azusa Street. The *REVIVAL was noteworthy also because of its interracial character. In the words of *FRANK BARTLEMAN, a contemporary, "The color line has been washed away by the blood."

By the end of 1906, Seymour had incorporated the ministry as the Pentecostal Apostolic Faith Movement; he also published a periodical, *Apostolic Faith,* which spread news of the *REVIVAL as well as the theological justifications that underlay it. Visitors came to Azusa Street from North America and from around the world and carried news of the *AZUSA STREET REVIVAL back to their homes.

Seymour, whose demeanor was that of a teacher more than a preacher, began to lose his grip on the *REVIVAL in 1908. Two of his followers, *FLORENCE CRAWFORD and Clara Lum, had opposed Seymour's marriage to Jenny Moore because, they said, the *RAPTURE of the Church was imminent. They took Seymour's mailing list for *Apostolic Faith* with them to Portland, Oregon, thereby leaving Seymour unable to communicate with his followers. Several years later, *WILLIAM H.

DURHAM, an early disciple of Seymour, returned to Los Angeles to promote his conviction that Seymour's teaching on *SANCTIFICATION was wrong, that believers could rely on the "finished work of Calvary" at the moment of *SALVATION.

Seymour's direct influence on the pentecostal movement began thereafter to wane, although he continued to conduct *REVIVAL campaigns. His vision of an interracial pentecostal movement also faded with the formation of various pentecostal denominations configured on either side of the racial divide. Seymour made himself "bishop" of the Pacific Apostolic Faith Movement in 1915 and stipulated that any successor be "a man of color."

References: Vinson Synan, *The Holiness-Pentecostal Movement in the United States* (1971); James T. Connelly, s.v. "William J. Seymour," in Charles H. Lippy, ed., *Twentieth-Century Shapers of American Popular Religion* (1989).

Shakarian, Demos (1913–) A member of a refugee family from the Armenian holocaust, Demos Shakarian grew up in the Armenian Pentecostal Church; when he received his Spirit *BAPTISM in 1926, he was also healed of impaired hearing. Shakarian went on to become a prosperous dairy farmer in California, using both his funds and his leadership skills to promote *PENTECOSTALISM. He befriended such pentecostal evangelists as *CHARLES S. PRICE, who was responsible for healing Shakarian's sister, and *ORAL ROBERTS. After helping to organize Roberts's 1951 *REVIVAL campaign in Los Angeles, Shakarian enlisted his support in the formation of the *FULL GOSPEL BUSINESS MEN'S FELLOWSHIP INTERNATIONAL.

Shaw, Anna Howard (1847–1919) Born in Newcastle-upon-Tyne, England, Anna Howard Shaw grew up in rural Michigan and was licensed to preach by the Methodists. She attended Albion College and the School of Theology at Boston University. Shaw was denied full ordination by church officials in 1880, whereupon she received ordination from a smaller Methodist body, the Methodist Protestants. She served congregations in East Dennis and Brewster, Massachusetts, while studying medicine and developing a concern for the wretched conditions in the slums of Boston. She became an ardent suffragist lecturer and served as president of the National American Woman's Suffrage Association from 1904 to 1915.

Shaw, Knowles (1834–1878) Knowles Shaw, the "singing *EVANGELIST," was born into poverty in Ohio and reared in rural Indiana. Lacking a formal education, he learned to play the violin his father gave him just before his death. Shaw became an active and energetic preacher, but his real metier was music; he would open his services with gospel hymns, many of which, including "Bringing In the Sheaves," he had written. Shaw, affiliated with the Christian Church (Disciples of Christ), itinerated widely, from Michigan to Texas, in a career that lasted for nearly two decades, until his untimely death in a train wreck in Texas.

Sheeks, E(lliott) J. (née Doboe) (1872–1946) Born in rural Kentucky, E. J. Doboe experienced an evangelical *CONVERSION at age eleven and joined the *CUMBERLAND PRESBYTERIAN CHURCH. She claimed to have been fourteen years old before she ever heard another woman pray in church, but her exposure to holiness teachings and the encouragement of others led her to consider preaching herself. While still a teenager, she married E. H. Sheeks, a salesman more than thirty years her senior. They moved to Memphis, Tennessee, where E. J. enrolled at the Old State Female College and attended the Methodist church. Shortly after the Sheekses attended a holiness *REVIVAL they relocated to Milan, Tennessee, and became charter members of the New Testament Church of Christ. Some time later, E. J. was reading sermons by *JOHN WESLEY when she claimed her experience of entire *SANCTIFICATION, and she began preaching during *REVIVAL services in Monett, Arkansas. In addition to her travels as an *EVANGELIST, she was involved in rescue missions. She enrolled in Peniel College (formerly Texas Holiness University) in 1915 and later joined the faculty of Bresee College in Hutchinson, Kansas.

Reference: Rebecca Laird, *Ordained Women in the Church of the Nazarene: The First Generation* (1993).

Sheldon, Louis P. (1934–) Louis P. Sheldon, founder of the *TRADITIONAL VALUES COALITION, was born in Washington, D.C., and graduated from Michigan State University and Princeton Theological Seminary. A pastor of evangelical churches for more than a quarter century, Sheldon founded *TRADITIONAL VALUES COALITION in 1980 as part of the so-called family values agenda of the *RELIGIOUS RIGHT. He has been an outspoken opponent of *ABORTION, pornography, and homosexuality, and has been equally outspoken in advocating "*REPARATIVE THERAPY" as a means of "treating" gays and lesbians. Sheldon and his organization produced and disseminated a rabidly homophobic videocassette, "The Gay Agenda," which warned that homosexuals were pursuing a program aimed at the corruption of American families and American society. In 1999, the *Orange County Register* reported that Sheldon's son, Steve, had secretly accepted money from casino gambling interests to persuade religious groups to oppose other forms of gambling. Lou Sheldon and the *TRADITIONAL VALUES COALITION then showed up at antigambling rallies. When Sheldon was asked about ten thousand dollars he had accepted from Hollywood Park Racetrack in 1994, he replied: "Politics makes strange bedfellows. The devil had that money long enough. It was about time we got our hands on it."

Shepherding Movement Also known as the discipleship movement, the shepherding movement arose out of the *CHARISMATIC RENEWAL, emphasizing accountability and submission to church leaders. In 1970, four charismatics from Florida—*DON BASHAM, *DEREK PRINCE, *CHARLES SIMPSON, and *BOB MUMFORD—established an organization called *CHRISTIAN GROWTH MINISTRIES in Fort Lauderdale. They persuaded dozens of churches to adopt their pyramid-like *AUTHORITY structure: Each church member submitted to the authority of an elder or "shepherd," who in turn submitted to the *AUTHORITY of the pastor. The lines of *AUTHORITY, however, continued beyond the congregation to regional shepherds and eventually to the leaders in Fort Lauderdale. Orders descended the pyramid, while tithes and offerings were to go up the pyramid.

Such a scheme quickly led to complaints about abuse and charges of cult-like manipulation; shepherds ruled on everything from marriage partners to domicile. Even *PAT ROBERTSON took umbrage with the shepherding movement, charging at one point that *CHRISTIAN GROWTH MINISTRIES was teaching "witchcraft" and remarking that the only difference between shepherding and Jonestown was "Kool-Aid," a reference to the mass suicide of People's Temple followers in Jonestown, Guyana, by drinking Kool-Aid laced with poison. While the leaders of the movement acknowledged some mistakes in the mid-1970s, "shepherding" spread to Roman Catholics—especially the Word of God Community in Ann Arbor, Michigan, and the People of Praise in South Bend, Indiana—and to the Crossroads movement, or the *INTERNATIONAL CHURCHES OF CHRIST. The shepherding movement disbanded in 1986, and in 1990 Mumford publicly asked forgiveness from those who were hurt by the movement. "Multiplied hundreds of pastors, like myself," *JACK HAYFORD wrote in 1990, "have spent large amounts of time over the past fifteen years picking up the broken lives that resulted from distortion of truth by extreme teachings and destructive applications on discipleship, *AUTHORITY and shepherding."

References: Bob Mumford, *The Problem of Doing Your Own Thing* (1973); "An Idea Whose Time Has Gone?" *Christianity Today*, March 19, 1990.

Sherrard, Samuel M. (1941–) Samuel M. Sherrard founded the Colombo chapter of *YOUTH FOR CHRIST in his native Sri Lanka in 1966. A member of the *CHRISTIAN AND MISSIONARY ALLIANCE, Sherrard was named executive director of *YOUTH FOR CHRIST in Hawai'i in 1974 and also served as pastor of Leeward Community Church in Pearl City, Oahu. Sherrard became area director of *YOUTH FOR CHRIST International Americas in 1994, and two years later the president and chief executive officer of *YOUTH FOR CHRIST INTERNATIONAL.

Shields, T(homas) T(odhunter) (1873–1955) Born in Bristol, England, to a Baptist preacher and his wife, T. T. Shields was reared in southwestern Ontario and soon began to exercise his gifts as a forceful and articulate preacher. Though he received no formal theological training, Shields became pastor of the Jarvis Street Baptist Church in Toronto in 1910, the largest Baptist church in Canada at the time. Throughout his career at Jarvis Street, which extended through the end of his life, Shields was known as the "Canadian Spurgeon," although his dogmatism and autocratic style occasionally placed him at odds with elements within his congregation.

An inveterate fundamentalist and an ardent separatist, Shields propagated his conservative theological views through the pages of the church's newspaper, *The Gospel Witness*, which reached thirty thousand subscribers in sixty countries. More significantly, Shields was one of the organizers—and the only president—of the *BAPTIST BIBLE UNION, a fundamentalist alliance that was the precursor to the *GENERAL ASSOCIATION OF REGULAR BAPTISTS. Shields was also one of the leaders of the International Council of Christian Churches. His leadership of fundamentalists in the Baptist Confederation of Ontario and Québec included attempts to block the appointment of theological liberals at McMaster University, a Baptist school. When that strategy failed, Shields bolted from the denomination in 1927 and formed the Union of Regular Baptist Churches of Ontario and Québec, which he served as president. That same year, he was designated president of the *BAPTIST BIBLE UNION's school, *DES MOINES UNIVERSITY, but a revolt by the faculty and a riot by the students forced the school's closure within two years.

In 1941, after having delivered some hysterical polemics against Roman Catholicism, Shields became president of the newly formed *CANADIAN PROTESTANT LEAGUE, an anti-Catholic organization, a post he held until 1950. Shields's autocratic leadership eventually wore thin with the Union of Regular Baptist Churches. Having ousted a large number of people in 1931, Shields himself was ousted as president in 1949 after he fired W. Gordon Brown as dean of Toronto Baptist Seminary. Shields bolted yet again, this time forming the Association of Regular Baptist Churches of Canada.

References: T. T. Shields, *The Inside of the Cup* (1921); idem, *Canadians Losing at Home the Freedom for Which They Are Fighting Abroad* (1943); George S. May, "Des Moines University and Dr. T. T. Shields," *Iowa Journal of History,* LIV (July 1956); C. Allyn Russell, "Thomas Todhunter Shields, Canadian Fundamentalist," *Ontario History,* LXX (1978); John G. Stackhouse Jr., s.v. "Thomas Todhunter Shields," in Charles H. Lippy, ed., *Twentieth-Century Shapers of American Popular Religion* (1989); David R. Elliott, "Knowing No Borders: Canadian Contributions to American Fundamentalism," in George A. Rawlyk and Mark A. Noll, eds., *Amazing Grace: Evangelicalism in Australia, Britain, Canada, and the United States* (1993).

Shiloh. *See* **Sandford, Frank W(eston).**

Shipps, Kenneth W(ayne) (1942–1996) An energetic and effective advocate for Christian higher education, Kenneth W. Shipps was born in Kansas City, Missouri. He graduated from *WHEATON COLLEGE and earned the Ph.D. in history from Yale University. He taught at Appalachian State University before his appointment to the history department at *TRINITY COLLEGE (now *TRINITY INTERNATIONAL UNIVERSITY) in Deerfield, Illinois. He served as dean of the faculty at *BARRINGTON COLLEGE in Rhode Island and became provost and dean at Phillips University, Enid, Oklahoma, in 1985. In 1992, Shipps moved to a similar position at Whitworth College in Spokane, Washington.

A formidable scholar in his own right, Shipps sought to raise the level of scholarship and teaching at Christian colleges and universities. He headed several initiatives under the auspices of the *COUNCIL FOR CHRISTIAN COLLEGES AND UNIVERSITIES, and his project on "The Integration of Faith and the Humanities" received funding from the National Endowment for the Humanities. Just before his untimely death Shipps had been named provost at *JOHN BROWN UNIVERSITY in Siloam Springs, Arkansas.

Shoemaker, Samuel Moor, (Jr.) (1893–1963) Samuel Moor Shoemaker entered Princeton University in 1912, where he became active in the school's religious life. After graduation, he taught at Princeton's extension campus in Beijing, China, where he met Frank Buchman, the Lutheran minister who founded the Moral Re-Armament movement. Shoemaker was ordained a deacon in the Episcopal Church in 1920, studied at General Theological Seminary and at Union Theological Seminary, was ordained a priest in 1921, and joined the pastoral staff of Grace Episcopal Church in New York City. In 1925, he became rector of Calvary Episcopal Church, also in Manhattan, which opened a mission during his tenure and built a large parish center, Calvary House.

Shoemaker's passion for personal *EVANGELISM prompted him to work closely with Buchman's Moral Re-Armament initiative during the 1930s, and Calvary House effectively became the organization's North American headquarters. Shoemaker also met Bill W., the founder of Alcoholics Anonymous, during this period and helped him to refine the small-group philosophy that remains the hallmark of the organization.

Competing demands on his time forced Shoemaker to decide to concentrate more on his parish work. He expanded the reach of programs at Calvary House and initiated a training program for laity, called Faith at Work. Shoemaker ventured onto the radio in 1945 with *Faith in Our Time,* a weekly program, and later with a daily broadcast, *Gems for Thought.* Both programs showcased Shoemaker's evangelical sympathies and his conservative interpretation of the *BIBLE. He left New York to become rector of Calvary Episcopal Church in Pittsburgh in 1952, where he remained for the final decade of his life. In Pittsburgh, he founded what he called the Pittsburgh Experiment, a program to assist the laity, especially wealthy business leaders, in their efforts at personal *EVANGELISM.

References: Samuel Moor Shoemaker, *A Young Man's View of the Ministry* (1923); idem, *The Church Can Save the World* (1938); idem, *Revive Thy Church—Beginning with Me* (1948); idem, *The Experiment of Faith* (1957); Helen Smith Shoemaker, *I Stand by the Door: The Life of Samuel Shoemaker* (1978).

Shuler, Robert Pierce "Bob" (1880–1965) Bob Shuler, known as "Fighting Bob" Shuler, graduated from Emory and Henry College in 1903 and was ordained in the Methodist Episcopal Church, South. He served Methodist churches in Virginia, Tennessee, and Texas before moving to Los Angeles in 1920 to become pastor of Trinity Methodist Church. The congregation grew rapidly under his leadership, and Shuler established himself as a fiery and combative figure, railing against political corruption, Hollywood, theological *LIBERALISM, the Los Angeles chief of police, Roman Catholicism, the ordination of women, moral decay, and William Randolph Hearst. Another target was *AIMEE SEMPLE MCPHERSON, the Los Angeles preacher whose radio audience exceeded Shuler's.

The fundamentalist preacher's antics became increasingly bizarre. During the 1928 presidential campaign, when Alfred E. Smith, a Roman Catholic, was the Democratic nominee, Shuler charged that Catholics were plotting to murder Protestants in their beds. He publicly supported the *KU KLUX KLAN. After the Federal Radio Commission refused to renew KGEF's license in 1931, Shuler decided to run for the United States Senate the following year on the Prohibition Party ticket. Although he won five hundred thousand votes, he lost the election, whereupon he pronounced a curse on the entire state of California; according to popular legend the Long Beach earthquake of 1933 was due to "Fighting Bob" Shuler's curse.

Sider, Ronald J(ames) (1939–) Born into a *BRETHREN IN CHRIST household in Stevensville, Ontario, Ronald J. Sider had an evangelical *CONVERSION experience at "about age eight." Profoundly shaped by the Anabaptist and Wesleyan sensibilities of his upbringing, Sider has sought to remain faithful to those traditions throughout a career as a theologian and a social activist. At Waterloo Lutheran University, Sider has written, "the full force of modern secularism flooded into my comfortable life." His evangelical faith prevailed, however, albeit not without a struggle. He continued his studies at Yale University, where he received the Ph.D. in 1969. During his graduate school years, Sider felt called to become an evangelical social activist. "There was no loud voice or special experience," he wrote. "But I slowly developed a clear inner sense that I should work as a biblical Christian for peace and justice in society."

Sider taught at *MESSIAH COLLEGE from 1968 until 1978, when he joined the faculty at *EASTERN BAPTIST THEOLOGICAL SEMINARY. He organized a small group called Evangelicals for McGovern in 1972 and was one of the founders of *EVANGELICALS FOR SOCIAL ACTION, serving at various times as chair, executive director, and president. He has served on the boards of numerous evangelical organizations and publications, and he has been a tireless crusader for social justice and for what he calls a "consistent life ethic" that opposes *ABORTION-on-demand but also expands the "pro-life" ethic to include opposition to capital punishment, nuclear proliferation, poverty, and support for education. Sider is the author of many books and articles, but his best-known work is *Rich Christians in an Age of Hunger,* first published in 1977.

References: Ronald J. Sider, *Christ and Violence* (1979); idem, *Rich Christians in an Age of Hunger: A Biblical Study* (1977); Tim Stafford, "Ron Sider's Unsettling Crusade," *Christianity Today,* April 27, 1992.

Simonds, Robert L. *See* **Citizens for Excellence in Education.**

Simpson, A(lbert) B(enjamin) (1843–1919) Born on Prince Edward Island, A. B. Simpson had a *CONVERSION experience in 1858 and soon thereafter dedicated himself to the ministry in a written "covenant." He graduated from Knox College in Toronto in 1865 and accepted the pulpit at Knox Presbyterian Church, Hamilton, Ontario. In 1873, he went to the Chestnut Street Presbyterian Church in Louisville, Kentucky, where he experienced the *BAPTISM OF THE HOLY SPIRIT. He became pastor of the Thirteenth Street Presbyterian Church in New York City in 1879 and shortly thereafter professed divine healing of a weak heart. He was baptized by immersion and resigned his pulpit to begin his own church, the Gospel Tabernacle, which was incorporated in 1883. The ministry soon expanded to include a missionary agency, The Missionary Union for the Evangelization of the World, a "Home for Faith and Physical Healing" (Berachah Home), and the New York Missionary Training College, known today as *NYACK COLLEGE and *ALLIANCE THEOLOGICAL SEMINARY.

Simpson summarized his theology as "the Fourfold Gospel": "Christ our Savior, Sanctifier, Healer, and Coming King." In 1887, at the Methodist Campgrounds in Old Orchard, Maine, Simpson organized the Christian Alliance and the Evangelical Missionary Alliance, which merged a decade later to form the *CHRISTIAN AND MISSIONARY ALLIANCE. A controversy over *SPEAKING IN TONGUES wracked the denomination in 1906. Simpson determined that tongues-speaking was not evidence of the *BAPTISM OF THE HOLY SPIRIT, and many with contrary views left the *CHRISTIAN AND MISSIONARY ALLIANCE.

Simpson, Charles (Vernon) (1937–) Reared in a Baptist household, Charles Simpson graduated from William Carey College and New Orleans Baptist Theological Seminary. He was ordained a Southern Baptist in 1957 but received the *BAPTISM OF THE HOLY SPIRIT in 1964, which altered the direction of his ministry. Simpson joined with *BOB MUMFORD, *DEREK PRINCE, and *DON BASHON in 1970 to form *CHRISTIAN GROWTH MINISTRIES, a quasidenomination that became controversial because of its authoritarian structure and teachings, also known as the *SHEPHERDING MOVEMENT.

Simpson left his Southern Baptist congregation in 1971, and in 1973 he established the Gulf Coast Christian Fellowship in Mobile, Alabama. He took over the publication of *New Wine* magazine in 1978, which folded in 1986 and gave way to another publication, *Christian Conquest*. His church, which has its own radio broadcast, changed its name to Covenant Church of Mobile in 1987.

Reference: Charles Simpson, *The Challenge to Care* (1986).

Simpson, Matthew (1811–1884) A famous opponent of slavery, Matthew Simpson was born in Cadiz, Ohio, and grew up in western Pennsylvania. Although he had no formal education, he taught himself well enough to become a teacher at a private school run by his uncle and at Madison College in Uniontown, Pennsylvania. Simpson studied medicine and was admitted to practice, but his evangelical *CONVERSION turned him in the direction of the ministry, joining the Pittsburgh conference of the Methodist Episcopal Church in 1834. He became vice president and professor of natural science at Allegheny College in 1839 and two years later was appointed president of Indiana Asbury (now DePauw) University.

Simpson had vigorously opposed the Plan of Separation, where the Methodists divided North and South over the issue of slavery in 1844. His ardent opposition to slavery intensified when he resigned the college presidency in 1848 to devote his efforts to editing the *Western Christian Advocate*, which he made into an abolitionist periodical. Elected bishop in 1852, Simpson became president of Garrett Theological Seminary in 1859.

Simpson cultivated a friendship with Abraham Lincoln, even before Lincoln's election to the presidency. The bishop pushed for the appointment of Methodists to government offices and sought to ensure that abolitionist ideas would prevail in the Lincoln administration. Simpson eagerly supported the Union efforts during the Civil War, and he preached both of the funerals for Lincoln—in Washington, D.C., and in Springfield, Illinois. When the war ended, Simpson advocated harsh Reconstruction policies and even persuaded the secretary of war to allow northern Methodists to confiscate Methodist churches and institutions in the South. President Andrew Johnson rescinded that permission, however, and Simpson later supported Johnson's impeachment.

Reference: Matthew Simpson, *Lectures on Preaching* (1879).

Simpson College and Graduate School (Redding, California) Simpson College was founded in Seattle in 1921 as Simpson Bible Institute. The school was named for evangelist ***A. B. SIMPSON**, who founded the ***CHRISTIAN AND MISSIONARY ALLIANCE** as well as Nyack Bible Institute (***NYACK COLLEGE**) and the ***BOSTON MISSIONARY TRAINING INSTITUTE**.

Within twenty years, Simpson Bible Institute had developed programs of study in theology, missions, ***BIBLE**, and music and was officially known as the ***CHRISTIAN AND MISSIONARY ALLIANCE**'s western regional school. The school was granting bachelor's degrees by 1955, and the same year it moved to San Francisco and changed its name to Simpson Bible College to reflect its new status as a four-year institution. The name was again changed in 1971, this time to Simpson College, because the school had fully adopted a liberal arts curriculum in addition to its programs in religion. The college has been located in Redding, California, since 1989. In recent years, Simpson has more fully developed its division of graduate studies. The graduate school now grants master's degrees in Christian ministry, missiology, and education.

Reference: Simpson College 1995–1997 Catalog (1995).

Sinclair, John C(halmers) (1863–1936) Born in Lydster, Scotland, John C. Sinclair emigrated to the United States and settled in Wisconsin, where he met and married Mary Ellen Bie. The Sinclairs moved to Chicago and were converted and baptized in *JOHN ALEXANDER DOWIE's Zion Tabernacle. John Sinclair was ordained as pastor of an independent mission located at 328 West Sixty-third Street, and on November 20, 1906, he spoke in *TONGUES, a pentecostal experience that was reportedly the first in Chicago. Sinclair was named to the executive presbytery of the *ASSEMBLIES OF GOD in 1914, but he soon withdrew, citing fears of denominationalism. Five years later, while pastor of the Christian Apostolic Assembly, he became the first general chairman of the Pentecostal Assemblies of the U.S.; again he withdrew. Sinclair became an itinerant preacher in his later years.

Sinner's Prayer The Sinner's Prayer, evangelicals believe, marks the transition from *SIN to *SALVATION. Although theologies surrounding *SALVATION differ, most evangelicals hold that, when offered with sincere intention, the Sinner's Prayer signifies an individual's acceptance of Christ as savior and thereby assures the new convert of a place in heaven. The prayer is usually formulaic and generally consists of the following elements: confession of *SIN, recognizing one's need for *SALVATION, acknowledging Jesus as savior, and a profession of one's determination to live a holy life. Many *EVANGELISTS, such as *BILLY GRAHAM, line out the prayer for those who have expressed interest in being *BORN AGAIN; the new convert repeats each phrase, and the *EVANGELIST assures her or him of a new status as a *BORN-AGAIN Christian.

Sioux Falls University. *See* **University of Sioux Falls.**

Skaggs, Ricky (1954–) Born in Cordell, Kentucky, Ricky Skaggs pursued his career as a country and bluegrass musician at an early age, performing with members of his family at age three. He taught himself the mandolin by the age of five, appeared on stage with Bill Monroe at six, and within another four years he had learned the fiddle and the guitar. After a stint with Ralph Stanley's Clinch Mountain Boys, Skaggs started his own group, Boone Creek, which lasted from 1975 to 1977. By 1982, Skaggs was inducted into the *GRAND OLE OPRY, at that time the youngest performer so honored. He has received many music awards, and he hosts his own television show, *Silent Witness,* on the *TRINITY BROADCASTING NETWORK. In 1991, Skaggs and his wife, Sharon White, founded a nonprofit evangelical organization, Teens in Trouble, to provide assistance to young people in crisis situations.

Skinner, Thomas "Tom" (1942–1994) The son of a Baptist minister in Harlem, New York, Tom Skinner was a precocious child who came to believe that Christianity was a tool of white oppression. "All the pictures of Christ I saw were the pictures of an Anglo-Saxon, middle-class, Protestant Republican," he remarked in 1970. "And I said, 'There is no way I can relate to that kind of Christ. . . . He doesn't look like he could survive in my neighborhood.'" Skinner became a leader of the

Harlem Lords, a local gang. As he was preparing for a large gang fight, he heard an uneducated radio preacher and was converted to evangelical Christianity. Skinner became a street preacher in Harlem and gradually began preaching in neighborhood churches. Together with other church and community leaders, Skinner organized the Harlem Evangelistic Association; he conducted an eight-month evangelistic crusade in 1962 at Harlem's redoubtable Apollo Theater, which earned him a reputation as the "black *BILLY GRAHAM."

Skinner's renown as a preacher soon spread beyond Harlem, in part because of his foray into radio. He formed another evangelistic organization, Tom Skinner Radio Crusades, which changed its name to Skinner Crusades in 1966, and was joined two years later by *WILLIAM PANNELL, author of *My Friend the Enemy,* a book that upbraided white evangelicals for their negligence of a holistic approach to the *GOSPEL.

By the early 1970s, after the assassinations of Malcolm X and Martin Luther King Jr. and with the rise of the Black Panther movement, Skinner's rhetoric turned more radical. White evangelicals became more and more uncomfortable and sought to distance themselves from him. Skinner's rhetoric, however, was still able to leave its mark, especially among younger evangelicals. He addressed InterVarsity's *URBANA '70 missions conference, chiding evangelicals for their nationalism and for their white-bread conservatism. "I disassociate myself from any argument which says God sends troops to Asia," Skinner thundered, "that God is a capitalist, that God is a militarist, that God is the worker behind our system." He challenged the predominantly white audience to "proclaim liberty to the captives" and to address their energies to "a world that is filled with hunger and poverty and racism."

Skinner's address at *URBANA received a standing ovation, but his endorsement of George McGovern over Richard Nixon in the 1972 presidential election angered white evangelicals. When Skinner, a member of a group calling itself Evangelicals for McGovern, introduced McGovern to students at *WHEATON COLLEGE's Edman Chapel, October 11, 1972, both Skinner and the Democratic candidate were met with boos, catcalls, and heckling. Skinner's travel schedule also took its toll on his family; he and his wife, Vivian, separated and eventually divorced. Many white evangelical leaders, already disenchanted with Skinner, used his divorce as a pretext to distance themselves further. By 1975, his organization was a shambles.

Skinner made something of a comeback in the early 1980s. A longtime chaplain for the Washington Redskins football team, Skinner was able to widen his circle of friends to include such well-known figures as Jesse Jackson and Maya Angelou. Skinner married Barbara Williams, an attorney and secretary for the Black Congressional Caucus, in 1981. In 1993, just a year before his death from leukemia, Skinner helped to found still another organization, Mission Mississippi.

His death, at age fifty-two, was mourned by people as diverse as Louis Farrakhan, head of the Nation of Islam, and Patrick Morley, a white business executive from Orlando, Florida. "Tom Skinner had the clearest understanding of the *GOSPEL of anyone that I've ever heard," said *JOHN M. PERKINS, another African American evangelical. "He was a prophet without honor because he was hitting at themes of reconciliation that were too radical for blacks and whites alike."

References: Tom Skinner, *Black and Free* (1968); idem, *How Black Is the Gospel* (1970); Edward Gilbreath, "A Prophet Out of Harlem," *Christianity Today,* September 16, 1996.

Slavic Gospel Association The Slavic Gospel Association was founded in 1923 by a Russian immigrant, Peter Deyenka, as an attempt to bring *EVANGELICALISM to the Soviet Union. In order to counteract the official atheism of the Soviet government, the Slavic Gospel Association used two tactics: They beamed radio broadcasts into the Soviet Union and smuggled millions of *BIBLES across the Soviet border. The collapse of the Soviet empire allowed the association to operate much more freely. The organization, which has its headquarters in Loves Park, Illinois, took on the task of training hundreds of national pastors and missionaries by means of seminaries, *BIBLE INSTITUTES, and conferences. With the cooperation of *MOODY BIBLE INSTITUTE, the Slavic Gospel Association has developed correspondence courses on the *BIBLE, and they have supported the planting of evangelical churches throughout the former Soviet Union.

Slavic Missionary Service Slavic Missionary Service, which has its headquarters in South River, New Jersey, was founded in 1945. The organization produces evangelistic materials, audiocassettes, and a radio program, *Slavic Missionary Service,* as a missionary outreach to the former Soviet Union.

Smith, Amanda Berry (Devine) (1837–1915) An African American *EVANGELIST in the holiness tradition, Amanda Berry was born into slavery in Long Green, Maryland, but her father purchased the family's freedom and they moved to York, Pennsylvania. Amanda married Calvin Devine in 1854 and experienced a religious *CONVERSION two years later. After her husband died fighting for the Union during the Civil War, she relocated to Philadelphia, where she met and married James Smith, a deacon in the African Methodist Episcopal Church. When the couple moved to New York City, Amanda Smith attended *PHOEBE PALMER's *TUESDAY MEETINGS, gatherings of women who were learning about the holiness doctrine of entire *SANCTIFICATION. Smith had her own experience of *SANCTIFICATION in September 1868 while listening to a sermon by John Inskip. After the death of her second husband the following year, Smith became an itinerant holiness *EVANGELIST.

Initially she preached to black congregations in New York and New Jersey, but after she addressed a *CAMP MEETING of white Methodists in 1870, Smith enlarged her itinerations to both white and black congregations on the *CAMP MEETING circuit. She went to Great Britain in 1878 and then a year later to India, where she worked on a Methodist mission for two years, returning to England in 1881. Smith did mission work in Liberia for eight years and returned to the United States on September 5, 1890. She settled for a time in Harvey, Illinois, where she wrote her autobiography and used her own resources to build the Amanda Smith Orphan's Home for Colored Children, which opened in 1899. Smith retired to Sebring, Florida, in 1912.

References: Amanda Smith, *An Autobiography of Mrs. Amanda Smith, The Colored Evangelist* (1893); M. H. Cadbury, *The Life of Amanda Smith* (1916).

Smith, Charles "Chuck," (Jr.) (1927–) Born in Ventura, California, Chuck Smith's family had been profoundly affected by the healing of a daughter a few months before Chuck was born. Committing his life at age seventeen to becoming a pastor, Smith entered *L.I.F.E. BIBLE COLLEGE, the school founded by *AIMEE SEMPLE MCPHERSON, where he graduated in 1948 with a degree in theology. Never comfortable in the pentecostal mold of the Foursquare denomination, Smith struggled through a number of pastorates over the course of seventeen years. It was a period of time he referred to later as the "desert years."

Having tired of an endless routine of church-growth gimmicks to boost membership, Smith became pastor of the despairing *CALVARY CHAPEL, a nondenominational congregation in 1965, and resolved simply to teach the *BIBLE. On the brink of closing down, the woeful core group of twenty-five had turned to Smith as a last-ditch effort to salvage the church. Under Smith's guidance, the tiny church grew steadily over the next few years, relocating several times as the membership quadrupled.

As the growing hippie population began to infiltrate Orange County, Smith and his wife, Kay, sensed an opportunity to reach these youth with the message of the *GOSPEL. They asked their teenage children to "bring home a real live hippie" so they could better understand the counterculture mentality. Their introduction to the counterculture came in the person of *LONNIE FRISBEE, a recent convert who had been involved in the first street Christian community in San Francisco. Smith asked Frisbee and his wife to join their church to head up a similar hippie outreach program. Smith's openness to the counterculture radically transformed *CALVARY CHAPEL as thousands of young hippies started to flock to services. One estimate has it that over a two-year period *CALVARY CHAPEL was spiritual midwife to eight thousand *BAPTISMS (by total immersion) and over twenty thousand *CONVERSIONS. In 1971, at the height of the *JESUS MOVEMENT, Smith, Frisbee, and *CALVARY CHAPEL were featured in articles that appeared in *Time, Newsweek,* and other magazines.

Smith became a father figure to the hippie generation. His expository preaching and his commonsense approach to doctrine have brought extraordinary growth, not only in the original *CALVARY CHAPEL but in other congregations that now make up a worldwide federation of *CALVARY CHAPELS (Smith dislikes the term "denomination"). Typically, home Bible studies grew into fledgling congregations, while other churches began looking to Smith for entrance into what became the *CALVARY CHAPEL movement.

References: Chuck Smith and Hugh Steven, *The Reproducers: New Life for Thousands* (1972); Chuck Smith, *Harvest* (1987); Randall Balmer, *Mine Eyes Have Seen the Glory: A Journey into the Evangelical Subculture in America,* 3d ed. (2000); Donald E. Miller, *Reinventing American Protestantism: Christianity in the New Millennium* (1997).

Smith, Gerald L(yman) K(enneth) (1898–1976) Born in rural Wisconsin, Gerald L. K. Smith worked his way through Valparaiso University in Indiana and graduated at the age of nineteen. Ordained in the Christian Church (Disciples of Christ), Smith served several small congregations; in 1928, he was called to the King's Highway Christian Church, in Shreveport, Louisiana, where he became active in politics.

Smith supported populist political causes and participated in far-right organizations such as William Dudley Pelley's Silver Shirts, which he joined in 1933. By the next year, however, he had left Pelley's organization, resigned his church, and begun traveling around the state organizing Huey Long's "Share Our Wealth" clubs. Smith was deeply disturbed by Long's assassination in 1935. He signed on with Francis Everett Townsend and his Old Age Revolving Pension Plan and allied himself briefly with Father Charles Coughlin, a Roman Catholic opponent of Franklin Roosevelt, in support of William Lemke for president in 1936. The following year Smith organized the Committee of One Million, a group dedicated to fighting communism, and lectured across the country.

In 1942, Smith began publishing a periodical, *The Cross and the Flag,* which railed against the "evils" of democracy. After World War II, Smith broadened his attacks to the United Nations, Jews, and blacks. He organized the Christian Nationalist Crusade in 1947, which preached racial purity and argued that Christian character was "the basis of all real Americanism." In 1964, Smith founded the Elna F. Smith Foundation in Eureka Springs, Arkansas, which supported the erection of a seven-story statue of Jesus, known as the Christ of the Ozarks. The foundation also supports a passion play every summer, based on the one in Oberammergau, Germany.

References: Gerald L. K. Smith, *The Great Issues* (1959); Ellsworth Perkins, *The Biggest Hypocrite in America: Gerald L. K. Smith Unmasked* (1949); Alan Brinkley, *Voices of Protest: Huey Long, Father Coughlin, and the Great Depression* (1983); Michael Barkun, *Religion and the Racist Right: The Origins of the Christian Identity Movement* (1994).

Smith, Hannah Whitall (1832–1911) Born in Philadelphia into an affluent Quaker household, Hannah Whitall married *ROBERT PEARSALL SMITH, also a Quaker, in 1851. Late in the 1850s the Smiths experienced religious *CONVERSIONS during the *URBAN AWAKENING and became more and more enamored of evangelical doctrines, especially as expressed in *CAMP MEETINGS. They broke with the Society of Friends; Robert affiliated with the Presbyterians and Hannah with the *PLYMOUTH BRETHREN. Although she had long sought it, Hannah Whitall Smith finally experienced the *BAPTISM OF THE HOLY SPIRIT in 1867, and husband and wife began to address holiness gatherings, enlarging their peregrinations to the United Kingdom in 1873 and 1874.

Robert was implicated in an extramarital affair in 1875, the same year that Hannah published *The Christian's Secret of a Happy Life,* an enormously popular devotional manual that remains in print. It anticipated in many ways the *KESWICK theology that would emerge in subsequent decades. "In order for a lump of clay to be made into a beautiful vessel," she wrote, "it must be entirely abandoned to the potter, and must lie passive in his hands."

As Robert's star faded—he spent the final twenty-five years of his life in virtual seclusion—Hannah's soared, despite her universalist theological leanings (the doctrine that everyone will be saved). She was dubbed "the angel of the churches," and she emerged as a strong advocate for women in education and in the ministry. Smith was one of the founders of the Women's Christian Temperance Union and became superintendent of its evangelistic department in 1883. She returned to England in 1895, where she wrote several books, continued her advocacy for women, and worked with the British Woman's Temperance Union.

References: Hannah Whitall Smith, *The Christian's Secret of a Happy Life* (1875); idem, *The Unselfishness of God and How I Discovered It: My*

Spiritual Autobiography (1903); idem, *Living in the Sunshine* (1906); Marie Henry, *The Secret Life of Hannah Whitall Smith* (1984).

Smith, J. Harold (1910–) A Baptist minister, radio broadcaster, and ardent fundamentalist, J. Harold Smith went on the radio from Greenville, South Carolina, in 1935. His message was doggedly conservative, criticizing the theological *MODERNISM of the day as well as the proclivities on the part of fellow believers to "*WORLDLINESS." After moving to a larger station in Knoxville, Tennessee, Smith's *Radio Bible Hour* diatribes came to the attention of the Federal Council of Churches, which sought to ban him from the airwaves. Such an action merely confirmed Smith's suspicions of the "liberal" body, which he excoriated as "a demoniac vulture sitting upon the pinnacles of our churches."

Smith started his own station, WBIK-radio, in 1947, but the Federal Communications Commission forced him from the airwaves in 1953. He promptly set up shop in Ciudad Acuña, Mexico, just across the Texas border and covered much of the United States with a one-hundred-thousand-watt signal. When the Mexican government banned all English-language religious broadcasts from within its borders in the 1980s, Smith was again forced off the air.

Reference: J. Gordon Melton, Phillip Charles Lucas, and Jon R. Stone, *Prime-Time Religion: An Encyclopedia of Religious Broadcasting* (1997).

Smith, Michael W. (1957–) Michael W. Smith, also known as "Smitty" to his fans, is practically synonymous with inspirational pop music, and the singer's rise to success closely parallels that of the Christian music industry. The West Virginia native arrived in Nashville, Tennessee, in 1978 with hopes of starting a singing career; he was recording albums by the mid-1980s. Numerous *GOSPEL MUSIC ASSOCIATION Dove Awards followed. Within a few years, however, Smith saw his appeal widen broadly as he became one of the most successful "crossover artists" into the mainstream market. The single "Place in This World" made it to number six on *Billboard*'s Pop Music chart in 1991. The following year sealed the singer's successful penetration of the mainstream market: Not only was his seventh album, *Go West Young Man,* certified as gold, but Smith won the American Music Award for Best New Artist. That year he was also chosen as one of *People* magazine's "50 Most Beautiful People." The singer is married and has five children.

Smith's 1994 album, *Change Your World,* included the songs "Place in this World" and "I Will Be There for You," which made it to, respectively, numbers six and twenty-seven on *Billboard*'s Hot 100 Singles. In 1995, his album *I'll Lead You Home* made a debut at number sixteen on the *Billboard* 200. With first-week sales of more than fifty thousand, the album achieved, at the time, the second highest debut for an inspirational album (after *House of Love* by Amy Grant).

Smith continued to record on Reunion Records, now partially owned by BMG, but has also signed a contract with Geffen Records, a decision that has helped his career in the mainstream market. In addition, the singer also owns his own independent recording company, Rocketown, which maintains a distribution agreement with Word Records.

References: Brian Q. Newcomb, "Mainstream Splash Doesn't Distract Michael W. Smith," *Billboard,* September 19, 1992; Deborah Evans Price, "Smith Goes 'Home' for a Reunion," *Billboard,* July 15, 1995; idem, "Christian Biz Hails Smith's Chart Bow," *Billboard,* September 9, 1995.

Smith, Oswald J(effrey) (1889–1986) Reared in rural Ontario, Oswald J. Smith studied at *TORONTO BIBLE COLLEGE and aspired to be a missionary. The Presbyterian Church of Canada, however, rejected him on the grounds of poor health and deficient academic training. Smith began preaching in rural areas and pursued theological training at McCormick Seminary in Chicago, where he became associated with *PAUL RADER, pastor of *MOODY CHURCH. Although he was ordained a Presbyterian in 1915, Smith eventually resigned his ordination and started his own church in Toronto, which merged with a struggling *CHRISTIAN AND MISSIONARY ALLIANCE congregation in 1921. Smith, a powerful preacher, a leader in Canadian *FUNDAMENTALISM, and the author of thirty-five books, maintained his zeal for missions throughout his life. He traveled overseas beginning in 1924 and returned to Canada to raise money and recruit missionaries. In 1928, he started another independent church, the People's Church, in downtown Toronto. *BILLY GRAHAM preached Smith's funeral in 1986, calling him "the greatest combination pastor, hymn writer, missionary statesman, and *EVANGELIST of our time."

References: Oswald J. Smith, *The Country I Love Best* (1934); idem, *The Passion for Souls* (1952); idem, *When the King Comes Back* (1957); David R. Elliott, "Knowing No Borders: Canadian Contributions to American Fundamentalism," in George A. Rawlyk and Mark A. Noll, eds., *Amazing Grace: Evangelicalism in Australia, Britain, Canada, and the United States* (1993).

Smith, Robert Pearsall (1827–1899) Robert Pearsall Smith, born in Philadelphia, married *HANNAH WHITALL in 1851, and both were converted to evangelical Christianity during the *URBAN AWAKENING of 1858. After their *BAPTISMS in the Holy Spirit, they began to address holiness gatherings both in the United States and in the United Kingdom. In 1875, the same year that *HANNAH WHITALL SMITH published her influential devotional volume, *The Christian's Secret of a Happy Life*, Robert Smith was implicated in an extramarital affair, amid rumors of a nervous breakdown. Although his wife continued her work as a holiness *EVANGELIST, Smith spent the remaining quarter century of his life in virtual seclusion.

Reference: Robert Pearsall Smith, *Holiness through Faith: Light on the Way to Holiness* (1870).

Smith, Rodney "Gipsy" (1860–1947) Born to Gypsy parents in England, Rodney Smith's mother died when he was a child. His father's *CONVERSION to Christianity and the change that the son observed deeply impressed the young boy. He converted in 1876 at a Primitive Methodist chapel in Cambridge. Although largely self-educated, Smith's desire to enter the ministry led him to *WILLIAM BOOTH, who enlisted Smith in his Christian Mission. At Booth's urging, Smith became an *EVANGELIST, preaching in various venues throughout England, usually for no more than six months at a time. During his assignment at Hull, he became known as "Gipsy" Smith, a moniker that stayed with him for the remainder of his life.

In 1882, Smith broke with Booth's organization, now known as the *SALVATION ARMY, over a minor infraction of Booth's rule. Smith settled in Hanley, England, and formed a congregation, and he soon began to travel and preach more widely. Beginning in 1892 his ministry was called the Gipsy Gospel Wagon Mission, and he made the first of many preaching tours to the United States in 1897. Although an independent *EVANGELIST, he often appeared before Methodist groups. In addition to his preaching, he was a gifted singer. He died at sea in 1947 while heading to America to preach.

References: Rodney "Gipsy" Smith, *As Jesus Passed By, and Other Addresses* (1905); idem, *Gipsy Smith's Best Sermons* (1907); idem, *The Beauty of Jesus* (1932); Harold Murray, *Sixty Years an Evangelist* (1937).

Smith, Wilbur M(oorehead) (1894–1976) Wilbur M. Smith studied at *MOODY BIBLE INSTITUTE for a year and then at the College of Wooster, but he earned no academic degrees. He served as pastor to a number of Presbyterian congregations before returning to Moody in 1937, where he remained as a teacher for a decade. Smith, having been part of the planning for the new *FULLER THEOLOGICAL SEMINARY in Pasadena, California, agreed to join the faculty there in 1947. He left in 1963, however, amid a dispute over biblical *INERRANCY. A strong inerrantist, Smith felt that Fuller was becoming "liberal" on the issue of biblical *AUTHORITY. He accepted a half-time appointment at the more conservative *TRINITY EVANGELICAL DIVINITY SCHOOL, Deerfield, Illinois, where he remained until his retirement in 1971.

Smith, a noted bibliophile and collector of theological books, was also a popular lecturer and a prolific author. In addition to writing more than two dozen books, he published articles in such magazines as *Moody Monthly, The Sunday School Times,* and **CHRISTIANITY TODAY*. From 1954 to 1963, he served on the revision committee for the **SCOFIELD REFERENCE BIBLE*.

References: Wilbur M. Smith, *The Supernaturalness of Christ* (1941); idem, *World Crises and the Prophetic Scriptures* (1950); idem, *Before I Forget* (1971); George M. Marsden, *Reforming Fundamentalism: Fuller Seminary and the New Evangelicalism* (1987).

Snake Handling. *See* **Serpent Handling.**

Social Gospel The rapid industrialization and urbanization late in the nineteenth century created vast inequities in the distribution of wealth. Nowhere were these inequities more apparent than in northern cities, especially New York, where the ravages of unbridled capitalism gave rise to the exploitation of labor and harsh living conditions. The Social Gospel movement—also known by various names, including social Christianity and Christian socialism—sought to address these ills, emphasizing the doctrine of the kingdom of God as a distinct historical possibility and calling upon Christians to seek the "*CONVERSION" not only of individuals, but of sinful social institutions as well.

The Social Gospel had many theorists and practitioners, including Washington Gladden, Josiah Strong, Richard T. Ely, Charles M. Sheldon, *JANE ADDAMS, and Reverdy C. Ransom, but Walter Rauschenbusch was one of the most forceful advocates. Rauschenbusch, recently graduated from Rochester Theological Seminary, arrived in New York in 1886 as pastor of the Second German Baptist Church on West Forty-fifth Street, at the edge of Hell's Kitchen. He soon became an impassioned defender of the poor and the working classes, seeking ways to improve their lot. His *Christianity and the Social Crisis,* published in 1907 after he returned to Rochester Seminary as professor, became a manifesto of the Social Gospel movement.

Evangelicals were profoundly ambivalent about the Social Gospel. The zeal for social reform comported well with the postmillennial sentiment of evangelicals in the earlier part of the nineteenth century, but evangelicals had grown suspicious of the cities late in the nineteenth century, viewing them as seedbeds of sinfulness. Many evangelicals abandoned the cities in the face of mounting social problems, preferring to emphasize individual, rather than social, regeneration. In response to Martin Luther King Jr.'s famous "I Have a Dream" speech, for example, *BILLY GRAHAM offered a more typical evangelical scenario: "Only when Christ comes again will the little white children of Alabama walk hand in hand with little black children."

Reference: Robert T. Handy, *The Social Gospel in America, 1870–1920: Gladden, Ely, Rauschenbusch* (1966).

Society for Promotion of Collegiate and Theological Education at the West Also known as the Western College Society, the Society for the Promotion of Collegiate and Theological Education in the West was founded in New York in 1843 to promote Christian education on the American frontier and to thwart the spread of Roman Catholicism. The organization, which numbered *LYMAN BEECHER among its founders, provided financial support for Lane Theological Seminary and for several colleges. *NATHAN S. S. BEMAN, one of the principals in the organization, addressed the society's annual meeting in 1846, arguing that education was the key to Protestant dominance as the nation expanded westward. "Let the colleges, and academies, and schools, and Orthodox Churches of the best portions of the East," Beman intoned, "be spread all over our Western country, and, under the Divine protection, they are safe, and we are safe, and this land will send forth, under the banner of the Son of God, a trained and mighty army to the peaceful and bloodless subjugation of the world." The society was one example of a widespread attempt by Americans in the East to "civilize" the West by means of Christianity.

Reference: George M. Marsden, *The Soul of the American University: From Protestant Establishment to Established Nonbelief* (1994).

Society for the Suppression of Vice. *See* **Wilberforce, William.**

Society of Christian Philosophers The Society of Christian Philosophers was founded in 1978 by a group of professional philosophers who reflect the resurgence of Christian faith in the ranks of academic philosophy. This resurgence is somewhat remarkable, since the field of philosophy was dominated for most of the twentieth century by various forms of skepticism, positivism, and humanism. An organizational gathering was convened during the annual Central Division meeting of the American Philosophical Association, which was held in Cincinnati. The society's stated purpose was to promote fellowship among Christian philosophers and to stimulate study and discussion of issues that arise from their joint Christian and philosophical commitments. Both in its original conception and in its historical experience, the society is broadly ecumenical in composition with respect to Christian denomination, theological perspective, and philosophical orientation. Membership is open to any person who classifies himself or herself as both a philosopher and a Christian.

The elected presidents of the society over the years constitute a list of highly respected and prestigious philosophers. In order, they are *WILLIAM P. ALSTON (Syracuse University), Robert M. Adams (Yale

University), *ALVIN PLANTINGA (University of Notre Dame), Marilyn Adams (Yale University), George Mavrodes (University of Michigan), *NICHOLAS WOLTERSTORFF (Yale Divinity School), and Eleonore Stump (St. Louis University). The membership of the society grew from approximately two hundred to about twelve hundred in 1997, symbolizing a changing trend in the profession.

The society holds meetings of various sorts in several regions of the United States. In addition, it holds meetings in conjunction with all divisions of the American Philosophical Association, the American Catholic Philosophical Association, and the Canadian Philosophical Association. From time to time, the society sponsors workshops and conferences on topics of special interest to Christian philosophers. The society has also stimulated a large number of books in philosophy of religion and related areas, making this academic field one of the most energetic of all academic professions. The activity of the society also led to the creation or reinstatement of courses in philosophy of religion both in undergraduate and graduate curricula across the United States. In 1984, the society launched its own scholarly journal, **FAITH AND PHILOSOPHY*, published from the campus of *ASBURY COLLEGE, Wilmore, Kentucky.

References: "Modernizing the Case for God," *Time,* April 7, 1980; Kenneth Konyndyk, "Christianity Reenters Philosophical Circles," *Perspectives,* November 1992; Kristine Christlieb, "Suddenly, Respect: Christianity Makes a Comeback in the Philosophy Department," *Christianity Today,* April 17, 1987.

Sojourners. *See* **Sojourners Community.**

Sojourners Community Sojourners is an ecumenical community, located in Washington, D.C., which represents something of an anomaly in evangelical circles: While fully grounded in Christian faith and theology, members of the community also work tirelessly for a generally "left-wing" political agenda of ending violence, racism, war, and poverty. The group sees itself as having deep historical connections to the "radical mission" of Christianity, a sense of action-based theology that makes it distinctive from both evangelical conservatives and secular liberals. The group has, for example, gained national attention as a voice against the arms race, apartheid in South Africa, and racism in the United States.

Sojourners began in the early 1970s with a group of students at *TRINITY EVANGELICAL DIVINITY SCHOOL in Deerfield, Illinois, who made a fledgling attempt to create a communitarian community. Their publication, the *Post American,* which first appeared in 1971, was unique in its time for its position as both evangelical and firmly committed to peace and social justice. Although the *Post American* continued, the community itself was short-lived.

In 1975, however, in an effort to renew its early vision, the group moved to Washington, D.C., where both it and the magazine were renamed *Sojourners.* There, under the direction of founder *JIM WALLIS, who still leads the group, the new community re-created its lifestyle of communal economics. Also, in addition to publishing the magazine, Sojourners launched the unprecedented endeavor of branching out into action-oriented ministry in the inner-city neighborhoods of Washington. At first, members visited people in their homes, but in 1983 the community acquired a building in Southern Columbia Heights and opened the Sojourners Neighborhood Center.

Today, Sojourners continues in its original mission of "radical discipleship . . . *EVANGELISM, social justice, spirituality and politics, prayer and peacemaking" and works toward these goals at both the national and local levels. The neighborhood center currently operates in three main areas—children's services, feeding programs, and adult computer literacy—but has other projects such as adult job-training and community organizing as well. Sojourners offers young adults the opportunity to volunteer at the site in a one-year internship program.

Nonetheless, in spite of the successful outreach of the center, the Sojourners Community is still best known for the publication that bears its name. Edited by Wallis, *Sojourners* is grounded in an action-oriented theology, and, contrary to the *RELIGIOUS RIGHT, it has been willing to take unpopular positions on issues as diverse as the morality of capital punishment and China's repressive regime in Tibet. The magazine has printed the opinions of environmental activist Winona LaDuke and United Farm Workers leader César Chavez, supported the charges that the Central Intelligence Agency was aware of the Contras' role in the Latin American drug trade, and has even printed pieces in support of gay rights. These views make it tempting to align *Sojourners* with the political left, although its influences are highly eclectic, ranging from St. Francis of Assisi to the Anabaptists, from Clarence Jordan to Dorothy Day.

Because the Sojourners Community draws its strength from its interpretation of Christian service, however, in some instances its agenda can be at odds with that of most liberals. For example, the group seeks to restore spiritual priorities to the traditional categories of liberal and conservative. It also advocates a "comprehensive pro-life agenda," which opposes *ABORTION even while it also rejects euthanasia, capital punishment, nuclear weapons, poverty, pollution, and racism.

Sojourners takes its role as an alternative to evangelical conservative politics quite seriously. Among the books and study guides the community has published is a title called *Recovering the Evangel: A Guide to Faith, Politics, and Alternatives to the Religious Right.* In 1995, under the leadership of Wallis, the Sojourners Community helped convene a new political organization, *CALL TO RENEWAL. This broad-based movement, which has a four-point agenda—rebuilding family and community, affirming life in every respect, ending poverty, and dismantling racism—includes representatives from the Children's Defense Fund, Bread for the World, and Maryknoll Justice and Peace. *JAMES FORBES, pastor of the Riverside Church in New York City, *TONY CAMPOLO of the Evangelical Association for the Promotion of Education, and Calvin Morris of the Interdenominational Theological Seminary in Atlanta all serve on the coordinating committee. *CALL TO RENEWAL publishes a newsletter and hosts conferences across the country on topics such as welfare reform. *CALL TO RENEWAL held a conference virtually across the street from the 1996 convention of the *CHRISTIAN COALITION.

Reference: Information provided by the Sojourners Community.

Sola Scriptura The doctrine of *sola scriptura,* or the *BIBLE alone, is perhaps the most important foundation of evangelical theology. Following the lead of Martin Luther, who railed against the theological accretions of the Roman Catholic Church, evangelicals profess to rely solely on the *BIBLE as their source of *AUTHORITY rather than the twin pillars of Scripture and tradition, as in Catholicism.

Because the *BIBLE, a wonderfully complex book, admits of so many interpretations, however, evangelicals—and Protestants generally—have used the doctrine of *sola scriptura* as their warrant to run in many theological directions, unchecked by the restraints of tradition.

Son City Revival The Son City Revival, which lasted from 1972 until 1978, was the immediate precursor of *WILLOW CREEK COMMUNITY CHURCH. South Park Church, in Park Ridge, Illinois, hired a gifted young musician, Dave Holmbo, as assistant minister of music in 1972. Holmbo started several musical groups among the high school youth in the church. He introduced contemporary music, including rock, into the church's worship services and organized a high school choir, The Son Company. Holmbo asked a friend, *BILL HYBELS, to come to Son Company rehearsals and offer Bible study.

The sessions evolved into an evangelistic outreach to students in the community, luring them to church with music, games, and Bible study. By January 1974, the gatherings exceeded four hundred. Conflicts with the church board, however, led to the resignations of Holmbo and Hybels during the summer of 1975. The church hired Jim Griffith, a third-year student at *TRINITY EVANGELICAL DIVINITY SCHOOL, as minister of youth, assisted by Don Cousins, a student at *TRINITY COLLEGE, who eventually left to join Hybels in his new venture. The *REVIVAL continued under Griffith and a new youth minister, Gary Jorian, but it eventually sputtered when Griffith and Jorian resigned in 1978. Hybels, meanwhile, was busy putting into practice many of the things he learned from the Son City Revival. His new project, which would be called *WILLOW CREEK COMMUNITY CHURCH, evolved into the premier megachurch in North America.

Reference: Fred W. Buettler, "Revivalism in Suburbia: The 'Son City' Revival, 1972–1978" (unpublished paper).

Southeast Association of Christian Schools. *See* **Association of Christian Schools International.**

Southern Baptist College. *See* **Williams Baptist College.**

Southern Baptist Convention Baptists first came to what would become the United States in the early seventeenth century. The first Baptist church in America was founded by *ROGER WILLIAMS in Providence, Rhode Island, in 1638. The first mission society was founded in 1814. Until that time, the majority of Baptists in America had been Particular Baptists, subscribing to a strict Calvinist doctrine that did not allow for mission work; the Calvinist emphasis on predestination and election had precluded the need to undertake the mission enterprise. The number of General Baptists, who held a more Arminian view, grew throughout the colonial and early republic years, especially with the Arminian theology that pervaded the *SECOND GREAT AWAKENING. Along with the growing influence of the General Baptists came the emphasis on the necessity of mission work. Finally, in 1814, Baptists in America were confronted with a decision.

Two years earlier, a Congregationalist minister and his party sailed from Salem, Massachusetts, for India to begin a Congregationalist mission there. During the voyage the missionary, *ADONIRAM JUDSON, became convinced through his study of the *BIBLE of Baptist doctrine, especially adult believers' *BAPTISM. Unable by reason of conscience to continue as Congregationalists, the party agreed to send one of their number, *LUTHER RICE, back to the United States to try to raise funds for the support of a Baptist mission endeavor in Burma. (Judson and his wife, Ann, did not want to compete with an existing Baptist mission station in India.) Upon his return, Rice began to raise money for the work. His efforts led to the founding of the General Missionary Convention of the Baptist Denomination in the United States of America for Foreign Missions, or the American Baptist Foreign Mission Society. This group met every three years and was known popularly as the *TRIENNIAL CONVENTION.

After the *TRIENNIAL CONVENTION was formed, Baptists added, in 1824, the American Baptist Home Mission Society and the American Baptist Tract and Publication Society in 1832. While there was no formal organization for Baptists, the three societies fulfilled many of the functions of a denomination.

By the 1840s, the issue that was to divide the nation was also felt among the Baptist churches. Both the foreign and home mission societies refused to appoint slave-holders as missionaries. This led, in 1845, to Baptist churches in the South withdrawing to form a separate denomination, the Southern Baptist Convention (SBC). From the beginning, the SBC had a much more centralized form of government, with headquarters in Atlanta. The work of both the foreign and home mission boards was placed under the direction of the convention, and the centralized government allowed the denomination to coordinate efforts efficiently. In the first years after the separation, the SBC grew slowly. By the end of the nineteenth century and the beginning of the twentieth, however, the convention grew dramatically. In 2000 the Convention reported 15.85 million members in over forty thousand local congregations.

Southern Baptist *POLITY is congregational, typical of the Baptist denominations and bodies. The local church is autonomous and acts as the locus of ecclesiastical authority. The congregations work together as associations, state conventions, and the national convention. Associations are often a single county. The national convention meets annually, and each local congregation is allowed to send delegates, called "messengers," to the annual convention meeting. The number of messengers depends on the size of the congregation. The national convention has direct oversight of the mission boards, the publishing house (Broadman Press), the *SUNDAY SCHOOL board, and several seminaries. The work of the convention is supported by contributions from the churches, especially through the Cooperative Program. In the Cooperative Program, local churches give to the convention a set percentage of the donations, tithes, and offerings they receive.

Theologically, the Southern Baptist Convention has historically been conservative and evangelical. The theological and doctrinal position of the Convention has been the cause of no little dispute in recent years. Beginning in 1979, a group of fundamentalists within the denomination organized to return the convention to its fundamentalist roots. The fundamentalists felt that the Southern Baptist Convention had lost its moorings and was drifting perilously close to the brink of a disastrous fall into *LIBERALISM. The conflict in many ways resembled a second fundamentalist-modernist controversy. In fact, both sides of the controversy described themselves as conservative, and both were ("liberal Southern Baptist" being something of an oxymoron). In the early days of the struggle for control of the

SBC, the sides were often identified by the terms "fundamental conservatives" and "moderate conservatives."

The issue of biblical *INERRANCY became the rallying point and Damocles' sword hanging over the head of the denomination. On the one hand the conservatives, as the fundamentalists came to be called, uphold a belief in the verbal, plenary inspiration of Scripture and in its infallibility and *INERRANCY in the original manuscripts. The conservatives wanted to root out the use of higher criticism in the seminaries and to require seminary professors and convention employees to subscribe to the doctrine of *INERRANCY. The members on the other side of the conflict were known finally as moderates. The moderates, many of whom are also fundamentalist conservatives, wanted the seminaries to be left alone, and to allow individuals, in the best Baptist tradition, to come to and hold their own beliefs. The moderates felt that the conservatives were abandoning the historical Baptist distinctive of soul liberty, which holds that every believer has the right and responsibility to read and to interpret Scripture according to the guiding of the Holy Spirit and to arrive at theological positions based on conscience rather than creeds.

The conservatives had, for many years, felt ignored by what they saw as the liberal convention leadership. They were aware that, within the SBC structure, the president of the convention has a great deal of authority to appoint leaders to various boards and committees. These positions are on the mission boards, the *SUNDAY SCHOOL board, and the boards of trustees of the seminaries, among others. By actively campaigning and using other political tactics, the conservatives were successful in having a conservative candidate, *ADRIAN ROGERS, elected president in 1979. They have also been successful in electing their candidate every year since 1979. The boards of every cooperating seminary and the mission boards were by the late 1980s firmly under the control of the conservatives.

For their part, the moderates have conceded this control to the conservatives. Many of the moderate Southern Baptist members and congregations have withdrawn from the Cooperative Program. In 1991, several moderates formed the Cooperative Baptist Fellowship (CBF). While the CBF has thus far remained within the SBC, it has not yet reached a decision on whether or not it will remain in the convention. The CBF supports its own missionaries, has formed a moderate seminary, and has given approval to a publishing concern. The CBF may not be a separate denomination, but it certainly has taken steps in that direction.

Reflecting the conservative turn the denomination has taken, the SBC has withdrawn support from the Baptist Joint Committee on Public Affairs, an interdenominational Baptist lobbying group in Washington, D.C. The convention has never joined the National Council of Churches in Christ or the World Council of Churches. It has thus far remained a participant in the *BAPTIST WORLD ALLIANCE.

A significant footnote to the controversy that has shaken the SBC is that in 1995 the convention adopted a resolution of apology for its racist roots and for its founders' defense of slavery. The resolution called on all Southern Baptists to denounce racism as *SIN and to repent of "racism of which we have been guilty whether consciously or unconsciously."

References: Frank S. Mead and Samuel S. Hill, *Handbook of Denominations in the United States,* 10th ed. (1996); J. Gordon Melton, *The Encyclopedia of American Religions,* 3d ed. (1993); *1997 Yearbook of American and Canadian Churches;* Arthur

E. Farnsley 2d, *Southern Baptist Politics: Authority and Power in the Restructuring of an American Denomination* (1994); Nancy Tatom Ammerman, *Baptist Battles: Social Change and Religious Conflict in the Southern Baptist Convention* (1990).

Southern Baptist Founders Conference Organized in 1982, the Southern Baptist Founders Conference is a loose confederation of pastors and theologians in the *SOUTHERN BAPTIST CONVENTION who advocate Reformed or Calvinist theology. They contend that early Baptist leaders were Calvinist but that the Southern Baptists have strayed from that position and have embraced Arminian theology. The group, which includes *R. ALBERT MOHLER JR., president of Southern Baptist Theological Seminary, and Mark T. Coppenger of Midwestern Baptist Theological Seminary, publishes *The Founders Journal*, a quarterly.

Reference: Keith Hinson, "Calvinism Resurging among SBC's Young Elites," *Christianity Today*, October 6, 1997.

Southern California College (Costa Mesa, California) Established in 1920, Southern California College was chartered and is owned by the Southern California District of the *ASSEMBLIES OF GOD. It is the largest liberal arts college affiliated with a pentecostal denomination west of the Rocky Mountains. Southern California College grants master's degrees in religion and education. The minority student enrollment is significantly higher than the average for evangelical colleges; more than 20 percent of the students are people of color. The college has a Division I athletic program.

Southern Nazarene University (Bethany, Oklahoma) In the early twentieth century the *CHURCH OF THE NAZARENE created so many colleges that they found themselves in competition with each other for funds and enrollment. The denomination responded to this problem by consolidating many schools. Southern Nazarene University is the end product of several such mergers.

The school was established in 1899 near Greenville, Texas, as Texas Holiness University. Named for the site where Jacob wrestled with an angel, Peniel, Texas, grew up around the holiness college, which became Peniel University and then Peniel College. Within ten years, four other colleges had joined Peniel—Arkansas Holiness College (founded in 1900 at Vilonia, Arkansas), Bresee College (Hutchinson, Kansas, 1905), Beulah Heights College (begun in 1906 in Oklahoma City, moved to Bethany, Oklahoma, and renamed Oklahoma Holiness College), and Central Nazarene University (Hamlin, Texas, 1910). These combined schools were known as Bethany-Peniel College. The name was changed in 1955 to Bethany Nazarene College. Southern Nazarene University adopted its current name in 1986, when the college reorganized its graduate and undergraduate programs into five distinct schools.

In addition to more than seventy different undergraduate programs, Southern Nazarene University offers master's degrees in religion, psychology, education, and business management. The library's special collections include the R. T. Williams Holiness Collection and Church Archives as well as a collection of *BIBLES. A variety of parietal rules apply to the students; social *DANCING, for instance, is considered unacceptable both on and off campus.

References: *Southern Nazarene University Catalog 1995–1997* (1995); Thomas C. Hunt and James C. Carper, eds., *Religious Higher Education in the United States: A Source Book* (1996).

Southern Wesleyan University (Central, South Carolina) Founded by the *WESLEYAN CHURCH, Southern Wesleyan University began in 1906 as a small *BIBLE INSTITUTE. Three years later it was chartered as Wesleyan Methodist College. By 1973, the school had evolved into a fully accredited four-year liberal arts college.

Southern Wesleyan University has graduate programs in ministry and management. It maintains a cooperative agreement with nearby Clemson University, allowing students to take classes at both schools.

The guidelines for student life are comparable to those of other *CHRISTIAN COLLEGES. In addition, however, students are formally admonished to keep their dorm rooms clean. Special holdings in the library include the Wesleyana Collection.

Reference: Southern Wesleyan University 1996–97 Catalog (1996).

Southwestern Baptist University. *See* **Union University.**

Southwestern Collegiate Institute. *See* **John Brown University.**

Sparks, Jack (Norman) (1928–) Born and reared in rural Indiana, Jack Sparks graduated from Purdue University (B.Sc.) and the University of Iowa (M.A. and Ph.D.) and worked as a professor of statistics at the University of Northern Colorado and Pennsylvania State University in the early 1960s. He joined *CAMPUS CRUSADE FOR CHRIST in 1961, eventually becoming a full-time staff member in January 1968. In April 1969, however, he moved his family to Berkeley to begin a radical Christian community on the campus of the University of California. Sparks was the founding member of the Christian World Liberation Front, whose various outreach programs included a number of communal houses, an underground street paper called *Right On!*, a street theater troupe, an alternative Christian educational program, and an apologetic ministry called the Spiritual Counterfeits Project. During this time, Sparks was also instrumental in providing a street translation of some of the New Testament books, called *Letters to Street Christians.*

In 1973, along with a number of *CAMPUS CRUSADE colleagues, Sparks embarked on a quest to rediscover the roots of the historic Christian faith. After deciding that the closest resemblance to New Testament Christianity was the Eastern Orthodox Church, the group formed the New Covenant Apostolic Order. They changed their name in 1979 to the Evangelical Orthodox Church and were accepted into the Antiochan Orthodox Christian Archdiocese of North America in February 1986. Sparks was consecrated a bishop in this church and has been active in the publication of early church documents and the *Orthodox Study Bible* and in leading the St. Athanasius Academy of Orthodox Training.

Reference: Jack Sparks, *God's Forever Family* (1974).

Speaking in Tongues. *See* **Glossolalia.**

Special Number A peculiar dimension of evangelical jargon, "special number" refers to a musical selection or performance offered during a worship service by an individual or group other than the choir. The pastor might say, for example, "After our offering this morning, Alice Thomasen will favor us with a special number."

Speer, Robert E(lliott) (1867–1947) Robert E. Speer, a Presbyterian layman, exerted an enormous influence over

Protestant missions around the turn of the twentieth century. Influenced by the Northfield Conferences organized by *DWIGHT L. MOODY and *JOHN R. MOTT, Speer worked briefly as traveling secretary for the *STUDENT VOLUNTEER MOVEMENT before going on to study at Princeton Theological Seminary. He left seminary during his second year to become secretary of the Board of Foreign Missions of the Presbyterian Church U.S.A., a post he held for nearly five decades.

Speer traveled around the world, especially to Latin America and the Far East. He insisted that mission enterprises in foreign countries move toward self-sufficiency. Although Speer recognized that some mission efforts might veer dangerously close to cultural imperialism, he nevertheless believed in the salutary effects of Christianity, not only for the spiritual welfare of others but also because Christianity brought in its wake "progress and free government." He resisted efforts on the part of theological liberals to acknowledge the integrity of other religions and, as a consequence, largely rejected the conclusions of the Hocking Commission, as set forth in *Re-Thinking Missions*, which urged missionaries to be less culturally imperialistic. As the fundamentalist-modernist controversy gathered force in the 1920s, however, Speer found it increasingly difficult to walk a middle course. *J. GRESHAM MACHEN criticized him for allowing liberals onto the mission field, and Machen eventually left the denomination to form his own mission board. The General Assembly, however, stood behind Speer, and he was elected moderator of the denomination in 1927.

References: Robert E. Speer, *Missionary Principles and Practice* (1902); idem, *Christianity and the Nations* (1910); idem, *The Church and Missions* (1926); idem, *"Re-Thinking Missions" Examined* (1933); W. Reginald Wheeler, *A Man Sent from God: A Biography of Robert E. Speer* (1956); William R. Hutchison, *Errand to the World: American Protestant Thought and Foreign Missions* (1987); John F. Piper Jr., *Robert E. Speer, Prophet of the American Church* (2000).

Spencer, Ivan Q(uay) (1888–1970) Ivan Q. Spencer, founder of *ELIM BIBLE INSTITUTE, was reared in *METHODISM and experienced a religious *CONVERSION at the age of twenty-one. Answering a call to the ministry, he studied briefly at Wyoming Seminary near Scranton, Pennsylvania. He contracted typhoid fever, boarded a train for home, and was miraculously healed while on board. He worked on a farm in Macedon, New York, attended Elim Tabernacle in nearby Rochester, and enrolled in Rochester Bible Training School in 1911. While a student he was baptized in the Holy Spirit. Spencer joined the *ASSEMBLIES OF GOD in 1920; started a church in Hornell, New York; and four years later founded *ELIM BIBLE INSTITUTE, which he intended as a replacement for Rochester Bible Training School, which had closed.

Elim moved about considerably in its early years—from Rochester to Red Creek to Hornell. Spencer also formed the Elim Ministerial Fellowship in 1932 in order to confer clerical credentials. *ELIM BIBLE INSTITUTE moved once again in 1951, this time to Lima, New York. Spencer, who was associated with the New Order of the Latter Rain in the 1940s, was named to the board of the Pentecostal Fellowship of North America when it was founded in 1948.

Sports World Ministries, Inc. In 1967, *IRA LEE ESHELMAN, founder of *BIBLETOWN CONFERENCE/RETREAT CENTER in

Boca Raton, Florida, retired from the day-to-day administration of Bibletown in order to devote himself to the task of establishing regular pregame chapel programs among all of the football teams in the National Football League. Florida's congressional delegation supported Eshelman's efforts and, armed with a letter of introduction from Pete Rozelle, the league commissioner, Eshelman soon succeeded in organizing chapels for every team. Sports World Ministries, the organization he established, has also set up similar programs in the Canadian Football League, Major League Baseball, and professional soccer.

Spring Arbor University (Spring Arbor, Michigan) Spring Arbor University was founded in 1873 by the *FREE METHODIST CHURCH as Spring Arbor Seminary, an academy for elementary and secondary grades, which was intended to be open to all children, "regardless of religious conviction or belief." The initiative to establish the school was led by evangelist Edward Payson Hart, who began preaching in Michigan in 1863, three years after the Free Methodist denomination was founded in the Northeast.

By 1907, enrollment had climbed to two hundred, but it declined during World War I. After the war, the school recovered, and in 1923, the fiftieth anniversary of its founding, Spring Arbor's trustees voted to add a junior college. Classes were introduced over the next few years, and the school changed its name in 1929 to Spring Arbor Seminary and Junior College. The following year, the elementary and intermediate classes were discontinued.

In 1960, Spring Arbor earned regional accreditation and became Spring Arbor College. Soon after, the high school was eliminated, and the trustees adopted plans to change over to a four-year college program. Senior college classes were introduced beginning in 1963, with the first bachelor's degrees awarded two years later. Spring Arbor introduced its first master's degree program in 1994, in management. Since then, the college has introduced graduate programs in education and teaching.

Spring Arbor University operates both television and radio stations under the call letters WSAE. The on-campus enrollment is approximately one thousand students, but Spring Arbor's nontraditional degree programs reach many more. Its extension courses in men's and women's prisons enroll more than two hundred inmates in degree programs. Spring Arbor's School of Adult Education operates nine extension centers in urban areas around the state, serving an additional nine hundred students.

Spring Arbor University's "College Affirmations" proscribe "excessive noise and disregard for quiet hours." These guidelines also make it clear that no resources, in the form of money or space, are to go toward sponsoring social *DANCING. No smoking is allowed on campus, and off-campus smoking is prohibited for degree-seeking students.

Reference: *Peterson's Choose a Christian College: A Guide to Academically Challenging Colleges Committed to Christ-Centered Campus Life,* 4th ed. (1992).

Springfield Presbytery. *See* **Christian Churches.**

Sproul, R(obert) C(harles) (1939–) R. C. Sproul, known for his strict *CALVINISM and unflagging commitment to biblical *INERRANCY, was born in Pittsburgh. He earned degrees in such Reformed settings as Westminster College (New Wilmington, Pennsylvania), Pittsburgh Theological Seminary, and the Free University of Amsterdam. Ordained into the United Presbyterian Church in 1965, Sproul, who claims Martin Luther, John Calvin, and *JONATHAN EDWARDS as his theological mentors, has taught in a number of evangelical settings, including *GORDON COLLEGE, Reformed Theological Seminary, and *D. JAMES KENNEDY'S *KNOX THEOLOGICAL SEMINARY. In 1971, he began a study center, now known as *LIGONIER MINISTRIES, in Stahlstown, Pennsylvania, and from 1977 until 1983 Sproul served on the executive committee of the International Council on Biblical Inerrancy.

References: R. C. Sproul, *God's Inerrant Word* (1975); idem, *Knowing Scripture* (1978); idem, *Ethics and the Christian* (1983); idem, *Johnny Come Home* (1984); idem, *Classical Apologetics* (1984); idem, *The Holiness of God* (1985); idem, *Surprised by Suffering* (1989).

Spurgeon, Charles Haddon (1834–1892)
Born in Kelvedon, England, Charles Haddon Spurgeon studied at All Saints Agricultural College, immersed himself in the New Testament, and, at the age of sixteen, was baptized by a retired Baptist missionary. Spurgeon began preaching and soon was offered the pastorate of the New Park Street Church in London, where his exceptional preaching skills began to attract attention; the small congregation grew into one of the city's largest churches, and soon Spurgeon was preaching in more and more commodious venues in order to accommodate the crowds. On the Day of National Humiliation in 1858, for example, he preached to an audience of twenty-three thousand at the Crystal Palace, perhaps the largest religious gathering to that time in the history of Europe. In 1861, the church erected a new building, the Metropolitan Tabernacle, where Spurgeon, who emerged as the preeminent Baptist in England, preached until the end of his career.

Spurgeon, known as "the prince of preachers," was unabashedly evangelistic and, in many ways, a nineteenth-century Puritan. He established Pastor's College in 1856 to train other evangelical leaders. In 1887, wary of evolutionary theory and of intellectual attacks on the integrity of the *BIBLE, Spurgeon decried the encroachment of "*LIBERALISM" into the Baptist Union. He demanded that the union adopt a creed to defend itself against such evils. When other Baptist leaders refused, Spurgeon withdrew from the union, thereby prompting a split among British Baptists as well as a foreshadowing of divisions among American Protestants four decades later.

References: Charles H. Spurgeon, *The Metropolitan Pulpit*, 37 vols. (1980); George C. Heedham, *The Life and Labors of Charles H. Spurgeon* (1886).

Stanley, Charles (Frazier), (Jr.) (1932–)
A fixture in the conservative wing of the *SOUTHERN BAPTIST CONVENTION and a principal in the fundamentalist takeover of the denomination, Charles Stanley is a popular preacher and the senior pastor of the First Baptist Church in Atlanta, which claims thirteen thousand members. He was educated at the University of Richmond, Southwestern Baptist Theological Seminary, and Luther Rice Seminary. Stanley's national television and radio program, *In Touch*, is broadcast throughout the United States, and he was twice elected president of the *SOUTHERN BAPTIST CONVENTION.

Stanley was a segregationist; as late as the 1970s he had guards stationed outside the church to keep African Americans out. He again became a controversial figure in 1992 when his wife, Anna, filed for divorce. In 1996, Stanley relinquished his administrative duties at the church and declared that he would resign immediately "if my wife divorces me." When the divorce was finalized in May 2000, however, Stanley remained in his post at the church.

References: Charles Stanley, *Eternal Security: Can You Be Sure?* (1990); Warren Bird, "Stanley Dilemma Underscores Troubled Clergy Marriages," *Christianity Today,* October 23, 1995.

Stanley, Sara G. (1836–?) Born in New Bern, North Carolina, Sara G. Stanley, an African American, matriculated at Oberlin College at the age of sixteen, receiving a teacher's certificate in 1857. A Presbyterian, she joined the American Missionary Association in 1864 for the purpose of assisting freed slaves in the South. Assigned as a teacher first to Norfolk, Virginia, she also taught in St. Louis; Louisville, Kentucky; and Mobile, Alabama. Throughout her career with the American Missionary Association (which ended when she married Charles Woodward, a white war veteran, in 1868), Stanley fought racism within the organization.

Reference: Judith Weisenfeld, "'Who Is Sufficient for These Things?': Sara G. Stanley and the American Missionary Association, 1864–1868," *Church History,* LX (1991).

Stapleton, Ruth Carter (1929–1983) Ruth Carter Stapleton, an *EVANGELIST, author, and faith healer, was born into a Southern Baptist family in Archery, Georgia, the younger sister of *JIMMY CARTER, thirty-eighth president of the United States. After a severe mental depression in the 1950s, Stapleton began to practice and to promote "inner healing," a holistic approach that included spiritual rebirth, prayer, meditation, psychology, diet, and exercise, although she insisted that "the psychiatric therapy part is a drop in the bucket compared to the flood of healing that comes from the Holy Spirit." Stapleton became an *EVANGELIST and headed Behold, Inc., a nonprofit organization promoting her views; people as diverse as Larry Flynt, publisher of *Hustler* magazine, and her brother Jimmy credited her with prompting their religious transformations.

References: Ruth Carter Stapleton, *The Gift of Inner Healing* (1976); idem, *Experiencing Inner Healing* (1977); idem, *Brother Billy* (1978).

Stearns, Shubal (1706–1771) Reared in New England, Shubal Stearns was converted in 1745 under the preaching of *GEORGE WHITEFIELD. His study of the *BIBLE convinced him of the truth of believer's *BAPTISM, however, and prompted him to take his *CONVERSION one step further. He was baptized in 1751 and persuaded enough of his fellow congregants of this view that they broke off from the Congregational church in Tolland, Connecticut, to form a Separate Baptist congregation, which Stearns served as pastor. Seized by a missionary impulse, Stearns and his family relocated to Virginia and then in 1755 to North Carolina. Joining with Daniel Marshall, his brother-in-law, Stearns organized the Sandy Creek Church. Due to the effectiveness of Stearns and Marshall as itinerant preachers, the Sandy Creek Association grew rapidly. According to Morgan Edwards, a contemporary, Stearns's voice was "musical and strong," and the Sandy Creek Church grew from sixteen to six hundred members. The Sandy Creek Association, according to Edwards, expanded to forty-three congregations in the span of Stearns's ministry.

Reference: Morgan Edwards, *Materials Towards a History of the Baptists,* 2 vols. (1770–1792).

Stebbins, George Coles **(1846–1945)** Reared in upstate New York, George Coles Stebbins exhibited a gift for music early in life and studied in Buffalo and Rochester. After marrying Elma Miller in 1867, he moved to Chicago, where he worked for the famous Lyon & Healy music store and as music director for the First Baptist Church. In 1874, Stebbins moved to ***A. J. GORDON**'s Clarendon Street Baptist Church in Boston and two years later to Tremont Temple. About this time, Stebbins began spending summers at ***DWIGHT L. MOODY**'s Northfield Conferences, an association that put him in touch with other evangelical musicians such as ***IRA D. SANKEY** and George C. Lorimer. Stebbins coedited several editions of *Gospel Hymns* and compiled *The Northfield Hymnal* in 1904. His many contributions to evangelical hymnody include "Take Time to Be Holy," "Jesus Is Tenderly Calling," and "Have Thine Own Way."

Stedman, Ray C. **(1917–1992)** Ray C. Stedman was born in Temvik, North Dakota, and attended ***WHITWORTH COLLEGE** and ***DALLAS THEOLOGICAL SEMINARY**. After a tour of duty with the navy and working as an assistant office manager at Libby Pineapple Plantations in Hawai'i, Stedman became pastor of Peninsula Bible Church in Palo Alto, California, in 1950. The congregation grew dramatically under his evangelical preaching, and the church's "Body Life" worship became especially popular with young people during the ***JESUS MOVEMENT** of the late 1960s and early 1970s.

References: Ray C. Stedman, *What on Earth's Going to Happen?* (1970); idem, *Body Life*, rev. ed. (1972); idem, *Riches in Christ* (1976); idem, *Triumphs of the Bible* (1980).

Stelzle, Charles **(1869–1941)** Born into poverty in New York City's famous Bowery, Charles Stelzle became a Presbyterian minister and one of the most forceful proponents of the ***SOCIAL GOSPEL**. He began working in a sweatshop at the age of eight and later became a machinist and a leader in the International Association of Machinists. Beginning in 1895, Stelzle studied for two years at the Bible Institute of Chicago (now, ***MOODY BIBLE INSTITUTE**) and then served as a lay assistant to congregations in New York and Minneapolis, Minnesota, before his ordination as a Presbyterian in 1900. After a brief pastorate in St. Louis, Stelzle was commissioned by the Presbyterian Board of Home Missions to work with urban laborers, and in 1906 he was named the first superintendent of the Presbyterian Department of Church and Labor. He was active in the Men and Religion Forward Movement, an interdenominational initiative to lure men back to the churches; he lectured and conducted surveys that formed the basis for the denomination's strategy for social amelioration in the cities, and he formed the Labor Temple on New York City's east side in 1910.

Stelzle belies the stereotype of evangelical indifference toward social ills. Although he promoted a political agenda that would generally be considered liberal, his theology was conservative, and he possessed a warm piety. The threat of budget cuts in 1913 forced him to resign from his Presbyterian post, but he continued his activities under the auspices of the American Red Cross and the Federal Council of Churches.

References: Charles Stelzle, *The Working Man and Social Problems* (1903); idem, *Christianity's Storm Center: A Study of the Modern City* (1907); idem, *The Church and Labor* (1910); idem, *A Son of the Bowery* (1926).

Stephan, Martin (1777–1846) Although the *LUTHERAN CHURCH—MISSOURI SYNOD prefers officially to trace its founding to a group of German immigrants to the Midwest led by *C. F. W. WALTHER, their roots go back to Saxony and a charismatic leader who was eventually discredited, Martin Stephan. Born in Moravia to Catholic parents in 1777, Stephan was educated by pietists at the Universities of Halle and Leipzig. After a brief stint as pastor of a church in Bohemia, he became pastor of St. John's (Lutheran) in Dresden, where he eventually took on additional roles as leader in the Saxon Bible Society, the Dresden Mission Society, and the local chapter of the German Society for the Promotion of Pure Doctrine and Holy Life. His charisma and his advocacy of *PIETISM attracted many followers, and he began also to attract scrutiny from state officials for conducting conventicles, small pietist gatherings that were officially illegal because they undermined the state church.

Stephan was unhappily married, and rumors circulated about his womanizing. Nevertheless, his followers remained loyal, and in the early 1830s a group of theology students at the University of Leipzig joined the movement, which became known as Stephanism. Stephan began to demand more and more deference, and when the new congregation issued its statement of faith, it read in part: "We alone have the correct, pure doctrine through Stephan and we alone constitute a proper, pure Lutheran church under Stephan."

Because of growing pressure from the authorities, Stephan began to make plans to emigrate to the United States, particularly to Missouri (because of some promotional literature). Following Stephan's arrest for immoral conduct and for holding conventicles, the planning intensified. The group met on December 6, 1837, and agreed that the leadership of their new church, once constituted in America, would consist of nine deacons and one bishop, who would wear "sacerdotal attire." The group also set up a Credit Fund, a pool of resources that would cover the expenses of emigration and setting up the new community in Missouri.

The Stephanites, 665 in all, migrated in November 1838, although one of their five vessels was shipwrecked; Stephan himself left his wife and children behind. On the way to New Orleans people aboard one of the ships held an investiture ceremony for Stephan, and when the group arrived in Missouri he became more authoritarian. He demanded unconditional allegiance, he alone controlled the Credit Fund, and he spent lavishly on himself and on a new bishop's residence in Perry County, Missouri. His followers grew restive under his *AUTHORITY, especially when renewed evidence emerged of Stephan's dalliances. A council of clergy and laymen convicted him of false teaching and having "committed *SINS of fornication and adultery, as well as of profligate malfeasance with alien properties."

On May 31, 1839, Stephan was exiled to the eastern side of the Missouri River. He spent the remainder of his years living in Horse Prairie, Illinois, with his housekeeper. The Saxon community regrouped under the leadership of Walther and eventually became the *LUTHERAN CHURCH—MISSOURI SYNOD.

Reference: Mary Todd, *Authority Vested: A Story of Identity and Change in the Lutheran Church—Missouri Synod* (2000).

Sterling College (Sterling, Kansas) The Synod of Kansas of the Presbyterian

Church of North America established Sterling College in 1887 under the name Cooper Memorial College. From the beginning, the school had a liberal arts curriculum, at first offering both a high school preparatory course and a liberal arts and vocational track that was designed in part to train school teachers and administrators.

Cooper Memorial College was renamed Sterling College in 1920. Although the Presbyterian Church of North America was incorporated into the Presbyterian Church in the United States, the college is affiliated by covenant relationship with the former denomination. It is, however, controlled by an independent board of trustees.

Perhaps because it never was a *BIBLE INSTITUTE, Sterling's lifestyle guidelines are in certain respects more lenient than most *CHRISTIAN COLLEGES. The school sponsors social dances and hosts several "Christian Rock" concerts each year. In addition, the theater department teaches dance classes, which is somewhat unusual in evangelical settings. The Crebbs Museum, located in Sterling's library, holds a small collection of American Indian artifacts and materials on local history.

Reference: *Sterling College 1996–1998 Catalog* (1996).

Stewart, Lyman **(1840–1923)** A devout and wealthy Presbyterian, Lyman Stewart had aspired to become a missionary as a child but entered the oil business instead at Titusville, Pennsylvania, site of America's first oil boom. Stewart enjoyed moderate success buying and selling oil leases, and in 1882 sold his holdings and headed for California, where he was later joined by his brother, Milton. The burgeoning oil boom in California brought success and wealth to the Stewart brothers and their business, the Union Oil Company of California, in part because of their forward-looking approach to research, exploration, refining, and marketing.

Stewart was an active layman in the Immanuel Presbyterian Church in Los Angeles, and as the controversies began to build over liberal or "modernist" theology in Protestant circles, Stewart threw his support—and his money—firmly behind the conservatives. In 1908, Stewart provided the bulk of the funding to start the ***BIBLE INSTITUTE OF LOS ANGELES (BIOLA)** and was instrumental in luring ***RUBEN A. TORREY** from ***MOODY CHURCH** in Chicago to become Biola's dean. Stewart also financed the Church of the Open Door, an evangelical congregation in downtown Los Angeles, which also enlisted Torrey as its first pastor.

Stewart's most significant contribution to American *EVANGELICALISM was the financing he and his brother provided for the compilation, publication, and distribution of twelve booklets entitled **THE FUNDAMENTALS; OR, TESTIMONY TO THE TRUTH*, a biting attack on theological *LIBERALISM. People who supported the very conservative doctrines propounded by **THE FUNDAMENTALS*, which were published between 1910 and 1915, became known as fundamentalists.

Stinson, Benoni **(1798–1869)** Benoni Stinson, reared on the frontier in Kentucky and Indiana, felt a call to the ministry at the age of twenty-two. As a Baptist and a member of the Wabash District Association (Indiana), Stinson objected to what he regarded as the harsh *CALVINISM of his fellow Baptists. He advocated a general view of the *ATONEMENT—that God's *GRACE was available to everyone, not only the elect—and formed a new congregation. In 1824, he organized his followers, who were called General Baptists or Stinsonites, into the Liberty Association of General Baptists, a group known today as the General Association of General Baptists.

Reference: William Henry Brackney, *The Baptists* (1988).

Stinsonites. *See* **Stinson, Benoni,** *and* **General Association of General Baptists.**

St. James, Rebecca (1977–) Pop-rock inspirational singer Rebecca St. James was born in Australia. Her father was a Christian-concert promoter who moved his wife and seven children to the United States in 1991. Shortly after they arrived, the job he had been promised fell through, and in a desperate effort to rescue the family from poverty, he began to develop the music career of his oldest daughter. Rebecca St. James released a debut album, *Rebecca St. James,* in 1994, which sold more than one hundred thousand copies, and the following year she was nominated for a Dove Award for Best New Artist by the *GOSPEL MUSIC ASSOCIATION. A second recording, *GOD,* came out in 1996. It included the singles "Me without You" and "God." Some of the musical stylings on the album, however, also brought the charge that St. James was little more than an evangelical imitation of the secular singer Alanis Morissette, but St. James claims she does not listen to non-Christian music.

St. James acts as a spokesperson for the relief organization Compassion International and also has published a book of devotions, *40 Days with God,* which grew out of entries from her journal.

Reference: Information provided by ForeFront Commuication Group, Inc.

Stoddard, Solomon (1643–1729) A Congregational minister in the Connecticut Valley of western Massachusetts, Solomon Stoddard was born in Boston and educated at Harvard. He assumed the Congregational pulpit at Northampton, Massachusetts, in 1672, and in the course of his forty-seven-year tenure the church grew to be the largest congregation outside of Boston. A good preacher and a commanding presence, Stoddard is best known for the theological innovation known as "Stoddardeanism." In response to the spiritual declension in Massachusetts, Stoddard decided that the *LORD'S SUPPER should no longer be restricted to church members, that it might be a "converting ordinance" for bringing the unchurched under the influence of evangelical preaching.

Stoddardeanism, which came in for extreme criticism from the Boston clergy, apparently succeeded. Late in the seventeenth century Stoddard reported several "harvests," or *REVIVALS, a source of irritation to some of the divines in Boston, who derided Stoddard as the "pope of the Connecticut Valley." In 1727, he brought his grandson, *JONATHAN EDWARDS, to Northampton as his associate. When Stoddard died two years later, Edwards took over the pulpit and presided over the *REVIVALS known collectively to historians as the *GREAT AWAKENING.

Stokes, Ellwood (1815–1897) Born in Medford, New Jersey, into a Quaker household, Ellwood Stokes converted to *METHODISM in 1834. He became an itinerant minister for the New Jersey Conference of the Methodist Episcopal Church and was appointed to the church at Lambertville in 1847, the first of several charges around the state. In 1867, Stokes was named presiding elder of the shore district; two years later he became president of the *OCEAN GROVE CAMP MEETING ASSOCIATION, a post he held until his death.

Reference: Ellwood Stokes, *Footprints in My Own Life* (1898).

Stone, Barton W(arren) (1772–1844) Born near Port Tobacco, Maryland, Barton W. Stone experienced an evangelical *CONVERSION at age nineteen and applied to the Orange Presbytery for a license to preach. He preached in North Carolina, Virginia, and Tennessee, but enjoyed his greatest success in Concord and *CANE RIDGE, Kentucky, the center of the *GREAT REVIVAL. Stone had long expressed reservations about the Calvinist doctrine of election, which he viewed as a hindrance to *REVIVAL. In 1803, he and four other revivalists withdrew from the Presbyterian Synod of Kentucky rather than face censure for their views. They took the name Springfield Presbytery (from the town in southern Ohio where they convened) and explicitly rejected creedal formulations as a test of fellowship, preferring simple adherence to the New Testament. They were convinced by 1804 that all denominational labels were inimical, adopted the name Christian, and dissolved the Springfield Presbytery by signing "The Last Will and Testament of the Springfield Presbytery."

By 1811, Stone became the sole leader of the group when two of the other founders joined the Shakers and another two returned to the Presbyterians. In the 1830s, he moved toward union with the Disciples, led by *THOMAS and *ALEXANDER CAMPBELL. The group became known as the Christian Church (Disciples of Christ).

Stone, Jean. *See* **Willans, Jean Stone.**

Stone Church (Chicago, Illinois) The Stone Church was founded in December 1906 by *WILLIAM H. PIPER, a disaffected follower of *JOHN ALEXANDER DOWIE and formerly one of Dowie's lieutenants in *ZION CITY, Illinois. Because of his disaffection Piper initially eschewed pentecostal preaching in his church, which consisted largely of other erstwhile members of the *ZION CITY community. By June 1907, however, after attendance had fallen off dramatically, Piper relented. "Nothing is better calculated to make a minister examine himself than a decrease in his audiences," he recalled later. "After long days and nights of agony of spirit in earnest prayer, I was finally brought to the decision that what was claimed as the *BAPTISM OF THE HOLY SPIRIT and the *SPEAKING IN TONGUES was really of God." After weeks of nightly services the pentecostal fervor took hold. Piper's wife, Lydia Markley Piper, was baptized in the Spirit in July 1907; Piper himself succumbed the following February. With the monthly publication of the *Latter Rain Evangel,* beginning in October 1908, the influence of the Stone Church on *PENTECOSTALISM in North America increased dramatically, and the congregation's central location in Chicago made it into a kind of crossroads for pentecostal preachers and missionaries passing though the Midwest. When Piper died late in 1911, his wife served briefly as pastor before moving to southern California. The Stone Church eventually affiliated formally with the *ASSEMBLIES OF GOD.

Reference: Edith L. Blumhofer, *Restoring the Faith: The Assemblies of God, Pentecostalism, and American Culture* (1993).

Stonehill, Randy (1952–) One of the pioneers of Christian rock music, Randy Stonehill grew up in a home where his father was Jewish and his mother Roman Catholic. He was interested in music from an early age, and he traces his *CONVERSION to evangelical Christianity to August 12, 1970. Soon thereafter he and fellow musician *LARRY NORMAN visited *PAT BOONE, who gave them three thousand dollars to produce their first albums; Norman released *Street Level,* and Stonehill released *Born Twice.* For more than two decades, Stonehill has continued his artistic creativity, all the while demonstrating his social concern through his involvement with Compassion International. "Even though the doors that have opened for me to be heard are more within the walls of the church," he said in a 1998 interview, "I've still tried not to be too self conscious about creating product to make the right noise and tickle the ears of the Christian record-buying audience."

Reference: Dwight Ozard, "Randy Stonehill: The Prism Interview," *Prism,* July/August 1998.

Stonehouse, Ned B(ernard) (1902–1962) Ned B. Stonehouse was born in Grand Rapids, Michigan. He graduated from *CALVIN COLLEGE, Princeton Theological Seminary, and the Free University of Amsterdam, where he earned a doctorate in New Testament in 1929. Stonehouse was one of the original faculty members at *WESTMINSTER THEOLOGICAL SEMINARY, where he taught for his entire career. An expert on the Synoptic Gospels, Stonehouse was also an active churchman within the *ORTHODOX PRESBYTERIAN CHURCH.

References: Ned B. Stonehouse, *The Witness of Matthew and Mark to Christ* (1944); idem, *The Witness of Luke to Christ* (1951); idem, *J. Gresham Machen: A Biographical Memoir* (1954); idem, *Origin of the Synoptic Gospels* (1963); Mark A. Noll, *Between Faith and Criticism: Evangelicals, Scholarship, and the Bible in America* (1986).

Stookey, Noel Paul (1937–) Best known as "Paul" in the folk group Peter, Paul & Mary, Noel Paul Stookey was born in Baltimore and used his skills as a guitarist to help pay tuition at Michigan State University. He and his family moved to Pennsylvania after graduation, but he soon decided to try to make his living as an entertainer. Relocating to New York City, he faced tough times, but by the end of 1960 he had established himself as a stand-up comic in Greenwich Village clubs. Stookey linked up with Mary Travers, a folk singer, and the addition of Peter Yarrow in 1961 created Peter, Paul & Mary. Their eponymous debut album was released in May 1962, and by the end of the year "Lemon Tree" and "If I Had a Hammer" were hit singles.

Throughout the turbulent 1960s, the group, which cast itself in the folk-protest tradition of Pete Seeger, became enormously popular, with hit singles, gold albums, and sold-out concerts. The grind of fame and travel, however, took its toll, especially on Stookey. He was charged with having illicit relations with a minor, which led to a religious awakening in 1968, which had been prompted in part by *BOB DYLAN's encouragement to read the *BIBLE. "After the discovery that I needed God in my life, it became obvious that I had allowed a great distance to develop between me and my family," Stookey recounted, "but since my body moves about two years after my mind, it wasn't until 1970 that I spoke about retiring."

As Peter, Paul & Mary each went separate ways, Stookey and his family finally settled in rural Maine in 1973, where he pursued a number of creative projects. His music and his interests became more religious and confessional. Stookey's "Wedding Song (There Is Love)," written for the marriage of Yarrow to Marybeth McCarthy, was probably the best example of willingness to embroider his faith into his music. The composition became very popular among evangelicals (and others), especially among those contemplating marriage.

Story, John Huntington (1926–) The notorious "rape doctor" of Lovell, Wyoming, John Huntington Story graduated from *WHEATON COLLEGE and from the medical school at the University of Nebraska. After his residency he practiced medicine for a year in Crawford, Nebraska, before moving to Lovell, Wyoming, to open a general practice. Through a series of circumstances in the 1980s it became apparent that Story regularly asked his female patients to undergo pelvic examinations, even for conditions that had no apparent connection to the physical complaints that brought them to his office. These exams were invariably conducted, contrary to standard procedure, with no one in the room other than Story and the patient.

As the women of Lovell learned that their own violations in Story's office were not unique, they banded together to convince their husbands and fathers and, finally, law enforcement officials that Story had indeed raped dozens of women in his examination room. The accusations polarized the community, generally along religious lines: Mormon women comprised a majority of Story's victims, while Story enlisted the support of the town's fundamentalist church, of which he was a respected member, and insisted that he was a victim of a "Mormon plot." Story was acquitted in his first trial but convicted on new evidence in the second trial. On August 4, 1986, he began serving a ten-to-fifteen-year sentence for multiple counts of assault and rape.

Reference: Jack Olsen, *"Doc": The Rape of the Town of Lovell* (1989).

Stott, John R(obert) W(almsley) (1921–) Throughout a pastoral career that spanned more than a half century, John R. W. Stott, a graduate of Trinity College, Cambridge, was pastor of a single parish, All Souls, Langham Place, in London, which he assumed in 1950. Yet his influence on *EVANGELICALISM reached around the world through his preaching and his writings (he is the author of more than forty books, including *Basic Christianity,* which has been translated into fifty languages). Among evangelicals in the United States, Stott's renown has been somewhat anomalous. American evangelicals generally look askance at the liturgy and the *LIBERALISM of the Church of England, and yet they admire Stott for his unflagging allegiance to the *AUTHORITY of the *BIBLE. He has often criticized American evangelicals for their cultural arrogance. "Some missionary endeavor has been a thinly disguised form of imperialism," he told the InterVarsity Student Missions Convention at *URBANA in 1979, "a hunger for the prestige of our country or our church or our organization or ourselves." Stott has been a contributing editor for **SOJOURNERS*, a magazine whose politics generally lean to the left of center.

Appointed honorary chaplain to the Queen of England in 1959, Stott, who was ordained in 1945, has resisted any attempts by evangelical Anglicans to separate from the Church of England. At a meeting of the National Assembly of Evangelicals in 1966, for example, Stott publicly refuted a call from Martyn Lloyd-Jones, another respected evangelical preacher, for evangelicals to leave the

Church of England. A kind of evangelical ecumenist, Stott was the principal drafter of the *LAUSANNE COVENANT, which grew out of the 1974 *INTERNATIONAL CONGRESS ON WORLD EVANGELIZATION. The Covenant reminded evangelicals of their twofold responsibility in the world: *EVANGELISM and social action.

References: John R. W. Stott, *Basic Christianity* (1958); idem, *Understanding the Bible* (1972); idem, *Between Two Worlds* (1982); idem, *Evangelical Truth: A Personal Plea for Unity, Integrity, and Faithfulness* (1999); Timothy Dudley-Smith, *John Stott: The Making of a Leader* (1999); David F. Wells, "Guardian of God's Word," *Christianity Today,* September 16, 1996; Peter Williams, s.v. "John R. W. Stott," in Walter A. Elwell, ed., *Handbook of Evangelical Theologians* (1993); John W. Yates 3d, "Pottering and Prayer," *Christianity Today,* April 2, 2001.

Stowe, Harriet (Elizabeth) Beecher (1811–1896) Best known as the author of *Uncle Tom's Cabin,* Harriet Beecher Stowe was the daughter of *LYMAN BEECHER. When the family moved from Litchfield, Connecticut, to Cincinnati, so that *LYMAN BEECHER could assume the directorship of Lane Theological Seminary, young Harriet was profoundly affected by her exposure to slavery. She visited a slave plantation across the river in Kentucky, she imbibed the abolitionist sentiments at Lane, and she eventually married one of the school's professors, Calvin E. Stowe, in 1836.

In 1850, the Stowes moved to Maine, where Calvin took a position at Bowdoin College. Harriet underwent a perfectionist *CONVERSION, mediated through the writings of *THOMAS UPHAM. After bearing seven children, she wrote *Uncle Tom's Cabin,* a novel depicting the depredations of slavery. First published serially in *National Era* in 1852, an antislavery newspaper, the work was extraordinarily successful and helped to focus the moral debate over slavery. According to tradition, when President Abraham Lincoln met Harriet Beecher Stowe, he remarked that this was the little lady who brought about the Civil War.

References: Harriet Beecher Stowe, *Uncle Tom's Cabin* (1852); idem, *Dred: A Tale of the Great Dismal Swamp* (1856); idem, *The Minister's Wooing* (1859); Calvin Stowe, *Life of Harriet Beecher Stowe* (1889); Marie Caskey, *Chariot of Fire: Religion and the Beecher Family* (1978); John Hedrick, *Harriet Beecher Stowe: A Life* (1994); Patricia R. Hill, "Harriet Beecher Stowe (1811–1896)," in Mark G. Toulouse and James O. Duke, eds., *Makers of Christian Theology in America* (1997).

Strachan, R(obert) Kenneth (1910–1965) Reared in a missionary household in Latin America, R. Kenneth Strachan studied at *WHEATON COLLEGE, *DALLAS THEOLOGICAL SEMINARY, and Princeton Theological Seminary. Following the death of his father, Strachan took over the leadership of the Latin American Mission, a post he retained from 1945 to 1965. During his tenure, Strachan sought to transfer control of the organization into Latin American hands, a task finally accomplished in 1971. He also began a program called Evangelism-in-Depth, which aimed to concentrate evangelistic activities in a single, highly visible Latin American republic. Nicaragua was the first target, beginning in 1960, and the initiative was extended to other Latin American countries over the course of the decade.

Reference: Elisabeth Elliot, *Who Shall Ascend: The Life of R. Kenneth Strachan of Costa Rica* (1968).

Strader, Karl (David) (1929–) A powerful preacher who is capable of quoting long passages of Scripture from memory, Karl Strader was reared in western Oklahoma and was influenced by the pentecostal ministry of *ORAL ROBERTS. Strader, however, attended a fundamentalist school, *BOB JONES UNIVERSITY, and then returned to the pentecostal fold. In 1966, he became pastor of the First Assembly of God in Lakeland, Florida, which has seen remarkable growth under his ministry. The congregation built a ten-thousand-seat auditorium, known as the Carpenter's Home Church, in 1985.

Straton, John Roach (1875–1929) An intense, firebrand fundamentalist, John Roach Straton was born in Evansville, Indiana, and grew up in the deep South. He studied at Mercer University, where he quickly distinguished himself as an orator, and at Southern Baptist Theological Seminary. Ordained as a Southern Baptist in 1900, Straton served churches in Kentucky, Illinois, Maryland, Virginia, and Texas before accepting a call to Calvary Baptist Church, New York City, in 1918, which necessitated a transfer to the Northern Baptist Convention.

In New York, the media soon became enamored of Straton, in part because of his campaigns calling for the censorship of entertainment; his colorful condemnations of *MODERNISM, which culminated in Straton's withdrawal from the Northern Baptist Convention in 1926, earned him the sobriquet "pope of *FUNDAMENTALISM." A forceful opponent of the *SOCIAL GOSPEL, Straton preached the importance of individual rather than social *SALVATION: "regeneration, not reform; soteriology, not sociology." Straton found opponents in evolution and Al Smith, the Roman Catholic governor of New York and Democratic candidate for president in 1928. Attacking Smith as an enemy of moral progress, Straton campaigned against him throughout the South. His regimen, however, took a toll. Straton suffered a stroke in 1929 and died on October 29, the day of the stock market crash.

References: John Roach Straton, *The Battle over the Bible* (1924); idem, *The Famous New York Fundamentalist-Modernist Debates* (1925); idem, *Fighting the Devil in Modern Babylon* (1929); idem, *God's Prophetic Calendar* (1987); C. Allyn Russell, *Voices of American Fundamentalism: Seven Biographical Studies* (1976).

Strong, Augustus H(opkins) (1836–1921) Born in Rochester, New York, the son of the publisher of the *Rochester Democrat,* Augustus H. Strong graduated from Yale College in 1857 and Rochester Theological Seminary in 1859. After serving as pastor of Baptist churches in Haverhill, Massachusetts, and Cleveland, where he numbered John D. Rockefeller among his congregants, Strong returned to Rochester in 1872 and spent the next forty years as president and professor of systematic theology at the seminary. Over the course of a long and distinguished career, Strong emerged as one of the most influential figures in the Northern Baptist Convention and as an articulate spokesman for conservative Protestant theology at the turn of the century.

Strong's *Systematic Theology,* first published in 1876, passed through eight editions and became the point of departure for many a Baptist seminarian's education. Although he sought to avoid theological controversy, Strong became concerned about the inroads of "modernist" theology after the turn of the century. He published *A Tour of the Missions: Observations and Conclusions* in 1918, a polemic that sounded the alarm about theological drift among Baptist foreign missionaries and contributed to the fundamentalist-modernist controversy. At the same time, however, Strong recognized the historical contingencies of all theology.

References: Augustus H. Strong, *Systematic Theology* (1886); idem, *Philosophy and Religion* (1888); idem, *Christ in Creation and Ethical Monism* (1899); idem, *Miscellanies,* 2 vols. (1912); Grant Wacker, *Augustus H. Strong and the Dilemma of Historical Consciousness* (1985).

Stryper Stryper was a Christian rock band that gained a considerable following in the 1980s. The band was formed in 1983 in Orange County, California, by brothers Michael and Robert Sweet and guitarist Oz Fox. Originally known as Roxx Regime, the trio played the Los Angeles "metal club" circuit. In 1984, bass player Timothy Gaines joined them and they were offered a contract with Enigma Records. At that time, the band changed its name to Stryper, which they said stands for "Salvation Through Redemption, Yielding Peace, Encouragement and Righteousness." At other times, however, they claimed that the name came from a passage in Isaiah 53:5: ". . . by His stripes we are healed."

Stryper's debut album, *The Yellow and Black Attack,* came out in 1984, but with their second release the group saw its popularity soar. *Soldiers under Command* came out in 1985 on Hollywood Records. The album sold more than half a million copies and stayed on the *Billboard* 200 for forty weeks. With hair weaves and loud guitars, Stryper's members rivaled the group ***Whiteheart** in their ability to adopt the "glam rock" popular at the time. They adopted a trademark style of wearing only black and yellow, often in the form of studded leather clothing. Like ***Whiteheart**, however, Stryper also took seriously their Christian commitments, and were known to toss ***Bibles** into the audience at their concerts.

Stryper hit its peak in 1986 with *To Hell with the Devil.* The album made history as the first for a Christian band—as opposed to a single artist—to go platinum. *To Hell with the Devil* generated a top-forty hit with the single "Honestly," which was at one point the most requested song on MTV.

The band's next project was almost as successful. When *In God We Trust* came out in 1988, it approached platinum status and won heavy airplay on MTV. Yet with the band's 1990 recording, *Against the Law,* fans were confused because the band had abandoned its trademark appearance. Stryper had changed its musical style as well, in favor of a cleaner, more "nineties" sound. Some fans objected to the changes in the music. Others questioned the sincerity of the musicians' faith.

Stryper went on to release one more album before the group split. An anthology album, *Can't Stop the Rock: The Stryper Collection,* came out the following year, with a couple of new singles done in the band's original style. The musicians seemed to have abandoned their bid for artistic freedom, however, and soon went on to other projects. Michael Sweet left to pursue a solo career and has released two albums on Benson Records. After several years of holding regular jobs and trying to make ends meet, Timothy Gaines and Oz Fox formed a new band called Sin Dizzy.

Stuart, George Hay (1816–1890) George Hay Stuart, businessman, philanthropist, and head of the ***United States Christian Commission**, was born in Ireland and emigrated to the United States at the age of fifteen. He quickly attained success as a dry goods wholesaler and a banker, despite the lack of a formal education. When the ***United States Christian Commission** was formed from a meeting of ***YMCA** delegates in 1861, Stuart was chosen to chair the new relief organization, which looked after the spiritual and the physical well-being of Union soldiers during the Civil War. After the war, Stuart refused several offers to join Ulysses S. Grant's cabinet but finally consented to an appointment to the Board of Indian Commissioners; as purchasing agent, he worked to limit corruption. Stuart's real interests, however, lay with urban *EVANGELISM. He became an enthusiastic supporter of *DWIGHT L. MOODY, and when Moody's church was destroyed by the Chicago fire of 1871, Stuart raised money to reconstruct the building.

Reference: George Hay Stuart, *The Life of George Hay Stuart* (1890).

Stuck, Hudson (1863–1920) Born in the United Kingdom and educated at King's College, London, Hudson Struck migrated to the United States in 1885 and settled in San Angelo, Texas. He studied theology at the University of the South (Sewanee, Tennessee) beginning in 1889. He was ordained into the Episcopal priesthood after graduation and appointed rector of Grace Episcopal Church in Cuero, Texas. In 1894, he became dean of St. Matthew's Cathedral in Dallas.

Stuck's career took a dramatic turn in 1904 when he resigned his post and accepted an appointment as archdeacon in the diocese of Alaska, a missionary diocese. Hudson worked in Alaska for the rest of his life, combining missionary efforts with intrepid adventure and exploration, including the first ascent of Mount Denali (McKinley). Stuck's writings portray the challenge of mission work in Alaska, and he emerged as something of an advocate for native Alaskans. He also established a library in Fairbanks and a hospital in Fort Yukon.

References: Hudson Stuck, *Spirit of Missions* (1909); idem, *Ten Thousand Miles with a Dog Sled* (1914); idem, *The Ascent of Denali* (1914); idem, *Voyages on the Yukon and Its Tributaries* (1917); idem, *A Winter Circuit of Our Arctic Coast* (1920); idem, *The Alaskan Missions of the Episcopal Church* (1920).

Student Volunteer Movement for Foreign Missions The Student Volunteer Movement for Foreign Missions, a nondenominational movement, originated in the summer of 1886 at Mount Hermon, Massachusetts, at a conference for *YMCA leaders organized by *DWIGHT L. MOODY. In the course of the gathering, exactly one hundred students, who became known as the *MOUNT HERMON HUNDRED, expressed their desire to become foreign missionaries. The sentiment spread to colleges and seminaries across North America, primarily through the agency of *ROBERT P. WILDER, a student at Princeton who had founded the Princeton Foreign Missionary Society in 1883. Within a year, Wilder had persuaded a thousand students to sign a pledge: "It is my purpose, if God permit, to become a foreign missionary." By 1888, the Student Volunteer Movement was formally organized with the motto "the evangelization of the world in this generation." *JOHN R. MOTT, one of the original *MOUNT HERMON HUNDRED, was designated chair of the group and *ROBERT E. SPEER the traveling secretary.

Over the course of its existence the Student Volunteer Movement sent about twenty thousand missionaries to foreign lands. It sponsored study programs and produced missionary literature. After 1920, however, the original fervor began to wane, and the organization went through several incarnations. It merged with other groups in 1959 to form the National Student Christian Federation, which in turn became the University Christian Movement in 1966. That body disbanded in 1969.

References: Robert P. Wilder, *The Student Volunteer Movement* (1935); William R. Hutchison, *Errand to the World: American Protestant Thought and Foreign Missions* (1987).

Subscription Controversy Among Presbyterians in the eighteenth century a controversy arose over the demand that candidates for church membership and especially candidates for ordination subscribe to the *WESTMINISTER STANDARDS. Would American Presbyterians define themselves by a mere intellectual assent to dogmatic and creedal definitions set forth in the Westminster documents, or would Presbyterians pay more attention to religious piety?

The issue profoundly divided American Presbyterians, with the Scots-Irish, led by John Thomson, generally lining up behind strict subscription, and the New Englanders, following the lead of *JONATHAN DICKINSON, arguing for more flexibility. The two sides eventually compromised. The *ADOPTING ACT of 1729 distinguished between the essential and the nonessential elements of the *WESTMINSTER STANDARDS. Any ministerial candidate who had reservations about the Westminister articles was required to state his scruples at the time of his examination. Members of the presbytery would then judge whether or not the reservations were of sufficient weight to merit denial of ordination. The *ADOPTING ACT, which had been drafted primarily by Dickinson, held American Presbyterians together for a time, at least until the *GREAT AWAKENING divided them into *NEW LIGHT and Old Light factions.

Reference: Randall Balmer and John R. Fitzmier, *The Presbyterians* (1993).

Summer Institute of Linguistics. *See* **Wycliffe Bible Translators.**

Summer of Mercy. *See* **Operation Save America.**

Summerfield, Glendel Buford "Glenn" In the fall of 1991, Glenn Summerfield, pastor of a *SERPENT-HANDLING congregation—The Church of Jesus with Signs Following, outside of Scottsboro, Alabama—was arrested for trying to murder his wife, Darlene, with snakes. According to court testimony Summerfield, who frequently handled snakes, drank strychnine, and poked his fingers into live electrical sockets to demonstrate his faith to the congregation, had fallen into a drunken, jealous rage and, at gunpoint, forced his wife to write a suicide note and then to plunge her hand into one of the cages where he kept the rattlesnakes he used in church services. Summerfield was convicted of attempted murder and sentenced to ninety-nine years in prison.

Reference: Dennis Covington, *Salvation on Sand Mountain: Snake Handling and Redemption in Southern Appalachia* (1995).

Sumner Academy. *See* **Whitworth College.**

Sumrall, Lester (Frank) (1913–1996) Born in New Orleans, Louisiana, Lester Sumrall was miraculously cured of tuberculosis at the age of seventeen and began preaching shortly thereafter. He began a church in Green Forest, Arkansas, and, having been ordained by the *ASSEMBLIES OF GOD, Sumrall traveled around the world as an itinerant *EVANGELIST. In the course of a *REVIVAL campaign in the Philippines, Sumrall founded what would become the largest church in that country. Sumrall and his wife, Louise, settled in South Bend, Indiana, in 1963, where he began a church that became known as Cathedral of Praise. Sumrall eventually separated from the *ASSEMBLIES OF GOD and formed the Lester Sumrall Evangelistic Association, which operates several radio and television stations, a home for orphans, and World Harvest Bible College, and publishes *World Harvest* magazine.

References: Lester Sumrall, *Miracles Don't Just Happen* (1979); idem, *The Gifts and Ministries of the Holy Spirit* (1982); idem, *My Story to His Glory* (1983); idem, *Faith to Change the World* (1983); "No Glitter for Lester," *Christianity Today*, February 3, 1989.

Sunday, William Ashley "Billy" (1862–1935) Born in Ames, Iowa, Billy Sunday spent his early years in various orphanages around the state until his athletic prowess, especially his running speed, earned him a baseball contract with the Chicago White Stockings, with whom he played until 1891. While in Chicago, Sunday underwent a *CONVERSION experience in 1886 at the *PACIFIC GARDEN MISSION, and soon afterward he joined the Jefferson Park Presbyterian Church, where he met and eventually married Helen Amelia Thompson. Under the auspices of the ***YMCA**, Sunday began his work as a part-time *EVANGELIST. He was traded to the Pittsburgh Alleghenies following the 1887 season and, late in the 1890 season, traded again to Philadelphia. Although he still had talent for the game—Sunday's single-season record of ninety-five stolen bases lasted until Ty Cobb broke it in 1915—Sunday quit baseball and joined the staff of the ***YMCA** in Chicago. Sunday began serving as an advance man for the itinerant revivalist *J. WILBUR CHAPMAN in 1893. When Chapman accepted a call to become pastor of Bethany Presbyterian Church in Philadelphia in 1895, Sunday struck out on his own in what he would call the "kerosene circuit" of small towns in the Midwest, beginning with an evangelistic campaign in Garner, Iowa, on January 7, 1896.

By the turn of the century, Sunday had taken his *REVIVAL campaigns to the cities. He would often use vaudeville antics to attract attention; he spoke in the folksy, salty vernacular of the day and would often taunt his audiences. "I put the cookies and jam on the lower shelf," he said, "so an audience don't have brain fag when they sit and listen to me." Sunday was a vigorous proponent of prohibition; one of his lines was, "I'm trying to make America so dry that a man must be primed before he can spit." Especially during World War I, Sunday trotted out patriotic and nativistic rhetoric, arguing that "Patriotism and Christianity are synonymous terms." He routinely condemned alcohol, gambling, and licentiousness but cared little for the niceties of theology. "I don't know any more about theology than a jackrabbit knows about ping-pong," he would say, "but I'm on my way to glory."

References: Billy Sunday, *Great Love Stories from the Bible and Their Lesson for Today* (1917); idem, *Wonderful, and Other Sermons* (1940); Lyle W. Dorsett, *Billy Sunday and the Redemption of Urban America* (1991); Douglas Frank, *Less Than Conquerors: How Evangelicals Entered the Twentieth Century* (1986); John Pahl, s.v. "Billy Sunday," in Charles H. Lippy, ed., *Twentieth-Century Shapers of American Popular Religion* (1989).

Sunday school The Sunday school movement originated in Great Britain in the eighteenth century as an effort to provide the rudiments of literacy and education to urban children, many of whom were working the other six days of the week. Sunday schools were established in Virginia as early as 1785, and by the 1790s Boston, Philadelphia, and New York City all had Sunday schools. Factory owners sometimes allowed teachers to operate schools on their premises.

After the turn of the nineteenth century, especially with the rise of the common school (public school) movement, Sunday schools gradually shifted their attention to religious instruction. The *AMERICAN SUNDAY-SCHOOL UNION was established in 1824, providing curricular materials as well as the organizational structure for expansion; mission Sunday schools did evangelistic work in urban and rural areas. Beginning in the 1820s and 1830s, individual denominations set up their own Sunday schools, which provided religious instruction from a particular confessional perspective. By the early twentieth century, a large number of Sunday school organizations had been formed, including the International Sunday School Conventions (1875), the *RELIGIOUS EDUCATION ASSOCIATION (1903), the International Sunday School Association (1905), and the Sunday School Council of Evangelical Denominations (1910). Among evangelicals, Sunday schools still play an important role in both the transmission of doctrine as well as socialization in the norms of godliness.

References: Jack L. Seymour, *From Sunday School to Church School: Continuities in Protestant Church Education in the United States, 1860–1929* (1982); Ann M. Boylan, *Sunday School: The Formation of an American Institution* (1988).

Swaggart, Jimmy (Lee) (1935–) One of the more colorful figures in twentieth-century *EVANGELICALISM, Jimmy Swaggart was born in Ferriday, Louisiana, to parents who were both *EVANGELISTS in the *ASSEMBLIES OF GOD. Swaggart himself began preaching at age six; he experienced a religious *CONVERSION and *BAPTISM OF THE HOLY SPIRIT at eight. Although he dropped out of high school, Swaggart followed a call to be an *EVANGELIST. His success derived not only from his extraordinary, highly emotional preaching but from his singing ability, which he had honed with his cousin, Jerry Lee Lewis, and with another cousin, Mickey Gilley, both of whom went on to successful (if controversial) careers as musicians. Swaggart himself has released several recordings of *GOSPEL MUSIC.

Swaggart, an itinerant preacher, was ordained by the *ASSEMBLIES OF GOD in 1958 (after initially being turned down), and his fame spread as he publicized his relationship to Lewis. In 1969, Swaggart launched a radio program, *The Camp Meeting Hour,* which he financed with royalties from his record albums. The success of his radio venture prompted Swaggart and his organization, Jimmy Swaggart Ministries, Inc., to venture into television in 1973, when relaxed FCC regulations allowed evangelical preachers to exploit the medium. By the early 1980s, the heyday of *TELEVANGELISM, *The Jimmy Swaggart Telecast* was the most popular, bringing in millions and millions of dollars annually and fueling the expansion of his empire in Baton Rouge to include Jimmy Swaggart Bible College, a printing plant, a recording studio, a television production center, a church sanctuary—the Family Worship Center, with seating for seven thousand—and a magazine, *The Evangelist.* (His success on television prompted Swaggart to drop the radio broadcasts in 1981.)

Swaggart's downfall began in 1987, when he was accused of plotting to destroy the ministry of a televangelist rival and fellow *ASSEMBLIES OF GOD minister, *JIM BAKKER. Swaggart and his minions leaked news of Bakker's adulterous tryst, but Swaggart himself soon faced accusations of voyeuristic liaisons with a prostitute. On his television broadcast of February 21, 1988, Swaggart offered a dramatic confession of guilt and a plea for forgiveness. He submitted to discipline by the *ASSEMBLIES OF GOD, which demanded that he refrain from preaching for a year. Swaggart adhered to that proscription for a few weeks, but the survival of his empire demanded large influxes of cash from his television program. Defrocked by the *ASSEMBLIES OF GOD in April 1988, he resumed his telecasts, but this time to sharply diminished ratings. Additional accusations of scandal have whittled his audiences further.

References: Jimmy Lee Swaggart, *To Cross a River* (1977); idem, *The Great White Throne Judgment* (1979); idem, *The Baptism in the Holy Ghost* (1981); idem, *Four Conditions for Being Included in the Rapture* (1981); idem, *God's Psychiatry* (1982); idem, *Sodom and Gomorrah* (1984); Richard N. Ostling, "Offering the Hope of Heaven," *Time,* March 16, 1987; idem, "TV's Unholy Row," *Time,* April 6, 1987; Paul G. Chappell, s.v. "Jimmy Swaggart," in Charles H. Lippy, ed., *Twentieth-Century Shapers of American Popular Religion* (1989); Randall Balmer, *Mine Eyes Have Seen the Glory: A Journey into the Evangelical Subculture in America,* 3d ed. (2000); Ann Rowe Seaman, *Swaggart: The Unauthorized Biography of an American Evangelist* (1999).

Swift, Wesley (1913–1970) Born in New Jersey, the son of a Methodist minister, Wesley Swift became one of the most important figures in the emergence of the *CHRISTIAN IDENTITY movement. He was converted to evangelical Christianity at the age of seventeen; he was licensed to preach in the Methodist Church the following year and headed west to Los Angeles to attend Kingdom Bible College. He was loosely associated with the *INTERNATIONAL CHURCH OF THE FOURSQUARE GOSPEL and perhaps with *CHARLES FOX PARHAM; he started his own church in Lancaster, California, in the mid-1940s, about the same time that he sought to revive the *KU KLUX KLAN in southern California.

Swift supported McCarthyism and was linked with various paramilitary groups in California; he was probably among the founders of the militant, supremacist Christian Defense League in the late 1950s and early 1960s. The league continued to publish Swift's sermons and writings even after his death in 1970. A compelling preacher and an associate of *GERALD L. K. SMITH, Swift popularized *CHRISTIAN IDENTITY ideology by combining *BRITISH ISRAELISM with a demonic anti-Semitism and political extremism.

Reference: Michael Barkun, *Religion and the Racist Right: The Origins of the Christian Identity Movement* (1994).

Swindoll, Charles Rozell "Chuck" (1934–) Born in El Campo, Texas, Chuck Swindoll originally aspired to become an engineer. He attended the University of Houston Trade School, but in the course of military service he concluded that he was called to be a pastor. Profoundly influenced by the dispensational teachings of *R. B. THIEME, Swindoll entered *DALLAS THEOLOGICAL SEMINARY in the fall of 1959 and graduated *summa cum laude* four years later. Beginning in 1963, he served as a pastor with *J. DWIGHT PENTECOST at Grace Bible Church in Dallas and then moved to the *EVANGELICAL FREE CHURCH in Waltham, Massachusetts, in 1965 for another two-year pastorate. Swindoll, a gifted expository preacher who was ranked by a 1995 *BAYLOR UNIVERSITY poll as one of the nation's twelve most effective preachers, moved to Irving Bible Church in Irving, Texas, in 1967 before becoming the senior pastor of the First *EVANGELICAL FREE CHURCH in Fullerton, California, in 1971.

Over the course of a twenty-three-year tenure in Fullerton, Swindoll's reputation within *EVANGELICALISM grew considerably through his books and through his nationally syndicated *Insight for Living* radio broadcast, which began in 1977. Swindoll left the Fullerton church to assume the presidency of *DALLAS THEOLOGICAL SEMINARY in the fall of 1994. He also started a new church, Stonebriar Community Church in Frisco, Texas, north of Dallas, in October 1998, and in 2000 he was appointed chancellor of Dallas Seminary.

References: Chuck Swindoll, *Improving Your Serve* (1977); idem, *Hope Again* (1996); Jim Jones, "Swindoll Starts Instant Megachurch," *Christianity Today*, April 26, 1999.

Sword Drill A common exercise in evangelical circles, especially among young people, a sword drill tests one's knowledge of the *BIBLE, at least the location of the various books. Typically, a leader calls out a biblical reference and those assembled compete with one another to see who can find the passage in her or his *BIBLE first and read it to the rest of the group. The term comes from the evangelical synonym for the *BIBLE, which is derived from Hebrews 4:12 (KJV): "For the word of God is quick, and powerful, and sharper than any twoedged sword, piercing even to the dividing asunder of soul and spirit, and of the joints and marrow, and is a discerner of the thoughts and intents of the heart."

■ ■ ■

Tabor College (Hillsboro, Kansas) Henry W. Lohrenz and J. K. Hiebert convinced the Mennonite Brethren and Krimmer Mennonite Brethren Churches to establish a church college in 1907. Tabor College, named after the biblical Mount Tabor, opened a year later. The Dust Bowl farm crisis and Great Depression nearly forced the college out of operation in the 1930s, and in 1934 the Tabor College Corporation transferred ownership of the college to the board of trustees of the Conference of the Mennonite Brethren Church of North America. Nonetheless, the college managed to pull through. Tabor was on more solid footing by the 1940s and gained additional stability at that time with regional accreditation. Tabor now operates under its own charter, independent of the church's national board.

In its early years, Tabor had a seminary, but in the 1950s the College of Theology was moved to Fresno Pacific College. Tabor's library houses the Center for Mennonite Brethren Studies. It also maintains collections of materials on writers *C. S. LEWIS, Madeleine L'Engle, and Flannery O'Connor.

References: Tabor College Academic Catalog 1995–1996 (1995); Thomas C. Hunt and James C. Carper, eds., *Religious Higher Education in the United States: A Source Book* (1996).

Tada, Joni Eareckson (1950–) A diving accident in July 1967 left Joni Eareckson a quadriplegic in a wheelchair, unable to use her hands. During two years of rehabilitation, she questioned God and struggled with a new identity as a disabled person. She also spent long months learning how to paint, holding a brush between her teeth. Today, she is an internationally known mouth artist, and she has appeared with *BILLY GRAHAM and other *EVANGELISTS to tell her story of tragedy and faith.

Eareckson's autobiography (she married after her accident and took the name Tada, and she pronounces her first name "Johnny") reached a wide audience among evangelicals. It was made into a motion picture, *Joni,* by World Wide Pictures and has been translated into numerous languages. Tada has also been an advocate for the disabled, serving on the National Council on Disability for three and a half years, during which time the Americans with Disabilities Act became law.

Tada founded JAF Ministries (formerly Joni and Friends), based in Agoura Hills, California, an "organization accelerating Christian ministry in the disability community." Her daily five-minute radio program, *Joni and Friends,* provides information and encouragement to people with disabilities.

Reference: Joni Eareckson [Tada], *Joni* (1976).

Talbot, Louis T(hompson) (1889–1976) Reared in Australia, Louis T. Talbot graduated from Newington College in Australia and from *MOODY BIBLE INSTITUTE in Chicago. He also studied at McCormick Theological Seminary. Talbot served as pastor of churches in Paris, Texas; Oak Park, Illinois; Keokuk, Iowa; and Minneapolis, Minnesota. In 1929, he accepted a call to the Philpott Tabernacle in Hamilton, Ontario, before moving on to Los Angeles in 1932.

Talbot was pastor of Church of the Open Door from 1932 until 1948, and he served simultaneously as president of the *BIBLE INSTITUTE OF LOS ANGELES (now *BIOLA UNIVERSITY), a post he held until 1952. Talbot's fund-raising efforts kept Biola afloat; a radio fund drive in 1938, for instance, saved the school from bankruptcy. In addition to his pastoral and educational efforts, Talbot wrote several books and promoted foreign missions.

References: Louis T. Talbot, *God's Plan of the Ages* (1936); idem, *The Prophecies of Daniel in Light of the Past, Present and Future Events* (1940); idem, *For This I Was Born: The Captivating Story of Louis T. Talbot* (1977).

Talbot School of Theology. *See* **Biola University.**

Talmage, T(homas) DeWitt (1832–1902) Born into a farm family near Bound Brook, New Jersey, T. DeWitt Talmage studied law briefly but then transferred to New Brunswick Theological Seminary. He graduated in 1856 and was soon ordained into the *REFORMED CHURCH IN AMERICA. Talmage served Reformed churches in Belleville, New Jersey; Syracuse, New York; and Philadelphia, where he began to establish himself as a powerful and flamboyant preacher. He accepted a call in 1869 to the Central Presbyterian Church in Brooklyn, New York, a deeply divided congregation. He remained there until 1895 and in the process built the church into one of the largest congregations in North America.

Talmage's preaching drew wide attention; he held considerable appeal to middle- and upper-class urbanites in the Gilded Age. His sermons appeared in more than three thousand newspapers across the country, and he published a number of popular books, many of them compilations of his sermons. He served as editor of several publications, including *Christians at Work* (1874–1876), *Frank Leslie's Sunday Magazine* (1881–1889), and **CHRISTIAN HERALD* (1890–1902). In order to accommodate the growing crowds in Brooklyn, the church built several new buildings, all of which were destroyed by fire. The final two buildings (each known as the Tabernacle) seated in excess of five thousand.

Talmage's critics contended that his florid, sensational sermons treated the

Scriptures out of context and therefore consisted of "falsehood and deceit." He was brought before the Brooklyn Presbytery in 1879 and accused of "using improper methods of preaching which tend to bring religion into contempt." He was acquitted of those charges (on a close vote), but controversy continued to swirl around him. After the Tabernacle burned again in 1894, Talmage moved the following year to the First Presbyterian Church, in Washington, D.C., where he remained until his retirement from the pulpit in 1899.

References: T. DeWitt Talmage, *The Abominations of Modern Society* (1872); idem, *Around the Tea Table* (1874); idem, *The Night Sides of New York* (1878); Charles Eugene Banks, *Authorized and Authentic Life and Works of T. DeWitt Talmage* (1902).

Tappan, Arthur (1786–1865) Born in Northampton, Massachusetts, Arthur Tappan settled in New York City in 1826 and became successful in the silk-jobbing business, which he ran with his brother *LEWIS. The Tappan brothers used their wealth to support various humanitarian reforms, including *TEMPERANCE, the *SUNDAY SCHOOL movement, and the distribution of tracts and *BIBLES. They leased the Chatham Street Theater and later built the Broadway Tabernacle for the use of *CHARLES GRANDISON FINNEY.

Arthur Tappan also gave money to Kenyon College, *ANDOVER SEMINARY, Auburn Seminary, and Yale. With the promise of financial support, Tappan persuaded *LYMAN BEECHER to accept the presidency of Lane Theological Seminary in Cincinnati, but when Finney went to Oberlin College, Tappan redirected his money there.

Tappan first supported colonization as an answer to the slavery issue, but he later became an outright abolitionist, aligning himself, at least briefly, with William Lloyd Garrison. He became president of the *AMERICAN ANTI-SLAVERY SOCIETY, partook in the formation of the American and Foreign Anti-Slavery Society in 1840, and assisted in the founding of the American Missionary Association in 1846.

Reference: Lewis Tappan, *The Life of Arthur Tappan* (1870).

Tappan, Lewis (1788–1873) Lewis Tappan, born in Northampton, Massachusetts, flirted briefly with Unitarianism before returning to his religious roots in *EVANGELICALISM. He joined his brother *ARTHUR in the silk-jobbing business in New York City in 1828 and also took over management of the *Journal of Commerce,* which Arthur had founded. Lewis Tappan withdrew from the partnership in 1841 and established the first commercial credit rating agency in the United States, a venture so successful that he retired in 1849 and devoted his energies to humanitarian causes.

The Tappan brothers underwrote such causes as tract and *BIBLE distribution, *SUNDAY SCHOOLS, missions, *REVIVALS, *TEMPERANCE, and sabbatarianism. Both were engaged in the antislavery movement and contributed to the formation of the *AMERICAN ANTI-SLAVERY SOCIETY, the American and Foreign Anti-Slavery Society, and the American Missionary Association. In addition to his support for *CHARLES GRANDISON FINNEY, Lewis Tappan also supported those involved in the Underground Railroad.

Reference: Bertram Wyatt-Brown, *Lewis Tappan and the Evangelical War Against Slavery* (1969).

Tate, Randy (1965–) Born in Pullayup, Washington, Randy Tate worked at his father's trailer park and went to school at Tacoma Community College and Western

Washington University, where he received a degree in political science. He claims to have recognized at a young age "the failed policies of *JIMMY CARTER, that *LIBERALISM didn't work, and big government didn't solve the problems." Tate was elected to the state legislature in 1988 and to the U.S. House of Representatives in 1994, after running a vicious campaign in which he implied that his Democratic opponent, a former state superintendent of schools, was a pedophile. In Congress, Tate quickly earned a reputation as one of the most loyal partisans of the *RELIGIOUS RIGHT, compiling a perfect voting record from the *CHRISTIAN COALITION. He defended gun rights, opposed environmental protections and federal assistance to the poor, and supported a constitutional amendment to outlaw flag-burning. In June 1997, following his defeat in the 1996 elections, Tate, who had been a Robertson delegate to the 1988 Republican National Convention, was named executive director of the *CHRISTIAN COALITION by *PAT ROBERTSON.

Reference: Michael Sayre, "The Chosen One," *Icon Thoughtstyle Magazine,* February 1988.

Taylor, Clyde W. (1904–1988) Best known for his work with the *NATIONAL ASSOCIATION OF EVANGELICALS, Clyde W. Taylor graduated from *NYACK MISSIONARY INSTITUTE, *GORDON COLLEGE, and Boston University. Under the auspices of the *CHRISTIAN AND MISSIONARY ALLIANCE, he was a missionary to Peru and Colombia, and he served as pastor of Central Baptist Church, Quincy, Massachusetts, before signing on with the newly formed National Association of Evangelicals.

Over the course of a career that spanned four decades, Taylor lobbied Congress, assisted foreign mission agencies, and traveled throughout the world as a goodwill ambassador for the *NATIONAL ASSOCIATION OF EVANGELICALS in particular and *EVANGELICALISM generally. In the realm of broadcasting, he fought successfully against the attempts on the part of the Federal Council of Churches to have a monopoly on the free air time earmarked for religious programming. Known as "Mr. NAE," Taylor also served as general secretary of the *WORLD EVANGELICAL FELLOWSHIP from 1970 to 1974.

Reference: James DeForest Murch, *Cooperation without Compromise: A History of the National Association of Evangelicals* (1956).

Taylor, Herbert J(ohn) (1893–1978) An evangelical businessman and philanthropist, Herbert J. Taylor was born in Pickford, Michigan, converted in a Methodist church, and graduated from Northwestern University in 1917. He worked in France under the auspices of the *YMCA during the years surrounding World War I. Upon his return to the United States, Taylor entered the oil and the real estate business in Oklahoma and in 1924 began work at the Jewel Tea Company in suburban Chicago, working his way up to executive vice president. In 1930, he moved to Club Aluminum Company, which he rescued from bankruptcy, becoming president in 1932 and chairman of the board in 1952. In the course of his business career, Taylor developed the "Four-Way Test," which Rotary International adopted in 1942: Is it the truth? Is it fair to all concerned? Will it build goodwill and better friendships? Will it be beneficial to all concerned?

As a philanthropist, Taylor's influence was far-reaching. In addition to Rotary

International, he supported such evangelical organizations as *FULLER THEOLOGICAL SEMINARY, Child Evangelism, the American Institute of Holy Land Studies, Christian Life, Creation House Publishers, and the National Methodist Foundation for Higher Education. He also founded the Christian Workers Foundation and served as chairman of the board of *YOUNG LIFE.

Reference: Herbert J. Taylor, *The Herbert J. Taylor Story* (1968).

Taylor, J(ames) Hudson (1832–1905) Venerable missionary to China and founder of the China Inland Mission, J. Hudson Taylor was born in Yorkshire, England, into a devout Methodist family. He experienced an evangelical *CONVERSION at age seventeen, whereupon he determined that God had called him to China as a missionary. He sailed for China in 1853, at age twenty-one, under the aegis of the Chinese Evangelization Society. Upon his arrival in Shanghai, Taylor decided to wear Chinese clothes and grow a pigtail. After two years he moved to Ningpo. He resigned from the Chinese Evangelization Society in 1857, married, and formed a church with twenty-one members. Taylor established the China Inland Mission in 1865, which eventually took the name Overseas Mission Fellowship (now OMF International). Taylor insisted that his new organization be open to any worker, no matter how qualified. The mission field was "so extensive," he declared, "and the need of laborers of every class so great, that 'the eye cannot say to the hand, I have no need of thee'; nor yet again the head to the feet, 'I have no need of you.' Therefore persons of moderate ability and limited attainments are not precluded from engaging in the work."

References: A. J. Broomhall, *Hudson Taylor and China's Open Century,* 7 vols. (1981–1990); John C. Pollack, *Hudson Taylor and Maria: Pioneers in China* (1962).

Taylor, John (1752–1835) Born in Fauquier County, Virginia, John Taylor attended a Baptist gathering at the age of seventeen "with the same view, that I would have gone to a frolic." The preacher's words, however, jolted him like "an electric shock," and after wrestling with the devil Taylor finally was converted. He joined a Baptist church and began preaching. Moving west to Kentucky in 1779, Taylor started a number of churches, including those at Clear Creek, Bullittsburg, Corn Creek, Frankfort, and Buck Run. His *History of Ten Baptist Churches,* published in 1823, offers insight into the character of frontier religion in the early republic.

References: John Taylor, *History of Ten Baptist Churches* (1823); Christine Leigh Heyrman, *Southern Cross: The Beginnings of the Bible Belt* (1997).

Taylor, Kenneth N. *See* **Tyndale House Publishers.**

Taylor, Nathaniel William (1786–1858) One of the most influential theologians of the nineteenth century, Nathaniel William Taylor was born in New Milford, Connecticut, and educated at Yale College, where he graduated in 1807 and then worked as a secretary and amanuensis to *TIMOTHY DWIGHT, president of the school. After serving as pastor of the First Congregational Church in New Haven from 1812 until 1822, Taylor became the first Dwight Professor of Didactic Theology at the newly formed Yale Divinity School, a post he held until 1857.

Taylor's theology, which became known as "Taylorism" or "*NEW HAVEN

THEOLOGY," sought to harmonize the Calvinist theology of a *JONATHAN EDWARDS and the Arminian revivalism of a *CHARLES FINNEY. Taylor wanted to remain true to the rudiments of Reformed, or Calvinist, theology, but he also tried to make room for the aggressive revivalism characteristic of the Arminian theology made so popular by Finney and other theologians. In his *Concio Ad Clerum*, delivered before a gathering of Congregational clergy in 1828, Taylor disowned the classical Calvinist notion that all humanity inherited Adam's *SIN. He argued that this doctrine not only was at odds with the prevailing democratic ethos of the new nation, its determinism also inhibited *EVANGELISM. *SIN and depravity, Taylor insisted, were not innate; rather, they were a consequence of individual moral choices: "there is no such thing as sinning without acting."

Taylor's pragmatic new theology met with resistance from conservatives, who contended that it represented a departure from orthodox *CALVINISM and from the theology of New England Puritanism. Others viewed it as a warrant for revivalism and social reform, and the *NEW HAVEN THEOLOGY served as the doctrinal basis for New School Presbyterianism.

References: Nathaniel William Taylor, *Practical Sermons* (1858); idem, *Lectures on the Moral Government of God* (1859); Sidney E. Mead, *Nathaniel William Taylor, 1786–1858: A Connecticut Liberal* (1942).

Taylor, William (1821–1902) A Methodist missionary for whom *TAYLOR UNIVERSITY is named, William Taylor was born in Virginia and converted in a *CAMP MEETING. In 1847, he was assigned as a missionary to San Francisco, California, where his ministry met with good results in the era of the California Gold Rush. Taylor conducted open-air meetings, preached outside of saloons and brothels, and organized the city's first Methodist congregation.

Taylor, known to some as "California" Taylor, also embarked on missionary sorties to England, Australia, South Africa, and India. He worked in Latin America from 1877 until 1884, when he was elected missionary bishop of Africa, a post he held until his retirement in 1896.

References: William Taylor, *Seven Years' Street Preaching in San Francisco* (1856); idem, *Story of My Life* (1896).

Taylor University (Upland, Indiana, and Fort Wayne, Indiana) Although it is now interdenominational, Taylor University began as Fort Wayne Female College, founded by the North Indiana Conference of the Methodist Episcopal Church in Fort Wayne. The first meeting of the board of trustees took place in 1846, and the Indiana State legislature granted a charter the following year. When the school opened for classes that fall, approximately one hundred girls were enrolled in levels ranging from primary school to college. Each student paid $22.50 in tuition per year. By 1855, the school had become coeducational.

The financial troubles with which the college struggled in its early years dramatically affected its future. Evidence suggests that the trustees twice tried to offer the college for sale. By the 1880s, the debt had climbed to fifteen thousand dollar. The school was rescued when, with the help of board member Christian B. Stemen, pastor of the Wayne Street Methodist Church, the college became the training school of the National Association of Local Preachers. This association, of which Stemen happened to be president, agreed to support the college in exchange for the free use of its facilities, and many association members joined the board of trustees.

In 1889, the newly reorganized college agreed to change its name to Taylor University, in honor of *WILLIAM "CALIFORNIA" TAYLOR. Taylor was a legendary figure for the pastors of the National Association of Local Preachers. Although he was a lay pastor like many of the association's members, Taylor was also the first lay pastor to be named a bishop of the Methodist Church, and he was known for both his energy and enthusiasm. In 1849, when Taylor sailed around Cape Horn to San Francisco, he was one of the first Methodist missionaries to California. Taylor witnessed there for seven years to frontiersmen and gold prospectors and became famous for preaching on top of whiskey barrels outside the saloons, brothels, and gambling halls in San Francisco. "California" Taylor's religious outlook was also reflected in the college that bore his name; in the 1890s, the school became very involved in the *HOLINESS MOVEMENT.

The following year, Taylor University merged with Fort Wayne College of Medicine. With the merger, as well as the transfer to the National Association of Lay Preachers, Taylor University would seem to have attained more financial security, but by 1892 the school was ordered to sell its campus and was forced to hold classes in a rented building. With the help of two local citizens in Upland, Indiana, however, the trustees were able to negotiate an agreement with the Upland Land Company, by which the college was given ten acres of land in Upland along with ten thousand dollars. In 1893, the college moved to Upland and was debt-free within five years.

Taylor University was one of the founding members of the *CHRISTIAN COLLEGE CONSORTIUM. In 1992, the school reestablished a presence in Fort Wayne when it acquired Summit Christian College, a school previously known as Fort Wayne Bible College. Summit Christian College's campus now functions as Taylor University's Fort Wayne campus.

Reference: Thomas C. Hunt and James C. Carper, eds., *Religious Higher Education in the United States: A Source Book* (1996).

Taylorism. *See* **Taylor, Nathaniel William.**

Teen Challenge Teen Challenge grew out of attempts by *DAVID WILKERSON, a young, pentecostal preacher from Philipsburg, Pennsylvania, to preach the *GOSPEL to gang members in New York City. Wilkerson had been moved by a 1958 article in *Life* magazine regarding seven boys on trial for murder. Though unsuccessful in reaching them, Wilkerson organized Teen Challenge with the help of other New York clergy in 1960. Since then, the organization has opened Teen Challenge Centers across North America and in several foreign countries. These centers offer help with drug and alcohol addiction, drug prevention programs, vocational training, and instruction in the *BIBLE. The organization claims an unusually high rate of cure for drug addiction.

Reference: David Wilkerson, *The Cross and the Switchblade* (1963).

Teens in Trouble. *See* **Skaggs, Ricky.**

Televangelism Televangelism, the propagation of the *GOSPEL over the airwaves, was a natural extension of *EVANGELICALISM's exploitation of communications technology. Throughout American history, evangelicals have been pioneers in mass communications, from *GEORGE WHITEFIELD's open-air preaching in the eighteenth century to *CHARLES GRANDISON FINNEY's use of newspapers in the nineteenth century to the radio programs of *AIMEE SEMPLE MCPHERSON and *CHARLES E. FULLER early in the twentieth century. When *BILLY GRAHAM emerged as a cultural phenomenon at mid-century, he turned first to radio and then to television to reach the masses.

Because of changes in the television industry, *EVANGELISTS began to have an even larger influence on the medium in the 1970s. The Federal Communications Commission (FCC) had mandated that all local stations allocate time to religious broadcasting, but network policy had forbidden local affiliates to accept money for such programming. With the increased independence of local stations, however, and with the blessings of the FCC, local stations began accepting money for religious broadcasts.

*EVANGELISTS pounced on the opportunity, recognizing that they could draw in donations that would more than pay for the inexpensive airtime available in the "religious ghetto" of Sunday mornings. The nature of religious programming changed dramatically. Whereas religious broadcasts had once been dominated by the staid liturgies of Roman Catholicism and mainline Protestantism, evangelicals, drawing on the long evangelical tradition of mixing religion and entertainment, translated the *GOSPEL into show business. The "electronic church" took many forms: the pentecostal and healing emphases of *KATHRYN KUHLMAN, *ORAL ROBERTS, and *ERNEST ANGLEY; the positive-thinking, Jesus-will-make-you-rich message of *REX HUMBARD, *ROBERT SCHULLER, and *ROBERT TILTON; the inimitable theatrics of *JIMMY SWAGGART; the conservative political cant of *JAMES ROBISON and *JERRY FALWELL; and the talk-show format of *PAT ROBERTSON and, later, his erstwhile lieutenant, *JIM BAKKER, whose programs were modeled explicitly after Johnny Carson's *Tonight Show.*

Televangelism became immensely profitable, with many of the televangelists drawing in millions of dollars every year, amounts far exceeding the budgets of entire denominations. Robertson's ability to garner large audiences, for instance, together with his financial acumen made his network, the *CHRISTIAN BROADCASTING NETWORK (CBN), into a formidable organization that provided the foundation for Robertson's campaign for the Republican presidential nomination in 1988.

By the middle of the 1980s, however, scandal caught up with many of the televangelists. Bakker's flamboyant lifestyle and his dreams of empire led to financial improprieties that eventually sent him to prison. Swaggart was caught in several dalliances with prostitutes in Louisiana. Roberts declared that God would "call me home" unless God's people ponied up several million dollars to save his flagging empire. Early in the 1990s, Tilton was reeling from an ABC News exposé that cast serious doubts on his integrity.

The cumulative effect of the scandals was a severe sag in ratings and, consequently, revenues. Many of the larger televangelist organizations cut back on their operations, but the proliferation of cable television has opened the doors for new televangelists and new networks.

References: Quentin J. Schultze, *Televangelism and American Culture: The Business of Popular Religion* (1991); J. Gordon Melton, Phillip Charles Lucas, and Jon R. Stone, *Prime-Time Religion: An Encyclopedia of Religious Broadcasting* (1997).

Temperance As the word applies to the temperance movement, the term "temperance" is really a misnomer because advocates for temperance reform more often than not called for total abstinence from alcohol, not temperance. Although Benjamin Rush, a renowned physician, had warned against the dangers of alcohol consumption as early as 1784, Americans drank liberally, especially in the frontier areas of the new nation, replete with grain. The ravages of alcohol soon became apparent in violence, sloth, and abuse.

When the American Temperance Society was established in Boston in 1826, seven of the sixteen founding members were clergymen. The society served as a kind of clearinghouse for other temperance initiatives, and the notion of temperance was in large measure an evangelical one; many of the biggest pushes came in the wake of *REVIVAL activity, and Protestants came to see abstinence from alcohol as a sign of devotion to evangelical ideals. Some reformers sought the repeal of state license laws, which permitted the sale of liquor. The passage of the "Maine Law" provided a model for other initiatives in the 1850s, although most were declared unconstitutional in 1857. Following the Civil War, the temperance cause was taken up by such groups as the *ANTI-SALOON LEAGUE and the Women's Christian Temperance Union. Temperance (read *abstinence*) remained an important component of evangelical, especially fundamentalist, social mores throughout most of the twentieth century.

References: W. J. Rorabaugh, *The Alcoholic Republic: An American Tradition* (1979); Joseph R. Gusfield, *Symbolic Crusade* (1963).

Templeton, Charles B. (1915–2000) One of *EVANGELICALISM's most notorious apostates, Charles B. Templeton was one of *BILLY GRAHAM's fellow *EVANGELISTS in the early years of *YOUTH FOR CHRIST; many observers at the time, in fact, thought that Graham was the inferior preacher. Templeton's intellectual restlessness, however, prompted him to attend Princeton Theological Seminary, and before enrolling he challenged Graham, who also had no formal theological training, to accompany him. Templeton's challenge caused something of a crisis in young Graham; he pondered the offer at some length but finally decided, just prior to his Los Angeles crusade in 1949, to set aside intellectual questions and simply to "preach the *GOSPEL."

Templeton, on the other hand, attended Princeton Seminary from 1948 to 1951, whereupon he became an itinerant *EVANGELIST for the National Council of Churches. His reservations about the truth of Christianity, however, overwhelmed him. "I came to a point finally where to go on would have meant preaching things I didn't believe," he recalled. In 1957, he returned to his native Toronto and embarked on an illustrious career as a journalist, sports cartoonist, editor, television news director, author, novelist, playwright, and screenwriter.

Graham still laments Templeton's lapse from the evangelical faith. "He was one of the greatest preachers I ever heard," Graham said in a 1993 television documentary. "He just had all-around ability. But somehow it didn't grip his heart the way I think it should have, like I wish it had, like I've often prayed—as many other people have prayed for him—because he would be a mighty servant of the Lord." Templeton describes himself as an agnostic, drawing a careful distinction between an atheist and an agnostic. "An atheist says there is no God," he said in an interview in 1980. "In my view that is presumptuous. How do you know? Have you examined all the evidence that you can flatly say there is no God? I wouldn't dare say that." Templeton, who acknowledges his admiration for Graham, also declared his indebtedness to Christianity. "The man, Jesus Christ, is still the biggest influence in my life. I think he is a spiritual and moral genius. I think his understanding of human beings and the human dilemma is far more profound than anyone else I've ever read," he continued, "but I don't worship him."

References: Charles B. Templeton, *Life Looks Up* (1955); idem, *Evangelism for Tomorrow* (1957); idem, *Jesus* (1973); idem, *The Kidnapping of the President* (1974); idem, *The Third Temptation* (1980); William Martin, *A Prophet with Honor: The Billy Graham Story* (1991); *Crusade: The Life of Billy Graham*, PBS documentary (1993).

Temptation Any attraction, enticement, or deception to do evil on the part of a believer is temptation. "Temptation" also describes a state in which one is constantly encouraged to act against the precepts of God, as defined by the Scriptures. Human desire to act willfully and independently of God is the locus of temptation's strongest attraction and leads to estrangement from God. Evangelicals believe that individuals must account for their sinfulness and willfulness, which is itself a *SIN in the eyes of many evangelicals.

Ten Boom, Corrie (1892–1983) Born in Amsterdam and reared in Haarlem, the Netherlands, Corrie ten Boom was the daughter of a clockmaker and learned her father's trade. When the Nazis invaded the Netherlands in 1940, however, she and her family became active in the Dutch Resistance. Their home became "the Hiding Place" for Jews until she and her family were arrested in February 1944 and eventually sent to the Ravensbruck concentration camp. Despite witnessing Nazi atrocities and the death of her own sister, Corrie organized a highly successful Bible study group, and Barracks 28 became known as "the crazy place where there is hope." Corrie was the only member of her family to survive imprisonment. Released on account of a clerical error, she returned to Holland to assist those displaced by the war. Her remarkable story, however, soon gained international attention. She became very popular with American evangelicals after the publication of her autobiography, *The Hiding Place,* in 1971, which was made into a motion picture by World Wide Pictures in 1975.

References: Corrie ten Boom, *The Hiding Place* (1971); idem, *Tramp for the Lord* (1974); idem, *Each New Day* (1977); Carole C. Carlson, *Corrie ten Boom: Her Life, Her Faith* (1983).

Tennent, Gilbert (1703–1764) The eldest son and a student of *WILLIAM TENNENT, Gilbert Tennent, born in County Armagh, Ireland, is generally regarded as the first "graduate" of his father's *LOG COLLEGE; he learned theology from his father, even though he had completed his studies by the time the log building itself was erected. The younger Tennent was licensed by the presbytery of Philadelphia in 1726 and briefly served the church at New Castle, on the Delaware River. That autumn he accepted a call from the Presbyterian church at New Brunswick, New Jersey, where he became acquainted with the nearby Dutch minister *THEODORUS JACOBUS FRELINGHUYSEN.

Tennent and Frelinghuysen became good friends, and Tennent credited Frelinghuysen with schooling him in the rudiments of *PIETISM. The two exchanged pulpits on occasion and contributed mightily to the *GREAT AWAKENING in the Middle Colonies. Emboldened by his new understanding and experience of piety, Tennent became an evangelistic firebrand, traveling throughout the Middle Colonies and into New England. He earned the respect and praise of *GEORGE WHITEFIELD, who admired Tennent's "searching" sermons and dubbed him "a son of thunder" for his powerful preaching. Tennent delivered his most famous sermon, "The Danger of an Unconverted Ministry," at Nottingham, Pennsylvania, on March 8, 1740. Later published and widely circulated, this sermon lambasted orthodox but impious clergy who, Tennent insisted, had the form of religion, but no substance. He urged his auditors to seek ministers who could claim *CONVERSION and a warmhearted piety. Even so dedicated and ardent a defender of Tennent as *ARCHIBALD ALEXANDER, who produced a hagiography of *LOG COLLEGE graduates, described the Nottingham sermon as "one of the most severely abusive sermons which was ever penned."

Tennent's censoriousness and his *ITINERANCY contributed greatly to the Old Side–New Side schism among American Presbyterians in 1741, when the revivalistic New Brunswick presbytery was effectively expelled from the synod. Tennent and other New Side Presbyterians eventually formed the synod of New York. As the *REVIVAL fervor waned, however, Tennent became more accommodating toward his erstwhile adversaries. He moved to Philadelphia in 1743 to serve as pastor of the Second Presbyterian Church, and in 1758 he presided as moderator over the reunified New York and Philadelphia synods.

References: Milton J. Coalter Jr., *Gilbert Tennent, Son of Thunder* (1986); Randall Balmer and John R. Fitzmier, *The Presbyterians* (1993).

Tennent, William (1673–1746) William Tennent graduated from the University of Edinburgh and was ordained deacon and, later, priest in the Church of Ireland, although he never served a parish. After emigrating to Philadelphia about 1718 Tennent acknowledged misgivings about the episcopal *POLITY and Arminian theology in the Anglican Communion and requested admission to the Presbyterian ministry. The synod deliberated on his past ordination and finally acceded, but not before directing the moderator to "give him a serious exhortation to continue steadfast in his now holy profession."

After serving several churches in New York and Pennsylvania, Tennent became pastor at Neshaminy, Pennsylvania, in 1726, where he remained until his death in 1746. Far more significant than his pastoral career, however, was the tutoring he provided for young protégés in the rudiments of evangelical theology and piety. In 1736, he erected what his critics derisively called the *LOG COLLEGE, which is generally regarded as the precursor to the College of New Jersey (now Princeton University). Tennent's students included his own sons, notably *GILBERT TENNENT, and such important eighteenth-century evangelical leaders as *SAMUEL FINLEY and *SAMUEL BLAIR.

Reference: Archibald Alexander, *The Log College* (1851).

Terry, Randall. *See* **Operation Save America.**

Testimony For evangelicals, the word "testimony" refers to a believer's open declaration of her or his faith, often in a gathering of other believers or, preferably, in a venue that includes nonbelievers. A testimony generally takes the form of a narrative, where someone tells others about how he or she was converted or how God had delivered him or her from danger, illness, or *TEMPTATION. The notion of testimony can also be interpreted more generally; someone who lives a godly life in the presence of others is being a "good testimony." Beginning in the 1990s many evangelicals, especially younger evangelicals, preferred to use the term "faith journey" when referring to testimony in the narrative sense of the word.

Texas Association of Christian Schools. *See* **Association of Christian Schools International.**

Texas Holiness University. *See* **Southern Nazarene University.**

Theonomy. *See* **Reconstructionism.**

Thieme, R(obert) B(unger), Jr. (1918–) Born in Fort Wayne, Indiana, R. B. Thieme Jr. graduated from the University of Arizona in 1940 and received a commission as a second lieutenant in the army reserves. Known to his followers as "Colonel Thieme" because of his military service during World War II, Thieme attended *DALLAS THEOLOGICAL SEMINARY, where he learned dispensational theology under *LEWIS SPERRY CHAFER. He earned the Th.M. degree in 1949. Thieme left Dallas before completing his doctorate, however, and assumed the pastorate of Berachah Church, a fundamentalist congregation in Houston. Thieme promptly dismissed the church board and instituted a regimen of lectures—four evenings a week and twice on Sunday—on his own idiosyncratic interpretations of the *BIBLE. For example, Thieme, a premillennialist who believes the end of the world is at hand, teaches that the references to one's heart in the Scriptures refer to the right lobe of the brain. He admires David as "a perfect combat soldier," and he finds a prefiguration of the United Nations in the collusion between Roman and Jewish authorities in the death of Jesus.

Despite the fact that he is reclusive and has very little commerce even with members of his own congregation, Thieme has exerted considerable influence in some corners of *FUNDAMENTALISM by means of his lectures, his books, and his "tape ministry," which distributes approximately thirty thousand audiotapes every month under the auspices of Operation Grace World Missions. Those who claim Thieme as their mentor include *HAL LINDSEY, author of *The Late Great Planet Earth*; *CHUCK SWINDOLL, a popular writer and lecturer; and *DAN and Marilyn QUAYLE, the former vice president of the United States and his wife.

Thieme has a history of exaggerated claims about his knowledge and his accomplishments. He claims, for example, to have a command of ancient languages, something that experts dispute. He once boasted that he had turned down a Rhodes Scholarship in order to take the church in Houston, although he was never offered such a scholarship. He claimed that he was "in charge of all Army Air Forces cadet military training" during World War II, when in fact he had written two short manuals, one on strategy and another on military etiquette. In 1988, when the connection with the Quayles came to light in the course of the presidential campaign, Garry Wills of Northwestern University, a journalist, critic, and classics scholar, went to Houston to learn more about Thieme. "I cannot judge his (or anybody's) Hebrew; but if it is no better than his Greek, it is a sham," Wills concluded. "Perhaps Thieme once had intellectual gifts; he certainly aspired to an eminence only they could give him. But he has chosen a way of life certain to obliterate them—surrounding himself with sycophants; avoiding for decades any new idea or challenge; dealing always with minds he considers inferior to his; putting on display a learning whose credentials need never be renewed; condescending to his own followers; refusing to deal with those whose submission is not predictable."

References: R. B. Thieme Jr., *Levitical Offerings* (1973); idem, *The Integrity of God* (1979); idem, *Christian Suffering* (1987); Garry Wills, *Under God: Religion and American Politics* (1990).

Third Day Third Day, a Christian rock band from Georgia, is the newest project of Reunion Records, which had enjoyed considerable success with *JARS OF CLAY. The band, whose five members were all in their early twenties, was founded in 1992 by lead singer Mac Powell and guitarist Mark Lee. Powell and Lee teamed up with bass player Tai Anderson and drummer David Carr, who had been playing in another band, and the quartet began performing together in Atlanta. Guitarist Brad Avery joined in 1994, the year the group released an independent compact disc. The following year Third Day released a self-titled debut album on an independent Atlanta label, and in December 1995 Reunion Records bought that recording, along with the group's contracts. The band cut two new songs, *Third Day* was remixed, and a new version of the album was released in early 1996. Third Day's sound incorporates elements from country, bluegrass, and *GOSPEL MUSIC. The singles from their first album include "Nothing at All," "Blackbird," "Consuming Fire," "Thief," and "Mama."

Reference: Information provided by Reunion Records.

Third Wave If the first wave of pentecostal renewal in the twentieth century can be traced to *AGNES OZMAN and *AZUSA STREET at the turn of the century and the second wave is the *CHARISMATIC RENEWAL of the 1960s, the so-called Third Wave refers to a movement that began to attract attention in the early 1980s. Those associated, wittingly or not, with the Third Wave generally are evangelicals who recognize the role of the Holy Spirit in divine healing, receiving prophecies, even casting out demons. These evangelicals, however, deny the pentecostal teachings about the "*SECOND BLESSING" and insist that believers are baptized in the Holy Spirit at the moment of *CONVERSION. People associated with the Third Wave (a term coined by C. Peter Wagner, a church growth expert, in 1983) also resist the schismatic tendencies apparent in previous pentecostal movements. They play down the practice of raising hands in worship and public *GLOSSOLALIA, for example, so as not to create divisiveness within their congregations.

References: C. Peter Wagner, "The Third Wave," *Christian Life* (September 1984); Vinson Synan, *In the Latter Days* (1984).

Thomas, B(illy) J(oe) (1942–) Born in Hugo, Oklahoma, B. J. Thomas took country and *GOSPEL MUSIC as his earliest influences; he idolized Hank Williams and sang in his church choir. In 1965, he joined a rock 'n' roll band called the Triumphs (the group eventually changed its name to B. J. Thomas and the Triumphs). His 1966 recording of a Williams classic, "I'm So Lonesome I Could Cry," catapulted him into the top-ten charts in both the United States and Australia. Other hits followed, including "Raindrops Keep Falling on My Head," the theme song from *Butch Cassidy and the Sundance Kid.*

Despite his success and his popularity on the concert circuit, Thomas fell deeper and deeper into depression and drugs, becoming almost suicidal. In the mid-1970s Thomas became a *BORN-AGAIN Christian, in part through the influence of his estranged wife. "That experience really brought everything into focus," he declared. "It set my priorities right—making records, my personal life, everything." Thomas continued his popular recording, but he also did a gospel album for Myrrh Records, *Home Where I Belong,* in 1977. He followed with several more gospel albums and in 1978 won a Grammy for "best inspirational performance." Thomas continued to mix popular songs with gospel, both in his concerts and in his recordings. "I'm not a Christian entertainer, I'm an entertainer who is a Christian," he explained. "I definitely have the freedom to do any kind of music I want to do. But I sing contemporary Christian songs because they have a positive and uplifting message. And more importantly, especially when discussing secular markets, I feel that *CONTEMPORARY CHRISTIAN MUSIC makes a positive statement while not always making a Christian statement."

Reference: Mark Joseph, *The Rock & Roll Rebellion: Why People of Faith Abandoned Rock Music—and Why They're Coming Back* (1999).

Thomas, W(illiam) H(enry) Griffith (1861–1924) W. H. Griffith Thomas was born in England, educated at King's College, London, and at Oxford, and was ordained a priest in the Church of England in 1885. After serving several parishes he became principal of Wycliffe Hall, Oxford, in 1905. Five years later Thomas migrated to Canada and, from 1910 to 1919, was professor of Old Testament and systematic theology at Wycliffe College in Toronto. Thomas was one of the contributors to **THE FUNDAMENTALS*, and he held to such fundamentalist doctrines as dispensational *PREMILLENNIALISM and *KESWICK teachings. He produced both scholarly works and popular devotional materials, and he was a regular contributor to *Moody Monthly, The Sunday School Times,* and *Bibliotheca Sacra.*

In order to devote more time to his *ITINERANCY, Thomas left Wycliffe College in 1919 and became increasingly active in fundamentalist causes, including the World Conference on Christian Fundamentals. He also became enamored of the *BIBLE INSTITUTE movement as a means of combating *MODERNISM. He joined the faculty of *MOODY BIBLE INSTITUTE and was slated to be one of the founding faculty members at *DALLAS THEOLOGICAL SEMINARY, but he died prior to the opening of the school.

References: W. H. Griffith Thomas, *The Holy Spirit of God* (1913); idem, *Grace and Power: Some Aspects of the Spiritual Life* (1916); idem, *The Christian Life and How to Live It* (1919); David R. Elliott, "Knowing No Borders: Canadian Contributions to American Fundamentalism," in George A. Rawlyk and Mark A. Noll, eds., *Amazing Grace: Evangelicalism in Australia, Britain, Canada, and the United States* (1993).

Thomas Road Baptist Church (Lynchburg, Virginia). *See* **Falwell, Jerry.**

Thompson, Donald W(hitney) (1937–) Born and reared in western New York, Donald W. Thompson became enamored of the media early in life, especially radio and motion pictures. He worked as a radio disk jockey for a number of stations, and he produced television programs (including specials for *EVANGELIST Lowell Lundstrom) and short, motivational films. In the early 1970s, he left Iowa Public Television to form *MARK IV PICTURES, in partnership with Russell S. Doughten Jr., and in 1973 Thompson produced and directed *A Thief in the Night,* a feature-length film depicting life on earth after the *RAPTURE. Despite its low budget and infelicities in acting, *A Thief in the Night* revolutionized the evangelical film industry and became the most popular such film ever. Thompson produced three sequels on the apocalypse—*A Distant Thunder, Image of the Beast,* and *Prodigal Planet*—as well as a number of other evangelistic films. His films have won many awards, and Thompson was named "Director of the Decade" for the 1970s by the Christian Film Distributors Association.

In addition to his filmmaking, Thompson has remained active in radio. An extraordinarily devout and energetic man, his Saturday morning program on KWKY, an evangelical station in Norwalk, Iowa, became quite popular among evangelicals in the Midwest. In 1996, Thompson began hosting a second program, a Sunday morning slot on WHO. His cinematic successes brought him notoriety in evangelical circles, and he was much in demand as a speaker among evangelicals, especially in the 1970s and 1980s.

Reference: Randall Balmer, *Mine Eyes Have Seen the Glory: A Journey into the Evangelical Subculture in America,* 3d ed. (2000).

Thompson, Frank C(harles) (1858–1940) Frank C. Thompson was born in Elmira, New York, and studied at Boston University School of Theology. He was licensed as a preacher by the Methodists in 1879 and served a number of congregations, including the Asbury Methodist Church in Rochester, New York. Thompson's most notable contribution to American *EVANGELICALISM was the *Thompson Chain Reference Bible,* which emerged from the glosses in his *Oxford Wide Margin Bible.* The first edition, published by the Chain Reference Bible Publishing Company, appeared in 1908, but an agreement with the B. B. Kirkbride Bible Company of Indianapolis, Indiana, in 1915 increased sales and distribution dramatically. The *Thompson Bible* was revised in 1929 and again in 1934; a concordance, outlines, and maps were added.

Among the most avid admirers of the *Thompson Bible* was *AIMEE SEMPLE MCPHERSON, who offered a warm endorsement for the publisher's advertisements. When Thompson retired to California, he taught at McPherson's *L.I.F.E. BIBLE COLLEGE and held the title of honorary dean.

Thompson Chain Reference Bible. *See* **Thompson, Frank C(harles).**

Tilton, Robert (Gibson) (1946–) One of the most brazen proponents of the so-called *PROSPERITY GOSPEL (the notion that God will reward believers with affluence) in the 1980s and early 1990s, Robert Tilton was born in McKinney, Texas, and attended Cook County Junior College and Texas Technological University. He claimed to be converted by young *EVANGELISTS who visited his home at a time when he was using drugs and his marriage was in trouble. Tilton went on to start Word of Faith Outreach Center in Dallas, Texas, a congregation that grew to approximately eight thousand. His television shows featured stream-of-consciousness preaching, punctuated by what appeared to be sudden messages from the Holy Spirit. He appealed unabashedly for funds, promising blessings proportionate to the size of the gift. An ABC News exposé on November 21, 1991, showed that the envelopes containing letters and prayer requests Tilton had solicited lay in the trash heap after the checks had been removed. One of Tilton's friends from college testified that Tilton had often mimicked revivalists and speculated on how easy it would be to fleece the faithful. The program also presented evidence that money raised for an orphanage in Haiti never reached its destination, while Tilton and his confederates lived in style.

Although Tilton vigorously denied the allegations, the charges prompted investigations from state and federal authorities, including the Federal Bureau of Investigation and the Internal Revenue Service. By October 29, 1993, Tilton's audience had diminished so much that he was forced off the air. Attendance at his church had dropped precipitously, and Tilton filed for divorce from his wife of twenty-five years. In addition, he faced lawsuits from several widows who claimed that Tilton had sent letters promising healing for their already deceased husbands. Tilton filed for divorce from his second wife in November 1995, after a marriage that lasted only twenty-one months.

Reference: John W. Kennedy, "End of the Line for Tilton?" *Christianity Today*, August 1993.

Tom Skinner Associates. *See* **Skinner, Thomas "Tom."**

Tomlinson, A(mbrose) J(essup) (1865–1943) Born in rural Indiana, A. J. Tomlinson became a *COLPORTEUR for the *AMERICAN BIBLE SOCIETY and in the course of his travels in western North Carolina was exposed to holiness teachings and practices. He learned the doctrine of divine healing from a publication written by *CARRIE JUDD MONTGOMERY, and in 1903 he and his family moved from Indiana to North Carolina, where Tomlinson soon became leader of a small band of holiness congregations. When Tomlinson moved on to Cleveland, Tennessee, he persuaded an independent church to affiliate with the North Carolina group, thereby creating—in nascent form, at least—the *CHURCH OF GOD denomination. In 1908, under the ministry of ***G. B.** CASHWELL, recently returned from the *AZUSA STREET REVIVAL, Tomlinson began speaking in *TONGUES, and in 1909 he was chosen general moderator of the fledgling denomination, which became known as the *CHURCH OF GOD (CLEVELAND, TENNESSEE).

Tomlinson steadily assumed more and more power in the denomination, including the authority to appoint pastors. Although he was designated general overseer for life in 1914, Tomlinson was accused of financial mismanagement, tried, and impeached in 1923. He left the denomination to form another group, which eventually became known as the Church of God of Prophecy.

Tomlinson, Homer A(ubrey) (1893–1968) The son of ***A. J.** TOMLINSON, Homer A. Tomlinson initially entered the advertising business and did not become involved in ecclesiastical matters until his father organized a new denomination, eventually known as the Church of God of Prophecy, in 1923. Homer then founded a new congregation in Jamaica, New York, where he was especially effective among immigrant groups.

After his father's death in 1943, Homer struggled with his brother, Milton, for leadership of the denomination. Milton prevailed in court, winning the right to the denomination's properties and trademarks. Like his father before him, Homer organized his followers into another denomination, the Church of God (World Headquarters). He also inherited his father's ambition and flamboyance. He was crowned "King of All Nations of Men in Righteousness" at his denomination's annual convention in 1954, and he ran for president of the United States on the Theocratic Party ticket.

Reference: Homer A. Tomlinson, *The Shout of a King* (1968).

Tongues. *See* **Glossolalia.**

Toronto Airport Christian Fellowship (Toronto, Ontario). *See* **Toronto Blessing.**

Toronto Bible College. *See* **Ontario Bible College and Theological Seminary.**

Toronto Blessing On a Thursday evening, January 20, 1994, Randy Clark, pastor of the *VINEYARD CHRISTIAN FELLOWSHIP in St. Louis, preached a *REVIVAL sermon at a small church called the Toronto Airport Vineyard, near the end of a runway of Pearson International Airport. In the course of the meeting more than one hundred congregants "fell all over the floor under the power of the Holy Spirit, laughing and crying." Clark, who was preaching at the invitation of the congregation's pastor, John Arnott, that night triggered what became known as the Toronto Blessing. Also known as the "laughing *REVIVAL" because many of those under the influence of the Holy Spirit laugh convulsively, the Toronto Blessing is a manifestation of the pentecostal-charismatic movement. Those affected by the *REVIVAL speak in *TONGUES, shake wildly, fall silently to the floor, roll and shake, or generally give the appearance of inebriation. Many claim healing—spiritual, emotional, or physical.

The Toronto Airport Vineyard, the locus of this *REVIVAL, grew rapidly, as word spread across North America and the world (similar to the renown of the *AZUSA STREET REVIVAL). By January 1995, they had purchased new facilities, with seating for more than three thousand, to accommodate large congregations of both the faithful and the curious. The Toronto Blessing, which has spread to other churches around the world, especially in the United Kingdom and such American churches as the Brownsville *ASSEMBLIES OF GOD in Pensacola, Florida, and Harvest Rock Church in Pasadena, California, is very much indebted to *JOHN WIMBER's "signs and wonders" theology. Although the congregation had been affiliated with the *ASSOCIATION OF VINEYARD CHURCHES, it was ousted from the denomination early in December 1995, ostensibly for violation of "Vineyard values" (the terms of the separation were "release and recognition of a different calling" rather than "expulsion"). Early in 1996 the Toronto congregation, which had taken the name Toronto Airport Christian Fellowship after dissolving its ties to the Vineyard movement, led in the formation of a new quasidenomination called Partners in Harvest. Arnott announced in 1999 that God was miraculously transforming dental amalgam into gold fillings. "This is a miracle you don't have to get sick to get," he said.

References: John Arnott, *The Father's Blessing* (1996); James A. Beverley, *Holy Laughter and the Toronto Blessing: An Investigative Report* (1995); idem, "Dental Miracle Reports Draw Criticism," *Christianity Today*, May 24, 1999; Margaret M. Paloma, "The 'Toronto Blessing': Charisma, Institutionalization, and Revival," *Journal for the Scientific Study of Religion*, 36 (1997).

Torrey, Reuben A(rcher) (1856–1928) Reuben A. Torrey, born in Hoboken, New Jersey, was educated at Yale University and Yale Divinity School before being ordained as a Congregationalist minister in 1878 and taking a church in Garrettsville, Ohio. During the academic year 1882–1883, Torrey studied at Leipzig and Erlangen, Germany. Upon his return he assumed the pastorate at Open Door Congregationalist Church in Minneapolis, where he remained until 1886; he then took on the superintendency of the City Missionary Society and the pastorate of the People's Church.

Torrey moved to Chicago in 1889 as superintendent of *D. L. MOODY's Chicago Training Institute (later known as *MOODY BIBLE INSTITUTE). Beginning in 1894, Torrey also served as pastor of the Illinois Street Church (*MOODY CHURCH), holding both positions until 1906, when he surrendered the pulpit and remained at the institute until 1908. Torrey became increasingly active during these years as both an *EVANGELIST and a polemicist on behalf of conservative *EVANGELICALISM. He conducted evangelistic crusades around the world; his 1905 campaign at Royal Albert Hall in London lasted five months.

Torrey founded the Montrose Bible Conference (Montrose, Pennsylvania) in 1908. He accepted the position of dean at the *BIBLE INSTITUTE OF LOS ANGELES (BIOLA) in 1912. He contributed to **THE FUNDAMENTALS* as editor of the final two volumes, continued a broad preaching ministry, and served concurrently as pastor of the Church of the Open Door in Los Angeles, beginning in 1915. In the course of his career Torrey edited two fundamentalist magazines—*The Institute Tie* (Moody) and *The King's Business* (*BIOLA)—and was one of the founders of the *WORLD'S CHRISTIAN FUNDAMENTALIST ASSOCIATION.

Torrey left the deanship at *BIOLA and the pastorate of Church of the Open Door in 1924. He continued as an itinerant preacher and made his home in Biltmore, North Carolina, until his death in 1928.

References: Reuben A. Torrey, *How to Promote and Conduct a Successful Revival* (1901); idem, *The Bible and Its Christ* (1906); idem, *The Person and Work of the Holy Spirit* (1910); idem, *The Christ of the Bible* (1924).

Total Woman, Inc. *See* **Morgan, Marabel (née Hawk).**

Townsend, (William) Cameron (1896–1982) Cameron Townsend, the founder of *WYCLIFFE BIBLE TRANSLATORS and the Summer Institute of Linguistics, became involved with the *STUDENT VOLUNTEER MOVEMENT while a student at Occidental College in Los Angeles. Responding to an appeal from the Bible House of Los Angeles, he sold *BIBLES in Guatemala beginning in 1917, but he became discouraged when he learned that the Cakchiquel Indians could not read Spanish. "If your God is so smart," one of the natives inquired, "why doesn't he speak Cakchiquel?"

Townsend and his wife, Elvira Malmstrom, returned to Guatemala under the auspices of the Central American Mission to work among the Cakchiquels. Although Townsend had no training in linguistics, he proceeded to learn the language and, over the course of a decade, to translate the New Testament into Cakchiquel. In 1934, wanting to expand on the work of translation, Townsend and I. I. Letgers founded Camp Wycliffe in Arkansas, out of which emerged both *WYCLIFFE BIBLE TRANSLATORS and the Summer Institute of Linguistics. By the time of "Uncle Cam's" death in 1982, approximately five thousand missionaries and translators were working around the world under Wycliffe's auspices.

Tozer, A(iden) W(ilson) (1897–1963) A self-educated man, A. W. Tozer was ordained in the *CHRISTIAN AND MISSIONARY ALLIANCE in 1920 and served churches in West Virginia, Ohio, Indiana, and Illinois before becoming pastor of the Avenue Road Alliance Church in Toronto. A vice president of the alliance, he resigned in 1950 to assume the editorship of the *Alliance Weekly* (now *Alliance Life*). A prolific writer with an almost mystical bent, Tozer nudged members of the alliance away from the pentecostal practice of *SPEAKING IN TONGUES with his oft-repeated dictum "Seek not, forbid not."

References: A. W. Tozer, *The Pursuit of God* (1948); idem, *The Knowledge of the Holy* (1961); idem, *The Christian Book of Mystical Verse* (1963); David J. Fant, *A. W. Tozer: A Twentieth Century Prophet* (1964); Edith L. Blumhofer, *Restoring the Faith: The Assemblies of God, Pentecostalism, and American Culture* (1993).

Traditional Values Coalition Founded in 1980 by *LOUIS P. SHELDON, the Traditional Values Coalition claims to articulate a "pro-family" agenda in the political arena. Sheldon, formerly an aide to *PAT ROBERTSON, has been one of the *RELIGIOUS RIGHT's most vociferous opponents of *ABORTION, pornography, and, in particular, civil rights for homosexuals. The organization, with offices in Washington, D.C., and Anaheim, has been effective in lobbying Congress and state legislatures on matters of concern to politically conservative evangelicals. Its sister organization, Traditional Values Coalition Education & Legal Institute, seeks to educate and support "churches in their efforts to restore America's cultural heritage."

Training School for Christian Workers. *See* **Azusa Pacific University.**

Trans World Radio Trans World Radio was founded in 1954 by *PAUL FREED, a *YOUTH FOR CHRIST director in Greensboro, South Carolina, who was concerned about the plight of evangelical Christians in Spain. In 1952, Freed and *BEN ARMSTRONG produced *Banderilla*, a documentary of the persecution these evangelicals were suffering under the right-wing Catholic rule of Francisco Franco. The film helped Freed raise money for a radio station in Tangiers, Morocco, which first sent out its twenty-five-hundred-watt signal on February 22, 1954.

Freed's fund-raising efforts soon allowed the ministry—and the signal—to expand. A fifty-thousand-watt transmitter blanketed Europe and northern Africa, beginning in 1959, broadcasting in more than thirty languages. That same year, however, the Moroccan government forced the station to relocate; it found a new home in Monaco, and the ministry changed its name from Voice of Tangiers to Trans World Radio.

Trans World Radio added a facility in Sri Lanka in 1978 and the following year a station on the island of Bonaire in the Netherlands Antilles. The organization, with headquarters in Cary, North Carolina, claims that its shortwave transmitters on Guam reach over a billion people in Asia, including most of China.

Reference: J. Gordon Melton, Phillip Charles Lucas, and Jon R. Stone, *Prime-Time Religion: An Encyclopedia of Religious Broadcasting* (1997).

Trevecca Nazarene University (Nashville, Tennessee) The Pentecostal Alliance, a Tennessee holiness group led by J. O. McClurkan, founded Trevecca Nazarene University in 1901 under the name Pentecostal Literary and Bible Training School for Christian Workers. In 1910, the curriculum was reorganized into a liberal arts program. At that time, the school took the name Trevecca College for Christian Workers, after a Wesleyan Methodist school established in Wales in the eighteenth century.

Trevecca College moved to east Nashville in 1914. The following year the Pentecostal Alliance merged with the *CHURCH OF THE NAZARENE, and by 1917 the college had become affiliated with the Nazarenes. At the encouragement of the denomination, Trevecca absorbed two additional colleges for financial reasons. In spite of this effort, however, the college still struggled to make ends meet and eventually lost its campus during the Great Depression. Nevertheless, the college held on in temporary facilities, taking the name Trevecca Nazarene College in 1934. A year later, in 1935, Trevecca was able to move onto part of its current campus. Seven years later, the first four-year students graduated.

Since 1969, master's degree programs in education, religion, and organizational management have been added, and the college is now known as Trevecca Nazarene University. The board of trustees is elected by the Southeast Educational Region of the *CHURCH OF THE NAZARENE.

References: *Trevecca Nazarene University Catalog 96–97* (1996); William C. Ringenberg, *The Christian College: A History of Protestant Higher Education in America* (1984); Thomas C. Hunt and James C. Carper, eds., *Religious Higher Education in the United States: A Source Book* (1996).

Triennial Convention Known officially as the General Missionary Convention of the Baptist Denomination in the United States for Foreign Missions, the Triennial Convention, the first national association of Baptists, was gaveled to order in Philadelphia on May 18, 1814. The immediate catalyst was *LUTHER RICE, who had challenged Baptists to organize their efforts in support of *ADONIRAM and *ANN JUDSON, missionaries to India and, later, Burma. The Triennial Convention, which met every three years (hence the name), chose Richard Furman of Charleston, South Carolina, as its first president. The organization also expanded into home missions in 1817 and into education the following year, with the founding of Columbian College (now George Washington University) in Washington, D.C. In 1845, the same year that Baptists in the South separated to form the *SOUTHERN BAPTIST CONVENTION, the Triennial Convention took the name American Baptist Missionary Union. In 1910, the name changed again to American Baptist Foreign Missionary Society.

Reference: William Henry Brackney, *The Baptists* (1988).

Trilateral Commission A major target for premillennialist paranoia, the Trilateral Commission was formed in 1972 by banker David Rockefeller and Zbigniew Brzezinski, who taught in the School of International Affairs at Columbia University. The purpose of the organization was to bring together the political, economic, and intellectual elites (hence, *Tri*lateral) of Europe, Japan, and the United States. One of the early members of the Trilateral Commission was the former governor of Georgia, *JIMMY CARTER, who was recruited in order to expand the organization's base in the South. After his election to the presidency, Carter appointed Brzezinski as one of his top foreign affairs advisors, and others affiliated with the Trilateral Commission assumed policy positions in the Carter administration.

Politically conservative premillennialists seized on the Trilateral Commission as a pernicious force in American foreign policy, one that would introduce alien influences into the United States and subjugate Americans to the machinations of a shadowy network of individuals, bankers, and evil organizations seeking to control the world. Premillennialists viewed Carter's election itself (because his candidacy had been such a long shot) as the result of a larger conspiracy that involved the media. Some conspiracy theorists expanded their target to include the Council on Foreign Relations, and they believed that their suspicions were realized with George Bush's rhetoric about a "*NEW WORLD ORDER" following the collapse of the Soviet Union.

Reference: Paul Boyer, *When Time Shall Be No More: Prophecy Belief in Modern American Culture* (1992).

Trinity Bible College (Ellendale, North Dakota) Founded in 1948 and affiliated with the *ASSEMBLIES OF GOD, Trinity Bible College offers the associate's and bachelor's degrees and enrolls approximately four hundred students. The campus has single-sex and freshmen-only dormitories, and students need special permission to live off-campus. Trinity offers academic programs in religion, fine arts, business, education, and general studies.

Trinity Broadcasting Network (TBN) Trinity Broadcasting Network (TBN), one of *EVANGELICALISM's most successful and far-reaching media enterprises, was founded in 1973 by *PAUL and *JAN CROUCH, with the cooperation of *JIM and *TAMMY FAYE BAKKER. Their first television station was in Santa Ana, California, which remains the headquarters for the network. The programming on TBN is generally pentecostal, but it is also broadly eclectic. Its programs range from *BENNY HINN and *GENE SCOTT to an apologetics talk show, *Reasons to Believe.* Although the décor of its main set in Santa Ana resembles something akin to a cross between trailer park chic and 1930s funeral parlor, TBN has been enormously influential as an outlet for religious and evangelistic programming.

Reference: J. Gordon Melton, Phillip Charles Lucas, and Jon R. Stone, *Prime-Time Religion: An Encyclopedia of Religious Broadcasting* (1997).

Trinity Christian College (Palos Heights, Illinois) Ten local Illinois business people met in 1952 to begin studying the possibility of founding a two-year religious college. Four years later they drafted a constitution and became incorporated as the Trinity Christian College Association, and three years after that the association bought an old golf course for the new campus. They renovated the clubhouse and pro shop to serve as the first buildings and were able to open for classes in the fall of 1959. Thirty-seven students enrolled.

By 1966, the board of trustees began to consider the expansion of Trinity's program to a four-year program. The college introduced a baccalaureate curriculum over the next three years, awarding the first bachelor's degrees in the spring of 1971.

Most students at Trinity Christian College are from the *CHRISTIAN REFORMED CHURCH or *REFORMED CHURCH IN AMERICA. Mindful of the Dutch Reformed heritage of the region, the college has a program in Dutch language, and students can take cultural courses on the Netherlands in cooperation with Dordt College in Iowa. Nonetheless, Trinity remains interdenominational, with students from many Christian groups enrolled. The Presbyterian churches in particular enjoy high representation.

Library archives include a collection of periodicals and curriculum materials to teach grades K–12. The college also maintains two cultural centers that have archives: the Dutch Heritage Center and the Elton Williams Collection on African American history.

References: *Trinity Christian College 1995/96 Catalog* (1995); *Peterson's Choose a Christian College: A Guide to Academically Challenging Colleges Committed to Christ-Centered Campus Life,* 4th ed. (1992).

Trinity College. *See* **Trinity International University.**

Trinity Episcopal School of Ministry (Ambridge, Pennsylvania) The newest Episcopal seminary, Trinity Episcopal School of Ministry was founded in 1975 by a group of clergy and laypeople, including *JOHN GUEST, with a vision to "equip the saints for the work of ministry." *JOHN R. W. STOTT, *J. I. PACKER, and other evangelical Anglican leaders helped write the school's statement of faith, and a retired missionary bishop, Alfred Stanway, was called as the founding dean. Trinity has become an influential center for evangelical theology and teaching within the Episcopal Church.

Trinity Evangelical Divinity School (Deerfield, Illinois) Trinity Evangelical Divinity School emerged in 1963 from a reorganization of Trinity Seminary and Bible College and its relocation from the north side of Chicago to Deerfield, Illinois, in Chicago's northern suburbs. Under the direction of *HARRY L. EVANS, president of both *TRINITY COLLEGE and Trinity Evangelical Divinity School, and with the guidance of *KENNETH S. KANTZER, who left *WHEATON COLLEGE to become dean of the Divinity School, Trinity became one of the leading evangelical seminaries of the 1970s and 1980s. Kantzer assembled a faculty, many of whom were drawn from Wheaton and from *FULLER THEOLOGICAL SEMINARY, who professed unwavering commitment to the doctrine of biblical *INERRANCY. For the seminary's faculty, especially for Kantzer, *D. A. CARSON, and *JOHN D. WOODBRIDGE, *INERRANCY became the touchstone of evangelical orthodoxy.

As Trinity Evangelical Divinity School grew and hewed more and more closely to the Reformed side of evangelical theology, it prompted a theological redirection within its parent denomination, the *EVANGELICAL FREE CHURCH OF AMERICA. Although the Free Church had strong roots in the holiness tradition and in Scandinavian *PIETISM, the faculty and graduates of the seminary gradually forced it toward a kind of rationalistic *FUNDAMENTALISM, which denied ordination for women and tended to attenuate expressions of the Holy Spirit.

Trinity International University (Deerfield, Illinois) Trinity International University traces its history back to 1897. The school was created with the merger of the Norwegian-Danish Free Church Association and the Swedish Evangelical Free Church of America. When these Scandinavian denominations combined as the *EVANGELICAL FREE CHURCH, their *BIBLE INSTITUTES also combined their resources into one school. In 1946, the school, by then known as the Evangelical Free Church Seminary and Bible Institute of Chicago, merged with Trinity Seminary and Bible Institute of Minneapolis, Minnesota. It remained in Chicago, however, until 1965, when it moved to nearby Deerfield, in Chicago's affluent northern suburbs and took the names Trinity College and *TRINITY EVANGELICAL DIVINITY SCHOOL.

*TRINITY EVANGELICAL DIVINITY SCHOOL was the birthplace of the *SOJOURNERS COMMUNITY in the early 1970s, now based in Washington, D.C. *SOJOURNERS, a group of left-wing evangelical activists, are best known for their publication of **SOJOURNERS* magazine. Today, *TRINITY EVANGELICAL DIVINITY SCHOOL offers several master of arts degrees and also has programs in divinity, theology, and religious education. The Divinity School grants doctorates in ministry, education, theological studies, and intercultural studies.

Trinity International University came into being in 1995, when Trinity College and *TRINITY EVANGELICAL DIVINITY SCHOOL of Deerfield, Illinois, merged with Trinity College in Miami. Trinity's Florida campus operates a one-hundred-thousand-watt radio station, WMCU in Miami. Trinity took over the Simon Greenleaf Law School in Anaheim, California, in 1998, renaming it Trinity Law School.

The Deerfield campus is home of Trinity's Center for Bioethics and Human Dignity, which runs an annual international conference as well as sponsoring research projects and educational programs in the area of bioethics. In addition, the center develops a variety of resource materials on the subject, including the journal *Ethics and Medicine.* Trinity also sponsors the Bannockburn Institute for Christianity and Contemporary Culture, a center that hosts conferences, offers courses, and runs programs that impart a biblical perspective to understanding contemporary social issues.

Trinity International University is a member of both the *CHRISTIAN COLLEGE CONSORTIUM and the *COUNCIL OF CHRISTIAN COLLEGES AND UNIVERSITIES. The library's archives include materials from the *EVANGELICAL FREE CHURCH OF AMERICA and the libraries of evangelical scholars *CARL. F. H. HENRY and *WILBUR SMITH. Although Trinity does not permit social *DANCING, its statement of conduct stipulates that during official school breaks, students are not expected to conform to the standards of conduct unless they are representing the school in some capacity.

References: Thomas C. Hunt and James C. Carper, eds., *Religious Higher Education in the United States: A Source Book* (1996); Virginia Lieson Brereton, *Training God's Army: The American Bible School, 1880–1940* (1990).

Trinity Seminary and Bible College. *See* **Trinity International University.**

Trinity Western Seminary (Langley, British Columbia). *See* **Trinity Western University** *and* **Associated Canadian Theological Schools.**

Trinity Western University (Langley, British Columbia) In 1984, Trinity Western College, which had been founded in 1962 as Trinity Junior College, was admitted into regular membership in the Association of Universities and Colleges of Canada, the congress of Canada's internationally recognized degree-granting universities. In October 1985, the British Columbia legislature changed the name to Trinity Western University and further expanded its degree granting powers. Trinity Western University maintains strong ties with its founding denomination, the *EVANGELICAL FREE CHURCH, and a fraternal relationship with that denomination's other school, *TRINITY INTERNATIONAL UNIVERSITY. Trinity Western University's theological school,

Trinity Western Seminary, is part of the *ASSOCIATED CANADIAN THEOLOGICAL SCHOOLS.

Trotman, Dawson (Earle) (1906–1956) Born in Bisbee, Arizona, Dawson Trotman became a Presbyterian after his *CONVERSION, although he withdrew from the Presbyterian Church in 1931 because of its drift toward *MODERNISM. After studying at the *BIBLE INSTITUTE OF LOS ANGELES and at Los Angeles Baptist Seminary, Trotman and his wife, Lila, began an evangelization campaign among the seamen in Los Angeles, one that emphasized the importance of Bible memorization, prayer, and Christian discipleship. The movement expanded and by 1934 was known as *THE NAVIGATORS (it was incorporated under that name in 1943). During World War II, Trotman shifted his energies to military personnel in the United States armed forces and then to university and college campuses after the war.

Trotman's energy and charisma accounted for much of the success and growth of *THE NAVIGATORS. He died suddenly, however, in 1956 after rescuing a swimmer at a Navigators camp at Schroon Lake, New York, in the Adirondacks.

Trotter, Mel(vin) (Ernest) (1870–1940) An alcoholic in his early years, Mel Trotter was converted in 1897 under the preaching of Harry Monroe at Chicago's *PACIFIC GARDEN MISSION. After doing volunteer work at the Mission, he began traveling with Monroe as an *EVANGELIST. They eventually started a city mission in Grand Rapids, Michigan, which later took the name *MEL TROTTER MISSION. Trotter continued as an itinerant preacher and established urban missions in several states, including Michigan, Ohio, Minnesota, and California.

True Love Waits The True Love Waits campaign is an interdenominational program that promotes premarital *CHASTITY. Begun in 1993 by the Southern Baptist Sunday School Board, it enlists the cooperation of twenty-seven other Christian evangelical, fundamentalist, pentecostal, and holiness groups. As many as one million young people in the United States, most of them between eleven and fifteen years old, are thought to have signed the True Love Waits pledge, which reads as follows: "Believing that true love waits, I make a commitment to God, myself, my family, my friends, my future mate, and my future children to be sexually abstinent from this day until the day I enter a biblical marriage relationship."

The target membership is not American teenagers in general, but rather "churched" teenagers already within the conservative Protestant fold. Survey research has shown that sexual activity among "churched" youth increased from the 1960s to the 1980s and then soared to a peak in 1987. Since 1987, although the proportion of sexually active "churched" youth has declined, so has the proportion believing that premarital sexual contact, including intercourse, is "always morally wrong." The True Love Waits campaign thus concentrates on chastity in the individual while cultivating an increased sense of moral commitment and solidarity within the church community. However, the campaign pursues no larger social or political goals; it has stayed out of the sex education controversy in public schools.

The True Love Waits campaign does not exclude teenagers who are already sexually active but rather specifically targets these teenagers by emphasizing chastity rather than virginity. The campaign creates a category of "secondary virginity" that allows—indeed, welcomes—

young people who have been sexually active to alter their behavior.

Truett, George W(ashington) (1867–1944) George W. Truett, one of the most influential leaders of the *SOUTHERN BAPTIST CONVENTION, was reared in rural North Carolina and read widely in the classics of Protestant spirituality. He was converted in 1886 and ordained four years later. At the age of twenty-four he went to *BAYLOR UNIVERSITY, not as a student but as the school's chief financial officer. Within two years the young preacher had erased the school's debt of nearly one hundred thousand dollars, all the while building his reputation among Baptists in Texas.

Truett stayed on at Baylor and earned the bachelor's degree at the same time that he served as pastor of the East Waco Baptist Church. Upon graduation in 1897 he became pastor of the First Baptist Church in Dallas, Texas, where he remained for forty-seven years. Over the course of his tenure the church grew from 715 to 7,804 members. Truett was an eloquent preacher as well as an influential leader in the denomination. He raised prodigious sums of money for Southern Baptist causes and served as president of the convention from 1927 to 1929. One of Truett's most famous sermons, "Baptists and Religious Liberty," was delivered on the steps of the U.S. Capitol on May 16, 1920.

References: George W. Truett, *We Would See Jesus* (1915); idem, *Baptists and Religious Liberty* (1920); idem, *Revival Sermons* (1959); James W. Powhatan, *George W. Truett: A Biography* (1939); Edward L. Queen II, s.v. "George W. Truett," in Charles H. Lippy, ed., *Twentieth-Century Shapers of American Popular Religion* (1989).

Trumbull, Charles G(allaudet) (1872–1941) A renowned leader and promoter of the *KESWICK MOVEMENT in America, Charles G. Trumbull was born in Hartford, Connecticut, and graduated from Yale in 1893. He worked with his father, *HENRY CLAY TRUMBULL, on the *Sunday School Times* publication and succeeded his father as editor in 1903. Charles Trumbull converted to *KESWICK *SANCTIFICATION in 1910 and thereafter became one of the movement's most impassioned *EVANGELISTS, arguing that surrender to the Holy Spirit provided victory over *SIN. His organization, Victorious Life Testimony, held summer conferences at various locations until it settled at Keswick Grove, New Jersey, in 1924.

Trumbull promoted *KESWICK teachings to American and Canadian evangelicals through various media, including the summer conferences, his own *ITINERANCY, and his weekly *SUNDAY SCHOOL lessons. A fervent fundamentalist, Trumbull also wrote a biography of *CYRUS INGERSON SCOFIELD.

Reference: Douglas Frank, *Less Than Conquerors: How Evangelicals Entered the Twentieth Century* (1986).

Trumbull, Henry Clay (1830–1903) One of the pioneers in the *SUNDAY SCHOOL movement, Henry Clay Trumbull attended Stonington Academy and Williston Seminary and then worked for a time for the railroad. He was ordained a Congregationalist minister in 1862 and served as a chaplain in the Union Army during the Civil War, in the course of which he was captured and held prisoner for four months. Following the war he became secretary for the New England department of the *AMERICAN SUNDAY SCHOOL UNION. Through his many publications and through his editorship of the *Sunday School Times*, beginning in 1875, Trumbull urged standardization of *SUNDAY

SCHOOL curricula. His *LYMAN BEECHER Lectures at Yale in 1888 were published as *The Sunday School: Its Origin, Mission, Methods, and Auxiliaries.*

References: Henry Clay Trumbull, *Teaching and Teachers* (1884); idem, *The Sunday School: Its Origin, Mission, Methods, and Auxiliaries* (1888); idem, *How to Deal with Doubts and Doubters* (1903); Philip Eugene Howard, *The Life Story of Henry Clay Trumbull* (1905).

Truth, Sojourner (née Baumfree, Isabella) (c. 1797–1883) An African American itinerant *EVANGELIST and abolitionist, Isabella Baumfree was born into slavery in Ulster County, New York. She was separated from her family and sold twice before the age of twelve. Her master manumitted her in 1827, and she supported herself as a domestic worker in New York City for several years. Responding to a vision from God, Baumfree left New York on June 1, 1843, and began to "travel up an' down the land showin' the people their *SINS an' bein' a sign unto them." About this time God gave her a new name, Sojourner Truth. Although illiterate, Sojourner Truth was a commanding preacher; she quoted Scripture extensively in support of *ABOLITION and women's rights. She met with Abraham Lincoln in 1864, and she was active in the National Freedman's Relief Association after the Civil War.

References: Arthur Huff Fauset, *Sojourner Truth: God's Faithful Pilgrim* (1971); Nell Irvin Painter, *Sojourner Truth: A Life, a Symbol* (1996).

Tuesday Meetings for the Promotion of Holiness Shortly after *SARAH LANKFORD's experience of entire *SANCTIFICATION on May 21, 1835, she began the Tuesday Meetings for the Promotion of Holiness in the home that she and her husband shared with her sister, *PHOEBE PALMER, and her husband in New York City. The Tuesday Meetings, initially open to women only, consisted of Bible study, prayer, and testimonies of people who had been sanctified. The meetings grew in popularity and became a major source for the propagation of holiness ideas. The admission of men to the gatherings spread the ideas further and contributed to the *PRAYER MEETING REVIVAL of 1858. Through the agency of Lankford, Palmer, and others, the Tuesday Meetings also expanded beyond New York City across North America and to Great Britain.

Tyler, Bennet (1783–1858) Born to a poor family in Middlebury, Connecticut, Bennet Tyler was able to attend Yale College where, under the preaching of Yale's president, *TIMOTHY DWIGHT, he experienced an evangelical *CONVERSION in 1802. Tyler studied for the Congregational ministry under Asahel Hooker in Goshen, Connecticut. He was licensed to preach in 1806 and the following year accepted the pastorate of the small Congregational church in South Britain, Connecticut, where he remained until his election to the presidency of Dartmouth College in 1822.

Tyler left Dartmouth in 1828 for the Second Congregational Church in Portland, Maine, where he became embroiled in a theological debate known as the *TYLER-TAYLOR CONTROVERSY. Tyler, one of the last proponents of the *NEW DIVINITY, a system of Calvinist theology that claimed the legacy of *JONATHAN EDWARDS, objected to what he saw as the *LIBERALISM inherent in the writings of *NATHANIEL WILLIAM TAYLOR. "Taylorism," also known as the *NEW HAVEN THEOLOGY, taught that humanity was not, as Calvin has claimed, morally disabled by Adam's *SIN; instead, "sin was in the sinning." Each transgression made an individual culpable before God, not the *SIN we inherited from Adam.

Taylor's views, edging toward *ARMINIANISM, comported better with the cultural climate of antebellum America than those of Tyler and his confrères, who tried to resurrect the writings of Edwards and the Puritans. Tyler and other conservatives sought to combat the *NEW HAVEN THEOLOGY by forming a new seminary in 1833. The Theological Institute of Connecticut (later renamed Hartford Theological Seminary and known today as the Hartford Seminary) was opened in East Windsor, Connecticut (Edwards's birthplace), and later moved to Hartford. Tyler served as president of the seminary from 1834 until his death.

References: Bennet Tyler, *Letters on the Origin and Progress of the New Haven Theology* (1837); idem, *New England Revivals* (1846); Allen C. Guelzo, *Edwards on the Will* (1989).

Tyler-Taylor Controversy The Tyler-Taylor Controversy of the 1830s pitted *BENNET TYLER, pastor of the Second Congregational Church of Portland, Maine, and an advocate of the *NEW DIVINITY, against *NATHANIEL WILLIAM TAYLOR of Yale, who propounded a new understanding of the notion of *SIN. "Taylorism," also known as the *NEW HAVEN THEOLOGY, taught that humanity's culpability before God should be reckoned in individual acts of transgression rather than as something inherited from Adam. Tyler and Taylor engaged in a paper war over the issue, and Tyler eventually formed the Theological Institute of Connecticut (now the Hartford Seminary Foundation) to counteract the *NEW HAVEN THEOLOGY.

Tyndale College and Seminary. *See* **Ontario Bible College and Ontario Theological Seminary.**

Tyndale House Publishers Tyndale House Publishers was founded in 1962 by Kenneth N. Taylor, who had been unable to find a publisher for his paraphrases of the *BIBLE. Taylor, a graduate of *WHEATON COLLEGE, had begun paraphrasing the *BIBLE in 1954 into more contemporary English for the benefit of his ten children. By 1962, Taylor and his wife, Margaret, used their own money to publish *Living Letters,* Taylor's paraphrase of the New Testament epistles. The book became enormously popular when the *BILLY GRAHAM EVANGELISTIC ASSOCIATION purchased large quantities and gave them away as promotional incentives during their crusade telecasts.

Tyndale House (named after the sixteenth-century translator of the *BIBLE, William Tyndale) soon grew too large for Taylor's home in suburban Chicago. The press, now located in Carol Stream, Illinois, published the remainder of Taylor's paraphrases as well as the completed project, called **THE LIVING BIBLE,* which has sold more than forty million copies in North America alone. In addition to various versions of the *BIBLE, Tyndale House publishes an extensive list of books by evangelical authors.

Tyng, Stephen Higginson, Jr. (1839–1898) Son and namesake of a prominent leader of evangelical Episcopalians, Stephen Higginson Tyng Jr. graduated from Williams College in 1858 and studied theology at the Protestant Episcopal Seminary of Virginia before the outbreak of the Civil War cut short his education. He was nevertheless ordained a deacon in the Episcopal Church in 1861 and served as an assistant to his father at St. George's Church in New York City. Two years later Tyng was ordained a priest and became rector of the Church of the Mediator, also in New York. Tyng, who shared his father's convictions about *EVANGELICALISM and about social reform efforts directed toward the poor, started a new parish in New York, the Church of the Holy Trinity, following the Civil War. He became enamored (like his father) of dispensational *PREMILLENNIALISM and organized the first International Prophetic Conference in 1878. The conference was held in the younger Tyng's church, and his father delivered the opening address.

Reference: Stephen Higginson Tyng Jr., *He Will Come* (1877).

Tyng, Stephen Higginson, Sr. (1800–1885) Born in Newburyport, Massachusetts, to an elite New England family, Stephen Higginson Tyng graduated from Harvard College in 1817 and began a career in business. His evangelical *CONVERSION the following year, however, prompted a change in vocation. He began studying theology in August 1819 under *ALEXANDER VIETS GRISWOLD in Bristol, Rhode Island; Tyng was ordained a deacon in the Episcopal Church in 1821 and a priest in 1824. He went on to serve prominent parishes in the District of Columbia, Maryland, Philadelphia, and New York City.

An impassioned and dramatic preacher—St. George's Church in New York became known as "Tyng's Theatre"—Tyng was an outspoken leader of the evangelical Episcopalians. He resisted the incursion of Tractarianism into the Episcopal Church, and he was active in the *SUNDAY SCHOOL movement, missions work, and antislavery societies. Tyng supported the Union cause during the Civil War. Following the war, he resisted the incursions of theological *LIBERALISM and became a foe of Darwinism. Although he never abandoned his vision for social amelioration, Tyng advocated dispensational *PREMILLENNIALISM and participated in the prophecy conference movement.

References: Stephen Higginson Tyng, *Lectures on Law and the Gospel* (1832); idem, *The Connexion Between Early Religious Instruction and Mature Piety* (1837); idem, *Forty Years Experience in Sunday Schools* (1860).

Tyson, Tommy (1922–) Born in Farmville, North Carolina, and educated at Duke University and Duke Divinity School, Tommy Tyson was converted in 1947 and soon thereafter pursued a call to preach. After six years as pastor in the North Carolina conference of the United Methodist Church, Tyson was named an *EVANGELIST under the conference's auspices. His Spirit *BAPTISM in 1952 and his continued affiliation with the United Methodists made him one of the leaders of the *CHARISMATIC RENEWAL MOVEMENT. He has worked for ecumenical causes, and from 1965 until 1968 he was director of spiritual life at *ORAL ROBERTS UNIVERSITY.

■ ■ ■

Union Gospel Mission (Akron, Ohio). *See* **McKinney, Claude A(dams).**

Union University (Jackson, Tennessee) Union University began in 1823 with the founding of a boy's school, Jackson Male Academy, in Jackson, Tennessee. Two years later, the school received a charter from the state legislature.

The North Carolina Compact, which ceded Tennessee to the United States government, had provided for the establishment of two colleges within the new territory, one in the east and one in the west. West Tennessee College was chartered by legislative enactment in 1844. At that time, all of the Jackson Male Academy's property was given over to the trustees of the new college.

In 1874, West Tennessee College was offered to the Tennessee Baptists, who reopened it as an academy. A year later, however, the school was rechartered and given the new name Southwestern Baptist University. The college became known as Union University in 1907; in 1925, the board of trustees deeded all property to the Tennessee Baptist Convention.

In 1975, Union moved to a new campus in Jackson, Tennessee, where most of the new physical plant is part of a single "shopping center" complex, with classes and academic and student services all housed under one roof. The university has offered master's degree programs in business and education since the early 1990s. Although Union does not condone social *DANCING, it does allow fraternities and sororities, and in fact, there are six Greek groups on campus.

References: *Union University 1996–97 Academic Catalog* (1996); Thomas C. Hunt and James C. Carper, eds., *Religious Higher Education in the United States: A Source Book* (1996).

United Baptist Bible Training School. *See* **Atlantic Baptist University.**

United Christian Endeavor Society. *See* **Christian Endeavor** *and* **Clark, Francis E(dward).**

United College of Gordon and Barrington (Wenham, Massachusetts). *See* **Gordon College.**

United Evangelical Church. *See* **Evangelical Congregational Church.**

United Mennonite Brethren of North America. *See* **Fellowship of Evangelical Bible Churches.**

United Methodist Church. *See* **Methodism.**

United Missionary Church. *See* **Missionary Church.**

United States Christian Commission The United States Christian Commission was organized in New York City on November 14, 1861, during a convention of *YMCA delegates from across the North. The new organization, chaired by *GEORGE HAY STUART, a lay Presbyterian and philanthropist, set as its goal "the spiritual good of the soldiers in the army, and incidentally their intellectual improvement and social and physical comfort." From a core of twelve men, the Commission grew to nearly five thousand delegates, lay and clerical, who took it upon themselves to provide religious and charitable assistance to the Union Army during the Civil War. They preached 55,304 sermons, conducted 77,744 prayer meetings, and wrote countless letters on behalf of men within the Union ranks who were sick or wounded. They tended the sick, buried the dead, and distributed millions of *BIBLES, hymnals, tracts, and library books to Union soldiers. The Commission's diet kitchen program, headed by Annie Wittenmyer, staved off malnutrition for countless wounded soldiers. The organization collected and dispersed over $6 million over the course of the war, and the United States Christian Commission represented an extraordinary venture of nineteenth-century interdenominational benevolence.

Reference: James Moorhead, *American Apocalypse: Yankee Protestants and the Civil War, 1860–1869* (1978).

Universal Fellowship of Metropolitan Community Churches The Universal

Fellowship of Metropolitan Community Churches traces its history to a gathering of twelve worshipers in Huntington Park, California, in October 1968. *TROY PERRY, who had been excommunicated from the *CHURCH OF GOD (ANDERSON, INDIANA) for his homosexuality, wanted a religious gathering that would be tolerant and inclusive. Within a year the gathering had grown large enough to fill a Los Angeles theater. By 1996, membership in the denomination stood at thirty-two thousand in the United States and forty-six thousand worldwide. Its largest congregation is the Cathedral of Hope in Dallas, Texas.

Reference: John Dart, "Gay and Mainline," *Christian Century*, March 21–28, 2001.

University of Sioux Falls (Sioux Falls, South Dakota) In 1872, pastors and delegates from the nine Baptist churches in the Dakota Territory assembled in Vermillion for the first meeting of the Territory's Baptist Association. At that convocation, the members adopted a resolution to begin to take steps to establish a religious school. Classes started at the Dakota Collegiate Institute eleven years later; the school first used the basement of the First Baptist Church in Sioux Falls. That fall, land was selected for a campus site along the pioneer Old Yankton Trail. By 1885, the first building was completed. That same year, the school was also reorganized as Sioux Falls University, marking the beginning of the transition to a full baccalaureate program. The first four-year class graduated in 1904, but the new school continued to run its academy until 1925.

When *DES MOINES UNIVERSITY closed in 1929, Sioux Falls University assumed control of that school's records and materials. In 1931, it merged with another school, Grand Island of Nebraska, and became known as Sioux Falls College. At that time the Baptist State Convention of North and South Dakota, Iowa, Nebraska, and Minnesota passed a resolution recognizing the college as denominationally affiliated and promising it financial support; this resolution was reaffirmed in 1956. Throughout the 1970s the college developed increasing ties to North American Baptist Seminary in Valley Stream, South Dakota, and in 1994, the board of trustees voted to change the name of the school to University of Sioux Falls, in recognition of its development and plans for further growth. The school now offers master's degrees in business administration and education.

Although an American Baptist institution, the University of Sioux Falls is open to students of all creeds and denominations. Furthermore, the school is arguably located on the more liberal end of the evangelical spectrum with regard to behavioral standards. Although alcohol is forbidden, the use of tobacco is not regulated at all. The university sponsors social *DANCING, and formal chapel services are held only once a week. Most important is the fact that participation in religious life is not mandatory. The policy on spiritual life reads: "All students are challenged to consider the importance of spiritual life but participation in spiritual life programming is a matter of personal choice."

References: *University of Sioux Falls 1995–1997 Catalog* (1995); *Peterson's Choose a Christian College: A Guide to Academically Challenging Colleges Committed to Christ-Centered Campus Life*, 4th ed. (1992).

Upham, Thomas C(ogswell) (1799–1872) Thomas C. Upham, born in Deerfield, New Hampshire, graduated from Dartmouth College in 1818, having experienced a spiritual awakening there three years earlier. He attended *ANDOVER THEOLOGICAL SEMINARY, whereupon he became an associate pastor of the Congregational church at Rochester, New Hampshire, in 1823. Two years later, he accepted an appointment to the faculty at Bowdoin College, where he remained until his retirement in 1867.

Upham, a philosopher, published *Elements of Intellectual Philosophy* in 1826, which became a standard introductory textbook. His *Philosophical and Practical Treatise on the Will,* which appeared in 1834, drew on the works of *JONATHAN EDWARDS and Thomas Reid and offered a disquisition on the subject from the perspective of *SCOTTISH COMMON SENSE REALISM. Two years later, Upham published *The Manual of Peace,* offering biblical and philosophical arguments for pacifism and urging a "congress of nations" to foster an end to belligerence.

Upham visited New York City in December 1839 and sat in on the *TUESDAY MEETING FOR THE PROMOTION OF HOLINESS, which to that point had been open only to women. Upham's wife, Phebe Lord Upham, had been influenced by a visit to the *TUESDAY MEETING earlier that year, and her husband was curious about this talk of entire *SANCTIFICATION. Upham soon had his own experience of *SANCTIFICATION and became one of the principal apologists for the *HOLINESS MOVEMENT, connecting contemporary manifestations with earlier mystics, including Madame Guyon, a French Quietist.

Upham continued a prodigious output of books throughout his life, including works on psychology and theology. He supported missionary causes and the *TEMPERANCE movement, and worked for the abolition of capital punishment.

References: Thomas C. Upham, *Elements of Intellectual Philosophy* (1826); idem, *The Manual of Peace* (1836); idem, *Mental Philosophy* (1841); idem, *Principles of the Interior and Hidden Life, Designed Particularly for the Consideration of Those Who are Seeking Assurance of Faith and Perfect Love* (1843); idem, *Life of Faith* (1845); idem, *Life and Religious Opinions and Experience of Madame de La Mothe Guyon* (1846).

Urban Alternative, The. *See* **Evans, Anthony "Tony."**

Urban Awakening. *See* **Prayer Meeting Revival.**

Urbana. *See* **InterVarsity Christian Fellowship.**

Utley, Uldine (Maybelle) (1912–?) Born in Durant, Oklahoma, and converted at the age of nine at a *REVIVAL in Fresno, California, Uldine Utley's decision to preach came after she reported seeing a vision of Jesus standing within an unfolding red rose. She had no formal education but was known to hold an audience spellbound from the time of her first public sermon in 1923, at the age of eleven. Utley wore a white pulpit dress and carried a large edition of the *BIBLE, a pose of childhood innocence in an era when many preachers excoriated urban women for their "loose" morals. At the age of twelve, Utley began publication of *Petals from the Rose of Sharon,* a magazine that included sermon reprints and reports of the crusades she led throughout the United States. From 1926 until 1928, the teenaged Utley appeared at a series of *REVIVALS in New York City. Utley preached at Madison Avenue Baptist Church, Fifth Avenue Presbyterian Church, and Calvary Baptist Church, the home of her mentor, the noted fundamentalist *JOHN ROACH STRATTON. In addition, under the sponsorship of the Evangelistic Committee of New York City, Utley held *REVIVAL services on a platform during lunch hour on Wall Street, at Carnegie Hall and in Madison Square Garden, and in gospel tents in Brooklyn, the Bronx, and Queens. Utley continued touring the United States until her career as child evangelist ended with her 1937 marriage to Eugene Langkop.

Reference: Uldine Utley, *Why I Am a Preacher* (1931).

Utterbach, Sarah **(1937–)** Sarah Utterbach, one of only a few African American women in religious broadcasting, was born into a ghetto in Norfolk, Virginia. She managed to escape poverty but found herself one day on the balcony of a high-rise apartment, contemplating suicide. Instead, she rededicated her life to Christ. She and her husband, Clinton Utterbach, began a Bible study and then enrolled at *KENNETH HAGIN's Rhema Bible Training Center in Tulsa, Oklahoma. In 1980, the Utterbachs founded Redeeming Love Christian Center in Nanuet, New York, and the following year went on the radio with *The Word Alive.* The ministry publishes *Horizons Unlimited,* a quarterly magazine, and the radio program is now called *Listen to Jesus.*

Reference: J. Gordon Melton, Phillip Charles Lucas, and Jon R. Stone, *Prime-Time Religion: An Encyclopedia of Religious Broadcasting* (1997).

■ ■ ■

Valdez, A. C., Sr. **(1896–1988)** A. C. Valdez Sr. was reared in a Roman Catholic household that had strong affinities with Franciscan spirituality, including a belief in *GLOSSOLALIA. He and his family attended the *AZUSA STREET REVIVAL in Los Angeles, and A. C. Valdez was ordained in 1916, thereby beginning a long career as a pentecostal leader. He preached around the world, often with his son, A. C. Valdez Jr., and the two men also were leaders of the Milwaukee (Wisconsin) Evangelistic Temple. The senior Valdez founded a periodical, *Evangelistic Times,* in 1958 and in 1963 cooperated with *GORDON LINDSAY to form the Full Gospel Fellowship of Churches and Ministers International.

Reference: A. C. Valdez Sr., *Fire on Azusa Street* (1980).

Van Cott, Margaret Ann Newton "Maggie" **(1830–1914)** Born in New York City and reared as an Episcopalian, Maggie Van Cott became the first American woman licensed to preach by the Methodist Episcopal Church. Van Cott had an evangelical *CONVERSION during the *URBAN AWAKENING of 1857–1858 and began attending the Duane Street Methodist Church. Only after her husband's death in 1866, however, did Van Cott transfer her membership, whereupon she became a leader of the Five Points Mission in a slum area, a mission begun by *PHOEBE PALMER. In 1868, Van Cott's success prompted an invitation to lead *REVIVAL services at the Methodist church in Durham, New York.

Van Cott was granted an exhorter's license in 1868; the following year she was given a local preacher's license by the Stone Ridge Methodist Episcopal Church, Ellenville, New York. (Only one other woman, Emma Richardson, of Canada, had been similarly licensed, in 1864.) Though never formally ordained, Van Cott supplied pulpits and traveled extensively throughout the course of a career that exceeded thirty years. She retired in 1902.

Van Impe, Jack (Leo) (1931–) A man of Belgian heritage who was baptized and reared as a Roman Catholic, Jack Van Impe was born in Freeport, Michigan, and moved with his family to Detroit in 1933, where his father supplemented his automobile worker's wages by performing as a musician in Belgian-American taverns. At an early age, Jack played the accordion in these beer gardens. His father's evangelical *CONVERSION in 1943, however, had a profound affect on Jack. He, too, was converted. Jack joined the Liberal Avenue Baptist Church and attended Detroit Bible College, where he graduated in 1951.

Van Impe was ordained as an independent Baptist minister and soon put his musical talents to work at *YOUTH FOR CHRIST gatherings. As a missionary to Belgium with a *YOUTH FOR CHRIST team, Van Impe met and eventually married *REXELLA SHELTON, and they became a popular musical and evangelistic team. Van Impe, who has memorized long passages of Scripture and is sometimes known as "The Walking Bible," gradually dropped the musical component of his appearances and began to concentrate on preaching, especially on prophetic and apocalyptic texts. He established Jack Van Impe Crusades, Inc., based in Royal Oak, Michigan, in 1970 and has expanded his reach to radio and to television.

References: Jack Van Impe, *Israel's Final Holocaust* (1979); idem, *11:59 . . . and Counting!* (1987); Roger F. Campbell, *They Call Him the Walking Bible: The Story of Dr. Jack Van Impe* (1988).

Van Impe, Rexella (née Shelton) (1932–) Born and reared in Pontiac, Michigan, Rexella Shelton was baptized at the age of twelve and was active in the music program of First Baptist Church. She studied for a year at *BOB JONES UNIVERSITY and met *JACK VAN IMPE at a *YOUTH FOR CHRIST function. The couple married in 1952 and formed an evangelistic troupe, Ambassadors for Christ. In 1970, they reorganized as Jack Van Impe Crusades, based in Royal Oak, Michigan. Jack did most of the preaching, emphasizing prophetic themes, and Rexella provided the music. The two moved into television, *Jack Van Impe Presents!*, in 1980. Rexella Van Impe, dubbed the "First Lady of Sacred Music," would open with a musical rendition, chat briefly with her husband, and then give way to his meditation about the biblical implications of some contemporary issue.

Reference: J. Gordon Melton, Phillip Charles Lucas, and Jon R. Stone, *Prime-Time Religion: An Encyclopedia of Religious Broadcasting* (1997).

Van Kampen, Robert (1938–1999) An evangelical financier and biblical scholar, Robert Van Kampen was born in Evergreen Park, Illinois, and graduated from *WHEATON COLLEGE in 1960, whereupon he joined the John Nuveen investment company in Chicago. He succeeded in both the real estate and the investment businesses and used some of his considerable wealth to pursue his avocation, a collection of *BIBLES and biblical manuscripts, which he housed in what he called a Scriptorium, a museum, library, and research center founded in 1994 near his home in Grand Haven, Michigan. Van Kampen himself was particularly interested in *ESCHATOLOGY, a study of the *END TIMES.

Van Til, Cornelius (1895–1987) Cornelius Van Til, an influential apologist among Reformed evangelicals, was born in Grootegast, the Netherlands, and emigrated to the United States with his family in 1905. He graduated from *CALVIN COL-

LEGE and *CALVIN THEOLOGICAL SEMINARY, schools affiliated with the *CHRISTIAN REFORMED CHURCH, Van Til's denomination. He also studied at Princeton Theological Seminary and Princeton University. Van Til was ordained in 1927 and taught briefly at Princeton Seminary before joining *J. GRESHAM MACHEN's revolt from Princeton to form *WESTMINSTER THEOLOGICAL SEMINARY and the *ORTHODOX PRESBYTERIAN CHURCH.

Van Til is famous for "presuppositionalism," which he derived from some combination of Abraham Kuyper, Herman Bavinck, and *B. B. WARFIELD. Van Til held that believers must presuppose the triune God, knowing full well that nonbelievers will find this presupposition preposterous. He asserted that the *BIBLE, God's special revelation, was the beginning of all philosophical inquiries about God, and that believers should be unapologetic about using Scripture as their point of departure.

Reference: Cornelius Van Til, *The Defense of the Faith* (1955); John M. Frame, *Cornelius Van Til: An Analysis of His Thought* (1995).

Vancouver Bible Training School (Vancouver, British Columbia) Organized in 1918, the Vancouver Bible Training School was the first *BIBLE INSTITUTE in western Canada. It drew students from a variety of denominational backgrounds, including Baptists, Presbyterians, Anglicans, and *PLYMOUTH BRETHREN, among others. Under the long-term leadership of Walter Ellis, who served as principal from 1918 until 1944, the school trained its students for missionary work (both home and foreign missions), for children's ministries, and for lay leadership. In addition to its classes, the Vancouver Bible Training School also conducted missions conferences, *KESWICK "deeper life" conferences, and various lectures for the public. It functioned, then, as a kind of fulcrum for evangelical activity in British Columbia.

Reference: Robert K. Burkinshaw, "Conservative Evangelicalism in the Twentieth-Century 'West': British Columbia and the United States," in George A. Rawlyk and Mark A. Noll, eds., *Amazing Grace: Evangelicalism in Australia, Britain, Canada, and the United States* (1993).

Vanhoozer, Kevin J(on) (1957–) Kevin J. Vanhoozer graduated from *WESTMONT COLLEGE and *WESTMINSTER THEOLOGICAL SEMINARY. He earned his doctorate at Cambridge University and landed his first teaching job at *TRINITY EVANGELICAL DIVINITY SCHOOL. From there he accepted a post at the University of Edinburgh but returned to Trinity in 1998 as research professor of systematic theology. Vanhoozer regards himself as an expert on postmodernism, which he believes opens the door for a serious reconsideration of theology. Postmodernism's repudiation of Enlightenment rationalism, he argues, should force evangelicals to rethink their infatuation with propositional truth, which itself is an Enlightenment construct. Vanhoozer, a gifted pianist, uses music as an example: "Brahms says a lot, but if you try to sum it up in a proposition, the way we often try to sum up the *BIBLE in a proposition, you lose so much."

References: Kevin J. Vanhoozer, *Is There Meaning in This Text?: The Bible, the Reader, and the Morality of Literary Knowledge* (1998); Tim Stafford, "Kevin Vanhoozer: Creating a Theological Symphony," *Christianity Today,* February 8, 1999.

Venn, Henry (1724–1797) Born in Surrey, England, and educated at Cambridge, Henry Venn was ordained in the Church of England in 1749. After serving as curate in

West Horsley and Clapham, he went to Huddersfield as vicar in 1759, where he remained until 1771, moving on to Yelling for the remainder of his career. Venn was friendly with such important evangelicals as *JOHN WESLEY and *GEORGE WHITEFIELD; his preaching was extemporaneous and evangelical. His devotional guide, *The Complete Duty of Man*, published in 1763, became quite popular among evangelicals and was meant to replace the enormously successful *The Whole Duty of Man*, which had been published anonymously.

References: Henry Venn, *The Complete Duty of Man* (1763); Kenneth Hylson-Smith, *Evangelicals in the Church of England, 1734–1984* (1989).

Vincent, John Heyl (1832–1920) A man who believed fervently in the importance of religious education, John Heyl Vincent was born in Tuscaloosa, Alabama, and was ordained a Methodist elder in 1857. He organized the first Sunday School Teacher's Institute in 1861 and five years later was appointed the general agent of the Methodist Episcopal Sunday School Union. Vincent was always looking for ways to improve religious instruction. He wrote *SUNDAY SCHOOL materials, introduced the idea of "lesson leaves" as a pedagogical tool, and, most important, was the cofounder, with Lewis Miller, of the *CHAUTAUQUA INSTITUTION in 1874, the most extensive lay education movement in American history.

Reference: L. H. Vincent, *John Heyl Vincent: A Biographical Sketch* (1925).

Vineyard Christian Fellowship In July 1974, Kenn Gullicksen, who had been reared a Lutheran, founded the first Vineyard congregation. Gullicksen had been ordained by *CALVARY CHAPEL in 1971, led a ministry in El Paso, Texas, and returned to Costa Mesa, California. He traces the origins of Vineyard to a meeting of five people in Chuck Girard's house, which soon expanded. "I played guitar and sat on a stool and led some worship and taught the *BIBLE," he explained later, "answered questions in homes, and at the end invited anyone who wanted to receive Christ to come for prayer, which they did in droves." Weekly attendance soon numbered into the thousands, and a half-dozen other Vineyards were formed.

The other strand of Vineyard Christian Fellowship history dates to October 1976 and a home fellowship conducted by Carol Wimber, wife of *JOHN WIMBER, then pastor of *CALVARY CHAPEL in Yorba Linda, California. As the group began more and more to emphasize spiritual gifts, what *JOHN WIMBER called "Signs and Wonders," the head of *CALVARY CHAPEL, *CHUCK SMITH, became more and more uneasy. Wimber left the *CALVARY CHAPEL umbrella in 1982 to join the group of six Vineyard churches, and Gullicksen quickly surrendered the reins of leadership to Wimber. In 1985, the *ASSOCIATION OF VINEYARD CHURCHES was formed, with Wimber's congregation in Anaheim at the head of the movement. By 1997, over four hundred congregations were associated with Vineyard in the United States and nearly two hundred more around the world.

Reference: Donald E. Miller, *Reinventing American Protestantism: Christianity in the New Millennium* (1997).

Voice of Calvary Ministries Voice of Calvary Ministries is the name of two evangelical organizations begun by *JOHN M. PERKINS, an African American, in his home state of Mississippi. Both are devoted to *EVANGELISM, social amelioration, and racial reconciliation. The first was established in Mendenhall shortly after Perkins returned to Mississippi from California in 1960. Perkins shifted his base of operations to Jackson, the state capital, in 1978. A new organization there took the name Voice of Calvary Ministries, while the group in Mendenhall adopted the name *MENDENHALL MINISTRIES.

References: John Perkins, *Let Justice Roll Down* (1976); Randall Balmer, *Mine Eyes Have Seen the Glory: A Journey into the Evangelical Subculture in America,* 3d ed. (2000).

Voice of Healing. *See* **Lindsay, Gordon.**

Voice of Tangiers. *See* **Trans World Radio.**

Volf, Miroslav (1956–) A professor of theology at Yale Divinity School, Miroslav Volf was born in Osijek (now in Serbia), the son of a pentecostal pastor. He earned the master of divinity degree from *FULLER THEOLOGICAL SEMINARY and the doctorate from the University of Tübingen. Volf, who has been called the "Croation Theology Wonder," describes his theology as "classical Protestant Christianity, with a dose of Anabaptist sensibilities."

References: Miroslav Volf, *Work in the Spirit: Toward a Theology of Work* (1991); idem, *Exclusion and Embrace: A Theological Exploration of Identity, Otherness, and Reconciliation* (1996); idem, *After Our Likeness: The Church as the Image of the Trinity* (1998).

■ ■ ■

Walker, David (Davillo) "Little David" (1934–) A son of itinerant *EVANGELISTS, David Walker claimed a call to preach at the age of nine. His parents had been healed—his mother of cancer, his father of burns—and David sought healing for himself of poisonous snakebites and eye infection that had led to blindness. His healing and Spirit *BAPTISM came after three days of fasting prayer.

At the age of nine, "Little David" Walker preached his first sermon in Colton, California, and then embarked on a preaching career that took him from Mexico to Paris to London for a two-week *REVIVAL campaign at the Royal Albert Hall. He began a church in Lansing, Michigan, at the age of seventeen and in 1958 joined with *R. W. CULPEPPER, another healing *EVANGELIST. In 1976, he was ordained by the *ASSEMBLIES OF GOD.

Walker, Samuel (1714–1761) Born in Exeter, England, on the same day as *GEORGE WHITEFIELD, Samuel Walker graduated from Oxford in 1736, was ordained in the Church of England the following year, and became the curate of Truro in 1746, where he remained for the balance of his career. Walker experienced an evangelical *CONVERSION in 1749, whereupon his preaching took on a new urgency. He denounced frivolity and the lack of Sunday observance, and soon the entire town, it seemed, attended his preaching. In 1754, amid a spiritual *REVIVAL in Truro, Walker set up small-group meetings, similar to pietist conventicles and to Methodist class meetings, for prayer and spiritual nurture. Walker, a loyal Anglican who was acquainted with both *CHARLES and *JOHN WESLEY, urged the latter not to separate from the Church of England and expressed his strong reservations about Wesley's use of itinerant lay preachers. Walker's ministry was marked by his sermons; Charles Simeon, a fellow evangelical, considered them "the best in the English language."

References: Samuel Walker, *The Christian* (1755); idem, *Fifty-two Sermons* (1763); G. C. B. Davies, *The Early Cornish Evangelicals 1735–60: A Study of Walker of Truro and Others* (1951).

Wallis, Jim (1948–) Born into a *PLYMOUTH BRETHREN household outside of Detroit, Jim Wallis was "*BORN AGAIN" at age six and for several years reflected the evangelical, patriotic values of his parents. At age thirteen, however, as he recalled in his autobiography *Revive Us Again: A Sojourner's Story,* "the world I had grown up in went sour on me." His family moved to Southfield, an upper-middle-class suburb, and Wallis became sullen and withdrawn, uncomfortable with the accouterments of his affluent surroundings.

In 1967, the summer of racial disturbances in Detroit, Wallis began to ask questions of his evangelical church and parents. His search led him into Detroit, where he met African American congregations of *PLYMOUTH BRETHREN. "I was beginning to see," he recalled later, "that to stand with those who suffered I would have to shed myself of the assumptions of privilege and comfort on which I had been raised." Wallis's growing impatience with what he believed was the hypocrisy of *EVANGELICALISM, especially on the issue of race, led to a break with the church over the Vietnam War, which Wallis deemed an extension of America's racism and its callousness toward the poor. As a student at Michigan State University, Wallis led protests against American policies in Southeast Asia, but as the antiwar fervor began to dissipate early in the 1970s, Wallis returned to the *BIBLE. In the Sermon on the Mount, Wallis found a biblical warrant for his own concerns about justice, and in the twenty-fifth chapter of Matthew, he "was deeply struck by a God who had taken up residence among the poor, the oppressed, the outcasts."

Seeking to deepen his understanding of theology, Wallis enrolled at *TRINITY EVANGELICAL DIVINITY SCHOOL in the fall of 1970, a seminary of the *EVANGELICAL FREE CHURCH OF AMERICA located in the affluent Bannockburn section of Deerfield, Illinois. There, amid a climate of theological conservativism, Wallis nevertheless found a handful of kindred spirits interested in "recovering the prophetic biblical tradition, the authentic evangelical message, and applying it to our historical situation." The group organized as the People's Christian Coalition, which in turn would form the core of what would eventually become the *SOJOURNERS Fellowship. At the seminary, however, this "radical discipleship" met with resistance from administration, faculty, even fellow students. Wallis and his confrères became known as the *BANNOCKBURN SEVEN; they conducted demonstrations, passed out leaflets on campus, and conducted forums on such issues as racism, the war in Vietnam, militarism, and discrimination against women.

While attempting to survive various attempts by the seminary to expel them, Wallis and others began to explore connections with other radical evangelicals. During the summer of 1971, they edited and published the first issue of the *Post-American,* a sixteen-page tabloid so named, Wallis recounted, because it "tried to put forward a Christian faith that broke free of the prevailing American civil religion." As the *Post-American* began to appear quarterly, people involved in its production gradually lost interest in the seminary and relocated to form a Christian community among the poor in the Rogers Park section of Chicago.

Wallis and the *Post-American* relocated to a poor neighborhood in Washington, D.C., in the fall of 1975. Both the community and the magazine took the name **SOJOURNERS*. Wallis, editor of the magazine, also maintains a demanding schedule of travel and lectures; he also serves as leader of *CALL TO RENEWAL, an organization that offers an alternative religious activism to the agenda of the *RELIGIOUS RIGHT. Under Wallis's direction, **SOJOURNERS* magazine has reflected an eclectic mix of theology and spirituality, ranging from Dorothy Day and Thomas Merton to Dietrich Bonhoeffer, Jacques Ellul, and John Howard Yoder.

References: Jim Wallis, *Agenda for Biblical People* (1976); idem, *The Call to Conversion* (1981); idem, *Revive Us Again: A Sojourner's Story* (1983); idem, *The Soul of Politics: A Practical and Prophetic Vision for Change* (1994); Randall Balmer, s.v. "Jim Wallis," in Charles H. Lippy, ed., *Twentieth-Century Shapers of American Popular Religion;* John Wilson, "Mr. Wallis Goes to Washington," *Christianity Today,* June 14, 1999.

Walther, C(arl) F(erdinand) W(ilhelm) (1811–1887) Born in Saxony and graduated from the University of Leipzig in 1833, C. F. W. Walther, influenced by *PIETISM, became disillusioned with hyperrationalism that had come to characterize Lutheran theology. Together with several hundred other German Lutherans, he emigrated to the United States in 1838 and settled in Perry County, Missouri. When the leader of the group, *MARTIN STEPHAN, was expelled, Walther became one of the founders of what would become the *LUTHERAN CHURCH—MISSOURI SYNOD. He moved to St. Louis in 1842 to take over the congregation of his deceased brother and started a religious periodical, *Der Lutheraner,* and also served as editor of *Lehre and Wehre,* begun in 1853.

Walther's leadership took many forms—editor, pastor, president of the denomination, president of *CONCORDIA SEMINARY, and author of several books, including *The Proper Distinction between Law and Gospel.* A vigorous opponent of theological *LIBERALISM, Walther, arguably the most important Lutheran leader of the nineteenth century, maintained a high view of God's *GRACE, an unswerving dedication to biblical *AUTHORITY, and a fidelity to Lutheran confessions.

Reference: August R. Suelflow, ed., *Selected Writings of C. F. W. Walther,* 6 vols. (1981).

Walvoord, John F(lipse) (1910–) One of the leading proponents and popularizers of dispensational *PREMILLENNIALISM, John F. Walvoord was born in Sheboygan, Wisconsin, and educated at *WHEATON COLLEGE, *DALLAS THEOLOGICAL SEMINARY, and Texas Christian University. A minister with the Independent Fundamental Churches of America, Walvoord once aspired to be a foreign missionary but spent his entire career at *DALLAS THEOLOGICAL SEMINARY instead, rising from registrar in 1935 to president in 1945. Most of his writings have been on apocalyptic themes, offering a dispensational spin on current events. Although he had retired from the Dallas presidency by then, Walvoord was consulted by the media as something of an expert witness during the Persian Gulf War because of his willingness to place the conflict into a larger apocalyptic scheme of biblical interpretation; he capitalized on the interest by quickly revising one of his earlier books to account for Saddam Hussein's actions and to speculate on how the war figured into the *END TIMES.

References: John F. Walvoord, *The Doctrine of the Holy Spirit: A Study in Pneumatology* (1943); idem, *The Return of the Lord* (1955); idem, *Inspiration and Interpretation* (1957); idem, *The Millennial Kingdom* (1959); idem, with John E. Walvoord, *Armageddon, Oil and the Middle East Crisis: What the Bible Says about the Future of the Middle East and the End of Western Civilization* (1974); idem, *The Blessed Hope and the Tribulation: A Biblical and Historical Study of Posttribulationism* (1976).

Wanamaker, John **(1838–1922)** Born into an abolitionist family, John Wanamaker, a Presbyterian, experienced a religious *CONVERSION in 1856. He formed the Bethany Sunday School in a poor area of Philadelphia in 1858 and remained as its superintendent for over sixty years; late in the 1850s, he became the first full-time secretary of the *YMCA in the United States. Wanamaker and his brother-in-law began their own mercantile in 1861, which by 1880 would become the largest retail establishment in the country. Wanamaker became a pioneer in retailing, using such devices as sales, advertisements, money-back guarantees, and seductive merchandising to lure shoppers into his store.

Wanamaker's economic success, however, did not dim his religious fervor; he gave generously to evangelical causes, including mission societies, the *YMCA, and the *SUNDAY SCHOOL movement. Under the aegis of Bethany Presbyterian Church, he led in the organization of a Penny Savings Bank that would accept the small deposits of urban workers, deposits spurned by larger banks. He provided the land in 1875 for a temporary tabernacle used by *DWIGHT L. MOODY in his evangelistic campaign in Philadelphia. He supported the urban *REVIVALS of *BILLY SUNDAY and helped to establish a number of popular magazines, including the *Sunday School Times*, the *Scholars' Quarterly*, and *Ladies' Home Journal*. Wanamaker also dabbled in politics. He served as postmaster-general under President Benjamin Harrison and later pushed for prohibition and for laws that would prohibit doing business on Sundays.

Reference: William R. Glass, "Liberal Means to Conservative Ends: Bethany Presbyterian Church, John Wanamaker, and the Institutional Church Movement," *American Presbyterians*, LXVIII (1990).

Ward, C(harles) M(orse) **(1909–1996)** An *EVANGELIST and radio preacher, C. W. Ward was a fixture on the *ASSEMBLIES OF GOD radio program *Revivaltime* from 1953 until 1978, a half-hour paid broadcast over the ABC network. Ward was also a president of Bethany College and a prolific writer, having published more than 25 books and 250 evangelistic booklets.

Reference: C. M. Ward, with Doug Wead, *The C. M. Ward Story* (1976).

Ward, William **(1769–1823)** A missionary to India under the auspices of the Baptist Missionary Society, William Ward was born in Derby, England, and became editor of the Derby *Mercury* in 1790 and, later, the Staffordshire *Advertiser* and the Hull *Advertiser*. Ward abandoned his political advocacy on behalf of democracy after his *BAPTISM on August 28, 1796. He enrolled in John Fawcett's seminary near Leeds and made plans to join *WILLIAM CAREY as a missionary to India, arriving there in 1799. After the East India Company denied him permission to settle in Bengal, Ward stayed in Serampore, where he was joined by Carey and *JOSHUA MARSHMAN to comprise the so-called *SERAMPORE TRIO.

Ward's major role in the Serampore mission was running Mission Press, which published tracts, journals, newspapers, and translations. He was also a compelling preacher and a gifted administrator, who helped to form the British India Society in 1821, while on furlough.

References: William Ward, *Account of the Writings, Religion, and Manners, of the Hindoos* (1811); idem, *The Love of Christ Bearest Us Away* (1820); idem, *Farewell Letters to a Few Friends in Britain and America* (1821); John Clark Marshman, *The*

Life and Times of Carey, Marshman, and Ward, 2 vols. (1859).

Warfield, B(enjamin) B(reckinridge) (1851–1921) A theologian in the Reformed tradition who has had a considerable influence on evangelical theology, B. B. Warfield was born into a wealthy Virginia family and graduated from the College of New Jersey and from Princeton Theological Seminary, where he studied under *CHARLES HODGE. After a brief pastorate in Baltimore, Warfield accepted a teaching appointment at Western Seminary (now Pittsburgh Theological Seminary), where he remained until 1887, when he succeeded *A. A. HODGE at Princeton Seminary as professor of didactic and polemic theology.

As theological and intellectual heir of *CHARLES and *A. A. HODGE, Warfield assumed responsibility for carrying the torch of *PRINCETON THEOLOGY into the twentieth century and thereby to retard the spread of theological *LIBERALISM. In the face of encroaching "*MODERNISM," Warfield fiercely defended Calvinistic ideas, especially as represented in the Westminster Confession of Faith, which he regarded as "the final crystallization of the very essence of evangelical religion." Along with *A. A. HODGE, Warfield wrote the 1881 "Inspiration" article in the *Presbyterian Review,* which insisted on the *INERRANCY of the *BIBLE in the original autographs, a position Warfield maintained throughout his career and which has been echoed by other evangelical inerrantists throughout the twentieth century.

Warfield, however, has not been a perfect champion for twentieth-century fundamentalists. He disappointed them on two counts: his attempt to reconcile Darwinism with revealed Christianity and his insistence on *POSTMILLENNIALISM rather than *PREMILLENNIALISM. His death in 1921, however, marked the end of an era at Princeton Theological Seminary. "It seemed to me," *J. GRESHAM MACHEN, one of the lone remaining conservatives at Princeton, remarked, "that the old Princeton—a great institution it was—died when Dr. Warfield was carried out."

Reference: Mark A. Noll, ed., *The Princeton Theology,* 1812–1921 (1983).

Warner, Anna (1820–1915) Though little known in evangelical circles, Anna Warner was a nineteenth-century novelist and the author of "Jesus Loves Me," a children's lullaby taught in *SUNDAY SCHOOLS around the world. The ditty first appeared in one of her novels, *Say and Seal,* when Johnny, a sickly character, asks his Sunday school teacher to sing. She responds with an impromptu rendition of "Jesus Loves Me," which calmed the feverish, fictional child. When the aging Karl Barth, probably the premier theologian of the twentieth century, was asked to summarize decades of thinking and his many volumes of theology, he responded: "Jesus loves me! this I know / For the Bible tells me so."

Reference: Evelyn Bence, *Spiritual Moments with the Great Hymns* (1997).

Warner, Daniel S(idney) (1842–1925) Born in Ohio, Daniel S. Warner was converted in 1865 and joined the Churches of God of North America (Winebrennerian). He was licensed to preach in 1872 and served as pastor and as a missionary in Ohio and Nebraska. In July 1877, having come under the influence of holiness teachings, Warner experienced entire *SANCTIFICATION, which eventually led to his ouster from the Winebrenner Church in 1878.

Warner hooked up with the Northern Indiana Eldership of the Churches of God and began to edit the group's periodical, *Herald of Gospel Freedom* (later called *Gospel Trumpet*). Warner's tireless advocacy for nonsectarian holiness eventually alienated him from denominational officials. He began to organize a new movement throughout the 1880s and 1890s by means of both literature and itinerant *EVANGELISTS. Eventually this confederation of believers incorporated as the *CHURCH OF GOD (ANDERSON, INDIANA).

Warner, Kurt(is) (1971–) A professional football quarterback and evangelical Christian, Kurt Warner was born in Burlington, Iowa, and attended Regis High School in Cedar Rapids, Iowa, where he lettered in football, baseball, and basketball. Warner attended the University of Northern Iowa, where he sat on the bench for three years, finally earning the starting quarterback spot in his senior year. His modest success—offensive player of the year in the Gateway Conference—led him to try for a professional career. For the next decade, a lifetime in professional sports, Warner sought to break onto a National Football League roster, but he was always deemed inadequate. He worked the graveyard shift as a stockboy for the Hy-Vee supermarket in Cedar Falls, Iowa, for $5.50 an hour. He was turned down by the Canadian Football League before catching on with the Iowa Barnstormers of the Arena Football League. Finally, after years of perseverance, he made the St. Louis Rams roster in the fall of 1999, where he was penciled in as the backup quarterback. Injuries to the starter, however, gave Warner his long-awaited opportunity. He took control of the offense, guided the hitherto hapless Rams to the Super Bowl and, in the process, was named the league's most valuable player.

The human-interest side of Warner's quest made his story even more appealing, especially for a league whose players routinely faced drug, assault, and even murder charges. He had married an older, divorced woman on food stamps with two children, one of them legally blind. Warner was a *BORN-AGAIN Christian, and he wanted everyone to know it. "I know I do a lot of preaching," he conceded, "but I live my life for Jesus, and my goal is to share him with as many people as possible. I want to spread the peace and joy I've achieved with as many people as I can." At the beginning of the 2000–2001 season, Warner told a reporter for the *Des Moines Register*, "What I love to do is share my faith and play football."

When the Rams beat the Tennessee Titans, 23–16, in Super Bowl XXXIV, Warner gave God the credit. "With the Lord," Warner said after the game, "all things are possible. I believe in him. I believe in myself. With the two of us together, there's nothing I feel we can't accomplish." Warner does a lot of work for charity, including the Red Cross and Camp Barnabas, a Christian summer camp for children with disabilities.

Reference: Randall Balmer, "Is God a Rams Fan?" *Sojourners*, January–February 2001.

Warner Pacific College (Portland, Oregon) Warner Pacific College was founded in 1937 by leaders of the *CHURCH OF GOD (ANDERSON, INDIANA) and is still operated under the auspices of that denomination. Originally located in Spokane, Washington, and known as Pacific Bible College, it was a training school for the Church of God. Seeking a more central location in the Pacific Northwest, the college moved to Portland, Oregon, in 1940. Over the next twenty years, the school's liberal arts program evolved, and Pacific Bible College was renamed

Warner Pacific College in 1959 both to honor *DANIEL S. WARNER, one of the early founders of the denomination, and to reflect the new emphasis of the curriculum. Today, Warner Pacific offers a master's degree in religion in addition to undergraduate programs.

Rather than mandatory chapel services for all undergraduates, Warner Pacific has an unusual system of "spiritual life" credits. Each student enrolled in eight or more hours of class is required to complete twenty-five credits each semester, but individual students are able to choose how they wish to earn them. They can choose to attend campus chapel services, go on retreats, or participate in a variety of community service projects.

Warner Southern College (Lake Wales, Florida) In 1964, some southern *CHURCH OF GOD (ANDERSON, INDIANA) congregations formed the Southeastern Association of the Church of God with the idea of establishing a church college. The association's board of trustees bought the campus in Lake Wales in 1965, and over the next three years they appointed an administrative staff and broke ground for construction. Warner Southern College admitted its first freshman class in 1968; an additional class was added each year for the next four years, so that by 1971 the college offered a four-year program. The first class graduated in the spring of 1972. The college achieved full regional accreditation in 1977.

References: *Warner Southern College Catalog,* 1996–98 (1996); *Peterson's Choose a Christian College: A Guide to Academically Challenging Colleges Committed to Christ-Centered Campus Life,* 4th ed. (1992).

Warnke, Mike (1950–) Mike Warnke was a comedian who recorded several comic albums on Word Records. At the top of his career, more than one million copies of his audio and video releases had been sold. His career came to a halt, however, in 1992 when several publications began to print allegations of personal misconduct, reporting on his lifestyle, ministry, financial practices, and multiple divorces. Warnke's claim to fame and notoriety was that he had been a drug fiend and a "satanic high priest"; he also claimed extensive academic credentials that could not be verified. When the scandal grew too big to contain, Word Records terminated its agreement with Warnke; it no longer sells or markets his products. The company's decision to end its relationship with the comedian sent ripples through the Christian recording industry, and it is one of the more graphic examples of the reason many companies now require new artists to sign a "morality contract" as part of their recording deals, attesting that they will maintain certain standards of probity.

References: Don Cusic, "Mike Warnke, Jester in the King's Court," *Contemporary Christian Music,* July 1979; Mike Hertenstein and Jon Trott, *Selling Satan: The Tragic History of Mike Warnke* (1993).

Water Street Mission Founded in 1872 by *JEREMIAH MCAULEY, an Irish immigrant and ex-convict from Sing Sing Prison, the McAuley Water Street Mission provided food, shelter, and the *GOSPEL to the indigent of Manhattan's Lower East Side. The mission, with the financial backing of A. S. Hatch, a Wall Street banker, moved into a formerly notorious dance hall at 316 Water Street, where it became a model for other urban missions, including the *BOWERY MISSION.

Reference: Norris Magnuson, *Salvation in the Slums: Evangelical Social Work, 1865–1920* (1977).

Waters, Ethel (1896–1977) A renowned vaudeville performer, actress, dancer, and singer, Ethel Waters was born in Chester, Pennsylvania, to an African American mother who had been raped by a white man. Her mother, who was only twelve, married another man and left Ethel in the care of her maternal grandmother, Sally Anderson. Waters consciously dissociated herself from the vice all around her in the neighborhoods where she grew up, and she made her first singing appearance in a Philadelphia church at the age of five. Her enrollment for two years in a Roman Catholic school instilled a sense of the importance of faith, although her spiritual awakening occurred at age twelve in a black pentecostal church. The next year, 1910, Waters married Merritt "Buddy" Purnsley. The marriage had been arranged by her mother against Ethel's wishes; she was only thirteen. She left Purnsley after a year and began *DANCING in a saloon in Wildwood, New Jersey, the beginning of her career in show business.

Waters did a vaudeville gig in Baltimore under the stage name "Sweet Mama Stringbean" and toured the South with another vaudeville company, where she felt the sting of racism. Her reputation as a blues singer, however, grew rapidly; she played in Philadelphia, Harlem, Chicago, and London, and her distinctive style of rhythm, phrasing, and elocution would influence such singers as Billie Holiday, Ella Fitzgerald, and Sarah Vaughn. Waters appeared in several revues and in 1933 recorded "Stormy Weather," which led to a stint on Broadway in Irving Berlin's *As Thousands Cheer.* Waters played several dramatic roles in the theater, and she was nominated twice for Academy Awards—for the films *Pinky* and *The Member of the Wedding.*

Waters attended *BILLY GRAHAM's crusade in New York's Madison Square Garden in May 1957. She joined the choir, rededicated her life to Christ, and was asked to sing her trademark song, "His Eye Is on the Sparrow," for several of the television broadcasts of the crusade. Although she continued her career in film and the theater, Waters devoted more and more of her time to singing in churches, at *YOUTH FOR CHRIST meetings, and at Graham's crusades. Graham hosted a testimonial dinner for Waters in California on October 6, 1972. "Ethel Waters," he said, "is one of the most beloved, remarkable, and *electric* women of the century."

References: Ethel Waters, *His Eye Is on the Sparrow* (1951); idem, *To Me It's Wonderful* (1972); Marsha C. Vick, s.v. "Ethel Waters," in Jessie Carney Smith, ed., *Notable Black American Women* (1992).

Watt, James G(aius) (1938–) A graduate of the University of Wyoming with both the B.S. and J.D. degrees, James G. Watt moved to Washington, D.C., in 1962 as an aide to Senator Milward Simpson. After his evangelical *CONVERSION two years later, he became a member of the *ASSEMBLIES OF GOD. While working in various posts in the U.S. Department of the Interior, Watt became associated with the so-called sagebrush rebellion, a coalition of western ranchers who wanted to open more wilderness areas to development and who opposed any efforts to alter their favorable grazing rights on federal lands.

Following *RONALD REAGAN's election to the presidency, Watt became secretary of the Interior and proceeded to earn a reputation as an implacable foe of environmental protection. In the course of a famous exchange before astounded members of the House Interior Committee, Watt allowed as how he was not terribly concerned about preserving the environment because the imminent *SECOND

COMING of Christ would render all such efforts irrelevant. "I don't know how many future generations we can count on before the Lord returns," he said.

Watts, Isaac (1674–1748) One of the formative writers of evangelical hymnody, Isaac Watts was born in Southampton, England, and he demonstrated his facility with English verse at an early age. Watts turned down an opportunity to study at the university in favor of a dissenting academy at Stoke Newington, under the direction of Thomas Rowe. Watts became affiliated with Rowe's church and began to write hymns. In 1702, Watts became pastor of an evangelical chapel, but poor health hampered his ability to discharge his duties. Watts turned more and more of his energies to writing: hymns, poetry, and popular theology.

Watts's hymns—approximately six hundred, all told—found a niche among evangelicals and dissenters. John Calvin's refusal to countenance any music other than metrical psalms and canticles in public worship had by the early eighteenth century stifled expressions of piety. Watts and a few others defied that embargo at about the same time that *JOHN WESLEY was urging a warmhearted piety and an Arminian theology. The hymns of Watts, with their fervent piety, joyfulness, and triumphalism, caught the *Zeitgeist* of *EVANGELICALISM perfectly, and they continue to shape evangelical piety centuries later.

References: Isaac Watts, *Hymns* (1707); idem, *Divine Songs* (1715); idem, *The Christian Doctrine of the Trinity* (1722); idem, *Essays towards the Encouragement of Charity Schools among the Dissenters* (1728); idem, *Useful and Important Questions concerning Jesus, the Son of God* (1746).

Watts, J(ulius) C(aesar), Jr. (1957–) Born in Eufala, Oklahoma, J. C. Watts Jr. graduated from the University of Oklahoma in 1981, where he was also a star quarterback for the Sooners football team, leading them to consecutive victories at the Orange Bowl in 1980 and 1981. Watts then played professional football for several years in the Canadian Football League and was a member of the *FELLOWSHIP OF CHRISTIAN ATHLETES. He was ordained a Southern Baptist youth minister in 1983.

Watts was elected to a seat on the Oklahoma Corporation Commission in 1990, a statewide board that regulates oil and gas utilities. Although he was never formally charged, Watts came under suspicion of soliciting campaign contributions from a utility lobbyist. Watts was elected to Congress from Oklahoma's fourth district in 1994, thereby becoming the first black Republican from south of the Mason-Dixon Line elected to Congress since Reconstruction. When asked during his campaign if he would accept help from the Christian Right, Watts replied, "I am the Christian Right." His fellow Republicans seized on the anomaly of an African American who was both a Republican and a conservative; Watts, a polished speaker, addressed the 1996 Republican National Convention and provided the Republican response to President Bill Clinton's State of the Union address in 1997. The following year he was chosen chair of the House Republican Conference, and in 1999 he used his influence to oppose campaign finance reform.

Reference: David Stout, "A Republican of Firsts: Julius Caesar Watts Jr.," *New York Times*, November 19, 1998.

Way International, The In 1957, *VICTOR PAUL WEIRWILLE, formerly a minster in the Evangelical and Reformed Church, left that denomination to devote his energies to an organization he called The Way.

Weirwille had developed a twelve-part series of lectures, called *Power for Abundant Living,* which articulated a heavily dispensationalist theology that identifies Jesus as the son of God while denying that he was God the Son. At the conclusion of the *Power for Abundant Living* course, participants are taught to speak in *TONGUES.

The organization, which changed its name to The Way International in 1975, is generally considered a cult because of its insularity from other groups and because of the financial demands on its followers. Its headquarters are located on the Weirwille family farm just outside of New Knoxville, Ohio, where adherents gather every summer for their Rock of Ages festival. The Way International, which had some ties to the *JESUS MOVEMENT, also has operations in Rome City, Indiana; Gunnison, Colorado; Emporia, Kansas; and Tinnie, New Mexico.

Wayland, Francis (1796–1865) Francis Wayland, a Baptist minister, theologian, and educator, was born in New York City and graduated from Union College in 1813. He studied medicine for a time, had an evangelical *CONVERSION, and then enrolled at *ANDOVER SEMINARY. He taught at Union College from 1817 until 1821, was ordained, and then became pastor of the First Baptist Church in Boston from 1821 until 1826. He returned briefly to Union College and then assumed the presidency of Brown University in 1827, a post he held for nearly three decades.

Wayland was an innovative educator, a gifted administrator, and, by the measure of his contemporaries, the preeminent Baptist intellect of the antebellum era. He taught and wrote on moral philosophy, he strongly advocated public education and prison reform, and he produced a biography of *ADONIRAM JUDSON. In the best Baptist tradition, Wayland insisted on the autonomy of local congregations. In addition, he crusaded against slavery and campaigned on behalf of Abraham Lincoln in the 1860 presidential election.

References: Francis Wayland, *Elements of Moral Science* (1835); idem, *Thoughts on the Present Collegiate System in the United States* (1842); idem, *Domestic Slavery Considered as a Scriptural Institution* (1845); idem, *A Memoir of the Life and Labors of the Rev. Adoniram Judson, D.D.,* 2 vols. (1853); idem, *Notes on the Principles and Practices of Baptist Churches* (1856); James O. Murray, *Francis Wayland* (1891); William Henry Brackney, *The Baptists* (1988).

Welch, Robert (H.) (W.), (Jr.) (1899–1985) Robert Welch, founder of the *JOHN BIRCH SOCIETY, came from a fundamentalist Baptist background. He graduated from the University of North Carolina and attended the U.S. Naval Academy and Harvard Law School. After success in the candy business, Welch became obsessed with the idea that a communist conspiracy was overtaking the United States. He and eleven other businessmen formed the *JOHN BIRCH SOCIETY in 1958, named after a Baptist missionary to China who had been killed by the communist government at the end of World War II. Welch believed that everything from Dwight Eisenhower's election to the presidency to *RONALD REAGAN's administration was the workings of a communist conspiracy; he once labeled Eisenhower "a dedicated, conscious agent of the communist conspiracy." Welch stepped down as president of the society in 1983, two years before his death.

Weld, Theodore Dwight (1803–1895) Born in Hampton, Connecticut, and reared in western New York, Theodore Dwight Weld was converted under the preaching of *CHARLES GRANDISON FINNEY in 1825, while Weld was a student at Hamilton College. Weld became a *TEMPERANCE lecturer two years later, and his *ITINERANCY came to the attention of *ARTHUR and *LEWIS TAPPAN, who provided the funds for Weld to attend Lane Theological Seminary and join the struggle against slavery. In the spring of 1834, Weld staged the Lane Debates over the issue of slavery. Weld succeeded in converting a majority of the students to the abolitionist cause, and their defiance of the seminary's trustees by crusading against slavery led to the *LANE REBELLION and the expulsion of Weld from the seminary. Weld went to Oberlin College (thirty-two Lane Rebels joined him), and he became an agent of the newly founded *AMERICAN ANTI-SLAVERY SOCIETY.

In the course of his travels promoting the antislavery cause, Weld met and eventually married another abolitionist preacher, *ANGELINA GRIMKÉ. Weld's tireless preaching eventually damaged his voice, so he devoted more and more of his energies to writing and editing material in support of abolition; his *Slavery As It Is,* published in 1839, provided *HARRIET BEECHER STOWE with much of her material for *Uncle Tom's Cabin.* Having tired of the public arena, the Welds retired to a farm in Belleville, New Jersey, in 1840. By 1854, however, Weld was teaching school in Perth Amboy, New Jersey, and in 1864 he taught in Lexington, Massachusetts, before finally retiring to Hyde Park, Massachusetts, three years later.

References: Theodore Dwight Weld, *The Bible Against Slavery* (1837); idem, *Slavery As It Is* (1839); R. H. Abzug, *Passionate Liberator: Theodore Dwight Weld and the Dilemma of Reform* (1980).

Wells, David F(alconer) (1928–) David F. Wells was born in Bulawayo, Southern Rhodesia (now Zimbabwe) and taught at Georgia State University until moving to *TRINITY EVANGELICAL DIVINITY SCHOOL and then to *GORDON-CONWELL THEOLOGICAL SEMINARY. Although he began his career as a church historian, Wells shifted to systematic theology at about the same time that he moved to Gordon-Conwell. Wells, one of the signers of the *CAMBRIDGE DECLARATION, has persistently lamented what he sees as a kind of abdication of the theological enterprise by evangelicals. His eloquent jeremiads castigate evangelicals for succumbing to the style and blandishments of the larger therapeutic culture. Wells was academic dean of Gordon-Conwell's Charlotte, North Carolina, campus from 1998–2000.

References: David F. Wells, *Revolution in Rome* (1972); idem, *The Search for Salvation* (1978); idem, *No Place for Truth: Or, Whatever Happened to Evangelical Theology?* (1993).

Welsh Revival A pentecostal outpouring that preceded the *AZUSA STREET REVIVAL, the Welsh Revival began in November 1903 at New Quay on Cardigan Bay, Wales, and lasted for more than a year. It was characterized by singing, *BAPTISM OF THE HOLY SPIRIT, prayer in concert, and something called the *Hwyl,* a spontaneous half-spoken, half-sung hymn. The most famous convert of the Welsh Revival was Evan Roberts, a miner and blacksmith who became the prime mover behind the spread of the *REVIVAL. Some of those who participated in the Welsh Revival also became part of the *AZUSA STREET REVIVAL of 1906.

Reference: Robert Mapes Anderson, *Vision of the Disinherited* (1979).

Wesley, Charles (1707–1788) The younger brother of *JOHN WESLEY, Charles Wesley matriculated at Christ Church, Oxford University in 1726 and became a member of the Holy Club, a group of serious, pious students. Wesley graduated in 1730 with the baccalaureate degree, earned the M.A. in 1733, and was ordained in 1735. He and his brother sailed for Georgia that same year to set up a mission to the Indians. The mission was short-lived, but the Wesleys' encounter with Moravians, a group of pietists, during the voyage had a profound effect on both men; John sought to appropriate their piety, and Charles was especially impressed with their hymns. Charles Wesley experienced an evangelical *CONVERSION on May 21, 1738. Shortly thereafter he began preaching in the open air and composing hymns (about nine thousand, all told) for use in Methodist society meetings.

Wesley, John (1703–1791) Born in Epworth, Lincolnshire, England, John Wesley attended Christ Church, Oxford University on a scholarship, where he earned the B.A. in 1724 and the M.A. in 1727. After assisting his father, the rector of Epworth, as curate, Wesley returned to Oxford in 1729; he led the Holy Club, a group of students intent on both their studies and on their piety. Shortly after his father's death in 1735, Wesley embarked on a missionary journey to Georgia, where he encountered the piety of the Moravians during the voyage. Wesley stayed only briefly, his mission to the Indians largely unsuccessful. Back in London, he underwent a *CONVERSION at a Methodist society on Aldersgate Street on May 24, 1738, when he felt his heart "strangely warmed."

Wesley's Aldersgate experience became the ideal of the fledgling Methodist movement. He traveled extensively, preaching an estimated forty thousand sermons, urging a warmhearted piety and organizing Methodist societies. Wesley steadily moved away from Calvinist theology to *ARMINIANISM; he preached that entire *SANCTIFICATION was available in this life. Wesley's teachings were embodied in the Methodist Episcopal Church, which was organized at Baltimore in 1784.

References: Robert G. Tuttle Jr., *John Wesley, His Life and Theology* (1978); Timothy L. Smith, *Whitefield and Wesley on the New Birth* (1986).

Wesleyan Church The Wesleyan Church was formed in 1968 by the merger of the Wesleyan Methodist Church and the *PILGRIM HOLINESS CHURCH. The Wesleyan Methodists had come into being in 1843 when twenty-two ministers and six thousand members withdrew from the Methodist Episcopal Church, one year before the split between North and South in the Methodist Church. The issues that led to the formation of the Wesleyan Methodists were slavery and the episcopacy (they opposed both). The American Civil War settled the slavery issue, but the Methodist episcopacy and other issues—most notably the sale and use of alcoholic beverages and belief among the Wesleyans in entire *SANCTIFICATION—prevented reconciliation.

The *PILGRIM HOLINESS CHURCH was a product of the *HOLINESS MOVEMENT of the late nineteenth century. It was organized as a completely Wesleyan union of churches, with an emphasis on holiness.

The theological stances of the two constituent bodies were nearly identical. The merger did not require any modification of the theological positions of either church. Entire *SANCTIFICATION is still central to Wesleyan belief. Prospective members are required to sign a statement disavowing the use, sale, or manufacture of tobacco products and alcoholic beverages. Members are not allowed to hold membership in any secret society.

The *POLITY of the Wesleyan Church,

which has its headquarters in Indianapolis, Indiana, is a modified episcopacy. The church is led by a general superintendent, who is elected to a four-year term by the general conference. A general board of administration operates between sessions of the general conference. In 1995, the Wesleyan Church reported 1,624 churches with a total membership of 115,867.

References: Frank S. Mead and Samuel S. Hill, *Handbook of Denominations in the United States*, 10th ed. (1996); J. Gordon Melton, *Encyclopedia of American Religions*, 3d ed. (1993).

Wesleyan/Holiness Women Clergy, International The first meeting of the Wesleyan/Holiness Women Clergy, International took place in Glorieta, New Mexico, in 1994. The group was formed "to equip and encourage divinely called women in vocational ministry and professional leadership positions." It is sponsored by the following denominations: *BRETHREN IN CHRIST, *CHURCH OF GOD (ANDERSON, INDIANA), *CHURCH OF THE NAZARENE, Evangelical Friends, *FREE METHODISTS, the *SALVATION ARMY, and the *WESLEYAN CHURCH. The organization is also endorsed by the Christian Holiness Association and the Wesleyan Theological Society.

Reference: Catherine Wessinger, ed., *Women's Institutions and Women's Leadership* (1996).

Wesleyan Methodist Church. *See* **Wesleyan Church.**

Wesleyan Methodist College. *See* **Southern Wesleyan University.**

West Tennessee College. *See* **Union University.**

Westboro Baptist Church (Topeka, Kansas) Westboro Baptist Church, which identifies itself as an Old School (Primitive) Baptist church, was founded in 1955 by *FRED PHELPS, who became one of the most vociferous antigay crusaders of the 1990s. Phelps, who was ordained in Utah in 1947, and members of his congregation (most of whom appear to be family members) travel throughout North America and stage demonstrations protesting homosexuality and civil rights for gays and lesbians. They march with signs and banners with such slogans as "God Hates Fags," "Fags Hate God," and "Matt in Hell," a reference to Matthew Shepard, a gay college student in Wyoming who was brutally beaten and left for dead in 1998. Phelps, who describes leaders of the *RELIGIOUS RIGHT as "lukewarm cowards," also picketed Shepard's funeral.

Western Association of Christian Schools. *See* **Association of Christian Schools International.**

Western Baptist College (Salem, Oregon) Established in 1935, Western Baptist College began as a *BIBLE INSTITUTE in Phoenix. In 1946, the institute moved to Oakland, California, where it became affiliated with the Baptist Church. The school moved again ten years later, this time to El Cerrito, California; Western Baptist College has been at its current location since 1969.

Affiliated with the archconservative *GENERAL ASSOCIATION OF REGULAR BAPTISTS, Western Baptist goes to greater lengths than many *CHRISTIAN COLLEGES to codify traditional family relationships, such as those between married couples or parents and children. In the standard of conduct statement, all members of the community are charged to "observe the Scriptural injunctions of love, obedience, and fidelity within their home (depending upon their position in the home)." The college's Prewitt-Allen Archeological Museum contains a small teaching collection of artifacts from the Near East and the Americas.

References: *Western Baptist College Catalog 1995–96* (1995); William C. Ringenberg, *The Christian College: A History of Protestant Higher Education in America* (1984).

Western Bible College. *See* **Colorado Christian University.**

Western Pilgrim College. *See* **Bartlesville Wesleyan College.**

Westminster Standards The Westminster Assembly of Divines, held from 1643 to 1652 at the request of Parliament and with the support of the Scottish Kirk and several Reformed divines from the Continent, drew up a series of documents, known collectively as the Westminster Standards. These documents became the definitive doctrinal statement for Presbyterians in England, Scotland, and North America. The documents, hammered out at the Westminster Assembly, include the following: *The Form of Presbyterian Church Government* (1644); *The Directory of Public Worship* (1644); *The Westminster Confession of Faith* (1647); *The Larger Catechism* (1647); and *The Shorter Catechism* (1647).

For evangelicals who place themselves in the Reformed tradition, the Westminster Standards became a kind of touchstone of orthodoxy, and any departure was viewed as a plunge into heresy. When the northern Presbyterians, for example, allowed something other than a strict subscription to the Westminster Standards in the 1920s, conservatives regarded this as a movement toward *LIBERALISM or "*MODERNISM."

References: John T. McNeill, *The History of Character of Calvinism* (1954); John H. Leith, *An Introduction to the Reformed Tradition: A Way of Being in the Christian Community*, rev. ed. (1977).

Westminster Theological Seminary. *See* **Machen, J(ohn) Gresham.**

Westmont College (Santa Barbara, California) Westmont College opened in Los Angeles in 1940 as an interdenominational liberal arts college. Within four years, the college had outgrown its Los Angeles facilities and began to seek a new campus. Westmont's trustees bought the former Dwight Murphy estate in Santa Barbara, California, in 1945.

Westmont enjoys a reputation as one of the most academically solid members of the *CHRISTIAN COLLEGE COALITION. It was rated "highly selective" by the Carnegie Foundation for the Advancement of Teaching.

Weyrich, Paul (1942–) Paul Weyrich, one of the architects of the *RELIGIOUS RIGHT, was born in Racine, Wisconsin, and reared in a blue-collar Roman Catholic household. As a far-right conservative, Weyrich saw the electoral potential for bringing conservative evangelicals into the political arena, where they might unite with conservative Catholics on issues like *ABORTION, anticommunism, and prayer in public schools. From the platform of his organization, the Committee for the Survival of a Free Congress (later known as the *FREE CONGRESS RESEARCH AND EDUCATION FOUNDATION), Weyrich helped to unite disparate elements to form the *RELIGIOUS RIGHT late in the 1970s. At a meeting with *JERRY FALWELL at the Holiday Inn in Lynchburg, Virginia, in the spring of 1979, Weyrich coined the phrase "moral majority," which Falwell used as the name for his own lobbying organization.

Weyrich was ordained a deacon in the Melkite Greek Eparchy of Newton in

1990. In the late 1990s, Weyrich invested much of his energies into the impeachment case against President Bill Clinton. When the Senate failed to convict Clinton, Weyrich complained bitterly. "Politics itself has failed," he wrote. "And politics has failed because of the collapse of the culture. The culture we are living in becomes an ever-wider sewer."

Wheaton College (Wheaton, Illinois) Founded in 1848 by Wesleyan Methodists as the Illinois Institute, Wheaton College took its present name on January 9, 1860, when it was rechartered by the Congregationalists. *JONATHAN BLANCHARD became president, and twenty-nine students gathered on a campus donated by Warren Wheaton, one of the founders of Wheaton, Illinois, west of Chicago.

Blanchard was a fervent advocate of social reform in the nineteenth century; he crusaded against slavery, alcohol, and secret societies. Wheaton's original curriculum prepared students for the ministry, but it broadened and diversified by the turn of the twentieth century. Today it is recognized as one of the elite Christian liberal arts colleges (a small graduate school was added in 1936), and many of the leaders of twentieth-century evangelicalism—*EDWARD J. CARNELL, *BILLY GRAHAM, *JIM ELLIOT, and *CARL F. H. HENRY, among others—are graduates of Wheaton. Theologically, the college hewed closely to *FUNDAMENTALISM earlier in the twentieth century, thereby betraying its socially activist, holiness origins, but Wheaton became a center for *NEO-EVANGELICALISM in the middle decades of the twentieth century. The board's selection of a dispensationalist as president, Duane Litfin, who took office in 1993, signaled at least the stirrings of a return to *FUNDAMENTALISM, although that move met with resistance from some of Wheaton's faculty, especially from *MARK A. NOLL of the history department. On September 29, 2000, in an uncharacteristic bow to political correctness, the college announced that it was changing the name of its athletic teams from the Wheaton Crusaders to the Wheaton Thunder.

References: Paul M. Bechtel, *Wheaton College: A Heritage Remembered, 1860–1985* (1984); Mark A. Noll, *The Scandal of the Evangelical Mind* (1994).

Wheaton Declaration Nearly a thousand evangelical delegates gathered in Wheaton, Illinois, in 1966 for a Congress on the Church's Worldwide Mission, sponsored jointly by the Interdenominational Foreign Missions Association and the Evangelical Foreign Missions Association. The congress adopted what became known as the Wheaton Declaration, which reiterated the urgency of *EVANGELISM throughout the world and condemned both universalism (the doctrine of universal salvation) and syncretism (acceptance of different deities and religious traditions). Meeting a year after the close of the Second Vatican Council, the declaration sounded a note of caution about the supposed reforms within the Roman Catholic Church and urged evangelical unity on the matter of missions.

Wheelock, Eleazar (1711–1779) Born in Windham, Connecticut, Eleazar Wheelock graduated from Yale College in 1733, was licensed the next year, and was ordained the following year, 1735, as pastor of the Second Congregational Church in Lebanon, Connecticut. Wheelock became one of the most effective of the itinerant preachers during the *GREAT AWAKENING, but his real contribution was in the field of education. In order to supplement his salary, Wheelock opened a school. The enrollment of *SAMSON OCCOM, a Mohegan from New London, Connecticut, in 1743 triggered Wheelock's interest in educating Native Americans for missionary work. With the donation of buildings and land from Joshua Moor, a neighbor, Wheelock opened Moor's Charity School in 1754. He was moderately successful in raising money for this enterprise, and in 1770 he moved the school to Hanover, New Hampshire, and renamed it Dartmouth College, in honor of one of his benefactors, the Earl of Dartmouth.

Reference: J. D. McCallum, *Eleazar Wheelock* (1969).

White, Alma (née Bridewell) (1862–1946) Born into poverty in rural Kentucky, Alma Bridewell had an evangelical *CONVERSION during a Methodist *REVIVAL meeting, led by William Godbey, at the age of sixteen. She earned a certificate in teaching and a baccalaureate degree from Millersburg Female College in 1881 but continued to believe that she had been called to the ministry. Her pastor encouraged her to marry a minister as the only socially acceptable way to pursue that call. She moved to Montana in 1882, where she became a pioneer school teacher and met a ministerial student, Arthur Kent White. The two married in December 1887 and soon thereafter moved to Denver, Colorado, where he studied at the University of Denver and she assisted him in his pastoral duties at a Methodist congregation.

Alma White experienced the *BAPTISM OF THE HOLY SPIRIT in 1893, which emboldened her to overcome her "man-fearing spirit" and begin preaching, first to her husband's congregations and then to holiness *CAMP MEETINGS. Her preaching, however, soon attracted opposition from officials of the Methodist Episcopal Church. She broke with the Methodists in 1901 and formed a new group, the Pentecostal Union, assuming the role of bishop in 1910. The denomination changed its name to Pillar of Fire, which had been the name of her periodical, in 1917.

Alma White's husband became a pentecostal in 1909, but her refusal to countenance *SPEAKING IN TONGUES eventually led to an estrangement. He moved to Great Britain and joined the Apostolic Faith Church, a British pentecostal denomination. Alma White moved to Zarephath, New Jersey, in 1907, where a donation of land made possible the relocation of Pillar of Fire's headquarters. She founded Alma White College (since renamed Zarephath Bible College) there in 1921 and established radio stations in both Zarephath and Denver. White was a forceful advocate of women's rights, and she also taught *PREMILLENNIALISM, pacifism, and vegetarianism. Her strong anti-Catholic sentiments led her to support the *KU KLUX KLAN in the 1920s, although she eventually distanced herself from the group. Both Zarephath Bible College and Pillar of Fire Ministries now represent mainstream *EVANGELICALISM.

References: Alma White, *The New Testament Church* (1929); idem, *Why I Do Not Eat Meat* (1938); idem, *Guardians of Liberty*, 2 vols. (1943); idem, *The Everlasting Life* (1944); idem, *Hymns and Poems* (1946).

White, Ellen Gould (née Harmon) (1827–1915) One of the more important and colorful figures in the history of American religion, Ellen Gould Harmon was born in Gorham, Maine, and reared in Portland, where her father was a milliner. Ellen was hit by a rock at the age of nine, an incident that left her unconscious for three weeks, kept her out of school because reading made her dizzy, and caused recurring health problems. She had a religious *CONVERSION as a teenager and was baptized by immersion in 1842 and joined the Methodist Church.

The Harmon family, however, became enamored of *WILLIAM MILLER's predictions about the *SECOND COMING of Christ. Miller's arcane calculations led him to assert that Jesus would return either in 1843 or 1844, and thousands of his followers, known as Adventists or *MILLERITES, had to endure ridicule after what is still known in Adventist circles as the *GREAT DISAPPOINTMENT. Ellen, however, held firm. She had the first of what would be thousands of visions over her lifetime and began to teach that Christ had indeed returned in 1844 but not to earth; he had cleansed the heavenly sanctuary for his final return. In the course of her travels propagating these Adventist ideas, she met *JAMES WHITE, another Adventist. The two married in 1846.

They founded a periodical, absorbed sabbatarianism from another Adventist, James Bates, and Ellen White published a pamphlet in 1851: *A Sketch of the Christian Experience and Views of Ellen G. White*. The Whites moved to Battle Creek, Michigan, in 1855, where they started the Seventh-day Publishing Association in 1861 and formally constituted the Seventh-day Adventist General Conference two years later, the precursor of the *SEVENTH-DAY ADVENTIST CHURCH.

In 1863, White began having visions about health, ideas that became part of *SEVENTH-DAY ADVENTIST teachings and formed the basis of the Western Health Reform Institute, later known as Battle Creek Sanitarium. White advocated vegetarianism and water treatments, as well as eschewing tobacco, alcohol, and drug-dispensing doctors. Her ideas about education were put into practice at Battle Creek College, beginning in 1875, a school now known as Andrews University. White also advocated dress reform and designed clothes for women that were intended to curb sexual passions.

References: Ellen G. White, *The Great Controversy Between Christ and His Angels and Satan and His Angels* (1858); idem, *Early Writings of Ellen G. White* (1882); idem, *Steps to Christ* (1892); *Christ's Object Lessons* (1900); Ronald L. Numbers, *Prophetess of Health: A Study of Ellen G. White* (1976); Paul K. Conkin, *American Originals: Homemade Varieties of Christianity* (1997).

White, James (1821–1881) Born in Palmyra, Maine, James White was ordained in the Christian Church in 1843, at the same time that his fascination with *WILLIAM MILLER's predictions about the imminent *SECOND COMING of Christ kept him occupied as an Adventist lecturer. Shortly after the *GREAT DISAPPOINTMENT, White met another Adventist apologist, *ELLEN GOULD HARMON; they married in 1846. He began publishing a periodical, *Present Truth* (later known as *Review and Herald*) in 1849. The couple moved to Battle Creek, Michigan, in 1855, where James White expanded his publishing operation, and the Whites organized what became the *SEVENTH-DAY ADVENTIST CHURCH in 1863. Ellen White provided the theological and inspirational leadership for the couple's various enterprises, including the Western Health Reform Institute, and James White contributed his editorial and administrative skills.

References: James White, *Life Incidents in Connection with the Great Advent Movement* (1868); idem, *Sketches of the Christian Life and Public Labors of William Miller* (1875); idem, *The Early Life and Later Experience and Labors of Elder Joseph Bates* (1878); idem, *Life Sketches of Elder James White, and His Wife, Mrs. Ellen G. White* (1880).

White, Mel (1940–) Born and reared in an evangelical household, Mel White struggled with his sexual identity for decades. He was married in 1962, worked for *YOUTH FOR CHRIST in Portland, Oregon, and pursued careers as a pastor, a filmmaker, and a ghostwriter for such *RELIGIOUS RIGHT figures as *JERRY FALWELL, *PAT ROBERTSON, *W. A. CRISWELL, and Oliver North. White underwent various forms of therapy, including shock therapy, in the hopes of being "cured" of his homosexuality. He finally embraced his identity in the 1980s, divorced his wife of twenty-five years (with whom he remained on good terms), and came out of the closet late in 1991. In 1993, he was named dean of the Cathedral of Hope in Dallas, Texas, and on February 15, 1995, he was arrested after refusing to leave Robertson's *CHRISTIAN BROADCASTING NETWORK headquarters. White promptly embarked on a hunger strike, demanding a meeting with Robertson. The hunger strike, which lasted three weeks, ended March 8, 1995, after Robertson met with his erstwhile ghostwriter; Robertson, however, refused to grant White's request that he condemn hate crimes against homosexuals.

Reference: Mel White, *Stranger at the Gate: To Be Gay and Christian in America* (1994).

White, Reginald "Reggie" (1962–) Dubbed the "minister of defense" for his skills as a defensive end in the National Football League, Reggie White holds the National Football League's career record for quarterback sacks and helped lead the Green Bay Packers to the Super Bowl championship in January 1997. White is also an associate pastor of Inner City Community Church in Knoxville, Tennessee, having started preaching at the age of seventeen and having been ordained in 1992. When Inner City Church fell victim to the rash of racist-inspired church burnings on January 8, 1996, White emerged as a national spokesperson against racism. "Burning churches sends a message to African Americans because the black church is more than a place of worship," he commented. "It was a safe haven our leaders met in during the civil rights movement. It's a place where we historically have come to find repose and restore self-respect." White raised money, including money from other professional football players, to rebuild the churches. "The only thing that overcomes racism," White declared, "is the love of God and the unity amongst the 'brethren.'"

In 1998, White attracted a great deal of attention—and criticism—for his public attacks on homosexuality, including an address before the Wisconsin state legislature. While leaders of the *RELIGIOUS RIGHT defended White's statements, others condemned them. White retired from football following the 1998–99 season, but he returned to play for the Carolina Panthers in 2000. He announced his second retirement on March 2, 2001.

References: Reggie White, *In the Trenches: The Autobiography* (1996); Johnette Howard, "Up from the Ashes," *Sports Illustrated,* September 2, 1996.

White, Stanley J(ames) (1962–) Stanley J. White, pastor of Christ the King Episcopal Church in Valdosta, Georgia, studied at Berean University, Valdosta State University, and the University of the South. In the late 1980s, he was assisting his father, James White, as pastor of Evangel Assembly of God in Valdosta. Stan White, who had a restless intellect, had become somewhat disillusioned with the relentless novelty of evangelical worship and sought some kind of grounding in the traditions and practices of church history.

He introduced liturgical prayers and even a processional to Evangel Assembly of God, an innovation that met with mixed response.

On August 12, 1988, seeking to be more connected with what he called "historic Christianity," White resigned his ordination in the *ASSEMBLIES OF GOD and two days later organized a new church, which would become Church of the King (later, Christ the King). The new, interracial congregation maintained its roots in pentecostal expression but gravitated steadily toward liturgy as well. White then became convinced to take the fateful step of affiliation with the Episcopal Church; on January 14, 1990, he was confirmed as an Episcopalian, and the congregation officially became an Episcopal mission. On Easter Sunday evening, April 15, 1990, 222 members of the congregation were accepted into the Episcopal Church in a roisterous service that exhibited all manner of pentecostal enthusiasm but within the rubric of the Book of Common Prayer. White was ordained a deacon in October of that year and a priest on June 9, 1991.

Reference: Randall Balmer, *Mine Eyes Have Seen the Glory: A Journey into the Evangelical Subculture in America,* 3d ed. (2000).

Whitefield, George (1714–1770) The "grand itinerant" of the *GREAT AWAKENING, George Whitefield was born in Gloucester, England, and early in life developed a love for the theater. He entered Pembroke College, Oxford University, in November 1732, where he met and befriended *CHARLES and *JOHN WESLEY, and joined their "Holy Club," a regular Methodist gathering. Whitefield experienced an evangelical *CONVERSION in 1735, graduated from Pembroke in July 1736, and was ordained a deacon in the Church of England the same year. Whitefield soon established a reputation as an extraordinary preacher. His sermons were all extemporaneous, and he used his stentorian voice and dramatic training to full effect. A contemporary once declared that Whitefield could bring tears to the eyes simply by saying "Mesopotamia."

Whitefield accompanied the Wesleys to Georgia in 1738, where he established an orphanage called Bethesda. When Whitefield returned to England to raise funds for the orphanage, he was ordained a priest at Christ Church, Oxford, on January 14, 1739. He went on a preaching tour of Wales in March, and his irregular, open-air preaching aroused the opposition of some fellow Anglicans.

Whitefield found a warmer reception across the Atlantic, arriving in America on October 30, 1739. The colonists, already in the throes of a nascent *REVIVAL, were captivated by the Anglican preacher, and in a culture with, as yet, no dramatic tradition, his theatrical flourishes were all the more effective. Whitefield's peregrinations along the Atlantic seaboard knit together the various disparate *REVIVALS to unleash what both contemporaries and historians called the *GREAT AWAKENING.

As Whitefield fanned the *REVIVAL fires, his opponents sought to muzzle him. Alexander Garden, the Church of England commissary in Charleston, South Carolina, brought ecclesiastical charges against Whitefield for preaching to dissenting congregations and for neglect of his putative charge in Georgia. Old Lights attacked Whitefield for his enthusiasm, for the *REVIVAL excesses, and for challenging the social order in New England by preaching outside of the meetinghouses. Even Whitefield's relationship with the Wesleys became strained when he clung to the Calvinist doctrine of election and refused to adopt the Wesleys' Arminian leanings and their emerging notion of Christian perfection; Whitefield became leader of the Calvinist Methodists as against the Wesleyan Methodists.

Whitefield's popularity overwhelmed his critics. In the course of his many preaching tours in England, Wales, Scotland, Ireland, and North America he preached approximately eighteen thousand sermons. He preached his final sermon in Exeter, New Hampshire, on September 29, 1770, and expired the following morning in Newburyport, Massachusetts.

References: George Whitefield, *George Whitefield's Journals* (1960); William H. Kenney, "George Whitefield, Dissenter Priest of the Great Awakening," *William and Mary Quarterly,* 3d Ser., XXVI (1969); Harry S. Stout, *The Divine Dramatist: George Whitefield and the Rise of Modern Evangelicalism* (1991).

Whitehead, John W(ayne) (1946–) As a student at the University of Arkansas, both as an undergraduate and in the law school, John W. Whitehead was a political leftist who edited an alternative newspaper and worked for the election of George McGovern in 1972. Two years later, after reading *The Late, Great Planet Earth,* by *HAL LINDSEY, Whitehead had an evangelical *CONVERSION and gradually moved to the far right of the political spectrum. *The Separation Illusion: A Lawyer Examines the First Amendment,* written in 1977, alleges that the separation of church and state in the United States is a myth perpetuated by people who want to impose a secularist order. The book also refers to public schools as "satanic imitations of the true God's institutional church."

Whitehead, with the help of *ROUSAS JOHN RUSHDOONY, founded the *RUTHERFORD INSTITUTE in 1982 to provide legal assistance for right-wing causes. He formed alliances with several leaders of the *RELIGIOUS RIGHT, including *JERRY FALWELL, who characterizes Whitehead as "a fine Christian man who has dedicated his life to securing the rights of Christians in this age of politically correct persecution." Whitehead and the *RUTHERFORD INSTITUTE assisted Paula Corbin Jones in her lawsuit in 1996 alleging sexual harassment by Bill Clinton, whom Whitehead had accused of "quietly constructing a despotic government and a new society of intolerance to traditional values."

References: John W. Whitehead, *The Separation Illusion: A Lawyer Examines the First Amendment* (1977); idem, *Religious Apartheid* (1994); Ted Olsen, "The Dragon Slayer," *Christianity Today,* December 7, 1998.

Whiteheart The Christian rock band Whiteheart was formed in 1982 by Mark Gersmehl and Billy Smiley, two musicians who had performed with the Bill Gaither Trio. Another founding member was lead vocalist *STEVE GREEN, who gave the group its name in opposition to secular groups like Joan Jett and the Blackhearts. Although their lyrics were unmistakably evangelical, Whiteheart heralded a new direction in *CONTEMPORARY CHRISTIAN MUSIC. With rhythm guitars and a "stacked vocals" sound, Whiteheart's music paralleled the "glamour rock" of 1980s secular artists more closely than it did that of other inspirational performers. At a time when most inspirational singers were almost uniformly clean-cut, the band members sported long hair and wore blue jeans, peace-sign T-shirts, and leather clothing.

Whiteheart has had thirty-five top-ten singles on the Christian Contemporary charts, including "Desert Rose," "Independence Day," "Heaven of My Heart," and "Let the Kingdom Come." The group has never won a Dove Award from the *GOSPEL MUSIC ASSOCIATION, however, and none of their eleven albums has been certified gold. That these standards of commercial success have proven elusive may be attributed to Whiteheart's rapid turnover in band members. Only twice has the band managed to record consecutive albums with the same lineup. *STEVE GREEN left after only one album, moving on to a far more conventional career in *CONTEMPORARY CHRISTIAN MUSIC. Green was replaced by Scott Douglas, whose position as lead singer was equally short-lived; Douglas was sentenced to fifteen years in prison in 1985 for sexually related crimes. After Douglas's departure, a former Whiteheart roadie and bus driver named Rick Florian became the new lead vocalist. While Florian is still with Whiteheart, other slots in the band's lineup have witnessed similar changes. In fact, Gersmehl and Smiley were the only two remaining original members by the late 1990s.

Whiteheart had equally strong connections in the Christian and mainstream music industries. One of the untold success stories of Whiteheart has been that several of the former band members have gone on to thriving careers as backup musicians in pop music. At the same time, Whiteheart does not wish to burn its bridges to *CONTEMPORARY CHRISTIAN MUSIC. The band maintains its ties to inspirational singers like *BILL GAITHER, who was so influential in their formation. In 1994, Whiteheart was featured on a Gaither *Homecoming* tribute album.

Reference: Information by Whiteheart's fan club.

Whitman, Marcus (1802–1847) A pioneer missionary in the Oregon Territory, together with his wife *NARCISSA, Marcus Whitman studied and practiced medicine before offering his services as a missionary under the auspices of the *AMERICAN BOARD OF FOREIGN MISSIONS. The Whitmans arrived at Fort Vancouver in the spring of 1836 and then headed out to establish a mission among the Cayuse at Waiilatpu, in the Oregon Territory.

After some initial success, the Whitmans' efforts were eroded somewhat by the steady arrival of white settlers on the Oregon Trail. The growing ill will between the groups was doubtless exacerbated by the spread of diseases among the Cayuse, diseases that Whitman had neither the skill nor the medicine to cure. When an epidemic of measles decimated the tribe in November 1847, the Cayuse attacked the mission station, killing the Whitmans and twelve of their colleagues and taking others captive. The territorial government suspended mission work in the territory in order to protect the missionaries and settlers. In 1850, the Cayuse turned over five men who, they said, had conducted the massacre. They were tried, found guilty, and hanged in June 1850 but, ironically, only after they had requested the ministrations of a local Roman Catholic missionary.

The missionary story of the Whitmans became something of a classic in the nineteenth century. Whitman College, in Walla Walla, Washington, near the mission, is named in their honor.

References: Archer B. Hulbert and Dorothy P. Hulbert, eds., *Marcus Whitman, Crusader,* 3 vols. (1936–1941); Clifford M. Drury, *Marcus Whitman, M.D.* (1937).

Whitman, Narcissa (née Prentiss) (1808–1847) Reared in Plattsburgh, New York, Narcissa Prentiss studied at Emma Willard's Female Academy and became interested in missions work among Native Americans. Because she was unmarried, however, she could not find a missions board to support her. Her marriage to *MARCUS WHITMAN in February 1836 provided her ticket to the Northwest, and Narcissa Whitman went with the attitude that it was "more my privilege than duty to labor for the *CONVERSION of the heathen."

The journey to Fort Vancouver, in the Oregon Territory, was arduous; Narcissa Whitman and her companion, Eliza Spaulding, were the first white women to travel so far west. After their arrival in Vancouver, the Whitmans began a mission among the Cayuse, near present-day Walla Walla, Washington. Two years after their arrival, the Whitmans' only child, Alice, drowned. Despite some early evangelistic successes, the encroachment of white settlers brought diseases and a growing suspicion of the missionaries. A band of Cayuse attacked the mission station in November 1847 and massacred the Whitmans and twelve of their colleagues. The publication of Narcissa Whitman's journal and correspondence, however, helped keep their memory alive and served as inspiration for other missionaries.

References: Narcissa Whitman, *Journal and Letters* (1893–1894); Jeanette Eaton, *Narcissa Whitman* (1941); Opal S. Allen, *Narcissa Whitman* (1959); Julie Roy Jeffrey, "The Making of a Missionary: Narcissa Whitman and Her Vocation," *Idaho Yesterdays*, spring/summer 1987.

Whitsitt, William H(eth) (1841–1911) William H. Whitsitt, who served as president of Southern Baptist Theological Seminary from 1895 until 1899, studied at *UNION UNIVERSITY, the University of Virginia, and Southern Baptist Seminary, as well as at universities in Berlin and Leipzig. Once in office as president of the seminary, Whitsitt created a controversy by suggesting that Baptists had borrowed the practice of total immersion from Dutch Anabaptists, thereby challenging traditional Baptist belief in an unbroken line of connection to believer's *BAPTISM in the New Testament. In the ensuing controversy, Whitsitt was forced to defend himself and his school against conservatives within the *SOUTHERN BAPTIST CONVENTION who called for his ouster. Whitsitt was eventually forced from office, whereupon he became professor of philosophy at Richmond College.

References: William H. Whitsitt, *The History of the Rise of Infant Baptism* (1878); idem, *A Question in Baptist History* (1896); William Henry Brackney, *The Baptists* (1988).

Whittemore, Emma Mott (1850–1931) The founder of the Door of Hope homes for "fallen and unfortunate women," Emma Mott Whittemore and her husband, Sidney, were converted at the *WATER STREET MISSION in New York City in 1875. After working at several missions, Whittemore opened the first Door of Hope on East Sixty-first Street in New York on October 25, 1890. Convinced that welfare workers could only do so much to reclaim lost lives, Whittemore placed a great deal of emphasis on *EVANGELISM. Other agencies, she declared, might bring women "out of the dens of vice, but only Jesus can get the vice out of the girls."

By the time of Whittemore's death in 1931, the movement grew to ninety-seven homes, called, collectively, the Door of Hope Union. Despite poor health, Whittemore established herself as a leader in the rescue mission movement, serving as vice president and then as president of the National Federation of Gospel Missions, which in 1913 became the International Union of Gospel Missions.

Reference: Norris Magnuson, *Salvation in the Slums: Evangelical Social Work, 1865–1920* (1977).

Whitworth College (Spokane, Washington) George Whitworth, a minister from the Ohio Valley, set off for the West in 1853 with the dream of establishing a Christian college. He brought thirty families with him when he embarked, but only his own family remained with him by the time he reached Oregon. Even after his family's arrival, Whitworth would have to wait until 1883 to see his dream materialize. That year, he founded Sumner Academy in the village of Sumner in Washington Territory. Seven years later, the school was chartered as Whitworth College, a coeducational institution affiliated with the Presbyterian Church but nonsectarian in its policies. In 1899, the college moved to Tacoma. Fifteen years later, it was again in need of more space and accepted a donation of land offered by a developer in Spokane.

Since its early years, the college has grown to offer graduate programs in education, business and management, and nursing. Whitworth does not have a graduate program in religion, but it offers a religion major leading to a certificate in church ministry. The college remains true to its original religious vision. Though affiliated with the Synod of Alaska-Northwest of the Presbyterian Church (U.S.A.), Whitworth admits not only evangelicals but students from any religious background. Other areas of college life also reflect a sense of openness. Whitworth has a major in peace studies, and the biology department offers an advanced course on evolution. Its promotional literature on student life lists rock concerts in downtown Spokane as one of the many off-campus activities available to prospective students. Furthermore, Whitworth's standards of conduct are underscored by only three major regulations, all of which are limited to the boundaries of campus: no drinking or illegal drugs are allowed; violence, vandalism, and personal harassment of any kind are absolutely forbidden; and on-campus "cohabitation" is prohibited. Whitworth is remarkably explicit about "cohabitation," which is understood to be "genital sexual participation outside marriage, and/or the spending of a night together by two people of the opposite sex who are not married to each other." Smoking, social *DANCING, and life during school breaks are not regulated.

References: *Whitworth College Catalog, 1995–1997* (1995); *Peterson's Choose a Christian College: A Guide to Academically Challenging Colleges Committed to Christ-Centered Campus Life,* 4th ed. (1992).

Wickham, John A., Jr. (1928–) An evangelical military man who rose to be chief of staff of the army, John A. Wickham Jr. was reared in an Episcopal household, but his "Christian experience" took place when he was wounded in Vietnam in 1967. Convinced that God had spared his life, Wickham dedicated himself to moral reform within the army. "I almost lost my life in Vietnam," he said. "So I tried to make a difference in terms of moral values." After Wickham's promotion to chief of staff, he and John O. Marsh, secretary of the army, declared "Values" the theme for the year 1986; Wickham sought to "deglamorize" alcohol consumption and to discourage smoking at army bases. He repeatedly urged army commanders to exercise "caring leadership," a quality that many found exemplified in the general himself. "I am a man of great faith, but quiet faith," he declared in a 1984 interview. "And I believe in prayer and pray every day, pray for all the help I can get." Wickham was commander-in-chief of the U.S. forces in Korea from 1979 to 1983 and chief of staff of the army from 1983 to 1987.

References: Ann C. Loveland, *American Evangelicals and the U.S. Military, 1942–1993* (1996).

Wierwille, Victor Paul (1916–1985) A graduate of Princeton Theological Seminary and ordained in the Evangelical and Reformed Church, Victor Paul Wierwille, after suffering through "spiritual frustrations," claimed in the summer of 1942 to have had an encounter with God that was to change the course of his life. He recounted that God told him that God "would teach me the Word as it had not been known since the first century if I would teach it to others." Wierwille obtained radio air time in Lima, Ohio, for a show that would eventually be known as *Chimes Hour Youth Caravan,* directed toward youth. Over the course of the next nine years, Wierwille developed what he called the *Power for Abundant Living* (PFAL) course, which would become the cornerstone of his teaching ministry. In 1951, he learned the gift of *TONGUES from pentecostal *EVANGELIST J. E. Stiles, who claimed to have a technique for inducing *GLOSSOLALIA. Wierwille's twelve-part *Power for Abundant Living* course concluded with the participants *SPEAKING IN TONGUES.

In 1955, Wierwille incorporated his ministry as *THE WAY (which later became *THE WAY INTERNATIONAL). He soon expanded his vision to include television and print media in an effort to educate young men and women in the "correct way of biblical education." He resigned as pastor of his church in Van Wert, Ohio, in 1957 and moved his entire ministry and followers to New Knoxville, Ohio, to a family-owned farm. By 1963, Wierwille was touring the country offering the PFAL course and supplementing it with a videotaped version. Wierwille's teaching seminars were moderately successful throughout the 1960s in recruiting a number of young leaders.

In 1968, a magazine article reporting on some "psychedelic *EVANGELISTS" reaping spiritual successes in San Francisco's Haight-Ashbury district captured Wierwille's attention. Astride his Harley-Davidson motorcycle, the midwestern *EVANGELIST made several trips to California in an attempt to persuade members of the House of Acts community to join his evangelistic entourage, arguing that he was the most powerful teacher since the Apostle Paul. The charismatic Wierwille was able to recruit two of the community's members, Jim Doop and Steve Heefner, thereby dividing the House of Acts community. In 1968, these two converts set up the Way West (in the San Francisco Bay Area) and the Way East (in Rye, New York). The growth of *THE WAY INTERNATIONAL benefited greatly from the recruitment of these two *JESUS PEOPLE leaders.

Where Wierwille drew most of the ire from other Christian groups was his provocative denunciation of the Trinitarian doctrine, the Nicean declaration in A.D. 325 that the Godhead (Father, Son, and Holy Spirit) existed in triunity. In his book *Jesus Christ Is Not God,* Wierwille claimed that the doctrine of the Trinity was agreed upon by a minority of leaders at Nicea, who were mistaken to do so. Christianity, he argued, had lain captive to this false doctrine for over sixteen centuries, awaiting Wierwille to release the church from error. As Wierwille's doctrines and his tactics became more widely known, cult experts charged that Wierwille exerted an ironhanded control over the regimented ministry. One of the largest of all the extremist groups associated with the *JESUS MOVEMENT, *THE WAY INTERNATIONAL boasted over twenty thousand active members by the mid-1970s. Wierwille died in 1986, leaving the organization in a state of disarray and having to deal with financial mismanagement, accusations that he had plagiarized some of his writings, and sexual immorality. *THE WAY INTERNATIONAL still operates outside of New Knoxville, Ohio, but on a much smaller scale than during its heyday in the 1970s.

References: Victor Paul Wierwille, *Power for Abundant Living* (1971); idem, *Witnessing and Undershepherding* (1974); *Jesus Christ Is Not God* (1975); Randall Balmer, *Grant Us Courage: Travels along the Mainline of American Protestantism* (1996).

Wilberforce, William (1759–1833) Born in Yorkshire, England, William Wilberforce was reared by an evangelical aunt and uncle and attended St. John's College, Cambridge. He was elected to Parliament in September 1780 at the age of twenty-one, and his political career advanced quickly, in part because of his friendship with William Pitt, British prime minister. After tours of Europe in 1784 and 1785 and a careful reading of the Greek New Testament and Philip Doddridge's *The Rise and Progress of Religion in the Soul,* Wilberforce became a crusader for an end to slavery and for a moral reformation among the "Higher and Middle Classes" in England. He formed an organization that became known as the Society for the Suppression of Vice and, after years of parliamentary maneuvering, Wilberforce secured a resolution in the House of Commons to abolish the slave trade in June 1806.

Wilberforce also urged evangelistic efforts in India, despite the hostility of the East India Company, and worked for the progress of *EVANGELICALISM within the Church of England. He was a man of extraordinary piety, and his political importance was such that Parliament insisted he be buried in Westminster Abbey following his death in 1833.

References: William Wilberforce, *A Practical View of the Prevailing Religious System of Professed Christians in the Higher and Middle Classes in this Country, Contrasted with Real Christianity* (1797); idem, *An Appeal to the Religion, Justice and Humanity of the Inhabitants of the British Empire on Behalf of the Negro Slaves in the West Indies* (1823); David Newsome, *The Wilberforces and Henry Manning* (1966); John Pollack, *Wilberforce* (1977).

Wilder, Robert Parmelee (1863–1938) A leader in the *STUDENT VOLUNTEER MOVEMENT, Robert Parmelee Wilder was born in India to missionary parents. While a student at Princeton University, he helped to organize the Princeton Foreign Missionary Society in 1883. The motto of this group, "The Evangelization of the World in This Generation," later became the watchword for the student missions initiative in America and abroad. Upon graduating from Princeton in 1886, Wilder participated in the launching of the *MOUNT HERMON HUNDRED, a student missions group later renamed the *STUDENT VOLUNTEER MOVEMENT FOR FOREIGN MISSIONS. He recruited students for missions while completing his theological studies at Union Theological Seminary, New York. Wilder also organized the Student Volunteer Missionary Union of Great Britain and Ireland. After poor health cut short his own missionary work in India, he returned to the United States to work with the ***YMCA** and as general secretary of the *STUDENT VOLUNTEER MOVEMENT. Wilder concluded his career with six years in Egypt as executive secretary of the Near East Christian Council.

Reference: Randall Balmer and John R. Fitzmier, *The Presbyterians* (1993).

Wildmon, Donald E(llis) (1938–) Donald E. Wildmon, an ordained United Methodist minister, earned his master of divinity degree from Candler School of Theology in 1965. After military service, he pastored churches from 1965 until he founded the National Federation for Decency in 1977, which in 1988 became the *AMERICAN FAMILY ASSOCIATION. According to his own account, the organization began shortly after he had sat in front of the television one night: "On one channel was adultery, on another cursing, on another a man beating another over the head with a hammer. I asked the children to turn off the TV. I sat there, got angry, and said, 'They're going to bring this into my home, and I'm going to do all I can to change it.'"

Wildmon's call for evangelicals to boycott television programs or motion pictures with "objectionable" content made him a highly visible figure in the *RELIGIOUS RIGHT. In addition to leading the *AMERICAN FAMILY ASSOCIATION, Wildmon serves as executive director of Christian Leaders for Responsible Television (CleaR-TV).

Wiley, Henry Orton (1877–1961) Born in Marquette, Nebraska, Henry Orton Wiley was pastor of a *CHURCH OF THE NAZARENE congregation in Berkeley, California, before becoming president of two Nazarene colleges: Pasadena College (1910–1916) and Northwest Nazarene College (1916–1926). Influenced by *CHARLES WESLEY and planted firmly in the holiness tradition, Wiley produced a three-volume *Christian Theology,* published in 1941, which became the standard systematic theology for the *CHURCH OF THE NAZARENE denomination. Wiley emphasized the importance of "Christian Perfection or Entire *SANCTIFICATION" in the *SALVATION process.

References: Henry Orton Wiley, *Christian Theology* (1941); idem, *Epistle to the Hebrews* (1959).

Wilkerson, David (Ray) (1931–) Reared in a pentecostal household as the son of two pentecostal preachers, David Wilkerson attended Central Bible Institute and assumed his first pastorate in the small town of Philipsburg, Pennsylvania. While engaging in intensive prayer in 1958, Wilkerson came upon a story in *Life* magazine about seven urban youths on trial for the murder of a crippled boy. The story prompted Wilkerson to wonder if the young men standing trial had ever heard the *GOSPEL. Wilkerson drove to New York City, trying to gain access to the defendants. He was ejected from the courtroom, but his picture appeared on the front page of the *New York Daily News* the next day (March 1, 1958).

The front-page headline served as a kind of passport into New York street life; gang members recognized Wilkerson as "the guy the cops don't like." Wilkerson preached to them and won some converts, including the notable *CONVERSION of *NICKY CRUZ, a gang leader from Puerto Rico who went on to his own evangelistic ministry. Wilkerson's success among gang members and drug addicts led to the formation of an organization called *TEEN CHALLENGE, which Wilkerson headed as executive director.

Wilkerson also wrote an account of his early years in New York, *The Cross and the Switchblade,* published in 1963. The book was made into a motion picture for theatrical release, with the improbable casting of *PAT BOONE in the role of the streetwise preacher. Wilkerson's book, with its unabashed accounts of *SPEAKING IN TONGUES, had a significant influence on the emergence of the *CHARISMATIC MOVEMENT. Students and teachers at Duquesne University read the book and became curious about speaking in *TONGUES, a gift they appropriated during the famous *DUQUESNE WEEKEND, which marked the beginning of the *CATHOLIC CHARISMATIC RENEWAL.

*TEEN CHALLENGE's success and Wilkerson's notoriety led to opportunities to expand the range of his ministry. He established World Challenge in 1972, and the organization has spread to Europe. Wilkerson returned to New York in 1987 to start a church in Midtown. The Times Square Church grew rapidly and now occupies Broadway's Mark Hellinger Theater.

References: David Wilkerson, *The Cross and the Switchblade* (1963); idem, *The Untapped Generation* (1971); idem, *The Vision* (1974).

Wilkerson, Ralph A. (1927–) Born in Ponca, Oklahoma, and educated at the University of Tulsa, Ralph A. Wilkerson received his ordination from the *ASSEMBLIES OF GOD in 1948. He is the author of several books and the founder of Melodyland Christian Center, a charismatic church begun in 1961 and now located next to the parking lot of Disneyland, in Anaheim, California.

References: Ralph A. Wilkerson, *Loneliness: The World's Number One Killer* (1978); idem, *Beyond and Back* (1977).

Willans, Jean Stone (1924–) Founder of the *BLESSED TRINITY SOCIETY, Jean Stone Willans had been a high-church Episcopalian at St. Mark's Episcopal Church in Van Nuys, California, when her rector, *DENNIS J. BENNETT, received his Spirit *BAPTISM. During the ensuing uproar, which culminated in Bennett's resignation in April 1960, Willans orchestrated the media coverage of the controversy, including stories in *Time* and *Newsweek*. For Willans, Bennett's removal illustrated the precarious position of charismatics who wished to remain in mainline denominations. The *BLESSED TRINITY SOCIETY, organized in 1960, sought to assist such clergy as well as to promote the *CHARISMATIC RENEWAL by means of conferences, tracts, and publicity, especially through a quarterly magazine, *Trinity*.

Willans worked for the charismatic cause tirelessly in the early 1960s, but a divorce in 1966 and subsequent remarriage to Richard Willans diminished her influence somewhat. The Willanses relocated to Hong Kong in 1968, where they promoted the *CHARISMATIC MOVEMENT until their return to the United States in 1983.

Willard, Frances (Elizabeth) (Caroline) (1839–1898) Born in Churchville, New York, Frances Willard graduated from North Western Female College (Evanston, Illinois) in 1859. She became a teacher and in 1871 accepted the presidency of the Evanston College for Ladies, a post she held for two years. In the winter of 1874, Willard began preaching at *TEMPERANCE meetings in Chicago. She became president of the Chicago and the Illinois chapters of the Women's Christian Temperance Union in 1874.

Beginning in 1877, Willard led women's *REVIVAL meetings in Boston under the auspices of *DWIGHT L. MOODY; she repeatedly expressed her desire for ordination but her denomination, the Methodist Episcopal Church, denied ordination to women. Willard became national president of the Women's Christian Temperance Union in 1879, a post she held for the remainder of her life. In addition to her crusade against alcohol, Willard sought other social reforms in the late nineteenth century under the banner of "home protection," and her espousal of a kind of Christian socialism in the last years of her life made her one of the forerunners of the *SOCIAL GOSPEL movement.

References: Frances Willard, *Woman in the Pulpit* (1889); Ruth Bordin, *Frances Willard* (1986).

William Tyndale College (Farmington Hills, Michigan) In 1945, the Christian Business Men's Committee in Detroit recognized the need for an interdenominational religious school in their area. In response, they organized the Detroit Bible Institute, using the facilities of the Missionary Workers Tabernacle. The institute later held classes in Detroit's Highland Park Baptist Church and Elim Baptist Church before building their own campus in northwest Detroit starting in 1950.

In its early years, William Tyndale granted a Christian Worker's Certificate. Starting in the 1950s, however, the college added four-year programs in theology, music, and religious education, becoming known as Detroit Bible College in 1960. The college sold its original campus in 1976 and moved to a larger site in Farmington Hills.

It was not until 1980, however, that the school introduced a liberal arts curriculum. The college earned regional accreditation for its associate degree in liberal arts in 1985, and authorization to award bachelor's degrees followed four years later. To reflect the new direction of its curriculum, Detroit Bible College changed its name to William Tyndale College in 1981, in honor of William Tyndale (1494–1536), the English martyr whose translation of the *BIBLE into English formed the basis of the King James Version. In spite of its shift toward four-year studies, the college has not abandoned its original mission as a *BIBLE INSTITUTE. In addition to the college's liberal arts offerings, the Tyndale Bible Institute runs nondegree Bible study courses in local churches throughout the Detroit area.

William Tyndale's library has a large collection on evangelical religion. The school has an unusually successful rate of enrollment for students of color. In 1995, the latest year available for reporting, nearly one third of William Tyndale's enrollment came from minority groups.

Reference: William Tyndale College 1996–97 Catalog (1996).

Williams, Roger (1603–1683) Roger Williams, born in London, read law and attended Cambridge University, at that time a hotbed of Puritanism. Dissatisfied with the progress of reform within the Church of England, Williams arrived in Salem, Massachusetts, in 1631, where he became pastor of the congregation and quickly emerged as a critic of the Puritan hierarchy. Williams warned against the Puritan encroachment onto Indian lands and urged complete separation from the Church of England. Haled several times before the General Court, Williams was banished from the colony on October 9, 1635.

After purchasing land from the Naragansetts, Williams settled what would become Rhode Island as a haven from religious coercion and persecution. "God requireth not an uniformity of Religion," Williams declared. His intellectual restlessness and his pursuit of "soul liberty" led him to embrace the Baptist tradition because of its reliance on Scripture and its generally irenic posture back in England. Ezekiel Holliman baptized Williams, who in turn baptized Holliman and others, thereby forming the first Baptist congregation in America. Some time later, however, Williams seems to have rejected Baptist beliefs as well, declaring himself a "Seeker."

The real significance of Roger Williams, however, lies in his conviction that the state and the church should be entirely separate entities. Williams worried that the "garden" of the church would be sullied by the "wilderness" of the world. His language about a "wall of separation" was eventually picked up by Thomas Jefferson in the formulation of religious disestablishment in the new nation.

References: Roger Williams, *The Bloudy Tenet of Persecution for Cause of Conscience Discussed* (1644); idem, *George Fox Digg'd Out of his Burrowes* (1676); Perry Miller, *Roger Williams: His Contribution to the American Tradition* (1953); Edmund S. Morgan, *Roger Williams: The Church and the State* (1967); Edwin S. Gaustad, *Liberty of Conscience: Roger Williams in America* (1999).

Williams Baptist College (Walnut Ridge, Arkansas) Williams Baptist College opened as a junior college in 1941 under the name Southern Baptist College. Its founder and future namesake was Hubert Ethridge Williams, pastor of First Baptist Church in Pocahontas, Arkansas. The college was first located in Pocahontas but moved to a vacant military base in Walnut Ridge in 1946, after the main building of the first campus was destroyed by fire. Beginning in 1948, Southern Baptist College was included in the annual budget of the Arkansas State Convention of the Southern Baptists and was officially adopted by the state convention twenty years later. The college began to award bachelor's degrees in 1984. The name was changed to Williams Baptist College in honor of its founder in 1991, the fiftieth year of the school's existence.

Reference: Williams Baptist College 1995–1997 Catalog (1995).

Williamsburg Mission. *See* **Chosen People Ministries.**

Willow Creek Association. *See* **Willow Creek Community Church.**

Willow Creek Community Church (South Barrington, Illinois) In 1975, *BILL HYBELS, then a student at *TRINITY COLLEGE, Deerfield, Illinois, set out to design an evangelical church that would appeal to residents of the northwest suburbs of Chicago, people he called "unchurched Harry and unchurched Mary." Hybels had considerable success running a youth ministry, which he called *SON CITY, in a church in Park Ridge, Illinois, but strained relations with the congregation's elders prompted him to strike out on his own.

In planning the new church, Hybels found—on the basis of a market-research survey—that suburbanites were bored by church, that they were put off by traditional religious symbols, and that they preferred to remain anonymous when they attended church. They disliked being dunned for money, so Hybels made it clear that visitors should consider themselves guests and not feel any pressure to contribute. Hybels's invention, which drew considerable inspiration from *ROBERT SCHULLER's Garden Grove Community Church (now the Crystal Cathedral), became known as Willow Creek Community Church, which first met at the Willow Creek Theater in Palatine, Illinois, on October 12, 1975, and grew rapidly; a year later the attendance had soared to one thousand. They moved into a new building on February 15, 1981, and by 2000 approximately fifteen thousand suburbanites flocked to the church's six weekend services—three on Saturday and three on Sunday—at the church's massive facility in South Barrington, Illinois.

The weekend services are calculated to bring people Hybels calls "seekers" into the ambit of *EVANGELICALISM. The services, which entail very little in the way of congregational participation, feature musical ensembles, dramatic presentations, and a sermon by Hybels or one of his associates. Both the auditorium and the programming resemble entertainment more than traditional evangelical worship. "We may use up-to-date language, music, and drama to communicate God's Word for today's culture," the church says, "but our message is as old as the *BIBLE itself. We embrace historic Christian teaching on all doctrines, emphasizing Jesus Christ's atoning death; *SALVATION through repentance and faith as a work of divine *GRACE; and the *AUTHORITY of the unique, God-inspired *BIBLE." The church is organized around five "core values": *GRACE, groups, growth, gifts, and good stewardship.

In addition to the weekend services, Willow Creek runs nearly three thousand specialized cell groups, such as for people with eating disorders, parents of junior-high students, hairdressers, young mothers, singles, and the like. Hybels insists that the real connections are made here in the cell groups, not in the "seeker" services. In keeping with the aversion to religious symbols and consonant with its suburban environment, Willow Creek resembles a shopping center or a corporate office park, complete with a duck pond and a fountain and acres of parking lots. The auditorium seats up to five thousand, and the facility includes classrooms, meeting rooms, conference facilities, several gymnasiums, and a food court similar to that of a shopping mall. The volume of traffic on weekends is so large that the church has an elaborate system of traffic control.

The success of Willow Creek Community Church has inspired imitators. Hybels is much in demand as an author and a conference speaker. An organization called Willow Creek Association was established in 1992 as a kind of network of churches—a denomination, really—operating on the Willow Creek model; by the end of the decade, membership in the Willow Creek Association had grown to more than fifty-six hundred congregations.

References: Lynne and Bill Hybels, *Rediscovering Church: The Story and Vision of Willow Creek Community Church* (1995); *Mine Eyes Have Seen the Glory,* three-part PBS documentary (1992); Gregory A. Pritchard, *Willow Creek Seeker Services: Evaluating a New Way of Doing Church* (1997); Kimon Howland Sargeant, *Re-Forming the Church: Evangelical Seeker Churches, Institutional Innovation, and Cultural Change* (1999); Verla Gillmor, "Community Is Their Middle Name," *Christianity Today,* November 13, 2000.

Wilson, J. Christy, (Sr.) (1881–1973) Born in Columbus, Nebraska, J. Christy Wilson earned the baccalaureate degree at the University of Kansas before receiving the M.A. from Princeton University and divinity degrees from Princeton Theological Seminary. He was a missionary to Iran for twenty years, beginning in 1919, working under the auspices of the Presbyterian Board of Foreign Missions. In addition, he chaired both the Near East Christian Council and the Near East Relief Committee for Iran. He wrote a regular missions column for *The Presbyterian Magazine* as well as a number of books on Islam and related subjects, including *Introducing Islam* (1958) and *The Christian Message to Islam* (1950).

Wilson returned to the United States and to Princeton Seminary in 1939, where he taught ecumenics and directed field work until 1962. He remained active in retirement, first as pastor of visitation at the First Presbyterian Church in Princeton and then in a similar post at the First Presbyterian Church in Monrovia, California.

Wilson also taught missions courses at *FULLER THEOLOGICAL SEMINARY while in California.

References: J. Christy Wilson, *Apostle to Islam: The Biography of Samuel M. Zwemer* (1952); idem, *Ministers in Training* (1957).

Wilson, John (?–1871) The son of an Irish weaver, John Wilson was one of the earliest proponents of *BRITISH ISRAELISM, the doctrine that northern Europeans were the "ten lost tribes" of ancient Israel. Wilson, a self-educated man, relied on biblical prophecy for his views, and he sought to demonstrate that the ten tribes migrated from the Middle East to Europe. He traveled and lectured in Ireland and England, propagating his views; Wilson's book on the topic, *Lectures on Our Israelitish Origin,* went through five editions.

References: John Wilson, *Lectures on Our Israelitish Origin* (1840); Michael Barkun, *Religion and the Racist Right: The Origins of the Christian Identity Movement* (1994).

Wilson, Robert Dick (1856–1930) Educated at the College of New Jersey (Princeton University), Western Theological Seminary, and the University of Berlin, Robert Dick Wilson, a Presbyterian, taught Old Testament and Semitic languages first at Western Seminary and, beginning in 1900, at Princeton Theological Seminary. A staunch defender of biblical *AUTHORITY and the Old *PRINCETON THEOLOGY, Wilson took on the modernists and the higher critics in 1922 with a volume entitled *Is the Higher Criticism Scholarly?* When Princeton Seminary was reorganized in 1929, thereby prompting *J. GRESHAM MACHEN to leave the faculty and start *WESTMINSTER THEOLOGICAL SEMINARY, Wilson, who had been *CARL MCINTIRE's mentor at Princeton, joined the new school at the age of seventy-four.

References: Robert Dick Wilson, *Studies in the Book of Daniel* (1917); idem, *Is the Higher Criticism Scholarly?* (1922); Mark A. Noll, *Between Faith and Criticism: Evangelicals, Scholarship, and the Bible in America* (1986).

Wimber, John (1934–1997) John Wimber, born in Kirksville, Missouri, and converted to evangelical Christianity in 1963, was a successful musician—keyboards for the Righteous Brothers—who decided to enter the ministry. He graduated from *AZUSA PACIFIC UNIVERSITY and became a pastor of the Yorba Linda (California) Friends Church in 1970. Five years later, he joined with C. Peter Wagner as a consultant on church growth, a relationship that evolved into the *CHARLES E. FULLER Institute of Evangelism and Church Growth. After an association with the *CALVARY CHAPEL movement, Wimber started the *VINEYARD FELLOWSHIP in Anaheim, California, in 1977, and broke with *CHUCK SMITH, head of *CALVARY CHAPEL. Under Wimber's leadership, the Anaheim Vineyard became famous for a phenomenon Wimber called "signs and wonders," miraculous cures and outpourings of the Holy Spirit; the congregation grew to five thousand. Wimber's personal charisma helped to spread news of "signs and wonders," and a denomination, the Association of Vineyard Churches, now claims several hundred congregations.

References: Tim Stafford, "Testing the Wine from John Wimber's Vineyard," *Christianity Today,* August 8, 1986; Donald E. Miller, *Reinventing American Protestantism: Christianity in the New Millennium* (1997); Joe Maxwell, "Vineyard Founder Wimber Dies," *Christianity Today,* January 12, 1998.

Winans, BeBe and CeCe BeBe and CeCe Winans are one of the few African

American musical groups to penetrate *CONTEMPORARY CHRISTIAN MUSIC. Since 1987, BeBe and CeCe Winans have earned a total of seven Grammy Awards, seven Dove Awards from the *GOSPEL MUSIC ASSOCIATION, five Stellar Awards, and three Image Awards from the NAACP. They have enjoyed repeated success on both the R&B and Christian/Inspirational charts.

Born Benjamin and Priscilla Winans (in 1962 and 1964, respectively), they grew up in Detroit with eight other siblings. Four of their older brothers formed the award-winning gospel group The Winans in the 1980s. BeBe and CeCe started performing with two of their brothers in a group called The Winans Part II, but they soon realized they worked better as a duo. BeBe and CeCe's first hit single was a gospel rendition of "Up Where We Belong." Their debut album, *BeBe and CeCe Winans,* came out in 1987. The album's singles, "I.O.U. Me" and "For Always," kept the recording on *Billboard*'s Inspirational chart for sixty-three weeks.

BeBe and CeCe's second recording, *Heaven,* released in 1988, was certified gold and became the first gospel album to reach the Top Ten on *Billboard*'s Black Album/Urban Chart. Among other commendations, *Heaven* earned BeBe and CeCe Grammy Awards for the Best Gospel Performance, Male, and Best Gospel Performance, Female categories. The pair's 1991 release, *Different Lifestyles,* was even more successful, going platinum and rising to the top of both *Billboard*'s R&B and Gospel album sales charts. Two songs from the album "Addictive Love" and "I'll Take You There," were hit R&B singles. In 1993 and 1994, respectively, BeBe and CeCe released two more recordings, *First Christmas* and *Relationships,* which also were well-received.

While BeBe and CeCe Winans have tried to break down racial barriers in the world of *CONTEMPORARY CHRISTIAN MUSIC, they have been no less successful in crossing over into non-Christian circles, with a style that blends rhythm and blues, jazz, and pop elements. BeBe and CeCe have been featured in a McDonald's commercial and sang with Ernie and Bert on *Sesame Street.* As well-known a musical producer as a musician, BeBe Winans has produced gospel songs by Whitney Houston and her husband, Bobby Brown, as well as Stephanie Mills and Gladys Knight. He received a Grammy Award with Houston for his work on the soundtrack for *The Bodyguard;* Houston, in turn, appeared as a guest artist on one of their albums. BeBe and CeCe occasionally faced criticism for both their modern style and their collaboration with non-Christian artists such as Houston and M. C. Hammer, but they counter by singing and producing only *GOSPEL MUSIC, although in a contemporary format. The brother and sister live with their families in Nashville, Tennessee, in order to be close to their recording company, Sparrow/Capitol.

Reference: Information provided by Sparrow Media Communications.

Winchester, A(lexander) B(rown) (1858–1943) Born in Scotland, A. B. Winchester migrated with his family to Woodstock, Ontario, where he encountered the preaching of James Robertson, Presbyterian superintendent of missions. Winchester studied at the University of Manitoba, preparing for a missionary career to western Canada, but changed his focus to China, where he went in 1887 under the auspices of the American Presbyterian Board. When he returned to Canada because of ill health, Winchester accepted his denomination's challenge to organize mission work among the Chinese in Vancouver and Victoria, British Columbia.

Winchester accepted the pulpit at Knox Church, Toronto, in 1901. During his pastorate, the church relocated from the center city to Spadina Avenue, where it doubled in size. Winchester opposed church union (which eventuated in the United Church of Canada in 1925) and just as fervently held to fundamentalist doctrines, including *PREMILLENNIALISM. After 1921, he became an itinerant Bible teacher and was active in the *WORLD'S CHRISTIAN FUNDAMENTALS ASSOCIATION. Winchester, one of the founders of *DALLAS THEOLOGICAL SEMINARY, taught there frequently.

Winchester, Elhanan (1751–1797) An influential Baptist and Universalist *EVANGELIST, Elhanan Winchester was born in Brookline, Massachusetts. He was converted in 1769 and admitted into a Separate Congregationalist church in his hometown, but he was baptized by immersion later that same year and moved his affiliation to a Baptist congregation in Canterbury, Connecticut. Winchester's oratorical skills were formidable; he preached to audiences on both sides of the Atlantic and in 1780 became pastor of the First Baptist Church, Philadelphia.

A self-educated man, Winchester's restless intellect led him from *ARMINIANISM to a hyper-*CALVINISM to a belief in universal restoration, which holds that Christ's atonement was for all people, not merely the elect, and that all humanity would eventually be restored to righteousness. Winchester's views did not sit well with some members of his Philadelphia congregation, however. Winchester and his followers were locked out of the church building, whereupon they continued their meetings at the University of Pennsylvania. Winchester, perhaps the premier universalist of the eighteenth century, was the author of numerous books and several volumes of hymns.

References: Elhanan Winchester, *The Universal Restoration* (1788); Stephen A. Marini, *Radical Sects of Revolutionary New England* (1982).

Winebrenner, John (1797–1860) John Winebrenner was born and reared in Maryland, educated at Dickinson College, and studied theology under the tutelage of Samuel Helffenstein, pastor of the Race Street Reformed Church in Philadelphia. In the course of his studies, Winebrenner had a *CONVERSION experience. He was ordained into the Reformed Church in 1820 and assigned to Harrisburg, where his revivalistic techniques, reminiscent of *CHARLES GRANDISON FINNEY's "*NEW MEASURES," alienated some of those under his charge. In April 1823, the vestry denied Winebrenner access to the church, which led to a split in the congregation. When the Reformed Synod of 1825 refused to back him, Winebrenner left the German Reformed Church. He and his supporters constructed Union Bethel Church in Harrisburg, which would become the fulcrum of a new fellowship of congregations called the Churches of God.

Sitting squarely in the primitivist tradition, Winebrenner sought to restore the true New Testament church free of the accretions of centuries of church history and divisiveness. He concluded that the true church was congregational in *POLITY and that *BAPTISM by immersion was the only biblical view. He added foot washing as a third ordinance for the church (in addition to *BAPTISM and communion).

Winebrenner was an effective preacher (both in English and German), a gifted organizer, and a prolific author. Like other evangelicals in the antebellum period,

Winebrenner was devoted to social reform, including the *TEMPERANCE crusade, the peace movement, and the *ABOLITION of slavery. He founded and edited *The Gospel Publisher* in 1835, one of the oldest church periodicals in the United States (now known as *The Church Advocate*), and the denomination he founded, known today as Churches of God, General Conference, has two schools, both in Findlay, Ohio: the University of Findlay and Winebrenner Theological Seminary.

References: John Winebrenner, *A Brief View of the Formation, Government, and Discipline of the Church of God* (1829); idem, *A Prayer Meeting and Revival Hymn Book* (1825).

Winnipeg Bible Training School. *See* **Providence College and Theological Seminary.**

Winona Lake Bible Conference Taking its inspiration from the *CHAUTAUQUA movement, the organization that became the Winona Lake Bible Conference began in 1894, offering correspondence courses and lecture series. By the turn of the twentieth century, the conference grounds on the shores of Winona Lake in Indiana had become a gathering place for evangelicals from a variety of denominations. The program included Bible studies, preaching, and informal socialization, all laced with dispensational premillennialist theology. Winona Lake was the summer home of *BILLY and "Ma" SUNDAY. It billed itself as a wholesome environment and a "tired mothers' paradise," and Winona Lake, along with the **SCOFIELD REFERENCE BIBLE* and the *NIAGARA and other Bible conferences, became one of the primary vehicles for the propagation of *DISPENSATIONALISM. *GRACE THEOLOGICAL SEMINARY moved there from Akron, Ohio, in 1939.

Reference: Vincent H. Gladdis and Jasper A. Huffman, *The Story of Winona Lake: A Memory and a Vision* (1960).

Winrod, Gerald Burton (1900–1957) Born in Wichita, Kansas, Gerald Burton Winrod became enamored of *EVANGELICALISM in his teens and himself became an *EVANGELIST at the age of twenty-one, although he never had any theological training, held no pastorate, and was not a member of any denomination. His influence was such, however, that when he called a meeting in Salina, Kansas, in 1925 "for the defense of the Christian faith" against the scourge of *MODERNISM, Winrod was able to rally about one hundred fundamentalists. An organization called *DEFENDERS OF THE CHRISTIAN FAITH emerged, with Winrod as leader, *Faith of Our Fathers* as the official hymn, and a statement of objectives derived from the book of Jude: "Contend for the faith which was once delivered unto the saints." Winrod founded *The Defender* magazine the next year and remained its editor until his death in 1957.

Winrod used his platform as editor and as executive director of *DEFENDERS OF THE CHRISTIAN FAITH to rail against *MODERNISM in its various guises, including the consumption of alcohol and the teaching of evolution in public schools. By the early 1930s and increasingly throughout his career, Winrod expanded his barrage to include Franklin Roosevelt and the New Deal, communism, and what he was convinced was a worldwide Jewish conspiracy.

To underscore his opposition to Roosevelt, Winrod, a gifted preacher whose oratorical skills were often compared to *WILLIAM JENNINGS BRYAN, mounted a race for the U.S. Senate in 1938. He used his weekly radio broadcasts over WIBW in Topeka to publicize his platform of "fundamental Americanism," and he made extensive use of his mailing list to distribute campaign literature throughout the state. Winrod's candidacy, however, which he characterized as "a holy crusade," drew criticism from many of the state's newspapers and politicians, who accused Winrod of reviving the spirit of the *KU KLUX KLAN. Winrod blamed his defeat on "the most powerful combination of communist and New Deal agencies ever assembled," which drew on "inexhaustible sums of Jewish money."

Winrod's anti-Catholic and anti-Semitic sentiments, which he had tried to modulate during the campaign, resurfaced when he was indicted in 1942, the first of three times, on charges of sedition, specifically for distributing Nazi propaganda. Winrod and twenty-nine others went to trial in April 1944; after the judge's death in late November (which Winrod characterized as an act of God), a mistrial was declared and the indictment eventually dismissed. Winrod continued his anti-Semitic campaigns after World War II and expanded still further his list of enemies. He opposed communism (which he traced back to Cain), the National Conference of Christians and Jews, Masons, the United Nations, the Federal Council of Churches, chain stores, and the medical profession. He regarded even fellow Kansan Dwight D. Eisenhower as a tool of the Jews.

Reference: Clifford R. Hope Jr., "Strident Voices in Kansas between the Wars," *Kansas History,* 2 (1979).

Wisconsin Evangelical Lutheran Synod
The Wisconsin Synod was formed in Milwaukee in 1850 as the First German Evangelical Lutheran Synod. The synod became a stout defender of conservative Lutheran doctrine and tradition against what it saw as the compromises that were developing in the larger Lutheran bodies. In 1892, the synod federated with synods in Michigan and Minnesota to form the Evangelical Lutheran Joint Synod of Wisconsin, Minnesota, and Michigan. A formal merger of the three groups in 1917 created the Evangelical Lutheran Joint Synod of Wisconsin and Other States. The synod adopted its current name in 1959.

Theologically, the Wisconsin Synod has remained true to its orthodox Lutheran roots. The synod takes a stance that is more conservative than the *LUTHERAN CHURCH—MISSOURI SYNOD. It maintains a belief in the infallibility and *INERRANCY of the Scriptures. It opposes fellowship with other bodies unless there is complete agreement on all matters of doctrine and practice. Due to the decided emphasis on proper fellowship, the synod warns its members against participation in the Boy Scouts and Girl Scouts and in secret societies, such as the Freemasons. The Wisconsin Synod is strictly Trinitarian. The denomination believes in the verbal inspiration of Scripture but distinguishes between what the synod believes and an understanding that is merely "mechanical dictation." The synod holds firmly to an understanding of the biblical creation and is amillennial with regard to the *END TIMES. An active mission program has work ongoing in twenty-six countries.

The synod is divided into twelve districts, and it meets biennially. The home offices are in Milwaukee. The synod reports 1,235 churches in the United States, Canada, Antigua, and St. Lucia. There are 413,839 baptized members and 315,127 communicant members.

References: Frank S. Mead and Samuel S. Hill, *Handbook of Denominations in the United States,*

10th ed. (1996); J. Gordon Melton, *The Encyclopedia of American Religions*, 3d ed. (1993).

Wise, Ted (1936–) Often cited as the first hippie convert to Christianity and what eventually became the *JESUS MOVEMENT, Ted Wise and his wife, Liz, had become extremely dissatisfied with their life at the center of San Francisco's emerging hippie counterculture in the mid-1960s. Wise claims that his evangelical *CONVERSION occurred while he was on LSD, driving over the San Francisco Bay Bridge. "Jesus knocked me off my metaphysical ass," he recounted. "I could choose him or literally suffer a fate worse than death." After the two converted in 1966, they naturally began to tell their friends what had happened to them. Within a few short months, they had gathered an initial group of four married couples to form a community to promote the *GOSPEL through street *EVANGELISM, food sharing, and offering needy hippies a place to crash.

Helped by a group of Baptist pastors who set up an umbrella organization to oversee their activities, the group opened the first Christian communal house of the *JESUS MOVEMENT, staffed by converted hippies. Located in the heart of the Haight-Ashbury district, The Living Room made evangelistic contact with thousands of young hippies in its brief life span. While studying the *BIBLE, one of the members noticed that the early Christians had sold their possessions and lived together in community. Taking the *BIBLE as a literal guidebook, the group decided to sell their possessions and move in together, renting a small house in Novato, California. The four families thereby established the House of Acts community. The Living Room mission and House of Acts communal house remained in operation for eighteen months, after which the families went their separate ways.

Ted Wise was recruited by *RAY STEDMAN of the Peninsula Bible Church to join in a Think and Pray Group. In addition to his work with the church, he has organized drug rehabilitation programs.

Reference: John A. MacDonald, *The House of Acts* (1970).

Witherspoon, John (1723–1794) Born in Yester, Scotland, John Witherspoon matriculated at the University of Edinburgh at the age of thirteen. He studied theology and was ordained to the ministry of the Scottish Kirk in 1745. Witherspoon's fame as a staunch defender of the faith drew the attention of Presbyterians in the Middle Colonies. In 1766, following the death of *SAMUEL FINLEY, president of the College of New Jersey (now Princeton University), the school's trustees invited Witherspoon to become the sixth president of the fledgling college. Witherspoon initially declined the offer but reconsidered and became president of the College of New Jersey in 1768.

Witherspoon's arrival in North America was significant on several counts. His traditional theology (which appealed to Old Side Presbyterians) and his warmhearted piety (of equal importance to New Side clergy) allowed him to effect a rapprochement between the two contentious factions of eighteenth-century Presbyterianism. His commitment to *SCOTTISH COMMON SENSE REALISM was quickly adopted by colonial clergy who were suspicious of radical forms of Enlightenment thought. Witherspoon's political ideas may have been even more important to colonial Presbyterians than his theological and philosophical convictions. A Scot who abhorred the imperialism of the British crown, Witherspoon became a vocal apologist for American independence. He fostered the spirit of liberty in his students and allowed the college to become a hotbed of patriotism; he signed the Declaration of Independence; he preached sermons and published tracts on behalf of the Patriot cause; he helped force the ouster of the Loyalist governor of New Jersey and served in the new state legislature; he served as a member of Congress; and he participated in the discussion that led to the formulation of the Articles of Confederation.

Witherspoon's prominence as a statesman in both church and state made him an influential figure in ecclesiastical affairs after the Revolution. During the first decade of independence, he was one of the movers behind the organization of American Presbyterians into a national body. Witherspoon was elected moderator of the new denomination at its first general assembly in 1789.

References: John Witherspoon, *Ecclesiastical Characteristics* (1753); idem, *Essay on the Connection Between the Doctrine of Justification by the Imputed Righteousness of Christ and Holiness of Life* (1756); idem, *Essays on Important Subjects* (1764); V. L. Collins, *President Witherspoon*, 2 vols. (1925); Mark A. Noll, *Princeton and the Republic, 1768–1822: The Search for a Christian Enlightenment in the Era of Samuel Stanhope Smith* (1989).

Witmarsum Theological Seminary. *See* **Bluffton College and Bluffton Theological Seminary.**

Witnessing For evangelicals, "witnessing" means sharing the faith with another, either through direct means (talking with a nonbeliever about Christianity) or indirectly (by living an exemplary life). Witnessing is a form of *EVANGELISM.

Wittenburg Door, The. *See* **Youth Specialties.**

Wolf, Frank R(udolph) (1939–) An evangelical and a member of the House of Representatives, Frank R. Wolf was born in Philadelphia and studied at the University of Mississippi, Pennsylvania State University, and Georgetown University Law School. After practicing law and working for various agencies in Washington, Wolf was elected to Congress from Virginia in 1980. Wolf, a Republican, has maintained close ties to *PAT ROBERTSON and the *CHRISTIAN COALITION, although he numbers *TONY HALL, fellow evangelical and Democratic congressman from Ohio, among his close friends.

Wolterstorff, Nicholas P. (1932–) Nicholas P. Wolterstorff earned the bachelor's degree from *CALVIN COLLEGE, where he taught philosophy for thirty years after completing his M.A. and Ph.D. degrees from Harvard University. He joined the faculty of Yale University Divinity School in 1989. He has written a number of books on philosophy of religion, aesthetics, and political philosophy, and he has served as president of the American Philosophical Association and the *SOCIETY OF CHRISTIAN PHILOSOPHERS. In 1987, following the tragic death of his son Eric in a mountain-climbing accident in 1983, Wolterstorff published a poignant memoir of reflections on grief, *Lament for a Son*.

References: Nicholas P. Wolterstorff, *Reason within the Bounds of Religion* (1976); idem, *Art in Action: Toward a Christian Aesthetic* (1980); idem, *Lament for a Son* (1987); idem, *Divine Discourse: Philosophical Reflections on the Claim That God Speaks* (1995); idem, *John Locke and the Ethics of Belief* (1996).

Women of Faith One of the organizations that sought both to imitate and to capitalize on the success of *PROMISE KEEPERS, Women of Faith was formed in

1996 by Steve Arterburn, a businessman from southern California who heads a chain of Christian counseling centers called *New Life Treatment Centers. Women of Faith, a for-profit organization, holds rallies for women—primarily evangelical women—across the nation. The rallies, called Joyful Journey, encourage women in their roles as wife and mother in Christian households.

Women's Aglow Fellowship A nondenominational evangelical organization providing worship, fellowship, and encouragement, Women's Aglow Fellowship was begun in Seattle in 1967 by a group of women meeting for lunch and prayer. The organization grew to more than thirteen hundred chapters around the world. The organization publishes a magazine, *Aglow,* and distributes evangelical literature and Bible study materials throughout the world under the auspices of World Literature Thrust.

Reference: R. Marie Griffith, *God's Daughters: Evangelical Women and the Power of Submission* (1997).

Women's Bible Society of New York Organized May 11, 1816, as the New York Female Auxiliary Bible Society of New York—a complement to the *American Bible Society, which was founded three days earlier—the Women's Bible Society of New York sent its members into the neighborhoods of immigrants, either donating or selling *Bibles, distributing tracts, and urging church attendance. During the Civil War, the Women's Bible Society gave *Bibles to soldiers heading off to battle, and by 1877 the organization shed its "auxiliary" status and became an independent entity. The Women's Bible Society sends children and teenagers to Bible camps in the summer and dispatches its "Bible Readers" to hospitals and shelters.

Reference: Women's Bible Society of New York brochure.

Wood 'n' Ware Controversy. *See* **Woods, Leonard.**

Woodbridge, Charles (Jahleel) (1902–1995) Born in China to missionary parents, Charles Woodbridge earned degrees at Princeton University, Princeton Theological Seminary, and Duke University. Ordained as a Presbyterian minister in 1927, he served as a pastor in Flushing, New York, and as a missionary to the French Cameroons from 1932 to 1934. Upon his return, Woodbridge became secretary for the Independent Board for Presbyterian Foreign Missions, the fundamentalist missions organization associated with Woodbridge's seminary mentor, *J. Gresham Machen. Woodbridge served as one of Machen's lawyers when the latter was tried by the New Brunswick Presbytery; both men eventually were suspended from the Presbyterian Church because of their refusal to countenance what they regarded as liberal or "modernist" ideas in the denomination.

After serving churches in North Carolina and Georgia, Woodbridge taught church history at *Fuller Theological Seminary and spent his summers as a Bible teacher, principally at *Jack Wyrtzen's Word of Life organization, in Schroon Lake, New York. Woodbridge became a fervent separatist, especially after *Billy Graham's 1957 crusade at Madison Square Garden in New York, when Graham enlisted the cooperation of liberal Protestant clergy. He left Fuller in 1958 because he believed that it was becoming apostate. He remained critical of the so-called "*NEW EVANGELICALISM," which sought to cooperate with other, nonfundamentalist believers in *EVANGELISM. Woodbridge's book, *The New Evangelicalism,* published in 1969, was a full-throated defense of doctrinal purity, *SEPARATISM, and biblical *INERRANCY, causes that his son, John D. Woodbridge, has continued to champion as professor of church history at *TRINITY EVANGELICAL DIVINITY SCHOOL, Deerfield, Illinois.

Reference: George M. Marsden, *Reforming Fundamentalism: Fuller Seminary and the New Evangelicalism* (1987).

Woodbridge, John D(unning) (1941–) Born in Salisbury, North Carolina, John D. Woodbridge grew up in a devout home; his father, *CHARLES WOODBRIDGE, was a leader in the fundamentalist movement and an ardent separatist. John Woodbridge graduated from *WHEATON COLLEGE in 1963 with a degree in history. He continued his studies at Michigan State University and earned the doctorate at the University of Toulouse. He began a long association with *TRINITY EVANGELICAL DIVINITY SCHOOL in 1966, first as a master of divinity student and then as a professor of church history. Though his primary scholarship lies in the field of French history, Woodbridge emerged in the 1970s as one of *EVANGELICALISM's most tenacious defenders of the doctrine of biblical *INERRANCY, and in 1997 he was named one of the senior editors of **CHRISTIANITY TODAY*.

A gentle man with an irenic spirit, Woodbridge tried in 1995 to rein in some of the more unruly and intolerant spirits on the *RELIGIOUS RIGHT. In an article that appeared in **CHRISTIANITY TODAY*, Woodbridge cautioned that "culture-war rhetoric leads us to distort others' positions, to see enmity in place of mere disagreement." Political intransigence, he continued, had led to divisions within *EVANGELICALISM because it "leaves no room for nuanced positions, or for middle ground." The article drew a quick and angry response from *JAMES DOBSON, who defended his use of militaristic rhetoric and "fighting words" in his engagement at the front lines of the "culture wars."

References: John D. Woodbridge, *Biblical Authority* (1982); idem, *Revolt in Pre-Revolutionary France: The Prince de Conti's Conspiracy against Louis XV, 1755–1757* (1995); idem, "Culture War Casualties: How Warfare Rhetoric Is Hurting the Work of the Church," *Christianity Today*, March 6, 1995; William Martin, *With God on Our Side: The Rise of the Religious Right in America* (1996).

Woodrow, James (1828–1907) Born in Carlisle, England, James Woodrow studied at Jefferson College, Harvard College, and the University of Heidelberg, where he earned the doctorate in 1856. A scientist, Woodrow in 1860 became the first incumbent of the Perkins Professorship of Natural Science in Connection with Revelation at Columbia Theological Seminary. The appointment, the first of its kind at any theological seminary in the United States, was controversial among southern Presbyterians from the outset. Conservatives, led by *ROBERT LEWIS DABNEY, feared that it would lead to the ascendance of natural science over revealed religion.

Woodrow gave such fears credence with his arguments that the *BIBLE was never meant as a scientific text, and that there was, in fact, no real contradiction between revelation and natural science. Although he stressed that evolution was only a theory, Woodrow's enemies, led by Dabney, seized on his apparent sympathy for Darwinism and sought his ouster.

Woodrow responded with *An Examination of Certain Recent Assaults on Physical Science,* which appeared in 1873. In the course of the ensuing pamphlet war between Dabney and Woodrow, the Columbia board of trustees gave Woodrow a vote of confidence in 1884, but denominational conservatives finally forced his ouster two years later. Woodrow continued his academic career at South Carolina College (now the University of South Carolina) as professor, dean, and president. In 1905, long after Woodrow's expulsion, the trustees of Columbia Theological Seminary passed several conciliatory resolutions praising Woodrow's piety and service to the denomination.

References: James Woodrow, *An Examination of Certain Recent Assaults on Physical Science* (1873); Randall Balmer and John R. Fitzmier, *The Presbyterians* (1993).

Woods, C(harles) Stacy (1909–1983) Born in Australia, C. Stacy Woods came to the United States in 1930 and earned degrees at *WHEATON COLLEGE and *DALLAS THEOLOGICAL SEMINARY. In 1934, at the age of twenty-five, he assumed leadership of the *INTERVARSITY CHRISTIAN FELLOWSHIP of Canada and in 1940 became the first general secretary of the organization for America. A skilled and ambitious administrator, Woods concurrently became the first general secretary of the International Fellowship of Evangelical Students in 1947. He also helped to organize InterVarsity's first student missionary convention, held in Toronto between Christmas and New Year's 1946–1947, and later in *URBANA, Illinois, on a triennial basis.

Reference: C. Stacy Woods, *The Growth of a Work of God* (1978).

Woods, Leonard (1774–1854) Born in Princeton, Massachusetts, Leonard Woods became one of the most influential Reformed theologians of the nineteenth century. He graduated from Harvard College in 1796 and studied for the ministry under *NATHANIEL EMMONS and Charles Backus, both of them *NEW DIVINITY theologians. Woods was ordained into the Congregationalist ministry in 1798. He was selected ten years later to be professor of theology at the newly formed *ANDOVER THEOLOGICAL SEMINARY, begun as a Calvinist counterpart to Harvard, which had recently become Unitarian.

Woods remained at Andover for the rest of his career. His dogged defenses of Calvinist theology placed him at loggerheads with both the *ARMINIANISM of *CHARLES FINNEY and *NATHANIEL WILLIAM TAYLOR and the Unitarianism of William Ellery Channing and Henry Ware, whose appointment as Hollis Professor of Divinity at Harvard had precipitated the founding of Andover. After Woods published *Letters to Unitarians* in 1820, which laid out the Calvinist doctrine of human depravity over the optimistic humanism of Channing, Ware engaged Woods in a literary war, which lasted until 1824. Known popularly as the Wood 'n' Ware Controversy, the debate centered on the issue of human nature, and it remains one of the most significant—and substantive—theological exchanges in American history.

References: Leonard Woods, *Letters to Unitarians* (1820); idem, *An Essay on Native Depravity* (1835); idem, *History of the Andover Seminary* (1885); Bruce Kuklick, ed., *The Unitarian Controversy, 1819–1823,* 2 vols. (1987).

Woodworth-Etter, Maria B(eulah) (1844–1924) Born near Lisbon, Ohio,

Maria B. Woodworth-Etter was converted at age thirteen. Shortly thereafter, she believed that she had been called to the ministry, although the responsibilities of child-rearing delayed her preaching until about 1880, when she began conducting *REVIVALS. She preached under the auspices of the United Brethren and, later, the Churches of God (Winebrenner). She divorced her husband, P. H. Woodworth, in 1891, charging him with adultery. The next year she married Samuel Etter and added his name to her own. By 1904, Woodworth-Etter had become so controversial that the Churches of God revoked her ministerial credentials, and she drifted toward *PENTECOSTALISM, including *SPEAKING IN TONGUES. In 1912, she held a major *REVIVAL at *F. F. BOSWORTH's church in Denver, Colorado, which provided a great deal of publicity, especially in pentecostal circles.

Woodworth-Etter believed in the gifts of the Holy Spirit. Auditors at her services would often be "slain in the Spirit," which she referred to as "receiving the power." During a campaign in Hartford City, Indiana, in 1885, she enjoyed success as a healer, which only served to swell attendance at her gatherings. By 1889, she traveled with a tent that seated eight thousand, but even that was often too small to accommodate the crowds as she traveled through the South and the Midwest. A reporter estimated one crowd in Indiana at twenty thousand.

Woodworth-Etter wrote a number of books on spirituality, and she founded the congregation known today as the Lakeview Christian Center, in Indianapolis. She was one of the most visible of the pentecostal preachers at the turn of the century, and her success paved the way for other women preachers like *AIMEE SEMPLE MCPHERSON and *KATHRYN KUHLMAN.

Reference: Wayne E. Warner, *The Woman Evangelist: The Life and Times of Maria B. Woodworth-Etter* (1986).

Wooster, Hezekiah Calvin (1771–1798) A leader of the Methodist expansion into Upper Canada in the 1790s, Hezekiah Calvin Wooster was "*BORN AGAIN" in December 1791 and experienced *SANCTIFICATION two months later. He became a Methodist missionary, appointed by the New York Conference to the Oswegotchie circuit in what is now eastern Ontario. A fiery and charismatic preacher with piercing eyes, Wooster was described by his contemporary *NATHAN BANGS as "a man of mighty prayer and faith." He, more than any other figure, was responsible for what another contemporary described as the "wildfire Methodist *REVIVAL" in Upper Canada. Bangs would later credit Wooster as the catalyst for the *REVIVAL that eventually became known as the *SECOND GREAT AWAKENING: "This great work may be said to have been, in some sense, the beginning of that great *REVIVAL of religion which soon spread through various parts of the United States." Though he died of tuberculosis at a young age, Wooster inspired other revivalists, including Bangs and *LORENZO "CRAZY" DOW.

Reference: G. A. Rawlyk, *The Canada Fire: Radical Evangelicalism in British North America, 1775–1812* (1994).

Word of Faith Outreach Center (Dallas, Texas). *See* **Tilton, Robert G(ibson).**

Word of God For most evangelicals, the term "Word of God" ("W" in *word* is usually capitalized) is synonymous with the *BIBLE—more particularly the sixty-six canonized books of the Old Testament (Hebrew Bible) and the New Testament. Whereas Martin Luther and other

Reformers understood that God's word comes to us in many forms—the sacraments, Scriptures, preaching—evangelicals, at least since the nineteenth century, have insisted that the word of God—God's revelation to humanity—is wholly contained in the *BIBLE.

Word of Knowledge A term used almost exclusively in pentecostal and charismatic circles, "word of knowledge" derives from a single reference in the New Testament, where it appears in a list of nine "manifestations of the Spirit" in 1 Corinthians 12:7–10. Charismatics and pentecostals use the word of knowledge to discern the physical or spiritual condition of someone else. A pentecostal healer, for example, would be able to place her hand on someone's head or take someone's hand and, under the power of the Holy Spirit, tick off a succession of physical maladies in need of healing or identify a particular spiritual problem—an unconfessed *SIN, perhaps—that needs to be addressed.

Word of Life, Inc. *See* **Wyrtzen, Jack.**

Word of Life Bible Institute (Schroon Lake, New York) Word of Life Bible Institute is the Bible school established by and affiliated with Word of Life Fellowship, Inc., an organization dedicated to the international *EVANGELISM of young people. The school dates its founding to the 1960s, when the fellowship's ministry in Brazil established a *BIBLE INSTITUTE and urged its New York–based home office to open a similar school in the United States. The founder of Word of Life, *JACK WYRTZEN, did not want to foster competition with other Bible colleges, so he asked the presidents of several other schools to consider creating a concentrated, one-year program of practical study. His colleagues countered by encouraging Wyrtzen to go ahead and establish such a program himself. In the fall of 1970, the winterized buildings of Word of Life's camp in the Adirondacks of upstate New York opened to seventy-three students. In 1981, a second year was added to the curriculum for students hoping to continue studies in youth work, missions, and *EVANGELISM. By 1994, the Bible Institute had grown to an enrollment of more than six hundred students.

Word of Life Bible Institute only offers Bible and Bible-related courses and does not grant degrees, only diplomas for completed study. Although service projects are required, students can choose from a variety of activities, including evangelizing other athletes by participating on the school's basketball team, assisting in local church outreach or prison ministries, or open-air witnessing in New York City and Boston. Word of Life *BIBLE INSTITUTE does not have regional accreditation, but it has authorization from the state of New York and is seeking accreditation with the Transnational Association of Christian Colleges, a federally recognized agency.

Word of Life Bible Institute is—like its parent organization, Word of Life Fellowship—a fundamentalist institution. The statement of faith published by the school limits the authenticity of spiritual gifts such as healing and *SPEAKING IN TONGUES to the period of the early church and holds their current practice to be unacceptable. Three hours of quiet study time are imposed each school night. Social *DANCING is forbidden, although there is a mandatory aerobics program to provide for physical activity. The school closely monitors entertainment, with television, music, and books all subject to regulation. Students and faculty may not attend commercial movies or stage productions.

Reference: Information provided by Word of Life Bible Institute.

WordAlone Network. *See* **Lutheran Congregations in Mission for Christ.**

Wordless Book In 1866, *CHARLES H. SPURGEON preached a simple sermon at the Metropolitan Tabernacle in London, where he told of an old preacher who had assembled a book of three pages, one black (to remind him of his sinfulness), another red (for the blood of Christ that provides satisfaction for *SIN), and the third white (the purity of the redeemed). The *Wordless Book* was picked up by other evangelicals, including *DWIGHT L. MOODY, *FANNY J. CROSBY, and *HARRY A. IRONSIDE. At some point a gold page was added to symbolize heaven, and a green page was added still later to represent Christian growth.

The *Wordless Book* has been adopted as an evangelistic tool by many *EVANGELICALS. Child Evangelism Fellowship distributes it among its workers, along with instructions on how to use it. The book has been used as an instructional tool in *SUNDAY SCHOOLS and as an evangelistic tool on the mission field.

World Evangelical Fellowship The World Evangelical Fellowship, an international network of evangelical organizations, traces its history to 1846 and the founding of the World Evangelical Alliance in Great Britain. In 1951, following the Second World War, *J. ELWIN WRIGHT and *HAROLD J. OCKENGA, evangelical leaders from the United States, convened the International Convention of Evangelicals in the Netherlands, at which time a doctrinal statement was adopted and the World Evangelical Fellowship established. The general assembly of the World Evangelical Fellowship convenes every six years, and the organization seeks the cooperation of more than fifty member organizations on such matters as missions and the defense of persecuted Protestants. Since 1987, the group has been based in Singapore.

Reference: David M. Howard, *The Dream That Would Not Die* (1986).

World Harvest Bible College (South Bend, Indiana). *See* **Sumrall, Lester (Frank).**

World Harvest Church. *See* **Parsley, Rod(ney).**

World Literature Thrust. *See* **Women's Aglow Fellowship.**

World Radio Congregation. *See* **Brown, R(obert) R.**

World Vision International World Vision International is the largest and most well-known evangelical relief organization. With a paid staff of more than seventy-seven hundred workers and an annual budget of more than $300 million, World Vision operates nearly five thousand programs in more than one hundred countries, including eight hundred projects in the United States alone.

World Vision was founded in 1950 by *BOB PIERCE, an *EVANGELIST who originally served as a rally leader for *YOUTH FOR CHRIST in the 1940s. Pierce was also a filmmaker and served as a United Nations war correspondent. His experience covering the war in Korea inspired him to found a relief agency for Korean war orphans. In 1953, Pierce's organization established one of the first child sponsorship programs; within ten years, this endeavor had expanded to serve nineteen thousand orphans in eighteen countries.

The child sponsorship program is the project for which World Vision has become most famous; it enrolled 1.1 million children in 1995. Yet World Vision also offers disaster relief and wartime emergency aid, and sponsors numerous community development projects. The organization, however, sees itself as having a dual purpose: to fulfill the Great Commandment and the Great Commission. By providing food, medicine, and economic assistance, World Vision sees itself as carrying out Christ's injunction to love one's neighbor; in its Christian outreach, World Vision seeks to carry out the mandate to "make disciples of all people." For this reason, the organization does "strategic Christian outreach," which includes *BIBLE distribution, church planting, and missions research. Thus, while World Vision may rival secular relief agencies like Save the Children and CARE in the size of its budget or the number of people served, the organization has maintained its evangelical character.

World Vision was located in Monrovia, California until 1995. At that time, however, under the leadership of *ROBERT A. SEIPLE, the organization moved its headquarters to Federal Way, Washington, thereby saving several million dollars a year in overhead costs.

Worldliness Among evangelicals, the most damning thing that one can say about another believer is that she has become "worldly." Evangelical suspicions of "the world" and "worldliness" find their biblical warrant in Paul's injunction to the Romans to be "in the world, but not of the world." Among twentieth-century evangelicals, warnings against worldliness intensified after the *SCOPES TRIAL of 1925, as evangelicals suspected that the broader culture had turned against them. Many evangelicals became separatists, pulling away from the culture and even from other Protestants whom they regarded as too liberal or "modernist," in order to avoid the perils of worldliness. As evangelicals retreated into their subculture, the world seemed distant indeed, but as they emerged from the subculture in the 1980s, lured by *RONALD REAGAN's presidency, the rhetoric about worldliness dissipated considerably.

World's Christian Endeavor Union. *See* **Clark, Francis E(dward).**

World's Christian Fundamentals Association The first interdenominational organization of fundamentalists, the World's Christian Fundamentals Association was formed at a 1919 meeting in Philadelphia by premillennialists who insisted on biblical *INERRANCY and who sought to combat "*MODERNISM" and evolution through Bible conferences and Bible schools. *WILLIAM BELL RILEY's magazine, *Christian Fundamentals in School and Church* (later known as the *Christian Fundamentalist*) became the official publication of the organization. At the group's meeting in Fort Worth, Texas, in 1923, a meeting hosted by *J. FRANK NORRIS, the World's Christian Fundamentals Association conducted a trial of Texas colleges, charging them with teaching rationalism, higher criticism, and evolution. The organization gradually lost some of its fervor after the *SCOPES TRIAL of 1925 and eventually dissolved in the 1940s.

References: George W. Dollar, *A History of Fundamentalism in America* (1973); George M. Marsden, *The Soul of the American University: From Protestant Establishment to Established Nonbelief* (1994).

World's Faith Missionary Association The World's Faith Missionary Association was incorporated in Shenandoah, Iowa, in 1896 by Charles and Minnie Hanley. Charles Hanley had been a deacon in the Congregational church and editor of the highly successful *Shenandoah Post.* The Hanleys experienced what Minnie Hanley called "special illuminations of the Spirit," whereupon they decided to devote their energies to full-time ministry. Subscribers to the *Post* suddenly found themselves receiving a newspaper that conformed to what the Hanleys considered a Christian paper. Charles Hanley could no longer "conscientiously advertise cigars and tobacco, theaters, publish town gossip, and engage in party and wire pulling politics." The Hanleys changed the name of the paper to *The Firebrand,* with the motto, "holiness unto the Lord," emblazoned on the front page.

The Hanleys cooperated for a time with the *FREE METHODISTS, but they launched their own enterprises, including rescue missions and a missionary training school. The World's Faith Missionary Association offered ministerial credentials and provided support for foreign missionaries and for itinerant *EVANGELISTS.

World's Folk Art Church, Inc., The. *See* **Finster, Howard.**

Worldwide Church of God The genesis of the Worldwide Church of God lies in the seventh-day sabbatarian movement as it existed in what is known today as the General Conference of the Church of God (Seventh Day), which had its headquarters in Stanberry, Missouri. The Church of God (Seventh Day) had, and still has, a strong emphasis on the Old Testament. The church believes that Old Testament law is still binding on Christians—including observance of the Ten Commandments, especially the fourth commandment concerning the Sabbath. The Church considers the traditional holy days of other churches—Christmas, Lent, Good Friday, Easter, and Sunday—pagan holidays.

In the years of the American Great Depression, the Oregon Conference of the Church of God (Seventh Day) separated from the headquarters in Missouri to form a distinct group. It was among these people that Herbert W. Armstrong began his work in the late 1920s. After his ordination in 1921, Armstrong became the pastor of a group in Eugene, Oregon. While still a member of the Church of God (Seventh Day), Armstrong started an independent radio ministry, *The World Tomorrow,* and began publishing *The Plain Truth.* The ministry was incorporated as the Radio Church of God. Armstrong, during this time, also came to accept a belief in *BRITISH ISRAELISM, which identifies the ancient tribes of Israel with the Anglo-Saxon nations. The belief was present among the ministers of the Church of God (Seventh Day) but had never been accepted by the church as a whole.

About this same time, a controversy arose in the Church of God over the observance of Old Testament feast days and the form of church government, a controversy that would eventually split the denomination. Armstrong favored observing the feast days and wanted the church to move to a less democratic form of *POLITY.

The group with which Armstrong was in agreement formed a separate branch of the Church of God (Seventh Day) in Salem, West Virginia. By 1937, the Salem branch had dropped the observance of the Old Testament holy days and denounced *BRITISH ISRAELISM. Armstrong withdrew from the Church of God (Seventh Day) but continued his ministry with the Radio Church of God.

In the 1960s, a television ministry was added, with Garner Ted Armstrong, the founder's son, as its spokesman. The name of the church was changed to the Worldwide Church of God in 1968. Through the 1970s the church endured a scandal involving Garner Ted Armstrong that led to his breaking away to start a competing ministry, the Church of God International. The Worldwide Church of God was also sued by ex-members, a case that was dismissed after a few months.

The Worldwide Church of God has been strongly criticized and attacked by conservative evangelical bodies as a "cult." These groups have produced a great deal of negative literature on the Church. The criticisms have focused primarily on what has been seen as a departure from traditional Christian positions on issues such as the Trinity. After Armstrong's death in 1986, the Church undertook a monumental revision of its doctrine to bring it in line with orthodox evangelical Christianity. In its "Statement of Beliefs," the Worldwide Church of God now asserts that God "is one divine Being in three eternal, co-essential, yet distinct Persons—Father, Son, and Holy Spirit." The Church further affirms many of the traditional beliefs of evangelical Christianity concerning the virgin birth of Jesus, the nature of humanity, *SIN, the need for repentance and justification, the *SECOND COMING of Christ, and *BAPTISM, among others. The Church maintains the ordinances of *BAPTISM and an annual observance of the *LORD'S SUPPER and foot washing. The seventh-day Sabbath, which is not believed to be required of Christians, is the tradition and practice of the church. The Old Testament festivals of Unleavened Bread, Passover, Pentecost, Atonement, Tabernacles, and the New Year are observed, but the traditionally Christian festivals of Christmas and Easter are held to be pagan. The Worldwide Church of God joined the *NATIONAL ASSOCIATION OF EVANGELICALS in 1997.

During his lifetime, Herbert W. Armstrong had absolute authority in the church. He ordained and appointed its ministers and saw himself as God's chosen apostle-messenger for the last days. When Armstrong died in 1986, he was replaced as pastor general by Joseph Tkach, who anointed his son, Joseph Jr., as his successor; the younger Tkach assumed the position after his father's death in 1995. In addition to being the chief administrative officer of the church, the pastor general is publisher of *The Plain Truth;* chancellor of the church-sponsored college, Ambassador College; executive producer of *The World Tomorrow;* and chairman and president of the Ambassador International Cultural Foundation, which sponsors a variety of cultural, humanitarian, and educational events. The Worldwide Church of God claims sixty-seven thousand members in the United States. *The Plain Truth* is read by more than five million people each month. The radio and television versions of *The World Tomorrow* air on 148 stations around the world.

References: Frank S. Mead and Samuel S. Hill, *Handbook of Denominations in the United States,* 10th ed. (1996); J. Gordon Melton, *Encyclopedia of American Religions,* 3d ed. (1993).

Wright, J(ames) Elwin (1890–1973) Born in Corinth, Vermont, J. Elwin Wright studied at the Missionary Training Institute (now *NYACK COLLEGE) and then became affiliated with Park Street Church in Boston. Wright, wanting to forge an alliance among evangelicals in New England, formed the New England Fellowship in 1929. The idea was so successful that Wright began to explore the notion of a similar organization on a national scale. In April 1942, he convened a National Conference for United Action among Evangelicals in St. Louis, a gathering that gave birth to the *NATIONAL ASSOCIATION OF EVANGELICALS. Wright, a tireless advocate for evangelical cooperation, remained active in the new organization for many years and, in addition, became cosecretary of the *WORLD EVANGELICAL FELLOWSHIP in 1951.

References: J. Elwin Wright, *Old Fashioned Revival Hour* (1940); idem, *Manna in the Morning* (1943).

Wright, N(icholas) T(homas) (1948–) An Anglican priest and New Testament scholar, N. T. Wright studied at Oxford University, earning the doctorate. He served as chaplain at Downing College in Cambridge and then taught at McGill University in Montréal. In 1999, after a stint as dean of Lichfield Cathedral in Staffordshire, England, Wright joined the faculty of Harvard Divinity School.

Wright's scholarship has emphasized the placing of Jesus into the flow of Jewish history, and he has tried to mediate between liberal and evangelical biblical scholarship, even though he steadfastly insists that he is theologically conservative and orthodox. "The *BIBLE is the book of my life," he declared in a 1998 interview. "It's the book I live with, the book I live by, the book I want to die by. How emphatic can I get about what the *BIBLE means to me? But the *BIBLE is God's book for God's people, and the security of God's people is ultimately in God. To get overprotective about particular readings of the *BIBLE is always in danger of idolatry." Wright went on to explain his professional aspirations: "I struggle to show again and again that when you really do business with the *BIBLE at the fullest historical and theological level, then it is passionately and dramatically relevant, life changing, and community changing."

References: N. T. Wright, *Evangelical Anglican Identity: The Connection between Bible, Gospel, and Church* (1980); idem, *The New Testament and the People of God* (1992); idem, *The Crown and the Fire* (1995); idem, *Following Jesus: Biblical Reflections on Discipleship* (1995); Tim Stafford, "N. T. Wright: Making Scholarship a Tool for the Church," *Christianity Today*, February 8, 1999.

W. W. J. D. W.W.J.D. stands for "What would Jesus do?" a phrase taken from Charles M. Sheldon's 1896 novel *In His Steps*, in which a businessman approaches everyday decisions by posing the question, "What would Jesus do?" In the late 1990s, the initials became something of a rage among Christian, especially evangelical, youth, who wore various items—necklaces, buttons, hats, T-shirts, bracelets—emblazoned with the initials. In January 1989, the youth pastor of Central Wesleyan Church of Holland, Michigan, approached Ken and Mike Freestone, local businessmen, about getting buttons printed with the initials. They provided them and then also had some fabric bracelets made. By 1992, the company was selling about two thousand items a year, primarily by regional marketing. The items became more and more popular, and in 1997 the company sold approximately 15 million items, about two thirds of the total volume.

Wyatt, Thomas (?–1964) Born into poverty in Jasper County, Iowa, Thomas Wyatt was converted in the Methodist Church. After a brush with death, he claimed to have heard a divine voice: "I am the Lord that healeth thee." During the Great Depression, Wyatt became an itinerant healer throughout the Midwest. In

1937, having broken with the Methodists, he moved to Portland, Oregon, where he continued his healing ministry, established Wings of Healing Temple, and in 1942 began a radio program, *Wings of Healing*. By 1953, the broadcast was carried by both the Mutual Broadcasting Company and the ABC network. Wyatt founded a monthly paper, *March of Faith*, in 1945 and moved into television in 1957 with *Global Frontiers Telecast*, which celebrated patriotism and lambasted communism. His Bethesda Bible Institute and Bethesda World Training Center sent "Gospel invasion teams" around the world to evangelize and to slow the spread of communism.

Wyatt moved his offices to Los Angeles in 1959, while his son, Max, remained in Portland. After Thomas Wyatt's death in 1964, Evelyn, his widow, capably assumed the reins of leadership.

Reference: David Edwin Harrell Jr., *All Things Are Possible: The Healing and Charismatic Revivals in Modern America* (1975).

Wycliffe Bible Translators Named for John Wycliffe, who translated the *BIBLE into English in the fourteenth century, Wycliffe Bible Translators was founded in 1934 by I. I. Letgers and *CAMERON TOWNSEND as a summer training program in linguistics. Townsend, who had served as a missionary to Guatemala, had taken upon himself the task of translating the New Testament into Cakchiquel. Wycliffe soon sent field workers into Mexico, Latin America, Asia, and eventually into Africa to learn native languages and to undertake the task of Bible translation. A sister institution to Wycliffe Bible Translators, the Summer Institute of Linguistics, founded in 1942, provides training in linguistics for both religious and secular purposes. By the 1980s, Wycliffe, an evangelical, interdenominational organization, had about five thousand missionaries and translators working under its auspices.

Wyrtzen, Jack (1924–1996) Jack Wyrtzen became a trombonist in a dance orchestra in the 1930s. According to his own *CONVERSION narrative, which he repeated many times, Wyrtzen began reading the *BIBLE and eventually was converted to fundamentalist Christianity. Wyrtzen, like many other fundamentalists, was fond of belittling liberal or mainline Protestants. He claimed that he never learned about Christianity in the mainline churches he attended. It was only in the army that he developed his "personal relationship with Jesus Christ," and Wyrtzen liked to quip that the army was "the greatest denomination in the U.S."

After his *CONVERSION, Wyrtzen began preaching on a weekly radio show, and in 1942 he founded the not-for-profit Word of Life organization. Under these auspices, Wrytzen conducted religious rallies beginning in the late 1940s. Most of them were directed toward youth, and some were so large that he used Madison Square Garden and Radio City Music Hall. Under Wyrtzen's leadership, Word of Life expanded to the Adirondacks, where it purchased large parcels of land in and around Schroon Lake for youth camps. Wyrtzen and his organization sponsored youth clubs in thirty-two countries throughout the world and a *BIBLE INSTITUTE. Near the end of his life, Wyrtzen also added a compound in Florida to his Word of Life empire.

Reference: Randall Balmer, *Mine Eyes Have Seen the Glory: A Journey into the Evangelical Subculture in America*, 3d ed. (2000).

■ ■ ■

Xenoglossolalia. *See* **Xenolalia.**

Xenolalia A variation of *GLOSSOLALIA (speaking in tongues), *xenolalia* refers to the speaking of a recognizable foreign language by someone who has never before learned that language. The term was coined by a French scholar in 1905, and the gift of *xenolalia* was especially sought after early in the twentieth century by prospective pentecostal missionaries who wanted to preach the *GOSPEL abroad without taking the time or the trouble to learn a foreign language.

Reference: H. Newton Malony and A. Adams Lovekin, *Glossolalia: Behavioral Science Perspectives on Speaking in Tongues* (1985).

■ ■ ■

Yaconelli, Michael Charles "Mike" (1942–) Born in Van Nuys, California, Mike Yaconelli has spent much of his career in youth ministry—as developer of curricular materials for youth workers, as a speaker on youth ministry to evangelical groups, and as lay pastor of a small-town church in Yreka, California. He is owner of *YOUTH SPECIALTIES, which produces and distributes materials for youth ministry and which, until 1997, published the *Wittenburg Door,* evangelicalism's version of *Mad* magazine.

Yancey, Philip D(avid) (1949–) Perhaps the most literate and thoughtful writer of popular evangelical literature, Philip D. Yancey was born in Atlanta and earned degrees from Columbia Bible College, *WHEATON COLLEGE, and the University of Chicago. Though reared in a fundamentalist setting, an atmosphere where "anything you could think of that was fun was wrong," Yancey came to reject strict *FUNDAMENTALISM in favor of a more temperate *EVANGELICALISM. He became editor of *Campus Life* in 1971 and remained there until 1979, having served those final years as publisher. Yancey became a freelance writer in 1980. His articles have appeared in such magazines as *Reader's Digest,* the *Saturday Evening Post,* and **CHRISTIANITY TODAY,* where he is also editor-at-large and a regular columnist. His books have won several awards, and his 1977 treatise on the problem of evil, *Where Is God When It Hurts?,* had sold more than half a million copies by the mid-1990s.

References: Philip D. Yancey, *After the Wedding* (1976); idem, *Where Is God When It Hurts?* (1977); idem, *Disappointment with God: Questions Nobody Asks Aloud* (1989); idem, *I Was Just Wondering* (1990); idem, *What's So Amazing about Grace?* (1997).

Yeatman, James (Erwin) (1818–1901) The son of a wealthy manufacturer in St. Louis, James Yeatman became a businessman and a philanthropist. During the Civil War, he headed the Western Sanitary Commission, a counterpart to the United States Sanitary Commission; both organizations addressed the physical and the spiritual needs of Union soldiers. Yeatman supervised the disbursement of medical and sanitary supplies to troops in Missouri, Kentucky, Tennessee, and Arkansas. Following the war, Yeatman was one of the forces behind the formation of the American Christian Commission, which sought to assess and to amelioriate the conditions in the cities.

YMCA. *See* **Young Men's Christian Association.**

Yoakum, Finis (Ewing) (1851–1920) Finis Yoakum, the son of a Texas physician, became a medical doctor himself and the chair of mental diseases at the Gross Medical College in Denver. On July 18, 1894, Yoakum was struck by a buggy driven by a drunken man. Badly injured, Yoakum nearly died and was severely weakened by infections in the ensuing months. He moved to Los Angeles and experienced divine healing on February 5, 1895, whereupon he determined to devote his life to healping the sick, the poor, and the destitute.

Yoakum participated in holiness churches and *CAMP MEETINGS in the Los Angeles area, spoke in *TONGUES, and attended the *AZUSA STREET REVIVAL. Yoakum referred to his own ministries as Pisgah, located in what is now North Hollywood. He published a periodical, *Pisgah,* and preached across the United States, Canada, and Great Britain. In 1914, Yoakum purchased more than three thousand acres northeast of Los Angeles in Lime Valley, where he wanted to construct a utopian community called Pisgah Grande. Yoakum's death in 1920, however, cut short the experiment.

Yoder, John Howard (1927–1997) Born into a Mennonite household in Smithville, Ohio, John Howard Yoder earned the baccalaureate degree from *GOSHEN COLLEGE and directed the relief efforts of the Mennonite Central Committee in Europe after World War II. He studied theology with Karl Barth at the University of Basel (Switzerland) and was active in a number of ecumenical and peace efforts. Upon his return to the United States, Yoder worked for his father's greenhouse in Wooster, Ohio, for a year before joining the faculty of Goshen Biblical Seminary in Elkhart, Indiana, where he remained until 1984. Yoder, a theologian and a pacifist, published his influential book on Christian pacifism, *The Politics of Jesus,* in 1972 and was part of the 1973 gathering that gave rise to the *CHICAGO DECLARATION OF SOCIAL CONCERN. He served for years as a contributing editor for **SOJOURNERS* magazine. In addition to his various duties at Goshen, which included a stint as president from 1970 to 1973, Yoder also taught at the University of Notre Dame for a number of years and joined their faculty of theology in 1984.

References: John Howard Yoder, *The Christian Witness to the State* (1964); idem, *The Politics of Jesus* (1972); idem, *He Came Preaching Peace* (1985); idem, *For the Nations* (1997).

Yoida Full Gospel Church (Seoul, Korea). *See* **Cho, Paul Yonggi.**

Young Life In the fall of 1938, a student at *DALLAS THEOLOGICAL SEMINARY, James C. Rayburn Jr., sought to enhance his evangelistic work with high school students in Gainsville, Texas. He started with a Bible study club after school but the next year moved the meetings to private homes and soon developed a formula that brought considerable growth: make meetings fun, aim for school leaders, hold meetings in private homes, and establish personal relationships.

Rayburn recruited other seminarians, who also saw success in their evangelistic efforts. With the help of a seminary friend, Rayburn gained the financial backing of *HERBERT J. TAYLOR, a Chicago businessman, which made possible the expansion of the program to other states. Taylor also purchased a number of camps that the Young Life organization uses for summer conferences. The organization, with headquarters in Colorado Springs, Colorado, estimates that approximately seventy thousand teenagers attend Young Life clubs.

Young Men's Christian Association The Young Men's Christian Association (YMCA) was founded in London in 1844 by George Williams in order to provide a refuge from the perils of urban life. The organization offered Bible classes, meeting rooms with edifying reading materials, and clean, safe lodging. The YMCA expanded to Montréal and Boston in 1851, and it quickly established itself in various forms of social amelioration—feeding the poor, caring for the sick, working for *TEMPERANCE, organizing *SUNDAY SCHOOLS—in addition to its evangelistic work. *DWIGHT L. MOODY began his evangelistic work under the aegis of the YMCA. The organization also sponsored military missions, the *STUDENT VOLUNTEER MOVEMENT, and various educational programs. In order to keep young men off the streets and out of trouble, the YMCA provided recreational facilities; the games of volleyball and basketball were both devised by people associated with the YMCA.

Though unmistakably evangelical in tenor, the YMCA over the decades has become a community service organization that now transcends religious boundaries; the three-part emphasis on mind, body, and spirit (derived from John 17:21) now finds expression in the small triangle imbedded in the "Y" logotype. It remains the largest health and social service agency in the United States and has a presence in nearly one hundred nations around the world.

Reference: C. H. Hopkins, *History of the YMCA in North America* (1951).

Young Women's Christian Association Modeled after the *YOUNG MEN'S CHRISTIAN ASSOCIATION, the Young Women's Christian Association (YWCA) was begun in 1866 to assist those young women and girls who were "dependent on their own exertions for support," aiming to encourage "those ideals of personal and social living" consistent with Christianity. Like the *YMCA, the YWCA has become increasingly secular over the decades. Although it maintains a separate leadership from the *YMCA and each local YWCA is independent, the YWCA frequently cooperates and shares facilities with local chapters of the *YMCA.

References: Mary S. Sims, *The Natural History of a Social Institution—The Young Women's Christian Association* (1936); Judith Weisenfeld, *African American Women and Christian Activism: New York's Black YWCA, 1905–1945* (1997).

Youth for Christ, International Youth for Christ is an independent, nonsectarian, interdenominational youth organization whose mission is to evangelize teenagers and young adults. The organization developed out of one of the mass rallies held in the 1940s by young *EVANGELISTS in England, the United States, and Canada; Youth for Christ was the name of the Indianapolis-based rallies. In 1944, at the *WINONA LAKE BIBLE CONFERENCE in Winona Lake, Indiana, a group including Roger Malsbury, J. Palmer Mintz, and Arthur McKee met to discuss planning for new rallies. Out of a second meeting came a temporary organization, which elected Chicago pastor *TORREY JOHNSON as chairman; a summer convention was planned for 1945.

Founded in the same period as the *NATIONAL ASSOCIATION OF EVANGELICALS, Youth for Christ was another organization that helped evangelicals gain a sense of national identity, after having been cast off from mainline Protestantism. The organization received its biggest boost, however, with the affiliation of two young, energetic preachers, *BILLY

GRAHAM and *CHARLES TEMPLETON. The first rally was held in 1945, and within two years more than nine hundred more meetings had been staged. These events became a Saturday-night social gathering for teenagers and young adults, as well as older people. Graham's dynamic preaching made large auditoriums commonplace, and one Chicago meeting in 1945 drew seventy thousand people to Soldiers Field.

With the rallies successfully underway, Youth for Christ began to expand to other ministry ventures. *BOB COOK succeeded Johnson as president of the organization in 1948. Cook shifted the focus to high school Bible clubs, which became known as Campus Life, as a more effective means for the *EVANGELISM of teenagers. The organization approached Kansas City youth leader Jack Hamilton, who had launched the school-based Bible Club movement in 1949 with YOB, Youth on the Beam. Hamilton had equipped several buses with pianos and sent them to schools as "portable clubhouses." Within a few years of being hired by Youth for Christ to take his idea nationally, Hamilton had organized thirty-six hundred Youth for Christ Clubs. The creation of these Bible clubs marked a key transition into youth ministry for the organization, but it had much in common with the earlier rallies. Both endeavors sought to witness to young people in ways they would find accessible—hence, the organization's slogan: "Geared to the times, anchored to the Rock."

In the decades that followed, Youth for Christ has continued to show an ability to adopt the trappings of modern youth culture in an effort to further its *EVANGELISM. In the 1960s, Youth for Christ Clubs were renamed Campus Life, because the name was seen as "less threatening." In a similar fashion, when Lifeline Ministries, Youth for Christ's outreach program to at-risk youth, was expanded in the 1960s, it became Youth Guidance. In the present day, Youth for Christ continues to keep its finger on the pulse of America's youth. The "witnessing merchandise" offered through its catalog includes leather-beaded bracelets, and the organization draws on the resources of the most popular Christian pop musicians to advance its cause.

With headquarters in Denver, Colorado, Youth for Christ has several divisions of ministry: Campus Life, for high school–age students; Campus Life/JV, for junior high and middle school students; Youth Guidance, for at-risk children and youth; DC Ministries, which teaches young people how to witness to non-Christian friends; World Outreach, which sponsors regular programs in twenty-three countries and periodic initiatives in many more; and Project Serve, which runs service projects in the United States and abroad. The organization publishes *Impact,* a four-page, two-color newsletter, as well as several smaller, scaled-down newsletters for its different divisions, including "Campus Life," "JV News," and "Whazzup?" In spite of this extensive national structure, each local Youth for Christ chapter is separately incorporated and has its own board of directors from the local community.

Starting in 1959, Youth for Christ began holding periodic "Capital Teen Conventions," which drew thousands of adolescents. More recently, the organization has hosted "Youth Evangelism SuperConferences" that teach ministry and witnessing techniques to teenagers and encourage them to affirm their lifelong commitment to *EVANGELISM. Held every three years, the 1994 conferences in Washington, D.C., and Los Angeles had a combined attendance of twenty-six thousand. Youth for

Christ also sponsors a National Leadership Training Institute each summer for approximately 150 students.

Youth for Christ International was born in 1968, with an outreach project to Jamaica. This sister organization sponsors mission trips and has launched an AIDS prevention campaign in Africa, "Worth the Wait," which promotes sexual abstinence until marriage.

Reference: Robert Wuthnow, *The Restructuring of American Religion* (1988).

Youth on the Beam. *See* **Youth for Christ, International.**

Youth Specialties Founded in San Diego in 1969 by Wayne Rice and *MIKE YACONELLI, Youth Specialties publishes resource materials for evangelical youth ministers and lay leaders. Its real contribution to *EVANGELICALISM, however, lay in its publication of a bimonthly magazine, *The Wittenburg Door,* *EVANGELICALISM's answer to *Mad* magazine. *The Wittenburg Door* (the misspelling was initially inadvertent, but it stuck) regularly lampooned evangelicals, their foibles, and their pretensions. It gave its coveted "green weenie" to its loser of the month, and past "theologians of the year" have included *TAMMY FAYE BAKKER and Woody Allen. *The Door* was acquired by Trinity Foundation, based in Dallas in 1995.

Youth with a Mission An evangelistic organization begun in 1960 by *LOREN CUNNINGHAM, then a student at an *ASSEMBLIES OF GOD college, Youth with a Mission operates in more than one hundred countries throughout the world. Cunningham had tried to enlist the support of the *ASSEMBLIES OF GOD in his idea of sending young people on short-term missions, but when the denomination demurred, Cunningham elected to make the organization interdenominational. Youth with a Mission relies on short-term missionaries who raise their own financial support. The organization, which operates a college—Pacific and Asia Christian University, in Kailua-Kona, Hawai'i—distributes *BIBLES and conducts evangelistic meetings, often with the help of drama troupes or musical ensembles. In addition to a full-time staff of approximately six thousand workers, the organization every summer sends out about fifty thousand volunteers for short-term mission work throughout the world.

Reference: Loren Cunningham, *Is That Really You, God?* (1984).

■ ■ ■

Z Music Z Music bills itself as a "24-hour Christian Rock Channel." In many respects, the station mimics MTV, except, as a reporter from the *National Review* observed, "The girls keep their clothes on and the messages are ethereal, not suicidal." Z Music began in the early 1990s but was taken over in 1994 by Gaylord Entertainment Company, the parent of Country Music Television. Within seven months, Z Music's new management had increased its subscriber base 50 percent, and by 1996 the station reached 17 million homes. Since the change in management, Z Music has launched several new ventures, including sponsoring tours by Christian artists like *AMY GRANT and releasing sample albums to promote the music the station airs. These promotional albums, produced in partnership with Benson Music and called "Z'ing is Believing," sold more than two hundred thousand copies in 1995. Z Music also has introduced "Cross Country," a Christian country music show that airs on Z Music and other cable stations. It broadcasts Z *Buzz Radio* in more than seventy markets across the United States.

References: Robert La Franco and Lisa Gubernick, "Rocking with God," *Forbes,* January 2, 1995; Deborah Evans Price, "From SoundScan to Christian Label Acquisitions, It Was a Notable Year," *Billboard,* December 23, 1995; David Scott, "Notes from the Alternative Nation," *National Review,* June 17, 1996.

Zacharias, Ravi (Kumar) (1946–) Born in Madras (now Chennai), India, and reared in Delhi, Ravi Zacharias migrated to Canada with his family in the mid-1960s. He graduated from *ONTARIO BIBLE COLLEGE (now Tyndale College) and earned the M.Div. from *TRINITY EVANGELICAL DIVINITY SCHOOL. An *EVANGELIST and an apologist, he is head of Ravi Zacharias Minstries, based in Atlanta. He has a weekly radio program, *Let My People Think,* and in January 2000 he added a daily radio program, *A Slice of Infinity.*

References: Ravi Zacharias, *A Shattered Visage: The Real Face of Atheism* (1994); idem, *Can Man Live without God?* (1994); idem, *Deliver Us from Evil* (1996); *Jesus among Other Gods* (2000).

Zarephath Bible College **(Zarephath, New Jersey).** *See* **White, Alma (née Bridewell).**

Zeisberger, David (1721–1808) A Moravian missionary to the Indians, David Zeisberger was born in Zauctentahal, Moravia, and emigrated with his parents to Herrnhut, Count *NIKOLAUS VON ZINZENDORF's haven for Moravians in Saxony. In 1736, he sailed for Savannah, Georgia, to join the Moravian colony there. He moved on to Bethlehem, Pennsylvania, several years later and embarked on a missionary career to the Delawares of Pennsylvania, New York, and Ohio, a career that lasted more than six decades. He established numerous Christian communities of Native Americans on the frontier; one such community, in Gnadenhütten, Ohio, was destroyed by American troops during the Revolutionary War, and ninety Indians were massacred. Zeisberger did linguistic work in the Delaware and Onondaga languages. He produced several grammars, a book of sermons, several collections of hymns, and translations of Moravian liturgies.

Zimmerman, Thomas F(letcher) (1912–1991) Born in Indianapolis, Indiana, Thomas F. Zimmerman had a *CONVERSION experience at the age of seven and received his Spirit *BAPTISM four years later. He resolved to enter the ministry, perhaps as a foreign missionary, but financial hardship forced him to drop out of school after only one year at Indiana University. After several years as an assistant pastor to John Price of Indianapolis, Zimmerman was ordained as an *ASSEMBLIES OF GOD minister in 1936. He served churches in Indiana, Illinois, Missouri, and Ohio before moving to a succession of administrative posts within the *ASSEMBLIES OF GOD. Beginning in 1945 he headed the radio department for the denomination and became one of the founders of *NATIONAL RELIGIOUS BROADCASTERS, an organization he later served as vice president and as president. Following a stint as assistant general superintendent for the denomination, Zimmerman was elected general superintendent in 1959, a position he held until 1985. By almost any index—members, followers, clergy—the *ASSEMBLIES OF GOD doubled in size during the quarter century of his leadership. Zimmerman also worked to improve relations with nonpentecostal evangelicals, and he was the first pentecostal elected president of the *NATIONAL ASSOCIATION OF EVANGELICALS.

Zinzendorf, Nikolaus Ludwig von (1700–1760) Born in Dresden, Germany, Nikolaus Ludwig von Zinzendorf studied at the pietist school in Halle and at the University of Wittenberg. He served as a counselor to the king of Saxony from 1721 to 1728. In 1722 he acquired an estate in Saxony, which he opened to exiles from Bohemia and Moravia. Zinzendorf relinquished his court duties to devote his energies to renewing the *Unitas Fratrum,* also known as the Moravian Church or the Church of the Brethren. The settlement became known as Herrnhut ("the Lord's protection"), and Zinzendorf was ordained by the group in 1735, later becoming bishop.

Zinzendorf was active in Moravian missions, including those to North America. He presided at the famous Christmas Eve service in Bethlehem, Pennsylvania, in 1741, which established the Moravians in northeastern Pennsylvania. He wrote approximately two thousand hymns and remained involved in Moravian enterprises in England, Germany, and North America his entire life.

Zion Bible Institute. *See* **Zion Evangelistic Fellowship** *and* **Gibson, Christine A(melia).**

Zion City On New Year's Day, 1900, JOHN ALEXANDER DOWIE, pastor of Chicago's *CHRISTIAN CATHOLIC CHURCH, unveiled his plans for a utopian community on more than six thousand acres of land situated along Lake Michigan, forty miles north of Chicago. Like Salt Lake City, Zion City was to be free of alcohol and tobacco but also without pork or drugstores. Dowie, who believed in divine healing and exhorted his followers to avoid all medicines, became the leader of this community, declaring himself Elijah in June 1901. Such a claim undermined his credibility in the eyes of his followers, especially as the experiment slid into financial ruin.

Dowie was partially paralyzed by a stroke in September 1905; the next year, while he was in Mexico City preparing for another utopia, Zion City leaders stripped him of his powers. The utopian experiment continued for a time under Dowie's successor, Wilbur Glenn Volivia, but Dowie's theocratic laws were eventually repealed and the experiment itself dissipated.

Reference: Philip Cook, *Zion, Illinois: Twentieth-Century Utopia* (1996).

Zion Evangelistic Fellowship The Zion Evangelistic Fellowship was established in 1935 by *CHRISTINE A. GIBSON, head of Zion Bible Institute in East Providence, Rhode Island. The group consisted of a loose federation of independent churches in the Northeast; by 1953, ninety-six congregations were members of the fellowship. Gibson formed the organization as a support network for the school and for foreign missions. Although Zion Evangelistic Fellowship collapsed in 1956, a year after Gibson's death, a remnant of the group formed another federation called Apostolic Challenge.

Zola Levitt Ministries. *See* **Levitt, Zola.**

Zoller, John (1888–1979) John Zoller's program, *Christ for Everyone,* first aired over WWJ-radio in Detroit in 1922, amid a violent thunderstorm. He was unsure that the signal had been heard until a letter arrived from a listener, informing Zoller that the radio homily had changed his life.

"At once I asked God to open the door so I could broadcast the *GOSPEL," Zoller later recounted. In 1938, he started a new program, *American Back to God Hour,* geared toward those in the military. Zoller's radio career reached its zenith during World War II when his programs were broadcast over War Department stations and the Mutual Network, as well as independent stations. His coverage declined after the war, however, and Zoller thereafter devoted his energies to the distribution of evangelistic tracts and literature.

Reference: J. Gordon Melton, Phillip Charles Lucas, and Jon R. Stone, *Prime-Time Religion: An Encyclopedia of Religious Broadcasting* (1997).

Zwemer, Samuel M(arinus) (1867–1952) Born near Vriesland, Michigan, and educated at Hope College and New Brunswick Theological Seminary, Samuel M. Zwemer was ordained in 1890 by the classis of Iowa of the *REFORMED CHURCH IN AMERICA. Influenced by *ROBERT P. WILDER and the *STUDENT VOLUNTEER MOVEMENT, Zwemer decided to become a missionary to the Muslims. He went to the Middle East under the auspices of the Syrian Mission of the Presbyterian Church and earned the sobriquet "apostle to Arabia."

Zwemer wrote a number of books about Islam and founded a periodical, *The Moslem World,* in 1911. He traveled around the world and also served as professor of missions and the history of religion at Princeton Theological Seminary.

References: Samuel M. Zwemer, *Islam, a Challenge to Faith* (1907); idem, *The Cross above the Crescent* (1941).

ABOUT THE AUTHOR

Randall Balmer is the Ann Whitney Olin Professor of American Religion at Barnard College, Columbia University. He has taught at Columbia since 1985, the year he earned the Ph.D. from Princeton University, and he has been a visiting professor at Rutgers, Yale, Drew, Princeton, and Union Theological Seminary, where he is also an adjunct professor of church history. He is the author of several books, including *Blessed Assurance: A History of Evangelicalism in America* and *Mine Eyes Have Seen the Glory: A Journey into the Evangelical Subculture in America,* which was made into an award-winning PBS series.

230 E92ba
Balmer, Randall Herbert.
Encyclopedia of
evangelicalism / Randall